BIBLIOGRAPHY OF AMERICAN LITERATURE

VOLUME 6

BIBLIOGRAPHY OF

American Literature

COMPILED BY JACOB BLANCK

for the Bibliographical Society of America

VOLUME SIX

AUGUSTUS BALDWIN LONGSTREET to THOMAS WILLIAM PARSONS

NEW HAVEN AND LONDON: *Yale University Press*

1973

The compilation of the manuscript of *Bibliography of American Literature*
was made possible by a grant from the Lilly Endowment, Inc., of
Indianapolis, Indiana, to the Bibliographical Society of America.

Published in Great Britain, Europe, and Africa by
Yale University Press, Ltd., London.
Distributed in Latin America by Kaiman & Polon,
Inc., New York City; in Australasia and Southeast
Asia by John Wiley & Sons Australasia Pty. Ltd.,
Sydney; in India by UBS Publishers' Distributors Pvt.,
Ltd., Dehli; in Japan by John Weatherhill, Inc., Tokyo.

This sixth volume of

Bibliography of American Literature

is dedicated to the memory of

M E R L E

Merle DeVore Johnson

Oregon City, Oregon, 1874 – New York City, 1935

Illustrator, Artist, Bibliographer, Teacher, Friend

Contents

Authors in Volume Six

Illustrations

Acknowledgments

*They helped every one his neighbour; and every
one said to his brother, Be of good courage.*

—*Isaiah, xxxxi: 6*

Many—libraries and librarians, collectors, antiquarian booksellers, fellow-bibliographers and others—have, in one way or another, in large part or in small, contributed to this compilation. The list is long—far longer than that given here or of the sum total of the names published in the preceding volumes of the *Bibliography* under *Location Symbols* or *Acknowledgments*.

If it were practical, this list would include (with grateful thanks) the names of the anonymous catalogers, page-boys, deck attendants, and all those others who, methodically and efficiently, make modern libraries the remarkable instruments they are. To all these silent contributors the *Bibliography* is deeply grateful.

With each passing year (the *Bibliography* is now in its twenty-ninth year) the list—and the debt of gratitude—grows.

First and foremost the *Bibliography* is grateful to the Lilly Endowment, Inc., of Indianapolis, Indiana, whose continued support has brought the *Bibliography* this far;

The members of the *Bibliography's* Supervisory Committee: Frederick B. Adams, Jr., who retired as Chairman and was succeeded by William H. Bond; C. Waller Barrett; Douglas C. Ewing; Herman W. Liebert; David A. Randall. And, *in memoriam:* James T. Babb, Clarence S. Brigham, William A. Jackson, Carroll A. Wilson;

The editorial aides who assisted in bringing this volume to publication: Colin Clair, Theodor M. Hauri, Suellen Mutchow, Fisher H. Nesmith, Jr., Lenore Putnam, Susan Riddell—with particular thanks to Miss Mutchow for her continued devotion to what sometimes seems an endless task;

Donald C. Gallup, curator of the Aldis Collection (and others) at Yale University Library, whose constant cooperation is of immeasurable value. Mr. Gallup, among other self-imposed tasks, read the galley proofs of the *Bibliography* and thereby prevented many a misstatement;

Messrs. Paul Goren and Perry O'Neil, tireless contributors of information relating to materials in The New York Public Library;

Houghton Mifflin Company, surely a pillar of American literature, which generously permitted examination of its earlier manufacturing records;

Leslie Mahin Oliver, whose proofing of this volume prevented many an error;

And all these whose cooperation has been of immeasurable value:

John Alden, The Boston Public Library

James Belliveau, The Boston Athenæum

Mary E. Brown, The American Antiquarian Society

Frank X. Cox, The Houghton Library

Julia E. Harty, The Library of Congress

Christine D. Hathaway, Brown University Library

Carolyn E. Jakeman, The Houghton Library

Richard Colles Johnson, The Newberry Library

Joseph P. McCarthy, The Houghton Library

William H. Runge, The Alderman Library

William Sartain, The Library of Congress

Marte Shaw, The Widener Library

Roger J. Trienens, The Library of Congress

And to all those libraries named in the *List of Locations* where the *Bibliography's* searchers have been made welcome, is the Project grateful. At risk of appearing partial, where partiality is not intended, let it again be recorded that the *Bibliography* is particularly grateful to The Houghton Library where, for so many years, the *Bibliography* has been a welcome, sometimes trying, guest.

JB

General References

The following references are mentioned in the lists under the designations given.

Allibone
: A Critical Dictionary of English Literature, and British and American Authors . . . , by S. Austin Allibone, 3 Vols.; two supplementary volumes compiled by John Foster Kirk, 1858–1891.

Am Cat
: The American Catalogue . . . , 1880–1911.

Appleton
: Appletons' Cyclopaedia of American Biography . . . , 1887–1901.

B A L
: Bibliography of American Literature Compiled by Jacob Blanck for the Bibliographical Society of America, 1955–   .

BMu Cat
: The British Museum Catalogue of Printed Books, 1881–1905. And, British Museum General Catalogue of Printed Books . . . , 1931–   .

C H A L
: The Cambridge History of American Literature . . . , 1917–1921.

D A B
: Dictionary of American Biography . . . , 1928–   .

D N B
: The Dictionary of National Biography . . . , 1885–   .

English Cat
: The English Catalogue of Books . . . Issued in the United Kingdom . . . , 1864–   .

Evans
: American Bibliography . . . , by Charles Evans, 1903–1934. Continued by Clifford K. Shipton, 1955. Supplement, by Roger P. Bristol, 1970.

Foley
: American Authors 1795–1895 a Bibliography of First and Notable Editions . . . , by P. K. Foley, 1897.

Griffin
: American Historical Association. Bibliography of American Historical Societies . . . , by Appleton Prentiss Griffin, 1896.

Johannsen
: The House of Beadle and Adams and Its Dime and Nickel Novels . . . , by Albert Johannsen, 1950.

Johnson
: American First Editions . . . , by Merle Johnson, 1929, 1932. And, editions of 1936, 1942, revised by Jacob Blanck.

Kaser
: The Cost Book of Carey & Lea 1825–1838, edited by David Kaser ⟨1963⟩.

Kelly
: See below under *Roorbach*.

L C Printed Cat
: . . . A Catalog of Books Represented by Library of Congress Printed Cards . . . , 1942–   .

Leon Brothers
: Catalogue of First Editions of American Authors, Poets, Philosophers, Historians . . . Compiled . . . and for Sale by Leon & Brother, New York, 1885.

Livingston
: The Chamberlain Bibliographies. A Bibliography of . . . Henry Wadsworth Longfellow . . . by Luther S. Livingston, 1908.

Roorbach
: Bibliotheca Americana. Catalogue of American Publications,

	Including Reprints and Original Works . . . Compiled and Arranged by O. A. Roorbach, 1852–1861. Continued by James Kelly, 1866–1871.
Sabin	A Dictionary of Books Relating to America, from its Discovery to the Present Time, by Joseph Sabin; concluded by Wilberforce Eames and R. W. G. Vail, 1868–1936.
Stone	First Editions of American Authors a Manual for Book-Lovers . . . , by Herbert Stuart Stone, 1893.
Thompson	American Literary Annuals & Gift Books 1825–1865, by Ralph Thompson, 1936.
U S Cat	The United States Catalog ⟨of⟩ Books in Print . . . , 1900–
Wegelin	The bibliographical studies of Oscar Wegelin, pioneer worker in the field of American literature, are cited by title within the lists.
Wilson	Thirteen Author Collections of the Nineteenth Century and Five Centuries of Familiar Quotations, edited by Jean C. S. Wilson and David A. Randall, 1950.
Wright	American Fiction 1774–1850 a Contribution toward a Bibliography, by Lyle H. Wright, 1939, 1948. *Or:* American Fiction 1851–1875 a Contribution toward a Bibliography, by Lyle H. Wright, 1957. *Or:* American Fiction 1876–1900 a Contribution toward a Bibliography, by Lyle H. Wright, 1966.

Principal Periodicals Consulted

A L B	Appleton's Literary Bulletin: A Monthly Record of New Books, English, French, German, and American (New York)
A L G	American Literary Gazette and Publishers' Circular (New York)
A M	Analectic Magazine (Philadelphia)
A Me	American Mercury (Hartford)
A Mi	American Minerva (New York)
A M M	American Monthly Magazine (New York)
A M R	American Monthly Review (Cambridge, Boston)
A P C	American Publishers' Circular and Literary Gazette (New York)
A Q R	American Quarterly Review (Philadelphia)
A R	Analytical Review; or, History of Literature, Domestic and Foreign (London)
Arc	Arcturus, a Journal of Books and Opinion (New York)
A R L J	The American Review and Literary Journal (New York)
Ath	Athenaeum; a Journal of Literature, Science, the Fine Arts, Music and the Drama (London)
A W R	American Review: A Whig Journal of Politics, Literature, Art and Science (New York)
B C	British Critic, and Quarterly Theological Review (London)
B F	Bibliographie de la France, ou Journal Général de l'Imprimerie et de la Librairie (Paris)
B J	Brother Jonathan (New York)
B Jl	Broadway Journal (New York)
Bkr	Bookseller (London)
B M	Bookseller's Medium and Publisher's Advertiser (New York)
B M L A	Bent's Monthly Literary Advertiser (London)
C	Critic; a Record of Literature, Art, Music, Science and the Drama (London)
C M	Canadian Monthly and National Review (Toronto)
C R	Critical Review; or, Annals of Literature (London)
C R N	Criterion, Literary and Critical Journal (New York)
E R	Eclectic Review (London)
G R R	General Repository and Review (Cambridge, Mass.)
H	The Harbinger (New York and Boston)
K	Knickerbocker, or New York Monthly Magazine (New York)
L A	Literary American (New York)
L G	Literary Gazette. A Weekly Journal of Literature, Science and the Fine Arts (London)
L G A A	Literary Gazette and American Athenaeum (New York)
L M	Literary Magazine and British Review (London)

L M A R   Literary Magazine, and American Register (Philadelphia)
L S R   Literary and Scientific Repository, and Critical Review (New York)
L W   Literary World (New York)
M   The Minerva; or, Weekly Literary, Entertaining, and Scientific Journal (New York)
M A   Monthly Anthology, and Boston Review (Boston)
M M   The Monthly Magazine and American Review (New York)
M R   Monthly Review (London)
N & A   Nation and Athenaeum (London)
N A R   North American Review (Boston, New York)
N E   New Englander (New Haven, Conn.)
N E M   New-England Magazine (Boston)
N L A   Norton's Literary Advertiser (New York)
N L G   Norton's Literary Gazette and Publishers' Circular (New York)
N L R   New London Review (London)
N W   New World. A Weekly Family Journal of Popular Literature, Science, Art and News (New York)
N Y L G   New York Literary Gazette (New York), Sept. 1825–March, 1826. New York Literary Gazette and Journal of Belles Lettres, Arts, Sciences, &c., (New York), Sept. 1834–March, 1835. New York Literary Gazette (New York), Feb.–July, 1839.
N Y M   New-York Mirror: a Weekly Gazette of Literature and The Fine Arts (New York)
N Y R   New York Review (New York)
P   The Panoplist (Boston)
P C   Publishers' Circular and Booksellers' Record (London)
P F   Port Folio (Philadelphia)
P W   Publishers' Weekly (New York)
S L M   Southern Literary Messenger (Richmond, Va.)
S R   Southern Review (Charleston, S. C.)
S W M   Simm's Monthly Magazine, Southern and Western Monthly Magazine and Review (Charleston, S. C.)
T L S   Times Literary Supplement (London)
U A   Universal Asylum and Columbian Magazine (Philadelphia)
U S D R   United States Democratic Review (Washington, D. C.)
U S L A   United States Literary Advertiser, Publishers' Circular, and Monthly Register of Literature and Art (New York)
U S L G   United States Literary Gazette (Boston); United States Review and Literary Gazette (Boston, New York)
U S M D R   United States Magazine and Democratic Review (Washington, D. C., 1837–1840; New York, 1841–1851)
W M R   Western Monthly Review (Cincinnati, Ohio)
W P L N L   Wiley & Putnam's Literary News-Letter, and Monthly Register of New Books, Foreign and American (New York)
W T C   The Publishers' and Stationers' Weekly Trade Circular (New York)
W V   Wöchentliches Verzeichnis der erschienenen und der vorbereiteten Neuigkeiten des deutschen Buchhandels (Leipzig)

Location Symbols

A A S	American Antiquarian Society, Worcester, Mass.
A H	Mr. Arthur Amory Houghton, Jr., Queenstown, Maryland.
A L	Mr. Arthur Lovell, Chicago, Illinois.
A M	The Adirondack Museum, Blue Mountain Lake, N. Y.
A N C	Academy of the New Church Library, Bryn Athyn, Pa.
A W	Mr. Ames W. Williams, Alexandria, Va.
B	Brown University Library, Providence, R. I.
B A	Boston Athenæum, Boston, Mass.
B D	Bowdoin College, Brunswick, Maine.
B M L	Boston Medical Library, Boston, Mass.
B Mu	The British Museum, London.
B P L	Boston Public Library, Boston, Mass.
C	Cornell University Library, Ithaca, N. Y.
C A W	The late Carroll A. Wilson, New York, N. Y.
C C	The Century Association Library, New York, N. Y.
C F	Concord Free Public Library, Concord, Mass.
C H	Craigie-Longfellow House, Cambridge, Mass.
Ch H S	Chicago Historical Society, Chicago, Illinois.
C Ho	Mr. Charles Honce, New York, N. Y.
C H S	Connecticut Historical Society, Hartford, Conn.
C O	Colby College, Waterville, Maine.
C P	Cleveland Public Library, Cleveland, Ohio.
C P L	Cambridge Public Library, Cambridge, Mass.
C S S	Charles Scribner's Sons, New York, N. Y.
C U	Columbia University Libraries, New York, N. Y.
C U A	Catholic University of America Libraries, Washington, D. C.
C W B	Mr. Clifton Waller Barrett, Charlottesville, Virginia.
D	Dartmouth College Library, Hanover, N. H.
De V	Mr. Thomas H. de Valcourt, Cambridge, Mass.
D P L	Detroit Public Library, Detroit, Mich.
D U	Duke University Libraries, Durham, N. C.
E M	Edward Morrill & Son, Boston, Mass.
E M O R Y	Emory University Library, Atlanta, Ga.
F C W	The late Frank C. Willson, Melrose, Mass.
F H B	The late Francis Hyde Bangs, Ogunquit, Maine.
F L P	The Free Library of Philadelphia, Philadelphia, Pa.
F M	The Rev. Frederick M. Meek, Chestnut Hill, Mass.
G	The Grosvenor Library, Buffalo, N. Y.

Gd	Goodspeed's Book Shop, Boston, Mass.
G E	The late Gabriel Engel, New York, N. Y.
Gi	Girard College Library, Philadelphia, Pa.
G M A	The late George Matthew Adams, New York, N. Y.
G O	Gilman's Old Books, Crompond, N. Y.
H	Harvard University Library, Cambridge, Mass.
H A	Haverford College Library, Haverford, Pa.
H C	Hamilton College Library, Clinton, N. Y.
H Cr	College of the Holy Cross, Dinand Memorial Library, Worcester, Mass.
H E H	Henry E. Huntington Library & Art Gallery, San Marino, Cal.
H M	Mr. Howard S. Mott, Sheffield, Mass.
H M L	Howard-Tilton Memorial Library, Tulane University, New Orleans, La.
H S P	The Historical Society of Pennsylvania, Philadelphia, Pa.
H U	Howard University Library, Washington, D. C.
H U C	Hebrew Union College Library, Cincinnati, Ohio.
I H S	Indiana State Historical Society, Indianapolis, Indiana.
I S L	Indiana State Library, Indianapolis, Indiana.
I U	Indiana University Library, Bloomington, Indiana.
J B	Mr. Jacob Blanck, Chestnut Hill, Mass.
J C	John Crerar Public Library, Chicago, Illinois.
J D G	The late John D. Gordan, New York, N. Y.
J F D	James F. Drake, Inc., New York, N. Y. *Note:* This distinguished firm of antiquarian booksellers ceased operation as of Dec. 31, 1965.
J H	Johns Hopkins University Libraries, Baltimore, Md.
J K L	The late J. K. Lilly, Indianapolis, Indiana.
J N	Mr. Jack Neiburg, Boston, Mass.
J N B	Mr. Jack N. Bartfield, New York, N. Y.
J S K	Mr. John S. Kebabian, New York, N. Y.
J T S	Jewish Theological Seminary of America Library, New York, N. Y.
J T W	The late John T. Winterich, Springfield, Mass.
J Z	Mr. Jacob Zeitlin, Los Angeles, Cal.
K	Kansas State Historical Society, Topeka, Kansas.
L B	Lever Brothers, Ltd., Port Sunlight, Cheshire, England.
L C	Library of Congress, Washington, D. C.
L C P	Library Company of Philadelphia, Philadelphia, Pa.
L S	Stanford University Libraries, Palo Alto, Cal.
L W C	Lloyd W. Currey, Elizabethtown, N. Y.
Md H S	Maryland Historical Society, Baltimore, Md.
M F	The late Mason Foley, Hingham, Mass.
M H	Mr. Maxwell Hunley, Beverly Hills, Cal.
M H S	Massachusetts Historical Society Library, Boston, Mass.
M I C	Midwest Inter-Library Center, Chicago, Illinois.
Mi H S	Minnesota Historical Society, St. Paul, Minn.
M L	The Pierpont Morgan Library, New York, N. Y.
M S L	Massachusetts State Library, Boston, Mass.

N	Newberry Library, Chicago, Ill.
N H S L	New Hampshire State Library, Concord, N. H.
N J H	The New Jersey Historical Society, Newark, N. J.
N K	Mr. Norman Kane, Pottstown, Pa.
N L M	The National Library of Medicine, Washington, D. C.
N Y H S	The New-York Historical Society Library, New York, N. Y.
N Y P L	The New York Public Library, New York, N. Y.
N Y S	New York State Library, Albany, N. Y.
N Y S L	New York Society Library, New York, N. Y.
N Y U	New York University Libraries, New York, N. Y.
O	Oberlin College Library, Oberlin, Ohio.
O H S	The Ohio Historical Society, Columbus, Ohio.
O S	Ohio State University Libraries, Columbus, Ohio.
P	Princeton University Library, Princeton, N. J.
P B	Peabody Institute Library, Baltimore, Md.
P D H	Mr. Parkman D. Howe, Needham, Mass.
P H S L	Presbyterian Historical Society, Philadelphia, Pa.
P L	Portland Public Library, Portland, Me.
P P L	Providence Public Library, Providence, R. I.
P S U	Pennsylvania State University Library, University Park, Pa.
R	Rutgers University Library, New Brunswick, N. J.
R B	Mr. Robert K. Black, Upper Montclair, N. J.
R E S	Mr. Roger E. Stoddard, Concord, Mass.
R G	The late Rodman Gilder, New York, N. Y.
R I H	Rhode Island Historical Society Library, Providence, R. I.
R L	Redwood Library & Athenaeum, Newport, R. I.
R L W	Prof. Robert Lee Wolff, Cambridge, Mass.
S	Swarthmore College Library, Swarthmore, Pa.
S G	Seven Gables Bookshop, New York, N. Y.
S M	Smithsonian Institution Libraries, Washington, D. C.
S N S	Mr. Simon Nowell-Smith, Headington, Oxford, England.
S R L	Sondley Reference Library, Pack Memorial Public Library, Asheville, N. C.
S U I	State University of Iowa Libraries, Iowa City, Iowa.
S W J	The late Stuart W. Jackson, Gloucester, Va.
U C	University of Chicago Library, Chicago, Ill.
U C B	University of California, General Library, Berkeley, Cal.
U C L A	University of California at Los Angeles, University Library, Los Angeles, Cal.
U G	The University of Georgia Libraries, Athens, Ga.
U I	University of Illinois Library, Urbana, Illinois.
U K	University of Kentucky Libraries, Lexington, Ky.
U Mi	University of Michigan Library, Ann Arbor, Mich.
U Mn	University of Minnesota Library, Minneapolis, Minn.
U N B	University of New Brunswick Library, Fredericton, New Brunswick, Canada.

U N C	University of North Carolina Library, Chapel Hill, N. C.
U P	University of Pennsylvania Library, Philadelphia, Pa.
U R	University of Rochester Library, Rochester, N. Y.
U S C	University of Southern California Library, Los Angeles, Cal.
U S Ca	University of South Carolina, Columbia, S. C.
U S D A	United States Department of Agriculture Library, Washington, D. C.
U T	The University of Texas, Austin, Texas.
U Tn	University of Tennessee, James D. Hoskins Library, Knoxville, Tenn.
U V	University of Virginia, Alderman Library, Charlottesville, Va.
U W	University of Wisconsin, General Library, Madison, Wis.
U Wa	University of Washington, Seattle, Wash.
V	Vassar College Library, Poughkeepsie, N. Y.
V P	The late Nathan Van Patten, Palo Alto, Cal.
V S L	Virginia State Library, Richmond, Va.
W	Wellesley College Library, Wellesley, Mass.
W C	Williams College Library, Williamstown, Mass.
W C L	Washington Cathedral Library, Washington, D. C.
W F P L	Worcester Free Public Library, Worcester, Mass.
Wh	Wheaton College Library, Norton, Mass.
W H C	Mr. Warder H. Cadbury, Albany, N. Y.
W L P	Mr. Walter L. Pforzheimer, Washington, D. C.
W M G	Mr. William M. Gibson, Upper Montclair, N. J.
W R	Western Reserve University Libraries, Cleveland, Ohio.
W S L	Washington University Libraries, St. Louis, Mo.
W U L	Wesleyan University, Olin Memorial Library, Middletown, Conn.
Y	Yale University Library, New Haven, Conn.

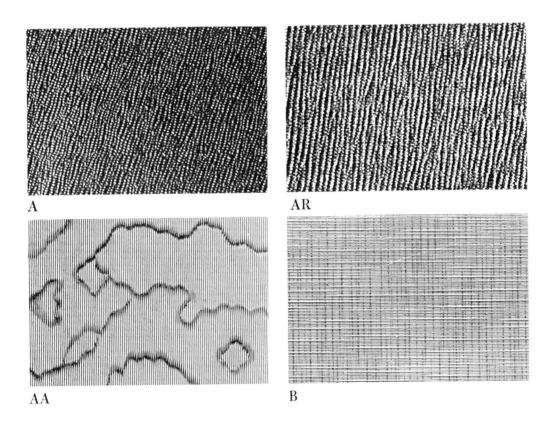

A

AR

AA

B

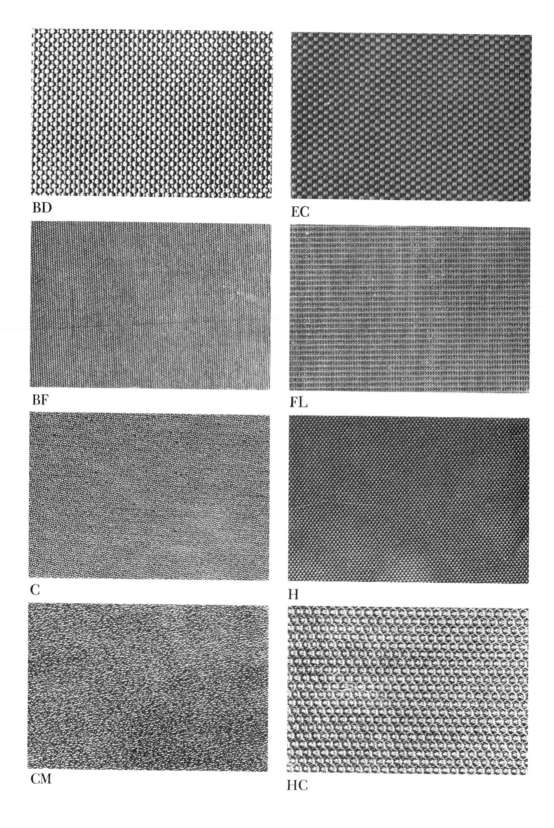

BD

EC

BF

FL

C

H

CM

HC

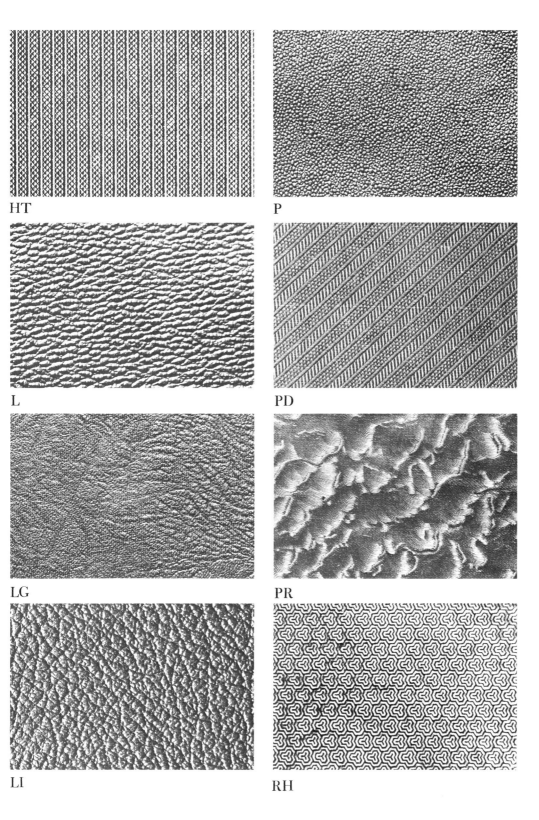

HT

P

L

PD

LG

PR

LI

RH

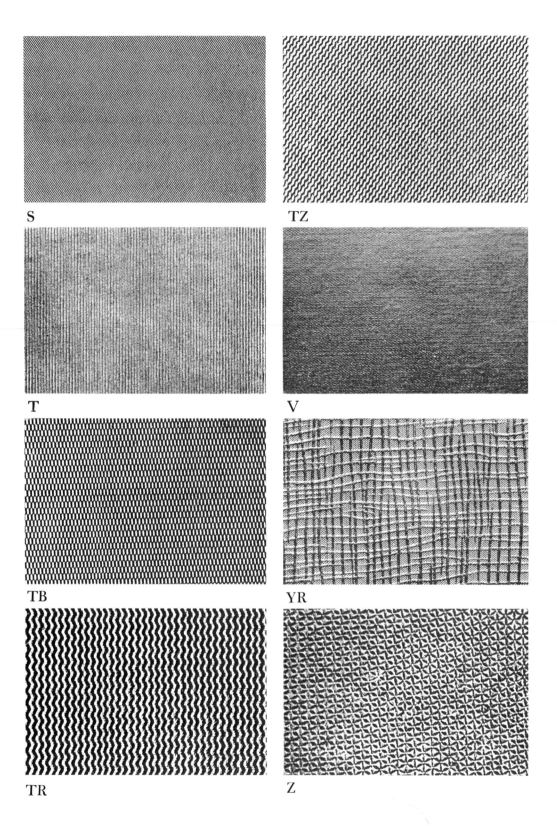

S

TZ

T

V

TB

YR

TR

Z

AUGUSTUS BALDWIN LONGSTREET

1 7 9 0 – 1 8 7 0

12944. ... AN ORATION, DELIVERED BE-FORE THE DEMOSTHENIAN & PHI KAPPA SOCIETIES, OF THE UNIVER-SITY OF GEORGIA, AT THE COM-MENCEMENT OF AUGUST, 1831 ...

AUGUSTA: PRINTED BY W. LAWSON. 1831.

⟨1⟩-23. $7\frac{11}{16}''$ × $4\frac{5}{8}''$.

Signature collation in doubt.

Issued in printed self-wrapper?

DU

12945. AN ORATION DELIVERED IN THE CITY OF AUGUSTA, ON THE CENTENNI-AL BIRTH-DAY OF GEORGE WASHING-TON ...

AUGUSTA: PRINTED BY W. LAWSON. 1832.

⟨1⟩-23. $7\frac{3}{4}''$ scant × $4\frac{7}{8}''$.

⟨-⟩⁴, A², B⁴, B2².

Issued in printed self-wrapper?

HEH

12946. GEORGIA SCENES, CHARACTERS, INCIDENTS, &C. IN THE FIRST HALF CENTURY OF THE REPUBLIC. BY A NATIVE GEORGIAN.

AUGUSTA: PRINTED AT THE S. R. SENTINEL OFFICE. 1835.

⟨i⟩-iv, ⟨5⟩-235. $7\frac{1}{4}''$ × $4\frac{3}{8}''$.

⟨-⟩², a-s⁶, t².

Tan paper boards, purple muslin shelfback, the purple usually faded to brown. Printed paper label on spine. Flyleaves.

In all examined copies: *Georiag* for *Georgia*, in the running head, pp. 73, 87.

Reviewed SLM March, 1836.

There were several reprintings (ignored in this list) from the same plates with the statement *Second Edition* on the title-page. The first of these noted by BAL was issued by Harper & Brothers, New York, 1840; deposited for copyright May 22,

1840. Other so-called *Second Editions* were issued with altered imprints and appropriate dates, but the copyright notice is invariably dated 1840. The latest Harper printing noted is dated 1897. Another reprint was issued under date 1894 by J. O. Culpepper, Quitman, Georgia; deposited July 6, 1894.

H   UV   Y

12947. ADDRESS DELIVERED BEFORE THE FACULTY AND STUDENTS OF EMORY COLLEGE, OXFORD, GA. BY AUGUSTUS B. LONGSTREET, PRESIDENT OF THAT INSTITUTION, AT HIS INAUGURATION, 10TH FEBRUARY, 1840.

AUYUSTA, ⟨*sic*⟩ GA. W. T. THOMPSON, PRINTER. 1840

⟨1⟩-22, blank leaf. $7\frac{5}{16}''$ × $4\frac{1}{2}''$.

⟨1-2⁶⟩.

Issued in printed self-wrapper?

B   Y

12948. EULOGY ON THE LIFE AND PUBLIC SERVICES OF THE LATE REV. MOSES WADDEL, D. D., FORMERLY PRESIDENT OF THE UNIVERSITY OF GEORGIA DELIVERED IN THE COLLEGE CHAPEL, ON THE THIRD DAY OF AUGUST, 1841 ...

AUGUSTA: PUBLISHED AT THE CHRONICLE AND SENTINEL OFFICE. MDCCCXLI.

⟨1⟩-18. $9''$ × $5\frac{3}{16}''$.

⟨1⟩-2⁴, 3¹.

Issued in printed self-wrapper?

8-line errata notice inserted.

DU

12949. LETTERS ON THE EPISTLE OF PAUL TO PHILEMON, OR THE CONNEC-TION OF APOSTOLICAL CHRISTIANITY WITH SLAVERY ...

CHARLESTON, S.C. PRINTED BY B. JENKINS, 100 HAYNE-STREET. 1845.

⟨1⟩-47. 8⅝″ × 5⁷⁄₁₆″.

⟨1-2⟩, 3⁸.

Probably issued in printed paper wrapper.

LC Y

12950. A VOICE FROM THE SOUTH: COMPRISING LETTERS FROM GEORGIA TO MASSACHUSETTS, AND TO THE SOUTHERN STATES. WITH AN APPENDIX CONTAINING AN ARTICLE FROM THE CHARLESTON MERCURY ON THE WILMOT PROVISO...

BALTIMORE: WESTERN CONTINENT PRESS. 1847.

Anonymous.

⟨1⟩-72. 9⅞″ full × 6³⁄₁₆″.

⟨1-4⁸, 5⁴⟩.

Printed paper wrapper, both blue and yellow noted.

According to Wade, p. 285, there were "eight editions" by 1849. BAL has noted at least two printings issued under date 1847. The presumed first was issued in a printed paper wrapper dated 1847; the presumed second printing was issued in a printed paper wrapper dated 1848. The 1848 wrapper has at the top of the front: EIGHTH EDITION. Stripped of the wrapper one printing may be taken for the other; both are from the same setting, both are dated 1847. However, certain variations are present indicating re-imposition and some rearrangement of the types. The following is sufficient for identification:

ORIGINAL PRINTING

The letterpress on the title-page is set 6³¹⁄₃₂″ deep. The letter A (in AND, line 6 of the title-page) is set below the letters MA (in MASSACHUSETTS).

P. 11: Lines 24-30 are not pied.

LATER PRINTING

The letterpress on the title-page is set 6⅞″ deep. The letter A (in AND, line 6 of the title-page) is set below the M (in MASSACHUSETTS)

P. 11: The endings of lines 24-30 are pied.

Listed NAR Oct. 1847.

H (both)   LC (both)   Y (both)

12951. ... THE LETTERS OF PRESIDENT LONGSTREET ... THE ALIEN AND SEDITION LAWS AND VIRGINIA AND KENTUCKY RESOLUTIONS OF 1798 AND 1799 ... THE DEMOCRATIC PLATFORM OF 1852 ...

⟨PRINTED AT THE OFFICE OF THE LOUISIANA COURIER, CUSTOMHOUSE STREET, NEW ORLEANS, n.d., 1852?⟩

The above on p. ⟨1⟩. Imprint at foot of p. 16. At head of title: *Campaign Document No. 2, Issued by the Democratic State Central Committee of Louisiana* ...

⟨1⟩-16. 8⅞″ × 5¹¹⁄₁₆″.

⟨-⟩⁸.

Printed self-wrapper? Printed paper wrapper?

LC

12952. KNOW NOTHINGISM UNVEILED. LETTER OF JUDGE A. B. LONGSTREET, OF MISSISSIPPI, ADDRESSED TO REV. WILLIAM WINANS, IN REPLY TO A COMMUNICATION PUBLISHED BY HIM IN THE NATCHEZ (MISSISSIPPI) COURIER, AND ADDRESSED TO JUDGE LONGSTREET, ON THE SUBJECT OF KNOW NOTHINGISM. UNIVERSITY OF MISSISSIPPI, DECEMBER 19, 1855...

⟨WASHINGTON, D. C., 1855?⟩

Caption-title. The above at head of p. ⟨1⟩.

⟨1⟩-8. 9¹⁄₁₆″ × 5¹⁵⁄₁₆″.

⟨-⟩⁴.

Single cut sheet folded to eight pages.

Below text, p. 8: *Printed at the Office of the Congressional Globe.*

H   LC   NYPL

12953. Annals of the American Pulpit; or Commemorative Notices of Distinguished American Clergymen ... by William B. Sprague, D. D. Volume IV.

New York: Robert Carter & Brothers, 530 Broadway. 1858.

Cloth?

"Moses Waddel, D. D. 1792–1840," pp. 63-67. Being a letter written at the request of the editor, dated *Jackson, La., May 1, 1849.*

H

12954. FAST-DAY SERMON: DELIVERED IN THE WASHINGTON STREET METHODIST EPISCOPAL CHURCH, COLUMBIA, S.C., JUNE 13, 1861 ...

COLUMBIA, S.C.: TOWNSEND & NORTH, PUBLISHERS. 1861.

⟨1⟩-14, blank leaf. 8¹³⁄₁₆″ × 5¹¹⁄₁₆″.

⟨1⟩-2⁴.

Printed blue paper wrapper.

LC

12955. SHALL SOUTH CAROLINA BEGIN THE WAR? . . .

⟨n.p., n.d., CHARLESTON, S. C., 1861⟩

Not seen. Entry on the basis of a Xerox copy and correspondence with UG. Place and date according to Richard Harwell: *More Confederate Imprints*, 1957, entry No. 1074.

Caption-title. The above on p. ⟨1⟩.

⟨1⟩-4. 8½″ × 5½″.

Single cut sheet folded to make four pages.

UG

12956. MASTER WILLIAM MITTEN: OR, A YOUTH OF BRILLIANT TALENTS, WHO WAS RUINED BY BAD LUCK. BY THE AUTHOR OF "GEORGIA SCENES."

MACON, GA.: BURKE, BOYKIN & COMPANY. 1864.

⟨1⟩-239. 8⁷⁄₁₆″ × 5⅛″.

⟨A⟩², B-O⁸, P⁶.

Printed pale tan paper wrapper.

LC UV Y

12957. VALUABLE SUGGESTIONS ADDRESSED TO THE SOLDIERS OF THE CONFEDERATE STATES . . .

⟨MACON, GA.: THE SOLDIERS' TRACT ASSOCIATION OF THE M.E. CHURCH, SOUTH, n.d., 1864?⟩

Caption-title. The above on p. ⟨1⟩. Imprint at foot of p. 16.

⟨1⟩-16. 5⁵⁄₁₆″ × 3½″ scant.

⟨-⟩⁸.

Printed self-wrapper.

Note: Also appears in, probably reprinted: *The Rebellion Record: A Diary of American Events . . .*, edited by Frank Moore, Vol. 8, pp. 433-437. For fuller information see entry No. 11531.

DU

12958. Judge Longstreet. A Life Sketch. By Bishop O. P. Fitzgerald . . .

Printed for the Author. Publishing House of the Methodist Episcopal Church, South. Barbee & Smith, Agents, Nashville, Tenn. 1891.

Contains many letters by Longstreet; and earliest located publication of "Darby Anvil," pp. 211-241. Also contains the following material by Longstreet here reprinted: "Ned Brace," otherwise "A Native Georgian"; and, "The Debating Society," "The Song," "The Shooting-Match."

Y

12959. STORIES WITH A MORAL HUMOROUS AND DESCRIPTIVE OF SOUTHERN LIFE A CENTURY AGO BY AUGUSTUS B. LONGSTREET . . . COMPILED AND EDITED BY FITZ R. LONGSTREET

1912 THE JOHN C. WINSTON COMPANY PHILADELPHIA

⟨1⟩-396, 2 blank leaves. Paper watermarked *Chester Wove M. & G. Co.* 7½″ × 5″.

⟨1⟩-9, ⟨10⟩, 11-20, ⟨21⟩-22, ⟨23⟩, 24-25⁸.

T cloth: brown.

". . . The following sketches are presented by the compiler after a tedious research in the old literary publications of prominence during the antebellum period, excepting one or two from *Georgia Scenes*, that are brought in to complete the series . . ."---p. ⟨5⟩.

Deposited June 11, 1912.

H NYPL

REPRINTS

The following publications contain material by Longstreet reprinted from other books.

The Lady's Annual Register and Housewife's Memorandum-Book, for 1838. By Caroline Gilman.

Boston: Published by T. H. Carter, 147 Washington Street. ⟨1837⟩

Printed paper boards, cloth shelfback.

Half-Hours with the Best Humorous Authors. Selected and Arranged by Charles Morris . . .

Philadelphia: J. B. Lippincott Company. 1889.

4 Vols.

A Pocket Book of the Early American Humorists Selections from the Best Writings of Benjamin Franklin, Joseph C. Neal . . . and Others

Boston Small, Maynard & Company 1907

Library of Southern Literature . . .

. . . New Orleans Atlanta Dallas ⟨1909–1913⟩

For fuller description see No. 7164.

REFERENCES AND ANA

Patriotic Effusions; by Bob Short.

New-York: Published by L. and F. Lockwood, No. 154 Broadway. J. & J. Harper, Printers. 1819.

Printed tan paper wrapper.

Not by Longstreet. "For many years Longstreet was thought to have been the author of *The*

Olio, because *The Olio* was written 'by the author of *Patriotic Effusions*' . . . and *Patriotic Effusions* was written by *Bob Short*———and Longstreet used the pseudonym *Bob Short* in his newspaper, the Augusta *States Rights Sentinel* in the 1830's, and also was nicknamed *Bob Short* when president of Emory College, at Oxford, Ga. Actually, Longstreet probably never heard of either volume, both having been written by William B. Gilley, of New York."———*Georgia 1800–1900 A Series of Selections* . . . , Atlanta Public Library ⟨1955⟩, p. 85.

"Occasionally he would write poetry. This interest of his, his use of the pseudonym *Bob Short*, and his later association with the Harpers in New York apparently connect him with a slight book of verse, *Patriotic Effusions by Bob Short*, published in New York in 1819. The pseudonym is indisputable. In the 1830's Longstreet's newspaper carried over a long period of time a series of comments by a Bob Short whose identity with the editor of the paper ⟨*i.e.*, Longstreet⟩ was generally acknowledged; later, while Longstreet was president of Emory College, it was a humored joke in the college community to refer to him as Bob Short, it being vaguely believed to this day by one who can remember old times in Oxford (where Emory College was situated) that the President assumed this name on becoming a member of some secret society or other which required its members upon entering to give themselves new identifications.

"But Edward Mayes, Longstreet's grandson-in-law and literary executor, was very definite in his feeling that Longstreet had no connection with the *Effusions*; never had the Judge mentioned to him any such work . . . Longstreet's failure to mention the *Effusions* was probably due to the fact that he died in happy ignorance of that book's existence.

"In 1823 there appeared in New York *The Olio*, a collection of verse similar in physical make-up, in spirit, and in technique to the *Effusions*———published, indeed, 'By the author of *Patriotic Effusions*.' . . . It is stated that some of the 'pieces' in *The Olio* 'were written on the other side of the Atlantic . . .' Longstreet did not see Europe until 1860 . . ."———Wade, pp. 89–90.

Franklin's Way to Wealth; or, "Poor Richard Improved, &c." A New Edition: Corrected and Enlarged by Bob Short . . .

London: Printed by W. Darton, Jun. 58, Holborn Hill. ⟨1819⟩

Printed paper wrapper. For comment on *Bob Short* see preceding entry.

The Olio, Being a Collection of Poems, Fables, Epigrams, &c. Including Tributes to the Memory of Lieut. Allen, The Hon. Wm. W. Van Ness, and the Hon. Brockholst Livingston. By the the ⟨*sic*⟩ Author of "Patriotic Effusions," &c.

New-York: Published by the Author. 1823.

Paper boards. For comment see *Patriotic Effusions*, 1819, above.

Hoyle Abridged. A Treatise on Back-Gammon; or Short Rules for Short Memories, with the Laws of the Game. Adapted Either for the Head or Pocket. By Bob Short . . . First American Edition.

New-York. Published by Caleb Barlett, No. 76 Bowery. 1828.

Paper wrapper, printed paper label on front. For comment on *Bob Short* see *Patriotic Effusions*, 1819, above.

The Olio: Collected by a Literary Traveller . . .

Boston. 1833.

Decorated paper boards. Sometimes attributed to Longstreet, possibly on the basis of *The Olio*, 1823, above.

In Memoriam. Rev. Bishop James Osgood Andrew . . . Rev. Augustus B. Longstreet . . . Rev. William A. Smith . . .

New York: Compiled and Published by Wm. T. Smithson. 1871.

Printed paper wrapper. Two issues noted: 1: The poems on pp. 33-36 are credited to *Sallie A. Broek;* 2: To *Sallie A. Brock*.

Judge Longstreet . . . by Bishop O. P. Fitzgerald . . .

. . . Nashville, Tenn. 1891.

For fuller entry see above in main list.

Augustus Baldwin Longstreet A Study of the Development of Culture in the South by John Donald Wade

New York The Macmillan Company 1924 . . .

Address Delivered at His Inauguration, 10th February, 1840 by Augustus B. Longstreet . . . Edited by Judson C. Ward, Jr. . . .

The Library Emory University Atlanta, Georgia 1955

Printed paper wrapper. *Emory University Publications Sources & Reprints*, Series IX, No. 2. See in main list for a description of the first printing of this address.

Georgia 1800–1900 A Series of Selections from the Georgiana Library of a Private Collector Public Exhibition

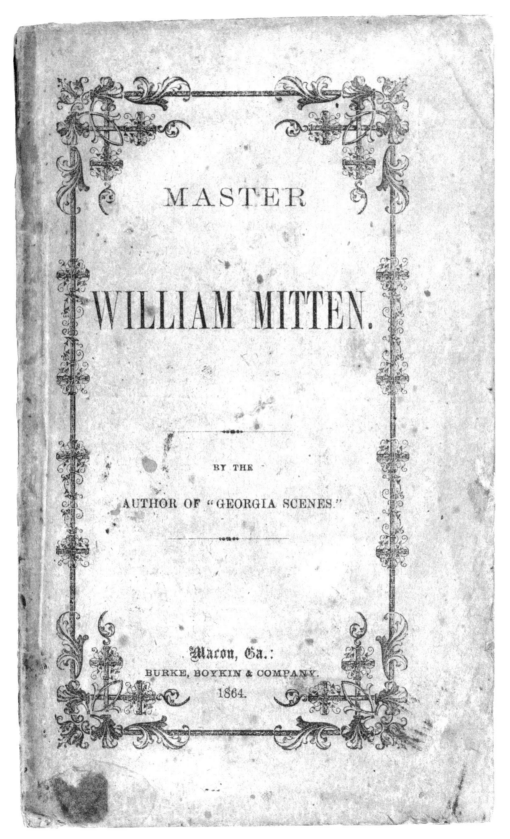

MASTER

WILLIAM MITTEN.

BY THE

AUTHOR OF "GEORGIA SCENES."

Macon, Ga.:
BURKE, BOYKIN & COMPANY.
1864.

Atlanta Public Library ⟨1955⟩

Cover-title. Printed paper wrapper. Paged: ⟨81⟩-98. A bibliography of Longstreet. *Series Four Augustus Baldwin Longstreet: Pater Litterarum* ---p. ⟨85⟩.

Note: Fitzgerald, p. 164, credits the following publications to Longstreet; further information wanting; *Letters to Clergymen of the Northern Methodist Church;* and, *A Review of the Decision of the Supreme Court in the Case of McCulloch vs. the State of Maryland.*

AMY LOWELL

(A Dreamer, A Poker of Fun)

1 8 7 4 - 1 9 2 5

12960. DREAM DROPS OR STORIES FROM FAIRY LAND BY A DREAMER

PRINTED FOR THE AUTHOR BY CUPPLES AND HURD BOSTON ⟨n.d., 1887⟩

Title-page in red and black. In collaboration with Amy Lowell's mother, Katherine Bigelow Lawrence Lowell, and sister, Elizabeth Lowell.

⟨i⟩-iv, ⟨1⟩-118, blank leaf. Laid paper. $7\frac{1}{8}$" × $4\frac{3}{4}$" (in wrapper); $6\frac{13}{16}$" × $4\frac{5}{8}$" (in cloth). The following leaves are cancels: pp. ⟨iii⟩-iv, ⟨5⟩-6, 27-28, 89-⟨90⟩, 99-102; pp. 99-102 are conjugate leaves.

⟨1², 2-8⁸, 9⁴⟩. The following leaves are cancels: ⟨1⟩₂, ⟨2⟩₃, ⟨3⟩₆, ⟨7⟩₅, ⟨8⟩₂₋₃. Leaves ⟨8⟩₂₋₃ are conjugates.

Note: In a copy in UV leaves ⟨3⟩₄₋₅ are not conjugates. Significance if any not known; possibly nothing more than a repair.

Printed mustard-yellow laid paper wrapper folded over white paper wrapper. Also issued in white muslin decorated in colors with a floral pattern; white vellum shelfback; top edges gilt; end papers of laid paper watermarked *Derby Mills Royal Linen.*

A NOTE ON FLYLEAVES

Copies in cloth noted as follows; no sequence is suggested, the designations are completely arbitrary.

A: No flyleaves.

B: At front a gathering of four leaves of laid paper watermarked *Derby Mills Royal Linen,* with one leaf used as the pastedown, the others present as free leaves. No flyleaves at back.

C: At front and at back a gathering of four leaves of white wove paper, with one leaf used as the pastedown, the others present as free leaves.

A single copy in wrapper has been noted as follows: A gathering of four leaves of wove paper at front, all four leaves being free. At back: A single flyleaf of wove paper; and, a true end paper of white wove paper. Usually: No end papers; quadruple flyleaves or none.

"... The books were delivered on December 19 and 20 (250 copies, 99 bound in half white and half flowered cloth, the rest in brown paper) ..."---Damon, p. 75.

AAS B BA H LC UV Y

Weeping Pierrot and Laughing Pierrot ...

Boston ... New York ... Paris ... ⟨1899⟩

See below under 1914.

12961. ... TWO LYRICS BY AMY LOWELL FOR A SOLO VOICE WITH PIANO ACCOMPANIMENT 1. THE SEA-SHELL ...

NEW YORK: G. SCHIRMER BOSTON: THE BOSTON MUSIC CO. LONDON: SCHOTT & CO. ⟨1911⟩

Sheet music. Cover-title. Cover printed in blue and black. Plate numbers: 22885 (on p. ⟨1⟩), 22885C (on p. 2), 22885 (on pp. 3-4).

At head of title: *Carl Engel*

Note: A reprint has been seen with the front printed in green only, not in blue and black; imprinted: *G. Schirmer, Inc., New York* ⟨1911⟩.

Collected in *A Dome of Many-Coloured Glass,* 1912.

Deposited Nov. 7, 1911.

H (1st) LC (1st) Y (reprint)

12962. ... TWO LYRICS BY AMY LOWELL FOR A SOLO VOICE WITH PIANO ACCOMPANIMENT ... 2. THE TROUT ...

NEW YORK: G. SCHIRMER BOSTON: THE BOSTON MUSIC CO. LONDON: SCHOTT & CO. ⟨1911⟩

Sheet music. Cover-title. Cover printed in blue and black. Plate numbers: 22886 (on p. ⟨1⟩), 22886C (on p. 2), 22886 (on pp. 3-4).

At head of title: *Carl Engel*

AMY LOWELL
Entry No. 12960
(Harvard University Library)

Query: Does this occur in a reprint with front cover printed in green only?

Collected in *A Dome of Many-Coloured Glass*, 1912.

Deposited Nov. 7, 1911.

AAS BPL H Y

12963. A DOME OF MANY-COLOURED GLASS . . .

BOSTON AND NEW YORK   HOUGHTON MIFFLIN COMPANY 1912

⟨i⟩-⟨xii⟩, ⟨1⟩-139; printer's imprint, p. ⟨140⟩.

7¹⁄₁₆″ × 4³⁄₈″. Laid paper.

⟨1-9⁸, 10⁴⟩.

Gray-blue laid paper boards sides, tan V cloth shelf back. Printed paper labels. White laid end papers. Also issued in leather?

On copyright page: *Published October 1912*

Noted for *today* PW Oct. 26, 1912. BPL copy received Oct. 28, 1912. Deposited Oct. 30, 1912. Listed PW Nov. 9, 1912. The London (Constable) edition listed Bkr April 18, 1913. According to the publisher's records 530 copies were printed Oct. 14, 1912; 25 copies bound Oct. 18, 1912; 497 copies bound Oct. 23, 1912.

AAS B BPL H UV Y

12964. BALLADS FOR SALE   FRESH, NEW BALLADS, WITH THE INK SCARCE DRIED UPON THEM . . .

SUNWISE TURN BROADSIDE NO. 1 ⟨n.p., New York, n.d., 1913? 1914?⟩

Single cut sheet of laid paper. 14½″ scant × 8″.

Printed on recto only. The circular vignette at the head of sheet occurs either plain; or, colored by hand.

Collected in *Ballads for Sale*, 1927.

According to a note from Witter Bynner (Feb. 22, 1962, in H) *Sunwise Turn Broadside No. 5* was issued in New York in 1913 or 1914. A copy of No. 1, the Lowell broadside, was received by H on Jan. 3, 1917.

H NYPL

12965. Des Imagistes An Anthology ⟨floret⟩

New York Albert and Charles Boni 96 Fifth Avenue 1914

Edited by Ezra Pound.

"In a Garden," p. 38. Collected in *Sword Blades and Poppy Seed*, 1914 (October).

Inserted at the front of some copies is a printed slip: *The following poems, contained in DES IMAGISTES, were first printed in POETRY, A MAGAZINE OF VERSE . . . and are here reprinted by permission . . .*

Note: The publication history of this book is such that the following account is all but imperative; the sequence is as follows; for a fuller discussion of these issues see Donald C. Gallup's *A Bibliography of Ezra Pound*, London, 1969, pp. 139-142.

PERIODICAL PUBLICATION

Des Imagistes An Anthology ⟨*The Glebe* device⟩

New York Albert and Charles Boni 96 Fifth Avenue 1914

Printed gray-green paper wrapper. Front: *Des Imagistes   The Glebe Volume I Number 5 February 1914* . . .

Gallup No. C125.

FIRST BOOK PUBLICATION

Des Imagistes An Anthology ⟨floret⟩

New York Albert and Charles Boni 96 Fifth Avenue 1914

See at head of this entry for fuller description. Bound in blue V cloth. Printed from the setting of *The Glebe* with altered title-page. Listed PW March 28, 1914. Deposited Aug. 1, 1914. Published March 2, 1914, according to Gallup, p. 140.

Gallup No. B7.

LONDON ISSUE

Des Imagistes An Anthology ⟨floret⟩

London: The Poetry Bookshop 35 Devonshire Street Theobalds Rd., W.C. ⟨lazy O⟩ New York Albert and Charles Boni 96 Fifth Avenue 1914

The London imprint appears to have been inserted after the printing of the sheets. Printed green paper boards. Sheets of the *First Book Publication* with the *Poetry Bookshop* imprint added to the title-page and to p. ⟨1⟩. *Note:* Also occurs without the lazy O present in the imprint. Listed Bkr April 24, 1914.

Gallup No. B7b.

SHAY REISSUE A

Des Imagistes An Anthology

New York Frank Shay, Publisher 1917

Sheets of *The Glebe* with cancel title-page. Issued in printed gray-blue paper wrapper. Listed PW Nov. 24, 1917.

Gallup No. B7c.

SHAY REISSUE B

Des Imagistes An Anthology ⟨*The Glebe* device⟩

New York Albert and Charles Boni 96 Fifth Avenue 1914

Sheets of *The Glebe* stripped of the original paper wrapper and reissued (probably by Frank Shay) in orange on white paper wrapper. Imprinted on outer front: *Des Imagistes   An Anthology*

Gallup B7d.

BA (*First Book Publication*) H (*London Issue*) Y (*all forms*)

12966. Weeping Pierrot and Laughing Pierrot . . . A Comedy with Music in One Act French Text by Edmond Rostand English Version by Amy Lowell Music by Jean Hubert Vocal Score with Dialogue . . .

Boston, Mass. The Boston Music Company New York: G. Schirmer, Inc. Paris: Heugel & Cie. *Copyright, 1914, by Heugel & Cie.*

Note: The material italicised is rubber-stamped and is not always present. When present it appears on either the title-page, the front wrapper, or the verso of the title-page.

⟨i-ii⟩, ⟨i⟩-⟨xviii⟩, ⟨1⟩-89; advertisement, p. ⟨90⟩; blank leaf. 11″ × 7½″.

Plate number 4048.

Printed cream paper wrapper.

Printed copyright notice present, dated 1899, in the name of Heugel & Cie.

On some copies the price, *n. 1.25*, has been erased from the title-page and the front wrapper.

Deposited Sept. 17, 1914.

H LC NYPL Y

12967. SWORD BLADES AND POPPY SEED . . .

NEW YORK THE MACMILLAN COMPANY 1914 ALL RIGHTS RESERVED

⟨i⟩-xviii, ⟨1⟩-246; publisher's catalog, pp. ⟨247–252⟩; blank leaf. Laid paper. 7¹⁄₁₆″ × 4³⁄₈″.

⟨1-17⁸⟩.

Green-gray laid paper boards sides, green V cloth shelf back. Paper labels. White laid end papers. Also issued in leather?

On copyright page: *Published October, 1914.*

The author's personal copy (in H) inscribed by her Sept. 22, 1914. Deposited Oct. 1, 1914. A copy in UV inscribed by the author Oct. 10, 1914. Listed PW Oct. 17, 1914. BA copy received Oct. 21, 1914. Listed Bkr Nov. 13, 1914.

AAS B H UV

12968. Some Imagist Poets An Anthology

Boston and New York Houghton Mifflin Company The Riverside Press Cambridge 1915

Printed paper wrapper.

Two editions noted:

1 : *Bibliography*, p. ⟨95⟩.

2 : *Bibliography*, pp. 95-⟨96⟩.

The London (Constable) edition made up of sheets of the first American edition with cancel title-page.

"Venus Transiens," pp. 81-⟨82⟩; "The Travelling Bear," pp. 83-⟨84⟩; "The Letter," p. 85; "Grotesque," p. 86; "Bullion," p. 87; "Solitaire," p. 88; all the preceding collected in *Pictures of the Floating World*, 1919. "The Bombardment," pp. 89-⟨92⟩, collected in *Men, Women and Ghosts*, 1916.

On copyright page: *Published April 1915*

Deposited April 19, 1915. Listed Bkr (Constable) June 11, 1915.

H (1st) Y (both)

12969. SIX FRENCH POETS STUDIES IN CONTEMPORARY LITERATURE . . .

NEW YORK THE MACMILLAN COMPANY 1915 ALL RIGHTS RESERVED

⟨i⟩-⟨xiv⟩, ⟨1⟩-488; publisher's catalog, pp. ⟨489-494⟩; 2 blank leaves. Laid paper. Frontispiece and 5 plates inserted. 8⅝″ × 5⅞″.

⟨1-32⁸⟩. *Signed:* ⟨A⟩⁸, ⟨B⟩⁷, C-D, ⟨E⟩, F-I, K-N, ⟨O⟩, P-U, X-Z, 2A-2D, ⟨2E⟩, 2F-2I⁸, ⟨2K⟩¹.

V cloth: blue.

Note: In some copies a page of errata (30 lines) inserted between pp. ⟨xiv-xv⟩. The corrections indicated have been seen in the May, 1916 (so marked) printing.

On copyright page: *Published November, 1915.*

The author's personal copy (in H) inscribed by her Nov. 10, 1915. Deposited Nov. 26, 1915. Listed PW Dec. 11, 1915. The London printing advertised as *ready* Ath Jan. 1916; listed Bkr Feb. 1916.

AAS BA H

12970. Anthology of Magazine Verse for 1915 . . . Edited by William Stanley Braithwaite

New York Gomme & Marshall 1915

Reprint save for "Patterns," pp. 22-25; and, "The Fruit Shop," pp. 145-150; both collected in *Men, Women and Ghosts*, 1916.

For fuller description see entry No. 11107.

12971. Some Imagist Poets 1916 An Annual Anthology

Boston and New York   Houghton Mifflin
Company   The Riverside Press   Cambridge
1916

Printed wrapper.

Reprint save for "Spring Day," pp. 82-⟨86⟩; and,
"Stravinsky's Three Pieces, 'Grotesques' for
String Quartet," pp. 87-⟨91⟩; both collected in
Men, Women and Ghosts, 1916 (October).

On copyright page: *Published May 1916*

A copy in UV presented to William Stanley Braith-
waite May 9, 1916. Deposited May 12, 1916.
The London (Constable) edition advertised in
Bkr Oct. 1916; listed by Ath Jan. 1917.

H NYPL UV

12972. MEN, WOMEN AND GHOSTS...

NEW YORK THE MACMILLAN COMPANY 1916 ALL
RIGHTS RESERVED

⟨i⟩-⟨xvi⟩, ⟨1⟩-363; blank, p. ⟨364⟩; publisher's
catalog, pp. ⟨365-368⟩; plus: ⟨369-370⟩. Laid
paper. 7″ scant × 4⅜″. *Note:* Pp. ⟨369-370⟩ are
sometimes reversed, producing the following
states of no known sequence, if any:

STATE A

P. ⟨369⟩: *Important New Poetry Spoon River Anthology* . . .

P. ⟨370⟩: *A Dome of Many-Coloured Glass* . . .

STATE B

P. ⟨369⟩: *A Dome of Many-Coloured Glass* . . .

P. ⟨370⟩: *Important New Poetry Spoon River Anthology* . . .

⟨A-B⟩, C-I, K-U, X-Z, 2A⁸, plus ⟨-⟩¹.

Blue paper boards sides, green V cloth shelfback.
Paper labels. White laid end papers. Also issued
in leather?

On copyright page: *Published October, 1916.*

The author's personal copy (in H) inscribed by
her Oct. 18, 1916. A copy in UV inscribed by the
author Oct. 18, 1916. Deposited Oct. 19, 1916.
Listed PW Nov. 4, 1916. The London edition
advertised as though published Ath Dec. 1916;
listed Bkr Jan. 1917.

AAS B H NYPL UV

12973. Some Imagist Poets 1917   An Annual
Anthology

Boston and New York   Houghton Mifflin
Company   The Riverside Press   Cambridge
1917

Printed wrapper.

"Lacquer Prints," pp. 79-⟨86⟩, comprising:
"Streets," "Near Kioto," "Desolation," "Sun-

shine," "Illusion," "A Year Passes," "A Lover,"
"To a Husband," "The Fisherman's Wife," "From
China," "The Pond," "Autumn," "Ephemera,"
"Document," "The Emperor's Garden," "One of
the 'Hundred Views of Fuji' by Hokusai," "Disil-
lusion," "Paper Fishes," "Meditation," "The
Camellia Tree of Matsue." Collected in *Pictures
of the Floating World*, 1919.

On copyright page: *Published April 1917*

Deposited April 16, 1917.

H NYPL

12974. TENDENCIES IN MODERN AMER-
ICAN POETRY...

NEW YORK THE MACMILLAN COMPANY 1917 ALL
RIGHTS RESERVED

⟨i⟩-⟨xvi⟩, ⟨1⟩-349; blank, p. ⟨350⟩; publisher's
catalog, pp. ⟨351-352⟩; plus: ⟨353-357⟩; blank,
pp. ⟨358-360⟩. Laid paper. Frontispiece and 5
plates inserted. 8¹¹⁄₁₆″ × 5⅞″.

⟨A-B⟩, C-I, K-U, X-Z⁸, plus ⟨-⟩⁴.

V cloth: green.

On copyright page: *Published October, 1917.*

The author's copy (in H) inscribed by her Oct.
4, 1917. Presentation inscriptions (H, Y) dated
Oct. 10, 1917. Deposited Oct. 11, 1917. Listed
PW Oct. 20, 1917. The earliest London edition
(Oxford: Blackwell) noted listed by N & A Dec.
3, 1921.

AAS H UV Y

12975. A Book of Yale Review Verse...

New Haven: Yale University Press   London:
Humphrey Milford   Oxford University Press
MDCCCCXVII

"William Blake," p. 57. Collected in *Pictures of
the Floating World*, 1919.

For fuller entry see No. 3049.

12976. Anthology of Magazine Verse for 1917...
Edited by William Stanley Braithwaite

Boston Small, Maynard & Company Publishers
⟨1917⟩

Boards, cloth shelfback, paper labels.

"A Bather," pp. 16-18; "On a Certain Critic,"
pp. 213-215; both collected in *Pictures of the
Floating World*, 1919. "Guns as Keys: And the
Great Gate Swings," pp. 137-162; collected in
Can Grande's Castle, 1918.

Listed PW Dec. 29, 1917.

H

12977. ... Defenders of Democracy ... Edited by the Gift Book Committee of the Militia of Mercy ...

New York: John Lane Company London: John Lane, The Bodley Head MCMXVIII

"The Breaking out of the Flags," pp. 270-272.

Deposited Dec. 6, 1917. For fuller entry see No. 9856.

12978. The Masque of Poets A Collection of New Poems by Contemporary American Poets Edited by Edward J. O'Brien

New York Dodd, Mead and Company 1918

"The Ring and the Castle," pp. 73-80; collected in *Legends*, 1921. "Shore Grass, " p. 81; collected in *Pictures of the Floating World*, 1919.

Deposited April 2, 1918.

H   NYPL

12979. CAN GRANDE'S CASTLE ...

NEW YORK THE MACMILLAN COMPANY 1918 ALL RIGHTS RESERVED

⟨i⟩-⟨xviii⟩, ⟨1⟩-232; publisher's catalog, pp. ⟨233-238⟩; plus: ⟨239-240⟩. 7″ × 4⅜″.

⟨1-16⁸, plus 17¹⟩.

Drab brown laid paper boards sides, red-brown V cloth shelf back. Printed paper labels.

The author's personal copy (in H) inscribed by her Sept. 18, 1918. Presentation inscriptions (AAS, H, UV) have been seen dated Sept. 19, 1918. Deposited Sept. 25, 1918. Listed PW Oct. 19, 1918. The earliest noted English edition (Oxford: Blackwell) listed by Ath Oct. 15, 1920.

AAS   B   H   NYPL   UV

12980. ... A SPRIG OF ROSEMARY ...

J. FISCHER & BROTHER, NEW YORK FOURTH AVENUE AND EIGHTH STREET (ASTOR PLACE) ⟨1919⟩

Sheet music. Cover-title. At head of title: *Fischer Edition Louis Koemmenich*

Plate number 4646-2 (low voice). Also issued for high voice; not seen.

Collected in *Pictures of the Floating World*, 1919 (September).

Deposited May 29, 1919.

B

12981. New Voices   An Introduction to Contemporary Poetry by Marguerite Wilkinson

New York The Macmillan Company 1919 All Rights Reserved

Reprint save for "The Cornucopia of Red and Green Comfits," pp. 265-268. Otherwise unlocated.

On copyright page: *Published June, 1919*

UV

12982. PICTURES OF THE FLOATING WORLD ...

NEW YORK THE MACMILLAN COMPANY 1919 ALL RIGHTS RESERVED

⟨i⟩-xx, ⟨1⟩-257; blank, p. ⟨258⟩; publisher's catalog, pp. ⟨259-266⟩; blank leaf. 6⅞″ × 4⅜″.

⟨1-18⁸⟩.

Green-gray laid paper boards sides, orange V cloth shelf back. Paper labels.

On copyright page: *Published September, 1919.*

Author's personal copy (in H) inscribed by her Sept. 24, 1919. Inscribed copies (AAS, UV) dated *Sept. 1919.* Deposited Oct. 3, 1919. H copy received Oct. 10, 1919. Listed PW Nov. 1, 1919.

AAS   H   UV   Y

12983. Poems by a Little Girl by Hilda Conkling with a Preface by Amy Lowell ...

New York   Frederick A. Stokes Company Publishers ⟨1920⟩

Boards, cloth shelf back.

"Preface," pp. vii-xix.

Deposited May 3, 1920.

H   NYPL   UV

12984. A Miscellany of American Poetry 1920

New York Harcourt, Brace and Howe 1920

"Night Clouds," p. 67; "Wind and Silver," p. 68; "Meeting-House Hill," pp. 71-72; "Once Jericho," pp. 73-74; all the preceding collected in *What's O'Clock*, 1925. "Granadilla," p. 69; "Old Snow," p. 70; "New Heavens for Old," pp. 75-76; all three collected in *Ballads for Sale*, 1927. "Funeral Song for the Indian Chief Blackbird ...," pp. 77-85; collected in *Legends*, 1921.

Deposited Sept. 23, 1920.

BA

12985. Anthology of Magazine Verse for 1920 and Year Book of American Poetry Edited by William Stanley Braithwaite

Boston Small, Maynard & Company Publishers ⟨1920⟩

Boards, cloth shelf back, label on spine.

Reprint save for: "Gavotte in D Minor," pp. 27-29; collected in *Legends*, 1921. "Merely Statement," pp. 37-38; collected in *What's O'Clock*, 1925.

Deposited Nov. 10, 1920. Listed PW Jan. 29, 1921.

H

12986. Diaries of Court Ladies of Old Japan Translated by Annie Shepley Omori and Kochi Doi . . . with an Introduction by Amy Lowell . . .

Boston and New York   Houghton Mifflin Company   The Riverside Press   Cambridge 1920

Printed paper boards, cloth shelf back.

"Introduction," pp. xi-⟨xxxiii⟩.

Deposited Nov. 23, 1920. BA copy received Nov. 23, 1920. Listed PW Dec. 4, 1920. The London (Constable) edition listed N&A Sept. 3, 1921; Bkr Oct. 1921.

B   BA   H

12987. Development   A Novel by W. Bryher ⟨*i.e.*, Annie Winifred Ellerman⟩ with a Preface by Amy Lowell

New York   The Macmillan Company   1920

"Preface," pp. ix-xvi.

Note: Made up the sheets of the London (Constable & Co., Ltd.), 1920, printing with altered front matter. The London edition does not contain the preface by Amy Lowell.

The London edition was issued in June, 1920. The New York edition was listed by PW Sept. 25, 1920.

B   LC   Y

12988. The Enchanted Years   A Book of Contemporary Verse Dedicated by Poets of Great Britain and America to the University of Virginia on the Occasion of its One-Hundredth Anniversary Edited by John Calvin Metcalf . . . and James Southall Wilson . . .

New York Harcourt, Brace and Company 1921

"The Enchanted Castle," p. 26; collected in *What's O'Clock*, 1925.

Deposited June 6, 1921.

H   NYPL

12989. LEGENDS . . .

BOSTON AND NEW YORK   HOUGHTON MIFFLIN COMPANY   THE RIVERSIDE PRESS   CAMBRIDGE 1921

⟨i⟩-⟨xvi⟩, ⟨1⟩-259: blank, p. ⟨260⟩; publisher's catalog, pp. ⟨261-269⟩; blank, p. ⟨270⟩; blank leaf. Paper watermarked *Flemish Book*. 6⅞″ × 4½″.

⟨1-18⁸⟩.

Brown-gray laid paper boards sides, red-orange V cloth shelf back. Printed paper labels.

Two states of undetermined sequence have been noted; the designations are completely arbitrary:

STATE A

P. ⟨268⟩: *Six French Poets . . . Third edition . . .*

P. ⟨269⟩: *Tendencies in Modern American Poetry . . . Third edition . . .*

Locations: B H: The author's personal copy, inscribed by her May 19, 1921; *but see below under State B*. H: A copy with an inserted note of presentation dated May 19, 1921.

STATE B

P. ⟨268⟩: *Tendencies in Modern American Poetry . . . Third edition . . .*

P. ⟨269⟩: *Six French Poets . . . Third edition . . .*

Locations: AAS BA H: The author's personal copy, inscribed by her May 19, 1921; *but see above under State A.* LC: Both deposit copies have the advertisements in this order. UV Y

The author's personal copies in H were inscribed by her on May 19, 1921. The first printing (2500 copies) was recorded by the publisher on May 31, 1921. Deposited June 9, 1921. Listed PW June 11, 1921. The second printing (1051 copies) was recorded by the publisher Nov. 16, 1921. The date was presumably removed from the imprint of the second printing.

For locations see above under *State A* and *State B*.

12990. Breezes by Lucy Gibbons Morse

⟨Boston and New York⟩ Houghton Mifflin Company   1921

Printed paper boards, cloth shelf back, label on spine. Printed on one side of leaf only.

"Foreword," pp. vii-⟨ix⟩.

BA copy received Oct. 11, 1921. Deposited Nov. 1, 1921.

AAS   B   BA   H

12991. Year Book of the Poetry Society of South Carolina for 1921

Charleston, So. Ca., U.S.A. ⟨1921⟩

Printed paper wrapper.

Message to the society, p. 17.

Issued under date *October 1921.*

H   NYPL

12992. Anthology of Magazine Verse for 1921 and Year Book of American Poetry Edited by William Stanley Braithwaite

Boston Small, Maynard & Company Publishers ⟨1921⟩

Paper boards, cloth shelf back, paper labels.

"The House with the Marble Steps," pp. 105–107; collected in *East Wind*, 1926. "Texas," pp. 107–109; "A Rhyme out of Motley," p. 111; "A Grave Song," p. 111; all three collected in *What's O'Clock*, 1925. "Flute-Priest Song for Rain," pp. 109–110; collected in *Ballads for Sale*, 1927.

Deposited Nov. 17, 1921.

H

12993. Fir-Flower Tablets Poems Translated from the Chinese by Florence Ayscough . . . English Versions by Amy Lowell

Boston and New York Houghton Mifflin Company The Riverside Press, Cambridge 1921

"Preface," pp. v–x.

⟨i⟩-⟨xcvi⟩, 1-227; printer's imprint, p. ⟨228⟩; plus publisher's catalog, pp. ⟨229-238⟩, blank leaf. 2-page map and 2 plates inserted. $7\frac{7}{8}'' \times 5\frac{1}{8}''$.

Printed paper boards sides, V cloth (blue; or, black) shelf back.

The author's personal copy (in H) inscribed by her Dec. 10, 1921. BA copy received Dec. 20, 1921. Listed PW Jan. 14, 1922. Deposited Jan. 17, 1922. The London (Constable) edition listed Bkr June, 1922.

B BA H

12994. A REVIEW BY AMY LOWELL––– SEPTEMBER 28, 1921 THE NEW REPUB- LIC 139 MARIONETTES OF FATE PUNCH: THE IMMORTAL LIAR, BY CONRAD AIKEN . . . [REPRINTED FROM THE NEW REPUBLIC OF SEPTEMBER 28, 1921.]

⟨NEW YORK: ALFRED A. KNOPF, 1921⟩

Caption-title. The above on the recto of a single cut sheet. $13\frac{1}{2}'' \times 8\frac{1}{4}''$. Printed on both sides.

Offprint of pp. 139-140 of *The New Republic*, New York, Sept. 28, 1921.

H

12995. American Poetry 1922 A Miscellany

New York Harcourt, Brace and Company ⟨1922⟩

Printed paper boards sides, cloth shelf back.

"Lilacs," pp. 3-7; "Twenty-Four Hokku on a Modern Theme," pp. 8-12; "The Swans," pp. 13-15; "Prime," p. 16; "Vespers," p. 17; "In Excelsis," pp. 18-19; "La Ronde du Diable," pp. 20-21. All collected in *What's O'Clock*, 1925.

H copy received Sept. 9, 1922. Deposited Sept. 12, 1922. The London (Cape) edition listed Bkr May, 1923.

BA H

12996. . . . A CRITICAL FABLE . . . A SE- QUEL TO THE "FABLE FOR CRITICS" . . . BY A POKER OF FUN . . .

HOUGHTON MIFFLIN AND COMPANY BOSTON AND NEW YORK PUBLISHED SEPTEMBER, 1922

Title-page in black and orange. At head of title: *Dear Sir (or Dear Madam) who happen to glance at this TITLE-PAGE* . . .

⟨i⟩-⟨x⟩, ⟨1⟩-99; blank, pp. ⟨100-102⟩. $8\frac{7}{16}'' \times 5\frac{5}{8}''$.

⟨1², 2-7⁸, 8⁶⟩.

Printed stiff, off-white, paper wrapper.

The author's personal copy (in H) inscribed by her *August, 1922*. Deposited Sept. 16, 1922.

AAS B BA H UV

12997. The Bookman Anthology of Verse 1922 Edited by John Farrar

New York George H. Doran Company ⟨1922⟩

Printed paper boards.

Reprint with the exception of "Purple Grackles," pp. 30-33; collected in *What's O'Clock*, 1925.

The first printing has the publisher's monogram and the figure *I* on the copyright page.

Deposited Nov. 16, 1922.

H

12998. The Year Book of the Poetry Society of South Carolina

Published by the Poetry Society of South Carolina The Carolina Press Charleston, South Carolina MDCCCCXXII

Printed paper wrapper. Edited by Hervey Allen, DuBose Heyward, John Bennett.

"Silhouette with Sepia Background," p. 35. Collected in *Ballads for Sale*, 1927.

Issued under date *November 1922*.

H NYPL

12999. Anthology of Magazine Verse for 1922 and Yearbook of American Poetry Edited by William Stanley Braithwaite

Boston Small, Maynard & Company Publishers ⟨1923⟩

Paper boards, cloth shelf back, paper labels.

"The Revenge," pp. 124-127; "The Book of Stones and Lilies," pp. 127-128; "Miniature," p. 129; "Aquatint Framed in Gold," pp. 130-131. All collected in *Ballads for Sale*, 1927.

Deposited Feb. 13, 1923.

H NYPL

13000. The Best Poems of 1922 Selected by Thomas Moult . . .

    Jonathan Cape, Eleven Gower Street London ⟨1923⟩

Boards, paper label on spine.

"Orientation," pp. 120-121. Collected in *What's O'Clock*, 1925.

Issued May, 1923, according to *The English Catalogue of Books*.

H NYPL

13001. Anthology of Magazine Verse for 1923 and Yearbook of American Poetry Edited by William Stanley Braithwaite

    Boston B. J. Brimmer Company 1923

Paper boards, cloth shelf back, printed paper labels.

On copyright page: *First Impression, November, 1923*

Reprint save for: "Song for a Violo ⟨*sic*⟩ d'Amore," pp. 220-222; "The Middleton Place," pp. 222-223; "The Vow," pp. 224-227; all collected in *What's O'Clock*, 1925. "And So, I Think, Diogenes," pp. 223-224; "The Immortals," pp. 228-230; both collected in *Ballads for Sale*, 1927.

Deposited Jan. 28, 1924.

H NYPL

13002. What I Read as a Child ⟨by⟩ Witter Bynner Joseph Hergesheimer Rupert Hughes Stephen Leacock Amy Lowell Hugh Walpole with a Complete Bookshelf by Kate Douglas Wiggin

    ⟨Chicago: Marshall Field & Co., n.d., *ca.* 1923⟩

Cover-title. Printed self-wrapper.

"What I Read as a Child," pp. 14-20.

Y

13003. The Best Poems of 1923 Edited by L. A. G. Strong . . .

Boston Small, Maynard & Company Publishers ⟨1924⟩

"Easel Picture: Decoration Day," p. 135. Collected in *Ballads for Sale*, 1927.

In his introduction to *The Best Poems of 1924* the editor states that because of certain errors in the first printing of the 1923 compilation "the edition . . . was at once called in and destroyed, and a new edition issued" in corrected state. All examined copies of the first 1923 edition contain the errors, the following being sufficient for identification:

FIRST PRINTING

In the table of contents, p. xi, the first name listed is *Aiken*. No reprint notice on the copyright page.

SECOND PRINTING

In the table of contents, p. xi, the first name listed is *Abercrombie*. On copyright page: *Second printing, April, 1924*.

Deposited Feb. 8, 1924.

H (both)

13004. The Best Poems of 1924 Edited by L. A. G. Strong . . .

    Boston Small, Maynard & Company Publishers ⟨1924⟩

"Exercise in Logic," p. 138. Collected in *What's O'Clock*, 1925.

Deposited Jan. 2, 1925.

H NYPL

13005. Robert Frost the Man and His Work . . .

    Henry Holt and Company New York ⟨n.d., 1924-1925⟩

Cover-title. Printed self-wrapper.

"A Biographical Sketch," pp. ⟨2-6⟩. Reprinted "from *Tendencies in Modern American Poetry* ⟨1917⟩ . . . with a few emendations of fact."

Three issues noted:

FIRST ISSUE

Imprint: As above.

P. ⟨6⟩: The initial *H*, last paragraph, erroneously placed at the right.

SECOND (THIRD?) ISSUE

Imprint: As above.

P. ⟨6⟩: The initial *H*, last paragraph, correctly placed at the left.

THIRD (SECOND?) ISSUE

Imprint: *Hampshire Bookshop, Inc. Northampton, Massachusetts*

P. ⟨6⟩: The initial *H*, last paragraph, correctly placed at the left.

Listed in US Cat for July, 1924–June, 1925.

AAS (2nd)   D (all)   H (2nd)

13006. JOHN KEATS...

> BOSTON AND NEW YORK   HOUGHTON MIFFLIN COMPANY   THE RIVERSIDE PRESS   CAMBRIDGE 1925

1: ⟨i⟩-xx, ⟨1⟩-631. Frontispiece and 17 plates inserted. Laid paper. 8⅞″ × 5⅞″.

2: ⟨i⟩-viii, ⟨1⟩-662, blank leaf. Frontispiece and 13 plates inserted.

1: ⟨1-40⁸, 41⁶⟩.

2: ⟨1-42⁸⟩.

V cloth: red. White laid end papers.

NYPL copy received Feb. 13, 1925. *Published yesterday*---PW Feb. 14, 1925. BPL copy received Feb. 14, 1925. Deposited Feb. 16, 1925. Author's personal copy (in H) inscribed Feb. 1925. Listed PW March 14, 1925. The London (Jonathan Cape) edition announced in PC Oct. 4, 1924. *Probably ... in January*---TLS Dec. 25, 1924. Listed TLS Feb. 19, 1925. Advertised as though published TLS Feb. 26, 1925. Listed PC Feb. 28, 1925. Reviewed TLS March 19, 1925. Again listed PC May 2, 1925.

AAS   H   NYPL   UV   Y

13007. WHAT'S O'CLOCK...

> BOSTON AND NEW YORK   HOUGHTON MIFFLIN COMPANY   THE RIVERSIDE PRESS   CAMBRIDGE 1925

Edited by Ada Dwyer Russell.

⟨i⟩-x, ⟨1⟩-240, blank leaf. 6⅞″ × 4⁵⁄₁₆″.

⟨1-15⁸, 16⁶⟩.

Gray-blue laid paper boards sides, blue V cloth shelf back. Printed paper labels.

Release date for review is Aug. 21, 1925---from a tipped-in notice to reviewers in the AAS copy. BPL copy received Aug. 22, 1925. Deposited Aug. 26, 1925. H copy received Aug. 29, 1925. Listed PW Sept. 5, 1925. The London (Cape) edition advertised as *just published* TLS Feb. 4, 1926; listed PC Feb. 6, 1926; reviewed TLS Feb. 18, 1926.

AAS   H   UV   Y

13008. American Poetry 1925 A Miscellany

> New York   Harcourt, Brace and Company ⟨1925⟩

"A Communication," pp. 123-124; "The Sibyl," p. 125; "Pastime," pp. 126-127; "Apotheosis,"

pp. 128-132; "Mesdames Atropos and Clio Engage in a Game of Slap-Stick," pp. 133-136. All collected in *Ballads for Sale*, 1927.

On copyright page: *First edition, August, 1925*

Listed PW Sept. 5, 1925.

BA   NYPL

13009. The Best Poems of 1925 Edited by L. A. G. Strong...

> Boston Small, Maynard & Company Publishers ⟨1925⟩

"The Conversion of a Saint," pp. 124-136. Collected in *East Wind*, 1926.

Advertised for Nov. 4, PW Sept. 26, 1925.

H   NYPL

13010. The Work of Stephen Crane Edited by Wilson Follett... The Black Riders and Other Lines...

> New York   Alfred A Knopf ⟨1926⟩

Issued as Vol. VI of Stephen Crane's collected works. For fuller entry see No. 4101.

"Introduction," pp. ix-xxix.

13011. EAST WIND...

> BOSTON AND NEW YORK   HOUGHTON MIFFLIN COMPANY THE RIVERSIDE PRESS CAMBRIDGE 1926

Edited by Ada Dwyer Russell.

⟨i-viii⟩, ⟨1⟩-240, blank leaf. 6⅞″ × 4⁵⁄₁₆″.

⟨1¹, 2-16⁸, 17⁴⟩.

Ecru laid paper boards sides, black V cloth shelf back. Printed paper labels.

Note: In some copies ⟨1⟩ is not present. In one copy deposited for copyright the leaf is present; in the other deposit copy the leaf is absent.

Release date for review is Aug. 27, 1926---from a tipped-in notice to reviewers in the AAS copy. Listed PW Aug. 28, 1926. Deposited Aug. 30, 1926. BA copy received Aug. 31, 1926.

AAS   BA   H   NYPL   Y

13012. THE MADONNA OF CARTHAGENA ...

> PRIVATELY PRINTED: MCMXXVII

Title-page in black and brown-orange.

⟨1-22⟩, blank leaf. Laid paper. 7¹³⁄₁₆″ × 4⅝″.

⟨-⟩¹².

Issued in unprinted robin's-egg blue Japan paper, flecked with gold, French-folded.

50 Copies Privately Printed February Mcmxxvii---p. ⟨22⟩.

Collected in *Ballads for Sale*, 1927.

NYPL Y

13013. BALLADS FOR SALE ...

BOSTON AND NEW YORK   HOUGHTON MIFFLIN COMPANY   THE RIVERSIDE PRESS   CAMBRIDGE 1927

Edited by Ada Dwyer Russell.

⟨i⟩-xii, ⟨1⟩-311. 6⅞″ × 4⅜″ full.

⟨1-19⁸, 20¹⁰⟩.

Lavender laid paper boards sides, purple-blue V cloth shelf back. Paper labels.

Release date for review is Sep 16 1927---from a tipped-in notice to reviewers in the AAS copy. Listed PW Sept. 17, 1927. Deposited Sept. 19, 1927. BA copy received Sept. 19, 1927.

AAS   H   NYPL   UV

13014. Percy MacKaye   A Symposium on His Fiftieth Birthday 1925 Foreword by Amy Lowell

The Dartmouth Press Hanover, N. H. 1928

Boards, cloth shelf back, paper labels. 300 copies only.

"Percy MacKaye and the Poetry of America," pp. xi-⟨xii⟩.

H   NYPL   Y

13015. POETRY AND POETS   ESSAYS ...

BOSTON AND NEW YORK   HOUGHTON MIFFLIN COMPANY   THE RIVERSIDE PRESS   CAMBRIDGE 1930

Edited by Ferris Greenslet.

⟨i⟩-⟨viii⟩, ⟨1⟩-232. 6⅞″ full × 4⅜″ full.

⟨1-15⁸⟩.

Gray-green paper boards, black V cloth shelf back. Paper labels.

Deposited May 3, 1930. Listed PW May 3, 1930. BA copy received May 5, 1930.

AAS   B   BA   H   NYPL

13016. Designed for Reading   An Anthology Drawn from the Saturday Review of Literature 1924-1934 by the Editors of the Saturday Review of Literature ...

The Macmillan Company New York 1934

Reprint with the exception of "Open the Door," pp. 587-591, a letter to the editor regarding the magazine's review of Hilda Conkling's *Ship's Log*.

On copyright page: *Published April, 1934*

Deposited April 11, 1934.

H

13017. FLORENCE AYSCOUGH & AMY LOWELL   CORRESPONDENCE OF A FRIENDSHIP EDITED ... BY HARLEY FARNSWORTH MACNAIR

UNIVERSITY OF CHICAGO PRESS CHICAGO ILLINOIS ⟨1945; *i.e.*, 1946⟩

⟨1⟩-⟨289⟩, blank leaf. Watermarked *Warren's Olde Style*. 5 plates inserted; other illustrations in text. 9″ × 5¹⁵⁄₁₆″.

⟨1-7¹⁶, 8¹⁸, 9¹⁶⟩.

Red balloon cloth. End papers imprinted in green with a picture map of Shanghai. Top edges stained yellow.

Advertised for *December* PW Sept. 22, 1945. NYPL copy received Jan. 8, 1946. Deposited Jan. 9, 1946. Published Jan. 14, 1946 (publisher's statement).

B   H   NYPL   Y

13018. The Complete Poetical Works of Amy Lowell with an Introduction by Louis Untermeyer

Houghton Mifflin Company   Boston   The Riverside Press Cambridge 1955

Reprint save for six uncollected poems, pp. ⟨591⟩-593: "On *The Cutting of an Agate* by W. B. Yeats," "A Rainy Night," "A Comparison," "May Evening in Central Park," "The Road to the Mountain," "Eleonora Duse."

Note: "Eleonora Duse" begins *The talk is hushed* ...; not to be confused with another poem of the same title which begins *Seeing's believing* ...

Deposited Oct. 7, 1955.

BA   H   Y

AMY LOWELL

SECTION II

In this section are listed those publications which bear Amy Lowell's name as author but are reprinted from earlier primary books. For a list of books by authors other than Amy Lowell which contain reprinted material see *Section III*.

13019. Three Poems by Amy Lowell Composed by Carl Engel . . . A Decade . . .

> G. Schirmer, Inc. New York ⟨1922⟩

Sheet music. Cover-title. Reprinted from *Pictures of the Floating World*, 1919. Plate numbers 30772C, 30772. Deposited June 13, 1922.

13020. Three Poems by Amy Lowell Composed by Carl Engel . . . Opal . . .

> G. Schirmer, Inc. New York ⟨1922⟩

Sheet music. Cover-title. Reprinted from *Pictures of the Floating World*, 1919. Plate numbers 30773C, 30773. Deposited June 13, 1922.

13021. Three Poems by Amy Lowell Composed by Carl Engel . . . A Sprig of Rosemary

> G. Schirmer, Inc. New York ⟨1922⟩

Sheet music. Cover-title. Reprinted from *Pictures of the Floating World*, 1919. Plate numbers 30771C, 30771. Deposited June 13, 1922.

13022. Patterns . . .

> ⟨New York⟩ The Unbound Anthology. ⟨n.d., ca. 1922⟩

Four leaves in a printed wrapper. Cover-title. Reprinted from *Men, Women and Ghosts*, 1916.

13023. . . . Two Poems by Amy Lowell . . . Reflections . . .

> G. Schirmer, Inc., New York ⟨1924⟩

Sheet music. Cover-title. At head of title: *Camille W. Zeckwer* Reprinted from *Pictures of the Floating World*, 1919. Plate numbers 31770C, 31770. Deposited April 8, 1924.

13024. . . . Two Poems by Amy Lowell . . . The Shower . . .

> G. Schirmer, Inc., New York ⟨1924⟩

Sheet music. Cover-title. At head of title: *Camille W. Zeckwer* Reprinted from *Pictures of the Floating World*, 1919. Plate numbers 31769C, 31769.

13025. Song Sea Shell . . . Music by Felix White . . .

> Boston: Oliver Ditson Company New York: Chas. H. Ditson & Co. Chicago . . . London . . . ⟨1926⟩

Sheet music. Cover-title. Reprinted from *A Dome of Many-Coloured Glass*, 1912. Plate number 75305-3 (low voice); 75250-3 (medium voice); one of each deposited for copyright March 10, 1926.

13026. . . . Falling Snow . . .

> J. Fischer & Bro. 119 West 40th Street New York 3, New Street, Birmingham, England . . . ⟨1926⟩

Sheet music. Cover-title. Reprinted from *Pictures of the Floating World*, 1919. At head of title: *J. Bertram Fox* . . . Plate number J.F.&B. 5762-4 (low voice). Also issued for high voice?

13027. Fool o' the Moon . . .

> Privately Printed by John S. Mayfield ⟨Austin, Texas, 1927⟩

4 pp. Watermarked *Dresden Pamphlet*. Printed paper wrapper, tied with blue cord. Reprinted from *What's O'Clock*, 1925. Certificate of issue: *Printed October 29, 1927 at Austin, Texas. Only forty-one copies made.*

13028. Christmas Greetings from Walter and Millicent Bingham

> 1927 . . . 110 Washington Place New York

Caption-title. The above on p. ⟨1⟩ of a four-page leaflet. Laid paper watermarked *Strathmore* . . . A printing of "To a Gentleman Who Wanted to See the First Drafts of my Poems . . ."; issued as a Christmas token. Reprinted from *Ballads for Sale*, 1927 (Sept.).

13029. Selected Poems of Amy Lowell Edited by John Livingston Lowes

> Boston and New York Houghton Mifflin Company The Riverside Press Cambridge 1928

NYPL copy received April 23, 1928; H copy received April 28, 1928. Listed PW May 5, 1928. Reprinted under date ⟨1927⟩.

13030. . . . Four Lacquer Prints   Words by Amy Lowell . . .

Éditions Maurice Senart 20, Rue du Dragon, 20   Paris . . . 1932 . . . Elkan-Vogel Co. Inc. 1716, Sansom Street Philadelphia, Pa. Imprimeries Française de Musique E.M.S. 8274 I.F.M. 9680

Sheet music. Cover-title. At head of title: *Alexander Steinert* Text reprinted from *Pictures of the Floating World*, 1919. Deposited Feb. 1, 1933.

13031. Madonna of the Evening Flowers . . . Music by Celius Dougherty . . .

Boosey & Hawkes ⟨New York, 1949⟩

Sheet music. Cover-title. Plate number B.&.H. 16512. Reprinted from *Pictures of the Floating World*, 1919.

13032. . . . Music . . .

R. D. Row Music Company Boston, Massachusetts . . . ⟨1953⟩

Sheet music. Cover-title. At head of title: *Celius Dougherty* Plate number: 809-6. Reprinted from *Sword Blades and Poppy Seed*, 1914.

13033. . . . Portrait of a Lady . . .

R. D. Row Music Company Boston, Massachusetts . . . ⟨1953⟩

Sheet music. Cover-title. At head of title: *High Voice* . . . *Celius Dougherty* Plate number: 825-5 (high voice). Also issued for low voice; not seen. Otherwise "A Lady," *Sword Blades and Poppy Seed*, 1914.

13034. Selected Poems of Amy Lowell A Shard of Silence Edited by G. R. Ruihley

New York: Twayne Publishers, Inc. ⟨1957⟩

Deposited May 9, 1957.

AMY LOWELL

SECTION III

In this section are listed books by authors other than Amy Lowell which contain material by her reprinted from earlier books. See *Section II* for a list of publications issued under Lowell's name which contain no first edition material by her.

Programme

> Sevenels Brookline March 25th 1913
>
> Cover-title. Printed self-wrapper.

Poems of the Great War Selected by J. W. Cunliffe . . .

> New York The Macmillan Company 1916 . . .
>
> On copyright page: *Published November, 1916.*

Anthology of Magazine Verse for 1916 . . . Edited by William Stanley Braithwaite

> New York Laurence J. Gomme 1916
>
> Boards, cloth shelf back, paper labels. Listed PW Jan. 20, 1917.

The Answering Voice . . . Selected by Sara Teasdale . . .

> Boston . . . 1917
>
> For comment see BAL, Vol. 2, p. 453.

Des Imagistes An Anthology

> New York . . . 1917
>
> See above in *Section I* under year 1914.

A Book of Verse of the Great War Edited by W. Reginald Wheeler . . .

> New Haven: Yale University Press MDCCCXCVII
>
> On copyright page: *First Published, November, 1917*

Pleiades Club Year Book 1917–'18 . . .

> ⟨New York, 1918⟩
>
> Printed paper boards. 500 numbered copies only.

The Second Book of Modern Verse . . . Edited by Jessie B. Rittenhouse

> Boston and New York Houghton Mifflin Company The Riverside Press Cambridge 1919

A Treasury of War Poetry . . . Second Series Edited, with Introduction and Notes, by George Herbert Clarke . . .

> Boston and New York Houghton Mifflin Company The Riverside Press Cambridge 1919

The John Keats Memorial Volume Issued by the Keats House Committee, Hampstead . . .

> London: John Lane, The Bodley Head, Vigo Street, W. New York: John Lane Company. February 23, 1921
>
> The NYPL copy received Feb. 23, 1921, the presumed day of publication.

1845–1920 The Diamond Jubilee A Record of the Seventy-Fifth Anniversary of the Founding of Baylor University Prepared by Henry Trantham for the University

> ⟨Dallas, Texas⟩ The Baylor University Press 1921
>
> Bound in limp imitation leather.

Anthology of Massachusetts Poets by William Stanley Braithwaite

> Boston Small, Maynard & Company Publishers ⟨1922⟩

. . . Free Verse Songs . . .

> G. Schirmer, Inc., New York ⟨1922⟩
>
> Printed paper wrapper. At head of title: ⟨*Music by*⟩ *Rupert Hughes* Plate numbers 30763, 30763C. "Falling Leaves," pp. 14-16; extracted from "The City of Falling Leaves," *Men, Women and Ghosts,* 1916.

American Poets An Anthology of Contemporary Verse by Leonora Speyer

> Kurt Wolff Verlag München ⟨1923⟩

The Soul of the City . . . Compiled by Garland Greever and Joseph M. Bachelor

Boston . . . 1923

For comment see BAL, Vol. 3, p. 288.

. . . Today's Poetry ⟨Edited by⟩ Nelson Antrim Crawford and David O'Neil

Haldeman-Julius Company   Girard, Kansas 1923

Printed paper wrapper. At head of title: *Ten Cent Pocket Series No. 298* . . . "Published January 29, 1923. First issue has two advertisements on back cover, with *In the Maytime Pear Orchard* by Grace Hazard Conkling on pp. 19-20, *Water* by Hilda Conkling on p. 20, and *Trees* by Joyce Kilmer on p. 63. Second issue as above with copyright date routed from verso of title-page. Third and subsequent issues have the poems by the Conklings and Kilmer routed from the plates. Cover series changed to *Little Blue Book no. 298* with fourth issue." *Not seen.* Entry courtesy of Dr. Gene DeGruson, Curator of the Haldeman-Julius Collection, Kansas State College of Pittsburg, Pittsburg, Kansas.

The Magic Carpet Poems for Travellers Selected by Mrs. Waldo Richards . . .

Boston and New York   Houghton Mifflin Company   The Riverside Press   Cambridge 1924

Leather. "Venice," pp. 337-338; "Rome," pp. 377-378; both reprinted from "The Bronze Horses," *Can Grande's Castle*, 1918. "Naples," p. 393; reprinted from "Sea-Blue and Blood-Red," *Can Grande's Castle*, 1918.

Modern American Lyrics An Anthology Compiled by Stanton A. Coblentz

New York   Minton, Balch & Company   1924

Printed paper labels.

May Days An Anthology of Verse from Masses-Liberator Chosen and Edited by Genevieve Taggard . . .

Boni & Liveright New York MCMXXV

Boards, cloth shelf back.

The Best Poems of 1926 Edited by L. A. G. Strong . . .

Dodd, Mead & Company New York 1926

The Best Poems of 1926 Selected by Thomas Moult . . .

London   Jonathan Cape, Thirty Bedford Square 1927

Boards, paper label.

The Best Poems of 1926 Selected by Thomas Moult . . .

New York   Harcourt, Brace & Company   383 Madison Avenue ⟨n.d., 1927⟩

Boards, cloth shelf back, paper label. Listed PW Feb. 26, 1927.

The Bookman Anthology of Verse   Second Series Edited by John Farrar

New York   George H. Doran Company ⟨1927⟩

First printing has the publisher's monogram and symbol *A* on copyright page.

The Third Book of Modern Verse . . . Edited by Jessie B. Rittenhouse

Boston and New York   Houghton Mifflin Company   The Riverside Press   Cambridge 1927

Prize Poems 1913 1929 Edited by Charles A Wagner . . .

1930   Charles Boni Paper Books New York

Printed paper wrapper. On copyright page: *Published April, 1930*

Shorter Modern Poems 1900–1931 [American-Irish-English] Compiled by David Morton

Harper & Brothers Publishers   New York and London   1932

On copyright page: *First Edition;* and, code letters *D-G,* signifying *printed April, 1932.*

The Smart Set Anthology Edited by Burton Rascoe and Groff Conklin

. . . New York ⟨1934⟩

For fuller entry see No. 11135.

Gentlemen, Scholars and Scoundrels A Treasury of the Best of Harper's Magazine from 1850 to the Present Edited by Horace Knowles

Harper & Brothers   New York ⟨1959⟩

Code letters *I-I* on copyright page, signifying *printed Sept. 1959.*

REFERENCES AND ANA

Literature in the Making by Some of its Makers Presented by Joyce Kilmer

. . . New York . . . ⟨1917⟩

For fuller entry see No. 11111.

Amy Lowell   A Sketch of Her Life and Her Place in Contemporary American Literature by Richard Hunt

The Macmillan Company 64-66 Fifth Avenue New York ⟨n.d., after Oct. 1917⟩

Printed self-wrapper. Cover-title.

Amy Lowell   A Critical Appreciation by W. Bryher ⟨*i.e.*, Annie Winifred Ellerman⟩

London: Eyre and Spottiswoode, Ltd   1918 Price Half-a-Crown

Printed paper wrapper.

Amy Lowell Sketches Biographical and Critical by Richard Hunt and Royall H. Snow

⟨Boston and New York: Houghton Mifflin Company, 1921⟩

Printed paper wrapper. Cover-title. For an earlier appearance of the Hunt sketch see above under 1917.

The House in Main Street   Narrative Poem by Amy Lowell Decorative Woodcuts by John J. A. Murphy

⟨n.p., n.d., 1922⟩

Seven leaves extracted from *Century Magazine*, Feb. 1922, and amateurishly stitched together. There is no evidence that this poem was ever so prepared for publication. In Y.

Amy Lowell a Mosaic by George H. Sargent

New York William Edwin Rudge 1926

Boards, cloth shelf back. 450 copies only.

Amy Lowell ⟨by⟩ Clement Wood

New York Harold Vinal 1926

The Poetry of Amy Lowell by Charles Cestre . . . Translated by Dana Hill . . .

⟨n.p., n.d., Boston: Houghton Mifflin Company, 1926⟩

Cover-title. Printed paper wrapper. Unpaged.

Two printings noted: 1: Last entry penultimate page is *East Wind*. 2: Last entry penultimate page is *The Selected Poems*.

"The Bronze Horses" A Comment on the Prose-Poem of Amy Lowell ⟨by⟩ H. C. Hoskier

Portland Maine The Mosher Press MDCCCCXXX

Printed paper boards. "Five Hundred Copies . . . Printed . . . July MDCCCCXXX"———Colophon. Deposited Oct. 6, 1930.

Amy Lowell a Chronicle with Extracts from Her Correspondence by S. Foster Damon . . .

Boston and New York   Houghton Mifflin Company The Riverside Press   Cambridge 1935

Deposited Nov. 11, 1935.

JAMES RUSSELL LOWELL

(Homer Wilbur, A Wonderful Quiz)

1819–1891

As ambassador to Spain and to Great Britain, Lowell published some items of an official nature. No attempt has been made to locate and to describe such material. A representative selection is given at the end of these lists.

This list is presented in seven sections as follows:
An index to Lowell's undated publications.
A list of unlocated Lowell publications.

Section I: Primary books in first or revised edition; books containing first book publication, including contributions to the books of others.

Section II: Reprints of Lowell's own books, including poems reprinted from Lowell's books and issued as sheet music.

Section III: Books by authors others than Lowell containing material by him reprinted from earlier books.
Official publications.
References and ana.

AN INDEX TO UNDATED LOWELL PUBLICATIONS

Arranged alphabetically by title; under title arranged alphabetically by publisher.

Alone . . . the Music by Elizabeth Philp . . .
    London: R. Mills & Sons . . .
See in *Section II under* 1855.

. . . American Humorous Poetry . . .
    "Review of Reviews" Office . . .
See in *Section II under* 1897.

Among My Books. Second Series . . .
    London   Sampson Low, Marston, Searle & Rivington . . .
See in *Section II under* 1876.

. . . The Biglow Papers, Edited, with an Introduction, Notes, Glossary, and Copious Index . . .
    London: S. O. Beeton . . .
See in *Section II under* 1865.

. . . The Biglow Papers, Edited . . . by Homer Wilbur . . .
    New York: Hurst & Company . . .
See in *Section II under* 1886.

The Biglow Papers . . . Author's Unabridged Edition.
    London   George Routledge and Sons . . .
See in *Section II under* 1863.

The Biglow Papers . . . with an Introduction by George Augustus Sala . . .
    London: George Routledge and Sons . . .
See in *Section II under* 1868.

The Biglow Papers . . . with a Prefatory Note by Ernest Rhys.
    London: Walter Scott . . .
See in *Section II under* 1885.

. . . The Biglow Papers . . .
    London: Ward, Lock, & Tyler . . .
See in *Section II under* 1873.

Early Poems . . .
    Chicago   W. B. Conkey Company . . .
See in *Section II under* 1900.

Early Poems . . .
    New York and Boston   Thomas Y. Crowell and Company
See in *Section II under* 1891.

Early Poems . . .
  Chicago: Donohue, Henneberry & Co. . . .
See in *Section II* under 1890.

Early Poems . . .
  New York Home Book Company . . .
See in *Section II* under 1893.

Early Poems . . .
  New York Hurst & Company . . .
See in *Section II* under 1887; and, 1910.

Early Poems . . .
  New York: John W. Lovell Company . . .
See in *Section II* under 1890.

Early Poems . . .
  The F. M. Lupton Publishing Company, New York
See in *Section II* under 1891.

Extract from a Letter to Mrs. Francis G. Shaw . . .
  ⟨n.d., 1893?⟩
See in *Section II* under 1893.

. . . From the Close Shut Window . . .
  Boston . . . Oliver Ditson . . .
See in *Section II* under 1855.

Il Pesceballo. Opera Seria: In un Atto . . .
  ⟨n.p., n.d., 1862⟩
See in *Section I* under 1862.

Lowell's Poems
  Chicago M. A. Donohue & Co. . . .
See in *Section II* under 1900.

On the Capture of Certain Fugitive Slaves . . .
  ⟨n.p., n.d., 1845?⟩
See in *Section I* under 1845.

. . . On Religion . . .
  ⟨Philadelphia, n.d., *ca.* 1886⟩
See in *Section I* under 1886.

An Open Letter to Readers of Books . . .
  ⟨New York, n.d., *ca.* 1888⟩
See in *Section I* under 1888.

Pesceballo, Il. Opera Seria: In un Atto . . .
  ⟨n.p., n.d., 1862⟩
See in *Section I* under 1862.

Pierpont
  See in *Section I*, note under *Poems*, 1844.

Poems . . .
  Philadelphia Henry Altemus
See in *Section II* under 1890.

Poems . . .
  New York Hurst and Company Publishers
See in *Section II* under 1897; 1900.

Poems . . .
  The Mershon Company Rahway, N. J. New York
See in *Section II* under 1897.

The Poetical Works . . . Introduction by William Michael Rossetti
  Ward, Lock & Co., Limited London . . .
See in *Section II* under 1900.

Poetical Works . . . Including the Biglow Papers with Prefatory Memoir, Notes Glossary, etc.
  London Frederick Warne and Co . . .
See in *Section II* under 1900.

Select Poems . . .
  Dodge Publishing Company . . . New York
See in *Section II* under 1900.

. . . To J. R. L. sur la Pipe Cassée . . .
  ⟨n.p., n.d., *ca.* 1890⟩
See in *Section I* under 1890.

UNLOCATED PUBLICATIONS

The following Lowell publications have not been located. BAL presumes that none contains any first edition material. The order of presentation is alphabetical by title.

The Biglow Papers and the Petroleum V. Nasby Papers.
  London and Halifax: Milner & Sowerby, 1867.
  The only record seen up to 1868 is inclusion in a full list of *The Cottage Library*, Bkr Dec. 12, 1867.

Possibly projected but not published. Not in *The English Catalogue*.

The Biglow Papers. Second Series.

London: Trübner & Co., 1866.

Advertised as *now ready* Ath Dec. 8, 1866. Advertised Ath Dec. 22, 1866, with the comment "consisting of eleven new pieces, an introduction on the Yankee dialect, and an index, pp. 200, cloth, 2/6." Listed Ath Dec. 22; PC Dec. 31, 1866, as 250 pp., cloth, 2/6.

The Biglow Papers. Second Series.

London: John Camden Hotten, 1869.

Listed PC Dec. 18, 1869, as 142 pp., sewed, 1/–.

Brother Jonathan's Best Things.

London: S. O. Beeton, 1867.

Listed PC Aug. 15, 1867, 292 pp., cloth 3/6. Two of the "things" are *The Biglow Papers* and Lowell's poetical works.

Poems.

London: Thomas Delf, 1851.

2 Vols. Described as an importation. Advertised PC April 15, 1851. Listed PC May 1, 1851. Advertised by Delf and Trübner Ath April 24, 1852.

A Russell Lowell Treasury. Selected by A. Broadbent.

Manchester: A. Broadbent; ⟨London:⟩ F. R. Henderson, 1905.

Listed Bkr Aug. 1905, pp. 44.

Six Songs. Music by Elizabeth Philp.

London: Cramer & Co., 1855.

Noticed by Ath Sept. 1, 1855. One of the songs is "O, Moonlight Deep and Tender," which had prior publication in *Poems*, 1844.

The Singing Leaves. Set to Music by Grace Mayhew.

Boston: H. B. Stevens Company, 1897.

Entry from Chamberlain-Livingston, p. 128. The poem had prior publication in *Under the Willows*, 1869. Deposited March 19, 1897.

SECTION I

Primary books in first or revised edition; books containing first book publication, including contributions to the works of others.

13035. TO THE CLASS OF '38, BY THEIR OSTRACIZED POET, (SO CALLED,) J.R.L. ...

⟨n.p., n.d., Concord, Mass.(?), 1838⟩

Single leaf. $9^{13}/_{16}'' \times 7^{7}/_{8}''$. Printed on recto only.

Collected in *Uncollected Poems*, 1950.

". . . The meeting ⟨class day exercises, July 17, 1838⟩ had to be held without him ⟨Lowell⟩, and although he sent in a little *Supper Song* which was printed as a broadside and distributed on the occasion, the ambitious class poem was not completed until nearly commencement time . . ." –––*Victorian Knight-Errant* . . . , by Leon Howard, 1952, p. 55.

Published July 17, 1838.

H

13036. CLASS POEM ...

⟨CAMBRIDGE PRESS: METCALF, TORRY, AND BALLOU⟩ M DCCC XXXVIII.

Anonymous.

⟨1⟩-52. $9^{1}/_{8}''$ scant $\times 5^{5}/_{8}''$.

⟨1⟩-5⁴, 6², 7⁴.

Printed tan paper wrapper.

"Lowell had insisted when he went to Concord that he would write no more for *Harvardiana*, but the July issue, like his own *Class Poem*, was late in appearing and apparently was published for the commencement at the end of August rather than for the undergraduate exercises held six weeks before."–––*Victorian Knight-Errant* . . . , by Leon Howard, 1952, p. 71.

Collected in *Uncollected Poems*, 1950.

Earliest located dated inscription: Aug. 27, 1838; copy in H. Listed NAR Oct. 1838.

AAS   H   LC   MHS   NYPL   UV   Y

13037. A YEAR'S LIFE ...

BOSTON: C. C. LITTLE AND J. BROWN. M DCCC XLI.

⟨i⟩-viii, ⟨1⟩-182, blank leaf. $7^{1}/_{16}'' \times 4^{7}/_{16}''$.

⟨-⟩⁴, 1-11⁸, 12⁴.

Tan paper boards, printed paper label on spine. Flyleaves. Inserted at back: A 7-line errata slip. In all examined copies all the errors save one are present. The exception: P. 41, line 9. According to the errata notice there is present at end of the line an offending exclamation point instead of a period. Copies occur either with or without the exclamation point; no copy examined has a period. A copy in NYPL has the period skilfully inserted by hand in ink.

"The book was issued in January, 1841 . . . On February 18 Lowell wrote: *My book . . . is out . . .*" –––Livingston, p. 6. "Published January, 1841." –––Cooke, p. 74.

AAS   H   NYPL   UV   Y

13038. The Token and Atlantic Souvenir, an Offering for Christmas and the New Year.

Boston: Published by David H. Williams . . . 1842.

"The Ballad of the Stranger," pp. ⟨133⟩-137. Collected in *Four Poems*, 1906; *Uncollected Poems*, 1950.

"The Lesson of a Moment," pp. ⟨9⟩-21. Probably by Lowell. A letter (in H) from George Stillman Hillard, ⟨Boston⟩ July 14 ⟨1841?⟩, to Lowell: ". . . When I consented to edit *The Token*, Mr. Williams put a number of pieces of prose and verse into my hands among which were two of yours. One of these I printed . . . As to the other piece, I had it for some time under consideration, and being desirous of having a second piece of yours, I said a few days ago that this piece was too peculiar to be popular . . . and asked him ⟨William Wetmore Story⟩ if you had not some other piece which might not be submitted . . . ⟨Story⟩ said that you had a number and would undoubtedly be willing to substitute some other . . ."

Ralph Thompson in *American Literary Annuals & Gift Books 1825–1865*, p. 69: ". . . Whether Lowell did so is not definitely known, but it may be that an unsigned story called *The Lesson of a Moment* is his. The tale is based on the thesis that one's own lot often seems unfortunate when compared to that of others, but *were all the houses of our friends unroofed by another Asmodeus, we should find that none of them was without its dark shadow*. The hero is a young man of old New England family, yet of humble station, who has achieved thru his own efforts *the best education which the institutions of our country afford*. He had, moreover, won literary distinction and was in love with a girl named Mary. This description of a youth full of literary zeal, poor, and in love with his Mary is significant when it is remembered that Lowell himself, a few years out of Harvard College, poor, became engaged to Maria White shortly before this story was published. What is more striking is that Lowell had written to his friend Loring a few years before as follows: 'Among other plans that have been fermenting in my brain is one of writing a tale founded upon the idea of a man's having the power given him of seeing into the minds of other men and women, as Asmodeus did into their houses.'"

For fuller entry see No. 1005.

13039. The Liberty Bell. By Friends of Freedom
. . .

Boston: Massachusetts Anti-Slavery Fair. M DCCC XLII.

Printed paper boards. Also cloth?

"Sonnets," pp. 37-38, as follows:

Great Truths are portions of the Soul of man; collected in *Poems*, 1844.

If ye have not the one great lesson learned; Livingston, p. 9, reports this as "apparently never reprinted by the author." The statement is erroneous. Under the title "Reformers" it was reprinted in *Poems*, 1844.

Also contains "Pierpont. Sonnet," printed on the recto of a leaf of coated paper; inserted opposite p. 152. Collected in *Poems*, 1844, as "The Fiery Trial."

An advertisement in *The Daily Evening Transcript* (Boston), Dec. 21, 1841, says that the fair was scheduled to open Dec. 22, 1841 and that "*The Liberty Bell* will be published the first morning of the Fair . . ."

H   NYPL

13040. Order of Services at the Dedication of the New Church, Erected by the Congregational Society, in Watertown, August 3, 1842 . . .

J. Howe, Printer, No. 39, Merchants Row, Boston.

Single leaf. Printed on recto only. Issued as a program. 9⅝" full × 7⅞".

Prints an "Original Hymn," *One house, our God, we give to thee . . .* Collected in *Uncollected Poems*, 1950.

HEH   PDH

13041. The Liberty Bell. By Friends of Freedom
. . .

Boston: Massachusetts Anti-Slavery Fair. MDCCCXLIII.

Cloth; and, printed paper boards.

"Elegy on the Death of Dr. Channing," pp. 12-17. Collected in *Poems*, 1844.

The fair opened Dec. 20, 1842; closed Dec. 28, 1842. See *The Daily Evening Transcript*, Boston.

H   NYPL

13042. Anniversary of West-India Emancipation, August 1st, 1843 . . .

⟨n.p., Dedham, Mass., 1843⟩

Single cut sheet. Printed on recto only 13⅜" × 7"; measurements approximate. Issued as a program and song sheet.

Contains (with other material) Lowell's "Hymn," *Men! whose boast it is, that ye . . .* Collected in

TO THE CLASS OF '38,

BY THEIR OSTRACIZED POET, (SO CALLED,)

J. R. L.

I.

Classmates, farewell! our journey's done,
 Our mimic life is ended,
The last long year of study 's run,
 Our prayers their last have blended!

CHORUS.

 Then fill the cup! fill high! fill high!
  Nor spare the rosy wine!
  If Death be in the cup, we 'll die!
  Such death would be divine!

II.

Now forward! onward! let the past
 In private claim its tear,
For while *one* drop of wine shall last,
 We 'll have no sadness here!

CHORUS.

 Then fill the cup! fill high! fill high!
  Although the hour be late,
  We 'll hob and nob with Destiny,
  And drink the health of Fate!

III.

What though Ill-luck may shake his fist,
 We heed not him or his,
We 've booked our names on Fortune's list,
 d—n his grouty phiz!

CHORUS.

 Then fill the cup! fill high! fill high!
  Let joy our goblets crown,
  We 'll bung Misfortune's scowling eye,
  And knock Foreboding down!

IV.

Fling out youth's broad and snowy sail,
 Life's sea is bright before us!
Alike to us the breeze or gale,
 So hope shine cheerly o'er us!

CHORUS.

 Then fill the cup! fill high! fill high!
  And drink to future joy,
  Let thought of sorrow cloud no eye,
  Here 's to our eldest boy!

V.

Hurrah! Hurrah! we 're launched at last,
 To tempt the billows' strife!
We 'll nail our pennon to the mast,
 And DARE the storms of life!

CHORUS.

 Then fill the cup! fill high once more!
  There 's joy on time's dark wave;
  Welcome the tempest's angry roar!
  'T is music to the brave.

Poems, 1844, as "Stanzas Sung at the Anti-Slavery Picnic in Dedham, 1843."

H   ML

13043. The Gift: A Christmas and New Year's Present. MDCCCXLIV.

Philadelphia: Carey and Hart. 1844.

"A Requiem," pp. ⟨37⟩-38. Collected in *Poems*, 1844.

For fuller entry see No. 4021.

13044. The Liberty Bell. By Friends of Freedom.

Boston: Massachusetts Anti-Slavery Fair. MDCCCXLIV.

Cloth; and, printed paper boards.

"A Chippewa Legend," pp. 17-29. Collected in *Poems*, 1844.

The Daily Evening Transcript (Boston), Dec. 19, 1843, reported that the fair would open on Dec. 19, 1843, and that "... *The Liberty Bell* ... will be published at the fair."

H   NYPL

13045. POEMS ...

CAMBRIDGE: PUBLISHED BY JOHN OWEN. M DCCC XLIV.

LARGE PAPER FORMAT

⟨i⟩-xii, ⟨1⟩-279. 10⅛″ × 6¼″.

⟨a⁴, b², 1-35⁴⟩. *Signed:* ⟨a⟩⁴, ⟨b⟩², 1-17⁸, 18⁴.

Brown paper boards, printed paper label on spine.

SMALL PAPER FORMAT

⟨i⟩-xii, ⟨1⟩-279. 7⁷⁄₁₆″ full × 4¾″.

⟨-⟩², a*⁴, 1-17⁸, 18⁴.

Brown paper boards, printed paper label on spine. Flyleaves.

Note: The poem "In Absence" herein also appears in *The Poems of Maria Lowell*, Cambridge, 1855, which was edited by James Russell Lowell. Hence, by Maria Lowell. In Maria Lowell's *Poems* the poem appears on p. ⟨60⟩ titled "Sonnet."

The UV copy inscribed by Lowell *Christmas Day, 1843.* Deposited Dec. 27, 1843. Listed as a Dec. 1843 publication in ALB Feb. 1844. A copy in AAS inscribed by Lowell Jan. 1, 1844. A copy in H received Jan. 12, 1844. Listed WPLNL Feb. 1844 as a Jan. 1844 publication. A third edition listed in WPLNL Feb. 1845 as issued in Jan. 1845.

Note: "Pierpont," a sonnet published herein under the title "The Fiery Trial," has been seen in a separate leaflet printing issued by *N. E. B. Note Co.* ⟨*i.e.*, the New England Bank Note Company⟩. The text varies somewhat from that in *Poems*, 1844. Single leaf of cream-coated paper; printed on one side of leaf only, 6⁹⁄₁₆″ × 3¹⁵⁄₁₆″. Date of publication not known. The only located example is in NYPL. Almost certainly removed from *The Liberty Bell*, 1842.

AAS (small paper)   H (small paper)   NYPL (both) UV (small paper)

13046. The Liberty Minstrel ... by Geo. W. Clark.

New-York: Leavitt & Alden ⟨*sic*⟩, 7 Cornhill, Boston: Saxton & Miles, 205 Broadway, N.Y.: Myron Finch, 120 Nassau St., N.Y.: Jackson & Chaplin, 38 Dean St., Albany, N.Y.: Jackson & Chaplin, Corner Genessee and Main St., Utica, N.Y. 1844.

"Rouse Up, New England," words by a Yankee, pp. 70-72. A truncated version of "A Rallying-Cry for New-England, against the Annexation of Texas." Collected, in full, *Uncollected Poems*, 1950.

"Are Ye Truly Free?," pp. 126-127; otherwise "Stanzas Sung at the Anti-Slavery Picnic in Dedham ... August 1, 1843"; reprinted from *Poems*, 1844 (Dec. 1843).

Deposited Jan. 6, 1845.

CAW NYPL

13047. Voices of the True-Hearted ...

Philadelphia ... J. Miller M'Kim, No. 31 North Fifth Street ...

For fuller description see entry No. 12072.

Reprint save for the following contributions:

"Song Writing," *Part 2*, pp. 23-27. Issued Nov. 1844. A truncated version. Collected in full in *Conversations on Some of the Old Poets*, third edition, enlarged, 1893.

"The Ghost-Seer," *Part 6*, pp. 95-96. Issued April, 1845. Collected in *Poems*, 1848.

"The Contrast," *Part 14*, p. 215. Issued Oct.–Dec. 1845? Also in *Liberty Chimes*, 1845 (Dec. ?), below. Collected in *Poems*, 1848.

"Hunger and Cold," *Part 15*, p. 240. Issued 1845? 1846? Collected in *Poems*, 1848.

"A Lyric for the Times," *Part 17*, pp. 258-259. Issued 1846. Collected in *Poems*, 1848, as "The Present Crisis."

"An Interview with Miles Standish," *Part 17*, pp. 264-265. Issued 1846. Collected in *Poems*, 1848.

Note: In the table of contents "From *Dream Love*" is erroneously credited to Lowell; the true author was William Wetmore Story.

13048. The Liberty Bell. By Friends of Freedom ...

Boston: Massachusetts Anti-Slavery Fair. MDCCCXLV.

"The Happy Martyrdom," pp. 147-150. Collected in *Uncollected Poems*, 1950.

For fuller entry see No. 12076.

13049. CONVERSATIONS ON SOME OF THE OLD POETS . . .

CAMBRIDGE: PUBLISHED BY JOHN OWEN. M DCCC XLV.

⟨i⟩-viii, ⟨1⟩-263. $7\frac{1}{16}'' \times 4\frac{7}{8}''$ (wrappered copies). $6\frac{3}{4}'' \times 4\frac{1}{4}''$ scant (cloth-bound copies).

⟨-⟩⁴, 1-16⁸, 17⁴.

White paper wrapper lithographed in gilt (usually oxidized to brown) and colors; *see below*. Also issued in S-like cloth, yellow-coated end papers, triple flyleaves, edges gilded; *see below*.

The wrappers vary; the following forms have been seen; the designations are for identification only and do not represent a sequence. Reference is to the front of the wrapper.

A WRAPPER

At upper left and right: The florets are not decorated with an arrangement of dots.

LOWELL's printed in green.

Conversations. printed in green.

Spine dated 1845.

Locations: H

B WRAPPER

At upper left and right: The florets are not decorated with an arrangement of dots.

LOWELL's printed in gold.

Conversations. printed in green.

Spine dated 1845.

Locations: H (2 copies, including one presented to Ralph Waldo Emerson, Jan. 1, 1845) NYPL Y

C WRAPPER

At upper left and right: The florets are decorated with an arrangement of dots.

LOWELL's printed in green.

Conversations. printed in green.

Spine dated 1845.

Locations: NYPL Y

D WRAPPER

At upper left and right: The florets are decorated with an arrangement of dots.

LOWELL's printed in gold.

Conversations. printed in green.

Spine: Lacking.

Location: NYPL

CLOTH

Heavy-grained S-like cloth, blue, embossed with a scattering of dots and flowers. Yellow-coated end papers. Edges gilded. Triple flyleaves.

Location: Y

Note: It will be observed that Livingston, p. 19, errs in reporting that the cover was printed "in red, green and gold"; the covers were printed in red, green, blue and gold. Livingston also reports a copy bound in "stiff boards" with *Lowell's Conversations* printed in gold. BAL has seen no copy in boards, nor a copy with the lettering cited in gold. Further citing Livingston, p. 19: "I have also seen a copy printed in red and gold only"; not located by BAL. Also unlocated by BAL is the following described by Livingston: "One copy examined has the date 1846 in green below *Lowell's Conversations* on the front cover, and is without the date 1845" on the spine "but this cover, without much doubt, was prepared for the second edition, though used on some unsold copies of the first edition."

A copy in H (binding variant B) inscribed by Lowell Jan. 1, 1845. Deposited Jan. 7, 1845. Listed WPLNL Feb. 1845 as a January publication. The Wiley and Putnam importation listed PC May 1, 1845. The London (Clarke) printing advertised as in *Clarke's Library of Choice Reading* PC Oct. 15, 1845; listed Ath Nov. 22, 1845; listed LG Nov. 29, 1845; listed PC Dec. 1, 1845. For the second edition, revised, see below under year 1846; for extended edition see below under year 1893.

Locations: See above under bindings.

13050. ON THE CAPTURE OF CERTAIN FUGITIVE SLAVES NEAR WASHINGTON . . .

⟨n.p., n.d., 1845?⟩

Caption-title. The above on p. ⟨1⟩.

⟨1⟩-4. $6\frac{1}{2}'' \times 4\frac{5}{8}''$ scant.

Single cut sheet of white, unwatermarked, wove paper, folded to make four pages.

Also in (reprinted from?) *Poems*, 1848.

The poem also occurs in the following publication:

. . . The Branded Hand. By John G. Whittier . . .

⟨Philadelphia: E. M. Davis; and, Anti-Slavery Office, 31 North Fifth Street, n.d., 1845⟩

Also issued: ⟨Salem, Ohio: The Anti-Slavery Bugle, n.d., 1845⟩

Caption-title. The above at head of p. ⟨33⟩. At head of title: [*No. 9.*] *Read and circulate* . . .

⟨33⟩-36. 9″ scant × 5⅞″. *Measurements approximated.*

Single cut sheet of white, unwatermarked, wove paper folded to make four pages.

"Lines . . . on Reading of the Capture of Certain Fugitive Slaves near Washington," pp. 35-36.

Note: T. F. Currier (*Bibliography of John Greenleaf Whittier*, p. 57) on sufficiently reasonable evidence states that the Davis printing was issued during the period Aug. 6–21, 1845.

AAS (Davis)   H (n.p., n.d.; Anti-Slavery Bugle)

13051. Liberty Chimes . . .

    Providence. Ladies' Anti-Slavery Society. 1845.

"The Contrast," pp. 70-71. Collected as "A Contrast," *Poems*, 1848. See *Voices of the True-Hearted*, 1844–1846, above.

Cloth. Also(?) boards, leather shelf back, printed paper label on spine.

H copy inscribed Dec. 7, 1845.

H   NYPL

13052. Poems by Alexander H. Everett.

    Boston: James Munroe & Co. 1845.

Cloth? Paper boards?

Extract from Lowell's review of Everett's *The Hermitage*, pp. ⟨9⟩-10; reprinted from *The Boston Miscellany*, Oct. 1842.

Deposited Dec. 18, 1845.

H

13053. The Singer's First Book; Consisting of Simple Rules and Easy Music for Common Schools. By J. & H. Bird. Second Edition.

    Cambridge: Published by John Owen. 1845.

Printed paper boards, cloth shelf back.

Testimonial, *Elmwood, Oct. 29, 1845*, p. 3.

H

13054. Conversations on Some of the Old Poets . . . Second Edition.

    Cambridge: Published by John Owen. 1846.

For first edition see above under year 1845; for extended edition see below under year 1893.

". . . A few corrections and verbal alterations have been made . . ."–––*Note to the Second Edition*, p. viii, dated *Sept. 20, 1845.*

Cloth. Also issued in lithographed paper wrapper according to Livingston, p. 22.

BPL   H   Y

13055. The Missionary Memorial: A Literary and Religious Souvenir . . .

    New York: E. Walker, 114 Fulton Street. M DCCC XLVI.

Noted only in publisher's leather. According to Livingston, p. 21, also issued in cloth.

"The Captive," 17 stanzas, pp. ⟨47⟩-51. Revised and somewhat abbreviated collected in *Poems*, 1848.

For fuller entry see No. 1341.

13056. The Liberty Bell. By Friends of Freedom . . .

    Boston: Massachusetts Anti-Slavery Fair. MDCCCXLVI.

"The Falconer," pp. 241-244. Collected in *Poems*, 1848.

For fuller information see entry Nos. 6495; 11151.

13057. The Ladies' Casket; Containing a Gem, together with its Sentiment, and a Poetical Description, for Each Day in the Week, and Each Month in the Year. By J. Wesley Hanson . . .

    Lowell: Merrill and Heywood. Boston: B. B. Mussey. 1846.

"Sapphire," pp. 56-57. Extracted from "Farewell," *Graham's Magazine*, June, 1842. The whole collected in *Early Poems*, 1887.

Deposited Dec. 26, 1846.

B

13058. The American Anti-Slavery Almanac, for 1847 . . .

    New York: Published by The American Anti-Slavery Society, 142 Nassau St.; Boston . . . Philadelphia . . . Salem, Columbiana Co., Ohio. ⟨1846⟩

Cover-title. Printed self-wrapper. Unpaged.

Contains the earliest located appearance, periodical publication excepted, of any of the "Biglow Papers"; credited to Ezekil ⟨*sic*⟩ Bigelow ⟨*sic*⟩. Reprinted from *The Boston Courier*. Collected in *The Biglow Papers*, Cambridge, 1848, pp. ⟨1⟩-11, as No. I of the letters.

BA   NYPL   UV

Voices of the True-Hearted . . .

    Philadelphia . . . 1846.

See above under year 1844–1846.

13059. The Liberty Bell. By Friends of Freedom . . .

Boston: National Anti-Slavery Bazaar. MDCCCXLVII.

Cloth; and, printed paper wrapper.

"Extreme Unction," pp. 240-245. Collected in *Poems*, 1848.

Two formats noted: Thin paper (sheets bulk ⅝"); and, thick paper (sheets bulk 1" scant).

Prepared for publication at the 13th annual fair held in Boston, Dec. 22, 1846–Jan. 1, 1847.

BA H NYPL

13060. The Estray: A Collection of Poems . . .

Boston: William D. Ticknor & Co. 1847.

"To a Pine-Tree," pp. 33-35. Collected in *Poems*, 1848.

For fuller description see entry No. 12088.

13061. The Young American's Magazine of Self-Improvement . . . Edited by George W. Light . . . First Volume.

Boston: Charles H. Peirce, 3 Cornhill. 1847.

"Above and Below," pp. 54-55; "Hebè," pp. 143-144; "Study for a Head," pp. 268-270. All three also in (reprinted from?) *Poems*, 1848.

For publication note see BAL, Vol. V, p. 595.

13062. . . . A FABLE FOR CRITICS . . . BY A WONDERFUL QUIZ . . .

SET FORTH IN OCTOBER, THE 21ST DAY, IN THE YEAR '48, BY G. P. PUTNAM, BROADWAY.

Title-page in black and red. At head of title: *READER! walk up at once* . . . See next two entries. Also see under year 1890.

⟨i-iv⟩, ⟨i⟩-⟨iv⟩, ⟨5⟩-78. 7⅝" × 5".

⟨-⟩², 1², 2-7⁶, 8¹.

Unprinted tan paper boards, printed paper label on spine. TB cloth: purple. Fine-grained TR cloth: purple. Tan end papers. Flyleaves.

Four states noted, possibly in the following sequence:

A: P. 63 mispaged 64. P. 64 mispaged 63.

B: P. 63 properly paged. P. 64 mispaged 63.

C: P. 63 mispaged 64. P. 64 properly paged.

D: Pp. 63 and 64 correctly paged.

Note: In all four of the preceding the following line does not appear on the title-page: A VOCAL AND MUSICAL MEDLEY

Advertised for Oct. 21 LW Oct. 14, 1848. Advertised as *just published* LW Oct. 21, 1848. According to a letter from Charles F. Briggs to Lowell (text from Livingston, pp. 28-29) 1000 copies were printed and published on Oct. 25, 1848. Advertised LW Oct. 28, 1848, as available in cloth; and, paper boards. Deposited Oct. 28, 1848. Listed as issued during the period Oct. 28–Nov. 4, in LW Nov. 4, 1848. The London (Chapman importation) issue advertised as *just received*. Ath Dec. 9, 1848; advertised without comment Ath Dec. 23, 1848. Reviewed Ath April 21, 1849. Advertised PC May 15, 1849, as in boards; Ath May 19, 1849, as in cloth. Listed PC June 1, 1849. The Putnam importation was advertised Ath May 11, 1850.

AAS (State D) H (States C,D) NYHS (State D) NYPL (States A,D) UV (all) Y (State C)

13063. . . . A Fable for Critics . . . A Vocal and Musical Medley . . . by a Wonderful Quiz . . . ⟨Second Printing⟩

Set Forth in October, the 21st Day, in the Year '48: G. P. Putnam, Broadway.

At head of title: *Reader! walk up at once* . . .

See preceding entry; also see next entry.

Corrected edition. Contains minor revisions or corrections in the text. Does not contain "A Preliminary Note to the Second Edition."

⟨i⟩-⟨vi⟩, ⟨7⟩-80.

⟨1-3¹², 4-5²⟩.

Cloth; and, tan paper boards, printed paper label on spine.

BPL H UV

13064. . . . A Fable for Critics . . . A Vocal and Musical Medley . . . by a Wonderful Quiz . . . ⟨Second Edition⟩

Set Forth in October, the 21st Day, in the Year '48: G. P. Putnam, Broadway.

At head of title: *Reader! walk up at once* . . .

Second edition. Extended by the addition of a six-page "A Preliminary Note to the Second Edition." See preceding two entries.

Pagination: 7 preliminary leaves (including an initial blank leaf, inserted title-leaf, and three inserted leaves comprising the "A Preliminary Note to the Second Edition"); followed by: ⟨7⟩-80; publisher's advertisements, pp. ⟨81-88⟩. The advertisements are paged 9-16. Final page of advertisements dated *November, 1848*.

⟨1¹⁶ (the title-leaf inserted; "A Preliminary Note to the Second Edition," printed on three leaves, also inserted); 2-3¹², 4⁸⟩.

Note: Copies with the publisher's address given as *10 Park Place* were issued not before May, 1852. One such set of sheets (in H) has present Ticknor & Fields's inserted catalog dated *June, 1854*.

BINDER'S VARIANT A

T cloth: slate. Sides blindstamped with a strap-work frame. "A Preliminary Note to the Second Edition," inserted immediately following the copyright notice; pasted in although sawed for sewing. The note consists of ⟨I², 2¹⟩.

BINDER'S VARIANT B

T cloth: brown; slate. Sides blindstamped with a strapwork frame. Tan paper boards, printed paper label on spine. "A Preliminary Note to the Second Edition" inserted immediately following the copyright notice; pasted in; printed on three singleton leaves; saw marks present on some copies.

Inserted at front of some copies there is a single leaf advertisement for Layard's *Nineveh and its Remains*, which is described as "in press and will shortly publish." The Layard was issued not before 1849.

BINDER'S VARIANT C

Tan paper boards, printed paper label on spine. "A Preliminary Note to the Second Edition" inserted, by pasting, immediately following the copyright notice; no saw marks present. The three leaves collate: ⟨I², 2¹⟩.

Inserted at front is a single leaf advertisement for Layard's *Nineveh and its Remains*, which is described as "in press and will shortly publish." The Layard was issued not before 1849.

BINDER'S VARIANT D

TB cloth: purple. "A Preliminary Note to the Second Edition" inserted immediately before p. ⟨7⟩; saw marks present; the three leaves collate: ⟨I², 2¹⟩. Sides blindstamped with a single rule frame, publisher's monogram at the center. The H copy inscribed by Longfellow: *Henry W. Long-fellow from the Author. 1851.* Also noted in tan paper boards, printed paper label on spine.

BINDER'S VARIANT E

Tan calf. Sides stamped with a border in gold and blind. At center, in blind, the ornate upright oval so frequently used during this period by William D. Ticknor. Advertisements removed. "A Preliminary Note to the Second Edition" inserted immediately before p. ⟨7⟩. Saw marks present. The three leaves collate: ⟨I², 2¹⟩. H copy inscribed by Lowell Dec. 24, 1853.

BPL (Variants B, D)   H (Variants A-E)   LC (Variant B)   Y (Variant A)

13065. The Liberty Bell. By Friends of Free-dom . . .

Boston: National Anti-Slavery Bazaar. MDCCCXLVIII.

"An Extract," *Force never yet gained one true victory*, pp. 180-183. Collected in *Uncollected Poems*, 1950.

H   NYPL

13066. POEMS . . . SECOND SERIES.

CAMBRIDGE: PUBLISHED BY GEORGE NICHOLS. BOSTON: B. B. MUSSEY AND COMPANY. 1848.

⟨i⟩-viii, ⟨I⟩-184. $7\frac{7}{16}$″ × $4\frac{11}{16}$″ full (untrimmed). $7\frac{1}{8}$″ × $4\frac{1}{2}$″ (cloth, plain edges). $6\frac{11}{16}$″ × $4\frac{3}{8}$″ (cloth, edges gilt). $7\frac{1}{4}$″ × $4\frac{9}{16}$″ (boards).

⟨-⟩⁴, I-11⁸, 12⁴.

Noted in the following bindings. Sequence not determined. The order of presentation is com-pletely arbitrary and the designations are for identification only.

A

A cloth: blue; white. S cloth: white, printed in red with horizontal stripes. Sides stamped in gold with a multiple rules frame enclosing an elaborate leafy scroll frame. Yellow end papers. Flyleaves. Edges gilt.

B

H cloth: black; purple. T cloth: black; blue; plum. Sides blindstamped with a triple rule frame, a floral ornament at each inner corner. Yellow end papers. Flyleaves. Edges plain.

C

Tan paper boards. Printed paper label on spine. Flyleaves. Edges plain. Also issued in glazed yellow boards.

D

T cloth: plum. Sides blindstamped with a triple rule frame, a filigree at each inner corner. At center, also blindstamped, an ornament composed of an upright decorated diamond. Yellow end papers. Flyleaves. Edges plain.

E

T cloth: brown. With the spine imprint: TICKNOR & CO. Inserted catalog (Ticknor, Reed & Fields) dated *July, 1852.* Copy in LC.

Note: "The Morning-Glory," pp. 131-134 was written by Maria Lowell.

A rebound copy in H inscribed by Lowell Dec. 24, 1847. Copies in binding C have been seen inscribed by Lowell Dec. 25, 1847. Advertised as *just published* LW Dec. 25, 1847. Deposited Jan. 6, 1848. Reviewed LW Jan. 8, 1848. Listed LW Jan. 15, 1848. The London importation listed PC May 1, 1848.

AAS   B   BA   H   NYPL   UV   Y

13067. Water Celebration, Boston, October 25, 1848, Exercises at the Fountain. I. Hymn. By George Russell, Esq. . . . III. Ode. By James Russell Lowell, Esq., to be Sung by the School Children . . .

⟨n.p., n.d., Boston, 1848⟩

Broadside. $11\frac{3}{4}'' \times 9''$ scant. Printed on recto only.

"Ode," beginning: *My name is water . . .* Collected in *Poems*, 1849.

Two states (probably printings) noted. The sequence has not been established and the designations are for identification only.

STATE A

Double rule below the line *Boston, October 25, 1848.* Exclamation point present at end of fourth line of George Russell's "Hymn."

STATE B

Wavy rule present below the line *Boston, October 25, 1848.* Exclamation point not present at end of fourth line of George Russell's "Hymn." Two copies of this printing were received by Harvard on Oct. 25, 1848; one of these being inscribed in a contemporary hand: *Printed in the Street & distributed while the Procession was passing.*

The poem also appears in *Celebration of the Introduction of the Water of Cochituate Lake into the City of Boston. October 25, 1848*, Boston ⟨not before Nov. 2, 1848⟩. Copies in AAS, H, Y.

AAS (A)   H (A,B)   BPL (B)   UV (B)   Y (B)

13068. . . . THE BIGLOW PAPERS, EDITED, WITH AN INTRODUCTION, NOTES, GLOSSARY, AND COPIOUS INDEX, BY HOMER WILBUR . . .

CAMBRIDGE: PUBLISHED BY GEORGE NICHOLS. 1848.

At head of title: *Melibœus-Hipponax.*

Also noted with the following imprints:

CAMBRIDGE: PUBLISHED BY GEORGE NICHOLS. NEW YORK: GEORGE P. PUTNAM, 155 BROADWAY. 1848.

CAMBRIDGE: PUBLISHED BY GEORGE NICHOLS. LONDON: PUTNAM'S AMERICAN LITERARY AGENCY, J. CHAPMAN, 142 STRAND. 1848.

⟨1⟩-12, ⟨i⟩-xxxii, ⟨1⟩-163. $7\frac{1}{4}''$ full $\times 4\frac{9}{16}''$.

a-b⁸, c⁶, 1-10⁸, 11².

Noted in the following bindings; the designations are for identification only; no sequence is suggested.

BINDING A

A cloth: purple. H cloth: brown, green, purple. T cloth: black, brown, plum. Sides blindstamped with a triple rule frame, a filigree at each inner corner, a filigree measuring $3\frac{1}{8}''$ tall at center. Yellow end papers. Tan end papers. Flyleaves.

BINDING B

Gray-brown paper boards, printed paper label on spine. White end papers.

BINDING C

Glazed yellow paper boards, printed paper label on spine. Yellow-coated end papers.

BINDING D

Moiréd S cloth. Sides blindstamped with a floral frame (within rules), a filigree measuring $3\frac{3}{4}''$ tall at center. White end papers. Noted only on sheets bearing the Cambridge and London imprint. Probably produced in England.

Sheets were also issued in London with leaf a₈ (the title-leaf) excised; and, a cancel title-leaf, probably printed in England, inserted preceding leaf a₁. The insert is imprinted: CAMBRIDGE, U.S. / PUBLISHED BY GEORGE NICHOLS. / LONDON: / JOHN CHAPMAN, 142, STRAND. / 1849. Locations: B, Y.

Livingston, p. 34, quotes a letter from Charles F. Briggs, to Lowell, *Oct. 1848*, as follows: "Putnam says that you may put his name into 100 copies for his London agency and 500 for New York, if you would like for him to attend to the sale and distribution here ⟨New York⟩." BAL has been unable to locate the original letter.

Noticed by *Daily Evening Transcript*, Boston, Nov. 20, 1848. The BA copy (now rebound) received Nov. 22, 1848. Listed by LW Nov. 25, 1848. The London issue advertised Ath Dec. 23, 1848; listed LG Dec. 23, 1848. Advertised PC May 15, 1849; listed PC June 1, 1849. For a somewhat extended edition see below under 1859.

AAS   B   H   NYHS   NYPL   UV   Y

13069. THE VISION OF SIR LAUNFAL . . .

CAMBRIDGE: PUBLISHED BY GEORGE NICHOLS. 1848.

⟨i-vi⟩, ⟨1⟩-27; leaf excised or pasted under the end paper. $7\frac{1}{4}'' \times 4\frac{7}{16}''$.

⟨1⟩-3⁶. Leaf 3₆ excised or pasted under the end paper. *Also signed:* ⟨A⟩-B⁸, C².

Printed glazed yellow paper boards. Yellow end papers. Flyleaf at front.

A Boston news letter dated Nov. 24, 1848, in LW Dec. 2, 1848, reports the book in press, to be issued about the middle of November. Livingston (p. 35) states "published on December 18." Noted as *just published* in a Boston news letter dated Dec. 21, 1848, in LW Dec. 30, 1848. BA copy received Dec. 20, 1848. UV copy inscribed by early owner Jan. 1, 1849. Deposited Jan. 18, 1849.

AAS   H   NYPL   UV   Y

13070. The Liberty Bell. By Friends of Freedom . . .

Boston: National Anti-Slavery Bazaar. MDCCCXLIX.

Cloth; and, leather.

"The Burial of Theobald," pp. 269-274. Collected in *Uncollected Poems*, 1950.

H

13071. The Gallery of Mezzotints: An Annual for 1849 . . .

New-York: M. H. Newman & Company, 199 Broadway. MDCCCXLIX.

Leather.

"To Lamartine," pp. ⟨9⟩-13. Collected in *Poems*, 1849 (Dec. 1849).

Precise date of publication not known. As an 1849 annual presumably issued in late 1848.

"It is but just to say that a volume substantially like the present, but with fewer embellishments, was published in the autumn of last year, under the title of the *Gem of the Season*."–––p. 4. Reference is to *The Gem of the Season, for 1848*, New York, 1848, which does not contain the Lowell poem.

H

13072. Hymns and Songs, for the Anti-Slavery Celebration of the Declaration of Independence, at Abington, July 4, 1849 . . .

Broadside. Printed on one side only.

Contains the following material by Lowell:

"Hymn," *Men! whose boast it is that ye;* otherwise "Stanzas Sung at the Anti-Slavery Picnic in Dedham . . . ," *Poems*, 1844.

"Song," *Friends of Freedom! ye who stand* . . . The earliest located book publication is in *Proceedings of the Anti-Slavery Meeting Held in Stacy Hall, Boston, on the Twentieth Anniversary of the Mob of October 21, 1835* . . . , by J. M. W. Yerrinton, Boston, 1855. Collected in *Uncollected Poems*, 1950, p. 108, as "Hymn".

H

13073. Poems by James Russell Lowell. In Two Volumes . . .

Boston: Ticknor, Reed, and Fields. M DCCC XLIX.

1: ⟨i⟩-xii, ⟨1⟩-251. 2: ⟨i⟩-⟨viii⟩, ⟨1⟩-254, blank leaf. 7³⁄₁₆″ × 4⁹⁄₁₆″ (paper boards). 7″ × 4⁷⁄₁₆″ (cloth). See note below for comment on bindings.

Reprint with the exception of the following poems which are here in their earliest located book publication; or, here first collected.

"Ambrose," "Beaver Brook," "Bibliotres," "Eurydice," "Freedom," "Kossuth," "Lines Suggested by the Graves of Two English Soldiers on Concord Battle-Ground," "Ode to France," "Ode Written for the Celebration of the Introduction of the

Cochituate Water into the City of Boston," "A Parable" (*Said Christ our Lord* . . .), "She Came and Went," "The Sower," "Thistle-Downs," "To–––" (*We, too, have autumns* . . .), "To John G. Palfrey," "To Lamartine," "To the Memory of Hood," "To W. L. Garrison," "Trial."

"The poem called *The Morning-Glory*, on page 131, it is proper to state, is by another hand." Vol. 2, p. vii.

BINDINGS

Noted in the following bindings. The designations are for identification only and no sequence is suggested.

BINDING A

Tan paper boards, printed paper label on spine. Light buff end papers. Flyleaves. Publisher's catalog, pp. ⟨1⟩-4, dated *December, 1849*, inserted at front of Vol. 1. Edges plain.

BINDING B

T cloth: brown; green; slate. On the sides: A gold-stamped rococo floral arrangement within a gold-stamped triple-rule frame. Yellow end papers. Flyleaves. Edges gilt.

BINDING C

T cloth: slate. On the sides: A goldstamped rococo floral arrangement within a blindstamped triple rule frame. Yellow end papers. Flyleaves. Edges gilt.

BINDING D

T cloth: brown. Sides blindstamped at center with an ornate medallion measuring 3½″ tall. Yellow end papers. Single; or, double flyleaves. Publisher's catalog, pp. ⟨1⟩-4, dated *December, 1849*, inserted at front of Vol. 1.

A copy in *Binding D* (in H) inscribed by Lowell Dec. 25, 1849. Listed in LW Jan. 5, 1850.

AAS (Binding C)   BA (Binding D)   H (Bindings B, D)   NYPL (Binding B)   UV (Bindings A, B)

13074. The Works of the Late Edgar Allan Poe: With Notices of His Life and Genius. By N. P. Willis, J. R. Lowell, and R. W. Griswold. In Two Volumes. Vol. 1. Tales.

New York: J. S. Redfield, Clinton Hall. 1850.

Two printings noted; the following is sufficient for identification:

1

Fly-title leaf not present. ⟨-⟩₁₂ᵣ is a divisional title-page.

2

Fly-title leaf: ⟨-⟩₂ᵣ. Divisional title-page not present.

Location: BPL

"Edgar A. Poe," pp. vii-xiii. ". . . Written . . . five years ago . . . published in Graham's Magazine for February, 1845. It is here reprinted with a few alterations and omissions." This version collected in *The Function of the Poet*, 1920. For earliest located book publication of the magazine text see *The Complete Works of Edgar Allan Poe . . . ⟨1902⟩*, below.

For fuller comment see entry No. 6684.

13075. The Liberty Bell. By Friends of Freedom . . .

Boston: National Anti-Slavery Bazaar. MDCCCLI.

"Yussouf," pp. 303-304. Collected in *Under the Willows*, 1869.

A copy in H inscribed by early owner 1850.

H

13076. Memory and Hope.

Boston: Ticknor, Reed, and Fields. MDCCCLI.

Cloth; and, leather.

"The First Snow-Fall," pp. 19-21. Collected in *Under the Willows*, 1869.

Noticed in LW Jan. 18, 1851.

BA   H   NYPL   UV   Y

13077. The Woodbine: A Holiday Gift. Edited by Caroline May . . .

Philadelphia: Lindsay and Blakiston. ⟨1851⟩

"The Tortoise Shell," by James Russel ⟨*sic*⟩ Lowell, pp. ⟨21⟩-22. Collected in *Under the Willows*, 1869, as "The Finding of the Lyre."

Listed LW Nov. 22, 1851.

Y

13078. Celebration of British West India Emancipation, at Framingham, August 3, 1852 . . .

Prentiss & Sawyer, Printers, No. 11 Devonshire, near State Street, Boston. ⟨1852⟩

Single cut sheet. Printed on recto only. $19\frac{5}{8}''$ × $11\frac{13}{16}''$.

Issued as a song sheet; six songs, including "Lines," by James Russell Lowell; *Let others strive or fame and gold* . . .

Otherwise unlocated.

BPL

13079. Thalatta: A Book for the Sea-Side . . .

Boston: Ticknor, Reed, and Fields. MDCCCLIII.

Reprint save for: "Appledore," pp. 61-63; collected in *Under the Willows*, 1869.

For comment see Nos. 1380, 8217.

13080. The Poetical Works of William Wordsworth . . .

Boston: Little, Brown, and Company. New York: Evans and Dickerson. Philadelphia: Lippincott, Grambo, and Co. M.DCCC.LIV.

7 Vols.

"Sketch of Wordsworth's Life," Vol. 1, pp. ⟨ix⟩-xl. Anonymous. Collected in *Among My Books, Second Series*, 1876, in somewhat revised form.

Deposited Nov. 28, 1854. Advertised NLG Dec. 15, 1854.

BPL   H   Y

13081. The Poetical Works of John Keats. With a Life.

Boston: Little, Brown and Company. New York: Evans and Dickerson. Philadelphia: Lippincott, Grambo and Co. M.DCCC.LIV.

"The Life of Keats," pp. ⟨vii⟩-xxxvi. Collected (revised) in *Among My Books, Second Series*, 1876.

Two forms of the binding noted:

Cloth gilt: Sides stamped in blind, edges plain.

Cloth extra gilt: Sides stamped in blind and gold, edges gilt.

Livingston, p. 42, reports "issued in cloth with paper label, *The | British Poets. | Poems of | Keats, 1855.*" Not located by BAL.

Deposited Jan. 15, 1855. Reviewed NLG March 1, 1855.

H

13082. The Knickerbocker Gallery: A Testimonial to the Editor of the Knickerbocker Magazine from Its Contributors . . .

New-York: Samuel Hueston, 348 Broadway. MDCCCLV.

"Masaccio. Brancacci Chapel, Florence," pp. ⟨381⟩-382. Collected in *Under the Willows*, 1869.

For fuller description see entry No. 1033.

13083. The Poems of Maria Lowell.

Cambridge: Privately Printed. 1855.

Edited anonymously by Lowell.

Cloth; and, morocco.

". . . Fifty copies were printed for presentation . . ."---Livingston, p. 46. BAL has been unable to verify the statement.

Lowell presented a copy to E. A. Duycinck May 1, 1855; in NYPL.

AAS   H   NYPL   Y

13084. The Poetical Works of Percy Bysshe Shelley, Edited by Mrs. Shelley . . .

Boston: Little, Brown and Company. New York: James S. Dickerson. Philadelphia: Lippincott, Grambo and Co. M.DCCC.LV.

3 Vols. Cloth, printed paper label on spine; stamped cloth.

"Memoir of Shelley," Vol. i, pp. ⟨xvii⟩-xli. Anonymous.

Deposited June 25, 1855. Advertised as *just published* NLG July 2, 1855. Noted as issued *since June 15*, NLG July 2, 1855.

AAS BPL H

13085. The Poetical Works of Dr. John Donne, with a Memoir.

Boston: Little, Brown and Company. Shepard, Clark and Co. New York: James S. Dickerson. Philadelphia: J. B. Lippincott and Co. M.DCCC.LV.

Edited by Lowell.

Cloth, printed paper label on spine.

Listed APC Dec. 29, 1855.

PDH

13086. Pictures and Readings from American Authors, Being the Choice Volume of Putnam's Magazine.

New York: Leavitt and Allen. 1855.

"Fireside Travels," pp. 473-482. Being part two of two parts. Collected in *Fireside Travels*, 1864, as part of "Cambridge Thirty Years Ago." See *Favorite Authors*, 1861, below.

"Our Own, His Wanderings and Personal Adventures," pp. 533-535. Being part two of three parts. Collected in *Uncollected Poems*, 1950.

"Simpkins on His Baldness," p. 299. Otherwise unlocated.

For comment see No. 11179.

13087. The Poetry and Mystery of Dreams. ⟨Compiled⟩ by Charles G. Leland . . .

Philadelphia: Published by E. H. Butler & Co. M.DCCC.LVI.

Untitled lines, pp. 90-91, *Who hath not been a poet?* . . . Extracted from "The Parting of the Ways," collected in *Under the Willows*, 1869.

Untitled lines, pp. 122-123; otherwise "The Fountain," *Poems*, 1844.

For fuller entry see No. 11527.

13088. The Poetical Works of Andrew Marvell. With a Memoir of the Author.

Boston: Little, Brown and Company. Shepard, Clark and Brown. Cincinnati: Moore, Wilstach, Keys and Co. M.DCCC.LVII.

Edited by Lowell.

Listed APC May 30, 1857.

BPL

13089. Tales and Sketches for the Fire-Side, by the Best American Authors. Selected from Putnam's Magazine.

New York: A. Dowling, 36 Beekman Street 1857.

"The Windharp," "Auf Wiedersehen! Summer," "Palinode. Autumn," all in the issue of Dec. 1854. All collected in *Under the Willows*, 1869.

Irregular pagination. For fuller comment see entry No. 8239.

13090. The Poetical Works . . . Complete in Two Volumes . . .

Boston: Ticknor and Fields. M DCCC LVIII.

Blue and Gold Edition.

Reprint save for:

"The Courtin'," Vol. 2, pp. 104-105, here present in 12 stanzas. In *The Biglow Papers*, 1848, the poem appears in 6 stanzas.

"The Two Gunners," Vol. 2, pp. 125-127.

"The Unhappy Lot of Mr. Knott, 1850," Vol. 2, pp. ⟨281⟩-309.

"An Oriental Apologue," Vol. 2, pp. ⟨311⟩-322.

Deposited Jan. 9, 1858. What may be this edition is listed as an importation Ath May 15, 1858.

AAS BPL H Y

13091. . . . AN AUTOGRAPH . . .

CAMBRIDGE, 7th MARCH, 1858.

Single leaf of personal stationery folded to make four pages. At upper left: Small oval embossed stationer's stamp displaying a crown, BATH, within a wreath. Page: 6¼″ × 3⅞″. Text on p. ⟨1⟩, otherwise unprinted.

At head of title: *Written in Aid of the Fair for the Poor, at the Boston Music Hall, March, 1858.*

The fair was held March 9-12, 1858.

Collected in *Under the Willows*, 1869, as "For an Autograph."

H

13092. Poetry of the Bells Collected by Samuel Batchelder, Jr

Riverside Press Printed in Aid of the Cambridge Chime by H. O. Houghton and Company 1858

Reprint save for "Godminster Chimes," pp. ⟨57⟩-60. Collected in *Under the Willows*, 1869.

H NYPL Y

13093. The Poets of the Nineteenth Century. Selected and Edited by the Rev. Robert Aris Willmott . . . with English and American Additions, Arranged by Evert A. Duyckinck . . .

New York: Harper & Brothers, Publishers, Franklin Square. 1858.

Reprint with the exception of "The Singing Leaves," pp. 584-588. Collected in *Under the Willows*, 1869.

H NYPL

13094. Report of the Committee of the Association of the Alumni of Harvard College, Appointed to Take into Consideration the State of the College Library, in Accordance with a Vote of the Association Passed at the Annual Meeting, July 16, 1857.

Cambridge: Metcalf and Company, Printers to the University. 1858.

Printed paper wrapper.

"Statement . . . ," dated *7th June, 1858*, pp. 20-21.

H Y

13095. The New American Cyclopædia: A Popular Dictionary of General Knowledge. Edited by George Ripley and Charles A. Dana . . .

New York: D. Appleton and Company, 346 & 348 Broadway. London: 16 Little Britain. M.DCCC.LVIII. ⟨-M.DCCC.LXIII.⟩

"Dante," Vol. 6, pp. 247-258. Anonymous. For attribution to Lowell see Longfellow's translation of Dante's *The Divine Comedy*, Vol. 1, 1867, p. 356. Not to be confused with Lowell's "Dante" in *Among My Books, Second Series*, 1876.

For comment see entry No. 3715.

(Privately Printed.) To J.R.L. Sur la Pipe Cassée . . . 1858

See below under *ca.* 1890.

To Mr. John Bartlett. On Sending Me a Seven-Pound Trout. 1858.

See below under the year 1866.

13096. ALL SAINTS . . . WRITTEN FOR HARRIET RYAN'S FAIR. MARCH 20th, 1859.

⟨n.p., n.d., 1859⟩

Single leaf. Folded to make four pages. Page: 6¼″ × 4″. Printed on p. ⟨1⟩ only.

Collected in *Under the Willows*, 1869.

H

13097. The Biglow Papers . . . Edited . . . by the Author of "Tom Brown's School-Days." Reprinted, with the Author's Sanction, from the Fourth American Edition.

London: Trübner & Co. 60, Paternoster Row. 1859.

Reprint save for a seven-line letter from Lowell, *14th September, 1859*, p. ⟨v⟩. Edited by Thomas Hughes. For first edition of the American edition see above under year 1848.

Noted in the following states:

STATE A

In the imprint an umlaut is either present or absent in the name Trübner. When present it appears either over the letter *u*; or, slightly to the left. BAL theorizes that the typesetters improvised and used a colon (set sideways) instead of a true umlaut.

The reprint notice on the title-page set in capital letters only.

P. viii, in the footnote, the word *secrecy* is misspelled *secresy*.

P. x, lines 5-6 from bottom: . . . 'Ents- | " tchungs-weise' . . .

P. xv, line 8 from bottom: . . . *most*

Terminal catalog not present.

STATE B

In the imprint an umlaut is present in the name Trübner and appears either over the letter *ü*; or, slightly to the left. BAL theorizes that the typesetters improvised and used a colon (set sideways) instead of a true umlaut.

The reprint notice on the title-page is set in capitals and lower case.

P. viii, in the footnote, the word *secrecy* is correctly spelled.

P. x, lines 5-6 from bottom: . . . 'Ent- | " stehungs-weise' . . .

P. xv, line 8 from bottom: . . . *mos⟨t⟩*

Terminal catalog present.

Note: Sheets of *State B* have been seen with a cancel title-leaf dated 1861 and imprinted *Third English Edition*. Copy in B.

Advertised for *the 28th inst.*, Bkr Oct. 1859. Listed in both Ath and LG Oct. 29, 1859. Listed Bkr Oct. 1859. Advertised for *this day* PC Nov. 1, 1859; Ath Nov. 5, 1859. Listed PC Nov. 15, 1859.

B (State A)   H (States A,B)   NYPL (State B)

13098. Gifts of Genius: A Miscellany of Prose and Poetry, by American Authors.

New York: Printed for C. A. Davenport. ⟨1859⟩

"Sea-Weed," pp. 89-90. Collected in *Under the Willows*, 1869.

For comment see entry No. 3717.

13099. Celebration of the Hundredth Anniversary of the Birth of Robert Burns, by the Boston Burns Club. January 25th, 1859.

Boston: Printed by H. W. Dutton and Son, Transcript Building. 1859.

"Poem," *A hundred years!* ..., pp. 55-59. Collected in *Heartsease and Rue*, 1888, as "At the Burns Centennial."

For comment see entry No. 8783.

13100. Folk Songs Selected and Edited by John Williamson Palmer ...

New York: Charles Scribner, 124 Grand Street. London: Sampson Low, Son and Company. M DCCC LXI.

Reprint save for "Without and Within," pp. 108-110. Collected in *Under the Willows*, 1869.

For comment see entry No. 11312.

13101. Favorite Authors. A Companion-Book of Prose and Poetry ...

Boston: Ticknor and Fields. M DCCC LXI.

Edited by James T. Fields.

"Cambridge Worthies———Thirty Years Ago," pp. ⟨270⟩-293. Previously in *Pictures and Readings* ..., 1855, a twilight book, above, *q.v.*, under the title "Fireside Travels." Collected in *Fireside Travels*, 1864.

H

13102. The Victoria Regia: A Volume of Original Contributions in Poetry and Prose. Edited by Adelaide A. Procter.

London: Printed and Published by Emily Faithfull and Co., Victoria Press, (for the Employment of Women,) Great Coram Street, W. C. 1861 ...

"The Fatal Curiosity," pp. 83-84. Collected in *Uncollected Poems*, 1950.

Cloth; and, leather.

AAS   BPL   H   Y

13103. ... MASON AND SLIDELL: A YANKEE IDYLL. TO THE EDITORS OF THE ATLANTIC MONTHLY, JAALAM, 6th JAN., 1862 ...

⟨n.p., n.d., Boston, 1862⟩

Caption-title. The above at head of p. 1. At head of title: *From the Atlantic Monthly.*

1-12. 9 11/16″ × 6 1/16″.

⟨-⟩⁶.

Printed self-wrapper.

Printed from the altered plates of *The Atlantic Monthly*, Feb. 1862. Collected in *The Biglow Papers, Second Series*, 1867. See next entry.

AAS   H   NYHS   NYPL   UV   Y

13104. THE BIGLOW PAPERS ... SECOND SERIES. PART I ... BIRDOFREDUM SAWIN, ESQ. TO MR. HOSEA BIGLOW ... MASON AND SLIDELL: A YANKEE IDYLL. AUTHORIZED EDITION.

LONDON: TRÜBNER & CO. 60, PATERNOSTER ROW. 1862.

Issued in three parts. For Parts II and III see below under year 1862. For extended editions see below under years 1864, 1865. For first American edition see below under year 1867.

⟨1⟩-52. 6 13/16″ full × 4 7/8″.

⟨A⟩-C⁸, D².

Printed paper wrapper. Two states of the wrapper noted:

STATE A WRAPPER

Blue-gray paper. The statement *Price One Shilling* not present.

STATE B WRAPPER

Rose paper. The statement *Price One Shilling* added to front of wrapper.

CONTENTS

"Birdofredum Sawin, Esq. to Mr. Hosea Biglow ... Jaalam, 15th Nov., 1861." Originally in *The Atlantic Monthly*, Jan. 1862. Collected in *The Biglow Papers, Second Series*, Boston, 1867.

"Mason and Slidell: A Yankee Idyll ... Jaalam, 6th Jan., 1862." Originally in *The Atlantic Monthly*, Feb. 1862. Also issued as a separate; see preceding entry. Collected in *The Biglow Papers, Second Series*, Boston, 1867.

A copy of *State A* in PDH inscribed by Trübner Feb. 12, 1862. Listed Ath Feb. 15, 1862. Reviewed Ath Feb. 22, 1862. Listed PC March 1, 1862.

H (State B)   UI (State A)   UV (State A)   Y (State B)

13105. Only Once. Original Papers, by Various Contributors.

Published for the Benefit of the New York Infirmary for Women and Children, No. 126 Second Avenue. 1862 ...

"Before the Embers," p. 6. A truncated and revised version collected in *Heartsease and Rue*, 1888, under the title "My Portrait Gallery." Collected in full in *Uncollected Poems*, 1950.

For fuller entry see No. 11183.

13106. THE BIGLOW PAPERS . . . SECOND SERIES. PART II . . . BIRDOFREDUM SAWIN, ESQ. TO MR. HOSEA BIGLOW . . . A MESSAGE OF JEFF DAVIS IN SECRET SESSION. AUTHORIZED EDITION.

LONDON: TRÜBNER & CO. 60, PATERNOSTER ROW. 1862.

Issued in three parts. For comment see under *Part I*, above, under year 1862.

⟨i-ii⟩, ⟨53⟩-90. $6^{15}/_{16}'' \times 4^{3}/_{4}''$.

⟨E⟩-F⁸, G⁴.

Printed rose paper wrapper. Inserted at front is a slip advertising *Mr. Charles Lever's Works* . . .

CONTENTS

"Birdofredum Sawin, Esq., to Mr. Hosea Biglow . . . Jaalam, 7th Feb., 1862." Originally in *The Atlantic Monthly*, March, 1862. Collected in *The Biglow Papers, Second Series*, Boston, 1867.

"A Message of Jeff Davis in Secret Session . . . Jaalam, 10th March, 1862." Originally in *The Atlantic Monthly*, April, 1862. Collected in *The Biglow Papers, Second Series*, Boston, 1867.

Note: It is probable that the copies first through the press have page 73 so numbered; later, paged 7.

Listed Ath April 19, 1862.

H (p. 73 paged 7)   PDH (p. 73 so paged)

13107. IL PESCEBALLO. OPERA SERIA: IN UN ATTO. MUSICA DEL MAESTRO ROSSIBELLI-DONIMOZARTI . . .

⟨n.p., n.d., Cambridge, 1862⟩

Anonymous. Italian text by Francis J. Child; English text by Lowell.

Caption-title. The above at head of p. ⟨1⟩.

⟨1⟩-31. $7'' \times 4^{5}/_{16}''$.

1-4⁴.

Printed self-wrapper.

Three printings noted; printings 2 and 3 vary textually from the first printing.

PRINTING 1

As collated above. Printed on wove paper. Issued in printed self-wrapper.

PRINTING 2

⟨1⟩-31. Printed on laid paper. Issued in printed self-wrapper. 1-2⁸. Signature mark 1 appears directly below the *ec* in *specialmente*. Signature mark 2 appears below the *h* in *had*.

PRINTING 3

⟨1⟩-31. Printed on laid paper. Issued in printed gray-green paper wrapper. 1-2⁸. Signature mark 1 appears directly below the *p* in *specialmente*. Signature mark 2 appears below the space in *had so*. Text as in the second printing.

A copy of the second printing in H inscribed by early owner May 8, 1862.

AAS (all three)   BA (1st, 2nd)   H (all three) BPL (1st, 2nd)   UV (1st, 2nd)   Y (1st, 2nd)

13108. THE BIGLOW PAPERS . . . SECOND SERIES. PART III . . . SPEECH OF HONOURABLE PRESERVED DOE IN SECRET CAUCUS . . . SUNTHIN' IN THE PASTORAL LINE. AUTHORIZED EDITION.

LONDON: TRÜBNER & CO. 60, PATERNOSTER ROW. 1862.

Issued in three parts. For comment see under *Part I*, above, under year 1862.

⟨i-ii⟩, ⟨91⟩-120. $6^{5}/_{8}''$ full $\times 4^{13}/_{16}''$.

H-I⁸. Signature mark H on p. ⟨91⟩.

Printed rose paper wrapper.

CONTENTS

"Speech of Honourable Preserved Doe in Secret Caucus." Originally in *The Atlantic Monthly*, May, 1862. Collected in *The Biglow Papers, Second Series*, Boston, 1867.

"Sunthin' in the Pastoral Line." Originally in *The Atlantic Monthly*, June, 1862. Collected in *The Biglow Papers, Second Series*, Boston, 1867.

Listed Ath June 21, 1862; PC July 17, 1862.

HEH

13109. War-Songs for Freemen. Dedicated to the Army of the United States . . . ⟨Edited by Francis J. Child⟩

Boston: Ticknor and Fields. 1862 . . .

"A Compromise," pp. 34-36. Uncollected. Anonymous. For authority of ascription to Lowell see *The Scholar-Friends Letters of Francis James Child and James Russell Lowell*, edited by M. A. DeWolfe Howe and G. W. Cottrell, Jr., 1952, p. 13.

For fuller description see entry No. 8818.

13110. Songs for the Times. 1. A New Plantation Song. 2. Negro Boatmen's Song. 3. Song of the Sneak. 4. Soldier's Oath . . .

⟨n.p., n.d., probably Boston: Ticknor & Fields, 1863⟩

Issued in printed self-wrapper? The above at head of p. ⟨1⟩.

4 lines beginning *Thet's wut we want,———we want to know* . . . , p. ⟨1⟩.

8 lines beginning *Ther's critters yit thet talk an' act* . . . , p. ⟨1⟩.

Both extracted from "Latest Views of Mr. Big-low," which was collected as "Letter No. 7" in *The Biglow Papers, Second Series*, Boston, 1867. Originally published in *The Atlantic Monthly*, Feb. 1863.

Note: This publication appears as BAL entry No. 1405, misdated *n.d., 1862.*

H   Y

13111. . . . THE PRESIDENT'S POLICY . . . FROM THE NORTH AMERICAN RE-VIEW, JANUARY, 1864.

⟨n.p., n.d., PHILADELPHIA: CRISSY & MARKLEY FOR THE UNION LEAGUE OF PHILADELPHIA, 1864⟩

At head of title: *No. 16.* Cover-title.

⟨1⟩-22, blank leaf. $8^{13}/_{16}''$ × $5^{7}/_{8}''$.

⟨-⟩[12]. Signed: ⟨1⟩[8], 2[4].

Printed salmon wrapper.

Note: All examined copies have the reading *crisises*, p. ⟨1⟩, line 1.

Extensively revised and rewritten and collected in *My Study Windows*, 1871, as "Abraham Lincoln."

Each of the following sources states that there were two printings of *The President's Policy:* John Russell Bartlett's *A Catalogue of Books and Pamphlets Relating to the Civil War in the United States* . . . , Boston & Providence, 1866, p. 252; P. K. Foley's *American Authors* . . . , Boston, 1897, p. 183; George Willis Cooke's *A Bibliography of James Russell Lowell*, Boston & New York, 1906, pp. 109-110. The imprints as given by these sources vary. BAL has seen but one printing, that here described, and believes that but a single printing was done. Livingston describes a single printing.

For a full account of the publication of the pamphlet see Theodore Wesley Koch's "Lowell's Pamphlet *The President's Policy,* 1864," in *The Bibliographer* (New York), Vol. II, No. 2, Feb. 1903, pp. 107-112. Koch, on the basis of documentary evidence, correctly states that the pamphlet was printed for the Union League of Philadelphia, by Crissy & Markley; that the pamphlet was ordered printed Jan. 28, 1864.

The heading, *No. 16,* continues to mystify; no reasonable explanation has been seen. According to *Chronicle of the Union League of Philadelphia 1862 to 1902*, Philadelphia, 1902, p. 156, the pamphlet

was issued in March, 1864, and was the league's 71st pamphlet.

AAS   B   BA   H   LC   MHS   NYHS   NYPL   UV   Y

13112. The Spirit of the Fair . . .

New York . . . 1864.

"To a Friend Who Sent Me a Meerschaum," No. 7, April 12, 1864, pp. 79-80. Extensively revised and collected in *Heartsease and Rue*, 1888, as "To C. F. Bradford on the Gift of a Meerschaum Pipe."

For fuller entry see No. 11186. Also see (*Privately Printed.*) *To J.R.L.* . . . ⟨n.p., n.d., *ca.* 1890⟩, below.

13113. Autograph Leaves of Our Country's Authors.

Baltimore, Cushings & Bailey 1864.

"The Courtin'," pp. 107-112. This is the earliest located book publication of the 24-stanza version; collected in *The Biglow Papers, Second Series*, Boston, 1867. Previous publication: 6-stanza version in *The Biglow Papers*, Cambridge, 1848; 12-stanza version *Poetical Works*, Boston, 1858.

For fuller entry see No. 2418.

13114. Memorial RGS ⟨Robert Gould Shaw⟩

Cambridge University Press 1864

Letter, August 28, 1863, pp. 148-149. "Memoriæ Positum R.G.S.," pp. 188-191. Collected in *Under the Willows*, 1869.

For comment see entry No. 3197.

13115. National Sailors' Fair. Boston, (Mass.,) Sept. 1, 1864 . . .

⟨Boston, 1864⟩

Single leaf. Wove paper. Printed on recto only. $8''$ × $5''$.

"In November next a *National Sailors' Fair* is to be held in Boston, for the purpose of establishing a Home for Sailors and Marines . . . It is proposed, during the period for which the Fair shall be open, to publish . . . a daily paper . . ."

Signed at end by Lowell and others. See *The Boatswain's Whistle*, 1864, below.

H

13116. The Biglow Papers . . . Second Series. Authorized Edition.

London: Trübner & Co. 60, Paternoster Row. 1864.

Printed paper wrapper. See above under year 1862.

Made up of the sheets of the previously issued Parts 1, 2, 3 (see above under 1862) with the original front matter excised and new front matter for this issue inserted; plus the following textual matter inserted at the back:

"Latest Views of Mr. Biglow." Originally in *The Atlantic Monthly*, Feb. 1863. Collected in *The Biglow Papers, Second Series*, Boston, 1867. This added matter comprises pp. ⟨121⟩-133 (Sig. K). *Note:* Sig. K is an 8vo gathering with the final leaf, a blank, used as a pastedown.

Occurs in the following forms:

1

Made up of the 1862 sheets with alterations in the sheets as described above. Clay-Taylor imprint on verso of the title-leaf; and, on pp. 52, 90, 133.

2

Wholly reprinted from the original setting, the alterations being done at press, not at the bindery. Clay-Taylor imprint on verso of the title-leaf and on p. 133; not present on pp. 52, 90.

Noticed by Ath Sept. 17, 1864. Listed Ath Sept. 17, 1864; Bkr Sept. 30, 1864; PC Oct. 1, 1864. The second printing listed PC Oct. 15, 1864; Bkr Oct. 31, 1864.

HEH (1st, 2nd)

13117. FIRESIDE TRAVELS . . .

BOSTON: TICKNOR AND FIELDS. 1864.

⟨i-xii⟩, ⟨1⟩-324. 7$\frac{1}{16}$" × 4$\frac{1}{2}$".

⟨-⟩⁶, 1-13¹², 14⁶. *Also signed:* ⟨-⟩⁶, A-T⁸, U².

BD cloth: purple. C cloth: purple. LI cloth: slate. LP cloth: green. P cloth: purple. Purple cloth embossed with an arrangement of horizontal ribs and rows of beads. Brown-coated end papers. Gray-coated end papers. Flyleaves. Inserted at back of some copies is a publisher's catalog, pp. ⟨1⟩-⟨23⟩, dated *September, 1864*.

Two binder's states noted. The variation was caused at the bindery and it is entirely likely that no sequence is involved. The designations are completely arbitrary and no sequence is suggested.

STATE A

The first three pages are blank; a list of *Mr. Lowell's Writings* . . . appears on the fourth page.

STATE B

The first page is blank; a list of *Mr. Lowell's Writings* . . . appears on the second page.

The Boston Daily Evening Transcript, July 2, 1862, carried a quite premature advertisement in which the book was described as *in press*. 2500 copies printed Aug. 31, 1864 (publisher's records). Advertised as *now ready* ALG Sept. 15, 1864.

Deposited Sept. 20, 1864. Listed ALG Oct. 1, 1864. BA copy received Oct. 6, 1864. The second printing (516 copies) recorded by the publishers March 17, 1865. The London (Macmillan) edition was advertised for *next week* Ath Sept. 17, 1864, and Sept. 24, 1864; listed Ath Oct. 1, 1864.

AAS   H   MHS   NYPL   UV   Y

13118. The Boatswain's Whistle. Published at the National Sailors' Fair . . .

Boston, November 9-19, 1864.

Lowell was a member of the Editorial Council. See *National Sailors' Fair* . . . , above under ⟨1864⟩.

For fuller entry see No. 1416.

13119. The Bryant Festival at "The Century," November 5, M.DCCC.LXIV.

New York: D. Appleton and Company, 443 & 445 Broadway. M.DCCC.LXV.

Extract from a letter, p. 59.

"On Board the Seventy-Six," pp. 59-61. Collected in *Under the Willows*, 1869.

For comment see entry No. 1692.

13120. ODE RECITED AT THE COMMEMORATION OF THE LIVING AND DEAD SOLDIERS OF HARVARD UNIVERSITY, JULY 21, 1865 . . .

CAMBRIDGE: PRIVATELY PRINTED. 1865.

Title-page in black and red.

⟨i-ii⟩, ⟨1⟩-25. 9$\frac{5}{8}$" × 6$\frac{7}{8}$". Laid paper.

⟨1⟩², ⟨2⟩-4⁴.

Gray paper boards, printed paper label on front. Green-coated on white end papers. Laid paper flyleaves. Top edges gilt.

Fifty copies printed. No.––– Certificate of issue.

Reprinted in *Harvard Memorial Biographies*, 1866. Collected in *Under the Willows*, 1869.

Copies have been seen (AAS, H, NYPL, UV, Y) inscribed by Lowell Sept. 3, 1865.

AAS   H   NYPL   UV   Y

13121. The Biglow Papers . . . Second Series. Authorized People's Edition.

London: Trübner & Co. 60, Paternoster Row. 1865.

See above under year 1862.

Printed paper wrapper. Pp. ⟨i-ii⟩, ⟨1⟩-141.

Reprint save for: "Mr. Hosea Biglow to the Editor of the Atlantic Monthly," pp. ⟨134⟩-141. Originally in *The Atlantic Monthly*, April, 1865.

Collected in *The Biglow Papers, Second Series*, Boston, 1867.

Advertised for *this day* PC Nov. 1, 1865. Listed Ath Nov. 4, 1865; PC Nov. 15, 1865.

BPL   LC   Y

13122. Good Company for Every Day in the Year . . .

Boston: Ticknor and Fields. 1866.

"Dara," pp. ⟨16⟩-18. Collected in *Under the Willows*, 1869.

For comment see entry No. 5950.

13123. [No. 310.] New England Loyal Publication Society. Office, No. 8 Studio Building, Boston. April 23, 1866 . . .

⟨Boston, 1866⟩

Single cut sheet. Printed on one side only. Issued for the use of editors. Prints, with other material:

"A Speech That Mr. Johnson Might Make. [From an article entitled 'The President on the Stump,' in the April number of the North American Review.]" Collected in *Political Essays*, 1888.

MHS

13124. CHRISTMAS CAROL, 1866

Three separate and distinct printings noted. Is it possible that but one of these was printed for the 1866 celebration? And the others done during later years but with the statement *Written for the Children's Festival at the Church of the Disciples, 1866,* retained for historic reasons? The designations are for identification only and no sequence is suggested.

Collected in *Heartsease and Rue*, 1888.

A

A CHRISTMAS CAROL, WRITTEN FOR THE CHRISTMAS FESTIVAL AT THE CHURCH OF THE DISCIPLES, 1866. BY JAMES RUSSELL LOWELL. [NOT PUBLISHED] ⟨Text: 7 numbered quatrains⟩

⟨n.p., Boston, Mass., 1866⟩

Single cut sheet. Unwatermarked wove paper. Printed on recto only. 9¾″ scant × 7⁹⁄₁₆″.

B

A CHRISTMAS CAROL, WRITTEN FOR THE CHILDREN'S FESTIVAL AT THE CHURCH OF DISCIPLES, 1866. BY JAMES RUSSELL LOWELL. [NOT PUBLISHED] ⟨Text: 7 numbered quatrains⟩

⟨n.p., Boston, Mass., 1866⟩

Single cut sheet. Unwatermarked wove paper.

Printed on recto only. 9¾″ × 7⅝″ full.

C

A CHRISTMAS CAROL. (WRITTEN FOR THE CHILDREN'S FESTIVAL AT THE CHURCH OF DISCIPLES, 1866.) BY JAMES RUSSELL LOWELL. [NOT PUBLISHED.] ⟨Text: 7 numbered quatrains; followed by "Christmas Hymn," 2 numbered stanzas beginning *Silent Night! Peaceful Night!*⟩

⟨n.p., Boston, Mass., 1866⟩

Single cut sheet. Unwatermarked laid paper.

Printed on recto only. 9¾″ × 7⁹⁄₁₆″.

B (B)   H (B)   MHS (A)   Y (C)

13125. TO MR. JOHN BARTLETT. ON SENDING ME A SEVEN-POUND TROUT

Two separate printings have been located. Sequence not known. The following is a record of the known printings and texts, exclusive of collected appearances. Each text varies from the other. Collected in *Under the Willows*, 1869.

"It is with some uncertainty that I insert this leaflet under the date 1858. The trout was certainly sent and the poem *written* in that year, though it was not published until 1866, when it appeared in the *Atlantic Monthly* for July . . . We know that Bartlett reprinted the poem in 1882 as a single quarto leaf for insertion in copies of his *Catalogue of Books on Angling* published in that year. It there bears the same date at end, *Elmwood, 1858* . . ."———Livingston, p. 51.

1

First publication. *The Atlantic Monthly*, July, 1866, pp. 47-48.

2

TO / MR. JOHN BARTLETT. / ON SENDING ME A SEVEN-POUND TROUT. / ⟨diamond rule⟩ / ⟨text⟩

At end of text: J. R. LOWELL. / ELMWOOD, 1858.

Single cut sheet folded to make four pages. Text on pp. ⟨1-4⟩. Laid paper. Watermarked WHITING PAPER CO Leaf: 6½″ × 4⅞″ full.

Printed not before 1866. The Whiting Paper Company was organized in 1865. See *A History of Paper-Manufacturing in the United States, 1690–1916*, by Lyman Horace Weeks, New York, 1916, p. 247.

3

TO MR. JOHN BARTLETT, / WHO HAD SENT ME A SEVEN-POUND TROUT. / ⟨diamond rule⟩ / ⟨text⟩

At end of text: J. R. LOWELL. / ELMWOOD, 1858.

Single cut sheet folded to make four pages. Text on pp. ⟨1-2⟩; pp. ⟨3-4⟩ blank. Unwatermarked wove paper. Leaf: 10³⁄₁₆″ full × 7¾″ full.

Presumably the "single quarto leaf" referred to by Livingston in the note quoted above.

4

Facsimile of an unlocated *ms*; in: *Bibliographical Contributions. Edited by Justin Winsor. No. 51. The Bartlett Collection . . . by Louise Rankin Albee*, Cambridge, Mass., 1896.

BA (2)   H (3)

13126. . . . THE BIGLOW PAPERS. SECOND SERIES . . .

BOSTON: TICKNOR AND FIELDS. 1867.

Anonymous. For prior publication see above under year 1862 (for London issue in three parts); and, see under years 1864 and 1865 for extended editions.

At head of title: MELIBŒUS-HIPPONAX.

Three printings of the trade format noted; for large paper printings see below.

1ST PRINTING, TRADE FORMAT

⟨i-iv⟩, ⟨i⟩-lxxx, ⟨1⟩-258; three blank leaves, the third being excised or pasted under the end paper. 7⅛″ × 4½″.

⟨a-c⟩¹², ⟨d⟩⁶, 1-3, ⟨4⟩, 5-10¹², 11⁸, ⟨12⟩⁴. Leaf ⟨12⟩₄ excised or pasted under the lining paper. *Also signed:* ⟨-⟩², ⟨A⟩, B-C, ⟨D⟩, E⁸, A, ⟨B⟩, C-N, ⟨O⟩, P⁸, ⟨Q⟩⁴. In addition to the above signing the following signatures are present in the front matter (pp. ⟨i-iv⟩, ⟨i⟩-lxxx): ⟨-⟩², ⟨a⟩, b-c¹², d⁴.

P. xvi, line 5: *are getting . . .*

P. xviii, line 4 from bottom: *pas faite . . .*

P. xxviii, line 3: . . . *heames . . .*

P. xxix, last line: . . . *toutes . . .*

P. xxxii, line 9 from bottom: . . . *Brampton* |

P. xxxiii, line 6: . . . *suggerins!*) |

P. lxv, line 9: . . . *speech-gilders . . .*

Noted only with the *Ticknor & Fields* device at foot of spine.

2ND PRINTING, TRADE FORMAT

⟨i-iv⟩, ⟨i⟩-lxxx, ⟨1⟩-258, blank leaf.

⟨1-5⟩⁸, ⟨6⟩², A, ⟨B⟩, C-N, ⟨O⟩, P⁸, ⟨Q⟩². *Also signed:* ⟨-⟩², ⟨a⟩, b-c¹², d⁴, 1-3, ⟨4⟩, 5-10¹², 11¹⁰. In addition the following signatures are present in the front matter (pp. ⟨i-iv⟩, ⟨i⟩-lxxx): ⟨-⟩², ⟨A⟩, B-C, ⟨D⟩, E⁸.

P. xvi, line 5: *are beginning . . .*

P. xviii, line 4 from bottom: *pas fait . . .*

P. xxviii, line 3: . . . *beames . . .*

P. xxix, last line: . . . *toute . . .*

P. xxxii, line 9 from bottom: . . . *So the good* |

P. xxxiii, line 6: . . . *suggerens!*) |

P. lxv, line 9: . . . *speech-gelders . . .*

Noted only with the *Ticknor & Fields* device at foot of spine.

Note: The sheets bulk ¹¹⁄₁₆″. A copy, pagination and signature collation as above, has been noted (in H) printed on thick paper; the sheets bulk 1″ scant. Leaf 7¹⁄₁₆″ full × 4½″. Status not known.

Query: By any chance is this one of the lost large paper copies? See below for comment on the large paper printings. Are these sheets of the first large paper printing inadvertently mixed in with the sheets of the regular trade printing?

3RD PRINTING, TRADE FORMAT

⟨i-iv⟩, ⟨i⟩-lxxx, ⟨1⟩-258, 3 blank leaves. The final leaf excised or pasted under the end paper.

⟨a-c⟩¹², ⟨d⟩⁶, 1-3, ⟨4⟩, 5-10¹², 11⁸, ⟨12⟩⁴. Leaf ⟨12⟩₄ excised or pasted under the end paper. *Also signed:* ⟨-⟩², ⟨A⟩, B-C, ⟨D⟩, E⁸, A, ⟨B⟩, C-N, ⟨O⟩, P⁸, ⟨Q⟩⁴. In addition the following signatures are present in the front matter (pp. ⟨i-iv⟩, ⟨i⟩-lxxx): ⟨-⟩², ⟨a⟩, b-c¹², d⁴.

Text as in *2nd Printing, Trade Format*, above.

Noted with the *Ticknor & Fields* device at foot of spine; and, with the spine imprint of *Fields, Osgood & Co.*

C cloth: green; purple; terra-cotta. Brown-coated end papers. Flyleaf at front. *Ticknor & Fields* device at foot of spine.

According to the publisher's records the first printing of 2500 copies was done by Oct. 23, 1866; all copies put in binding by Oct. 30, 1866. A copy of the first printing presented to H by the publishers Oct. 27, 1866. Listed ALG Nov. 1, 1866. Plates corrected Nov. 19, 1866. The second printing consisted of 514 copies on Jan. 4, 1867; all copies bound by March 4, 1867. The third printing consisted of 520 copies, April 5, 1867; 300 copies bound by Sept. 6, 1867; 165 copies bound Aug. 14, 1869; 104 copies bound Aug. 16, 1869. The two binding lots of August, 1869, have the Fields, Osgood & Company imprint at foot of spine since the firm's name changed in Nov. 1868.

LARGE PAPER PRINTINGS

A large paper printing, *title-page printed in black only*, was bound in full morocco and presented by Lowell to E. R. Hoar, the dedicatee. Leaf: 7¾″ × 5¾″. Sheets bulk 1″ plus. Inscribed: *To E. R. Hoar, this edition (of one copy only) is inscribed with renewed esteem & affection by H. Biglow. Jaalam*

Jany 29, 1867. Inserted is a letter from Lowell to Hoar, *29th Jany, 1867,* which reads: *I send you at last* your *copy of the* Biglow Papers. *It is worth more than I expected, for, out of an edition of twelve, it is the only one left* ... *The other eleven being sent to a different binder were all lost on their way* ... In NYPL

To compensate for the loss referred to by Lowell, there was prepared another large paper printing (12 copies? 11 copies?) with *the title-page printed in black and red.* Sheets bulk 1″ plus. Leaf: 7$\frac{11}{16}$″ × 5$\frac{3}{4}$″. Noted only in purple C cloth, bevelled covers. Copies in H, NYPL.

Neither large paper printing precedes the first printing of the trade format; both large paper printings are of the revised text.

The above entry made on the basis of copies in:

AAS   B   H   NYHS   NYPL   UV

13127. ⟨Printed letter⟩ Boston, Dec. 4, 1867. J. K. Paine, Esq. Dear Sir, We have heard with much pleasure of the approbation with which your Mass was received by the severely critical audience of the Berlin Sing-Academie ...

Boston, Jan. 1, 1868 ...

Single leaf. Printed on recto only. 8″ scant × 5$\frac{1}{16}$″.

Issued as an advertisement for Paine's announced concert, Boston Music Hall, April 12, 1868.

Signed by Lowell and others.

H

13128. The Atlantic Almanac 1869 Edited by Donald G. Mitchell ...

Boston: Ticknor and Fields, Office of The Atlantic Monthly ... 1868 ...

"My Garden Acquaintance," pp. 32-37. Collected in *My Study Windows,* 1871.

For comment see entry No. 4037.

13129. UNDER THE WILLOWS AND OTHER POEMS ...

BOSTON: FIELDS, OSGOOD, & CO., SUCCESSORS TO TICKNOR AND FIELDS. 1869.

⟨i⟩-viii, ⟨9⟩-286, blank leaf. Laid paper. 6$\frac{7}{8}$″ × 4$\frac{1}{2}$″ full.

⟨1⟩-4, 7 (*sic*), 6-12^{12}. *Also signed:* ⟨A⟩-R^8. *See notes below.*

C cloth: green; purple; terra-cotta. Bevelled covers. Brown-coated end papers. Top edges gilt. In some copies an erratum slip is inserted at pp. 286-⟨287⟩. *See notes below.*

According to the publisher's records there were five printings during the period 1868–1869 as follows:

1st printing: Nov. 10, 1868. 1000 copies. The records show that an erratum slip was printed in time for insertion in the copies first shipped. Slight variations in the slip indicate multiple setting of type. An erratum slip is present in the surviving deposit copy.

2nd printing: Nov. 28, 1868. 1000 copies.

3rd printing: Dec. 18, 1868. 1000 copies.

4th printing: Jan. 25, 1869. 450 copies.

5th printing: April 16, 1869. 1000 copies.

BAL has been able to identify but three states of the sheets (probably printings); it is probable that one or more of the following represents not one state (or printing) but two or more.

STATE A

P. 97 erroneously signed 7.

P. 224, line 3, second stanza: *Thy* ...

STATE B

P. 97 correctly signed 5.

P. 224, line 3, second stanza: *Thy* ...

The surviving copyright deposit copy thus.

STATE C

P. 97 correctly signed 5.

P. 224, line 3, second stanza: *Its* ...

Four bindings noted; the following sequence appears correct:

BINDING A

Publisher's spine imprint stamped from small and large capital letters, roman; the ampersand has a round top. Brown-coated on white end papers; laid or wove paper flyleaves; top edges gilded. The surviving copyright deposit copy thus.

BINDING B

Publisher's spine imprint stamped from a curious face; the s has exaggerated vertical serifs; the initial o in OSGOOD has two vertical rules within the letter; the ampersand has a flat top. Brown-coated on white end papers; laid paper flyleaves; top edges gilded.

BINDING C

Publisher's spine imprint stamped from small and large capital letters, the initial o in OSGOOD has thickened sides; all other letters, save for the initials, are from a sans-serif face; the ampersand has a flat top. Brown-coated on white end papers; laid paper flyleaves; top edges gilded. In some copies: A laid paper flyleaf at front, a wove paper flyleaf at back.

BINDING D

Publisher's spine imprint stamped from large and small capital letters; all the o's have thickened sides; the ampersand has a flat top. Brown-coated on white end papers; wove paper flyleaves; top edges gilded.

A copy (Sheets A, Binding A) in H presented to William Dean Howells by Lowell Nov. 20, 1868. A copy (Sheets B, Binding A) in H presented to "Mr. Bartlett" by Lowell Nov. 20, 1868. Deposited Nov. 21, 1868. A copy (Sheets A, Binding A) in H presented to Thomas Bailey Aldrich by Lowell Nov. 21, 1868. A copy (Sheets B, Binding A) in H presented to Ralph Waldo Emerson by Lowell Nov. 21, 1868. Listed ALG Dec. 1, 1868. Listed PC Jan. 16, 1869.

AAS (Sheets A, Binding A; Sheets B, Binding A; Sheets C, Binding A; Sheets C, Binding C) BPL (Sheets B, Binding A) H (Sheets A, Binding A; Sheets B, Binding A; Sheets C, Binding B; Sheets C, Binding C; Sheets C, Binding D) LC (Sheets B, Binding A, being a deposit copy; Sheets C, Binding C) UV (Sheets A, Binding A; Sheets B, Binding A) Y (Sheets A, Binding A; Sheets C, Binding B)

13130. The Atlantic Almanac 1870 . . .

Boston: Fields, Osgood, & Co., Office of The Atlantic Monthly . . . 1869 . . .

"A Good Word for Winter," pp. 39-47. Collected in *My Study Windows*, 1871.

For comment see entry No. 1708.

13131. The Poetical Works . . . Complete Edition.

Boston: Fields, Osgood, & Co. 1869.

Cloth; and, leather. On cloth binding: *Diamond Edition*

Reprint with the exception of "Anti-Apis," pp. 95-96; and, the brief dedication to George William Curtis.

Deposited Nov. 3, 1869. Listed Ath Nov. 27, 1869; PC Dec. 8, 1869.

AAS   B   BA   BPL   H   UV

13132. Sixty-Third Anniversary Celebration of the New-England Society in the City of New York at Delmonico's Dec. 22, 1868.

⟨n.p., n.d., New York, 1869⟩

Printed paper wrapper.

Letter, Dec. 17, 1868, p. 63.

H   NYPL

13133. Tobacco and Alcohol . . . by John Fiske . . .

New York: Leypoldt & Holt. 1869.

Testimonial, p. ⟨172⟩ of the second printing.

For fuller comment see entry No. 5993.

13134. George W. Minns' Scientific, Classical and Commercial School for Boys.

Boston, 1869.

Not seen; not found. Entry from Livingston, p. 80: "A pamphlet printed as an advertisement . . . contains, on p. 6, a short testimonial letter from J. R. Lowell."

13135. THE CATHEDRAL . . .

BOSTON: FIELDS, OSGOOD, & CO. 1870.

Title-page in black and red.

⟨i-ii⟩, ⟨1⟩-⟨53⟩. $6^{15}/_{16}'' \times 4^{1}/_{2}''$.

⟨1-3⁸, 4⁴⟩.

C cloth: green; purple; terra-cotta. Brown-coated end papers. Flyleaf at front and at back; these may be of book stock; a lighter weight wove paper; laid paper. Apparently the binders used whatever came to hand in inserting the flyleaves. In some copies one finds that the preliminary flyleaf varies from the terminal flyleaf. Covers bevelled.

According to the publisher's records 3016 copies were printed Dec. 17, 1869; bound during the period Dec. 18, 1869–Feb. 25, 1870. No further printings from these plates recorded; plates melted down June 5, 1901. Copies (in H) have been seen with Lowell's presentation inscription dated Dec. 18, 1869. Deposited Dec. 21, 1869. Listed ALG Jan. 1, 1870; PC Feb. 1, 1870; Bkr March 1, 1870; Ath April 9, 1870.

AAS   H   MHS   NYHS   NYPL   UV   Y

13136. AMONG MY BOOKS . . .

BOSTON: FIELDS, OSGOOD, & CO. 1870.

According to the publisher's records there were six printings during the year 1870. BAL has been able to identify three printings only. It is possible that the reprints described below represent not single printings but two.

FIRST PRINTING

On the basis of dated inscriptions the first printing collates as follows:

⟨i-viii⟩, ⟨1⟩-380. $7^{1}/_{4}''$ scant $\times 4^{3}/_{4}''$.

⟨a-b⟩², A-W⁸, X⁶. *Also signed:* ⟨-⟩⁴, 1-15¹², 16¹⁰.

Front matter:

P. ⟨i⟩: Blank

P. ⟨ii⟩: *James Russell Lowell's Writings* . . .

P. ⟨iii⟩: Title-page

P. ⟨iv⟩: Copyright notice

P. ⟨v⟩: Dedication

P. ⟨vi⟩: Blank

P. ⟨vii⟩: *Contents* . . .

P. ⟨viii⟩: Blank

REPRINT A (B?)

⟨i-viii⟩, ⟨1⟩-380.

⟨a-b⟩², A-W⁸, X⁶. *Also signed:* ⟨-⟩⁴, 1-15¹², 16¹⁰.

Front matter:

P. ⟨i⟩: Title-page

P. ⟨ii⟩: Copyright notice

P. ⟨iii⟩: Dedication

P. ⟨iv⟩: Blank

P. ⟨v⟩: Blank

P. ⟨vi⟩: *James Russell Lowell's Writings* . . .

P. ⟨vii⟩: *Contents* . . .

P. ⟨viii⟩: Blank

REPRINT B (A?)

⟨i-viii⟩, ⟨1⟩-380.

⟨-⟩⁴, A-W⁸, X⁶. *Also signed:* ⟨-⟩⁴, 1-15¹², 16¹⁰.

Front matter:

P. ⟨i⟩: Blank

P. ⟨ii⟩: *James Russell Lowell's Writings* . . .

P. ⟨iii⟩: Title-page

P. ⟨iv⟩: Copyright notice

P. ⟨v⟩: Dedication

P. ⟨vi⟩: Blank

P. ⟨vii⟩: *Contents* . . .

P. ⟨viii⟩: Blank

C cloth: green; purple; terra-cotta. Covers bevelled. Brown-coated end papers. Laid paper flyleaves. Also wove flyleaves in first printing?

Title-page entered Jan. 18, 1870. First printing, 1500 copies, recorded Feb. 5, 1870. BA copy (first printing) received Feb. 15, 1870. Listed ALG March 1, 1870. Second printing, 280 copies, recorded March 14, 1870. Third printing, 500 copies, recorded March 23, 1870. Fourth printing, 500 copies, recorded May 11, 1870. Fifth printing, 500 copies, recorded June 24, 1870. Sixth printing (imprint dated 1871?), 500 copies, recorded Nov. 19, 1870. The London (Macmillan) edition advertised as *this day* PC March 1, 1870; again, PC March 15, 1870. Listed Ath March 5, 1870.

The present entry made on the basis of copies in: AAS, B, H, NYPL, UV, Y.

13137. Tributes to the Memory of Hon. John Pendleton Kennedy.

Reprinted ⟨*i.e.*, preprinted⟩ from the Proceedings of the Massachusetts Historical Society. ⟨n.p., Boston, 1870⟩

Cover-title. Printed paper wrapper.

Comments, pp. 12-14. Appears also in *Proceedings of the Massachusetts Historical Society, 1869–1870*, Boston, 1871.

H copy received Oct. 4, 1870.

B H NYPL

13138. The Poets and Poetry of Europe. With Introductions and Biographical Notices. By Henry Wadsworth Longfellow. A New Edition, Revised and Enlarged . . .

Philadelphia: Porter and Coates, 822 Chestnut Street. 1871.

"To Madame du Chatelet," p. 841; *From the French of Voltaire*. Collected in *Uncollected Poems*, 1950.

For comment see entry No. 9554.

13139. MY STUDY WINDOWS . . .

BOSTON: JAMES R. OSGOOD AND COMPANY, LATE TICKNOR & FIELDS, AND FIELDS, OSGOOD, & CO. 1871.

⟨i-viii⟩, ⟨1⟩-433, blank leaf. 7³⁄₁₆″ × 4³⁄₄″.

⟨-⟩⁴, 1-4, ⟨5⟩, 6-18¹², ⟨19⟩². *Also signed:* ⟨-⟩⁴, A-E, ⟨F-G⟩, H-Z, AA⁸, ⟨-⟩².

According to the publisher's records there were four printings during the period Jan. 20–Aug. 21, 1871. BAL has been unable to identify four printings but offers the following notes:

FIRST PRINTING

2100 copies printed Jan. 20, 1871. All were in binding by Jan. 30, 1871.

Features of the first printing (printings?):

Publisher's list on p. ⟨i⟩; not on p. ⟨ii⟩.

FO monogram (not JRO monogram) at foot of spine.

P. 274, line 5: . . . *Certainly with* . . .

P. 293, line 12: . . . *unkinged* . . .

Undoubtedly the first printing has the features outlined above. However, there is some likelihood that these features are present also in the second and third printings. It is also certain that the first printing (printings?) has unbattered type in lines 5-6 of the dedication (. . . *shall* / . . . *to* /).

On the basis of publisher's records, and other evidence presented below, it becomes clear that any copy with the above features which is distinguished by an inscription dated prior to Feb. 2, 1871, the date of the second printing, is indisputably a copy of the first printing.

Locations: H

1022 copies printed Feb. 2, 1871. Bound during the period Feb. 28–March 31, 1871. 200 copies (in sheets?) sent to Sampson Low, London, Feb. 7, 1871. Not identified by BAL.

THIRD PRINTING

518 copies printed May 13, 1871. All copies bound during the period June 7–30, 1871, with the exception of 50 copies (in sheets?) sent to Sampson Low, London, on June 5, 1871; and, returned to Boston from London Aug. 26, 1871, by which time Low had his own printing on the market which appears to explain the return.

BAL has seen a copy that may be of this printing. The types in the dedication are battered; and, the JRO monogram is present on the spine. Equally, it could well be a copy of the second printing. With the exception of the battered types and the spine monogram all the features of the known first printing are present.

Locations: H

JULY 31, 1871

On this date Lowell wrote to Leslie Stephen (*Letters . . .* , 1894, Vol. 2, pp. 72-74): . . . *I should have sent* My Study Windows . . . *but was waiting for a new edition, in which the misprints are corrected* . . . (Livingston, p. 84, errs in stating that the letter was addressed to Charles Eliot Norton, unless Lowell employed the same statement in writing to Norton on the same day he wrote to Stephens.)

FOURTH PRINTING

518 copies printed Aug. 21, 1871. All were in binding by Jan. 23, 1872. In this printing the revised readings are present:

P. 274, line 5: . . . *Certainly not with* . . .

P. 293, line 12: . . . *discrowned* . . .

In this printing the publisher's list is on p. ⟨ii⟩, not on p. ⟨i⟩.

JRO monogram at foot of spine.

In the dedication the types are battered.

Locations: H

Note: The publisher's records show that the first and second printings were done on 80 lb. paper; the third and fourth printings on 60 lb. paper.

C cloth: green; star-sprinkled purple. FL cloth: purple; terra-cotta. Brown-coated end papers. Flyleaves. Bevelled covers. The earliest cases have the FO monogram at foot of spine; see comments on this feature under descriptions of the printings, above.

Publication notes: See above under the separate printings for publisher's records. Copies inscribed by Lowell (in H, NYPL) with date Jan. 20, 1871. Published in Jan. 1871, according to a note in

ALG Feb. 2, 1871. Listed ALG Feb. 15, 1871. American edition listed PC March 1, 1871. Low's edition listed Ath March 11, 1871.

The present entry made on the basis of copies in: AAS H NYPL UV Y

13140. Catalogue of the School of Modern Languages. Seventh Year. 1872–73.

The Riverside Press. 1872.

Printed paper wrapper.

Testimonial, *Cambridge, May 24, 1872*, p. 24. The testimonial was reprinted in the catalogs for 1873, 1874.

BPL

13141. His Imperial Highness the Grand Duke Alexis in the United States of America during the Winter of 1871–72 . . . for Private Distribution

Cambridge Printed at the Riverside Press 1872

Leather. Also cloth? Edited by William W. Tucker?

Address, pp. 102-104. Otherwise unlocated.

The name of the editor is not present on the title-page. Livingston, p. 84, reports a variant issue, the most notable variation being the presence of the following lines on the title-page: *By | William W. Tucker |*

The MHS copy received from Tucker Oct. 24, 1872.

H MHS

13142. Prophetic Voices Concerning America . . . by Charles Sumner . . .

Boston: Lee and Shepard, Publishers. New York: Lee, Shepard, and Dillingham. 1874.

Testimonial, p. 7 of the terminal advertisements.

Note: The testimonial is for *The Works of Charles Sumner*, issued 1870–1883. It is probable that the testimonial had publication prior to 1874. For a comment on Sumner's *Works* see entry No. 12154.

Listed PW May 9, 1874.

H

13143. Jeffries Wyman. Memorial Meeting of the Boston Society of Natural History, October 7, 1874.

⟨n.p., n.d., 1874⟩

Printed paper wrapper.

"Jeffries Wyman," p. ⟨3⟩. Collected in *Heartsease and Rue*, 1888.

B H NYPL Y

13144. Parnassus Edited by Ralph Waldo Emerson . . .

Boston: James R. Osgood and Company, (Late Ticknor and Fields, and Fields, Osgood, and Co.) 1875.

Reprint save for "Origin of Didactic Poetry," p. 483. Collected in *Heartsease and Rue*, 1888.

For comment see entry No. 5269.

13145. . . . ⟨Extracts from⟩ The Atlantic for July . . .

H. O. Houghton and Company, Boston. Hurd and Houghton, New York. ⟨n.d., 1875⟩

Contains "Sonnet from over Sea. On Being Asked for an Autograph in Venice." Collected in *Heartsease and Rue*, 1888, as "On Being Asked for an Autograph in Venice."

For comment see entry No. 282.

13146. Sheets for the Cradle . . .

Boston . . . 1875 . . .

An occasional newspaper. For comment see entry No. 4048.

"An Anecdote of Walter Savage Landor," Vol. 1, No. 5, p. ⟨1⟩. For another version of this anecdote see "Some Letters of Walter Savage Landor" in *Latest Literary Essays*, 1892.

3147. Cambridge in the "Centennial." Proceedings, July 3, 1875, in Celebration of the Centennial Anniversary of Washington's Taking Command of the Continental Army, on Cambridge Common.

Cambridge: Printed by Order of the City Council. M DCCC LXXV.

Printed paper wrapper; and, cloth.

"Poem," pp. ⟨27⟩-38. Collected as "Under the Old Elm" in *Three Memorial Poems*, 1877, somewhat revised.

Response, p. 87.

BA   H

13148. The Harvard Book. A Series of Historical, Biographical, and Descriptive Sketches. By Various Authors . . . Collected and Published by F. O. Vaille and H. A. Clark, Class of 1874. Vol. II.

Cambridge: Welch, Bigelow, and Company, University Press. 1875.

"Class Day," pp. ⟨157⟩-172. Otherwise unlocated.

For comment see entry No. 4045.

13149. JOSEPH WINLOCK. DIED JUNE 11, 1875 . . .

⟨n.p., presumably Boston, 1875⟩

Single cut sheet of laid paper folded to make four pages. P. ⟨1⟩ as above, otherwise blank. Page: $7^{15}/_{16}''$ full × $5''$ full.

Collected in *Heartsease and Rue*, 1888.

PDH

13150. THE WORLD'S FAIR, 1876, AND TEMPORA MUTANTUR . . . FROM "THE NATION."

⟨New York: Kilbourne Tompkins, Agent. Book, Law and Job Printing, of Every Description. 16 Cedar St., n.d., 1875? 1876? Not after 1879⟩

Cover-title.

⟨1-8⟩. Laid paper. $4^{7}/_{8}'' \times 4^{11}/_{16}''$.

⟨-⟩⁴.

Printed self-wrapper. Single sheet folded to make eight pages.

"The World's Fair, 1876," *The Nation*, Aug. 5, 1875. Also in *Star Selections* . . . , 1877; see below. Collected in *Uncollected Poems*, 1950.

"Tempora Mutantur," *The Nation*, Aug. 26, 1875. Collected in *Heartsease and Rue*, 1888.

PDH

13151. Laurel Leaves. Original Poems, Stories, and Essays . . .

Boston: William F. Gill and Company, 309 Washington Street. 1876.

"Gloria Mundi," p. 103. Much revised, collected in *Heartsease and Rue*, 1888, under the title "The Eye's Treasury."

"To a Friend, Who Gave Me a Group of Weeds and Grasses," p. ⟨401⟩. Collected in *Heartsease and Rue*, 1888.

For comment see entry No. 116.

13152. AMONG MY BOOKS. SECOND SERIES . . .

BOSTON: JAMES R. OSGOOD AND COMPANY, LATE TICKNOR & FIELDS, AND FIELDS, OSGOOD, & CO. 1876.

⟨i-viii⟩, ⟨1⟩-327. $7^{1}/_{4}''$ scant × $4^{3}/_{4}''$ full.

⟨-⟩⁴, 1-13¹², ⟨14⟩⁸. *Also signed:* ⟨-⟩⁴, A-I, ⟨J⟩, K-L, ⟨M⟩, N-O, ⟨P⟩, Q-S, ⟨T⟩⁸, ⟨U⟩⁴.

Two issues noted:

FIRST ISSUE

On the title-page: . . . BELLES-LETTERS . . .

Copyright notice dated 1875.

SECOND ISSUE

On the title-page: . . . BELLES-LETTRES . . .

Copyright notice dated 1876.

C cloth: green. FL cloth: terra-cotta. Covers bevelled. Brown-coated end papers. Flyleaves. JRO monogram at foot of spine. A late binding has been seen (on first issue sheets) with the Houghton, Osgood spine imprint.

According to the publisher's records there was but one printing of this book: 3212 copies, completed Dec. 31, 1875. Sheets were being bound as late as May 31, 1879, by which time the firm's name had changed to Houghton, Osgood & Co. A copy of the second issue (in H) inscribed by Lowell Jan. 13, 1876. A surviving copyright deposit copy, deposited Jan. 15, 1876, is of the second issue. Listed PW Jan. 22, 1876. The London (Low) edition advertised as *ready* Ath May 27, 1876; listed Ath May 27, 1876.

AAS (1st, 2nd) H (2nd) BPL (1st, in Houghton Osgood binding) LC (2nd, being a deposit copy NYPL (2nd) UV (1st, 2nd) Y (2nd)

13153. Proceedings at the Centennial Celebration of Concord Fight April 19, 1875.

Concord, Mass. Published by the Town. 1876.

Cloth; and, printed paper wrapper.

"Ode," pp. 82-88. Collected in *Three Memorial Poems*, 1877.

Issued *ca.* May, 1876.

BA BPL H LC

13154. THREE MEMORIAL POEMS . . .

BOSTON: JAMES R. OSGOOD AND COMPANY, LATE TICKNOR & FIELDS, AND FIELDS, OSGOOD, & CO. 1877.

Title-page in black and red.

⟨i-ii⟩, ⟨1⟩-92; blank, save for a decorative red rule box, pp. ⟨93-94⟩. $6\frac{11}{16}'' \times 5\frac{1}{16}''$.

⟨1-12⁴⟩.

C cloth: green; terra-cotta. S cloth: blue; blue-gray; mauve; terra-cotta. Brown-coated on white end papers. Flyleaves. Edges stained red.

Advertised for *next week* PW Dec. 9, 1876. Copies (in H) presented to Longfellow and to Emerson by Lowell, inscriptions dated Dec. 15, 1876. Listed PW Dec. 23, 1876.

AAS BA H NYHS NYPL UV Y

13155. Golden Songs of Great Poets . . .

New York: Sarah H. Leggett, No. 1184 Broadway. 1877.

Unpaged. Contains "The Fire-Fly: A Parable." Revised and extended, collected in *Heartsease and Rue*, 1888, as "The Lesson."

For comment see entry No. 1760.

13156. Old South Meeting-House. Report of a Meeting of the Inhabitants of Cambridge, in Harvard Hall, Harvard College, January 18th, 1877. Addresses by . . . Charles W. Eliot . . . James Russell Lowell . . . ⟨and Others⟩

Boston: Press of George H. Ellis. 1877.

Printed paper wrapper.

"Address . . . ," pp. 6-10. Elsewhere unlocated.

AAS BA H NYPL UV Y

13157. Star Selections, 1876. A Fresh Collection of Patriotic Readings, in Prose and Poetry. By Professor J. E. Goodrich.

New York: Sheldon & Company, No. 8 Murray Street. 1877.

Printed boards, cloth shelf back.

"Character of Washington," pp. 35-36. Extracted from "Under the Old Elm," the text being that as published in *Cambridge in the "Centennial"* . . . , 1875. Here reprinted.

"The World's Fair, 1876," p. 93. Also in (reprinted from?) *The World's Fair, 1876* . . . , described above under ⟨n.d., 1875? 1876?⟩.

H

13158. Tribute of the Massachusetts Historical Society to the Memory of Edmund Quincy and John Lothrop Motley

Boston Massachusetts Historical Society 1877

Printed paper wrapper.

Remarks, pp. 9-11. Also in (reprinted) the society's *Proceedings*, 1878.

H NYPL Y

13159. . . . A Masque of Poets. Including Guy Vernon, a Novelette in Verse.

Boston: Roberts Brothers. 1878.

"My Heart, I Cannot Still it," p. 142. Extended and revised, collected in *Heartsease and Rue*, 1888, as "Auspex."

"Red Tape," p. 153. Revised, collected in *Heartsease and Rue*, 1888, as "The Brakes."

For comment see entry No. 118.

13160. Johnson's New Universal Cyclopædia . . . Volume IV . . .

Alvin J. Johnson & Son, 11 Great Jones Street, New York . . . MDCCCLXXVIII.

"Trouvères," pp. 951-952. Presumably written for this publication; not located elsewhere.

For comment see entry No. 11595.

13161. American Poems Longfellow: Whittier: Bryant: Holmes: Lowell: Emerson With Biographical Sketches and Notes

Boston Houghton, Osgood and Company The Riverside Press, Cambridge 1879

Reprint with the exception of "Agassiz," pp. 395-415. Collected in *Heartsease and Rue*, 1888.

CH

13162. . . . True Manliness. From the Writings of Thomas Hughes. Selected by E. E. Brown. With an Introduction by James Russell Lowell.

Boston: D. Lothrop and Co., Franklin Street, Corner of Hawley. ⟨1880⟩

At head of title: *Spare Minute Series*.

"Preliminary Note," pp. v-vi.

Listed PW Oct. 23, 1880. Reprinted and reissued by D. Lothrop Company ⟨1880; *i.e.*, not before 1887⟩.

AAS   BA   H   LC

13163. New Year's Address and Messages to Blackfriar's Bible Class, Edited by John Leith.

1881

Not seen; not located; entry on the basis of the following note in *The Scottish Congregationalist* (Edinburgh), Feb. 1881.

"In *New Year's Address and Messages* to Blackfriar's Bible Class, Aberdeen, Mr John Leith, who has conducted this class for twelve years, reviews the work of the class for the year, and gives wise and loving counsel to his pupils. He has this year been fortunate in securing *Messages* to the class from three men of mark, viz., Mr Peter Bayne, Mr J. Russell Lowell, and the Bishop of Manchester . . ."

13164. The Dante Society, of Cambridge, Massachusetts, proposes to print the hitherto inedited Latin Comment on the Divine Comedy by Benvenuto da Imola . . .

Cambridge, Mass., June, 1881.

Signed at end by Lowell and others.

For fuller entry see No. 12226.

13165. In a Circular issued in June last, the Dante Society of Cambridge, Massachusetts, announced its intention of publishing the hitherto inedited Comment on the Divine Comedy . . .

Cambridge, Mass., December, 1881.

Signed at end by Lowell and others.

For fuller entry see No. 12232.

13166. Death of President Garfield Meeting of Americans in London at Exeter Hall 24 September 1881 . . .

London: Benjamin Franklin Stevens 4 Trafalgar Square Charing Cross 1881

White cloth, printed on laid paper watermarked *Elzevir Press*. Printed blue-gray paper wrapper, printed on wove paper.

Edited anonymously by Lowell.

Preface, pp. ⟨5⟩-7.

Remarks, pp. 11-21.

In addition to copies printed on paper there were also copies printed on vellum, almost certainly in 1883. In PDH is a vellum copy inscribed by Lowell: (*Five copies printed on vellum at the suggestion & under the superintendence of Mr Stevens.*) *No 2.* Laid in at the front is a letter from Lowell to Stevens, London, Sept. 10, 1883: *One of the Copies belongs naturally to you & if it didn't I should prefer to give it that destination . . .* Also laid in are several *ms* leaves of the preface in Lowell's hand.

Note: In all examined copies of the printings on paper, p. ⟨5⟩, line 7, reads: . . . *sincere* . . . ; in the vellum printing the text reads: . . . *spontaneous* . . .

A copy in wrapper (NYPL) inscribed by early owner Nov. 7, 1881.

BA (cloth)   BPL (cloth)   H (wrapper, vellum) LC (cloth)   NYPL (cloth, wrapper)   Y (cloth, wrapper)

13167. Exercises in Celebrating the Two Hundred and Fiftieth Anniversary of the Settlement of Cambridge Held December 28, 1880 . . .

Cambridge University Press: John Wilson and Son 1881

Letter, p. 127, *Legation of the United States, London, Dec. 5, 1880.*

H

13168. ⟨Review of John James Piatt's *Poems*, Cincinnati, 1868⟩

Lowell's review appeared in NAR Oct. 1868; it has not been collected in full; the major portion of it appears in *The Function of the Poet . . .*, edited by Albert Mordell, 1920, under the assigned title "Poetry and Nationality." In a footnote Mordell states: *The brief, concluding portion of the review is of little value and is omitted here.*

The final portion, however, was considered of sufficient importance to be used in advertising Piatt's poems. The sequence of the following publications has not been determined and the designations are for identification only.

PRINTING A

Mr. Piatt's Poems Extracts from General Critical Notices.

⟨Boston: James R. Osgood & Co., n.d., *ca.* 1881⟩

Self-wrapper. Cover-title. Preceding at head of p. ⟨1⟩. Lowell's review on pp. 3-4.

PRINTING B

Mr. Piatt's Poems . . . Extracts from Letters . . .

⟨n.p., n.d., after Sept. 19, 1881⟩

Four-page leaflet. The above at head of p. ⟨1⟩. Comment, p. 2.

NYPL (A)   WMG (B)

13169. . . . Selections for School Exhibitions and Private Reading, Illustrating and Advocating Kindness to All Creatures. Nos. 1, 2, 3 . . .

Boston: Wright & Potter Printing Company. No. 18 Post Office Square, 1882.

At head of title: *Gen. I, 31.*

Inserted slip: . . . "*Selections from the Poems of Longfellow,*" *printed by permission* . . .

Reprint with the exception of:

"Phoebe," pp. 126-127. In revised and extended form collected in *Heartsease and Rue,* 1888.

"Loyalty," p. 167, extracted from *Ode Recited at the Commemoration* . . . , 1865. "A June Day," p. 70, extracted from *The Vision of Sir Launfal,* 1848.

H

13170. Sir Walter Raleigh and America. A Sermon Preached at St. Margaret's Church, Westminster, on May 14, 1882, by the Rev. Canon Farrar . . .

London: Printed at the "Anglo-American Times" Press, 127, Strand, W C ⟨n.d., 1882⟩

Printed paper wrapper. Cover-title.

Lines written for the Raleigh Window, p. 7; and, the same lines used as caption for the frontispiece. Collected in *Heartsease and Rue,* 1888, as "For a Memorial Window to Sir Walter Raleigh, Set up in St. Margaret's, Westminster, by American Contributors."

H

13171. ADDRESS ⟨*On Democracy*⟩ DELIVERED BEFORE THE BIRMINGHAM AND MIDLAND INSTITUTE . . .

This address has been noted in the following forms. For an exhaustive bibliographical study see "James Russell Lowell *On Democracy,*" by James C. Armstrong and Kenneth E. Carpenter, in *Papers of the Bibliographical Society of America,* Vol. 59, 4th Quarter, 1965, pp. 385-399.

PRIVATE PRINTING

ADDRESS DELIVERED BEFORE THE BIRMINGHAM AND MIDLAND INSTITUTE, AT BIRMINGHAM, ON MONDAY, OCTOBER 6th, 1884 . . .

⟨Harrison and Sons, Printers, St. Martin's Lane, London, n.d., 1884⟩

Cover-title.

⟨1⟩-24. 9³⁄₁₆″ × 7½″ scant.

⟨A⟩-F⁴.

Printed on one side of leaf only. Issued in printed self-wrapper.

Privately printed for the author's use. The copy from which Lowell read, inscribed by him Oct. 6, 1884, is in H.

Locations: H   WC

PUBLISHED EDITION

. . . ON DEMOCRACY: AN ADDRESS DELIVERED IN THE TOWN HALL, BIRMINGHAM, ON THE 6th OF OCTOBER, 1884 . . .

BIRMINGHAM: PRINTED BY COND BROS., PATERNOSTER ROW, MOOR STREET. ⟨n.d., 1884⟩

At head of title: *Birmingham And Midland Institute.*

Cover-title.

Two states noted; see note below.

⟨1⟩-15. 8½″ × 5½″.

⟨1⟩⁸.

Printed self-wrapper.

Note: Two states of undetermined sequence have been noted; the designations are completely arbitrary:

PUBLISHED EDITION, STATE A

The statement PRICE SIXPENCE not present at upper left, p. ⟨1⟩. A comma follows the word ROW in the imprint. Prepared for distribution to members of the Birmingham and Midland Institute.

PUBLISHED EDITION, STATE B

The statement PRICE SIXPENCE present at upper left, p. ⟨1⟩. No comma following the word ROW in the imprint. Prepared for public distribution.

"The ledgers of the Birmingham and Midland Institute record that the bill for printing the address was paid on 30 Nov. 1884."–––Armstrong and Carpenter, *op. cit.* The same authorities locate a copy inscribed by Lowell Nov. 13, 1884.

Collected in *Democracy and other Addresses,* 1887.

Locations: AAS (A) B (B) BA (A) H (A, B) LC (A) NYPL (A,B) Y (A,B)

13172. ...BROWNING SOCIETY. MONTH-LY ABSTRACT OF PROCEEDINGS. TWENTY-FOURTH MEETING, FRIDAY, APRIL 24, 1884...

⟨London: The Browning Society, 1884⟩

Caption-title; the above on p. 113*. At head of title: *113*

113*-124*. 8⁹⁄₁₆″ full × 5½″ scant.

⟨-⟩⁶.

Printed self-wrapper.

Preprinted from *The Browning Society's Papers, 1881-4, Part V,* London, 1884. Collected in *American Ideas for English Readers* ⟨1892⟩, in revised form, as "On Robert Browning."

Y

13173. Transactions of the Wordsworth Society. Edited by the Hon. Secretary. No. 6.

⟨Edinburgh, 1884⟩

Printed paper wrapper, cloth shelfback.

Remarks, May 10, 1884, pp. 12-24. Collected in *Democracy and Other Addresses,* 1887.

BA UV

13174. Birmingham Health Lectures, with Preface by...James Russell Lowell...Second Series.

Birmingham: Hudson and Son, Edmund Street. London: Hamilton, Adams, and Co., Paternoster Row. 1884. ⟨*i.e.,* 1885⟩

Not seen. Entry from Livingston, p. 103.

"On pp. ⟨v⟩-vii will be found the *Preface,* signed *J. R. Lowell,* and dated January 5th, 1885."---Livingston, p. 103.

13175. Wensley and Other Stories by Edmund Quincy...

Boston James R. Osgood and Company 1885

"Bankside," pp. ⟨v⟩-vii. Collected in *Heartsease and Rue,* 1888.

The following pencilled note appears on p. 107 of the H copy of Livingston: *"Bankside" printed separately, a little broadside.* Further information wanting.

Deposited Feb. 11, 1885. Listed PW Feb. 14, 1885. A copy in H inscribed by the editor Feb. 14, 1885.

H

13176. Records of the Tercentenary Festival of the University of Edinburgh Celebrated in April 1884 Published under the Sanction of the Senatus Academicus

William Blackwood and Sons Edinburgh and London MDCCCLXXXV...

Response to a toast, pp. 136-138.

Speech, p. 152. Not elsewhere located.

H copy received April 1, 1885, with covering printed presentation slip dated *February, 1885.* Reviewed Ath, May 9, 1885, which states that 150 copies (of the whole printing) were released for purchase by the public.

H

13177. Emmanuel College Cambridge Commemoration of the Threehundredth ⟨*sic*⟩ Anniversary of the Foundation MDCCCLXXXIV

⟨Cambridge, England, 1885⟩

Remarks, pp. 9-10.

Colophon: *Cambridge...At The University Press. MDCCCLXXXV.*

H copy received June 26, 1885.

BA H Y

13178. Celebration of the Two Hundred and Fiftieth Anniversary of the Incorporation of Concord, September 12, 1885...

Concord, Mass.: Published by the Town ⟨1885⟩

Printed paper wrapper; and, cloth.

"Mr. Lowell's Speech," pp. 65-69. Uncollected.

H NYPL Y

13179. Proceedings at the Presentation of a Portrait of John Greenleaf Whittier to Friends' School, Providence, R. I. Tenth Month, 24th, 1884

Cambridge Printed at the Riverside Press 1885

Printed paper wrapper. Some copies contain an inserted slip: *Compliments of Charles F. Coffin.* At least one copy (that presented to Whittier by Charles F. Coffin; in CAW) was bound in tree calf.

Letter, Sept. 11, 1884, pp. 81-82.

"To J. G. Whittier," p. 82. Revised and collected in *Heartsease and Rue,* 1888, as "To Whittier on His Seventy-Fifth Birthday."

According to the printer's records printed Jan. 20, 1885.

H NYPL

13180. The London Chamber of Commerce... Third Annual Report of the Council to the

Members of the Chamber Transactions of the Year 1884 . . .

London: Waterlow & Sons Limited, Printers, London Wall. 1885.

Response to a toast, "The Chambers of Commerce of the United Kingdom and of the Whole World," pp. 65-66. Collected in *American Ideas for English Readers* . . . ⟨1892⟩.

Y

13181. Life of Henry Wadsworth Longfellow with Extracts from His Journals and Correspondence Edited by Samuel Longfellow . . .

Boston Ticknor and Company 1886

"To H.W.L.," Vol. 2, pp. 433-434. Reprint save for an added stanza: *A gift of symbol-flowers I meant to bring* . . .

For fuller description see entry No. 12258.

13182. Belford's Annual 1886–7. Edited by Thomas W. Handford . . .

Chicago and New York: Belford Clarke & Co. ⟨1886⟩

"The Eighteenth Century," p. 182. Extracted from Lowell's "Gray," *New Princeton Review*, March, 1886; collected in *Latest Literary Essays and Addresses*, 1892.

See next entry. For fuller entry see No. 10467.

13183. Belford's Chatterbox December, 1886. Edited by Thomas W. Handford . . .

Chicago and New York: Belford Clarke & Co. ⟨1886⟩

"The Eighteenth Century," p. 182.

For comment see preceding entry. For fuller entry see No. 10468.

The History of the World's Progress . . .

. . . Boston . . . ⟨1886⟩

See below under 1888.

13184. Proceedings at the Dedication of the New Library Building Chelsea, Mass. December 22, 1885 with the Address by James Russell Lowell

Cambridge John Wilson and Son University Press 1886

Printed paper wrapper; cloth.

"Address," pp. ⟨16⟩-30. Collected in *Democracy and Other Addresses*, 1887.

Note: Extracts appear in *Commonplace Books——— Why and How Kept. A Lecture by Prof. James D. Butler . . . Madison, Wisconsin. With Suggestions on*

Object and Method in Reading, by Argyll . . . Lowell . . . ⟨and Others⟩, ⟨n.p., n.d., 1886?⟩ Cover-title? Printed self-wrapper? Copy in AAS.

Sequence of publication not determined.

AAS B BA H LC NYPL Y

13185. The Sonnets of Europe A Volume of Translations Selected . . . by Samuel Waddington . . .

London: Walter Scott, 24 Warwick Lane, Paternoster Row, and Newcastle-on-Tyne. 1886.

Probably issued in cloth, printed paper label on spine.

"From the Vita Nuova," by Dante, p. 19. Otherwise unlocated.

DE V

13186. . . . ON RELIGION . . .

⟨W. F. Geddes' Son, Printer, 716 Chestnut St., Philadelphia, n.d., *ca* 1886⟩

Cover-title. At head of title: *James Russell Lowell*

⟨1⟩-4. 4⅜″ × 3″. Imprint on p. 4.

Single leaf of tan paper folded to make four pages.

Text otherwise unlocated.

H

13187. DEMOCRACY AND OTHER ADDRESSES . . .

BOSTON AND NEW YORK HOUGHTON, MIFFLIN AND COMPANY THE RIVERSIDE PRESS, CAMBRIDGE 1887

Two printings noted:

FIRST PRINTING

⟨i-vi⟩, ⟨i⟩-vi, ⟨1⟩-245; blank, pp. ⟨246-248⟩; plus publisher's catalog, pp. ⟨1⟩-14, blank leaf. 7″ scant × 4⅝″ full (trade format). 7¼″ × 4¾ (so-called large paper format).

⟨1-21⁶, 22⁴, plus: 23⁸⟩.

P. 77, line 14: *Reformation* . . .

P. 83, line 9 from bottom: . . . *country* . . .

SECOND PRINTING

Pagination and signature collation as above.

P. 77, line 14: *Restoration* . . .

P. 83, line 9 from bottom: . . . *county* . . .

V cloth: blue; green. All edges trimmed, top edges gilt. White laid end papers. *Also:* V cloth: blue. Printed paper label on spine. Wholly untrimmed. White laid end papers. According to the publisher's records 100 copies only were done in the untrimmed format. The first printing (2538 copies) recorded Nov. 24, 1886; on the same date 1025 copies were sent to Macmillan (London). The first printing put in binding during the period Nov. 23–Dec. 1, 1886. Deposited Nov. 29, 1886. A charge for plate alteration recorded Nov. 29, 1886. 100 copies were bound untrimmed on Dec. 1, 1886. Second printing (1010 copies) recorded Dec. 1, 1886; bound during the period Dec. 2, 1886–Jan. 4, 1887. Listed PW Dec. 11, 1886. Third printing (1010 copies) recorded Jan. 1, 1887; apparently a reprint statement added to the copyright page of this printing. Fourth printing (1000 copies) recorded March 28, 1887; to this printing the statement *Sixth Thousand* was probably added to the copyright page.

AAS (1st)   H (1st, 2nd)   MHS (1st)   NYPL (1st, 2nd)   PSU (untrimmed, being first printing)

13188. Richard the Third and the Primrose Criticism ... ⟨by Frank M. Bristol⟩

Chicago A. C. McClurg and Company 1887

Fourteen-line extract from an address on *Richard III*, p. ⟨5⟩. The entire address collected in *Latest Literary Essays and Addresses*, 1892.

Deposited June 27, 1887. Listed PW July 9, 1887.

H NYPL

13189. A Collection of Letters of W. M. Thackeray 1847–1855 ...

London Smith, Elder & Co., 15, Waterloo Place 1887 ...

"In this final arrangement of the letters, and in some additional annotations, the publishers have enjoyed the privilege of advice and assistance from Mr. James Russell Lowell ..."––p. ⟨v⟩.

Listed PC Oct. 1, 1887. See next entry for first American issue.

H

13190. A Collection of Letters of Thackeray 1847–1855 ...

New York Charles Scribner's Sons MDCCCLXXX-VII

For comment see London issue, preceding entry.

Listed PW Dec. 15, 1888.

H

13191. EARLY POEMS ...

NEW YORK: JOHN B. ALDEN, PUBLISHER. 1887.

⟨3⟩-172. 7⁵⁄₁₆″ × 4″.

⟨1-7¹², 8¹⟩.

S cloth: blue; blue-green. Flyleaves.

Reprint with the possible exception of:

*"Sonnet," p. 27. *If some small favor creep into my rhyme* ...

"Hakon's Lay," pp. 69-71.

*"Out of Doors," pp. 73-75.

*"Farewell," pp. 78-81.

*"Fancies about a Rosebud, Pressed in an Old Copy of Spenser," pp. 86-88.

*"New Year's Eve, 1844. A Fragment," pp. 88-92

*"A Mystical Ballad," pp. 92-94.

*Collected in *Uncollected Poems*, 1950.

No contemporary notices found.

B   UWA

13192. ... A Record of the Commemoration, November Fifth to Eighth, 1886, on the Two Hundred and Fiftieth Anniversary of the Founding of Harvard College.

Cambridge, N. E.; John Wilson and Son. University Press. 1887.

At head of title: *1636. Harvard University. 1886.*

Reprint save for "Speech," pp. 300-302. Otherwise unlocated.

H   Y

13193. The West Church, Boston Commemorative Services on the Fiftieth Anniversary of its Present Ministry and the One Hundred and Fiftieth of Its Foundation on Tuesday, March 1, 1887 ...

Boston Damrell and Upham 1887

Printed presentation slip inserted at front of some copies.

"Address ...," pp. 58-64. Elsewhere unlocated.

H   NYPL   Y

13194. HEARTSEASE AND RUE ...

BOSTON AND NEW YORK HOUGHTON, MIFFLIN AND COMPANY THE RIVERSIDE PRESS, CAMBRIDGE 1888

The publisher's records show five printings during the year 1888; these are as follows:

FIRST PRINTING, FIRST STATE

⟨i-iv⟩, ⟨i⟩-⟨x⟩, ⟨1⟩-218. Laid paper. Portrait frontispiece inserted. 7″ × 4¹¹⁄₁₆″ (trade format, edges trimmed, top edges gilt). 7¼″ × 4¾″ (untrimmed).

⟨1-14⁸, 15⁴⟩.

P. 41, line 10: ... *should be* |

P. 63 ends: ... *blissful woe* |

P. 92, line 4: . . . *thy breath.* |

P. 144, line 7 from bottom: . . . *windward* . . .

Leaf ⟨5⟩7 (pp. 63-64) is an integral leaf, not a cancel.

Plates cast Jan. 31, 1888. 3060 copies (first printing) done by Feb. 8, 1888, including 1030 copies with the London imprint of *Macmillan and Company.* Feb. 17, 1888: Labels printed for the untrimmed format. Copies of the first printing (second state) have been seen (in H) inscribed by Lowell March 7, 1888. During the period Feb. 18–March 21, 1888, 250 copies were bound untrimmed. The London issue (Macmillan) noted for *next week* Ath March 3, 1888. Deposited (American issue) March 7, 1888, both copies being of the second state. Noted as *just issued* PW March 10, 1888. The London issue listed Ath March 10, 1888. The Boston issue listed PW March 24, 1888.

All located copies of the London (Macmillan) issue are of the first state of the first printing. The publisher's records suggest that copies may occur with p. 63 in the corrected state. Thus far no copy of the untrimmed state (the so-called large paper format) has been seen in first printing, first state but since some copies were put in binding prior to Feb. 28, 1888, the date on which the cancel was printed, untrimmed copies may yet be found in the earliest state.

Locations: EM (Boston issue, in boards, cloth shelfback) UV (a set of folded sheets; a copy of the London issue) B (London)

FIRST PRINTING, SECOND STATE

As above save for leaf ⟨5⟩7 (pp. 63-64) which is a cancel. P. 63 ends: *That women in their self-surrender know?* In some copies leaf ⟨5⟩7 is pasted to the original stub. In other copies leaf ⟨5⟩2, the conjugate of ⟨5⟩7, is a singleton, pasted to leaf ⟨5⟩3. This variation appears to be nothing more than the result of the method used by the individual binder in making the correction.

The corrected leaf was printed Feb. 28, 1888.

Locations: AAS (cloth, paper label; boards, cloth shelfback) H (cloth, paper label; boards, cloth shelfback) LC (boards, cloth shelfback; being the deposit copies) NYPL (boards, cloth shelfback) UV (cloth, paper label; boards, cloth shelfback) Y (cloth, paper label)

SECOND PRINTING

⟨i-ii⟩, ⟨i⟩-⟨x⟩, ⟨1⟩-218, blank leaf. Laid paper. Portrait frontispiece inserted. 7″ × 4¹¹⁄₁₆″. Pp. 63-64 is an integral leaf, not a cancel.

⟨1-14⁸, 15⁴⟩.

P. 41, line 10: . . . *should be* |

P. 63 ends: . . . *self-surrender know?* |

P. 92, line 4: . . . *thy breath.* |

P. 144, line 7 from bottom: . . . *windwaved* . . .

1015 copies printed March 26, 1888.

Note: A copy of this printing (in UV) was presented by Lowell to E. L. Godkin under date March 7, 1888. This printing was not done until March 26 and Lowell predated the inscription for reasons not known to BAL; perhaps to cover the fact that the presentation was made well after the day of publication.

Locations: H (boards, cloth shelfback) UV (boards, cloth shelfback)

THIRD PRINTING

Not identified by BAL.

1016 copies printed April 12, 1888.

Leaf ⟨5⟩7 (pp. 63-64) integral, not a cancel. P. 63 ends: . . . *self-surrender know?* |

FOURTH PRINTING

On copyright page: SIXTH THOUSAND.

P. 41, line 10: . . . *'t is for me* |

P. 63 ends: . . . *self-surrender know?* |

P. 92, line 4: . . . *your breath.* |

P. 144, line 7 from bottom: . . . *windwaved* . . .

Leaf ⟨5⟩7 (pp. 63-64) is an integral leaf, not a cancel.

1428 copies printed May 31, 1888 (June 2, 1888?). 500 copies shipped to Macmillan, London.

Locations: H (boards, cloth shelfback)

FIFTH PRINTING

On copyright page: EIGHTH THOUSAND.

P. 41, line 10: . . . *'t is for me* |

P. 63 ends: . . . *self-surrender know?* |

P. 92, line 4: . . . *your breath.* |

P. 144, line 7 from bottom: . . . *windwaved* . . .

Leaf ⟨5⟩7 (pp. 63-64) is an integral leaf, not a cancel.

1020 copies printed July 16, 1888.

Locations: H (boards, cloth shelfback)

Gray laid paper boards sides, white V cloth shelfback and corners. White laid end papers. Laid paper flyleaf at back. Top edges gilt. Edges trimmed. *Also:* 250 copies in blue V cloth, printed paper label on spine; all edges untrimmed. *Note:* The limited issue does not contain a certificate of issue; the figure 250 based on publisher's records.

Locations: See above under the separate printings.

13195. What American Authors Think about International Copyright

New-York American Copyright League 1888

"International Copyright," p. ⟨3⟩; here without title. For collected publication see *Poetical Works, Cabinet Edition*, pp. 560, ⟨1890; *i.e., ca.* 1895⟩; and, *The Complete Poetical Works, Cambridge Edition,* Boston ⟨1896⟩.

Statement before the Senate Committee on Patents, Jan. 29, 1886, pp. 10-11.

At pp. ⟨14⟩-15 is "An Open Letter to Readers of Books. Address of the American Copyright League, January, 1888," signed at end by Stedman, Lowell, Eggleston and others. The letter also had separate publication; see next entry.

For fuller comment see entry No. 218.

13196. An Open Letter to Readers of Books. Address of the American Copyright League.

⟨New York, n.d., *ca.* 1888⟩

A single leaf of blue; or, cream, paper, folded to make 8 pages. Signed at end by Lowell, Stedman, Eggleston and others. Also appears in the preceding entry.

H NYPL

13197. No. 19. Standard Recitations by Best Authors . . . Compiled . . . by Frances P. Sullivan . . . March, 1888 . . .

M. J. Ivers & Co., Publishers, 86 Nassau Street, N. Y. . . . ⟨1888⟩

Printed paper wrapper.

"Fancy or Fact," p. 6. Collected in (reprinted from?) *Heartsease and Rue*, 1888 (February) as "Fact or Fancy."

Two printings noted:

1: Imprint as above.

2: Publisher's address in imprint: *379 Pearl Street.*

Title entered for copyright Feb. 29, 1888. Further copyright and publication information wanting.

H (2nd)   LC (1st)   NYPL (1st)

13198. POLITICAL ESSAYS . . .

BOSTON AND NEW YORK   HOUGHTON, MIFFLIN AND COMPANY   THE RIVERSIDE PRESS, CAMBRIDGE   1888

Two binding variants noted. The sequence, if any, has not been determined and the designations are for identification only.

BINDING VARIANT A

⟨i-viii⟩, ⟨1⟩-326, blank leaf. Laid paper. $7\frac{7}{16}''$ full × $4\frac{7}{8}''$.

⟨1², 2-21⁸, 22⁶⟩.

BINDING VARIANT B

⟨i-vi⟩, ⟨1⟩-326. Laid paper. $7\frac{7}{16}''$ full × $4\frac{7}{8}''$.

The sheets appear to be the same as *Binding Variant A* but leaves ⟨1⟩₁ and ⟨22⟩₆ are excised.

S cloth: green. Covers bevelled. Blue-black coated end papers. Laid paper flyleaves. Top edges gilt.

UNTRIMMED FORMAT

V cloth: blue. Printed paper label on spine. Made up of untrimmed sheets of the first printing. Leaf: $7\frac{13}{16}'' × 5''$. ⟨1⟩₁ excised; ⟨22⟩₆ present. Laid paper flyleaf at front; in some copies a laid paper flyleaf inserted between ⟨22⟩₅₋₆. Reportedly but 75 copies were done in this untrimmed format but BAL has been unable to substantiate the statement.

2546 copies printed July 2, 1888; 520 copies shipped to London. Advertised for July 21 PW July 14, 1888. Deposited July 20, 1888. Advertised for *next week* Ath July 21, 1888. MHS copy (*Variant B*) inscribed by early owner July 24, 1888. BA copy (*Variant B*) received July 26, 1888. Listed Ath July 28, 1888; PW Aug. 4, 1888.

AAS (*Variant A;* untrimmed)   BA (*Variant B*)   H (*Variant B;* untrimmed)   LC (*Variant B,* being a deposit copy)   MHS (Variant B)   Y (*Variant B*)

13199. THE INDEPENDENT IN POLITICS

Precise date of publication not known. Also appears in (reprinted from?) *Political Essays*, 1888 (July 20); see preceding entry. Three formats noted; sequence not determined.

SMALL PAPER FORMAT

. . . THE INDEPENDENT IN POLITICS AN ADDRESS DELIVERED BEFORE THE RE-FORM CLUB OF NEW YORK, APRIL 13, 1888 . . .

NEW YORK   THE REFORM CLUB   12 EAST 33D STREET   1888

At head of title: *Reform Club Series.——I*

⟨1⟩-27. Wove paper. $8'' × 5\frac{1}{4}''$ full.

⟨-⟩¹⁴.

Printed blue-green laid paper wrapper.

Locations: AAS   H   NYHS   NYPL   UV   Y

LARGE PAPER FORMAT

Title-page: As above.

⟨1⟩-27. Laid paper. $9\frac{5}{8}'' × 7\frac{1}{4}''$.

⟨1², 2-3⁶⟩ (?).

On p. ⟨2⟩: LARGE PAPER EDITION 300 COPIES. NO. . . .

Binding: Noted only bound together with other publications in the series with general title-page: Reform Club Series / Nos. 1-4 / NEW YORK, 1888 /

Locations: AAS   LC

TRADE FORMAT

... THE INDEPENDENT IN POLITICS AN ADDRESS DELIVERED BEFORE THE REFORM CLUB OF NEW YORK, APRIL 13, 1888 ...

NEW YORK & LONDON G. P. PUTNAM'S SONS THE KNICKERBOCKER PRESS 1888

At head of title: *Questions of the Day. No. XLVIII.*

⟨i-ii⟩, ⟨1⟩-27; blank, p. ⟨28⟩; 2 pp. advertisements. Wove paper. 7⅝″ × 5⅜″.

⟨1-2⁸⟩.

Printed gray paper wrapper.

Locations: AAS H LC Y

Published in the *New York Evening Post*, April 17, 1888; *Civil Service Reformer* (Baltimore), May, 1888. Putnam edition deposited July 25, 1888.

13200. The English Poets: Lessing, Rousseau: Essays by James Russell Lowell, with "An Apology for a Preface."

London   Walter Scott, 24 Warwick Lane Toronto: W. J. Gage and Co. 1888

Reprint save for "An Apology for a Preface," pp. ⟨vii⟩-x, dated at end *October 13th, 1888.*

According to an advertisement in the back of the LC copy the books in this series, *The Camelot Series,* were available in two styles: Cloth, cut; and, cloth, uncut. *Noted as follows;* the designations are for identification only:

Binding A

Red V cloth, stamped in black and gold. All edges trimmed. *Locations:* LC NYPL

Binding B

Blue V cloth, printed paper label on spine. Wholly untrimmed. *Locations:* BA Y

Under the title *Essays on . . .* , advertised for Nov. 26, Ath. Nov. 17, 1888. Under the title *English Poets . . .* , advertised for Nov. 17, Ath Dec. 1, 1888. *Now ready* PC Dec. 6, 1888. Listed PC Dec. 6, 1888. Distributed in United States by Whittaker, New York (with their imprint?). Listed PW Jan. 12, 1889.

13201. Arbor Day . . . Edited and Compiled by Robert W. Furnas.

Lincoln, Neb.: State Journal Company, Printers. 1888.

Bound in imitation leather.

Letter, March 25, 1888, pp. 102-104.

BA

13202. The History of the World's Progress. A General History of the Earth's Construction, and of the Advancement of Mankind. With an Introduction by Hon. James Russell Lowell. Edited by Charles E. Beale . . .

World's Library Association: 592 Washington St., Boston, Mass. ⟨1886; *i.e.,* 1888⟩

Presumably a subscription book; issued in a variety of formats, with varying imprint? Noted as both a 2-volume work; and, two volumes bound in one.

"Introduction," Vol. 1, pp. ⟨i⟩-x. At foot of p. ⟨i⟩: *Copyright, 1888, By M. R. Gately.* The introduction does not appear in the 1886 printing. Collected in *Latest Literary Essays and Addresses,* 1892.

H (2 Vols. in 1)   Y (2 Vols.)

13203. Proceedings at the Meeting for the Formation of the International Copyright Association, Parker House, December 27, 1887.

Boston: Press of Rockwell and Churchill, 39 Arch Street. 1888.

Printed self-wrapper. Cover-title.

Remarks, pp. 11-12, and following.

NYPL Y

13204. Proceedings of the Massachusetts Historical Society. Vol. III.---Second Series. 1886-1887 . . .

Boston: Published by the Society. M. DCCC. LXXXVIII.

Tribute to Charles Francis Adams, pp. 149-152.

Cloth. Also issued in two paper-covered parts?

H NYPL

13205. Report of the Proceedings at the Dinner Given by the Society of Authors to American Men and Women of Letters at the Criterion Restaurant, on Wednesday, July 25, 1888.

London: Society of Authors, 4, Portugal Street, Lincoln's Inn Fields, W. C. 1888.

Cover-title. Printed paper wrapper.

Speech, pp. 18-25. Collected in *American Ideas . . .* ⟨1892⟩, under the title "At the Dinner to American Authors."

AAS BA H LC

13206. Appletons' Cyclopædia of American Biography Edited by James Grant Wilson and John Fiske . . .

New York D. Appleton and Company 1,3 and 5 Bond Street 1887 ⟨-1889⟩

"John Greenleaf Whittier," Vol. VI, pp. 493-494.

For comment see entry No. 6020.

13207. Library of Tribune Extras. Vol 1. May, 1889. No. 5. The Washington Centenary Celebrated in New-York April 29, 30–May 1, 1889 . . .

The Tribune Association, New-York.

Printed paper wrapper. Cover-title.

Extracts from "Remarks by Mr. Lowell," pp. 71-72. The whole collected in *Writings*, 1890–1892, Vol. 6.

For comment on another issue see entry No. 685.

AAS H Y

13208. The Complete Angler, or the Contemplative Man's Recreation, of Izaak Walton and Charles Cotton. With an Introduction by James Russell Lowell . . .

Boston: Little, Brown, and Company. 1889.

2 Vols.

Two printings noted:

FIRST PRINTING

Vol. 1, p. xx, line 10 from bottom: . . . *to have had Dryden's* . . .

Noted only in the format limited to 500 copies.

SECOND PRINTING

Vol. 1, p. xx, line 10 from bottom: . . . *to have read Dryden's* . . .

Noted only in the format limited to 150 copies.

Two formats issued: Limited to 500 numbered copies. Certificate of issue on copyright page, both volumes. Title-page vignettes and full-page plates printed on India paper and mounted (not tipped). Leaf 8″ scant tall. *And:* Limited to 150 numbered copies. Certificate of issue on copyright page, both volumes. Title-page vignettes and full-page plates printed on Japan paper and tipped down. Leaf 8³⁄₁₆″ tall.

"Introduction," Vol. 1, pp. ⟨xv⟩-lxv. Collected in *Latest Literary Essays*, 1892.

Advertised PW Sept. 14/21, 1889: ". . . The work will be issued in the following styles: Five hundred numbered copies (for America and England), with the plates on India paper. 2 vols., crown 8vo, cloth, uncut, $10.00 net; half levant morocco extra, gilt top, $16.00 net. One hundred and fifty numbered copies (for America and England), with the plates on Japan paper. 2 vols., medium 8vo, cloth, uncut, $15.00 net; half levant morocco extra, gilt top, $21.00 net." Deposited Oct. 10, 1889. Listed (as *not seen*) PW Oct. 19, 1889. The London issue (Macmillan) announced for *next week* Ath Oct. 5, 1889; noted as *ready* Ath Oct. 12, 1889; no listings noted in British trade periodicals.

AAS (1 of 500) BA (1 of 500) H (both) NYPL (1 of 150) Y (1 of 500)

13209. No. 25. Standard Recitations by Best Authors . . . Compiled . . . by Frances P. Sullivan . . . September, 1889 . . .

M. J. Ivers & Co., Publishers, 86 Nassau Street, N. Y. . . . ⟨1889⟩

"Extract from How I Consulted the Oracle of the Goldfishes," p. 10. Collected in *Last Poems*, 1895.

For comment see entry No. 348.

13210. 68 Beacon Street, Boston, 20th Feb., 1889. Dear Sir: I have just been reading with profound interest and emotion your Biographical Sketch of your remarkable kinswoman . . . I remain faithfully yours, J. R. Lowell . . .

Single leaf. Printed on recto only. Printed on *Crane's Japanese Linen, 1889.* 7³⁄₈″ scant × 4³⁄₄″.

Letter from Lowell to Theodore Bacon commenting on the latter's *Delia Bacon, a Biographical Sketch*, 1888. Presumably printed for insertion in copies of the book, wherein it is usually found. The letter was written under date *20th Feb., 1889*; the book was listed in PW Dec. 15, 1888. *Not located as a separate publication.*

NYPL UV

13211. The Art of Authorship . . . Compiled . . . by George Bainton.

London: James Clarke & Co., 13 & 14, Fleet Street. 1890.

Contribution, pp. 30-31.

For comment see entry No. 1271.

13212. The Writings of James Russell Lowell

Two formats issued:

Large-Paper Edition. The Writings of James Russell Lowell in Ten ⟨Twelve⟩ Volumes.

Cambridge Printed at the Riverside Press 1890 ⟨–1892⟩

Caption-title. Vols. 1-10 dated 1890; Vol. 11 dated 1891; Vol. 12 dated 1892. Limited to 300 numbered sets for America; 25 numbered sets for Great Britain.

Probably issued in a variety of custom bindings. A copy deposited for copyright was bound in three-quarters cloth, printed paper label on spine.

Riverside Edition. The Writings of James Russell Lowell

Boston and New York Houghton, Mifflin and Company The Riverside Press, Cambridge MDCCCXC ⟨–1892⟩

Caption-title. Vols. 1-10 dated MDCCCXC; Vols. 11-12 dated 1892.

Noted in cloth; half calf; half calf gilt extra; half levant.

"Contains some material collected for the first time. Though edited by Lowell himself, he made few if any revisions, and the text was mainly reprinted from earlier volumes . . ."–––Livingston, p. 121.

1: Literary Essays, I.

Reprint save for "Prefatory Note to the Essays," pp. ⟨v⟩-vii.

Large paper format printed May 17, 1890; 333 copies. Large paper format bound during the period May 24, 1890–Jan. 14, 1891. *Riverside* printed May 27, 1890; 1530 copies. 25 large paper copies shipped to London (Macmillan) May 28, 1890. 525 *Riverside* copies shipped to London (Macmillan) May 28, 1890. Large paper copies deposited May 29, 1890. *Riverside* copies bound during the period June 6, 1890–Dec. 6, 1890. 100 copies of the *Riverside* format were bound uncut June 7–9, 1890. *Riverside* format advertised as *recently published* PW Sept. 13, 1890; offered in two tyles: *gilt top* and *uncut*. Listed, both limited, trade formats, PW Sept. 13, 1890. London issue (Macmillan) noted as *ready September 25* Ath Sept. 13, 1890. Second printing (*Riverside*) Nov. 10, 1890; 514 copies. Third printing (*Riverside*) May 1, 1891; 518 copies.

2: Literary Essays, II.

Reprint.

Large paper format deposited May 29, 1890. Listed, both limited, trade formats, PW Sept. 13, 1890. *Riverside* advertised as *recently published* PW Sept. 13, 1890; offered in two styles: *gilt top* and *uncut*. London issue (Macmillan) listed Ath Oct. 25, 1890.

3: Literary Essays, III.

Reprint.

Large paper format deposited July 10, 1890. Listed, both limited, trade formats, PW Oct. 4, 1890. London issue (Macmillan) listed Ath Nov. 22, 1890.

4: Literary Essays, IV.

Reprint.

Large paper format deposited July 10, 1890. Listed, both limited, trade formats, PW Oct. 4, 1890. London issue (Macmillan) listed Ath Jan. 10, 1891.

5: Political Essays.

Reprint.

Large paper format deposited Nov. 24, 1890. Listed, trade format, not limited, PW Dec. 6, 1890. *Riverside* advertised for Nov. 19 PW Nov. 15, 1890; offered in two styles: *gilt*

top and *uncut*. London issue (Macmillan) listed Ath Jan. 10, 1891.

6: Literary and Political Addresses.

First book publication for:

"Tariff Reform Address . . . Tariff Reform League, Boston, December 29, 1887," pp. ⟨181⟩-189.

"'Our Literature.' Response to a Toast . . . April 30, 1889 . . . ," pp. ⟨222⟩-228. Extracts had prior publication in *Library of Tribune Extras. Vol I, May, 1889*, above.

Nov. 14, 1890, 1528 copies of *Riverside* format printed. 528 copies of *Riverside* format shipped to Macmillan (London) Nov. 14, 1890. Large paper format printed Nov. 15, 1890; 334 copies printed. *Riverside* format advertised for Nov. 19 PW Nov. 15, 1890; offered in two styles: *gilt top* and *uncut*. *Riverside* bound during the period Nov. 20, 1890–Jan. 6, 1891, including fifty copies bound uncut. Large paper copies bound during the period Nov. 20, 1890–Jan. 14, 1891. Large paper copies deposited Nov. 24, 1890. Listed, trade format, not limited, PW Dec. 6, 1890. Second printing (*Riverside*) Dec. 20, 1890; 506 copies. London issue (Macmillan) listed Ath March 7, 1891. Third printing (*Riverside*) June 9, 1891; 504 copies.

7: Poems, I.

Reprint save for "Prefatory Note to the Poems," pp. ⟨v⟩-vi.

Possibly here first in book form: "Letter from Boston," which also appears in: *Poetical Works*, Boston ⟨1890⟩, red line edition, publication date not known; and, *Poetical Works, Household Edition*, Boston ⟨1890⟩, pp. 507, published not before *ca.* Nov. 1890.

Sept. 4, 1890, 1532 copies of *Riverside* format printed. Sept. 18, 1890, 343 large paper copies printed. *Riverside* format bound during the period Oct. 14, 1890–Jan. 5, 1891. Large paper copies bound during the period Oct. 15, 1890–Jan. 14, 1891. Oct. 15, 1890, 524 copies (*Riverside*) shipped Macmillan (London). Oct. 16, 1890, fifty *Riverside* copies bound uncut. Oct. 27, 1890, large paper copies deposited for copyright. Listed, both limited, trade formats, PW Nov. 1, 1890. Second printing of *Riverside* format, Dec. 27, 1890, 516 copies. London (Macmillan) issue listed Ath April 25, 1891. Third printing of *Riverside* format, May 21, 1891, 518 copies. Fourth printing of *Riverside* format, Oct. 30, 1891, 520 copies.

8: Poems, II.

Reprint.

Oct. 27, 1890, large paper copies deposited. Listed, both limited, trade formats, PW Nov.

1, 1890. London (Macmillan) issue listed Ath May 2, 1891.

9: Poems, III.

Reprint with the possible exception of "Fragments of an Unfinished Poem," pp. ⟨126⟩-136, which appears also in *Poetical Works*, Boston ⟨1890⟩, red line edition, publication date not known; and, *Poetical Works, Household Edition*, Boston ⟨1890⟩, pp. 507; published not before *ca.* Nov. 1890.

Sept. 12, 1890, 1542 copies of *Riverside* format printed. Sept. 18, 1890, 342 copies of large paper format printed. Large paper copies bound Nov. 10, 1890–Jan. 14, 1891. *Riverside* copies bound Nov. 13, 1890–Jan. 5, 1891. Large paper copies deposited for copyright Nov. 15, 1890. Fifty copies of *Riverside* format bound uncut Nov. 19, 1890. Both limited and trade formats listed PW Dec. 6, 1890. *Note:* Listed ambiguously as *Vol. 3*, meaning Vol. 3 of the *Poems*, not Vol. 3 of the set. Second printing of *Riverside*, Jan. 6, 1891, 516 copies. London (Macmillan) issue listed Ath May 30, 1891. Third printing of *Riverside*, June 16, 1891, 518 copies. Fourth printing of *Riverside*, Nov. 7, 1891, 520 copies.

10: Poems, IV.

Reprint.

Large paper copies deposited Nov. 15, 1890. Listed, both limited, trade formats, PW Dec. 6, 1890. *Note:* Listed ambiguously as *Vol. 4*, meaning Vol. 4 of the *Poems*, not Vol. 4 of the set. London (Macmillan) issue listed Ath July 11, 1891.

11: Latest Literary Essays and Addresses.

See full entry, below, under year 1892.

12: The Old English Dramatists.

See full entry, below, under year 1892.

The above entry made on the basis of copies in H, LC, NYPL.

13213. The Art of Authorship . . . Compiled . . . by George Bainton

New York D. Appleton and Company 1890

Contribution, pp. 29-30.

For comment see entry No. 1272.

13214. A Fable for Critics . . .

Boston and New York Houghton, Mifflin and Company The Riverside Press, Cambridge M DCCC XCI ⟨*i.e.,* 1890⟩

"Prefatory Note," p. ⟨5⟩.

For first edition see under year 1848.

Deposited Oct. 6, 1890.

AAS B BA H MHS

13215. Areopagitica   A Speech of Mr. John Milton . . . with an Introduction by James Russell Lowell

New-York The Grolier Club MDCCCXC

Paper boards, printed paper label on spine.

"Introduction," pp. ⟨xi⟩-lvii. Collected in *Latest Literary Essays*, 1892.

325 copies on Holland paper, 3 copies on vellum. ". . . Printed . . . September and October, 1890." ———Certificate of issue.

Deposited Nov. 14, 1890.

AAS BA H Y

13216. MY BROOK . . . SUPPLEMENT TO THE NEW YORK LEDGER DECEMBER 13TH 1890

⟨New York: The New York Ledger, 1890⟩

Cover-title.

⟨19⟩-⟨22⟩. 16⅜″ × 11¼″.

Single cut sheet folded to make four pages. On p. ⟨22⟩: *Souvenir The New York Ledger Supplement Dec 13 1890*

Earliest located book publication: *James Russell Lowell and his Friends*, by Edward Everett Hale, 1899, pp. 285-286. Collected in *Uncollected Poems*, 1950.

Deposited Dec. 11, 1890.

BA BPL LC

13217. ADDRESS . . . BEFORE THE MODERN LANGUAGE ASSOCIATION OF AMERICA 1889 EXTRACTED FROM THE PUBLICATIONS OF THE MODERN LANGUAGE ASSOCIATION, VOL. V, NO. I.

⟨Baltimore: The Modern Language Association of America, 1890⟩

Cover-title.

⟨5⟩-22. Laid paper. 9⅛″ × 6⅛″.

Leaves extracted from *Publications of the Modern Language Association of America, 1890 . . . Vol. V*, Baltimore, 1890, and issued in printed paper wrapper.

Collected in *Latest Literary Essays*, 1892, as "The Study of Modern Languages."

AAS

13218. The Poetical Works of James Russell Lowell Household Edition with Illustrations

Boston and New York Houghton, Mifflin and Company The Riverside Press, Cambridge ⟨1890⟩

Pp. 507. Printed in two columns.

Reprint with the possible exception of "Letter from Boston" and "Fragments of an Unfinished Poem." For other book publication of these see next entry; also see *The Writings* . . . , 1890, Vols. 7, 9.

At least two printings have been identified:

A: In the preliminary advertisement the *Complete Works of James Russell Lowell* is described as in *10 Vols.* Issued not before *ca.* Nov. 1890.

B: In the preliminary advertisement the *Complete Works of James Russell Lowell* is described as in *11 Vols.* Issued not before *ca.* Nov. 1891.

H (A, B) UV (A)

13219. The Poetical Works of James Russell Lowell. With Numerous Illustrations.

Boston and New York: Houghton, Mifflin and Company. The Riverside Press, Cambridge. ⟨1890⟩

Red line edition.

Reprint with the possible exception of "Letter from Boston" and "Fragments of an Unfinished Poem." For other book publication of these see preceding entry.

B

13220. (Privately Printed.) To J.R.L. Sur la Pipe Cassée ⟨by Charles Frederick Bradford⟩ . . . To C. F. Bradford, on the Gift of a Meerschaum Pipe ⟨by James Russell Lowell⟩ . . . ⟨letter from Lowell to Bradford, *Cambridge, October, 1858*⟩

⟨n.p., n.d., *ca.* 1890.⟩

Single leaf. Printed on recto only. White wove paper watermarked *Westlock*. 19$\frac{5}{16}$″ × 3$\frac{3}{4}$″.

Lowell's poem first published in *The Spirit of the Fair*, 1864, *q.v.* Collected in *Heartsease and Rue*, 1888. The text varies in all three appearances. The Lowell letter is here in its earliest located appearance.

H

13221. The Soldier's Field June 10, 1890

⟨n.p., n.d., Cambridge: Harvard College, 1890⟩

Printed paper wrapper. Pp. ⟨1⟩-12.

An account of the dedication of Soldier's Field, Boston, Mass., June 10, 1890, being principally the text of an oration by Henry Lee Higginson, donor of the field. The oration embodies, p. 9, an epitaph written for this occasion by Lowell which incorporates Emerson's quatrain, "Sacrifice."

Note: Copies of the above, stripped of the wrapper, also occur stitched together with biographical sketches of the six soldiers memorialized by the field; pagination: ⟨1-6⟩, ⟨1⟩-12. Printed paper wrapper. Two states of the wrapper enclosing the enlarged form have been seen; sequence, if any, not determined: A: At upper left of the front of the wrapper is an embossed reproduction of a medal in gold and colors; B: At upper left a medal printed in purple.

H (all three forms)

13222. The Story of the Memorial Fountain to Shakspeare . . . Edited by L. Clarke Davis

Cambridge Printed at the Riverside Press 1890

Letter, pp. 35-38. Collected in *American Ideas for English Readers* ⟨1892⟩, as "At the Stratford Memorial Fountain Presentation."

H

The Poetical Works . . .

Boston and New York Houghton, Mifflin and Company The Riverside Press, Cambridge ⟨1890; *i.e., ca.* 1895⟩

On binding: *Cabinet Edition.*

See below under *ca.* 1895.

A Fable for Critics . . .

Boston . . . M DCCC XCI

See above under 1890 (Oct.).

LATEST LITERARY ESSAYS AND ADDRESSES . . .

CAMBRIDGE PRINTED AT THE RIVERSIDE PRESS 1891

See next entry.

13223. LATEST LITERARY ESSAYS AND ADDRESSES . . .

BOSTON AND NEW YORK HOUGHTON, MIFFLIN AND COMPANY THE RIVERSIDE PRESS, CAMBRIDGE 1892 ⟨*i.e.,* 1891⟩

Edited by Charles Eliot Norton.

Three printings noted:

FIRST PRINTING

⟨i-viii⟩, ⟨1⟩-184. Portrait frontispiece inserted. 7$\frac{5}{8}$″ × 5″.

⟨1⁴, 2-12⁸, 13⁴⟩. Leaves ⟨1⟩$_{2-3}$ (the title-leaf and *Note*) are inserts.

Editor's *Note*, p. ⟨v⟩, in one paragraph.

Noted in *Bindings A, Aa, B;* see below.

SECOND PRINTING

⟨i-viii⟩, ⟨1⟩-184, blank leaf. Portrait frontispiece inserted. 7″ scant × 4⅞″ full.

⟨1⁷, 2-16⁶⟩. Leaf ⟨1⟩₂ inserted.

Editor's *Note*, p. ⟨v⟩, in one paragraph.

Noted in *Bindings A, B;* see below.

THIRD PRINTING

⟨i-viii⟩, ⟨1⟩-184, blank leaf. Portrait frontispiece inserted. 7⅝″ × 5″.

⟨1⁷, 2-16⁶⟩. Leaf ⟨1⟩₂ inserted.

Editor's *Note*, p. ⟨v⟩, in two paragraphs.

Noted only in *Binding A;* see below.

Noted in the following bindings:

BINDING A

Coarse-grained S cloth: maroon. Sides blind-stamped with a single rule frame. All lettering on spine; front cover not lettered. Laid paper end papers. Flyleaves. Top edges gilt. Green ribbon marker. Prepared as *The Writings*, Vol. XI, although the sheets are not so identified.

BINDING Aa

Same as *Binding A* but the sides are wholly unstamped.

BINDING B

Green silk. Lettered on both spine and on front cover. Back cover stamped in blind with a frame of florets. Dark red-coated end papers. Flyleaves. Top edges gilt. Green ribbon marker.

LARGE PAPER FORMAT

Also issued in a large paper format as Vol. XI of *Lowell's Writings.*

Latest Literary Essays and Addresses . . .

Cambridge   Printed at the Riverside Press 1891

Title-page printed in black and red. Limited to 300 copies "printed for America" and fifty (?) copies printed for Great Britain. *Reprint.* See publication notes below.

Contemporary advertisements indicate that the trade format was available also in "half calf . . . half calf, gilt top . . . half levant."

On May 18, 1892, Charles Eliot Norton wrote Houghton, Mifflin & Company (letter in H) requesting that a correction be made on p. 149. According to the publisher's records the correction was made on May 31, 1892, well after production of the third printing which was recorded in the publisher's records on Dec. 28, 1891.

The original reading: *"Like the new-abashed nightingale | That slinteth first . . .*

The corrected reading: *"the new-abashed nightingale | That stinteth first . . .*

Nov. 18-25, 1891, 3822 copies printed, of which 730 copies were sent to London (Macmillan). Bound during the period Nov. 25–Dec. 21, 1891, including fifty copies bound uncut. Deposited Dec. 3, 1891. 368 large paper copies printed Dec. 4, 1891. Two copies of the large paper printing bound Dec. 11, 1891, for copyright deposit. Second printing, Dec. 11, 1891, 1568 copies. Large paper copies bound Dec. 12, 1891; seven additional copies bound 1892, 1893. Large paper copies deposited Dec. 14, 1891. Listed (trade format) PW Dec. 19, 1891. Third printing, Dec. 28, 1891, 2042 copies. The London (Macmillan) issue advertised as *a new volume of Lowell's Works. Just published . . . cloth*–––PC Jan. 2, 1892. Listed PC Jan. 9, 1892.

AAS (1st, *Binding B*)   BPL (1st, *Binding Aa*)   H (1st, *Binding A;* 1st, *Binding B;* 2nd, *Binding A;* 3d, *Binding A*)   LC (1st, *Binding A,* being a deposit copy)   Y (1st, *Binding A;* 2nd, *Binding B*)

13224. AMERICAN IDEAS FOR ENGLISH READERS . . . WITH INTRODUCTION BY HENRY STONE

PUBLISHED BY J, G, CUPPLES CO, 250 BOYLSTON ST. BOSTON ⟨1892⟩

⟨i⟩-⟨xvi⟩, ⟨1⟩-94; title-leaf for publisher's catalog; plus: 6 pp. advertisements, blank leaf. Portrait frontispiece inserted. 7″ scant × 3¹³⁄₁₆″.

⟨1-14⁴, plus 15⁴⟩.

S cloth: gray; lavender; tan; stamped in color. According to an advertisement on the end papers the book was available in two styles: "Cloth, $1.00; white and gold, $1.25." Not noted by BAL in white and gold. White end papers imprinted with advertisements; copies have been seen with the terminal end paper unprinted.

Deposited May 21, 1892.

AAS   BA   H   NYPL   Y

13225. THE OLD ENGLISH DRAMATISTS . . .

BOSTON AND NEW YORK   HOUGHTON, MIFFLIN AND COMPANY   THE RIVERSIDE PRESS, CAMBRIDGE 1892

Edited by Charles Eliot Norton.

Two formats issued:

TRADE FORMAT

⟨i-ii⟩, ⟨i-vi⟩, ⟨1⟩-132, blank leaf. Portrait frontispiece inserted. 7⅝″ × 5″ scant.

$\langle -^1, 1\text{-}11^6, 12^4 \rangle$.

Noted in two bindings; presumed simultaneous:

BINDING A

Coarse-grained S cloth: maroon. Sides blind-stamped with a single-rule frame. All lettering on spine; front cover not lettered. Laid paper end papers. Flyleaf at front. Top edges gilt. Green ribbon marker. Prepared as *The Writings*, Vol. XII, although not so identified.

BINDING B

Red silk. Lettered on both spine and on front cover. Back cover stamped in blind with a frame of florets. Olive-coated end papers. Flyleaf at front. Top edges gilt. Red ribbon marker. Leaf trimmed to 7″ × 5″ scant.

LARGE PAPER FORMAT

THE OLD ENGLISH DRAMATISTS . . .

CAMBRIDGE PRINTED AT THE RIVERSIDE PRESS 1892

Title-page in black and orange.

$\langle i\text{-}x \rangle$, $\langle 1 \rangle$-132, blank leaf. Laid paper. Watermarked *The Riverside Press* Frontispiece portrait inserted. $8\frac{7}{8}″ \times 5\frac{7}{8}″$.

$\langle 1^{10}, 2\text{-}8^8, 9^6 \rangle$. $\langle 1 \rangle_{2\text{-}3}$ inserted.

Blue-gray laid paper sides, white V cloth shelf back and corners, printed paper label on spine. End papers of book stock.

"Three Hundred Copies Printed for America No. . . ."---p. $\langle vi \rangle$.

Issued as Vol. XII, of the *Large-Paper Edition* of *The Writings*.

Contemporary advertisements indicate that the trade format was available also in "half calf . . . half calf, gilt top . . . half levant."

First published in *Harper's Monthly*, June–Nov. 1892. Printed Nov. 11, 1892, 3614 copies. Large paper format printed Nov. 19, 1892, 350 copies. Bound during the period Nov. 19–Dec. 9, 1892. Large paper copies bound during the period Nov. 26, 1892–April 21, 1893. Large paper copies deposited Nov. 29, 1892. Noted for *to-day* PW Dec. 3, 1892; presumably trade format since the note states ". . . there will also be a large-paper edition." Listed, presumably the trade format, PW Dec. 10, 1892. The London issue (Macmillan) listed Ath Dec. 24, 1892.

AAS (*Binding B; Large paper*) H (*Binding A; Large paper*) B (*Binding A*) NYPL (*Binding A*) UV (*Large paper*) Y (*Binding A; Large paper*)

13226. Conversations on Some of the Old Poets . . . with an Introduction by Robert Ellis Thompson . . . Third Edition Enlarged.

Philadelphia: David McKay, Publisher, 23 South Ninth Street. 1893.

For previous editions see above under years 1845, 1846.

"To this edition . . . have been appended the two papers on *Middleton* and on *The English Song-Writers* which Mr. Lowell contributed to the first two numbers $\langle$of *The Pioneer*$\rangle$."---p. x.

Two printings noted; the following sequence is probable:

PRINTING A

Printed on wove paper.

No terminal advertisements.

At foot of spine: DAVID MCKAY / PHILADELPHIA

PRINTING B

Printed on laid paper.

Single leaf of advertisements inserted at back, on p. $\langle 2 \rangle$ of which *Conversations on Some of the Old Poets* is blurbed with an extract from the *London Spectator* of April 22, 1893.

At foot of spine: AMERICAN / CLASSIC / SERIES

Deposited June 28, 1893. Listed PW July 8, 1893.

AAS (A, B) BA (A) H (A) LC (A, 2 copies, being deposit copies) Y (B)

13227. LETTERS . . . EDITED BY CHARLES ELIOT NORTON . . .

LONDON OSGOOD, MCILVAINE & CO. 45, ALBEMARLE STREET, W. 1894 [ALL RIGHTS RESERVED]

For (later?) American publication see next entry.

2 Vols.

1: $\langle i\text{-}ii \rangle$, $\langle i \rangle$-$\langle x \rangle$, $\langle 1 \rangle$-454, blank leaf. Laid paper. $8\frac{5}{8}″$ scant × $5\frac{15}{16}″$.

2: $\langle i \rangle$-$\langle viii \rangle$, $\langle 1 \rangle$-531.

1: $\langle - \rangle^2$, $\langle A \rangle^4$, B-I, K-U, X-Z^8, Aa-Ff^8, Gg^4.

2: $\langle A \rangle^4$, B-I, K-U, X-Z^8, Aa-Ii, Kk-Ll^8, Mm^2.

V cloth: green. Black-coated end papers. Top edges gilt.

Immediately---Ath Oct. 7, 1893. Listed Ath Oct. 14, 1893. *To be published Oct. 25*---Ath Oct. 21, 1893; PC Oct. 21, 1893. Reviewed Ath Oct. 28, 1893. Listed PC Nov. 4, 1893. Advertised Ath Nov. 25, 1893: *Two editions were rapidly disposed of; a third . . . is now ready.*

Caution: BAL has examined but a single copy of this publication; and the publishers claim three printings for it; see note extracted from Ath, Nov. 25, 1893, above. Are the reprints identified?

H

13228. LETTERS . . . EDITED BY CHARLES ELIOT NORTON . . .

NEW YORK   HARPER & BROTHERS PUBLISHERS
1894

For (earlier?) British publication see preceding entry.

2 Vols. Title-pages in black and brown.

1 : ⟨i-ii⟩, ⟨i⟩-viii, ⟨1⟩-418, blank leaf. Laid paper. Frontispiece and 1 plate inserted. 8¾″ × 5¾″.

2 : ⟨i-ii⟩, ⟨i⟩-⟨vi⟩, ⟨1⟩-464. Frontispiece inserted.

1 : ⟨-⟩⁵, 1-26⁸, 27². ⟨-⟩₂ inserted.

2 : ⟨-⟩², ⟨*⟩², 1-29⁸.

Dark blue rough linen. White laid end papers. Top edges gilt.

Will publish at once---pw April 15, 1893. *Nearly ready*---pw Aug. 26, 1893. Deposited Oct. 18, 1893. *Will issue at once*---pw Oct. 21, 1893. mhs copy received Oct. 30, 1893. ba copy received Nov. 2, 1893. Listed pw Nov. 4, 1893.

"An extract from a letter to Mrs. Francis G. Shaw, beginning *My dear Sarah:*, printed on pp. 195, 196 of Vol. I, was reprinted privately as a remembrance card, probably late in 1893, after the publication of these volumes. This extract was printed in black-letter type, with the initial letter in red, upon heavy cardboard, with beveled edges. The card measures 9³⁄₁₆″ by 7⅛ inches." ---Livingston, p. 125. Further information wanting.

AAS   B   H   MHS   NYPL

13229. The Harvard Crimson Supplement . . . Unpublished Fragments, Furnished by Charles Eliot Norton, from the College Lectures of James Russell Lowell . . .

Cambridge, Mass., . . . 1894 . . .

Caption-title.

6 parts. Dated March 23, 1894–May 4, 1894.

BA   H   LC

13230. LAST POEMS . . .

BOSTON AND NEW YORK HOUGHTON, MIFFLIN AND COMPANY   THE RIVERSIDE PRESS, CAMBRIDGE
M DCCC XCV

Title-page in black and red.

Edited by Charles Eliot Norton.

⟨i-vi⟩, 7-47; *i.e.*, ⟨i-vi⟩, 7-⟨88⟩, the leaves being printed on one side only save for the title-leaf which is printed on both sides. Portrait frontispiece inserted. Laid paper. 7½″ full × 5″ full.

⟨-¹, 1-7⁶, *¹⟩.

Buckram: green; red; tan. Laid end papers. Laid paper flyleaves. Top edges gilt.

2552 copies printed Sept. 4, 1895. Bound during the period Sept. 10–Oct. 3, 1895. Deposited Sept. 13, 1895. Advertised for Sept. 21, 1895, pw Sept. 7, 1895. Listed pw Oct. 5, 1895. Second printing, 2493 copies, Oct. 16, 1895; the second printing so marked; 520 copies shipped to London (Innes). Sixty sets of sheets (first printing) were pulped on July 13, 1903. The London (Innes) issue (American sheets) noted as *shortly* pc Oct. 19, 1895; listed Ath Nov. 16, 1895.

AAS   B   BA   H   NYPL   UV   Y

13231. The Poetical Works . . .

Boston and New York Houghton, Mifflin and Company The Riverside Press, Cambridge ⟨1890; *i.e., ca.* 1895⟩

Printed in two columns. Pp. 560. On binding: *Cabinet Edition.*

Precise date of publication not known. Reprint with the possible exception of "International Copyright," p. 543, which may be here first collected. Also in *The Complete Poetical Works . . . Cambridge Edition* ⟨1896⟩; see below.

See *What American Authors Think about International Copyright*, New York, 1888; and, *The Complete Poetical Works, Cambridge Edition*, Boston ⟨1896⟩.

Note: Cooke, p. 30, errs in stating that "International Copyright" was first collected in *Heartsease and Rue*, 1888.

H   UV

13232. THE POWER OF SOUND A RHYMED LECTURE . . .

PRIVATELY PRINTED ⟨at The Gilliss Press⟩ NEW YORK MDCCCXCVI

Title-page in black and red.

Edited by Charles Eliot Norton.

⟨i⟩-⟨xii⟩, 1-35; certificate of issue, p. ⟨36⟩. 8⅛″ scant × 5⅝″. Noted on paper; and, Japanese paper.

⟨1-6⁴⟩.

Marbled paper boards sides, mauve moiréd T cloth shelf back and corners.

". . . Only seventy-five copies . . . twenty-five are on Japanese paper and fifty on hand-made. No. . . ."---Certificate of issue.

"The only existing copy of the poem is in print on galley slips . . . It was put into type ⟨*ca.* 1862⟩ . . . for convenience of reading ⟨by Lowell⟩ in public . . ."---P. x.

Introductory note dated June, 1896. A hand-made paper copy in H received July 18, 1896.

Deposited July 28, 1896. Collected in *Uncollected Poems*, 1950.

AAS (hand-made paper) BA (hand-made paper) H (Japan; hand-made paper)

13233. The Complete Poetical Works . . . Cambridge Edition

Boston and New York Houghton, Mifflin and Company The Riverside Press, Cambridge ⟨1896⟩

Reprint with the possible exception of "International Copyright," p. 433, which may be here first collected. Also in *The Poetical Works . . .* ⟨1890; *i.e.*, *ca.* 1895⟩; see above.

Two printings noted:

FIRST PRINTING

⟨iii⟩-⟨xviii⟩, ⟨1⟩-492, blank, pp. ⟨493-496⟩.

No fly-title page.

SECOND (and later?) PRINTING

⟨i⟩-⟨xviii⟩, ⟨1⟩-492, blank pp. ⟨493-494.⟩

Fly-title page present.

According to contemporary notices available in cloth; and, in leather.

See *What American Authors Think about International Copyright*, New York, 1888; and, *The Poetical Works, Cabinet Edition* ⟨1890; *i.e.*, *ca.* 1895⟩.

Note: Cooke, p. 30, errs in stating that "International Copyright" was first collected in *Heartsease and Rue*, 1888.

Advertised for *this week* PW Jan. 27, 1897. Deposited Feb. 22, 1897. Listed PW March 16, 1897.

H (1st, 2nd)

13234. Francis Parkman

Boston Little, Brown, and Company 1896

Printed paper wrapper. Cover-title.

Extract from an essay on Parkman, p. 9. Originally in *Century Magazine*, Nov. 1892. Uncollected.

H

13235. LECTURES ON ENGLISH POETS . . .

CLEVELAND THE ROWFANT CLUB MDCCCXCVII

Title-page in black and red. Edited by S. A. Jones.

⟨i⟩-xvi, ⟨1⟩-210, printer's device, p. ⟨211⟩. 8¹⁵⁄₁₆″ × 6″.

⟨-⟩⁸, ⟨1⟩-12⁸, 13², 14⁸.

Tan T cloth sides, leather shelf back. At front and at back: A single gathering of four leaves of book

stock used as end papers and paste-downs; in some copies two leaves, not one, are pasted down.

"Two hundred and twenty-four copies printed in the month of March, 1897. This is No. . . ." ---Certificate of issue, p. ⟨i⟩.

Publication was contemplated as early as 1855; NLG Feb. 15, 1855, noted that the lectures "are to be published." Deposited April 19, 1897.

AAS B H NYPL UV

13236. The Old Rome and the New and Other Studies by W. J. Stillman . . .

London Grant Richards 9 Henrietta Street, Covent Garden 1897

"A Few of Lowell's Letters," pp. 128-167. Save for the following the letters had prior publication in *Letters*, 1894; the exceptions:

Pp. 155-156: Material beginning *When you come . . . ⟨to⟩ there are no lectures. And: Tell me what your plans are . . .⟨to end of page⟩.*

Pp. 161-162: . . . *Yes, my dear Stillman . . .* ⟨to end of letter⟩.

Cloth, printed paper label on spine.

H Y

13237. Old Cambridge by Thomas Wentworth Higginson . . .

New York The Macmillan Company London: Macmillan & Co., Ltd. 1899 All Rights Reserved

Extracts from "A Pepsyian Letter" sent to Charles F. Briggs, pp. 160-172; contains a poem which was collected under the title "Lady Bird . . . ," *Uncollected Poems*, 1950, p. 72. Letters to Higginson, pp. 176, 179-180, 182, 183-184.

For fuller description see entry No. 8429.

13238. IMPRESSIONS OF SPAIN . . . COMPILED BY JOSEPH B. GILDER WITH AN INTRODUCTION BY A. A. ADEE

BOSTON AND NEW YORK HOUGHTON, MIFFLIN AND COMPANY THE RIVERSIDE PRESS 1899

Title-page in black and red.

Two printings noted:

FIRST PRINTING

⟨i-iv⟩ (pp. ⟨iii-iv⟩ excised); ⟨i⟩-⟨x⟩ (pp. ⟨i-ii⟩ a single leaf, being the title-leaf); ⟨1⟩-107. Frontispiece and printed tissue inserted. Watermarked *Ruisdael* save for the title-leaf which is printed on paper watermarked *John Dickinson & Co.* 8″ scant × 5⅛″. *Query:* Was excised p. ⟨iii⟩ the original *Putnam* title-page?

⟨1⁷, 2-14⁴, 15²⟩. ⟨1⟩₂ excised; ⟨1⟩₃ inserted.

Folios present on the divisional title-pages: 21, 51, 73, 85, 93, 99.

On the protective tissue: *From a photograph by F. Gutekunst* is set 1⅞″ scant wide.

⟨i⟩-⟨x⟩, ⟨1⟩-107. Frontispiece and printed tissue inserted. Printed on paper watermarked *John Dickinson & Co.* 8″ × 5″.

⟨1¹, 2-8⁸, 9²⟩.

Folios not present on the divisional title-pages.

On the protective tissue: *From a photograph by F. Gutekunst* is set 1¾″ wide.

Printed tan paper boards, white vellum shelfback. Top edges gilt. *Two states of binding noted:*

A: Wove end papers, wove paper flyleaves. Publisher's imprint not present on spine.

B: Laid paper end papers, laid paper flyleaves. Publisher's imprint present on spine.

". . . Made up of selections from Lowell's letters to the Department of State, printed in *Papers Relating to the Foreign Relations of the United States, 1878-79*."---Livingston, p. 129.

The book was originally projected by G. P. Putnam's Sons and announced by them in PW Sept. 30, 1899. For reasons unknown to BAL the book was taken over by Houghton, Mifflin & Company who, on Nov. 28, 1899, recorded receipt of 1012 bound copies and 1101 copies in sheets. Deposited for copyright Nov. 14, 1899. Sheets put in binding during the period Dec. 6, 1899-Jan. 14, 1924. Listed PW Dec. 23, 1899. The London (Putnam) issue listed Ath Dec. 30, 1899. Plates melted down May 29, 1906. On Nov. 23, 1925 the remaining copies (526 perfect copies, 9 imperfect copies) were pulped by Houghton Mifflin Company.

H (both)

13239. Specimens of Printing Types in Use at the Marion Press Jamaica, Queensborough New-York . . .

⟨Jamaica, N. Y.⟩ September 1899

Printed self-wrapper. Cover-title. 300 copies printed.

Letter to Lord C., March 18, 1881; and the poem, "Cuiviscunque," p. ⟨9⟩. The poem collected in *Uncollected Poems*, 1950.

NYPL Y

13240. An American Anthology 1787-1899 . . . Edited by Edmund Clarence Stedman . . .

Boston and New York Houghton, Mifflin and Company The Riverside Press, Cambridge M DCCCC

Reprint with the possible exception of "An Autograph," p. 218. Dated at end *24th June, 1886*. Elsewhere unlocated.

For fuller description see entry No. 3082.

Modern Eloquence . . .

. . . Philadelphia ⟨1900⟩

See next entry.

13241. Modern Eloquence . . . ⟨Edited by⟩ Thomas B. Reed . . .

John D. Morris and Company Philadelphia ⟨1900; *i.e.,* 1901⟩

Reprint save for:

"Harvard Alumni," Vol. 2, pp. 737-741; delivered at the Harvard alumni dinner, June 30, 1875.

"National Growth of a Century," Vol. 2, pp. 741-745; delivered at the Harvard alumni dinner, June 28, 1876.

"The Stage," Vol. 2, pp. 745-748; delivered at the breakfast for American actors at the Savage Club, London, August, 1880.

"After-Dinner Speaking," Vol. 2, pp. 750-753; delivered at a banquet to Henry Irving, London, July 4, 1883.

"'The Return of the Native,'" Vol. 2, pp. 753-757; delivered at the Sanderson Academy dinner, Ashfield, Mass., Aug. 27, 1885.

Deposited April 19, 1901.

For fuller entry see No. 3467.

13242. The Complete Works of Edgar Allan Poe Edited by James A. Harrison . . . Volume I. Biography

New York Thomas Y. Crowell & Company Publishers ⟨1902⟩

Vignette title-page: *The Life of Edgar Allan Poe by James A. Harrison Virginia Edition* . . . Also issued in other formats?

"Edgar Allan Poe," pp. 367-383. Reprinted from *Graham's Magazine*, Feb. 1845. For another version see *The Works of the Late Edgar Allan Poe* . . . , New York, 1850, above.

Reprinted and reissued under date ⟨1903⟩ as Vol. 1 of *Life and Letters of Edgar Allan Poe*, by James A. Harrison; a 2-volume work; listed PW April 18, 1903.

H

13243. EARLY PROSE WRITINGS . . . WITH A PREFATORY NOTE BY DR. HALE, OF BOSTON, AND AN INTRODUCTION BY WALTER LITTLEFIELD

PUBLISHED BY JOHN LANE   THE BODLEY HEAD
LONDON & NEW YORK ⟨1902⟩

Title-page in black and green.

⟨i⟩-xxxviii, ⟨1⟩-248, blank leaf. Laid paper. Frontispiece. 7⁹⁄₁₆″ × 5¼″.

⟨1-18⁸⟩.

Two bindings of unknown sequence (if any) noted. The following designations are all but arbitrary and are not designed to suggest a sequence.

BINDING A

Green paper boards sides, ecru buckram shelf-back, printed paper label on spine. White wove end papers. Ribbon marker not present. Top edges plain. A copy thus deposited for copyright. A copy thus at H stamped *Review Copy*.

BINDING B

Green paper boards sides, ecru buckram shelf back, printed paper label on spine. White laid end papers. Green ribbon marker present. Top edges gilt. A copy thus in NYPL purchased Dec. 13, 1902.

On copyright page: *First Edition, September, 1902*

Deposited Oct. 28, 1902. Listed PW Nov. 15, 1902. The London edition (John Lane) listed Dec. 6, 1902.

AAS (A)   H (A)   LC (A)   NYPL (B)   UV (A)
Y (A)

13244. THE ANTI-SLAVERY PAPERS OF JAMES RUSSELL LOWELL...

BOSTON AND NEW YORK   HOUGHTON MIFFLIN AND COMPANY MDCCCCII

2 Vols. "Edited by William Belmont Parker..."
---Cooke, p. 137.

1: ⟨i-ii⟩, ⟨i⟩-⟨xiv⟩, ⟨1⟩-223. 9⁵⁄₁₆″ × 5¾″.

2: ⟨i⟩-⟨viii⟩, ⟨1⟩-203; colophon, p. ⟨204⟩, 2 blank leaves.

1: ⟨1-15⁸⟩.

2: ⟨1⁴, 2-14⁸⟩.

Gray, linen-weave, paper boards, printed paper label on spine. End papers of book stock. Flyleaves: Vol. 1, flyleaf at front, two flyleaves at back; Vol. 2, double flyleaf at front.

"... Five Hundred And Twenty-Five Copies... No. ..."---Colophon.

Deposited Nov. 15, 1902. H copy received Nov. 21, 1902. Listed PW Dec. 13, 1902.

B   BA   H   NYHS   NYPL   Y

13245. The Complete Writings of James Russell Lowell Edition de Luxe...

Cambridge   Printed at the Riverside Press
MCMIV

Title from divisional title-pages. Imprint on title-pages as given. Noted only in coarse linen, printed paper label on spine. Limited to 1000 numbered copies.

1: *Fireside Travels.*

Reprint. Printed Jan. 20, 1904. Deposited Jan. 30, 1904.

2: *My Study Windows.*

Reprint. Printed Jan. 21, 1904. Deposited Jan. 30, 1904.

3: *Among My Books. First and Second Series. Vol. 1.*

Reprint. Printed Jan. 30, 1904. Deposited Jan. 30, 1904.

4: *Among My Books. First and Second Series. Vol. 2.*

Reprint. Printed April 28, 1904. Deposited May 24, 1904.

5: *Among My Books. First and Second Series. Vol. 3.*

Reprint. Printed May 1, 1904. Deposited May 24, 1904.

6: *Political Essays.*

Reprint. Printed May 1, 1904. Deposited May 24, 1904.

7: *Literary and Political Addresses.*

Reprint. Printed April 30, 1904. Deposited May 24, 1904.

8: *Latest Literary Essays The Old English Dramatists.*

Reprint. Printed May 19, 1904. Deposited May 24, 1904.

9: *The Poetical Works. In Five Volumes. Vol. 1. Earlier Poems. Miscellaneous Poems. The Vision of Sir Launfal.*

Reprint. Printed Aug. 23, 1904. Deposited Aug. 30, 1904.

10: *The Poetical Works. In Five Volumes. Vol. 2. The Biglow Papers First Series.*

Reprint. Printed Aug. 23, 1904. Deposited Aug. 30, 1904.

11: *The Poetical Works. In Five Volumes. Vol. 3. The Biglow Papers Second Series.*

Reprint. Printed Aug. 23, 1904. Deposited Aug. 30, 1904.

12: *The Poetical Works. In Five Volumes. Vol. 4. A Fable for Critics. Under the Willows. Other Poems.*

Reprint. Printed July 30, 1904. Deposited Aug. 30, 1904.

13: *The Poetical Works. In Five Volumes. Vol. 5. Poems of the War. Heartsease and Rue. Last Poems.*

Reprint. Printed Aug. 23, 1904. Deposited Aug. 30, 1904.

14-16: *Letters. In 3 Vols.*

". . . In these three volumes are included many letters hitherto unpublished, which have been here inserted by Professor Norton in their proper chronological order . . ."–––*Publishers' Note*, Vol. 1 of the set.

Printed, respectively, Jan. 18, 1904; Jan. 15, 1904; Jan. 18, 1904. Deposited Jan. 30, 1904.

The Elmwood Edition (1020 copies printed) was produced as follows: Vols. 1-8 recorded as printed July 30, 1904; Vols. 9-16 printed not before Sept. 14, 1904.

Note: Livingston, p. 131, erroneously terms the *Edition de Luxe* the *Autograph Edition*.

LC

13246. FOUR POEMS THE BALLAD OF THE STRANGER KING RETRO THE ROYAL PEDIGREE AND A DREAM I HAD . . . (NOW FIRST COLLECTED)

HINGHAM   PRINTED FOR PRIVATE DISTRIBUTION THE VILLAGE PRESS 1906

⟨i-vi⟩, ⟨1⟩-32; colophon, p. ⟨33⟩; 2 blank leaves. Laid paper watermarked *Arches*. 9⅛″ × 5⅞″.

⟨a⟩⁶, b-e⁴.

Printed gray-blue laid paper boards, unbleached linen shelf back. End papers of book stock, being integral parts of the first and last gatherings.

50 numbered copies only.

Contents:

"The Ballad of the Stranger."* Previously in *The Token and Atlantic Souvenir for 1842.*

"King Retro."*

"The Royal Pedigree." Reprinted from *Poems,* 1848.

"A Dream I Had."*

* *Uncollected Poems,* 1950.

". . . Finished March 10, 1906 . . ."–––Colophon. BA copy received April 7, 1906.

AAS   BA   H   LC   NYPL   Y

13247. THE ROUND TABLE . . .

RICHARD G. BADGER THE GORHAM PRESS BOSTON ⟨1913⟩

⟨1⟩-241, blank leaf. 8⅞″ × 5¹¹⁄₁₆″.

⟨1-14⁸, 15¹⁰⟩.

Red buckram, printed paper label on spine.

". . . One thousand copies printed . . ."–––P. ⟨2⟩.

Listed PW Aug. 9, 1913; Bkr (Nisbet) Oct. 17, 1913.

AAS   BA   H   NYPL   Y

13248. . . . Poems . . .

Humphrey Milford   Oxford University Press London, Edinburgh, Glasgow   New York, Toronto, Melbourne, Bombay 1917

At head of title: *Oxford Edition*

Earliest located printing; issued prior to 1917?

Reprint with the exception of:

"Our Own   His Wanderings and Personal Adventures," pp. 538-553. This comprises material first published in *Putnam's Monthly Magazine,* April–June, 1853, as follows:

"Digression A": In *Uncollected Poems,* 1950.

"Digression B": In *Uncollected Poems,* 1950.

"Progression A.–––The Invocation": In *Uncollected Poems,* 1950.

"Progression B Leading to Digression C": The whole of this (with some variations in the text) appears in *Works,* Vol. 9, 1890. The following line inadvertently omitted from *Works: I have not sat these years in vain, the world is saved at length;–––* Also appears in *Uncollected Poems,* 1950.

"Digression D": A portion had prior publication in *Works,* Vol. 9, 1890. The whole in *Uncollected Poems,* 1950.

"Progression C": In *Uncollected Poems,* 1950.

"Progression D": In *Uncollected Poems,* 1950.

"Progression E": In *Uncollected Poems,* 1950.

"Progression F": This embodies, here untitled, "Aladdin," which was collected in *Under the Willows,* 1869. A portion of the other matter appears also in *Works,* Vol. 9, 1890; also in *Uncollected Poems,* 1950.

"Red Tape," p. 602. Previously in *A Masque of Poets,* 1878. With revisions, collected as "The Brakes," *Heartsease and Rue,* 1888.

H

13249. ⟨rule⟩ / James Fisk, Jr. / ⟨leaf⟩ / An Epitaph / ⟨rule⟩ / ⟨Boston: The Merrymount Press, 1918⟩

⟨1-8⟩. Laid paper. 7⁷⁄₁₆″ × 5⁵⁄₁₆″. Title on p. ⟨3⟩. ⟨-⟩⁴.

Edited by Worthington Chauncey Ford. From the prefatory note, p. ⟨5⟩: "The sonnet printed on the next leaf was written . . . in the first week of

January, 1872. It was printed in *The Nation*, New York, October 1, 1874 . . . ⟨Lowell⟩ intended to include a much altered form . . . ⟨in *Heartsease and Rue*, 1888⟩ but a lawyer advised against it . . . Both versions are now given."

On p. ⟨8⟩: THE MERRYMOUNT PRESS ⟨dot⟩ BOSTON

Fifty copies printed but not published---p. ⟨4⟩.

BA   H   NYPL   UV   Y

13250. THE FUNCTION OF THE POET AND OTHER ESSAYS . . . COLLECTED AND EDITED BY ALBERT MORDELL

BOSTON AND NEW YORK   HOUGHTON MIFFLIN COMPANY MDCCCCXX

⟨i-ii⟩, ⟨i⟩-⟨xii⟩, ⟨1⟩-⟨224⟩; blank, p. ⟨225⟩; printer's imprint, p. ⟨226⟩; blank leaf. 8″ full × 5 1/16″.

⟨1⁹, 2-15⁸⟩. ⟨1⟩₃ inserted.

Tan paper boards sides, yellow-tan T cloth shelf back, printed paper label on spine.

". . . five hundred and seventy-five copies . . ."---p. ⟨iii⟩.

Listed PW June 12, 1920. Deposited June 19, 1920.

AAS   BA   H   Y

13251. NEW LETTERS . . . EDITED BY M. A. DEWOLFE HOWE . . .

NEW YORK AND LONDON   HARPER & BROTHERS PUBLISHERS 1932

Title-page in black and orange.

⟨i⟩-⟨xx⟩, 1-364. Frontispiece and 7 plates inserted. Other illustrations in text. Laid paper. 8 5/8″ × 5 3/4″.

⟨1-24⁸⟩.

V cloth: blue.

On copyright page: *First Edition;* and, code letters *K-G*, signifying *printed October, 1932*.

Deposited Nov. 25, 1932. The BA copy received Nov. 26, 1932.

AAS   B   H   MHS   NYPL

13252. Lowell Essays, Poems and Letters Selected and Edited by William Smith Clark II . . .

The Odyssey Press   New York   ⟨1948⟩

Previously unpublished letters pp. 310-315, 327-331, 392-395, 401-403.

On copyright page: *First Edition*

Published Nov. 12, 1948 (publisher's statement). Deposited Nov. 22, 1948.

LC

13253. UNCOLLECTED POEMS . . . EDITED BY THELMA M. SMITH

UNIVERSITY OF PENNSYLVANIA PRESS PHILADELPHIA 1950

⟨i⟩-⟨xxvi⟩, ⟨1⟩-291, blank leaf. 2 facsimiles in text. 9 1/4″ × 6 1/16″.

⟨1-20⁸⟩.

V cloth: maroon. Stamped in gold. Also noted in a variant (remainder?) binding of blue-gray V cloth, spine stamped in black.

Deposited Dec. 20, 1950.

AAS   B   H   UV (variant)

13254. THE SCHOLAR-FRIENDS LETTERS OF FRANCIS JAMES CHILD AND JAMES RUSSELL LOWELL EDITED BY M. A. DEWOLFE HOWE AND G. W. COTTRELL, JR

CAMBRIDGE, MASSACHUSETTS   HARVARD UNIVERSITY PRESS 1952

⟨i-viii⟩, 1-84. Wove paper watermarked *Warren's Olde Style* 9 1/2″ scant × 6 1/2″ scant. 8 pages of plates on 4 leaves inserted.

⟨1-4⁸, 5⁶, 6⁸⟩.

Two bindings noted; sequence undetermined. The designations are for identification only.

BINDING A

V cloth: gray. Spine lettered in black. In a letter to BAL (Jan. 16, 1971) Mr. Cottrell reports that this gray V cloth binding is the only one known to him. The publishers report (letter to BAL Jan. 28, 1971) "we first issued . . . in gray cloth lettered in black . . ."

BINDING B

A cloth: red. Spine lettered in gold. The publishers state (letter cited): ". . . nobody at Harvard University Press knows about the . . . red cloth binding lettered in gold."

Contains some material reprinted from *The Letters of James Russell Lowell*, 1894, and material here first published in book form.

Deposited Oct. 6, 1952 (gray V cloth) H copy received Oct. 14, 1952 (gray V cloth) Listed PW Nov. 1, 1952.

AAS (red A)   BA (gray V)   H (gray V)   LC (being a deposit copy in gray V)   Y (gray V)

13255. UNDERGRADUATE VERSES RHYMED MINUTES OF THE HASTY PUDDING CLUB . . . EDITED BY KENNETH WALTER CAMERON

TRINITY COLLEGE, HARTFORD   THE THISTLE PRESS HARTFORD 1, CONN. 1956

⟨1⟩-119. 8½″ × 11″. Printed on rectos only; blank versos considered in the printed pagination. Facsimiles in text.

60 leaves. Side stitched.

Some copies issued with stiff blue paper wrapper, white paper label.

Prepared by offset from typewritten sheets with the addition of some letterpress.

". . . Selections from the early records of the Hasty Pudding Club"---p. ⟨5⟩. The selections are from the minutes kept by Lowell as secretary of the club.

Deposited April 23, 1956.

B   BA   UV

13256. TWENTY-SEVEN POEMS . . . ⟨Edited⟩ BY MARTIN B. DUBERMAN

REPRINTED FROM THE AMERICAN LITERATURE VOL. XXXV, NO. 3, NOVEMBER, 1963

Cover-title.

⟨321⟩-351. 9″ full × 5¹⁵⁄₁₆″.

14 leaves extracted from *The American Literature;* and, issued in printed paper wrapper of the same stock.

"The twenty-seven poems . . . gathered here come from a wide variety of public and private manuscript collections. None of them, so far as I have been able to ascertain, has previously been published, either during Lowell's lifetime or subsequently . . ."---p. ⟨322⟩.

H

COLLECTIONS of reprinted material issued under Lowell's name; separate editions, including sheet music, reprinted from Lowell's books. For a list of books by authors other than Lowell containing reprinted Lowell material see *Section III.*

13257. Poems . . .

London: C. E. Mudie, 28, Upper King Street, Bloomsbury Square. 1844.

"The present Volume, recently published in New York ⟨*sic*⟩ is now reprinted in London . . ."---P. ⟨iv⟩.

Advertised Ath March 9, 1844. Listed LG April 6, 1844; PC April 15, 1844.

13258. Poems . . . Second Edition.

Cambridge: Published by John Owen. M DCCC XLIV.

Boards, printed paper label on spine.

13259. Poems . . . Third Edition.

Cambridge: Published by John Owen. M DCCC-XLIV.

Illuminated paper wrapper. Date 1845 on spine.

13260. Where Is the True Man's Father Land . . . Music by Franz Petersilea.

Boston: Published by C. Bradlee & Co. 184 Washington St. . . . 1845 . . .

Sheet music. Otherwise "The Fatherland," *Poems,* 1844.

13261. Zeekel and Huldy or a Natural Courtship Written by Hosea Bigelow ⟨*sic*⟩ Music by J. J. Hutchinson . . .

Boston . . . G. P. Reed & Co. 17 Tremont Row . . . 1850 . . .

Sheet music. Cover-title. Reprinted from *The Biglow Papers,* first series, 1848.

13262. The Poetical Works . . . Edited . . . by Andrew R. Scoble.

London: George Routledge and Co., Farringdon Street. 1852.

13263. Poems . . . in Two Volumes . . . Fifth Edition.

Boston: Ticknor, Reed, and Fields. M DCCC LIII.

13264. The Poetical Works . . . Edited . . . by Andrew R. Scoble.

London: George Routledge and Co., Farringdon Street. 1853.

13265. . . . The Fountain . . . Music by L. H. Southard . . .

. . . Nathan Richardson . . . 282, Washington St. Boston . . . 1854 . . .

Sheet music. Cover-title. At head of title: *To Herr Regenbogen.* Plate No. 129. Reprinted from *Poems,* 1844.

13266. Poems . . . in Two Volumes . . . Sixth Edition.

Boston: Ticknor and Fields. M DCCC LIV.

13267. Alone . . . The Music by Elizabeth Philp . . .

London; R. Mills & Sons, 140, New Bond Street, W. ⟨n.d., *ca.* 1855⟩

Sheet music. Cover-title. A copy received at BMU March 12, 1855. Otherwise "Serenade," *A Year's Life,* 1841.

13268. . . . Music by Elizth Philp . . . From the Close Shut Window . . .

Boston . . . Oliver Ditson Washington St . . . ⟨n.d., *ca.* 1855⟩

Sheet music. Cover-title. Presumably a reprint of the preceding entry.

At head of title: *6 Songs Written by Longfellow, James Russell Lowell and Others*

Lowell's name misspelled *James Russel Lowell* at head of p. 2. Title at head of p. 2: *Serenade.* No plate numbers.

13269. . . . O Moonlight Deep and Tender . . . Music by L. H. Southard . . .

. . . Nathan Richardson . . . 282 Washington St Boston . . . 1855 . . .

Sheet music. Cover-title. At head of title: *To James Russell Lowell*. Plate number 118. Otherwise "Song," *Poems*, 1844.

13270. . . . From the Close Shut Window . . .

Boston . . . Oliver Ditson & Co. Washington St. . . . 1857 . . .

Sheet music. Cover-title. Plate No. 14147. At head of title: *Florence   A Collection of Songs . . . Music by F. Boott* . . . A reprint was issued with plate number 24539. Otherwise "Serenade," *A Year's Life*, 1841.

13271. Poems . . . in Two Volumes . . . Seventh Edition.

Boston: Ticknor and Fields. M DCCC LVII.

13272. The Poetical Works of Percy Bysshe Shelley, Edited by Mrs. Shelley. With a Memoir, by James Russell Lowell . . . in Two Volumes . . .

Boston: Little, Brown and Company. Shepard, Clark and Brown. M.DCCC.LVII.

Blue and Gold format. See in *Section I* under 1855 for first printing.

13273. . . . The Biglow Papers . . . with Additional Notes, an Enlarged Glossary, and an Illustration by George Cruikshank.

London: John Camden Hotten, Piccadilly 1859.

At head of title: *The Choicest Humorous Poetry of the Age*.

"The editor of the present edition ⟨John Camden Hotten⟩ has added here and there a few notes explanatory . . . These are enclosed within brackets, and bear his initials."―――Pp. vii-viii.

Lowell had nothing to do with this edition, although Sydney Howard Gay probably did. See Lowell's letter to Gay, *Letters* . . . , Vol. I, pp. 275-276, letter misdated Dec. 21, 1856 ⟨error for 1859⟩.

Advertised for Nov. 1, Bkr Oct. 1859. Advertised as *now ready* PC Nov. 1, 1859. Listed LG Nov. 5, 1859; PC Nov. 15, 1859.

13274. The Poetical Works . . . Complete in Two Volumes . . .

Boston: Ticknor and Fields. M DCCC LX.

Blue and Gold format.

13275. . . . The Biglow Papers . . . with Additional Notes, an Enlarged Glossary, and Coloured

Illustrations by George Cruikshank. Second English Edition.

Eondon ⟨sic⟩: John Camden Hotten, Piccadilly. 1861.

At head of title: *The Choicest Humorous Poetry of the Age*.

Reprint of the London, 1859, edition, above.

Advertised for *the 20th inst* PC Nov. 1, 1860: *adapted for the English reader*. Listed Ath Nov. 10, 1860; PC Nov. 15, 1860.

13276. The Poetical Works . . . Complete in Two Volumes . . .

Boston: Ticknor and Fields. M DCCC LXI.

Blue and Gold format.

13277. Jonathan to John. Words by Hosea Bigelow ⟨sic⟩ Music Composed by F. Boott.

Boston . . . Henry Tolman & Co. 291 Washn. St. . . . 1862 . . .

Sheet music. Cover-title. Plate number 2906. Deposited Sept. 4, 1862. Reprinted from *Mason and Slidell* . . . ⟨1862⟩.

13278. The Poetical Works . . . in Two Volumes . . .

Boston: Ticknor and Fields. M.DCCC.LXII.

Blue and Gold format.

13279. The Poetical Works . . . Complete in Two Volumes . . .

Boston: Ticknor and Fields. M DCCC LXIII.

Blue and Gold format.

13280. The Biglow Papers . . . Author's Unabridged Edition.

London   George Routledge and Sons   The Broadway, Ludgate ⟨n.d., after Dec. 1863⟩

Pp. 96. Issued in printed paper wrapper?

13281. . . . The Biglow Papers . . . with Additional Notes and Enlarged Glossary. Third English Edition.

London: John Camden Hotten, Piccadilly. 1864.

At head of title: *The Choicest Humorous Poetry of the Age*.

Printed paper wrapper. The "additional notes" were inserted by John Camden Hotten; see above under 1859.

Advertised for *this day* PC July 1, 1864. Listed PC Nov. 15, 1864.

13282. ... Alone! Alone! Serenade ... Music by Geo. Boweryem ...

New York ... Wm. A. Pond & Co 547 Broadway ... 1864 ...

Sheet music. Cover-title. At head of title: *To Miss Adrienne P. Webster*. Plate number 5775.

Otherwise "Serenade," *A Year's Life*, 1841.

13283. ... The Biglow Papers ... with Additional Notes and Enlarged Glossary. Fourth English Edition.

London: John Camden Hotten, Picadilly. 1864.

At head of title: *The Choicest Humorous Poetry of the Age*.

Cloth? Printed paper wrapper? The "additional notes" were inserted by John Camden Hotten; see above under 1859. A reprint was issued under date 1865.

13284. Four American Poems. The Raven. By Edgar Allan Poe ... The Rose. By James Russell Lowell. Metrically Translated into German by Charles Theodore Eben.

Philadelphia: Frederick Leypoldt. 1864.

English and German text on opposing pages. Printed paper wrapper; and, publisher's leather.

13285. The Biglow Papers ⟨First Series⟩ ... with an Introduction by George Augustus Sala Reprinted from the Original

London   Ward, Lock, and Tyler   158 Fleet Street   MDCCCLXV

Not seen. Entry on the basis of a photographic copy of the title-page of the original (in BMU) and correspondence. Listed PC Nov. 15, 1865.

13286. The Biglow Papers ... Second Series. Authorized Edition.

London: Trübner & Co. 60, Paternoster Row. 1865.

Printed paper wrapper. Pp. 133. Issued prior to Nov. 1865.

13287. ... The Biglow Papers, Edited, with an Introduction, Notes, Glossary, and Copious Index. By Homer Wilbur ...

London: S. O. Beeton, 248, Strand, W.C. ⟨n.d., 1865⟩

At head of title: *Melibœus-Hipponax*. Printed paper wrapper? Pp. 217. Contains both series. According to *The English Catalogue of Books* ... issued in 1865.

13288. ... Betrothal ... Music by S.D.S. ...

Philadelphia ... Chas. W. A. Trumpler 7th & Chestnut St. ... 1865 ...

Sheet music. Cover-title. At head of title: *To Miss Fanny Hewitt* Plate number 225-4. Otherwise "Song," (*O, moonlight deep and tender*) in *Poems*, 1844.

13289. The Poetical Works ... Complete in Two Volumes ...

Boston: Ticknor and Fields. M DCCC LXV.

Blue and Gold format.

13290. ... The Poetical Works ... Including a Fable for the Critics

London S. O. Beeton, 248 Strand, W. C. (Ten Doors from Temple Bar) 1865

Printed paper wrapper. At head of title: *Beeton's Companion Poets*

13291. ... The Biglow Papers ... by Homer Wilbur ... (Re-printed from the Latest Copyright Edition.)

Montreal: Published by R. Worthington. 1866.

Printed paper wrapper. At head of title: *Meliboeus Hipponax*.

13292. Poems ... in Two Volumes ... Eighth Edition.

Boston: Ticknor and Fields. M DCCC LXVI.

13293. The Poetical Works ... in Two Volumes ...

Boston: Ticknor and Fields. M DCCC LXVI.

13294. The Biglow Papers by James Russell Lowell and The Petroleum V. Nasby Papers by David Ross Locke

London and Halifax: Milner & Sowerby, 1867.

Presumed to be a reprint. Not located. Entry on the basis of inclusion in a list of Milner & Sowerby's *Cottage Library*, Bkr Dec. 12, 1867. Not found in *The English Catalogue of Books*. Possibly projected only, not published.

13295. The Biglow Papers ... with an Introduction by George Augustus Sala Reprinted from the Original

London: George Routledge and Sons, Broadway, Ludgate. ⟨n.d., 1868⟩

Printed paper wrapper. Sala's introduction dated at end *October, 1865*. Pp. 96.

At least two printings:

1: Imprint as above.

2: Imprinted: *London   George Routledge and Sons The Broadway, Ludgate ⟨n.d.⟩.*

Listed (this issue?) Bkr July 1, 1868.

13296. Under the Willows . . .

London: Macmillan and Co. 1869.

Advertised as *in a few days* Ath Dec. 12, 1868; as *this day* PC Dec. 18, 1868. Listed Ath Dec. 19, 1868; PC Dec. 31, 1868. Reviewed Ath April 17, 1869.

13297. The Poetical Works . . . Complete in Two Volumes . . .

Boston: Fields, Osgood, & Co., Successors to Ticknor and Fields. 1869.

Binding dated 1869.

13298. The Poetical Works . . . Complete Edition, with Illustrations.

Boston: Fields, Osgood, & Co. 1871.

Red Line edition. Printed in double columns. Pp. 453.

13299. The Poetical Works . . . Complete Edition.

Boston: James R. Osgood and Company, Late Ticknor & Fields, and Fields, Osgood, & Co. 1871

Cloth; also leather. Printed in double columns. Pp. 453. On binding: *Diamond Edition*

13300. The Poetical Works . . . Complete in Two Volumes . . .

Boston: James R. Osgood and Company, Late Ticknor & Fields, and Fields, Osgood, & Co. 1871.

Binding dated 1869.

13301. . . . The Biglow Papers . . .

London: Ward, Lock, & Tyler, Warwick House, Paternoster Row. ⟨n.d., 1873⟩

At head of title: *Meliboeus-Hipponax.* Printed paper wrapper. Announced PC Dec. 8, 1873 as No. 27 in *Beeton's Humorous Works.*

13302. The Poetical Works . . . Complete Edition.

Boston: James R. Osgood and Company, Late Ticknor & Fields, and Fields, Osgood, & Co. 1873

On binding: *Diamond Edition*   Printed in two columns. Pp. 453.

13303. The Poetical Works . . . Complete Edition, with Illustrations.

Boston: James R. Osgood and Company, Late Ticknor & Fields, and Fields, Osgood, & Co. 1873.

13304. The Poetical Works . . . Complete in Two Volumes . . .

Boston: James R. Osgood and Company, Late Ticknor & Fields, and Fields, Osgood, & Co. 1873.

Blue and Gold format.

13305. The Poetical Works . . . Complete Edition.

London: Macmillan and Co. 1873.

Pp. 453.

13306. The Courtin' . . . Illustrated by Winslow Homer

Boston James R. Osgood and Company Late Ticknor & Fields, and Fields, Osgood, & Co. 1874

Reprinted from *The Biglow Papers, Second Series,* 1867. Noted as *in a few days* WTC Nov. 28, 1872. Listed PW Nov. 22, 1873. Advertised by Low as *a new American book* PC Feb. 1, 1874.

13307. . . . Auf Wiedersehen . . . Music by Bern. Cecil Klein . . .

Philadelphia . . . F. A. North & Co. 1308 Chestnut St . . . 1874 . . .

Sheet music. Cover-title. At head of title: *Respectfully Dedicated to Mrs. Elizabeth Little.* Plate number 1828-4, save on p. 4 where the plate number is 1228-4. Reprinted from *Under the Willows,* 1869.

13308. The Poetical Works . . . Complete Edition, with Illustrations.

Boston: James R. Osgood and Company, Late Ticknor & Fields, and Fields, Osgood, & Co. 1875.

Red Line edition. Pp. 453.

13309. Silhouettes and Songs Illustrative of the Months . . . Edited by Edward E. Hale . . .

Boston . . . 1876.

Contains "May," an extract from *The Biglow Papers, Second Series,* 1867. For fuller description see entry No. 9130.

13310. Among My Books. Second Series . . .

London   Sampson Low, Marston, Searle & Rivington   St. Dunstan's House   Fetter Lane, Fleet Street, E.C. ⟨n.d., 1876⟩

Advertised as *ready* Ath May 27, 1876; listed Ath May 27, 1876.

13311. The Poetical Works . . . Household Edition.

Boston: James R. Osgood and Company, Late Ticknor & Fields, and Fields, Osgood, & Co. 1876.

Printed in two columns. Pp. 406. Cloth; and, leather.

13312. . . . The Vision of Sir Launfal The Cathedral. Favorite Poems . . .

Boston: Houghton, Mifflin and Company. The Riverside Press, Cambridge. ⟨1876; *i.e.*, not before 1880⟩

At head of title: *Modern Classics.*

13313. The Prophet Music by Miss Carrie A. Smith . . .

Boston, White, Smith & Company, 516 Washington Street . . . 1877 . . .

Sheet music. Cover-title. Dated 1876 on p. 3. Plate number 2962-5. Otherwise "A Parable," *Poems*, 1844.

13314. My Garden Acquaintance and a Good Word for Winter . . .

Boston: James R. Osgood and Company, Late Ticknor and Fields, and Fields, Oogood ⟨*sic*⟩, & Co. 1877.

Vest-Pocket Series. According to the publisher's records there were two printings in 1877; BAL has recognized but one printing. First printing, 1,000 copies, May 21, 1877. Listed PW June 2, 1877. Second printing, 500 copies, June 12, 1877. Reprinted from *My Study Windows*, 1871.

13315. A Moosehead Journal . . .

Boston: James R. Osgood and Company, Late Ticknor and Fields, and Fields, Osgood, & Co. 1877.

Vest-Pocket Series. Listed PW July 28, 1877. Reprinted from *Fireside Travels*, 1864.

13316. Favorite Poems . . .

Boston: James R. Osgood and Company, Late Ticknor & Fields, and Fields, Osgood, & Co. 1877.

Vest-Pocket Series. Listed PW Oct. 6, 1877.

13317. The Cathedral, and the Harvard Commemoration Ode . . .

Boston: James R. Osgood and Company, Late Ticknor & Fields, and Fields, Osgood, & Co. 1877.

Vest-Pocket Series.

13318. The Poetical Works . . . Complete Edition.

Boston: James R. Osgood and Company, Late Ticknor & Fields, and Fields, Osgood, & Co. 1877

On binding: *Diamond Edition*

13319. The Poetical Works . . . Household Edition.

Boston: James R. Osgood and Company, Late Ticknor & Fields, and Fields, Osgood, & Co. 1877.

Printed in two columns. Pp. 406. Cloth; and, leather.

13320. The Poetical Works . . . New Revised Edition . . .

Boston: James R. Osgood and Company, Late Ticknor & Fields, and Fields, Osgood, & Co. 1877.

Red Line edition. Pp. 406.

13321. The Rose . . .

Boston James R. Osgood and Company Late Ticknor & Fields, and Fields, Osgood, & Co. 1878

Reprinted from *Poems*, 1844. Issued in cloth; morocco; tree calf. Noted for *this week* PW Nov. 3, 1877. Listed PW Nov. 17, 1877.

13322. The Poetical Works . . . in Two Volumes . . .

Boston: Houghton, Osgood and Company. Cambridge: The Riverside Press. 1878.

Blue and Gold format.

13323. The Poetical Works . . . Complete Edition.

Boston: Houghton, Osgood and Company. The Riverside Press, Cambridge. 1879.

On binding: *Diamond Edition*

13324. The Poetical Works . . . Household Edition.

Boston: Houghton, Osgood and Company. The Riverside Press, Cambridge. 1879.

13325. Papyrus Leaves . . . Edited by William Fearing Gill . . .

New York . . . 1880.

Deposited Dec. 26, 1879. For comment see entry No. 2477.

13326. The Biglow Papers . . . with a Preface by Thomas Hughes . . . Authorised Copyright Edition.

London: Trübner & Co., Ludgate Hill. 1880.

Listed Ath Feb. 7, 1880; PC Feb. 17, 1880. For a comment on this printing see Ath March 13, 1880.

13327. American Prose Hawthorne: Irving: Longfellow: Whittier: Holmes: Lowell: Thoreau: Emerson With Introductions and Notes by the Editor of "American Poems" ⟨Horace Elisha Scudder⟩

Boston Houghton, Osgood and Company The Riverside Press, Cambridge 1880

13328. The Poetical Works . . . Complete Edition.

Boston: Houghton, Osgood and Company. The Riverside Press, Cambridge. 1880.

On binding: *Diamond Edition*

13329. The Poetical Works . . . Household Edition.

Boston: Houghton, Osgood and Company. The Riverside Press, Cambridge. 1880.

Reprinted and reissued by Houghton, Mifflin & Company, 1880.

13330. The Poetical Works . . . New Revised Edition. With Numerous Illustrations.

Boston: Houghton, Osgood and Company. The Riverside Press, Cambridge. 1880.

Red Line edition. Printed in two columns. Pp. 422.

13331. The Poetical Works . . . Complete Edition.

Boston: Houghton, Mifflin and Company. The Riverside Press, Cambridge. 1880.

On binding: *Diamond Edition*

13332. The Rose . . .

Boston: Houghton, Mifflin and Company. The Riverside Press, Cambridge. 1880.

13333. . . . The Vision of Sir Launfal The Cathedral. Favorite Poems . . .

Boston: Houghton, Mifflin and Company. The Riverside Press, Cambridge. 1880.

At head of title: *Modern Classics.*

13334. Aladdin . . . Music by Matilda Scott-Paine . . .

Detroit: C. J. Whitney . . . 40 Fort St. (West.) . . . 1881 . . .

Sheet music. Cover-title. Reprinted from *Under the Willows*, 1869.

13335. The Poetical Works . . . Household Edition.

Boston: Houghton, Mifflin and Company. The Riverside Press, Cambridge. 1881.

13336. The Poetical Works . . . New Revised Edition . . .

Boston: Houghton, Mifflin and Company. The Riverside Press, Cambridge. 1881.

13337. Poets and Etchers . . .

Boston James R. Osgood and Company 1882

Issued in a trade format, cloth; and a printing on China paper limited to 100 numbered copies. Listed PW Dec. 10, 1881.

13338. The Poetical Works . . . Complete Edition.

Boston: Houghton, Mifflin and Company. The Riverside Press, Cambridge. 1882.

Printed in two columns. Pp. 472.

13339. The Poetical Works . . . Complete Edition, with Illustrations.

Boston: Houghton, Mifflin and Company. The Riverside Press, Cambridge. 1882.

Red Line edition. Pp. 472. Printed in 2 columns.

13340. The Poetical Works . . . Household Edition.

Boston: Houghton, Mifflin and Company. The Riverside Press, Cambridge. 1882.

Printed in two columns. Pp. 422. Two formats noted; sequence not determined:

A: Green S cloth, covers bevelled. Front stamped in gold with a facsimile of Lowell's autograph.

B: Brown S cloth; mauve S cloth. Covers bevelled. Front stamped in brown and gold: LOWELL's POEMS and with florets, butterfly, *Household Edition* ⟨in intaglio⟩, etc., etc.

13341. The Poetical Works . . . New Revised Edition. With Numerous Illustrations.

Boston: Houghton, Mifflin and Company. The Riverside Press, Cambridge. 1882.

Red Line edition.

13342. The Lowell Birthday-Book . . .

Boston: Houghton, Mifflin and Company, New York: 11 East Seventeenth Street. The Riverside Press, Cambridge. 1883.

Deposited Feb. 21, 1883. Listed PW Feb. 24, 1883. The London (Chatto & Windus) issue advertised as though published Ath Oct. 20, 1883; listed Ath Oct. 20, 1883. A Routledge issue listed Ath Oct. 23, 1886; PC Nov. 1, 1886.

13343. . . . Auf Wiedersehn . . . Music by Sebastian B. Schlesinger . . .

Boston, Carl Prüfer, 34 West St. . . . 1883 . . .

Sheet music. Cover-title. At head of title: *To Miss Constance Rives*. Plate number CP 486. Reprinted from *Under the Willows*, 1869.

13344. . . . O Moonlight Deep and Tender . . . Music by Mrs. George E. Aiken . . .

New York. Edward Schuberth & Co. 23 Union Square . . . 1883 . . .

Sheet music. Cover-title. At head of title: *To Mr. Norton Berkley Wood*. Plate number E.S.&Co. 1322. Otherwise "Song," *Poems*, 1844.

13345. The Poetical Works . . . New Revised Edition. With Numerous Illustrations.

Boston: Houghton, Mifflin and Company. The Riverside Press, Cambridge. 1883.

Red Line edition. Pp. 422.

13346. *Entry cancelled.*

13347. . . . Auf Wiederseh'n . . . Music by M. R. Macfarlane . . .

New York Wm. A. Pond & Co. . . . 1884 . . .

Sheet music. Cover-title. At head of title: *Dedicated to the Baroness Ottilie von der Lühe*. Plate number 11311. Reprinted from *Under the Willows*, 1869.

13348. The Poetical Works . . . Complete Edition.

Boston: Houghton, Mifflin and Company. The Riverside Press, Cambridge. 1884.

13349. The Poetical Works . . . Household Edition.

Boston: Houghton, Mifflin and Company. The Riverside Press, Cambridge. 1884.

Printed in two columns. Noted in three-quarters morocco; and, three-quarters calf. Also issued in cloth?

13350. . . . Under the Old Elm, and Other Poems . . .

Houghton, Mifflin and Company Boston: 4 Park Street; New York: 11 East Seventeenth Street The Riverside Press, Cambridge 1885

At head of title: *The Riverside Literature Series* Printed paper wrapper. Issued as No. 15 of the series. Advertised for *next week* PW April 18, 1885. Deposited April 20, 1885. Listed PW June 6, 1885.

13351. The Poetical Works . . . Household Edition with Illustrations

Boston Houghton, Mifflin and Company New York: 11 East Seventeenth Street ⟨1885⟩

BAL suspects that this volume was prepared for copyright renewal purposes only; that it was made up of the sheets of an earlier printing and deposited with inserted, cancel, title-leaf. Deposited July 27, 1885. *Location:* LC (deposit copy).

13352. . . . Melibœus-Hipponax The Biglow Papers . . . by Homer Wilbur . . .

Boston Houghton, Mifflin and Company New York: 11 East Seventeenth Street The Riverside Press, Cambridge 1885

At head of title: *The Riverside Aldine Series*

13353. . . . Melibœus-Hipponax The Biglow Papers Second Series . . .

Boston Houghton, Mifflin and Company New York: 11 East Seventeenth Street The Riverside Press, Cambridge 1885

At head of title: *The Riverside Aldine Series*

Anonymous.

13354. The Poetical Works . . .

Boston and New York Houghton, Mifflin and Company The Riverside Press, Cambridge ⟨1885⟩

Printed in two columns. Pp. 472.

13355. The Poetical Works . . . Household Edition With Illustrations

Boston and New York Houghton, Mifflin and Company The Riverside Press, Cambridge ⟨1885⟩

Printed in two columns. Pp. 422. Noted in both cloth; and, three-quarters calf.

13356. . . . The Present Crisis . . .

⟨n.p., n.d., Boston: Old South Meeting House, 1885⟩

At head of title: *Third Series. No. 2. Old South Leaflets.* Caption-title; the above at head of p. ⟨1⟩. Printed self-wrapper. Reprinted from *Poems, Second Series,* 1848.

Also occurs as No. 1 of the series. Sequence not determined.

13357. The Biglow Papers . . . with a Prefatory Note by Ernest Rhys.

London: Walter Scott, 24 Warwick Lane, Paternoster Row. ⟨n.d., not before 1885⟩

Cloth?

13358. Old Lines in New Black and White Lines from Lowell Holmes Whittier With Illustrations by F. Hopkinson Smith

Boston & New York Houghton Mifflin and Co The Riverside Press Cambridge 1886

Contains extracts from *Under the Willows,* 1869.

On front: Printed paper label, sealing wax seal, ribbon.

According to the publisher's records there were three printings of the trade format during the years 1885–1886; and, a large paper printing in 1886. BAL has identified but one printing of the trade format. First printing, Nov. 1, 1885, 252 copies. Deposited Dec. 9, 1885. Listed PW Dec. 12, 1885. Second printing, Dec. 29, 1885, 150 copies. Large paper format printed, Oct. 19, 1886. Third printing Nov. 15, 1886, 270 copies. The large paper format was issued in a portfolio and carries the following statement: *This edition, printed on Japanese paper, is limited to One Hundred ⟨numbered⟩ Copies* . . .

13359. The Poetical Works . . . Household Edition with Illustrations

Boston and New York Houghton, Mifflin and Company The Riverside Press, Cambridge 1886

Pp. 422. On binding: *Household Edition of the Poets*

13360. The Poetical Works of James Russell Lowell.

Boston: Houghton, Mifflin and Company. The Riverside Press, Cambridge. 1886.

13361. The Poetical Works . . . with Numerous Illustrations.

Boston and New York: Houghton, Mifflin and Company. The Riverside Press, Cambridge. 1886.

Cloth? Red Line edition. Pp. 422.

13362. . . . Under the Old Elm . . .

⟨n.p., Boston: Old South Meeting House, 1886⟩

At head of title: *Fourth Series, 1886. No. 7. Old South Leaflets* Cover-title. Printed self-wrapper. Also occurs bound together with other publications in the series with general title-page: *The Old South Leaflets. Fourth Series, 1886. Boston: Old South Meeting House. 1886.* Previously in *Three Memorial Poems,* 1877.

13363. . . . The Biglow Papers, Edited . . . by Homer Wilbur . . .

New York: Hurst & Company, Publishers. ⟨n.d., not before 1886⟩

At head of title: *Meliboeus-Hipponax.*

13364. Democracy and Other Addresses . . .

London Macmillan and Company 1887 . . .

Advertised as *new* PC Dec. 15, 1886. Noted as *immediately* Ath Dec. 18, 1886. Listed Ath Dec. 25, 1886. A copy in NYPL presented to Lady Wemyss, Christmas, 1886. Advertised as *new* PC Dec. 31, 1886. Reviewed Ath Jan. 22, 1887.

13365. . . . The Vision of Sir Launfal and Other Poems . . .

Houghton, Mifflin and Company Boston: 4 Park Street; New York: 11 East Seventeenth Street The Riverside Press, Cambridge 1887

At head of title: *The Riverside Literature Series*

Printed paper wrapper. Issued as No. 30 of the series under date Nov. 1, 1887. Deposited Nov. 14, 1887. Reissued under date ⟨1887⟩.

13366. My Study Windows . . . Introduction by Richard Garnett . . .

London: Walter Scott, 24 Warwick Lane, Paternoster Row. 1887.

Probably issued in cloth, printed paper label on spine.

13367. The Poetical Works . . .

Boston and New York Houghton, Mifflin and Company The Riverside Press, Cambridge 1887

Printed in two columns. Pp. 472.

13368. The Poetical Works . . . with Illustrations

Boston and New York Houghton, Mifflin and Company The Riverside Press, Cambridge 1887

Printed in two columns. Pp. 422.

13369. The Poetical Works . . . Household Edition with Illustrations

Boston and New York Houghton, Mifflin and Company The Riverside Press, Cambridge 1887

Printed in two columns. Pp. 422.

13370. Early Poems . . .

New York: Hurst & Co., Publishers, 122 Nassau St. ⟨n.d., not before 1887⟩

On binding: *Arlington Edition.* Pp. 172. Not a Red Line printing.

The following reprints of the above have been seen; the order of presentation is purely arbitrary:

A

Imprint: *New York: Hurst & Co., Publishers, No. 122 Nassau Street.* ⟨*n.d.*⟩. Text enclosed by a red rule frame. Pp. 172.

B

Imprint: *New York Hurst & Company, Publishers 134-136 Grand Street* ⟨*n.d.*⟩. Text enclosed by a red rule frame. Pp. 172.

C

Imprint: *New York Hurst & Company Publishers* ⟨*n.d.*⟩. Not a Red Line printing. Pp. 100; *i.e.*, this is a partial reprint, done from the original plates. Issued in printed paper wrapper.

D

Issued in printed paper wrapper as No. 63 in *The Useful Knowledge Series*, under date Jan. 9, 1894, by *Hurst and Company, 135 Grand Street*.

13371. Early Poems . . .

New York Hurst & Company Publishers ⟨n.d., not before 1887⟩

Pp. 280. Printed portrait pasted to front cover.

13372. . . . The Gettysburg Speech and Other Papers by Abraham Lincoln and an Essay on Lincoln by James Russell Lowell . . .

Houghton, Mifflin and Company Boston: 4 Park Street; New York: 11 East Seventeenth Street The Riverside Press, Cambridge 1888

At head of title: *The Riverside Literature Series.* Printed paper wrapper. Issued as No. 32 of the series under date Jan. 1888. A reprint was issued under date ⟨1888⟩. Deposited Feb. 8, 1888.

13373. Selections from the Writings of James Russell Lowell Arranged under the Days of the Year, and Accompanied by Memoranda of Anniversaries of Noted Events and of the Birth or Death of Famous Men and Women

Boston and New York: Houghton, Mifflin & Co. The Riverside Press, Cambridge 1888

Flexible cloth. Deposited Aug. 2, 1888.

13374. The Poetical Works . . . with Illustrations

Boston and New York Houghton, Mifflin and Company The Riverside Press, Cambridge 1888

Printed in two columns.

13375. The Poetical Works . . . with Numerous Illustrations.

Boston and New York: Houghton, Mifflin and Company. The Riverside Press, Cambridge. 1888.

Red Line edition. Printed in two columns. Pp. 422.

13376. . . . Books and Libraries and Other Papers . . . with Notes

Houghton, Mifflin and Company Boston: 4 Park Street; New York: 11 East Seventeenth Street The Riverside Press, Cambridge 1889

At head of title: *The Riverside Literature Series*

Issued in printed paper wrapper as No. 39 of the series under date *December, 1888.* Deposited Jan. 7, 1889.

13377. An Indian Summer Reverie . . .

The Art Lith. Publ. Co., Munich & New York. Printed in Germany . . . ⟨1889⟩

Pictorial boards. Reprinted from *Poems, Second Series*, 1848. Deposited May 11, 1889.

13378. . . . A Prayer . . . Music by John Gernert . . .

Copyright 1890 by John Gernert.

Sheet music. Cover-title. At head of title: *Dedicated to Mrs J. Sharp McDonald* Reprinted from *Poems*, 1844.

A Fable for Critics . . .

New York . . . G. P. Putnam's Sons . . . ⟨1890⟩

See below under *ca.* 1903.

13379. Early Poems . . .

Chicago: Donohue, Henneberry & Co., 407–429 Dearborn Street. ⟨n.d., 1890–1900⟩

13380. Early Poems . . .

New York: John W. Lovell Company. 150 Worth Street, Mission Place. ⟨n.d., not before 1890⟩

Also occurs in bindings bearing the spine imprint of *T. Y. Crowell & Co., New York*.

13381. Poems . . .

  Philadelphia Henry Altemus ⟨n.d., *ca.* 1890⟩

Pp. 229. Reprinted several (perhaps many) times. Noted in the following forms; the order of presentation is all but arbitrary.

A: Title-page lettered in blue, decorated in red. No terminal advertisements.

B: Title-page lettered in red, decorated in green. No terminal advertisements.

C: Title-page lettered in red, decorated in green. Publisher's terminal catalog indicates publication not before 1897.

D: Title-page lettered in faded red, decorated in faded red and green. Publisher's terminal catalog indicates publication not before 1897.

E: Title-page lettered in faded red, decorated in faded red and green. No terminal advertisements. The B copy received Dec. 18, 1899.

13382. The Poetical Works . . .

  Boston and New York Houghton, Mifflin and Company The Riverside Press, Cambridge ⟨1890⟩

Pp. 550. Sheets of an unidentified printing with inserted, cancel, title-leaf. Possibly prepared for copyright renewal purposes.

13383. The Poetical Works . . . with Numerous Illustrations . . .

  Boston and New York: Houghton, Mifflin & Company. The Riverside Press, Cambridge ⟨1890⟩

Red Line edition.

13384. The Poetical Works of James Russell Lowell

  Boston and New York Houghton, Mifflin and Company The Riverside Press, Cambridge ⟨1890; *i.e.*, not before 1891⟩

Pp. 550. Date on the basis of the advertisement opposite the title-page wherein is offered (among other books) Lowell's *Latest Literary Essays and Addresses* which was first published in Dec. 1891.

13385. ⟨Standard Library Edition The Works of James Russell Lowell⟩

  Boston and New York Houghton, Mifflin and Company The Riverside Press, Cambridge ⟨1892; *i.e.*, 1893⟩

11 Vols. Vol. 11 printed April 24, 1893.

13386. Lowell Gems Illustrated by W. Goodrich Beal

  Boston Samuel E. Cassino 196 Summer Street ⟨1891⟩

Deposited Dec. 19, 1891. Decorated flexible boards.

13387. Early Poems . . .

  The F. M. Lupton Publishing Company, New York ⟨n.d., not before 1891⟩

13388. Early Poems . . .

  New York and Boston Thomas Y. Crowell and Company ⟨n.d., not before 1891⟩

On binding: *Gladstone Edition*

13389. Harvard College During the War. By Capt. Nathan Appleton. Harvard Memorial Poems, by Emerson, Longfellow, Holmes, Lowell, and S. F. Smith. Reproduced from the New England Magazine.

  ⟨Republished by the New England Magazine, 86 Federal Street, Boston, n.d., 1891⟩

Printed paper wrapper. Cover-title. Contains, untitled, *Ode* . . . , 1865.

13390. The Poetical Works . . . with Illustrations

  Boston and New York Houghton, Mifflin and Company The Riverside Press, Cambridge 1891

Pp. 507. Printed in two columns.

13391. The Poetical Works . . . with an Introduction by Thomas Hughes, Q.C.

  London Macmillan and Co. And New York 1891 All Rights Reserved

13392. Selections from Lord Macaulay, Robert Browning, George Eliot, and James Russell Lowell . . . by Thomas Harlin . . .

  Melbourne: Melville, Mullen and Slade, (Booksellers to the University). 1891.

13393. Odes, Lyrics, and Sonnets from the Poetic Works of James Russell Lowell

  Boston and New York Houghton, Mifflin and Company The Riverside Press, Cambridge M DCCC XCII

Three printings during the period 1891–1892. BAL has made no effort to distinguish the printings. First printing, Nov. 19, 1891, 1000 copies. Listed PW Dec. 19, 1891. Second printing, Dec. 19, 1891, 1000 copies. Third printing, April 13, 1892, 1000 copies.

13394. . . . Ah! When the Fight is Won . . . Music by F. Boott . . .

Boston . . . MDCCCXCII . . . Oliver Ditson Company . . .

Sheet music. Cover-title. At head of title: *To the Memory of Col. Robert G. Shaw* Plate number 35-55397-6. Deposited Feb. 18, 1892.

Extracted from "Memoriæ Positum," *Under the Willows*, 1869.

13395. Fireside Travels . . .

Boston and New York: Houghton, Mifflin and Company. The Riverside Press, Cambridge. 1892.

Sheets of an earlier printing deposited for copyright renewal with cancel title-leaf imprinted as above. Deposited May 18, 1892.

13396. The Beggar. Forgetfulness . . .

Boston: Samuel E. Cassino. Copyright 1892.

Printed pictorial wrapper. Deposited July 14, 1892. Reprinted from, respectively, *A Year's Life*, 1841; *Poems*, 1844.

13397. The Early Poems . . . with Biographical Sketch by Nathan Haskell Dole.

New York: 46 East 14th Street. Thomas Y. Crowell & Co. Boston: 100 Purchase Street. ⟨1892⟩

Pp. 364. Occurs with text enclosed by red rules; and, without that feature. A copy decorated with red rules was deposited for copyright Sept. 21, 1892.

13398. The Poetical Works . . . with an Introduction by Thomas Hughes . . .

London Macmillan and Co. And New York 1892 All Rights Reserved

13399. The Early Poems . . . with Biographical Sketch by Nathan Haskell Dole.

New York: 46 East 14th Street. Thomas Y. Crowell & Company. Boston: 100 Purchase Street. ⟨1893⟩

Also occurs (reprinted?) with the imprint: *New York Thomas Y. Crowell & Co. Publishers ⟨1893⟩*. A copy with the dual imprint was deposited Aug. 7, 1893.

13400. . . . The Vision of Sir Launfal and Other Poems . . .

New York: Maynard, Merrill, & Co., Publishers, 43, 45, and 47 East Tenth Street. New Series, No. 100. December 15, 1892 . . . ⟨1893⟩

At head of title: *English Classic Series---No. 129.* Printed paper wrapper. Copyright notice, p. ⟨2⟩, dated 1893. Deposited Jan. 11, 1894.

13401. . . . What Means that Star? . . .

Boston Everett E. Truette & Co. 149a Tremont St. ⟨1893⟩

Sheet music. Cover-title. At head of title: *Three Songs . . . by Benjamin Cutter* . . . Plate number 43-4.

For an earlier printing see *Christmas Carol*, in *Sec. I*, under year 1866. Collected in *Heartsease and Rue*, 1888.

13402. Extract from a Letter to Mrs. Francis G. Shaw

⟨n.d., 1893?⟩

Not seen; not located. Entry from Livingston, p. 125.

"An extract from a letter to Mrs. Francis G. Shaw, beginning *My dear Sarah:*, printed on pp. 195, 196 of Vol. I ⟨of the *Letters*⟩, was reprinted privately as a remembrance card, probably late in 1893, after the publication of ⟨*The Letters*⟩ . . . This extract was printed in black-letter type, with the initial letter in red, upon heavy cardboard, with beveled edges. The card measures 9³⁄₁₆″ by 7⅛″."

13403. Early Poems . . .

New York Home Book Company 45 Vesey Street ⟨n.d., not before 1893⟩

Noted only in three-quarters leather, marbled paper boards sides. Pp. 229.

13404. Early Poems . . .

New York: Hurst & Company, Publishers. ⟨1894⟩

Printed paper wrapper. Issued as No. 63 in *The Useful Knowledge Series* under date Jan. 9, 1894.

13405. Poems . . . Vignette Edition . . . Illustrations by Edmund M. Ashe

New York Frederick A. Stokes Company Publishers ⟨1894⟩

Decorated paper boards sides, cloth shelf back and corners. Deposited Sept. 24, 1894.

13406. . . . The Vision of Sir Launfal and Other Poems . . .

Houghton, Mifflin and Company Boston: 4 Park Street; New York: 11 East Seventeenth Street Chicago: 28 Lakeside Building The Riverside Press, Cambridge ⟨1894⟩

At head of title: *The Riverside Literature Series*

Copyright notice on reverse of title-page is multidated, the latest date being 1894. Issued as No. 30 of the series under date Nov. 1, 1887 ⟨*sic*⟩. Deposited Nov. 17, 1894.

13407. . . . The Broken Tryst . . .

Boston The B. F. Wood Music Co. ⟨1895⟩

Sheet music. Cover-title. At head of title: *To Miss Priscilla White A Group of Songs by Kenneth McKenzie* . . . Plate number B.F.W.132. Previously in *Heartsease and Rue*, 1888.

13408. Childhood's Sunny Days . . . ⟨by⟩ Lucy Larcom . . . and Others . . .

. . . 1895 . . . Chicago . . .

Contains an extract from "The Rose," *Poems*, 1844, under the title "Life is Joy." For comment see entry No. 4747.

13409. The Poems of John Donne . . . Revised by James Russell Lowell . . .

New-York The Grolier Club 1895

2 Vols. See under year 1855 for first printing.

13410. . . . Selected Poems, with "His Message, and How it Helped Me." . . .

"Review of Reviews" Office, Mowbray House, Temple, London, W. C. June 27, 1895.

At head of title: *The Masterpiece Library. IV.--- James Russell Lowell*. Edited by W. T. Stead. Printed paper wrapper. Issued as *The Penny Poets*, No. IV.

13411. . . . Sun-Worship . . .

Boston The B. F. Wood Music Co. ⟨1895⟩

Sheet music. Cover-title. At head of title: *To Miss Priscilla White A Group of Songs by Kenneth McKenzie* . . . Plate number B.F.W.134. Reprinted from *Heartsease and Rue*, 1888.

13412. The Poetical Works . . . Household Edition with Illustrations

Boston and New York Houghton, Mifflin and Company The Riverside Press, Cambridge ⟨1896⟩

Pp. 507. Deposited June 22, 1896. Issued in cloth?

13413. . . . The Vision of Sir Launfal and Other Poems . . .

Houghton, Mifflin and Company Boston: 4 Park Street; New York: 11 East Seventeenth Street Chicago: 158 Adams Street The Riverside Press, Cambridge ⟨1896⟩

At head of title: *The Riverside Literature Series* Printed paper wrapper. Issued as No. 30 of the series under date Nov. 1, 1887 ⟨*sic*⟩. Deposited Aug. 15, 1896.

13414. . . . Lowell Leaflets Poems and Prose Passages from the Works of James Russell Lowell . . . Compiled by Josephine E. Hodgdon . . .

Houghton, Mifflin and Company Boston . . . New York . . . Chicago . . . The Riverside Press, Cambridge ⟨1896⟩

At head of title: *Riverside Literature Series* Cloth; and, printed paper wrapper. Issued as No. 99, *Extra Double Number o*, under date Sept. 2, 1896. Possibly also issued as a set of individual leaves in printed paper box. Deposited (wrapper) Nov. 14, 1896.

13415. *Entry cancelled.*

13416. . . . Vision of Sir Launfal and Other Poems Edited by Mabel Caldwell Willard . . .

Leach, Shewell, & Sanborn, Boston. New York. Chicago. ⟨1896⟩

At head of title: *The Students' Series of English Classics.* Deposited Dec. 19, 1896. Reissued by Sibley & Ducker, Boston and Chicago.

13417. The Complete Poetical Works . . .

New York Grosset & Dunlap Publishers ⟨1896; *i.e.*, not before 1904⟩

Pp. 410. Printed in 2 columns.

13418. The Poetical Works . . . with Numerous Illustrations.

Boston and New York: Houghton, Mifflin and Company. The Riverside Press, Cambridge. ⟨1897⟩

Deposited Oct. 30, 1897. Pp. 515. Text not enclosed by red rules.

13419. The Complete Poetical Works . . . Cambridge Edition

Boston and New York Houghton, Mifflin and Company The Riverside Press, Cambridge ⟨1897⟩

Pp. 492.

13420. . . . O Moonlight Deep and Tender . . .

Boston Oliver Ditson Company, New York C. H. Ditson & Co. Philadelphia J. E. Ditson & Co. Chicago Lyon & Healy ⟨1897⟩

Sheet music. Cover-title. At head of title: *Songs by Ameircan Composers* . . . Music by Ferdinand Dunkley. Plate number (high voice) 4-37-61334-3. Also issued for medium voice in A. Otherwise "Song," *Poems*, 1844.

13421. The Poetical Works . . . Household Edition With Illustrations

Boston and New York Houghton, Mifflin and Company The Riverside Press, Cambridge ⟨1897⟩

13422. The Poetical Works . . . Popular Edition with Illustrations

Boston and New York Houghton, Mifflin and Company The Riverside Press, Cambridge ⟨1897⟩

Noted only in leather.

13423. The Poetical Works . . . with Numerous Illustrations.

Boston and New York: Houghton, Mifflin and Company. The Riverside Press, Cambridge. ⟨1897⟩

Red Line edition. Pp. 515. *Note:* The only located copies occur with the later spine imprint: *Houghton Mifflin Co.*

13424. Poems . . .

New York Hurst and Company Publishers ⟨n.d., not before 1897⟩

Two formats noted. Sequence not determined:

A: Leaf 6⁹⁄₁₆″ tall. Bound in cloth save for the front cover which is of printed board. Edges plain.

B: Leaf 5¾″ tall. Bound in padded imitation leather. Edges rounded, stained red.

13425. Poems . . .

The Mershon Company   Rahway, N. J. New York ⟨n.d., not before 1897⟩

Two printings noted. Sequence not determined:

A: Title-page in black and red. Leaf 6½″ tall.

B: Title-page in black. Leaf 5¹³⁄₁₆″ tall.

13426. Poems . . .

New York The Mershon Company Publishers ⟨n.d., not before 1897⟩

13427. . . . American Humorous Poetry . . . ⟨by⟩ John Hay . . . James Russell Lowell . . . Bret Harte . . . Oliver Wendell Holmes . . .

⟨London⟩ "Review of Reviews" Office. Entered at Stationers' Hall. ⟨n.d., 1897?⟩

At head of title: *The Masterpiece Library.* Printed paper wrapper. *The Penny Poets,* No. LVII.

13428. . . . Democracy and Other Papers . . .

Houghton, Mifflin and Company Boston: 4 Park Street; New York: 11 East Seventeenth Street Chicago: 378-388 Wabash Avenue The Riverside Press, Cambridge ⟨1898⟩

At head of title: *The Riverside Literature Series*

Printed paper wrapper. Issued as No. 123 of the series under date March 2, 1898. Deposited March 10, 1898.

13429. Poems . . . with Biographical Sketch by Nathan Haskell Dole

New York: 46 East 14th Street Thomas Y. Crowell & Company Boston: 100 Purchase Street ⟨1898⟩

Vignette title-page: *Early Poems* . . . Printed paper boards sides, cloth shelf back. Deposited June 22, 1898.

Also noted in cloth; on spine: *Gladstone Edition*

13430. . . . Books and Libraries Democracy and Other Papers . . .

Houghton, Mifflin and Company Boston: 4 Park Street; New York . . . Chicago . . . The Riverside Press, Cambridge ⟨1898⟩

At head of title: *The Riverside Literature Series*

13431. My Study Windows . . .

Boston: Houghton, Mifflin and Company New York: 11 East Seventeenth Street. The Riverside Press, Cambridge. 1899.

Made up of an unknown printing and deposited for copyright renewal with cancel title-leaf imprinted as above. Deposited Dec. 29, 1838. Cloth?

13432. The Complete Poetical Works . . . Cabinet Edition

Boston and New York Houghton, Mifflin and Company The Riverside Press, Cambridge M DCCC XCIX

Listed PW Dec. 2, 1899.

13433. Abraham Lincoln by Carl Schurz The Gettysburg Speech and Other Papers by Abraham Lincoln Together with Testimonies by Emerson Whittier, Holmes, and Lowell

New York Cleveland Chicago The Chautauqua Press ⟨1899⟩

Printed from the plates of earlier books. Three printings noted; the order of presentation is presumed correct. The following features are sufficient for identification:

First Printing

⟨i-iv⟩, ⟨1⟩-91; blank, p. ⟨92⟩; ⟨1⟩-100. Frontispiece inserted. Inserted between pp. ⟨6-7⟩ (of the second section) is a notice: *In the selection of books* . . . "Abraham Lincoln," by Lowell, pp. ⟨7⟩-36 (in the second section). Imprint as above.

Second Printing

⟨i-iv⟩, ⟨1⟩-91; blank, p. ⟨92⟩; ⟨1⟩-98. Frontispiece inserted. "Abraham Lincoln" by Henry Watterson, pp. ⟨3⟩-36 (in the second section). Imprint as above.

Third Printing

Issued not before 1908. Bears the imprint of *Houghton Mifflin Company*. Issued as Nos. 132-133 of *Riverside Literature Series*.

13434. . . . The Biglow Papers by Homer Wilber ⟨*sic*⟩ . . .

Philadelphia Henry Altemus ⟨1899⟩

At head of title: *James Russell Lowell* Date taken from copyright notice on inserted portrait frontispiece.

13435. . . . The Gettysburg Speech and Other Papers by Abraham Lincoln Lowell's Essay on Lincoln and Whitman's O Captain! My Captain! . . .

Houghton, Mifflin and Company Boston . . . New York . . . Chicago . . . The Riverside Press, Cambridge ⟨1899⟩

Printed paper wrapper. At head of title: *The Riverside Literature Series*

13436. Poems . . .

Philadelphia Henry Altemus ⟨1899⟩

Decorated paper boards, cloth shelf back. Date taken from copyright notice on inserted portrait frontispiece.

13437. The Poetical Works . . . Household Edition with Illustrations

Boston and New York Houghton, Mifflin and Company The Riverside Press, Cambridge 1899

13438. . . . The Vision of Sir Launfal and Other Poems . . . Edited . . . by Ellen A. Vinton . . .

Benj. H. Sanborn & Co., Boston, U.S.A. ⟨1899⟩

At head of title: *Number 4*

13439. The Early Poems . . . including the Biglow Papers with Biographical Sketch by Henry Ketcham

New York A. L. Burt, Publisher ⟨1900⟩

Deposited June 27, 1900.

13440. The Complete Poetical Works . . . Library Edition Illustrated with Photogravures

Boston and New York Houghton, Mifflin and Company The Riverside Press, Cambridge MDCCCC

Deposited Aug. 15, 1901. Cloth?

13441. Early Poems . . .

Chicago W. B. Conkey Company Publishers ⟨1900⟩

Deposited Aug. 27, 1900. Reprinted and reissued without date.

13442. Vision of Sir Launfal ⟨and Other Poems⟩ . . .

H. M. Caldwell Co. New York and Boston. ⟨1900⟩

Deposited Sept. 24, 1900. Cloth?

13443. . . . The Vision of Sir Launfal and Other Poems with Introduction and Notes by Francis R. Lane . . .

Boston Allyn and Bacon 1900

At head of title: *The Academy Series of English Classics*

A copy imprinted as above deposited for copyright Jan. 17, 1901. Also occurs with the imprint: *Allyn and Bacon Boston and Chicago ⟨1900⟩*.

13444. The Biglow Papers ⟨and Other Poems⟩ . . .

A. L. Burt Company, Publishers 52-58 Duane Street, New York ⟨1900⟩

Cloth?

13445. The Early Poems . . . Including the Biglow Papers with Biographical Sketch by Henry Ketcham

A. L. Burt Company, Publishers, 52-58 Duane Street, New York ⟨1900⟩

Padded leather.

13446. Poems . . . with Illustrations from Original Paintings and Engravings by Celebrated Artists

New York A. L. Burt, Publisher ⟨1900⟩

13447. Lowell's Poems

Chicago   M. A. Donohue & Co.   407-429
Dearborn St. ⟨n.d., not before 1900⟩

Imitation leather sides, cloth shelf back.

13448. Poems . . .

New York   Hurst & Company Publishers
⟨n.d., *ca.* 1900⟩

Padded cloth.

13449. Poetical Works . . . Including the Biglow
Papers with Prefatory Memoir, Notes Glossary,
Etc.

London   Frederick Warne and Co   Bedford
Street, Strand ⟨n.d., *ca.* 1900⟩

On spine: *Chandos Classics*

13450. The Poetical Works . . . Introduction by
William Michael Rossetti

Ward, Lock & Co., Limited   London and Melbourne ⟨n.d., *ca.* 1900⟩

13451. Select Poems . . .

Dodge Publishing Company Makers of Unique
Books at 40 West Thirteenth Street, New York
⟨n.d., *ca.* 1900⟩

Printed paper wrapper. Cover-title: *For Friendship's Sake*

13452. Democracy . . .

⟨Cambridge⟩ The Riverside Press 1902

Boards, cloth shelf back. 500 numbered copies
only. Deposited Feb. 21, 1902. Listed PW March
22, 1902.

13453. Memorials of Two Friends James Russell
Lowell . . . George William Curtis . . .

New York   Privately Printed   MCMII

The Lowell contribution reprinted from *Heartsease
and Rue*, 1888. Printed paper wrapper. 50 copies
only. Deposited Sept. 8, 1902. Listed PW Nov. 22,
1902.

13454. The Complete Poetical Works . . . Cabinet
Edition

Boston and New York   Houghton, Mifflin and
Company   The Riverside Press, Cambridge
M DCCCC II

13455. . . . James Russell Lowell with a Critical
and Biographical Introduction by Brander
Matthews . . .

The American Home Library Company, New
York City ⟨1902⟩

At head of title: *A Library of Poetical Literature in
Thirty-Two Volumes* Issued as Vol. 19.

13456. Auf Wiedersehn . . . Music by Max Ben-
dix . . .

The John Church Company, Cincinnati,
Chicago, New York, Leipsic, London. ⟨1903⟩

Sheet music. Cover-title. Plate number 14396-4
(low voice). Also issued for high voice. Reprinted
from *Under the Willows*, 1869.

13457. A Fable for Critics . . .

New York and London   G. P. Putnam's Sons
The Knickerbocker Press ⟨1890; *i.e.,* *ca.* 1903⟩

Flexible leather. *Ariel Booklets*, No. 68. Date on the
basis of *The United States Catalog.*

13458. . . . Vision of Sir Launfal, and Other
Poems. With . . . Notes by Margaret Hill
McCarter . . .

Crane & Company, Publishers   Topeka,
Kansas 1904

At head of title: *The Crane Classics* Deposited
Oct. 24, 1904.

13459. The Syrens . . . Music by W. W. Gilchrist
. . .

New York: G. Schirmer ⟨1904⟩

Printed paper wrapper. Reprinted from *A Year's
Life,* 1841.

13460. . . . Selected Poems   Longfellow, Macaulay, Lowell . . . with Introductions and Notes
. . .

Houghton, Mifflin and Company   Boston . . .
New York . . . Chicago . . . The Riverside Press,
Cambridge ⟨1905⟩

At head of title: *The Riverside Literature Series*

13461. . . . A Moosehead Journal   My Garden
Acquaintance   A Good Word for Winter . . .

Houghton, Mifflin and Company   Boston . . .
New York . . . Chicago . . . The Riverside Press,
Cambridge ⟨1907⟩

At head of title: *The Riverside Literature Series*
Printed paper wrapper. Issued as No. 169 of the
series. Deposited March 2, 1907.

13462. The Vision of Sir Launfal and Other
Poems . . . Edited . . . by Charles M. Stebbins
. . .

Brooklyn   The   English   Leaflet   Company
1907

Deposited Nov. 13, 1907.

13463. F. Morris Class   Six Songs . . . 6. The
Violet . . .

New York: G. Schirmer ⟨1907⟩

Sheet music. Cover-title. Reprint of "Song,"
(Violet! sweet violet!), *Poems*, 1844.

13464. . . . The Vision of Sir Launfal and
Other Poems . . . Edited . . . by Julian W. Aber-
nethy . . .

New York   Charles E. Merrill Co. 44-60 East
Twenty-Third Street ⟨1908⟩

At head of title: *Merrill's English Texts* Deposited
Nov. 3, 1908.

13465. Songs by William G. Hammond   A
Song of Autumn   Song of the Fountain . . .

The John Church Company   Cincinnati
New York Chicago Leipsic London ⟨1908⟩

Sheet music. Cover-title. Plate number 15940-4
(high voice). Plate number 15941-4 (low voice).
Reprinted from *Poems*, 1844.

13466. The Courtin . . .

Boston and New York   Houghton Mifflin
Company   The Riverside Press, Cambridge
⟨1909⟩

Printed paper boards sides, cloth shelf back.
Deposited Oct. 7, 1909.

13467. . . . The Lost Child . . . Music by Arthur
Shepherd . . .

Newton Center Massachusetts ⟨1909⟩

At head of title: *The Wa-Wan Press* . . . Sheet
music. Cover-title. Reprinted from *A Year's Life*,
1841.

13468. Cambridge Thirty Years Ago   1854 A
Memoir Addressed to the Edelmann Storg in
Rome . . .

Boston and New York   Houghton Mifflin
Company   The Riverside Press   Cambridge
1910

Printed paper wrapper. Reprinted from *Fireside
Travels*, 1864.

13469. Life's Song

Buffalo, N. Y.   The Hayes Lithographing
Company ⟨1910⟩

Pictorial paper boards. *Gift of Cheer* series. Extracted from *The Vision of Sir Launfal*, 1848.

13470. Early Poems . . .

New York   Hurst & Company Publishers
⟨n.d., *ca.* 1910⟩

Printed paper wrapper. Cover-title: *Lowell's
Poems*

13471. The Earlier Essays of James Russell
Lowell Edited . . . by Ernest Godfrey Hoffsten
. . .

New York The Macmillan Company 1916 . . .

On copyright page: *Published December, 1916.*
Deposited Jan. 11, 1917. Listed PW Feb. 24,
1917; Bkr Aug. 1917.

13472. The Complete Poetical Works . . . Cambridge Edition

Boston and New York   Houghton Mifflin
Company   The Riverside Press, Cambridge
⟨1924⟩

Printed in two columns. Pp. 492.

13473. The Complete Poetical Works . . . Cambridge Edition

Boston and New York   Houghton Mifflin
Company   The Riverside Press, Cambridge
⟨1925⟩

Printed in two columns. Pp. 492.

13474. Two Essays of James Russell Lowell On a
Certain Condescension in Foreigners and
Democracy Edited by Tucker Brooke . . .

New York Henry Holt and Company ⟨1927⟩

On copyright page: *October, 1927* Deposited
Nov. 19, 1927.

13475. The Shepherd of King Admetus Pastoral
Cantata . . . Poem by James Russell Lowell
Music by Earl Towner

C. C. Birchard & Company Boston New York
⟨1930⟩

Printed paper wrapper. Plate number 226.
Reprinted from *Poems*, 1844.

13476. The Present Crisis . . .

The University of Oregon   John Henry Nash
Fine Arts Press MCMXLI

Stamped vellum wrapper. According to the colophon apparently issued in a limited printing (the
number of copies not stated), each copy numbered.

IN THIS SECTION are listed books by authors other than Lowell containing material by him reprinted from earlier books. See *Section II* for reprints of Lowell's own books.

The Poets of America . . . Edited by John Keese. [Volume Second of the Series.]

New York . . . 1842.

For comment see entry No. 3280.

The Poets and Poetry of America . . . by Rufus W. Griswold . . .

Philadelphia . . . MDCCCXLII.

For comment see entry No. 6644.

Friendship's Offering, and Winter's Wreath. A Christmas and New Year's Present for MDCCCXLIII.

Philadelphia: Published by E. H. Butler. 1843.

Leather. Also issued with the imprint: *Boston: Published by Lewis and Sampson. 1843.*

The Mourner's Chaplet . . . Selected . . . by John Keese . . .

Boston . . . 1844.

For comment see entry No. 8548.

The Mourner Consoled . . . by . . . R. W. Griswold . . . John Keese.

Boston . . . ⟨1844⟩

For comment see entry No. 6661; and, BAL, Vol. V, p. 593.

The Odd-Fellow's Gem . . . Edited by a Lady . . .

Springfield: Benjamin F. Brown. Boston: R. H. Sherburne, Cornhill. 1845.

Deposited Nov. 23, 1844.

The Poet's Gift . . . Edited by John Keese.

Boston . . . 1845.

For fuller entry see BAL, Vol. I, p. 206.

Songs of Home and Happiness . . .

Thomas Nelson, Edinburgh, and VIII Paternoster Row, London. MDCCCXLV.

All Lowell material herein reprinted from other books. "Love Immortal," extracted from sonnet 28, *Poems*, 1844. "Love's Fidelity," extracted from "A Legend of Brittany," *Poems*, 1844.

. . . The Temperance Almanac, of the Massachusetts Temperance Union, for . . . 1845 . . .

Boston: Published by the Massachusetts Temperance Union Sold by Isaac Tompkins, at the Office of the Union, No. 9 Cornhill . . .

Printed self-wrapper. Cover-title. At head of title: *Vol. I. No. 7.*

Scenes in the Lives of the Apostles. Edited by H. Hastings Weld . . .

Philadelphia: Lindsay & Blakiston. ⟨1846⟩

Leather. Listed WPLNL Oct. 1845.

"The Way of Life," p. ⟨28⟩; otherwise sonnet XIV, *I saw a gate . . .* , *A Year's Life*, 1841.

A Book of Hymns for Public and Private Devotion.

Cambridge . . . 1846.

"Anti-Slavery Hymn," No. 437. Otherwise "Stanzas Sung at the Anti-Slavery Picnic in Dedham . . . ," *Poems*, 1844.

For fuller entry see No. 1630.

National Songs, Ballads, and Other Patriotic Poetry, Chiefly Relating to the War of 1846. Compiled by William M'Carty.

Philadelphia: Published by William M'Carty. 1846.

"My Father Land," p. 76; otherwise "The Fatherland," *Poems*, 1844.

The Odd-Fellow's Gem: Containing Sentiments of "Friendship, Love and Truth." Edited by a Lady . . .

Nashua: Charles T. Gill. 1846.

For an earlier printing see *The Odd-Fellow's Gem . . .* , 1845, above.

The Pioneer . . . by Henry Clapp, Jr. . . .

Lynn . . . 1846.

"The Times, the Manners, and the Men,"
pp. 172-173; otherwise an extract from "A
Glance behind the Curtain," *Poems*, 1844.

For fuller entry see No. 4854.

The Fountain: A Temperance Gift. Edited by
J. G. Adams and E. H. Chapin . . .

Boston: George W. Briggs, 403 Washington-
Street. 1847.

The Anti-Slavery Harp: A Collection of Songs for
Anti-Slavery Meetings. Compiled by William W.
Brown, a Fugitive Slave.

Boston: Published by Bela Marsh, No. 25
Cornhill 1848.

Printed paper wrapper. "Are Ye Truly Free?,"
pp. 44-45; anonymous; otherwise "Stanzas
Sung at the Anti-Slavery Picnic in Dedham
. . . ," *Poems*, 1844.

Christ's Messengers: Or, the Missionary Memorial
. . .

New York: E. Walker, 114 Fulton Street.
M DCCC XLVIII.

A reprint of *The Missionary Memorial* . . . ,
1846; see in *Section I*.

The Free Soil Minstrel . . .

New York: Martyn & Ely, 162 Nassau St.
1848.

"Are Ye Truly Free?," pp. 156-157. Otherwise
"Stanzas Sung at the Anti-Slavery Picnic in
Dedham . . . ," *Poems*, 1844.

Echoes of Infant Voices . . . ⟨Edited by M. A. H.⟩

Boston: Wm. Crosby and H. P. Nichols, 111
Washington Street. 1849.

Listed NAR July, 1849.

Gift-Leaves of American Poetry. Edited by Rufus
W. Griswold.

New-York . . . ⟨1849⟩

For fuller entry see No. 6682.

The Boston Miscellanies . . .

. . . Boston: 1849.

For fuller entry see No. 5925.

The Canzonet . . . by Bennett Palmer.

Montpelier . . . 1849.

"Lines on the Death of Rev. Charles T.
Torrey"; otherwise "On the Death of Charles
T. Torrey," *Poems, Second Series*, 1848. "The
Outcast," otherwise "The Forlorn," *Poems*,
1844.

For a fuller entry see BAL V, p. 595.

The Boston Book . . .

Boston . . . MDCCCL.

For comment see entry No. 5929.

Gems from the Spirit Mine . . .

London . . . MDCCCL.

For comment see BAL V, p. 596.

The Present, or a Gift for the Times. Edited by
F. A. Moore . . .

Manchester, N. H. Robert Moore. 1850.

"Love of the Beautiful and True," pp. 181-182.
Extracted from *Conversations* . . . , 1845, pp.
135-136.

The Youth's Poetical Instructor, Part II . . .

Belfast . . . 1851.

All Lowell material herein reprinted from
other books. "They are Slaves," p. 135, extracted from "Stanzas Sung at the Anti-
Slavery Picnic in Dedham . . . ," *Poems*, 1844.

For fuller entry see BAL, I, p. 373.

The Dew-Drop . . . for MDCCCLII.

Philadelphia . . . 1852.

For fuller entry see No. 1188.

Selections from the Writings and Speeches of
William Lloyd Garrison . . .

Boston: R. F. Wallcut, 21 Cornhill. 1852.

"The Day of Small Things," pp. ix-x; otherwise "To W. L. Garrison," *Poems*, 1849.

Garden Walks with the Poets. By Mrs. C. M.
Kirkland.

New-York . . . 1852.

"The Dandelion," pp. ⟨52⟩-54; otherwise "To
the Dandelion," *Poems, Second Series*, 1848.
The other two Lowell pieces herein, "A Day
in June" and "Winter Piece" are extracts from
The Vision of Sir Launfal, 1848.

For fuller entry see No. 1379.

The Evergreen. A Christmas, New Year, and
Birthday Gift.

New York: Leavitt & Allen, 379 Broadway. ⟨n.d., not before 1852⟩

Publisher's leather. A reprint of a portion of *The Missionary Memorial* ... , 1846; see above in *Section One*.

The String of Diamonds ... by a Gem Fancier.

Hartford ... 1852.

All Lowell material herein is reprint. "Signs of Revolution," p. ⟨186⟩, extracted from "The Present Crisis," *Poems*, 1848.

For fuller entry see No. 1190.

... The Unitarian Congregational Register, for ... 1853 ...

Boston: Crosby, Nichols, and Company, 111 Washington Street. Price 5 Cents. ⟨n.d., 1852⟩

Printed paper wrapper. At head of title: *Annual Series. No. 3.*

... The Garland of Freedom ...

London ... MDCCCLIII.

"They Are Slaves," Part II, p. 156. Extracted from "Stanzas Sung at the Anti-Slavery Picnic in Dedham ... ," *Poems*, 1844.

"The Happy Martyrdom," Part III, pp. 153-154; previously in *The Liberty Bell*, 1845; see above in *Section One*.

For fuller entry see BAL, I, p. 373; BAL, II, p. 155.

The Humorous Speaker ... by Oliver Oldham ...

New York ... 1853.

The Lowell material herein reprinted from *The Biglow Papers*, 1848.

For fuller entry see BAL v, p. 90.

The Wheat-Sheaf ...

Philadelphia ... 1853.

For comment see entry No. 3176.

The Rendition of Anthony Burns. Its Causes and Consequences. A Discourse on Christian Politics, Delivered in Williams Hall, Boston, on Whitsunday, June 4, 1854. By James Freeman Clarke ...

Boston: Crosby, Nichols, & Co., and Prentiss & Sawyer. 1854.

"Hymn," pp. 6-7; extracted from "Stanzas Sung at the Anti-Slavery Picnic in Dedham ... ," *Poems*, 1844.

Hymns for the Twentieth Anniversary of the Memorable Twenty-first of October, 1835 ...

⟨n.p., n.d., Boston, 1855⟩

Single cut sheet. Printed on recto only. 16½″ × 8⅛″.

Reprints Lowell's "Song," *Friends of Freedom! ye who stand* ... For an earlier printing see *Hymns and Songs, for the Anti-Slavery Celebration* ... *1849*, in *Section One*.

... Proceedings of the Anti-Slavery Meeting Held in Stacy Hall, Boston, on the Twentieth Anniversary of the Mob of October 21, 1835. Phonographic Report by J. M. W. Yerrinton.

Boston: Published by R. F. Wallcut. 1855.

Printed paper wrapper. At head of wrapper: *"Gentlemen of Property and Standing."*

Untitled hymn beginning *Friends of Freedom! ye who stand* ... , p. 31. Earliest located book publication; for an earlier printing see in *Section One* under 1849. Also see preceding entry.

Affection's Gift, a Christmas, New-Year and Birthday Present, for MDCCCLV.

Philadelphia: Published by E. H. Butler & Co. 1855.

"Sonnet———Truth," p. 256. Otherwise "Sub Pondere Crescit," *Poems*, 1844.

Cyclopædia of American Literature ... by Evert A. Duyckinck and George L. Duyckinck. In Two Volumes ...

New York ... 1855.

For fuller entry see No. 11092A.

Anti-Slavery Festival in Faneuil Hall. A Welcome to Parker Pillsbury, on His Safe Return to America. Wednesday Evening, May 28, 1856 ...

⟨Boston⟩ Prentiss & Sawyer, Printers, No. 19 Water Street.

Broadside. 19½″ × 12⅛″. Caption-title. Contains Lowell's "Song," *Friends of Freedom! ye who stand* ... For an earlier printing see above in *Section One* under the year 1849.

The Humorous Poetry of the English Language ... by J. Parton.

New York ... 1856.

All Lowell material herein reprinted from earlier volumes. The following material extracted from *The Biglow Papers*, 1848: "A Revolutionary Hero," p. 578; "Letter from Mr. Hosea Biglow ... ," pp. 619-623; "The Candidate's Creed," pp. 626-629; "The Courtin'," p. 629.

For fuller entry see BAL IV, p. 324.

The Harp of Freedom . . . by Geo. W. Clark . . .

New-York . . . 1856.

For fuller entry see No. 1660.

Margaret: A Tale of the Real and the Ideal, Blight and Bloom; Including Sketches of a Place Not Described, Called Mons Christi . . . by the Late Rev. Sylvester Judd . . .

Phillips, Sampson & Co., Publishers, 13 Winter Street, Boston. ⟨n.d., 1856?⟩

Single leaf. Printed on recto only. Laid paper. 7¹⁵⁄₁₆″ × 6⅛″. Issued as an advertisement. Embodies Lowell's lines on Judd extracted from *A Fable for Critics*, 1848.

Seen only inserted in copies of *Compositions in Outline by Felix O. C. Darley from Judd's Margaret* . . . , New York, 1856.

The Republican Campaign Songster: A Collection of Lyrics, Original and Selected . . .

New York and Auburn: Miller, Orton and Mulligan, New York: 25 Park Row. Auburn: 107 Genesee St. 1856.

Printed wrapper. "True Freedom," p. 93; otherwise "Stanzas Sung at the Anti-Slavery Picnic in Dedham . . . ," *Poems*, 1844.

The Wheat-Sheaf . . .

Philadelphia . . . ⟨1856⟩

For fuller entry see BAL, Vol. v, p. 599.

Leaflets of Memory. Compiled by the Editor of the "Oriental Annual." . . .

New York: Published by Leavitt & Allen, 379 Broadway. ⟨n.d., not before 1856⟩

Leather. Also in cloth?

Hymns and Songs for the Festival in Faneuil Hall, in Commemoration of the Twenty-Fifth Anniversary of the Massachusetts Anti-Slavery Society, Friday Evening, January 2, 1857 . . .

⟨Boston⟩ Prentiss & Sawyer, Printers, 19 Water Street.

Single sheet. Blue-gray wove paper. Printed on recto only. 13″ × 9¹¹⁄₁₆″.

Under the title "Song" reprints the hymn beginning *Friends of Freedom! Ye who stand* . . . See in *Section One* under year 1849.

The Psalms of Life . . . ⟨Compiled⟩ by John S. Adams . . .

Boston . . . ⟨1857⟩

All Lowell material herein reprinted from earlier books. Under the title "Friends of Freedom" reprints the hymn beginning *Friends of Freedom! Ye who stand* . . . See in *Section One* under the year 1849.

Poetry of the Age of Fable Collected by Thomas Bulfinch

Boston . . . ⟨1857⟩

See below under year 1863.

The Household Book of Poetry . . . Edited by Charles A. Dana.

New York . . . 1858.

For comment see entry No. 12120.

. . . The (Old) Farmer's Almanack . . . for the Year of Our Lord 1860 . . . by Robert B. Thomas . . .

Boston: Hickling, Swan & Brewer . . . 1859 . . .

Printed paper wrapper. At head of title: *Number Sixty-Eight*. "Charity," p. 40; extracted from "Heritage," *Poems*, 1844.

Deposited Nov. 21, 1859.

A Budget of Humorous Poetry . . .

Philadelphia . . . 1859.

Contains two extracts from *The Biglow Papers*, 1848. For fuller entry see No. 11529.

The Poets of the West . . .

London . . . 1859.

For comment see BAL, Vol. i, p. 101.

Proceedings of the Pennsylvania Yearly Meeting of Progressive Friends . . . 1859 . . .

New York: John F. Trow, Printer, 377 & 379 Broadway, Corner of White Street. 1859.

Printed paper wrapper. The material on inner back wrapper extracted from "A Glance behind the Curtain," *Poems*, 1844. "A Lesson for Creed-Makers," printed on the back wrapper, otherwise "Ambrose," *Poems*, 1849.

Irvingiana: A Memorial of Washington Irving . . .

New York . . . 1860.

For comment see entry No. 656; and, BAL, Vol. v, p. 94.

The Bobolink Minstrel: Or, Republican Songster, for 1860. Edited by George W. Bungay . . .

New York: O. Hutchinson, Publisher, 272 Greenwich Street. 1860.

... The Duty of Disobedience to the Fugitive Slave Act ... by L. Maria Child ...

Boston ... 1860.

For fuller description see entry No. 3190.

The Poets of the West ...

London ... 1859.

For comment see BAL, Vol. I, p. 101.

The Loves and Heroines of the Poets. Edited by Richard Henry Stoddard.

New York ... M D CCC LXI.

For fuller entry see BAL, Vol. I, p. 72.

Hymns of the Ages. Second Series ...

Boston ... M DCCC LXI.

For comment see entry No. 1397.

The Children's Garland from the Best Poets Selected and Arranged by Coventry Patmore

Macmillan and Co. London and Cambridge 1862

Choice Poems and Lyrics ...

London   Whittaker & Co., Ave Maria Lane 1862

The Lady's Almanac, for the Year 1863.

Boston, Issued by George Coolidge, 17 Washington Street. New York: Sold by Henry Dexter. ⟨1861; i.e., 1862⟩

"The Ice Palace," p. 37; otherwise an extract from "Prelude to Part Second," *The Vision of Sir Launfal*, 1848.

"We, Too, Have Our Autumns," pp. 70–71; otherwise "To———," *Poems*, 1849.

The Rebellion Record ... Edited by Frank Moore ... Second Volume ...

New York ... 1862.

For comment see entry No. 11531.

The Rebellion Record ... Edited by Frank Moore ... Fourth Volume ...

New York ... 1862.

For comment see entry No. 11531.

War-Songs for Freemen ... Fourth Edition.

Boston ... 1863 ...

For fuller description see No. 11535.

Poetry of the Age of Fable Collected by Thomas Bulfinch

Boston ... ⟨1863; i.e., 1864?⟩

All Lowell material herein reprinted from earlier books. "The Fortunate Isles," p. 186, extracted from "To the Past," *Poems, Second Series*, 1848. "Sybaris. To the Dandelion," p. 199, extracted from "To the Dandelion," *Poems, Second Series*, 1848.

For fuller entry see BAL, Vol. V, p. 602.

Cloud Crystals; a Snow-Flake Album ... Edited by a Lady ...

New York ... 1864.

All Lowell material herein reprinted from earlier books. "Frost Architecture," pp. ⟨125⟩-126; otherwise an extract from "Prelude to Part Second," *The Vision of Sir Launfal*, 1848.

For fuller entry see BAL, Vol. I, p. 295.

The School-Girl's Garland ... by Mrs. C. M. Kirkland. First Series ...

New York ... 1864.

For comment see entry No. 4837.

Lyrics of Loyalty ... Edited by Frank Moore

New York ... 1864

For comment see entry No. 1203.

The School-Girl's Garland. A Selection of Poetry, in Four Parts. By Mrs. C. M. Kirkland. Second Series ...

New York ... 1864.

For fuller entry see No. 11185.

Personal and Political Ballads ... Edited by Frank Moore

New York ... 1864

For comment see entry No. 1208.

Golden Leaves from the American Poets Collected by John W. S. Hows ...

New York ... ⟨1864; i.e., not before 1866⟩

See below under year 1865.

Life-Lights of Song. Songs of God and Nature. Edited by David Page ...

Edinburgh: William P. Nimmo, 1864.

Life-Lights of Song. Songs of Love & Brotherhood. Edited by David Page ...

Edinburgh: William P. Nimmo. 1864.

All Lowell material herein reprinted from other books. "Spotless Love," p. 88; otherwise "To---," *Poems*, 1844. "Love's Lowliness," pp. 145-146; otherwise "Love," *Poems*, 1844.

The Silver Bell ... by Charles Butler ...

Boston ... 1864.

For fuller entry see No. 4035.

Lyra Americana ... Selected ... by the Rev. George T. Rider ...

New York ... 1865.

For comment see entry No. 2827.

Golden Leaves from the American Poets Collected by John W. S. Hows

New York James G. Gregory 540 Broadway M DCCC LXV

"Act for Truth," pp. 302-304. Extracted from "A Glance behind the Curtain," *Poems*, 1844.

Reprinted with the imprint: *New York Bunce and Huntington* M DCCC LXV

Reprinted not before 1866 and issued with the imprint: *New York: George Routledge and Sons, 416 Broome Street* ⟨*1864*⟩

Home Ballads by Our Home Poets ...

New York ... 1865.

For comment see BAL, Vol. I, p. 248.

The Sunday Book of Poetry ... Arranged by C. F. Alexander ...

Cambridge ... 1865

"Seeds of Light," pp. 265-266; extracted from "An Incident in a Railroad Car," *Poems*, 1844.

For fuller entry see BAL, Vol. V, p. 603.

The Book of Rubies ...

New York ... 1866.

For comment see entry No. 5522.

Poetry Lyrical, Narrative, and Satirical of the Civil War ... Edited by Richard Grant White

New York ... 1866

For comment see entry No. 4604.

Anecdotes, Poetry and Incidents of the War ... Arranged by Frank Moore ...

New York ... 1866.

For comment see entry No. 3202.

Golden Leaves from the American Poets Collected by John W. S. Hows ...

New York: George Routledge and Sons, 416 Broome Street. ⟨1864; *i.e.*, not before 1866⟩

Hymns for Mothers and Children. Second Series. Compiled by the Editor of "Hymns of the Ages." ⟨Mrs. Caroline S. W. Guild⟩

Boston: Walker, Fuller, and Company. 1866.

Yankee Drolleries ...

London ... 1866.

For comment see entry No. 1542.

The Year-Book of the Unitarian Congregational Churches for 1867.

Boston: American Unitarian Association, 26, Chauncy Street. ⟨n.d., 1866⟩

Printed paper wrapper. "'Though He Be Not Far from Every One of Us,'" p. 89. Extracted from "Bibliolatres," *Poems*, 1849.

The Book of the Sonnet Edited by Leigh Hunt and S. Adams Lee ...

Boston ... 1867

For comment see entry No. 1218.

The Atlantic Almanac 1868 Edited by Oliver Wendell Holmes and Donald G. Mitchell ...

Boston ... 1867 ...

For comment see entry No. 266.

Christ and the Twelve ... Edited by J. G. Holland ...

Springfield ... 1867.

For comment see entry No. 8604.

Our Little One. The Little Shoe. Little Feet. Little Footsteps ...

Boston: Gould and Lincoln, 59, Washington Street. 1867.

"His Sandals Unsoiled," pp. 48-49; extracted from "Threnodia," *A Year's Life*, 1841.

A Thousand and One Gems of English Poetry ... Arranged by Charles Mackay ...

London ... 1867.

For fuller entry see BAL, Vol. V, pp. 604-605.

Yankee Drolleries ... with Introductions by George Augustus Sala.

London ... ⟨n.d., 1868⟩

For fuller comment see BAL, Vol. V, p. 429. Reprints *The Biglow Papers ... Author's Un-abridged Edition*, London: George Routledge and Sons, The Broadway, Ludgate ⟨n.d., after Dec. 1863⟩

Chimes for Childhood ...

Boston ... ⟨1868⟩

For comment see entry No. 11325.

... The Lady's Almanac, for the Year 1869.

Boston, Issued by George Coolidge, 3 Milk St. ... ⟨1868⟩

At head of title: *No. 16.*

"Margaret ... ," pp. ⟨28⟩-29. Extracted from "A Legend of Brittany," *Poems*, 1844.

The Sunday-School Speaker ... Arranged by O. Augusta Cheney.

... Boston. ⟨1869⟩

For comment see entry No. 1433A.

Tom Hood's Comic Readings in Prose and Verse ...

London ... ⟨n.d., 1869⟩

For comment see entry No. 1546.

More Yankee Drolleries ...

London ... ⟨n.d., 1869⟩

For comment see entry No. 1547.

The Piccadilly Annual of Entertaining Litera-ture ...

London ... ⟨1870⟩

For comment see entry No. 3323.

Songs of Life Selected from Many Sources ...

New York: Charles Scribner & Company. 1870.

Winter Poems by Favorite American Poets ...

Boston ... 1871

For comment see BAL, Vol. I, p. 377.

Public and Parlor Readings ... Humorous. Edited by Lewis B. Monroe.

Boston ... 1871.

For comment see entry No. 1550.

One Hundred Choice Selections No. 4 ... by Phineas Garrett ...

... Philadelphia ... 1871.

For comment see entry No. 2461.

Declamations and Dialogues for the Sunday-School. By Prof. J. H. Gilmore ...

Boston ... ⟨1871⟩

For comment see BAL, Vol. V, p. 318.

Child Life: A Collection of Poems, Edited by John Greenleaf Whittier ...

Boston ... 1872.

For comment see entry No. 11332.

Humorous Poems ... Edited by William Michael Rossetti ...

London ... ⟨n.d., 1872⟩

For comment see BAL, Vol. I, p. 207.

American Poems ... Edited by William Michael Rossetti ...

London ... ⟨n.d., after Nov. 1872⟩

For comment see BAL, Vol. V, p. 318.

The Buyers' Manual and Business Guide ... Com-piled by J. Price and C. S. Haley.

San Francisco ... 1872.

For comment see entry No. 7261.

The Garland of Poetry and Prose by Celebrated Authors ...

Boston D. Lothrop and Co. Dover, N. H.: G. T. Day & Co. 1872

Hymns for Mothers and Children. Second Series ...

Boston ... 1872.

For fuller entry see BAL, Vol. IV, p. 215.

The Poets of the Nineteenth Century ... Edited by ... Robert Aris Willmott ...

New York ... 1872.

For comment see BAL, Vol. V, p. 318.

Public and Parlor Readings ... Miscellaneous. Edited by Lewis B. Monroe.

Boston ... 1872.

"Appledore in a Storm," pp. 295-296; otherwise "Pictures from Appledore," *Under the Willows*, 1869. "Our Country Saved," pp. 329-330, extracted from *Ode Recited at the Commemoration . . .* , 1865.

For fuller entry see BAL, Vol. v, p. 318.

The World of Wit and Humour. Edited by George Manville Fenn.

... London ... ⟨n.d., 1871–1872⟩

"The First Mate," p. 169; extracted from *Fireside Travels*, 1864.

For fuller entry see BAL, Vol. iii, p. 470.

A Hand-Book of English Literature. Intended for the Use of High Schools ... by Francis H. Underwood ... American Authors.

Boston: Lee and Shepard, Publishers. New York: Lee, Shepard and Dillingham. 1873.

The Poets and Poetry of America. By Rufus Wilmot Griswold ...

New York ... 1873.

For comment see BAL, Vol. iv, p. 60.

Illustrated Library of Favorite Song . . . Edited by J. G. Holland ...

New York ... ⟨1873⟩

For comment see entry No. 2853.

The Poet's Gift of Consolation to Sorrowing Mothers.

A. S. Barnes & Co. New York. ⟨n.d., 1873⟩

Contains one poem by Lowell, here reprinted. Also contains "Lines to a Bereaved Parent," pp. 31-34, here miscredited to James Russell Lowell; the author was Maria Lowell in whose *Poems*, 1855, the poem is titled "The Alpine Sheep."

Sacred Poems . . . from the Poets . . .

Boston ... 1873

For fuller entry see BAL, Vol. v, p. 606.

Little People of God and What the Poets Have Said of Them Edited by Mrs George L Austin

Boston Shepard and Gill 1874

Listed PW Dec. 20, 1873.

Free Congregational Society of Florence. Programme of Dedicatory Exercises of Cosmian Hall, Beginning Wednesday Evening, March 25th . . .

⟨n.p., n.d., Florence, Mass., 1874⟩

Caption-title. The above at head p. ⟨1⟩. Single cut sheet folded to make four pages.

"True Freedom," p. ⟨4⟩; extracted from "Stanzas Sung at the Anti-Slavery Picnic ... 1843," *Poems*, 1844.

One Hundred Choice Selections No. 8 ...

... Philadelphia ... 1874.

For fuller entry see BAL, Vol. i, p. 84.

Sea and Shore ...

Boston ... 1874.

For comment see entry No. 4043.

The Muses of Mayfair ... by H. Cholmondeley-Pennell ...

London ... 1874

For comment see entry No. 279.

The Rose, Thistle and Shamrock ... Arranged by Ferdinand Freiligrath. Fifth Edition ...

Stuttgart ... ⟨1874⟩

For fuller entry see BAL, Vol. v, p. 607.

Vers de Société Selected ... by Charles H. Jones ...

New York ... 1875

For comment see BAL, Vol. i, p. 73.

The Ark ...

Boston ... 1875 ...

An untitled stanza, Vol. i, No. 4, p. ⟨1⟩; extracted from *The Vision of Sir Launfal*, 1848. For fuller entry see No. 281.

The Comic Poets of the Nineteenth Century ... by W. Davenport Adams ...

London ... ⟨n.d., 1875⟩

For comment see BAL, Vol. iii, p. 471.

... Little Classics. Edited by Rossiter Johnson. Minor Poems ...

Boston ... 1875.

For fuller entry see BAL, Vol. v, p. 608.

More Yankee Drolleries: A Second Series ...

London ... 1875.

For fuller entry see BAL, Vol. iv, p. 329.

The Sunny Side ... by Chas. W. Wendté and H. S. Perkins ...

New York ... ⟨1875⟩

For fuller entry see No. 178.

Worth Reading. An Ideal Reformer. From The Nation. ⟨Edited by Rowland Connor⟩

New York, 1875.

Not seen; not located. Entry from Livingston, p. 88: "An advertising pamphlet published by the *Nation*"; and, sale catalog of the Stephen H. Wakeman collection, American Art Association, Inc., New York, April 28-29, 1924, entry No. 918.

Songs of Three Centuries. Edited by John Greenleaf Whittier.

Boston . . . 1876.

For comment see entry No. 11341.

Golden Treasures of Poetry, Romance, and Art . . .

Boston . . . 1876

"Sonnet," p. 25; extracted from *The Vision of Sir Launfal*, 1848.

For fuller entry see No. 1749.

Troy Morning Whig 1876 New-Year Offering.

⟨Troy, N. Y., 1876⟩

Cover-title. Printed paper wrapper. All Lowell material herein reprinted from other books. "Freedom," pp. 4-5, extracted from "Freedom," *Poems*, 1849.

Theatrum Majorum. The Cambridge of 1776 . . . Edited . . . by A. G. . . .

Cambridge . . . M D CCCLXX VI.

"The River Charles in June," p. 110; extracted from "Under the Willows," *Under the Willows*, 1869. The untitled lines on p. 110 extracted from "An Indian-Summer Reverie," *Poems, Second Series*, 1848.

For fuller entry see No. 11417.

Yankee Drolleries Second Series . . .

London . . . ⟨n.d., 1876⟩

For comment see entry No. 1553.

The Mountains . . .

Boston . . . 1876.

For comment see entry No. 1239.

Roadside Poems for Summer Travellers. Edited by Lucy Larcom.

Boston . . . 1876.

For fuller entry see No. 11343.

Poetic Localities of Cambridge. Edited by W. J. Stillman . . .

Boston: James R. Osgood and Company, Late Ticknor & Fields, and Fields, Osgood, & Co. 1876.

Yankee Drolleries. The Most Celebrated Works of the Best American Humourists . . . with Introductions by George Augustus Sala.

London: Chatto and Windus, Piccadilly. 1876.

Autumn Leaves.

⟨n.p., n.d., 1876?⟩

For comment see entry No. 11344.

New-Year Offering Troy ⟨New York⟩ Morning Whig January 1, 1877.

Cover-title. Printed paper wrapper.

Poems of Places Edited by Henry W. Longfellow . . . France. Vol. I.

Boston . . . 1877.

"Chartres," pp. 114-120; extracted from *The Cathedral*, 1870.

For fuller entry see No. 12182.

Poems of Places Edited by Henry W. Longfellow . . . Italy. Vol. I.

Boston . . . 1877.

All Lowell material herein reprinted from other books. "Boyhood of Columbus," pp. 101-102 extracted from "Columbus," *Poems, Second Series*, 1848. For fuller entry see No. 12184.

Poems of Places Edited by Henry W. Longfellow . . . Italy. Vol. III.

Boston . . . 1877.

For fuller entry see No. 4050.

Hillside and Seaside in Poetry . . . Edited by Lucy Larcom

Boston . . . 1877

"Mountains from Appledore," pp. 233-235, extracted from "Pictures from Appledore," *Under the Willows*, 1869. Other Lowell material herein reprinted from other books.

For fuller entry see No. 11345.

One Hundred Choice Selections No. 14 . . .

. . . Philadelphia . . . 1877.

For comment see BAL, Vol. II, p. 104.

Dick's Recitations and Readings No. 6 . . .

New York . . . ⟨1877⟩

For comment see entry No. 3375.

Poems of Places Edited by Henry W. Longfellow
. . . Germany. Vol. I.

Boston . . . 1877.

For fuller entry see No. 12192.

Poems of the Life Beyond and Within . . . Edited
. . . by Giles B. Stebbins . . .

Boston . . . 1877.

"To William E. Channing," pp. 214-215; ex-
tracted from "Elegy on the Death of Dr.
Channing," *Poems*, 1844. For comment see entry
No. 9451.

Christmastide Containing Four Famous Poems . . .

Boston . . . 1878

For comment see BAL, Vol. I, p. 74.

Poems of Places Edited by Henry W. Longfellow
. . . Greece, and Turkey in Europe.

Boston . . . 1878.

For comment see entry No. 12198.

Latter-Day Lyrics . . . Selected . . . by W. Davenport Adams . . .

London . . . 1878 . . .

For comment see BAL, Vol. I, p. 74.

Poems of Places Edited by Henry W. Longfellow
. . . Russia.

Boston . . . 1878.

For fuller entry see No. 12201.

The Fireside Encyclopædia of Poetry . . . Compiled . . . by Henry T. Coates.

Porter & Coates, Philadelphia. ⟨1878⟩

Advertised PW Nov. 2, 1878, for *Nov. 5.* Advertised as *now ready* PW Nov. 16, 1878. Listed PW
Nov. 16, 1878, as in cloth; half calf; half
morocco; turkey morocco.

Garnered Treasures from the Poets . . .

Philadelphia . . . 1878.

"The Wife," pp. 37-39; otherwise "My Love,"
A Year's Life, 1841.

For fuller entry see No. 4772.

Golden Thoughts . . . Introduction by Rev. Theo.
L. Cuyler . . .

New-York . . . ⟨1878⟩

Contains a 4-line extract from "She Came and
Went," *Poems*, 1849.

For fuller comment see BAL, Vol. II, p. 104.

Our Children's Songs . . .

New York . . . 1878.

For comment see BAL, Vol. III, p. 471.

. . . Play-Day Poems Collected and Edited by
Rossiter Johnson . . .

New York Henry Holt and Company 1878

At head of title: *Leisure Hour Series.---No. 97*

All Lowell material herein reprinted from
earlier books. "Spring," pp. 85-88, extracted
from *The Biglow Papers, Second Series*, 1867, letter
six.

Poetry of America Selections from One Hundred
American Poets from 1776 to 1876 . . . by W. J.
Linton.

London: George Bell & Sons, York Street,
Covent Garden. 1878.

Proceedings of the Massachusetts Historical
Society. ⟨Vol. 15⟩ 1876-1877 . . .

Boston: Published by the Society. M.DCCC.-
LXXVIII.

Tears for the Little Ones . . . Edited by Helen
Kendrick Johnson . . .

Boston . . . 1878.

For fuller entry see BAL, Vol. V, p. 112.

Poems of Places Edited by Henry W. Longfellow
. . . New England. Vol. I.

Boston . . . 1879.

All Lowell material herein reprinted from
earlier books. "The United States," pp. 35-36,
extracted from "An Ode for the 4th of July
1876," *Three Memorial Poems*, 1877. "The
Washington Elm," pp. 126-128, extracted from
"Under the Old Elm," *Three Memorial Poems*,
1877. "Charles River Marshes," pp. 160-163,
extracted from "An Indian-Summer Reverie,"
Poems, Second Series, 1848.

For fuller entry see No. 12208.

Poems of Places Edited by Henry W. Longfellow
. . . New England. Vol. II.

Boston . . . 1879.

For fuller entry see No. 12209.

Poems of Places Edited by Henry W. Longfellow . . . Southern States.

Boston . . . 1879.

"Washington," pp. 8-9, extracted from "Under the Old Elm," *Three Memorial Poems*, 1877. For fuller entry see No. 12213.

Essays from the North American Review. Edited by Allen Thorndike Rice.

New York . . . 1879.

For comment see entry No. 679.

Tributes to William Lloyd Garrison, at the Funeral Services, May 28, 1879.

Boston: Houghton, Osgood and Company. The Riverside Press, Cambridge. 1879.

Cloth; and, printed paper wrapper.

"The Day of Small Things," pp. ⟨51⟩-52; otherwise "To W. L. Garrison," *Poems*, 1849.

In some copies is a printed slip reading: *From the Children of William Lloyd Garrison*.

The H copy received Aug. 4, 1879. Listed PW Aug. 9, 1879.

The Children's Book of Poetry: Carefully Selected . . . by Henry T. Coates . . .

Porter & Coates. Philadelphia. ⟨1879⟩

Poetry for Children Edited by Samuel Eliot . . .

Authorized for Use in the Boston Public Schools 1879

Scrap-Book Recitation Series, No 1 . . . Compiled by H. M. Soper . . .

Chicago . . . ⟨1879⟩

For comment see entry No. 2476.

The Elocutionist's Annual Number 7 . . . Edited by J. W. Shoemaker . . .

Philadelphia . . . 1880.

For comment see BAL, Vol. I, p. 74.

Ballads and Lyrics. Selected . . . by Henry Cabot Lodge.

Boston: Houghton, Osgood and Company. The Riverside Press, Cambridge. 1880.

Flower Songs for Flower Lovers. Compiled by Rose Porter . . .

New York: Anson D. F. Randolph & Company, 900 Broadway, Cor. 20th Street. ⟨1880⟩

The Union of American Poetry and Art A Choice Collection of Poems by American Poets Selected . . . by John James Piatt . . .

Cincinnati W. E. Dibble, Publisher 1880

"Under a Tree," pp. 72-73; extracted from "Under the Willows," *Under the Willows*, 1869.

According to The Library of Congress originally issued in 20 paper-covered parts. Seen only in three-quarters morocco. Quite probably issued as a subscription book and in a variety of bindings.

Harper's Cyclopædia of British and American Poetry Edited by Epes Sargent

New York . . . 1881

For fuller entry see No. 4336.

In Memoriam. James A. Garfield . . . Compiled by Henry J. Cookinham . . .

Utica . . . MDCCCLXXXI.

"James Abram Garfield," pp. 73–75. Otherwise extracts from "Elegy on the Death of Dr. Channing," *Poems*, 1844; and, from *Ode* . . . , 1865.

For fuller entry see No. 10448.

Gems for the Fireside . . . ⟨Compiled by⟩ Rev. O. H. Tiffany . . .

Boston . . . 1881.

For fuller entry see BAL, Vol. V, p. 610.

Indian Summer Autumn Poems and Sketches ⟨Compiled by⟩ L. Clarkson . . .

New York . . . 1881 . . .

For comment see entry No. 10449.

Favorite Poems . . .

New York . . . ⟨n.d., after May 1, 1881⟩

For fuller entry see BAL, Vol. V, p. 320.

The Cambridge Book of Poetry and Song . . . by Charlotte Fiske Bates . . .

New York . . . ⟨1882⟩

All Lowell material herein reprinted from earlier books. "The Storm at Appledore," p. 352, is an extract from "Pictures from Appledore," *Under the Willows*, 1869. For fuller description see entries 7887, 11490.

Poems of American Patriotism Chosen by J. Brander Matthews

　　New-York　Charles Scribner's Sons　1882

　　h copy received Nov. 25, 1882. Listed pw Dec. 2, 1882.

One Hundred Choice Selections No. 21 . . .

　　. . . Philadelphia . . . Chicago . . . 1882.

　　For comment see entry No. 2486.

Tender and True. Poems of Love . . .

　　Boston . . . 1882.

　　For fuller entry see bal, Vol. v, p. 112.

Memorials of the Class of 1833 of Harvard College Prepared . . . by . . . Waldo Higginson

　　Cambridge: John Wilson and Son. University Press. 1883.

Flowers from Hill and Dale　Poems Arranged . . . by Susie Barstow Skelding . . .

　　New York . . . 1883

　　For fuller entry see No. 11363.

Brilliant Diamonds of Poetry and Prose . . . ⟨Compiled by⟩ Rev. O. H. Tiffany . . .

　　Published for the Trade. ⟨n.p., 1883⟩

　　A truncated printing of *Gems for the Fireside* . . . , edited by Rev. O. H. Tiffany, Boston ⟨1883⟩.

Fifty Perfect Poems. Selected and Edited by Charles A. Dana and Rossiter Johnson . . .

　　New York: D. Appleton and Company, 1, 3, and 5 Bond Street. 1883.

Gems for the Fireside . . . ⟨Compiled by⟩ Rev. O. H. Tiffany . . .

　　Springfield . . . ⟨1883⟩

　　For fuller entry see bal, Vol. v, p. 611.

Picturesque American Scenery . . . with Text by N. P. Willis and Others . . .

　　Boston: Estes and Lauriat . . . 1883.

　　"Commemoration," p. ⟨37⟩, extracted from *Ode Recited at . . . Harvard University*, 1865. "Washington," p. 60, extracted from "Under the Old Elm," *Three Memorial Poems*, 1877.

Old South Leaflets. ⟨No. 2⟩ The Pilgrim Fathers. The Arrival in Cape Cod Harbor. From Bradford's Journal . . .

⟨Beacon Press: Thomas Todd, Congregational House, Boston, n.d., 1883⟩

　　4 pp. Title at head of p. ⟨1⟩. Imprint, p. 4. The nine lines from Lowell, p. 4, are extracted from "New England Two Centuries Ago," *Among My Books*, 1870.

Surf and Wave: The Sea as Sung by the Poets. Edited by Anna L. Ward . . .

　　New York: Thomas Y. Crowell & Co. 13 Astor Place. ⟨1883⟩

Wit and Humor of the Age . . .

　　Chicago: Western Publishing House. 1883.

　　For fuller entry see No. 11220.

Flowers from Glade and Garden　Poems Arranged . . . by Susie Barstow Skelding . . .

　　New York . . . 1884

　　For fuller entry see bal, Vol. ii, p. 39.

An Old Scrap-Book. With Additions . . .

　　⟨Cambridge⟩ February 8, 1884.

　　"The Wisest Man Could Ask No More," p. 382. Previously in *Jeffries Wyman* . . . , n.d., 1874; see in *Section One*. For fuller entry see No. 7763.

No. 3. Standard Recitations . . . March, 1884 . . .

　　. . . N. Y. . . . ⟨1884⟩

　　For fuller entry see in Joaquin Miller, *Section One*.

Belford's Chatterbox. December, 1884. Edited by Elmo . . .

　　Chicago . . . 1884.

　　"Life is Joy," p. 109; extracted from "The Rose," *Poems*, 1844. "When a Deed is Done," p. 240; otherwise "The Present Crisis," *Poems, Second Series*, 1848. For fuller description see bal, Vol. v, p. 320.

Roses and Forget-Me-Nots　A Valentine . . . Arranged . . . by Susie B. Skelding

　　New York　White, Stokes, & Allen　1884

　　Pictorial paper wrapper.

Flowers from Sunlight and Shade . . . Arranged . . . by Susie Barstow Skelding . . .

　　New York . . . 1885

　　For fuller entry see bal, Vol. v, p. 113.

... The Reading Club and Handy Speaker ... Edited by George M. Baker. No. 15.

Boston ... ⟨1885⟩

For fuller entry see No. 7894.

December Edited by Oscar Fay Adams ...

Boston ... ⟨1885⟩

For comment see entry No. 57.

January Edited by Oscar Fay Adams ...

Boston ... ⟨1885⟩

For comment see entry No. 58.

Flowers from Here and There Poems Arranged and Illustrated by Susie Barstow Skelding ...

New York White, Stokes, & Allen 1885

Childhood's Happy Days ... Edited by Edward Everett Hale.

New York ... ⟨n.d., ca. 1885⟩

For comment see BAL, Vol. IV, p. 381.

With the Poets in Smokeland.

Published by Allen & Ginter Richmond, Virginia. Lindner, Eddy & Clauss, Lith. N. Y. ⟨n.d., ca. 1885⟩

Printed paper wrapper. Cover-title. Unpaged. Contains "To a Friend Who Sent Me a Meer-schaum," reprinted from *The Spirit of the Fair*, 1864. Revised and collected in *Heartsease and Rue*, 1888.

February Edited by Oscar Fay Adams ...

Boston ... ⟨1886⟩

For comment see entry No. 59.

April Edited by Oscar Fay Adams ...

Boston ... ⟨1886⟩

For comment see entry No. 61.

Representative Poems of Living Poets ...

... New York 1886

For comment see entry No. 436.

May Edited by Oscar Fay Adams ...

Boston ... ⟨1886⟩

For comment see entry No. 63.

July Edited by Oscar Fay Adams ...

Boston ... ⟨1886⟩

For comment see entry No. 65.

August Edited by Oscar Fay Adams ...

Boston ... ⟨1886⟩

For comment see entry No. 66.

September Edited by Oscar Fay Adams ...

Boston ... ⟨1886⟩

For comment see entry No. 67.

November Edited by Oscar Fay Adams ...

Boston ... ⟨1886⟩

For comment see entry No. 69.

Bugle-Echoes ... Edited by Francis F. Browne

New York ... MDCCCLXXXVI

For comment see BAL, Vol. I, p. 75.

The Children of the Poets An Anthology ... Edited ... by Eric S. Robertson.

London: Walter Scott, 24 Warwick Lane, Paternoster Row, and Newcastle-on-Tyne. 1886.

Cloth, printed paper label on spine.

Fifth Annual Report of the Dante Society. May 18, 1886 ...

Cambridge: John Wilson and Son. University Press. 1886.

Printed paper wrapper.

Note: Lowell became president of the society in 1883 and continued in that office until his death in 1892. The society's reports, therefore, may contain some evidence of his hand.

Hymns and Anthems Adapted for Jewish Worship. Selected and Arranged by Dr. Gustav Gottheil ...

New York. 1886.

"True Freedom," pp. 111-112; otherwise "Stanzas Sung at the Anti-Slavery Picnic ... 1843," *Poems*, 1844.

Proceedings of the Dedication of the Fountain on Eaton Square, Ward 24, October 24, 1885, in Memory of Theodore Lyman, Jr. ...

Boston: Printed by Order of the City Council. MDCCCLXXXVI.

Reprints "The Fountain," p. 26. On p. 54 is a note, Oct. 23, 1885, here in its earliest located book appearance.

The Two Voices ... Selected by John W. Chad-wick ...

Troy ... 1886

All Lowell material herein reprinted from earlier books. "Not Only," p. 12, extracted from *The Vision of Sir Launfal*, 1848. "God, Give Us Peace," p. 95, extracted from "The Washers of the Shroud," *Under the Willows*, 1869. "The White Birch," p. 173, extracted from "The Birch-Tree," *Poems, Second Series*, 1848.

For fuller entry see BAL, Vol. V, p. 321.

Mark Twain's Library of Humor . . .

New York . . . 1888

For comment see entry No. 9636.

Franklin Square Song Collection . . . No. 5. Selected by J. P. McCaskey . . .

New York . . . ⟨1888⟩

"Peace on Earth," p. 127; otherwise "A Christmas Carol;" see above in *Section One*, under year 1866. For fuller entry see BAL, Vol. IV, p. 333.

Belford's Annual. 1888–9. Edited by Thomas W. Handford . . .

Chicago . . . ⟨1888⟩

"George Washington," p. 112; extracted from "Under the Old Elm," *Three Memorial Poems*, 1877. "The Heritage of the Rich and the Poor," p. 103; otherwise "The Heritage," *Poems*, 1844. For fuller entry see No. 5735.

American Sonnets. Selected . . . by William Sharp.

London . . . ⟨n.d., 1889⟩

All Lowell material herein reprinted from earlier books. "Love and Sorrow," p. 147, is a reprint of "To M.W.L.," *Poems*, 1848. For comment see BAL, Vol. III, p. 101.

Franklin Square Song Collection . . . No. 6 . . .

New York . . . ⟨1889⟩

"Castles in Spain . . . ," p. 54; otherwise "Aladdin," *Under the Willows*, 1869. For fuller entry see No. 9019.

. . . Harper's Fifth Reader American Authors

New York . . . 1889

For comment see entry No. 7917.

Belford's Annual. 1889–90 . . .

Chicago . . . ⟨1889⟩

For comment see BAL, Vol. V, p. 113.

The Elocutionist's Annual Number 17 . . . Compiled by Mrs. J. W. Shoemaker

Philadelphia . . . 1889

"The Poor and the Rich," pp. 188-190; otherwise "The Heritage," *Poems*, 1844. For fuller entry see No. 1270.

Beiträge von Literaten und Künstlern zum Deutschen Hospital Bazaar . . .

⟨New York, 1889⟩

Unpaged. Contains 14 untitled lines, facsimile autograph, extracted from "What Rabbi Jehosha Said," *Under the Willows*, 1869. For comment see entry No. 4369.

Half-Hours with the Best Humorous Authors. Selected and Arranged by Charles Morris . . .

Philadelphia: J. B. Lippincott Company. 1889.

4 Vols.

Wordsworthiana A Selection from Papers Read to the Wordsworth Society Edited by William Knight

London Macmillan & Co. and New York 1889

. . . Kings of the Platform and Pulpit by Melville D. Landon . . .

Chicago . . . 1890

"Lowell's Greatest Poem," pp. 502-503; otherwise "The Present Crisis," *Poems, Second Series*, 1848.

For fuller entry see BAL, Vol. II, p. 249.

The Poets' Year . . . Edited by Oscar Fay Adams . . .

Boston . . . ⟨1890⟩

All Lowell material herein reprinted from earlier books. "January," extracted from *The Vision of Sir Launfal*, 1848. For fuller entry see No. 80.

American Sonnets Selected . . . by T. W. Higginson and E. H. Bigelow

Boston . . . 1890

For comment see entry No. 8373.

Representative Sonnets by American Poets . . . by Charles H. Crandall

Boston . . . 1890

For comment see entry No. 8374.

Local and National Poets of America . . . Edited . . . ⟨by⟩ Thos. W. Herringshaw . . .

Chicago . . . 1890.

For fuller entry see BAL, Vol. II, p. 391.

God and Little Children . . . by Henry Van
Dyke . . .

> Published by Anson D. F. Randolph and Co.,
> 38 West Twenty-Third Street, New York.
> ⟨1890⟩
>
> Printed paper label on front cover.

The Speakers' Library . . . Edited by Daphne
Dale.

> 1890 . . . Chicago Philadelphia.
>
> For comment see entry No. 6324.

Out of the Heart Poems . . . Selected by John
White Chadwick . . . and Annie Hathaway Chadwick . . .

> Troy, N. Y. . . . 1891
>
> For comment see BAL, Vol. V, p. 114.

The Lover's Year-Book of Poetry . . . ⟨Compiled⟩
by Horace Parker Chandler Vol. I. January to
June

> Boston . . . 1891
>
> For comment see entry No. 4015.

The Lover's Year-Book of Poetry . . . ⟨Compiled⟩
by Horace Parker Chandler Vol. II. July to
December

> Boston . . . 1892
>
> For fuller entry see BAL, Vol. IV, p. 61.

The Lover's Year-Book of Poetry ⟨Second Series⟩
. . . Married-Life and Child-Life ⟨Compiled⟩ by
Horace Parker Chandler . . .

> Boston . . . 1893
>
> For comment see entry No. 10903.

American Lecturers and Humorists by Melville
D. Landon . . .

> . . . Akron . . . ⟨1893⟩
>
> See entry No. 11228.

Children's Souvenir Song Book Arranged by
William L. Tomlins . . .

> London and New York Novello, Ewer &
> Company ⟨1893⟩
>
> Printed paper wrapper.

Random Rhymes. ⟨Edited by Roland R. Conklin⟩

> ⟨n.p., Kansas City, Mo., 1893⟩

A Symphony of the Spirit Compiled by George S.
Merriam

Boston . . . 1894

> For fuller entry see BAL, Vol. V, p. 615.

Hymns. Supplemental to Existing Collections.
Selected and Edited by W. Garrett Horder . . .

> London: Elliot Stock, 62, Paternoster Row,
> E.C. ⟨n.d., 1894⟩
>
> Received BMU Feb. 5, 1894.

The World of Wit and Humour . . . ⟨New and
Enlarged Edition⟩

> . . . London . . . 1895 ⟨-1896⟩ . . .
>
> For comment see BAL, Vol. III, p. 400.

Through Love to Light A Selection . . . by John
White Chadwick and Annie Hathaway Chadwick

> Boston . . . 1896
>
> For comment see entry No. 2633.

The Lover's Year-Book of Poetry A Collection of
Love Poems for Every Day in the Year The Other
Life by Horace Parker Chandler Vol. I. January
to June

> Boston Roberts Brothers 1896
>
> All Lowell material herein reprinted from
> earlier books. "L'Envoi," p. 105, extracted from
> "L'Envoi. To M. W.," *Poems*, 1844. "April," p.
> ⟨120⟩ extracted from "A Foreboding," *Hearts-
> ease and Rue*, 1888.

The Treasury of American Sacred Song . . . Selected . . . by W. Garrett Horder . . .

> London . . . 1896
>
> For fuller entry see BAL, Vol. V, p. 323.

Voices of Doubt and Trust Selected by Volney
Streamer

> New York Brentano's 1897
>
> "God is Not Dumb," p. 109; extracted from
> "Bibliolatres," *Poems*, 1849. Deposited Sept. 2,
> 1897.

Library of the World's Best Literature Ancient and
Modern Charles Dudley Warner Editor . . . Vol.
XVI

> New York . . . ⟨1897⟩
>
> For comment see entry No. 10624.

Three Minute Readings for College Girls Selected
and Edited by Harry Cassell Davis . . .

> Copyright, 1897 . . . Hinds & Noble, Publishers
> 4-5-13-14 Cooper Institute New York City

Lyra Nicotiana . . . Edited . . . by William G. Hutchison . . .

London . . . ⟨n.d., 1898⟩

For comment see BAL, Vol. I, p. 77.

The International Library of Famous Literature . . . Introductions by Donald G. Mitchell . . . and Andrew Lang . . .

New York . . . ⟨1898⟩

For fuller entry see BAL, Vol. V, p. 204.

American Lecturers and Humorists by Melville D. Landon . . .

. . . Akron . . . ⟨1893; i.e., ca. 1898⟩

For fuller entry see No. 11228.

The Memory of Lincoln Poems Selected . . . by M. A. DeWolfe Howe

Boston Small Maynard & Company 1899

Alice Miller Rice. July 22, 1840–March 27, 1900.

⟨n.p., 1900?⟩

Flexible leather. Unpaged. Contains eight lines extracted from "Elegy on the Death of Dr. Channing," Poems, 1844.

The Young Folks' Library . . .

. . . Boston ⟨1901–1902⟩

For comment see entry No. 391.

Songs of Nature Edited by John Burroughs

New York . . . MCMI . . .

For comment see entry No. 2169.

The Heath Readers. Sixth Reader . . .

D. C. Heath & Co., Publishers Boston New York Chicago London ⟨1903⟩

American Familiar Verse Vers de Société Edited . . . by Brander Matthews . . .

Longmans, Green, and Co. 91 and 93 Fifth Avenue, New York London and Bombay 1904

Issued in The Wampum Library of American Literature series. Listed PW Nov. 5, 1904.

Masters of Mirth and Eloquence by Melville D. Landon . . .

The Golden West Publishing Company Seattle, Washington ⟨1906⟩

Our Girls Poems in Praise of the American Girl . . .

New York . . . 1907

For comment see entry No. 1945.

Through Italy with the Poets Compiled by Robert Haven Schauffler . . .

New York . . . 1908

"Boyhood of Columbus," pp. 76-77, extracted from "Columbus," Poems, Second Series, 1848.

For comment see BAL, Vol. IV, p. 446.

Stories of Humor . . . by Oliver Wendell Holmes . . . and Others

New York . . . ⟨1908⟩

For fuller entry see BAL, Vol. IV, p. 62.

Poems of American History Collected . . . by Burton Egbert Stevenson

Boston . . . 1908

All Lowell material herein reprinted from earlier books. "Flawless His Heart," p. ⟨128⟩, extracted from "An Ode for the Fourth of July, 1876," Three Memorial Poems, 1877. For a fuller entry see in Joaquin Miller, Section One.

The Little Book of Friendship . . . Edited . . . by Wallace and Frances Rice

. . . Chicago ⟨1910⟩

For comment see BAL, Vol. III, p. 65.

The Oxford Book of American Essays Chosen by Brander Matthews . . .

New York . . . 1914 . . .

For fuller entry see BAL, Vol. IV, p. 446.

International Perspective in Criticism . . . by Gustav Pollak

New York Dodd, Mead and Company 1914

On copyright page: Published, October, 1914

A Roycroft Anthology . . . Edited by John T. Hoyle . . .

. . . East Aurora, N. Y. MCMXVII

"Candor," p. 147. Extracted from "A Glance behind the Curtain," Poems, 1844. For fuller entry see No. 4099 (where this publication is misdated MCMVII).

The Poetry of Peace Selected by R. M. Leonard

Humphrey Milford Oxford University Press London . . . New York . . . 1918

"Peace, the Daughter of Victory," pp. 60-64; extracted from *The Biglow Papers, Second Series*, 1867. "Release," pp. 64-65; extracted from *Ode Recited ... 1865 ...* , 1865.

The Catholic Anthology by Thomas Walsh ...

New York The Macmillan Company 1927 ...

A Treasury of Fishing Stories Compiled by Charles E. Goodspeed ...

A. S. Barnes and Company New York 〈1946〉

Thoreau A Century of Criticism Edited by Walter Harding ...

Southern Methodist University Press: Dallas 1954

OFFICIAL PUBLICATIONS

As ambassador to Spain and to Great Britain some of Lowell's publications were of an official nature. No attempt has been made to locate and to describe such material. A representative selection is given herewith.

Papers Relating to the Foreign Relations of the United States, Transmitted to Congress, with the Annual Message of the President, December 3, 1877 ...

Washington: Government Printing Office. 1877.

Official letters, p. 521 and elsewhere.

Papers Relating to the Foreign Relations of the United States, Transmitted to Congress, with the Annual Message of the President December 2, 1878 ...

Washington: Government Printing Office. 1878.

Official letters, p. 764 and elsewhere.

Papers Relating to the Foreign Relations of the United States, Transmitted to Congress, with the Annual Message of the President, December 1, 1879 ...

Washington: Government Printing Office. 1879.

Official letters, p. 935 and elsewhere.

Papers Relating to the Foreign Relations of the United States, Transmitted to Congress, with the Annual Message of the President, December 6, 1880 ...

Washington: Government Printing Office. 1880.

Official letters, pp. 479-484; p. 588; pp. 887-890.

Papers Relating to the Foreign Relations of the United States, Transmitted to Congress, with the

Annual Message of the President, December 5, 1881 ...

Washington: Government Printing Office. 1882.

Official letters, p. 492 and elsewhere.

Papers Relating to the Foreign Relations of the United States, Transmitted to Congress, with the Annual Message of the President, December 4, 1882 ...

Washington: Government Printing Office. 1883.

Official letters, p. 192 and elsewhere.

Papers Relating to the Foreign Relations of the United States, Transmitted to Congress, with the Annual Message of the President, December 4, 1883 ...

Washington: Government Printing Office. 1884.

Official letters, p. 408 and elsewhere.

Papers Relating to the Foreign Relations of the United States, Transmitted to Congress, with the Annual Message of the President, December 1, 1884 ...

Washington: Government Printing Office. 1885.

Official letters, p. 214 and elsewhere.

Papers Relating to the Foreign Relations of the United States, Transmitted to Congress, with the Annual Message of the President, December 8, 1885 ...

Washington: Government Printing Office. 1886.

Official letters, p. 444 and elsewhere.

... In the Senate of the United States. May 21, 1886 ... Report: [To Accompany Bill S. 2496.] ...

〈Washington, D. C., Government Printing Office, 1886.〉

Printed self-wrapper. At head of title: *49th Congress, 1st Session. Senate. Report No. 1188.* Caption-title, the above at head of p. 〈1〉.

"Statement," pp. 34-44.

Impressions of Spain ...

Boston ... 1899

For a description of this publication see in *Section One*, above.

REFERENCES AND ANA

Prospectus Of The Pioneer, A Literary And Critical Magazine. Edited By J. R. Lowell And R. Carter. On the first of January, 1843, the

Subscribers will commence the publication of a Monthly Magazine, with the above title . . .

Boston. Leland & Whiting. October 15th, 1842 . . .

Single cut sheet folded to make four pages. P. ⟨1⟩ as above, otherwise unprinted.

The Nooning.

1849–1852

Never published.

Announced in LW Dec. 29, 1849. Advertised for *the forthcoming season* LW Jan. 5, 1850. Noted as *just ready* LW June 8, 1850, but advertised in the same issue and in succeeding issues as *in the press*. Advertised as *in preparation* LW Jan. 18, 1851 and other issues as late as Oct. 11, 1851. Noted as *in press* LW May 10, 1851.

"The design for ⟨*The Nooning*⟩ . . . was not carried out, though cherished for many years. See the prefatory note to *Fitzadam's Story* in *Heartsease and Rue*."———*Letters of James Russell Lowell*, 1894, Vol. 1, p. 168.

". . . And the *Nooning*. Sure enough, where is it? The *June Idyl* (written in '51 or '52) is a part of what I had written as the induction to it. The description of spring in one of the *Biglow Papers* is another fragment . . . So is a passage in *Mason and Slidell*, beginning *Oh, strange new world*. The *Voyage to Vinland*, the *Pictures from Appledore*, and *Fitz-Adam's Story* were written for the *Nooning* . . . Perhaps it will come by and by . . ."———Lowell's letter to James B. Thayer, Dec. 8 1868, *Letters of James Russell Lowell*, 1894, Vol. II, p. 11.

Ticknor, Reed and Fields continued to advertise the book as *in press* as late as Feb. 21, 1852. The advertisement for the following week, Feb. 28, 1852, does not list *The Nooning*. References are to LW.

The Baronet's Bride, Mrs. Washington Potts and its Sequel Mr. Smith, Mary Powell, The Disponent, and Twenty-five other Capital Stories . . .

Philadelphia: J. Van Court, Printer and Publisher, 243 Arch Street. 1858.

"Autumn," p. 88, signed at end *J.R.L.* Not found in Lowell's works; presumably not by him.

Associate Members Of The United States Sanitary Commission Meeting In Boston. Address To The Public. The United States Sanitary Commission was appointed by the War Department to aid and co-operate with the Medical Bureau, in providing for the Sanitary interests of the new raised Volunteer forces . . .

⟨Boston, Dec. 2, 1861⟩

Single cut sheet folded to make four pages. Lowell named as a member of the *Committee on Addresses*, p. 2.

Poems of Infancy . . .

Boston: George Coolidge, 13 Tremont Row. 1861.

"Lines to a Bereaved Parent," pp. 118-120. Not by James Russell Lowell but by Maria Lowell in whose *Poems*, 1855, the poem is titled "Alpine Sheep."

Essays. From Elizabethan Writers.

Boston: Little, Brown & Company, 1863.

Advertised as *in preparation* ALG Nov. 2, 1863; Nov. 16, 1863. Under the title *Essays from English Writers* advertised ALG Nov. 1, 1864. The book was never completed.

⟨The Works of the Old Dramatists⟩

⟨Boston: Little, Brown & Company, 1864⟩

Edited by Lowell. Unpublished. Announced ALG Nov. 16, 1863. Advertised ALG Nov. 16, 1863 as in ten volumes, in preparation. ALG Nov. 1, 1864 described Vol. 1 as "ready in December."

"An interesting venture was made by Little, Brown & Co. in the summer of 1864, which unfortunately proved too uncertain to be carried through. Lowell was to have edited a series of volumes illustrative of the Old Dramatists, from Marlowe down. He prepared one volume, which was put into type but never published. A set of proofs is in the library of Harvard University."———*James Russell Lowell a Biography*, by Horace Elisha Scudder, Boston, 1901, Vol. II, p. 78.

In a letter to Charles Eliot Norton (in H), Aug. 1, 1864, Lowell makes brief reference to the proofs.

A proof printing of part of the work in H bears the following inscription by Charles Eliot Norton: "This volume is made up of the sheets of the first volume of a proposed series of Old Plays to be edited by Mr. Lowell, and published by Little, Brown & Co. It was undertaken not long before the War (the exact date may be found in one of J.R.L.'s letters to me), and the project seems to have been brought to naught by the interference of greater interests.

"The notes to which reference is made by numerals on the pages were, so far as I know, never written.

"The proof sheets bound up in this volume are, I believe, the sole remnant of the work, with the exception of a parcel of similar, less complete, proofs which I gave to the ⟨Harvard⟩ College Library. ⟨Not found, July 17, 1964.⟩

"The pencil corrections on the first proofs of *Monsieur d'Olive* are in J.R.L.'s autograph . . . 27 April, 1892."

New England Two Centuries Ago

1865.

Not seen; not located. Presumably a ghost; based on Cooke, p. 41: *Reprinted as 8vo pamphlet, 1865.* First published NAR Jan. 1865. Collected in *Among My Books*, 1870.

A Look before and after. (Reprinted from the N. A. Review)

1867 ⟨*i.e.*, 1869⟩

Not seen; not located. Presumably a ghost. Entry on the basis of Underwood's *The Poet and the Man*, 1893, p. 131. The piece was first published in NAR Jan. 1869 and appears to be uncollected.

Witchcraft

1868

Not seen; not located. Presumably a ghost; based on Cooke, p. 70: *Reprinted as pamphlet, 1868.* First published NAR Jan. 1868. Collected in *Among My Books*, 1870.

Poetical Works. [Newly Revised.] Household Edition.

Boston, 1873.

Not seen; not located. Entry from Foley. Presumably a ghost. According to the publisher's records the first printing of the *Household Edition* was printed Aug. 1876.

⟨A selection of Lowell's poems⟩

⟨n.p., n.d., not before 1875⟩

14 leaves of laid paper. Leaf: 11⁵⁄₁₆″ × 8½″. Paged: ⟨1⟩-26, blank leaf. Printed without title-page.

The format is similar to that of William Cullen Bryant's *The Odyssey* . . . , Boston, 1871–1872. It is possible that these Lowell sheets represent some sort of an experimental printing; possibly a projected format of Lowell's poems which, so far as BAL knows, was never issued. In H.

If the date *ca.* 1875 may be accepted, contains no material here first in book form with the possible exception of an extract from "Under the Old Elm . . . ," for full printing of which see *Cambridge in the "Centennial"* . . . , 1875, in *Section One*.

A Life of Nathaniel Hawthorne.

Boston: Houghton, Mifflin & Company. London: Sampson Low. 1881–1890.

An abandoned project. *American Men of Letters Series.*

"On Houghton's agenda for his London trip of 1881 was a meeting with Lowell to secure his promise to write the life of Hawthorne . . . for a number of years he encouraged Houghton to believe he would finally write the biography and the firm repeatedly announced the book as forthcoming. At long last in 1889, Lowell said he was ready to undertake the project provided Houghton, Mifflin would pay him $3000. His price was too high. Ultimately the assignment fell to George E. Woodberry . . ."---Ellen B. Ballou: *The Building of the House Houghton Mifflin's Formative Years*, Boston, 1970, pp. 340-341.

For notices and advertisements see PC Dec. 7, 1885; Oct. 1, 1887; March 1, 1888; Oct. 1, 1889; Feb. 1, 1890; April 1, 1890, and, Ath Jan. 18, 1890.

Garfield . . . 1881.

⟨n.p., n.d.⟩

See below under 1887.

Stanley . . . 1881.

⟨n.p., n.d.⟩

See below under 1887.

To Mrs. Lois Dunlap, on Her Ninetieth Birth-Day, October 4, 1881 . . .

⟨n.p., 1881⟩

Anonymous. Single leaf. Printed on recto only. 9⅜″ × 5⅞″.

The copy in BD is inscribed in an unknown hand: *Written by James Russel ⟨sic⟩ Lowell*. BAL has been unable to identify the author of the poem.

James Russell Lowell a Biographical Sketch by Francis H. Underwood

Boston James R. Osgood and Company 1882

Sparks from the Philosopher's Stone. By James Lendall Basford . . .

London: David Bogue, 3 St. Martin's Place, Trafalgar Square, W. C. 1882.

Cooke, p. 185, states that this book "contains letter by Lowell." Examination of the book shows no such contribution.

The "Biglow Papers." An Essay by William Lenhart McPherson, Pennsylvania College, Class of '83.

Printed for Private Circulation. 1883.

Cover-title. Printed paper wrapper.

Wordsworth . . . 1884.

⟨n.p., n.d.⟩

See below under 1887.

Addresses at the Inauguration of Bryn Mawr College, by President Rhoads and President D. C. Gilman . . . Bryn Mawr, 1885.

Philadelphia: Printed by Sherman & Co., Seventh and Cherry Streets. 1886.

Cooke, p. 177, states that Lowell's address on the occasion is included in the above. Cooke in error. The address does not appear. A summary of the address appears in *Addresses at the Inauguration of Bryn Mawr College, Bryn Mawr, 1885*, Philadelphia, 1887, p. 4.

Concordance Of The Divina Commedia. The Dante Society has the pleasure of announcing that the Concordance Of The Divina Commedia, which has been mentioned in its recent annual reports . . . is now completed . . .

⟨Cambridge, July, 1887⟩

Caption-title. The above on p. ⟨i⟩. Pp. ⟨i-ii⟩, ⟨1⟩-2. Single cut sheet folded to make four pages. Lowell's name heads the list of members of the Council of the Dante Society, p. ⟨ii⟩.

Garfield. Spoken on the Death of President Garfield at the Memorial Meeting in Exeter Hall, London, 24 September, 1881.

⟨n.p., n.d., 1887⟩

Caption-title. Not a separate printing but pp. ⟨43⟩-56 of *Democracy and Other Addresses*, Boston, 1887, removed.

Life of James Russell Lowell by E E Brown . . .

Boston   D Lothrop Company   Franklin and Hawley Streets ⟨1887⟩

Stanley. Speech at the Meeting in the Chapter House of Westminster Abbey in Commemoration of Dean Stanley, 13 December, 1881.

⟨n.p., n.d., 1887⟩

Caption-title. Not a separate printing but pp. ⟨57⟩-63 of *Democracy and Other Addresses*, Boston, 1887, removed.

Wordsworth. Address as President of the Wordsworth Society, 10 May, 1884.

⟨n.p., n.d., 1887⟩

Caption-title. Not a separate printing but pp. ⟨135⟩-156 of *Democracy and Other Addresses*, Boston, 1887, removed.

Lowell's Mind and Art   A Criticism by John White Chadwick

⟨n.p., n.d., Boston, 1891⟩

Printed paper wrapper.

James Russell Lowell an Address by George William Curtis . . .

New York Harper and Brothers 1892

For fuller entry see No. 4394.

The Poet and the Man Recollections and Appreciations of James Russell Lowell by Francis H. Underwood . . .

Boston Lee and Shepard Publishers 10 Milk Street 1893

Reviewed by Ath July 15, 1893. The London (Bliss, Sands & Foster) edition listed by Ath Oct. 28, 1893.

Mr. Lowell in England. A Series of Familiar Letters Edited by George W. Smalley.

London: Macmillan & Company, 1894.

Ath Sept. 15, 1894, noted that a book of the above title "will shortly appear"; also see PC Oct. 20, 1894. The project appears to have been abandoned. An article by Smalley, "Mr. Lowell in England," was published in *Harper's New Monthly Magazine*, April, 1896.

James Russell Lowell a Biographical Sketch by Francis H. Underwood

Boston and New York Houghton, Mifflin and Company   The Riverside Press, Cambridge 1895

See under 1882 for first printing.

Memoir of James Russell Lowell, LL.D. by A. Lawrence Lowell. [Reprinted from the Proceedings of the Massachusetts Historical Society, June, 1896.]

Cambridge: John Wilson and Son. University Press. 1896.

Printed paper wrapper.

James Russell Lowell by Edward Everett Hale, Jr.

Boston Small, Maynard & Company MDCCCXCIX

The Beacon Biographies series.

James Russell Lowell and His Friends by Edward Everett Hale . . .

Boston and New York Houghton, Mifflin and Company The Riverside Press, Cambridge 1899

Noted and advertised PW March 11, 1899. Deposited April 15, 1899. Listed PW April 22, 1899. Second printing announced PW April 29, 1899.

Il Pesceballo Opera in One Act . . .

Chicago The Caxton Club 1899

Edited by Charles Eliot Norton. 207 copies on paper; 3 copies on Japan vellum. Deposited Jan. 27, 1900. For first edition see in *Section One* under year 1862.

James Russell Lowell a Biography by Horace Elisha Scudder . . .

Boston and New York Houghton, Mifflin and Company The Riverside Press, Cambridge 1901

2 Vols. Trade format imprinted as above, issued in cloth. Also a large paper format imprinted: *Cambridge Printed at the Riverside Press MCMI* limited to 350 numbered copies in paper boards, cloth shelf back, printed paper label on spine.

On copyright page: *Published November, 1901* Deposited Nov. 2, 1901. Listed Ath Dec. 14, 1901.

James Russell Lowell His Life and Work by Ferris Greenslet . . .

Boston and New York Houghton, Mifflin and Company The Riverside Press, Cambridge 1905

On copyright page: *Published October 1905* Deposited Oct. 6, 1905. Listed Ath Feb. 3, 1906.

A Bibliography of James Russell Lowell Compiled by George Willis Cooke

Boston and New York Houghton Mifflin and Company MDCCCCVI

Cloth, printed paper label on spine. *Five Hundred And Thirty Copies Printed———P. ⟨iv⟩.*

Lowell's "The Vision of Sir Launfal" a Study and Interpretation . . . by Lucy Adella Sloan . . .

Sloan Publishing Company Chicago, Illinois ⟨1913⟩

Printed paper wrapper. On copyright page: *Published August 1913*

. . . A Bibliography of the First Editions in Book Form of the Writings of James Russell Lowell Compiled Largely from the Collection Formed by the Late Jacob Chester Chamberlain with Assistance from His Notes and Memoranda by Luther S. Livingston

New York Privately Printed 1914

At head of title: *The Chamberlain Bibliographies*

Printed paper boards, printed label on spine. *Five Hundred ⟨numbered⟩ Copies Printed On Old Stratford Paper And Fifty Copies On Van Gelder———* P. ⟨ii⟩.

James Russell Lowell As a Critic by Joseph J. Reilly . . .

G. P. Putnam's Sons New York and London The Knickerbocker Press 1915

Letters of John Holmes to James Russell Lowell and Others Edited by William Roscoe Thayer . . .

Boston and New York Houghton Mifflin Company The Riverside Press Cambridge 1917

On copyright page: *Published November 1917*

Commemoration of the Centenary of the Birth of James Russell Lowell Poet, Scholar, Diplomat . . . Held under the Auspices of the American Academy of Arts and Letters in New York, February 19-22, 1919

Published for the Academy New York: Charles Scribner's Sons 1919

Printed paper boards, cloth shelf back.

Lowell's Religious Outlook a Dissertation . . . by Leo Martin Shea . . .

The Catholic University of America Washington, D. C. 1926

Printed paper wrapper.

James Russell Lowell by Richmond Croom Beatty

Nashville, Tennessee Vanderbilt University Press 1942

James Russell Lowell Representative Selections, with Introduction, Bibliography, and Notes by Harry Hayden Clark . . . and Norman Foerster . . .

American Book Company New York Cincinnati Chicago Boston Atlanta Dallas San Francisco ⟨1947⟩

On copyright page of the first printing: *E.P.I.* Deposited Jan. 4, 1947.

The Pioneer a Literary Magazine Edited by James Russell Lowell with an Introduction by Sculley Bradley . . .

   Scholars' Facsimiles and Reprints   New York 1947

Victorian Knight-Errant   A Study of the Early Literary Career of James Russell Lowell by Leon Howard

University of California Press   Berkeley and Los Angeles 1952

James Russell Lowell   *On Democracy* by James C. Armstrong and Kenneth E. Carpenter [Separate from the Papers of the Bibliographical Society of America]   Volume Fifty-Nine, Fourth Quarter, 1965

⟨n.p., New York⟩ Copyright 1965, by the Bibliographical Society of America.

Cover-title. Printed paper wrapper.

ROBERT TRAILL SPENCE LOWELL

1 8 1 6 – 1 8 9 1

Lowell "returned in 1847 to America ... He began a mission in a poor quarter of Newark, N. J., where he reestablished and rebuilt a neglected church. In 1859 he became rector of Christ Church, Duanesburg, N. Y. ..." where he remained until 1869. No attempt has been made to record Lowell's appearances in the annually issued *Journal of the Proceedings of the Convention of the Protestant Episcopal Church* of the New Jersey and New York dioceses.

There may also be official documents bearing his name during the period of his earlier ministry in Bermuda and Newfoundland and later during his period of teaching.

(Quoted material above extracted from DAB.)

13477. ... FIVE LETTERS, OCCASIONED BY PUBLISHED ASSERTIONS OF A ROMAN CATHOLIC PRIEST ...

NEWARK, N. J.: PRINTED AT THE DAILY ADVERTISER OFFICE. 1853.

At head of title: *The Papal Church Persecutes to Death and Dungeons Worse Than Death* ...

⟨i⟩-iv, ⟨5⟩-22, blank leaf. 9½″ × 6⅜″ full.

⟨1⟩⁸, 2⁴.

Printed purple paper wrapper.

Listed NLG May 15, 1853.

AAS H NYPL

13478. THE NEW PRIEST IN CONCEPTION BAY ...

BOSTON: PHILLIPS, SAMPSON AND COMPANY. M DCCC LVIII.

Anonymous. Title-page in black and red.

1: ⟨i-ii⟩, ⟨i⟩-viii, ⟨9⟩-309, blank leaf. 7⅛″ scant × 4⁹⁄₁₆″.

2: ⟨i⟩-vi, ⟨7⟩-339.

1: ⟨1¹³, 2-13¹²⟩. ⟨1⟩₃ inserted. *Signed:* ⟨1⟩⁹, 2-19⁸, 20⁴.

2: ⟨1², 2⁶, 3⁴, 4-16¹², 17²⟩. *Signed:* ⟨1⟩-2, 2⟨sic⟩, 4-21⁸, 22².

A-like cloth: brown; purple. BD cloth: black; slate-purple. Flyleaves. Yellow end papers imprinted with advertisements.

Announced BM Oct. 1, 1858. Deposited Nov. 22, 1858. Listed BM Dec. 1, 1858. Advertised as a Trübner importation Bkr April, 1859. Advertised as a Low importation PC June 1, 1859. For other editions see under 1864, 1889.

AAS BA NYPL UV Y

13479. Memorials of the Class of 1833, of Harvard College. Prepared for the Twenty-Fifth Anniversary of Their Graduation, by the Class Secretary, Waldo Higginson. ⟨Second Edition⟩

Cambridge: Metcalf and Company, Printers to the University. 1858.

Printed paper wrapper.

Note: The first edition (23 pp.) contains no Lowell material. The second edition, containing Lowell material, consists of 68 pages.

Note, *Newark, June 9, 1858*, p. 37.

Untitled poem, pp. 48-49. Collected in *Fresh Hearts* ..., 1860, under the title "The Little Years."

Note, *Newark, Wednesday evening, July 21st, 1858*, pp. 49-50.

"This classmate has lately achieved a distinguished success in his novel, *The New Priest in Conception Bay*."---p. 50.

H

13480. FRESH HEARTS THAT FAILED THREE THOUSAND YEARS AGO; WITH OTHER THINGS BY THE AUTHOR OF "THE NEW PRIEST IN CONCEPTION BAY."

BOSTON: TICKNOR AND FIELDS. M DCCC LX.

⟨i⟩-⟨viii⟩, ⟨1⟩-121, blank leaf. 7⅛″ × 4⅝″.

⟨-⟩⁴, 1-7⁸, 8⁶.

Three-line erratum notice, p. vi.

T-cloth: brown. Brown-coated on white end papers. Flyleaves.

Note: Four states of the binding have been seen; sequence, if any, not determined. The designations are wholly arbitrary and are for identification only.

Binding A

Publisher's spine imprint: $^3/_{32}''$ tall.

Publisher's inserted catalog dated *March, 1860.*

Inserted at front: A 4-page series of comments on *The New Priest in Conception Bay.*

A 5-line errata notice not inserted.

Binding B

Publisher's spine imprint: $^1/_8''$ tall.

Publisher's inserted catalog dated *March, 1860.*

Inserted at front: A 4-page series of comments on *The New Priest in Conception Bay.*

A 5-line errata notice not inserted.

Binding C

Publisher's spine imprint: $^1/_8''$ tall.

Publisher's inserted catalog dated *May, 1860.*

Inserted at front: A 4-page series of comments on *The New Priest in Conception Bay.*

A 5-line errata notice inserted.

Binding D

Publisher's spine imprint: $^1/_8''$ tall.

Publisher's inserted catalog not present.

Inserted at front: A 4-page series of comments on *The New Priest in Conception Bay.*

A 5-line errata notice not inserted.

Listed APC April 28, 1860. Deposited April 30, 1860. A copy in H (*Binding A*) received from the publisher April 30, 1860. Listed PC June 15, 1860. Reviewed Ath July, 14 1860.

AAS (*A*)   B (*B*)   BA (*A*)   H (*A,C*)   NYHS (*A*) UV (*A,C,D*)   Y (*C,D*)

13481. THE MASSACHUSETTS LINE

This poem has been seen in the following forms; sequence not determined. Collected in *Poems,* 1864. The assigned designations are completely arbitrary.

A

CAMP SONGS. 1861. THE MASSACHUSETTS LINE. FROM THE ATLANTIC MONTHLY. AIR.---YANKEE DOODLE ...

BOSTON: PUBLISHED AND FOR SALE BY WM. V. SPENCER, 94 WASHINGTON ST. RUSSELL & PATEE, 61 COURT ST. ⟨n.d., 1861?⟩

Printed in red and blue. Anonymous. Single leaf. Laid paper. $6^{15}/_{16}'' \times 5^1/_8''$. Printed on recto only. Also issued as sheet music?

EM

B

THE MASSACHUSETTS LINE. BY REV. R. T. S. LOWELL ...

⟨n.p., n.d., 1861?⟩

Single leaf. Printed on recto only. $7^{11}/_{16}'' \times 4^{15}/_{16}''$.

AAS

C

Chimes of Freedom and Union. A Collection of Poems for the Times, by Various Authors ...

Boston: Published by Benjamin B. Russell, 515 Washington Street. MDCCCLXI.

"The Massachusetts Line," pp. 56-57.

For fuller description see entry No. 8808.

D

National Hymns. How They Are Written and How They Are Not Written ... by Richard Grant White

New York: Rudd & Carleton, 130 Grand Street and George W. Elliott, 39 Walker Street. M DCCC LXI.

"The Massachusetts Line," pp. 20-21.

Deposited Oct. 9, 1861. Listed APC Oct. 14, 1861.

H   NYPL

E

The Rebellion Record: A Diary of American Events ... Edited by Frank Moore ... First Volume ...

New York: G. P. Putnam. C. T. Evans, General Agent. 1861.

"The Massachusetts Line," p. 122.

Issued after July, 1861.

For comment see entry No. 11531.

13482. The Rebellion Record: A Diary of American Events ... Edited by Frank Moore ... Second Volume ...

New York: G. P. Putnam. C. T. Evans, General Agent. 1862.

"Hymn for the Host in War," pp. 4-5. Collected in *Poems,* 1864.

For fuller entry see No. 11531.

13483. The Rebellion Record: A Diary of American Events . . . Edited by Frank Moore . . . Fourth Volume . . .

New York: G. P. Putnam, 532 Broadway. Chas. T. Evans, 448 Broadway. 1862.

"The Men of the Cumberland," p. 94. Collected in *Poems*, 1864.

For fuller entry see No. 11531.

13484. The Rebellion Record: A Diary of American Events . . . Edited by Frank Moore . . . Fifth Volume . . .

New York: G. P. Putnam, 441 Broadway. Chas. T. Evans, 448 Broadway. 1863.

"This Day, Countrymen!," p. ⟨1⟩. Collected in *Poems*, 1864.

"New-Orleans Won Back," pp. 5-6. Also in *Songs of the War*, 1863 (July). Collected in *Poems*, 1864.

"Call for True Men," pp. 47-48. Collected in *Poems*, 1864.

For fuller entry see No. 11531.

13485. Songs of the War . . .

Albany: J. Munsell, 78 State Street. 1863.

Reprint with the possible exception of "New Orleans Won Back," pp. 76-78, which appears also in *The Rebellion Record . . . Fifth Volume*, 1863, above.

For fuller entry see No. 259.

13486. THE POEMS OF ROBERT LOWELL . . . A NEW EDITION (WITH MANY NEW POEMS.)

BOSTON: E. P. DUTTON AND COMPANY. 1864.

Title-page in black and red.

⟨i-iv⟩, ⟨i⟩-vi, ⟨7⟩-182; 183*-184* (inserted), 183-206. 6¹¹⁄₁₆″ × 4⁷⁄₁₆″.

⟨1⟩⁹, 2-11⁸, 12⁹, 13⁸. ⟨1⟩₂ inserted; ⟨1⟩₅ a cancel; 12₅ inserted. Superfluous signature mark 5 on p. 65.

Polished V cloth: green. Buff-coated end papers; yellow-coated end papers; maroon end papers. Flyleaves. Top edges gilt. In some copies there is inserted a 16-page publisher's catalog. In some copies there is present a 7-line errata notice inserted opposite p. 206.

Announced ALG Dec. 1, 1863. Listed ALG April 1, 1864. Reviewed Ath May 28, 1864. Deposited Oct. 27, 1864. Listed Bkr Sept. 30, 1865; advertised *ib.*, by Trübner as a new importation.

AAS   B   BA   H   NYHS   UV   Y

13487. The Story of the New Priest in Conception Bay . . . a New Edition . . .

Boston: E. P. Dutton and Company. 1864.

For first edition see *The New Priest in Conception Bay*, 1858. For a revised edition see under 1889.

Cursory examination indicates no revisions save for deletions; three chapters have been omitted and at least two others truncated.

Announced ALG Dec. 1, 1863. Listed ALG June 1, 1864.

H   NYPL   Y

13488. Harvard College Commemoration. July 21, 1865. Order of Services in the Church . . .

⟨Cambridge, 1865⟩

Single cut sheet folded to make four pages. P. ⟨4⟩ blank.

"Hymn," *Thy work, O God, goes on, in earth . . .*, p. 3.

H

13489. Atlantic Tales. A Collection of Stories from the Atlantic Monthly

Boston: Ticknor and Fields. 1866.

"A Raft that No Man Made," pp. ⟨147⟩-161.

For fuller entry see No. 3775.

13490. SERMON BEFORE THE CONVOCATION OF NORTHERN NEW YORK . . .

HARTFORD: PUBLISHED BY THE CHURCH PRESS COMPANY. 1867.

Cover-title.

⟨1⟩-22, blank leaf. 6⅝″ × 4¼″.

Signed: ⟨1⟩⁸, 2⁴.

Printed self-wrapper.

NYPL

13491. ANTONY BRADE . . .

BOSTON: ROBERTS BROTHERS. 1874.

⟨i⟩-viii, ⟨1⟩-⟨416⟩, 8pp. advertisements. Laid paper. 6¹³⁄₁₆″ × 4⁹⁄₁₆″.

⟨-⟩⁴, 1-7, ⟨8⟩, 9-17¹², 18⁸. *Also signed:* ⟨-⟩⁴, A-Z⁸, ⟨a⟩⁴.

C cloth: green. FL-like cloth: blue; green; rust. Brown-coated end papers. Laid paper flyleaves.

Advertised for June 1 PW May 9, 1874. "Will not be ready before mid-summer"---PW June 13, 1874. BA copy received Sept. 29, 1874. Listed PW Oct. 3, 1874; PC Dec. 18, 1874. Noticed by Ath Dec. 26, 1874.

AAS   BPL   H   UV

13492. BURGOYNE'S LAST MARCH. POEM FOR THE CELEBRATION OF THE HUNDREDTH YEAR OF BEMIS HEIGHTS, (SARATOGA) SEPT. 19, 1877 . . .

1878.

On reverse of the title-page: *Printed by L. J. Hardham, Newark, N.J.*

Title-page printed in black and red.

⟨i-ii⟩, ⟨1⟩-⟨15⟩, blank leaf. Laid paper. 7⁷⁄₁₆″ × 4¾″ full.

⟨-⟩¹⁰.

Printed gray paper wrapper.

A copy in NYPL is inscribed March 30, 1878.

AAS   B   H   NYPL   UV   Y

13493. A STORY OR TWO FROM AN OLD DUTCH TOWN . . .

BOSTON: ROBERTS BROTHERS. 1878.

⟨1⟩-322, 2 pp. advertisements. Laid paper. 6¹³⁄₁₆″ × 4⁹⁄₁₆″.

⟨1⟩-13¹², 14⁶.

C cloth: blue; green; purple; terra-cotta. Brown-coated end papers. Laid paper flyleaves.

Noted for Oct. 15 PW Oct. 12, 1878. BA copy received Oct. 21, 1878. Listed PW Oct. 26, 1878. H copy received from the author Nov. 19, 1878. Noted Ath Nov. 23, 1878. Listed Bkr Jan. 1879.

AAS   H   NYHS   UV

13494. Memorials of the Class of 1833 of Harvard College Prepared . . . by . . . Waldo Higginson

Cambridge: John Wilson and Son. University Press. 1883.

Two statements "kindly furnished by Robert T. S. Lowell . . . ," pp. 128-130.

H

13495. The Acadians . . .

⟨Bangor, Maine, 1884⟩

Caption-title as above at head of p. ⟨1⟩.

Paged ⟨1⟩-8. Also paged 65-72. Laid paper. 8½″ × 6″.

Issued in printed terra-cotta paper wrapper as a number in *The Monograph, a Serial Collection of Indexed Essays, Published Monthly*, Bangor, Me., Q. P. Index; and, New York: J. W. Christopher.

"The Acadians," pp. ⟨1⟩-5. "From *The Nation*, 7, 8, 1884 ⟨i.e.,* Aug. 7, 1884⟩, being a review of *Acadia: A Lost Chapter in American History*. By Philip H. Smith . . . ⟨and⟩ *Over the Border. Acadia,*

the Home of Evangeline. By Eliza B. Chase . . ."--- p. 8. At head of text, p. ⟨1⟩, the author's name is given as *Robert S. T. Lowell.*

Published 1st October, 1884.---p. 8.

H

13496. The New Priest in Conception Bay . . .

Boston: Roberts Brothers. 1889.

"Preface to the Revised Edition," May 31, 1889, p. ⟨v⟩.

". . . The author has gone over it all, touching it in very many places, shading and lighting here and there,---making it, it is hoped, better."---P. ⟨v⟩. For other editions see under 1858, 1864.

Advertised as a summer book PW May 25, 1889. Listed (not received) PW June 22, 1889. Advertised for Nov. 15 PW Nov. 9, 1889. Deposited Nov. 15, 1889. Noted as *just ready* PW Nov. 16, 1889. H copy received Nov. 18, 1889. Listed PW Dec. 7, 1889.

AAS   H   LC   UV   Y

13497. Abraham Coles: Biographical Sketch, Memorial Tributes, Selections from His Works . . . Edited by His Son Jonathan Ackerman Coles . . .

New York: D. Appleton & Company. 1892

A one-sentence note, p. 63.

One-paragraph extract from the *Church Monthly*, p. ⟨286⟩.

Listed PW Feb. 18, 1893.

H   NYPL

13498. An American Anthology 1787-1899 . . . Edited by Edmund Clarence Stedman . . .

Boston and New York Houghton, Mifflin and Company The Riverside Press, Cambridge M DCCCC

Reprint save for "The After-Comers," p. 180.

For fuller entry see No. 3082.

REPRINTS

The following publications contain material by Robert T. S. Lowell reprinted from earlier books.

Lyrics of Loyalty . . . Edited by Frank Moore

New York . . . 1864

For comment see entry No. 1203.

. . . Soldiers' and Sailors' Patriotic Songs. New York, May, 1864.

New York . . . 1864

For comment see BAL, Vol. III, p. 156.

Songs of the Soldiers . . . Edited by Frank Moore

New York . . . 1864

For comment see entry No. 261.

Lyra Americana . . . Selected . . . by the Rev. George T. Rider . . .

New York . . . 1865.

For comment see entry No. 2827.

Lyra Americana: Hymns of Praise and Faith, from American Poets.

London: The Religious Tract Society . . . 1865.

Listed PC Oct. 2, 1865, Ath Oct. 7, 1865.

Modern Classics . . .

Philadelphia . . . ⟨1865⟩

See below under 1876.

Poetry Lyrical, Narrative, and Satirical of the Civil War . . . Edited by Richard Grant White

New York . . . 1866

For comment see entry No. 4604.

Anecdotes, Poetry and Incidents of the War . . . Arranged by Frank Moore . . .

New York . . . 1866.

For comment see entry No. 3202.

Christ and the Twelve . . . Edited by J. G. Holland . . .

Springfield . . . 1867.

"Christmas," p. 25; otherwise "A Song for Christmas," *Poems*, 1864. For comment see entry No. 8604.

Christian Lyrics: Chiefly Selected from Modern Authors . . . ⟨by Lucy Fletcher Massey⟩

London: Frederick Warne and Co. Bedford Street, Covent Garden. New York: Scribner, Welford, & Co. ⟨n.d., 1871⟩

Dated 1871 by *The English Catalogue of Books.*

Public and Parlor Readings . . . Miscellaneous. Edited by Lewis B. Monroe.

Boston . . . 1872.

For fuller entry see BAL, Vol. V, p. 318.

The Poets and Poetry of America. By Rufus Wilmot Griswold . . .

New York . . . 1873.

For comment see BAL, Vol. IV, p. 60.

The Elocutionist's Annual . . . by J. W. Shoemaker . . .

. . . Philadelphia. 1873.

For comment see entry No. 7268.

Parnassus Edited by Ralph Waldo Emerson . . .

Boston . . . 1875.

For fuller information see entry No. 5269.

. . . Little Classics. Edited by Rossiter Johnson. Mystery . . .

Boston: James R. Osgood and Company, Late Ticknor & Fields, and Fields, Osgood, & Co. 1875.

At head of title: *Eighth Volume.* Advertised for March 27, PW March 13, 1875. Listed PW March 20, 1875.

One Hundred Choice Selections No. 11 . . .

. . . Philadelphia . . . 1875.

For comment see entry No. 4046.

. . . Little Classics. Edited by Rossiter Johnson. Minor Poems . . .

Boston . . . 1875.

For fuller entry see BAL, Vol. V, p. 608.

Modern Classics . . . and Other Stories from the "Atlantic Monthly."

Philadelphia . . . ⟨1865; i.e., 1876⟩

For comment see BAL, Vol. II, p. 273.

Poems of Places Edited by Henry W. Longfellow . . . Asia. Persia . . .

Boston . . . 1878.

For comment see entry No. 12204.

Dick's Recitations and Readings No. 8 . . .

New York . . . ⟨1878⟩

For comment see entry No. 8626.

Poetry of America . . . ⟨Edited⟩ by W. J. Linton.

London . . . 1878.

For fuller entry see No. 7872.

The Centennial Celebrations of the State of New York. Prepared . . . by Allen C. Beach, Secretary of State.

Albany: Weed, Parsons & Co., Printers. 1879.

"Poem," pp. 165-170; otherwise *Burgoyne's Last March*, 1878.

Harper's Cyclopædia of British and American Poetry Edited by Epes Sargent

New York . . . 1881

For fuller entry see No. 4336.

Standard Recitations by Best Authors ⟨No. 1⟩ . . . Compiled . . . by Frances P. Sullivan.

M. J. Ivers & Co., Publishers, 86 Nassau Street, N. Y. ⟨1883⟩

Printed paper wrapper. Deposited April 20, 1883. The earliest printing (printings?) does not have a statement identifying the publication as No. 1 of the series.

American War Ballads and Lyrics . . . Edited by George Cary Eggleston . . .

New York . . . ⟨1889⟩

For fuller comment see BAL, Vol. V, p. 337.

Three Minute Readings for College Girls Selected and Edited by Harry Cassell Davis . . .

Copyright, 1897 . . . Hinds & Noble, Publishers 4-5-13-14 Cooper Institute New York City

The Little Book of Cheer Compiled and Edited with an Introduction by Wallace and Frances Rice

. . . The Reilly & Britton Co. Chicago ⟨1910⟩

Boards, paper labels. Listed PW March 19, 1910.

GEORGE BARR McCUTCHEON

(Richard Greaves)

1 8 6 6 – 1 9 2 8

13499. I trust that my friends / who read these verses / will not have to stretch / the imagination as far / as I did in getting the / good points ⟨5 dots⟩ / ⟨all the preceding in red, each line underlined in red; wholly enclosed by a double-rule box printed in blue⟩ / Several Short Ones, / ⟨3 dot-crosses⟩ FOUND BY ⟨3 dot-crosses⟩ ⟨preceding 2 lines in blue⟩ / ⟨dot⟩ Geo. B. McCutcheon, ⟨dot⟩ ⟨printed in red, enclosed by a single-rule box printed in blue⟩ / ⟨3 dot-crosses⟩ DURING ⟨3 dot-crosses⟩ / Flights of Imagination. / ⟨preceding 2 lines in blue⟩ / ⟨the following 7 lines in red, each underlined in red, the whole in a double-rule blue box⟩ / If the good points are / at first imperceptible, / do not hastily conclude / that they are absent / altogether. Perhaps / my imagination is bet- / ter than yours. / ⟨all of the preceding decorated with (in blue) dots, rules, scrolls; wholly enclosed by a single-rule box in red; below the box, in blue:⟩ MORNING JOURNAL PRINT. / ⟨n.p., n.d., Lafayette, Ind., *ca.* 1886–1890⟩

The above printed on the face of a single cut sheet of flexible cardboard to which are tied (through holes punched at the top, with a piece of golden-yellow silk rope) fourteen leaves of heavy paper, each imprinted on the face with the poetical contents of the publication. Text printed in black, within a red rule frame. Printed on rectos only. Wove paper watermarked *Germanic Royal Linen.*

Size of leaf and cover: 8³⁄₁₆″ × 5⁷⁄₈″ scant.

Privately printed when McCutcheon "was in the very early twenties . . . So far as I know, there are only three copies in existence. One belongs to me, one to my wife, and the third to my sister. The other forty-odd copies were never distributed . . . They were locked away in a drawer, where they remained in virgin condition until the would-be poet, arriving at years of discretion, took them out one day, and anticipating by a great many centuries the destruction of the world by fire . . . attended to the job himself. They burned very slowly, as all green things do, but they raised a lot of smoke."––*Books Once Were Men,* 1931, p. 58.

Y

13500. The Christmas Courier LaFayette, Ind., Dec. 25, 1897. A Magazine Supplement for Christmas Night Readers . . .

⟨Lafayette, Ind., *The Courier,* Dec. 25, 1897⟩

Caption-title. 4 pp. Complete thus?

"The Maid and the Blade," p. ⟨2⟩.

Y

13501. GRAUSTARK THE STORY OF A LOVE BEHIND A THRONE . . .

HERBERT S. STONE AND COMPANY   ELDRIDGE COURT, CHICAGO MDCCCCI

Title-page in black, orange and blind.

⟨i-viii⟩, 1-459, 2 blank leaves. Laid paper watermarked H S STONE & CO. NEW YORK & CHICAGO 7⁷⁄₁₆″ × 4³⁄₄″.

⟨1⁴, 2-30⁸⟩.

Four printings noted:

FIRST PRINTING

As collated above.

Paper watermarked H S STONE & CO. NEW YORK & CHICAGO

No printer's imprint, p. ⟨461⟩.

P. 150, line 6: . . . *Noble's* . . .

P. 334, last line: *lact . . . fata /*

P. 401, line 11: "*Ask Her Maiesty,*" *commanded the captain,/*

Noted in *Binding A;* see below.

INTERMEDIATE

Pagination and signature collation as above.

Paper not watermarked with the publisher's name and address.

Donnelley imprint, p. ⟨461⟩.

P. 150, line 6: . . . *Lorry's* . . .

P. 334, last line: *lact . . . fata /*

I trust that my friends who read these verses will not have to stretch the imagination as far as I did in getting the good points. . . . .

Several Short Ones,

+ + + FOUND BY + + +

Geo. B. McCutcheon,

+ + + DURING + + +

Flights of Imagination.

If the good points are at first imperceptible, do not hastily conclude that they are absent altogether. Perhaps my imagination is better than yours.

MORNING JOURNAL PRINT.

GEORGE BARR McCUTCHEON
Entry No. 13499
(Yale University Library)

P. 401, line 11: "*Ask Her Maiesty,*" *commanded the captain,* |

Noted in *Binding A;* see below.

SECOND PRINTING

Pagination and signature collation as above.

Paper not watermarked with the publisher's name and address.

No imprint, p. ⟨461⟩.

P. 150, line 6: . . . *Lorry's* . . .

P. 334, last line: *lact . . . fata* |

P. 401, line 11: "*Ask Her Maiesty,*" *commanded the captain,* |

Noted in *Binding B; Binding C; Binding D;* see below.

THIRD PRINTING

Pagination and signature collation as above.

Paper not watermarked with the publisher's name and address.

No imprint, p. ⟨461⟩.

P. 150, line 6: . . . *Lorry's* . . .

P. 334, last line: *act . . . fatal* |

P. 401, line 11: "*Ask Her Royal Highness,*" *commanded* |

Noted in *Binding B;* see below.

FOURTH PRINTING

Pagination and signature collation as above.

Paper not watermarked with publisher's name and address.

Donnelley imprint, p. ⟨461⟩.

P. 150, line 6: . . . *Lorry's* . . .

P. 334, last line: *act . . . fatal* |

P. 401, line 11: "*Ask Her Royal Highness,*" *commanded* |

Noted in *Binding B; Binding D;* see below.

Size-dyed V cloth: blue. White laid end papers, some showing portions of the watermarked publisher's name. Top edges gilt. *See the following note.*

Four bindings noted. The following notes are sufficient for ready identification. The sequence of *Bindings B-D* is not certain. Since the book was a best-seller there is every possibility that two or more of the bindings could have been simultaneous.

BINDING A

Publisher's spine imprint stamped from capital letters only.

Publisher's device present on back cover.

Noted on the first printing; and, intermediate printing. McCutcheon's personal copy (IU) inscribed: *This book was published today . . . March 16, 1901.*

BINDING B

Publisher's spine imprint stamped from capital letters only.

Back cover unstamped.

Noted on second printing, third printing, fourth printing.

BINDING C

Publisher's spine imprint absent.

Back cover unstamped.

Noted on the second printing.

BINDING D

Publisher's spine imprint stamped from upper and lower case letters.

Back cover unstamped.

Noted on the second printing; fourth printing.

McCutcheon's personal copy (IU) inscribed by him: *This book was published today . . . March 16, 1901.* "Published March 21, 1901, according to later advertisements . . ."---Sidney Kramer: *A History of Stone & Kimball . . .,* 1940, p. 335. NYPL copy (1st, *Binding A*) inscribed by author March 22, 1901. Listed PW March 23, 1901. Deposited April 10, 1901. The London (Richards) edition listed Ath April, 1902. The London (Hodder & Stoughton) edition issued without date *ca.* 1917.

AAS (2nd, *Binding D*) BA (2nd, *Binding C*) H (1st, *Binding A;* 4th, *Binding D*) IU (1st, *Binding A;* 3d, *Binding B*) NYPL (1st, *Binding A*) UV (1st, *Binding A;* intermediate, *Binding A;* 4th, *Binding B;* 4th, *Binding D*) Y (1st, *Binding A;* 2nd, *Binding D;* 3d, *Binding B;* 4th, *Binding D*)

13502. CASTLE CRANEYCROW . . .

CHICAGO   HERBERT S. STONE AND COMPANY
MCMII

Title-page in black, orange and blind.

⟨i-viii⟩, 1-391; blank, p. ⟨392⟩; printer's imprint, p. ⟨393⟩; blank, p. ⟨394⟩; three blank leaves. Laid paper. 7$\frac{7}{16}$″ × 4$\frac{13}{16}$″.

⟨1⁴, 2-26⁸⟩.

V cloth: green. Stamped in green, white, yellow. Top edges gilt; or, plain.

Three printings noted:

FIRST PRINTING

Pagination and signature collation as above.

P. ⟨393⟩: *Donnelley* imprint present; *Marsh, Aiken & Curtis* imprint not present.

Binding as above.

SECOND PRINTING

Pagination and signature collation as above.

P. ⟨393⟩: *Donnelley* imprint present; also present, imprint of *Marsh, Aiken & Curtis.*

Binding as above.

Note: A set of second printing sheets has been seen in a presumed experimental binding: Red V cloth with stamping unlike that described above, a principal variation being goldstamped lettering on the spine, not greenstamped lettering. Also present is an inserted frontispiece; the first printing contains no illustrations.

Also occurs in a binding with Grosset & Dunlap spine imprint.

THIRD PRINTING

Title-page printed in black only.

Paged: ⟨i-iv⟩, 1-391, 2 blank leaves. Laid paper.

⟨1-25⁸⟩.

P. ⟨393⟩ blank.

Noted only in a binding with the Grosset & Dunlap spine imprint.

Deposited Aug. 13, 1902. On copyright page: *Issued August 15, 1902* A copy of the first printing (in Y) inscribed by McCutcheon... *published... August 15, 1902.* A copy of the second printing (in Y) inscribed by McCutcheon... *published... August 15, 1902.* Listed PW Aug. 23, 1902. BA copy of the first printing received Sept. 27, 1902. The London (Richards) printing listed Ath Nov. 14, 1903.

AAS (1st) H (1st) UV (1st; 2nd; 2nd, variant binding of red V; 3rd) Y (1st; 2nd; 2nd, variant binding of red V; 2nd in Grosset & Dunlap binding)

13503. Indiana Writers of Poems and Prose. ⟨Edited by Edward Joseph Hamilton⟩

The Western Press Association, Publishers. Chicago, 1902.

Unpaged. Contains "When I Played the Part of Santa Claus."

Deposited Sept. 6, 1902.

ISL Y

13504. BREWSTER'S MILLIONS BY RICHARD GREAVES

CHICAGO HERBERT S. STONE & CO. MCMIII

Title-page in black, orange, blind.

⟨i-x⟩, 1-325; blank, p. ⟨326⟩; Donnelley imprint, p. ⟨327⟩; blank leaf. Laid paper. 7⁹⁄₁₆″ × 4¹³⁄₁₆″.

⟨1⁴, 2-21⁸, 22⁶⟩.

Two printings noted:

FIRST PRINTING

As described above.

SECOND PRINTING

⟨i-x⟩, 1-325; blank, p. ⟨326⟩; Donnelley imprint, p. ⟨327⟩; 3 blank leaves. Laid paper.

⟨1⁴, 2-22⁸⟩.

Rough red V cloth. Front lettered in gold: Brewster's / Millions / By / Richard / P. / Greaves / ⟨all the preceding on a circular black field enclosed by a goldstamped ring; to the left of the lettering, in gold, coins and wings⟩. White laid end papers. To edges gilt. *Note:* The first printing occurs in rough V cloth; second printing sheets, stamped as described, noted in smooth V cloth.

Note: A copy, printing not determined (the book has been extensively damaged and crudely repaired) has been seen in a Tabard Inn binding; see BAL, Vol. I, pp. xxxii-xxxiii. Front stamped in gold: BREWSTER'S MILLIONS / ⟨trefoil⟩ / RICHARD P. GREAVES

Also note: A copy of the second printing has been seen in smooth red V cloth with the spine imprint reading: Stone / Chicago In the first form of the binding the spine imprint reads: STONE / CHICAGO

On copyright page: *Issued April 20, 1903* Deposited April 20, 1903. Listed PW May 9, 1903. The London (Collier) edition listed Ath May 25, 1907; apparently the first British printing. As a play produced at the Seymour Hicks Theatre, London; see Ath May 11, 1907.

AAS (2nd) NYPL (2nd) UV (2nd; Tabard Inn) Y (1st)

13505. THE SHERRODS...

NEW YORK DODD, MEAD AND COMPANY 1903

Title-page in black and green.

Two printings noted; the following order is suggested:

PRINTING A

⟨i⟩-⟨viii⟩, ⟨9⟩-343, 2 blank leaves. 7⁷⁄₁₆″ × 5¹⁄₁₆″. Frontispiece and five plates inserted.

⟨1-14⟩, 15, ⟨16-20⟩⁸, 21⁴, ⟨22-23⟩¹, ⟨24⟩⁸. Note presence of signature marks 15 and 21.

PRINTING B

⟨i⟩-⟨viii⟩, ⟨9⟩-343. Frontispiece and five plates inserted. 7⁷⁄₁₆″ × 5¹⁄₁₆″.

Printing B consists of 21 gatherings in 8, with a final

gathering in 4. The signing occurs as follows with no established sequence:

PRINTING B, SIGNING A

⟨1-3⟩, 4-6, ⟨7-21⟩⁸, ⟨22⟩⁴.

PRINTING B, SIGNING B

⟨1-4⟩, 5-6, ⟨7-21⟩⁸, ⟨22⟩⁴.

PRINTING B, SIGNING C

⟨1-21⁸, 22⁴⟩. Copies thus have been noted in the original Dodd, Mead and Company binding; and, in the binding of Grosset & Dunlap.

V cloth: slate-blue. *Note:* The spine imprint occurs as follows; the sequence offered is probable:

A: DODD, MEAD & / COMPANY

B: DODD, MEAD / & COMPANY

On copyright page: *Published September, 1903* Published Sept. 15, 1903 (author's statement inscribed in a Y copy of *Printing B*. Listed PW Sept. 19, 1903. The London (Ward, Lock) edition listed Ath Feb. 11, 1905.

AAS (Printing A, Binding A) H (Printing B, Binding B, Signing A) Y (Printing B, Binding A, Signing C; Printing B, Binding B, Signing B)

13506. THE DAY OF THE DOG . . .

NEW YORK DODD MEAD & COMPANY 1904

⟨i-iv⟩, ⟨9⟩-137, blank leaf. Frontispiece and 4 plates inserted; other illustrations in text. 7⁹⁄₁₆″ × 5⅛″ full.

⟨1², 2-9⁸, 10²⟩.

Two states (printings?) noted:

FIRST STATE (PRINTING?)

On the copyright page the dog device is lettered CAVE CANUM . . .

SECOND STATE (PRINTING?)

On the copyright page the dog device is lettered CAVE CANEM . . .

Two bindings noted:

BINDING A

T cloth: red. Winged dog's head stamped on front. White end papers printed in orange with hero and heroine pursued by man, boy, dog, etc. Top edges gilt. Noted on both *First State (Printing?)* and *Second State (Printing?)*.

BINDING B

T cloth: green. Winged dog's head not present on front; replaced by the statement: *A Love Story* Noted only on *Second State (Printing?)*.

On copyright page: *Published March, 1904*

Advertised for *Spring* PW March 19, 1904. Deposited March 24, 1904. Advertised as

just published PW March 26, 1904. *This book was published today . . . March 29, 1904*---McCutcheon's inscription in his personal copy (in Y). Listed PW April 9, 1904.

AAS (2nd, *Binding A*) BA (1st, *Binding A*) H (1st, *Binding A*) NYPL (2nd, *Binding A;* 2nd, *Binding B*) Y (1st, *Binding A;* 2nd, *Binding B*)

13507. BEVERLY OF GRAUSTARK . . .

NEW YORK DODD, MEAD & COMPANY 1904

⟨i⟩-⟨viii⟩, 1-357, blank leaf. Frontispiece and 4 plates inserted. 7⅜″ × 5″ scant.

⟨1⁴, 2-23⁸, 24⁴⟩.

Two states noted; the sequence has not been determined and the designations are for identification only.

STATE A

The title-page reads: . . . *Author of "Graustark," "The Sherrods," etc. With Illustrations by Harrison Fisher* . . .

STATE B

The title-page reads: . . . *Author of "Graustark," "Castle Craneycrow," etc. With Illustrations by Harrison Fisher* . . . In some copies the *o* in *Harrison* is lacking.

S cloth: blue.

Noted for *early fall publication* PW June 11, 1904. Noted for *the 17th inst.,* PW Sept. 10, 1904; for *September 17th* PW Sept. 17, 1904. *Published September 17th*---PW Sept. 24, 1904. Noted as *just ready* PW Sept. 24, 1904. On copyright page: *Published September, 1904.* Listed PW Oct. 1, 1904. The London (Hodder & Stoughton) edition listed Ath March 25, 1905.

AAS (B) H (B) ISL (A,B) Y (B)

13508. THE PURPLE PARASOL . . .

NEW YORK DODD, MEAD AND COMPANY 1905

Two printings noted:

FIRST PRINTING

⟨1⟩-108. Frontispiece and 4 plates inserted. 7⅝″ × 5¼″.

⟨1-6⁸, 7⁶⟩.

On copyright page: *Published April, 1905* and *The University Press, Cambridge, Mass., U.S.A.*

SECOND PRINTING

⟨i-iv⟩, ⟨1⟩-108. Frontispiece and 4 plates inserted. ⟨1-7⁸⟩.

On copyright page: *Published April, 1905* Printer's imprint not present.

Noted in the following bindings. The order is all but completely arbitrary:

BINDING A

T cloth: green. Publisher's spine imprint (the whole set ⁵⁄₃₂″ deep): DODD MEAD / & COMPANY ⟨note absence of comma⟩ White paper end papers printed in purple with an all-over pattern of blocks and cupids. Double flyleaves at both front and at back. Top edges gilt. Noted on first printing sheets.

BINDING B

T cloth: green. Publisher's spine imprint (the whole set ⁵⁄₃₂″ deep): DODD MEAD / & COMPANY ⟨note absence of comma⟩ White paper end papers printed in yellow with an all-over pattern of blocks and cupids. No flyleaves at front; double flyleaf at back. Top edges gilt. Noted on second printing sheets.

BINDING C

S cloth: green. Publisher's spine imprint (the whole set ⁹⁄₃₂″ deep): DODD, MEAD / & COMPANY ⟨note presence of comma⟩ White paper end papers printed in purple with an all-over pattern of blocks and cupids. No flyleaves at front; double flyleaf at back. Top edges gilt. Noted on second printing sheets. Also occurs in green T cloth, the end papers printed in gray, or blue, with an all-over pattern of blocks and cupids.

BINDING D

T cloth: green. Publisher's spine imprint enclosed by a single rule frame: DODD, MEAD / & COMPANY ⟨note presence of comma⟩. White paper end papers printed in gray-blue with an all-over pattern of blocks and cupids. Flyleaves? Noted on second printing sheets.

Noted as *soon* PW March 4, 1905. Announced for *April 15* PW April 8, 1905. Advertised as *to-day* and noted as *just ready* PW April 15, 1905. The author's copy (in Y), second printing, binding B, inscribed by the author, *published . . . April 17, 1905.* Listed PW April 22, 1905. On the copyright page: *Published April, 1905.* Reprinted and reissued *ca.* 1908–1910 by A. L. Burt Company, New York, under date ⟨1905⟩.

BPL (2nd, *Binding C*) H (1st, *Binding A;* 2nd, *Binding C*) NYPL (2nd, *Binding D*) UV (1st, *Binding A*) Y (2nd, *Binding B*)

13509. NEDRA . . .

NEW YORK DODD, MEAD & COMPANY 1905

Two states (probably printings) noted. The sequence has not been firmly established.

STATE A

Letterpress of title-page enclosed by a rules frame consisting of four simple rules and a dotted rule.

P. ⟨ii⟩: Blank.

STATE B

Letterpress of title-page enclosed by a rules frame consisting of three simple rules and a dotted rule.

P. ⟨ii⟩: Imprinted with a boxed advertisement: OTHER BOOKS BY MR. MCCUTCHEON . . .

Note: The title-page of a Grosset & Dunlap reprint has the title-page in *State B.*

Both states collate as follows:

⟨i⟩-⟨x⟩, ⟨11⟩-343. Frontispiece and 4 plates inserted. 7⁵⁄₁₆″ full × 5″ scant.

⟨1-21⁸, 22⁴⟩.

S cloth: green. A color print of Nedra pasted to the front cover.

"In spare moments at the editorial office ⟨from *ca.* 1893–1901⟩ he wrote a romance, *Pootoo's Gods,* which at first sold poorly, but later, under the new title of *Nedra,* became a season's success."––– DAB. Sold only in periodical form under the title *Pootoo's Gods?*

On copyright page: *Published September, 1905* The statement is present in all examined copies including Grosset & Dunlap reprints.

Advertised and noted for Sept. 16 PW Sept. 2, 1905. Advertised for Sept. 16 PW Sept. 9, 1905. Advertised as *published to-day* PW Sept. 16, 1905. Advertised as published Sept. 16 PW Sept. 23, 1905. A copy of *State A* in H inscribed by early owner Sept. 27, 1905. Listed PW Sept. 30, 1905.

AAS (A) H (A,B) ISL (B) Y (B)

13510. . . . The Foolish Almanack for the Year of 1906 . . .

. . . Boston and London . . . John W. Luce and Company . . . 1905.

At head of title: *Vox Gallinae Mariti!*

Cloth, printed paper labels.

According to the foreword McCutcheon co-authored this publication.

Deposited Nov. 14, 1905. Listed PW Dec. 9, 1905.

H NYPL Y

13511. COWARDICE COURT . . .

NEW YORK 1906 DODD MEAD & COMPANY

⟨i-iv⟩, ⟨1⟩-140. Frontispiece and 4 plates inserted. 7⁵⁄₈″ × 5⅛″.

⟨1⁶, 2-8⁸, 9², 10⁸⟩. *Signed:* ⟨-⟩², 1-8⁸, 9⁶.

Two printings noted:

1: As above.

2: ⟨1-9⁸⟩. *Signed:* ⟨-⟩², 1-8⁸, 9⁶.

S cloth: green-gray. Oval portrait of the heroine, in colors, pasted to front cover. White end papers printed in green-gray with hearts and quatrefoils. Top edges gilt.

Two states of the binding noted:

1: On spine: *Coward | Ice* ⟨etc.⟩ End papers decorated as described above.

2: *Cowardice | ⟨etc.⟩* End papers unprinted.

Advertised for spring PW March 17, 1906. Noted for the *28th inst.* PW March 17, 1906. Noted for *this week* PW March 31, 1906. On copyright page: *Published March, 1906* Listed PW April 7, 1906. *Was published on March 31st*———PW April 7, 1906. The third edition advertised in PW April 21, 1906; BAL has identified two printings only.

AAS (1st) H (2nd) NYPL (1st) IU (1st) UV (2nd) Y (1st)

13512. JANE CABLE . . .

NEW YORK   DODD, MEAD & COMPANY   1906

⟨i-viii⟩, ⟨1⟩-336. Frontispiece and 4 plates inserted. 7⅜″ × 5¹⁄₁₆″.

⟨1-21⁸, 22⁴⟩.

S cloth: blue. Color print of the heroine pasted to front cover.

The author's personal copy in IU inscribed by him *published today . . . September 15, 1906. Published to-day*———PW Sept. 15, 1906. Noted for *this week* PW Sept. 15, 1906. BA copy received Sept. 19, 1906. Listed PW Sept. 22, 1906. ". . . The publishers found it necessary to print and bind a second large edition before publication . . ."———PW Sept. 22, 1906; BAL has recognized but one printing only. On copyright page: *Published September, 1906* The London (Richards) printing listed Ath June 8, 1907.

AAS BA H NYPL Y

13513. The Foolish Almanack for Anuthur Year . . .

John W. Luce and Company   Boston   1906 London

Cloth, paper labels.

"By that coterie of humorists . . . whose *Foolish Almanac* last year was such a tremendous success." ———Advertisement, PW Sept. 29, 1906, which offered the publication for Oct. 15, 1906. For comment on authorship see *The Foolish Almanack for . . . 1906*, above.

Deposited Nov. 21, 1906.

H

13514. THE FLYERS . . .

NEW YORK   1907   DODD MEAD & COMPANY

⟨i-viii⟩, ⟨1⟩-127. Frontispiece and 4 plates inserted. 7¾″ × 5⅛″ full.

⟨1⁴, 2-9⁸⟩.

S cloth: gray-blue. Color print of the heroine pasted to front cover. White end papers imprinted in gray-blue-green with decorations. Top edges gilt.

Advertised for *spring* PW March 16, 1907. Published March 23, 1907; author's inscription in the Y copy. *Published to-day*———PW March 23, 1907. Noted as *just ready* PW March 23, 1907. Deposited March 25, 1907. *Published March, 1907*———on copyright page. Listed PW April 13, 1907.

AAS H NYPL Y

13515. THE DAUGHTER OF ANDERSON CROW . . .

NEW YORK   DODD, MEAD AND COMPANY   1907

⟨iii⟩-⟨viii⟩, ⟨1⟩-346. Frontispiece and 14 plates inserted, other illustrations in text. 7⅜″ × 5″ scant.

⟨1-22⁸⟩.

S cloth: gray-blue. Color print of heroine pasted to front cover.

Noted for Sept. 14 PW Aug. 24, 1907; PW Aug. 31, 1907. Advertised for *to-day* PW Sept. 14, 1907. Noted for *to-day* PW Sept. 14, 1907. BA copy received Sept. 18, 1907. Listed PW Sept. 21, 1907. Advertised *now ready* PW Sept. 21, 1907. *Published September, 1907*———on copyright page. *Another edition* advertised in PW Nov. 2, 1907; BAL has identified one printing only. The London (Hodder & Stoughton) edition listed Ath Sept. 28, 1907.

AAS H IHS UV Y

13516. THE HUSBANDS OF EDITH . . .

NEW YORK   1908   DODD, MEAD & COMPANY

⟨i-viii⟩, 1-⟨127⟩. Frontispiece and 4 plates inserted. 7⅝″ × 5⅛″.

⟨-⟩⁴, 1-8⁸.

S cloth: gray. Portrait, in color, pasted to front cover. White end papers printed in gray-green with lion's-heads and theatrical masks. Top edges gilt.

Advertised for *spring* PW March 21, 1908. Noted for *April 28* PW April 18, 1908; PW April 25, 1908. *Published April, 1908* on copyright page. Listed PW May 2, 1908.

AAS H NYPL UV Y

13517. THE MAN FROM BRODNEY'S . . .

NEW YORK   DODD, MEAD & COMPANY   1908

⟨i⟩-⟨viii⟩, ⟨1⟩-355, 2 blank leaves, the second of

which is used as a pastedown. Frontispiece and 3 plates inserted. $7\frac{3}{8}'' \times 4\frac{15}{16}''$ full.

⟨1-23⁸⟩.

S cloth: orange. Color print pasted to front cover. White wove end papers at front; at back leaves ⟨23⟩₇₋₈ used as end papers.

Author's personal copy (Y) inscribed by McCutcheon . . . *published today . . . September 12, 1908.* Noted for *to-day* PW Sept. 12, 1908. Listed PW Sept. 26, 1908. *Published September, 1908* on copyright page. *3rd large edition on press*–––PW Dec. 5, 1908; BAL has noted a single printing only. The London (Hodder & Stoughton) edition listed Ath Oct. 31, 1908.

AAS H UV Y

13518. An Account of the Proceedings on the Occasion of the Fourth Annual Banquet of the Indiana Society of Chicago . . . December the Eleventh Nineteen Hundred and Eight . . .

Prepared for the Personal Use of the Members of the Society, under the Supervision of John T. McCutcheon Historian of the Indiana Society of Chicago ⟨1908? 1909?⟩

Printed paper wrapper.

Address, pp. 8-12.

JFD

13519. THE ALTERNATIVE . . .

NEW YORK: 1909 DODD, MEAD & COMPANY

⟨i-viii⟩, 1-⟨120⟩. Frontispiece and 3 plates inserted. $7\frac{1}{2}''$ full $\times 5\frac{1}{8}''$ full.

⟨1-8⁸⟩. *Signed* ⟨-⟩⁴, 1-7⁸, 8⁴.

S cloth: gray. Two diamond-shaped halftones, in color, pasted to front cover. White end papers printed in gray-green with decorations. Top edges gilt.

Advertised for *April* PW Feb. 27, 1909. Advertised as *soon* PW March 20, 1909. Published April 10, 1909 according to author's inscription in his personal copy in Y. Deposited April 12, 1909. Listed PW April 17, 1909. *Published, April, 1909* on copyright page.

AAS BA H NYPL Y

13520. TRUXTON KING   A STORY OF GRAUSTARK . . .

NEW YORK DODD, MEAD & COMPANY 1909

According to contemporary notices and advertisements (see publication notes below) there were five printings in 1909; BAL has identified three:

A

⟨i-xii⟩, ⟨1⟩-369, blank leaf. $7\frac{3}{8}'' \times 4\frac{7}{8}''$. Frontispiece and four plates inserted.

⟨1-24⁸⟩.

Leaf ⟨1⟩₆ (the list of illustrations) is an integral leaf; and, lists frontispiece and four plates. Country of origin statement not present on the copyright page. Copyright notice not present on either the inserted plates or the color print pasted to the front cover.

B

⟨i-xii⟩, ⟨1⟩-369, blank leaf. $7\frac{3}{8}''$ scant $\times 4\frac{7}{8}''$. Frontispiece and three plates inserted.

⟨1-24⁸⟩.

Leaf ⟨1⟩₆ (the list of illustrations) is a cancel and lists frontispiece and three plates. Country of origin statement not present on the copyright page. Copyright notice present (in some copies) on the color print pasted to the front cover; not present on the inserted plates.

C

⟨i-xii⟩, ⟨1⟩-369, blank leaf. $7\frac{5}{16}''$ full $\times 4\frac{7}{8}''$. Frontispiece and three plates inserted. On copyright page: *Printed In U.S.A.* Copyright notice on the color print pasted to the front cover and on each of the inserted plates.

S cloth: gray. *Note:* The earliest form of the binding does not have a copyright notice on the color print pasted to the front.

Noted for *next month* PW Aug. 14, 1909. Advertised and noted for *today* PW Sept. 11, 1909. Deposited Sept. 13, 1909. Listed PW Sept. 18, 1909. *Second edition started 5 days before publication*–––PW Sept. 25, 1909. On copyright page: *Published, September, 1909* A fifth edition advertised PW Jan. 1, 1910. The London (Everett) edition listed Bkr April 8, 1910.

AAS (*Printing B*, first binding)   H (*Printing B*, later binding)   Y (*Printing A*, first binding; *Printing C*, later binding)

13521. THE BUTTERFLY MAN . . .

NEW YORK DODD, MEAD & COMPANY 1910

⟨1⟩-121, blank leaf. Frontispiece and 3 plates inserted. $7\frac{9}{16}'' \times 5\frac{1}{8}''$ full.

⟨1⟩-7⁸, 8⁶.

C cloth: lavender. White end papers printed in lavender with butterflies, flowers, panels. *Also:* Unprinted end papers; sequence, if any, not known. Top edges gilt.

Published May 7, 1910, according to author's inscription in his personal copy (Y). Listed PW May 7, 1910. Advertised and noted for *today* PW May

7, 1910. Deposited May 9, 1910. *Published, May, 1910*---on copyright page.

AAS   BA   H   Y

13522. THE ROSE IN THE RING . . .

NEW YORK   DODD, MEAD AND COMPANY   1910

⟨iii⟩-⟨viii⟩, ⟨1⟩-425. Frontispiece and 3 plates inserted. 7⁵⁄₁₆″ × 5″.

⟨1-27⁸⟩. *Signed:* ⟨-⟩³, 1-11, ⟨12⟩, 13-26⁸, 27⁵.

C cloth: red.

Advertised for fall publication PW Aug. 13, 1910. Noted for Sept. 16 PW Aug. 20, 1910; PW Sept. 3, 1910; PW Sept. 10, 1910. Advertised for *today* PW Sept. 17, 1910. Listed PW Sept. 24, 1910. *Published, September, 1910* on copyright page. The London (Everett) edition listed Bkr Oct. 7, 1910.

AAS   H   IHS   Y

13523. BROOD HOUSE   A PLAY IN FOUR ACTS . . .

PRIVATELY PRINTED   NEW YORK, MCMX

Title-page in black and brown.

⟨i-iv⟩, ⟨1⟩-187. Wove paper watermarked *Old Stratford USA.* 9⁷⁄₁₆″ × 6³⁄₈″.

⟨1², 2-12⁸, 13⁶⟩.

Printed brown laid paper boards sides, white imitation vellum shelf back and corners. Sunburst end papers faintly tinted with brown and orange. Top edges gilt. Flyleaf at front.

Seventy-Five Copies . . . Printed For Private Distribution . . .---P. ⟨ii⟩.

Deposited Oct. 29, 1910. Copies have been seen inscribed by the author *October, 1910.* Listed PW Dec. 3, 1910.

AAS   B   UV   Y

13524. . . . "What's His Name" . . .

⟨New York: The New York Herald, 1910–1911⟩

Cover-title. At head of title: *The New York Herald. Special Fiction Section . . .*

9 eight-page parts. Printed self-wrappers. Issued weekly, Sunday, Dec. 25, 1910-Feb. 19, 1911. Also issued by other periodicals?

For book publication see next entry.

NYU

13525. WHAT'S-HIS-NAME . . .

NEW YORK . . . 1911

See preceding entry.

Two states of the imprint have been seen; sequence not determined. The designations are for identification only.

IMPRINT A

NEW YORK / DODD, MEAD AND COMPANY / 1911 /

IMPRINT B

NEW YORK / DODD, MEAD & COMPANY / 1911 /

⟨i-x⟩, ⟨1⟩-243, blank leaf. Frontispiece and 3 plates inserted. 7⁵⁄₁₆″ × 4¹⁵⁄₁₆″.

⟨1-16⁸⟩.

C cloth: orange-red; noted only on *Imprint A* copies. T cloth: orange-red; noted on *Imprint B* copies only.

To be published at an early date---PW Feb. 25, 1911. Advertised as *new* PW March 18, 1911. *Published March, 1911* on copyright page. Advertised as *ready*---*at last* PW April 8, 1911. Listed PW April 8, 1911. BA copy (*Imprint A*) received April 12, 1911.

AAS (Imprint B)   BA (Imprint A)   H (Imprint A)
ISL (Imprint B)   Y (Imprint A)

13526. MARY MIDTHORNE . . .

NEW YORK   DODD, MEAD AND COMPANY   1911

⟨i-viii⟩, 1-439. Frontispiece and 3 plates inserted. 7¼″ × 5″.

⟨1-28⁸⟩.

S cloth: blue-gray. Colored halftone pasted to front cover.

According to McCutcheon's inscription in his personal copy in Y published Sept. 16, 1911. Listed PW Sept. 16, 1911. On copyright page: *Published, September, 1911* The London (Bell) edition, prepared for export to the British colonies advertised without comment Bkr Feb. 7, 1913. The London (Everett) edition, with *Published, September, 1911,* on the reverse of the title-page appears to have been first issued in 1913; listed Bkr March 7, 1913.

AAS   H   Y

13527. HER WEIGHT IN GOLD . . .

INDIANAPOLIS THE BOBBS-MERRILL CO. PUBLISHERS ⟨1911⟩

For trade publication see next entry.

⟨i-viii⟩, 1-⟨78⟩, blank leaf. 7″ scant × 4¼″.

⟨1⁴, 2-6⁸⟩.

T cloth: red.

Also noted in limp leather with inserted general title-leaf: *Volume V The Hoosier Set Special Limited Edition in Twelve Volumes . . . This title page is signed by the Author and this volume is one of Set No. . . .*

The Indiana Society of Chicago 1912 Copy in Y. According to a letter from Miss Martha E. Wright, Indiana State Library, Sept. 22, 1970, to BAL, "this was a part of The Hoosier Set, 'a souvenir set of twelve volumes of original stories, poems, etc. by Hoosier authors, presented to each member and guest at the seventh annual dinner of the society, December 9, 1911'."

AAS   B   H   IU

13528. HER WEIGHT IN GOLD . . .

NEW YORK DODD, MEAD AND COMPANY 1912

First trade edition. For prior publication see preceding entry.

⟨i-ii⟩, ⟨1⟩-⟨121⟩, 2 blank leaves. Illustrated. 7¼″ × 4¾″.

⟨1-8⁸⟩.

C cloth: red.

Noted for April 27 PW April 20, 1912. *Published today* PW April 27, 1912. Deposited April 30, 1912. *Published April, 1912* on copyright page. Listed PW May 11, 1912.

Johnson (1941) reports "reissued, *New York, 1914,* with added material." No such extended edition found by BAL or otherwise reported.

AAS   IHS   NYPL   Y

13529. THE HOLLOW OF HER HAND

COPYRIGHT ISSUE

THE HOLLOW OF HER HAND . . .

NEW YORK DODD, MEAD AND COMPANY 1912

⟨i-x⟩, ⟨1⟩-422. Frontispiece and 4 plates inserted. 7¼″ × 4¹⁵⁄₁₆″.

⟨1-27⁸⟩. ⟨1⟩₁ is a cancel.

The statement *Published, September, 1912* does not appear on the copyright page.

T cloth: red. The publisher's spine imprint stamped from capital letters.

Deposited June 26, 1912. A copy in IU bearing McCutcheon's bookplate is inscribed in an unknown hand: "Copy Number 2 of an edition of six copies issued June 26th 1912, antedating the trade edition for copyright purposes. Dodd Mead & Co." Also inscribed by McCutcheon: "This book was published today . . . June 26, 1912."

PUBLISHED EDITION

Title-page, pagination, signature collation, as above, save for the title-leaf which is an integral leaf, not a cancel. On the copyright page: *Published, September, 1912* The publisher's spine imprint is stamped from capitals and lower case letters, not capitals only.

Note: Because the title-leaf in the copyright issue is a cancel it seems likely that the sheets of the trade edition were used for copyright deposit by cancelling the original title-leaf and inserting the cancel leaf lacking the statement *Published, September, 1912* If this is correct then the sequence is:

1: Published edition printed.

2: Six copies of the preceding prepared with cancel title-leaf for purposes of copyright.

3: Published edition issued.

4: Large-paper edition printed during the month of September, 1912.

To be published September 27th and ⟨sic⟩ just published PW Sept. 21, 1912. *Ready!* ---PW Sept. 28, 1912. Y copy stamped *Oct. 1, 1912.* Listed PW Oct. 5, 1912. According to the *English Catalogue of Books* the London (Collins) printing was issued in 1917.

LARGE PAPER EDITION

Title-page in black and orange; title-pages of copyright and published issues printed in black only.

⟨i-xii⟩, ⟨1⟩-422, blank leaf. Printed on Japanese vellum. Frontispiece and 4 plates, each with printed tissue, inserted. 9⅛″ × 6⅛″.

⟨1-27⁸, 28²⟩.

Orange paper boards, white vegetable vellum shelf back and corners, goldstamped. End papers of book stock.

"Twenty-five copies . . . on Imperial Japan Vellum were printed September, 1912, for private circulation. This is number . . ." ---P. ⟨ii⟩.

On copyright page: *Published, September, 1912*

Published Sept. 27, 1912, according to the author's inscription in his own copy in Y.

AAS (trade)   IHS (trade)   IU (copyright issue) UV (trade; large-paper)   Y (trade; large-paper)

13530. The Morris Book Shop Impressions of Some Old Friends in Celebration of the xxvth Anniversary

Chicago ⟨The Morris Book Shop⟩ 1912

Contains "A Letter."

For comment see entry No. 5799.

13531. The Hoosier Almanack and Family Magazine Containing Much Valuable Meteorological and Historical Information, together with Many Highly Interesting Literary Contributions

⟨Chicago: W. B. Conkey Company, The Hammond Press⟩ Indiana Society of Chicago 1912

Pictorial paper wrapper.

"Narcissus," p. 98.

Issued under date of Dec. 7, 1912. On front cover: ". . . A Souvenir of the Eighth Annual Banquet of the Indiana Society of Chicago."

Y

13532. A FOOL AND HIS MONEY

LARGE PAPER FORMAT

A FOOL AND HIS MONEY . . .

NEW YORK DODD, MEAD AND COMPANY 1913

Title-page in black and orange.

⟨i-x⟩, ⟨1⟩-373. Frontispiece and nine mounted plates inserted, each with a printed tissue. Paper watermarked *Arches (France)* $9^{15}/_{16}$" × $6^{1}/_{2}$".

⟨1-24^8⟩.

Printed green-gray laid paper boards sides, white vegetable vellum shelf back and corners. End papers of book stock.

This First Edition of Fifty Copies . . . printed September, 1913, for private circulation. This is Number . . . ––– Certificate of issue.

TRADE FORMAT

Title-page in black only.

⟨i-x⟩, 1-373. Frontispiece and 4 plates inserted. $7^{3}/_{8}$" × 5" scant.

⟨1-24^8⟩.

CM cloth: red. Two states of the binding have been noted. The sequence has not been established and the designations are for identification only.

BINDING A

Stamped in white and blind. The author's personal copy in Y thus.

BINDING B

Stamped in gold and blind.

On copyright page: *Published, September, 1913*

Trade format noted for Sept. 13 PW Sept. 6, 1913. The trade format published Sept. 13, 1913, according to the author's inscription in his personal copy in Y. Trade format listed PW Sept. 27, 1913.

AAS (trade, *Binding B*) H (trade, *Binding B*) IU (large paper) Y (large paper; trade, *Binding A*)

13533. BLACK IS WHITE . . .

NEW YORK DODD, MEAD AND COMPANY 1914

⟨i-x⟩, 1-389. Frontispiece and three plates inserted. $7^{5}/_{16}$" × $4^{7}/_{8}$" full.

⟨1-25^8⟩.

V cloth: gray.

To be published on March 14th–––PW March 7, 1914. According to the author's inscription in his personal copy (in Y) published March 14, 1914. BA copy received March 17, 1914. Listed PW March 21, 1914. On copyright page: *Published, March, 1914* The London (Everett) edition listed Bkr May 28, 1915.

AAS H UV Y

13534. THE PRINCE OF GRAUSTARK

ADVANCE PRINTING

THE PRINCE OF GRAUSTARK . . .

NEW YORK DODD, MEAD AND COMPANY 1914

Title-page in black only.

⟨i-x⟩, 1-394. $7^{1}/_{4}$" scant × $4^{15}/_{16}$". *Not illustrated.*

⟨1-25^8, 26^2⟩.

Printed off-white paper wrapper.

On wrapper: *. . . To be published September 12th. Completed book will have 404 pages . . .*

On copyright page: *Published, September, 1914*

The only located copy inscribed by the author: "This copy . . . was issued May 29, 1914, for reviewers and salespeople and lacks the illustrations, which were not finished at the time. May 29, 1914 . . ."

LARGE PAPER FORMAT

Title-page in black and orange.

⟨i-xii⟩, 1-394, blank leaf. Watermarked *Arches (France)*. Frontispiece and 4 plates, each with a printed protective tissue, inserted. $10^{1}/_{16}$" full × $6^{5}/_{8}$". The frontispiece and illustrations are mounted on inserted leaves of book stock.

⟨1-25^8, 26^4⟩.

Printed brown laid paper boards, white vegetable vellum shelf back and corners. End papers of book stock.

On copyright page: *Published, September, 1914*

This First Edition of Forty Copies . . . was printed September, 1914 . . . This is Number . . . ⟨*signed*⟩ *George Barr McCutcheon, August* ⟨*sic*⟩ *27, 1914*––– Certificate of issue.

TRADE FORMAT

Title-page in black only.

⟨i-x⟩, 1-394. Frontispiece and 3 plates inserted. $7^{7}/_{16}$" × $4^{7}/_{8}$".

⟨1-25^8, 26^2⟩.

Coarse B cloth: green-blue. Color print pasted to front cover.

On copyright page: *Published, September, 1914*

Listed PW Sept. 12, 1914. Noted for *today* PW Sept. 12, 1914.

AAS (trade) H (trade) IU (large paper) NYPL (trade) Y (advance; large paper; trade)

13535. MR. BINGLE ...

NEW YORK DODD, MEAD AND COMPANY 1915

⟨i-x⟩, 1-357. Frontispiece and 4 plates inserted. $7\frac{3}{8}'' \times 4\frac{7}{8}''$.

⟨1-23⁸⟩.

Rough-grained B cloth: blue-gray. Spine imprint: *Dodd, Mead & Company.*

Note: Also occurs in a remainder format with the spine imprint of *A. L. Burt Company;* frontispiece only; list of illustrations excised.

Listed PW Sept. 18, 1915. Deposited Sept. 22, 1915. The London (Nash) edition listed Bkr Aug. 1916.

AAS H NYPL Y (also remainder)

13536. THE LIGHT THAT LIES ...

NEW YORK DODD, MEAD AND COMPANY 1916

⟨i-vi⟩, 1-121. Frontispiece and 4 plates inserted. $7\frac{1}{2}'' \times 5\frac{3}{16}''$.

⟨1-8⁸⟩.

Two binding issues noted; the following sequence is presumed correct:

BINDING A

B cloth: blue. Lettered in gold. The following is sufficient for identification; spine lettered: The / Light / That / Lies / ⟨rule⟩ / McCutcheon / DODD, MEAD / AND / COMPANY

BINDING B

V cloth (size-dyed): blue. Lettered in blue. The following is sufficient for identification; spine lettered: The / Light That / Lies / ⟨rule⟩ / McCutcheon / Dodd Mead / & Company

A copy in UV (*Binding A*) inscribed by McCutcheon April 15, 1916. Listed PW April 15, 1916. Deposited April 18, 1916. The London (Jenkins) edition listed Bkr Nov. 1917.

AAS (*Binding A*) BA (*Binding A*) H (*Binding A*) NYPL (*Binding A; Binding B*) UV (*Binding A*) Y (*Binding A*)

13537. FROM THE HOUSETOPS ...

NEW YORK DODD, MEAD AND COMPANY 1916

⟨i-vi⟩, 1-442. Frontispiece and 4 plates inserted. $7\frac{7}{16}'' \times 4\frac{7}{8}''$.

⟨1-28⁸⟩.

B cloth: green.

Advertised for *today* PW Sept. 16, 1916. Listed PW Sept. 23, 1916. The London (Nash) edition listed Bkr March, 1917.

AAS Y

13538. The Day of the Dog ⟨and other stories⟩ ...

New York Charles Scribner's Sons 1916

Reprint.

H Y

13539. First Annual Run-in and Get-together of Former Indiana Newspaper Men

The National Press Club Washington, D. C. February 27, 1916

Printed paper wrapper.

Fifteen-line greeting, p. ⟨3⟩.

JFD

13540. GREEN FANCY ...

NEW YORK DODD, MEAD AND COMPANY 1917

⟨i⟩-⟨viii⟩, 1-355. Frontispiece inserted. $7\frac{5}{16}'' \times 5''$ scant.

⟨1-22⁸, 23⁶⟩.

B cloth: green.

Advertised for *today* PW Sept. 8, 1917. Listed PW Sept. 8, 1917. Deposited Sept. 11, 1917. The London (Hodder & Stoughton) edition listed Bkr June, 1918.

AAS H NYPL UV Y

13541. For France ...

Garden City New York Doubleday, Page & Company MCMXVII

"Courage," pp. 15-20. A set of proof sheets with title-page: *Courage ... First Proofs from the Printer New York July, 1917* is in Y; presumably prepared for the author's use.

For fuller entry see No. 485.

13542. ... Defenders of Democracy ... Edited by the Gift Book Committee of the Militia of Mercy ...

New York: John Lane Company London: John Lane, The Bodley Head MCMXVIII

"Pour la Patrie," pp. 275-285.

Deposited Dec. 6, 1917. For fuller entry see No. 9856.

13543. ... A PICTURE OF YOU ... ⟨text, set in two columns⟩

Single cut sheet. Printed on recto only. 12″ × 4⅞″. Prepared as copy for the use of editors.

At head of title: *Exclusive Service of The Vigilantes Release April 28* ⟨*1918*⟩

JFD

13544. SHOT WITH CRIMSON . . .

NEW YORK DODD, MEAD AND COMPANY 1918

⟨i-viii⟩, 1-161, blank leaf. Frontispiece and 3 plates inserted. 7⁷⁄₁₆″ × 5″.

⟨1-10⁸, 11⁶⟩.

B cloth: tan.

Deposited May 21, 1918. Listed PW May 25, 1918. The London (Jenkins) edition listed by Ath May 14, 1920.

AAS H NYPL Y

13545. OF WHAT ARE WE THINKING?

Two printings noted: sequence, if any, not determined. The designations are for identification only.

PRINTING A

. . . OF WHAT ARE WE THINKING? . . . ⟨text, set in one column⟩

Single cut sheet. Printed on recto only. 15½″ × 2⅝″ scant. Prepared as copy for the use of editors.

At head of title: *Exclusive Service of The Vigilantes Release July 28* ⟨*1918*⟩

PRINTING B

BY THE VIGILANTES ARTICLES ON THE WAR AND SUBJECTS RELATING THERE-TO BY THE BEST KNOWN AUTHORS AND WRITERS IN THE UNITED STATES. A PAGE WILL BE ISSUED EVERY THREE WEEKS. PRICE, $1.50 FOR USE OF PLATES.

WESTERN NEWSPAPER UNION ATLANTA . . . ⟨n.d., 1918?⟩

Single cut sheet. Printed on recto only. 22″ × 15¼″. Printed in six columns. Column 2: "Of What Are We Thinking?," by McCutcheon; the other five columns by others.

JFD (A) Y (B)

13546. THE CITY OF MASKS . . .

NEW YORK DODD, MEAD AND COMPANY 1918

⟨i-vi⟩, 1-314. Frontispiece inserted. 7⅜″ scant × 4⅞″ full.

⟨1-20⁸⟩.

B cloth: green. Front end papers printed in colors with a drawing-room scene; back end papers printed in colors with a kitchen scene.

Advertised for Sept. 14, 1918, PW Aug. 31, 1918. Published Sept. 14, 1918, according to author's inscription in his personal copy in IU. Listed PW Sept. 14, 1918. Deposited Sept. 19, 1918. For London printing see *The Court of New York*, 1919, *below.*

AAS H IU Y

13547. . . . THE LIVING MONUMENT . . . ⟨text, set in one column⟩

Single cut sheet. Printed on recto only. 14½″ × 2¾″. Prepared as copy for the use of editors.

At head of title: *Exclusive Service of The Vigilantes Release November 24* ⟨*1918*⟩

JFD

13548. ONE SCORE AND TEN A COMEDY IN FOUR ACTS . . .

THIRTY COPIES OF THIS EDITION HAVE BEEN PRINTED, BUT NOT PUBLISHED, FOR THE AUTHOR NEW YORK 1919

⟨i-viii⟩, 1-248. Paper watermarked *Flemish Book.* 9½″ × 6⁵⁄₁₆″.

⟨1-16⁸⟩.

Blue-gray paper boards. White paper boards. Printed blue paper label on spine.

A set of advance sheets (in Y) inscribed by McCutcheon July 3, 1919. McCutcheon's personal copy (in Y) inscribed by him *18 July 1919.* Deposited July 24, 1919.

AAS LC Y

13549. SHERRY . . .

NEW YORK DODD, MEAD AND COMPANY 1919

⟨i-viii⟩, 1-374, blank leaf. Frontispiece inserted. 7⅜″ × 4⅞″ full.

⟨1-24⁸⟩.

B cloth: gray.

Published Sept. 13, 1919, according to author's inscription in the IU copy. Deposited Sept. 16, 1919. Listed PW Sept. 20, 1919.

AAS H IU Y

13550. The Court of New York . . .

London: Andrew Melrose Ltd. 3 York Street, Covent Garden, W.C. 2 1919 ⟨*i.e.,* 1920⟩

Reprint of *The City of Masks*, 1918, above.

In a letter to BAL Oct. 20, 1953, the publishers state that the book was issued on May 11, 1920 and that they cannot explain the date 1919 on the title-page. According to *The English Catalogue* issued in April, 1920. Received at BMU May 11, 1920. Listed Bkr June, 1920.

Y

13551. ANDERSON CROW DETECTIVE...

NEW YORK DODD, MEAD AND COMPANY 1920

⟨i-x⟩, ⟨1⟩-353, 2 blank leaves. Frontispiece and 23 plates inserted. 7⅜″ scant × 4⅞″ full.

⟨1-23⁸⟩.

B cloth: green.

Published March 20, 1920, according to an inscription in the author's personal copy (in JFD). Deposited March 23, 1920. Listed PW April 3, 1920.

AAS   H   JFD   Y

13552. WEST WIND DRIFT...

NEW YORK DODD, MEAD AND COMPANY 1920

Two printings noted:

FIRST PRINTING

⟨i-x⟩, 1-368, 3 blank leaves. 7⅜″ × 5″ scant.

⟨1-24⁸⟩.

SECOND PRINTING

⟨i-vi⟩, 1-368, blank leaf.

⟨1-23⁸, 24⁴⟩.

Two bindings noted:

BINDING A

V cloth: blue. Spine imprint: DODD, MEAD / & COMPANY

BINDING B

V cloth: gray. Spine imprint: DODD, MEAD & / COMPANY

Advertised for Oct. 23 PW Oct. 2, 1920. Listed PW Oct. 2, 1920. Advertised for Oct. 23 PW Oct. 9, 1920. Published Oct. 23, 1920, according to the author's inscription in his personal copy (in Y). Deposited Oct. 27, 1920. The London (Nash) edition listed Bkr May, 1921.

AAS (2nd, *Binding B*) H (1st, *Binding A*) NYPL (1st, *Binding A*) Y (1st, *Binding A*)

13553. QUILL'S WINDOW...

NEW YORK DODD, MEAD AND COMPANY 1921

⟨i-viii⟩, 1-335. Frontispiece inserted. 7⅜″ × 5″.

⟨1-21⁸, 22⁴⟩.

B cloth: gray.

Advertised for Sept. 17 PW Sept. 10, 1921. Advertised for *today* PW Sept. 17, 1921. Deposited

Sept. 20, 1921. Listed PW Sept. 24, 1921. The London (Nash & Grayson) edition listed NA Jan. 21, 1922.

AAS   H   IHS   Y

13554. My Maiden Effort Being the Personal Confessions of Well-Known American Authors as to Their Literary Beginnings with an Introduction by Gelett Burgess

Published for the Authors' League of America by Doubleday, Page & Company Garden City, N.Y., and Toronto 1921

Contribution, pp. 171-174.

For fuller entry see No. 9358.

13555. The Second Book of the Authors Club Liber Scriptorum...

New York Published by the Authors Club MCMXXI

"How I Retired from the Stage," pp. 339-351.

For fuller entry see No. 7057.

13556. YOLLOP...

NEW YORK DODD, MEAD AND COMPANY 1922

⟨i-x⟩, 1-112, 3 blank leaves. Frontispiece inserted. 7⅜″ plus × 5⅛″.

⟨1-8⁸⟩.

T cloth: gray.

A copy in AAS presented by McCutcheon to Booth Tarkington Feb. 25, 1922. Deposited Feb. 28, 1922. Listed PW March 4, 1922.

AAS   H   NYPL   Y

13557. VIOLA GWYN

LARGE PAPER FORMAT

VIOLA GWYN...

NEW YORK DODD, MEAD AND COMPANY 1922

Title-page in black and red.

⟨i-viii⟩, 1-378. Laid paper watermarked *Old Stratford USA*. Frontispiece, with printed protective tissue, tipped to p. ⟨iv⟩. 9⁹⁄₁₆″ × 6¼″.

⟨1⁹, 2-24⁸⟩. Leaf ⟨1⟩₂ inserted.

Printed brown sunburst paper boards, white vegetable vellum shelf back and corners. White laid paper end papers.

This First Edition of Fifty Copies...was printed September, 1922, for private circulation. This is Number...---P. ⟨ii⟩.

TRADE FORMAT

Title-page in black only.

⟨i-vi⟩, 1-378. Frontispiece inserted. $7\frac{3}{8}'' \times 5\frac{1}{8}''$.
⟨1-24⁸⟩.

CM cloth: green-blue.

Advertised for Sept. 9, 1922 PW July 15, 1922; Aug. 19, 1922. According to McCutcheon's inscription in his own copy (in Y) published Sept. 9, 1922. Listed PW Sept. 9, 1922. Deposited Sept. 13, 1922. The London (Nash & Grayson) edition listed Bkr Dec. 1922.

AAS (large paper; trade) H (trade) NYPL (trade) UV (large paper) Y (large paper; trade)

13558. ... Norfolk Daily Prune A Journalistic Spasm

Vol. 1---No. 1---Never Again! Norfolk, Conn., Sunday, September 10, 1922. Price One Dollar

Caption-title. At head of title: *First Edition* Title flanked by *Weather ... More Weather ...*

A burlesque newspaper. McCutcheon listed as a contributing editor, p. 2.

"Under a Cloud or Love Will Find a Way If Necessary," by McCutcheon, p. 4.

Y

13559. OLIVER OCTOBER ...

NEW YORK DODD, MEAD AND COMPANY 1923

⟨i-viii⟩, 1-337, blank leaf. $7\frac{3}{8}''$ full $\times 5\frac{1}{8}''$.
⟨1-21⁸, 22⁶⟩.

B cloth: green.

Published Aug. 23, 1923, according to the author's inscription in his personal copy (IU). Deposited Aug. 30, 1923. BA copy received Sept. 29, 1923. Advertised for *today* PW Oct. 25, 1923. Listed PW Oct. 25, 1923. The London (Harrap) edition listed PC May 10, 1924.

AAS BA H IU NYPL Y

13560. Anthony, the Joker by George Barr McCutcheon A Great Man's Wife by Booth Tarkington The Unpresentable Appearance of Col. Crane by G. K. Chesterton

Blue Ribbon Fiction ⟨n.p., Chicago, 1924⟩

"Anthony, the Joker," pp. 7-39.

Binder's title: *Three Yarns.*

Issued on the occasion of the convention of American Newspaper Publishers Association, New York, April 24–26, 1924.

H IU NYPL UV Y

13561. EAST OF THE SETTING SUN A STORY OF GRAUSTARK ...

NEW YORK DODD, MEAD AND COMPANY 1924

⟨i-vi⟩, 1-350. $7\frac{3}{8}'' \times 5\frac{1}{8}''$.
⟨1-22⁸, 23²⟩.

YR cloth: blue-gray.

Deposited Aug. 23, 1924. The author's copy in Y inscribed by him: *Advance copy issued to the Author on August 14, 1924. The date of publication ... was October 4, 1924.* Listed PW Oct. 4, 1924. After several preliminary announcements for Sept. 21 and Sept. 27, 1924 publication, the publishers finally advertised publication for Oct. 4, 1924 in PW Sept. 6, 1924. The London (Harrap) edition listed PC April 25, 1925.

AAS H Y

13562. Bobbed Hair by Twenty Authors ...

G. P. Putnam's Sons New York & London The Knickerbocker Press 1925

"Chapter Sixteen," pp. 253-273.

According to the author's inscription in his personal copy (JFD) published March 11, 1925. The London edition listed PC May 23, 1925.

H

13563. ROMEO IN MOON VILLAGE ...

NEW YORK DODD, MEAD AND COMPANY 1925

⟨i⟩-⟨viii⟩, 1-344. $7\frac{3}{8}'' \times 5\frac{1}{8}''$.
⟨1-22⁸⟩.

V cloth: blue-gray.

Advertised for Sept. 19 PW Sept. 12, 1925. Deposited Sept. 24, 1925. Listed PW Sept. 26, 1925. The London (Nash & Grayson) edition listed PC Feb. 27, 1926.

AAS H IHS Y

13564. KINDLING AND ASHES ...

LARGE PAPER EDITION

KINDLING AND ASHES, OR THE HEART OF BARBARA WAYNE ...

DODD, MEAD AND COMPANY NEW YORK 1926

Title-page in black and blue.

⟨i-iv⟩, ⟨i⟩-⟨viii⟩, 1-395. Japan vellum. $8\frac{7}{8}'' \times 6''$.
⟨1-51⁴⟩.

Blue paper boards sides, white vegetable vellum shelf back. Printed paper label on spine. Blue end papers.

*Twenty-Five Copies ... Printed For The Author, Of Which This Is No.---*Certificate of issue.

TRADE EDITION

KINDLING AND ASHES OR, THE HEART OF BARBARA WAYNE...

NEW YORK DODD, MEAD AND COMPANY 1926

Title-page in black only.

⟨i⟩-⟨viii⟩, 1-395. 7$\frac{7}{16}$″ × 5$\frac{1}{8}$″ full.

⟨1-25⁸, 26²⟩.

B cloth: black. Top edges stained orange.

Advertised for Sept. 18 PW Sept. 4, 1926. According to the author's inscription in his personal copy (in Y) published Sept. 18, 1926. Deposited Sept. 22, 1926. Listed PW Sept. 25, 1926. The London (Lane) edition listed Bkr Feb. 11, 1927.

AAS (trade) NYPL (trade) UV (trade) Y (both)

13565. THE INN OF THE HAWK AND RAVEN A TALE OF OLD GRAUSTARK ...

DODD, MEAD AND COMPANY NEW YORK 1927

⟨i-viii⟩, 1-360. 7$\frac{7}{16}$″ × 5$\frac{1}{16}$″ full.

⟨1-23⁸⟩.

B cloth: blue. Top edges stained orange; or, unstained.

Noted for July 16th PW June 25, 1927. The B copy received at the Providence Athenaeum July 13, 1927. Advertised for July 26 PW July 16, 1927. Listed PW July 23, 1927. The London (Lane) edition listed Bkr Oct. 28, 1927.

AAS B H NYPL Y

13566. BLADES ...

DODD, MEAD & COMPANY NEW YORK MCMXXVIII

⟨i-viii⟩, 1-344. 7$\frac{3}{8}$″ × 5$\frac{1}{8}$″.

⟨1-22⁸⟩.

V cloth: black.

Published Aug. 24, 1928 according to McCutcheon's inscription in his personal copy (in UV). Listed PW Aug. 25, 1928. The London (Lane) edition listed PC Oct. 27, 1928.

AAS H NYPL UV

13567. THE MERIVALES ...

NEW YORK DODD, MEAD & COMPANY 1929

⟨i-viii⟩, 1-303. 7$\frac{3}{8}$″ × 5$\frac{1}{8}$″.

⟨1-19⁸, 20⁴⟩.

B cloth: old rose. Light buff end papers printed in old rose with an all-over pattern of sickle-like ornaments and dots. Top edges stained rose.

Listed PW Sept. 7, 1929. Deposited Sept. 11, 1929.

AAS H NYPL Y

13568. BOOKS ONCE WERE MEN AN ESSAY FOR BOOKLOVERS ... WITH AN INTRODUCTION BY WILLIAM DANA ORCUTT ...

NEW YORK DODD, MEAD & COMPANY MCMXXXI

⟨i-iv⟩, ⟨i⟩-x, ⟨1⟩-61, 2 blank leaves. Illustrated. Laid paper watermarked *Warren's Olde Style.* 7$\frac{7}{8}$″ × 5$\frac{1}{2}$″.

⟨1-5⁸⟩.

Black and gray sunburst boards, veined with gold, black V cloth shelf back. Black silk ribbon marker. Gray laid end papers. Top edges gilt.

"...One thousand copies..."---Certificate of issue.

Deposited Sept. 25, 1931.

H NYPL Y

REFERENCES AND ANA

The Old Dominion; or, the Banshee of Bathurst Hall, a Comedy Drama in Five Acts.

LaFayette, Indiana, 1887.

Presumably unpublished. A title-page as above was deposited for copyright Dec. 22, 1887. No record found of text deposit.

Graustark ... a Thrilling Romance of Love and Adventure ... Advertising Plates Free ...

American Press Association New York ... ⟨and elsewhere⟩ ⟨1901?⟩

Copyright notice dated 1901 in the name of Herbert S. Stone, p. 1.

Pp. ⟨i⟩, 1-15. Text, in six columns, of *Graustark* prepared as a prospectus by the American Press Association and offered to periodicals for serial publication. Size of page 22$\frac{1}{2}$″ × 15$\frac{1}{2}$″.

P. ⟨i⟩ is devoted to promotional argument including reviews of the book which suggest that this was issued after book publication.

Beverly of Graustark ⟨Dramatized by Robert M. Baker⟩

Published September, 1914 Copyright, 1914 by Klaw & Erlanger Copyrighted in Great Britain

Printed paper wrapper.

A dramatization of *Beverly of Graustark*, 1904. Dramatist's name not present.

Deposited Oct. 6, 1914. Prepared for copyright purposes only?

Literature in the Making by Some of its Makers Presented by Joyce Kilmer

Harper & Brothers   New York and London
⟨1917⟩

"Magazines Cheapen Fiction," pp. 157-⟨166⟩,
an interview with McCutcheon.

For fuller entry see No. 11111.

Paintings in the Collection of George Barr
McCutcheon

⟨n.p., n.d., *ca.* 1920⟩

A portfolio containing a series of twenty-eight
reproductions (on 27 sheets). Contains no
material by McCutcheon.

Cover-title. Presumably prepared by or for
McCutcheon's private use. The only located
copy is in Y.

Is this perhaps related to *My Pictures?* From
what BAL has been able to determine or deduce
(on the basis of the McCutcheon archive in
JFD, in 1946) this was a privately printed
collection of forty reproductions of paintings
owned by McCutcheon, produced serially
during the years 1916–1925, in a limited edition
of 15 copies. JFD contained reproductions 39 and
40: Willard L. Metcalf's *Spring Festival* and
Homer D. Martin's *A Glimpse of the Sea.* Each
printed on the third page of a 4-page cut sheet
of Umbria handmade Italian paper with
McCutcheon's comments on the second page.
Pp. ⟨1⟩ and ⟨4⟩ blank. Folded size: 15″ full ×
10″ full.

Brewster's Millions   A Comedy in Four Acts by
Winchell Smith and Byron Ongley . . .

Duly Copyrighted As a Play, 1907 and 1925 . . .
New York: Samuel French Publisher 25 West
45th Street   London: Samuel French, Ltd.
26 Southampton Street Strand

Printed paper wrapper. Deposited March 28,
1925.

Graustark . . . A Modern Romantic Comedy by
Grace Hayward Dramatized from the Novel . . .

. . . 1926 . . . New York   Samuel French Publisher 25 West 45th Street   London   Samuel
French, Ltd. 26 Southampton Street Strand

Printed paper wrapper. Deposited Jan 3, 1927.

The Renowned Collection of First Editions of
Thomas Hardy Rudyard Kipling Robert Louis
Stevenson Formed by George Barr McCutcheon
. . .

American Art Association Inc.   Madison
Avenue 56th to 57th Street   New York . . .
⟨1925⟩

Printed paper wrapper. Printed on laid paper.
McMurtrie imprint at foot of last page.

Note: A copy in Y is printed on China paper;
printed on one side of leaf only.

Also note: Both this and *The Renowned Collection
of First Editions of Charles Dickens* . . . , New York
⟨1926⟩, see below, were reprinted on wove
paper and issued together as a single cloth-
bound volume. The reprint was produced in
1931 by the late great New York bookseller, M.
Harzof.

The Renowned Collection of First Editions of
Charles Dickens and William Makepeace
Thackeray Formed by George Barr McCutcheon
. . .

American Art Association Inc.   Madison
Avenue 56th to 57th Street   New York . . .
⟨1926⟩

Printed paper wrapper. Printed on laid paper.
McMurtrie imprint at foot of final leaf.

See preceding entry.

JAMES McHENRY

(Solomon Secondsight)

1 7 8 5 – 1 8 4 5

Do not confuse the subject of this list with James McHenry (1753–1816), a Revolutionary War soldier, Secretary of War in Washington's cabinet. He was the author of *A Letter to the Honourable the Speaker of the House of Representatives . . . 28th December, 1802*, Baltimore, 1803; and compiled the *Baltimore Directory . . . for 1807*, Baltimore, 1807.

Caution

". . . Did he ⟨James McHenry⟩ not once determine to take the general applause by storm, and on the publication of one of his unhappy novels, ⟨a footnote reveals that the novel was *O'Halloran, the Insurgent Chief, 1824*⟩ repeatedly stop the press, and cause *second*, *third*, and *fourth* editions to be inserted in the title-page of the *same* impression? Was not the *third* edition for sale at the book-stores before the *first* was bound? Was not the same system adopted with several of his other works, the plagiarized *Pleasures of Friendship*, especially? Any Philadelphia bookseller can answer these queries, much more readily than our critic would like to admit them . . ."––– "American Poets, and Their Critics" in *The Knickerbocker, or New-York Monthly Magazine*, Vol. 4, 1834, p. 24. Anonymous. The author was Willis Gaylord Clark; collected in his *Literary Remains . . .*, New York, 1844 (BAL No. 3282), pp. 288–289.

13569. THE BARD OF ERIN, AND OTHER POEMS MOSTLY NATIONAL . . .

BELFAST: PRINTED BY SMYTH & LYONS, 115, HIGH-STEET. ⟨*sic*⟩ 1808.

Not seen. Entry on the basis of a photographic copy of the title-page of the BMU copy and correspondence.

Pp. viii, 80. $5\frac{7}{8}'' \times 3\frac{1}{2}''$.

13570. PATRICK: A POETICAL TALE, FOUNDED ON INCIDENTS WHICH TOOK PLACE IN IRELAND DURING THE UNHAPPY PERIOD OF 1798 . . .

GLASGOW: PRINTED BY D M'KENZIE. 1810.

⟨i⟩-vi, ⟨7⟩-28. $7\frac{5}{8}'' \times 4\frac{13}{16}''$.

⟨-⟩², A-C⁴.

Issued in printed paper wrapper?

H

13571. THE PLEASURES OF FRIENDSHIP, A POEM, IN TWO PARTS; TO WHICH ARE ADDED A FEW ORIGINAL IRISH MELODIES . . .

PITTSBURGH: PRINTED FOR THE AUTHOR, BY EICHBAUM AND JOHNSTON, MARKET-STREET. 1822.

For other editions see under 1825, 1828, 1830 (4th and 5th editions), 1834, 1836.

⟨1⟩-72; *Errata*, p. ⟨73⟩. $7\frac{3}{4}'' \times 4\frac{3}{4}''$.

⟨1⟩-6⁶, ⟨7⟩¹.

Unprinted drab paper boards. Flyleaf at front.

Title-page deposited Dec. 14, 1821. Listed LSR May, 1822. Reviewed PF Oct. 1822, with an apology "for not having reviewed it earlier."

B H HEH

13572. WALTHAM: AN AMERICAN REVOLUTIONARY TALE. IN THREE CANTOS . . .

NEW-YORK: PUBLISHED BY E. BLISS & E. WHITE. J. W. BELL PRINTER NO. 70 BOWERY. 1823.

⟨i⟩-⟨xii⟩, ⟨13⟩-70, blank leaf. $6\frac{1}{8}'' \times 3\frac{3}{4}''$.

⟨A⟩-F⁶.

Printed green paper wrapper. White paper end papers. Flyleaf at front and at back.

Title-page deposited Feb. 1, 1823. Advertisement on outer back wrapper dated Feb. 6, 1823.

B H MHS NYPL Y

13573. THE WILDERNESS; OR BRAD-DOCK'S TIMES. A TALE OF THE WEST . . .

NEW-YORK: PUBLISHED BY E. BLISS AND E. WHITE. J. SEYMOUR, PRINTER. 1823.

2 Vols. Anonymous. See next entry.

1 : ⟨i-ii⟩, ⟨i⟩-iv, ⟨5⟩-288. 7¹³⁄₁₆″ × 4⅝″.

2 : ⟨1⟩-292.

1 : ⟨-⟩¹, ⟨A⟩-I, K-U, X-Z, 2A⁶.

2 : ⟨1⟩-24⁶, 25².

Blue paper boards. Printed paper label on spine.

Title-page deposited Feb. 21, 1823. The manuscript reviewed by M March 8, 1823, "we observe ⟨it⟩ is announced for publication in a few weeks." Reviewed M April 12, 1823. The London (Newman) edition listed BC July, 1823; advertised LG July 12, 1823; advertised LG April 10, 1824, as "reprinted from the American edition." For another printing see below under year 1848.

UV

13574. The Wilderness; or the Youthful Days of Washington. A Tale of the West. In Three Volumes. By Solomon Secondsight . . .

London: Printed for A. K. Newman and Co. Leadenhall-Street. 1823.

Reprint of the preceding entry. Paper boards?

Listed as *recent* BC July, 1823. Advertised LG July 12, 1823. Again advertised LG April 10, 1824: "reprinted from the American edition."

LC

13575. THE SPECTRE OF THE FOREST, OR, ANNALS OF THE HOUSATONIC, A NEW-ENGLAND ROMANCE. BY THE AUTHOR OF "THE WILDERNESS." . . .

NEW-YORK: E. BLISS AND E. WHITE, NO. 128 BROADWAY. JOHNSTONE & VAN NORDEN, PRINTERS. 1823.

2 Vols. *Note:* Terminal quotation marks not present in Vol. II.

1 : ⟨i⟩-⟨xviii⟩, ⟨19⟩-226, blank leaf. P. xvii mispaged xvi. 7⅛″ × 4⅜″.

2 : ⟨1⟩-244.

1 : *Signed:* ⟨-⟩², 1-18⁶, 19⁴.

2 : *Signed:* ⟨-⟩², 1-20⁶.

Probably issued in paper boards, cloth shelf back, printed paper labels.

Note: Copies occur on both thick and thin papers. Sequence, if any, not determined:

Thin paper: Sheets bulk ⁷⁄₁₆″ to ½″ plus thick.

Thick paper: Sheets bulk ⅝″ scant to ⅝″.

Noted as *nearly ready for the press* M Aug. 2, 1823. Title-page deposited Sept. 6, 1823. Reviewed (from the manuscript) M Sept. 13, 1823: ". . . Messrs. Bliss and White, have ⟨it⟩ . . . in the press . . . the public may not for a few weeks have an opportunity of giving it their sanction." Noted for *October* NYM Sept. 20, 1823. A published copy reviewed M Oct. 4, 1823. The London (Newman) edition advertised LG Dec. 6, 1823; issued in December according to *The English Catalogue.*

AAS   H   NYPL   UV

13576. O'HALLORAN; OR, THE INSURGENT CHIEF. AN IRISH HISTORICAL TALE OF 1798. BY THE AUTHOR OF "THE WILDERNESS" . . .

PHILADELPHIA: PUBLISHED BY H. C. CAREY AND I. LEA. J. HARDING, PRINTER. 1824.

2 Vols.

1 : ⟨i⟩-⟨xvi⟩, ⟨17⟩-264. 7¾″ × 4⁹⁄₁₆″.

2 : ⟨1⟩-232.

1 : ⟨A⟩-I, K-U, X-Y⁶.

2 : ⟨A⟩-I, K-T⁶, U².

Gray paper boards, printed paper label on spine. Flyleaves.

In the press———M March 13, 1824. Noted as *for sale* USLG June 15, 1824. The London (Newman) edition issued under the title *The Insurgent Chief; or, O'Halloran,* with authorship ascribed to *Solomon Secondsight;* advertised as *now first published* BMLA Sept. 1824. For a revised edition see *The Insurgent Chief . . . ,* 1848, below.

In his preface to the London edition of *Hearts of Steel,* 1825, McHenry states that *O'Halloran* was published in mutilated form in three editions: Two in England and one in the United States. BAL has traced but one contemporary English edition (Newman). McHenry also states, in the preface cited, that "a more complete edition" to be called *The United Irishmen* is in contemplation; further information wanting.

NYPL   UV   Y

13577. The Pleasures of Friendship, a Poem, in Two Parts; to Which Are Added a Few Other Poems, and Original Melodies ⟨Second Edition⟩ . . .

Philadelphia: A. R. Poole, No. 66, Chestnut Street. 1825.

For first edition see under 1822; for other editions see under the years 1828 (3rd edition); 1830 (4th and 5th editions); 1834 (6th edition); 1836 (7th edition).

Reprint save for the following poems:

"Caithalore . . . ," previously in *The Bard of Erin*, Belfast, 1808.

"Cush La Ma Chree"

"Elegy Written at the Grave of a Rural Poet"

"A Monody," *In Carolina's fatal clime* . . .

"An Ode to Gen. Lafayette"

"The Rural Cot"

"To a Friend, Who Wished for Some Verses . . ."

"To My First Love"

⟨i-viii⟩, ⟨7⟩-10, 13-96. $6^{15}/_{16}$″ × $4^{3}/_{16}$″. Note irregular pagination. Drab paper boards, printed paper label on spine, flyleaves.

Listed USLG June 1, 1825.

UV   Y

13578. THE HEARTS OF STEEL, AN IRISH HISTORICAL TALE OF THE LAST CEN-TURY. BY THE AUTHOR OF "THE WILDERNESS," . . .

　　LONDON: PRINTED FOR WIGHTMAN AND CRAMP, PATERNOSTER-ROW. 1825.

Not seen. Entry on the basis of photographs of the title-pages (BMU) and correspondence. See below under 1825 for first American edition.

3 Vols.

1: ⟨i⟩-xii, ⟨1⟩-315. A trimmed copy measures 7″ × 5½″.

2: ⟨i⟩-⟨iv⟩, ⟨1⟩-321; blank leaf(?).

3: ⟨i⟩-⟨iv⟩, ⟨1⟩-346; blank leaf(?).

1: ⟨A⟩⁶, B-I, K-O¹², P².

2: ⟨A⟩², B-I, K-O¹², P⁶.

3: ⟨A⟩², B-I, K-P¹², Q⁶.

Possibly issued in paper boards, cloth shelf back, printed paper label on spine.

Advertised as *in . . . press* LG Aug. 13, 1825; as *shortly* BMLA Sept. 1825. Reviewed LG Oct. 15, 1825. Listed LG Nov. 5, 1825. A Belfast, Dublin and London edition (Henderson, Cumming & Ferguson, Gilbert) advertised Ath Feb. 20, 1847; listed PC April 1, 1847. A London (Routledge) edition listed Ath Sept. 9, 1854. A Glasgow (Cameron, Ferguson) edition advertised PC Feb. 26, 1898.

13579. The Blessings of Friendship, and Other Poems . . .

　　London: Printed for Wightman and Cramp, Paternoster-Row. 1825.

Not seen. Entry on the basis of a photographic copy of the title-page of the BMU copy and correspondence.

Paper boards?

Reprint with the exception of:

"Battle of Trafalgar"

"Battle of Waterloo"

"The Dying Soldier"

"On My Birthday"

"A Scene on the Coast of the County of Antrim"

"Stanzas Written at Sea, When Returning from America in 1825"

"To a Comet"

Advertised as *in press* BMLA Sept. 1825. Listed LG Nov. 5, 1825. Reviewed LG Dec. 3, 1825.

13580. THE HEARTS OF STEEL. AN IRISH HISTORICAL TALE OF THE LAST CEN-TURY. BY THE AUTHOR OF "THE WILDERNESS," . . .

　　PHILADELPHIA: A. R. POOLE, 66 CHESNUT STREET. J. HARDING, PRINTER. 1825

2 Vols. For prior publication see above under 1825.

The statement *In Two Volumes* present in Vol. 1; not present Vol. 2.

1: ⟨i⟩-⟨xii⟩, ⟨1⟩-326. $7^{3}/_{4}$″ × $4^{3}/_{4}$″.

2: ⟨1⟩-411.

1: *Signed:* ⟨-⟩⁶, A-I, K-T⁶, U², X-Z, 2A-2D⁶, 2E⁵.

2: *Signed:* ⟨A⟩-I, K-U, X-Z, 2A-2I, 2K-2L⁶, 2M².

Paper boards, cloth shelf back, printed paper label on spine?

Neither volume contains a copyright notice.

Listed USLG Jan. 1, 1826.

AAS   NYPL

13581. The Atlantic Souvenir; a Christmas and New Year's Offering. 1828.

　　Philadelphia: Carey, Lea & Carey. Sold in Boston by Hilliard, Gray, & Co. ⟨1827⟩

"Literature," pp. 83-87. Collected as "Knowl-edge," *Pleasures of Friendship*, 1830.

For fuller entry see No. 10122.

13582. The Atlantic Souvenir; a Christmas and New Year's Offering. 1829.

　　Philadelphia: Carey, Lea & Carey. ⟨1828⟩

"Chapeau de Paille," pp. 158-159; uncollected.

"Twilight Thoughts," pp. 116-117; collected in *The Pleasures of Friendship*, 1830.

"The Unwelcome Guest," pp. 294-295; uncollected.

Printed paper boards. For fuller entry see No. 843.

13583. The Pleasures of Friendship, and Other Poems . . . Third American Edition. . .

Philadelphia: John Grigg, South Fourth Street. 1828.

For first edition see under 1822; for other editions see under the years 1825 (2nd edition); 1830 (4th and 5th editions); 1834 (6th edition); 1836 (7th edition).

Reprint save for the following poems:

b "Corun and Lora"

a "The Dying Soldier"

b "Edward and Eliza"

c "Ellinor's Grave"

c "Lament of a Husband for His Deceased Wife"

c "Love's First Glance: A Song"

a "On My Birthday"

b "Ronard and Ella"

a "A Scene on the Coast of the County of Antrim"

a "Stanzas Written at Sea, in 1825"

a "To a Comet"

c "To an Infant Sleeping on its Mother's Bosom"

Key: a—Previously in *The Blessings of Friendship*, London, 1825; *b*—Previously in *The Bard of Erin*, Belfast, 1808; *c*—Here first located.

⟨1⟩-120. Frontispiece inserted. 5¾″ × 3⅛″ (untrimmed). 5″ × 2¾″ (all edges gilt). Paper boards, printed paper label on spine.

Listed NAR April, 1828, under the title *The Blessings of Friendship*.

B   LCP

13584. ADDRESS WRITTEN BY DR JAMES M'HENRY AT THE REQUEST OF THE ASSOCIATION OF THE FRIENDS OF IRELAND, AND DELIVERED AT THE CELEBRATION OF CATHOLIC EMANCIPATION, HELD 14 JULY 1829, IN THE HALL OF INDEPENDENCE.

PHILADELPHIA: PRINTED BY JAMES KAY, JUN. & CO. LIBRARY STREET. 1829.

Not seen. Entry on the basis of a photographic copy.

Cover-title?

⟨1⟩-8. 8″ × 5³⁄₁₆″.

⟨-⟩⁴.

"At a meeting . . . 3d of December 1829 . . . Resolved . . . that five hundred copies be printed . . ."---P. ⟨2⟩.

HSP

13585. The Jackson Wreath, or National Souvenir . . . Containing a Biographical Sketch of General Jackson until 1829. By Robert Walsh, Jr. Esqr. With a Continuation until the Present Day, Embracing a View of the Recent Political Struggle. By Dr. James M'Henry.

Philadelphia: Published by Jacob Maas, Franklin Engraving Office, 65, Arcade. William W. Weeks, Printer. 1829.

McHenry contributed the continuation of Jackson's biography, pp. 57-86; and, "Dirge to the Memory of Mrs. Jackson," pp. 84-85.

Printed boards, leather shelf back.

Variations have been noted. BAL has been unable to establish a firm sequence but suggests the following order:

STATE A

Title-page, line 10: . . . UNTIL 1829. /

P. 75, line 12: *Kentuckey* . . .

P. 86: Mispaged 66

STATE B

Title-page, line 10: . . . UNTIL 1819. /

P. 75, line 12: *Kentucky* . . .

P. 86: Correctly paged 86.

Copies occur with and without a footnote on p. vii. BAL suggests the following sequence. Reference is to line 3 from the bottom of the note:

A: *Any* . . .

B: *any* . . .

C: Footnote not present.

Intermediates appear to be the rule.

AAS   BA   UV

13586. THE USURPER, AN HISTORICAL TRAGEDY, IN FIVE ACTS . . .

PHILADELPHIA: JESPER HARDING, PRINTER. 1829

Cover-title?

⟨i⟩-⟨viii⟩, ⟨9⟩-65, 3 blank leaves. 6¼″ × 3⅞″ scant.

⟨A⟩-F⁶.

Printed self-wrapper?

Title-page deposited March 24, 1829. Listed NAR Oct. 1829. Reviewed by AQR Sept. 1830.

H   LC   UP

13587. The Atlantic Souvenir for MDCCCXXX.

Philadelphia: Carey, Lea & Carey, Chesnut Street. 1830.

Leather.

"The Temple of Egina," pp. ⟨292⟩-295. Collected in *The Pleasures of Friendship . . . Fourth American Edition*, 1830.

For fuller entry see No. 846.

13588. The Pleasures of Friendship, and Other Poems . . . Fourth American Edition . . .

Philadelphia: John Grigg, North Fourth Street. J. Harding, Printer. 1830

For first edition see under 1822; for other editions see under the years 1825 (2nd edition); 1828 (3rd edition); 1830 (5th edition); 1834 (6th edition); 1836 (7th edition).

Reprint save for the following poems:

a "Address, Spoken by Mr. Blake, at the Walnut Theatre . . ."

a "The Champion of Erin Has Broken Her Chains"

a "Dulrana, an Irish Legend"

e "Feelings of Age"

b "Knowledge"

a "My Mother's Grave"

a "On Poetry. Written in a Lady's Album"

a "Prize Address . . . Walnut Street Theatre . . . January 7th, 1829"

a "The Song of the Princess Moriat"

e "The Star of Love"

d "The Temple of Egina"

c "Twilight Thoughts"

a "Upon the Banks of Delaware"

a "Woman. Written for a Lady's Album"

Key: *a*—Here first located; *b*—Previously in *The Atlantic Souvenir . . . 1828*; *c*—Previously in *The Atlantic Souvenir . . . 1829*; *d*—Previously in *The Atlantic Souvenir for MDCCCXXX*; *e*—See entry No. 13590.

⟨i⟩-⟨viii⟩, ⟨11⟩-200. Frontispiece and 1 plate inserted. 5⁹⁄₁₆″ × 3³⁄₈″. *Pagination postulated.* Paper boards, printed label on spine?

B   H

13589. THE BETROTHED OF WYOMING. AN HISTORICAL TALE . . .

PHILADELPHIA: SOLD BY THE PRINCIPAL BOOK-SELLERS; AND IN NEW YORK, BOSTON, BALTIMORE, AND WASHINGTON. 1830.

Anonymous. Presumably by McHenry. Blanc, pp. 80-81, submits circumstantial evidence both *pro* and *con*. Wright (second revised edition, 1969) credits the book to McHenry without comment.

⟨i⟩-viii, ⟨9⟩-231. 8¹⁄₁₆″ × 5″. See note below for comment on p. 230.

⟨A⟩-I, K-T⁶, U².

Tan paper boards, tan linen shelf back, printed paper label on spine. Flyleaves.

Note: Copies occur with p. 230 either mispaged 203; or, correctly paged 230. Presumably the sequence is as here presented. *Also:* Copies occur with one or the other of the following statements on the title-page: *Second Edition*; or, *Third Edition*. Because of internal evidence (see below) BAL believes that the statements are pure fiction intended to suggest a popularity for the book that did not exist. The book has been seen in the following forms; the designations are completely arbitrary and no sequence is suggested or implied:

ISSUE A

No edition statement on the title-page.
P. 230 mispaged 203.
Locations: NYPL Y

ISSUE Aa

No edition statement on the title-page.
P. 230 correctly paged.
Locations: NYPL

ISSUE B

The statement *Second Edition* on the title-page.
P. 230 mispaged 203.
Locations: AAS

ISSUE Ba

The statement *Second Edition* on the title-page.
P. 230 correctly paged.
Locations: UV Y

ISSUE C

The statement *Third Edition* on the title-page.
P. 230 mispaged 203.
Locations: Y

ISSUE Ca

The statement *Third Edition* on the title-page.
P. 230 correctly paged.
Locations: AAS LC

Title-page deposited Sept. 9, 1830. Listed NAR Jan. 1831.

See excerpt from Willis Gaylord Clark at head of this list.

Locations: See above under description of issues.

13590. THE FEELINGS OF AGE, TO WHICH IS ADDED THE STAR OF LOVE: POEMS . . . SECOND EDITION . . .

PHILADELPHIA: BANKS & BROTHER, 76, SOUTH THIRD STREET. S. NEALL & CO. PRINTERS. 1830.

⟨1⟩-36. 5⁵⁄₁₆″ × 3⁵⁄₈″. Engraved vignette title-page inserted.

Signature collation:

Printed paper wrapper? Printed paper boards?

Contents: "The Feelings of Age" and "The Star of Love," both of which are also in (reprinted from? collected in?) *The Pleasures of Friendship . . . Fourth American Edition*, 1830; see above.

Query: Does this occur without the statement *Second Edition* on the title-page?

Entry on the basis of a rebound, imperfect copy at B; and correspondence with The American Philosophical Society Library.

B

13591. The Pleasures of Friendship, and Other Poems . . . Fifth American Edition . . .

Philadelphia: John Grigg, North Fourth Street. J. Harding, Printer. 1830

Cloth? Probably sheets of the *Fourth American Edition*, 1830, with altered, cancel title-leaf. The only located copy has been rebound and the state of the title-leaf cannot be determined.

For other editions see under years 1822 (1st edition); 1825 (2nd edition); 1828 (third edition); 1830 (4th edition); 1834 (6th edition); 1836 (7th edition).

". . . We cannot say much in praise of the *Pleasures of Friendship*, a volume of poems recently received from Philadelphia; though we observe that it has reached a 'fifth American edition'."--- LG Jan. 7, 1832.

LC

13592. The Atlantic Souvenir for MDCCCXXXI.

Philadelphia: Published by Carey and Lea. 1831.

Publisher's leather.

"Time," pp. ⟨278⟩-280. Uncollected. For publication of an extract see the title-page of *The Feelings of Age . . .* , 1830, above.

Title deposited Aug. 10, 1830. Published in 1830?

H NYPL

13593. MEREDITH; OR, THE MYSTERY OF THE MESCHIANZA. A TALE OF THE AMERICAN REVOLUTION. BY THE AUTHOR OF "THE BETROTHED OF WYOMING." . . .

PHILADELPHIA: SOLD BY THE PRINCIPAL BOOK-SELLERS; AND IN NEW YORK, BOSTON, BALTIMORE, AND WASHINGTON. 1831.

Presumably by McHenry. Blanc, pp. 80-81, submits circumstantial evidence both *pro* and *con*. Wright (second revised edition, 1969) credits the book to McHenry without comment.

⟨1⟩-260. 7¹³⁄₁₆″ × 4⁵⁄₈″.

⟨A⟩-I, K-U, X⁶, Y⁴.

Drab paper boards, printed paper label on spine. Also: drab paper boards, unbleached linen shelf-back, printed paper label on spine. Flyleaf at back; or, flyleaves.

Title-page deposited Dec. 28, 1830. Listed NAR July 1831.

AAS BA UV

13594. The Pleasures of Friendship, and Other Poems . . . Sixth American Edition . . .

Philadelphia: Grigg & Elliott, North Fourth Street. John Young, Printer. 1834.

Cloth? On the basis of a single copy examined made up of the sheets of the *Fourth American Edition*, 1830, issued with altered cancel title-leaf as above.

For other editions see under the years 1822 (first edition); 1825 (second edition); 1828 (3rd edition); 1830 (4th and 5th editions); 1836 (7th edition).

LC

13595. The Pleasures of Friendship, and Other Poems . . . Seventh American Edition . . .

Philadelphia: Grigg & Elliott, North Fourth St. Stereotyped by L. Johnson. 1836.

Noted in leather; and, cloth.

Reprint with the exception of:

"The Bard's Retrospect"

"The Fisherman's Wife"

"The Drama of Britain: A Song"

"Eveline O'Neal"

"To Ellen: A Song"

"To Miss M. W. of Philadelphia"

"The Vale of My Birth"

"War and Love; a Canzonet"

For other editions see under years: 1822 (1st edition); 1825 (2nd edition); 1828 (3rd edition); 1830 (4th and 5th editions); 1834 (6th edition).

B LC Y

13596. THE ANTEDILUVIANS, OR, THE WORLD DESTROYED; A NARRATIVE POEM, IN TEN BOOKS . . .

LONDON: PRINTED FOR T. M. CRADOCK, 48, PATERNOSTER ROW. 1839.

For American edition see under year 1840.

⟨i-iv⟩, ⟨i⟩-⟨xvi⟩, ⟨1⟩-272. 6¾″ × 4¼″.

⟨-⟩², a⁸, B-I, K-S⁸.

H cloth: blue; blue-green. Yellow-coated end papers.

"It will be remembered . . . that . . . in the *Knickerbocker* for July, 1834, reference was made to a manuscript volume . . . *The Antediluvians* . . . by Dr James M'Henry . . . which he had been compelled to send to London to be printed, because the publishers on this side of the water could not see its merits. Well, after five years . . . the great work has appeared. No copy of it has yet found its way to the United States, to our knowledge . . ."---K Sept. 1839, p. 286.

Described as *in press* BMLA Nov. 1838. Advertised for *December* BMLA Dec. 1838. Listed LG Jan. 12, 1839; Ath. Jan. 12, 1839; PC Jan. 15, 1839; BMLA Jan. 1839.

B   BA

13597. TO BRITANNIA: AN ODE . . . DEDICATED TO THE MEMBERS OF THE LITERARY FUND SOCIETY . . .

LONDON: PUBLISHED BY W. STEPHENSON, 12 & 13, PARLIAMENT STREET. PRICE SIXPENCE. H. ROBERTSON, PRINTER, RUSSELL COURT, COVENT GARDEN. ⟨1839⟩

Not seen. Entry on the basis of a photographic copy of the title-page of the original in BMU.

⟨1⟩-8. 7⅞″ × 4⅞″.

Issued in printed paper wrapper?

13598. THE ANTEDILUVIANS, OR THE WORLD DESTROYED; A NARRATIVE POEM, IN TEN BOOKS . . . FIRST AMERICAN EDITION.

PHILADELPHIA: J. B. LIPPINCOTT, & CO., S. W. CORNER RACE AND FOURTH STREETS. 1840.

For prior London publication see above under year 1839.

⟨1-2⟩, ⟨i⟩-⟨xvi⟩, ⟨3⟩-272. 6¼″ full × 3¹³⁄₁₆″.

⟨1⟩-2⁶, 3⁴, 4-24⁶, 25².

T cloth: green; purple. Also noted in a purple cloth embossed with an all-over pattern resembling link armour on an underlying T-grain base. Flyleaves. Neither publisher's device nor spine imprint present.

Title-page deposited May 16, 1838 ⟨*sic*⟩.

Unsold sheets were issued, not before Jan. 1, 1850, with the device of Lippincott, Grambo & Company blindstamped on the sides. Copies in LC, Y.

B   BPL   H

13599. The Poems of the Pleasures . . . The Pleasures of Imagination, by Mark Akenside . . . The Pleasures of Memory, by Samuel Rogers . . . The Pleasures of Hope, by Thomas Campbell . . . The Pleasures of Friendship, by James M'Henry . . .

Philadelphia: J. B. Lippincott & Co., Corner of Fourth and Race St. 1841.

Reprint. Contains an anonymous biographical sketch of McHenry written by a knowledgeable person.

B   H   LC

13600. The Household Book of Select Songs, with Numerous Critical Explanatory Observations . . .

Philadelphia: Printed & Published at Young's Office, Black Horse Alley. For Sale at the Principal Book Stores in the United States. 1842.

Reprint with the exception of the following:

"As Late I Stood beside Her Grave," pp. 65-66.

"Ellen's Place of Rest," p. 33.

"For Maids with Gold When Young Men Sigh," pp. 51-52.

"I Have No Joy but Mourning," pp. 42-43.

"When from the Orient Herb Ascends," p. 117.

"Why to Yon Ruin's Gray?," pp. 143-144.

"Th' Yankee in London," pp. 155-156.

Other poems appear herein under altered titles:

"Love and War," p. 162; otherwise "War and Love; a Canzonet," *The Pleasures of Friendship* . . . *Seventh American Edition*, 1836.

"The Lover's Lament," pp. 137-138; otherwise "Lament of a Husband for His Deceased Wife," *The Pleasures of Friendship* . . . *Third American Edition*, 1828.

"Our Ship How Beauteous to Survey," p. 136; otherwise "Stanzas Written at Sea, in 1825," *The Pleasures of Friendship* . . . *Third American Edition*, 1828.

Query: Was this compilation edited by McHenry?

UV

13601. The Dramatic Authors of America. By James Rees . . .

Philadelphia: G. B. Zieber & Co. 1845.

Printed paper wrapper.

Extract from "The Maid of Wyoming," pp. 106-107. The only known fragment of this unlocated play; probably otherwise unpublished. See under *ca.* 1826 in the section of *References and Ana* below.

Two issues of the front wrapper noted:

A: Cover-title: *The Dramatig ⟨sic⟩ Authors . . .*

B: Cover-title: *The Dramatic Authors . . .*

Issued after April 25, 1845; this on the basis of the latest entry in the "Chronological Table," p. 142.

H (both)

13602. The Insurgent Chief; a Tale of the United Irishmen . . . A New Edition Revised by the Author.

 Glasgow: Published by R. Griffin & Co. MDCCCXLVIII.

The earliest revision noted.

A revision of *O'Halloran; or, the Insurgent Chief . . .*, 1824.

Y

13603. The Wilderness; or, Braddock's Times. A Tale of the West . . . Two Volumes in One . . .

 Pittsburgh: M. P. Morse, 85 Fourth Street. John B. Kennedy, Book Publisher, Federal Street, Allegheny. 1848.

Title-page for Vol. 2 follows p. ⟨230⟩, Vol. 1. The line *M. P. Morse, 85 Fourth Street* appears on the title-page for Vol. 1 only.

Reprint. For first printing see above under year 1823. Deposited for copyright Feb. 12, 1848. Unsold sheets were reissued in 1876 by J. R. Weldin & Co., Pittsburgh; front matter removed and replaced by two leaves of matter including an "Advertisement" by Weldin, whence the following: ". . . Some copies . . . which had been stored away and neglected, have been recently found. These have been re-bound, and are now offered in the present shape . . ." The reissued sheets have stab marks which suggest they were originally bound in printed paper wrappers, not in cloth.

Cloth; and, printed paper wrapper.

AAS (1848; 1876) Y (1848; 1876)

13604. William Cullen Bryant Representative Selections, with Introduction, Bibliography, and Notes by Tremaine McDowell . . .

 American Book Company New York . . . ⟨1935⟩

Part of an article, "American Lake Poetry," pp. 372-374; originally in AQR March, 1832.

For fuller entry see No. 1810.

REPRINTS

The following publications contain material by McHenry reprinted from earlier books.

The Lady's Cabinet Album . . .

 New-York . . . MDCCCXXXII.

 For fuller entry see No. 6793.

The Lady's Cabinet Album . . .

 New-York . . . MDCCCXXXIV.

 For fuller entry see BAL, Vol. V, p. 88.

The Philadelphia Book . . .

 Philadelphia . . . 1836.

 For comment see entry No. 1158.

The Lady's Cabinet Album . . .

 New-York: E. Sands. MDCCCXXXVII.

 Cloth? Reissued as *The Moss Rose*, n.d., *ca.* 1845.

The Moss Rose, or an Annual Gift . . .

 New-York: Published by Nafis & Cornish. ⟨n.d., *ca.* 1845⟩

 Leather? See preceding entry.

REFERENCES AND ANA

A Letter to the Honourable the Speaker of the House of Representatives . . . Read . . . on the 28th December, 1802. By James M'Henry . . .

 Baltimore: Printed by John W. Butler, Corner of Gay & Water Streets. 1803.

 Printed paper wrapper. Erroneously attributed to the subject of this list by Sabin. It was written by James McHenry, 1753-1816.

An Essay on Knowledge, by James McHenry.

 Belfast: A. Mackay, 1804.

 Not seen. Entry from *Catalogue of Early Belfast Printed Books, 1694 to 1830. Supplementary to the Third Edition, Published 1890,* compiled by John Anderson, Belfast, 1902, p. 19.

 The preface to McHenry's *The Bard of Erin . . .*, 1808, suggests that *The Bard of Erin* was McHenry's first book. *An Essay on Knowledge* was presumably written by another James McHenry.

Baltimore Directory, and Citizens' Register, for 1807 . . . by James M'Henry.

Printed by Warner & Hanna, Corner of Gay and Baltimore Streets. ⟨n.d., 1807⟩

Paper boards?

Sometimes credited to the subject of this list.

DAB credits this publication to James McHenry, 1753–1816. Since the subject of this list didn't emigrate until 1817 the book could not have been done by him.

"... During this year, McHenry ⟨1753–1816⟩ employed his leisure by compiling and publishing the *Baltimore Directory and Citizens Register for 1807* ..."———Bernard C. Steiner: *The Life and Correspondence of James McHenry, Secretary of War under Washington and Adams*, Cleveland, 1907, p. 535.

It Would Be So; a Vision. By Solomon Second-sight.

Dublin, 1811.

Attributed to McHenry by Halkett & Laing, probably because of the pseudonym which McHenry used on the London printing of *The Wilderness*, 1823: *Solomon Secondsight*.

BAL has been unable to establish the authorship of *It Would Be So*.

The Maid of Wyoming. A Tragedy.

Philadelphia, *ca.* 1826.

Presumably unpublished save for a fragment which appears in *The Dramatic Authors of America*, by James Rees; see above in *Section One* under the year 1845.

"... He wrote ... the tragedies of *The Usurper* and *Wyoming*, and the novels of *The Betrothed of Wyoming* and *Meredith*. Both of the tragedies were performed in Philadelphia. *The Usurper*, and the two novels ... were published in the same city ..."——— *The Poems of the Pleasures ... by Mark Akenside ... Samuel Rogers ... Thomas Campbell ... James M'Henry ...*, Philadelphia, 1841, p. 280.

"*The Maid of Wyoming.* Acted January 28 and 31, February 4, 7 and 11, 1831. Not extant ..." ———Blanc, p. 123.

According to Arthur Hobson Quinn: *A History of the American Drama*, second edition, New York ⟨1951⟩, p. 462, the play was presented at the Arch Street Theatre, Philadelphia, Jan. 28, 1831.

Love and Poetry; or a Modern Genius. A Play

1829

Not seen. Entry from Blanc, p. 123, who states *not extant*.

Which Shall I Marry? Or, Who Loves Best? A Musical Interlude in One Act.

1835.

Reviewed by K Nov. 1835: "Never performed ... it was written in April"; but K fails to make clear whether the piece is in manuscript or in book form. Blanc, p. 116, locates the interlude as a manuscript only.

Memoirs of Major Robert Stobo, of the Virginia Regiment ...

Pittsburgh: Published Ry ⟨*sic*⟩ John S. Davidson, No. 65 Market Street. Printed at the Office of Kennedys' Bank Note Review, Third St. 1854.

Sometimes misattributed to McHenry. "... No one knows who wrote it, or when, or where, or why. ... ⟨It⟩ was first published in London by J. Skirven, Ratcliff-Highway, in 1800 ... carries no name of author or editor ... Sometime before 1854, Neville B. Craig of Pittsburgh ... searched out a few basic facts about Stobo's career ... and then ... obtained from the British Museum a hand-written ... copy of the Skirven edition ... This he published in Pittsburgh ..."———Robert C. Alberts: *The Most Extraordinary Adventures of Major Robert Stobo*, Boston, 1965, p. ⟨347⟩.

James McHenry ... Playwright and Novelist A Dissertation in English ... ⟨by⟩ Robert E. Blanc

Philadelphia ⟨University of Pennsylvania⟩ 1939

Printed paper wrapper.

Anthony Wayne A Name in Arms ... The Wayne-Knox-Pickering-McHenry Correspondence Transcribed and Edited by Richard C. Knopf

University of Pittsburgh Press ⟨1960⟩

The McHenry of this correspondence is James McHenry, 1753–1816.

CHARLES MAJOR

(Edwin Caskoden)

1 8 5 6 – 1 9 1 3

13605. WHEN KNIGHTHOOD WAS IN FLOWER OR THE LOVE STORY OF CHARLES BRANDON AND MARY TUDOR ... REWRITTEN AND RENDERED INTO MODERN ENGLISH FROM SIR EDWIN CASKODEN'S MEMOIR BY EDWIN CASKODEN

INDIANAPOLIS AND KANSAS CITY THE BOWEN-MERRILL COMPANY M DCCC XCVIII

Title-page in black and red.

⟨i-xiv⟩, 1-⟨249⟩; 3 blank leaves. Frontispiece and 17 plates inserted. Laid paper. 7½″ full × 5″. Final blank leaf used as a pastedown.

⟨-⟩⁷, ⟨1⟩-16⁸. ⟨-⟩₂ inserted.

T cloth: gray-blue; green. White wove end paper at front; at back: leaf 16₈ used as pastedown. Top edges gilt.

Advertised PW Nov. 26, 1898. Listed (not received) PW Dec. 3, 1898. The London (Sands) edition listed Ath July 15, 1899; Bkr Aug. 1899.

AAS H IU UV Y

13606. THE BEARS OF BLUE RIVER ...

NEW YORK DOUBLEDAY & McCLURE CO. 1901

⟨i⟩-viii, ⟨1⟩-277, blank leaf. Frontispiece and 14 plates inserted; other illustrations in text. 7¾″ × 5³⁄₁₆″ full.

⟨1-18⁸⟩.

T cloth: mottled green.

Note: A copy has been seen (in the Doubleday & McClure binding) with cancel title-leaf imprinted: *New York   The Macmillan Company ... 1902 ...   Prepared for distribution in Great Britain?*

Noted as *in press* PW Aug. 3, 1901. Deposited Aug. 30, 1901. Noted for *this week* PW Aug. 31, 1901. Listed PW Sept. 7, 1901. On copyright page: *September, 1901.* The London (Macmillan) edition

listed Ath May 10, 1902; Bkr June, 1902; reviewed Ath Nov. 1, 1902.

AAS IU UV

13607. DOROTHY VERNON OF HADDON HALL

Two printings noted:

COPYRIGHT PRINTING

DOROTHY VERNON OF HADDON HALL BY CHARLES MAJOR AUTHOR OF "WHEN KNIGHTHOOD WAS IN FLOWER," "THE BEARS OF BLUE RIVER," ETC. WITH ILLUSTRATIONS

NEW YORK THE MACMILLAN COMPANY LONDON: MACMILLAN & CO., LTD. 1902 ALL RIGHTS RESERVED

Prepared for copyright only.

⟨i-ii⟩, 1-367. Printed on wove paper. 7½″ × 5⅛″. No illustrations present.

⟨A⟩¹, B-I, K-U, X-Z, 2A⁸.

T cloth: blue. Stamped in gold only. Top edges gilt.

PUBLISHED EDITION

DOROTHY VERNON OF HADDON HALL BY CHARLES MAJOR AUTHOR OF "WHEN KNIGHTHOOD WAS IN FLOWER," "THE BEARS OF BLUE RIVER," ETC. WITH ILLUSTRATIONS BY HOWARD CHANDLER CHRISTY

NEW YORK THE MACMILLAN COMPANY LONDON: MACMILLAN & CO., LTD. 1902 ALL RIGHTS RESERVED

⟨i⟩-⟨x⟩, 1-369, blank, p. ⟨370⟩; 4 pages of advertisements. Frontispiece and 7 plates inserted. Printed on laid paper. 7½″ × 5⅛″.

⟨1-24⁸⟩. *Signed:* ⟨A⟩⁵, B-I, K-U, X-Z, 2A⁸, 2B³.

V cloth: gray-blue. Stamped in gold and colors. Top edges gilt.

Copies occur with a label printed in gold-colored ink pasted to the inner front cover: *The first edition of this book comprises 100,000 copies, of which 500 copies were used for presentation by the publishers. This is No. ...*

A copy has been seen with a label pasted inside the front cover: *This Edition Is Limited To One Thousand Copies, Numbered And Signed By The Author. This Is No. ...* Status unknown.

Copyright printing deposited Jan. 3, 1902. The following dates refer to the published edition: Announced for *spring* PW Jan. 18, 1902. Deposited April 12, 1902. "Will publish towards the end of this month"---PW April 12, 1902. On copyright page: ... *April, 1902*. Listed PW May 3, 1902. Listed Ath June 7, 1902.

The following variations are present:

COPYRIGHT PRINTING   PUBLISHED EDITION

Title-page

Title is set in three lines.   Title is set in two lines.

Reverse of title-leaf

Month of publication not present.

Month of publication, *April*, present.

Caption-title, p. 1

The Life and Adventures of Dorothy Vernon A Touch of Black Magic

A Touch of Black Magic

Pagination

Text ends on p. 367.   Text ends on p. 369.

Not present: Dedication, table of contents, list of illustrations.

Present are the following features: Dedication, table of contents, list of illustrations.

P. 336

Superfluous signature mark Z is not present.

Superfluous signature mark Z is present.

Running Heads

Life and Adventures of Dorothy Vernon

Dorothy Vernon ...

AAS (trade) B (trade) CU (copyright) H (trade)
IU (trade) UV (trade)

13608. Indiana Writers of Poems and Prose. ⟨Edited by Edward Joseph Hamilton⟩

The Western Press Association, Publishers. Chicago, 1902.

Unpaged. Contains "The Fatal Milk Can."

Deposited Sept. 6, 1902.

ISL Y

13609. A FOREST HEARTH A ROMANCE OF INDIANA IN THE THIRTIES ...

NEW YORK THE MACMILLAN COMPANY LONDON: MACMILLAN & CO., LTD. 1903 ALL RIGHTS RESERVED

⟨1⟩-354; advertisements, pp. ⟨1⟩-8; 3 blank leaves, the final blank used as a pastedown. Laid paper. Frontispiece and 7 plates inserted and reckoned in the printed pagination. $7\frac{9}{16}'' \times 5\frac{1}{4}''$.

⟨1-22⁸⟩. Signed: ⟨A⟩⁵, B², C⁷, D-F⁸, ⟨G⟩⁷, H⁸, ⟨I⟩⁷, K-M⁸, N⁷, O-P, ⟨Q⟩⁸, R⁷, S-U⁸, X⁷, Y⁸, Z⁷, 2A⁸.

T cloth: green. White wove end paper at front; ⟨22⟩₈ used as terminal pastedown. Top edges gilt.

Listed PW Oct. 31, 1903. On copyright page: ... *October, 1903*. Advertised for Nov. 7 PW Nov. 7, 1903. The London edition advertised for Dec. 8 Ath Dec. 5, 1903; listed Ath Dec. 19, 1903.

AAS NYPL

13610. YOLANDA MAID OF BURGUNDY ...

THE MACMILLAN COMPANY NEW YORK MCMV LONDON: MACMILLAN & CO., LTD.

Two printings noted:

FIRST PRINTING

⟨i⟩-⟨x⟩, 1-407; blank, p. ⟨408⟩; advertisements, pp. ⟨409-411⟩; blank, p. ⟨412⟩; blank leaf. Laid paper. Frontispiece and 4 plates inserted. $7\frac{9}{16}'' \times 5\frac{1}{8}''$.

⟨1-26⁸, 27⁴⟩. Signed: ⟨A⟩⁵, B-I, K-U, X-Z, 2A-2C⁸, 2D⁷.

On copyright page: ... *Published October, 1905*. Imprint of the *Norwood Press*.

T cloth: blue. Stamped in blue and gold. Spine imprint: THE MACMILLAN / COMPANY Top edges stained yellow.

SECOND PRINTING

⟨i⟩-⟨x⟩, 1-407. Wove paper. Frontispiece and 4 plates inserted.

⟨1-26⁸, 27¹⟩. Signed: ⟨A⟩⁵, B-H, ⟨I⟩, K, ⟨L⟩, M-Q, ⟨R-T⟩, U, X-Z, 2A-2C⁸, 2D⁴.

On copyright page: Statement *Published October, 1905* not present. The statement *Printed in the United States of America* present; the statement is not present in the first printing.

C cloth: gray. Stamped in black and gold. Spine imprint: MACMILLAN / ⟨4 dots⟩ Top edges plain.

Advertised for Oct. 25 PW Sept. 16, 1905. Listed PW Nov. 11, 1905; Ath Dec. 16, 1905; Bkr Jan. 1906.

AAS (1st) IU (1st; 2nd) UV (1st) Y (1st)

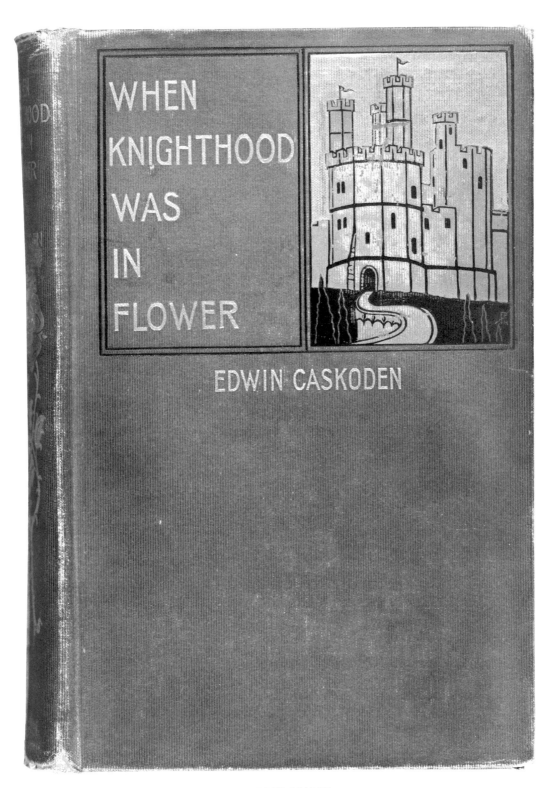

WHEN KNIGHTHOOD WAS IN FLOWER

EDWIN CASKODEN

13611. What's Next or Shall a Man Live Again? ... Compiled by Clara Spalding Ellis ...

Boston   Richard G. Badger   The Gorham Press 1906

Statement, p. 38.

EM

13612. UNCLE TOM ANDY BILL   A STORY OF BEARS AND INDIAN TREASURE ...

NEW YORK   THE MACMILLAN COMPANY   1908   ALL RIGHTS RESERVED

⟨i⟩-⟨xii⟩, 1-344, 2 blank leaves. Laid paper. $7\frac{1}{2}''$ scant × $5\frac{1}{8}''$ scant. Frontispiece and 23 plates inserted; one 2-page map inserted.

⟨1-22⁸, 23⁴⟩. *Signed:* ⟨A⟩⁶, B-I, K-U, X-Y⁸, Z⁶.

Two bindings noted. The sequence, if any, has not been determined; the designations are for identification only:

BINDING A

T cloth: blue-gray. Front stamped in blue. Spine stamped in gold and blue. White wove paper end papers. A copy thus in IU inscribed by Major *1908*.

BINDING B

T cloth: mottled green. Stamped in white only. White wove paper end papers.

Deposited Oct. 1, 1908. Announced as *just ready* PW Oct. 3, 1908. On copyright page: ... *October, 1908.* Listed PW Nov. 7, 1908. The London edition listed Ath Dec. 5, 1908.

H (*Binding B*)   IU (*Binding A*)

13613. A GENTLE KNIGHT OF OLD BRANDENBURG ...

NEW YORK   THE MACMILLAN COMPANY   1909

⟨i-viii⟩, 1-378; advertisements, pp. ⟨379-382⟩; blank leaf. Frontispiece and 7 plates inserted. $7\frac{3}{8}'' × 5\frac{1}{8}''$. Laid paper.

⟨-⟩⁴, ⟨1⟩-24⁸.

V cloth: blue-gray.

Noted as *nearly ready* PW June 19, 1909. Advertised for Oct. 6 PW Sept. 25, 1909. On copyright page: ... *September, 1909* Noted as *making ready rapidly* PW Oct. 2, 1909. Noted as *issued this week* PW Oct. 9, 1909. Listed PW Nov. 6, 1909; Ath Nov. 27, 1909; Bkr Dec. 3, 1909.

AAS   H   UV   Y

13614. Sun-Ways of Song by Alonzo L. Rice with an Introduction by Charles Major ...

Boston   Sherman, French & Company   1910

"Introduction," pp. ⟨v-vi⟩.

Listed PW Sept. 10, 1910.

B   IU

13615. THE LITTLE KING   A STORY OF THE CHILDHOOD OF LOUIS XIV KING OF FRANCE ...

NEW YORK   THE MACMILLAN COMPANY   1910   ALL RIGHTS RESERVED

⟨i⟩-⟨x⟩, ⟨1⟩-249; blank, p. ⟨250⟩; advertisements, pp. ⟨251-254⟩. Frontispiece and 5 plates inserted; other illustrations in text. $7\frac{9}{16}'' × 5\frac{1}{8}''$.

⟨1-16⁸, 17⁴⟩. *Signed:* ⟨-⟩⁵, ⟨1⟩-15⁸, 16⁷.

V cloth: blue.

Advertised for Nov. 2 PW Oct. 1, 1910. Received by BA Nov. 15, 1910. Listed PW Nov. 19, 1910. On copyright page: ... *November, 1910.* The London edition listed Ath Dec. 3, 1910; Bkr Dec. 9, 1910. The *Colonial Edition* noted in Bkr Jan. 20, 1911 as *recently* added to the list.

AAS   H

13616. SWEET ALYSSUM ...

INDIANAPOLIS   THE BOBBS-MERRILL CO. PUBLISHERS ⟨1911⟩

⟨i-viii⟩, 1-⟨54⟩, blank leaf. $7'' × 4\frac{1}{4}''$.

⟨1-4⁸⟩.

T cloth: red.

Sheets were also issued with inserted general title-page imprinted: *The Indiana Society of Chicago 1912* Flexible suède leather binding. Issued as Vol. 7 of *The Hoosier Set* with the inserted general title-page signed by the author and numbered. Copy in Y.

AAS   B   H

13617. THE TOUCHSTONE OF FORTUNE BEING THE MEMOIR OF BARON CLYDE, WHO LIVED, THRIVED, AND FELL IN THE DOLEFUL REIGN OF THE SO-CALLED MERRY MONARCH, CHARLES II ...

NEW YORK   THE MACMILLAN COMPANY   1912   ALL RIGHTS RESERVED

⟨i⟩-⟨viii⟩, 1-299, blank, p. ⟨300⟩; 12-page catalog. Frontispiece inserted. $7\frac{9}{16}'' × 5\frac{1}{8}''$.

⟨1-20⁸⟩. *Signed:* ⟨A⟩⁴, B-I, K-U⁸, ⟨X⟩⁴.

V cloth: blue.

Deposited March 22, 1912. On copyright page: ... *March, 1912.* Listed PW April 13, 1912; Bkr May 10, 1912.

AAS   H   NYPL   UV

13618. The Hoosier Almanack and Family Magazine ...

⟨Chicago: W. B. Conkey Company, The Hammond Press⟩ Indiana Society of Chicago 1912

"Tommy's Historical Novel," pp. 63-64.

For fuller entry see above in *George Barr McCutcheon* list.

13619. ROSALIE . . .

NEW YORK THE MACMILLAN COMPANY 1925 ALL RIGHTS RESERVED

⟨i⟩-⟨viii⟩, 1-331. 7$\frac{7}{16}$" × 5$\frac{1}{8}$".

⟨1-21⁸, 22²⟩.

S cloth: green.

Deposited June 10, 1925. On copyright page: *Published June, 1925.*

AAS   B   LC

REFERENCES AND ANA

Mistress Dorothy of Haddon Hall Being the True Love Story of Dorothy Vernon of Haddon Hall by Henry Hastings

R. F. Fenno & Company   9 and 11 East Sixteenth Street, New York   1902

"A novel founded on an incident of the Elizabethan era, namely the elopement of Dorothy Vernon and John Manners. This episode was likewise the theme of the latest novel by the author of *When Knighthood Was in Flower*."---PW July 5, 1902.

A Forest Hearth   A Romance of Indiana in the Thirties by Charles Major . . .

New York: The Macmillan Company London: Macmillan & Co., Ltd. 1903

Printed paper wrapper. A series of comments, extracts from reviews, etc. Issued as an advertisement.

A Madcap Princess Comedy Opera in Three Acts Founded upon Charles Major's New Novel "When Knighthood Was in Flower" The Libretto by Harry B. Smith The Music by Ludwig Englander . . .

Jos. W. Stern & Co.   34 East Twenty-First Street, New York . . . MCMIV . . .

Printed paper wrapper.

Dorothy Vernon of Haddon Hall   A Romantic Drama in Four Acts by Paul Kester . . .

Copyright, 1929 . . . New York Samuel French Publisher 25 West 45th Street London Samuel French, Ltd. 26 Southampton Street Strand, W. C. 2

Printed paper wrapper.

Note: A comment in Ath Jan. 5, 1907, suggests that the dramatization was done by Kester in collaboration with Major; further information wanting.

The Charles Major Manuscripts in the Purdue University Libraries by William M. Hepburn . . .

⟨Bloomington, Indiana⟩ 1946

Cover-title. Printed paper wrapper. Offprint from *The Indiana Quarterly for Bookmen*, July, 1946.

CORNELIUS MATHEWS

(The Late Ben Smith)

1817-1889

13620. THE MOTLEY BOOK: A SERIES OF TALES AND SKETCHES. BY THE LATE BEN. SMITH. WITH ILLUSTRATIONS FROM DESIGNS LEFT BY THAT GENTLEMAN WITH HIS LITERARY EXECUTOR.

NEW YORK: JAMES TURNEY, JR. 55, GOLD STREET. MDCCCXXXVIII.

Probably issued in seven tan or green paper-covered parts. Pagination and signature collation postulated.

PART I

⟨1⟩-24. 2 plates inserted. 8⅞″ × 5¹³⁄₁₆″.

⟨1⟩-3⁴.

Preface dated at end Jan. 12, 1838. . . .*On the third day of February . . . to issue . . . the first number of . . . The Motley Book . . . The first Number will be followed by a second on the 15th of February, and thence forward on the 1st and 15th of each month . . . each number containing two illustrations . . . January 20, 1838.*---From the front wrapper, Part I. Reviewed by *The New-Yorker* Feb. 24, 1838. AMM Feb. 1838, noted that Turney announces it for "3rd Feb. . . . It will appear in similar form with *Pickwick Papers* on the 1st and 15th of each month till completed." Noted by K March 1838. Listed NYR April 1838. See below under years 1838, 1840.

PART II

25-48, 6 (8?) pp. advertisements. 2 plates inserted.

4-6⁴, ⟨-⟩⁴ (?).

PART III

49-72. 2 plates inserted.

7-9⁴.

PART IV

73-96. 2 plates inserted.

10-12⁴.

Reviewed AMM May, 1838; listed NAR July, 1838.

PART V

97-120. 2 plates inserted.

13-15⁴.

Reviewed AMM May, 1838; listed NAR July, 1838.

PART VI

121-144. Illustrated?

16-18⁴.

PART VII

145-190; blank leaf. Illustrated?

19-24⁴.

The present entry made on the basis of an incomplete set (NYPL) in binding, and, reprints.

13621. The Motley Book . . . by the Late Ben. Smith . . . New Edition.

New-York: J. & H. G. Langley, 57 Chatham-Street. Boston: Weeks, Jordan & Co. Philadelphia: Orrin Rogers. MDCCCXXXVIII.

Almost certainly a reprint but inability to locate a complete set of the first printing in parts (see preceding entry) prevents a positive statement. Probably reprinted from the setting of the first printing but there is a possibility that unsold parts of the first printing may have been used in preparing this one-volume issue.

Reviewed by K Dec. 1838. Deposited Jan. 25, 1839.

AAS   B   H   Y

13622. BEHEMOTH: A LEGEND OF THE MOUND-BUILDERS.

NEW-YORK: J. & H. G. LANGLEY. BOSTON: WEEKS, JORDAN & CO. 1839.

Anonymous.

Two binding states noted; sequence, if any, not known. The designations are for identification only.

STATE A

⟨i-iv⟩, ⟨i⟩-⟨viii⟩, ⟨1⟩-192. $7\frac{3}{8}''$ scant × $4\frac{1}{2}''$.

⟨a⟩², ⟨b⟩⁴, 1-16⁶. Signature mark 7* (for 11*) on p. 125 of all examined copies. Sig. ⟨a⟩ is devoted to advertisements. The surviving copyright deposit copy thus.

STATE B

⟨i⟩-⟨viii⟩, ⟨1⟩-192; plus: 4 pp. advertisements.

⟨a⟩⁴, 1-16⁶, ⟨17⟩². Signature mark 7* (for 11*) on p. 125 of all examined copies. Sig. ⟨17⟩ (which occurs as signature ⟨a⟩ in *State A*) is devoted to advertisements.

Muslin: blue. T cloth: green; purple. Printed paper label on spine. Flyleaves.

Deposited April 5, 1839. Reviewed NYR April, 1839. *Reached us too late for perusal*---K June, 1839. Listed NAR July, 1839.

AAS (A) B (B) H (A) NYHS (A) UV (A) Y (A)

13623. THE TRUE AIMS OF LIFE: AN ADDRESS DELIVERED BEFORE THE ALUMNI OF THE NEW-YORK UNIVERSITY...JULY 16, 1839...

NEW-YORK: WILEY & PUTNAM, J. & H. G. LANGLEY. 1839.

⟨1⟩-41. $5\frac{3}{4}''$ × $3\frac{7}{8}''$.

⟨A⟩-B⁹, C², ⟨D⟩¹. Leaves ⟨A⟩₅ and B₅ inserted.

T cloth: green. Flyleaves.

Reviewed K Nov. 1839.

NYPL

13624. The Motley Book...by the Author of "Behemoth, a Legend of the Mound-Builders,"...Third Edition---Revised.

New-York: Benj. G. Trevett, 28 Ann Street; Boston: George O. Bartlett, 133 Washington-Street. 1840.

For first edition see above under year 1838.

Reprint save for:

"Preface to the Third Edition," pp. ⟨i⟩-ii.

"Noadiah Bott; or, Adventures with a Governor and a Widow," pp. ⟨3⟩-16.

Listed NAR Jan. 1840.

AAS B UV Y

13625. THE POLITICIANS: A COMEDY...

Two printings noted. Sequence, if any, not determined. The designations are for identification only.

PRINTING A

THE POLITICIANS: A COMEDY, IN FIVE ACTS.

NEW-YORK: 1840.

Anonymous.

⟨1⟩-118, blank leaf. $7\frac{7}{16}''$ × $4\frac{9}{16}''$.

⟨1⟩-10⁶.

Printed buff paper wrapper.

Privately printed for the use of actors.

PRINTING B

THE POLITICIANS: A COMEDY, IN FIVE ACTS. BY CORNELIUS MATHEWS...

NEW-YORK: BENJAMIN G. TREVETT, 28 ANN-STREET, BARTLETT & WEFFORD ⟨sic⟩, 2 ASTOR HOUSE, BROADWAY, TURNER & FISHER, 52 CHATHAM-STREET. 1840.

⟨1⟩-118, blank leaf. $7\frac{3}{16}''$ × $4\frac{3}{16}''$.

⟨1⟩-10⁶.

Printed buff paper wrapper.

Note: Not to be confused with *The School for Politicians*..., New York, 1840, a comedy based on Scribe's *Bertrand et Raton*.

Reviewed NYR Oct. 1840. *It will be produced at the National Theatre as soon as it can be done efficiently.*--- Arc Dec. 1840. Listed NAR Jan. 1841. Deposited (*Printing B*) Dec. 22, 1841.

B (A) BPL (A) H (B) LC (B) NYHS (B) NYPL (A)

13626. WAKONDAH; THE MASTER OF LIFE. A POEM.

NEW-YORK: GEORGE L. CURRY & CO., 167 BROADWAY. MDCCCXLI.

Anonymous.

SMALL PAPER

⟨1⟩-24. $7\frac{15}{16}''$ × $5\frac{7}{16}''$.

⟨1⟩-3⁴.

Undecorated tan paper boards. Also black paper boards decorated in gold with an all-over pattern of stylized stars. Printed paper label on front. White wove end papers. Flyleaves. Top edges plain.

LARGE PAPER

⟨1⟩-24. $9\frac{5}{16}''$ × 6''.

⟨1⟩-3⁴.

Black paper boards sides imprinted in gold with an all-over pattern of stylized stars, goldstamped morocco shelfback; brown and red leather shelf-back noted. Yellow-coated end papers. Triple flyleaves. Top edges gilt. No cover label.

Small paper copy deposited Nov. 23, 1841. A large paper copy (in H) presented by Mathews to James Russell Lowell Dec. 8, 1841. Listed NYR Jan. 1842.

B (large) H (both) BPL (small) LC (small) Y (small)

13627. ... THE CAREER OF PUFFER HOP-KINS ... (CONTINUED IN ARCTURUS FOR DECEMBER, 1841, AND THE NUM-BERS FOLLOWING.)

NEW-YORK: GEORGE L. CURRY & CO., 167 BROADWAY, MDCCCXLI. C. R. LINCOLN, PRINTER, ST. THOMAS' HALL PRESS, FLUSHING.

Cover-title. At head of title: SUPPLEMENT TO ARCTURUS.

⟨9⟩-86; excised leaf. 2 plates inserted. $8^{15}/_{16}''$ × $5^{1}/_{2}''$ full.

2-11^4. 11_4 excised.

Printed yellow paper wrapper.

Contains chapters 1 to 10 only; for publication of the whole see below under 1842. The whole, chapters 1-22, first published in Arc June 1841–May 1842.

NYHS

13628. A SPEECH ON INTERNATIONAL COPYRIGHT, DELIVERED AT THE DIN-NER TO CHARLES DICKENS, AT THE CITY HOTEL, NEW YORK, FEBRUARY 19, 1842 ...

NEW YORK: PUBLISHED AT THE OFFICE OF 'ARCTURUS,' BY GEORGE L. CURRY AND COMPANY. MDCCCXLII.

Cover-title.

⟨1⟩-16. $8^{1}/_{4}''$ × $5^{1}/_{8}''$.

⟨1⟩⁶, 2^2. *Signed:* ⟨-⟩², 1^4, 2^2.

Self-wrapper.

Listed NAR April 1842. Reviewed K April 1842.

BPL H NYPL

13629. AN APPEAL TO AMERICAN AUTHORS AND THE AMERICAN PRESS, IN BEHALF OF INTERNATIONAL COPY-RIGHT. [REPUBLISHED FROM GRA-HAM'S MAGAZINE.] ...

NEW-YORK AND LONDON: WILEY & PUTNAM. MDCCCXLII.

⟨1⟩-16. $7^{3}/_{4}''$ × $4^{3}/_{4}''$.

⟨1⟩⁶, 2^2.

Self-wrapper?

Reviewed BJ Aug. 13, 1842; LG Nov. 26, 1842.

BA H NYPL UV

13630. THE CAREER OF PUFFER HOPKINS ...

NEW-YORK: D. APPLETON AND CO. MDCCCXLII.

For prior publication of the first ten chapters see above under year 1841.

⟨i⟩-viii, ⟨9⟩-319. 3 plates inserted. $8^{7}/_{8}''$ × $5^{9}/_{16}''$. *Note:* In some copies p. 171 is paged 71; sequence not determined.

⟨1⟩-40⁴.

Coarse T-grained cloth: black; blue-green; slate. Pale salmon end papers. Flyleaves.

A copy in H presented by the author to Long-fellow Nov. 8, 1842. Reviewed NYM Nov. 26, 1842; USDR Dec. 1842.

Note: Also issued in printed paper wrapper as a supplement to *Brother Jonathan*, New York, Nov. 26, 1842; copies in H, UV. Below text, p. 52: *An Illustrated Octavo Edition of this work is just published by D. Appleton & Co., 200 Broadway. It is printed in beautiful letter press, with original illustrations by H. K. Browne, Esq. (Phiz.).* The *Brother Jonathan* edition was advertised in BJ Nov. 19, 1842 as *in a few days.*

AAS H NYHS UV

13631. THE BETTER INTERESTS OF THE COUNTRY, IN CONNEXION WITH IN-TERNATIONAL COPY-RIGHT: [A LEC-TURE DELIVERED AT THE LECTURE-ROOM OF THE SOCIETY LIBRARY, FEB. 2, 1843.] ...

NEW-YORK AND LONDON: WILEY & PUTNAM. MDCCCXLIII.

⟨1⟩-30; blank, p. ⟨31⟩; advertisement, p. ⟨32⟩. $7^{3}/_{8}''$ × $4^{1}/_{2}''$.

⟨1⟩², 2-3^6, 4^2.

Issued in self-wrapper?

BPL H LC NYPL

13632. The Various Writings of Cornelius Mathews.

New York: The Sun Office, 1843.

Not seen. The present entry on the basis of a single part (*Part III*) and the Harper one-volume edition of 1843 (misdated MDCCCLXIII).

Advertised BJ April 8, 1843: "Now Publishing At The Sun Office: A uniform Edition of the various Writings of Cornelius Mathews ... To be published in 8 octavo Numbers, at 12½ cents per No.---- averaging 48 closely printed pages each --- the first number to be published on Wednes-day, April 5th, 1843, and to follow at regular intervals---

"I. The Motley Book: with a general intro-duction. Fourth edition.

"II. Behemoth: A Legend of the Mound-builders. A revised edition.

"III. The Politicians: A Comedy in five acts. Heretofore unpublished.

"IV. Wakondah, The Master of Life; and other Poems. Second edition.

"V. The Career of Puffer Hopkins. Fourth edition.

"VI. Miscellanies on various Subjects; with Selections from Arcturus . . ."

It is presumed, but presumed only, that the Harper, 1843, one-volume edition was printed from the same setting as the 8-part issue. The prefatory note that appears in *Part III* does not appear in the one-volume printing; were other like notes omitted in the reprint? All statements regarding first appearances in the parts issue must be considered tentative since such statements (save for *Part III*) are based on the text of the Harper, 1843, issue.

PART I

The Motley Book.

Pp. 87?

Reprint save for a "General Introduction" dated at end *March 1st, 1843.*

Noticed BJ April 8, 1843.

PART II

Behemoth: A Legend of the Mound-Builders.

⟨89⟩-115? The text varies somewhat from the 1839 text.

Reviewed BJ June 24, 1843.

PART III

The Politicians: A Comedy. In Five Acts.

Anonymous.

Cover-title. Printed self-wrapper.

⟨117⟩-150.

Reprint save for a brief note, p. ⟨118⟩: "In the melancholy condition of the drama, at this time, the author presents the following Comedy, with the hope of rendering an humble service . . . A few copies . . . were printed at the date of the following preface, to facilitate its production upon the stage. The play is now, however, first published. May, 1843." For other printings see under year 1840.

"Will be published in the beginning of June"––– BJ May 27, 1843. Reviewed BJ June 10, 1843; K Nov. 1843.

UI

PART IV

Poems on Man, in His Various Aspects under the American Republic; and, *Wakondah, the Master of Life.*

⟨151⟩-166?

Definitely a reprint of *Wakondah* but possibly issued prior to *Poems on Man . . . ,* 1843, which was deposited for copyright Sept. 20, 1843.

In the normal course of publishing this fourth number would have been issued after *Part III* (June 10, 1843) and before publication of *Part V* (Aug. 12, 1843) but BAL has been unable to find any evidence that *Part IV* was indeed so issued. Some significance may attach to the fact that BJ Nov. 4, 1843, reviewed *Parts III, V, VI* without mention of *Part IV*. The same review includes comments on "a volume of poems" but the review fails to state whether the volume referred to is *Part IV* (which seems unlikely since it is not identified as such) or the Wiley & Putnam publication (Sept. 20, 1843). Until further information is found, the primacy of one or of the other, *Part IV* vis-à-vis the Wiley & Putnam issue, cannot be determined.

PARTS V-VI

The Career of Puffer Hopkins; and, *Miscellanies.*

⟨293⟩-316?

See under years 1841, 1842 for first printing of *The Career of Puffer Hopkins.*

Issued in two parts. BJ Aug. 12, 1843, noted *Part V* as *issued.* BJ Sept. 23, 1843, reported *Part VI* as issued, commenting that the part contains the conclusion of *The Career of Puffer Hopkins* and "some miscellaneous pieces." BJ Sept. 9, 1843, reviews *Puffer Hopkins* but says nothing of parts.

PART VII

Selections from Arcturus.

⟨317⟩-352?

Issued as a separate?

PART VIII

International Copyright.

⟨353⟩-370.

Issued as a separate?

ONE-VOLUME PRINTING

The Various Writings of Cornelius Mathews . . .

New York: Harper & Brothers, 82 Cliff Street. MDCCCLXIII. ⟨*sic*⟩

Listed ALB Jan. 1844, as a Dec. 1843, publication. Deposited Feb. 10, 1844. Reviewed Ath March 23, 1844; LG March 30, 1844.

Copies of the one-volume Harper printing in: AAS, B, H, NYHS, Y.

13633. POEMS ON MAN, IN HIS VARIOUS ASPECTS UNDER THE AMERICAN REPUBLIC...

NEW-YORK. WILEY AND PUTNAM. MDCCCXLIII.

Copies were prepared for publication in Great Britain with the following imprint: LONDON: / WILEY AND PUTNAM. / MDCCCXLIII. Copies in B, H.

⟨1⟩-112; advertisements, p. ⟨113⟩; blank, p. ⟨114⟩; blank leaf. 6¾″ × 4½″. Longfellow's copy (in H) measures 8⁷⁄₁₆″ × 5″, wholly untrimmed.

⟨1⟩-9⁶, 10⁴.

Note: The divisional title-page for "The Father" occurs on both ⟨1⟩₆ᵣ and on 2₁ᵣ. The fault was remedied in some copies by excision of ⟨1⟩₆.

Also note: The divisional title-page for "The Soldier" printed on 45ᵥ. In some copies the correction was effected by excision of the leaf; and, by reinsertion in correct position; *i.e.*, with *The Soldier* appearing on the recto. It is entirely possible that the original leaf was discarded and the correction done by reprinting the leaf.

The following errors are present in all examined copies:

P. 23, line 3: *Least . . .* for *Lest . . .*

P. 44 (mispaged 43), line 2: *. . . unabled . . .* for *. . . unbabied . . .*

P. 64, line 8: *. . . crost . . .* for *. . . coast . . .*

Brown-orange paper boards; gray paper boards. Printed paper label on spine.

Deposited Sept. 20, 1843. Listed as an October publication ALB Nov. 1843. Listed as an importation PC Jan. 15, 1844. Reviewed Ath Feb. 3, 1844. For a revised edition see *Man in the Republic . . .*, 1846. Also see *The Various Writings . . .*, 1843, Vol. IV.

Foley, p. 190, erroneously lists an 1842, London, edition.

AAS B H NYHS Y

13634. An Address to the People of the United States in Behalf of the American Copyright Club, Adopted at New-York, October 18th, 1843.

New-York: Published by the Club. MDCCCXLIII.

For fuller entry see No. 1625.

13635. The Opal: A Pure Gift for the Holy Days. Edited by N. P. Willis . . .

New-York: John C. Riker 15 Ann Street. 1844.

"To a Reverend Friend, Departing for Maryland," p. 74.

For comment see entry No. 6648.

13636. A Drama of Exile: And Other Poems. By Elizabeth Barrett Barrett . . .

New-York: Henry G. Langley, No. 8, Astor-House. M.DCCC.XLV.

2 Vols.

AWR Jan. 1845: ". . . It is published simultaneously with the English ⟨edition⟩ under the care of an American author." In her preface the author makes special note of "Mr Mathews . . . whose success in the construction of fossil romances . . . does not interfere with the freshness of his cordialities." The volumes contain no known contributions by Mathews but he appears to have had a part in their production.

Noted in the following bindings. Sequence, if any, not known; the designations are for identification only.

A

T cloth: black. Sides stamped in blind, the central ornament being a filigree measuring 3³⁄₁₆″ tall.

B

T cloth: black. Sides stamped in blind, the central ornament being a figure measuring 1¹⁄₁₆″ tall.

C

T cloth: green-blue. Sides stamped in blind, the central ornament being a decorated lyre 2½″ tall.

D

T cloth: black. Sides stamped in blind, the central ornament being a cartouche 2¼″ tall.

E

Yellow paper boards, printed paper label on spine.

H (all)

13637. BIG ABEL, AND THE LITTLE MANHATTAN...

NEW YORK: WILEY AND PUTNAM, 161 BROADWAY. MDCCCXLV.

Two printings noted. The sequence has not been firmly established.

PRESUMED FIRST PRINTING

⟨i-viii⟩, ⟨1⟩-93; blank, pp. ⟨94-96⟩; plus 8 pages of advertisements. 7³⁄₈″ scant × 5³⁄₁₆″.

⟨-⟩⁴, 1, 3-7⁸, plus ⟨8⟩⁴.

Printed tan paper wrapper. Front: . . . WILEY AND PUTNAM'S / LIBRARY OF AMERICAN BOOKS. / ⟨wavy rule⟩ / NO. V. / ⟨wavy rule⟩ / BIG ABEL / AND / THE LITTLE MANHATTAN . . . Outer back wrapper: WILEY AND PUTNAM'S LIBRARY OF AMERICAN BOOKS . . . ⟨Nos. I-V⟩ LIBRARY OF CHOICE READING . . . ⟨Nos. I-XVII⟩

Terminal advertisements, p. ⟨1⟩: *Correspondence of Schiller and Goethe . . .* Note: Copies have been seen in which the terminal advertisements are so folded as to have p. ⟨1⟩ read: *New Work on the East* . . .

PRESUMED SECOND PRINTING

⟨i-viii⟩, ⟨1⟩-93; blank, p. ⟨94⟩; *New and Valuable Books* . . . , p. ⟨95⟩; *Vegetable Physiology* . . . , p. ⟨96⟩. 7⁷⁄₁₆″ × 5⅛″.

⟨a-b⟩², 1, 3-7⁸.

Printed tan paper wrapper. Front: . . . WILEY AND PUTNAM'S / LIBRARY OF AMERICAN BOOKS. / ⟨wavy rule⟩ / NO. V. / ⟨wavy rule⟩ / BIG ABEL. / AND / THE LITTLE MANHATTAN . . . Outer back wrapper: WILEY AND PUTNAM'S LIBRARY OF AMERICAN BOOKS . . . ⟨Nos. I-VII⟩ IN IMMEDIATE PREPARATION . . . ⟨7 titles⟩

Listed as an October publication WPLNL Nov. 1845. Advertised by Wiley under *New American Books* and listed PC Sept. 1, 1845. Listed as in cloth (not seen by BAL) Ath Sept. 6, 1845.

BPL (1st) NYHS (1st) UV (1st, 2nd) Y (1st)

13638. AMERICANISM. AN ADDRESS DE-LIVERED BEFORE THE EUCLEIAN SOCIETY OF THE NEW-YORK UNIVER-SITY, 30th JUNE, 1845 . . .

NEW-YORK: PAINE AND BURGESS, NO. 62 JOHN-STREET. MDCCCXLV.

⟨1⟩-34, blank leaf. 6¹⁵⁄₁₆″ × 4⅝″.

⟨1⟩², 2-2⁶ ⟨sic⟩, 3⁴.

Printed fawn paper wrapper.

Noted as issued *Aristidean* (N.Y.), Nov. 1845.

NYHS NYPL Y

13639. Man in the Republic: A Series of Poems . . . a New Edition.

New York: Paine & Burgess, 62 John-Street. MDCCCXLVI.

A revised edition of *Poems on Man* . . . , 1843. Contains a new preface dated at end *28th October, 1845*, pp. ⟨vii⟩-viii.

Listed ALB Feb. 1846. Reviewed Ath May 30, 1846: . . . *A new edition, faults have not been corrected.*

B H

13640. MONEYPENNY . . .

Issued in the following forms:

PART I

MONEYPENNY, OR, THE HEART OF THE WORLD. A ROMANCE OF THE PRESENT DAY. ILLUSTRATED BY DARLEY.

NEW YORK: DEWITT & DAVENPORT, TRIBUNE BUILDINGS, NASSAU STREET. 1849.

Anonymous.

⟨1⟩-155; blank, p. ⟨156⟩. *See note below.* Frontispiece inserted. 9¾″ × 6¼″.

⟨1-9⁸, 10⁶⟩. *Signed:* ⟨1⟩-19⁴, 20².

Printed buff paper wrapper.

Contains Chapters I-XVII.

Two printings noted: the following order is presumed correct:

1: As above. P. ⟨156⟩ blank.

2: As above save for p. ⟨156⟩ which is imprinted with advertisements.

PART II

. . . MONEYPENNY OR THE HEART OF THE WORLD. A ROMANCE OF THE PRESENT DAY. EMBRACING . . . WITH VARIOUS OTHER CHARACTERS FROM THE UPPER AND LOWER WALKS OF LIFE. IN TWO PARTS—PART II. BY CORNELIUS MATHEWS.

NEW YORK: DEWITT & DAVENPORT, TRIBUNE BUILDINGS. 1850.

At head of title: PRICE 25 CENTS.

Cover-title. Issued without title-page?

155-270; table of contents, p. ⟨271⟩; advertisements, pp. ⟨272-290⟩. 9⁹⁄₁₆″ × 5¹¹⁄₁₆″.

Signed: ⟨-⟩³, 21¹, 22³, 22¹, 23⁷, 23-27⁸, 28⁴; plus(?): ⟨29⟩⁹.

Printed buff paper wrapper.

Contains Chapters XVIII-XXXIII.

ONE-VOLUME EDITION

MONEYPENNY, OR, THE HEART OF THE WORLD. A ROMANCE OF THE PRESENT DAY. ILLUSTRATED BY DARLEY.

NEW YORK: DEWITT & DAVENPORT, TRIBUNE BUILDINGS, NASSAU STREET. 1849. ⟨i.e., 1850; copyright notice dated 1848⟩

Anonymous.

⟨1⟩-271; advertisements, p. ⟨272⟩, plus: pp. ⟨273-278⟩. Frontispiece inserted. 9¾″ × 6¼″.

⟨1-9⁸, 10-11¹, 12², 13-19⁸, 20⁴; plus: 21¹, 22².⟩ *Signed:* ⟨1⟩-21⁴, 22¹, 23⁷, 23-27⁸, 28⁷.

Printed tan paper wrapper.

Issued simultaneously with *Part II?* See publication notes below.

PUBLICATION NOTES

Nov. 18, 1848: Announced in LW.

Nov. 25, 1848: *Part I* advertised LW for Dec. 1, 1848.

Dec. 2, 1848: *First Part . . . has been published*——— LW.

Dec. 2, 1848: Advertisement of Nov. 25, 1848 repeated, LW.

Dec. 9, 1848: Advertisement of Nov. 25, 1848 repeated, LW.

Dec. 9, 1848: *Part I* reviewed LW.

Dec. 16, 1848: The *second edition* of *Part I* listed LW.

Jan. 27, 1849: "It gives us pleasure to state that Cornelius Mathews is recovering from his late serious accident from a fall on the ice, though it will be some time before he will have the use of his arm . . ."---LW.

Feb. 2, 1850: LW noted that *Part II* would be published *immediately*.

March 9, 1850: Advertisement in LW "preparing for immediate publication. *Moneypenny* . . . In Two Parts, 25 cts, Each. Complete, 50 cts."

March 30, 1850: LW reports *Part II* to be *issued shortly*.

April 6, 1850: LW reports that "after the long and unavoidable delay . . . *Moneypenny* . . . is announced for publication . . . in the course of the coming week, in a complete form . . ."

April 12, 1850: Advertised in *New York Tribune* as "ready . . . after a long delay . . . announce the completion . . . published (in 270 8vo pages) at the low price of 50 cents a copy . . ."

April 13, 1850: Advertisement in LW: "Will be published Saturday April 13 . . . Complete. Fifty Cents."

April 16, 1850: Advertisement in *New York Tribune*: ". . . now ready, complete, price 50 cents . . ."

April 18, 1850: Advertisement in *New York Tribune*: ". . . now ready . . . Price, 50 cents--- complete . . ."

April 20, 1850: Advertisement in *New York Tribune*: ". . . complete, 50 cents . . . the First Edition of three thousand copies was immediately exhausted; a new edition will be ready . . . today . . ."

April 20, 1850: Reviewed LW: "Mr. Mathews' novel . . . the first volume of which our readers will remember was reviewed in this journal a year or two since, and the conclusion of which was interrupted by an accident to the author of a severe character, now appears before us in its complete form . . . two hundred and seventy octavo pages . . ."

May 1850: As a complete work reviewed SLM.

June 1850: As a complete work reviewed AWR.

Sept. 1850: As a complete work reviewed USDR.

The London (Clarke, Beeton) edition advertised as *now ready* Ath July 16, 1853; listed Ath July 16, 1853.

AAS (*One-Volume Edition*) B (*Part I*, 2nd) NYHS (*Part I*, 1st) NYPL (*Part II*) Y (*Part I*, 2nd)

13641. . . . "EAGLESTONE, A VISION OF GOOD COMPANY . . . THE SONG OF UNION . . .

At head of title: *OFFICE OF THE WEEKLY REVIEW, New York, Feb., 1850. WE publish, as appropriate to the times, the following poem, from a volume shortly to be issued from the Press in this city, entitled . . .*

Single leaf. Printed on recto only. $7^{15}/_{16}''$ × 5".

Elsewhere unlocated.

NYPL

PRICE 25 CENTS. MONEYPENNY . . . PART II . . .

NEW YORK . . . 1850.

See above under 1849.

13642. CHANTICLEER: A THANKSGIVING STORY OF THE PEABODY FAMILY.

BOSTON: B. B. MUSSEY & CO.   NEW-YORK: J. S. REDFIELD. 1850.

Anonymous.

⟨1⟩-155. $7^3/_8''$ × $4^5/_8''$.

⟨1⟩-6¹², 7⁶.

Noted in the following bindings; sequence, if any, not determined. The designations are for identification only.

BINDING A

T-like cloth: green, printed in black and yellow with an all-over floral pattern. V cloth: blue, embossed with a herringbone pattern.

Front: Stamped in blind.

Back: Stamped in blind.

End papers: White, printed in blue with an all-over pattern of small square units. Also, plain yellow.

Flyleaves.

Edges: Gilt.

BINDING B

A cloth: blue. T cloth: brown.

Front: Stamped in gold and blind.

Back: Stamped in blind; the name *Chanticleer* present.

End papers: Yellow

Flyleaves.

Edges: Plain.

A cloth: blue.

Front: Stamped in gold and blind.

Back: Stamped in blind; the name *Chanticleer* not present.

End papers: Yellow.

Flyleaves.

Edges: Plain.

T cloth: red, printed in black and yellow with an all-over floral pattern. V cloth: blue, embossed with a herringbone pattern.

Front: Stamped in gold.

Back: Stamped in gold.

End papers: White, printed in blue with an all-over pattern of small square units. Also: Plain yellow end papers.

Flyleaves; or, flyleaf at front only.

Edges: Gilt.

Advertised for Nov. 1 LW Oct. 19, 1850. Noted as *published* LW Nov. 16, 1850. Advertised as *just published* LW Nov. 30, 1850. Deposited (a copy of the *Second Edition*, so identified on the title-page) Dec. 6, 1850. Second edition advertised as *now ready* LW Dec. 28, 1850. Listed Ath July 26, 1851.

AAS (C)   B (B)   BPL (D)   NYPL (A)   UV (A,D)   Y (B,D)

Moneypenny, or, the Heart of the World. A Romance of the Present Day by Cornelius Mathews.

New York: Dewitt & Davenport, Tribune Buildings. 1850.

Reprint. Copyright notice dated 1850. See above under year 1849.

13643. WITCHCRAFT: A TRAGEDY, IN FIVE ACTS . . .

LONDON: DAVID BOGUE. 1852.

See next entry for American printing.

Cancel title-leaf?

⟨1⟩-99. 6″ × 3¹³⁄₁₆″.

⟨1-8⁶, 9²⟩. *Signed:* ⟨1⟩-4¹², 5².

Probably issued in printed paper wrapper.

". . . Now first published, in England and not in the country of the Author, for reasons with which it is not necessary to trouble the reader . . ."——— P. ⟨3⟩.

It "has not yet appeared in an American Edition." ———SLM Dec. 1852.

Listed Ath June 5, 1852; PC June 15, 1852.

B

13644. WITCHCRAFT: A TRAGEDY, IN FIVE ACTS . . .

NEW-YORK: S. FRENCH, 1852.

See preceding entry for prior publication.

⟨1⟩-99. 5⅞″ × 3⅞″.

⟨1-8⁶, 9²⟩. *Signed:* ⟨1⟩-4¹², 5².

Printed paper wrapper, both green and yellow noted. White end papers.

Deposited June 24, 1852.

Note: Copies occur with an inserted notice (on a slip 1¹³⁄₁₆″ × 3½″): *As ⟨it is⟩ thought it might be a matter of curiosity to some persons ⟨to⟩ look through a copy . . . printed and acted . . . nearly twenty years ago, especially ⟨as⟩ the subject has attracted fresh attention in anticipation ⟨of the⟩ publication announced for the present month (Oct. 1868,) ⟨of The⟩ New England Tragedy . . . by Mr. Longfellow ⟨the⟩ author has exhumed from a box, where they have lain in the dust some sixteen years, the "remainder" of the Edition of Witchcraft, printed in 1852, a copy of which ⟨is⟩ now in your hands . . . C. Mathews, Oct. 1, 1868.*

H   NYHS

13645. CALMSTORM, THE REFORMER. A DRAMATIC COMMENT.

NEW YORK: W. H. TINSON, 22 SPRUCE STREET. 1853.

Anonymous. Presumed to be by Mathews. "Probably by Mathews."———*Later American Plays* . . . , by Robert F. Roden, New York, 1900, p. 82. Attributed to Mathews without comment by Arthur Hobson Quinn in *A History of the American Drama* . . . , New York, 1923, p. 425.

⟨1⟩-71. 5¹⁵⁄₁₆″ × 3¹³⁄₁₆″.

⟨-⟩², 1-5⁶, 6⁴.

Printed cream-white wrapper.

Deposited July 11, 1853.

H   LC   NYHS   NYPL   Y

13646. A PEN-AND-INK PANORAMA OF NEW-YORK CITY . . .

NEW-YORK: JOHN S. TAYLOR, 17 ANN-STREET. 1853.

⟨i⟩-iv, ⟨5⟩-209; blank, p. ⟨210⟩; advertisements, pp. ⟨13⟩-⟨18⟩. 5⅞″ × 3¾″ scant.

⟨1², 2⁴, 3-19⁶⟩.

A cloth: purple; slate. Pale yellow end papers. Flyleaves.

Note: The surviving copyright deposit copy, as well as an ex-Smithsonian Institution copy, have the copyright notice revised by means of a pasted slip. In the copyright notice as printed originally the name of the copyright claimant is *John S. Taylor*; the slip, imprinted BY CORNELIUS MATHEWS, is pasted over Taylor's name.

Reviewed LW Aug. 27, 1853. Deposited Sept. 26, 1853. Noticed Ath Jan. 7, 1854. Reviewed LG Jan. 7, 1854.

B   UV

13647. FALSE PRETENCES; OR, BOTH SIDES OF GOOD SOCIETY. A COMEDY IN FIVE ACTS ... EACH COPY OF THIS PLAY IS THE PRIVATE PROPERTY OF THE AUTHOR.

NEW YORK: 1856.

Cover-title.

⟨i⟩-⟨vi⟩, 7-88. 6⁵⁄₁₆″ × 4³⁄₁₆″.

⟨1⟩-3¹², 4⁶, ⟨5⟩².

Printed self-wrapper.

Printed for the author's use and distributed by him to theatre managers in an effort to have the play produced.

Extract from the author's prefatory note, pp. ⟨iii⟩-iv: "[Private.] 142 Broadway, New York, ⟨space for date⟩ th, 1856. The Comedy of *False Pretences* is now printed, not for publication, but for the convenience of presenting it to managers with a view to its production at different theatres ... To save the necessity of individual correspondence with each ⟨manager⟩, it may be here stated, that a copy ... is addressed to various managers, with the privilege of producing it for any number of nights to the end of the present theatrical season, at $ ⟨space⟩ per night ... managers who do not desire to produce the play, are requested to return the copy to my address ..." The date April 9, 1856, inserted in LC copy; Sept. 27, 1856, in AAS copy.

Title deposited for copyright Oct. 27, 1856. "... Performed at Burton's Theatre, N. Y., Dec. 3d, 1856."---P. ⟨v⟩.

AAS   H   LC

13648. The Indian Fairy Book. From the Original Legends ...

New York: Published by Mason Brothers. 1856.

Edited anonymously by Mathews.

⟨i⟩-vi, ⟨7⟩-338; 10 pp. advertisements. Frontispiece and 3 plates inserted. 7³⁄₈″ scant × 4¹³⁄₁₆″.

"The Editor has been so fortunate as to be able to separate from a large mass of Indian material--- placed at his disposal by the generous friendship of Henry R. Schoolcraft, Esq.---a number of fairy and magical stories ..."---P. ⟨iii⟩.

Copyright notice dated 1855. Advertised for *this day* APC Dec. 15, 1856. Deposited Jan. 15, 1857. For other editions see this title under the year 1869; *The Enchanted Moccasins ...*, 1877; *Hiawatha and Other Legends ...*, ⟨n.d., 1882⟩.

Dated 1854 by Sabin (No. ⟨46832⟩) with the statement "reprinted in 1856." No 1854 printing has been located by BAL.

Y

The Various Writings of Cornelius Mathews ...

New York ... MDCCCLXIII.

See above under year 1843.

13649. The Indian Fairy Book ...

New-York: Published by Allen Brothers. 1869.

A reprint of the 1856 edition with the exception of the "Preface" (dated at end *October, 1868*) which is a truncated version of the original. For other editions see *The Enchanted Moccasins ...*, 1877; *Hiawatha and Other Legends ...* ⟨n.d., 1882⟩.

Title-page entered Sept. 18, 1868. Listed ALG Jan. 1, 1869. Listed PC Feb. 15, 1869.

AAS

13650. The Enchanted Moccasins and Other Legends of the Americans ⟨*sic*⟩ Indians ... by Cornelius Matthews ⟨*sic*⟩ ...

New York   G. P. Putnam's Sons   182 Fifth Avenue   1877

Save for "Preface to the Third Edition," pp. ⟨iii⟩-iv, a reprint of *The Indian Fairy Book ...*, 1856; 1869. See next entry.

The misspelling *Matthews* occurs on both title-page and on binding.

Listed PW Oct. 20, 1877.

AAS   NYPL   Y

13651. Hiawatha and Other Legends of the Wigwams of the Red American Indians ...

London: W. Swan Sonnenschein & Co. Paternoster Row ⟨n.d., 1882⟩

Reprint of *The Indian Fairy Book*, 1856, with the following additional material:

"The Hill of the Little People," pp. ⟨339⟩-342.

"Compact with the Evil One," pp. ⟨343⟩-344.

"Manabozho, the Mischief-Maker" appears herein with slight revisions as "Hiawatha, the Mischief-Maker."

Listed Ath April 1, 1882; PC April 1, 1882.

H NYPL

REPRINTS

The following publications contain material by Mathews reprinted from earlier books.

The Prose Writers of America . . . by Rufus Wilmot Griswold . . .

Philadelphia . . . 1847.

For comment see entry Nos. 3158, 6676.

Cyclopædia of American Literature . . . by Evert A. Duyckinck and George L. Duyckinck. In Two Volumes . . .

New York . . . 1855.

Contains no material by Mathews here first published. "Little Trappan," Vol. 2, pp. 648-649, extracted from *A Pen-and-Ink Panorama . . .*, 1853, pp. 56-66.

For fuller comment see entry No. 11092A.

The Poets and Poetry of America. By Rufus Wilmot Griswold . . .

New York . . . 1873.

For comment see BAL, Vol. 4, p. 60.

An American Anthology 1787-1899 . . . Edited by Edmund Clarence Stedman . . .

Boston . . . M DCCCC

For fuller entry see No. 3082.

REFERENCES AND ANA

. . . The Tragedy of Jacob Leisler: The Patriot Hero of New-York. A Sketch of His Life, and the Struggles of the Early Colonists of the Empire State, against Arbitrary Power. With the Cast of the Piece to Be Produced at the Bowery Theatre . . .

New York; William H. Graham, Tribune Buildings. 1848.

Cover-title. Pp. 8. Printed self-wrapper. An advertisement; text of the play not included.

At head of title: *Tot-het-huys von Leisler!*

No record of publication found. K April 1848 noted that the play was offered to a New York actor who refused it. K May 1848 reported the play a "mosaic of several hands . . . recently brought out ⟨in⟩ Philadelphia." K June 1848

reported the play produced "at the Bowery . . . was a great failure."

The Prompter; a Weekly Miscellany, Devoted to Public Amusements. Edited by Cornelius Mathews . . .

⟨n.p., presumably New York, 1850⟩

Issued biweekly. Four issues (all published?) noted, June 1, 1850 to Aug. 5, 1850. The preceding bear Mathews's name as editor. Superseded by *The Prompter's Whistle. A Weekly Miscellany, Devoted to Public Amusements*, "edited by the Man behind the Curtain"; suspended Sept. 28, 1850.

From *The Prompter's Whistle*, Aug. 31, 1850:

A CARD.

"The Prompter not being at his post of duty, *The Prompter's Whistle* has fallen into other hands, and now for the first shrill note———

"*The Prompter* was published by W. Taylor and Cornelius Mathews, under an agreement, in which each was to bear an equal half of the losses, and to share an equal half of the profits; the settlement to be made monthly, after four numbers were published. The loss was about $200, and *one* of the parties having failed to pay up his half of the losses, the other party refused to advance any more money to carry it on; and hence the death of *The Prompter*."

The absence of Mathews's name from the successor periodical suggests that he was not editor.

The Modern Standard Drama and *The Minor Drama*, 1850.

"The Editorship of *The Modern Standard Drama* and *The Minor Drama* (efficiently published by William Taylor & Co.) has, we understand, been assigned to Cornelius Mathews, whose dramatic position before the public, as the author of the Tragedies of *Witchcraft* and *Jacob Leisler*, is the guarantee of a right sympathy and understanding in the premises."———LW March 30, 1850.

Examination of the series indicates that LW overstated the facts in ascribing the editorship to Mathews. The only Mathews contributions that may be definitely ascribed to him are listed below.

The following list is for the record only. The imprints are of the earliest (or only) copies thus far noted and are not necessarily the earliest issued. All entries are subject to correction.

A list of the plays known to contain Mathews contributions:

Modern Standard Drama, No. LXXX. Goldsmith, Oliver: *She Stoops to Conquer.* New York: Wm. Taylor & Co., 18 Ann Street ⟨n.d., 1850⟩. Noted in LW April 20, 1850. A reprint was issued with the publisher's later address: *151 Nassau Street.*

Modern Standard Drama, No. LXXXI. Shakespeare, William: *Julius Caesar.* New York: Wm. Taylor & Co., 18 Ann Street ⟨n.d.⟩.

Modern Standard Drama, No. LXXXII. Goldsmith, Oliver: *The Vicar of Wakefield.* New York: Wm. Taylor & Co., 18 Ann Street ⟨n.d.⟩. A reprint has been seen with the publisher's later address: *151 Nassau Street.*

Modern Standard Drama, No. LXXXIII. Buckstone, J. Baldwin: *Leap Year; or, the Ladies' Privilege.* New York: Wm. Taylor & Co., 18 Ann Street ⟨n.d.⟩.

Modern Standard Drama, No. LXXXIV. Jerrold, Douglas: *The Catspaw.* New York: Wm. Taylor & Co., 18 Ann Street ⟨n.d.⟩. A reprint has been seen with the publisher's later address: *151 Nassau Street.*

Modern Standard Drama, No. LXXXV. Bernard, Bayle: *The Passing Cloud.* New York: Wm. Taylor & Co., 18 Ann Street ⟨n.d.⟩. A reprint has been seen with the publisher's later address: *151 Nassau Street.*

The Minor Drama, No. XXXVII. Kenney, James: *The Irish Ambassador.* New York: Wm. Taylor & Co. (S. French, General Agent) 151 Nassau Street ⟨n.d., 1850⟩. Reviewed LW May 11, 1850.

The Minor Drama, No. XXXIX. Allingham, J. T.: *The Weathercock.* New York: Wm. Taylor & Co. (S. French, General Agent) 151 Nassau Street ⟨n.d.⟩.

The Minor Drama, No. XXXVIII. Dance. Charles: *Delicate Ground; or, Paris in 1793.* New York: Wm. Taylor & Co. (S. French, General Agent) 151 Nassau Street ⟨n.d.⟩.

REFERENCE

Big Abel and the Little Manhattan by Cornelius Mathews with a New Foreword by Donald J. Yannella, Jr.

Garrett Press, Inc. New York, 1970

Note: In a letter to BAL (Aug. 17, 1970) the editor states: "... Garrett has also reissued *Puffer Hopkins* and *Behemoth,* both prefaced with the same *Foreword* ..."

HERMAN MELVILLE

1819–1891

13652. NARRATIVE OF A FOUR MONTHS'
RESIDENCE AMONG THE NATIVES OF
A VALLEY OF THE MARQUESAS
ISLANDS; OR, A PEEP AT POLYNESIAN
LIFE . . .

LONDON: JOHN MURRAY, ALBEMARLE STREET.
1846.

For first American edition see next entry, *Typee.*
Also see under year 1968.

Issued in two parts, printed paper wrapper, as
Nos. XXX-XXXI of *Murray's Home and Colonial
Library* series; also two parts in a single cloth-
bound volume, No. XV of the same series.

FIRST ISSUE, WRAPPERS, ORIGINAL STATE OF
SHEETS

1: ⟨iii⟩-⟨xviii⟩, ⟨1⟩-144; plus: publisher's catalog,
pp. ⟨1⟩-16, dated on p. ⟨1⟩ *March, 1846.* $7\frac{1}{8}''$ ×
$4\frac{7}{8}''$ scant. *Note:* The title-page is p. ⟨iii⟩; map is
p. ⟨xviii⟩. The title-page present in Vol. 1 only.

2: 145-285; Clowes imprint, p. ⟨286⟩; fly-title-
page, p. ⟨287⟩; blank, p. ⟨288⟩; plus: publisher's
catalog, pp. ⟨1⟩-16, dated on p. ⟨1⟩ *March, 1846.*

1: ⟨A⟩-I, K⁸; plus: ⟨-⟩⁸. *Note:* The title-page is
⟨A⟩1r; the map is ⟨A⟩8v.

2: L-T⁸; plus ⟨*⟩⁸. *Note:* The fly-title-page is
T8r.

P. 19, line 1: . . . *Pomarea* . . .

Printed tan paper wrappers.

Inner front wrapper: *Mr. Murray's List Of New
Works Just Published* . . . ⟨Nos. I-XVI⟩

Inner back wrapper: *New Editions of Standard
Works* . . . ⟨Nos. I-XVIII⟩

Outer back wrapper, Part 1: . . . *No. XXXI. Will
Contain A Residence In The Marquesas. Part II* . . .
On Part 2: . . . *No. XXXII. Will Be Published
May 1* . . .

Spine of Vol. 1 lettered up: THE MARQUESAS ISLANDS.

Spine of Vol. 2 lettered up: THE MARQUESAS
ISLANDS.――PART II

Locations: UV Y (wrappers missing in part)

FIRST ISSUE, CLOTH, BINDER'S VARIANT A

⟨i⟩-⟨xviii⟩, ⟨1⟩-285; Clowes imprint, p. ⟨286⟩;
pp. ⟨287-288⟩ excised. 7″ × 4¾″. Noted with and
without publisher's inserted terminal catalog,
pp. 16; see note below. The fly-title-leaf, pp. ⟨i-ii⟩,
was printed as pp. ⟨287-288⟩ and brought
forward by the binder. Title-page, p. ⟨iii⟩; map,
p. ⟨xviii⟩.

⟨-⟩¹ (=T8), ⟨A⟩-I, K-T⁸ (-T8). T8 is the fly-
title-leaf; *i.e.,* ⟨-⟩.

P. 19, line 1: . . . *Pomarea* . . .

A cloth: red. Spine lettered in gold: COLONIAL /
AND / HOME / LIBRARY / VOL. / XV / MELVILLE'S /
MARQUESAS / ISLANDS / MURRAY

Yellow-coated end papers.

The Terminal Catalog

The terminal catalog has been noted as follows;
the designations are all but wholly arbitrary.

A

Terminal catalog not present.

B

Terminal catalog dated *March, 1846.*

C

Terminal catalog dated *September, 1846.*

Note: A copy has been seen (Y) with the spine
lettered as follows: MELVILLE'S / MARQUESAS /
ISLANDS / MURRAY Also noted on a set of 1847
sheets, inserted terminal catalog dated *May, 1848.*
Also on a set of 1847 sheets, inserted terminal
catalog dated *January, 1851.* The 1847 copies
located in H.

Locations: N UV

FIRST ISSUE, CLOTH, BINDER'S VARIANT B

⟨i-ii⟩, ⟨i⟩-xvi, ⟨1⟩-285; Clowes imprint, p. ⟨286⟩;
pp. ⟨287-288⟩ excised; plus: publisher's catalog,
pp. ⟨1⟩-16, dated on p. ⟨1⟩ *March, 1846.* The fly-
title-leaf (the very first leaf in the book) was
printed as pp. ⟨287-288⟩ and brought forward by
the binder. The map appears opposite the title-
page. 7″ × 4¾″.

⟨a⟩¹ (= T8), ⟨b⟩², ⟨A⟩⁶, B-I, K-T⁸ (-T8); plus: ⟨*⟩⁸. T8 is the fly-title-leaf; *i.e.*, ⟨a⟩. Leaves ⟨A⟩1,8, removed from the gathering as originally printed, to become ⟨b⟩2 and ⟨b⟩1 respectively.

P. 19, line 1 : . . . *Pomarea . . .*

A cloth: red. Spine lettered in gold: COLONIAL / AND / HOME / LIBRARY / VOL. / XV / MELVILLE'S / MARQUESAS / ISLANDS / MURRAY

Yellow-coated end papers.

Locations : UV

SECOND ISSUE, WRAPPERS, ORIGINAL STATE OF SHEETS

1 : ⟨iii⟩-⟨xviii⟩, ⟨1⟩-144; plus: publisher's catalog, pp. ⟨1⟩-16, dated on p. ⟨1⟩: *March, 1846*. 7″ scant × 4¾″.

2 : 145-285; Clowes imprint, p. ⟨286⟩; fly-title, p. ⟨287⟩; blank, p. ⟨288⟩; plus: publisher's catalog, pp. ⟨1⟩-16, dated on p. ⟨1⟩: *March, 1846*.

1 : ⟨A⟩-I, K⁸; plus: ⟨-⟩⁸.

2 : L-T⁸; plus: ⟨-⟩⁸.

Leaf T8 is the fly-title-leaf, designed to be brought forward by the binder. The map is leaf ⟨A⟩8v.

Printed tan paper wrapper.

Outer back wrapper, Part 1: *Cheap Pocket Volumes for the Country . . . No. XXXI. Will Contain A Residence In The Marquesas. Part II . . .*

Spine, Part 1, lettered up: THE MARQUESAS ISLANDS.---PART I.

Outer back wrapper, Part 2: *Cheap Pocket Volumes for the Country . . . No. XXXII. Will Be Published May 1 . . .*

Spine, Part 2, lettered up: THE MARQUESAS ISLANDS.---PART II.

P. 19, line 1 : . . . *Pomare . . .*

Locations : H

SECOND ISSUE, WRAPPERS, BINDER'S VARIANT A

1 : ⟨i⟩-xvi, ⟨1⟩-144. 7¹/₁₆″ × 4⅞″.

2 : 145-285; Clowes imprint, p. ⟨286⟩.

1 : ⟨-⟩², ⟨A⟩⁶, B-I, K⁸. Leaves ⟨A⟩1,8 (as originally printed) removed from the gathering to become, respectively, ⟨-⟩2 and ⟨-⟩1. Map appears opposite the title-page.

2 : L-T⁸. Leaf T8, presumably the fly-title-leaf, removed and discarded.

Printed tan paper wrapper. The following is sufficient for identification:

Inner front, Part 1: *Mr. Murray's List Of New Works . . .* ⟨Nos. I-XII⟩

Inner back, Part 1: *Mr. Murray's List of Works . . .* ⟨Nos. XIII-XXIV⟩

Outer back, Part 1: *Mr. Murray's Monthly Library . . .*

Spine lettered up, Part 1: THE MARQUESAS ISLANDERS. ⟨*sic*⟩

Inner front, Part 2: *Books for Presents . . .* ⟨Nos. I-VIII⟩

Inner back, Part 2: *Lord Byron's Life And Works . . .* ⟨10 numbered volumes⟩

Outer back, Part 2: *Published Monthly . . . The Home And Colonial Library . . .* ⟨Nos. 1-31⟩

Spine lettered up, Part 2: THE MARQUESAS ISLANDS. ---PART II.

Note : The wrapper is probably considerably later than the sheets. The extended list on the outer back of Part 2 includes, among other titles, Melville's *Omoo* which was issued by Murray in 1847.

P. 19, line 1 : . . . *Pomare . . .*

Locations : H

SECOND ISSUE, CLOTH, BINDER'S VARIANT B

⟨i⟩-⟨xviii⟩, ⟨1⟩-285; Clowes imprint, p. ⟨286⟩; pp. ⟨287-288⟩ excised; plus: publisher's catalog, pp. ⟨1⟩-16, dated on p. ⟨1⟩: *March, 1846*; or, *September, 1846*. *Note :* The fly-title-leaf, pp. ⟨i-ii⟩, was printed as pp. ⟨287-288⟩, and brought forward by the binder. Title-page, p. ⟨iii⟩; map, p. ⟨xviii⟩. 7″ × 4¹¹/₁₆″.

⟨-⟩¹ (= T8), ⟨A⟩-I, K-T⁸ (-T8); plus: ⟨*⟩⁸. T8 is the fly-title-leaf; *i.e.*, ⟨-⟩.

A cloth: red. Spine lettered in gold: COLONIAL / AND / HOME / LIBRARY / VOL. / XV / MELVILLE'S / MARQUESAS / ISLANDS / MURRAY

Yellow-coated end papers.

P. 19, line 1 : . . . *Pomare . . .*

A copy has been seen (in N) with "The Story of Toby" inserted at back. In all likelihood the insertion was done by a private owner, not by a professional binder.

AAS (March catalog) H (March catalog) LC (September catalog)

SECOND ISSUE, CLOTH, BINDER'S VARIANT C

⟨i-ii⟩, ⟨i⟩-xvi, ⟨1⟩-285; Clowes imprint, p. ⟨286⟩; pp. ⟨287-288⟩ excised; plus: publisher's catalog, pp. ⟨1⟩-16, dated on p. ⟨1⟩: *March, 1846*. Note: The fly-title-leaf was printed as pp. ⟨287-288⟩ and brought forward by the binder. Title-page, p. ⟨iii⟩; map, p. ⟨ii⟩, *i.e.*, leaf ⟨b⟩1v. 7″ × 4¾″.

⟨a⟩¹ (= T8), ⟨b⟩², ⟨A⟩⁶, B-I, K-T⁸ (-T8); plus: ⟨*⟩⁸. T8 is the fly-title-leaf; *i.e.*, ⟨a⟩. Leaves ⟨A⟩1,8, removed from the gathering as originally folded to become ⟨b⟩2 and ⟨b⟩1 respectively.

P. 19, line 1 : . . . *Pomare . . .*

A cloth: red. Spine lettered in gold: COLONIAL / AND / HOME / LIBRARY / VOL. / XV / MELVILLE'S / MARQUESAS / ISLANDS / MURRAY

Yellow-coated end papers.

A copy thus presented by Gansevoort Melville to Mrs. Bancroft March 3, 1846; in UV.

Locations: N UV

SECOND ISSUE, CLOTH, BINDER'S VARIANT D

⟨i⟩-⟨xviii⟩, ⟨1⟩-285; Clowes imprint, p. ⟨286⟩; pp. ⟨287-288⟩ excised. No terminal catalog present. *Note:* The fly-title-leaf, pp. ⟨i-ii⟩, was printed as pp. ⟨287-288⟩, and brought forward by the binder. Title-page, p. ⟨iii⟩; map, p. ⟨xviii⟩. $6^{15}/_{16}'' \times 4^{11}/_{16}''$.

⟨-⟩¹ (=T8), ⟨A⟩-I, K-T⁸ (-T8). T8 is the fly-title-leaf; *i.e.,* ⟨-⟩.

P. 19, line 1: . . . *Pomare* . . .

A cloth: red. Spine lettered in gold: MELVILLE'S / MARQUESAS / ISLANDS / 15 / MURRAY Yellow-coated end papers.

Location: N

SUMMARY

First issue, original state of sheets:

P. 19, line 1: . . . *Pomarea* . . .

Map on p. ⟨xviii⟩

Fly-title on p. ⟨287⟩

Noted in paper only.

First issue, cloth, binder's variant A:

P. 19, line 1: . . . *Pomarea* . . .

Map on p. ⟨xviii⟩

Fly-title on p. ⟨i⟩

Spine numbered *XV*

First issue, cloth, binder's variant B:

P. 19, line 1: . . . *Pomarea* . . .

Map opposite the title-page

Fly-title on p. ⟨i⟩

Spine numbered *XV*

Second issue, original state of sheets:

P. 19, line 1: . . . *Pomare* . . .

Map on p. ⟨xviii⟩

Fly-title on p. ⟨287⟩

Noted in paper only.

Second issue, binder's variant A:

P. 19, line 1: . . . *Pomare* . . .

Map opposite the title-page

Fly-title excised and discarded

Noted in paper only.

Second issue, cloth, binder's variant B:

P. 19, line 1: . . . *Pomare* . . .

Map on p. ⟨xviii⟩

Fly-title on p. ⟨i⟩.

Spine numbered *XV*

Second issue, cloth, binder's variant C:

P. 19, line 1: . . . *Pomare* . . .

Map opposite the title-page

Fly-title on p. ⟨i⟩

Spine numbered *XV*

Second issue, cloth, binder's variant D:

P. 19, line 1: . . . *Pomare* . . .

Map on p. ⟨xviii⟩

Fly-title on p. ⟨i⟩

Spine numbered *15*

PUBLICATION NOTES

No wholly satisfactory publication sequence has been established for the London issues of this book. In the United States it was issued under the title *Typee . . .* ; in England as *Narrative of a Four Months' Residence among the Natives of a Valley of the Marquesas Islands.* In October, 1846 (the year of first publication) it was issued in London under the more familiar title, *Typee . . . .* The history is further complicated by the publication of an additional chapter, "The Story of Toby," which was first published (not as a separate) in the United States in August, 1846; and, in London (as pamphlet) in October, 1846.

The following dates demonstrate the problem.

Part 1. London. Announced for Feb. 28, 1846, PC Feb. 16, 1846.

———: Announced for Feb. 28, 1846, LG and Ath Feb. 21, 1846.

———: First part of a review of Part I Ath Feb. 21, 1846.

Cloth: ". . . Mr. Murray sent me 6 bound copies of Herman's book . . ."———extracted from Gansevoort Melville's diary, entry for Feb. 24, 1846, as reported by Victor Hugo Paltsits in "Herman Melville's Background and New Light on the Publication of *Typee*," in *Bookmen's Holiday Notes and Studies Written and Gathered in Tribute to Harry Miller Lydenberg,* New York, 1943. See below under March 3, 1846.

Feb. 26, 1846. The title-page for the New York printing deposited for copyright. *Melville Log,* p. 204.

London: "...Herman's book will appear tomorrow..."———Paltsits, *op. cit.*, entry for Feb. 26, 1846.

Part 1. London: "This day is published"———Ath Feb. 28, 1846.

Part 1. London: Advertised without comment LG Feb. 28, 1846.

Parts 1-2. London: Reviewed Ath Feb. 28, 1846, pp. 218-220.

———: Reviewed *Spectator* (London) Feb. 28, 1846, pp. 209-210.

Part 1. London: Advertised as *this day is published* PC March 2, 1846.

Cloth. London: Gansevoort Melville presented a copy to Mrs. Bancroft March 3, 1846. Copy in UV. See above under Feb. 24, 1846.

Part 1. London: Advertised without comment LG March 7, 1846.

Cloth. London: Advertised as *just issued* Ath March 14, 1846.

———: Advertised as though published LG March 14, 1846.

———: Listed PC March 16, 1846. Described as in cloth, pp. 302, Vol. 15 of the series.

Part 1. London: Listed PC March 16, 1846 as *Home & Colonial Library*, No. 30, pp. 144.

Parts 1-2, New York: Deposited March 17, 1846.

New York: Melville presented a copy of the New York edition to Mrs. Tomlinson, March 18, 1846. *Melville Log*, p. 207.

New York. Cloth: Melville presented a copy to the dedicatee, Chief Justice Shaw, March 19, 1846. Copy in H.

New York. Cloth: A copy in NYPL inscribed by Melville March 19, 1846.

———: A copy in NYPL inscribed by Melville March 20, 1846.

Cloth. London: Advertised as *this day is published* LG March 21, 1846.

———: *This day is published*———PC April 1, 1846.

Part 1. New York: A copy in NYPL inscribed by Henry Gansevoort, April 3, 1846.

Cloth. London: This day is published———PC April 15, 1846.

Part 2. London: Listed PC April 15, 1846.

Parts 1-2. London: This day is published, as Nos. 30-31 of the series, LG April 18, 1846.

Cloth and paper. New York: Advertised NYM April 18, 1846.

Parts 1-2. New York: Noted as received NAR April, 1846.

Cloth. London: Noted in PC May 1, 1846 as No. 20 ⟨*sic*⟩ of the series.

Cloth. New York: A copy in UV inscribed by Allan Melville May 29, 1846.

Cloth. London: Noted PC July 1, 1846, as Vol. 15 of the series.

New York: A new edition, with "The Story of Toby" added, announced WPLNL July, 1846.

Aug. 1, 1846: Melville "sent Murray the Sequel ⟨'The Story of Toby'⟩ by steamer on August 1 with the statement that it 'will not be published here ⟨USA⟩, until at least ten days hence——— owing to the backwardness in getting out the *Revised Edition* in which the Sequel will first appear.'" Leon Howard, "Historical Note," in *Typee*, Chicago, 1968, p. 287.

Revised edition. New York: Wiley & Putnam accounts show first printing of the *Revised Edition* (with "The Story of Toby") on July 31; issued Aug. 6, 1846. Leon Howard, *op. cit.*, pp. 287-288.

Revised edition. New York: Advertised NYM Aug. 15, 1846, as one volume in cloth; two volumes in paper.

Revised edition. New York: By Sept. 2, 1846, the *Revised Edition* had gone through a second printing. Leon Howard, *op. cit.*, p. 288.

———: By Sept. 2, 1846, Wiley & Putnam "had probably issued 250 copies of the earlier version (for which they printed extra covers of the *Revised Edition* on July 31) with *The Story of Toby* bound in." Leon Howard, *op. cit.*, p. 288.

The Story of Toby, as a pamphlet. London: "...A concluding chapter, added... It is printed as a few pages of addition..."———Ath Oct. 3, 1846.

———: Listed PC Oct. 15, 1846.

Typee. London: Under this title noted as *ready* PC Oct. 15, 1846.

———: Advertised as *now ready* Ath Oct. 17, 1846.

———: Advertised as *now ready* LG Oct. 17, 1846.

The Story of Toby, as a pamphlet. London: Listed Ath, LG Oct. 31, 1846.

———: Advertised PC Nov. 2, 1846.

Typee. London: Advertised PC Dec. 1, 1846, "with the story of Toby's escape." Earliest located advertisement of a printing with the sequel.

Locations: See above under the several forms of the book.

13653. TYPEE: A PEEP AT POLYNESIAN LIFE. DURING A FOUR MONTHS' RESIDENCE IN A VALLEY OF THE MARQUESAS WITH NOTICES OF THE FRENCH OCCUPATION OF TAHITI AND THE PROVISIONAL CESSION OF THE

SANDWICH ISLANDS TO LORD PAULET ...

NEW YORK: WILEY AND PUTNAM. LONDON: JOHN MURRAY, ALBEMARLE STREET 1846.

For the English edition see preceding entry. For revised edition see next entry: also see under the year 1968.

2 Vols. The title-page of Vol. 2 varies from the above as follows: A semi-colon follows MARQUESAS and a period follows STREET.

The following binding variants noted. The sequence, if any, not established and the designations are for identification only.

BINDING VARIANT A, CLOTH

Two volumes bound in one.

1: ⟨i-ii⟩, being a blank leaf, excised from some copies; ⟨iii-iv⟩, the fly-title leaf; ⟨i⟩-⟨xvi⟩, ⟨1⟩-166; one leaf excised, being a leaf of advertisements. Frontispiece map, being an integral leaf. $7\frac{3}{8}'' \times 5\frac{1}{16}''$.

2: ⟨i-iv⟩, ⟨167⟩-325; blank, p. ⟨326⟩; plus: 6 pp. advertisements paged ⟨v⟩-x. *Note:* In some copies pp. ix-x of the advertisements, a singleton leaf, is misbound causing the pagination to be: ⟨v⟩-viii, x, ix; in some copies the leaf (pp. ix-x) is not present.

1: ⟨1⟩^{10}, 2-3, ⟨4⟩, 5-8^{12}. In some copies leaf ⟨1⟩$_1$ excised; leaf 8$_{12}$ excised.

2: ⟨-⟩^{2}, 9-11, ⟨12⟩, 13-14^{12}, 15^6, ⟨16⟩^{2}; plus: ⟨17^2, 18^1⟩. In some copies ⟨18⟩ is not present.

T cloth: blue; brown; green; slate blue. Pale peach end papers. Buff end papers. Pale tan end papers decorated in red with a pattern of dots and rosettes. Flyleaves. Spine lettered in gold: LIBRARY / OF / AMERICAN / BOOKS / TYPEE / HERMAN / MELVILLE / WILEY & PUTNAM

Locations: AAS   H   LC   NYPL   UV   Y

BINDING VARIANT B, CLOTH

Two volumes bound in one.

1: ⟨i-iv⟩, excised, comprising a blank leaf and the fly-title leaf; ⟨i⟩-⟨xvi⟩, ⟨1⟩-166; one leaf excised, being a leaf of advertisements. Frontispiece map, being an integral leaf. $7\frac{3}{16}'' \times 5''$.

2: ⟨i-iv⟩, ⟨167⟩-325; blank, p. ⟨326⟩; plus: 6 pp. advertisements paged ⟨v⟩-x.

1: ⟨1⟩^{10}, 2-3, ⟨4⟩, 5-8^{12}. Leaves ⟨1⟩$_{1-2}$ and 8$_{12}$ excised.

2: ⟨-⟩^{2}, 9-11, ⟨12⟩, 13-14^{12}, 15^6, ⟨16⟩^{2}; plus: ⟨17^2, 18^1⟩.

T cloth: blue; slate-blue. Pale buff end papers. Flyleaves. Spine lettered in gold: TYPEE / HERMAN / MELVILLE / WILEY & PUTNAM

Locations: H (extensively restored; not collated; presented by Melville to the dedicatee, Chief Justice Shaw, March 19, 1846) NYPL (presented by Melville to Susan Gansevoort, March 20, 1846)

PAPER WRAPPER

1: ⟨i-iv⟩, ⟨i⟩-⟨xvi⟩, ⟨1⟩-166; 2 pp. advertisements paged x, ix. $7\frac{3}{8}'' \times 5''$ scant.

2: ⟨i-iv⟩, ⟨167⟩-325; blank, p. ⟨326⟩; plus: advertisements, pp. ⟨v⟩-viii.

1: ⟨1⟩^{10}, 2-3, ⟨4⟩, 5-8^{12}.

2: ⟨-⟩^{2}, 9-11, ⟨12⟩, 13-14^{12}, 15^6, ⟨16⟩^{2}; plus: ⟨17⟩^{2}.

Printed pale tan paper wrapper. The wrapper for *Part 1* has been noted in two forms; the sequence presented is presumed correct:

A: Identified on the front as *Nos. XIII. & XIV.* of the series.

B: Identified on the front as *No. XIII.* of the series. The surviving copyright deposit copy thus.

Note: Reportedly the first printing has p. 163 mispaged; the reference does not apply to the first printing. See *Revised Edition* below. All examined copies of the first printing have folio *ix* at the left side of the page.

Publication: For publication notes see under preceding entry.

AAS (Cloth, *Variant A*) H (Cloth, *Variant A*) LC (Cloth, *Variant A*) NYPL (Cloth, *Variant A*; Cloth, *Variant B*; Wrapper, *State A*; Wrapper, *State B*) UV (Cloth, *Variant A*; Wrapper, *State B*) Y (Cloth, *Variant A*)

13654. TYPEE---REVISED EDITION

1846

Text revised and extended by the addition of "The Story of Toby," pp. 293-307. The addition is preceded by a "Note to the Sequel," dated *July, 1846*, p. ⟨292⟩.

For first edition see preceding entry. Noted as follows:

FIRST PRINTING---PART I

Typee: A Peep at Polynesian Life. During a Four Months' Residence in a Valley of the Marquesas by Herman Melville. Part I.

New York: Wiley and Putnam. London: John Murray, Albemarle Street 1846.

Note absence of the statement *The Revised Edition, with a Sequel;* absence of semi-colon following *Marquesas;* absence of a period following *Street.*

⟨i-ii⟩, ⟨i⟩-xiv, ⟨1⟩-149; blank, pp. ⟨150-152⟩. $7\frac{5}{8}'' \times 5''$. Frontispiece map not present. The title-leaf is integral, not an insert.

⟨1⟩^{8}, 2-7^{12}, 8^4.

Front matter:

⟨i-ii⟩: Blank

⟨i⟩: Fly-title-page

⟨ii⟩: Blank

⟨iii⟩: Title-page

⟨iv⟩: Copyright notice; and, imprints of R. Craighead's Power Press; and, T. B. Smith, Stereotyper.

⟨v⟩: Dedication

⟨vi⟩: Blank

⟨vii⟩: *Preface to the Revised Edition*

⟨viii⟩: Blank

⟨ix⟩-x: Preface, being a truncated version of the preface in the first edition.

⟨xi⟩-xiv: Table of contents

Note presence of dedication; absence of map.

P. 101, line 3 from bottom: *. . . groves.* /

FIRST PRINTING – – – PART 2

Typee: A Peep at Polynesian Life during a Four Months' Residence in a Valley of the Marquesas; the Revised Edition, with a Sequel. By Herman Melville. Part II.

New York: Wiley and Putnam. London: John Murray, Albemarle Street. 1846.

Note presence of the *Revised* statement; presence of the semi-colon following *Marquesas;* presence of the period following *Street.*

⟨xi⟩-⟨xxvi⟩, ⟨151⟩-307; blank, p. ⟨308⟩; publisher's advertisements: p. ⟨309⟩: *. . . Books of Travels . . .* ; p. ⟨310⟩: *. . . Library of American Books . . .*

⟨-⟩², ⟨*⟩⁶, 9-14¹², ⟨15⟩⁶, ⟨16⟩².

Front matter:

⟨xi⟩: Fly-title-page

⟨xii⟩: Blank

⟨xiii⟩: Title-page

⟨xiv⟩: Blank

⟨xv⟩-xxiii: *(Revised Edition.) Publishers' Advertisement . . .*

⟨xxiv-xxvi⟩: Blank

Noted only in printed tan paper wrapper. Issued as Nos. XIII-XIV of *Wiley and Putnam's Library of American Books.* Also issued in cloth, two volumes in one?

Location: UV

FIRST PRINTING – – – SECOND STATE

The title-page for Part I is a cancel and reads:

Typee: A Peep at Polynesian Life. During a Four Months' Residence in a Valley of the Marquesas;

the Revised Edition, with a Sequel. By Herman Melville. Part I.

New York: Wiley and Putnam. London: John Murray, Albemarle Street. 1846.

Note presence of the statement *The Revised Edition, with a Sequel;* presence of the semi-colon following *Marquesas;* presence of a period following *Street.*

⟨i-ii⟩, ⟨i⟩-xiv, ⟨1⟩-149; p. ⟨150⟩ blank; one leaf excised; ⟨xv-xviii⟩; ⟨151⟩-307; blank, p. ⟨308⟩; publisher's advertisements: p. ⟨309⟩: *. . . Books of Travels . . .* ; p. ⟨310⟩: *. . . Library of American Books . . . 7¼″ × 5″.*

⟨1⟩⁸, 2-7¹², 8⁴, ⟨-⟩², 9-14¹², ⟨15⟩⁶, ⟨16⟩². It will be observed that gathering ⟨*⟩, *(Revised Edition.) Publishers' Advertisement,* is not present. Leaf 8₄ excised.

Front matter:

⟨i-ii⟩: Blank

⟨i⟩: Fly-title-page

⟨ii⟩: Blank

⟨iii⟩: Title-page

⟨iv⟩: Copyright notice; and, imprints of R. Craighead's Power Press; and, T. B. Smith, Stereotyper.

⟨v⟩: Dedication

⟨vi⟩: Blank

⟨vii⟩: *Preface to the Revised Edition*

⟨viii⟩: Blank

⟨ix⟩-x: Preface, being a truncated version of the preface in the first edition.

⟨xi⟩-xiv: Table of contents

Note presence of dedication; absence of map.

P. 101, line 3 from bottom: *. . . groves.* /

TITLE-PAGE – – – PART 2

Paged ⟨xvii-xviii⟩

Typee: A Peep at Polynesian Life during a Four Months' Residence in a Valley of the Marquesas; the Revised Edition, with a Sequel. By Herman Melville. Part II.

New York: Wiley and Putnam. London: John Murray, Albemarle Street. 1846.

Note presence of the *Revised* statement; presence of the semi-colon following *Marquesas;* presence of the period following *Street.*

Noted only in cloth, two volumes in one. Also issued in printed paper wrapper?

Location: N

SECOND PRINTING – – – PART I

Typee: A Peep at Polynesian Life. During a Four Months' Residence in a Valley of the Marquesas;

the Revised Edition, with a Sequel. By Herman Melville. Part i.

New York: Wiley and Putnam. London: John Murray, Albemarle Street. 1846.

⟨xi⟩-⟨xxvi⟩, ⟨1⟩-149; blank, p. ⟨150⟩; p. ⟨151⟩: ... *Library of American Books* ... ; p. ⟨152⟩: ... *Books of Travels* ... ; plus (in some copies) 4 pp. advertisements. 7⁹⁄₁₆″ × 5¹⁄₁₆″. Frontispiece map inserted.

⟨-⟩², ⟨1⟩⁶, 2-7¹², 8⁴; plus (in some copies) ⟨9⟩².

Front matter:

⟨xi-xii⟩: Blank

Inserted map

⟨xiii⟩: Title-page

⟨xiv⟩: Copyright notice; and, imprints of R. Craighead's Power Press; and, T. B. Smith, Stereotyper.

⟨xv⟩-xxiii: (*Revised Edition.*) Publishers' Advertisement ...

⟨xxiv-xxvi⟩: Blank

Note absence of dedication and prefaces.

P. 101, line 3 from bottom: ... *groves.*/

SECOND PRINTING ——— PART 2

Typee: A Peep at Polynesian Life during a Four Months' Residence in a Valley of the Marquesas; the Revised Edition, with a Sequel. By Herman Melville. Part ii.

New York: Wiley and Putnam. London: John Murray, Albemarle Street. 1846.

⟨i-iv⟩, ⟨151⟩-307; blank, p. ⟨308⟩; p. ⟨309⟩: ... *Library of American Books* ... ; p. ⟨310⟩: ... *Books of Travels* ... ; plus (in some copies) 4 pp. advertisements.

⟨-⟩², 9-14¹², ⟨15⟩⁶, ⟨16⟩²; plus (in some copies) ⟨17⟩². In some copies signature mark 11 is present as a ghost; or, is completely absent.

Front matter:

⟨i⟩: Fly-title-page

⟨ii⟩: Blank

⟨iii⟩: Title-page

⟨iv⟩: Blank

Noted only in printed tan paper wrapper. Issued as Nos. XIII-XIV of *Wiley and Putnam's Library of American Books*. Also issued in cloth, two volumes in one?

Locations: bpl (incomplete) h (incomplete) uv (incomplete)

THIRD PRINTING

The title-page for Part i is not a cancel and reads:

Typee: A Peep at Polynesian Life. During a Four

Months' Residence in a Valley of the Marquesas; the Revised Edition, with a Sequel. By Herman Melville. Part i.

New York: Wiley and Putnam. London: John Murray, Albemarle Street. 1846.

Note presence of the statement *The Revised Edition, with a Sequel;* presence of the semi-colon following *Marquesas;* presence of a period following *Street.*

⟨i-ii⟩, ⟨i⟩-xiv, ⟨1⟩-149; blank, p. ⟨150⟩; leaf excised; ⟨xv-xviii⟩; ⟨151⟩-307; blank, p. ⟨308⟩; plus publisher's advertisements, (*Revised Edition.*) Publishers' Advertisement, pp. ⟨xv⟩-xxiii; blank, p. ⟨xxiv⟩; leaf excised; plus publisher's catalog, dated 1846, 8 pp., irregularly paged. 7⁵⁄₁₆″ full × 5¹⁄₁₆″. Frontispiece map an integral leaf, not an insert.

⟨1⟩⁸, 2-7¹², 8⁴, ⟨-⟩², 9-14¹², ⟨15⟩⁶, ⟨16⟩¹; plus: ⟨17⟩⁶, ⟨18⟩⁴. Leaves 8₄ and ⟨17⟩₆ excised.

Front matter:

⟨i⟩: General title-page

⟨ii⟩: Blank

⟨i⟩: Blank

⟨ii⟩: Frontispiece map

⟨iii⟩: Title-page

⟨iv⟩: Copyright page; following imprints present: R. Craighead's Power Press; and, T. B. Smith, Stereotyper.

⟨v⟩: Dedication

⟨vi⟩: Blank

⟨vii⟩: *Preface to the Revised Edition*

⟨viii⟩: Blank

⟨ix⟩-x: Preface, being a truncated version of the preface in the first edition.

⟨xi⟩-xiv: Table of contents

Note presence of dedication; presence of map, being an integral leaf.

P. 101, line 3 from bottom: ... *groves. /*

Noted in cloth only, two volumes in one. Also issued in printed paper wrapper?

Location: n

FOURTH PRINTING

Typee: A Peep at Polynesian Life. During a Four Months' Residence in a Valley of the Marquesas; the Revised Edition, with a Sequel ...

New York: Wiley and Putnam. London: John Murray, Albemarle Street. 1847.

Note presence of the statement *The Revised Edition, with a Sequel;* presence of the semi-colon following *Marquesas;* presence of a period following *Street.*

⟨i-ii⟩, ⟨i⟩-xiv, ⟨1⟩-149; blank, p. ⟨150⟩; ⟨151⟩-307; blank, p. ⟨308⟩; publisher's advertisements,

(Revised Edition.) Publishers' Advertisement, pp. ⟨xv⟩-xxiii; blank, p. ⟨xxiv⟩. Frontispiece an integral leaf, not an insert.

⟨1⟩⁸, 2-7¹², 8², ⟨8*⟩¹, 9-14¹², ⟨15⟩¹².

Front matter:

⟨i⟩: General title-page

⟨ii⟩: *Now Publishing . . . March, 1846.*

⟨i⟩: Blank

⟨ii⟩: Frontispiece map

⟨iii⟩: Title-page

⟨iv⟩: Copyright page; the following imprints present: R. Craighead's Power Press; and, T. B. Smith, Stereotyper

⟨v⟩: Dedication

⟨vi⟩: Blank

⟨vii⟩: *Preface to the Revised Edition*

⟨viii⟩: Blank

⟨ix⟩-x: Preface, being a truncated version of the preface in the first edition

⟨xi⟩-xiv: Table of contents

Note presence of the dedication; presence of map, being an integral leaf.

P. 101, line 3 from bottom: . . . *grove.* /

Noted in cloth only, two volumes in one. Also issued in printed paper wrapper?

Location: NYPL

For publication notes see above under *Narrative . . .*, London, 1846.

Note: In all examined copies of the above printings p. 163 is mispaged 463. In the fourth printing (see below) the error is corrected.

Also note: The "Preface to the Revised Edition" appears in the first, third and fourth printings of the revised edition; it is not present in the second printing. The preface is present in the 1847, 1848, 1849 printings.

13655. OMOO: A NARRATIVE OF ADVEN-
TURES IN THE SOUTH SEAS; BEING A
SEQUEL TO THE "RESIDENCE IN THE
MARQUESAS ISLANDS." . . .

LONDON: JOHN MURRAY, ALBEMARLE STREET.
1847.

For American edition see next entry. Also see under year 1968.

WRAPPERS

1: ⟨i⟩-⟨xiv⟩, ⟨1⟩-160. Map, p. ⟨ii⟩. 7″ × 4⅞″ scant.

2: 161-321; printer's imprint, p. ⟨322⟩; plus: Publisher's catalog, pp. ⟨1⟩-16.

1: ⟨-⟩¹, ⟨A⟩⁶, B-I, K-L⁸.

2: M-U, X⁸, Y¹; plus ⟨Z⟩⁸.

Printed tan-gray paper wrapper. Inserted at back of Vol. 2: Publisher's catalog, pp. ⟨1⟩-16.

CLOTH

⟨i⟩-⟨xiv⟩, ⟨1⟩-321; printer's imprint, p. ⟨322⟩; plus: Publisher's catalog, pp. ⟨1⟩-16. 7″ full × 4¾″ full.

⟨-⟩¹, ⟨A⟩⁶, B-I, K-U, X⁸, Y¹; plus: ⟨Z⟩⁸.

A cloth: red. Cream-coated end papers.

Note: Some copies of the cloth-bound format occur with a leaf of advertisements printed on one side only inserted at the front. The advertisement is for Murray's *Home and Colonial Library*, Nos. 1-24, *Omoo* being No. 22 of the series.

Also note: Signature mark P (p. 209) occurs in the following states of undetermined sequence; the designations are for identification only:

A: Present and perfectly printed.

B: Present as a printed vestige.

C: Present in blind, with a tiny portion printed.

Advertised for March 31 in Ath and LG March 6, 13, 20, 1847; PC March 15, 1847. Advertised as *this day is published* LG April 3, 1847. Reviewed Ath April 10, 1847. Listed PC April 15, 1847. Reviewed LG May 29, 1847.

AAS (cloth) H (cloth) LC (cloth) NYPL (paper) UV (both)

13656. OMOO: A NARRATIVE OF ADVEN-
TURES IN THE SOUTH SEAS . . .

NEW YORK: HARPER & BROTHERS, PUBLISHERS.
LONDON: JOHN MURRAY. 1847.

Title-page in black and red.

For prior publication see preceding entry. Also see under year 1968.

WRAPPERS

1: ⟨i⟩-⟨xvi⟩, ⟨17⟩-196. Frontispiece map inserted; 1 illustration in text. 7⅜″ × 5″.

2: 197-389; blank, p. ⟨390⟩; 2 pp. advertisements, paged ⟨-⟩, xvi; plus: 24 pp. advertisements, paged: xvii-xxiii; blank, p. ⟨xxiv⟩, ⟨1⟩-16.

1: ⟨-⟩⁴, A*⁸, B-H¹², I². Sig. I cut from the full 12mo gathering; see initial gathering of *Part 2* below.

2: ⟨I⟩¹⁰, K-Q¹², R⁴; plus: ⟨-⟩¹². Sig. ⟨I⟩ was printed as a 12mo, the first two leaves excised and bound in *Part 1*, see above.

Printed cream-white paper wrappers. White wove end papers.

⟨i⟩-⟨xvi⟩, ⟨17⟩-389; blank, p. ⟨390⟩; advertisements, ⟨xv⟩-xvi; plus: xvii-xxiii; blank, p. ⟨xxiv⟩; ⟨1⟩-16. Fontispiece map inserted; one illustration in text. 7³/₈″ full × 4¹⁵/₁₆″.

⟨-⟩⁴, A*⁸, B-I, K-Q¹², R⁴, plus: ⟨S⟩¹².

A cloth: brown; purple; red. H cloth: black; slate. V cloth, moiréd: slate. T cloth, moiréd: black; slate. TB cloth: green. Marbled end papers. Double flyleaves; see note below. A principal feature of the stamping is a goldstamped ship at the center of the front cover. Spine lettered in gold: OMOO. / MELVILLE. / NEW-YORK. / HARPER & BROTHERS See below for comment on a variant binding.

A note on the flyleaves: As in certain other books issued by the Harpers at this time, the binders inserted at both front and back a gathering of four blank leaves; one leaf pasted to the end paper as a lining; another leaf pasted under the pastedown; the other two leaves present as free flyleaves.

A variant binding of unknown status has been seen (NYPL): Leaves ⟨-⟩1 and ⟨S⟩5-12 lacking. Bound in H-like cloth; the ornamental ship not stamped on the side. Spine lettered with the title only: OMOO.

Advertised LW April 3, 1847, as *in a few days.* Noted as *just ready* LW April 10, 1847. Passages printed in LW April 24, 1847, where the book is described as *forthcoming.* Advertised as *now ready* LW May 1, 1847. Reviewed LW May 1, 1847. Deposited May 5, 1847. Listed LW May 29, 1847. The fourth thousand advertised in LW May 29, 1847; listed LW June 5, 1847.

AAS (cloth)　H (paper)　NYPL (cloth; paper)　UV (cloth; paper)　Y (cloth)

13657. MARDI: AND A VOYAGE THITHER . . . IN THREE VOLUMES . . .

LONDON: RICHARD BENTLEY, NEW BURLINGTON STREET. 1849.

Title-page in black and red.

For first American edition see next entry.

1: ⟨i⟩-x, ⟨1⟩-336. 7³/₄″ × 4⅞″.

2: ⟨i⟩-x, ⟨1⟩-335.

3: ⟨i⟩-viii, ⟨1⟩-348.

1: ⟨-⟩², a², a¹ ⟨sic⟩, B-I, K-P¹².

2: ⟨a⟩-b², b¹ ⟨sic⟩, B-I, K-P¹².

3: ⟨b⟩-c², B-I, K-P¹², Q⁶.

A cloth: pale green. White wove end papers printed in blue with an all-over pattern and advertisements.

Announced for the *15th inst* Ath March 3, 1849, as in two volumes; Ath March 10, 1849, as in

three volumes. Advertised as *now ready* Ath March 17, 1849. Listed Ath March 17, 1849. Reviewed Ath March 24, 1849. Listed PC April 2, 1849.

UV

13658. MARDI: AND A VOYAGE THITHER . . . IN TWO VOLUMES . . .

NEW YORK: HARPER & BROTHERS, PUBLISHERS, 82 CLIFF STREET. 1849.

For prior publication see preceding entry.

1: ⟨i⟩-xii, ⟨13⟩-365, 2 blank leaves, the second of which is used as lining for the terminal end paper; leaf excised or pasted under the end paper. 7⁷/₁₆″ × 5″ full.

2: ⟨v⟩-xii, ⟨9⟩-387; blank, p. ⟨388⟩; advertisements, pp. ⟨1⟩-8.

1: ⟨A⟩-I, K-P¹², Q⁶. Leaf Q6 excised or pasted under the end paper.

2: ⟨A⟩-I, K-Q¹², R⁶.

A cloth: blue-green; green; purple. T cloth: blue-green; brown. Fine-grained TR cloth: green. Yellow-coated end papers. Vol. 1: Double flyleaf at front; at back: Q5 used as lining for the terminal end paper. Vol. 2: Double flyleaves. For a comment on double flyleaves see note under *Omoo,* New York, 1847.

Note: Copies occur either with or without a blind-stamped rule about ⅛″ from the top of the spine. Significance not determined. Do not confuse with normal wear at the top of spine, nor with the blindstamped ornamented fillet which is about ³/₄″ from top of spine.

Advertised for *immediate publication* LW March 3, 10, 1849. ". . . Will be immediately issued, being published simultaneously by Messrs. Harper in this city, and Bentley in London."———LW April 7, 1849. Advertised as *in a few days* LW April 7, 1849. Deposited April 13, 1849. Reviewed LW April 14, 1849. Advertised as *now ready* LW April 14, 1849.

H　LC　NYPL　UV　Y

13659. REDBURN: HIS FIRST VOYAGE. BEING THE SAILOR-BOY CONFESSIONS AND REMINISCENCES OF THE SON-OF-A-GENTLEMAN, IN THE MERCHANT SERVICE . . . IN TWO VOLUMES . . .

LONDON: RICHARD BENTLEY, NEW BURLINGTON STREET. 1849.

For first American edition see next entry. Also see under year 1969.

1: ⟨i⟩-viii, ⟨1⟩-316. 7³/₄″ full × 4⅞″.

2: ⟨i⟩-viii, ⟨1⟩-314.

1: ⟨A⟩⁴, B-I, K-O¹², P².

2: ⟨A⟩⁴, B-I, K-O¹², P¹.

A cloth: blue. The end papers have been noted as follows; sequence, if any, not determined and the designations are for identification only:

End papers A: White end papers printed in blue with an all-over pattern and with advertisements at front, p. ⟨ii⟩: . . . *History and Biography. Correspondence of Schiller . . .* ⟨to⟩ *Rollo and His Race . . .* ; advertisements at back, p. ⟨iii⟩: . . . *Voyages and Travels. Mackay's Western World . . .* ⟨to⟩ *Paddiana . . .*

End papers B: Yellow-coated end papers printed with advertisements at front, p. ⟨ii⟩: *History and Biography. Memoirs of the House of Orleans . . .* ⟨to⟩ *Louis XIV . . .* ; p. ⟨iii⟩: *History and Biography. Memoirs of the Reigns of Edward VI. and Mary . . .* Back, p. ⟨ii⟩: *Voyages and Travels. Wayside Pictures . . .* ; p. ⟨iii⟩: *Voyages and Travels. Letters from the Danube . . .*

Advertised as *immediately* Ath Sept. 8, 1849. Advertised for Sept. 20 Ath Sept. 15, 1849. Advertised for *Friday next* ⟨*i.e.*, Sept. 28⟩ Ath Sept. 22, 1849. Listed Ath Sept. 29, 1849; LG Sept. 29, 1849; PC Oct. 1, 1849. Advertised as *now ready* Ath Oct. 13, 1849. Reviewed LG Oct. 20, 1849. Advertised for *October* PC Nov. 1, 1849. A copy in UV inscribed by Melville Nov. 8, 1849. Reviewed Ath Nov. 10, 1849.

Note: Sheets, presumably of the first printing, have been seen, two volumes bound in one (red A cloth); original title-leaves cancelled and newly printed title-leaves inserted: LONDON: / RICHARD BENTLEY, NEW BURLINGTON-STREET. / ⟨*rule*⟩ / 1853. Copy in UV.

BPL (end papers A) H (end papers A) NYPL (end papers B) UV (end papers A)

13660. REDBURN: HIS FIRST VOYAGE. BEING THE SAILOR-BOY CONFESSIONS AND REMINISCENCES OF THE SON-OF-A-GENTLEMAN, IN THE MERCHANT SERVICE . . .

NEW YORK: HARPER & BROTHERS, PUBLISHERS, 82 CLIFF STREET. 1849.

For prior publication see preceding entry.

WRAPPER

⟨i⟩-⟨xii⟩, ⟨13⟩-390; advertisements, pp. ⟨i-iv⟩, ⟨1⟩-10. 7¾″ scant × 5⅜″.

⟨A⟩-I, K-Q¹², R¹⁰.

Printed white paper wrapper. Quadruple flyleaves.

CLOTH

Pagination and signature collation as above. Leaf: 7⁷⁄₁₆″ × 5″.

A cloth: blue; purple. Yellow-coated end papers. Double flyleaves; for a comment on the flyleaves see note under *Omoo,* New York, 1847. Sides blindstamped with a Grolieresque frame, publisher's monogram at center. Both printings (see below) noted thus.

Two printings noted:

FIRST PRINTING

As above. The advertisements end at p. 10.

SECOND PRINTING

⟨A⟩-I, K-R¹². The advertisements are extended and are paged: ⟨i-iv⟩, ⟨1⟩-11, 14, ⟨1⟩-2.

Sometimes found in a black TZ binding, the sides blindstamped with a chain-like frame.

Noted for *immediate* publication LW Nov. 10, 1849. Reviewed LW Nov. 17, 1849. Advertised as *now ready* (cloth and paper) LW Nov. 17, 1849. Deposited (2nd printing) Nov. 23, 1849. Listed LW Dec. 1, 1849.

AAS (cloth, 2nd) H (cloth, 2nd) LC (cloth, 2nd) NYPL (cloth, 1st; cloth, 2nd; 2nd in variant binding) UV (cloth, 1st; 1st in wrapper; cloth, 2nd) Y (cloth, 2nd)

13661. WHITE JACKET; OR, THE WORLD IN A MAN-OF-WAR . . .

LONDON: RICHARD BENTLEY, NEW BURLINGTON STREET. 1850.

2 Vols.

For first American edition see next entry. Also see under years, 1967, 1970.

1: ⟨i⟩-⟨vi⟩, ⟨1⟩-322. 7⅞″ × 4¾″ full.

2: ⟨i⟩-iv, ⟨1⟩-315.

1: ⟨a⟩¹, b², B-I, K-O¹², P⁵. *Note:* P6 probably used as ⟨a⟩.

2: ⟨A⟩², B-I, K-O¹², P².

A cloth: blue. Cream-coated end papers imprinted with publisher's advertisements.

Note: Unsold sheets were issued by Bentley, two volumes in one, the original title-leaves excised and replaced by title-leaves dated 1853. Copy in HM.

Advertised as *immediately* LG Jan. 19, 1850. Advertised for *the present month* Ath Jan. 19, 1850. Advertised as *now ready* Ath Jan. 26, 1850. Listed Ath Jan. 26, 1850; LG Jan. 26, 1850; PC Feb. 1, 1850. Reviewed Ath Feb. 2, 1850. Advertised as *just published* Ath Feb. 2, 1850. Reviewed LG Feb. 9, 1850. Advertised as *now ready* Ath Feb. 9, 1850. Advertised as *published this day* Ath Feb. 23, 1850. Advertised as *now ready* PC March 15, 1850.

H   UV

13662. WHITE-JACKET; OR THE WORLD
IN A MAN-OF-WAR . . .

NEW YORK: HARPER & BROTHERS, PUBLISHERS,
82 CLIFF STREET. LONDON: RICHARD BENTLEY.
1850.

*For prior publication see preceding entry. Also see under
years 1967, 1970.*

CLOTH

⟨i⟩-⟨viii⟩, ⟨9⟩-465; blank, p. ⟨466⟩; 6 pp.
advertisements. $7\frac{7}{16}'' \times 5\frac{1}{16}''$.

⟨A⟩-I, K-P, Q*, R-S, ⟨T⟩¹², U⁸. All examined
copies, both first and second printings: P. ⟨9⟩
erroneously signed C* for A*.

Two printings noted:

FIRST PRINTING

Pagination: As above.

Signature collation: As above.

P. ⟨iii⟩: Extract from Fuller's *Good Sea-Captain.*

P. ⟨iv⟩: *Note*, dated *New York, March, 1850.*

P. ⟨361⟩: Missigned *Q*.*

P. 433: Signature mark *T* not present.

Six pp. terminal advertisements.

SECOND PRINTING

⟨i⟩-⟨viii⟩, ⟨9⟩-465; blank, p. ⟨466⟩; 14 pp.
advertisements.

⟨A⟩-I, K-U¹².

P. ⟨iii⟩: *Note*, dated *New York, March, 1850.*

P. ⟨iv⟩: Extract from Fuller's *Good Sea-Captain.*

P. ⟨361⟩: Correctly signed *Q*.

P. 433: Signature mark *T* present.

Fourteen pp. terminal advertisements.

Three cloth bindings noted; the following variations
are sufficient for identification:

FIRST CLOTH BINDING

A cloth: gray-green; slate. FL-like cloth: black;
brown. Sides blindstamped with an ornate frame
with a device at center lettered *Harper and Brothers
New-York.* Yellow-coated end papers. At front and
at back a gathering of four blank leaves used in one
of the following ways; no sequence known; the
designations are for identification only:

A: One of the four leaves pasted under the
pastedown, the remaining three leaves present as
free flyleaves.

B: One of the four leaves pasted under the
pastedown; another leaf pasted to the free
portion of the end paper; the other two leaves
present as free flyleaves.

SECOND CLOTH BINDING

FL-like cloth: brown. Sides blindstamped with an
ornate frame with a device at center lettered
Harper and Brothers New-York. Plain white wove
end papers. Single flyleaves; or: at front and at
back a gathering of four leaves with two of the
leaves pasted to the cover, two leaves free and
used as flyleaves.

THIRD CLOTH BINDING

A cloth: slate. Sides blindstamped with a grolieresque frame; sides not lettered. White wove end
papers. Flyleaves.

INTERMEDIATE CLOTH

⟨i⟩-⟨viii⟩, ⟨9⟩-465; blank, p. ⟨466⟩; 14 pp.
advertisements. *Note:* In the only located copy the
final leaf of the terminal advertisements has been
excised.

⟨A⟩-I, K-U¹².

P. ⟨iii⟩: Extract from Fuller's *Good Sea-Captain.*

P. ⟨iv⟩: *Note*, dated *New York, March, 1850.*

P. ⟨361⟩: Signed *Q*, not *Q*.*

P. 433: Signature mark *T* present.

Noted in the second cloth binding, purple A cloth.

WRAPPERS

1: ⟨i⟩-⟨viii⟩, ⟨9⟩-240. $7\frac{7}{16}'' \times 5\frac{1}{8}''$ (trimmed).
$7\frac{3}{4}'' \times 5\frac{1}{2}''$ (untrimmed).

2: ⟨241⟩-465; blank, p. ⟨466⟩; 6 pp. advertisements.

1: ⟨A⟩-I, K¹².

2: L-P, Q*, R-S, ⟨T⟩¹², U⁸.

Two printings noted; see above.

Printed pale tan paper wrapper. Double flyleaves.
The wrappers have been noted in two forms:

PART 1, FIRST WRAPPER

Back wrapper: *The Great Histories* . . . ⟨Hume,
Macaulay and Gibbon advertised as *in immediate
preparation*⟩

PART 1, SECOND WRAPPER

Back wrapper: . . . *May, 1850* . . . *Book List For
The Present Season* . . .

PART 2, FIRST WRAPPER

Back wrapper: *Valuable Works* . . .

PART 2, SECOND WRAPPER

Back wrapper: *New Books* . . .

Noted as *nearly ready* LW Feb. 23, 1850. Reviewed
LW March 16, 1850. Advertised as *just published*
LW March 23, 1850. Deposited March 26, 1850.
Listed LW March 30, 1850. The *Fifth Thousand*
advertised LW April 13, 1850.

AAS (cloth, 2nd printing, 2nd binding) H (cloth, 1st printing, 1st binding; cloth, 2nd printing, 3rd binding) IU (wrappers, second printing, 1st form wrappers) LC (cloth, intermediate sheets) NYPL (cloth, 1st printing, 1st binding; wrappers, 2nd printing, 2nd form wrappers) UV (cloth 1st printing, 1st binding; cloth, 1st printing, 2nd binding; wrappers, 1st printing, 1st form wrappers; wrappers, 2nd printing, 1st form wrappers) Y (cloth, 1st printing, 1st binding; cloth, 1st printing, 2nd binding)

13663. THE WHALE ... IN THREE VOL-UMES ...

LONDON: RICHARD BENTLEY, NEW BURLINGTON STREET. 1851.

For first American edition see next entry. Also see under years 1922, 1952, 1967.

1: ⟨i⟩-viii, ⟨1⟩-312. 7¾″ full × 4¹⁵⁄₁₆″.

2: ⟨i⟩-iv, ⟨1⟩-303.

3: ⟨i⟩-iv, ⟨1⟩-328. P. 325 paged 32.

1: ⟨A⟩⁴, B-I, K-O¹². P. 177 missigned 12.

2: ⟨A⟩², B-I, K-N¹², O⁶, P².

3: ⟨A⟩², B-I, K-O¹², P⁸.

Blue V cloth sides embossed either vertically or horizontally with an arrangement of fine, wavy, ribs, white A cloth shelf back. At center of sides is a blindstamped filigree. Spine lettered in gold: THE WHALE / HERMAN MELVILLE / VOL. I. ⟨II.⟩ ⟨III.⟩ / LONDON / BENTLEY. Cream-coated end papers.

Note: Also occurs in a remainder binding of purple T cloth. The sides, while decorated, do not have a blindstamped filigree at the center. Spine lettered in gold: THE / WHALE. / VOL. I. ⟨II.⟩ ⟨III.⟩ / *Note:* Certain of the numerals are overstamped; hence, the transcription as here given is not wholly precise. Yellow-coated end papers.

Advertised for *October* Ath Oct. 4, 1851; for *this month* Ath and LG Oct. 11, 1851; for the *16th* PC Oct. 15, 1851. Listed Ath Oct. 18, 1851. Advertised as *now ready* Ath and LG Oct. 18, 1851. Listed LG Oct. 25, 1851. Advertised as *just published* Ath Oct. 25, 1851. Reviewed Ath Oct. 25, 1851. Listed PC Nov. 1, 1851. Advertised as *now ready* PC Dec. 1, 1851. Reviewed LG Dec. 6, 1851.

H   UV (first binding; remainder) Y

13664. MOBY-DICK; OR, THE WHALE ...

NEW YORK: HARPER & BROTHERS, PUBLISHERS. LONDON: RICHARD BENTLEY. 1851.

For prior publication see preceding entry. Also see under years 1952, 1964, 1967.

⟨i⟩-⟨xxiv⟩, ⟨1⟩-⟨635⟩; blank, p. ⟨636⟩; 6 pp. advertisements, blank leaf. *Note:* P. ⟨x⟩ is paged 9-10; p. xi is paged 11. For a comment on the front matter see below. 7⅜″ full × 5″ scant.

A Note on the Front Matter

All examined copies have the front matter in the following form:

P. ⟨ix⟩: ETYMOLOGY / ⟨rule⟩ / *"While you take ...*

P. ⟨x⟩: Paged 9-10. Headed: EXTRACTS. / (*Supplied by a Sub-Sub-Librarian.*) ...

P. 11: EXTRACTS. / ⟨rule⟩ / *"And God created ...*

P. xii: ... *Scarcely had we proceeded ...*

Two leaves exist (in N) which indicate that at least one copy of Sig. ⟨A⟩ was printed from mis-imposed plates. Identification by leaf has been rendered impossible; nor is it possible to distinguish recto from verso; for explanation of this condition see below. In the following note the words *recto* and *verso* are used arbitrarily.

Leaf: Recto: ETYMOLOGY / ⟨rule⟩ / *"While you take ...*

Verso: EXTRACTS. / ⟨rule⟩ / *"And God created ...*

Leaf: Recto: Paged 9-10. Headed: EXTRACTS. / (*Supplied by a Sub-Sub-Librarian.*) ...

Verso: ... *"Scarcely had we proceeded ...*

Dr. Harrison Hayford (who was good enough to bring this information to BAL) reports "the history of the copy is this. It belonged to the University of Chicago; when in the late 1940's H. P. Vincent was editing the Hendricks House *Moby-Dick* he was using it there and persuaded the librarian to sell it to him ... Vincent made his collation with *The Whale* in pencil right on the pages, and then marked these pages as printer's copy for his edition. The printers sliced off the whole back of the pile of gatherings, so it became a pile of single leaves. They set from it and returned the pile to him. He sold it to me when the Melville Project began in 1965 and I gave it to The Newberry Library, where it is now ..."

⟨A⟩¹², 1-26¹², 27¹⁰.

Three bindings noted:

FIRST BINDING

A cloth: black; blue; gray; green; drab purple-brown; red; slate. T cloth: black. Sides stamped in blind with a heavy rule frame; and, publisher's circular device at center. *End papers: See note below.* Double flyleaves at front and at back; for a comment on the flyleaves see the note in entry for *Omoo*, New York, 1847.

A Note on the End Papers, First Binding

It is frequently claimed that the book was first issued with orange-coated end papers. The fact is that the book was first issued with orange-coated end papers (of varying shades) and also maroon end papers veined with gold; brown-orange end papers; marbled end papers. A single copy has been seen by BAL with plain white wove end papers. A single copy has been seen with the publisher's device on the sides stamped upside down.

BAL theorizes that the claim for orange end papers originated with Michael Sadleir's *Excursions in Victorian Bibliography*, London, 1922, p. 229, where Mr. Sadleir's copy of *Moby-Dick* is described as with "orange end-papers." Mr. Sadleir was not the originator of the myth which resulted from overlooking his note on p. 221: "Collectors should observe the fact that it was the custom of American publishers in the fifties and sixties to bind one edition in cloths of various colours for the purposes of window display. Consequently Melville's first American editions are met with in a variety of colourings which, in the matter of date of issue, rank equally."

SECOND BINDING

Noted in A cloth: blue; gray. Also other colors?

The publisher's circular device is not present on the sides. Sides decorated with a blindstamped grolieresque frame. White wove end papers, single flyleaves.

The end papers and flyleaves are as follows: At both front and at back is a single gathering of four leaves of white wove paper. *At front:* Leaf 1 excised or pasted under the pastedown; leaf 2 used as the pastedown; leaf 3 occurs as the free portion of the end paper; leaf 4 present as a flyleaf. *At back:* Leaf 1 present as a flyleaf; leaf 2 is the free portion of the end paper; leaf 3 is the pastedown; leaf 4 excised or pasted under the pastedown.

THIRD BINDING

Noted only in brown TZ cloth. The sides stamped in blind with a frame of rules, beads and a braid-like rule. BAL has noted two copies only in this binding; in each leaf 27_{10} had been excised. Yellow-coated end papers. Triple flyleaves. The flyleaves at both front and at back are parts of a single gathering of four leaves of white wove paper. *At front:* Leaf 1 excised or pasted under the paste-down; leaves 2-4 present as flyleaves; note that leaf 2 is not pasted to the end paper. *At back:* Leaves 1-3 present as flyleaves; leaf 4 excised or pasted under the pastedown; note that leaf 3 is not pasted to the end paper.

Query: Is this style of binding contemporary?

NLA Dec. 15, 1851, listed the book as in both cloth; and, printed paper wrapper. No copy in printed paper wrapper has been seen or otherwise reported.

A NOTE ON THE TEXT

The publishers used as their text Melville's original manuscript. *The Whale*, as issued in London, was set from New York sheets, with Melville's alterations.

A copy in UV (first binding) inscribed by early owner Nov. 15, 1851. Advertised as *just published* LW Nov. 15, 1851. Reviewed LW Nov. 15, 1851. Deposited Nov. 19, 1851. Listed NLA Dec. 15, 1851.

AAS (first binding) H (first binding) NYPL (first binding) UV (all three bindings) Y (first and third bindings)

13665. Memorial of James Fenimore Cooper
New York G P Putnam 1852

Letter, p. 30.

For comment see entry No. 1650.

13666. PIERRE; OR, THE AMBIGUITIES . . .

NEW YORK: HARPER & BROTHERS, PUBLISHERS 329 & 331 PEARL STREET, FRANKLIN SQUARE. 1852.

$\langle i \rangle$-viii, $\langle 1 \rangle$-495. $7\frac{3}{8}''$ full $\times$ 5$''$.

$\langle - \rangle^4$, A-H, $\langle I \rangle$, K-T, $\langle U \rangle^{12}$, X^8.

T cloth: black. A cloth: green; purple; slate. Double flyleaves; for a comment on the flyleaves see note under *Omoo*, New York, 1847. Brown-coated; green-coated; orchid-coated; orange-coated; slate-coated end papers.

Also in printed paper wrapper according to an advertisement LW Aug. 21, 1852; BAL has seen no copies in wrapper, no copies thus reported.

Deposited Aug. 9 (11?), 1852. Listed LW Aug. 14, 1852; NLG Aug. 15, 1852. Advertised LW Aug. 21, 1852. The London (Sampson Low) edition (American sheets): Ath Oct. 2, 1852 reports from *America* that Melville has published *Pierre*. Advertised as an importation Ath Nov. 6, 1852. Listed LG Nov. 13, 1852; PC Nov. 15, 1852.

B H UV Y

13667. ISRAEL POTTER: HIS FIFTY YEARS OF EXILE . . .

NEW YORK: G. P. PUTNAM & CO., 10 PARK PLACE. 1855.

Three printings noted:

FIRST PRINTING

$\langle 1 \rangle$-276. $7\frac{5}{16}'' \times 5''$ full.

$\langle 1 \rangle$-11^{12}, 12^6.

P. 141: The heading reads: CHAPTER XVI.

P. 237, line 23: . . . *by---! You* . . .

P. 238, line 2: ... *the d---d |*

P. 238, line 3: *soul* ...

P. 239, line 6: ... *by---! Every* ...

SECOND PRINTING

Pagination and signature collation as above. No reprint notice on the title-page.

P. 141: The heading reads: CHAPTER XIV.

P. 237, line 23: ... * * * *You* ...

P. 238, line 2: ... *the* * * * |

P. 238, line 3: * * ...

P. 239, line 6: ... * * * *Every* ...

THIRD PRINTING

Pagination and signature collation as above. Readings as in the *Second Printing*. On title-page: THIRD EDITION.

Two bindings noted:

FIRST BINDING

On the spine the initials F, Y and E ⟨in *Fifty Years Exile*⟩ are ornamented with pendants. Noted on first printing only.

SECOND BINDING

On the spine the initials F, Y and E ⟨in *Fifty Years Exile*⟩ are not ornamented with pendants. Noted on the second and third printings.

Note: A reprint in The Newberry Library has the joint imprint of G. P. Putnam & Co., New York; and, Low, Son & Co., London.

A cloth: green; red. T cloth: purple. TZ cloth: purple. Yellow end papers. Flyleaves.

Deposited March 10, 1855. Noted as *published since March 1* NLG March 15, 1855. Noted as *lately issued* PC April 16, 1855. Listed by Low (as an importation) PC April 16, 1855. Advertised by Low PC May 15, 1855, as *new*. A Routledge edition listed by Ath April 21, 1855; advertised Ath April 28, 1855; listed PC May 1, 1855.

AAS (2nd) H (1st, 2nd, 3rd) NYPL (1st, 2nd, 3rd) UV (1st) Y (1st, 2nd)

13668. Pictures and Readings from American Authors, Being the Choice Volume of Putnam's Magazine.

New York: Leavitt and Allen. 1855.

"The Encantadas, or, Enchanted Isles," pp. 460-466; comprises sketches ten and eleven only. Collected in *Piazza Tales*, 1856.

For fuller description see in James Russell Lowell list.

13669. THE PIAZZA TALES ...

NEW YORK; DIX & EDWARDS, 321 BROADWAY. LONDON: SAMPSON LOW, SON & CO. 1856.

⟨i-iv⟩, ⟨1⟩-431; blank, p. ⟨432⟩; plus: 7 pp. advertisements. $7\frac{1}{16}'' \times 4\frac{3}{4}''$.

⟨-⟩², 1-18¹², plus: ⟨19⟩⁴. In some copies signature mark 14 is lacking.

A cloth: blue. T cloth: black; brown; green; purple; slate. Moiréd T-like cloth: purple. TZ cloth: brown. End papers: blue-coated; lavender; old rose-coated; yellow. Flyleaves.

Advertised *Criterion* May 3, 1856. Deposited May 20, 1856. Listed *Criterion* May 31, 1856. *London:* Announced Ath May 31, 1856; PC June 2, 1856. Listed PC June 16, 1856. Advertised as *now ready* PC July 1, 1856; Ath July 12, 1856; PC July 16, 1856. Reviewed Ath July 26, 1856.

AAS B BA H LC NYPL UV Y

13670. THE CONFIDENCE-MAN: HIS MASQUERADE ...

NEW YORK: DIX, EDWARDS & CO., 321 BROADWAY. 1857.

See next entry; also see publication notes below.

⟨i-vi⟩, ⟨i⟩-vi, ⟨1⟩-394, blank leaf. $7\frac{1}{2}''$ full $\times$ 5″. The initial leaf excised or pasted under the end paper.

⟨a⟩⁶, 1-16¹², 17⁶. ⟨a⟩1 excised or pasted under the end paper.

T cloth: brown; green; purple. Blue-coated, brown-coated, olive-coated, yellow-tan end papers. Flyleaf at back.

Issued simultaneously with the London edition? The following publication notes indicate the problem; see next entry for first London printing. Page reference numbers refer to *The Melville Log* ... ⟨1951⟩.

New York: Advertised as *in press* APC March 28, 1857. P. 562.

New York: March 31, 1857. "Evert Duyckinck writes to his brother, George: Allan Melville has just this moment sent me Herman's *Confidence Man* ..." P. 563.

London: Advertised for *Friday next* ⟨April 3⟩ Ath Mar. 28, 1857.

---: Advertised as *now ready* PC April 1, 1857.

---: Listed Ath April 4, 1857.

---: Listed LG April 4, 1857.

New York: April 6, 1857. "The *Salem Register* quotes the *Albany Evening Journal's* review ..." P. 566.

---: April 8, 1857. Noticed by the *Boston Daily Advertiser*. P. 568.

London: Reviewed Ath April 11, 1857.

———: Reviewed LG April 11, 1857.

———: Listed PC April 15, 1857.

———: Reviewed Ath April 11, 1857. P. 570.

———: Reviewed *The Critic* April 15, 1857. P. 572.

New York: Deposited May 2, 1857.

Note: All examined copies have the imprint of *Miller & Holman* on the copyright page. Unsubstantiated report has it that a second printing, dated 1857, exists with the imprint of *Curtis & Miller* on the copyright page; further information wanting.

B   H   NYPL   UV   Y

13671. THE CONFIDENCE-MAN: HIS MASQUERADE . . . AUTHORISED EDITION.

LONDON: LONGMAN, BROWN, GREEN, LONGMANS, & ROBERTS. 1857. THE RIGHT OF TRANSLATION IS RESERVED.

Issued simultaneously with the New York edition? See preceding entry.

⟨i⟩-vi, ⟨1⟩-354. 6¾″ × 4³⁄₁₆″.

⟨-⟩², a¹, B-I, K-U, X-Z⁸, AA¹.

TZ cloth: orange. Brown-coated end papers, imprinted with publisher's advertisements; *see below.* Publisher's catalog inserted at back; *see below.*

The end papers have been noted in four forms; sequence not determined.

A

At front, p. ⟨2⟩: *Mrs. Jameson's Works* . . .

At back, p. ⟨3⟩: *List of Works by Contributors to the Edinburgh Review* . . .

P. 24 of terminal catalog dated *September, 1855.*

B

At front, p. ⟨3⟩: *Books on Rural Sports* . . .

At back, p. ⟨2⟩: *Books on Rural Sports* . . .

P. 24 of terminal catalog dated *September, 1855.*

C

At front, p. ⟨2⟩: *Historical Works* . . .

At back, p. ⟨3⟩: *Works on the Arts* . . .

P. 24 of terminal catalog dated *September, 1855.*

D

At front, p. ⟨2⟩: *Acton's Cookery-Book* . . .

At back, p. ⟨3⟩: *Approved Works of Reference* . . .

P. 24 of terminal catalog dated *March, 1856.*

For publication notes see preceding entry.

N (A,B,C)   UV (A)   Y (D)

13672. Autograph Leaves of Our Country's Authors.

Baltimore, Cushings & Bailey 1864.

"Inscription for the Slain at Fredericksburgh," p. 189. Collected in *Collected Poems* ⟨1947⟩.

For fuller entry see No. 2418.

13673. BATTLE-PIECES AND ASPECTS OF THE WAR . . .

NEW YORK: HARPER & BROTHERS, PUBLISHERS, FRANKLIN SQUARE. 1866.

⟨i⟩-x, ⟨11⟩-272. 7⁷⁄₁₆″ × 4¹⁵⁄₁₆″.

⟨A⟩-I, K-L¹², M⁴.

C cloth: blue; brown; green; purple. C-like cloth: red-purple. V cloth: brown; green. Covers bevelled. Brown-coated end papers. Double flyleaves; see note regarding flyleaves under *Omoo,* New York, 1847.

Note: In all examined copies the word *hundred* in the copyright notice is misspelled *hnndred.*

Johnson (1941): "Blue cloth, gold monogram on the sides; green cloth, blind-stamped monogram on the sides." BAL believes Johnson in error; all examined copies have the monogram blind-stamped on the sides.

Deposited Aug. 17, 1866. Listed ALG Sept. 1, 1866. Reviewed ALG Sept. 1, 1866. Advertised by Trübner as an importation Bkr Oct. 31, 1866.

B   BA   H   NYPL   UV   Y

13674. CLAREL A POEM AND PILGRIMAGE IN THE HOLY LAND . . . IN FOUR PARTS . . . JERUSALEM . . . MAR SABA . . . THE WILDERNESS . . . BETHLEHEM . . .

NEW YORK   G. P. PUTNAM'S SONS   NO. 182 FIFTH AVENUE   1876

2 Vols.

1: ⟨i-iv⟩, ⟨i⟩-⟨iv⟩, ⟨7⟩-300. Laid paper. 6¾″ × 4¹⁵⁄₁₆″.

2: ⟨i⟩-iv, ⟨301⟩-571.

1: ⟨1⁹, 2-18⁸, 19⁶⟩. ⟨1⟩₂ inserted. *Note:* ⟨19⟩ is an 8vo gathering the final two leaves excised; probably used in making Vol. 2. *Signed:* ⟨1⟩¹³, ⟨2⟩, 3-4, ⟨5-6⟩, 7, ⟨8⟩, 9-10, ⟨11⟩, 12¹², 13⁶.

2: ⟨1², 2-3¹, 4-19⁸, 20⁶⟩. *Signed:* ⟨13⟩⁸, ⟨14-17⟩, 18, ⟨19⟩, 20-21, ⟨22⟩, 23¹², ⟨24⟩¹⁰. ⟨2-3⟩ probably originally ⟨19⟩₇₋₈, Vol. 1.

Note: It is probable that the publishers originally planned a one-volume production; later decided on a two-volume production; hence the irregularities in pagination and signature collation.

Also note: All examined copies have *banks* for *blanks*, p. 395, line 23. All examined copies have the following superfluous signature marks: Vol. 1, p. 65, *2**; p. 255, *8**; Vol. 2, p. 359, *13;* p. 557, *18.*

S cloth: green; mauve; olive; tan; terra-cotta. Covers bevelled. Brown-coated end papers. Laid paper flyleaves.

A copy (in H) presented by Melville to his wife June 6, 1876. A copy in NYPL inscribed by early owner June 9, 1876. Listed PW June 10, 1876. For a revised edition see below under year 1960.

AAS B BPL H NYPL UV Y

13675. The History of Pittsfield, (Berkshire County,) Massachusetts, from the Year 1800 to the Year 1876. Compiled and Written . . . by J. E. A. Smith . . .

Springfield: Published by C. W. Bryan & Co., 1876.

"Article, Major Thomas Melville, in J. E. A. Smith's *The History of Pittsfield*, Pittsfield ⟨*sic*⟩, 1876."——Minnigerode, p. 194. The article referred to, while not set apart from other text by quotation marks or otherwise, appears on pp. 206-208; presumably Melville supplied material for it. On pp. 399-400 is a direct quotation from a "relative" of Thomas Melville, identified in the text as a nephew, *i.e.,* Herman Melville.

Cloth?

H NYPL

13676. JOHN MARR AND OTHER SAILORS WITH SOME SEA-PIECES

NEW YORK THE DE VINNE PRESS 1888

Anonymous.

⟨i-iv⟩, ⟨1⟩-103. Laid paper. 6¾″ × 4½″ full.

⟨-⟩², ⟨1⟩-13⁴.

Printed light tan stiff paper wrapper.

On front of wrapper: *25 Copies . . .*

Deposited Sept. 7, 1888.

AAS B H NYPL UV Y

13677. TIMOLEON ETC.

NEW YORK THE CAXTON PRESS 1891

Anonymous.

⟨i⟩-vi, ⟨7⟩-70, blank leaf. Laid paper. 7″ × 4⅝″.

⟨1-9⁴⟩.

Printed tan-gray paper wrapper.

Privately printed; presumably 25 copies only.

Deposited June 16, 1891.

AAS B H NYPL UV Y

13678. Some Personal Letters of Herman Melville and a Bibliography by Meade Minnigerode

Edmond Byrne Hackett: The Brick Row Book Shop, Inc. New York New Haven Princeton 1922

Paper boards, cloth shelfback, printed paper label on spine.

On copyright page: *First Printing November, 1922 1500 Copies*

Deposited Dec. 9, 1922.

AAS B BA H LC NYPL Y

13679. Moby Dick or the White Whale . . .

New York   Dodd, Mead and Company, MCMXXII

The earliest located American printing of the English text of *Moby-Dick, i.e., The Whale*, London, 1851.

H

13680. The Works of Herman Melville Standard Edition . . . ⟨fly-title⟩

Constable and Company Ltd London Bombay Sydney 1922 ⟨-1924⟩

1: *Typee . . .*

Dated 1922.

2: *Omoo . . .*

Dated 1922.

3-4: *Mardi . . . in Two Volumes . . .*

Dated 1922.

5: *Redburn . . .*

Dated 1922.

6: *White Jacket . . .*

Dated 1922.

7-8: *Moby-Dick . . . in Two Volumes . . .*

Dated 1922.

9: *Pierre . . .*

Dated 1923.

10: *The Piazza Tales . . .*

Dated 1923.

11: *Israel Potter . . .*

Dated 1923.

12: *The Confidence-Man . . .*

Dated 1923. Contains a bibliography of the first editions of the prose works, by Michael Sadleir.

13: *Billy Budd and Other Prose Pieces . . . Edited by Raymond W. Weaver . . .*

Dated 1924. See full collation below under 1924.

14-15: *Clarel a Poem and Pilgrimage in the Holy Land . . . in Two Volumes . . .*

Dated 1924.

16: *Poems . . .*

Dated 1924. See full collation below under 1924.

Numbered certificate of issue in Vol. 1. No certificate in Vols. 2-12. Unnumbered certificate in Vol. 13. No certificate in Vols. 14-16.

750 copies.

Reissued New York, 1963; see below under 1963.

BA H LC NYPL

13681. THE APPLE-TREE TABLE AND OTHER SKETCHES . . . WITH AN INTRODUCTORY NOTE BY HENRY CHAPIN

PRINCETON PRINCETON UNIVERSITY PRESS LONDON: HUMPHREY MILFORD OXFORD UNIVERSITY PRESS MCMXXII ⟨*i.e.*, 1923?⟩

TRADE FORMAT

Title-page in black only.

⟨i-vi⟩, ⟨1⟩-329; blank, p. ⟨330⟩; colophon, p. ⟨331⟩; blank, pp. ⟨332-338⟩. 8¹¹⁄₁₆″ × 5½″ full. Unwatermarked laid paper.

⟨1-21⁸, 22⁴⟩. Leaves ⟨1⟩₁ and ⟨22⟩₄ used as pastedowns.

Green paper boards, tan V cloth shelf back.

FRENCH PAPER FORMAT

Title-page in black and orange.

Pagination and signature collation as above. Printed on laid paper watermarked *Glaslan . . .* 8¾″ × 5½″.

Green marbled paper boards sides, black V cloth shelf back.

Colophon: . . . *Sixteen Hundred Seventy-Five Copies . . . Printed And One Hundred Seventy-Five Copies Are On French Hand-Made Paper And Numbered . . .*

Trade format listed PW Feb. 10, 1923. Trade format deposited March 28, 1923. Listed Bkr April, 1923.

B (trade) NYPL (trade) UV (both) Y (both)

13682. BILLY BUDD AND OTHER PROSE PIECES . . . EDITED BY RAYMOND W. ⟨*sic*⟩ WEAVER

CONSTABLE AND COMPANY LTD LONDON BOMBAY SYDNEY 1924

Title-page in black and blue.

Issued as *The Works of Herman Melville Standard Edition,* Vol. 13.

⟨i⟩-viii, ⟨1⟩-399. Laid paper. 9″ full × 5¾″.

⟨-⟩⁴, ⟨A⟩-I, K-U, X-Z, 2A-2B⁸.

LP cloth: blue. Maroon-coated end papers. Top edges gilt.

This Edition is limited to 750 copies---p. ⟨ii⟩.

The following pieces here first located in book form:

"Billy Budd, Foretopman." . . . *Never before published* . . .---p. v.

"The Cincinnati"

"Daniel Orme"

"Fragment"

"Fragments from a Writing-Desk"

"Jack Gentian"

"Major Gentian and Colonel J. Bunkum"

"The Marquis de Grandvin"

"Portrait of a Gentleman"

"To Major John Gentian, Dean of the Burgundy Club"

"The Two Temples"

"Under the Rose"

For other editions of *Billy Budd* see below under years 1928, 1948, 1962, 1963, 1965.

Advertised for *March* NA March 15, 1924. Listed TLS April 3, 1924; PC April 5, 1924. For first American printing of this collection see below under the year 1963.

H NYPL Y

13683. POEMS . . . BATTLE-PIECES JOHN MARR AND OTHER SAILORS TIMOLEON AND MISCELLANEOUS POEMS . . . ⟨Edited by Michael Sadleir and Raymond M. Weaver⟩

CONSTABLE AND COMPANY LTD LONDON BOMBAY SYDNEY 1924

Title-page in black and blue.

Issued as *The Works of Herman Melville Standard Edition,* Vol. 16.

⟨i⟩-xii, ⟨1⟩-434, blank leaf. Laid paper. 9¹⁄₁₆″ × 5¾″.

⟨-⟩⁶, ⟨A⟩-I, K-U, X-Z, 2A-2D⁸, 2E². Signature mark b2 on p. ⟨v⟩.

LP cloth: blue. Maroon-coated end papers. Top edges gilt.

Presumably limited to 750 copies.

The following material here first located in book form:

"Author's Note," p. 192.

"Miscellaneous Poems," pp. ⟨297⟩-349.

"At the Hostelry," pp. ⟨351⟩-434.

Advertised for *March* NA March 15, 1924. Listed
TLS April 3, 1924; PC April 5, 1924. For first
American printing see below under year 1963.

BA H NYPL Y

13684. Shorter Novels of Herman Melville with
an Introduction by Raymond Weaver

Horace Liveright New York ⟨1928⟩

First American book publication of "Billy Budd,
Foretopman," pp. 229-328. For first publication
see under year 1924. For other editions see below
under the years 1948, 1962, 1963, 1965.

Deposited Oct. 30, 1928.

H LC NYPL UV

13685. Family Correspondence of Herman Melville 1830-1904 in the Gansevoort-Lansing
Collection Edited by Victor Hugo Paltsits

New York The New York Public Library
1929

Printed paper wrapper.

According to the printer's code 500 copies were
printed Aug. 30, 1929.

B H NYPL UV Y

13686. JOURNAL OF MELVILLE'S VOYAGE
IN A CLIPPER SHIP . . . [REPRINT FROM
THE NEW ENGLAND QUARTERLY,
VOLUME II, NUMBER 1, 1929]

⟨PORTLAND, MAINE⟩ COPYRIGHT 1929 BY THE
SOUTHWORTH PRESS

Cover-title.

120-125, blank leaf. 9⁵⁄₁₆″ × 6⅛″. Watermarked
Flemish Book.

⟨-⁴⟩.

Printed green paper wrapper.

H

13687. MELVILLE'S "AGATHA" LETTER
TO HAWTHORNE EDITED BY S. E.
MORISON [REPRINT FROM THE NEW
ENGLAND QUARTERLY, VOLUME II,
NUMBER 2, 1929]

⟨PORTLAND, MAINE⟩ COPYRIGHT 1929 BY THE
SOUTHWORTH PRESS

⟨295⟩-307, blank leaf. 9⁵⁄₁₆″ × 6⅛″. Watermarked *Flemish Book.*

⟨-⁸⟩.

Printed green paper wrapper.

H

13688. A BOOK REVIEW BY HERMAN
MELVILLE ⟨Edited by⟩ JOHN HOWARD
BIRSS [REPRINT FROM THE NEW
ENGLAND QUARTERLY, VOLUME V,
NUMBER 2, 1932]

⟨PORTLAND, MAINE⟩ COPYRIGHT 1932 BY THE
SOUTHWORTH PRESS

⟨i-ii⟩, 347-348. 9⁵⁄₁₆″ × 6³⁄₁₆″. Watermarked
Flemish Book.

⟨-²⟩.

Printed green paper wrapper.

H

13689. "TRAVELLING" A NEW LECTURE
BY HERMAN MELVILLE ⟨Edited by⟩
JOHN HOWARD BIRSS

⟨BALTIMORE: THE NEW ENGLAND QUARTERLY,
n.d., 1934⟩

Cover-title.

725-728. 9⅜″ scant × 6¹⁄₁₆″. Watermarked
Warren's Olde Style.

⟨-²⟩.

Printed green paper wrapper.

H

13690. . . . JOURNAL UP THE STRAITS
OCTOBER 11, 1856–MAY 5, 1857 EDITED
WITH AN INTRODUCTION BY RAY-
MOND WEAVER

NEW YORK PUBLISHED BY THE COLOPHON 1935

At head of title: HERMAN MELVILLE

⟨i⟩-⟨xxxii⟩, ⟨1⟩-182; blank, p. ⟨183⟩; colophon,
p. ⟨184⟩. Frontispiece and one 2-page facsimile
inserted. 9″ × 5⅞″ full.

⟨1-13⁸, 14⁴⟩.

Marbled muslin. Goldstamped black leather label
on spine. At front and at back: A gathering of
four blank leaves used as end papers and flyleaves.

. . . Completed in May 1935---colophon; size of
printing not given. According to Johnson the
printing was limited to 650 copies.

For another edition see *Journal of a Visit to
Europe . . .* , below, under the year 1955.

BPL copy received June 24, 1935. Deposited Oct.
4, 1935.

B BPL H LC NYPL UV Y

13691. Herman Melville Representative Selections, with Introduction, Bibliography, and
Notes by Willard Thorp . . .

American Book Company New York Cincinnati Chicago Boston Atlanta ⟨1938⟩

Reprint save for the following material:

"[Criticism] from *The Literary World* (March 6, 1847)," pp. 320-345.

"To Daniel Shepherd," pp. 346-348. Collected in *Collected Poems*, Chicago ⟨1947⟩.

Letters, pp. 368-404.

"In the following pages will be found . . . new biographical material from the Duyckinck Collection of the New York Public Library, an unknown review by Melville, an unpublished poem of considerable personal interest, five unpublished letters, three letters from which only fragments have previously been quoted and nine which have not before been given in a correct and complete text."---P. v.

The first printing has the code *W.P.I.* on the copyright page.

Deposited July 7, 1938.

H   LC   NYPL

13692. . . . TWO NEW LETTERS OF HERMAN MELVILLE ⟨Edited⟩ BY HARRISON HAYFORD . . .

⟨BALTIMORE, MARYLAND, 1944⟩

Caption-title. The above at head of first page of text. At head of title: [*Reprinted from ELH, A Journal of English Literary History, Vol. 11, No. 1, March, 1944.*]

76-83. Laid paper. Watermarked *Warren's Olde Style*. 8⅞″ × 6″ scant. Pp. ⟨75⟩ and ⟨84⟩ blank.

5 leaves; stapled.

H

13693. . . . Selected Poems Edited by F. O. Matthiessen

The Poets of the Year New Directions Norfolk Connecticut ⟨n.d., 1944⟩

At head of title: *Herman Melville*

Printed paper wrapper; also, printed paper boards.

Reprint save for the following poems which are here first in an American book; each had prior publication in *Poems*, London, 1924.

"Gold in the Mountain"

"Immolated"

"The Lake Pontoosuc"

"Time's Long Ago"

Published Oct. 16, 1944; date from a review copy in Y.

BA   H   NYPL   UV   Y

13694. Collected Poems . . . Edited by Howard P. Vincent

Chicago Packard and Company Hendricks House ⟨1947⟩

The material at pp. 259-398, with the exceptions noted, is here first in an American book; all had prior publication in *Poems*, London, 1924. The exceptions are: "Immolated," "Time's Long Ago," "Gold in the Mountain" and "Pontoosuce" ⟨*sic*⟩; these four had prior American publication in *Selected Poems* ⟨n.d., 1944⟩.

Here first collected:

"Inscription for the Slain at Fredericksburgh"; previously in *Autograph Leaves* . . . , 1864.

Here first located in book form:

"Adieu"

"The Admiral of the White"

"The Continents"

"A Ditty of Aristippus"

"The Dust-Layers"

"In a Nutshell"

"Puzzlement"

"A Rail Road Cutting near Alexandria in 1855"

"Rammon"

"A Reasonable Constitution"

"Suggested by the Ruins of a Mountain-temple in Arcadia"

"To Tom"

"Specks, Tiny Specks." This had prior publication in *Billy Budd*, London, 1924. Here in its earliest located American book publication.

Deposited April 28, 1947. Received at PW June 2, 1947.

B   BA   H   LC   Y

13695. JOURNAL OF A VISIT TO LONDON AND THE CONTINENT . . . 1849-1850 EDITED BY ELEANOR MELVILLE METCALF

HARVARD UNIVERSITY PRESS CAMBRIDGE, MASSACHUSETTS 1948

Title-page in black and red-brown.

⟨i⟩-xx, ⟨1⟩-189; colophon, p. ⟨190⟩; blank leaf. 5 plates inserted. 8¼″ scant × 5½″.

⟨1-12⁸, 13¹⁰⟩.

Red-brown balloon cloth. Pink laid end papers. Top edges stained blue-gray.

Deposited Oct. 14, 1948. Published Oct. 22, 1948 (publisher's statement). The London (Cohen &

West) edition advertised in *The New Statesman* Oct. 8, 1949.

BA   BPL   H   LC   MHS   UV   Y

13696. Melville's Billy Budd Edited by F. Barron Freeman . . .

Published by Harvard University Press ⟨1948⟩

In addition to the text of *Billy Budd* contains the following material:

"Baby Budd, Sailor," pp. ⟨285⟩-342.

"Related Fragments Found in the Manuscripts," pp. ⟨343⟩-356.

"Unrelated Fragments," pp. ⟨357⟩-370.

In some copies there is a slip of *Corrigenda* inserted.

Deposited Nov. 17, 1948. Published Nov. 22, 1948 (publisher's statement). For other editions see under the years 1924, 1928, 1962, 1963, 1965.

BA   BPL   H   LC   UV   Y

13697. A THOUGHT ON BOOKBINDING . . .

⟨BOSTON: THE BOSTON BOOKBUILDERS WORKSHOP, 1948⟩

Cover-title.

⟨i-iv⟩, 1-3; colophon, p. ⟨4⟩; 2 blank leaves. 6″ × 4⅝″.

⟨-⁶⟩. Leaves 1 and 6 used as pastedowns.

Rough-toothed purple-brown paper, printed paper label on front.

"This review ⟨of Cooper's *The Red Rover*⟩ appeared, unsigned, in *The Literary World*, VI (March 16, 1850) . . . It was reprinted for the first time, in slightly emended form, by John Howard Birss in an article written for *The New England Quarterly*, V (April, 1932) . . . The text given here is taken from the . . . *Literary World* . . ."--- Colophon.

BA

13698. The Complete Stories . . . Edited . . . by Jay Leyda

Random House   New York   ⟨1949⟩

First located American book publication of "The Two Temples," pp. 149-165. For prior publication see *Billy Budd* . . . , London, 1924.

Deposited April 18, 1949.

BA   H   LC   UV   Y

13699. Moby-Dick or, the Whale . . . Edited by Luther S. Mansfield and Howard P. Vincent

Hendricks House   New York, 1952

An "elaborately annotated edition . . ."---P. xxxiii.

For first edition see under year 1851; also see under years 1922, 1967.

Deposited March 20, 1952.

LC

13700. The Portable Melville Edited . . . by Jay Leyda

New York   1952   The Viking Press

On copyright page: *Published By The Viking Press In January 1952*

Contains some material here first published. For comment see the editor's "Notes on Manuscripts and Textual Sources," pp. 743-745.

Deposited Jan. 31, 1952.

H   LC   UV

13701. Journal of a Visit to Europe and the Levant October 11, 1856–May 6, 1857 . . . Edited by Howard C. Horsford . . .

Princeton, New Jersey   Princeton University Press 1955

Princeton Studies in English, No. 35. For an earlier edition see *Journal up the Straits* . . . , 1935.

". . . It only remains here to say something about the reasons for redoing this work when an edition already exists---*Journal up the Straits* . . . , edited by Raymond Weaver and published . . . in 1935. As well as being a very limited edition and therefore now difficult to obtain, Mr. Weaver's effort was one of the first to attempt the painful task of deciphering Melville's handwriting and suffers from a number of errors in detail . . . which demanded correction."---P. viii.

Deposited Feb. 7, 1955.

B   BPL   H   LC   UV   Y

13702. Melville As Lecturer by Merton M. Sealts, Jr.

Harvard University Press   Cambridge, Massachusetts   1957

Contains, pp. ⟨127⟩-185, texts of Melville's three lectures "based on contemporary newspaper reports" and other material.

Deposited Nov. 7, 1957.

BA   H   LC   Y

13703. Clarel   A Poem and Pilgrimage in the Holy Land . . . Edited by Walter E. Bezanson

Hendricks House, Inc.   New York   1960

For first edition see above under year 1876.

"... The present text is that of the first American, with typographical errors corrected, inconsistencies reduced, and Melville's own minor revisions (for the first time) incorporated..." ---P. ⟨i⟩.

Deposited Dec. 19, 1960.

B BA BPL LC

13704. THE LETTERS OF HERMAN MELVILLE EDITED BY MERRELL R. DAVIS AND WILLIAM H. GILMAN

NEW HAVEN: YALE UNIVERSITY PRESS, 1960

⟨i-ii⟩, ⟨i⟩-⟨xxxii⟩, ⟨1⟩-398. Frontispiece and 5 facsimiles inserted. 9$\frac{3}{16}$″ full × 6$\frac{1}{16}$″ full.

⟨1-12^{16}, 13^8, 14^{16}⟩.

V cloth: blue.

Deposited July 18, 1960.

B BA BPL LC MHS

13705. Billy Budd Sailor (An Inside Narrative) ... Reading Text and Genetic Text, Edited from the Manuscript with Introduction and Notes by Harrison Hayford and Merton M. Sealts, Jr.

The University of Chicago Press ⟨1962⟩

Cloth. Also issued in printed paper wrapper with the following imprint: *Phoenix Books   The University of Chicago Press ⟨1962⟩*; and with the following note on reverse of the title-leaf: *This book is also available from The University of Chicago Press in a clothbound edition containing an analysis and transcription of the manuscript...First Phoenix Edition 1962...*

For other editions see under years 1924, 1928, 1948, 1963, 1965.

B (cloth)   BA (cloth)   UV (paper)

13706. Narrative of the Most Extraordinary and Distressing Shipwreck of the Whaleship Essex by Owen Chase with Supplementary Accounts of Survivors and Herman Melville's Notes Introduction by B. R. McElderry, Jr. ...

Corinth Books New York ⟨1963⟩

Issued in printed paper wrapper?

"Herman Melville's Notes," pp. 137-141.

The notes reprinted from the original *ms* in The Houghton Library.

B

13707. The Works of Herman Melville Standard Edition ... ⟨fly-title⟩

New York Russell & Russell Inc 1963

16 Vols. A reprint of the *Constable Edition*, 1922–1924, above. Vols. 13 and 16 contain some material here first printed in an American book. See separate entries, below, for *Billy Budd...*, 1963; and *Poems...*, 1963.

H

13708. Billy Budd and Other Prose Pieces... Edited by Raymond W. ⟨*sic*⟩ Weaver

New York Russell & Russell Inc 1963

The Works of Herman Melville Standard Edition, Vol. 13.

A facsimile reprint of the London, 1924, printing. First American book publication of:

"The Cincinnati"

"Daniel Orme"

"Fragment"

"Fragments from a Writing-Desk"

"Jack Gentian"

"Major Gentian and Colonel J. Bunkum"

"The Marquis de Grandvin"

"Portrait of a Gentleman"

"To Major John Gentian, Dean of the Burgundy Club"

"Under the Rose"

H

13709. Poems   Containing Battle-Pieces   John Marr and Other Sailors   Timoleon and Miscellaneous Poems ... ⟨Edited by Michael Sadleir and Raymond M. Weaver⟩

New York Russell & Russell Inc 1963

The Works of Herman Melville Standard Edition, Vol. 16.

A facsimile reprint of the London, 1924, printing. First American book publication of:

"Author's Note"

"Angel o' the Age!"

"Preface" to "At the Hostelry"

"To M. de Grandvin," being the dedication to "At the Hostelry."

H

13710. Billy Budd   Benito Cereno ... with an Introduction by Maxwell Geismar ...

Printed for the Members of the Limited Editions Club New York 1965

"... The present edition, for the most part, follows the Harvard University Press text established by F. Barron Freeman in 1948 and corrected by Elizabeth Treeman in 1956 . . ."---"A Note on the Text of Billy Budd," p. xv.

". . . Fifteen hundred copies . . ."---Colophon.

For other editions of *Billy Budd* see under years 1924, 1928, 1948, 1962, 1963. "Benito Cereno" reprinted from *Piazza Tales*, 1856.

Deposited June 2, 1965.

BPL   LC

13711. . . . Moby-Dick   An Authoritative Text   Reviews and Letters by Melville   Analogues and Sources   Criticism   Edited by Harrison Hayford   Hershel Parker . . .

W W Norton & Company Inc   New York ⟨1967⟩

At head of title: *A Norton Critical Edition   Herman Melville*

On copyright page: *First Edition*

". . . Unlike any previous edition in that it is not a slightly corrected reproduction of the first American text but a *critical*, constructed text--- that is, one which attempts to come closer than the first edition did to the author's final intention by correcting errors and adopting his own later revisions . . ."---P. x.

For first edition see under year 1851; also see under years 1922, 1952.

Cloth; and, printed paper wrapper.

LC

13712. White-Jacket or the World in a Man-of-War . . . Edited by Hennig Cohen . . .

Holt, Rinehart and Winston   New York   Chicago   San Francisco   Toronto   London ⟨1967⟩

Printed paper wrapper.

For first edition see under year 1850; also see under year 1970.

". . . Based on the first American edition collated with the first English edition. Passages which were altered from the first American edition have been inserted in square brackets. Passages which were omitted from the English edition are bracketed and marked with an asterisk and footnote."---P. vii.

LC

13713. Typee   A Peep at Polynesian Life . . .

Northwestern University Press and The Newberry Library   Evanston and Chicago   1968

The Writings of Herman Melville   The Northwestern-Newberry Edition, Vol. 1. Edited by Harrison Hayford, Hershel Parker and G. Thomas Tanselle.

For first edition see above under year 1846.

"The . . . text is *critical* in the sense that it does not correspond exactly to any one existing document; but it is closer to the author's intentions---insofar as they are recoverable---than any single documentary form of the text."---P. 304.

H   LC

13714. Omoo   A Narrative of Adventures in the South Seas . . .

Northwestern University Press and The Newberry Library   Evanston and Chicago   1968

The Writings of Herman Melville   The Northwestern-Newberry Edition, Vol. 2. Edited by Harrison Hayford, Hershel Parker and G. Thomas Tanselle.

For first edition see above under year 1847.

"The . . . text is *critical* in the sense that it does not correspond exactly to any one existing document; but it is closer to the author's intentions ---insofar as they are recoverable---than any single documentary form of the text."---P. 346.

H

13715. Redburn   His First Voyage . . .

Northwestern University Press and The Newberry Library   Evanston and Chicago   1969

The Writings of Herman Melville   The Northwestern-Newberry Edition, Vol. 4. Edited by Harrison Hayford, Hershel Parker and G. Thomas Tanselle.

For first edition see above under year 1849.

"The . . . text is *critical* in that it does not correspond exactly to any authorized edition, but it is closer to the author's intentions---insofar as they are recoverable---than any single authorized edition."---P. 354.

H

13716. Mardi and a Voyage Thither . . .

Northwestern University Press and the Newberry Library   Evanston and Chicago   1970

The Writings of Herman Melville   The Northwestern-Newberry Edition, Vol. 3. Edited by Harrison Hayford, Hershel Parker and G. Thomas Tanselle.

For first edition see above under year 1849.

"The . . . text is *critical* in that it does not correspond exactly to any authorized edition, but it is closer to the author's intentions---insofar as they are recoverable---than any single authorized edition."---P. 684.

LC

13717. White-Jacket or the World in a Man-of-War . . .

Northwestern University Press and The Newberry Library Evanston and Chicago 1970

The Writings of Herman Melville The Northwestern-Newberry Edition, Vol. 5. Edited by Harrison Hayford, Hershel Parker and G. Thomas Tanselle.

For first edition see under year 1850. Also see under year 1967.

"The . . . text is *critical* in that it does not correspond exactly to any single authorized edition, but it is closer to the author's intentions———insofar as they are recoverable———than any such edition."———P. 442.

H

Reprints of Melville's books; sheet music and separate editions; *i.e.*, pieces reprinted from Melville's works and issued in separate form. For a list of books by authors other than Melville containing reprinted Melville material see in *Section Three*.

13718. The Story of Toby, a Sequel to "Typee." By the Author of That Work. ⟨Signature mark:⟩ U

⟨London: John Murray, Albemarle Street. Price Threepence, n.d., 1846⟩

Printed paper wrapper. For publication information see in *Section One* under *Narrative of a Four Months' Residence* . . . , London, 1846.

"It was first printed on or before September 30, 1846, in an edition of 1,000 copies. Of these, 250 were in wrappers for separate sale as a pamphlet . . . Most of the remaining 750 could have been distributed with the copies of the original edition of the *Narrative* . . ."---*Typee* . . . , Evanston & Chicago, 1968, edited by Harrison Hayford and others, p. 298.

"The pamphlet sale was sufficiently successful to call for another printing of 250 copies in wrappers on March 31, 1847."---*Ibid.* BAL has not identified two printings.

Copies, without the wrapper, have been found inserted in *Narrative of a Four Months' Residence among the Natives of a Valley of the Marquesas Islands*, London, 1846. See, as an example, the N copy of the second issue, cloth, binder's variant B; almost certainly inserted by an amateur, not by a professional binder. Also noted in the N copy of the London, 1847, printing of *Typee;* terminal advertisements dated March, 1849.

Issued after Aug. 1, 1846, on which date Melville sent Murray the text. The New York edition of *Typee* containing the addition was issued Aug. 6, 1846. For fuller publication notes see in *Section One* under *Narrative* . . . , London, 1846.

13719. Narrative of a Four Months' Residence among the Natives of a Valley of the Marquesas Islands; or, a Peep at Polynesian Life . . .

London: John Murray, Albemarle Street. 1846.

"The Story of Toby . . . ," pp. ⟨287⟩-301.

The earliest located mention of the book with the added material is in PC Dec. 1, 1846, by which time the title of the book is given as *Typee.*

13720. Typee; or, a Narrative of a Four Months' Residence among the Natives of a Valley of the Marquesas Islands . . .

London: John Murray, Albemarle Street. 1847.

The statement *New Edition* not present on the title-page. Copies have been seen with inserted terminal catalog dated *May, 1848;* also, *February, 1856.*

13721. Typee; or, a Narrative of a Four Months' Residence among the Natives of a Valley of the Marquesas Islands; or, a Peep at Polynesian Life . . . New Edition.

London: John Murray, Albemarle Street. 1847.

A copy has been reported with terminal catalog dated *January, 1851.*

13722. Typee: A Peep at Polynesian Life . . . The Revised Edition, with a Sequel . . .

New York: Wiley and Putnam. London: John Murray, Albemarle Street 1847.

Cloth; and, two paper-covered parts.

13723. Typee: A Peep at Polynesian Life . . . The Revised Edition, with a Sequel . . .

New York: Harper & Brothers, Publishers. London: John Murray. 1849.

Cloth; and, printed paper wrapper.

13724. The Refugee . . .

Philadelphia: T. B. Peterson & Brothers, 306 Chestnut Street. ⟨1865⟩

Reprint of *Israel Potter*, 1855.

A copy in NYPL inscribed by Susan Gansevoort March 17, 1865. Deposited April 11, 1865. Advertised ALG Sept. 15, 1865, as *just out;* offered in both cloth; and, in printed paper wrapper. Copies in the binding of *Peterson's Dollar Series* are presumed late.

13725. John Marr and Other Poems . . . with an Introductory Note by Henry Chapin

Princeton Princeton University Press London: Humphrey Milford Oxford University Press MCMXXII ⟨*i.e.*, 1923?⟩

175 copies on French handmade paper: Title-page printed in black and orange. Paper watermarked *Glaslan*. Certificate of issue numbered. Marbled paper boards sides, black V cloth shelf back.

1675 copies in trade format: Title-page printed in black only. Paper unwatermarked. Certificate of issue not numbered. Mottled green paper boards sides, tan V cloth shelf back.

Trade format listed PW Feb. 10, 1923. Trade format deposited for copyright March 28, 1923.

13726. Benito Cereno . . .

MCMXXVI The Nonesuch Press 16 Great James Street, London

1650 numbered copies only. Reprinted from *Piazza Tales*, 1856. Reviewed TLS March 3, 1927.

13727. Romances of Herman Melville . . .

The Pickwick Publishers, Inc. New York MCMXXVIII

Flexible leather.

13728. Romances of Herman Melville . . .

Tudor Publishing Co. New York ⟨1931⟩

Printed from the plates of the preceding entry.

13729. The Encantadas or, Enchanted Isles . . . with an Introduction, Critical Epilogue & Bibliographical Notes by Victor Wolfgang Von Hagen

1940 William P. Wreden: Burlingame California

Boards, cloth shelf back, printed paper label. 550 copies only.

Reprinted from *Piazza Tales*, 1856. Deposited April 22, 1940.

13730. . . . Billy Budd, Benito Cereno and the Enchanted Isles . . .

The Press of the Readers Club, New York ⟨1942⟩

At head of title: *Three shorter novels by the author of "Moby Dick"*

Deposited Sept. 17, 1942.

13731. Moby Dick; or, the Whale . . . with an Introduction by Clifton Fadiman and Illustrations by Boardman Robinson

⟨New York⟩ The Limited Editions Club 1943

2 Vols. Leather.

13732. Selected Poems . . . Edited by William Plomer . . .

The Hogarth Press 37 Mecklenburgh Square London, W.C. 1 ⟨1943⟩

The New Hogarth Library, Vol. 10. Printed paper boards; and, cloth.

13733. Billy Budd Foretopman . . . with an Introduction by William Plomer

John Lehmann London 1946

13734. Contemporary American Songs . . . Second Series . . . Epitaph . . .

Associated Music Publishers, Inc. New York . . . ⟨1946⟩

Sheet music. Cover-title. Plate number A.M.P. 194542. *Note:* The plate number varies with the key. Music by David Diamond. Reprinted from *Battle-Pieces*, 1866.

13735. 7 Songs by David Diamond Billy in the Darbies (Herman Melville) . . .

Elkan-Vogel Co. Inc., Philadelphia, Pa. ⟨1946⟩

Sheet music. Cover-title. Reprinted from *Billy Budd*.

13736. . . . Billy Budd and Other Stories with an Introduction by Rex Warner

London John Lehmann ⟨1951⟩

At head of title: *Herman Melville*

13737. The Martyr ⟨Music by⟩ David Diamond . . .

Southern Music Publishing Company, Inc. New York ⟨1951⟩

Sheet music. Cover-title. Plate number 62-6. Reprinted from *Battle-Pieces*, 1866.

13738. Selected Writings . . . Complete Short Stories . . .

The Modern Library New York ⟨1952⟩

Deposited Jan. 18, 1952.

13739. The Mask of Cain . . . The Portent . . . ⟨Music by⟩ Robert Evett . . .

Peer International Corporation New York ⟨1953⟩

Sheet music. Cover-title. Plate number 217-4. A full suite includes the above together with "Youth is the Time When Hearts Are Large" and "Shiloh."

Reprinted from *Battle-Pieces*, 1866.

See next two entries.

CHEAP LITERATURE FOR ALL CLASSES.

MURRAY'S

HOME AND COLONIAL LIBRARY.

THE STORY OF TOBY,

A SEQUEL TO "TYPEE."

BY THE AUTHOR OF THAT WORK.

LONDON:

JOHN MURRAY, ALBEMARLE STREET.

Price Threepence.

W. CLOWES AND SONS,   STAMFORD STREET.

13740. The Mask of Cain . . . "Youth Is the Time When Hearts Are Large" ⟨Music by⟩ Robert Evett . . .

Peer International Corporation   New York ⟨1953⟩

Sheet music. Cover-title. Plate number 218-8. Otherwise "On the Slain Collegians," *Battle-Pieces*, 1866.

See preceding entry; see next entry.

13741. The Mask of Cain . . . Shiloh ⟨Music by⟩ Robert Evett . . .

Peer International Corporation   New York ⟨1953⟩

Sheet music. Cover-title. Plate number 219-6. Reprinted from *Battle-Pieces*, 1866.

See preceding two entries.

13742. Encantadas Two Sketches from Herman Melville's Enchanted Isles with Woodcuts by Rico Lebrun

Printed at the Gehenna Press in Northampton MCMLXIII

Portfolio. Reprinted from *Piazza Tales*, 1856.

13743. Selected Poems of Herman Melville Edited by Hennig Cohen

Anchor Books   Doubleday & Company, Inc. Garden City, New York 1964

Printed paper wrapper. Received at LC Jan. 8, 1964. See next entry.

13744. Selected Poems of Herman Melville Edited by Hennig Cohen

Southern Illinois University Press   Carbondale ⟨1964⟩

Printed from the same setting as the preceding entry.

13745. Moby-Dick or, the Whale . . . Edited . . . by Charles Feidelson, Jr. . . .

The Bobbs-Merrill Company, Inc. A Subsidiary of Howard W. Sams & Co., Inc. Publishers Indianapolis New York Kansas City ⟨1964⟩

". . . The text is that of the first American edition (November 1851), supplemented by one short passage that appears only in the first English edition (October 1851) . . ."---P. viii. The passage referred to is a footnote that appears on pp. 9-10 of *The Whale*, London, 1851, Vol. 3. Its publication in the United States has been traced to the edition of *Moby-Dick* issued in New York by Dodd, Mead & Company, 1922, p. 355.

In this section are listed books by authors other than Melville which contain material by him reprinted from earlier books. See *Section II* for reprinted material issued under Melville's name.

Tales and Sketches for the Fire-Side . . .

New York . . . 1857.

For fuller entry see No. 8239.

Life in the South Seas. History of the Whale Fisheries . . . by Capt. E. C. Williams . . .

New York: Polhemus & De Vries, Printers, 66 Courtlandt Street. 1860.

Printed paper wrapper.

The Poets and Poetry of America. By Rufus Wilmot Griswold . . .

New York . . . 1873.

A proof printing of Melville's contributions to this anthology is in H. For fuller entry see BAL, Vol. 4, p. 60.

. . . Little Classics. Edited by Rossiter Johnson. Tragedy . . .

Boston . . . 1874.

For fuller entry see No. 4610.

Poetry of America . . . ⟨Edited⟩ by W. J. Linton.

London . . . 1878.

For fuller entry see No. 7872.

American War Ballads and Lyrics . . . Edited by George Cary Eggleston . . .

New York . . . ⟨1889⟩

For fuller comment see BAL, Vol. 4, p. 337.

A Century of American Literature Benjamin Franklin to James Russell Lowell . . . Chosen . . . by Huntington Smith

New York Thomas Y. Crowell & Co. 13 Astor Place ⟨1889⟩

. . . Harper's Fifth Reader American Authors

New York Harper & Brothers, Franklin Square 1889

"Whale-Fishing in the Indian Ocean," pp. 99-104, reprinted from *Moby-Dick*, 1851, Chapter 61.

Note: Reprinted and reissued not before 1890 by The American Book Company under date ⟨1889⟩. For fuller entry see No. 7917.

Capital Stories by American Authors.

Published by the Christian Herald, Louis Klopsch, Proprietor, Bible House, New York. ⟨1895⟩

The Memory of Lincoln Poems Selected with an Introduction by M. A. DeWolfe Howe

Boston Small Maynard & Company 1899

Capital Stories by American Authors

The Christian Herald Louis Klopsch, Proprietor Bible House, New York City . . . 1903 . . .

Poems of American History Collected . . . by Burton Egbert Stevenson

Boston . . . 1908

For fuller entry see in Joaquin Miller, *Section One*.

Gentlemen, Scholars and Scoundrels . . . Edited by Horace Knowles

. . . New York ⟨1959⟩

For fuller entry see in Amy Lowell, *Section Three*.

Future Perfect American Science Fiction of the Nineteenth Century ⟨by⟩ H. Bruce Franklin

New York Oxford University Press 1966

Life and Remarkable Adventures of Israel R. Potter . . . Who Was a Soldier in the American Revolution . . .

Providence: Printed by Henry Trumbull--- 1824. (Price 28 Cents.)

Boards, leather shelf back?

A corrected printing was issued with the imprint: *Providence: Printed by J. Howard, for I. R. Potter---1824. (Price 31 Cents.)*

Sometimes associated with Melville because of his *Israel Potter*, 1855. Not by Melville.

The Romancist, and Novelist's Library: The Best Works of the Best Authors . . .

London: Printed by C. Reynell, Little Pulteney Street. J. Clements, Nos. 21 and 22 Little Pulteney Street, Regent Street. MDCCCXXXIX. ⟨-MDCCCXL.⟩

"Mocha Dick or, the White Whale of the Pacific. (A Leaf from a Manuscript Journal)," by J. N. Reynolds, Vol. 3, pp. 61-64.

Here for the record.

Redburn: Or the Schoolmaster of a Morning.

New-York: Wm. M. Christy, No. 2, Astor House. M DCCC XLV.

Anonymous. Not by Melville. Sometimes associated with Melville because of his *Redburn*, 1849.

Unprinted paper boards.

Missionary Operations in Polynesia: A Review (In Part) of the Historical Passages of Melville's "Omoo." By Wm. Oland Bourne. From the New Englander for January.

New-York: Wm. Oland Bourne, Printer, 6 Cortlandt Street 1848.

Cover-title. Printed paper wrapper.

The Golden Present . . . Edited by Mrs. J. Thayer.

Nashua . . . 1849.

"Autumn," p. 85. Credited thus: *Melville*. BAL has found no evidence of Herman Melville's authorship.

For fuller description see BAL, Vol. 4, p. 201.

One Hundred Cottage Stories for Boys. By Melville . . .

Portland: William Hyde & Son. 1851.

Author not known; certainly not by the subject of this list.

Two Journeys to Japan. 1856-7. By Kinahan Cornwallis . . . in Two Volumes . . .

London: Thomas Cautley Newby, Publisher, 30, Welbeck Street. 1859 . . .

". . . What is essentially *Typee* appears in Vol. 2, pp. 209-300 . . ." --- Richard Colles Johnson in *Melville in Anthologies*, Chicago: The Newberry Library, n.d.

Life and Adventure in the South Pacific. By a Roving Printer.

New York: Harper & Brothers, Publishers, Franklin Square. 1861.

Contains some passages extracted from *Moby-Dick*. For a discussion of this publication see George Clark's "Notes on a Roving Plagiarist," in *Alumni News of Hanover College*, fall, 1968.

Typee . . . with Biographical and Critical Introduction by Arthur Stedman . . .

New York   American Publishers Corporation 310-318 Sixth Avenue. ⟨1892⟩

Noted only with the imprint of the United States Book Company on the spine.

Biographical Sketch of Herman Melville. 1891. ⟨By J. E. A. Smith⟩

⟨n.p., n.d., probably Pittsfield, Mass., 1897⟩

Printed paper wrapper. At head of text, p. ⟨1⟩: *Written for the Evening Journal, Pittsfield, Mass., by J. E. A. Smith, 1891.*

Herman Melville Mariner and Mystic by Raymond M. Weaver

New York   George H. Doran Company ⟨1921⟩

The first printing has the publisher's *GHD* monogram on the copyright page.

Some Personal Letters of Herman Melville and a Bibliography by Meade Minnigerode

Edmond Byrne Hackett . . . 1922

For fuller entry see in *Section One* above.

The Art of Crystal Gazing. New Edition Revised.

Chicago: Regan Publishing Corporation, 1925 ⟨1926?⟩

Not seen. Not located. Entry from *The Cumulative Book Index . . . 1925 . . . 1926 . . .*, New York, 1927, where a book of this title is erroneously credited to Melville.

Herman Melville by John Freeman

New York   The Macmillan Company   1926
All Rights Reserved

Also issued with a London imprint.

Herman Melville ⟨by⟩ Lewis Mumford

Harcourt, Brace & Company New York ⟨1929⟩

Also issued with the imprint of The Literary
Guild, New York.

Journal of a Cruise to the Pacific Ocean, 1842–
1844, in the Frigate United States with Notes on
Herman Melville Edited by Charles Roberts
Anderson . . .

Durham   North Carolina   Duke University
Press 1937

The Meaning of Moby Dick by William S. Gleim

Edmond Byrne Hackett The Brick Row Book
Shop, Inc. Fifty-Five Fifth Avenue New York
1938

Boards, cloth shelf back, printed paper label on
spine. On copyright page: *First Printed January
1938*

Melville in the South Seas by Charles Roberts
Anderson . . .

New York: Morningside Heights   Columbia
University Press . . . 1939

Melville's Religious Thought An Essay in Interpretation by William Braswell

Duke University Press Durham, North Carolina
1943

Herman Melville   The Tragedy of Mind ⟨by⟩
William Ellery Sedgwick

Cambridge, Massachusetts Harvard University
Press 1944

. . . An Index of Herman Melville's Mardi, Moby-
Dick, Pierre, and Billy Budd . . . by Gordon H.
Roper

Chicago, Illinois 1944

Printed paper wrapper. At head of title: *The
University of Chicago*

. . . Call Me Ishmael

Reynal & Hitchcock New York ⟨1947⟩

At head of title: *Charles Olson*

Herman Melville a Critical Study by Richard
Chase

1949 The Macmillan Company New York

On copyright page: *First Printing*

Melville's Use of the Bible ⟨by⟩ Nathalia Wright

Duke University Press Durham, North Carolina
1949

The Trying-Out of Moby-Dick ⟨by⟩ Howard P.
Vincent . . .

Houghton Mifflin Company   Boston   The
Riverside Press Cambridge 1949

A Collection of Published Melville Letters Prepared by English 378

University of Chicago   Summer Quarter,
1949 . . .

Mimeographed.

Herman Melville ⟨by⟩ Newton Arvin . . .

⟨New York⟩ William Sloane Associates ⟨1950⟩

On copyright page: *First Printing*

. . . Herman Melville   A Check List of Books
and Manuscripts in the Collections of the New
York Public Library Compiled . . . by Herbert
Cahoon . . .

New York The New York Public Library 1951

Cover-title. At head of title: *Gordon Lester Ford
Memorial Study No. 4*

Printed self-wrapper. 300 copies printed according to the printer's certificate of issue.

Herman Melville A Biography by Leon Howard

University of California Press Berkeley & Los
Angeles ⟨1951⟩

. . . The Melville Log   A Documentary Life of
Herman Melville 1819-1891 . . .

Harcourt, Brace and Company, New York
⟨1951⟩

2 Vols. At head of title: *Jay Leyda*

On copyright: *first edition*

. . . Melville's Early Life and Redburn by William
H. Gilman

New York New York University Press, Washington Square London Geoffrey Cumberlege,
Oxford University Press 1951

At head of title: "*Divine imaginings . . . Redburn*

Deposited Aug. 13, 1951.

Herman Melville   Cycle and Epicycle ⟨by⟩ Eleanor Melville Metcalf...

Harvard University Press   Cambridge   1953

Melville and the Comic Spirit ⟨by⟩ Edward H. Rosenberry

Harvard University Press   Cambridge   1955

Melville Bibliography   1952–1957   Including Published Works and Research Completed or in Progress during the Years 1952–1957 about

Herman Melville Compiled by the Bibliographical Committee of the Melville Society   John H. Birss ... Gordon Roper ... Stuart C. Sherman ...

Multilithed by the Providence (R.I.) Public Library 1959

Cover-title.

Battle-Pieces and Aspects of the War by Herman Melville   A Facsimile Reproduction with an Introduction by Sidney Kaplan...

Gainesville, Florida   Scholars' Facsimiles & Reprints 1960

JOAQUIN MILLER

(Cincinnatus Hiner Miller)

1 8 3 7 – 1 9 1 3

"The baby . . . was named Cincinnatus Hiner (not Heine) Miller . . . Joaquin always asserted that his parents had bestowed on him the middle name of Heine because at his birth they astutely sensed that someday he would possess the lyrical gifts of the great German poet. In reality, Joaquin borrowed the *Heine* in signing his first two works; he owed the *Hiner* to an obscure doctor by that name who attended him at birth."–––Marberry, p. 3.

Miller's "diary on three occasions revealed his birthdate to be September 8, 1837, and not November 10, 1841 or 1842."–––Marberry, p. 19.

For a list of unlocated (unpublished?) productions see *Section Three* below.

For a list of undated publications see immediately below.

INDEX TO CERTAIN UNDATED PUBLICATIONS

The following publications were issued without date and are here listed alphabetically by title. Unless otherwise noted these will be found in *Section One* of this list.

After the Snow and the Shroud. Ca. 1893.

American Poems. Selected . . . by William Michael Rossetti, London, n.d., 1872. See in *Section Four*.

The Battle of Castle Crags. 1894?

Christmas Wishes. Ca. 1885.

Masterpieces of American Humor, Girard, Kansas, n.d., 1926. See in *Section Four*.

〈*Mothers of Men*〉. Untitled poem beginning *The bravest battle that ever was fought* . . . See *The Elocutionist's Annual Number 17* . . . , 1889, in *Section One*.

Oakland. See *Songs by Juanita and Joaquin Miller* . . . 〈1914〉, in *Section One*.

Panama, Union of the Oceans. Ca. 1912.

Paquita, the Indian Heroine. See under 1881 in *Section Two*.

Peace on Earth. Ca. 1885.

Readings from California Poets 〈*Selected by*〉 *Edmund Russell.* See under 1893 in *Section Four*.

Sack Cloth and Ashes. See under 1869.

Song of the Centennial. Ca. 1876.

Stories of the Sierras and Other Sketches. See under 1872.

Thompson's Prodigal and Other Sketches. By Bret Harte . . . with a Story of Wild Western Life. By Joaquin Miller. See in *Section Two* under n.d., 1885.

The Tree by the Well. See under 1884.

Where Rolls the Oregon. See under 1876.

13746. SPECIMENS

〈CANYON CITY, O., APRIL 1st 1868〉

Place and date taken from the preface.

〈1〉-54; blank leaf. $5^{13}/_{16}'' \times 4^{3}/_{16}''$.

〈1-7⁴〉.

Unprinted lavender paper wrapper. Copies also occur in black leather. Letter (in LC) from Miller to his sister, April 28, 1868: ". . . Last week I sent you a small volume of my poems. I desire that you have them *bound* so that you can keep them while you live. You will direct the binder to put heavy state and fly leaves on the sides so as to give it bulk. If finely bound with the title 'Specimens' and the authors name on the side it will be a nice ornament for your centre table. They can be bound in Portland."

Preface signed at end: *C. H. Miller. Canyon City, O*〈*regon*〉*., April 1st 1868.*

H NYPL UV Y

13747. JOAQUIN, ET AL., BY CINCINNATUS H MILLER.

PORTLAND OREGON: S. J. McCORMICK, PUBLISHER, 105 FRONT STREET, 1869.

⟨1⟩-112. $5^{11}\!\!/_{16}''\times4''$ full.

⟨1-14⁴⟩.

C cloth: green. Pale buff end papers. Flyleaves.

Deposited April 16, 1869.

AAS B H HEH LC UV Y

13748. SACK CLOTH AND ASHES . . .

⟨n.p., n.d., probably Eugene City, Oregon, 1869⟩

Date on the basis of postmarked envelope in which the production was mailed.

Galley proof. Not prepared for publication thus. Elsewhere unlocated. At end of text: *C. H. Miller.*

$23\frac{1}{2}''\times3\frac{1}{2}''$.

Not after July 6, 1869.

UV

13749. PACIFIC POEMS . . .

LONDON: WHITTINGHAM AND WILKINS. 1871.

⟨i⟩-⟨xii⟩, ⟨1⟩-107. See under bindings for leaf size.

⟨A⟩⁶, B-G⁸, H⁶.

Noted in the following bindings. Sequence, if any, not determined. The designations are for identification only. The following features are sufficient to identify:

BINDING A

C cloth: green. Covers bevelled. Edges not gilded. Leaf $6\frac{3}{4}''\times4\frac{1}{4}''$. Tan-coated end papers. On the spine the initials in PACIFIC POEMS are $\frac{1}{4}''$ scant tall.

BINDING B

C cloth: green. Covers bevelled. Edges gilded. Leaf $6\frac{1}{2}''$ scant $\times\ 4\frac{1}{16}''$. Tan-coated end papers. On the spine the initials in PACIFIC POEMS are $\frac{1}{4}''$ scant tall.

BINDING C

C cloth: green. Covers bevelled. Top edges gilded. Leaf $6\frac{1}{2}''$ full $\times\ 4\frac{1}{16}''$. Tan-coated end papers. On the spine the initials in PACIFIC POEMS are $\frac{1}{8}''$ tall.

According to Marberry, pp. 79-80, the book "was put out anonymously, and did not even bear the publisher's imprint. The edition was limited to one hundred copies; one was given to a bookseller as a token that the book was on sale to the public, and the remaining ninety-nine were sent to reviewers and to people of prominence . . ." All examined copies bear Miller's name as author; all bear the imprint of Whittingham and Wilkins, the printers, as publisher.

". . . One hundred were printed, bearing the name of my printer as publisher . . ."---*Joaquin Miller's Poems*, Vol. 1, San Francisco, 1909, p. 177.

Rumors of an anonymous issue persist; no anonymous printing has been found by BAL. Under date March 26, 1871*, Miller states: "Eureka! The *St. James* ⟨sic⟩ *Gazette* says *Arizonian* is by Browning!" which suggests that Miller issued something anonymously and sent it out for review. A partial printing of *Pacific Poems?* However, since the *St. James's Gazette* was first issued on May 31, 1880, and Miller's journal would have the periodical in existence in 1871, the journal becomes suspect. Was the journal written in 1871?

"The more the critics examined . . . ⟨the journal⟩ the more they were convinced that (a) Joaquin's original diary entries had been cut or expanded or doctored for publication, or, (b) the diary jottings had been entirely manufactured---written shortly before publication time. A close examination of the entries today tends to confirm the reviewers' judgment and makes it seem likely that their first supposition is probably correct; but the evidence is by no means conclusive."---Marberry, p. 182.

A copy in *Binding B* (in H) inscribed by Miller Jan. 12, 1871. A copy in *Binding C* (in Y) inscribed by Miller Jan. 12, 1870 ⟨*i.e.,* 1871⟩.

The following reading is present in all examined copies, p. x, line 3: *me not to publish. I shall follow his advice, for* |

AAS B H HEH NYPL UV Y

13750. SONGS OF THE SIERRAS . . .

LONDON: LONGMANS, GREEN, READER, AND DYER. 1871.

For American edition see next entry. Also see under 1892.

A revised and enlarged edition of *Pacific Poems,* 1871.

⟨i-ii⟩, ⟨i⟩-⟨xiv⟩, ⟨1⟩-301; leaf, either present; or, excised or pasted under the end paper. $7\frac{1}{2}''\times5''$.

A-I, K-U⁸. U8 either present; or, excised or pasted under the end paper.

Two bindings noted; sequence, if any, not determined. The designations are for identification only. The following features are sufficient for identification:

BINDING A

C cloth: green. Covers bevelled. Gold stamping on both sides. Tan-coated end papers. Edges gilt.

* In his journal, *Memorie and Rime,* 1884, p. 26.

BINDING B

C cloth: green. Covers bevelled or plain. Gold stamping on front, blind stamping on back. Tan-coated end papers. Edges not gilded.

Note: Sheets have been seen with the following imprint: NEW YORK: / PUBLISHED FOR THE AUTHOR. / ⟨*rule*⟩ / 1871. The title-leaf is a cancel. Noted in *Binding B*. The only located copies (two) were deposited for American copyright in the name of *Cincinnatus Miller*. Location: LC.

Advertised for publication *on Thursday next, i.e.,* April 20, in Ath April 15, 1871. Listed PC May 1, 1871. Reviewed PC May 1, 1871. Listed Bkr May 1, 1871; Ath May 6, 1871.

H ⟨*Binding B*⟩ LC ⟨*Binding B*⟩ UV (both) Y ⟨*Binding A*⟩

13751. SONGS OF THE SIERRAS . . .

BOSTON: ROBERTS BROTHERS. 1871.

For London edition see preceding entry. The texts vary considerably. Also see under 1892.

⟨i-xii⟩, ⟨1⟩-299. Laid paper. 6⅞″ full × 4¾″.

⟨1², 2⁴, 3-14¹², 15⁶⟩. *Signed:* ⟨a⟩⁶, ⟨1⟩-18⁸, ⟨b⟩¹, 19⁵.

Two issues (printings?) noted, probably in the order as here given:

ISSUE A

⟨i⟩: *Thoughts about Art* . . .

⟨ii⟩: *Pink and White Tyranny* . . .

⟨iii⟩: . . . *The Earthly Paradise* . . .

⟨iv⟩: *The Handy Volume Series* . . .

ISSUE B

⟨i⟩: . . . *The Earthly Paradise* . . .

⟨ii⟩: *The Handy Volume Series* . . .

⟨iii⟩: *Pink and White Tyranny* . . .

⟨iv⟩: *Thoughts about Art* . . .

C cloth: terra-cotta. FL cloth: blue; green; purple. Brown-coated end papers. Laid paper flyleaves. Top edges gilt.

Two states of the binding noted; the order of presentation is probably correct.

BINDING A

At foot of spine: R ⟨*star*⟩ B

BINDING B

At foot of spine: ROBERTS / ⟨*wheel hub*⟩ / BROS The printings of 1872, 1888 noted thus.

Contains the following poems not present in the London edition:

"Even So"

"Kit Carson's Ride"

"Myrrh"

Noted for *this week* ALG July 1, 1871. Noted for July 15 ALG July 1, 1871. ". . . About to be re-published in the U.S. . . . Considerable alterations and additions . . . have been made . . ."---Ath July 15, 1871. Advertised for September ALG Sept. 15, 1871. "Ready. Our advance orders have already exhausted two large editions"---ALG Sept. 15, 1871. Listed and reviewed ALG Sept. 15, 1871.

Note: Copies have been seen (*Binding B, Sheets A*) with an inserted terminal catalog, pp. 1-24. On p. 2 appears a publisher's notice dated *September, 1871.* P. 24 dated at end: *Boston, July 26, 1871.*

AAS (*Sheets A, Binding B*) B (*Sheets A, Binding B*) BA (*Sheets A, Binding B*) BPL (*Sheets A, Binding A; Sheets A, Binding B*) H (*Sheets A, Binding A; Sheets A, Binding B*) NYPL (*Sheets A, Binding B; Sheets B, Binding B*) UV (*Sheets A, Binding A*) Y (*Sheets A, Binding A; Sheets A, Binding B*)

13752. The Christmas Locket A Holiday Number of Old & New

Boston: Roberts Brothers, 143 Washington Street. 1871.

"The Wanderer's Poem," pp. 5-6. Collected in *Songs of the Sunlands,* London, 1873, as "At Bethlehem"; and, *Complete Poetical Works,* San Francisco, 1897.

For fuller entry see No. 10417.

13753. . . . Stories of the Sierras and Other Sketches. By Bret Harte . . . with a Story of Wild Western Life by Joaquin Miller . . .

London: John Camden Hotten, 74 & 75, Piccadilly . . . ⟨n.d., 1872⟩

"The Last Man of Mexican Camp," pp. ⟨9⟩-36.

For fuller entry see No. 7259.

13754. SONGS OF THE SUN-LANDS . . .

LONDON: LONGMANS, GREEN, READER AND DYER. 1873.

For American edition see below under year 1873. The London and Boston editions vary textually. Also see under 1878 and 1892.

SMALL PAPER FORMAT

⟨i-ii⟩, ⟨i⟩-⟨viii⟩, ⟨1⟩-243; printer's imprint, p. ⟨244⟩; . . . *Songs of the Sierras* . . . *Opinions of the Press* . . . , pp. ⟨1-17⟩. 8¾″ × 5½″ full.

⟨-⟩¹, ⟨A⟩⁴, B-I, K-R⁸, S², T¹.

C cloth: green. Blue-black-coated end papers; cream-coated end papers. Edges plain.

LARGE PAPER FORMAT

⟨i-ii⟩, ⟨i⟩-⟨viii⟩, ⟨1⟩-243; printer's imprint, p. ⟨244⟩; ... *Songs of the Sierras* ... *Opinions of the Press* ..., pp. ⟨1-17⟩. Laid paper watermarked with a circular device. $9\frac{3}{4}'' \times 7\frac{3}{4}''$.

⟨-⟩¹, ⟨A⟩⁴, B-I, K-R⁸, S², T¹.

C cloth: green. Blue-coated end papers. Top edges gilt.

Note: Sheets of the trade edition were prepared with a cancel title-leaf, n.p., n.d. Possibly prepared for American copyright purposes. The only located copy is in LC.

Advertised as *just published* Ath April 19, 1873. Listed Ath April 26, 1873. Reviewed Ath April 26, 1873. Listed Bkr May 1, 1873; PC May 1, 1873.

AAS (trade) B (trade) LC (large paper) NYPL (trade) UCLA (trade) UV (large paper) Y (both)

13755. LIFE AMONGST THE MODOCS: UNWRITTEN HISTORY ...

LONDON: RICHARD BENTLEY AND SON, PUBLISHERS IN ORDINARY TO HER MAJESTY, NEW BURLINGTON STREET. 1873.

For first American edition see below under year 1874, *Unwritten History.*

⟨i⟩-viii, ⟨1⟩-400. $8\frac{5}{8}''$ scant $\times$ $5\frac{9}{16}''$.

⟨A⟩⁴, B-I, K-U, X-Z, AA-CC⁸.

Two cloth bindings noted. Sequence, if any, not determined. The following is sufficient for identification:

BINDING A

C cloth: orange-brown. Covers bevelled. Brown-coated end papers. Spine lettered: LIFE / AMONGST / THE / MODOCS / JOAQUIN / MILLER / *R. Bentley & Son.*

BINDING B

S cloth: cocoa-brown. Covers not bevelled. Spine lettered: LIFE / AMONGST THE / MODOCS / J MILLER. / Yellow-coated end papers.

"... *Life amongst the Modocs* ... purported to be an autobiography. This book at first was not regarded with much pride by Joaquin, for Prentice Mulford had been hired to manufacture the volume after listening to Joaquin's tales of adventure--- '*Mulford did all the work,*' Joaquin freely admitted. The book was called *Life amongst the Modocs* ... Today this 'autobiography' is indexed in many libraries (the New York Public Library, for instance) under the heading of fiction."--- Marberry, pp. 119-120.

Miller "is said to be correcting for the press a prose work ⟨that⟩ is autobiographical. In it he gives ⟨his⟩ experiences of the Modoc Indians." ---Ath June 7, 1873. Advertised for July 9 Ath June 28, 1873. Advertised for July 14 Ath July 12, 1873. Advertised for *next week* Ath July 19, 1873. Advertised without comment Ath July 26, 1873. Listed Ath July 26, 1873; Bkr Aug. 1, 1873; PC Aug. 1, 1873. Reviewed Ath Aug. 9, 1873.

B (*Binding A*)   LC (*Binding A*)   UV (*Binding B*)

13756. SONGS OF THE SUN-LANDS ...

BOSTON: ROBERTS BROTHERS. 1873.

For prior London publication see above under year 1873. Also see under years 1878, 1892.

⟨i⟩-vi, ⟨7⟩-212; advertisements, pp. 1-4. $6\frac{7}{8}'' \times 4\frac{5}{8}''$.

⟨1⟩-9¹². Also signed: ⟨A⟩-M⁸, N⁴.

FL cloth: green; purple; terra-cotta. Gray-green-coated end papers; brown-coated end papers. Top edges gilt. Flyleaves of either laid or wove paper.

Listed PW Oct. 25, 1873.

B   BPL   H   USC   UV   Y

13757. UNWRITTEN   HISTORY: LIFE AMONGST THE MODOCS

For prior London publication see *Life Amongst the Modocs,* 1873.

Note: The present entry is tentative and is based on copies, some in original binding, in: AAS, H, HEH, LC, NYPL, UV, Y.

Examination indicates that this book went into an undetermined number of reprintings. The copies first printed do not have a *Publisher's Announcement* on the reverse of the dedication leaf; nor is there present, p. ⟨442⟩, a footnote reading: **American Edition.* Copies with these features present are reprints and are here ignored.

UNWRITTEN HISTORY: LIFE AMONGST THE MODOCS ... SOLD BY SUBSCRIPTION ONLY.

HARTFORD, CONN.: AMERICAN PUBLISHING COMPANY. 1874.

⟨i-viii⟩; inserted, unpaged, leaf; ⟨ix⟩-xvi, 17-445; advertisements, pp. ⟨446-452⟩. Portrait frontispiece and 23 plates inserted. Also inserted: Facing the portrait frontispiece, a plate. This latter is a duplicate of any one of the 23 full-page plates. $8\frac{5}{8}''$ full $\times$ $5\frac{5}{8}''$.

⟨A⟩⁹, B-Z⁸, A-⁸, B-¹⁰. ⟨A⟩5 inserted. *Note:* The surviving copyright deposit copy (rebound, imperfect, uncollatable) does not have ⟨A⟩5 present but does have all the other features of the earliest printing described below.

C cloth: black. Off-white; peach; buff end papers. Triple flyleaves. Edges sprinkled brown; or, gilded. Also issued in leather? This publisher usually offered books in a variety of cloth and leather bindings. *The United States Catalog . . .* offers the book at $3.00 (presumably cloth, edges plain); $3.50 (presumably cloth, edges gilded); and in "half calf" at $4.50.

Three states noted; the order of presentation is probable:

STATE A

As above. ⟨A⟩5 is printed on recto only with a *Publisher's Announcement: In offering this book . . .* ⟨A⟩4v is blank. The lower half of p. ⟨447⟩ devoted to an advertisement of *Life amongst the Modocs.*

STATE B

Same as the preceding but the lower half of p. ⟨447⟩ is devoted to an advertisement of *Everybody's Friend.*

STATE C

⟨i⟩-xvi, 17-445; advertisement, pp. ⟨446-452⟩.

⟨A⟩-Z⁸, A-⁸, B-¹⁰.

The *Publisher's Announcement* appears on ⟨A⟩4v. Lower half of p. ⟨447⟩ contains an advertisement for *Everybody's Friend.*

A rebound copy at BPL (*State A? State B?*) inscribed by early owner Oct. 22, 1874. Listed (cloth only) PW Nov. 14, 1874. A set of 1875 sheets (in HEH) has been seen with binder's title: *Paquita the Indian Heroine.* See *My Own Story,* 1890, in *Section One.* Also see *Paquita . . . ,* 1881, in *Section Two.*

AAS (*State B*) H (*State A*) HEH (*State B*) NYPL (*State C*) Y (*State B*)

13758. FIRST FAM'LIES IN THE SIERRAS . . .

LONDON: GEORGE ROUTLEDGE AND SONS, THE BROADWAY, LUDGATE. 1875.

For first American edition see *First Fam'lies of the Sierras* under year 1876. Also see *The Danites in the Sierras,* 1881, 1889.

⟨i-viii⟩, ⟨1⟩-151. 6⅜" × 4".

⟨A⟩⁴, B-I, K⁸, L⁴.

Yellow paper boards, printed in colors. White end papers imprinted with advertisements.

Listed by Ath May 22, 1875. Noticed by Ath June 26, 1875. Listed by PC and Bkr June, 1875.

H LC UV Y

13759. THE SHIP IN THE DESERT . . .

LONDON: CHAPMAN AND HALL, 193, PICCADILLY. 1875.

For first American edition see next entry.

⟨i-iv⟩, ⟨i⟩-viii, ⟨1⟩-140. 6¾" × 4³⁄₁₆".

A⁶, B-I⁸, K⁶.

S cloth: green. Covers bevelled. Cream-coated end papers.

Advertised as *this day* Ath June 5, 1875. Listed Ath June 12, 1875. A copy in Y contains an inserted presentation slip dated June 23, 1875. Listed PC July 1, 1875. Described as *new* PC July 1, 1875. Reviewed Ath July 10, 1875.

UV Y

13760. THE SHIP IN THE DESERT . . .

BOSTON: ROBERTS BROTHERS. 1875.

For prior publication see preceding entry.

⟨i⟩-⟨xii⟩, ⟨13⟩-205; blank, p. ⟨206⟩; advertisements, paged: 1-3, 1, 3-8. Laid paper. 6⅞" full × 4⅝".

⟨1⟩-9¹². *Also signed:* ⟨A⟩-M⁸, ⟨-⟩⁴. In some copies signature mark C is not present.

S cloth: green; purple; terra-cotta. Brown-coated end papers. Laid paper flyleaves. Top edges gilt.

Listed PW Oct. 23, 1875.

AAS B BA BPL H NYPL UV Y

13761. Tom Hood's Comic Annual for 1876. Edited by Henry Sampson . . .

London: Published for the Proprietors at the Fun Office, 80 Fleet Street, E. C. ⟨1875⟩

"A Practical Poet," pp. ⟨45⟩-47. Elsewhere unlocated.

For fuller entry see No. 1103.

13762. Mae Madden, by Mary Murdoch Mason, with an Introductory Poem, by Joaquin Miller . . .

Chicago: Jansen, McClurg & Co. 1876.

"A Dream of Italy. An Allegory Introducing *Mae Madden,*" pp. ⟨3⟩-10. Elsewhere unlocated.

Announced for *immediate publication* PW Dec. 4, 1875. Listed PW Dec. 4, 1875.

AAS B BA H LC NYPL UCLA UV Y

13763. Songs of Three Centuries. Edited by John Greenleaf Whittier.

Boston: James R. Osgood and Company, Late Ticknor & Fields, and Fields, Osgood, & Co. 1876.

"Sunrise in Venice," p. 314. Collected in *Songs of Italy,* 1878.

For fuller entry see No. 11341.

13764. THE ONE FAIR WOMAN ... IN THREE VOLUMES ...

LONDON: CHAPMAN AND HALL, PICCADILLY. 1876. (ALL RIGHTS RESERVED.)

For American edition see below under year 1876.

1: ⟨i-ii⟩, ⟨i⟩-vi, ⟨1⟩-296. 7½″ scant × 5″ scant.

2: ⟨i-ii⟩, ⟨i⟩-vi, ⟨1⟩-307.

3: ⟨i⟩-vi, ⟨1⟩-309.

1: A⁴, B-I, K-T⁸, U⁴.

2: A⁴, B-I, K-U⁸, X².

3: ⟨A⟩⁴, B-I, K-U⁸, X².

S cloth: mauve. Cream-coated end papers.

Announced Ath Sept. 25; Bkr Nov. 1875. Advertised for *Monday* ⟨*i.e.*, Feb. 28⟩ Ath Feb. 26, 1876. Listed Ath March 4, 1876. Advertised as *new* Ath March 11, 1876. Reviewed Ath March 25, 1876.

Y

13765. FIRST FAM'LIES OF THE SIERRAS ...

CHICAGO: JANSEN, MCCLURG & CO. 1876.

For prior publication see First Fam'lies in the Sierras, *above, under 1875. The Chicago edition is much revised. For other revisions see* The Danites in the Sierras, *1881, 1889.*

⟨i-ii⟩, ⟨1⟩-iv, 5-258; advertisements, pp. ⟨1⟩-4. 6⅞″ full × 4⁹⁄₁₆″.

⟨1⟩-11¹². *Note:* Superfluous signature mark 2 on p. 17.

S cloth: green; maroon; purple; terra-cotta. Brown-coated end papers. Flyleaves.

Noted as *nearly ready* PW Feb. 19, 1876, with the comment that it "is issued simultaneously in London ..." Listed PW March 11, 1876.

HEH   NYPL   UV   Y

13766. THE ONE FAIR WOMAN ... THREE VOLUMES IN ONE.

NEW YORK: G. W. CARLETON & CO., PUBLISHERS. LONDON: CHAPMAN & HALL. MDCCCLXXVI.

For prior publication see above under the year 1876.

⟨i⟩-⟨x⟩, ⟨11⟩-548; advertisements, pp. ⟨1⟩-4. 7³⁄₁₆″ × 4⅞″.

⟨1⟩-7, ⟨8⟩, 9-23¹².

Noted on two weights of paper, probably representing two printings:

A: Sheets bulk 1⅜″. A copyright deposit copy thus.

B: Sheets bulk 1⅛″ to 1³⁄₁₆″.

FL-like cloth: green. Blue end papers. Flyleaves.

Two states of the binding noted; the sequence has not been firmly established:

A: The square unit in the publisher's spine imprint measures ⅜″ × ⅜″. A copyright deposit copy thus.

B: The square unit in the publisher's spine imprint measures ⁷⁄₁₆″ × ⁷⁄₁₆″.

Listed PW April 8, 1876. A second edition noted PW April 29, 1876.

AAS (*Sheets A, Binding A*)   B (*Sheets B, Binding A*) LC (*Sheets A, Binding A, being a deposit copy*) UV (*Sheets A, Binding A*)   Y (*Sheets A, Binding A; Sheets B, Binding B*)

13767. WHERE ROLLS THE OREGON.

⟨n.p., n.d., Hanover, N. H. (?), 1876⟩

Not seen. Entry on the basis of a photographic copy. Caption-title. The above at head of text. Anonymous.

Note: Not to be confused with another poem of the same title which begins: *See once these stately scenes, then roam no more ...* The printing here described begins: *In a land so far that you wonder whether | The God would know it should you drop dead ...*

22 printed slips, prepared for the author's use in reading at Dartmouth College commencement, 1876. The only known copy thus; *i.e.*, 22 printed slips. Quite probably a lesser number (8?) of galley-proofs cut to smaller size for convenience.

Later published in somewhat altered form as the first part of *The Baroness of New York,* 1877. Further altered and reprinted in *Songs of the Mexican Seas,* 1887, under the title "The Sea of Fire."

D

13768. ... MY SHIP COMES IN ... MUSIC BY H. MILLARD ...

NEW YORK ... SPEAR & DENHOFF 717 BROADWAY ... 1876 ...

Sheet music. Cover-title. At head of title: *To Mrs. Hester A. Spades ...*

Note: The only located copy bears the following statement on the front: *10th Edition.*

Not found elsewhere save in *Surf and Wave* ⟨1883⟩, *q.v.*

AAS

13769. SONG OF THE CENTENNIAL ...

⟨n.p., n.d., 1876⟩

Caption-title. The above at head of text.

⟨1-4⟩. Illustrated. 15¹⁄₁₆″ × 10⅞″.

Presumably originally a single sheet; the only located copy comprises two sheets stapled together.

Issued thus? Extracted from a periodical?

UV

13770. Poems of Places Edited by Henry W. Longfellow ... France and Savoy. Vol. II.

Boston: James R. Osgood and Company, Late Ticknor & Fields, and Fields, Osgood, & Co. 1877.

"In Père la Chaise," pp. 70-71. Collected in *Songs of Italy*, 1878.

For fuller entry see No. 12183.

13771. THE BARONESS OF NEW YORK ...

NEW YORK: G. W. CARLETON & CO., PUBLISHERS. MDCCCLXXVII. [DRAMATIC RIGHTS RESERVED.]

⟨1⟩-244. 7³⁄₁₆″ × 4¹⁵⁄₁₆″.

⟨1-10¹², 11²⟩. *Signed:* ⟨1⟩-15⁸, 16².

S cloth: green; terra-cotta. Purple end papers. Flyleaves.

Note: All examined copies save one have the publisher's circular device stamped at the center of the back cover. The exception, one of the two copyright deposit copies, does not have the device present. The other copyright deposit copy has the device present.

Listed PW Sept. 29, 1877.

B   BPL   H   LC   NYPL   UV

13772. The Danites: And Other Choice Selections from the Writings of Joaquin Miller ... Edited by A. V. D. Honeyman.

New York: The American News Company, 1878.

Basically a reprint but contains the following material here first located in book form:

The poems at pp. ⟨139⟩-146. All, with the exception of "To the American Flag," p. 146, collected in *Songs of Italy*, 1878. "To the American Flag" had prior publication in *Song of the Centennial* ⟨1876⟩.

"General Custer," pp. 156-157. Elsewhere unlocated.

"The Capitol at Washington," p. 157. Collected in *In Classic Shades*, 1890, as the first eight lines of "The New President."

"A Race for Love and Life," pp. 159-160. Extracted from "The Sioux Chief's Daughter," collected in *In Classic Shades*, 1890.

Note: Certain of the brief prose passages published herein have not been located in Miller's writings; further investigation required.

Listed PW Dec. 29, 1877.

B   H   HEH   NYPL   Y

13773. SONGS OF ITALY ...

BOSTON: ROBERTS BROTHERS. 1878.

See also next entry.

⟨1⟩-186; 6 pp. advertisements, paged: 1, 1-⟨5⟩. Laid paper. 6⅞″ × 4¹¹⁄₁₆″.

⟨1-8¹²⟩. *Signed:* ⟨1⟩-12⁸.

FL cloth: green; purple; terra-cotta. Green-coated end papers. Top edges gilt. Laid paper flyleaves.

BA copy received Oct. 8, 1878. Listed PW Oct. 12, 1878.

BA   BPL   H   UV   Y

13774. SONGS OF FAR-AWAY LANDS ...

LONDON: LONGMANS, GREEN, READER, AND DYER. 1878.

⟨i⟩-viii, ⟨1⟩-301; blank, p. ⟨302⟩; blank leaf. 7″ × 5¹⁄₁₆″.

⟨A⟩⁴, B-I, K-U⁸.

S cloth: green. Three binding variants have been noted; the following is sufficient to identify. Sequence not determined; the order of presentation is wholly arbitrary.

BINDING A

Spine imprint: LONGMANS & Cº   Gray-tan coated end papers. Double flyleaves.

BINDING B

Spine imprint: LONGMAN & CO. Gray-tan coated end papers. No flyleaves.

BINDING C

Spine imprint: LONGMANS   Cream-coated end papers. Double flyleaves.

Note: Y has a set of folded sheets, presumably a proof printing, with the author's name misspelled *Joaquim* on the title-page.

Thirteen of the poems herein had prior publication in other of Miller's books; some of these as here published underwent revision. The remaining poems also appear in *Songs of Italy*, Boston, 1878, which may have issued simultaneously with this book; see preceding entry. Louise Chandler Moulton in Ath Nov. 9, 1878, reported that *Songs of Far-Away Lands* was the same as *Songs of Italy*, Boston, 1878.

Noted for September Ath June 22, 1878. A copy in BPL (*Binding C*) inscribed by Miller Aug. 15,

1878; advance copy? Announced Ath Sept. 28, 1878; PC Oct. 2, 1878. Advertised as *now ready* Ath Oct. 12, 1878. Listed Ath Oct. 12, 1878. Reviewed Ath Oct. 19, 1878. Listed Bkr Nov. 2, 1878; PC Nov. 2, 1878.

B (*Binding A*)   BPL (*Binding C*)   LC (*Binding A; Binding B*)   UV (*Binding A*)

13775. Songs of the Sierras and Sunlands. Two Volumes in One . . . Revised Edition.

 London: Longmans, Green, Reader, and Dyer. 1878.

For other editions see under years 1871, 1873, 1892.

Basically a complete reprint. A cursory comparison with earlier texts reveals some revisions. Many of the pieces herein appear under altered titles, some being extracts from longer, previously collected, poems.

Announced PC Oct. 2, 1878. Advertised as *now ready* Ath Oct. 12, 1878. Reviewed Ath Oct. 19, 1878. Listed PC Nov. 2, 1878.

B

13776. The Society of the Army of the Potomac. Report of the Eleventh Annual Re-Union, at Burlington, Vermont, June 16, 1880.

 New York: Macgowan & Slipper, Printers, 30 Beekman Street. 1880.

Printed paper wrapper.

'"Beyond the River,"' pp. 12-14. Here present in nine stanzas. For another version, truncated, see *Representative Poems . . .*, 1886, below. Otherwise unlocated.

"Address of Mr. Joaquin Miller," pp. 58-59.

Note: Johnson, p. 367, records a broadside printing of "Beyond the River"; not located by BAL; further information wanting.

B   H   NYPL

13777. The Elocutionist's Annual Number 8 . . . Edited by Mrs. J. W. Shoemaker . . .

 Philadelphia: National School of Elocution and Oratory. 1881.

"The Sioux Chief's Daughter," pp. 82-85. For a partial printing see *The Danites*, 1878, pp. 159-160. Collected in *In Classic Shades*, 1890.

For fuller entry see No. 434.

13778. SHADOWS OF SHASTA . . .

 CHICAGO: JANSEN, MCCLURG & COMPANY. 1881.

Three printings noted:

FIRST PRINTING

⟨1⟩-184; 8 pp. advertisements; plus: 8 pp. advertisements. 6¹⁵⁄₁₆″ × 4⅝″.

⟨1⟩-12⁸; plus: ⟨13⟩⁴.

P. ⟨200⟩: "*This book places its author . . .*"

Spine imprint: JANSEN.McCLURG & CO.

SECOND (THIRD?) PRINTING

⟨1⟩-184; plus 16 pp. advertisements.

⟨1-15⁸·⁴; plus: 16-17⁴⟩. Signed: ⟨1⟩-12⁸, ⟨13⟩⁴.

P. ⟨200⟩: JUST PUBLISHED. BELLE AND THE BOYS . . .

Spine imprint: JANSEN.McCLURG & CO.

THIRD (SECOND?) PRINTING

⟨1⟩-184; plus: 8 pp. advertisements.

⟨1-16⁸·⁴⟩. Signed: ⟨1⟩-12⁸.

Spine imprint: JANSEN,McCLURG & CO.

S cloth: blue; brown; olive. Covers bevelled. Brown-coated end papers. Flyleaves. For a comment on the spine imprint see above.

Noted for *this week* PW April 9, 1881. Deposited April 12, 1881. Listed PW April 30, 1881.

BPL (1st)   LC (1st)   NYPL (2nd)   UV (1st; 2nd)   Y (3rd)

13779. The Danites in the Sierras . . .

 Chicago: Jansen, McClurg & Company. 1881.

For first edition see *First Fam'lies in the Sierras*, 1875.

"This little book was first brought out . . . under the name of *The First Fam'lies of the Sierras* . . . my maturer judgment, advised by the better sense of my American publishers, disapproves of some of its realistic features and I have here swept them away . . ."———From the author's preface, dated at end *March 1st, 1881.*

A cursory examination indicates that this 1881 edition was printed from the altered plates of *First Fam'lies of the Sierras*, Chicago, 1876, the principal variations being the addition of a "Preface" to this revised edition; revision of the material at pp. 154-163 of *First Fam'lies of the Sierras*.

Note: Johnson (1942), p. 365, reports a Chicago, 1878, printing; not located by BAL and Johnson presumed to be in error. Very likely this title was confused with *The Danites: And Other Choice Selections . . .*, New York, 1878.

Also note: Miller claimed about fifty editions of *The Danites in the Sierras:* "... In this last of nearly half a hundred editions ..."———Preface, p. ix, *The Danites . . .*, Chicago, 1889. One is free to either accept or reject Miller's claim.

Deposited May 11, 1881. Listed PW June 4, 1881. For another revised edition see below under year 1889.

AAS   B   BA   H   HEH   LC   NYPL   UV   Y

13780. The Poets' Tributes to Garfield   The Collection of Poems Written for the Boston Daily Globe, and Many Selections . . . ⟨First Edition⟩

Cambridge, Mass. Published by Moses King Harvard Square 1881

"Rejoice," pp. 31-32. Collected as "Garfield," *In Classic Shades*, 1890.

For a fuller entry see No. 8955. The poem under its original title, "Rejoice," was first published in *The Boston Daily Globe*, Vol. xx, No. 89, Sept. 27, 1881, p. ⟨1⟩. For a comment on a special printing of the newspaper see entry No. 8955.

13781. One Hundred Choice Selections No. 20 . . .

Published by P. Garrett & Co., 708 Chestnut Street, Philadelphia, Pa., and 116 E. Randolph Street, Chicago, Ill. 1881.

"Tantalus: Texas," pp. 172-173. Not found in the collected works.

For fuller entry see No. 5120.

13782. MY DARLING HAVE YOU MONEY. WORDS BY JOAQUIN MILLER. MUSIC BY MARION T. FORTESCUE . . .

PUBLISHED FOR THE AUTHOR BY WM. A. POND & CO. 25 UNION SQUARE NEW-YORK. CHICAGO MUSIC CO. 152 STATE ST. CHICAGO. COPYRIGHT 1881 BY MARION T. FORTESCUE.

Title at head of p. 3. Imprint at foot of p. ⟨1⟩.

⟨1⟩-5. A trimmed example, removed from a bound volume, measures $13\frac{3}{16}''\times10\frac{5}{16}''$.

Sheet music. Pp. ⟨2⟩ and ⟨6⟩ blank. Text and music, pp. 3-5.

Plate number 0460.

Otherwise unlocated.

The only located example was seen Nov. 1946, in the New York book shop of Edward Eberstadt & Sons.

13783. . . . The Reading Club and Handy Speaker . . . Edited by George M. Baker. No. 9.

Boston: Lee and Shepard, Publishers. New York: Charles T. Dillingham. ⟨1881⟩

At head of title: . . . *No. 9* . . .

Should be dated 1881? Presumably issued in both cloth; and, in printed paper wrapper.

"The Tramp of Shiloh," pp. 40-42. Collected in *In Classic Shades*, 1890, as "After the War."

H

13784. FORTY-NINE: A CALIFORNIA DRAMA and DANITES IN THE SIERRAS: A DRAMA

Sheets of the above plays have been noted in the following forms. The sequence of *A* and *B* is tentative but BAL suspects that the order given is correct.

FORM A

FORTY-NINE: A CALIFORNIA DRAMA IN FOUR ACTS . . .

SAN FRANCISCO: THE CALIFORNIA PUBLISHING COMPANY, 408 CALIFORNIA STREET. 1882.

Note: The above is leaf ⟨-⟩.

DANITES IN THE SIERRAS: A DRAMA IN FOUR ACTS . . .

SAN FRANCISCO: THE CALIFORNIA PUBLISHING COMPANY, 408 CALIFORNIA STREET. 1882.

Note: The above is leaf 7_3.

⟨i-ii⟩, ⟨1⟩-102; blank, pp. ⟨103-104⟩; ⟨i⟩-⟨viii⟩, ⟨105⟩-203. $6\frac{1}{8}''\times4\frac{1}{2}''$.

⟨-⟩^{1}, ⟨*⟩^{2}, 1-6^8, 7^{12}, 8-12^8, 13^4. Sig. 7 is an 8vo gathering inserted in which is a 4to gathering as follows:

Leaf 3r: Title-page for *Danites in the Sierras*.

Leaf 3v: Extract from *Genesis*.

Leaf 4r: Dedication *To Marion*.

Leaf 4v: Blank

Leaves 5r,v; 6r: "Preface," dated at end *New York, Dec. 30, 1881*. This preface does not appear in other forms of the publication; the leaves are lacking in the Y copy.

Leaf 6v: Blank

No copyright notices present.

Forty-Nine dedicated *To Juanita*.

Danites dedicated *To Marion*.

Danites contains a 3-page preface.

S cloth: blue. Top edges gilt. Gray-tan end papers.

Locations: AAS   Y (lacking leaves 7_{5-6})

FORM B

'49 FORTY-NINE: A CALIFORNIA DRAMA IN FOUR ACTS . . .

SAN FRANCISCO: THE CALIFORNIA PUBLISHING COMPANY, 408 CALIFORNIA STREET. 1882. ENTERED ACCORDING TO ACT OF CONGRESS, IN

THE YEAR 1882, BY C. H. MILLER, IN THE OFFICE OF THE LIBRARIAN OF CONGRESS AT WASHINGTON. ALL RIGHTS RESERVED.

Note: The above is leaf ⟨-⟩.

THE DANITES IN THE SIERRAS: A DRAMA IN FOUR ACTS . . .

SAN FRANCISCO: THE CALIFORNIA PUBLISHING COMPANY, 408 CALIFORNIA STREET. 1882. ENTERED ACCORDING TO ACT OF CONGRESS, IN THE YEAR 1882, BY C. H. MILLER, IN THE OFFICE OF THE LIBRARIAN OF CONGRESS AT WASHINGTON. ALL RIGHTS RESERVED.

Note: The above is leaf 7_3.

⟨i-ii⟩, ⟨1⟩-102; blank, pp. ⟨103-104⟩; ⟨i-ii⟩, ⟨105⟩-203. $6\frac{1}{8}'' \times 4\frac{1}{2}''$.

⟨-⟩^{1}, ⟨*⟩^{2}, 1-6^8, 7^9, 8-12^8, 13^4. Leaf 7_3 (the title-leaf for *The Danites in the Sierras*) is an inserted singleton.

Note presence of copyright notices on the title-pages.

Forty-Nine dedicated *To Juanita.*

The dedication leaf for *The Danites in the Sierras* not present.

Does not contain the 3-page preface to *The Danites in the Sierras.*

S cloth: Blue. Top edges gilt. Gray-tan end papers.

Copies thus were deposited for copyright June 8, 1882.

Locations: B (being a deposit copy) LC (being a deposit copy)

FORM C

'49: FORTY-NINE: AN IDYL DRAMA OF THE SIERRAS, IN FOUR ACTS . . . (SECOND EDITION.)

SAN FRANCISCO: THE CALIFORNIA PUBLISHING COMPANY, 408 CALIFORNIA STREET. 1882.

Note: The above is leaf ⟨-⟩$_1$.

THE DANITES IN THE SIERRAS: AN IDYL DRAMA, IN FOUR ACTS. THE ORIGINAL LONDON VERSION . . . (SECOND EDITION.)

SAN FRANCISCO: THE CALIFORNIA PUBLISHING COMPANY, 408 CALIFORNIA STREET. 1882.

Note: The above is leaf 7_3.

⟨i-ii⟩, ⟨1⟩-102; blank, pp. ⟨103-104⟩; ⟨i-iv⟩, ⟨105⟩-203. $6\frac{13}{16}'' \times 4\frac{5}{8}''$ scant.

⟨-⟩^{2}, ⟨*⟩^{1}, 1-6^8, 7^{10}, 8-12^8, 13^4. Leaves 7_{3-4} are inserted conjugates and comprise:

Leaf 7_{3r}: Title-page.

Leaf 7_{3v}: Copyright notice.

Leaf 7_{4r}: A rhymed dedication to "my fellow pioneers of the Sierras."

Note presence of the copyright notice on the verso of each title-leaf.

Forty-Nine dedicated to Ina D. Coolbrith.

Danites dedicated to "my fellow pioneers of the Sierras."

Danites does not contain the 3-page preface which is found only in *Form A.*

Printed tan paper wrapper. Front: "'49": "Danites": Idyl Dramas . . .

Locations: BPL Y

FORMS D and E

The plays, as they occur in *Form C,* issued separately, each in a printed paper wrapper. The separate (NYPL, Y) of *The Danites* is printed on the front: *The Danites in the Sierras: An Idyl Drama of the Sierras* . . . The separate of *'49* (LC) is printed on the front: *"'49" Forty-Nine: An Idyl Drama of the Sierras* . . .

Note: Ath Feb. 5, 1881, reports a "revival" of *The Danites;* no further information found. Possibly a reference to a public reading for purposes of British copyright.

Also note: According to Marberry, p. 158, *The Danites* was written in collaboration with "P. A. Fitzgerald, a Philadelphia playwright."

13785. Katy's Birthday by Sara ⟨*sic*⟩ O. Jewett. With Other Stories by Famous Authors

Boston D. Lothrop and Company 32 Franklin Street ⟨1883⟩

Contains "Mr. Tennyson's Fairies."

Deposited Nov. 24, 1883. For comment see entry No. 3792.

13786. THE SILENT MAN: A COMEDY-DRAMA, IN FOUR ACTS . . .

ENTERED ACCORDING TO ACT OF CONGRESS, IN THE YEAR 1883, BY JOAQUIN MILLER, IN THE OFFICE OF THE LIBRARIAN OF CONGRESS AT WASHINGTON, D. C.

⟨1⟩-61, blank leaf. $9''$ scant $\times 5\frac{11}{16}''$.

⟨1-4^8⟩.

Printed pale peach paper wrapper.

Presumably printed for copyright purposes only. Deposited July 12, 1883. The H copy inscribed by Miller ". . . Not published . . . 20 July 83"

H LC

13787. WILLIAM BROWN OF OREGON . . .

1883. THE ALDEN PRINTING COMPANY, 74
FRANKFORT STREET. CLEVELAND, OHIO.

⟨1⟩-20. *Note:* The pagination is irregular. 4⅞″ ×
6³⁄₁₆″. Printed on mixed laid papers of various
colors: gray, pink, salmon, tan, aqua.

⟨-¹⁰⟩.

Printed flexible green cardboard wrapper tied
with red cord.

Issued primarily as an advertisement, with text
and advertisements run together.

Collected in *In Classic Shades*, 1890.

The LC copy inscribed Aug. 13, 1883.

LC   Y

13788. "TALLY-HO!" A MUSICAL DRAMA,
IN THREE ACTS . . .

ENTERED, ACCORDING TO ACT OF CONGRESS,
SEPTEMBER, 1883, BY "JOAQUIN" C. H. MILLER,
IN THE OFFICE OF THE LIBRARIAN OF CONGRESS,
AT WASHINGTON, D. C.

⟨1⟩-37, blank leaf. 9¹⁄₁₆″ full × 5¾″ scant.

⟨1-2⁸, 3⁴⟩.

Printed blue paper wrapper.

Presumably printed for coyright purposes only.
Deposited Sept. 20, 1883.

According to the Library of Congress music for
this drama was composed by John Philip Sousa.

LC   Y

13789. California-Album. Eine Errinnerung vom
Strande des Stillen Meeres. Für Deutsch-
Amerikaner. Herausgegeben von C. I. Brick . . .

San Francisco: Druck von Rosenthal & Roesch.
1883.

"The Jewess," pp. 100-101.

"Peter Cooper," p. 105.

Both the preceding collected in *Memorie and Rime*,
1884.

"Princess Lillie," pp. 107-108. Otherwise "Unica-
Aeterna," *Songs of Italy*, 1878.

UV

13790. 1884 The Independent Almanac

⟨New York: The Independent, 1883⟩

Printed paper wrapper. Cover-title.

"The Brown Earth," p. 29. Otherwise unlocated
save in *The Independent*, May 10, 1883.

H

13791. Lost in Pompeii by H. H. Clark, U.S.N.
with Other Stories of Adventure

Boston D. Lothrop and Company 32 Franklin
Street ⟨1883⟩

Unpaged.

Contains "Robin Hood's Ghost."

On binding: *Peace Island Series*

UV

13792. SONGS OF E. CATENHUSEN . . .
OVER THE MOUNTAINS . . .

NEW-YORK. WM. A. POND & CO. 25 UNION SQ. . . . .
⟨1883⟩

Sheet music. Cover-title. Plate number: 10912.

Text otherwise unlocated. *Over the mountains and
down by the sea, | A dear old mother is waiting for me . . .*

B

13793. Surf and Wave: The Sea As Sung by the
Poets. Edited by Anna L. Ward . . .

New York: Thomas Y. Crowell & Co. 13 Astor
Place. ⟨1883⟩

"My Ship Comes in," p. 91. Otherwise unlocated
save in sheet music form; see above under 1876.

"Unloved and Alone," pp. 14-15; otherwise "To
Carrie A.S.," *Songs of Italy*, 1878.

EM

13794. Parker's Choice Selections No. 1 . . .
Readings & Recitations . . . Compiled . . . by
C. C. Parker . . .

Sedalia, Mo.: J. West Goodwin, Steam Printer,
Engraver, and Book-Binder. 1884.

Printed paper wrapper.

Reprint save for "The Girl of Long Ago," p. 206.
Collected in *Memorie and Rime*, 1884; see next
entry.

Deposited Feb. 4, 1884.

LC

13795. MEMORIE AND RIME . . .

NEW YORK FUNK & WAGNALLS, PUBLISHERS 10
AND 12 DEY STREET 1884

PAPER

19-20; ⟨i⟩-⟨viii⟩, ⟨9⟩-237; advertisements (paged
21), p. ⟨238⟩. Laid paper. 7⁵⁄₁₆″ × 4⅞″.

⟨1-7¹⁶, 8⁸⟩.

Printed tan paper wrapper, as No. 108 of the
Standard Library; issued under date Feb. 11, 1884.

CLOTH

⟨i⟩-⟨viii⟩, ⟨9⟩-237; blank, p. ⟨238⟩; advertisements, pp. ⟨239-240⟩. Wove paper. $7\frac{7}{16}'' \times 4\frac{15}{16}''$.

⟨1-15⁸⟩.

S cloth: gray. V cloth: ecru. Covers bevelled. Yellow end papers. Flyleaves.

Issued as the *Standard Library*, No. 3.

Note: Also occurs in green V cloth, covers not bevelled; and, in three-quarters brown marbled paper sides, tan V cloth shelf back and corners. A principal variation on these later bindings is the style in which the publisher's name occurs: *Funk & Wagnalls Company*. In the known early binding the name is given as: *Funk & Wagnalls*. Later bindings in: LC, UCLA, Y.

Deposited (paper) Feb. 11, 1884. BA copy (cloth) received Feb. 19, 1884. Listed PW (both formats) March 1, 1884.

AAS (paper) B (paper) BA (cloth) H (cloth) LC (paper) NYPL (paper) UV (cloth) Y (paper)

13796. No. 3. Standard Recitations by Best Authors . . . Compiled . . . by Frances P. Sullivan . . . March, 1884 . . .

M. J. Ivers & Co., Publishers, 86 Nassau Street, N. Y. . . . ⟨1884⟩

Printed paper wrapper.

"The Battle Flag at Shenandoah," pp. 46-47. Collected in *In Classic Shades*, 1890.

A later printing has the publisher's revised street address: *379 Pearl Street, New York*.

Deposited April 24, 1884.

LC NYPL

13797. THE TREE BY THE WELL

OREGON UNIVERSITY: CLASS 1884.

Anonymous.

Caption-title. Otherwise unlocated.

Single leaf. Printed on recto only. 10″ full × $3\frac{5}{8}''$.

LC

13798. The Elocutionist's Annual Number 12 . . . Compiled by Mrs. J. W. Shoemaker.

Publication Department, National School of Elocution and Oratory. Philadelphia. 1884.

Reprint save for "Luther," p. 140; otherwise unlocated.

For fuller entry see No. 10454.

13799. '49 THE GOLD-SEEKER OF THE SIERRAS . . .

FUNK & WAGNALLS NEW YORK: 1884. 10 AND 12 DEY STREET. LONDON: 44 FLEET STREET. ALL RIGHTS RESERVED.

Note: The imprint as here presented has been regularized.

PAPER

114-115; ⟨i⟩-viii, ⟨9⟩-148; advertisements, pp. 116-125. Laid paper. $7\frac{3}{8}''$ scant × $4\frac{15}{16}''$.

⟨1-3¹⁶, 4-7⁸⟩.

Printed buff paper wrapper, as No. 123 of the *Standard Library;* issued under date Sept. 8, 1884.

CLOTH

⟨i-ii⟩, ⟨i⟩-viii, ⟨9⟩-148; 10 pp. advertisements. Laid paper. $7\frac{3}{8}'' \times 4\frac{13}{16}''$.

⟨1-10⁸⟩.

S cloth: red. Covers bevelled. Yellow end papers. Laid paper flyleaves. Issued as *Standard Library*, No. 18.

Note: Also occurs in green V cloth, covers not bevelled; and, marbled paper boards sides, tan V cloth shelf back and corners, covers not bevelled. A principal variation of these later bindings is the style in which the publisher's name occurs: *Funk & Wagnalls Company*. In the known early bindings the name is given as *Funk & Wagnalls*. Later bindings seen in: LC, Y.

Deposited (paper) Sept. 8, 1884. BA copy (cloth) received Sept. 30, 1884. Both formats listed PW Oct. 4, 1884. The London issue (J. Bordon Hunt) listed Ath March 14, 1885.

AAS (cloth; paper) BA (cloth) H (paper) LC (cloth; paper) NYPL (paper) Y (cloth; paper)

13800. White Elephant Chimes. Selections from over One Thousand Poems Written on Barnum, Bailey & Hutchinson's Royal Sacred White Elephant for Their Offered Five Hundred Dollar Prize.

Buffalo, N. Y. Published by the Courier Company. 1884.

Printed paper wrapper. Cover-title.

Letter, Miller to P. T. Barnum, June 6, 1883, p. 5.

"The Sacred White Elephant---Toung Taloung," pp. 6-7. Elsewhere unlocated.

AAS

13801. We Young Folks Original Stories for Boys and Girls by Harriet Beecher Stowe . . . and Others . . .

Boston D. Lothrop and Company Franklin and Hawley Streets. ⟨1886; *i.e.,* 1885⟩

Pictorial boards. Unpaged.

Reprint save for "The Little Gold Miners of the Sierras." See *The Little Gold Miners of the Sierras ...* ⟨1886⟩, below.

Deposited Aug. 15, 1885.

LC

13802. No. 9. Standard Recitations by Best Authors ... Compiled ... by Frances P. Sullivan ... Sept. 1885 ...

M. J. Ivers & Co., Publishers, 86 Nassau Street, N. Y. ... ⟨1885⟩

Printed paper wrapper.

"The Fortunate Isles," pp. 15-16. Collected in *In Classic Shades*, 1890.

A later printing was issued with the publisher's revised address: *379 Pearl Street, New York.*

Deposited for copyright Sept. 22, 1885.

LC   NYPL

13803. CHRISTMAS WISHES ...

⟨Boston: L. Prang & Co., n.d., *ca.* 1885⟩

Caption-title. The above at head of text.

Single card, lithographed in colors. $9\frac{1}{16}'' \times 7''$. A two-dimensional "book"; that is, a depiction. The face of the card lettered on the "spine": *A Christmas Carol. Vol. I. L. Prang & Co. Boston.* "Front cover" lettered: *Merrie Christmas* On reverse of card: The "verso leaf" imprinted with a floral decoration; the "recto leaf" with Miller's poem beginning: *This book should hold a hundred leaves / And every leaf a song as dear ...*

Otherwise unlocated.

HM

13804. PEACE ON EARTH ...

⟨n.p., n.d., probably Boston: L. Prang & Co., *ca.* 1885⟩

Caption-title. The above at head of text.

Single leaf of flexible white card stock. Printed on recto only, on a light tan background, in darker tan, silver and green-gray. All lettering in green-gray; decorations in silver and tan: Wings, stars, crescent moon. $9\frac{1}{2}''$ full $\times 7\frac{7}{16}''$.

We bring the Peace, the Saviour Saith: / The white unfolded wings of Faith ...

Otherwise unlocated.

HM

We Young Folks Original Stories for Boys and Girls by Harriet Beecher Stowe ... and Others ...

Boston ... ⟨1886⟩

See above under 1885.

13805. Bugle-Echoes a Collection of Poems of the Civil War ... Edited by Francis F. Browne

New York White, Stokes, & Allen MDCCCLXXXVI

"The Last Regiment," pp. 261-263. Otherwise "The Lost Regiment," *In Classic Shades*, 1890.

Cloth; half calf; and, tree calf, advertised for *March or April* PW March 13, 1886. Listed PW May 1, 1886.

H

13806. No. 11. Standard Recitations by Best Authors ... Compiled ... by Frances P. Sullivan ... March, 1886 ...

M. J. Ivers & Co., Publishers, 86 Nassau Street, N. Y. ... ⟨1886⟩

Printed paper wrapper.

"Ballad of a Brave Cattle-Man," pp. 29-30; otherwise a version of "That Faithful Wife of Idaho," *In Classic Shades*, 1890.

A later printing was issued with the publisher's revised address: *379 Pearl Street, New York.*

Deposited March 27, 1886.

LC   NYPL

13807. Representative Poems of Living Poets American and English Selected by the Poets Themselves with an Introduction by George Parsons Lathrop

Cassell & Company, Limited   739 & 741 Broadway, New York 1886

Reprint save for:

"Sophie Perowskaja," pp. 479-481. Collected in *In Classic Shades*, 1890, as "To the Czar"; in *Joaquin Miller's Poems*, Vol. 1, 1909, as "The Dead Czar."

"To the Army of the Potomac," pp. 476-478. A revised, truncated, version of "Beyond the River," *The Society of the Army of the Potomac. Report ...*, 1880.

For fuller comment see entry No. 436.

13808. THE DESTRUCTION OF GOTHAM ...

FUNK & WAGNALLS. NEW YORK: 10 AND 12 DEY STREET. LONDON: 44 FLEET STREET. 1886.

Note: The imprint as here presented has been regularized.

⟨i⟩-iv, ⟨5⟩-214; 10 pp. advertisements. Laid paper. $7\frac{7}{16}'' \times 4\frac{15}{16}''$ full.

⟨1-14⁸⟩.

It is possible that the book was issued (simultaneously?) in two types of hard binding; the sequence presented is purely arbitrary.

HARD BINDING A

V cloth: gray-blue. Publisher's monogram at foot of spine. White end papers printed in olive with a floral pattern. Laid paper flyleaves.

HARD BINDING B

Marbled boards sides, tan S cloth shelf back and corners. At foot of spine: FUNK & WAGNALLS Manila end papers. Laid paper flyleaves.

PAPER

Also issued in printed paper wrapper as No. 139 of the *Standard Library;* wrapper dated May 28, 1886. A heavily restored copy, uncollatable, is in BPL.

Also noted in a later binding: V cloth, green; spine imprint: FUNK & WAGNALLS COMPANY. Location: Y.

Deposited (*Hard Binding A*) May 29, 1886. Listed, cloth only, PW June 12, 1886. The BA copy (*Hard Binding B*) received July 14, 1886.

B (*Hard Binding A*) BA (*Hard Binding B*) H (*Hard Binding B*) LC (*Hard Binding A*, being a deposit copy) NYPL (*Hard Binding A; Hard Binding B*) UV (*Hard Binding B*) Y (*Hard Binding A*)

13809. The Little Gold Miners of the Sierras by Joaquin Miller and Other Stories . . .

Boston D. Lothrop & Company Franklin and Hawley Streets ⟨1886⟩

"The Little Gold Miners of the Sierras," pp. 7-22. For prior publication see *We Young Folks . . .* ⟨1886; *i.e.,* 1885⟩, above.

Deposited Oct. 7, 1886.

AAS B NYPL Y

13810. The Elocutionist's Annual Number 14 . . . Compiled by Mrs. J. W. Shoemaker.

Publication Department, The National School of Elocution and Oratory. Philadelphia: 1886.

Cloth; and, printed paper wrapper.

"The Soldiers' Home, Washington," pp. 102-105. Collected in *In Classic Shades,* 1890.

Deposited Oct. 26, 1886.

LC

13811. Beecher Memorial Contemporaneous Tributes to the Memory of Henry Ward Beecher Compiled and Edited by Edward W. Bok

Privately Printed Brooklyn, New York 1887

A one-paragraph tribute, p. 64.

For fuller comment see No. 2148.

13812. SONGS OF THE MEXICAN SEAS . . .

BOSTON ROBERTS BROTHERS 1887

Three issues postulated. The following sequence is presumed correct.

FIRST ISSUE

Not seen. Postulated.

Pp. ⟨1⟩-132. Author's note in the front matter occurs on a page other than p. ⟨7⟩. The dedication leaf not conjugate with pp. 11-12 of text.

SECOND ISSUE

Sheets of the above corrected at the bindery.

⟨3⟩-⟨133⟩. Laid paper. $6^{13}/_{16}''$ × $4^{5}/_{8}''$. Author's note, p. ⟨133⟩.

⟨1^7 (see note below); 2-$10^{4.8}$, 11^6, 12^1⟩. *Signed:* ⟨1⟩^{7}, 2-8^8, 9^3. *Note:* Sig. ⟨1⟩ originally in 8; a leaf (author's note) excised and bound in at the back as Sig. ⟨12⟩. Sig. ⟨1⟩ is present as follows:

Leaves 1 & 7 (fly-title-leaf and pp. 15-16) conjugate.

Leaves 2 & 6 (title-leaf and pp. 13-14) conjugate.

Leaves 3 & 4 (dedication leaf and pp. ⟨9⟩-10) conjugate.

Leaf 5 (pp. 11-12) is a singleton.

THIRD ISSUE

Presumably corrected by reprinting Sig. ⟨1⟩.

⟨1⟩-132. Laid paper. $6^{13}/_{16}''$ full × $4^{5}/_{8}''$.

⟨1-$10^{8.4}$, 11^6⟩.

Author's *Note* on p. ⟨7⟩.

V cloth: brown; mustard; turquoise. Laid end papers. Laid paper flyleaves. Top edges gilt.

Deposited Sept. 12, 1887. Advertised for Oct. 8 PW Oct. 1, 1887. Listed PW Oct. 15, 1887.

LC (2nd; 3rd) UV (2nd; 3rd)

13813. Belford's Annual. 1888-9. Edited by Thomas W. Handford . . .

Chicago, New York and San Francisco. Belford Clarke & Co. ⟨1888⟩

Reprint save for the following pieces which BAL has been unable to locate elsewhere:

"The Legend of the Loom and the Hammer," pp. 146-148.

"Twilight in Nazareth," p. 78.

For fuller entry see No. 5735.

13814. No. 21. Standard Comic Recitations by Best Authors . . . Compiled . . . by Frances P. Sullivan . . . September, 1888 . . .

M. J. Ivers & Co., Publishers, 86 Nassau Street, N. Y. . . . ⟨1888⟩

Printed paper wrapper.

"That Gentleman from Boston Town. [An Idyl of Oregon]," pp. 13-14. Collected in *In Classic Shades*, 1890.

Reprinted and reissued with the publisher's later address: *379 Pearl Street, New York.*

Deposited Oct. 10, 1888.

LC

13815. Arbor Day . . . Edited and Compiled by Robert W. Furnas.

Lincoln, Nebr.: State Journal Company, Printers. 1888.

Imitation leather.

On pp. 181-182, a poem read by Miller at the first festival of tree-planting, celebrated early in 1887, at Yerba Buena, California. Collected in *Complete Poetical Works*, 1897, as "Arbor Day."

BA

13816. Picturesque California and the Region West of the Rocky Mountains, from Alaska to Mexico. Edited by John Muir . . .

The J. Dewing Company, Publishers. San Francisco and New York. MDCCCLXXXVIII.

Issued in various formats. For fuller entry see in *John Muir.*

"Game Regions of the Upper Sacramento," pp. 111-120.

"Early California Mining and the Argonauts," pp. ⟨233⟩-240.

"The San Joaquin Valley," pp. ⟨257⟩-264.

"The New City by the Great Sea (San Francisco)," pp. ⟨353⟩-368.

"Yellowstone Park," pp. ⟨421⟩-432.

13817. The Elocutionist's Annual Number 17 . . . Compiled by Mrs. J. W. Shoemaker

Philadelphia The Penn Publishing Company 1889

"Army of the Potomac," pp. 71-73. Reprint; otherwise an extract from "Beyond the River," *The Society of the Army of the Potomac. Report . . .*, 1880.

"The Bravest Battle That Ever Was Fought," pp. 104-105. Collected in *Complete Poetical Works*, 1897.

Also noted as a 20th century postcard, printed together with Ella Wheeler Wilcox's poem, "The Coming Man."

For fuller entry see No. 1270.

13818. The Danites in the Sierras . . .

Chicago: Belford-Clarke Co., Publishers. 1889.

Printed paper wrapper.

Cover-title: *The Danites of the Sierras.*

Issued as No. 2, Vol. 6, of *The Household Library*, under date Dec. 9, 1889.

Revised. For earlier editions see *First Fam'lies in the Sierras*, 1875; *First Fam'lies of the Sierras*, 1876; *The Danites in the Sierras*, 1881.

Contains a preface, pp. ⟨vii⟩-x, not present in the edition of 1881.

HEH LC

13819. . . . Some Famous Pseudonyms. Well-Known Authors Tell the Stories of Their Nom de Plumes . . . ⟨Edited by Edward W. Bok⟩

. . . Copyrighted . . . 1889, by the Bok Syndicate Press of New York . . .

Caption-title. The above at head of column ⟨1⟩. At head of sheet: *This Article Is Furnished by the Bok Syndicate Press* . . .

Single cut sheet. $18\frac{3}{8}'' \times 14\frac{11}{16}''$. Printed on recto only with a series of autobiographical and biographical statements. Printed in five columns.

Contains an autobiographical statement by Miller.

H

13820. My Own Story . . .

Chicago: Belford-Clarke Co., Publishers. 1890.

Printed paper wrapper; and, cloth. Wrapper imprinted: *The Household Library, No. 4, Vol. 7, April 23, 1890.*

A revised edition of *Unwritten History*, 1874.

Copies in cloth deposited May 12, 1890. A copy (now rebound) received by BPL May 14, 1890.

AAS LC NYPL UV

13821. IN CLASSIC SHADES AND OTHER POEMS . . .

CHICAGO: BELFORD-CLARKE CO. 1890.

⟨i-iv⟩, ⟨1⟩-154, blank leaf. $7\frac{1}{4}'' \times 4\frac{7}{8}''$.

⟨1-20⁴⟩.

S cloth: blue; brown; green; terra-cotta. White end papers printed in gray with a pattern of small ornaments.

Deposited May 16, 1890.

B H NYPL UV

13822. Werner's Reading and Recitations. No. 2. Compiled . . . by Elsie M. Wilbor.

New York: Edgar S. Werner, 28 West 23d Street. 1890.

Printed paper wrapper. Front wrapper dated *Sept. 1890.*

"Joaquin Miller's Bear Story," pp. 30-32. Elsewhere unlocated.

Reprinted and reissued with the imprint: *Edgar S. Werner & Company.*

H

13823. ⟨At head of first column:⟩ HOW TO HANDLE A HORSE. JOAQUIN MILLER ON HOW TO RIDE AND MANAGE THE HORSE . . .

(COPYRIGHT, 1890, BY THE BOK SYNDICATE PRESS, NEW YORK.) . . .

Single sheet. Printed on recto only. 16⅜″ × 9⅞″. Printed in three columns.

At head of sheet: *Famous Men and Women Series 1890-91. This Article Is Furnished by The Bok Syndicate Press, No. 23 Park Row, New York . . .*

HEH

13824. Eleven Possible Cases . . .

New York Cassell Publishing Company 104 & 106 Fourth Avenue ⟨1891⟩

"A Lion and a Lioness," pp. 58-82.

For comment see entry No. 5657.

13825. Shoemaker's Best Selections for Readings and Recitations Number 19 Compiled by Mrs. Anna Randall-Diehl

Philadelphia The Penn Publishing Company 1891

Reprint with the possible exception of "Twilight at Nazareth," pp. 194-197; elsewhere unlocated.

For fuller entry see No. 5562.

13826. Songs of the Sierras and Sunlands (Two Volumes in One.) . . .

Chicago: Morrill, Higgins & Co. 1892.

Reprint save for a few notes. For other editions see under 1871, 1873, 1878.

"This is made up of revised and shortened poems from *Songs of the Sierras*, etc."---Miller's annotation in the BPL copy.

Deposited July 14, 1892.

AAS BPL LC NYPL UV Y

13827. No. 36. Standard Recitations by Best Authors . . . Compiled . . . by Frances P. Sullivan . . . June 1892 . . .

M. J. Ivers & Co., Publishers, 379 Pearl Street, N. Y. . . . ⟨1892⟩

Reprint save for "Columbus," p. 22. Collected in *Songs of the Soul,* 1896.

For fuller entry see No. 5748.

13828. Werner's Readings and Recitations No. 7. Compiled and Arranged by Elsie M. Wilbor

New York Edgar S. Werner & Co. Copyright, 1892 . . .

Probably issued in printed paper wrapper.

"How We Hung Red Shed," pp. 40-46. Elsewhere unlocated.

NYPL

13829. The Story of the Files A Review of Californian Writers and Literature by Ella Sterling Cummins.

Issued under the Auspices of the World's Fair Commission of California, Columbian Exposition, 1893 . . . ⟨San Francisco⟩

Part of a sketch on Robert Browning, pp. 137-138.

"The Passing of Tennyson," pp. 139-140. Collected in *Songs of the Soul,* 1896.

Paragraph on Madge Morris Wagner, p. 283.

For fuller entry see No. 1113.

13830. THE BUILDING OF THE CITY BEAUTIFUL . . .

CAMBRIDGE & CHICAGO PUBLISHED BY STONE & KIMBALL IN THE YEAR MDCCCXCIII

Title-page in black and orange.

SMALL PAPER

⟨i-iv⟩, ⟨i⟩-iv, ⟨1⟩-196; colophon, p. ⟨197⟩; blank, p. ⟨198⟩; blank leaf. Laid paper. 6½″ scant × 4¼″.

⟨-⟩⁴, 1-12⁸, 13⁴.

V cloth: slate. Covers bevelled. White laid end papers. Top edges gilt. Flyleaf of book stock at front.

". . . Limited to five hundred copies."---⟨-⟩1r.

LARGE PAPER

Leaf: 7⅞″ full × 5⅞″. Wove paper.

Pagination and collation otherwise as above.

Gray paper boards, printed paper label on spine. Flyleaf at front.

"This is Number ⟨space⟩ Of the Large Paper Edition. Fifty Copies Only Were Printed"––– ⟨-⟩1r.

Noted as *in press* PW Oct. 28, 1893. Listed PW Dec. 2, 1893. The London (Lane) issue listed Ath Oct. 6, 1894; advertised as *ready* PC Oct. 13, 1894. See under 1905 for a revised edition.

B (large) BPL (small) H (small) UV (small) Y (small; large)

13831. In Re Walt Whitman: Edited by ... Horace L. Traubel, Richard Maurice Bucke, Thomas B. Harned ...

Published by the Editors Through David McKay 23 South Ninth Street Philadelphia 1893

Five-line note, p. 366.

For a fuller entry see No. 2155.

13832. AFTER THE SNOW AND THE SHROUD ...

OAKLAND, CAL. ⟨n.d., *ca.* 1893⟩

Printed as proof only?

Single leaf. Printed on recto only. 5″ scant × 5″ scant.

Here reprinted? Reprinted from (?) *The Building of the City Beautiful*, 1893, where the poem appears as the introduction to Chapter XXIII.

LC

13833. Selections from the Youth's Companion for Supplementary Reading. Number 3. The American Tropics ...

Copyright, 1894. Perry Mason & Company, Boston, Mass.

Printed paper wrapper.

"In the Grand Plaza of Mexico," pp. 38-45.

Deposited Aug. 20, 1894. Reprinted as *The American Tropics. The Companion Library. Number Three* ..., copyright, 1894, Perry Mason Company, Boston, Mass.

LC

13834. TO THE CALIFORNIA PIONEERS ...

HIGHTS, OKLAND ⟨*sic*⟩, CAL., SEPT. '94.

Single cut sheet. Caption-title; imprint at foot of sheet. 12″ × 6″. Printed on recto only.

The poem also appears in: ⟨*Celebration of the*⟩ *Forty-Fourth Anniversary of the Society of California Pioneers September 10, 1894* ... ⟨San Francisco⟩ 1894. Copies in HEH, UV. Collected in *Complete Poetical Works*, 1897.

LC

13835. An Illustrated History of the State of Montana, Containing a History of the State of Montana from the Earliest Period of its Discovery to the Present Time, together with Glimpses of its Auspicious Future ... by Joaquin Miller ...

Chicago: The Lewis Publishing Co. 1894.

2 Vols.

A subscription book and as such issued in a variety of formats.

"Introduction," Vol. 1, pp. ⟨iii-iv⟩.

Peterson, 1937, assumes that Miller wrote most of the book and quotes from it to illustrate Miller's life in Montana, pp. 43, 44, 45. P. 172, last paragraph, gives the *History* as an example of Miller's colloquial prose style. P. 101: "In 1894 he was commissioned to write *The History of the State of Montana* ... The textual narrative is by Joaquin Miller, and the biographical notices of Montana's leading citizens were in some cases written, in other cases edited, by him ... The subject matter is in the poet's best pictorial style ..."

Marberry, 1953, p. 251: "... Some of the text was written by Joaquin, but what the publishers wanted primarily was his 'name' ..."

BPL LC NYPL Y

13836. SONGS BY CHARLES DENNÉE ... GOODNIGHT ...

BOSTON; ARTHUR P. SCHMIDT, ⟨*sic*⟩ ⟨1894⟩

Sheet music. Cover-title. Plate number: *A.P.S. 3326-4* (high voice).

Otherwise unlocated.

B

13837. THE BATTLE OF CASTLE CRAGS ...

⟨San Francisco: Published by the Traveler, No. 602 Market Street, n.d., 1894?⟩

Cover-title.

⟨1-20⟩. 5″ × 6½″. Illustrated.

⟨-10⟩.

Printed self-wrapper.

Issued as an advertisement for the Tavern of Castle Crag, "near the junction of Soda Creek and the Sacramento River," California.

LC UCLA Y

13838. SONGS OF THE SOUL...

SAN FRANCISCO THE WHITAKER & RAY COMPANY
(INCORPORATED) 1896

TRADE FORMAT

⟨i-iv⟩, ⟨1⟩-162; pp. ⟨163-164⟩ inserted; 2 blank
leaves; leaf excised or pasted under the end paper.
P. ⟨163⟩ is a note from, and a picture of, Miller.
In some copies pp. ⟨i-ii⟩ are excised. $7\frac{9}{16}''$ ×
$4\frac{15}{16}''$. Wove paper.

⟨1⁴, 2², 3-11⁸, 12⁹⟩. In some copies leaf ⟨1⟩₁ is
excised. Leaf ⟨12⟩₉ excised or pasted under the
end paper; leaf ⟨12⟩₆ inserted.

S cloth: gray; white. Usually without flyleaves; a
copy has been seen with a double flyleaf at front.

DE LUXE FORMAT

⟨i-ii⟩, ⟨1⟩-162; 2 blank leaves; leaf excised or
pasted under the end paper. Laid paper. $8\frac{1}{8}''$
6″. Frontispiece inserted.

⟨1², 2¹, 3², 4-13⁸⟩. Leaf ⟨13⟩₈ excised or pasted
under the end paper.

S cloth: white. White laid end papers. Top edges
gilt.

A set of de luxe printing sheets have been seen in
full padded leather; inscribed by Miller: *With
love ... Joaquin Miller ... May 15/96 No 28*
Location: UV. Another set of de luxe printing
sheets, no inscription present, has been seen (B)
in three-quarters leather; so issued?

A set of sheets (trade format) has been seen in
printed paper wrapper; copy in UV. Advertisements on the wrapper indicate a late form of
binding, *ca.* 1897-1898.

Noted as *at once* PW March 28, 1896. Deposited
May 7, 1896. A copy (UV) of the de luxe printing
has been seen inscribed by Miller May 15, 1896.
Listed PW (both formats) May 23, 1896.

B (trade) BA (trade) BPL (de luxe) H (de
luxe) LC (trade) NYPL (trade) UV (both) Y
(trade)

13839. ... STAY HAND, GOLD TORIES!

... SAN FRANCISCO ... DIERS PRINT. ⟨1896⟩

Caption-title. At head of title: *Joaquin Miller's
Latest and Best ...*

Not seen. Entry on the basis of a photographic
copy.

Single leaf. Printed on recto only. 11″ × $7\frac{1}{8}''$.

At end of text: *El Dorado, Cal., October 24, 1896.*

Preceding the text of Miller's poem is a letter,
dated *San Francisco, Cal., Oct. 27, 1896,* signed by
Oscar T. Shuck: *You probably read in The Examiner's Silver Edition of October 25th this exhilarating
production ...*

Otherwise unlocated. Place taken from printer's
union device at foot of sheet.

UCB

13840. Later American Poems Edited by J. E.
Wetherell ...

Toronto: The Copp, Clark Company, Limited.
1896.

Reprint save for "Dakota," p. 61; otherwise unlocated.

JH

13841. The Complete Poetical Works ...

San Francisco: The Whitaker & Ray Co.
(Incorporated) 1897

Contains a number of poems here first collected;
also contains much material here first collected in
an American publication.

Noted as *in press* PW March 20, 1897. Noted for
December PW Nov. 13, 1897. Deposited Dec. 15,
1897. Listed PW Jan. 8, 1898; again listed Feb. 5,
1898.

"Joaquin's *Complete Poetical Works* was published
in London in 1897. It was issued in the United
States in 1900, and in a revised edition two years
later. It was a fairly large volume of 330 pages
printed in double columns, selling at $2.50 and
$4.50 for trade and deluxe copies, with auto-
graphed copies priced at $7.50."---Marberry,
pp. 251-252. BAL has found no London, 1897,
printing of Miller's poems; nor an American
printing of 1900. The only periodical reference
found (PC Nov. 20, 1897) states that Routledge
"will shortly issue it in one volume." Routledge
imported the San Francisco, 1897, printing which
is listed by PC Feb. 26, 1898.

AAS B BPL H LC UV Y

13842. The Literature of America and Our
Favorite Authors ... Choice Selections from
Their Writings ... Compiled and Edited by
William Wilfred Birdsall ... Rufus M. Jones ...
and Others ...

John C. Winston & Co., Philadelphia Chicago
Toronto ⟨1897⟩

Reprint with the exception of "Joaquin Miller's
Alaska Letter," p. 164, an "extract from a syndi-
cate⟨d⟩ letter clipped from the *Philadelphia In-
quirer.*"

Issued as a subscription book with varying imprints; a copy as above was deposited for copyright Jan. 18, 1898.

H LC

13843. Transactions of the Twenty-Fourth Annual Reunion of the Oregon Pioneer Association for 1896 . . .

Portland, Oregon Geo. H. Himes and Company, Printers McKay Building, 248 1/2 Stark Street 1897

Printed paper wrapper.

"The Pioneers to New Oregon, the Great Emerald Land," pp. ⟨41⟩-42. Also in (reprinted from?) *The Complete Poetical Works*, 1897.

H

13844. Poems of American Patriotism 1776-1898 Selected by R. L. Paget

Boston L. C. Page and Company (Incorporated) MDCCCXCVIII

"The Defence of the Alamo," pp. 99-101. Collected in *The Complete Poetical Works*, 1902.

For fuller entry see BAL, Vol. 1, p. 249.

13845. Anthology of Living American Poets, 1898. Arranged by Deborah Ege Olds.

Cincinnati. The Editor Publishing Company. 1898.

"Give Me the Desert," p. 8. Otherwise unlocated.

H   NYPL

13846. Just back from Dawson and Other Doggerel ⟨By Sam C. Dunham⟩

⟨W. F. Roberts: The Perfect Press, Washington, 1899⟩

Cover-title. Printed paper wrapper. Unpaged. 8 pp.

"Comrades of the Klondike," p. ⟨2⟩. Dated at end: *Circle City, Oct. 19, 1897*. Collected in *Poems*, Vol. 1, 1909, as "Chilkoot Pass."

B

13847. CHANTS FOR THE BOER . . .

SAN FRANCISCO THE WHITAKER & RAY COMPANY (INCORPORATED) 1900

Title-page in black and red.

⟨i-ii⟩, ⟨1⟩-28, 2 pp. advertisements. Laid paper. 7⅝″ × 5⅝″ full.

⟨1-2⁸⟩.

Printed red paper wrapper tied with red cord.

Deposited Feb. 5, 1900. Listed PW May 12, 1900.

AAS   BA   BPL   H   NYPL   UV   Y

13848. TRUE BEAR STORIES . . . WITH INTRODUCTORY NOTES BY DR. DAVID

STARR JORDAN . . . TOGETHER WITH A THRILLING ACCOUNT OF THE CAPTURE OF THE CELEBRATED GRIZZLY "MONARCH." . . .

CHICAGO AND NEW YORK: RAND, McNALLY & COMPANY, PUBLISHERS. ⟨1900⟩

Title-page in black and orange.

Three printings noted:

FIRST PRINTING

⟨i-vi⟩, 1-259; blank, p. ⟨260⟩; 3 blank leaves. 20 plates inserted. Laid paper. 7¹¹⁄₁₆″ × 5¼″. *Note:* In some copies there is present a frontispiece; *i.e.*, there is a total of twenty-one inserted plates including the frontispiece. The copyright deposit copies do not contain the frontispiece; contain 20 plates only. The AAS copy (sophisticated?) has a total of 20 plates including a frontispiece, possibly a plate brought forward and used as frontispiece.

⟨1⟩-17⁸. *Also signed:* ⟨-⟩¹, ⟨1⟩-7, ⟨8⟩, 9-15, ⟨16⟩⁸, ⟨17⟩⁷. *Note:* leaves 17₆₋₇ present as blanks; leaf 17₈ used as a pastedown.

SECOND PRINTING

⟨i-vi⟩, 1-259; blank, p. ⟨260⟩; blank leaf. Frontispiece and 19 plates inserted. 7⅝″ × 5⅛″. Wove paper.

⟨1⟩-5, ⟨6⟩, 7-16⁸, 17⁶. *Also signed:* ⟨-⟩¹, ⟨1⟩-7, ⟨8⟩, 9-15, ⟨16⟩⁸, ⟨17⟩⁵.

THIRD PRINTING

⟨i-vi⟩, 1-259; blank, p. ⟨260⟩; 3 blank leaves. 6(?) illustrations inserted. 7½″ × 5″ full. Wove paper.

⟨1⟩, 2-3, ⟨4⟩, 5-17⁸. *Also signed:* ⟨-⟩¹, ⟨1⟩, 2-3, ⟨4⟩, 5-7, ⟨8⟩, 9-15, ⟨16⟩⁸, ⟨17⟩⁷.

The binding has been noted as follows:

BINDING A

T cloth: tan. Stamped in black ⟨dark brown?⟩, brown, green, red. In the spine imprint a comma is present; spine imprint stamped from letters ⅛″ scant tall. At front: True binder's end papers of laid paper; at back, leaf 17₈ used as the pastedown. Top edges stained orange. Front lettered: TRUE / BEAR / STORIES / ⟨etc., etc.⟩ Noted only on first printing sheets.

BINDING B

T cloth: tan. Stamped in black ⟨dark brown?⟩, brown, green, red. In the spine imprint a comma is present; spine imprint stamped from letters ⅛″ tall. At front and at back: True binder's end papers of wove paper. Top edges stained pale yellow. Front lettered: TRUE / BEAR / STORIES / ⟨etc., etc.⟩ Noted only on second printing sheets.

BINDING C

T cloth: green. The stamping is quite unlike that of *Binding A* or *Binding B*, a notable variation being the absence of the comma from the spine imprint which indicates a later style of the firm's name. Front cover lettered: TRUE / BEAR STORIES / ⟨*etc., etc.*⟩

At front and at back: True binder's end papers of wove paper. Top edges not stained. Noted only on third printing sheets.

Deposited Sept. 13, 1900. Listed PW Dec. 1, 1900.

AAS (1st)   LC (1st, being deposit copies; 3rd)   UV (1st; 2nd)   Y (1st)

13849. JOAQUIN MILLER *vs.* THE CHINESE EXCLUSION ACT. (PUBLISHED BY PERMISSION) LOMPOC, CAL. OCT. 6th, 1901. REV. N. R. JOHNSTON, OAKLAND, CAL. MY DEAR NEIGHBOR JOHNSTON . . .

⟨n.p., 1901⟩

Caption-title.

Single leaf folded to make 4 pp. Unpaged. Size of page: $5^{13}/_{16}$″ × $4^{5}/_{8}$″.

Originally in NAR Dec. 1901, under the title "The Chinese and the Exclusion Act."

HEH

13850. The Complete Poetical Works . . .

San Francisco: The Whitaker & Ray Co. (Incorporated) 1901 ⟨*i.e.*, 1902⟩

Reprint save for the "Preface," pp. v-xiii, dated at end *June 1, 1902.* The preface is a revision of that in the 1897 edition.

B

13851. The Golden Poppy by Emory Evans Smith

Palo Alto, California 1902 ⟨Copyright 1901⟩

"God's Gold," p. 142. Collected in *Complete Poetical Works*, 1902, as "The California Poppy."

"Frémont," p. 175.

H

13852. The Grand Canyon of Arizona Being a Book of Words from Many Pens, about the Grand Canyon of the Colorado River in Arizona.

Published by the Passenger Department of the Santa Fe. 1902.

"A New Wonder of the World," pp. 58-60.

Deposited Nov. 22, 1902.

H

13853. The Complete Poetical Works . . . Revised Edition . . .

San Francisco The Whitaker & Ray Company (Incorporated) 1902

Reprint save for the following:

"Boston to the Boers"

"The California Poppy." Previously in *The Golden Poppy*, see above under 1902; *i.e.*, 1901.

"Californians"

"The Defense of the Alamo." Here first collected; previously in *Poems of American Patriotism*, 1898.

"England's Lion"

"The Fourth of Our Fathers"

"Usland to England"

Deposited Dec. 9, 1902. Listed PW Dec. 13, 1902.

LC

13854. The Awakening of Poccalito A Tale of Telegraph Hill, and Other Tales. ⟨By⟩ Eugenia Kellogg

The Unknown Publisher San Francisco 1903.

Letter, Miller to the author, Nov. 7, 1903, p. ⟨7⟩.

Two issues (printings?) noted: the order is presumed correct:

1st

Index on verso of title-leaf. A copy thus deposited for copyright Sept. 30, 1904 ⟨*sic*⟩. The word *copyright*, in the copyright notice, correctly spelled.

2nd

Index on p. ⟨3⟩. The word *copyright*, in the copyright notice, misspelled *copywright.*

Noted in cloth only. Reported (not seen by BAL) in printed paper wrapper.

LC (both)

13855. AS IT WAS IN THE BEGINNING. A POEM . . . DEDICATED TO THE MOTHERS OF MEN.

⟨SAN FRANCISCO: A. M. ROBERTSON, 1903⟩

⟨1⟩-99. $11^{3}/_{8}$″ × $5^{11}/_{16}$″.

50 sheets, each folded to the above size, the inner fold unprinted; bound in Japanese fashion.

Printed yellow paper wrapper.

Deposited July 9, 1903. Listed PW Aug. 1, 1903.

NYPL   Y

13856. Laurel Leaves for Little Folk Edited . . . by Mary E. Phillips

Boston Lee & Shepard MCMIII

"Nina," p. ⟨44⟩. A version of "To the Jersey Lily," *Songs of Faraway Lands*, London, 1878; *Complete Poetical Works*, 1897.

"God's Flowers," pp. ⟨133-135⟩. Otherwise unlocated.

According to the table of contents both of these were "written for *Laurel Leaves*."

On copyright page: *Published September, 1903* Listed PW Nov. 21, 1903.

EM

13857. A Biographical Sketch of the Life of Charles Algernon Sidney Vivian Founder of the Order of Elks ... by Imogen Holbrook Vivian

San Francisco The Whitaker & Ray Company Incorporated 1904

"Charles Algernon Sidney Vivian in Memoriam," p. 9.

B

13858. CHRISTMAS 1904 ...

⟨n.p., 1904⟩

Card. Printed on recto only. Text, 6 lines, printed in brown. Decorated in colors. $3\frac{1}{2}'' \times 5\frac{1}{2}''$ scant. Otherwise unlocated.

B

13859. JAPAN OF SWORD AND LOVE BY JOAQUIN MILLER AND YONE NOGUCHI

PUBLISHERS KANAO BUNYENDO TOKYO 1905

Title-page in black and red.

⟨i⟩-⟨xviii⟩, 1-74; Japanese colophon, p. ⟨75⟩; list in Japanese, p. ⟨76⟩. Frontispiece inserted. $7\frac{3}{8}'' \times 5''$.

⟨1^5, 2^4, 3-6^8, 7^4, 8^2⟩. Leaf ⟨1⟩$_2$ inserted.

Printed green paper wrapper. White end papers.

According to the colophon printed Jan. 21, 1905; published Feb. 15, 1905.

H LC Y

13860. The Building of the City Beautiful ...

Albert Brandt: Publisher Trenton, New Jersey 1905

Revised. For first edition see above under 1893. Contains a brief prefatory note written for this edition, p. 7.

"Albert Brandt ... will bring out this fall ..." ---PW Sept. 2, 1905. Deposited Nov. 7, 1905. BA copy received Nov. 28, 1905. Listed PW Dec. 9, 1905.

B BA LC UV Y

13861. LIGHT A NARRATIVE POEM ...

HERBERT B. TURNER & CO. BOSTON 1907

Title-page in black and green.

⟨i⟩-vi, ⟨1⟩-153. $7\frac{1}{2}'' \times 4\frac{9}{16}''$.

⟨1^4, 2^2, 3-4^8, 5^2, 6-7^8, 8^6, 9^2, 10-11^8, 12-13^2, 14^8, 15^4⟩.

Printed slate-blue boards sides, white imitation vellum shelf back. Printed mottled black boards sides, white imitation vellum shelf back. Two black paper labels on spine. Top edges gilt.

Note: Both deposit copies, each rebound, appear to have the titles inserted as cancels. No other copies examined show the title-leaf as a cancel. Significance not determined.

On copyright page: *Published, March, 1907* Deposited April 3, 1907. Listed PW June 1, 1907. BA copy received June 5, 1907. See *A Song of Creation*, 1899, in *Section Three* of this list.

B BA BPL H UV Y

13862. Western Frontier Stories Retold from St. Nicholas

New York The Century Co. 1907

"A Race with Idaho Robbers," pp. 3-17.

Deposited Sept. 13, 1907. Listed PW Oct. 5, 1907.

LC

13863. Poems of American History Collected ... by Burton Egbert Stevenson

Boston and New York Houghton Mifflin Company The Riverside Press Cambridge 1908

Reprint save for:

"Resurge San Francisco," p. 658. Collected as "Resurgo San Francisco," Miller's collected works, Vol. 3; see next entry.

"San Francisco," p. 657.

On copyright page: *Published November, 1908* Deposited Nov. 21, 1908. Listed PW Dec. 12, 1908.

H

13864. ⟨Collected Works⟩

⟨San Francisco: The Whitaker & Ray Company, 1909–1910⟩

See below for comment on formats.

1: *An Introduction, etc.* 1909. *Bear Edition* deposited April 7, 1909.

2: *Songs of the Sierras.* 1909. *Bear Edition* deposited May 24, 1909.

3: *Songs of the Sunlands.* 1909. *Bear Edition* deposited June 7, 1909.

4: *Songs of Italy and Others.* 1909. *Bear Edition* deposited June 29, 1909.

5: *Songs of the American Seas.* 1909. *Bear Edition* deposited June 29, 1909.

6: *Poetic Plays.* 1910. *Bear Edition* deposited May 5, 1910.

BEAR EDITION

Printed paper boards, imitation vellum shelf back. Also blue T cloth. At head of title: *Bear Edition*

AUTHOR'S DE LUXE EDITION

Three-quarters leather, marbled paper boards sides. Also full leather. 250 numbered sets, signed by Miller. At head of title: *Author's De Luxe Edition*

Contains some material here first published or collected. Reissued by DeWitt & Snelling in the *Oakland Edition.*

"This will doubtless be the final revision of the poet's works, and will be known as the *Author's Edition,* in five ⟨*sic*⟩ volumes. It will be printed on deckle paper ... The first volume will contain almost entirely new matter, and ... an autobiography of the writer ... A limited edition de luxe, on fine paper ... bound in leather ..." ———PW Dec. 5, 1908.

B   BA   H   LC

13865. The Journal of Columbus' First Voyage "Columbus" by Joaquin Miller ...

Copyright, 1912, by The Inventors' Outlook, Washington, D. C.

Cover-title. Printed paper wrapper.

Reprint with the possible exception of "To My Log Cabin Lovers," which appears on an inserted folded leaf. "Written ... by Joaquin Miller for the dedication exercises of the Log Cabin, held on June 2, 1912 ..."

LC

13866. PANAMA, UNION OF THE OCEANS ...

⟨n.p., n.d., *ca.* 1912⟩

Note: Printed throughout in brown ink on brown paper.

⟨1-15⟩. 8⅝″ × 5⅝″.

⟨-⁸⟩.

Printed self-wrapper. Illustration tipped to p. ⟨1⟩. Collected in *Poetical Works,* 1923, as "Light of the Southern Cross."

B   USC   Y

13867. The Men Who Blaze the Trail and Other Poems by Sam. C. Dunham with an Introduction by Joaquin Miller ...

New York Barse & Hopkins Publishers ⟨1913⟩

Reprint save for "The Poet Laureate of Alaska," pp. 9-12.

AAS   H   HEH   NYPL   UV

13868. Out of the North by Howard V. Sutherland with a Foreword by Joaquin Miller

New York Desmond FitzGerald, Inc. MCMXIII

Boards, cloth shelf back.

"Foreword," p. ⟨xiii⟩.

Deposited Sept. 11, 1913.

H   NYPL

13869. Songs by Juanita and Joaquin Miller Only One To-Day. Oakland. God's Garden.

Published by the Song Shop Oakland, Cal. ... ⟨1914⟩

Sheet music. Cover-title.

"Only One Today"; otherwise "The Voice of the Dove," *The Building of the City Beautiful,* 1893.

"Oakland"; see next entry.

"God's Garden"; otherwise "Nina" in *Laurel Leaves ...,* 1903.

Deposited Jan. 17, 1914.

LC

13870. OAKLAND ...

⟨n.p., n.d., *ca.* 1914⟩

Not seen. Entry on the basis of a photographic copy.

Single leaf. Printed on recto only. 9⅜″ × 6⅞″.

Text illustrated with illustrations of Miller, Miller's home; Miller's monument to Frémont; view of Oakland.

Text not found elsewhere save as a song; see preceding entry.

UCB

13871. Anecdotes of the Hour by Famous Men as Told by Winston Churchill ... Jack London ... and about 100 Other Notable Men ...

New York Hearst's International Library Co. 1914.

Anecdote, p. 48.

Deposited April 13, 1914.

H

13872. The Shoes of Happiness and Other Poems . . . by Edwin Markham . . .

Garden City New York Doubleday, Page & Company 1915

Brief comment, p. 191.

Listed PW March 27, 1915.

H

13873. Walt Whitman, As Man, Poet and Friend . . . Being Autograph Pages from Many Pens, Collected by Charles N. Elliot

Boston: Richard G. Badger The Gorham Press ⟨1915⟩

Contribution, pp. 199-200.

For fuller entry see No. 6635.

13874. Poems of Charles Warren Stoddard . . . Collected by Ina Coolbrith

New York: John Lane Company London: John Lane, The Bodley Head MCMXVII

"Say, Charlie," p. 7. Otherwise unlocated.

Trade format in blue buckram; also 50 de luxe copies in light yellow buckram.

Deposited Aug. 6, 1917.

H   NYPL

13875. . . . BERKELEY . . . MUSIC BY JUANITA MILLER

EARL MUSIC PUBLISHING CO. ⟨n.p., 1917⟩

Sheet music. Cover-title. At head of title: *As Sung by Miss Goldie Hulin, at the Greek Theatre.*

"Joaquin published his last poem in 1912. It was called *Berkeley* . . . closely modeled on a poem he had penned years before, *San Diego*."---Marberry, p. 272. BAL has found no printing prior to 1917.

Y

13876. Literary California   Poetry Prose and Portraits Gathered by Ella Sterling Mighels . . .

Harr Wagner Publishing Co.   San Francisco, California 1918

Reprint save for an unlocated piece, "Good-Bye, Bret Harte," p. 360.

For fuller entry see BAL, Vol. 1, p. 226.

13877. The Eighteenth Year Book 1919

Printed for Members Only   The Bibliophile Society Boston Massachusetts MCMXIX

Boards, printed paper label on spine.

Six lines of verse, p. 122; otherwise unlocated save for publication in *My Father* . . . , by Juanita J. Miller, Oakland ⟨1941⟩, pp. 194-195.

500 copies only.

H   NYPL

13878. TRELAWNY WITH SHELLEY AND BYRON . . .

1922 THE BIBLIO COMPANY   POMPTON LAKES, NEW JERSEY

⟨1⟩-24. Watermarked *Alexandra, Made in U.S.A.* 9⅛″ × 5¹⁄₁₆″.

⟨-¹²⟩.

Printed self-wrapper.

The Ramapo Press Publications, No. 1.---P. ⟨3⟩.

Limited Edition of 300 Numbered Copies . . .---P. ⟨4⟩.

Written at The Heights ⟨sic⟩, Oakland, California January 1, 1893---P. ⟨4⟩.

B   H   LC   NYPL   UV   Y

13879. Overland in a Covered Wagon An Autobiography . . . Edited by Sidney G. Firman . . .

D. Appleton and Company New York London 1930

Trade edition. Pp. 130. Bound in yellow-orange B cloth, stamped in green only. Symbol (I) on p. ⟨130⟩. Note presence of date, 1930, on the title-page.

NYPL copy received Oct. 21, 1930. BPL copy received Nov. 6, 1930. A copy of this printing deposited Nov. 15, 1930.

A version of Miller's "An Introduction," works, Vol. 1, San Francisco, 1909.

". . . Contains, one is told, not a syllable of truth!" ---Van Wyck Brooks as quoted by Marberry, p. 269. "Mr. Brooks' statement to the contrary, the volume is one of the most believable of all of Joaquin's prose work."---Marberry, p. 269.

Also issued in a school edition. Pp. 131. Bound in tan V cloth, stamped in black and yellow. Symbol (I) on p. ⟨131⟩. Issued under the imprint: *New York D. Appleton and Company ⟨1930⟩*

Save for some typographic variations in the front matter, and the presence of a page (p. ⟨131⟩) of *Topics for One-Paragraph Accounts* and *Subjects for Longer Compositions*, printed from the same setting as the *trade* edition.

BPL (trade) H (school) LC (trade) NYPL (trade) UV (school) Y (trade)

13880. A ROYAL HIGHWAY OF THE
WORLD . . .

1932 METROPOLITAN PRESS, PUBLISHERS PORT-
LAND, OREGON

⟨i-vi⟩, ⟨i⟩-⟨xviii⟩, ⟨1⟩-23; blank, p. ⟨24⟩; colophon, p. ⟨25⟩; blank, pp. ⟨26–32⟩. Laid paper
watermarked *Roxburghe*. 10¹³⁄₁₆″ × 8″. Frontispiece (tipped to leaf ⟨1⟩₂ᵥ; 1 facsimile in text; 1
plate inserted (leaf ⟨3⟩ᵣ); 1 plate inserted between
⟨5⟩₃₋₄.

⟨1⁷ (leaf 2 inserted), 2⁴, 3¹, 4–7⁴⟩.

Blue balloon cloth. Lining papers of book stock.
Double flyleaf of book stock at front. Top edges
gilt.

"A Royal Highway of the World," being a letter,
Canyon City, Oregon, July 17, 1907, addressed *To
the Hon., the Co. Judges and Commissioners of Grant
and Harney Counties*, pp. 3-14.

245 numbered copies only.

Deposited July 14, 1932.

AAS   B   BPL   H   NYPL   UV   Y

13881. ADAH ISAACS MENKEN . . .

YSLETA   EDWIN B. HILL   1934

⟨1-13⟩, blank leaf. Laid paper watermarked
Utopian. 7½″ × 5¼″.

⟨-⁸⟩.

Wire saddle-stitched. Some copies, unstitched,
laid in the printed wrapper.

Printed wrapper of stiff green or gray paper.

"In . . . 1892 . . . Miller wrote an appreciation of
Adah Isaacs Menken which duly appeared in
'The Morning Call' of San Francisco . . ."---
P. ⟨13⟩.

AAS   H   NYPL   Y

13882. The Letters of Western Authors A Series
of Letters . . . in Facsimile . . .

. . . Book Club of California   San Francisco
1935

Letter dated *9-25-6*, here included.

For comment see entry No. 4488.

13883. JOAQUIN MILLER HIS CALI-
FORNIA DIARY BEGINNING IN 1855 &
ENDING IN 1857 EDITED, & WITH AN
INTRODUCTION BY JOHN S RICHARDS
. . .

NOW FIRST PUBLISHED BY FRANK MCCAFFREY AT
HIS DOGWOOD PRESS IN SEATTLE 1936

Title-page in black, red and green.

⟨i-ii⟩, ⟨1⟩-106; 4 blank leaves. Illustrated. Tan
paper. 9⁵⁄₁₆″ × 6¼″.

⟨1-5⁸, 6¹⁰, 7⁸⟩.

Rough V cloth: yellow-tan. End papers of book
stock.

". . . 700 copies have been printed. This is copy
No. . . ."---Certificate of issue.

Deposited Aug. 15, 1936.

H   NYPL   UV   Y

13884. My First Publication Edited . . . by James
D. Hart . . .

The Book Club of California   1961

Printed paper boards, cloth shelf back, printed
paper label on spine.

"How I Came to Be a Writer of Books," pp.
35-40. Reprinted from *Lippincott's Monthly Magazine*, July, 1886.

AAS   BA   H

Collections of reprinted material issued under Miller's name; separate editions (*i.e.*, pieces reprinted from Miller's books and issued in separate form). For a list of books by authors other than Miller containing reprinted Miller material see in *Section IV*.

13885. Songs of the Sierras . . .

Toronto: The Canadian News and Publishing Co. 1871.

13886. Songs of the Sierras . . . a New Edition.

London: Longmans, Green, and Co. 1872.

Sheets of the Boston, 1871, edition issued with title-page as above. Advertised (this edition?) as a *new edition, revised*, Ath Dec. 2, 9, 1871; PC Dec. 8, 1871. Listed Bkr Dec. 2, 1871; PC Dec. 8, 1871.

13887. Joaquin, et Al. (From the Original Edition Published at Oregon.)

London: John Camden Hotten, Piccadilly. 1872.

Note: By removing the title-leaf (⟨A⟩1) this publication may be mistaken by the unwary for the genuine first edition. At least one copy so sophisticated has been noted. Knowledge of the following features of the Hotten reprint may prevent such imposition. *Pagination:* ⟨i-viii⟩, ⟨1⟩-124; *signature collation:* ⟨A⟩⁴, B-H⁸, I⁴, K². For collation of the genuine 1869 printing see above in *Section One*.

Also note: The imprint of *John Strangeways* is present, pp. ⟨ii⟩ and 124, of the Hotten reprint.

Listed Ath June 29, 1872. Advertised Ath June 29, 1872: "A few copies only issued for admirers of the Poet . . . The original little volume . . ." Advertised for *this day* Bkr Aug. 3; Sept. 2, 1872, where the title is given as *Oregon Poems*. Ath Nov. 30, 1872: "We are requested to state that the edition of ⟨Miller's⟩ early poems, advertised by Mr Hotten, is issued without the sanction of the author, and, indeed, that its publication is quite contrary to his wishes."

13888. The Pacific Tourist. Williams' Illustrated Trans-Continental Guide of Travel, from the Atlantic to the Pacific Ocean . . . Henry T.

Williams, Editor. With Special Contributions by Prof. F. V. Hayden, Clarence King, Capt. Dutton, A. C. Peale, Joaquin Miller . . .

New York: Henry T. Williams, Publisher. 1876 . . .

"The Great Plains and Desert," p. 188. Extracted from *The Ship in the Desert*, Boston, 1875, p. 102.

Advertised for May 23 in PW May 20, 1876; offered in both cloth and flexible cloth. Listed PW May 27, 1876.

13889. Songs of the Sierras . . .

Boston: Roberts Brothers. 1877.

13890. Songs of the Sun-Lands . . .

Boston: Roberts Brothers. 1877.

13891. Paquita, the Indian Heroine . . .

Hartford, Conn.: American Publishing Company. 1881.

Otherwise *Unwritten History: Life amongst the Modocs*, 1874.

Deposited Nov. 3, 1881.

Noted in the following forms. Sequence not determined and the designations are for identification only.

A

Imprint: As above.

The title-leaf is a cancel.

First page of text: A cancel. Headed: *Shadows of Shasta* . . .

B

Imprint: *Hartford, Conn.: American Publishing Company.* ⟨n.d.⟩.

The title-leaf may be a cancel; BAL has been unable to determine.

The first page of text is not a cancel and is headed: *Life Amongst the Modocs* . . .

13892. The Pacific Tourist. Adams & Bishop's Illustrated Trans-Continental Guide of Travel, from the Atlantic to the Pacific Ocean . . .

Henry T. Williams, Editor . . . Contributions by . . . Joaquin Miller . . . ⟨and Others⟩

New York: Adams & Bishop, Publishers. 1881 . . .

13893. Songs of the Sun-Lands . . .

Boston: Roberts Brothers. 1881.

13894. Poems . . .

Boston Roberts Brothers 1882

Printed from the plates of earlier books; unaltered pagination.

13895. Thompson's Prodigal and Other Sketches. By Bret Harte . . . with a Story of Wild Western Life. By Joaquin Miller.

Ward, Lock and Co. London: Warwick House, Salisbury Square, E. C. New York: Bond Street. ⟨n.d., 1885⟩

Printed paper wrapper. Announced Ath Sept. 26, 1885. Listed PC Dec. 7, 1885.

13896. The Pacific Tourist. Adams & Bishop's Illustrated Trans-Continental Guide of Travel, from the Atlantic to the Pacific Ocean . . . Frederick E. Shearer, Editor. With Special Contributions by . . . Clarence King . . . Joaquin Miller . . .

New York: Adams & Bishop, Publishers, 1885.

According to a statement on the title-page available in flexible covers, 332 pages; and, cloth, stiff covers, 364 pages.

13897. Poems . . .

Boston Roberts Brothers 1889

Printed from the plates of earlier books; unaltered pagination.

13898. Joaquin Miller's Romantic Life amongst the Red Indians An Autobiography.

London: Saxon & Co., Publishers. 23 Bouverie St. Fleet St., E. C. ⟨1890⟩

Printed paper wrapper. Also cloth. Printed from the same setting as *My Own Story*, 1890.

The date ⟨1890⟩ is questionable. Listed by Ath Sept. 12, 1891. Further, the only examined copies of this publication could not have issued prior to 1897; see inner wrapper with extracts from reviews dated 1897. A Saxon printing listed by PC Jan. 22, 1898.

13899. My Life among the Indians . . .

Chicago: Morrill, Higgins & Co. 1892.

Printed paper wrapper. *The Midland Series*, Vol. II, No. 16; issued under date June 9, 1892. Copies at LC, NYPL, numbered *16;* the Y copy numbered *6.*

13900. Songs of Summer Lands . . .

Chicago Morrill, Higgins & Co. 1892.

In some copies leaf 2₅ (pp. 25-26) is a cancel; significance not known.

Reissued with the following imprints:

W. B. Conkey Company, Chicago ⟨n.d., 1893⟩

W. B. Conkey Company, Chicago ⟨1893⟩

Chicago W. B. Conkey Company ⟨n.d.⟩

Morrill, Higgins & Company sheets have been seen in later Conkey bindings.

Noted for June PW May 28, 1892. Deposited July 14, 1892. Advertised and listed as a "new revised edition" PW Aug. 13, 1892.

13901. . . . He Blessed Them A Song for Children's Sunday . . . Music by T. H. H. . . .

Boston Louis H. Ross & Co. 32 West St. ⟨1892⟩

Sheet music. Cover-title. At head of title: *To Dorothy H.* Plate number: L.H.R. & CO. 159.

Otherwise "Beyond Jordan," *Songs of the Sun-Lands,* Boston, 1873.

13902. Autumn Leaves: A Pictorial Library of Prose, Poetry and Art, by . . . Eminent Authors . . . Celia Thaxter . . . Paul Hamilton Hayne . . . Lucy Larcom . . . Joaquin Miller . . . Mary E. Wilkins . . . and Many Others . . . Edited by Daphne Dale.

⟨n.p.⟩ 1893. National Book Mart

13903. The River of Rest Chorus for Women's Voices . . . Music by A. W. Platte Vocal Score . . .

New York G. Schirmer ⟨1898⟩

Printed paper wrapper. In: *G. Schirmer's Collection of Oratorios and Cantatas.* Deposited Sept. 10, 1898. Reprinted from *In Classic Shades,* 1890.

13904. The Voice of the Dove . . . ⟨Music⟩ by Charles Willeby . . .

The John Church Company. Cincinnati . . . ⟨1905⟩

Sheet music. Cover-title. Plate number 14845-3 (high voice). Reprinted from *The Building of the City Beautiful,* 1893.

13905. . . . Four Songs with Piano Accompaniment . . . No. 4. To Russia . . .

New York: G. Schirmer ⟨1906⟩

Sheet music. Cover-title. At head of title: *Sidney Horner* Plate numbers: 18499 (high voice); 18500 (low voice). Reprinted from *In Classic Shades*, 1890.

13906. Kindergarten Gems for Home and Kindergarten by Joaquin Miller . . . and Other Popular Juvenile Authors . . .

The Saalfield Publishing Company New York Akron, Ohio Chicago ⟨1907⟩

Unpaged. Deposited July 22, 1907.

13907. The Danites in the Sierras (In Four Acts) . . .

San Francisco Whitaker & Ray-Wiggin Co. 1910

Purple linen-weave paper wrapper, printed paper label on front.

Sheets extracted from *Poetic Plays*, 1910; *i.e.*, Joaquin Miller's works, Vol. 6, 1910, and issued with cancel title-leaf.

13908. Forty-Nine an Idyl Drama of the Sierras (In Four Acts) . . .

San Francisco Whitaker & Ray-Wiggin Co. 1910

Blue linen-weave paper wrapper, printed paper label on front.

Sheets extracted from *Poetic Plays*, 1910; *i.e.*, Joaquin Miller's works, Vol. 6, 1910, and issued with cancel title-leaf.

13909. . . . The Voice of the Dove . . . Music by Charles S. Burnham . . .

White-Smith Music Publishing Co. Boston New York Chicago ⟨1912⟩

Sheet music. Cover-title. At head of title: *To Cecil Fanning* Plate number 14273-5 (low voice); 14256-5 (medium voice); 14274-5 (high voice). Reprinted from *The Building of the City Beautiful*, 1893.

13910. Columbus . . . Music by Carlos Troyer . . .

Philadelphia Theodore Presser Co. 1712 Chestnut Str. ⟨1915⟩

Sheet music. Cover-title. Plate No. 13387. Reprinted from *Songs of the Soul*, 1896.

13911. Magnolia Blooms . . . Music by Charles Wakefield Cadman . . .

White-Smith Music Publishing Co. Boston . . . ⟨1916⟩

Sheet music. Cover-title. Plate number 14881-4. Reprinted from *In Classic Shades*, 1890.

13912. Song . . . ⟨In men whom men condemn as ill⟩

⟨n.p.⟩ Kohler & Chase ⟨1917⟩

Sheet music. Cover-title. Extracted from "Burns and Byron," *Songs of the Sierras*, 1871.

Deposited April 4, 1917. At head of p. ⟨2⟩: "*Judge Not*" . . . ⟨*Music by*⟩ *Juanita Miller* . . .

13913. Columbus A Short Cantata for Mixed Voices Music by E. S. Hosmer . . .

Boston: Oliver Ditson Company New York: Chas. H. Ditson & Co Chicago: Lyon & Healy ⟨1917⟩

Sheet music. Cover-title. Plate number: 5-149-72055-14. For an earlier setting see under ⟨1915⟩.

13914. . . . Joaquin Miller's Poems [In Six Volumes] . . .

San Francisco Harr Wagner Publishing Co. 1917

At head of title: *Bear Edition*

Cloth, printed paper labels.

Vol. 1 only located; presumably all published.

13915. The Poetical Works . . . Edited with an Introduction and Notes by Stuart P. Sherman . . .

G. P. Putnam's Sons New York & London The Knickerbocker Press 1923

"I have added more than fifty poems which he discarded or overlooked . . ."———P. iii. BAL has been unable to find a poem herein which had not been published in an earlier book.

Deposited April 10, 1923. The H copy received April 27, 1923; listed Bkr Aug. 1923.

13916. Columbus A Short Cantata for Women's Voices . . . Music by E. S. Hosmer

Boston: Oliver Ditson Company New York: Chas. H. Ditson & Co. Chicago: Lyon & Healy, Inc. London: Winthrop Rogers, Ltd. Made in U.S.A. ⟨1926⟩

Printed paper wrapper. For an earlier setting see above under year ⟨1915⟩. Deposited Jan. 3, 1927.

13917. . . . Columbus . . . Music by E. S. Hosmer . . .

Boston: Oliver Ditson Company New York: Chas. H. Ditson & Co. Chicago: Lyon & Healy, Inc. London: Winthrop Rogers, Ltd. Made in U.S.A. ⟨1929⟩

Printed paper wrapper. At head of title: *A Short School Cantata for Soprano, Alto and Bass* For an earlier setting see above under the year ⟨1915⟩. Deposited Nov. 23, 1929.

13918. Seven   Songs...Music   by   Juanita Miller...

Souvenir Shop at "The Hights" Joaquin Miller Road Oakland, California ⟨1935⟩

Cover-title. Printed paper wrapper.

Deposited April 22, 1935. All material herein had prior book publication. "Indian"; extracted from "Loua Ellah," *Specimens*, 1868, p. 15. "California.

A Saraband"; otherwise "California's Christmas," Joaquin Miller's works, 1909, Vol. 4.

13919. Selections from Joaquin Miller's Poems Arranged and Copyrighted 1945 by Juanita Joaquina Miller...

Tooley-Towne, Printers Oakland

Printed paper boards, cloth shelf back, printed paper label on front.

"In this compilation of selections from my father's poems I have given only excerpts from some of his long descriptive poems . . ."---P. 3.

SECTION III

The following have not been located. Some, perhaps all, never existed in separate form.

Valedictory Class Poem

Eugene, Oregon: Columbia College, 1859.

"The first thing of mine in print was the valedictory class poem, Columbia College, Eugene, Oregon, 1859."——*The Complete Poetical Works* . . . , San Francisco, 1897, p. vi.

For a four-line extract see Wagner, p. 48; the earliest located publication. The text extracted from an interview with Miller's youngest brother, George Melvin Miller, published in the *Oregonian*, Oct. 23, 1928.

Songs of the Sunlands.

Boston: Roberts Brothers, 1871.

Entry from Wagner, p. 307. Presumably an erroneous entry for *Songs of the Sun-Lands*, Boston: Roberts Brothers, 1873.

Beyond the River.

⟨n.p., n.d., *ca.* 1880?⟩

Broadside. Entry from Johnson (1942), p. 367. For a printing of the poem see in *Section One: The Society of the Army of the Potomac. Report of the Eleventh Annual Re-Union* . . . , New York, 1880.

For the Right.

⟨New York, 1883⟩

Broadside. Entry from Johnson (1942), p. 367. For a printing of the poem see Miller's *Shadows of Shasta*, 1881.

Oregon Idyl.

⟨n.p.?, 1883?⟩

Entry from Johnson (1942), p. 366, where the entry appears with the note: *Details not available.*

Perhaps a manuscript deposited for copyright? For a published version see *Poetic Plays*, being Vol. 6, of Miller's works, 1909–1910.

Fifty-Eight Short Stories from American Sources. Complete Stories by Joaquin Miller . . . &c. &c.

London: Saxon & Company, 1888.

Pp. 186. Probably issued in printed paper wrapper. Entry from the listing in PC Sept. 15, 1888, p. 1073.

A Song of Creation

1899

"In 1899 Joaquin published *A Song of Creation*, his longest poem . . ."——Marberry, p. 253.

BAL has found no 1899 publication of this poem. Issued under the title *Light*, 1907. With additions collected as "A Song of Creation," Miller's works, Vol. 5, 1909; *Poetical Works*, 1923.

Happy Days. By Joaquin Miller and Others.

Akron, Ohio: Saalfield Publishing Company, 1912.

Entry from *The United States Catalog of Books in Print January 1, 1912* . . .

Autobiography and Favorite Poems.

San Francisco: Harr Wagner, 1919.

Entry from *The United States Catalog . . . 1918 . . . 1921* . . . , New York, 1921. Perhaps reprinted from Joaquin Miller's works, 1909–1910?

In this section are listed books by authors other than Miller containing material by him reprinted from earlier books. See *Section Two* for reprints of Miller's own books.

Public and Parlor Readings . . . Miscellaneous. Edited by Lewis B. Monroe.

Boston . . . 1872.

For fuller entry see BAL, Vol. V, p. 318.

The Buyers' Manual and Business Guide . . . Compiled by J. Price and C. S. Haley.

San Francisco . . . 1872.

"A Fragment," p. 23; extracted from "With Walker in Nicaragua," *Songs of the Sierras*, 1871.

For comment see entry No. 7261.

American Poems. Selected and Edited by William Michael Rossetti . . .

London: E. Moxon, Son, & Co., Dover Street, and 1 Amen Corner, Paternoster Row. ⟨n.d., after Nov. 1872⟩

Cloth?

A Hand-Book of English Literature. Intended for the Use of High Schools . . . by Francis H. Underwood, A. M. American Authors.

Boston: Lee and Shepard, Publishers. New York: Lee, Shepard and Dillingham. 1873.

One Hundred Choice Selections No. 8 . . .

. . . Philadelphia . . . 1874.

For fuller entry see BAL, Vol. I, p. 84.

Sea and Shore . . .

Boston . . . 1874.

"At Sea," reprinted from *Songs of the Sun-Lands*, 1873. "I stand beside the Mobile Sea," extracted from "Californian," *Songs of the Sierras*, 1871.

For fuller entry see No. 4043.

The Elocutionist's Annual Number 3 . . . Edited by J. W. Shoemaker . . .

. . . Philadelphia. 1875.

For fuller entry see BAL, Vol. V, p. 607.

Poems of Places Edited by Henry W. Longfellow . . . Scotland. Vol. I.

Boston . . . 1876.

For fuller entry see No. 12177.

The Mountains . . .

Boston . . . 1876.

"A Morning in Oregon," pp. 32-33; extracted from "By the Sun-Down Seas," *Songs of the Sun-Lands*, 1873. "Shasta," p. 89; extracted from "The Tale of the Tall Alcalde," *Songs of the Sierras*, 1871.

For a fuller entry see No. 1239.

Poems of Places Edited by Henry W. Longfellow . . . Italy. Vol. III.

Boston . . . 1877.

For fuller entry see No. 4050.

Latter-Day Lyrics . . . Selected . . . by W. Davenport Adams . . .

London . . . 1878 . . .

Untitled six lines, p. ⟨182⟩; otherwise the proem to "Myrrh," *Songs of the Sierras*, 1871.

For fuller entry see BAL, Vol. I, p. 74.

Dick's Recitations and Readings No. 8 . . .

New York . . . ⟨1878⟩

For comment see entry No. 8626.

Poems of Places Edited by Henry W. Longfellow . . . Africa.

Boston . . . 1878.

"In Africa," pp. 24-25. Extracted from "Africa," *The Ship in the Desert*, Boston, 1875.

For fuller entry see No. 12206.

Notes of a Voyage to California via Cape Horn . . . by Samuel C. Upham . . .

Philadelphia: Published by the Author. 1878.

Letter of regret (here in its earliest located book appearance) and an untitled poem, pp. 449-450. The poem reprinted from *The Baroness of New York*, 1877, p. 22.

Poetry of America . . . by W. J. Linton.

London . . . 1878.

For fuller entry see No. 7872.

Poems of Places Edited by Henry W. Longfellow . . . Southern States.

Boston . . . 1879.

For fuller entry see No. 12213.

Poems of Places Edited by Henry W. Longfellow . . . Western States.

Boston . . . 1879.

"California," pp. 32-35; "The Cañon," pp. 36-39; both the preceding extracted from *Songs of the Sierras*, 1871. "The Plains of Arizona," pp. 42-44; extracted from *The Ship in the Desert*, 1875; the text varies somewhat. "The Plains," pp. 152-154; extracted from *Joaquin et Al.*, 1869. "The Plains," p. 159; extracted from *Songs of the Sierras*, 1871.

For fuller entry see No. 12214.

Poems of Places Edited by Henry W Longfellow . . . British America . . .

Boston . . . 1879.

For fuller entry see No. 12215.

Sketches and Reminiscences of the Radical Club of Chestnut Street, Boston. Edited by Mrs. John T. Sargent.

Boston . . . 1880.

Six lines of poetry, p. 399; extracted from the proem to Part v, "Isles of the Amazons," *Songs of the Sun-Lands*, 1873.

For fuller entry see No. 8950.

The Union of American Poetry and Art . . . by John James Piatt . . .

Cincinnati . . . 1880

For fuller entry see in James Russell Lowell, *Section Three*.

One Hundred Choice Selections No. 19 . . .

. . . Philadelphia . . . 1881.

For fuller entry see No. 3392.

Harper's Cyclopædia of British and American Poetry Edited by Epes Sargent

New York . . . 1881

All Miller material herein reprinted from other books. "For Pauline," *Songs of Italy*, 1878, appears herein under the title "Love Me, Love."

For fuller entry see No. 4336.

In Memoriam. Gems of Poetry and Song on James A. Garfield . . .

Columbus . . . 1881.

For fuller entry see No. 122.

Gems for the Fireside . . . ⟨Compiled by⟩ Rev. O. H. Tiffany . . .

Boston . . . 1881.

For fuller entry see BAL, Vol. v, p. 610.

Indian Summer Autumn Poems and Sketches ⟨Compiled by⟩ L. Clarkson . . .

New York . . . 1881 . . .

For fuller entry see No. 10449.

Echoes of the Aesthetic Society of Jersey City

New-York   Thompson & Moreau, Printers Nos. 51 & 53 Maiden Lane MDCCCLXXXII.

In the Saddle A Collection of Poems on Horse-back-Riding ⟨Edited by Annie Allegra Long-fellow⟩ . . .

Boston Houghton, Mifflin and Company New York: 11 East Seventeenth Street The River-side Press, Cambridge 1882

Advertised PW June 24, 1882, as for *June 24*. Listed PW July 22, 1882.

The Poets' Tributes to Garfield . . . ⟨Second Edition⟩

Cambridge . . . 1882

For comment see entry No. 1248.

. . . The Reading Club and Handy Speaker . . . Edited by George M. Baker. No. 11.

Boston . . . ⟨1882⟩

For fuller entry see BAL, Vol. 3, p. 399.

One Hundred Choice Selections No. 22 . . .

. . . Philadelphia . . . 1883.

For comment see entry No. 4738.

No. 2. Standard Recitations by Best Authors . . . Compiled . . . by Frances P. Sullivan.

M. J. Ivers & Co., Publishers, 86 Nassau Street, N. Y. ⟨1883⟩

Printed paper wrapper. Deposited Nov. 14, 1883. Reprinted and reissued with the publisher's revised address: *379 Pearl Street, New York.*

Brilliant Diamonds of Poetry and Prose . . . ⟨Compiled by⟩ Rev. O. H. Tiffany . . .

Published for the Trade. ⟨n.p., 1883⟩

Gems for the Fireside . . . ⟨Compiled by⟩ Rev. O. H. Tiffany . . .

Springfield, Mass. . . . ⟨1883⟩

For fuller entry see BAL, Vol. V, p. 611.

One Hundred Choice Selections No. 23 . . .

. . . Philadelphia . . . 1884.

"The Old Soldier Tramp," pp. 114-115; otherwise "The Tramp of Shiloh," *The Reading Club . . . No. 9 . . .* ⟨1881⟩, above.

For fuller entry see No. 2490.

Illustrated Stories from Wide Awake with Episodes from Serials

Boston . . . ⟨1884⟩

For fuller entry see No. 6307.

Excelsior Recitations and Readings No. 3 . . .

New York . . . ⟨1884⟩

For fuller entry see BAL, Vol. 2, p. 472.

Fenno's Favorites . . . ⟨Compiled⟩ by Frank H. Fenno . . . ⟨No. 1⟩

Philadelphia . . . ⟨1884⟩

For comment see entry No. 11193.

The Children of the Poets An Anthology . . . Edited . . . by Eric S. Robertson.

London: Walter Scott, 24 Warwick Lane, Paternoster Row, and Newcastle-on-Tyne. 1886.

Cloth, printed paper label on spine.

Dick's Recitations and Readings No. 16 . . .

New York . . . ⟨1886⟩

For comment see BAL, Vol. 2, p. 96.

At Gettysburg. By Rowland B. Howard.

⟨Boston: Published by the American Peace Society, No. 1 Somerset Street. 1887. J. E. Farwell, Printer, 45 Pearl St., Boston.⟩

Single cut sheet folded to four pages. "The People's Song of Peace," p. ⟨4⟩. Previously in *The Song of the Centennial* ⟨1876⟩.

The Elocutionist's Annual Number 15 . . . Compiled by Mrs. J. W. Shoemaker.

Publication Department, the National School of Elocution and Oratory. Philadelphia: 1887.

"The People's Song of Peace," pp. 30-31. Previously in *The Song of the Centennial* ⟨1876⟩.

Wide Awake Pleasure Book Gems of Literature and Art . . .

Boston . . . ⟨1887⟩

For fuller entry see BAL, Vol. 5, p. 113.

. . . Irish Dialect Recitations . . . Edited by George M. Baker . . .

Boston . . . 1888

For fuller entry see BAL, Vol. 3, p. 370.

Poems of Wild Life . . . Edited by Charles G. D. Roberts . . .

London . . . 1888

For comment see BAL, Vol. 1, p. 380.

Tennyson's Fairies and Other Stories . . .

Boston . . . ⟨1889⟩

For fuller entry see BAL, Vol. 5, p. 203.

. . . Harper's Fifth Reader American Authors

New York Harper & Brothers, Franklin Square 1889

Note: Reprinted and reissued by The American Book Company not before 1890. For fuller entry see No. 7917.

Belford's Annual. 1889-90 . . .

Chicago . . . ⟨1889⟩

"Christ and the Children," p. 24; extracted from "Beyond Jordan," *Songs of the Sun-Lands,* 1873. "The Closing Hymn in the upper Room," p. 40; otherwise "The Last Supper," *Songs of the Sun-Lands,* 1873.

For fuller entry see BAL, Vol. V, p. 113.

Boys' and Girls' New Pictorial Library . . . Introduction by . . . Rev. W. H. Milburn . . .

Chicago . . . 1889.

For comment see entry No. 6319.

Borrowings . . .

San Francisco . . . 1889

Untitled poem, p. 60; otherwise the proem to "Olive Leaves," *Songs of the Sun-Lands*, 1873.

For fuller entry see No. 5300.

Half-Hours with the Best Humorous Authors. Selected and Arranged by Charles Morris . . .

Philadelphia: J. B. Lippincott Company. 1889.

4 Vols.

Local and National Poets of America . . . Edited . . . ⟨by⟩ Thos. W. Herringshaw . . .

Chicago . . . 1890.

For fuller entry see BAL, Vol. 2, p. 391.

Younger American Poets 1830–1890 Edited by Douglas Sladen . . .

. . . London . . . 1891

For fuller entry see No. 6557.

Younger American Poets 1830–1890 Edited by Douglas Sladen . . .

. . . New York 1891

For fuller entry see No. 6558.

The Proved Practicability of International Arbitration. — — 1891.

Issued by the Peace Society, 47, New Broad Street, London, E.C. . . .

Caption-title. The above at head of p. ⟨1⟩. 8 pp. pamphlet. Printed self-wrapper.

"The Dying Soldier," p. 8; extracted from "To Die for the Country," *In Classic Shades*, 1890.

Christopher Columbus and His Monument Columbia . . . Compiled by J. M. Dickey.

Chicago and New York: Rand, McNally & Company, Publishers. 1892.

Printed paper boards. Deposited Oct. 17, 1892.

Scrap Book Recitations No. 9. By H. M. Soper . . .

Chicago   T. S. Denison, Publisher   163 Randolph Street ⟨1893⟩

Printed paper wrapper. Deposited May 27, 1893.

Shoemaker's Best Selections . . . Number 21 . . .

Philadelphia . . . 1893

For fuller entry see BAL, Vol. 3, pp. 138-139.

Sun Prints in Sky Tints . . . by Irene E. Jerome

Boston . . . 1893

For fuller entry see BAL, Vol. 2, p. 452.

Readings from California Poets ⟨Selected by⟩ Edmund Russell

. . . San Francisco . . . ⟨n.d., 1893⟩

Contains much material by Miller, including some extracts and altered titles; none here first published in book form.

For fuller entry see BAL, Vol. 3, p. 474.

No. 40. Standard Recitations . . . Compiled . . . by Frances P. Sullivan . . . June 1893 . . .

. . . N. Y. . . . 1893

"O'er the Llano Estacado," p. 25; previously in *One Hundred Choice Selections No. 20* . . . , 1881, under the title "Tantalus: Texas." For fuller entry see BAL, Vol. 3, p. 370.

Martial Recitations . . . Collected . . . by James Henry Brownlee . . .

Chicago . . . ⟨1896⟩

All Miller material herein reprinted from other books. "Peace," p. 5, extracted from *The Song of the Centennial* ⟨1876⟩. For fuller entry see BAL, Vol. 5, p. 338.

The Treasury of American Sacred Song . . . Selected . . . by W. Garrett Horder . . .

London . . . 1896

For fuller entry see BAL, Vol. 5, p. 323.

Shoemaker's Best Selections . . . Number 25 . . .

Philadelphia . . . 1898

For fuller entry see BAL, Vol. 3, p. 139.

Dew Drops and Diamonds . . .

. . . 1898 . . . Chicago . . .

For fuller entry see BAL, Vol. 1, p. 77.

Spanish-American War Songs . . . Compiled . . . by Sidney A. Witherbee.

. . . Detroit . . . 1898.

For comment see entry No. 738.

War Poems 1898 Compiled by the California
Club . . .

    The Murdock Press San Francisco ⟨1898⟩

    For publication notes see under entry No. 738.

War-Time Echoes Patriotic Poems . . . of the
Spanish-American War Selected . . . by James
Henry Brownlee . . .

    The Werner Company New York Akron, Ohio
Chicago ⟨1898⟩

    Listed PW April 8, 1899.

Voices of Peace. Compiled by H. Livinia Bailey . . .

    Published by the Peace Committee of the
National Council of Women of the United
States. Mrs. H. J. Bailey, Chairman, Winthrop
Centre, Maine. ⟨n.d., not before 1899⟩

    Printed paper wrapper?

An American Anthology . . . Edited by Edmund
Clarence Stedman . . .

    Boston . . . M DCCCC

    For comment see entry No. 3082.

Poets and Poetry of Indiana . . . Compiled . . . by
Benjamin S. Parker and Enos B. Heiney . . .

    . . . New York . . . ⟨1900⟩

    All Miller material herein reprinted from other
books. "The Great Discoverer," pp. 339-340;
otherwise "Columbus," *Songs of the Soul*, 1896.
For fuller entry see No. 2974.

. . . By Land and Sea

    1900 Perry Mason & Company Boston, Mass.

    At head of title: *The Companion Series*

. . . Strange Lands near Home

    Boston, U.S.A. Ginn & Company, Publishers
The Athenæum Press 1902

    At head of title: *Youth's Companion Series*

    Deposited Sept. 29, 1902.

Home and School Stories by George C.
Eggleston . . .

    Akron . . . 1904 . . .

    For comment see entry No. 6373.

Little Lads by George Cary Eggleston . . .

    Akron . . . 1904 . . .

    For comment see entry No. 6375.

San Diego and Vicinity Tributes Paid by Well
Known Poets . . . Edited by Allen H. Wright

    1907 San Diego, California Press of San Diego
Herald

    Printed paper wrapper.

Through Italy with the Poets Compiled by Robert
Haven Schauffler . . .

    New York . . . 1908

    For comment see BAL, Vol. 4, p. 446.

"A Book of Verses"

    Published by P.C.: A.C. 1910

    Printed paper wrapper. Unpaged. Contains
"Above the Clouds," extracted from "Isles of
the Amazons," *Songs of the Sun-Lands*, 1873.

Pathway to Western Literature ⟨Edited⟩ by
Nettie S. Gaines . . .

    Stockton, California Nettie S. Gaines All
Rights Reserved ⟨1910⟩

Poems of Country Life . . . ⟨Edited⟩ by George S.
Bryan . . .

    New York . . . 1912

    "The Song of Peace," pp. 166-167; extracted
from *The Song of the Centennial* ⟨1876⟩. For comment see entry No. 7906.

Path Breaking An Autobiographical History of
the Equal Suffrage Movement in Pacific Coast
States. By Abigail Scott Duniway

    ⟨Portland, Oregon: James, Kerns & Abbott
Co., 1914⟩

    On copyright page: *Published June 4, 1914*

One Hundred Choice Selections Number 40 . . .
Edited by Henry Gaines Hawn

    Philadelphia . . . 1914

    For comment see BAL, Vol. 1, p. 77.

A Collection of Verse by California Poets from
1849 to 1915 Compiled by Augustin S. Macdonald . . .

    A. M. Robertson San Francisco 1914

    Erratum slip, pp. 34-35. Printed boards.

300 Latest Stories by 300 Famous Story Tellers . . .

    . . . New York ⟨1914⟩

    For fuller entry see No. 12001.

San Francisco's Welcome from the Panama-Pacific International Exposition . . .

⟨San Francisco: Bolte & Braden Co., n.d., 1915?⟩

Caption-title. The above at head of p. ⟨1⟩. Printed paper wrapper. Cover-title: *Undaunted*

"San Francisco Bay," p. ⟨15⟩; extracted from *Light*, 1907.

Not seen. Entry on the basis of a photographic copy.

Golden Songs of the Golden State Selected by Marguerite Wilkinson

Chicago A. C. McClurg & Co. 1917

On copyright page: *Published November, 1917*

A Roycroft Anthology Selected and Edited by John T. Boyle . . .

The Roycrofters East Aurora, N. Y. MCMXVII

Marbled paper boards, leather shelf back and corners.

St. Nicholas Book of Verse Edited by Mary Budd Skinner and Joseph Osmun Skinner . . .

. . . New York . . . MCMXXIII

. . . Masterpieces of American Humor

Haldeman-Julius Company Girard, Kansas ⟨n.d., 1926⟩

Printed paper wrapper. At head of title: *Little Blue Book No. 959 Edited by E. Haldeman-Julius* Published March 17, 1926; date supplied by Dr. Gene DeGruson, curator, The Haldeman-Julius Collection, Kansas State College.

Songs and Stories Selected . . . by Edwin Markham . . .

Powell Publishing Company San Francisco Los Angeles Chicago ⟨1931⟩

Ballads of Eldorado Selected, with an Introduction by Earle V. Weller . . .

The Book Club of California San Francisco 1940

The St. Nicholas Anthology Edited by Henry Steele Commager . . .

Random House New York ⟨1948⟩

Listed PW Nov. 20, 1948.

REFERENCES AND ANA

Songs of the Sierras. By Joaquin Miller. Extracts from Some Reviews of the New American Poet, Which Have Appeared in the English Literary Journals — — — the Criticisms of Some of the Most Learned Critics of the Day . . .

⟨Boston: Roberts Brothers, 1871⟩

Caption-title. The above on p. 1. Printed self-wrapper.

P. 2: . . . *This selection of Notices from the English Press, of the Poems of Joaquin Miller, a voluntary tribute to American talent and genius, is presented to the American public, with a feeling of national pride, by the Publishers, Roberts Brothers. Boston, September, 1871.*

Songs of the Sand Hills. By Walking Hiller.

San Francisco: A. L. Bancroft and Company, Printers. 1873.

A burlesque. Sometimes misattributed to Miller. Written by Joseph Ross.

Joaquin Miller's Arizonian. Deutsch von Eduard Leyh.

Baltimore, Fischer & Rossmässler, 1874.

Printed paper wrapper. Caption-title, p. 3: *Der Goldgräber von Arizona* . . .

A translation into German. Erroneously listed by Johnson (1942, p. 365) as though an original Miller production.

. . . Chez les Peaux-Rouges Scènes de la Vie des Mineurs et des Indiens de Californie par Joaquin Miller . . .

⟨Paris: Revue Britannique, 1879⟩

Caption-title. At head of title: *Ethnographie* . . .

Not a separate publication as sometimes suggested, but a translation into French of *Life Amongst the Modocs* . . . , London, 1873, and published as pp. ⟨57⟩-118, ⟨343⟩-400, ⟨103⟩-148, ⟨451⟩-488, of *Revue Britannique*, Paris.

The Christmas Bell . . .

New York: Anson D. F. Randolph & Company, 900 Broadway, Cor. 20th St. ⟨1879⟩

A novelty booklet cut in the outline of a bell. Illuminated paper wrapper.

By Joaquin Miller? Untitled two eight-line stanzas beginning: *The Christmas bells as sweetly chime / As in the day when first they rung* . . . , p. 7. Here credited to *Miller*.

How to Win in Wall Street: By a Successful Operator.

New York . . . 1881 . . . G. W. Carleton & Co., Publishers. London: S. Low, Son & Co. MDCCCLXXXI.

Printed paper wrapper; and, cloth.

Sometimes attributed to Joaquin Miller. BAL has been unable to support the attribution. Author unknown.

. . . A Conversation with Joaquin Miller

Reprinted from The Coming Age   Boston April, 1899 . . .

At head of title: *Topics of the Hour*

Cover-title. Printed self-wrapper.

. . . A Little Journey to the Home of Joaquin Miller by Elbert Hubbard Also a Study of the Man and His Work by George Wharton James . . . with Sundry Selected Poems by the Poet . . .

. . . The Roycrofters . . . East Aurora, N. Y. ⟨1903⟩

At head of title: *So Here Then Is*

Flexible suède. Trade printing on paper; also a limited edition (100 copies) on Japanese vellum.

According to the colophon printed Oct. 1903.

Little Lassies by Mary E. Wilkins . . . Joaquin Miller . . .

Akron, Ohio   The Saalfield Publishing Company   New York, 1904 Chicago

Although the title-page lists Miller as one of the contributing authors, the book contains nothing identifiable as his. For a fuller entry see No. 6374.

The Rubaiyát of Omar Kháyyám Translated into English Verse by Edward Fitzgerald; with Illustrations Photographed from Life Studies by Adelaide Hanscom and Blanche Cumming

Published in New York   Dodge Publishing Co. 214-220 East Twenty-Third St. ⟨1912⟩

Leather. "Adelaide Hanscom and Blanche Cumming Express Their Gratitude To Joaquin Miller, George Sterling . . . And Others Who Have Rendered Valuable Assistance In Posing For These Illustrations . . ."---*Preliminary Note.*

A Rare First Edition   Being the Story of Joaquin Miller's Pacific Poems (1871) . . .

Walter M. Hill Chicago 1915

Printed paper wrapper. 100 numbered copies only.

About "The Hights" with Juanita Miller Illustrated by the Author

⟨From the Press of Chas. P. MacLafferty, Oakland, Cal., 1917⟩

Printed stiff paper wrapper. Deposited May 25, 1917.

Joaquin Miller and His Other Self by Harr Wagner

Harr Wagner Publishing Company   San Francisco, California ⟨1929⟩

". . . First Printing Limited to 1100 Copies" ---Certificate of issue. Deposited Oct. 28, 1929.

. . . Joaquin Miller Frontier Poet by Merritt Parmelee Allen

Harper & Brothers Publishers   New York and London 1932

At head of title: *The Long-Rifle Series.*

On copyright page: *First Edition;* and, code letters *G-G*, signifying: *Printed July, 1932.*

Joaquin Miller Literary Frontiersman by Martin Severin Peterson

Stanford University Press Stanford University, California London: Humphrey Milford Oxford University Press ⟨1937⟩

Deposited Aug. 11, 1937.

. . . Bret Harte, Joaquin Miller, and the Western Local Color Story: A Study in the Origins of Popular Fiction . . . Dissertation . . . by Roger Rilus Walterhouse

Private Edition, Distributed by The University of Chicago Libraries Chicago, Illinois 1939

Printed paper wrapper. At head of title: *The University of Chicago*

My Father C. H. Joaquin Miller Poet by Juanita J. Miller.

Tooley-Towne   Oakland Calif. ⟨1941⟩

Limp leather.

Splendid Poseur   Joaquin Miller---American Poet by M. M. Marberry

Thomas Y. Crowell Company   New York ⟨1953⟩

Joaquin Miller by O. W. Frost . . .

Twayne Publishers, Inc. New York ⟨1967⟩

DONALD GRANT MITCHELL

(Jno. Crowquill; Ik. Marvel; An Opera Goer)

1822 – 1908

13920. THE DIGNITY OF LEARNING

1841

Two printings of this oration have been noted. The sequence, if any, has not been determined and the designations are for identification only.

A

THE DIGNITY OF LEARNING. A VALEDIC-TORY ORATION . . . PRONOUNCED BEFORE THE SENIOR CLASS OF YALE COLLEGE, JULY 7, 1841. PUBLISHED BY REQUEST OF THE CLASS.

NEW HAVEN: PRINTED BY B. L. HAMLEN. 1841.

⟨1⟩-30. 9⁵/₁₆″ × 5¹¹/₁₆″.

⟨1⟩¹, 2-4⁴, 5². *Note:* Sig. 5 was originally in 4; as bound leaves 3-4 have been excised.

Printed paper wrapper, both cream and blue papers noted.

Printed from the setting (with alterations in pagination and signing) of the following:

B

POEM, BY GUY BRYAN SCHOTT, AND THE VALEDICTORY ORATION, BY DONALD G. MITCHELL. PRONOUNCED BEFORE THE SENIOR CLASS OF YALE COLLEGE, JULY 7, 1841. PUBLISHED BY REQUEST OF THE CLASS.

NEW HAVEN: PRINTED BY B. L. HAMLEN. 1841.

⟨1⟩-48. 9⁵/₁₆″ × 5¹³/₁₆″.

⟨1⟩-6⁴.

Printed paper wrapper: blue, brown, cream, peach papers noted.

Mitchell's oration, pp. ⟨19⟩-44.

BPL (B)   H (B)   UV (B)   Y (A,B)

13921. Transactions of the New-York State Agricultural Society, together with an Abstract of the Proceedings of the County Agricultural Societies, for the Year 1842. Vol. II.

Albany: E. Mack, Printer to the Senate. 1843. "Plans of Farm Buildings," pp. 125-130.

H

13922. FRESH GLEANINGS; OR, A NEW SHEAF FROM THE OLD FIELDS OF CONTINENTAL EUROPE. BY IK. MARVEL . . .

NEW YORK: HARPER & BROTHERS. 1847.

Title-page in black and red.

PAPER

Note: Title-page in *Part One* only.

1: ⟨i-iv⟩, ⟨i⟩-iv, ⟨1⟩-168. 8⁷/₁₆″ × 5¼″. Wholly untrimmed.

2: ⟨i-iv⟩, 169-336.

1: ⟨-⟩⁴, ⟨A⟩-G¹².

2: ⟨-⟩², H-I, K-O¹².

Printed green paper wrapper.

Note: In *Part Two* ⟨-⟩2r is imprinted with a divisional title-page for *Part Two*; printed in black and red. This feature is not present in the cloth-bound format. ⟨-⟩1 is a blank.

CLOTH

Presumably of the same printing as the two parts format. The divisional title-page and its blank conjugate, present in *Part Two* of the paper format, are not present.

⟨i-iv⟩, ⟨i⟩-iv, ⟨1⟩-336. See under bindings (below) for leaf size.

⟨-⟩⁴, ⟨A⟩-I, K-O¹².

Noted in the following cloth bindings. The sequence has not been established and the designations are all but completely arbitrary.

CLOTH BINDING A

A cloth: brown. TB cloth: green.

218

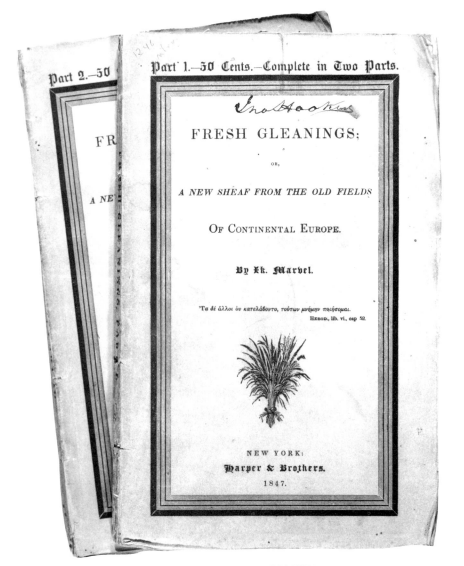

Part 2.—50

Part 1.—50 Cents.—Complete in Two Parts.

FRESH GLEANINGS;

OR,

A NEW SHEAF FROM THE OLD FIELDS

OF CONTINENTAL EUROPE.

By Ik. Marvel.

Τὰ δέ ἄλλοι ὁν κατελάβοντο, τούτων μνήμην ποιήσομαι.
HEROD., lib. vi., cap 52.

NEW YORK:
Harper & Brothers.
1847.

DONALD G. MITCHELL
Entry No. 13922
Reduced
(Harvard University Library)

Front: Blindstamped with a rules frame, a gold-stamped wheat sheaf at center.

Back: All the preceding repeated in blind.

Spine goldstamped: FRESH / GLEANINGS. / ⟨*rule*⟩ / MARVEL. / NEW-YORK. / HARPER & BROTHERS Spine decorated with an arrangement of three blind-stamped fillets and blindstamped rules.

End papers: Pale yellow. Also: White end papers.

Flyleaves: At both front and at back, a gathering of four leaves; one leaf pasted under the end paper; a leaf pasted to the end paper as a lining; two leaves left free. Also noted with single flyleaves.

Leaf: 8½″ scant × 5⅛″ (wholly untrimmed). 8¹⁄₁₆″ × 5″ (top edges untrimmed, other edges lightly trimmed).

CLOTH BINDING B

T cloth: black.

Front: Blindstamped with a rules frame, a gold-stamped wheat sheaf at center.

Back: All the preceding repeated in blind.

Spine goldstamped: FRESH / GLEANINGS. / ⟨*rule*⟩ / MARVEL. / NEW-YORK, / HARPER & BROTHERS Spine decorated with an arrangement of three blind-stamped fillets and blindstamped rules.

End papers: White end papers.

Flyleaves: Two at front, one at back.

Leaf: 8″ × 5″ scant (top edges untrimmed, other edges trimmed).

CLOTH BINDING C

A cloth: black.

Front: Blindstamped with a rules frame, a gold-stamped wheat sheaf at center.

Back: All the preceding repeated in blind.

Spine goldstamped: FRESH / GLEANINGS. / ⟨*rule*⟩ / MARVEL. / NEW-YORK, / HARPER & BROTHERS Spine decorated with an arrangement of three blind-stamped fillets and blindstamped rules.

End papers: Yellow-coated.

Flyleaves: Triple.

Leaf: 7¹¹⁄₁₆″ × 5″ (all edges trimmed).

CLOTH BINDING D

A cloth: slate.

Sides: Blindstamped with a rococo frame, enclosed by a triple rule frame.

Spine goldstamped: FRESH / GLEANINGS. / ⟨*rule*⟩ / MARVEL. / NEW-YORK, / HARPER & BROTHERS. Spine decorated in blind with an arrangement of rules and fillets.

End papers: White.

Flyleaves: Single.

Leaf: 7⅝″ × 4¹⁵⁄₁₆″ (all edges trimmed).

Note: Erroneous sig. mark F* is present on p. 105 of all examined copies, including an 1851 reprint.

Listed (1 vol., cloth; 2 parts in paper) LW Aug. 14, 1847. Reviewed NYM Aug. 14, 1847; LW Aug. 21, 1847; AWR Aug. 1847. Deposited Sept. 16, 1847. For another edition see below under year 1851.

AAS (paper; *Cloth A*) B (*Cloth A*) BA (*Cloth D*) H (paper; *Cloth A; Cloth B*) NYPL (paper; *Cloth A; Cloth C*) UV (*Cloth A*) Y (paper; *Cloth A*)

13923. Transactions of the New-York State Agricultural Society. With an Abstract of the Proceedings of the County Agricultural Societies. Vol. VII. 1847.

Albany: C. Van Benthuysen, Public Printer. 1848.

Report by Mitchell and others, pp. 107-109.

H

13924. THE BATTLE SUMMER: BEING TRANSCRIPTS FROM PERSONAL OB-SERVATION IN PARIS, DURING THE YEAR 1848. BY IK. MARVEL . . .

NEW YORK: BAKER AND SCRIBNER. 1850.

⟨i-iv⟩, ⟨i⟩-⟨x⟩, ⟨v⟩-⟨x⟩, ⟨1⟩-289, blank leaf. Frontispiece and vignette title-page inserted. 7⁵⁄₁₆″ × 4¹⁵⁄₁₆″.

⟨1⁸, 2¹, 3-26⁶, 27²⟩. Leaf ⟨1⟩₇ inserted. *Signed:* ⟨-⟩¹⁰, 1-12¹², ⟨13⟩².

Two printings noted; the order as here given is presumed correct:

1

As above.

Vignette title-page dated 1850.

Between pp. 288-289 is an inserted slip imprinted: PUBLISHERS' NOTICE. *The sequel to the "Battle Summer," to be entitled "Reign of Bourgeois," will be published early in the spring.*

2

⟨-⟩¹⁰, 1-12¹², ⟨13⟩².

Vignette title-page undated.

Publishers' Notice not present.

Two bindings noted; the following variations are sufficient for identification:

STATE A BINDING

H cloth: black. T cloth: brown. TB cloth: blue; blue-gray; green. B&S device blindstamped at center of covers. Yellow end papers. Flyleaves. Edges plain. Noted only on first printing sheets.

STATE B BINDING

AR cloth: purple; slate-blue. T cloth: brown. A goldstamped coat of arms at center of sides. Yellow end papers. Top edges gilt; or, all edges stained red. Flyleaves. Noted only on second printing sheets with the exception of the following:

Note: A binding variant has been seen (BA): Sheets of the first printing; vignette title-page undated; bound in *State B* binding.

Advertised for *this week* LW Dec. 15, 1849. Published Dec. 21, 1849 (Dunn). A copy in UV (restored, not here located) inscribed by the author Dec. 24, 1849; in *State A Binding.* Listed LW Jan. 5, 1850. Reviewed LW Jan. 5, 1850. Deposited Jan. 7, 1850 (first printing). A new edition, uniform with *Reveries of a Bachelor,* advertised NLA Sept. 15, 1851. The London edition advertised by Bentley for *the present month* Ath Feb. 23, 1850. Under *importations* noted as *recent* Ath Feb. 23, 1850; PC March 1, 1850. Again announced by Bentley Ath March 2, 1850; no further Bentley notes. As an importation listed PC June 1, 1850.

AAS (1st, 2nd) BPL (1st, 2nd) H (1st, 2nd) LC (1st) Y (1st)

13925. .... THE LORGNETTE OR STUDIES OF THE TOWN BY AN OPERA GOER ...

Cover-title.

Issued in 24 paper-covered parts. The wrappers vary in color from buff to pale yellow. Size of leaf (largest noted): $8\frac{1}{2}'' \times 5\frac{3}{16}''$. Size of leaf (smallest noted): $7\frac{3}{4}'' \times 5\frac{1}{8}''$.

Each part dated and numbered in the heading, first page of text.

For a revised edition see next entry.

Part 1

At head of title: *No. 1. One Shilling.*

Imprint: NEW-YORK: HENRY KERNOT, 633 BROADWAY. MDCCCL.

Date of issue: Jan. 20.

⟨1⟩-22, blank leaf.

1-2⁶.

Locations: AAS   CC   H   Y

Part 2

At head of title: *No. 2. One Shilling.*

Imprint: NEW-YORK: HENRY KERNOT, 633 BROADWAY. MDCCCL.

Date of issue: Jan. 30.

⟨23⟩-41.

3⁶, 4⁴.

Locations: CC   H   Y

Part 3

At head of title: *No. 3. One Shilling.* The CC, NYPL, Y copies thus. The copy in H is in a wrapper imprinted *No. 5,* the *5* altered by hand (pen and ink) to *3.*

Imprint: NEW-YORK: HENRY KERNOT, 633 BROADWAY. MDCCCL.

Date of issue: Feb. 7.

⟨43⟩-64; blank leaf.

5-6⁶.

Locations: CC   H   NYPL   Y

Part 4

At head of title: *No. 4. One Shilling.*

Imprint: NEW-YORK: HENRY KERNOT, 633 BROADWAY. MDCCCL.

Date of issue: Feb. 14.

⟨65⟩-85; blank, pp. ⟨86-88⟩.

7-8⁶.

Locations: CC   H   Y

Part 5

At head of title: *No. 5. One Shilling.*

Imprint: NEW-YORK: HENRY KERNOT, 633 BROADWAY. MDCCCL.

Date of issue: Feb. 21.

⟨87⟩-110.

9-10⁶.

Locations: H

Part 6

At head of title: *No. 6. One Shilling.*

Imprint: NEW-YORK: HENRY KERNOT, 633 BROADWAY. MDCCCL.

Date of issue: Feb. 28.

⟨111⟩-133.

11-12⁶.

Locations: CC   H   Y

Part 7

At head of title: *No. 7. One Shilling.*

Imprint: NEW-YORK: HENRY KERNOT, 633 BROADWAY. MDCCCL.

Date of issue: March 7.

⟨135⟩-160.

13⁶, 14*⁶, 15¹.

Locations: AAS   CC   H   Y

Part 8

At head of title: *No. 8. One Shilling.*

Imprint: NEW-YORK: HENRY KERNOT, 633 BROAD-
WAY. MDCCCL.

Date of issue: March 14.

⟨161⟩-186.

16-17⁶, 18¹.

Locations: CC   H   Y

Part 9

At head of title: *No. 9. One Shilling.*

Imprint: NEW-YORK: HENRY KERNOT, 633 BROAD-
WAY. MDCCCL.

Date of issue: March 28.

⟨187⟩-212.

19-20⁶, 21¹.

Locations: CC   H   Y

Part 10

At head of title: *No. 10. One Shilling.*

Imprint: NEW-YORK: HENRY KERNOT, 633 BROAD-
WAY. MDCCCL.

Date of issue: April 4.

⟨213⟩-237.

22-23⁶, 24¹.

Locations: CC   H   Y

Part 11

At head of title: *No. 11. One Shilling.*

Imprint: NEW-YORK: HENRY KERNOT, 633 BROAD-
WAY. MDCCCL.

Date of issue: April 11.

⟨239⟩-266.

25-26⁶, 27².

Locations: AAS   CC   H   Y

Part 12

At head of title: *No. 12. One Shilling.*

Imprint: NEW-YORK: HENRY KERNOT, 633 BROAD-
WAY. MDCCCL.

Date of issue: April 24.

⟨267⟩-294.

28-29⁶, 30².

Locations: AAS   CC   H   Y

Part 13

At head of title: *No. 13. New Series, No. 1. CNE*
⟨sic⟩ *SHILLING.*

Imprint: NEW-YORK: HENRY KERNOT, 633 BROAD-
WAY. MDCCCL. Also noted with the following
imprint: NEW-YORK: STRINGER & TOWNSEND,
222 BROADWAY. MDCCCL.

Date of issue: May 10.

⟨1⟩-24.

1-2⁶.

Locations: AAS (Kernot imprint)   CC (Stringer &
Townsend imprint)   H (Kernot imprint)
Y (Kernot imprint)

Part 14

At head of title: *No. 14. New Series, No. 2. ONE*
SHILLING.

Imprint: NEW-YORK: STRINGER & TOWNSEND, 222
BROADWAY. MDCCCL.

Date of issue: May 25.

⟨25⟩-48.

3-4⁶.

Locations: AAS   CC   H   Y

Part 15

At head of title: *No. 15. New Series, No. 3 ONE*
SHILLING.

Imprint: NEW-YORK: STRINGER & TOWNSEND, 222
BROADWAY. HENRY KERNOT, 633 BROADWAY.
MDCCCL.

Date of issue: June 10.

⟨49⟩-79.

5-6⁶, 7⁴.

Locations: CC   H   Y

Part 16

At head of title: *No. 16. New Series, No. 4. ONE*
SHILLING.

Imprint: NEW-YORK: STRINGER & TOWNSEND, 222
BROADWAY. HENRY KERNOT, 633 BROADWAY.
MDCCCL.

Date of issue: June 24.

⟨81⟩-106.

8-9⁶, 10¹.

Locations: CC   H   Y

Part 17

At head of title: *No. 17. New Series, No. 5. ONE*
SHILLING.

Imprint: NEW-YORK: STRINGER & TOWNSEND, 222
BROADWAY. HENRY KERNOT, 633 BROADWAY.
MDCCCL.

Date of issue: July 8.

⟨107⟩-129.

11-12⁶.

Locations: CC   Y

Part 18

At head of title: *No. 18. New Series, No. 6. ONE*
SHILLING.

Imprint: NEW-YORK: STRINGER & TOWNSEND, 222 BROADWAY. HENRY KERNOT, 633 BROADWAY. MDCCCL.

Date of issue: July 20.

⟨131⟩-150; 2 blank leaves.

13-14⁶.

Locations: AAS   CC   H   Y

Part 19

At head of title: *No. 19. New Series, No. 7. ONE SHILLING.*

Imprint: NEW-YORK: STRINGER & TOWNSEND, 222 BROADWAY. HENRY KERNOT, 633 BROADWAY. MDCCCL.

Date of issue: August 4.

⟨151⟩-174.

15-16⁶.

Locations: CC   Y

Part 20

At head of title: *No. 20. New Series, No. 8 ONE SHILLING.*

Imprint: NEW-YORK: STRINGER & TOWNSEND, 222 BROADWAY. HENRY KERNOT, 633 BROADWAY. MDCCCL.

Date of issue: August 18.

⟨175⟩-200. 4-line errata notice at foot of p. 200.

17-18⁶, 19¹.

Locations: AAS   CC   H   Y

Part 21

At head of title: *No. 21. New Series, No. 9 ONE SHILLING.*

Imprint: NEW-YORK: STRINGER & TOWNSEND, 222 BROADWAY. HENRY KERNOT, 633 BROADWAY. MDCCCL.

Date of issue: August 31.

⟨201⟩-227.

20-21⁶, 22².

Locations: CC   Y

Part 22

At head of title: *No. 22. New Series, No. 10. ONE SHILLING.*

Imprint: NEW-YORK: STRINGER & TOWNSEND, 222 BROADWAY. HENRY KERNOT, 633 BROADWAY. MDCCCL.

Date of issue: September 11.

⟨229⟩-250; blank leaf. 10-line errata notice at foot of p. 250.

23-24⁶

Locations: CC   H   Y

Part 23

At head of title: *No. 23. New Series, No. 11. ONE SHILLING.*

Imprint: NEW-YORK: STRINGER & TOWNSEND, 222 BROADWAY. HENRY KERNOT, 633 BROADWAY. MDCCCL.

Date of issue: September 25.

⟨251⟩-271; blank, pp. ⟨272-274⟩.

25-26⁶.

Locations: CC   H   Y

Part 24

At head of title: *No. 24 Last Number. ONE SHILLING.*

Imprint: NEW-YORK: STRINGER & TOWNSEND, 222 BROADWAY. HENRY KERNOT, 633 BROADWAY. MDCCCL.

Date of issue: October 9.

⟨273⟩-298; *Press notices,* pp. ⟨1⟩-6. Portrait frontispiece inserted.

27-28⁶, 29⁴.

Locations: CC (incomplete; Sig. 29 in proof)   H   Y

Publication notes: Part 1 advertised for Jan. 23, LW Jan. 26, 1850. A New York letter dated Oct. 18, 1850, in SLM Nov. 1850: "The last number has just been issued." Noted as "recently brought to a close" K Jan. 1850. See next entry. Also see under year 1851.

13926. The Lorgnette: Or, Studies of the Town. By an Opera Goer . . . Second Edition . . .

New York. Printed for Stringer and Townsend, and for Sale at 222 Broadway, and All Respectable Book-Shops. ⟨1850⟩

For first edition see preceding entry. See below under year 1851 for the *Fourth Edition.*

2 Vols.

VOL. I

"To My Readers," pp. ⟨iii⟩-vi. Dated at end *July the 10th, MDCCCL.* Written for this edition.

"Carefully revised" according to an advertisement LW Aug. 17. 1850.

Two printings noted:

VOL. I, FIRST PRINTING

Preliminary gathering in 6. Imprint of *Edward O. Jenkins* and copyright notice on verso of the title-leaf.

VOL. I, SECOND PRINTING

Preliminary gathering in 12. Copyright notice only on verso of the title-leaf.

Advertised as *ready* LW Aug. 17, 1850. Listed LW Aug. 24, 1850. Deposited Sept. 21, 1850. The Thomas Delf (London) importation listed PC March 1, 1851. The Newby (London) edition noted as *in press* Ath Dec. 13, 1851; listed PC Jan. 1, 1852. *Note:* Although the Newby edition is described as *in press* it was in fact made up of American sheets with cancel title-leaf imprinted: *London: Thomas Cautley Newby . . . 1852.*

VOL. 2

"To My Readers," pp. ⟨iii⟩-iv, dated at end *December the 4th, MDCCCL.* Written for this edition.

Vols. 1-2 noted in SLM Nov. 1850.

AAS (Vol. 1, 1st; Vol. 1, 2nd; Vol. 2) BA (Vol. 2) BPL (Vol. 2) H (Vol. 1, 1st; Vol. 1, 2nd; Vol. 2) NYPL (Vol. 2) UV (Vol. 1, 1st; Vol. 2) Y (Vol. 1, 1st; Vol. 1, 2nd; Vol. 2)

13927. REVERIES OF A BACHELOR: OR A BOOK OF THE HEART. BY IK. MARVEL
. . .

NEW YORK: BAKER & SCRIBNER. 1850.

⟨i⟩-⟨xiv⟩, ⟨15⟩-298; advertisements, p. ⟨299⟩; blank, p. ⟨300⟩. Frontispiece and vignette title-page inserted. See below under bindings for leaf size.

⟨1-25⁶⟩. Signed: ⟨1⟩-4, ⟨5⟩-⟨7⟩, 8-12¹², 13⁶.

Contemporary notices suggest that the book went into two or more printings before alteration of the title-page. BAL has been unable to identify more than a single printing. Evidence of worn plates supports the belief of several printings. The following notes may be an aid in the further investigation indicated:

P. ⟨29⟩, last line: Note the word *sleep*

P. 43, last line: Note the word *escapes*

In known reprints the words cited are printed from battered metal.

Sheets have been noted in the following styles of binding. A sequence has not been established and the designations, intended only for identification, are all but arbitrary. Yellow end papers, single flyleaves.

TENTATIVE BINDING A

A cloth: brown; blue; green; green-gray; purple-brown.

Edges: Top edges gilded.

Sides: Frame stamped in blind, cluster stamped in gold.

Spine: Decorated with four goldstamped acorn clusters; the stems point as follows: right, left, right, left.

Leaf size: 7½″ full × 4¹⁵⁄₁₆″.

Locations: AAS BPL NYPL UV Y (including a copy inscribed Dec. 13, 1850)

TENTATIVE BINDING B

A cloth: blue.

Edges: All edges stained red.

Sides: Frame stamped in blind, cluster stamped in gold.

Spine: Decorated with four goldstamped acorn clusters; the stems point as follows: right, left, right, left.

Leaf size: 7⁵⁄₁₆″ × 4¾″ full.

Locations: NYPL Y

TENTATIVE BINDING C

A cloth: blue. H cloth: brown.

Edges: All edges gilded.

Sides: Frame stamped in gold, acorn cluster stamped in gold.

Spine: Decorated with four goldstamped acorn clusters; the stems point as follows: right, left, right, left.

Leaf size: 7⁵⁄₁₆″ × 4¾″ full.

Locations: UV Y

Note: A copy at UV, presumably the publisher's personal copy, has end papers unlike those noted on any other copy: Blue-coated, printed in gold with a pattern of maltese cross-like ornaments. (Usual end papers are plain yellow.)

TENTATIVE BINDING D

A cloth: blue-green; gray-green.

Edges: Top edges gilded.

Sides: Frame stamped in blind, acorn cluster stamped in gold.

Spine: Decorated with four goldstamped acorn clusters; the stems point as follows: left, right, left, right.

Leaf size: 7⅜″ × 4⅞″.

Locations: H Y

TENTATIVE BINDING E

A cloth: blue. H cloth: brown.

Edges: Top edges gilded.

Sides: Frame stamped in blind, acorn cluster stamped in gold.

Spine: Decorated with four goldstamped acorn clusters; the stems point as follows: right, left, left, right.

Leaf size: 7⁵⁄₁₆″ × 4⅞″.

Locations: Y

TENTATIVE BINDING F

A cloth: purple-brown. H cloth: brown.

Edges: All edges plain.

Sides: Frame stamped in blind, acorn cluster stamped in gold.

Spine: Decorated with four goldstamped acorn clusters; the stems point as follows: left, right, left, right.

Leaf size: $7\frac{3}{8}'' \times 4\frac{7}{8}''$.

Locations: AAS   NYPL

PERSONAL BINDINGS

According to the publisher's records eight copies were custom bound for the use of the author. The following designations are wholly arbitrary and are for identification only. All eight bindings were billed to Mitchell on Dec. 31, 1850.

A: Extra gilt morocco. See description below. Three copies bound thus.

B: Half morocco. Two copies bound thus. Unlocated by BAL.

C: Three-quarters leather. See description below. Three copies bound thus.

PERSONAL BINDING A

Full brown morocco. Covers bevelled. Sides stamped in gold and blind with a rules frame enclosing a filigree. Spine lettered in gold: REVERIES / OF / A BACHELOR / BY / IK. MARVEL Spine decorated with four boxed filigrees in gold, blindstamped rules, five false bands. Cream-coated end papers. Dentelles. Leaf: $7\frac{3}{16}'' \times 4\frac{11}{16}''$ scant. All edges gilded. Flyleaves.

Locations: Y

PERSONAL BINDING B

Unlocated.

PERSONAL BINDING C

Brown A cloth sides, brown morocco shelfback and corners. Spine lettered in gold: REVERIES / OF / A BACHELOR / BY / IK. MARVEL Cream-coated end papers. Leaf: $7\frac{3}{8}''$ full $\times 4\frac{7}{8}''$. Top edges gilded.

Locations: NYPL

Noted as *in press* LW March 23, 1850. Deposited Nov. 25, 1850 (publisher's records). Noted as *just appeared* LW Dec. 7, 1850. A copy (in GD, *Tentative Binding B*) inscribed by the author Dec. 7, 1850. A copy (in Y, *Tentative Binding A*) inscribed by an early owner Dec. 13, 1850. The *5th thousand* advertised LW Feb. 1, 1851. "Scarcely a month out and now in its fifth edition of a thousand copies each"———K Feb. 1851. The *10th thousand* advertised NLA June, 1851. LW Nov. 8, 1851, noted receipt of a newly stereotyped printing with illustrations by Darley; cloth and morocco bindings advertised as *in a few days* LW Nov. 15, 1851.

NLA Nov. 15, 1851 reported fifteen printings of the book. The Darley edition listed LW Dec. 13, 1851; NLA Dec. 15, 1851. The *20th thousand* advertised NLG March 15, 1852. See next entry. Also see under years 1863, 1884, 1895.

LONDON PUBLICATION

The John Chapman importation reviewed LG June 7, 1851. The *9th edition*, illustrations by Darley, no publisher mentioned, noted by Ath July 26, 1851. The Delf & Trübner importation advertised as *new* Ath March 6, 1852. The Bogue edition listed by Ath May 8, 1852; LG May 8, 1852; PC May 15, 1852. A Simpkin, Marshall edition listed by *The English Catalogue of Books* . . . , 1852. The Clarke, Beeton & Company edition advertised Ath Dec. 18, 1852; listed Ath Jan. 1, 1853; PC Jan. 17, 1853. A Simpkin, Marshall edition listed PC Feb. 1, 1862.

13928. A BACHELOR'S REVERIE: IN THREE PARTS. I. SMOKE———SIGNIFYING DOUBT. II. BLAZE———SIGNIFYING CHEER. III. ASHES———SIGNIFYING DESOLATION. BY IK: MARVEL.

WORMSLOE ⟨Georgia⟩. MDCCCL.

⟨1⟩-40; colophon, p. ⟨41⟩. $10\frac{1}{4}'' \times 6\frac{1}{4}''$.
⟨1⟩-5⁴, ⟨6⟩¹.

Noted in Roxburghe binding only; no two being precisely the same.

"This edition of twelve copies . . . hath been: by the Authour's Leave: printed Privately for George Wymberley-Jones."———Colophon.

A reprint of the text as published in SLM Sept.–Oct. 1849; not a printing of the text as published in the preceding entry.

Precise date of publication not known. In the Y copy is a typed transcript of a letter, Winthrop Sargent to Mitchell, Nov. 8, 1850, requesting permission for an unnamed friend to reprint the piece in this limited edition. The issue of SLM containing the text was issued under date *Sept.–Oct. 1849.*

H   NYPL   Y

13929. The Lorgnette . . . by an Opera Goer . . . Fourth Edition . . .

New York. Printed for Stringer and Townsend, and for Sale at 222 Broadway, and All Respectable Book-Shops. 1851.

For first and second editions see above under year 1850.

2 Vols.

"Preface to the Fourth Edition," Vol. 1, pp. ⟨iii⟩-x.

Noted as *just ready* NLA April 15, 1851. Advertised as *lately issued* LW June 21, 1851. Reviewed Ath June 28, 1851; AWR June 1851. Advertised as *just published* LW July 15, 1851.

Using the word 'edition' as used by the publishers in their advertising, the publication history of this book appears to be:

Vol. 1 (*i.e.*, First Series)

1st edition: Issued in parts. See above under year 1850.

2nd edition: 1 Vol., cloth. Marked *Second Edition*. The first printing has the *Jenkins* imprint on the copyright page. See above under year 1850.

3rd edition: 1 Vol., cloth. Marked *Second Edition*. Being the second printing of the immediate preceding. Does not have the *Jenkins* imprint on the copyright page.

4th edition: Title-page marked: *Fourth Edition*.

Query: Was this ever issued with the statement *Third Edition* on the title-page? Presumably not.

Vol. 2 (*i.e.*, Second Series)

1st edition: Issued in parts. See above under year 1850.

2nd edition: 1 Vol., cloth. Marked *Second Edition*. See above under 1850.

3rd edition: 1 Vol., cloth. Marked *Third Edition*. Reprint.

4th edition: Title-page marked *Fourth Edition*.

AAS   BPL   Y

13930. Fresh Gleanings; or, a New Sheaf from the Old Fields of Continental Europe. By Ik. Marvel . . .

New York: Charles Scribner. 1851.

For first edition see above under year 1847.

Contains "A New Preface," dated at end *May 30, 1851*.

Several printings have been noted.

FIRST PRINTING

The first printing may be identified by the presence of horizontal rules on the copyright page.

REPRINTS

The book went into at least five reprints, none of which have horizontal rules on the copyright page.

At least three bindings have been noted. The following designations are for identification only and are all but completely arbitrary.

BINDING A

A cloth: blue; slate; purple; gray-green. T cloth: blue-green; gray-green. Sides stamped in blind with a rustic frame; a wheat sheaf stamped in gold at center. Edges plain. All edges trimmed. Noted on first printing sheets; also noted on reprints.

BINDING B

A cloth: blue; gray-green. H cloth: slate-purple. Sides blindstamped with a rustic frame; a wheat sheaf stamped in gold at center. All edges trimmed and stained red. Noted on first printing sheets; also noted on reprints.

BINDING C

A cloth: blue; brown. Sides stamped in gold with a rustic frame and a wheat sheaf at the center. Edges trimmed and gilded. Noted on reprints only.

Listed LW June 28, 1851. A surviving deposit copy (rebound, uncollatable) was received Oct. 6, 1851; clearly a reprint since it lacks the horizontal rules on the copyright page.

AAS (1st in *Binding A*; reprints in *Binding A*, *Binding C*) BPL (reprint in *Binding A*) H (1st in *Binding A*; reprint in *Binding A*) UV (reprint in *Binding A*) Y (reprint in *Binding A*, reprint in *Binding B*)

13931. DREAM LIFE: A FABLE OF THE SEASONS. BY IK. MARVEL . . .

NEW YORK: CHARLES SCRIBNER. 1851.

Four printings noted:

FIRST PRINTING

It will be observed that the title-leaf is a cancel; the reason for this has not been determined. Further investigation wanted.

⟨i-ii⟩, ⟨i⟩-⟨viii⟩, ⟨11⟩-286; blank leaf. Frontispiece inserted. For leaf size see below. Also see below regarding a leaf of advertisements found in some copies. For other editions see under years 1863, 1884,

Leaf: $7\frac{7}{16}'' \times 4\frac{7}{8}''$ full (top edges gilded, other edges plain). $7\frac{5}{16}''$ full $\times 4\frac{7}{8}''$ scant (all edges gilded).

⟨1-24⁶⟩. *Signed:* ⟨1⟩-3, ⟨4⟩-12¹². Leaf ⟨1⟩₁ is a cancel.

Inserted between ⟨24⟩₅₋₆ of some copies is a leaf of advertisements: Recto: *Darley's Illustrated Edition of Reveries of a Bachelor . . .* ; verso: *Fresh Gleanings . . .*

TYPOGRAPHIC FEATURES

Benedict imprint on copyright page.

P. ⟨v⟩: The word PAGE is present at head of column of references.

P. ⟨v⟩: Six dots (not five) before number 56.

P. vi: The word WORLD (entry for p. 150) unbroken in copies first printed.

P. ⟨31⟩: The *O* in *Or* is $\frac{1}{16}''$ full tall.

P. 207, last line: The word *dignity* is unbroken. In a known reprint the word is printed from battered metal. In an 1852 printing the word has been replaced and reads: *diginty* ⟨sic⟩.

Noted in the following bindings (see below): A, B, Ba, D.

Locations: AAS (*Binding A*) B (*Binding B*) H (*Binding B*) LC (*Bindings B, Ba*) NYPL (*Binding B*) UV (*Bindings A, B; the B binding inscribed by the author Dec. 24, 1851*) Y (*Bindings A, B, D*)

SECOND PRINTING

⟨i-ii⟩, ⟨i⟩-⟨viii⟩, ⟨11⟩-286; blank leaf. Frontispiece inserted. The title-leaf (⟨1⟩₁) is not a cancel. See below for leaf size.

⟨1⟩-3, ⟨4⟩, 5-12¹².

TYPOGRAPHIC FEATURES

Benedict imprint on copyright page.

P. ⟨v⟩: The word PAGE is present at head of column of references.

P. ⟨v⟩: Five dots (not six) before number 56.

P. vi: The word WORLD printed from battered metal.

P. ⟨31⟩: The *O* in *Or* is $\frac{1}{16}''$ full tall.

P. 207, last line: The word *dignity* is unbroken.

Leaf size: $7\frac{3}{8}''$ full × $4\frac{7}{8}''$ (top edges gilded, other edges trimmed). $7\frac{3}{8}''$ full × $4\frac{7}{8}''$ full (all edges stained red).

Noted in the following bindings (see below): B, D.

Locations: AAS (*Binding B*) H (*Binding B*) NYPL (*Bindings B, D*) UV (*Binding B*) Y (*Bindings B, D*)

THIRD PRINTING

⟨i-ii⟩, ⟨i⟩-⟨viii⟩, ⟨11⟩-286; blank leaf. Frontispiece inserted. The title-leaf (⟨1⟩₁) is not a cancel. See below for leaf size.

⟨1⟩-3, ⟨4⟩, 5-12¹².

TYPOGRAPHIC FEATURES

Printer's imprint not present on copyright page.

P. ⟨v⟩: The word PAGE is not present at head of column.

P. ⟨v⟩: Five dots (not six) before number 56.

P. vi: The word WORLD broken.

P. ⟨31⟩: The *O* in *Or* is $\frac{1}{16}''$ full tall.

P. 207, last line: The word *dignity* is broken.

Leaf size: $7\frac{3}{8}'' \times 4\frac{15}{16}''$ (top edges gilded, other edges trimmed).

Noted in the following bindings (see below): B, C.

Locations: AAS (*Binding B*) BPL (*Binding B*) H (*Binding B*) NYPL (*Binding B*) UV (*Binding C*)

FOURTH PRINTING

⟨i-ii⟩, ⟨i⟩-⟨viii⟩, ⟨11⟩-286; blank leaf. Frontispiece inserted. The title-leaf (⟨1⟩₁) is not a cancel. See below for leaf size.

⟨1⟩-3, ⟨4⟩, 5-12¹².

TYPOGRAPHIC FEATURES

Printer's imprint not present on copyright page.

P. ⟨v⟩: The word PAGE is not present at head of column.

P. ⟨v⟩: Five dots (not six) before number 56.

P. vi: The word WORLD broken.

P. ⟨31⟩: The *O* in *Or* is $\frac{1}{8}''$ scant tall.

P. 207, last line: The word *dignity* is broken.

Leaf size: $7\frac{5}{16}'' \times 4\frac{7}{8}''$ (top edges gilded, other edges trimmed).

Noted in the following binding: B

Locations: NYPL (*Binding B*)

Five bindings noted. The sequence has not been established and the following designations are all but arbitrary:

TENTATIVE BINDING A

A cloth: green; purple-brown. Stamped completely in gold. Yellow end papers. Flyleaves. All edges gilt.

Noted only on the *First Printing.*

Locations: AAS   UV   Y

TENTATIVE BINDING B

A cloth: black; blue; brown; purple; purple-brown; slate; slate-green. Sides blindstamped with a rustic frame within a single rule box, a goldstamped cluster of grapes at center. Yellow end papers. Flyleaves. Top edges gilded, other edges plain.

Noted on: *First Printing* (one being inscribed by Mitchell Dec. 24, 1851); *Second Printing; Third Printing; Fourth Printing.* Also noted on the 1861 printing.

Locations: AAS (2nd, 3rd printings) B (1st printing) BPL (3rd printing) NYPL (1st, 2nd, 3rd, 4th printings) Y (1st, 2nd printings)

TENTATIVE BINDING Ba

Same as *Tentative Binding B* but all edges stained red.

Noted on: *First Printing.*

Locations: LC

TENTATIVE BINDING C

Same as *Tentative Binding B* save for one exception: The goldstamped grapes on the sides are inverted; *i.e.*, the stem is at the bottom, not at the top.

Noted on: *Third Printing.*

Locations: UV

TENTATIVE BINDING D

A cloth: blue. Sides blindstamped with a rustic frame within a single rule box, a goldstamped cluster of grapes at center. Yellow end papers. Flyleaves. All edges stained red.

Noted on: *First Printing; Second Printing.*

Locations: NYPL Y

Advertised as *in press* and *for immediate publication* NLA Sept. 15, 1851. Advertised for Nov. 22 NLA Nov. 15, 1851. Advertised for *this week* LW Dec. 13, 1851. Listed as a November publication (prematurely?) NLA Dec. 15, 1851. A copy in UV (first printing) inscribed by Mitchell Dec. 24, 1851. Listed LW Dec. 27, 1851. The *10th thousand* advertised NLG Feb. 15, 1852. The *14th thousand* advertised NLG March 15, 1852.

LONDON PUBLICATION

As an importation: Advertised by Delf & Trübner PC March 1, 1852. Listed PC March 1, 1852. Delf & Trübner importation advertised Ath March 3, 1852. The John Chapman importation reviewed Ath May 1, 1852.

British produced editions: A *T. Nelson & Sons* issue published under date MDCCCLIII. *Edward Howell* (*Liverpool*): Listed Ath Sept. 16, 1853. *Routledge* (?): Listed PC May 2, 1853. *Ward & Lock:* Listed PC Aug. 1, 1857.

13932. The Knickerbocker Gallery: A Testimonial to the Editor of the Knickerbocker Magazine from Its Contributors . . .

New-York: Samuel Hueston, 348 Broadway. MDCCCLV.

"The Bride of the Ice-King," pp. ⟨39⟩-57.

For comment see entry No. 1033.

13933. FUDGE DOINGS: BEING TONY FUDGE'S RECORD OF THE SAME. IN FORTY CHAPTERS. BY IK. MARVEL . . .

NEW YORK: CHARLES SCRIBNER. 1855.

1: ⟨i-vi⟩, ⟨i⟩-xii, ⟨19⟩-235; blank, pp. ⟨236-240⟩. *Note:* The initial and terminal blank leaves excised or pasted under the end papers. Frontispiece inserted. $7\frac{3}{16}''$ full × $4\frac{7}{8}''$ scant.

2: ⟨i⟩-viii, ⟨9⟩-257; blank, pp. ⟨258-264⟩. *Note:* The final blank leaf excised or pasted under the end paper. Frontispiece inserted.

⟨1⟩-10^{12}. Leaves ⟨1⟩$_1$ and 10$_{12}$ excised or pasted under the end papers.

⟨1⟩-11^{12}. Leaf 11$_{12}$ excised or pasted under the end paper.

T cloth: gray-green. TZ cloth: brown; purple. Yellow end papers. Flyleaf at front of Vol. 2. Top edges gilt.

Deposited Dec. 15, 1854 (publisher's records). Listed NLG Jan. 1, 1855. A copy in H inscribed by early owner Jan. 5, 1855. Listed PC Jan. 16, 1855; no record of British printing found. Deposited Feb. 16, 1855 (Copyright Office records). A surviving copyright deposit copy has stamped date of receipt: Feb. 1, 1856⟨*sic*⟩.

AAS B BA BPL H NYPL Y

13934. AGRICULTURAL ADDRESS DELIVERED BEFORE THE CONNECTICUT STATE AGRICULTURAL SOCIETY, AT BRIDGEPORT . . .

PUBLISHED BY THE SOCIETY. 1858.

⟨1⟩-27. $8\frac{15}{16}'' \times 5\frac{11}{16}''$.

⟨1⟩-3^4, 4^2.

Printed yellow-coated paper wrapper.

The address was delivered Oct. 15, 1857.

AAS NYPL Y

13935. Report of the Proceedings of the Twenty-Fifth Anniversary of the Brotherhood of Alpha Delta Phi, Held in New York, 24th and 25th June, 1857. Issued by the Fraternity.

New York: Charles Scribner, 377 & 379 Broadway. M.DCCC.LVIII.

"The Oration," pp. 14-37.

Note: UV has a set of folded sheets, prior to binding, of the oration.

Collected in *Bound Together*, 1884.

H MHS NYPL Y

13936. The Norwich Jubilee. A Report of the Celebration at Norwich, Connecticut, on the Two Hundredth Anniversary of the Settlement of the Town, September 7th and 8th, 1859 . . . Compiled, Printed and Published by John W. Stedman . . .

Norwich, Conn. 1859.

Reply to an invitation, Nov. 10, 1858, p. 15.

"Address," pp. 175-186.

The address, with some revisions, collected in *Bound Together*, 1884, as "Beginnings of an Old Town."

Title deposited Nov. 18, 1859.

H Y

13937. MY FARM OF EDGEWOOD: A COUNTRY BOOK. BY THE AUTHOR OF "REVERIES OF A BACHELOR." . . .

NEW-YORK: CHARLES SCRIBNER. 1863.

Title-page printed in black and red.

⟨i-ii⟩, ⟨i⟩-⟨xii⟩, ⟨1⟩-319. $7\frac{3}{8}'' \times 4\frac{7}{8}''$ (edges stained red). $7\frac{11}{16}'' \times 5\frac{1}{16}''$ (edges unstained). Laid paper.

⟨-⟩⁷, 1-13¹², 14⁴. Leaf ⟨-⟩3 (the title-leaf) inserted.

Two printings noted; the following variations are sufficient for identification:

FIRST PRINTING

P. ⟨vii⟩: The initial *A* is $\frac{3}{16}''$ tall.

P. ⟨xi⟩: Numeral *I.* present.

P. ⟨111⟩: Numeral *III.* present.

P. ⟨219⟩: Numeral *IV.* present.

SECOND PRINTING

P. ⟨vii⟩: The initial *A* is $\frac{5}{16}''$ tall.

P. ⟨xi⟩: Numeral *I.* not present.

P. ⟨111⟩: Numeral *III.* not present.

P. ⟨219⟩: Numeral *IV.* not present.

Noted in the following bindings; the sequence is presumed correct:

BINDING A

A cloth: purple. HC cloth: purple. Covers bevelled. Sides blindstamped with a panel. Front stamped in gold: MY FARM / OF EDGEWOOD Spine stamped in gold: ⟨*fillet*⟩ / MY FARM ⟨*in a circular frame*⟩ / IK. MARVEL / ⟨*rule*⟩ / ⟨*fillet*⟩ Brown-coated end papers. Laid paper flyleaves. Edges stained red.

Noted on: *First Printing* only.

Locations: B   H   Y

BINDING Aa

A cloth: purple. Sides unstamped. Covers not bevelled. Printed paper label on spine, printed in black and red: MY FARM / OF / EDGEWOOD. / ⟨*rule*⟩ / BY THE AUTHOR OF / *"Reveries of a Bachelor."* / ⟨*rule*⟩ / NEW YORK:1863. / ⟨*all of the preceding in a box*⟩ Brown-coated end papers. Laid paper flyleaves. Top edges untrimmed; other edges either trimmed or rough-trimmed. Edges not stained, not gilded.

Noted on: *First Printing* only.

Locations: B   H   Y (the author's personal copy, inscribed: *Home copy. 1st edition*)

BINDING B

A cloth: purple. Covers bevelled. Sides blind-stamped with a panel. Front stamped in gold: MY FARM / OF EDGEWOOD Spine stamped in gold: MY FARM ⟨*in a circular frame*⟩ / IK. MARVEL / ⟨*rule*⟩ / Note absence of fillets. Brown-coated end papers. Laid paper flyleaves. Edges stained red.

Noted on: *Second Printing* only.

Locations: AAS   UV

BINDING C

A cloth: purple. Sides unstamped. Covers not bevelled. Spine stamped in gold: MY FARM / OF / EDGEWOOD. / ⟨*rule*⟩ / BY THE AUTHOR OF / *"Reveries of a Bachelor."* / ⟨*rule*⟩ / NEW YORK:1863. / ⟨*all the preceding in a goldstamped single rule frame*⟩ Brown-coated end papers. Wove, or laid, paper flyleaves. All edges trimmed. Edges not stained, not gilded.

Noted on: *Second Printing* only.

Locations: AAS   Y

Note: According to contemporary notices (*e.g.*, APC Oct. 1, 1863) the book was available also in half calf; and, morocco.

Advertised for *about the 20th September* APC Sept. 1, 1863. Advertised for Oct. 17 APC Oct. 1, 1863. Deposited (according to the publisher's records) Oct. 23, 1863. A copy of the second printing in UV inscribed by the author Oct. 29, 1863. Listed APC Nov. 2, 1863. Advertised as *just published* APC Nov. 2, 1863. Deposited Dec. 16, 1863 (Copyright Office records). The *8th edition* advertised APC Dec. 1, 1863. For another edition see under 1884.

London publication: Advertised (an importation?) by Low for Nov. 20 in PC Nov. 16, 1863. Advertised for *next week* Ath Nov. 21, 1863; as *just ready* Ath Nov. 28, 1863; for *Monday next* ⟨*i.e.*, Dec. 7⟩ Ath Dec. 5, 1863. Listed Ath Dec. 12, 1863; PC Dec. 15, 1863. Advertised without comment PC Dec. 31, 1863. Reviewed Ath Jan. 9, 1864.

13938. Dream Life . . . by Ik. Marvel . . . a New Edition.

New York: Charles Scribner, 124 Grand Street. 1863.

For first edition see above under year 1851; also see under year 1884.

"A New Preface," dated Sept. 1863, pp. ⟨iii⟩-xiv.

Listed ALG Nov. 16, 1863, as in both cloth; and, morocco. Listed as a *Trübner* importation PC Dec. 8, 1863. Deposited Dec. 16, 1863.

AAS   H

13939. Reveries of a Bachelor: Or a Book of the Heart. By Ik. Marvel . . . a New Edition.

New York: Charles Scribner, 124 Grand Street. 1863.

For first edition see above under 1850; also see under years 1884, 1895.

"A New Preface," dated *Edgewood, 1863*, pp. ⟨v⟩-viii.

Listed ALG Nov. 16, 1863, as in both cloth; and, morocco. Listed PC Dec. 8, 1863; Bkr June 30, 1864.

AAS H Y

13940. The Spirit of the Fair . . .

New York . . . 1864.

"A Soldier's Dream," No. 8, p. 89.

Extracts from *Seven Stories* . . . , 1864 (see next entry): No. 12, pp. 139-140; No. 13, pp. 151-152; No. 15, p. 176; No. 16, pp. 187-188; No. 17, pp. 198-199.

For fuller entry see No. 11186.

13941. SEVEN STORIES, WITH BASEMENT AND ATTIC. BY THE AUTHOR OF "MY FARM OF EDGEWOOD."

NEW-YORK: CHARLES SCRIBNER. 1864.

Title-page in black and red.

⟨i⟩-viii, ⟨1⟩-314; advertisement, p. ⟨315⟩. Laid paper. For leaf size see below under binding.

⟨-⟩^{4}, 1-8, 13⟨*sic*⟩, 10-13^{12}, 14^2.

Noted in the following bindings. The designations are more or less arbitrary and are designed for identification:

BINDING A

A cloth: purple-tan. Sides blindstamped with a rules panel. Front goldstamped: SEVEN STORIES / WITH BASEMENT / AND ATTIC Spine goldstamped: SEVEN / STORIES / ⟨*preceding two lines in a wreath*⟩ / IK. MARVEL / ⟨*rule*⟩ / ⟨*spine imprint?*⟩ Covers bevelled. Brown-coated end papers. Laid paper flyleaves. Edges stained red. Leaf: $7\frac{5}{16}''$ scant × $4\frac{7}{8}''$ scant. Blindstamped rules (triple?) at top and at bottom of spine.

Locations: H (inscribed by early owner May 25, 1864)

BINDING B

A cloth: blackish-slate; green. Printed paper label on spine in black and red: SEVEN / STORIES, / WITH / *Basement and Attic.* / ⟨*rule*⟩ / BY THE AUTHOR OF / "*Reveries of a Bachelor.*" / ⟨*rule*⟩ / NEW YORK:1864. / ⟨*all of the preceding in a box*⟩ Covers not bevelled. Top edges gilt. Brown-coated end papers. Laid paper flyleaves. $7\frac{1}{2}''$ × $5\frac{1}{8}''$. Sides not stamped.

Locations: UV (inscribed by Mitchell June 10, 1864) Y (inscribed by Mitchell June 10, 1864)

BINDING C

A cloth: blackish-slate; blue-gray; purple. HC cloth: purple. Sides blindstamped with a triple rule frame. Front cover not lettered. Spine goldstamped: SEVEN / STORIES, / WITH / *Basement and Attic* / ⟨*rule*⟩ / *By the Author of* / "*Reveries of a Bachelor*" / ⟨*rule*⟩ / NEW YORK:1864. / ⟨*all the preceding in a box*⟩ Blindstamped triple rule at top and at bottom of spine. Covers bevelled. Brown-coated end papers. Laid, or wove, flyleaves. Edges plain. Leaf: $7\frac{5}{16}''$ scant × $4\frac{7}{8}''$ scant.

Locations: AAS B (inscribed by an early owner Oct. 1864) H NYPL Y

BINDING D

A cloth: purple. Sides unstamped. Spine goldstamped: SEVEN / STORIES, / WITH / *Basement and Attic.* / ⟨*rule*⟩ / *By the Author of* / "*Reveries of a Bachelor.*" / ⟨*rule*⟩ / NEW YORK:1864. / ⟨*all the* preceding in a box⟩ Covers not bevelled. Top edges gilded. Brown-coated end papers. Laid paper flyleaves. $7\frac{7}{16}''$ × $4\frac{15}{16}''$.

Locations: Y

BINDING E

A cloth: purple. Covers bevelled. Sides stamped in blind with a panel but no lettering is present. Spine stamped in gold: SEVEN / STORIES, / WITH / *Basement and Attic* / ⟨*rule*⟩ / *By the Author of* / "*Reveries of a Bachelor.*" / ⟨*rule*⟩ / NEW YORK:1864/ ⟨*all the preceding in a box*⟩ At top and at bottom of spine, in blind, a triple rule. Brown-coated end papers. Laid paper flyleaves.

Locations: GD

BINDING F

C cloth: green. Probably *ca.* 1867. The following is sufficient for identification: Spine stamped in gold: ⟨*fillet*⟩ / SEVEN STORIES / WITH / BASEMENT & ATTIC. / ⟨*circular ornament decorated with ivy-like leaves*⟩ / *Donald G. Mitchell* / ⟨*fillet*⟩ Covers not bevelled. Yellow end papers. Laid paper flyleaves. Edges plain. $7\frac{5}{16}''$ × $4\frac{7}{8}''$.

Locations: BPL Y

BINDING G

A quite late binding. Basically the same as *Binding F* but the spine imprint of *Scribner, Armstrong & Co.* is present. Issued *ca.* 1872.

Locations: Y

"We understand that they are printing nine thousand of Ik Marvel's new book as the first edition."---ALG May 2, 1864. Deposited May 4, 1864 (publisher's records). Advertised for May 21 PW May 16, 1864. BA copy (rebound) received May 22, 1864. Listed PW June 1, 1864; PC July 15, 1864. Deposited July 29, 1864 (Copyright Office records).

13942. WET DAYS AT EDGEWOOD: WITH OLD FARMERS, OLD GARDENERS, AND OLD PASTORALS. BY THE AUTHOR OF "MY FARM OF EDGEWOOD."

NEW YORK: CHARLES SCRIBNER. 1865.

Title-page in black and red.

⟨i-iv⟩, ⟨i⟩-⟨viii⟩, ⟨1⟩-324. Laid paper. Illustrated. For leaf size see below under binding.

⟨-⁶, 1-13¹², 14⁶⟩. *Signed:* ⟨-⟩⁶, ⟨1⟩-3, 5⟨*sic*⟩, 5-20⁸, 21².

Noted in the following bindings; the sequence is presumed correct.

BINDING A

P cloth: purple. Sides blindstamped with a double rule frame. Spine goldstamped: WET DAYS / AT / EDGEWOOD. / ⟨*rule*⟩ / BY THE AUTHOR OF / *My Farm of Edgewood* / ⟨*rule*⟩ / NEW YORK 1865. / ⟨*all the preceding in a box*⟩ Brown-coated end papers; yellow paper end papers. Laid paper flyleaves. Top edges gilt. *Also:* Brown-coated end papers, all edges stained red. Leaf: 7³⁄₈″ full × 5″.

Locations: BPL (received Dec. 20, 1864) LC (being a deposit copy) Y

BINDING Aa

P cloth: purple. Sides unstamped. Printed paper label on spine, dated 1865. Yellow end papers. Laid paper flyleaves. Top edges gilt. Leaf: 7¹⁄₂″ scant × 5″ scant.

Locations: Gd (inscribed by Mitchell *Xmas 1864*)

BINDING B

C cloth: green. Sides blindstamped with a triple rule frame. Spine stamped in gold: ⟨*fillet*⟩ / WET DAYS / AT / EDGEWOOD. / ⟨*ornament*⟩ / *Donald G. Mitchell* / SCRIBNERS. / ⟨*fillet*⟩ Yellow end papers. Laid paper flyleaves. Leaf ⟨-⟩₁ excised. Top edges plain. Leaf: 7³⁄₈″ × 5″.

Locations: AAS Y

BINDING C

C cloth: green. Sides blindstamped with a triple rule frame. Spine stamped in gold: ⟨*fillet*⟩ / WET DAYS / AT / EDGEWOOD. / ⟨*ornament*⟩ / *Donald G. Mitchell* / ⟨*fillet*⟩ Pale peach end papers. Wove paper flyleaves.

Locations: UV Y

BINDING D

Not before *ca.* 1872. Issued with the spine imprint of *Scribner, Armstrong & Co.*

Locations: LC Y

Announced under the title *Wet Weather Work* ALG June 15, 1864. Advertised for *early in October* ALG Sept. 1, 1864; as *ready December 7* ALG Dec. 1, 1864. BPL copy (*Binding A*) received Dec. 20, 1864. Listed ALG Jan. 2, 1865. Deposited March 8, 1865. For another edition see below under year 1884.

London publication: Listed as an importation PC Feb. 1, 1865. Advertised by Low Ath Feb. 4,

1865, as an importation. Announced by Low for *Monday* (*i.e.,* June 5) PC June 1, 1865; Ath June 3, 1865. Listed PC June 15, 1865. Reviewed Ath July 15, 1865.

13943. DOCTOR JOHNS: BEING A NARRATIVE OF CERTAIN EVENTS IN THE LIFE OF AN ORTHODOX MINISTER OF CONNECTICUT. BY THE AUTHOR OF "MY FARM OF EDGEWOOD." . . .

NEW YORK: CHARLES SCRIBNER AND COMPANY. 654 BROADWAY. 1866.

2 Vols. Title-pages in black and red.

1: ⟨i-ii⟩, ⟨1⟩-300; 2 blank leaves, the second of which excised or pasted under the end paper. Laid paper. 7³⁄₈″ × 4⁷⁄₈″.

2: ⟨i-ii⟩, ⟨1⟩-295.

1: ⟨1¹, 2-13¹², 14⁸⟩. Leaf ⟨14⟩₈ excised or pasted under the end paper. *Signed:* ⟨-⟩¹, 1-18⁸, 19⁷.

2: ⟨1¹, 2-13¹², 14⁴⟩. *Signed:* ⟨-⟩¹, 1-18⁸, 19⁴.

Note: The *fifth thousand* advertised in ALG Oct. 1, 1866. BAL has been unable to identify two printings of this book.

Noted in the following bindings. No firm sequence has been established and the order of presentation is all but arbitrary. The designations are for identification only:

BINDING A

C cloth: green. Spine goldstamped: ⟨*triple rule*⟩ / DOCTOR / JOHNS. / ⟨*rule*⟩ / *Donald G. Mitchell* / VOL. I ⟨II⟩ / ⟨*triple rule*⟩ Brown-coated end papers. Laid paper flyleaf at front of Vol. 1; laid paper flyleaves in Vol. 2.

A copy thus deposited for copyright Sept. 21, 1866. A copy thus in H inscribed by an early owner *October 1866.* A copy thus in UV inscribed by Mitchell Dec. 20, 1866.

Locations: AAS H LC (Vol. 1 only) NYPL UV Y

BINDING B

C cloth: green. Spine goldstamped: ⟨*fillet with a leaf-like pendant*⟩ / DOCTOR / JOHNS. / ⟨*rule*⟩ / VOL. I ⟨II⟩ / ⟨*ornament: a circular device surmounted by a leafy spray*⟩ / *Donald G. Mitchell* / ⟨*fillet, surmounted by a leaf-like ornament*⟩

Locations: NYPL Y

BINDING C

C cloth: green. Spine goldstamped: ⟨*fillet with a leaf-like pendant*⟩ / DOCTOR / JOHNS. / ⟨*rule*⟩ / VOL. I. ⟨II.⟩ / ⟨*ornament: a circular device surmounted by a leafy spray*⟩ / *Donald G. Mitchell* / C. SCRIBNER & Cᵒ / ⟨*fillet, surmounted by a leaf-like ornament*⟩

Locations: NYPL

BINDING D

C cloth: green. Spine goldstamped: ⟨*fillet, with a leaf-like pendant*⟩ / DOCTOR / JOHNS. / ⟨*rule*⟩ / VOL. I. ⟨II.⟩ / ⟨*ornament: a circular device surmounted by a leafy spray*⟩ / *Donald G. Mitchell* / SCRIBNERS. / ⟨*fillet, surmounted by a leaf-like ornament*⟩

Locations: Y

BINDING E

Issued two-volumes-in-one. Green P cloth. The following spine imprint present: SCRIBNER, ARMSTRONG & CO. Issued not before *ca.* 1872.

Locations: UV

Nearly ready---ALG Aug. 15, 1866. Deposited Aug. 25, 1866 (publisher's records). Deposited Sept. 21, 1866 (Copyright Office records). Listed ALG Oct. 1, 1866. The *fifth thousand* advertised ALG Oct. 1, 1866. For another edition see below under the year 1884.

London publication: The American printing listed PC Oct. 1, 1866. Advertisements and notices of Low's edition indicate that it was printed in Great Britain; the following notes refer to Low's edition. Advertised PC Oct. 17, 1866; *just ready* Ath Oct. 20, 1866; *ready* PC Nov. 1, 15, 1866. Listed (as an English book) Ath Oct. 27, 1866; Bkr Oct. 31, 1866; PC Nov. 1, 1866. Reviewed Ath Nov. 3, 1866.

13944. RURAL STUDIES WITH HINTS FOR COUNTRY PLACES. BY THE AUTHOR OF "MY FARM OF EDGEWOOD."

NEW YORK: CHARLES SCRIBNER & CO. 1867.

Title-page in black and red.

⟨i-iv⟩, ⟨i⟩-iv, ⟨vii⟩-⟨x⟩, ⟨1⟩-295; blank, p. ⟨296⟩; plus 3 pp. advertisements. Illustrated. $7\frac{3}{8}'' \times 5''$. *See note below for a comment on the pagination.*

⟨a⟩⁴, ⟨b⟩², 1-12¹², 13⁴, plus ⟨c⟩². All examined copies have p. 55 missigned *2**; should be *3**.

Two states (printings?) noted:

1

The final page of the preface is paged *iv*.

2

The final page of the preface is paged *vi*.

C cloth: green. Brown-coated end papers. Flyleaves. Publisher's spine imprint not present; see comment below.

A copy of the first state has been seen in a variant binding, having the spine imprint of *Scribner, Armstrong & Co.* Issued thus not before 1872. Copy in Y presented by the author in 1876.

Listed ALG June 1, 1867, "308 pages." Deposited June 3, 1867. BPL copy (1st) received June 3, 1867. BA copy (1st) received June 4, 1867. Again

listed ALG July 1, 1867, "295 pages." See *Out-of-Town Places . . .* , 1884, below.

London publication: Listed (as an importation) PC July 1, 1867. Advertised as *Rural Essays* for *Monday next* (*i.e.*, July 8) Ath July 6, 1867. Advertised without comment Ath July 13, 1867. Listed as *Rural Studies* Ath July 13, 1867. As a British publication listed PC Aug. 1, 1867; ALG Aug. 1, 1867.

AAS (1st) B (2nd) BA (1st) BPL (1st) H (1st) LC (1st) NYPL (1st) UV (2nd) Y (1st, 2nd)

13945. The Atlantic Almanac 1868 Edited by Oliver Wendell Holmes and Donald G. Mitchell . . .

Boston: Ticknor and Fields, Office of the Atlantic Monthly . . . 1867 . . .

"A Talk about the Year. Winter Talk," pp. 15-17.

"Spring Talk," pp. 31-33.

"Summer Talk," pp. 35-37.

"Autumn Talk," pp. 53-57.

With some textual variations collected in *Bound Together*, 1884, as "Procession of the Months."

For fuller entry see No. 266.

13946. The Atlantic Almanac 1869 Edited by Donald G. Mitchell . . .

Boston: Ticknor and Fields, Office of The Atlantic Monthly . . . 1868 . . .

"Fireside," pp. 3-7. Collected in *Bound Together*, 1884, as "Fires and Fireside."

The following contributions have not been located elsewhere:

"Roadside," pp. 16-20.

"Brookside," pp. 25-28.

"Side by Side," pp. 37-40.

For fuller entry see No. 4037.

13947. PICTURES OF EDGEWOOD; IN A SERIES OF PHOTOGRAPHS, BY ROCKWOOD, AND ILLUSTRATIVE TEXT, BY THE AUTHOR OF "MY FARM OF EDGEWOOD."

NEW YORK: CHARLES SCRIBNER AND COMPANY. 1869.

⟨1⟩-65. Portrait frontispiece, 11 plates, 1 double-leaf plate inserted. $12\frac{1}{2}'' \times 10''$ scant.

⟨1⟩-16², 17¹.

C cloth: green. FL cloth: green. Green-coated end papers. Top edges gilt. Flyleaves; or, double flyleaves.

According to Mitchell's *ms* autobibliography "300 copies only" were prepared.

"Will be published in November"———ALG Nov. 2, 1868. Advertised by Trübner as an importation Bkr Dec. 12, 1868, *only 300 copies printed*. A copy in Y inscribed by Mitchell Oct. 1869. Advertised for Nov. 13 ALG Nov. 1, 1869. Listed ALG Dec. 1, 1869; PC Feb. 1, 1870.

H Y

13948. The Sayings of Dr. Bushwhacker, and Other Learned Men. By Frederic S. Cozzens . . .

New York: Published by Hurd and Houghton. Cambridge: Riverside Press. 1871.

Mitchell's sketch of Cozzens, pp. ⟨xxiii⟩-xxvii.

For fuller entry see No. 4011.

13949. Sixth Annual Report of the American Dairymen's Association . . . for the Year 1870. Published by the Association.

   Syracuse, N.Y.: Truair, Smith & Co., Printers, Daily Journal Office. 1871.

Printed paper wrapper.

"An Address Delivered before the American Dairymen's Association, at Utica, N. Y., on Wednesday, January 11th, 1871 . . . on Some of the Relations of Science to Farm Practice," pp. ⟨59⟩-74.

Y

13950. Alpha Delta Phi Reunion Dinner in New York 1875 with a Register of Members in New York

   New York Privately Printed 1876

Letter, pp. 14-15, *Edgewood, November 16 ⟨1875⟩*.

Printed paper wrapper.

H NYPL

13951. Alpha Delta Phi New England Graduate Association Proceedings and Dinner April 27th, 1876

   Boston Privately Printed 1876

Contains, p. 15, an inconsequential 5-line note of refusal, *Edgewood, April 26, 1876*.

Printed paper wrapper.

H

13952. . . . Ninth Annual Report of the Secretary of the Connecticut Board of Agriculture. 1875-'76 . . .

Hartford: Press of the Case, Lockwood & Brainard Co. 1876.

At head of title: *State of Connecticut*.

"Fences and Division of Farm Lands," pp. 171-186. Replies to questions, pp. 186–187.

Y

13953. Twenty-Fourth Annual Report of the Secretary of the Massachusetts Board of Agriculture . . . for 1876.

   Boston: Albert J. Wright, State Printer, 79 Milk Street (Corner of Federal). 1877.

"The Farmer's Homestead, and Its Relation to Farm Thrift," pp. 131-141.

Y

13954. ABOUT OLD STORY-TELLERS: OF HOW AND WHEN THEY LIVED, AND WHAT STORIES THEY TOLD . . .

   NEW YORK: SCRIBNER, ARMSTRONG, & CO. 1878.

Title-page in black and red.

⟨i-ii⟩, ⟨i⟩-⟨xvi⟩, 17-237, blank leaf. Frontispiece inserted; other illustrations in text. $7\frac{1}{4}'' \times 5\frac{1}{4}''$.

⟨1^9, 2-15^8⟩. ⟨1⟩$_3$ (the title-leaf) inserted.

Two printings noted:

FIRST PRINTING

On copyright page: Imprint of *Rand, Avery, and Company*.

SECOND PRINTING

On copyright page: Imprint of *Trow's Printing and Bookbinding Co.*

Reissued under date ⟨1877⟩ by *Charles Scribner's Sons*.

S cloth: blue; green; mauve; orange; red; terracotta. Brown-coated end papers. Top edges gilded. Flyleaves.

Advertised for *next week* PW Nov. 17, 1877. Listed PW Dec. 1, 1877.

AAS (2nd) B (1st) BA (1st) BPL (1st) H (1st) NYPL (1st) Y (1st, 2nd)

13955. Proceedings of the Harvard Club of New York City . . . Delmonico's February 21st, 1878

   New York G. P. Putnam's Sons 182 Fifth Avenue 1878

Printed paper wrapper.

Address, pp. 17-21. Elsewhere unlocated.

H

13956. The Atlantic Monthly Supplement. The Holmes Breakfast . . .

⟨n.p., n.d., Boston, February, 1880⟩

Letter, p. 21, *Edgewood, Thanksgiving Day, November, 1879.*

For fuller entry see No. 10440.

13957. DESCRIPTION OF LAFAYETTE COLLEGE AND VICINITY, EASTON, PA.

⟨n.p., n.d., *ca.* 1880⟩

⟨1⟩-14, blank leaf. Illustrated. $9^{13}/_{16}'' \times 6^{15}/_{16}''$.

⟨-⟩⁸.

Printed tan paper wrapper. *Note:* Two states of the wrapper have been seen; the sequence, if any, has not been established and the designations are for identification only:

WRAPPER A

The back wrapper is blank.

WRAPPER B

The back wrapper imprinted with an illustration captioned: *Lafayette College Gymnasium.*

A revision of "Lafayette College," *Scribner's Monthly,* Dec. 1876.

H (*Wrapper B*) NYPL (*Wrapper B*) Y (*Wrapper A*)

13958. A REPORT TO THE COMMISSIONERS ON LAY-OUT OF EAST ROCK PARK . . .

NEW HAVEN: L. S. PUNDERSON, BOOK AND JOB PRINTER. 1882.

⟨1⟩-20. Folded map inserted. $9^{5}/_{16}'' \times 5^{7}/_{8}''$.

⟨1-2⁴, 3²⟩.

Printed paper wrapper; blue, tan noted. Two states of the wrapper have been noted. Sequence, if any, not determined. The designations are for identification only.

WRAPPER A

Tan and blue noted.

Imprinted: NEW HAVEN: / L. S. PUNDERSON, PRINTER AND LITHOGRAPHER. / 1882.

WRAPPER B

Tan noted.

Imprinted: NEW HAVEN: / L. S. PUNDERSON, BOOK PRINTER AND LITHOGRAPHER. / 1882.

AAS (A) BA (B) H (B) Y (A,B)

13959. . . . The Woodbridge Record Being an Account of the Descendants of the Rev. John Woodbridge of Newbury, Mass. Compiled from the Papers Left by the Late Louis Mitchell, Esquire

Privately Printed at New Haven, 1883.

Edited by Donald G. and Alfred Mitchell. "Prefatory," by Donald G. Mitchell, pp. 1-3.

At head of title: *Viventes enim Sciunt se esse Morituros* . . .

Printed paper wrapper; and, vellum.

"Two Hundred Copies Only Of This Book Have Been Printed, Of Which This Is No. . . ."---Certificate of issue.

AAS   B   H   NYPL   Y

13960. Daniel Tyler: A Memorial Volume Containing His Autobiography and War Record . . .

Privately Printed at New Haven MDCCC LXXXIII

Edited by Mitchell. "The children of the late General Daniel Tyler have desired me to edit, and supervise the printing of the papers which make up this Memorial Volume . . ."---P. ⟨ix⟩.

Noted in the following bindings; sequence, if any, not known and the designations are for identification only:

BINDING A

S cloth: purple. Covers bevelled. Goldstamped. Leaf: $10^{3}/_{8}'' \times 8^{1}/_{2}''$. Top edges gilded.

BINDING B

V cloth: white. Covers bevelled. Sides stamped in blind. Printed paper label on spine. Leaf: $10^{5}/_{8}'' \times 8^{5}/_{8}''$. Wholly untrimmed, top edges not gilded. Copies thus have been noted (H, Y) inscribed by Mitchell Nov. 1883; Dec. 19, 1883.

AAS (A)   B (B)   BPL (A)   H (B)   NYPL (B)   Y (A,B)

13961. Reveries of a Bachelor or a Book of the Heart: By Ik Marvel . . . New and Revised Edition

New York   Charles Scribner's Sons   1884

For first edition see under the year 1850; also see under years 1863, 1895.

"A New Preface," dated *Aug., 1883,* pp. ⟨xiii⟩-xxi.

". . . I . . . have made, a few verbal emendations ---a little coy toning down of over-exuberance . . ."---P. xix.

Published Sept. 15, 1883 (publisher's records). Advertised PW Sept. 22, 1883. Listed PW Sept. 29, 1883. Advertised PW Nov. 17, 1883. A large paper printing, limited to 250 numbered copies, was advertised for Dec. 15 PW Dec. 8, 1883.

London publication: The Low edition advertised as *forthcoming* PC Dec. 31, 1883. Noted as *nearly ready*

PC Feb. 2, 1884; PC Feb. 15, 1884. Listed PC March 1, 1884.

H NYPL UV Y

13962. Dream Life: A Fable of the Seasons by the Author of "Reveries of a Bachelor." . . .

New York Charles Scribner's Sons 1884

For first edition see under year 1851; also see under year 1863.

"A New Preface," dated *Sept., 1883*, pp. ⟨v⟩-viii.

Published Oct. 23, 1883 (publisher's records). Deposited Oct. 29, 1883. Listed PW Nov. 24, 1883. A large paper printing, limited to 250 numbered copies, was advertised for Dec. 15, PW Dec. 8, 1883. The London (Low) edition was advertised PC Dec. 31, 1883; listed PC March 1, 1884.

NYPL UV Y

13963. Wet Days at Edgewood with Old Farmers, Old Gardeners, and Old Pastorals by the Author of "My Farm of Edgewood."

New York Charles Scribner's Sons 1884

For first edition see above under year 1865.

"Prefatory Note," dated *1883*, p. ⟨vii⟩.

Published Oct. 23, 1883 (publisher's records). Deposited Oct. 29, 1883. Listed PW Nov. 24, 1883. The London (Low) edition advertised PC Dec. 31, 1883; listed PC March 1, 1884.

AAS H LC NYPL UV Y

13964. Doctor Johns Being a Narrative of Certain Events in the Life of an Orthodox Minister of Connecticut by the Author of "Reveries of a Bachelor" New and Revised Edition

London Sampson Low, Marston, Searle & Rivington 1884

Not seen. For American printing see next entry.

Advertised PC Dec. 31, 1883. Listed PC March 1, 1884.

13965. Doctor Johns . . . by the Author of "Reveries of a Bachelor" New and Revised Edition

New York Charles Scribner's Sons 1884

For first edition see under year 1866. For prior publication see preceding entry.

Published March 15, 1884 (publisher's records). Deposited March 22, 1884. Listed PW March 22, 1884.

H Y

13966. BOUND TOGETHER: A SHEAF OF PAPERS BY THE AUTHOR OF "WET DAYS AT EDGEWOOD," . . .

NEW YORK CHARLES SCRIBNER'S SONS 1884

Title-page in black and red.

⟨i⟩-viii, ⟨1⟩-291. Laid paper. $7\frac{1}{4}'' \times 4\frac{7}{8}''$.

⟨a⟩², ⟨b⟩², ⟨1-2⟩, 3-10, ⟨11⟩-18⁸, 19².

Straw-colored buckram. White laid end papers. Single flyleaves of laid or wove paper. Top edges gilt.

Published March 22, 1884 (publisher's records). Deposited March 22, 1884. H copy received March 22, 1884. Listed PW March 29, 1884. The London (Low) edition announced PC April 15, 1884; listed PC Sept. 1, 1884.

AAS B BA H LC Y

13967. Out-of-Town Places: With Hints for Their Improvement by the Author of "Wet Days at Edgewood" [A Re-Issue of "Rural Studies"]

New York Charles Scribner's Sons 1884

For first edition see *Rural Studies . . .* , 1867.

"Prefatory Note," dated *April, 1884*, pp. ⟨iii⟩-iv.

Published May 15, 1884 (publisher's records). BPL copy received May 16, 1884. Deposited May 20, 1884. Listed PW May 24, 1884. The London (Low) edition noted as *in a few days* PC May 15, 1884; advertised as *now ready* PC July 1, 1884; listed PC Aug. 15, 1884.

AAS BPL H LC Y

13968. My Farm of Edgewood A Country Book by the Author of "Reveries of a Bachelor" . . .

New-York Charles Scribner's Sons 1884

"Avant-Propos," pp. ⟨iii⟩-iv. Dated at end: *Edgewood, October 28, 1884.*

For first edition see above under year 1863.

"This edition is limited to fifty copies. Each copy is numbered and registered. This is No. . . ."--- P. ⟨ii⟩.

Paper boards, imitation vellum shelf back.

Advertised for Oct. 18 PW Oct. 11, 1884.

Y

13969. . . . Readings from Macaulay. Italy. With an Introduction by Donald G. Mitchell . . .

Boston: Chautauqua Press, 117 Franklin Street. 1885.

At head of title: *Chautauqua Library Garnet Series.*

"Lord Macaulay," pp. iii-xiv.

Deposited Sept. 12, 1885. Noted as though published PW Oct. 3, 1885. Listed PW Oct. 24,

1885. Reprinted and reissued ⟨1889⟩ by *Educational Publishing Company*, Boston.

AAS   BPL   LC   NYPL   Y

13970. Appletons' Cyclopædia of American Biography Edited by James Grant Wilson and John Fiske . . .

New York D. Appleton and Company 1, 3 and 5 Bond Street 1887 ⟨–1889⟩

"Washington Irving," Vol. 3, pp. 360-363.

For comment see entry No. 6020.

13971. ENGLISH LANDS LETTERS AND KINGS FROM CELT TO TUDOR . . .

NEW YORK   CHARLES SCRIBNER'S SONS MDCCC-LXXXIX

Title-page in black and sepia.

For other volumes in this series see under 1890, 1895, 1897.

⟨i⟩-⟨xii⟩, ⟨1⟩-327. Laid paper; pp. ⟨i-iv⟩ on wove paper. $7\frac{3}{16}''$ × $4\frac{15}{16}''$.

⟨1^2, 2^2, 3-22^8, 23^6⟩. *Signed:* ⟨-⟩^{6}, 1-14, ⟨15⟩-16, ⟨17-19⟩, 20^8, 21^4.

V cloth: green. White laid end papers. Laid paper flyleaves. Top edges gilt.

Note: A copy in Y, presumably prepared for the author's private use: Black C cloth, hand-lettered label on spine. Leaf: $7\frac{9}{16}''$ × $5\frac{1}{8}''$.

Published Oct. 8, 1889 (publisher's records). Deposited Oct. 9, 1889. Noted and advertised as *just ready* PW Oct. 12, 1889. Listed PW Oct. 19, 1889. The London (Low) issue "will issue simultaneously with the American"---PC Nov. 1, 1889; listed Ath Dec. 7, 1889.

AAS   B   H   LC   NYPL   Y

13972. Alpha Delta Phi Addresses Delivered in New York City at the Semi-Centennial Convention, 1882 and at the 56th Annual Convention, 1888

Published by the Executive Council of the Fraternity 1889

"Fifty Years' Progress in Literature," pp. ⟨11⟩-20.

H   LC   Y

13973. . . . Some Famous Pseudonyms. Well-Known Authors Tell the Stories of Their Nom de Plumes . . . ⟨Edited by Edward W. Bok⟩

. . . Copyrighted . . . 1889, by the Bok Syndicate Press of New York . . .

Contains an autobiographical statement by Mitchell.

For a fuller description see above in the Joaquin Miller list.

13974. ENGLISH LANDS LETTERS AND KINGS FROM ELIZABETH TO ANNE . . .

NEW YORK   CHARLES SCRIBNER'S SONS MDCCCXC

Title-page in black and sepia.

For other volumes in this series see under 1889, 1895, 1897.

⟨i-ii⟩, ⟨i⟩-⟨x⟩, ⟨1⟩-347, blank leaf; leaf excised or pasted under the end paper. Laid paper; pp. ⟨i-iv⟩ on wove paper. $7\frac{3}{16}''$ full × $4\frac{7}{8}''$ full.

⟨-⟩^{6}, 1-6, ⟨7-8⟩, 9-21, ⟨22⟩^{8}. Leaves ⟨-⟩$_{2-3}$ inserted; leaf ⟨22⟩$_8$ excised or pasted under the end paper.

V cloth: green. White laid end papers. Laid paper flyleaf at front. Top edges gilt.

Note: Two copies in Y, prepared for the author's private use: Green V cloth, paper label on spine. Leaf: $7\frac{1}{2}''$ × $5\frac{1}{4}''$. One of these inscribed by Mitchell: *Home Copy. D.G.M. April 12, 1890*

Deposited April 7, 1890. Published April 9, 1890 (publisher's records). BPL copy received April 10, 1890. Listed PW April 12, 1890; PC April 15, 1890; Bkr July, 1890.

AAS   B   LC   NYPL   Y

13975. Semi-Centennial Historical and Biographical Record of the Class of 1841 in Yale University Printed for the Class

New Haven: Tuttle, Morehouse & Taylor, Printers 1892

"Preface," pp. ⟨iii⟩-viii.

NYPL   Y

13976. Homes in City and Country . . .

New York Charles Scribner's Sons 1893

"The Country House," pp. ⟨99⟩-136.

Deposited April 21, 1893. BPL copy received April 27, 1893. Listed PW April 29, 1893.

AAS   BA   H   Y

13977. Fame's Tribute to Children . . . ⟨Second Edition. Edited by Mrs. George L. Dunlap and Martha S. Hill⟩

Chicago ⟨Hayes and Company⟩ 1893

Sentiment, p. 28 of the second section.

For comment see entry No. 1284A.

13978. ENGLISH LANDS LETTERS AND KINGS QUEEN ANNE AND THE GEORGES . . .

NEW YORK CHARLES SCRIBNER'S SONS MDCCCXCV

Title-page in black and sepia.

For other volumes in this series see under 1889, 1890, 1897.

⟨i⟩-⟨x⟩, ⟨1⟩-354. Laid paper. 7⅛″ × 4⅞″.

⟨1², 2-23⁸, 24⁴⟩. *Signed:* ⟨-⟩⁵, 1-22⁸, ⟨23⟩¹.

V cloth: green. Top edges gilt.

Note: A copy in Y, presumably prepared for the author's private use: Paper boards sides, S cloth shelf back, printed paper labels on spine. Leaf: 7⁹⁄₁₆″ × 5¹⁄₁₆″.

Deposited Sept. 6, 1895. Published Sept. 7, 1895 (publisher's records). Noted as *just ready* PW Sept. 7, 1895. Listed PW Sept. 14, 1895. The London (Low) edition announced PC Sept. 28, 1895; advertised as *ready* PC Nov. 2, 1895; listed Ath Nov. 9, 1895.

AAS BA H LC NYPL Y

13979. . . . A NEW REVERIE BY IK MARVEL HE WRITES OF STUDENT LIFE AT YALE COLLEGE SIXTY YEARS AGO . . .

(COPYRIGHT, 1895, BY BACHELLER, JOHNSON & BACHELLER.) ⟨NEW YORK⟩ . . .

Caption title. The above at head of the first of four columns. At head of title: *For June 23*

Prepared for subscribers to The Bacheller, Johnson & Bacheller Syndicate.

Single sheet. Printed on recto only. Printed in four columns. Illustrated. Quite possibly the present example is but a portion of a larger sheet with text by another (Mitchell?) removed. 23″ × 9½″ scant.

Y

13980. AMERICAN LANDS AND LETTERS THE MAYFLOWER TO RIP-VAN-WINKLE . . .

NEW YORK CHARLES SCRIBNER'S SONS MDCCCXCVII

Title-page in black, orange, brown.

For another volume in this series see under year 1899.

Two printings noted:

FIRST PRINTING

⟨i-ii⟩, ⟨i⟩-⟨xxiv⟩, ⟨1⟩-402; 3 blank leaves. Frontispiece and chart inserted; other illustrations in text. 8³⁄₁₆″ × 5⁹⁄₁₆″.

⟨a⟩⁸, ⟨b⟩⁴, ⟨c⟩¹, 1-7, ⟨8-9⟩, 10, ⟨11⟩, 12-13, ⟨14⟩, 15-17, ⟨18-19⟩, 20-21, ⟨22⟩, 23, ⟨24-25⟩⁸, ⟨26⟩⁴.

SECOND PRINTING

⟨i⟩-⟨xxiv⟩, ⟨1⟩-402; 3 blank leaves.

⟨a⟩⁴, ⟨b⟩⁸, 1-7, ⟨8-9⟩, 10, ⟨11⟩, 12-13, ⟨14⟩, 15-17, ⟨18-19⟩, 20-21, ⟨22⟩, 23, ⟨24-25⟩⁸, ⟨26⟩⁴.

Rough linen: tan. Cream end papers. Top edges gilded.

Note: A set of first printing sheets (in Y) has been seen bound in smooth brown V cloth; status not determined. Experimental binding?

Published April 3, 1897 (publisher's records). Deposited April 3, 1897. Noted for *today* PW April 3, 1897. BA copy (1st) received April 6, 1897. BPL copy (1st) received April 8, 1897. Listed PW April 10, 1897. The London (Dent) edition listed Ath Nov. 20, 1897.

AAS (1st) B (2nd) BA (1st) BPL (1st) Y (1st)

13981. ENGLISH LANDS LETTERS AND KINGS THE LATER GEORGES TO VICTORIA . . .

NEW YORK CHARLES SCRIBNER'S SONS MDCCCXCVII

Title-page in black and brown.

For other volumes in this series see under 1889, 1890, 1895.

⟨i-ii⟩, ⟨i⟩-⟨xiv⟩, ⟨1⟩-294, blank leaf. Laid paper. 7³⁄₁₆″ × 4¹⁵⁄₁₆″.

⟨a-b⟩⁴, 1-18⁸, ⟨19⟩⁴.

V cloth: green. Top edges gilded.

Note: A copy in Y, inscribed by Mitchell, was presumably prepared for the author's private use. Unstamped green V cloth, printed paper labels on spine, top edges gilded. Leaf: 7⅝″ × 5⅛″.

Deposited Sept. 17, 1897. BA copy received Sept. 21, 1897. Listed PW Oct. 2, 1897. The London (Elkin Mathews) edition noted as *immediately* PC Sept. 18, 1897; listed Ath Oct. 30, 1897.

AAS BA H LC NYPL Y

13982. The International Library of Famous Literature Selections from the World's Great Writers . . . with Biographical and Explanatory Notes and with Introductions by Donald G. Mitchell . . . and Andrew Lang Compiled and Arranged by Nathan Haskell Dole, Forrest Morgan and Caroline Ticknor . . .

New York   Merrill and Baker Publishers ⟨1898⟩

"Introduction," Vol. 1, pp. ix-xxiii.

For fuller entry see BAL, Vol. 5, p. 204.

13983. The Library of Household Classics.

New York: Doubleday & McClure Company, 1898.

Not seen. Not located. Advertised PW Sept. 24, 1898, as in eighteen volumes.

"Introduction to a Series of Household Classics furnished by D.G.M. pp. xii. Doubleday & McClure Co., N. Y."———From Mitchell's *ms* autobibliography in Y.

"An Introduction to the Library of Household Classics. New York. Doubleday & McClure Co."———Dunn, p. 408, under the year 1898. Did Dunn get the entry from the autobibliography?

13984. AMERICAN LANDS AND LETTERS LEATHER-STOCKING TO POE'S "RAVEN" ...

NEW YORK   CHARLES SCRIBNER'S SONS MDCCCXCIX

Title-page in black, orange, brown.

For another volume in this series see under year 1897.

⟨i-ii⟩, ⟨i⟩-⟨xxvi⟩, ⟨1⟩-412. Frontispiece inserted; other illustrations in text. 8⅜″ × 5⁹⁄₁₆″.

⟨1⁴, 2², 3-28⁸, 29⁶⟩. *Note:* Signed irregularly and incompletely in 8.

Rough linen: tan. Cream end papers. Top edges gilded.

Deposited Sept. 19, 1899. Published Sept. 27, 1899 (publisher's records). BPL copy received Sept. 28, 1899. Listed PW Oct. 7, 1899. The London (Dent) edition announced PC Sept. 30, 1899; listed Ath Dec. 16, 1899.

B   BA   BPL   H   NYPL   Y

13985. Favorite Food of Famous Folk ...

... John P. Morton & Company ... Louisville, Kentucky ... MCM

Contribution, p. 27.

For fuller entry see No. 470.

13986. The Record of the Celebration of the Two Hundredth Anniversary of the Founding of Yale College ... October the Twentieth to October the Twenty-Third ... Nineteen Hundred and One

Published by the University New Haven 1902

Three-quarters leather, marbled boards sides.

"Dedicatory Address," pp. 419-427. Otherwise "Woodbridge Hall."

H

13987. Mary Pringle Mitchell. Born, February 1, 1831, at Charleston, South Carolina. Died, December 5, 1901, at Edgewood, New Haven, Connecticut.

⟨n.p., n.d., New Haven: The Tuttle, Morehouse & Taylor Press, 1903⟩

Introductory note, pp. 3-4, dated *Edgewood, Dec. 5, 1901;* and, a letter, July 19, 1903, addressed to *Dear Harry,* pp. 4-5.

AAS   Y

13988. LOOKING BACK AT BOYHOOD BY "IK MARVEL"

THE ACADEMY PRESS JUNE, 1906

⟨i-iv⟩, ⟨1⟩-21; blank, p. ⟨22⟩; 3 blank leaves. 5½″ × 2¹³⁄₁₆″.

⟨1-4⁴⟩.

Printed cartridge paper wrapper over flexible boards.

"Foreword" signed at end: *E.S.G.;* editor further unidentified.

"With ⟨Mitchell's⟩ ... permission an article which he wrote for the *Youth's Companion* ⟨April 21, 1892⟩ some years ago is here reprinted ... "———P. 3.

AAS   UV   Y

13989. The Works of Donald G. Mitchell ... ⟨Edgewood Edition⟩

Charles Scribner's Sons New York 1907

Issued in ecru sateen-like cloth. Also leather? Vols. 13 and 15 have been seen in a presumed remainder binding of tan V cloth.

15 Vols.

1: *Fresh Gleanings.* Reprint save for "Prefatory," pp. v-xi, dated August 10, 1907. Deposited Oct. 1, 1907.

2: *Reveries of a Bachelor.* Deposited Oct. 1, 1907.

3: *Dream Life.* Deposited Oct. 1, 1907.

4: *Wet Days at Edgewood.* Deposited Oct. 1, 1907.

5: *Bound Together.* Deposited Nov. 20, 1907.

6: *My Farm of Edgewood.* Deposited Nov. 20, 1907.

7: *Out-of-Town Places.* Deposited Nov. 20, 1907.

8: *Doctor Johns.* Deposited Nov. 20, 1907.

9: *Seven Stories.* Deposited Nov. 29, 1907.

10: *English Lands Letters and Kings. From Celt to Tudor.* Deposited Nov. 29, 1907.

11: *English Lands Letters and Kings. From Elizabeth to Anne.* Deposited Nov. 29, 1907.

12: *English Lands Letters and Kings. Queen Anne and the Georges.* Deposited Nov. 29, 1907.

13: *English Lands Letters and Kings. The Later Georges to Victoria.* Deposited Dec. 20, 1907.

14: *American Lands and Letters. The Mayflower to Rip Van Winkle.* Deposited Dec. 20, 1907.

15: *American Lands and Letters. Leather-Stocking to Poe's "Raven".* Deposited Dec. 20, 1907.

BA   H   LC   Y

13990. LOUIS MITCHELL A SKETCH . . .

    CLAREMONT PRIVATELY PRINTED MCMXLVII

Edited by Waldo H. Dunn.

⟨i-viii⟩, ⟨1⟩-27; blank, pp. ⟨28-32⟩. 6″ × 3¾″ full. Watermarked *Warren's Olde Style.*

⟨1-5⁴⟩.

Printed rough-toothed gray-green paper wrapper.

125 Copies Printed---P. ⟨iv⟩.

Y

DONALD GRANT MITCHELL

SECTION II

Collections of reprinted material issued under Mitchell's name or pseudonyms; separate editions (*i.e.*, pieces reprinted from Mitchell's books and issued in separate form). For a list of books by authors other than Mitchell containing reprinted Mitchell material see *Section III*.

13991. The Lorgnette: Or, Studies of the Town. By an Opera Goer . . . Volume II. ⟨*i.e.*, Second Series⟩ Third Edition . . .

New York. Printed for Stringer and Townsend . . . ⟨1850⟩

13992. The Opera Goer: Or, Studies of the Town. By Ike ⟨*sic*⟩ Marvell ⟨*sic*⟩ . . .

London: Thomas Cautley Newby, Publisher, Welbeck Street, Cavendish Square. 1852.

Caution: Entry on the basis of Vol. 2 only; issued in two volumes.

Sheets of *The Lorgnette* (New York printing) issued with cancel title-leaf as above.

13993. Reveries of a Bachelor: Or a Book of the Heart. By Ik. Marvel . . . Illustrated Edition.

New York: Charles Scribner. 1852.

For publication notes see under entry for the first edition, 1850.

Noted in both cloth; and, leather.

Not printed from the plates of the first edition; printed from a new setting. Contains a dedication to Mrs. E. L. Dixon which is not present in the first edition.

13994. Extracts from The Reveries of a Bachelor, by Ik. Marvel . . . E. Thomas Lyon, Chemist, and Manufacturer of Lyon's Kathairon, and Pure Jamaica Ginger . . . for Gratuitous Distribution.

New-York: Oliver & Brother, Book and Job Printers, 89 Nassau-Street, Sun Building. 1853.

Printed paper wrapper. Cover-title. Issued as an advertisement for E. Thomas Lyon's nostrums.

Sayings, Wise and Otherwise by the Author of the Sparrowgrass Papers . . . Introductory Note by Donald G. Mitchell.

New York . . . ⟨1870; *i.e.*, *ca.* 1892⟩

For fuller entry see below under year 1892. For first printing of Mitchell's note see above in *Section One* under the year 1871.

13995. Sayings, Wise and Otherwise by the Author of Sparrowgrass Papers, etc., with a Brief Autobiographic Sketch, and an Introductory Note by Donald G. Mitchell.

New York: American Book Exchange, Tribune Building. 1880.

Copyright notice dated 1870. For first printing see in *Section One* under the year 1871.

13996. My Farm of Edgewood: A Country Book by the Author of "Reveries of a Bachelor" . . .

New York   Charles Scribner's Sons   1884

Trade format. Does not contain the new foreword found in the large paper printing of this year. Leaf: $7\frac{1}{4}'' \times 4\frac{7}{8}''$.

13997. Seven Stories, with Basement and Attic. By the Author of "Reveries of a Bachelor."

New York: Charles Scribner's Sons. 1884.

Copyright notice dated 1883. The H copy received Dec. 1, 1883. The London (Low) issue advertised PC Dec. 31, 1883; listed PC March 1, 1884.

13997A. Washington Irving   Commemoration of the One Hundredth Anniversary of His Birth by the Washington Irving Association at Tarrytown-on-Hudson Tuesday Evening, April 3, 1883   Addresses by Judge Noah Davis, Charles Dudley Warner, Donald G. Mitchell . . . Etc.

G. P. Putnam's Sons   New York: 27 & 29 West 23d Street   London: 25 Henrietta Street, Covent Garden   1884

Preliminary note (not by Mitchell) dated *May, 1884*

Mitchell's address, pp. 37–47, had prior publication in *Bound Together*, 1884, entry No. 13966, published March 22, 1884.

Lays of Ancient Rome by Thomas Babington Macaulay with an Introduction by Donald G. Mitchell . . .

... Boston ... ⟨1885; *i.e., ca.* 1912⟩
See below under 1912.

13998. Reveries of a Bachelor or a Book of the Heart by Ik Marvel ...

London   Frederick Warne & Co. 1889 [All Rights Reserved]

Advertised as though ready Ath Dec. 1, 1888. Listed Ath Dec. 22, 1888; pc Dec. 31, 1888; Bkr Jan. 1889.

13999. Dream-Life ... by the Author of "Reveries of a Bachelor" ...

New York   Charles Scribner's Sons 1889

Johnson erroneously reports a new preface in this printing. A printing (this?) distributed in London by Dent; listed pc Dec. 31, 1889; advertised as *ready* Ath Jan. 4, 1890; listed Bkr Jan. 1890.

14000. Reveries of a Bachelor or a Book of the Heart by Ik Marvel ... with an Etching by Percy Moran.

New York   Charles Scribner's Sons 1889

Green V cloth, cameo on front cover. Leaf: 6½" × 4" full. Pp. 260.

Also issued in a large paper edition limited to 200 numbered copies; boards, vellum shelf back. Leaf: 8⅛" × 5".

The publishers report that at an unknown time 1500 copies were prepared for distribution by The Phœnix Insurance Company. These may be identified by the presence of the following statement at the lower left of the front cover: PRESENTED BY THE PHŒNIX INSURANCE CO. OF HARTFORD CONN.

A printing (this?) distributed in London by Dent. Listed pc Dec. 31, 1889; advertised as *ready* Ath Jan. 4, 1890; listed Bkr Jan. 1890.

Lays of Ancient Rome by Thomas Babington Macaulay. With an Introduction by Donald G. Mitchell ...

... Boston ... ⟨1889; *i.e.,* 1899⟩

See below under 1899.

14001. *Entry cancelled.*

14002. ... Reveries of a Bachelor

Philadelphia   Henry Altemus Company ⟨n.d., not before 1892⟩

At head of title: *Donald G. Mitchell*

14003. Sayings, Wise and Otherwise by the Author of the Sparrowgrass Papers, etc., with a Brief Autobiographic Sketch, and an Introductory Note by Donald G. Mitchell.

New York   United States Book Company Successors to John W. Lovell Company 142 to 150 Worth Street ⟨1870; *i.e., ca.* 1892⟩

See *The Sayings of Dr. Bushwhacker* ..., 1871, in *Section One.*

14004. ... Dream-Life ... by the Author of "Reveries of a Bachelor" ...

New York   Charles Scribner's Sons 1893

At head of title: *Author's Complete Edition*

14005. Reveries of a Bachelor or, a Book of the Heart. By Ik Marvel (Donald G. Mitchell) ...

New York: Optimus Printing Company 53 Rose Street. ⟨n.d., *ca.* 1890-1895⟩

14006. Reveries of a Bachelor: Or a Book of the Heart. By Ik Marvel ...

Philadelphia: The Rodgers Company. ⟨n.d., *ca.* 1895⟩

14007. Lays of Ancient Rome by Thomas Babington Macaulay. With an Introduction by Donald G. Mitchell ...

Educational Publishing Company, Boston. New York. Chicago. ⟨1889; *i.e.,* 1899⟩

Copyright notice dated 1885, 1889. Wrapper dated *November 15, 1899*. For first printing see in *Section One* under the year 1885: *Readings from Macaulay* ...

14008. Reveries of a Bachelor or a Book of the Heart by Ik Marvel with an Introduction by Arlo Bates ...

New York   Thomas Y. Crowell Company Publishers ⟨1900⟩

Flexible leather.

14009. Reveries of a Bachelor or a Book of the Heart by Ik Marvel (Donald G. Mitchell)

New York   The Mershon Company Publishers ⟨n.d., *ca.* 1900⟩

14010. Dream-Life: A Fable of the Seasons ...

New York: A. L. Burt, Publisher. ⟨n.d., *ca.* 1902⟩

14011. Reveries of a Bachelor or a Book of the Heart by Ik Marvel with Illustrations & Decorations by E. M. Ashe

Indianapolis   The Bobbs-Merrill Company Publishers ⟨1906⟩

On copyright page: *October*

14012. Reveries of a Bachelor or a Book of the Heart . . .

R. F. Fenno & Company   18 East Seventeenth Street, New York ⟨1906⟩

14013. By a City Grate . . .

R. F. Fenno & Company   18 East Seventeenth St., New York ⟨1907⟩

Two printings noted:

FIRST PRINTING

Date ⟨1907⟩ present. Bound in cloth. Leaf: $8^{15}/_{16}'' \times 6^{1}/_{4}''$.

SECOND PRINTING

Issued without date. Pictorial paper wrapper. Leaf: $7^{1}/_{8}'' \times 4^{5}/_{16}''$.

Reprinted from *Reveries of a Bachelor.*

14014. Evening . . .

R. F. Fenno & Company   18 East Seventeenth St., New York ⟨1907⟩

Reprinted from *Reveries of a Bachelor.*

14015. Morning . . .

R. F. Fenno & Company   18 East Seventeenth St., New York ⟨1907⟩

Reprinted from *Reveries of a Bachelor.*

14016. Noon . . .

R. F. Fenno & Company   18 East Seventeenth St., New York ⟨1907⟩

Reprinted from *Reveries of a Bachelor.*

14017. Over a Wood Fire . . .

R. F. Fenno & Company   18 East Seventeenth St., New York ⟨1907⟩

Two printings noted:

FIRST PRINTING

Date ⟨1907⟩ present. Bound in cloth. Leaf: $8^{15}/_{16}'' \times 6^{1}/_{4}''$.

SECOND PRINTING

Issued without date. Pictorial paper wrapper. Leaf: $7^{1}/_{8}'' \times 4^{5}/_{16}''$.

Reprinted from *Reveries of a Bachelor.*

14018. Over His Cigar . . .

R. F. Fenno & Company   18 East Seventeenth St., New York ⟨1907⟩

Two printings noted:

FIRST PRINTING

Date ⟨1907⟩ present. Bound in cloth. Leaf: $8^{15}/_{16}'' \times 6^{1}/_{4}''$.

SECOND PRINTING

Issued without date. Pictorial paper wrapper. Leaf: $7^{3}/_{16}'' \times 4^{5}/_{16}''$.

Reprinted from *Reveries of a Bachelor.*

14019. Lays of Ancient Rome by Thomas Babington Macaulay with an Introduction by Donald G. Mitchell . . .

Educational Publishing Company, Boston. New York. Chicago. ⟨1885; *i.e., ca.* 1912⟩

For first printing see in *Section One* under the year 1885: *Readings from Macaulay* . . .

DONALD GRANT MITCHELL

SECTION III

In this section are listed books by authors other than Mitchell which contain material by him reprinted from earlier books. See *Section II* for a list of reprints issued under Mitchell's name or pseudonyms.

The White Veil . . . Edited by Mrs. Sarah Josepha Hale . . .

> Philadelphia . . . 1854.
>
> "A Good Wife," pp. 255-257; extracted from *Dream Life*, 1851, pp. 182-185.
>
> "The Young Husband's Reveries," pp. 265-269; extracted from *Dream Life*, 1851, pp. ⟨234⟩-238.
>
> For fuller entry see No. 6883.

The Atlantic Souvenir, for 1859 . . .

> New York: Derby & Jackson, 119 Nassau Street. 1859.
>
> Noted only in publisher's leather.

The Mosaic. Edited by J.H.B.

> Buffalo . . . 1861.
>
> Extract, p. 38; extracted from *Reveries of a Bachelor*, p. 239.
>
> Extract, pp. 40-41; extracted from *Reveries of a Bachelor*, p. 224.
>
> Extract, pp. 42-43; extracted from *Reveries of a Bachelor*, p. 257.
>
> Extract, p. 65; extracted from *Dream Life*, p. 12.
>
> For fuller entry see BAL, Vol. 5, p. 90.

. . . Little Classics. Edited by Rossiter Johnson. Life . . .

> Boston . . . 1875.
>
> "A Bachelor's Revery," pp. ⟨126⟩-152; extracted from *Reveries of a Bachelor*.
>
> For fuller entry see No. 8576.

Vol. I. No. 2. The Quarterly Elocutionist . . . Edited and Published by Mrs. Anna Randall-Diehl . . . April, 1875 . . .

> . . . Anna Randall-Diehl, 27 Union Square, New York. Copyright . . . 1875.
>
> Printed paper wrapper. Cover-title.

. . . Harper's Fifth Reader American Authors

> New York Harper & Brothers, Franklin Square 1889
>
> *Note:* Reprinted and reissued by The American Book Company not before 1890. For fuller entry see No. 7917.
>
> "The Old-Time Thanksgiving-Day," pp. 174-180. Reprinted from *Bound Together*, 1884.

Capital Stories by American Authors.

> Published by the Christian Herald, Louis Klopsch, Proprietor, Bible House, New York. ⟨1895⟩
>
> "Clarence's Courtship," pp. 68-81; extracted from *Dream Life*, 1851, pp. ⟨219⟩-233.

The International Library of Famous Literature . . . Edited by Dr. Richard Garnett . . . in Twenty Volumes . . .

> London . . . 1899
>
> For comment see entry No. 10638.

. . . The Universal Anthology . . .

> . . . ⟨1899⟩
>
> See below under 1901.

. . . The Universal Anthology . . .

> . . . London . . . New York . . . Paris . . . Berlin ⟨1899; *i.e.*, 1901⟩
>
> "A Retrospect of the Anthology," Vol. 30, pp. xv-xxviii, is a truncated version of Mitchell's "Introduction" to *The International Library of Famous Literature*, New York, 1898.
>
> For comment see entry No. 10646.

Love-Story Masterpieces . . . Chosen by Ralph A. Lyon

> William S. Lord Evanston 1902
>
> Cloth? Deposited June 3, 1902.

Stories of Chivalry Retold from St. Nicholas

> New York The Century Co. 1909

"Ivanhoe," pp. 177-192; reprinted from *About Old Story-Tellers*, 1878.

Deposited June 28, 1909.

International Short Stories Edited by William Patten . . . American

   . . . New York ⟨1910⟩

"Over a Wood Fire," pp. 375-382; reprinted from *Reveries of a Bachelor*, 1850, pp. ⟨15⟩-28.

For fuller entry see No. 782.

REFERENCES AND ANA

A History of Venice

Allibone (II, p. 1326) reports that when a consul at Venice, 1853, Mitchell collected materials for such a history and implies that publication was projected. NLG May 15, 1855, reported Mitchell working on the project. An abandoned project.

"Long before he left Paris he had come to a realization that he had made only a small beginning upon Venice; that he had years of work ahead of him before he could complete the story in any satisfactory way."–––Dunn, p. 268.

A Freehold Villa for Nothing; or, How I Became My Own Landlord without Capital. By I. ⟨*sic*⟩ Marvel. To Which Is Appended How to Construct a Freehold Villa. By D. Smith . . .

London: John Kempster & Company, 9 & 10, St. Bride's Avenue, Fleet Street, E. C. ⟨n.d., 1873⟩

Printed paper boards?

Listed PC Aug. 1, 1873. In the listing and in Kempster's advertisements the implication is that the above work is not by D. G. Mitchell; not listed in the British Museum *Catalogue* as Mitchell's.

Listed in Foley as though by Mitchell. BAL has found no evidence to support the attribution. Johnson (p. 369) is incorrect in stating that the publication is a British piracy of *My Farm of Edgewood*.

Address before the Alpha Delta Phi Society, at the Academy of Music, N. Y.

New York, 1883.

Not located. Entry from Foley. Perhaps an erroneous entry for *Alpha Delta Phi Addresses* . . . , 1889, which Foley fails to list.

Standard Recitations by Best Authors ⟨No. 1⟩ . . . Compiled . . . by Frances P. Sullivan.

M. J. Ivers & Co., Publishers, 86 Nassau Street, N. Y. ⟨1883⟩

"The Water-Mill," pp. 31-32. Not by Mitchell although here credited to him. Written by Sarah Doudney, 1843–1926.

Printed paper wrapper. Deposited April 20, 1883. The earliest printing (printings?) does not have a statement identifying the publication as No. 1 of the series.

The Works of Donald G. Mitchell.

New York, 1888.

8 Vols. *Not seen. Not located.* Entry from Johnson, p. 371. A ghost?

Bibliography D.G.M. 1841-1902 Extending over Sixty-One Years

⟨n.p., n.d., New Haven, 1902⟩

Manuscript. Compiled by Mitchell. A highly interesting and reasonably accurate compilation. In Y.

The Life of Donald G. Mitchell . . . by Waldo H. Dunn . . .

New York Charles Scribner's Sons 1922

Published April 28, 1922 (publisher's records).

The First Editions of Donald G. Mitchell "Ik Marvel" A Checklist Compiled by Paul S. Seybolt

Privately Printed Boston 1930

Cover-title. Printed paper wrapper. 100 numbered copies only.

ISAAC MITCHELL

1 7 5 9 – 1 8 1 2

14020. . . . ALONZO AND MELISSA . . .

Two editions noted; sequence not known. The designations are completely arbitrary.

A

THE ASYLUM; OR, ALONZO AND MELISSA. AN AMERICAN TALE, FOUNDED ON FACT. BY I. MITCHELL . . . IN TWO VOLUMES . . .

POUGHKEEPSIE: PUBLISHED BY JOSEPH NELSON. C. C. ADAMS AND CO. PRINTERS. 1811.

1: ⟨i⟩-xxviii, ⟨29⟩-264. Frontispiece inserted. 7¾″ × 4⅝″.

2: ⟨1⟩-278, blank leaf. See below regarding the blank leaf.

1: ⟨A⟩-I, K-U, X-Y⁶.

2: ⟨A⟩-I, K-U, X-Z⁶, Aa². In some copies leaf Aa2 is pasted under the terminal end paper.

Printed blue-gray paper boards sides, white paper shelf back. Printed paper label on spine. Flyleaves in Vol. 1; flyleaf at front of Vol. 2. Also issued in leather?

". . . On Dec. 2, 1810, a copyright for the publication of the story in book form was obtained in the name of Joseph Nelson 'as proprietor' of the *Political Barometer*. That paper advertised, Sept. 25, 1811, *A New Novel, The Asylum or Alonzo and Melissa, will be ready for delivery to subscribers and others on Monday next*, while on Oct. 2, 1811, the *Republican Herald* of Poughkeepsie advertised: *New Novel just published by Joseph Nelson* . . .

"In the same year, 1811, there appeared at Plattsburg, N. Y., an extraordinary example of plagiarism, a one-volume novel entitled *Alonzo and Melissa or The Unfeeling Father*, of which Daniel Jackson, Jr. (b. May 31, 1790), a teacher at Plattsburg Academy, claimed to be author and proprietor. Jackson's story . . . is identical, except for a few verbal substitutions, with Isaac Mitchell's newspaper story in the *Political Barometer* of 1804 . . ."---DAB.

The text is a revision of the original as published in *The Political Barometer*, Poughkeepsie, N. Y.,

June 5–Oct. 30, 1804, under the title *Alonzo and Melissa, a Tale*.

There were many reprints, in some of which the text varies, issued under the title *Alonzo and Melissa*. Mitchell died in 1812 and it is unlikely that any of the revised texts are his. For a list of the printings under the several titles see Lyle H. Wright's *American Fiction 1774-1850* . . . , San Marino, Cal., 1969, Nos. 1886-1909.

For comments on the authorship see *Book Notes* . . . , Providence, R. I., Jan. 14, 1905, pp. ⟨1⟩-6; *The Nation*, New York, Dec. 8, 1904, p. 458; Feb. 2, 1905, pp. 91-92; Feb. 25, 1909, pp. 191-192.

Note: All examined copies have p. 120, Vol. 1, mispaged *201*.

AAS   H   UV

B

A SHORT ACCOUNT OF THE COURTSHIP OF ALONZO & MELISSA: SETTING FORTH THEIR HARDSHIPS AND DIFFICULTIES, CAUSED BY THE BARBARITY OF AN UNFEELING FATHER . . .

PLATTSBURGH, N.Y. PRINTED FOR THE PROPRIETOR. 1811.

Anonymous. Some copies have the following line added (by hand stamp?): BY DANIEL JACKSON, *Jun*. See below.

⟨1⟩-218, blank leaf. 8″ × 4⅞″.

⟨A⟩-I, K-U, W-Z⁴, Aa-Cc⁴, Dd².

Noted only in contemporary leather.

The text is that of the original appearance in *The Political Barometer*, Poughkeepsie, N. Y., June 5–Oct. 30, 1804. The Poughkeepsie issue of the book is revised.

Four issues noted; the sequence has not been established and the designations are for identification only.

Issue A

Issued anonymously. The name *Daniel Jackson* does not appear on the title-page.

Pp. 117-118: A cancel leaf.

Pp. 123-126: Cancel conjugate leaves.

Tail-piece: The lettering is black on white.

Location: AAS

Issue B

The following line appears on the title-page (added by hand stamp?): BY DANIEL JACKSON, *Jun.* This feature appears to have been inserted after the title-page had been printed.

Pp. 117-118, 123-126, are not cancels. The text appears to be the same as that of *Issue A*.

The tail-piece is printed from a reverse engraving; *i.e.*, the lettering is white on black.

Locations: AAS, B, IHS

Issue C

The following line appears on the title-page (added by hand stamp?): BY DANIEL JACKSON, *Jun.* This feature appears to have been inserted after the title-page had been printed.

Pp. 117-118, 123-126, are not cancels. The text appears to be the same as that of *Issue A*.

The tail-piece is lettered black on white.

Locations: HEH N UV

Issue D

Issued anonymously. The name *Daniel Jackson* does not appear on the title-page.

Pp. 117-118, 123-126, are not cancels. The text appears to be the same as that of *Issue A*.

The tail-piece is printed from a reverse engraving; *i.e.*, the lettering is white on black.

Location: B

Date of publication not known. "A search of the Plattsburgh papers of 1811 and 1812 has failed to uncover any local mention of the publication of Jackson's Plattsburgh edition. It seems impossible therefore to determine in what part of the year 1811 Jackson's book was published. It may have been prior to Mitchell's two-volume edition . . ." ———"Alonzo and Melissa," by Glyndon Cole, in *York State Tradition*, Saranac, N. Y., Vol. 20, No. 2, Spring, 1966.

JOHN AMES MITCHELL

1 8 4 5 – 1 9 1 8

14021. THE SUMMER SCHOOL OF PHILO-
SOPHY AT Mͭ͟ DESERT . . .

NEW YORK HENRY HOLT AND COMPANY 1881

Title-page in red and black.

⟨1-48⟩ paged ⟨1⟩-24. Except for the title-leaf
printed on one side of leaf only. Illustrated.
9⅜″ × 7⅝″ (in paper). 10⅝″ × 8½″ (in cloth).
⟨1-12²⟩.

Printed white paper wrapper. V cloth: ecru;
green. Cloth-bound copies have bevelled covers;
white end papers printed in green with a leafy
pattern; flyleaves.

Listed PW Dec. 3, 1881. Deposited Dec. 12, 1881.

BA BPL H LC Y

14022. The Good Things of Life . . .

New York White, Stokes, & Allen 1884

Edited by Mitchell?

Deposited Aug. 28, 1884.

LC

14023. The Good Things of Life Second Series
. . .

New York White, Stokes, & Allen 1885

Edited by Mitchell?

Deposited Aug. 20, 1885.

LC

14024. Life's Verses . . .

Published by Mitchell & Miller 1155 Broadway New York ⟨1885⟩

According to the Library of Congress edited by
Mitchell.

Printed paper boards, paper shelf back; also,
printed paper boards, cloth shelf back.

Deposited Sept. 22, 1885. Advertised as *now ready*,
Life, Sept. 24, 1885.

H LC NYPL

14025. THE ROMANCE OF THE MOON . . .

NEW YORK HENRY HOLT AND COMPANY 1886

Title-page in green and orange.

⟨1-32⟩. Printed on one side of leaf only save for
the title-leaf which is imprinted on the verso
with a copyright notice. Printed throughout in
green and orange. Illustrated. 5⁷⁄₁₆″ × 7″.
⟨1-4⁴⟩.

S cloth: blue; blue-gray; blue-green. Covers
bevelled. White end papers printed in ochre with
a floral pattern. Flyleaves.

Deposited June 9, 1886. Listed PW Oct. 30, 1886.

AAS B BPL LC Y

14026. Life's Verses Second Series . . .

New York Copyright, 1886, by White, Stokes, &
Allen 1886

According to the Library of Congress edited by
Mitchell.

"A Rendezvous," p. 17.

Deposited Aug. 30, 1886. Listed PW Oct. 23, 1886.

H LC NYPL Y

14027. The Good Things of Life Third Series . . .

New York White, Stokes, & Allen 1886

Edited by Mitchell?

Deposited Sept. 10, 1886.

LC

14028. The Good Things of Life Fourth Series . . .

New York Frederick A. Stokes Successor to
White, Stokes, & Allen 1887

Edited by Mitchell?

Deposited Aug. 4, 1887.

LC

14029. The Good Things of Life Fifth Series . . .

New York Frederick A. Stokes & Brother 1888

Edited by Mitchell?

Deposited Oct. 15, 1888.

LC

14030. THE LAST AMERICAN   A FRAG-
MENT FROM THE JOURNAL OF KHAN-
LI PRINCE OF DIMPH-YOO-CHUR AND
ADMIRAL IN THE PERSIAN NAVY
EDITED BY J. A. MITCHELL

NEW YORK   FREDERICK A. STOKES & BROTHER
MDCCCLXXXIX

See under year 1902 for a revised edition.

⟨1⟩-78, blank leaf. Illustrated. $7\frac{1}{16}''$ × $5\frac{7}{16}''$ full.
⟨1-5⁸⟩.

S cloth: blue.

Copies also occur as follows: Leaves ⟨1⟩₁ and ⟨5⟩₈
excised. Inserted at the back is a single leaf,
printed on recto only, being the menu of a dinner,
The Last Man's Club, Hotel Bellevue, Philadelphia, *Avril 22me 1889*. Edges gilded. Leaf:
$6\frac{15}{16}''$ × $5\frac{3}{8}''$. Bound in printed maroon paper
sides, white V cloth shelf back, covers bevelled,
moiréd white end papers.

Deposited March 11, 1889. Listed PW March 23,
1889. The earliest British notice observed is Gay &
Bird's announcement in PC March 4, 1893.

AAS   LC   HM (*Last Man's Club*)   NYPL   Y

14031. The Good Things of Life   Sixth Series . . .

New York   Frederick A. Stokes & Brother
MDCCCLXXXIX

Edited by Mitchell?

Deposited Aug. 2, 1889.

LC

14032. The Good Things of Life   Seventh Series
. . .

New York   Frederick A. Stokes Company
MDCCCXL ⟨*sic*⟩

Edited by Mitchell?

Deposited Aug. 11, 1890.

LC

14033. The Good Things of Life   Eighth Series
. . .

New York   Frederick A. Stokes Company
MDCCCXCI

Edited by Mitchell?

Deposited Aug. 12, 1891.

LC

14034. The Good Things of Life   Ninth Series . . .

New York   Frederick A. Stokes Company
MDCCCXCII

Edited by Mitchell?

Deposited Aug. 27, 1892. Listed PW Oct. 29, 1892.

LC

14035. LIFE'S FAIRY TALES . . .

NEW YORK   FREDERICK A. STOKES COMPANY
MDCCCXCII

⟨i⟩-⟨viii⟩, ⟨1⟩-117, blank leaf. Illustrated. $7''$
full × $5\frac{3}{8}''$ full.
⟨1-8⁸⟩.

S cloth: blue.

Deposited Oct. 17, 1892. Listed PW Dec. 3, 1892.
Distributed in London by Gay & Bird; see PC
March 4, 1893.

AAS   LC   Y

14036. The Good Things of Life   Tenth Series . . .

New York   Frederick A. Stokes Company
Publishers ⟨1893⟩

Edited by Mitchell?

Deposited July 15, 1893.

LC   UV

14037. Some Artists at the Fair . . .

New York   Charles Scribner's Sons   1893

Printed cloth folded over flexible boards.

"Types and People at the Fair," pp. ⟨43⟩-58.

Deposited Nov. 22, 1893. BPL copy received Nov.
22, 1893; BA copy Nov. 29, 1893. Listed PW
Dec. 9, 1893.

BA   BPL   NYPL

14038. AMOS JUDD . . .

CHARLES SCRIBNER'S SONS   NEW YORK, 1895

⟨i-iv⟩, ⟨1⟩-199. $6\frac{7}{16}''$ × $3\frac{3}{4}''$.
⟨1-12⁸, 13⁶⟩. *Signed:* ⟨-⟩², ⟨1⟩-4, ⟨5⟩, 6-7, ⟨8⟩, 9,
19 ⟨*sic*⟩, 11, ⟨12⟩⁸, ⟨13⟩⁴.

White buckram. Top edges gilt.

Deposited Nov. 23, 1895. BA copy received Nov.
26, 1895. Listed PW Dec. 7, 1895. The London
(Dent) edition announced PC March 7, 1896; Ath
Sept. 12, 1896; PC Oct. 3, 1896. Listed PC Dec. 5,
1896; Bkr Dec. 11, 1896.

AAS   H   LC   Y

14039. THAT FIRST AFFAIR AND OTHER
SKETCHES ...

NEW YORK CHARLES SCRIBNER'S SONS 1896

⟨i-iv⟩, ⟨i⟩-viii, ⟨1⟩-177, blank leaf. Illustrated.
7″ × 4¾″ full

⟨1², 2-12⁸, 13⁶⟩. *Signed:* ⟨-⟩⁶, ⟨1⟩-11⁸, 12².

Two printings noted:

FIRST PRINTING

As above.

Fly-title-page: That First Affair /

University Press imprint on copyright page.

SECOND PRINTING

⟨1-12⁸⟩. *Signed:* ⟨-⟩⁶, ⟨1⟩-11⁸, 12².

Fly-title-page: That First Affair / And Other
Sketches /

Trow imprint on copyright page.

V cloth: green; red. Top edges gilt.

Noted as *at once* PW Nov. 21, 1896. Deposited Nov.
28, 1896. Listed PW Dec. 12, 1896. The H copy
(first printing) received Dec. 15, 1896.

BA (1st) H (1st, 2nd) LC (1st, being a deposit
copy) Y (2nd)

14040. GLORIA VICTIS ...

NEW YORK CHARLES SCRIBNER'S SONS 1897

See *Dr Thorne's Idea* ... , 1910, for a revised
edition.

⟨i-viii⟩, 1-269; blank, p. ⟨270⟩; 3 blank leaves.
6¹⁵⁄₁₆″ × 4⅞″.

⟨1-17⁸, 18⁶⟩. *Signed:* ⟨-⟩⁴, 1-17⁸, ⟨18⟩².

Green rough V cloth. Top edges gilded.

Advertised for *today* PW Nov. 20, 1897. Deposited
Nov. 22, 1897. BA copy received Nov. 23, 1897.
Listed PW Dec. 4, 1897. The London (Nutt)
edition advertised Ath Feb. 5, 1898; listed Ath
Feb. 12, 1898.

LC NYPL UV Y

14041. THE PINES OF LORY ...

NEW YORK LIFE PUBLISHING COMPANY 1901

⟨1⟩-⟨230⟩; tail-piece, p. ⟨231⟩. Illustrated. 7⅝″ ×
5⅛″.

⟨1⟩-14⁸, 15⁴.

Two printings noted:

FIRST PRINTING

As above.

SECOND PRINTING

⟨1⁴, 2-15⁸⟩. *Signed:* ⟨1⟩-14⁸, 15⁴.

Green buckram. Top edges gilded. *Two states of
the binding noted:*

1

The oval vignette on the front cover is stamped in
black only. Noted only on first printing sheets,
including the deposit copies.

2

The oval vignette on the front cover is stamped in
black and gold. Noted on second printing sheets
only.

The BA copy (2nd) received Nov. 12, 1901.
Deposited Dec. 3, 1901. Listed PW Dec. 7, 1901.
The London (Henderson) edition listed Ath
April 5, 1902.

B (2nd) H (2nd) LC (1st, being deposit copies)
NYPL (2nd) Y (1st)

14042. The Last American A Fragment from the
Journal of Khan-Li ... Edition de Luxe ...

New York Frederick A. Stokes Company
Publishers ⟨1902⟩

Revised. For first edition see under 1889.

Two printings noted:

FIRST PRINTING

⟨i-viii⟩, ⟨1⟩-151; blank, pp. ⟨152-156⟩. In some
copies pp. ⟨155-156⟩ used as the pastedown.
Illustrations in text; and, inserted: Frontispiece
and 7 plates. 7½″ × 5⁷⁄₁₆″.

⟨1⁶, 2-4⁴, 5-12⁸⟩. *Signed:* ⟨-⟩⁴, ⟨1-2⟩, 3-5, ⟨6-7⟩, 8,
⟨9⟩⁸, ⟨10⟩⁶.

On copyright page: *University Press* imprint.

Issued in blue T cloth, stamped in gold, white,
yellow, red. Top edges stained yellow. White
wove end papers; but, in some copies leaf ⟨12⟩₈
is used as the terminal pastedown.

SECOND PRINTING

⟨i-viii⟩, ⟨1⟩-⟨151⟩. Illustrations in text; and,
inserted: Frontispiece and 7 plates. 7⁷⁄₁₆″ × 5⁷⁄₁₆″.

⟨1-10⁸⟩. *Signed:* ⟨-⟩⁴, ⟨1-2⟩, 3-5, ⟨6-7⟩, 8, ⟨9⟩⁸,
⟨10⟩⁴.

Printer's imprint not present on copyright page.

Issued in yellow-orange T cloth stamped in blue.
Top edges plain.

AAS (2nd) B (2nd) LC (1st) UV (1st, 2nd) Y (1st)

14043. THE VILLA CLAUDIA ...

NEW YORK LIFE PUBLISHING COMPANY 1904

⟨i-ii⟩, ⟨1⟩-306. Illustrated. 7⁹⁄₁₆″ full × 5³⁄₁₆″.

⟨-⟩⁸, ⟨1⟩², 2-19⁸.

T cloth: tan. Top edges gilt.

BA copy received May 3, 1904. Deposited May 7, 1904. Listed PW July 16, 1904.

AAS B H NYPL UV Y

14044. Th. Nast His Period and His Pictures by Albert Bigelow Paine

New York The Macmillan Company London: Macmillan & Co., Ltd. 1904 . . .

Extract from "Contemporary American Caricature," p. 549; reprinted from *Scribner's Magazine*, Dec. 1889.

NYPL copy received Nov. 26, 1904. Listed PW Dec. 17, 1904.

H

14045. THE SILENT WAR . . .

NEW YORK LIFE PUBLISHING COMPANY 1906

⟨1⟩-222, blank leaf. Frontispiece and 3 plates inserted. 7⁹⁄₁₆″ × 5³⁄₁₆″ scant.

⟨1-14⁸⟩.

T cloth: red.

Noted for *early autumn* PW Sept. 8, 1906. Advertised as *ready* PW Oct. 20, 1906. Deposited Oct. 26, 1906. BA copy received Oct. 30, 1906. Listed PW Dec. 8, 1906.

AAS BA H LC Y

14046. Dr Thorne's Idea Originally Published as "Gloria Victis" . . .

New York Life Publishing Company 1910

For the original version of this story see *Gloria Victis*, 1897, above.

"This tale, in its original form, was published in 1899 ⟨*sic*⟩ as *Gloria Victis*. With the addition of certain passages and the revision of others . . . the book is now presented . . ."---P. ⟨7⟩.

Two printings noted. The following variations are sufficient for identification:

FIRST PRINTING

⟨i-vi⟩, ⟨1⟩-244; blank, pp. ⟨245-250⟩. Pp. ⟨i-ii⟩ and ⟨249-250⟩ used as pastedowns. Frontispiece and 3 plates inserted.

P. 13: The third line is both redundant and textually incorrect and reads: *ious tugs as they darted hither and thither on* /

Noted in *Bindings A* and *B*. See below.

SECOND PRINTING

⟨i-iv⟩, ⟨1⟩-244; blank, pp. ⟨245-252⟩. The preliminary and terminal leaves are present as free blanks and are not used as pastedowns. Frontispiece and 3 plates inserted.

P. 13: The third line reads: *their breathless, never ending business. At last* / The redundant line is not present.

Noted in *Binding C*. See below.

BINDING

Noted in three states. The sequence of A and B not firmly determined. The following is sufficient for identification:

BINDING A

Stamped in gold only. Publisher's imprint not present on spine. Author's name as follows at foot of front of cover: MITCHELL The first and last leaves used as pastedowns. Noted on first printing sheets.

BINDING B

Stamped in gold and white. Publisher's imprint at foot of spine. Author's name as follows at head of front cover: JOHN AMES MITCHELL The first and last leaves used as pastedowns. Noted on first printing sheets.

BINDING C

Stamped in gold and white. Publisher's imprint at foot of spine. Author's name as follows at foot of front cover: JOHN AMES MITCHELL True binder's end papers; the first and last leaves are not used as pastedowns. Noted on second printing sheets.

Deposited June 7, 1910. Listed PW July 2, 1910. Reprinted and reissued by George H. Doran Company, New York, under date ⟨1910⟩.

B (1st, *Binding B*) H (1st, *Binding B*) LC (deposit copy: 1st, *Binding B*) UV (1st, *Binding A*; 2nd *Binding C*) Y (1st, *Binding B*)

14047. PANDORA'S BOX . . .

NEW YORK   FREDERICK A. STOKES COMPANY PUBLISHERS ⟨1911⟩

⟨i-x⟩, 1-390. Frontispiece and 3 plates inserted. 7⁵⁄₁₆″ full × 5″ full.

⟨1-25⁸⟩.

T cloth: blue.

Note: The second edition advertised PW Sept. 16, 1911; the third edition advertised PW Oct. 14, 21, Nov. 4, 1911; the fourth edition advertised and noted PW Dec. 9, 1911. BAL has been unable to identify the reprints. Reprinted and reissued by Grosset and Dunlap under date ⟨1911⟩.

On copyright page: *September, 1911* Noted for *early autumn* PW July 15, 1911. Advertised for Sept. 8 PW Aug. 26, 1911. The BA copy received Sept. 8, 1911. Advertised and noted as *just published* PW Sept. 9, 1911. Listed PW Sept. 16, 1911.

AAS BA H Y

14048. John Ames Mitchell . . . Reprinted from The Book News Monthly March, 1912

Compliments of Frederick A. Stokes Company Publishers New York ⟨1912⟩

Printed self-wrapper. Cover-title.

"Why *Pandora's Box* Was Written," pp. 10-13.

BA NYPL

14049. DROWSY . . .

NEW YORK   FREDERICK A. STOKES COMPANY PUBLISHERS ⟨1917⟩

⟨i-ii⟩, ⟨i⟩-⟨xii⟩, 1-301, 2 blank leaves. *See note below.* Frontispiece and 18 plates inserted. Printed on unwatermarked wove paper. $7\frac{3}{8}'' \times 5''$.

⟨1-20⁸⟩. *Note:* Leaf ⟨20⟩₈ is present as a free blank; or, excised; or, used as the terminal pastedown.

Two printings noted:

FIRST PRINTING

As above. Leaf ⟨1⟩₂ᵣ imprinted: DROWSY

SECOND PRINTING

Pagination and collation as above. Printed on wove paper watermarked SUEDE FINISH ⟨and the letter D in a lozenge⟩. Leaf ⟨1⟩₂ᵣ blank.

The following features are common to both printings:

P. 54, line 12: *financée* for *fiancée*

P. 112, line 8 up: *coacoa* for *cocoa*

P. 135, the final lines transposed.

B cloth: blue. White wove end papers, some showing the watermark: *Regal Antique* and the letter *D* in a lozenge. See above under collation for a comment on the end papers.

Deposited Oct. 6, 1917. Listed PW Oct. 6, 1917. Noted as *just published* PW Oct. 6, 1917.

H (1st) BA (1st) LC (1st) NYPL (1st) UV (1st) Y (2nd)

REFERENCES AND ANA

Part II. American Etchings, Edited by Ernest Knaufft. "A Poor Relation," . . .

New York: The Art Interchange Publishing Company, No. 140 Nassau Street. 1881

Printed paper wrapper. Contains no text by Mitchell; one etching by Mitchell herein.

Mitchell was not only a writer but an illustrator; for examples of his pictorial work see his *The Summer School of Philosophy at Mt. Desert*, 1881; *The Romance of the Moon*, 1886; *The Last American*, 1889; *That First Affair* . . . , 1896, etc., etc., etc.

John Ames Mitchell . . . Reprinted from The Book News Monthly March, 1912

Compliments of Frederick A. Stokes Company Publishers New York ⟨1912⟩

Cover-title. Printed self-wrapper.

SILAS WEIR MITCHELL

(Edward Kearsley)

1 8 2 9 – 1 9 1 4

Note: **Proceedings** and *transactions* of the societies to which Mitchell frequently contributed are serials and therefore not included in this list. See BAL, Vol. 1, p. xiv. For a record of such appearances see the bibliographies of Mitchell described at the end of this list. Offprints from such periodicals, being separate publications, are included here.

Also note: A number of Mitchell's offprints have been seen in unprinted drab paper wrappers, many of these being the author's own copies. BAL has been unable to determine whether or not these pieces were so issued, or whether the wrappers were applied by Mitchell himself. Hence the statement *unprinted paper wrapper* as applied to these publications must be considered tentative.

UNDATED PUBLICATIONS

The following publications were issued without date. They are here listed alphabetically by title with date assigned.

Address . . . Delivered . . . November 11th, 1909. See under 1909.

Address on Behalf of the Board of Trustees of the University of Pennsylvania . . . See under 1900.

Addresses at the Dinner Given to Dr. T. Gaillard Thomas . . . See under 1901.

Ave Pennsylvania! See under 1909.

The Birth and Death of Pain. See under 1896.

A Catalogue of the Scientific and Literary Work of S. Weir Mitchell . . . See under 1894.

The Christ of the Snow . . . See under 1887.

Dedicatory Address . . . ⟨University of Pennsylvania, Department of Medicine⟩. See under 1900.

The Eve of Battle, 1645. See under 1900.

Franklin Inn Club Song . . . See *Verses Read to the Franklin Inn Club . . . , 1903.*

The Influence of the Poet's Time on the Poet. See under 1898 in the section of *References and Ana.*

King Christmas and Master New Year. See under 1901.

The Memory of Franklin. See under 1906.

Nervous Diseases and Their Treatment. See under 1894.

Ode on a Lycian Tomb. See under 1899.

The Physician. See under 1900.

A Prayer. See under 1898.

Precision in the Treatment of Chronic Diseases. See under 1892.

The Rate of Growth of the Nails . . . See under 1874.

Recital of Compositions by Alexander MacFayden . . . See under 1903 in *Section Three.*

⟨Report to⟩ The College of Physicians of Philadelphia. See under 1885.

Verses Read to the Franklin Inn Club . . . See under 1903.

14050. Five Essays. By John Kearsley Mitchell, M. D. . . . Edited by S. Weir Mitchell . . .

Philadelphia: J. B. Lippincott & Co. 1859.

"Preface," pp. v-vi.

Deposited April 1, 1859. Listed PC June 15, 1859.

BPL   H   NYPL   UV   Y

14051. . . . NOTES UPON THE EFFECT OF ALCOHOL, GLYCERINE, WATER, GUM, AMMONIA, AND THE VACUUM UPON THE EXPOSED HEARTS OF FROGS, SNAPPING-TURTLES, AND STURGEONS . . . READ BEFORE THE ACADEMY OF NATURAL SCIENCES, BIOLOGICAL DEPARTMENT, DECEMBER 20, 1858 . . .

⟨n.p., PHILADELPHIA, 1859⟩

Caption-title. The above at head of p. ⟨1⟩. At head of title: [*Extracted from the American Journal of the Medical Sciences for April, 1859.*]

⟨1⟩-6, blank leaf. 8¼″ × 5⅜″ full.

1⁴.

Printed self-wrapper.

Y

14052. ... EXPERIMENTAL RESEARCHES RELATIVE TO CORROVAL AND VAO: TWO NEW VARIETIES OF WOORARA, THE SOUTH AMERICAN ARROW POISON. BY WILLIAM A. HAMMOND... AND S. WEIR MITCHELL... READ BEFORE THE ACADEMY OF NATURAL SCIENCES OF PHILADELPHIA, BIOLOGICAL DEPARTMENT, MAY 16, 1859. RECOMMENDED FOR PUBLICATION, MAY 31, 1859...

⟨n.p., PHILADELPHIA, 1859⟩

Caption-title. The above at head of p. ⟨1⟩. At head of title: [*Extracted from The American Journal of the Medical Sciences for July, 1859.*]

⟨1⟩-48. Illustrated. 8⅜″ scant × 5⁷⁄₁₆″.

1-3⁸.

Printed self-wrapper.

UP

14053. ... ON THE INHALATION OF CINCHONIA, AND ITS SALTS ...

⟨PHILADELPHIA, 1859⟩

Caption title. The preceding at head of p. ⟨1⟩. At head of title: *Read before the Biological Department of the Academy of Natural Sciences, Dec. 1858.*

⟨1⟩-2, blank leaf. 9³⁄₁₆″ × 5⅝″.

⟨-⟩².

Single leaf folded to make four pages.

Also in: *Proceedings of the Academy of Natural Sciences of Philadelphia. 1858*, Philadelphia, 1859. The *Proceedings* also contains Mitchell's "Observations on the Blood Crystals of the Sturgeon."

LC NYPL Y

14054. ON THE TREATMENT OF RATTLE-SNAKE BITES, WITH EXPERIMENTAL CRITICISMS UPON THE VARIOUS REMEDIES NOW IN USE ... [EXTRACTED FROM THE NORTH AMERICAN MEDICO-CHIRURGICAL REVIEW FOR MARCH, 1861.]

PHILADELPHIA: J. B. LIPPINCOTT & CO. 1861.

⟨1⟩-45; blank leaf. 9¼″ scant × 5⅞″.

⟨1⟩-3⁸.

Printed tan paper wrapper.

H Y

14055. ... RESEARCHES UPON THE VENOM OF THE RATTLESNAKE: WITH AN INVESTIGATION OF THE ANATOMY AND PHYSIOLOGY OF THE ORGANS CONCERNED ... [ACCEPTED FOR PUBLICATION, JULY, 1860.]

⟨WASHINGTON AND NEW YORK, 1861⟩

At head of title: *Smithsonian Contributions to Knowledge.*

⟨i⟩-⟨x⟩, ⟨1⟩-145. Illustrated. 13″ × 10″.

Signed: ⟨A⟩⁴, B¹, 1-18⁴, 19¹.

Printed drab paper wrapper. Imprinted: *Published by the Smithsonian Institution. January, 1861. New York: D. Appleton & Co.*

Also appears in *Smithsonian Contributions to Knowledge. Vol. XII ...*, Washington, 1860. For other papers on the same subject see *Experimental Contributions to the Toxicology of Rattle-Snake Venom, 1868*; and, *Researches upon the Venoms of Poisonous Serpents, 1886.*

H NYPL UV Y

14056. EXPERIMENTS AND OBSERVATIONS UPON THE CIRCULATION IN THE SNAPPING TURTLE, CHELONURA SERPENTINA, WITH ESPECIAL REFERENCE TO THE PRESSURE OF THE BLOOD IN THE ARTERIES AND VEINS ...

PHILADELPHIA: PRINTED BY C. SHERMAN & SON. 1862.

⟨1⟩-14, blank leaf. 11¾″ × 9⅜″.

⟨1⟩-2⁴.

Printed off-white paper wrapper.

Appears also in: *Transactions of the American Philosophical Society, Held at Philadelphia ... Vol. XII. New Series. Part I ...*, Philadelphia, 1862.

NYPL Y

14057. ... Report of a Committee of the Associate Medical Members of the Sanitary Commission on the Subject of Scurvy, with Special Reference to Practice in the Army and Navy. [Second Edition.]

Washington: M'Gill & Witherow, Printers 1863.

Cover-title. Printed self-wrapper. At head of title: *Sanitary Commission. N.*

Signed at end by Mitchell and others. *Mitchell* misspelled *Mitchel*, at end, p. 29.

Note: The first edition has not been located.

Y

14058. ... RESEARCHES UPON THE ANAT-
OMY AND PHYSIOLOGY OF RESPIRA-
TION IN THE CHELONIA. BY S. WEIR
MITCHELL ... AND GEORGE R. MORE-
HOUSE ... [ACCEPTED FOR PUBLICA-
TION, MARCH, 1863.]

⟨WASHINGTON AND NEW YORK, 1863⟩

At head of title: *Smithsonian Contributions to Knowledge. 169*

⟨i⟩-⟨viii⟩, ⟨1⟩-39. Illustrated. 13″ × 9⅞″.

⟨-⟩⁴, 1-5⁴.

Two editions noted:

FIRST EDITION

As above. Issued as No. 169 of the series. On p. ⟨v⟩
the *List of Wood-Cuts* is listed as on *p. viii*. Publication notice on p. 39.

SECOND EDITION

Text extended by the addition of an appendix,
pp. 41-42. Issued as No. 159 of the series. Pagination: ⟨i⟩-⟨viii⟩, ⟨1⟩-42, blank leaf. ⟨-⟩⁴, 1-5⁴, 6².
On p. v the *List of Wood-Cuts* is listed (incorrectly)
as on *p. ix*. Publication notice on p. 42. Pp. 41-42
devoted to an "Appendix": *Since committing to the
press the preceding paper* ...

Printed tan paper wrapper. Imprinted: *Washington
City: Published by the Smithsonian Institution. April,
1863. New York: D. Appleton & Co.*

Also in: *Smithsonian Contributions to Knowledge. Vol.
XIII* ..., Washington, 1863.

"Published ... April, 1863."---P. 39.

H (1st, 2nd)

14059. Summary of the Transactions of the College of Physicians of Philadelphia. Volume III.
–New Series ...

Philadelphia: Collins, Printer, 705 Jayne Street.
1863.

"A Case of Protracted Sleep," pp. 37-43.

"Improved Spirometer," pp. 254-255.

NYPL

14060. ... REFLEX PARALYSIS.

⟨WASHINGTON⟩ SURGEON GENERAL'S OFFICE,
MARCH 10, 1864.

Cover-title. At head of title: *Circular, No. 6.*

In collaboration with George R. Morehouse and
William W. Keen, Jr.

⟨i-ii⟩, ⟨1⟩-17. 7¾″ scant × 5¼″.

⟨-⟩¹⁰.

Printed self-wrapper.

H Y

14061. THE CHILDREN'S HOUR. BY E. W. S.
AND S.W.M. ...

PHILADELPHIA: PUBLISHED FOR THE BENEFIT OF
THE SANITARY COMMISSION. 1864.

See *Prince Little Boy*, 1888.

⟨i-ii⟩, ⟨i⟩-⟨viii⟩, 9-128. Frontispiece and 9 plates
inserted. 7⅜″ full × 5⁹⁄₁₆″. See *Note* below.

⟨1⟩⁹, 2-8⁸. Leaf ⟨1⟩₂ inserted. See *Note* below.

Note: The book is printed on wove paper. Leaf
⟨1⟩₂ is printed on laid paper and sometimes is
found inserted at the back of the book. To that
extent the pagination of some copies varies from
that given above. The leaf is not present in the
surviving copyright deposit copy. The leaf is
devoted to a series of acknowledgments: To the
printer, the stereotyper, the paper suppliers, etc.,
all of whom contributed materials and labor gratis.
The book was manufactured for the benefit of The
Sanitary Commission and sold at the Great Central Fair, Philadelphia, June 1864. (A trade format
was issued by J. B. Lippincott & Co., Philadelphia,
1866; possibly made up of unsold sheets with cancel title-leaf.) In the acknowledgments five binders
are mentioned by name which surely accounts for
the variety of bindings in which the book is found.
BAL has noted three bindings only, but clearly
there may be as many as five. The bindings have
been arbitrarily designated, and the designations
are for identification only.

BINDING A

BD cloth: blue-green; green; red. Sides blindstamped with a double-rule frame. Front stamped
in gold: ⟨2 classical children, running; repeated in
blind on the back⟩. Spine stamped in gold:
⟨fillet⟩ / THE / CHILDREN'S / HOUR / ⟨preceding
three lines in intaglio on a stylized ribbon, decorated with flowers⟩ / ⟨fillet⟩ White wove end
papers. Flyleaves. Edges stained purple.

BINDING B

TR cloth: blue. Sides blindstamped with a double
rule frame, an ornament at each inner corner. At
center of front: A goldstamped ornament; repeated in blind on the back. Spine stamped in
gold: ⟨fillet⟩ / THE / CHILDREN'S / HOUR / ⟨pre-
ceding three lines in intaglio on a stylized ribbon,
decorated with flowers⟩ / ⟨ornament⟩ / ⟨fillet⟩
Brown-coated on white end papers. Flyleaves;
sometimes triple flyleaves. Edges plain.

BINDING C

BD cloth: green. Sides blindstamped with a double
rule frame only. Spine stamped in gold: ⟨fillet⟩ /
THE / CHILDREN'S / HOUR / ⟨preceding three lines in
intaglio on a stylized ribbon, decorated with
flowers⟩ / ⟨fillet⟩ White wove end papers. No
flyleaves. Edges plain.

Letter, signed by Mitchell, Jan. 5, 1903; original in Y: "Dear Sir / The little book of which you speak *The Children's Hour* was written by Miss Elizabeth Stevenson and me for the benefit of the Sanitary Commission Fair of Philadelphia in 1864 and was edited by Mrs. Annie⟨?⟩ L. Wister, daughter of the Rev Dr Furness. It was the first publication from my hand. The stories are mine, and the introductory verses. The other verses are by Miss Stevenson." (Letter reprinted by courtesy of Yale University Library.)

Sold at Great Central Fair, Philadelphia, June, 1864. Deposited July 11, 1864.

H (B)   HM (C)   LC (B, being a deposit copy) UP (A)   UV (A)   Y (A)

14062. GUNSHOT WOUNDS AND OTHER INJURIES OF NERVES. BY S. WEIR MITCHELL . . . GEORGE R. MOREHOUSE . . . WILLIAM W. KEEN . . .

PHILADELPHIA: J. B. LIPPINCOTT & CO. 1864.

Two binder's variants noted. Sequence, if any, not determined. The designations are for identification only. The variations were caused by the binder, not by the printer.

VARIANT A

⟨i-ii⟩, ⟨1⟩-vi, 9-164. $7\frac{5}{8}'' \times 4\frac{13}{16}''$.

⟨a-b⟩², 2-14⁶.

Noted only in printed gray paper wrapper.

VARIANT B

⟨i⟩-⟨viii⟩, 9-164. $7\frac{7}{16}'' \times 4\frac{11}{16}''$.

⟨1⟩⁴, 2-14⁶.

Noted only in terra-cotta V cloth, covers bevelled, brown-coated on white end papers, flyleaves.

Deposited Oct. 4, 1864. Listed Bkr Dec. 31, 1864; again listed May 31, 1865; PC July 1, 1865.

H (both)

14063. . . . ON THE ANTAGONISM OF ATROPIA AND MORPHIA, FOUNDED UPON OBSERVATIONS AND EXPERIMENTS MADE AT THE U.S.A. HOSPITAL FOR INJURIES AND DISEASES OF THE NERVOUS SYSTEM. BY S. WEIR MITCHELL . . . WM. W. KEEN . . . AND GEORGE R. MOREHOUSE . . .

⟨N.P., PHILADELPHIA, 1865⟩

Caption-title. The above at head of p. ⟨1⟩. At head of title: *Extracted from the American Journal of the Medical Sciences for July, 1865.*

⟨1⟩-10, blank leaf. $9\frac{1}{2}'' \times 6''$. Illustrated.

1⁶.

Printed self-wrapper.

Y

14064. PARALYSIS FROM PERIPHERAL IRRITATION . . . EXTRACTED FROM THE NEW YORK MEDICAL JOURNAL.

NEW YORK: JOHN MEDOLE, PRINTER, 4 THAMES STREET. 1866.

⟨1⟩-67. $9\frac{11}{16}'' \times 6\frac{1}{4}''$.

⟨1⟩-4⁸, 5².

Printed off-white paper wrapper, white wove end papers.

LC NYPL

14065 THE WONDERFUL STORIES OF FUZ-BUZ THE FLY AND MOTHER GRABEM THE SPIDER.

PHILADELPHIA J. B. LIPPINCOTT & CO., 1867.

Title-page in black and red. Anonymous. See *Prince Little Boy,* 1888.

LARGE PAPER FORMAT

⟨i-ii⟩, ⟨1⟩-79. Frontispiece and 8 plates inserted; 1 illustration in text. $9\frac{1}{2}''$ full $\times$ $6\frac{7}{8}''$ full.

⟨1⁵, 2-10⁴⟩. Leaf ⟨1⟩₂ (the title-leaf) inserted. *Signed:* ⟨1⟩⁷, 2-6⁶, 7⁴. *Also signed:* ⟨A⟩¹³, B-C¹², D⁴.

Purple-brown paper boards sides, purple C cloth shelf back. Gray-coated on white end papers; gray-brown coated on white end papers. Flyleaves.

SMALL PAPER FORMAT

⟨i-ii⟩, ⟨1⟩-79. Frontispiece and 2 plates inserted; 1 illustration in text. See below under binding for leaf size.

⟨1⁹, 2-5⁸⟩. Leaf ⟨1⟩₂ (the title-leaf) inserted. *Signed:* ⟨1⟩⁷, 2-6⁶, 7⁴. *Also signed:* ⟨A⟩¹³, B-C¹², D⁴.

Noted in the following bindings of unknown sequence: the designations are for identification only.

SMALL PAPER FORMAT BINDING A

S cloth: brown. Covers bevelled. Front stamped in gold (at center): FUZ BUZ THE FLY / AND / MOTHER GRABEM / ⟨preceding three lines decorated with spider web, spiders, fly⟩ All the preceding repeated in blind on the back. Spine decorated in blind with an arrangement of rules. Edges plain. White wove end papers. Flyleaves. Leaf size: $6\frac{3}{4}'' \times 5\frac{1}{16}''$.

SMALL PAPER FORMAT BINDING B

S cloth: purple. Covers bevelled. Front stamped in gold (at center): FUZ BUZ THE FLY / AND /

THE

CHILDREN'S HOUR.

BY

E. W. S. AND S. W. M.

Between the dark and the daylight,
When the night is beginning to lower,
Comes a pause in the day's occupations,
That is known as the Children's Hour.

PHILADELPHIA:

PUBLISHED FOR THE BENEFIT OF THE SANITARY COMMISSION.

1864.

MOTHER GRABEM / ⟨preceding three lines decorated with spider web, spiders, fly⟩ All the preceding repeated in blind on the back. Spine decorated in blind with an arrangement of rules and quatrefoils. Edges plain. Brown-coated end papers. Flyleaves. Leaf size: 6¾″ × 5¹⁄₁₆″.

SMALL PAPER FORMAT BINDING C

C cloth: purple. Covers bevelled. Front stamped in gold (about 1″ from the top): FUZ BUZ THE FLY / AND / MOTHER GRABEM / ⟨preceding three lines decorated with a spider web, spiders, fly⟩ Back cover unstamped. Spine stamped in gold: FUZ-BUZ / *The Fly* / AND / *Mother* / *Grabem* / ⟨all the preceding in a box⟩ Edges plain. Pale peach wove end papers. Flyleaves. Leaf size: 6¾″ × 5″ full.

INTERMEDIATE FORMAT

Also occurs in an intermediate format; status not known. Possibly nothing more than an extra-illustrated form of the *Small Paper Format.*

⟨i-ii⟩, ⟨1⟩-79. Frontispiece and 8 plates inserted; 1 illustration in text. See below under binding for leaf size.

⟨1⁹, 2-5⁸⟩. Leaf ⟨1⟩₂ (the title-leaf) inserted. Signed: ⟨1⟩⁷, 2-6⁶, 7⁴. *Also signed:* ⟨A⟩¹³, B-C¹², D⁴.

Noted in the following bindings of unknown sequence; the designations are for identification only.

INTERMEDIATE FORMAT BINDING A

C cloth: green. Covers bevelled. Front stamped in gold at center: FUZ BUZ THE FLY / AND / MOTHER GRABEM / ⟨preceding three lines decorated with spider web, spiders, fly⟩ Back cover unstamped. Spine stamped in gold: ⟨squared rustic ornament⟩ / ⟨floral filigree⟩ Gray-brown coated end papers. Flyleaves. Top edges gilt. Leaf size: 6¾″ × 5¹⁄₁₆″.

INTERMEDIATE FORMAT BINDING B

C cloth: brown; purple. H-like cloth embossed with a series of vertical rules: blue. Fine-grained L cloth: green. T cloth: blue. Covers bevelled. Front stamped in gold at center: FUZ BUZ THE FLY / AND / MOTHER GRABEM / ⟨preceding three lines decorated with spider web, spiders, fly⟩ Blindstamped on both front and on back with a Greek fret frame. Spine stamped in blind: ⟨fillet⟩ / ⟨filigree⟩ / ⟨fillet⟩ Edges plain. Pale yellow end papers. Flyleaves. Leaf size: 6¾″ × 5¹⁄₁₆″.

INTERMEDIATE FORMAT BINDING C

C cloth: green. Covers bevelled. Front stamped in gold at center: FUZ BUZ THE FLY / AND / MOTHER GRABEM / ⟨preceding three lines decorated with spider web, spiders, fly⟩; sides otherwise unstamped. Spine unstamped save for blindstamped rules (double? triple?) at top and at bottom. Brown-coated end papers. Flyleaf at back. Edges plain. Leaf: 6¾″ × 5″.

Written and published for the benefit of The Children's Hospital, Philadelphia; see preface to *Prince Little Boy*, 1888. In all likelihood the binding was contributed by a number of binders, hence the variations. See, for a similar occurrence, the collation of *The Children's Hour*, 1864.

Deposited Dec. 3, 1866. Advertised as *just published* ALG Dec. 15, 1866. A copy in H (*Intermediate sheets, Binding B*) inscribed by early owner Dec. 25, 1866.

AAS (*Intermediate sheets, Binding C*) BA (*large paper*) H (*Intermediate sheets, Binding A; Intermediate sheets, Binding B*) NYPL (*large paper*) UV (*large paper; small paper, Binding A; small paper, Binding B; small paper, Binding C; Intermediate sheets, Binding A; Intermediate sheets, Binding B*) Y (*large paper; Intermediate sheets, Binding B*)

14066. Contributions Relating to the Causation and Prevention of Disease, and to Camp Diseases . . . Edited by Austin Flint . . .

New York: Published for the U.S. Sanitary Commission, by Hurd and Houghton, 459 Broome Street. 1867.

"On the Diseases of Nerves, Resulting from Injuries," pp. ⟨412⟩-468.

H

14067. . . . ON RETROGRESSIVE MOTIONS IN BIRDS PRODUCED BY THE APPLICATION OF COLD TO THE CERVICAL SPINE, WITH REMARKS ON THE USE OF THAT AGENT AS AN AID IN PHYSIOLOGICAL INVESTIGATIONS . . .

⟨n.p., PHILADELPHIA, 1867⟩

Caption-title. The above at head of p. ⟨1⟩. At head of title: [*Extracted from the American Journal of the Medical Sciences for January, 1867.*]

⟨1⟩-15. 9⁹⁄₁₆″ × 5⁷⁄₈″.

1⁸

Printed self-wrapper.

Y

14068. . . . EXPERIMENTAL CONTRIBUTIONS TO THE TOXICOLOGY OF RATTLE-SNAKE VENOM . . .

NEW YORK: MOORHEAD, SIMPSON & BOND. 1868.

Cover-title. At head of title: *From the New York Medical Journal, January, 1868.*

⟨1⟩-34. Laid paper. 9¼″ × 5⁷⁄₈″.

1-2⁸, 3¹.

Printed pale peach wrapper.

For other papers on the same subject see *Researches upon the Venom of the Rattlesnake* . . . ⟨1861⟩; and, *Researches upon the Venoms of Poisonous Serpents*, 1886.

BPL   H   LC   Y

14069. A LIST OF THE ORIGINAL MEMOIRS OF S. WEIR MITCHELL . . .

PHILADELPHIA: J. B. LIPPINCOTT & CO. 1868.

Anonymous. Presumably compiled by Mitchell.

⟨1⟩-8. $9\frac{1}{4}'' \times 5^{15}/_{16}''$.

⟨-⟩⁴.

Printed tan paper wrapper.

Y

14070. . . . ON THE PRODUCTION OF REFLEX SPASMS AND PARALYSIS IN BIRDS, BY THE APPLICATION OF COLD TO DEFINITE REGIONS OF THE SKIN . . .

⟨n.p., PHILADELPHIA, 1868⟩

Caption-title. The above at head of p. ⟨1⟩. At head of title: [*Extracted from the American Journal of the Medical Sciences for January, 1868.*]

⟨1⟩-7. $9^{11}/_{16}'' \times 6\frac{1}{16}''$.

⟨-⟩⁴.

Printed self-wrapper.

H   LC   NYPL   Y

14071. . . . RESEARCHES ON THE PHYSIOLOGY OF THE CEREBELLUM . . .

⟨n.p., PHILADELPHIA, 1869⟩

Caption-title. The above at head of p. ⟨1⟩. At head of title: [*Extracted from the American Journal of the Medical Sciences for April, 1869.*]

⟨1⟩-19. $9\frac{1}{8}'' \times 5\frac{3}{4}''$ full.

⟨1⟩⁸, 2².

Unprinted drab paper wrapper.

Y

14072. . . . ON THE EFFECT OF OPIUM AND ITS DERIVATIVE ALKALOIDS . . . (READ BEFORE THE BIOLOGICAL AND MICROSCOPICAL SECTION OF THE ACADEMY OF NATURAL SCIENCES, MARCH 1, 1869 . . .

⟨PHILADELPHIA, 1870⟩

Caption-title. The above at head of p. ⟨1⟩. At head of title: [*Extracted from the American Journal of the Medical Sciences for January, 1870.*]

⟨1⟩-16. $8^{13}/_{16}'' \times 5\frac{3}{8}''$.

⟨-⟩⁸.

Printed self-wrapper.

NYPL   Y

14073. Balloon Post . . .

Boston, Mass., April . . . 1871 . . .

An occasional newspaper. 6 numbers. For fuller comment see entry No. 4038.

"Verses," No. VI, p. 5. Extensively revised and collected in *The Hill of Stones*, 1883, as "A Tale Untold."

14074. WEAR AND TEAR, OR HINTS FOR THE OVERWORKED . . .

PHILADELPHIA: J. B. LIPPINCOTT & CO. 1871.

For other editions and printings see below (in *Section One*) under 1887; and, (in *Section Two*) under 1872, 1899.

Two states (probably printings) noted:

1

⟨1⟩-59. $6\frac{1}{2}'' \times 4\frac{3}{8}''$.

⟨1-5⁶⟩. *Signed:* ⟨1⟩-3⁸, 4⁶.

2

⟨A⟩-E⁶. *Also signed:* ⟨1⟩-3⁸, 4⁶.

C cloth: green; purple-brown; violet. Brown-coated end papers. Flyleaves.

Listed ALG July 1, 1871. A copy of the first in Y inscribed by early owner *July, 1871.* A copy of the second in BPL inscribed by early owner *July, 1871.* The *Third Edition* advertised as in both cloth; and, paper, ALG Aug. 15, 1871. Advertised as a Trübner importation Bkr Aug. 3, *1871*; listed Bkr Aug. 3, 1871; listed PC Aug. 15, 1871.

BPL (2nd)   H (1st)   LC (1st)   NYPL (2nd)   UV (1st)   Y (1st, 2nd)

14075. INJURIES OF NERVES AND THEIR CONSEQUENCES . . .

PHILADELPHIA: J. B. LIPPINCOTT & CO 1872.

⟨i⟩-viii, 9-377; blank, p. ⟨378⟩; blank leaf. $8\frac{1}{4}''$ full × $5\frac{1}{2}''$ scant.

⟨1⟩⁴, 2-23⁸, 24⁴, 25⁶.

Four bindings noted; the sequence of A and B not determined and the designations are for identification only.

BINDING A

P cloth: purple. Covers bevelled. Sides blind-stamped with a rule frame. Spine goldstamped: ⟨*ornate fillet*⟩ / INJURIES / OF / NERVES / ⟨*rule*⟩ / MITCHELL / J. B. LIPPINCOTT & CO. ⟨*in intaglio on a ribbon*⟩ | ⟨*ornate fillet*⟩ Brown-coated end papers. Flyleaves.

BINDING B

C cloth: purple. Covers bevelled. Sides blind-stamped with a rule frame. Spine stamped in gold: ⟨*triple rule*⟩ | INJURIES | OF | NERVES | ⟨*rule*⟩ | MITCHELL | J. B. LIPPINCOTT & CO. ⟨*in a lozenge frame*⟩ | ⟨*triple rule*⟩ Brown-coated end papers. Flyleaves.

BINDING C

C cloth: purple. Covers bevelled. Sides blind-stamped with a rule frame. Spine stamped in gold: ⟨*triple rule*⟩ | INJURIES | OF | NERVES | ⟨*rule*⟩ | MITCHELL | ⟨*ornament*⟩ | J B LIPPINCOTT & CO ⟨*in intaglio on a ribbon*⟩ | ⟨*triple rule*⟩ Brown-coated on white end papers. Flyleaves. Leaf 25₆ excised. Inserted at back is *J. B. Lippincott & Co.'s Catalogue of Medical and Surgical Works*, pp. 1-12. On p. 7 of the catalog the present title is listed, together with reviews.

BINDING D

The most notable variation is the publisher's spine imprint which is: J. B. LIPPINCOTT CO. Not prior to March, 1885, in which month J. B. Lippincott & Company became J. B. Lippincott Company.

A rebound copy in BPL received April 11, 1872. Listed WTC April 18, 1872.

B (*Binding B*)   LC (*Binding C, not a deposit copy*)   Y (*Bindings A, D*)

14076. . . . THE RATE OF GROWTH OF THE NAILS AS A MEANS OF DIAGNOSING CERTAIN FORMS OF PARALYSIS . . .

⟨n.p., n.d., 1872⟩

Caption-title. The above at head of p. ⟨2⟩. At head of title: *Original Communications.*

⟨1-4⟩. 8¹¹⁄₁₆″ scant × 5″ full.

Single leaf folded to make four pages; pp. ⟨1⟩ and ⟨4⟩ blank; text, pp. ⟨2-3⟩.

H   Y

14077. . . . CASES ILLUSTRATIVE OF THE USE OF THE OPHTHALMOSCOPE IN THE DIAGNOSIS OF INTRA-CRANIAL LESIONS. BY S. WEIR MITCHELL . . . AND WM. THOMSON . . .

⟨n.p., PHILADELPHIA, 1873⟩

Caption-title. The above at head of p. ⟨1⟩. At head of title: [*Extracted from the American Journal of the Medical Sciences for July, 1873.*]

⟨1⟩-15. 9⅛″ × 5⅞″. Illustrated.

⟨-⟩⁸.

Printed self-wrapper.

Y

14078. . . . THE INFLUENCE OF REST IN LOCOMOTOR ATAXIA . . .

⟨n.p., PHILADELPHIA, 1873⟩

Caption-title. The above at head of p. ⟨1⟩. At head of title: [*Extracted from the American Journal of the Medical Sciences for July, 1873.*]

⟨1⟩-3. 9⅛″ × 5⅞″ full.

Single cut sheet folded to make four pages.

LC   NYPL   Y

14079. . . . POST-PARALYTIC CHOREA . . .

⟨n.p., PHILADELPHIA, 1874⟩

Caption-title. The preceding at head of p. ⟨1⟩. At head of title: [*Extracted from the American Journal of the Medical Sciences for October, 1874.*]

⟨1⟩-11. 9¼″ full × 5¹⁵⁄₁₆″ scant.

⟨1⟩⁶.

Printed self-wrapper.

NYPL   Y

14080. Summary of the Transactions of the College of Physicians of Philadelphia. Vol. IV. New Series. From February, 1863, to May, 1874, Inclusive . . .

Philadelphia: Collins, Printer, 705 Jayne Street. 1874.

"Effects of Chloral, Chloroform, and Ether Hypodermically Employed," p. 316.

"Microscopical Examination," pp. 225-227.

"On Certain Forms of Neuralgia . . .," pp. 282-288.

"On the Growth of the Nails as a Prognostic Indication in Cerebral Paralysis," pp. 364-366.

"On the Use of Bromide of Lithium," pp. 350-352.

"Ulceration of the Skin as an Effect of the Use of Bromides," pp. 347-349.

Comments, pp. 346, 349, 350.

H

14081. . . . TRAUMATIC NEURALGIA; SECTION OF MEDIAN NERVE . . .

⟨n.p., PHILADELPHIA, 1874⟩

Caption-title. The preceding at head of p. ⟨1⟩. At head of title: [*Extracted from the American Journal of the Medical Sciences for July, 1874.*]

⟨1⟩-13, blank leaf. Illustrated. 9¼″ × 5⅞″ full.

1⁸.

Printed self-wrapper.

HSP   NYPL   Y

14082. ... REST IN THE TREATMENT OF NERVOUS DISEASE ...

NEW YORK: G. P. PUTNAM'S SONS, FOURTH AVE. AND 23d ST. 1875.

Cover-title. At head of title: *A Series of American Clinical Lectures Edited by E. C. Seguin, M.D. Volume I. No. IV.*

⟨i-ii⟩, ⟨1⟩-20. Also paged: ⟨i-ii⟩, ⟨83⟩-102. 9¹⁄₁₆″ × 5¾″ scant.

⟨1¹, 2¹⁰⟩.

Printed self-wrapper.

Preprinted from *A Series of American Clinical Lectures*, edited by E. C. Seguin, Vol. 1, Jan.-Dec., 1875, New York: G. P. Putnam's Sons, 1876.

H

14083. ... SPINAL ARTHROPATHIES ...

⟨n.p., PHILADELPHIA, 1875⟩

Caption-title. The above at head of p. ⟨1⟩. At head of title: [*Extracted from the American Journal of the Medical Sciences for April, 1875.*]

⟨1⟩-10, blank leaf. 9³⁄₁₆″ × 5⅞″.

1⁶.

Printed self-wrapper.

HSP NYPL Y

14084. ... ON SOME OF THE DISORDERS OF SLEEP ... REPRINTED FROM VIRGINIA MEDICAL MONTHLY, JANUARY, 1876.

RICHMOND: J. W. FERGUSSON & SON, PRINTERS. 1875.

Cover-title. At head of title: *Compliments of the Author.*

⟨1⟩-13, blank leaf. 9⁵⁄₁₆″ × 5⅝″ scant.

⟨-⟩⁸.

Printed wrapper of mottled blue-gray paper.

Y

14085. CASES ILLUSTRATING LOCAL INJURIES OF NERVES AND THEIR TROPHIC CONSEQUENCES, WITH COMMENTS ... [READ MAY 3, 1876.] ...

⟨PHILADELPHIA, 1876⟩

Caption-title. The above at head of p. ⟨115⟩.

⟨115⟩-138. 9⅝″ × 6⅛″. One plate inserted; other illustrations in text.

Presumably leaves extracted from the *Transactions* (see below) and issued in gray-green paper wrapper imprinted: *Extracted from the Transactions of the College of Physicians of Philadelphia, Third Series, Volume II.*

Also appears in: *Transactions of the College of Physicians of Philadelphia. Third Series. Volume the Second*, Philadelphia, 1876.

Y

14086. ... HEADACHES FROM EYE STRAIN ...

⟨n.p., PHILADELPHIA, 1876⟩

Caption-title. The above at head of p. ⟨1⟩. At head of title: [*Extracted from the American Journal of the Medical Sciences for April, 1876.*]

⟨1⟩-12. 9¼″ scant × 5¹³⁄₁₆″ full.

⟨-⟩⁶.

Printed self-wrapper.

NYPL Y

14087. ... NEUROTOMY. BY S. WEIR MITCHELL ... WITH AN EXAMINATION OF THREE GENERATED NERVES, AND NOTES UPON NEURAL REPAIR: BY R. M. BERTOLET ...

⟨n.p., PHILADELPHIA, 1876⟩

Caption-title. The above at head of p. ⟨1⟩. At head of title: [*Extracted from the American Journal of the Medical Sciences for April, 1876.*]

⟨1⟩-14, blank leaf. Illustrated. 9¼″ × 5¹⁵⁄₁₆″.

⟨-⟩⁸.

Printed self-wrapper.

Y

14088. ... ON FUNCTIONAL SPASMS ...

⟨n.p., PHILADELPHIA, 1876⟩

Caption-title. The above at head of p. ⟨1⟩. At head of title: [*Extracted from the American Journal of the Medical Sciences for October, 1876.*]

⟨1⟩-13, blank leaf. Illustrated. 9⅛″ × 5¾″ scant.

⟨-⟩⁸.

Printed self-wrapper.

Y

14089. FAT AND BLOOD: AND HOW TO MAKE THEM ...

PHILADELPHIA: J. B. LIPPINCOTT & CO. 1877.

For other editions and printings see below (in *Section One*) under 1878, 1884, 1885, 1891, 1898, 1900; and, (in *Section Two*) under 1879, 1888, 1902, 1911.

⟨1⟩-101, blank leaf. 7″ × 4⅝″.

⟨1⟩-8⁶, 9⁴.

A cloth: brown. C cloth: maroon. S cloth: brown. Gray-coated end papers. Flyleaves. Edges stained red.

A copy in BPL received Aug. 14, 1877. Listed PW Aug. 18, 1877.

AAS   NYPL   Y

14090. NURSE AND PATIENT, AND CAMP CURE ... [REPRINTED FROM LIPPIN-COTT'S MAGAZINE.]

PHILADELPHIA   J. B. LIPPINCOTT & CO. 1877.

⟨1⟩-73. 5⁵⁄₁₆″ × 3½″ full.

⟨A⟩-C, ⟨D⟩-F⁶, G¹.

Noted in four varying bindings; sequence, if any, not determined. The designations are for identifica-tion only.

BINDING A

C cloth: green; purple. S cloth: green; terra-cotta. Sides stamped in blind with a triple-rule frame. Front stamped in gold: *Nurse and Patient | and | Camp Cure.* Spine stamped in gold, up the spine: *Nurse and Patient* Flyleaves. Yellow-coated end papers. Cream end papers. Brown-coated end papers.

BINDING B

S cloth: maroon. Stamped in gold only. Front: *Nurse and Patient | and | Camp Cure.* Spine lettered down: *Nurse and Patient* Flyleaves. Brown-coated end papers.

BINDING C

S cloth: green. Stamped in gold only. Front: *Nurse and Patient | and | Camp Cure.* Spine lettered up: *Nurse and Patient* Flyleaves. Brown-coated end papers.

BINDING D

S cloth: brown. Stamped in gold only. Front: *Nurse and Patient | and | Camp Cure.* Spine lettered down: *Nurse and Patient* No flyleaves. White end papers.

Listed PW Sept. 8, 1877.

H (*Binding A*)   LC (*Binding A, being a deposit copy*) NYPL (*Binding A*)   Y (*Bindings A, B, C, D*)

14091. Advertisement Number. The Medical News and Library. December, 1877 ...

Henry C. Lea––––Philadelphia. ⟨1877⟩

The above on p. ⟨1⟩.

Prospectus, pp. 32, for the forthcoming 1878 issues of *The Medical News and Library*, Philadelphia.

"Clinical Lectures on Nervousness in the Male," pp. ⟨1⟩-3, 29–32; reprinted from *The Medical News and Library*, Dec. 1877.

Y

14092. ... THE ANNUAL ORATION BE-FORE THE MEDICAL AND CHIRURGI-CAL FACULTY OF MARYLAND, ⟨sic⟩ 1877 ... REPRINTED FROM THE TRANS-ACTIONS OF THE MEDICAL AND CHIRURGICAL FACULTY OF MARY-LAND, APRIL, 1877.

BALTIMORE: INNES & COMPANY, PRINTERS AND BINDERS 1877.

Cover-title. At head of title: *With the Author's Compliments.*

⟨1⟩-18. 8⅞″ scant × 5¹¹⁄₁₆″.

⟨1-2⁴, 3¹⟩.

Printed gray laid paper wrapper.

NYPL   UV   Y

14093. Johnson's New Universal Cyclopædia: A Scientific and Popular Treasury ...

A. J. Johnson & Son ... New York ... MDCCCLXXVII.

"Poison of Serpents," Vol. 3, p. 1302.

Deposited Sept. 4, 1876.

For fuller entry see No. 11595.

14094. ON THE TRANSMISSION OF ELEC-TRIC INFLUENCE ACROSS THE MIDDLE LINE OF THE BODY ... REPRINTED FROM THE TRANSACTIONS OF THE AMERICAN NEUROLOGICAL ASSOCIA-TION VOL. II., 1877

NEW YORK   G. P. PUTNAM'S SONS   182 FIFTH AVENUE 1877

Cover-title.

⟨1⟩-5, blank leaf. Illustrated. 9¼″ scant × 5⅞″.

⟨-⟩⁴.

Printed mottled blue-gray wrapper.

NYPL   Y

14095. ... THE RELATIONS OF PAIN TO WEATHER, BEING A STUDY OF THE NATURAL HISTORY OF A CASE OF TRAUMATIC NEURALGIA ...

⟨n.p., PHILADELPHIA, 1877⟩

Caption-title. The above at head of p. ⟨1⟩. At head of title: [*Extracted from the American Journal of the Medical Sciences for April, 1877.*]

$\langle 1 \rangle$-25. Illustrated. $9\frac{1}{4}''$ full $\times 5\frac{11}{16}''$.

1^8, 2^5. Leaf 2_3 (signed with an asterisk) inserted. *Collation tentative.*

Printed self-wrapper.

For a continuation of this study see below under year 1883.

Y

14096. Report of Harrison et al. vs. St. Mark's Church, Philadelphia. A Bill to Restrain the Ringing of Bells So As to Cause a Nuisance to the Occupants of the Dwellings in the Immediate Vicinity of the Church. In the Court of Common Pleas, No. 2. in Equity . . . Philadelphia, February, 1877.

> Printed by Allen, Lane & Scott, No. 233 South Fifth Street. $\langle$n.d., 1877?$\rangle$

Mitchell's testimony, pp. 97-100. ". . . The multiplication of needless noises in modern life is beginning to attract attention . . ."

Two letters, respectively dated *3d November, 1876;* and, *4th November* $\langle$n.y., 1876$\rangle$, p. 101.

Y

14097. Fat and Blood: And How to Make Them . . . Second Edition, Revised.

> Philadelphia: J. B. Lippincott & Co. London: 16 Southampton Street, Covent Garden. 1878.

See above under 1877 for first edition.

"Preface to the Second Edition," p. 7.

". . . I have made some few additions to the text." ---From the preface.

Listed PW Nov. 3, 1877. "The first edition was exhausted in a few weeks, and a new edition is now in preparation involving the resetting the entire work."---PW Nov. 3, 1877. The London (Lippincott) edition, marked *First English from the Second American Edition,* listed PC and Bkr April 1, 1878.

NYPL Y

14098. . . . ADDRESS DEDICATORY OF THE NEW BUILDINGS ERECTED BY THE UNIVERSITY OF PENNSYLVANIA FOR ITS DENTAL SCHOOL AND MEDICAL LABORATORIES . . . DELIVERED OCTOBER 2, 1878 . . .

> PHILADELPHIA: J. B. LIPPINCOTT & CO. 1878.

Cover-title. At head of title: *Compliments of the Author.*

1-16. $9\frac{3}{16}'' \times 5\frac{7}{8}''$.

$\langle 1 \rangle^8$.

Printed gray paper wrapper.

BPL H LC NYPL Y

14099. . . . ON A RARE VASO-MOTOR NEUROSIS OF THE EXTREMITIES,[1] AND ON THE MALADIES WITH WHICH IT MAY BE CONFOUNDED . . .

> $\langle$n.p., PHILADELPHIA, 1878$\rangle$

Caption-title. The above at head of p. $\langle 1 \rangle$. At head of title: [*Extracted from the American Journal of the Medical Sciences for July, 1878.*]

$\langle 1 \rangle$-20. $9\frac{3}{16}'' \times 5\frac{5}{8}''$. Laid paper. Illustrated.

1^8, 2^2.

Issued in $\langle$printed? unprinted?$\rangle$ drab paper wrapper.

Y

14100. THE CREMASTER-REFLEX . . . [REPRINTED FROM JOURNAL OF NERVOUS AND MENTAL DISEASE, OCTOBER, 1879.] . . .

> $\langle$n.p., CHICAGO, 1879$\rangle$

Caption-title. The above at head of p. $\langle 1 \rangle$.

$\langle 1 \rangle$-10. $9\frac{3}{8}'' \times 6\frac{3}{16}''$.

$\langle 1^4, 2^1 \rangle$.

Printed self-wrapper.

NYPL Y

14101. HEPHZIBAH GUINNESS; THEE AND YOU; AND A DRAFT ON THE BANK OF SPAIN . . .

> PHILADELPHIA: J. B. LIPPINCOTT & CO. 1880.

$\langle 1 \rangle$-199; blank, p. $\langle 200 \rangle$; 4 pp. advertisements. $7\frac{1}{2}'' \times 5''$ scant.

$\langle 1 \rangle$-17^6. *Also signed:* $\langle$a$\rangle$-i, k-m^8, n^6. *Also signed:* $\langle$A$\rangle$-H^{12}, I^6.

S cloth: brown; green. Covers bevelled. Stamped in gold. Brown-coated end papers. Flyleaves.

Note: A set of sheets (in Y) is bound in gray V cloth, stamped in brown. The following rubber-stamped notice appears on the copyright page: *Copyright Renewed 1908 by S. Weir Mitchell.*

Listed PW June 26, 1880. A London edition (an import?) listed Bkr July, 1880. The Lippincott edition listed PC Aug. 16, 1880. For a revised edition see under year 1897.

AAS NYPL Y

14102. LECTURES ON DISEASES OF THE NERVOUS SYSTEM, ESPECIALLY IN WOMEN . . . WITH FIVE PLATES.

> PHILADELPHIA: HENRY C. LEA'S SON & CO. 1881.

A copy in Y has the imprint concealed by a label reading: *London: J. & A. Churchill, New Burlington Street.*

For a second edition see below under 1885.

⟨i⟩-xii, ⟨13⟩-238; 2 pp. advertisements. Laid paper. Four charts and one folded chart inserted. $7^{13}/_{16}''$ full × $5^{1}/_{8}''$.

⟨1⟩-20⁶.

Noted in the following bindings. The sequence has not been determined and the designations are for identification only.

BINDING A

S cloth: brown; green. Sides blindstamped with a triple rule frame. Spine goldstamped: ⟨*double rule*⟩ / NERVOUS / DISEASES / ⟨*rule*⟩ / MITCHELL / ⟨*publisher's monogram in a shield*⟩ / ⟨*double rule*⟩ Blue-coated end papers printed in black with a leafy pattern. Also unprinted brown-coated end papers. Single laid paper flyleaves. No inserted catalog.

BINDING B

C cloth: bluish-blackish-green; green. Sides blindstamped with a double rule frame. Spine goldstamped: ⟨*double rule*⟩ / NERVOUS / DISEASES / ⟨*rule*⟩ / MITCHELL / ⟨*publisher's monogram; not in a shield*⟩ / ⟨*double rule*⟩ Brown-coated end papers. At front and at back: A gathering of four leaves of laid paper used as end papers as follows: Two leaves free, one leaf pasted under the end paper, one leaf used to line the end paper. Inserted at back: Publisher's catalog, 12 pp.

BINDING C

C cloth: bluish-blackish-green. Sides blindstamped with a double rule frame. Spine goldstamped: ⟨*double rule*⟩ / NERVOUS / DISEASES / ⟨*rule*⟩ / MIT-CHELL / ⟨*publisher's monogram in a shield*⟩ / ⟨*double rule*⟩ Brown-coated end papers. Triple laid paper flyleaves at front and at back; not the flyleaf arrangement described in *Binding B.* Inserted at back: Publisher's catalog, 12 pp.

Deposited April 11, 1881. Noted as *now ready* PW April 16, 1881. Listed PW May 21, 1881. The London (Churchill?) edition listed Ath May 14, 1881.

H (*Bindings A, C*) LC (*Binding A,* being a deposit copy) Y (*Bindings A, B*)

14103. The Cambridge Book of Poetry and Song ... by Charlotte Fiske Bates ...

New York: Thomas Y. Crowell & Co., No. 13 Astor Place. ⟨1882⟩

"The Quaker Graveyard," pp. 844-845. Collected in *The Hill of Stones* ... , 1883.

For comment see entry Nos. 7887, 11490.

14104. The Elocutionist's Annual Number 10 ... Edited by Mrs. J. W. Shoemaker ...

Philadelphia: National School of Elocution and Oratory. 1882.

"The Shriving of Guinevere," pp. 70-74. Collected in *The Hill of Stones* ... , 1883.

Cloth; and, printed paper wrapper.

Deposited Oct. 4, 1882.

LC

14105. THE HILL OF STONES AND OTHER POEMS ...

BOSTON HOUGHTON, MIFFLIN AND COMPANY NEW YORK: 11 EAST SEVENTEENTH STREET THE RIVERSIDE PRESS, CAMBRIDGE 1883

TRADE FORMAT

⟨i⟩-iv, ⟨1⟩-98; blank leaf. Laid paper. $6^{5}/_{8}''$ full × $4^{5}/_{16}''$. See note below regarding the final blank leaf.

⟨-⟩², 1-6⁸, 7². See below regarding leaf 7₂.

S cloth: blue-green; dark brown; gray; green; light brown; mauve. White laid end papers. Top edges gilt.

Two binding variants noted; the designations are for identification only. Sequence, if any, not determined.

BINDING VARIANT A

Leaf 7₂ excised. Laid paper flyleaf at front; one or two laid paper flyleaves at back.

BINDING VARIANT B

Leaf 7₂ present. Wove paper flyleaf at front. No flyleaf at back.

LARGE PAPER FORMAT

Leaf size: $8^{5}/_{8}''$ × $5^{7}/_{8}''$. Leaf 7₂ present. Pagination and signature collation as above. Noted in S cloth: blue-green; brown. Flyleaves.

According to the publisher's records 1008 copies of the *trade format* were printed Dec. 11, 1882; bound during the period Dec. 12, 1882 to July 20, 1893; on Aug. 31, 1897, "149 sheets sent to Dr. S. Weir Mitchell." On Dec. 16, 1882, the publisher's recorded the printing of 66 large paper copies; 62 copies bound Jan. 6, 1883; 1 copy bound Jan. 12, 1883. According to a letter from the publishers (in Y), Sept. 10, 1914, 63 large paper copies only were printed. The publisher's records show that the small paper format was first printed.

Advertised for *next week* PW Dec. 9, 1882. Deposited Dec. 15 (10?), 1882. A copy (*Binding Variant A*) in NYPL inscribed by George Bancroft Dec. 17, 1882. The BA copy (*Binding Variant A*) received Dec. 20, 1882. Listed PW Dec. 23, 1882.

b (*Binding Variant A*)　ba (*Binding Variant A*)　h (*Binding Variant A*)　lc (*Binding Variant A*) nypl (*Binding Variant A*)　uv (*large paper*)　y (*Binding Variants A, B; large paper*)

14106. A PARTIAL STUDY OF THE POISON OF HELODERMA SUSPECTUM . . .

Two printings have been seen; sequence, if any, not known; the designations are for identification only.

PRINTING A

A PARTIAL STUDY OF THE POISON OF HELODERMA SUSPECTUM (COPE)--- THE GILA MONSTER. BY S. WEIR MIT-CHELL . . . AND EDWARD T. REICHERT . . .

⟨PHILADELPHIA⟩ FROM THE MEDICAL NEWS, FEBRUARY 10, 1883.

Cover-title.

⟨1⟩-16. 6⁷⁄₁₆″ × 4⁷⁄₁₆″.

⟨-⟩⁸.

Printed self-wrapper.

PRINTING B

A PARTIAL STUDY OF THE POISON OF HELODERMA SUSPECTUM (COPE)--- THE GILA MONSTER. BY S. WEIR MIT-CHELL . . . AND EDWARD T. REICHERT . . . [READ FEBRUARY 7, 1882.] . . .

⟨n.p., n.d., PHILADELPHIA, 1883⟩

Caption-title. The above at head of p. ⟨255⟩.

⟨255⟩-266. 9½″ × 6¹⁄₁₆″.

Sheets extracted from the *Transactions* (see below) and issued in printed gray paper wrapper.

Appears also in: *Transactions of the College of Physicians of Philadelphia, Third Series, Volume the Sixth*, Philadelphia, 1883.

lc (both)　nypl (*Printing B*)　y (both)

14107. PRELIMINARY REPORT ON THE VENOMS OF SERPENTS. BY S. WEIR MITCHELL . . . AND EDWARD T. REICH-ERT . . . FROM THE MEDICAL NEWS APRIL 28, 1883.

⟨n.p., PHILADELPHIA, 1883⟩

Cover-title.

⟨1⟩-14, blank leaf. 7⁵⁄₈″ × 5¹⁄₁₆″.

⟨-⟩⁸.

Printed self-wrapper.

h　y

14108. The Relations of Pain to Weather

A continuation of a study published in 1877; see above.

Two printings noted; sequence, if any, not determined. The designations are for identification only. Both printings are from the same setting with some rearrangement of the types.

PRINTING A

The Relations of Pain to Weather, Studied during Eleven Years of a Case of Traumatic Neuralgia. By Captain R. Catlin . . . with Notes by S. Weir Mitchell . . . Read before the College of Physicians of Philadelphia, June 6, 1883. Extracted from the Transactions of the College of Physicians, Vol. vi.

Philadelphia: Collins, Printer, 705 Jayne Street. 1883.

Printed paper wrapper. True title-page (as above) present. Pp. ⟨1⟩-19. Two folded charts inserted; 1 single leaf chart inserted; other illustrative material in text.

PRINTING B

Issued without title-page. Caption-title, p. ⟨411⟩: The Relations of Pain to Weather, Studied during Eleven Years of a Case of Traumatic Neuralgia. By Captain R. Catlin . . . with Notes by S. Weir Mitchell . . .

Issued in printed paper wrapper: *Extracted from the Transactions of the College of Physicians of Philadelphia. Third Series, Volume VI.* ⟨1883⟩. Paged ⟨411⟩-427; two folded charts inserted; 1 single leaf chart inserted; other illustrative material in text.

h (A)　lc (B)　nypl (A)　y (A,B)

14109. Fat and Blood . . . Third Edition, Revised, with Additions.

Philadelphia: J. B. Lippincott & Co. London: 16 Southampton Street, Strand. 1884.

For first edition see under year 1877.

". . . I have taken the occasion to rewrite a good deal . . . to add many practical hints . . . and to insert a considerable matter in regard to the treatment of obesity, the use of milk as a diet . . ." ---"Preface to the Third Edition," dated at end *October, 1883*, p. 5.

Deposited Jan. 11, 1884.

Advertised as *just published* pw Jan. 12, 1884. Listed pw March 1, 1884; Oct. 11, 1884.

h　lc　y

14110. IN WAR TIME . . .

BOSTON HOUGHTON, MIFFLIN AND COMPANY NEW YORK: 11 EAST SEVENTEENTH STREET THE RIVERSIDE PRESS, CAMBRIDGE 1885

Note: All examined copies have the error *Hepzibah* for *Hephzibah* on the title-page.

⟨i-iv⟩, ⟨1⟩-423; plus: publisher's catalog, pp. ⟨1⟩-12. Laid paper. 7″ full × 4⅝″.

⟨1², 2-18¹², 19⁸; plus: 20⁶⟩. *Signed:* ⟨-⟩², 1-26⁸, 27⁴; plus: ⟨28⟩⁶.

V cloth: brown; red. White laid end papers. Laid paper flyleaves.

Note: In all likelihood there were two printings issued under the date *1885*; BAL has failed to identify two printings so dated. See publication notes below.

First printing: 1848 copies recorded in the publisher's records Nov. 24, 1884; bound during the period Nov. 26-Dec. 4, 1884. 250 copies shipped to David Douglas (Edinburgh) Nov. 29, 1884. Deposited Dec. 1, 1884. The H copy received Dec. 1, 1884. Listed PW Dec. 13, 1884. *Second printing:* 276 copies recorded in the publisher's records March 11, 1885; bound during the period March 20-June 8, 1885. *Third printing:* recorded Jan. 5, 1886, the date presumably altered. The *Edinburgh* issue (American sheets) advertised as *nearly ready* Ath Dec. 6, 1884; listed Ath Jan. 24, 1885.

AAS   LC   NYPL   Y

14111. Lectures on Diseases of the Nervous System, Especially in Women . . . Second Edition, Revised and Enlarged . . .

Philadelphia: Lea Brothers & Co. 1885.

For first edition see above under year 1881.

". . . I have altered considerably some of the early lectures, and have added others . . ."−−−"Preface to the Second Edition," p. ⟨v⟩.

Deposited March 10, 1885. Listed PW June 6, 1885.

BA   BPL   H   LC   Y

14112. Fat and Blood: An Essay on the Treatment of Certain Forms of Neurasthenia and Hysteria . . . Fourth Edition, Revised, with Additions.

Philadelphia: J. B. Lippincott Company. London: 15 Russell Street, Covent Garden. 1885.

For first edition see under year 1877.

Contains a dedication to Samuel Lewis, not present in the earlier editions.

"I have made some slight changes in this edition, and have added a few not unimportant points in regard to treatment."−−−"Preface to the Fourth Edition," p. 7.

Deposited Sept. 15, 1885.

LC   Y

14113. NOVEMBER ⟨1885. REPORT TO⟩ THE COLLEGE OF PHYSICIANS OF PHILADELPHIA . . .

⟨n.p., n.d., PHILADELPHIA, 1885⟩

Not seen. Entry on the basis of a photographic copy of an imperfect example.

Caption-title. The above at head of p. ⟨1⟩.

2 pp. 8¹⁵⁄₁₆″ × 6¾″.

"As there has been published by the American Antivivisection Society a pamphlet *Facts in regard to the Failure of the Bills presented to the Legislature for the Restriction of Vivisection . . .*"

At end: *S. Weir Mitchell. H. C. Wood.*

NLM

14114. . . . PHYSIOLOGICAL STUDIES OF THE KNEE-JERK, AND OF THE REACTIONS OF MUSCLES UNDER MECHANICAL AND OTHER EXCITANTS. BY S. WEIR MITCHELL . . . AND MORRIS J. LEWIS . . . FROM THE MEDICAL NEWS, FEBRUARY 13 and 20, 1886.

⟨n.p., PHILADELPHIA, 1886⟩

Cover-title. At head of title: *With the Compliments of the Authors.*]

⟨1⟩-35. 6½″ scant × 4⅝″.

⟨1⟩-2⁸, 3². *Collation postulated.*

Printed blue paper wrapper.

Y

14115. A System of Practical Medicine. By American Authors. Edited by William Pepper . . . Assisted by Louis Starr . . . Volume V . . .

Philadelphia: Lea Brothers & Co. 1886.

"Vertigo," pp. 416-428.

Noted in publisher's leather only.

Deposited July 5, 1886.

Y

14116. BEAULIEU

1886

Not located. Privately printed.

The Houghton, Mifflin & Company records show that on Sept. 28, 1886, thirty-six ⟨*sic*⟩ copies were printed on imported French laid paper; and that thirty-nine ⟨*sic*⟩ copies were folded. Further information wanting.

14117. THE TENDON-JERK AND MUSCLE-JERK IN DISEASE, AND ESPECIALLY IN POSTERIOR SCLEROSIS. BY S. WEIR

MITCHELL ... AND MORRIS J. LEWIS ... FROM THE AMERICAN JOURNAL OF THE MEDICAL SCIENCES. OCTOBER, 1886.

⟨n.p., PHILADELPHIA, 1886⟩

Cover-title.

⟨1⟩-10, blank leaf. Laid paper. 9⅝₁₆″ × 6″.

⟨-⟩⁶.

Printed blue paper wrapper. Two states of the wrapper have been noted; sequence, if any, not known. The designations are for identification only.

A: Outer back wrapper blank.

B: Outer back wrapper imprinted with an advertisement for *The Medical News* and *The American Journal of the Medical Sciences.*

NYPL (A)   Y (B)

14118. ROLAND BLAKE AND SOME OTHER PEOPLE ...

PHILADELPHIA (PRINTED NOT PUBLISHED) 1886

For published edition see below under year 1886.

⟨i-iv⟩, ⟨1⟩-377; blank, pp. ⟨378-380⟩. 9½″ scant 7⅟₁₆″.

⟨1², 2-48⁴, 49²⟩. *Signed:* ⟨-⟩², 1-23⁸, 24⁶.

Sewn, folded sheets.

Prepared for the author's use. The text varies from that of the published edition. See "S. Weir Mitchell at Work," by Lyon N. Richardson, *American Literature*, March, 1939.

Letter, Mitchell to Paul Lemperley (in Y), undated save for *14th;* envelope postmarked April 14, 1898: "... I had six copies printed on large paper for correction & not as an edition of what Lowell called de 'Looks'———(luxe)———Two I destroyed in altering the book———two I gave to the two critic friends who read it for me———one copy I have———one I do not account for ..."

Y

14119. ... RESEARCHES UPON THE VENOMS OF POISONOUS SERPENTS. BY S. WEIR MITCHELL ... AND EDWARD T. REICHERT ... [ACCEPTED FOR PUBLICATION, MAY, 1885.]

WASHINGTON: PUBLISHED BY THE SMITHSONIAN INSTITUTION. 1886.

At head of title: *Smithsonian Contributions to Knowledge. 647*

⟨i-ii⟩, ⟨i⟩-⟨x⟩, 1-186, blank leaf. 5 inserted plates; other illustrations in text. 13⅛″ × 9⅞″.

⟨A⟩², B⁴, 1-23⁴, 24². Signature mark B on p. ix.

Printed tan paper wrapper; and, cloth.

For other papers on the same subject see *Researches upon the Venom of the Rattlesnake ...* ⟨1861⟩; *Experimental Contributions to the Toxicology of Rattle-Snake Venom,* 1868.

Listed PW Nov. 13, 1886.

B   BA   BPL   H   Y

14120. ROLAND BLAKE ...

BOSTON AND NEW YORK HOUGHTON, MIFFLIN AND COMPANY THE RIVERSIDE PRESS, CAMBRIDGE 1886

For a privately printed edition see above under 1886.

On the title-page of all examined copies: *Hepzibah Guiness* for *Hephzibah Guinness.*

⟨i-iv⟩, ⟨1⟩-379; blank, p. ⟨380⟩; plus: publisher's catalog, pp. ⟨1⟩-12. 7″ × 4⅝″.

⟨1-24⁸; plus: 25⁶⟩. *Signed:* ⟨-⟩², 1, ⟨2-4⟩, 5-9, ⟨10-11⟩, 12-13, ⟨14⟩, 15-17, ⟨*⟩, 18, 20-⟨21⟩, 22-23⁸, 24⁶; plus: ⟨25⟩⁶.

V cloth: brown; green. White laid end papers. Flyleaves.

According to the publisher's records 1551 copies printed Oct. 25, 1886; bound during the period Oct. 26-Dec. 10, 1886. Deposited Oct. 29, 1886. Listed PW Nov. 13, 1886. An edition statement added to the second printing, Dec. 21, 1886. The Edinburgh edition (Douglas) consisted of 262 sets of American sheets; cancel title-page for which printed Oct. 29, 1886; listed Ath Dec. 11, 1886.

AAS   H   NYPL   UV   Y

14121. College of Physicians of Philadelphia. Centennial Celebration.

Philadelphia, November 20th, 1886 ...

Caption-title. The above at head of leaf.

Single leaf. 8″ × 4¹⁵₁₆″ full. Printed on recto only.

Announcement of a centennial celebration to be held Jan. 3, 1887. Signed at end by Mitchell and others as a committee.

Y

14122. A DOCTOR'S CENTURY

BAILEY, BANKS & BIDDLE, PHILADA. ⟨1887⟩

Cover-title. *Note:* The imprint is embossed; the title printed conventionally in black.

⟨1-10⟩. 6⅜″ × 5½″. Imitation deckled edges, save for left edge. Watermarked *Egyptian Papyrus Hand Made* Printed on rectos only.

5 leaves tied with blue ribbon.

"Read at the Centennial Dinner of the Fellows of the College of Physicians, of Philadelphia."———

p. ⟨3⟩. At end of text: *S. Weir Mitchell | January 4th, 1887*

Also in: Mitchell's *A Masque and Other Poems*, 1887 (Dec. 1887). And: *Transactions of the College of Physicians of Philadelphia. Centennial Volume*, Philadelphia, 1887. And: *Transactions of the College of Physicians of Philadelphia. Third Series. Volume the Ninth*, Philadelphia, 1887.

Y

14123. Wear and Tear, or Hints for the Overworked . . . Fifth Edition, Thoroughly Revised.

    Philadelphia: J. B. Lippincott Company. 1887.

For first edition see above under year 1871.

"The rate of change in this country in education, in dress, and in diet and habits of daily life surprises even the most watchful American observer. It is now but fifteen years since this little book was written . . ."---From the preface to this edition.

Deposited Feb. 4, 1887. Listed PW April 30, 1887.

H   LC   NYPL   Y

14124. A MASQUE AND OTHER POEMS . . .

    BOSTON AND NEW YORK HOUGHTON, MIFFLIN AND COMPANY THE RIVERSIDE PRESS, CAMBRIDGE 1887

⟨i-viii⟩, ⟨1⟩-63. Laid paper watermarked *The Riverside Press.* $8^{11}/_{16}''$ × $5^{7}/_{8}''$.

⟨1-5⁴, 6-7⁸⟩.

Pale tan laid paper boards sides, white V cloth shelfback, printed paper label on spine. Flyleaves and end papers of book stock. Top edges gilt.

According to the publisher's records 560 copies printed Dec. 1, 1887; 500 labels printed Dec. 6, 1887; bound during the period Dec. 14, 1887 to Jan. 27, 1890. Deposited Dec. 16, 1887. Advertised for Jan. 25, 1888, PW Jan. 14, 1888. Listed PW Feb. 4, 1888. Noted by Ath April 28, 1888.

AAS   B   BA   H   LC   NYPL   Y

14125. CENTENNIAL   ANNIVERSARY . . . COMMEMORATIVE ADDRESS

Two printings noted; sequence, if any, not established. The designations are for identification only.

A

CENTENNIAL ANNIVERSARY OF THE INSTITUTION OF THE COLLEGE OF PHYSICIANS OF PHILADELPHIA. COMMEMORATIVE ADDRESS . . . EXTRACTED FROM THE TRANSACTIONS OF THE COLLEGE OF PHYSICIANS OF PHILADELPHIA, JANUARY 3, 1887.

PHILADELPHIA: WM. J. DORNAN, PRINTER. 1887.

⟨1⟩-32. $8^{3}/_{4}''$ full × $5^{3}/_{4}''$.

⟨1⟩-2⁸.

Printed gray-green paper wrapper.

B

CELEBRATION OF THE CENTENNIAL ANNIVERSARY OF THE INSTITUTION OF THE COLLEGE OF PHYSICIANS OF PHILADELPHIA. COMMEMORATIVE ADDRESS . . . DELIVERED JANUARY 3, 1887.

⟨n.p., PHILADELPHIA, 1887⟩

⟨i-ii⟩, ⟨1⟩-40. Laid paper. $9^{3}/_{4}''$ scant × $6^{7}/_{8}''$.

⟨-⟩¹, ⟨1⟩-5⁴.

Printed tan laid paper wrapper.

Also appears in *Transactions of the College of Physicians of Philadelphia. Centennial Volume*, Philadelphia, 1887. And: *Transactions of the College of Physicians of Philadelphia. Third Series. Volume the Ninth*, Philadelphia, 1887.

H (A)   NYPL (B)   Y (A,B)

14126. NEURALGIC HEADACHES WITH APPARITIONS OF UNUSUAL CHARACTER . . . [READ JUNE 1, 1887]

    ⟨n.p., PHILADELPHIA, 1887⟩

Caption-title. The above at head of p. ⟨175⟩.

⟨175⟩-180. $9^{11}/_{16}''$ × $6^{1}/_{16}''$.

Signed: ⟨11⟩¹, 12².

Printed pale green paper wrapper.

Leaves extracted from *Transactions of the College of Physicians of Philadelphia. Third Series. Volume the Ninth*, Philadelphia, 1887.

NYPL   Y

14127. Preliminary Report of the Commission Appointed by the University of Pennsylvania to Investigate Modern Spiritualism in Accordance with the Request of the Late Henry Seybert

    Philadelphia J. B. Lippincott Company 1887

Co-edited by Mitchell.

Reissued in 1920.

H

14128. . . . A Record of the Commemoration, November Fifth to Eighth, 1886, on the Two Hundred and Fiftieth Anniversary of the Founding of Harvard College.

    Cambridge, N. E.: John Wilson and Son. University Press. 1887.

At head of title: *1636. Harvard University. 1886.*

Material by Mitchell, pp. 315-318.

H   Y

14129. THE CHRIST OF THE SNOW A NORWEGIAN LEGEND . . .

⟨n.p., Christmas, n.y., *ca.* 1887⟩

P. ⟨1⟩ as above.

Anonymous.

Single cut sheet folded to make four pages. Text on pp. ⟨1⟩ and ⟨3⟩; pp. ⟨2⟩ and ⟨4⟩ blank. Page: 7¼″ full × 5⁷⁄₁₆″. Wove paper water-marked *Whiting Paper Company.*

At end of text: *With Christmas Greetings from* ⟨Mitchell's autograph⟩

Also in (reprinted from?) *A Masque and Other Poems,* 1887.

Y

14130. PRINCE LITTLE BOY AND OTHER TALES OUT OF FAIRY-LAND . . .

PHILADELPHIA: J. B. LIPPINCOTT COMPANY. 1888.

"In 1864 I wrote . . . *The Children's Hour* . . . ⟨and⟩ the story of Fuz-Buz, the Fly . . . I have added certain stories of recent date . . ."———From the "preface." See above under 1864, 1867.

⟨i⟩-⟨x⟩, 7-157; blank, p. ⟨158⟩; leaf, excised or pasted under the end paper. Frontispiece and 10 plates inserted; other illustrations in text. 7⅞″ scant × 5¹⁵⁄₁₆″ full.

Note: Collation tentative. Two printings have been noted; the sequence is presumed correct:

FIRST PRINTING

Pagination as above.

⟨1¹, 2⁵, 3-21⁴⟩. Leaf ⟨2⟩₄ (the list of illustrations) inserted. Leaf ⟨21⟩₄ (the title-leaf?) excised. Signed: ⟨1⟩¹⁰, 2-10⁸.

V cloth: brown-orange; green. Blue-coated on white end papers. Flyleaves.

SECOND PRINTING

Pagination as above.

⟨1-2¹, 3-22⁴⟩. Leaves ⟨3⟩₂₋₃ (the contents leaf and the list of illustrations) are conjugate. Leaf ⟨22⟩₄ (the title-leaf?) excised. *Signed:* ⟨1⟩¹⁰, 2-10⁸.

V cloth: gray-green. Off-white end papers printed in brown with an all-over star-like pattern.

Deposited Oct. 24, 1887. Listed PW Oct. 29, 1887. A "new edition" was noted in PW Jan. 21, 1899; not seen by BAL.

AAS (1st)   UV (1st)   Y (2nd)

14131. DOCTOR AND PATIENT . . .

PHILADELPHIA: J. B. LIPPINCOTT COMPANY. LONDON: 10 HENRIETTA STREET, COVENT GARDEN. 1888.

⟨1⟩-177. Laid paper. 9½″ × 6″.

⟨a⟩-i, k-l⁸, ⟨m⟩¹. *Also signed:* ⟨1⟩-14⁶, 15⁵. *Also signed:* ⟨A⟩-G¹², H⁵.

S cloth: brown. Brown-coated on white end papers. Flyleaves. Top edges gilded.

The Y copy of the large paper format inscribed by Mitchell: ". . . This is one of twenty five large paper copies . . ."

⟨i-ii⟩, ⟨1⟩-177; leaf excised or pasted under the end paper. 7⅝″ × 5¹⁄₁₆″. Wove paper.

⟨-⟩¹, ⟨1⟩-15⁶. Leaf 15₆ excised or pasted under the end paper. *Also signed:* ⟨-⟩¹, ⟨a⟩-i, k-l⁸, ⟨m⟩¹. *Also signed:* ⟨-⟩¹, ⟨A⟩-G¹², H⁵.

S cloth: brown (several shades noted). White end papers printed in gray with a floral pattern; white end papers printed in black with a floral pattern; white end papers printed in ochre with a floral pattern. Flyleaves. Top edges plain.

A small paper printing was deposited Dec. 30, 1887. BPL copy (small paper) received Jan. 7, 1888. Listed PW Jan. 14, 1888. The Edinburgh & London (Pentland) edition listed PC May 15, 1888.

H (both)   LC (small)   NYPL (large)   Y (both)

14132. . . . LOCOMOTOR ATAXIA CONFINED TO THE ARMS: REVERSAL OF ORDINARY PROGRESS . . .

⟨n.p., CHICAGO, 1888⟩

Caption-title. The above at head of p. ⟨1⟩. At head of title: *Reprinted from the Journal of Nervous and Mental Disease, April, 1888.*

⟨1⟩-4. 9³⁄₁₆″ full × 5¹⁵⁄₁₆″.

Single cut sheet folded to make four pages.

LC   NYPL   Y

14133. ON THE MUSCULAR REACTIONS KNOWN AS TENDON-JERKS AND MUSCLE-JERKS. A LECTURE DELIVERED AT THE INFIRMARY FOR NERVOUS DISEASES, MAY 17, 1888 . . . FROM THE MEDICAL NEWS, JUNE 23, 1888.

⟨n.p., PHILADELPHIA, 1888⟩

Cover-title.

⟨1⟩-31. Illustrated. 7¹³⁄₁₆″ × 5⅜″.

⟨-⟩¹⁶.

Printed blue paper wrapper.

LC   NYPL   Y

14134. READ AT THE DINNER COM-MEMORATIVE OF THE FIFTIETH YEAR OF THE DOCTORATE OF D. HAYES AGNEW, M.D. APRIL 6, 1888.

⟨n.p., PHILADELPHIA, 1888⟩

Cover-title.

⟨1-12⟩. Laid paper. Printed on rectos only. $7^{15}\!/_{16}'' \times 5^{15}\!/_{16}''$.

⟨-⟩⁶.

Printed self-wrapper. Leaf ⟨-⟩₁ decorated with a bow of orange ribbon.

Untitled introductory poem, pp. ⟨3-5⟩: *Good Chairman, Brothers, Friends, and Guests, all ye who come with praise* . . . ; collected as the introduction to "Minerva Medica," *The Cup of Youth*, 1889.

"Minerva Medica," pp. 7-11. Collected in *The Cup of Youth*, 1889.

Y

14135. FAR IN THE FOREST. A STORY . . .

PHILADELPHIA: J. B. LIPPINCOTT COMPANY. 1889.

⟨1⟩-298, blank leaf. $7^{3}\!/_{8}''$ scant × 5″ full.

⟨1⟩-25⁶. *Also signed:* ⟨a⟩-i, k-s⁸, t⁶. *Also signed:* ⟨A⟩-I, K-M¹², N⁶.

V cloth: brown; gray; green. White end papers printed in brown with a floral pattern on a background of criss-crossed lines. Rule present below spine imprint. Flyleaves.

Also noted in a variant binding of unknown status: As above save for the absence of the rule below the spine imprint; white end papers printed in tan with a leafy pattern.

For a revised edition see below under 1899.

BA copy received May 3, 1889. Listed PW May 11, 1889.

AAS   NYPL (normal; variant)   Y

14136. THE CUP OF YOUTH AND OTHER POEMS . . .

BOSTON AND NEW YORK HOUGHTON, MIFFLIN AND COMPANY THE RIVERSIDE PRESS, CAMBRIDGE 1889

⟨i-vi⟩, ⟨1⟩-76. Laid paper watermarked: *The Riverside Press* $8^{5}\!/_{8}'' \times 5^{13}\!/_{16}''$.

⟨a⟩¹, ⟨b⟩², 1-4⁸, 5⁶.

Gray laid paper boards sides, white V cloth shelfback. Printed paper label on spine. Flyleaves and end papers of book stock. Top edges gilt.

518 copies printed April 30, 1889; bound during the period May 9, 1889 to Dec. 5, 1893; on May 20, 1889, six copies were bound in three-quarters

levant. Deposited May 16, 1889. BPL copy received May 16, 1889. Listed PW June 8, 1889.

B   BA   BPL   H   LC   NYPL   Y

14137. ANEURISM OF AN ANOMALOUS ARTERY CAUSING ANTEROPOSTER-IOR DIVISION OF THE CHIASM OF THE OPTIC NERVES AND PRODUC-ING BITEMPORAL HEMIANOPSIA . . . REPRINTED FROM THE JOURNAL OF NERVOUS AND MENTAL DISEASE, JANUARY, 1889.

M. J. ROONEY & CO., PRINTERS, CORNER BROAD-WAY AND 35TH STREET. NEW YORK. ⟨1889⟩

Cover-title.

⟨1⟩-19. Illustrated. $9^{5}\!/_{16}'' \times 6^{3}\!/_{8}''$ full.

⟨-⟩¹⁰.

Printed pinkish-tan wrapper.

NYPL   Y

14138. . . . AN IMPROVED FORM OF SUS-PENSION IN THE TREATMENT OF ATAXIA, ETC. . . .

⟨n.p., PHILADELPHIA, 1889⟩

Caption-title. The preceding at the head of p. ⟨1⟩. At head of title: [*Reprinted from the Medical News, April 13, 1889.*]

⟨1⟩-3. Illustrated. $6^{5}\!/_{8}'' \times 4^{1}\!/_{4}''$.

Single cut sheet folded to make four pages.

LC   NYPL   Y

14139. MARY REYNOLDS: A CASE OF DOUBLE CONSCIOUSNESS . . . RE-PRINTED FROM THE TRANSACTIONS OF THE COLLEGE OF PHYSICIANS OF PHILADELPHIA, APRIL 4, 1888.

PHILADELPHIA: WM. J. DORNAN, PRINTER. 1889.

⟨i-ii⟩, ⟨1⟩-19. $9^{3}\!/_{16}''$ full × $5^{15}\!/_{16}''$.

⟨1¹, 2¹⁰⟩.

Printed mottled blue-gray wrapper.

H   LC   NYPL   Y

14140. SUBJECTIVE FALSE SENSATIONS OF COLD . . . REPRINT FROM THE TRANSACTIONS OF THE ASSOCIA-TION OF AMERICAN PHYSICIANS, SEPTEMBER, 1889.

⟨n.p., PHILADELPHIA, 1889⟩

Cover-title.

⟨1⟩-12. $9^{5}\!/_{16}'' \times 5^{15}\!/_{16}''$.

⟨-⟩⁶.

Printed wrapper.

14141. A PSALM OF DEATHS AND OTHER POEMS . . .

BOSTON AND NEW YORK HOUGHTON, MIFFLIN AND COMPANY THE RIVERSIDE PRESS, CAMBRIDGE 1890

⟨i-viii⟩, ⟨1⟩-70, blank leaf. Laid paper watermarked: *The Riverside Press* $8\frac{5}{8}''$ × $5\frac{13}{16}''$.

⟨-⟩⁴, ⟨1⟩-4⁸, 5⁴. *See below.*

Note: The state of Sig. 2 (pp. 17-32) suggests that a misimposition required correction. The signature is made up as follows: Conjugates: 1,8; 2,7; 3,6. Leaves 4,5 singletons. Leaf 2 wholly blank. Leaf 5 (pp. 25-26) may be a cancel. All examined copies thus.

Gray laid paper boards sides, white V cloth shelf-back. Printed paper label on spine. Cream-white laid end papers. Top edges gilt.

According to the publisher's records 322 copies were printed Dec. 15, 1890; bound (201 copies) Jan. 10, 1891; bound (118 copies) Jan 12, 1891. A copy in H presented to James Russell Lowell by Mitchell Jan. 10, 1891. Deposited Jan. 12, 1891. Noted for *next week* PW Jan. 17, 1891. Listed PW Feb. 7, 1891.

MEMOIR OF JOHN CALL DALTON . . .

. . . 1890 . . .

See below under 1895.

14142. . . . SUSPENSION IN LOCOMOTOR ATAXIA . . .

⟨n.p., PHILADELPHIA, 1890⟩

Cover-title. At head of title: *Reprinted from the University Medical Magazine, April 1890.*

⟨1⟩-5. $10\frac{5}{16}''$ × $6\frac{3}{4}''$.

⟨1², 2¹⟩.

Printed tan laid paper wrapper.

14143. . . . UNUSUAL CASES OF CHOREA, POSSIBLY INVOLVING THE SPINAL CORD.[1] BY S. WEIR MITCHELL . . . AND CHARLES W. BURR . . .

⟨n.p., CHICAGO, 1890⟩

Caption-title. The above at head of p. ⟨1⟩. At head of title: *Reprinted from the Journal of Nervous and Mental Disease, July, 1890.*

⟨1⟩-4. $9\frac{3}{8}''$ × 6″ full.

⟨-⟩².

Single leaf folded to make four pages.

The footnote: *Read before the American Neurological Association, June, 1890.*

Also appears in *Transactions of the American Neurological Association, Sixteenth Annual Meeting . . . June . . . 1890*, New York, 1890.

14144. THE HISTORY OF INSTRUMENTAL PRECISION IN MEDICINE

Two printings noted; the sequence, if any, not known. The designations are for identification only.

PRINTING A

ADDRESS BEFORE THE CONGRESS OF AMERICAN PHYSICIANS AND SURGEONS SEPTEMBER 23d, 1891 THE HISTORY OF INSTRUMENTAL PRECISION IN MEDICINE . . .

PHILADELPHIA UNIVERSITY OF PENNSYLVANIA PRESS 1891

⟨1⟩-44. 9″ × $5\frac{3}{4}''$.

⟨1-2⁸, 3⁴, 5²⟩.

Unprinted gray paper wrapper, embossed with a pebbled finish.

Contains no appendices although references to them are made. For an extended edition with appendices see under 1892.

PRINTING B

REPRINTED FROM UNIVERSITY MEDICAL MAGAZINE, OCTOBER, 1891. THE HISTORY OF INSTRUMENTAL PRECISION IN MEDICINE . . .

⟨PHILADELPHIA: UNIVERSITY MEDICAL MAGAZINE, 1891⟩

Cover-title.

⟨1⟩-16. $9\frac{15}{16}''$ full × $6\frac{13}{16}''$.

⟨-⟩⁸.

Printed tan laid paper wrapper.

14145. . . . Atmospheric Electricity.

⟨n.p., Washington: National Academy of Sciences, 1891⟩

Cover-title. Printed paper wrapper. At head of title: *National Academy of Sciences. Vol. VI. Second Memoir.*

Brief introductory note by Mitchell, p. 27, to Robert Catlin's "A Study on the Relation of Atmospheric Electricity, Magnetic Storms, and

Weather Elements to a Case of Traumatic Neuralgia."

Y

14146. Fat and Blood: An Essay on the Treatment of Certain Forms of Neurasthenia and Hysteria . . . Sixth Edition.

Philadelphia: J. B. Lippincott Company. London: 10 Henrietta Street, Covent Garden. 1891.

See above under 1877 for first edition.

"The present edition has been carefully revised by my son, Dr. John K. Mitchell . . ."–––From S. Weir Mitchell's "Preface to the Sixth Edition," p. 3.

UV   Y

14147. THE   MOTHER   ⟨AND   OTHER POEMS⟩ . . .

⟨n.p., PRIVATELY PRINTED, 1891⟩

Caption-title. The above at head of p. ⟨1⟩.

For published edition see below under 1893.

⟨1⟩-22, blank leaf. 11⅞″ × 9⅜″ full.

⟨-⟩¹².

Tied. Printed self-wrapper.

According to the sales catalog of *The Library and Autograph Collection of Edmund Clarence Stedman, Part II*, The Anderson Auction Company, New York, 1911, Catalog No. 885, item No. 2015, there were 20 copies printed; no supporting evidence given. The only located copy inscribed by Mitchell: *No VIII S W M to T W*

Y

14148. CHARACTERISTICS . . .

NEW YORK   THE CENTURY CO. 1892

⟨i-viii⟩, ⟨1⟩-307; blank leaf; leaf excised or pasted under the end paper. 7¹¹⁄₁₆″ × 5⅛″.

⟨-⟩⁴, ⟨1⟩-26⁶. Leaf 26₆ excised or pasted under the end paper.

S cloth: blue-gray. Flyleaf at front. White wove end papers. Also: White wove end paper at front, white laid paper end paper at back. Top edges gilt. Reported, not seen, in publisher's leather.

Deposited Sept. 19, 1892. Listed PW Oct. 15, 1892. The earliest London notice seen is for the *sixth edition*, listed PC Aug. 5, 1899.

AAS   BPL   H   NYPL   Y

14149. ADDRESS ON OPENING OF THE INSTITUTE OF HYGIENE OF THE UNIVERSITY OF PENNSYLVANIA . . .

PHILADELPHIA   UNIVERSITY OF PENNSYLVANIA PRESS 1892

⟨1⟩-16. 9¼″ × 5⅞″.

⟨1⟩⁸.

Unprinted mottled blue-gray laid paper wrapper.

Also appears in *The Opening Exercises of the Institute of Hygiene of the University of Pennsylvania. Philadelphia, February 22, 1892*, Philadelphia, 1892.

H   NYPL

14150. . . . Cases of Unusual Forms of Spasm Reported from the Clinics of S. Weir Mitchell . . . by Charles W. Burr . . .

⟨n.p., Chicago, 1892⟩

Printed self-wrapper. Caption-title. The above at head of p. ⟨1⟩. At head of title: *Reprinted from the Journal of Nervous and Mental Disease, May 1, 1892*.

Remarks, pp. 3-4.

NYPL   Y

14151. The Early History of Instrumental Precision in Medicine. An Address before the Second Congress of American Physicians and Surgeons September 23rd, 1891 . . . ⟨Second Edition⟩

New Haven: Tuttle, Morehouse & Taylor, Printers. 1892

See above under 1891 for first edition.

Contains appendices, pp. ⟨27⟩-42, not present in the first printings, 1891.

Printed blue paper wrapper.

Also appears in *Transactions of the Congress of American Physicians and Surgeons. Second Triennial Session . . . 1891*, New Haven, 1892.

BPL   H   LC   NYPL   Y

14152. PRECISION IN THE TREATMENT OF CHRONIC DISEASES . . .

⟨n.p., NEW YORK, 1892⟩

Caption-title. The above at the head of p. ⟨345⟩.

⟨345⟩-359. 8¹¹⁄₁₆″ × 5⅜″.

Signed: ⟨-⟩⁴, AA⁴.

Unprinted yellow-green paper wrapper.

Footnote, p. ⟨345⟩: *A portion of an address delivered before the New York Academy of Medicine; published in full in the New York Medical Record, No. 26, vol. 42* ⟨Dec. 24, 1892⟩.

NYPL

14153. A TALK ABOUT NURSES AND NURSING ... DELIVERED BEFORE THE NURSES OF THE PHILADELPHIA ORTHOPÆDIC HOSPITAL AND INFIRMARY FOR NERVOUS DISEASES, MONDAY EVENING, APRIL 4th, 1892.

PHILADELPHIA: BILLSTEIN & SON, 41 NORTH TENTH STREET.

⟨1⟩-15. 9″ scant × 5¾″ scant.

⟨-⟩⁸.

Printed mottled blue-gray paper wrapper.

Y

14154. VERSES READ ON THE PRESENTATION ... TO THE PHILADELPHIA COLLEGE OF PHYSICIANS OF SARAH W. WHITMAN'S PORTRAIT OF OLIVER WENDELL HOLMES ... APRIL 30th 1892

⟨PHILADELPHIA: UNIVERSITY OF PENNSYLVANIA PRESS, 1892⟩

All the preceding printed in silver.

Cover-title.

6 unpaged leaves. 7″ × 7″. Printed on recto only.

Issued in a printed wrapper of heavy white paper, tied at the top with white silk cord.

H   NYPL   Y

14155. THE MOTHER AND OTHER POEMS ...

BOSTON AND NEW YORK HOUGHTON, MIFFLIN AND COMPANY THE RIVERSIDE PRESS, CAMBRIDGE 1893

Title-page in black and blind.

For a privately printed edition see above under 1891.

⟨i-ii⟩, ⟨i⟩-iv, ⟨1⟩-69. Laid paper. Watermarked: *The Riverside Press* 8⅝″ full × 5⅞″.

⟨1⁵, 2-9⁴, 10¹⟩. Leaf ⟨1⟩₂ inserted.

V cloth: green. Green-coated on white end papers. Laid paper flyleaf at back. Top edges gilded. Also three copies in full brown morocco: Leaf size 8⁵⁄₁₆″ × 5⅝″; all edges gilded.

Noted for *today* PW Dec. 3, 1892. According to the publisher's records 497 copies were printed Dec. 8, 1892; bound during the period Dec. 13-30, 1892; three copies bound in morocco Dec. 30, 1892. Deposited Dec. 16, 1892. Listed PW Dec. 24, 1892. Probably imported into Great Britain; advertised as *ready* by Gay & Bird PC Feb. 18, 1893. The Boston edition noted as *on our table* Ath April 29, 1893. Plates melted June 10, 1897.

B   BA   H   LC   NYPL   Y (cloth; morocco)

14156. FRANCIS DRAKE A TRAGEDY OF THE SEA ...

BOSTON AND NEW YORK HOUGHTON, MIFFLIN AND COMPANY THE RIVERSIDE PRESS, CAMBRIDGE 1893

Title-page in black and blind.

⟨i-ii⟩, ⟨i⟩-⟨viii⟩, ⟨1⟩-60, 2 blank leaves. Laid paper watermarked: *The Riverside Press* 8⅝″ × 5⅞″.

⟨1⁵, 2-9⁴⟩. Leaf ⟨1⟩₂ inserted.

V cloth: white. White end papers imprinted in gold with an all-over pattern. Top edges gilt. Also three copies in morocco; see publication notes below.

According to the publisher's records 494 copies printed Dec. 14, 1892; bound during the period Dec. 15-30, 1892. Three copies bound in morocco Dec. 30, 1892. Noted for *today* PW Dec. 3, 1892. Deposited Dec. 17, 1892. Listed PW Dec. 24, 1892. Advertised as *ready* PC Feb. 18, 1893; noted as *on our table* Ath May 13, 1893. Plates melted June 10, 1897.

AAS   B   H   LC   NYPL   Y

14157. MR. KRIS KRINGLE. A CHRISTMAS TALE ...

PHILADELPHIA: GEORGE W. JACOBS & CO., 103 SOUTH 15TH STREET, 1893.

SMALL PAPER FORMAT

Noted in the following forms:

Presumed First Printing

⟨1⟩-48. Five inserted plates. *Note:* The page reference on each plate is centered below the caption. *Printed on wove paper.* 7⁷⁄₁₆″ × 5¼″.

⟨1⟩-3⁸.

Pinkish-salmon paper boards; tan paper boards. White V cloth shelf back. White wove end papers.

Presumed Second Printing

⟨1⟩-48. Frontispiece and four plates, each inserted. *Note:* The page reference on each plate (and the frontispiece) is set at the lower right corner. *Printed on laid paper.* 7⁷⁄₁₆″ × 5¼″ full.

⟨1⟩-3⁸.

Tan paper boards. White V cloth shelf back. Laid paper end papers.

LARGE PAPER FORMAT

⟨1⟩-48. Frontispiece and four plates, each inserted. *Note:* The page reference on each plate (and the frontispiece) is centered below the caption. *Printed on wove paper.* 9⅝″ full × 7³⁄₁₆″.

⟨1-6⁴⟩. *Signed:* ⟨1⟩-3⁸.

White grosgrain silk, stamped in gold on front. No flyleaves. White wove end papers. Edges gilt.

Note: The author's personal copy of the large paper format differs somewhat from the above, a principal variation being the presence on the front cover of a goldstamped label. Location: Y, inscribed *Weir Mitchell from Weir Mitchell Xmas 1893.*

Deposited Nov. 29, 1893. Listed PW Dec. 9, 1893. For another edition see below under year 1904.

AAS (2nd) H (1st) LC (2nd, being a deposit copy) UV (1st, *Large Paper*) Y (1st, *Large Paper*)

14158. TWO LECTURES ON THE CONDUCT OF THE MEDICAL LIFE . . . ADDRESSED TO THE STUDENTS OF THE UNIVERSITY OF PENNSYLVANIA AND THE JEFFERSON MEDICAL COLLEGE

PHILADELPHIA   UNIVERSITY OF PENNSYLVANIA PRESS 1893

⟨1⟩-51. $7\frac{7}{16}'' \times 6\frac{3}{8}''$.

⟨1-3⁸, 4²⟩.

Printed terra-cotta paper boards, brown V cloth shelf back.

AAS UV Y

14159. HYSTERICAL RAPID RESPIRATION, WITH CASES; PECULIAR FORM OF RUPIAL SKIN DISEASE IN AN HYSTERICAL WOMAN . . . FROM THE AMERICAN JOURNAL OF THE MEDICAL SCIENCES, MARCH, 1893.

⟨n.p., PHILADELPHIA, 1893⟩

Cover-title.

⟨1⟩-12. Frontispiece inserted, other illustrations in text. $9\frac{5}{16}''$ full $\times 6\frac{1}{8}''$ scant.

⟨-⟩⁶.

Printed blue paper wrapper.

Also published in *Transactions of the College of Physicians of Philadelphia. Third Series. Volume the Fourteenth,* Philadelphia, 1892.

LC NYPL Y

14160. WHEN ALL THE WOODS ARE GREEN A NOVEL . . .

NEW YORK THE CENTURY CO. 1894

⟨i-viii⟩, 1-419; blank leaf; leaf excised or pasted under the end paper. Portrait frontispiece inserted. $7\frac{9}{16}'' \times 5\frac{1}{8}''$.

⟨-⟩⁴, 1-26⁸, 27⁴. Leaf 27₄ excised or pasted under the end paper.

V cloth: green. Flyleaf at front. Top edges gilt.

Deposited Sept. 21, 1894. Advertised for *October 10th* PW Sept. 29, 1894. Noted as *just ready* PW Oct. 13, 1894. Listed PW Oct. 20, 1894.

AAS BPL NYPL Y

14161. . . . ADDRESS BEFORE THE AMERICAN MEDICO-PSYCHOLOGICAL ASSOCIATION . . .

⟨NEW YORK, 1894⟩

At head of title: *Reprinted from the Journal of Nervous and Mental Disease, July, 1894.*

⟨i-ii⟩, ⟨1⟩-61, blank leaf. $9\frac{7}{16}'' \times 6\frac{1}{4}''$.

⟨1¹, 2-5⁸⟩.

Printed gray paper wrapper.

"Address before the Fiftieth Annual Meeting of the American Medico-Psychological Association, Held in Philadelphia, May 16th, 1894."

BPL Y

14162. A CATALOGUE OF THE SCIENTIFIC AND LITERARY WORK OF S. WEIR MITCHELL . . .

⟨n.p., n.d., PHILADELPHIA, 1894⟩

Caption-title. The above at head of p. ⟨1⟩.

⟨1⟩-40. $8\frac{1}{4}''$ full $\times 5\frac{7}{8}''$.

"Preface," pp. ⟨3⟩-4.

BPL LC NYPL UP Y

14163. NERVOUS DISEASES AND THEIR TREATMENT . . . BY S. WEIR MITCHELL . . . AND F. X. DERCUM . . .

⟨n.p., n.d., not before 1894⟩

Caption-title. The above at head of p. ⟨17⟩.

⟨17⟩-40. $9\frac{3}{8}'' \times 5\frac{7}{8}''$. Illustrated.

So issued? Possibly leaves extracted from a larger work. The only located example, S. Weir Mitchell's personal copy, is interleaved and in unprinted drab paper wrapper. *Signed:* 2⁸, 3⁴.

Y

14164. Suggestions to Hospital and Asylum Visitors. By John S. Billings . . . and Henry M. Hurd . . . with an Introduction by S. Weir Mitchell . . .

Philadelphia: J. B. Lippincott Company. 1895.

"Introduction," pp. 5-7.

Noted as *in press* PW Feb. 23, 1895. Deposited March 7, 1895. Listed PW March 16, 1895.

NYPL Y

14165. PHILIP VERNON A TALE IN PROSE
AND VERSE . . .

NEW YORK THE CENTURY CO. 1895

⟨i-ii⟩, 1-55. Laid paper. 7½″ × 5⅛″ scant.

⟨-⟩¹, 1-7⁴.

V cloth: green. Laid paper end papers. Laid paper
flyleaf at back. Top edges gilded.

Deposited May 7, 1895. Listed PW June 8, 1895.

AAS   B   H   NYPL   Y

14166. A MADEIRA PARTY . . .

NEW YORK THE CENTURY CO. 1895

Title-page in black and brown.

⟨i-viii⟩, ⟨1⟩-165, blank leaf. Frontispiece inserted.
5¹⁄₁₆″ × 2⅞″ scant.

⟨-⟩⁴, ⟨1⟩-10⁸, 11⁴.

Tan skiver. Brown marbled end papers. Flyleaf at
front. Edges gilded.

Deposited July 6, 1895. Advertised for Oct. 10 in
PW Sept. 28, 1895. Listed PW Oct. 12, 1895.

AAS   H   LC   NYPL   UV   Y

14167. . . . THE COMPOSITION OF EX-
PIRED AIR AND ITS EFFECTS UPON
ANIMAL LIFE. BY J. S. BILLINGS . . .
S. WEIR MITCHELL . . . AND D. H.
BERGEY . . .

CITY OF WASHINGTON: PUBLISHED BY THE
SMITHSONIAN INSTITUTION. 1895.

At head of title: *Smithsonian Contributions to Knowledge. 989 Hodgkins Fund.*

For an abstract see below under the year 1896.

⟨i⟩-⟨iv⟩, ⟨1⟩-81. Illustrated. 14⅛″ × 10½″
(wrapper). 12¾″ × 9⅝″ (cloth).

⟨1², 2-11⁴, 12¹⟩.

Printed tan paper wrapper. *Also:* S cloth: green;
laid yellow paper end papers; flyleaf at front.

The London (Wesley) edition listed PC Aug. 29,
1896.

LC   NYPL   Y

14168. MEMOIR OF JOHN CALL DALTON.
1825–1889 . . . READ BEFORE THE NA-
TIONAL ACADEMY, APRIL 16, 1890 . . .

⟨n.p., WASHINGTON, 1895?⟩

177-185. 9⅛″ × 5⅞″.

Signed: 23⁴, 24¹.

Printed blue-gray paper wrapper.

Offprint (preprint?) from *National Academy of
Sciences. Biographical Memoirs. Vol. III*, Washington,
1895.

H   Y

14169. Number One   The Year Book of the
Pegasus . . .

J. B. Lippincott Company   Philadelphia
MDCCCXCV

Printed paper wrapper.

"The Passing of Tennyson   Duty, Faith, and
Love," pp. 25-27. Collected in *The Wager*, 1900.

NYPL   UV

14170. A Text-Book on Nervous Diseases by
American Authors. Edited by Francis X.
Dercum . . .

Philadelphia: Lea Brothers & Co. 1895.

"General Considerations," pp. ⟨17⟩-50.

H   Y

14171. "Vivisection" a Statement in Behalf of
Science

⟨n.p.⟩ February, 1896

Cover-title.

Signed by Mitchell and others.

Printed paper wrapper.

Accompanying the BA copy is a printed letter,
Feb. 24, 1896, signed by Charles W. Eliot and
others, which refers to the publication as *now
published.*

BA   BPL   H   NYPL

14172. ADDRESS TO THE STUDENTS OF
RADCLIFFE COLLEGE DELIVERED
JANUARY 17, 1895 . . .

CAMBRIDGE, MASS 1896

Cover-title.

⟨1⟩-23. Laid paper. 9″ × 5⅞″.

⟨1⟩¹².

Printed self-wrapper.

Two states (printings?) have been seen, both from
the same setting. The only significant typographical variation noted occurs on p. ⟨1⟩ (the cover-
title), line 4. The designations are for identification
only.

A

Delivered January 17 1895 ⟨Note absence of comma.⟩

B

Delivered January 17, 1895 ⟨Note presence of comma.⟩

AAS (B)   H (A)   NYPL (A)   Y (A)

14173. THE BIRTH AND DEATH OF PAIN: A POEM READ OCTOBER SIXTEENTH, MDCCCXCVI, AT THE COMMEMORATION OF THE FIFTIETH ANNIVERSARY OF THE FIRST PUBLIC DEMONSTRATION OF SURGICAL ANÆSTHESIA . . .

⟨n.d., BOSTON, 1896?⟩

Cover-title.

⟨1-6⟩; blank, p. ⟨7⟩; *Merrymount Press* imprint, p. ⟨8⟩. Laid paper watermarked: *Van Gelder Zonen* $12\frac{3}{4}'' \times 9\frac{1}{4}''$.

⟨1⟩⁴.

Printed self-wrapper.

Appears also in *The Semi-Centennial of Anæsthesia . . . October 16, 1896*, Boston, 1897.

An undated reprint, *ca.* 1909, is printed on laid paper watermarked: *Etruria Italy*; $11\frac{1}{2}'' \times 8\frac{1}{4}''$. On p. ⟨8⟩: Imprint of *Vreeland Advertising Press, 117 West 31st Street, New York.*

Collected in *The Wager*, 1900.

H (1st)   NYPL (1st; 2nd)   Y (1st; 2nd)

14174. . . . The Composition of Expired Air and Its Effects upon Animal Life. Abstract of a Report on the Results of an Investigation Made for the Smithsonian Institution . . . by J. S. Billings . . . S. Weir Mitchell . . . and D. H. Bergey . . . from the Smithsonian Report for 1895, Pages 389-412.

Washington: Government Printing Office. 1896.

At head of title: 1047

For a full report see above under 1895.

Printed paper wrapper.

⟨i-ii⟩, 389-412. $9\frac{5}{8}'' \times 6\frac{1}{16}''$. Presumably leaves extracted from *Annual Report of the Board of Regents of the Smithsonian Institution . . . to July, 1895*, Washington, 1896.

Y

14175. MEMOIR OF OWEN JONES WISTER . . . FROM THE TRANSACTIONS OF THE COLLEGE OF PHYSICIANS OF PHILADELPHIA, 1896.

⟨PHILADELPHIA, 1896⟩

Cover-title.

⟨1⟩-15. $9\frac{1}{4}''$ full $\times 5\frac{15}{16}''$.

⟨-⟩⁸.

Printed tan paper wrapper.

Appears also in *Transactions of the College of Physicians of Philadelphia. Third Series. Volume the Eighteenth*, Philadelphia, 1896; also contains remarks by Mitchell, p. 149.

NYPL   Y

HUGH WYNNE FREE QUAKER . . .

. . . 1896

See below under 1897.

14176. CLINICAL LESSONS ON NERVOUS DISEASES

1897

Two formats issued:

AUTHOR'S EDITION

CLINICAL LESSONS ON NERVOUS DISEASES BY ⟨author's signature⟩ . . .

LEA BROTHERS & CO. PHILADELPHIA AND NEW YORK 1897 AUTHOR'S SIGNED COPY. NO.

Title-page in black and red.

⟨i⟩-⟨viii⟩, ⟨13⟩-305, blank leaf. $7\frac{3}{4}'' \times 5''$ full. Two plates inserted; other illustrations in text.

⟨1⟩⁴, 2-8, ⟨9⟩, 10-25⁶, 26⁴.

H cloth: green. Flyleaves. Top edges gilt.

TRADE FORMAT

CLINICAL LESSONS ON NERVOUS DISEASES . . .

LEA BROTHERS & CO. PHILADELPHIA AND NEW YORK 1897

Title-page in black, not black and red.

⟨i-viii⟩, ⟨13⟩-305, blank leaf. $7\frac{7}{8}'' \times 5\frac{1}{8}''$. Two plates inserted; other illustrations in text.

⟨1⟩⁴, 2-25⁶, 26⁴. *Note:* In some copies signature mark 9 is absent.

Two bindings noted; sequence, if any, not determined. The designations are for identification only. The variation given is sufficient to identify.

TRADE FORMAT, BINDING A

H cloth: green. An ornate fillet at top and at bottom of spine. Flyleaves. Top edges plain. Inserted at back: Publisher's catalog, pp. ⟨1⟩-16. Olive-drab end papers.

TRADE FORMAT, BINDING B

C cloth: green. A simple triple rule at top and at bottom of spine. Flyleaves. Top edges plain. Publisher's catalog not present. Olive-drab end papers.

Deposited April 8, 1897. Listed (trade format only) PW May 1, 1897.

AAS (*trade, Binding A*)   H (*author's; trade, Binding B*) Y (*author's; trade, Binding A*)

14177. Library of the World's Best Literature Ancient and Modern   Charles Dudley Warner Editor . . . Thirty Volumes Vol. XVII

New York   R. S. Peale and J. A. Hill Publishers ⟨1897⟩

Reprint save for "Andre's Fate," pp. 10124–10140. Extracted from *Hugh Wynne*, 1897.

Deposited Aug. 20, 1897. For fuller entry see No. 10624.

14178. HUGH WYNNE FREE QUAKER

1896–1897

About 1932 the late Perriton Maxwell, at one time associated with The Century Company, told Merle Johnson that after the book had been printed (and some copies bound) it was decided to postpone book publication and run the novel serially in *Century Illustrated Monthly Magazine*. This accounts for the existence of the prepublication 1896 title-page and the 1897 (cancel) title-leaf in copies first published. The book has been noted as follows:

PREPUBLICATION PRINTING

HUGH WYNNE FREE QUAKER SOME-TIME BREVET LIEUTENANT-COLONEL ON THE STAFF OF HIS EXCELLENCY GENERAL WASHINGTON . . .

NEW YORK   THE CENTURY CO. 1896

2 Vols. The title-leaf is not a cancel. Imprint dated 1896.

1: ⟨i-viii⟩, 1-306; leaf excised. $6^{13}/_{16}$″ × $4^{5}/_{8}$″ full. All edges trimmed. Not illustrated.

2: ⟨i-viii⟩, 1-261; leaf excised. Not illustrated save for a map, p. ⟨74⟩.

1: ⟨-⟩^{4}, 1-18^8. 19^2, 20^8. Leaf 20$_8$ excised.

2: ⟨-⟩^{4}, 1-16^8, 17^4. Leaf 17$_4$ excised.

Unrevised text. The following readings are sufficient for identification:

Vol. 1, p. 15, line 2 up: *arms.* /

Vol. 1, p. 54, last line: . . . *used to ride with her in* /

Vol. 1, p. 60, line 16: *dear* . . .

Vol. 2, p. 18, line 5 up: *it. Thus wisely counselled* . . .

Vol. 2, p. 34, line 9 up: *seemed in* . . .

Vol. 2, p. 95, line 17: *I bowed* . . .

Vol. 2, p. 176, line 14: *and of some* . . .

Vol. 2, p. 220, line 15: *set down; as to* . . .

Vol. 2, p. 255, line 8: *As for me* . . .

Vol. 2, p. 260, line 16: . . . *between* /

Noted in the following bindings. No sequence has been established and the designations are for identification only:

PREPUBLICATION BINDING A

V cloth: Tan.

Stamping: Brown only, not brown and blind.

In each volume: Two flyleaves at front, one flyleaf at back.

All edges trimmed.

Top edges plain.

PREPUBLICATION BINDING B

V cloth: Tan.

Stamping: Stamped in brown and blind, not in brown only.

Flyleaf at front of each volume.

All edges trimmed.

Top edges plain.

Note: A copy of Vol. 2 has been seen in gray V cloth, stamped in red only. (In H)

PUBLISHED FORMAT

HUGH WYNNE FREE QUAKER SOME-TIME BREVET LIEUTENANT-COLONEL ON THE STAFF OF HIS EXCELLENCY GENERAL WASHINGTON . . .

NEW YORK   THE CENTURY CO. 1897

Note: Each title-leaf is a cancel. Imprint dated 1897. 2 Vols.

1: ⟨i-viii⟩, 1-306; leaf excised. $6^{3}/_{4}$″ × $4^{9}/_{16}$″. All edges trimmed. Frontispiece inserted.

2: ⟨i-viii⟩, 1-261; leaf excised. Frontispiece inserted. Map, p. ⟨74⟩.

1: ⟨-⟩^{4}, 1-18^8, 19^2, 20^8. Leaf ⟨-⟩$_3$ (the title-leaf) is a cancel. Leaf 20$_8$ excised.

2: ⟨-⟩^{4}, 1-16^8, 17^4. Leaf ⟨-⟩$_3$ (the title-leaf) is a cancel. Leaf 17$_4$ excised.

Unrevised text. The readings are the same as those described above.

Noted in the following bindings.

PUBLISHED BINDING A

V cloth: Tan.

Stamping: Stamped in brown and blind.

At front of each volume: A gathering of four leaves of white wove paper used as end papers and flyleaf, one leaf being excised or pasted under the paste-down. At back of each volume: Normal end papers of white wove paper.

All edges trimmed.

Top edges plain.

PUBLISHED BINDING B

V cloth: Gray.

Stamping: Stamped in red only.

At front of each volume: A gathering of four leaves of white wove paper used as end papers and flyleaf, one leaf being excised or pasted under the paste-down. At back of each volume: Normal end papers of white wove paper.

All edges trimmed.

Top edges plain.

Summary: In short, the sheets of the *Prepublication Printing* and the *Published Format* are precisely the same save for the title-page and the inserted illustrations.

REVISED EDITION

Hugh Wynne . . .

New York The Century Co. 1897

2 Vols. The title-leaves are not cancels.

1: ⟨i-viii⟩, 1-306; leaf excised. 7$\frac{1}{16}$″ full × 4$\frac{3}{4}$″ full. Top edges gilt, other edges untrimmed. Frontispiece inserted.

2: ⟨i-viii⟩, 1-261; leaf excised. Frontispiece inserted. Map, p. ⟨74⟩.

1: ⟨-⟩^{4}, 1-18^8, 19^2, 20^8. 20$_8$ excised.

2: ⟨-⟩^{4}, 1-16^8, 17^4. 17$_4$ excised.

Text revised. The following readings are sufficient for identification:

Vol. 1, p. 15, line 2 up: *the picture . . .*

Vol. 1, p. 54, last line: *. . . used to ride with her |*

Vol. 1, p. 60, line 16: *fair-haired . . .*

Vol. 2, p. 18, line 5 up: *upon it . . .*

Vol. 2, p. 34, line 9 up: *riders . . .*

Vol. 2, p. 95, line 17: *I bent . . .*

Vol. 2, p. 176, line 14: *tion, and of some . . .*

Vol. 2, p. 220, line 15: *set down. The . . .*

Vol. 2, p. 255, line 8: *I picked up . . .*

Vol. 2, p. 260, line 16: *. . . lines of in- |*

BINDING --- REVISED EDITION

S cloth: Gray.

Stamped in red, gold and gray.

Top edges gilt, other edges untrimmed.

Flyleaf at front of each volume.

LARGE PAPER FORMAT

A large paper printing (revised text as of the second printing) was issued under date 1897. 2 Vols., paper boards, cloth shelf back and corners, printed paper label on spine. Leaf: 11$\frac{5}{16}$″ × 7$\frac{13}{16}$″. According to the certificate of issue limited to 60 numbered copies. One of Harvard's two copies has an inserted printed slip: *With the Author's Compliments . . .* Accompanying the large paper printing is an envelope of twelve illustrations by Howard Pyle. Copies in H, UV, Y.

First published ⟨*sic*⟩ in *The Century Illustrated Monthly Magazine*, Nov. 1896-Oct. 1897. As a book: Advertised for Sept. 24, 1897, PW Sept. 25, 1897. Listed PW Sept. 25, 1897. "The large first edition . . . was exhausted by advance orders some days ago. The work was at once put upon the press again, but the second edition has since been further increased in size, and this has made necessary the postponement of the date of issue until October 8."---PW Oct. 2, 1897. Advertised for Oct. 8 PW Oct. 9, 1897. "After issuing it as a serial in the *Century*, the American publishers struck off three editions ⟨totalling⟩ 14000 copies and are now going to press with an edition of 10000."---PC Nov. 20, 1897. The London (Unwin) edition listed Ath Oct. 2, 1897; see next entry. For a revised edition see under 1908.

AAS (published format, published binding B) BA (revised edition) BPL (prepublication printing, prepublication binding B; revised edition) H (published format, published binding B; large paper; prepublication printing, published binding B, Vol. 2 only) UV (prepublication printing, prepublication binding A; published format, published binding A; published format, published binding B) Y (revised edition; large paper).

14179. HUGH WYNNE FREE QUAKER SOMETIME BREVET LIEUTENANT-COLONEL ON THE STAFF OF HIS EXCELLENCY GENERAL WASHINGTON . . .

LONDON T. FISHER UNWIN PATERNOSTER SQUARE MDCCCXCVII

Title-page in black and red.

Issued simultaneously with the New York edition? See preceding entry.

Two states noted:

I

⟨i-viii⟩, 1-485; blank, p. ⟨486⟩; *The Gresham Press* imprint, p. ⟨487⟩; blank, p. ⟨488⟩. Frontispiece and 1 plate inserted. Map, p. ⟨323⟩. Laid paper. 7$\frac{15}{16}$″ full × 5$\frac{1}{8}$″.

⟨1⟩^{4}, 2-31^8, 32^4.

P. ⟨iv⟩: *Six-Shilling Novels ... The Grey Man ...* ⟨to⟩ *... The Outlaws of the Marches ...*

P. ⟨vii⟩: INTRODUCTORY / *The second title of this book ...* ⟨being a note written for this London edition⟩

P. 1: Text: *A Child's early life ...*

Note: It will be observed that this first London printing does not contain the "Introductory" present in the American edition which begins: *It is now many years since I began these memoirs ...*

2

Sheets of the first state but with a leaf inserted between ⟨1⟩₄ and 2₁, paged vii-viii ⟨*sic*⟩ devoted to an "Introductory Chapter" which begins: *It is now many years since I began these memoirs ...* Presumably in the second printing the leaf is not an insert. In the *Third Printing* (so identified) it appears on leaf ⟨1⟩₃.

T cloth: green. Top edges gilt. Tan (oxidized white?) wove paper end papers. Tan (oxidized white?) laid paper end papers in the second state.

Note: The text contains some of the original (prepublication) readings; some of the revisions. For a fuller note on the text see under preceding entry.

A copy of the first state was sent to Mitchell under date Aug. 26, 1897. Advertised for *next week* PC Oct. 2, 1897. Listed Ath Oct. 2, 1897.

UV (1st. Inscribed by Mitchell: *1st English copy with Introduction left out———Paris———Sept. 2, 1897*) Y (2nd)

14180. AN ANALYSIS OF 3000 CASES OF MELANCHOLIA ... REPRINTED FROM THE TRANSACTIONS OF THE ASSOCIATION OF AMERICAN PHYSICIANS.

⟨n.p., PHILADELPHIA⟩ 1897

Cover-title.

⟨1⟩-8. 9⁵⁄₁₆″ × 5¹⁵⁄₁₆″ scant.

⟨-⟩⁴.

Printed gray paper wrapper.

Also in: *Transactions of the Association of American Physicians. Twelfth Session ... Volume XII*, Philadelphia, 1897.

NYPL   Y

14181. Hephzibah Guinness; Thee and You; and a Draft on the Bank of Spain ... Third Edition.

Philadelphia: J. B. Lippincott Company. 1897.

For first edition see above under year 1880.

Contains a few minor revisions.

Y

14182. ... THE RELATIONS OF NERVOUS DISORDERS IN WOMEN TO PELVIC DISEASE ...

⟨n.p., PHILADELPHIA, 1897⟩

Cover-title. At head of title: *Reprinted from University Medical Magazine ... University of Pennsylvania ... March, 1897*

⟨1⟩-37. 9¹⁵⁄₁₆″ scant × 6¾″ full.

⟨1-2⁸, 3², 4¹⟩.

Printed tan laid paper wrapper.

Y

The Semi-Centennial of Anæsthesia ...

Boston ... 1897

See above: *The Birth and Death of Pain*, under the year 1896.

14183. Fat and Blood: An Essay on the Treatment of Certain Forms of Neurasthenia and Hysteria ... Seventh Edition.

Philadelphia: J. B. Lippincott Company. London: 6 Henrietta Street, Covent Garden. 1898.

For first edition see above under year 1877.

"... The present edition, like the last, has been carefully revised by my son, Dr. John K. Mitchell ..."———From S. Weir Mitchell's "Preface to the Seventh Edition," dated at end *September, 1897*, p. 5.

Deposited Jan. 10, 1898.

LC   Y

14184. THE ADVENTURES OF FRANÇOIS FOUNDLING, THIEF, JUGGLER, AND FENCING-MASTER DURING THE FRENCH REVOLUTION ...

NEW YORK   THE CENTURY CO.   1898

⟨i-ii⟩ (excised or pasted under the end paper), ⟨i⟩-⟨xiv⟩, 1-321; leaf, excised or pasted under the end paper. Frontispiece; and, fourteen inserted plates, each of these last reckoned in the printed pagination. 7⅝″ scant × 5⅛″ full.

⟨-⟩⁸, 1-18⁸, 19⁴. Leaves ⟨-⟩₁ and 19₄ excised or pasted under the end papers.

V cloth: orange. Stamped in green, black and gold. Spine lettered in gold: THE / ADVENTURES / OF / FRANÇOIS / S. WEIR / MITCHELL / THE / CENTURY / CO.

Also noted in a variant binding of unknown status. The sides stamped in blind with an all-over pattern of filigrees; the spine lettered in gold: THE ADVEN- / TURES OF / FRANÇOIS / ⟨*dot*⟩ S ⟨*dot*⟩ / WEIR / MITCHELL / THE / CENTURY / CO

Note: According to contemporary trade notices there were three printings in 1898; BAL has been unable to identify these.

Noted for October in PW Aug. 13, 1898; Sept. 24, 1898. A copy in Y inscribed by early owner Oct. 12, 1898. Listed PW Oct. 15, 1898. "The twenty-fifth thousand and third large edition . . . was on press before issue."---PW Nov. 26, 1898. A paper-covered printing was advertised PW July 15, 1899; listed PW Aug. 12, 1899; issued under date 1899. The London (Macmillan) issue advertised for Nov. 1, 1898 PC Oct. 29, 1898; listed Ath Nov. 5, 1898.

AAS   B   BPL   H (variant)   NYPL   Y

14185. A CLINICAL RE-EXAMINATION OF THE MOTOR-SYMPTOMS OF CHOREA. BY S. WEIR MITCHELL . . . AND J. H. WALLACE RHEIN . . . FROM THE PHILADELPHIA MEDICAL JOURNAL,

⟨n.p., PHILADELPHIA⟩ 1898.

Cover-title.

⟨1⟩-10. 8½″ × 5½″.

⟨1⁴, 2¹⟩.

Printed yellow paper wrapper.

Reprinted from *Transactions of the College of Physicians of Philadelphia. Third Series. Volume the Nineteenth*, Philadelphia, 1897.

NYPL   Y

14186. . . . A CONTRIBUTION TO THE STUDY OF THE EFFECT OF THE VENOM OF CROTALUS ADAMANTEUS UPON THE BLOOD OF MAN AND ANIMALS . . .

⟨Washington, D. C., Government Printing Office, 1898⟩

Title-page as above, p. 1. At head of title-page: *Memoirs National Academy of Sciences. Second Memoir.*

General title-page: *Memoirs of the National Academy of Sciences. Volume VIII. Washington: Government Printing Office. 1898.*

⟨i-ii⟩, 1-14. Six plates inserted. 11⅝″ × 9¼″.

⟨-⟩⁸.

Printed blue-gray paper wrapper.

In collaboration with Alonzo H. Stewart.

A preliminary study appeared in *Transactions of the College of Physicians of Philadelphia. Third Series. Volume the Nineteenth*, Philadelphia, 1897.

LC   Y

14187. A PRAYER

1898?

Two printings have been noted. The sequence may be as here presented:

PRINTING A

A Prayer | ⟨*rule*⟩ | ⟨*2 lines from the 45th psalm*⟩ | ⟨*rule*⟩ | ⟨*text*⟩ | S. WEIR MITCHELL.

Single leaf. Laid paper. No watermark. 10¼″ × 6¾″. Printed on recto only.

Text (save for the punctuation which varies somewhat) is that of the original appearance in *Harper's Weekly*, Aug. 13, 1898, p. 791.

Line 10: *Heroic competence of will*

Line 15: *When, high above the battle's shroud,*

PRINTING B

A Prayer | ⟨*rule*⟩ | ⟨*2 lines from the 45th psalm*⟩ | ⟨*rule*⟩ | ⟨*text*⟩

Single leaf. Laid paper. Watermarked: ⟨MERRY?⟩-MOUNT 11³⁄₁₆″ × 6¾″. Printed on recto only.

Text (save for the punctuation which varies somewhat) is essentially that of the printing in *The Wager*, 1900, pp. 20-21.

Line 10: *The steadfast heart, the quiet will*

Line 15: *When, high above the battle shroud,*

Does not bear the author's name; issued anonymously.

Written on the occasion of the Battle of Santiago, July 1-3, 1898.

A copy of printing B (in NYPL) inscribed in an unknown hand: . . . *This is one of a very few special prints made by the author. October, 1898.*

Note: Also appears in *War-Time Echoes Patriotic Poems . . . of the Spanish-American War Selected . . . by James Henry Brownlee . . .* , New York, 1898; listed PW April 8, 1899.

NYPL (B)   Y (A)

14188. Far in the Forest A Story . . .

New York The Century Co. 1899

For first edition see above under 1889.

Extended and somewhat revised.

Noted as *shortly* PW Aug. 6, 1898. Advertised for October PW Sept. 24, 1898. Listed PW Oct. 1, 1898. The London (Unwin) issue advertised as *ready* Ath Oct. 22, 1898; listed PC Oct. 22, 1898; reviewed Ath April 22, 1899.

B

14189. A CASE OF ERYTHROMELALGIA, WITH MICROSCOPICAL EXAMINATION OF THE TISSUE FROM AN AMPUTATED TOE. BY S. WEIR MITCHELL . . . AND

WILLIAM G. SPILLER...FROM THE AMERICAN JOURNAL OF THE MEDICAL SCIENCES, JANUARY, 1899.

⟨n.p., PHILADELPHIA, 1899⟩

Cover-title.

⟨1⟩-13, blank leaf. Illustrated. 9⅜″ full × 6³⁄₁₆″ scant.

⟨-⟩⁸.

Printed light blue paper wrapper.

LC   NYPL   Y

14190. ODE ON A LYCIAN TOMB...

⟨NEW YORK, 1899⟩

⟨1⟩-16. Laid paper. 7¹³⁄₁₆″ × 5⁵⁄₁₆″ full.

⟨1-2⁴⟩.

Printed laid blue-gray paper boards. End papers and flyleaves of book stock. Top edges gilt.

On verso of the title-leaf: PRIVATELY PRINTED BY / S. WEIR MITCHELL / THE DE VINNE PRESS.

According to an undated letter (in UV), Mitchell to F. J. Stimson, thirty-five copies were printed.

Collected in *Selections . . .*, 1901; *The Comfort of the Hills*, 1910.

AAS   H   NYPL   UV   Y

14191. THE WAGER AND OTHER POEMS...

NEW YORK   THE CENTURY CO.   1900

⟨i⟩-⟨viii⟩, 1-47. Laid paper. 7⅝″ × 5¼″ scant.

⟨-⟩⁴, 1-3⁸.

V cloth: blackish-green. Laid end papers. Top edges gilt.

A copy (NYPL) has been seen with a four-page insert, 6¼″ × 4⅛″, with p. ⟨1⟩ engraved: *With the Author's Compliments.*

Deposited Jan. 31, 1900. BA copy received March 27, 1900. Listed PW Jan. 5, 1901 ⟨*sic*⟩.

B   BA   BPL   H   LC   NYPL   Y

14192. THE   AUTOBIOGRAPHY   OF   A QUACK AND THE CASE OF GEORGE DEDLOW...

NEW YORK   THE CENTURY CO.   1900

⟨i⟩-⟨xii⟩, 1-149. Frontispiece inserted. Seven plates inserted and reckoned in the printed pagination. Laid paper. 6¹⁵⁄₁₆″ × 4⁹⁄₁₆″.

⟨-⟩⁶, 1-7⁸, 8⁴, 9⁸.

V cloth: blue-green. Stamped in gold. White laid end papers. Laid flyleaves. Top edges gilt.

Also noted in a variant (remainder?) binding: Blue-green V cloth, stamped in black only. Top edges plain. White laid end papers. Laid paper flyleaves. Leaf: 6⅞″ × 4½″.

Deposited March 12, 1900. NYPL copy received March 22, 1900; BA copy March 27, 1900; H copy March 29, 1900. Listed PW March 31, 1900. The London (Unwin) edition mentioned as *in the autumn* Ath Aug. 11, 1900; listed Ath Sept. 1, 1900. See under 1901 for another printing.

AAS   B   H   NYPL   Y (two copies, one being the variant described)

14193. DR. NORTH AND HIS FRIENDS...

NEW YORK   THE CENTURY CO.   1900

⟨i-xii⟩, 1-499. 7⅝″ full × 5¼″.

⟨-⟩⁶, 1-30⁸, 31², 32⁸.

V cloth: green. Top edges gilt.

Two printings noted:

1: As above.

2: ⟨1⟩-32⁸.

Deposited Sept. 24, 1900. BA copy (rebound; presumed to be first printing) received Oct. 23, 1900. Listed PW Oct. 27, 1900. The London (Macmillan) edition listed Ath Nov. 10, 1900.

B (1st)   BPL (1st, 2nd)   H (2nd)   NYPL (1st, 2nd) Y (1st, 2nd)

14194. Life and Letters of Phillips Brooks by Alexander V. G. Allen . . .

New York   E. P. Dutton and Company   31 West Twenty-Third Street   1900

2 Vols.

"An Appreciation of Phillips Brooks," Vol. 1, pp. 631-635.

Listed PW Dec. 29, 1900.

H

14195. ADDRESS   ON   BEHALF   OF   THE BOARD OF TRUSTEES OF THE UNIVERSITY   OF   PENNSYLVANIA...REPRINTED FROM THE AMER. PHILOS. SOC. MEMORIAL VOLUME.

⟨n.p., n.d., PHILADELPHIA, 1900⟩

The above on p. ⟨1⟩. The address was given in memory of William Pepper, M.D.

⟨1⟩-3. 9⁵⁄₁₆″ × 5¹⁵⁄₁₆″.

⟨-⟩².

Unprinted drab paper wrapper.

Also appears in *Proceedings of the American Philosophical Society . . . Memorial Volume I*, Philadelphia, 1900.

Y

14196. Fat and Blood . . . Eighth Edition. Edited, with Additions, by John K. Mitchell, M.D.

Philadelphia: J. B. Lippincott Company. London: 36 Southampton Street, Covent Garden. 1900.

For first edition see above under 1877.

"Preface to the Eighth Edition," by S. Weir Mitchell, pp. 5-6.

H

14197. DEDICATORY ADDRESS . . .

⟨n.p., n.d., PHILADELPHIA, *ca.* 1900⟩

Caption-title. The above at head of p. 1.

1-16. $8^{13}/_{16}'' \times 5^{9}/_{16}''$.

⟨-⟩⁸.

Printed self-wrapper? Printed paper wrapper?

"Gentlemen:——I have been asked as Chairman of the Committee of Trustees on ⟨*sic*⟩ the Department of Medicine ⟨of the University of Pennsylvania⟩ to receive the splendid gift of the new buildings just announced by the Provost . . ."———p. 1.

Y

14198. The Eve of Battle / 1645 / ⟨*preceding two lines in a vignette*⟩ / ⟨*text*⟩ / ⟨n.p., n.d., 1900?⟩

The above at head of p. ⟨1⟩.

Printed on two leaves, on rectos only. $8'' \times 5^{1}/_{2}''$. Probably printed as proof. At end of text, p. ⟨2⟩: *Copyright reserved by Dr. Mitchell. Illustrations by Alfred Morton Githens.*

Collected in *The Wager*, 1900.

UV

14199. THE PHYSICIAN

⟨n.d., BOSTON, 1900⟩

⟨i-iv⟩, 1-⟨8⟩; colophon, p. ⟨9⟩; blank leaf. Laid paper. Watermarked: *Unbleached Arnold* $9^{15}/_{16}'' \times 6^{7}/_{8}''$.

⟨-⟩⁸.

Printed blue-gray laid paper wrapper. Some examples show the watermark *Vidalon*.

On p. ⟨iv⟩: *With the Compliments of ⟨signature of the author⟩*

Sixty copies printed at the Merrymount Press, Boston——— Colophon.

Also in *Transactions of the Congress of American Physicians and Surgeons. Fifth Triennial Session, Held . . . 1900*, New Haven, 1900.

Printed in 1900 according to Julian Pearce Smith's *Notes on the Merrymount Press*, 1934, p. 83.

H   NYPL   Y

14200. Proceedings and Addresses at the Complimentary Dinner Tendered to Dr. A. J. Jacobi on the Occasion of the Seventieth Anniversary of his Birthday May Five, Nineteen Hundred

⟨n.p., n.d., New York, 1900⟩

"Abraham Jacobi . . . ," p. 15. Collected in *The Comfort of the Hills*, 1910. Also contains a letter, pp. 60-61.

CC   Y

14201. Selections from the Poems of S. Weir Mitchell . . .

London   Macmillan and Co., Limited 1901 . . .

Reprint save for a 4-line "Preface" and a few notes. "The poems herein presented are selections from eight thin volumes of verse published in the United States between the years 1886 and 1889." ———Preface.

Note: In all examined copies the title-leaf is a cancel.

". . . Published at my expense by Macmillan in London . . . In all, eighteen copies sold in the first year and, so far as I know, none since. Two years later I was asked to say what was to be done with the remaining volumes. Unfortunately, the English publishers had placed in them a statement that the book was copyrighted in America. This was true only as to a part of its contents, but it absolutely prevented the exportation to this country ⟨*i.e.*, United States⟩. Accordingly, I desired Mr. Macmillan to burn the rest of the volumes or to consign them afresh to the paper-mill to serve for reincarnation of the poems in some more fortunate form. I asked also that fifty bound copies be sent to America. They were promptly stopped in the New York Custom-House. A book said to be copyrighted in America, printed in England, returned to America, the law forbids to enter. I asked what should be done with them. Might I buy them? I could not. I believe it was finally concluded to cremate them . . ."——— *The Comfort of the Hills and Other Poems*, New York, 1910, pp. x-xi.

The BPL copy presented by Mitchell to Charles Eliot Norton July 16, 1901. Listed Ath July 20, 1901. Noted as a *new book* Bkr July, 1901.

BPL   H   NYPL   Y

14202. CIRCUMSTANCE . . .

NEW YORK THE CENTURY CO. 1901

⟨i-viii⟩, ⟨1⟩-495. 7⁹⁄₁₆″ full × 5³⁄₁₆″.

⟨-⟩⁴, ⟨1⟩-31⁸.

V cloth: maroon; red. Top edges gilt.

Note: All examined copies have a list of Mitchell's books on p. ⟨iv⟩; *i.e.*, opposite, and conjugate with, the fly-title-page. The conjugate of the title-leaf is wholly blank. In the surviving copyright deposit copy the list of books is not present; the conjugate of the title-leaf is imprinted on the recto with the fly-title. Further information wanting; the surviving copyright deposit copy was reported *not found* March 22, 1971.

Deposited July 30, 1901. Noted for October PW Aug. 24, 1901. Noted for Oct. 5 PW Sept. 21, 1901. BA copy received Oct. 8, 1901. Laid into the surviving deposit copy is a note from the publisher to the Librarian of Congress stating that the book "will not be issued until Oct 10th 1901." Listed PW Oct. 12, 1901. The London (Macmillan; American sheets with cancel title-leaf) advertised for Oct. 8 Ath Oct. 5, 1901; listed Ath Oct. 12, 1901.

BPL H NYPL Y

14203. TO THE YOUNGER READERS OF THE BAR HARBOR LIBRARY

⟨BAR HARBOR, MAINE, 1901⟩

The above at head of p. 1.

1-⟨3⟩. Laid paper. 7⅛″ × 4½″.

Single leaf folded to make four pages.

At end: *December, 1901.*

NYPL

14204. Addresses at the Dinner Given to Dr. T. Gaillard Thomas on His Seventieth Birthday . . . at Sherry's November Twenty-First Nineteen Hundred and One

⟨New York, n.d., 1901?⟩

Address, pp. 26-30.

Printed paper wrapper over unprinted boards.

On p. ⟨4⟩: Device and imprint of The Winthrop Press, New York.

H Y

14205. The Autobiography of a Quack and Other Stories . . .

New York The Century Co. 1901

A reprint of *The Autobiography of a Quack . . .*, 1900, with other stories also here reprinted. A complete reprint save for a minor alteration in the "Introduction," p. vii.

Issued in Great Britain with cancel title-leaf imprinted: *London Macmillan and Co., Limited 1901*

H

14206. Dedication of the New Building of the Boston Medical Library . . . January 12, 1901 . . .

Boston Printed by S. J. Parkhill & Co. 1901

Printed flexible paper boards, cloth shelfback.

Letter, Dec. 29, 1900, pp. ⟨38⟩-39.

H

14207. King Christmas and Master New Year / ⟨*text: 7 quatrains*⟩ / With Christmas Greetings / from / ⟨*Mitchell's signature*⟩ ⟨n.p., n.d., 1901?⟩

Card. Printed on recto only. 4⅜″ scant × 5⁹⁄₁₆″ full.

King Christmas from his house of ice, | Looked out across the snow . . .

Y

14208. New Samaria . . .

Philadelphia J. B. Lippincott Company 1902

Lippincott's Monthly Magazine, Aug. 1902, issued with title-page as above. For formal publication of this novel see below under 1904.

Deposited July 18, 1902.

LC

14209. AN AUTOBIOGRAPHY OF GEORGE WASHINGTON TO THE CLOSE OF GENERAL BRADOCK'S ⟨*sic*⟩ CAMPAIGN EDITED BY S. WEIR MITCHELL . . .

NEW YORK THE CENTURY CO. 1902

A version of *The Youth of Washington . . .* , 1904.

Unpublished. Proof sheets only. 138 leaves printed on recto only; unpaged. Leaf: 9⅝″ × 7⅞″.

DU

14210. . . . THE MUSCULAR FACTORS CONCERNED IN ANKLE-CLONUS . . .

⟨NEW YORK, 1902⟩

Cover-title. At head of title: *Reprinted from the "Journal of Nervous and Mental Disease,"* May, 02

⟨1⟩-3. 10¹⁄₁₆″ × 6¹³⁄₁₆″ scant.

⟨-⟩².

Printed gray paper wrapper.

NYPL

14211. . . . NURSES AND THEIR EDUCA-
TION . . .

⟨n.p., ROCHESTER, N. Y., 1902⟩

Caption-title. The preceding at head of p. ⟨1⟩. At head of title: *Reprinted from the American Journal of Nursing, August, 1902.*

⟨1⟩-9, blank leaf. $9^{13}\!/_{16}'' \times 6^{1}\!/_{2}''$.

⟨-⟩⁶.

Printed self-wrapper.

NYPL

14212. VERSE READ BEFORE THE
UNIVERSITY OF PENNSYLVANIA ON
THE BIRTHDAY OF WASHINGTON,
MDCCCCII . . .

⟨BOSTON: THE MERRYMOUNT PRESS, n.d., 1902⟩

⟨i-iv⟩, i-vii; blank, p. ⟨viii⟩; Merrymount Press imprint, p. ⟨ix⟩; blank leaf. Laid paper water-marked *Merrymount* $10^{3}\!/_{16}'' \times 6^{3}\!/_{4}''$.

⟨-⟩⁸.

Printed gray laid paper wrapper watermarked MBM⟨?⟩.

Appears also in *University of Pennsylvania Proceedings of "University Day" February 22, 1902* . . . , Philadelphia, 1902. Collected in *The Comfort of the Hills*, 1910.

According to Julian Pearce Smith's *Notes on the Merrymount Press*, 1934, printed in 1902.

Y

14213. Cooking in Old Créole Days . . . by Célestine Eustis with an Introduction by S. Weir Mitchell . . .

New York R. H. Russell 1903

Boards, cloth shelf back; and, three-quarters calf.

"Introduction," pp. 5-6.

Two printings noted:

1 : As above. Mitchell's contribution on pp. 5-6. *P. F. Collier & Son* imprint on copyright page. Deposit copy thus.

2 : Mitchell's contribution on pp. xiii-xiv. Printer's imprint not present on copyright page. Thus in 1904 printing.

Deposited Feb. 10, 1903. Listed PW April 4, 1903.

H (2nd)   LC (1st)   UV (2nd)

14214. VERSES READ TO THE FRANKLIN
INN CLUB ON THE BIRTHDAY OF
FRANKLIN JANUARY 6 O. S.

⟨n.p., PHILADELPHIA: THE LIPPINCOTT PRESS, n.d., 1903⟩

Not seen. Entry on the basis of a photographic copy.

Cover-title.

⟨1-7⟩. $14'' \times 8^{1}\!/_{2}''$.

Printed self-wrapper.

An extract from the above was issued as sheet music: *Franklin Inn Club Song Chorus by Dr. S. Weir Mitchell from the Loving Cup of the Club Words and Music by C. Wharton Stork Arranged for the Piano by Philip H. Goepp*, privately printed, n.d. A copy in Y.

HSP

14215. WASHINGTON IN HIS LETTERS AN
ADDRESS BEFORE THE UNIVERSITY
OF PENNSYLVANIA . . . THE BIRTHDAY
OF WASHINGTON NINETEEN HUN-
DRED AND THREE

THE LIPPINCOTT PRESS ⟨PHILADELPHIA, 1903⟩

Cover-title.

⟨one⟩-⟨twenty-two⟩, blank leaf. $11^{3}\!/_{16}'' \times 8''$. Watermarked: *Strathmore USA*

⟨-⟩¹².

Printed self-wrapper. Tied with cord.

According to NYPL 100 copies only were printed.

An incomplete copy was received at the United States Department of State on March 13, 1903; now LC

NYPL   UV   Y

14216. A COMEDY OF CONSCIENCE . . .

NEW YORK THE CENTURY CO. 1903

⟨i⟩-⟨vi⟩, ⟨1⟩-129. Frontispiece inserted. Four inserted plates reckoned in the printed pagination. $7''$ scant $\times 4^{9}\!/_{16}''$.

⟨1⟩-8⁸.

Two printings noted; the following sequence is probable:

1 : The title-page is printed in black and red.

2 : The title-page is printed in black only. The deposit copies thus.

V cloth: blue-green. Stamped in white.

Note: Copies (both printings) have been seen in goldstamped maroon T cloth. Presumably prepared for the use of The Tabard Inn Library. See BAL, Vol. 1, pp. xxxii-xxxiii.

About to publish--- PW Feb. 14, 1903. On copyright page: *Published March, 1903* Deposited March 20, 1903. Noted for March 28 PW March 21, 1903. Noted as *just published* PW March 28, 1903. Listed

PW April 4, 1903. The Edinburgh (Douglas) edition listed Bkr March, 1904.

AAS (2nd) B (2nd) H (1st) LC (2nd) NYPL (2nd) Y (1st; 2nd; Tabard)

14217. LITTLE STORIES . . .

NEW YORK THE CENTURY CO. MDCCCCIII

Title-page in black and green.

⟨i-viii⟩, ⟨1⟩-⟨110⟩, blank leaf. 7½″ scant × 4⁷⁄₁₆″. ⟨1-7⁸, 8⁴⟩.

V cloth: blue. Top edges gilt.

Advertised PW Sept. 26, 1903. Deposited Sept. 30, 1903. On copyright page: *Published, October, 1903* Listed PW Oct. 17, 1903. BA copy received Oct. 20, 1903. The London (Warne) edition listed Bkr Jan. 1919.

AAS B BA H Y

14218. Historical Notes of Dr. Benjamin Rush 1777 . . . Reprinted from the Pennsylvania Magazine of History and Biography, April, 1903

Philadelphia 1903

Cover-title. Printed paper wrapper.

Edited by Mitchell.

⟨1⟩-22. Laid paper. 9⁷⁄₈″ × 6⁹⁄₁₆″.

NYPL Y

14219. Leaders of Men or Types and Principles of Success As Illustrated in the Lives and Careers of Famous Americans of the Present Day . . . Edited by Henry W. Ruoff . . .

The King-Richardson Company Springfield: Massachusetts San Jose Chicago Toronto Indianapolis 1903

Presumably a subscription book and if so, issued in a variety of formats, possibly with varying imprints. Noted in cloth, leather shelf back; and, cloth.

Autobiographical comment, pp. ⟨369⟩-370.

H

14220. . . . THE RELATION OF NEURALGIC HEADACHES TO STORMS . . .

⟨n.p., PHILADELPHIA, 1903⟩

Caption-title. The above at head of p. ⟨1⟩. At head of title: [*Reprinted from American Medicine, Vol V, No. 26, pages 1023-1024, June 27, 1903.*]

⟨1⟩-4. 8¹⁄₁₆″ × 5⁵⁄₁₆″ scant.

Single cut sheet folded to make four pages.

LC NYPL

14221. Mr Kris Kringle A Christmas Tale . . .

Philadelphia George W Jacobs & Co ⟨1904⟩

For first edition see above under year 1893.

Revised. Contains a foreword written for this edition, pp. 15-21.

Deposited Sept. 1, 1904.

LC Y

14222. NEW SAMARIA AND THE SUMMER OF ST. MARTIN . . .

PHILADELPHIA & LONDON J. B. LIPPINCOTT COMPANY 1904

Title-page in black and red.

For prior publication of *New Samaria* see above under year 1902.

⟨i-ii⟩, ⟨1⟩-168. Frontispiece and four plates inserted. Laid paper. 7″ full × 4½″.

⟨1⟩⁹, 2-8, ⟨9⟩, 10⁸, 11⁴. ⟨1⟩₂ inserted.

EC cloth: red, stamped in red and gold. EC cloth: blue, stamped in blue and gold. Top edges gilt.

On copyright page: *Published September, 1904* Deposited Sept. 9, 1904. Noted as *at once* PW Sept. 17, 1904. Advertised PW Sept. 24, 1904. BA copy received Sept. 27, 1904. Listed PW Oct. 1, 1904; Ath Dec. 10, 1904.

B H LC NYPL Y

14223. THE YOUTH OF WASHINGTON . . .

. . . 1904

Issued in both trade and limited formats. For an extended edition see under *Works*, 1905. For an earlier printing see *An Autobiography of George Washington* . . . , 1902.

TRADE FORMAT

THE YOUTH OF WASHINGTON TOLD IN THE FORM OF AN AUTOBIOGRAPHY BY S. WEIR MITCHELL, M.D.

NEW YORK THE CENTURY CO. 1904

Title-page printed in black only.

⟨i-viii⟩, ⟨1⟩-290, blank leaf. 7⁹⁄₁₆″ × 5⅛″.

Noted in the following forms:

FIRST PRINTING, FIRST ISSUE

⟨-⟩⁴, ⟨1⟩-2, 2⟨*sic*⟩, 4-5, ⟨6⟩, 7-17⁸, 18², 19⁸. Leaf 12₆ (pp. 187-188) is an integral leaf. 13 lines of text, p. 187.

FIRST PRINTING, SECOND ISSUE

⟨-⟩⁴, ⟨1⟩-2, 2⟨*sic*⟩, 4-5, ⟨6⟩, 7-17⁸, 18², 19⁸. Leaf 12₆ (pp. 187-188) is a cancel. 12 lines of text, p. 187.

SECOND PRINTING (*1st printing, 3rd issue?*)

⟨-⟩⁴, ⟨1⟩-5, ⟨6⟩, 7-17⁸, 18², 19⁸. Leaf 12₆ (pp. 187-188) is a cancel. 12 lines of text, p. 187.

THIRD (*Second?*) PRINTING

⟨-⟩⁴, ⟨1⟩-17⁸, 18², 19⁸. Leaf 12₆ (pp. 187-188) is an integral leaf. 12 lines of text, p. 187.

Two bindings noted. Binding A noted on all forms of the book save for Third (Second?) Printing. The following variations are sufficient for identification:

BINDING A

V cloth: yellow. Stamped in blue, gold and blind. Spine imprint: *The | Century | Co.* Top edges gilt.

BINDING B

T cloth: orange. Stamped in blue and maroon. Spine imprint: A ⟨*dot*⟩ WESSELS / COMPANY / NEW YORK Top edges plain.

Deposited Sept. 10, 1904. Advertised PW Sept. 24, 1904. On copyright page: *Published October, 1904* Noted for *the 8th inst.*, PW Oct. 1, 1904. Advertised for Oct. 8, 1904 PW Oct. 8, 1904. Noted for *to-day* PW Oct. 8, 1904. Listed PW Oct. 15, 1904. The London (Unwin) edition noted as *about to publish* Ath Nov. 12, 1904; listed Ath Jan. 14, 1905.

LARGE PAPER FORMAT

THE YOUTH OF WASHINGTON TOLD IN THE FORM OF AN AUTOBIOGRAPHY BY S. WEIR MITCHELL, M.D. LL.D., HARVARD AND EDINBURGH

NEW YORK THE CENTURY CO. 1904

Title-page in black and blind.

⟨i-viii⟩, ⟨1⟩-290; blank leaf. Wove paper watermarked *Unbleached Arnold* 10½″ × 7⅜″.

⟨1⁴, 2-18⁸, 19², 20⁸⟩.

Leaf comprising pp. 187-188 is an integral, not a cancel. 12 lines of text, p. 187.

Blue-gray cartridge paper sides, white imitation vellum shelf back and corners. Printed blue-gray cartridge paper label on spine. End papers and single flyleaves of book stock.

"... One Hundred Printed ... New York, October, M CM IV"---P. ⟨i⟩.

Listed PW Dec. 24, 1904.

BPL (1st printing) 2nd issue; 3rd ⟨2nd?⟩ printing) H (2nd printing ⟨first printing, 3rd issue?⟩) LC (1st printing 1st issue) UV (large paper) Y (large paper)

14224. A CASE OF UNCOMPLICATED HYSTERIA IN THE MALE LASTING THIRTY YEARS, WITH POST-MORTEM EXAMINATION. BY S. WEIR MITCHELL ... AND WILLIAM G. SPILLER ... FROM

THE TRANSACTIONS OF THE ASSOCIATION OF AMERICAN PHYSICIANS,

⟨PHILADELPHIA⟩ 1904.

Cover-title.

⟨1⟩-13, blank leaf. 9⁵⁄₁₆″ × 6″.

⟨-⟩⁸.

Printed gray paper wrapper.

Also appears in: *Transactions of the Association of American Physicians. Nineteenth Session ... Volume XIX*, Philadelphia, 1904.

LC NYPL Y

14225. ... DR. WEIR MITCHELL'S RESPONSE TO THE TOAST "THE ADMIRAL AND HIS FRIENDS"

⟨n.p., n.d., PHILADELPHIA, 1904⟩

At head of title: *Dinner to Admiral Charles E. Clark at the Union League Club Philadelphia October 21, 1904*

⟨i-ii⟩, ⟨1⟩-8, blank leaf. Laid paper watermarked *Van Gelder Zonen.* 9⅛″ × 6³⁄₁₆″.

⟨-⟩⁶.

Printed self-wrapper.

DeVinne Press device, p. ⟨2⟩.

NYPL Y

14226. THE EVOLUTION OF THE REST TREATMENT ... REPRINTED FROM THE JOURNAL OF NERVOUS AND MENTAL DISEASE, JUNE, 1904

⟨n.p., CHICAGO, 1904⟩

Cover-title.

⟨1⟩-6, blank leaf. 9½″ × 6¾″ full.

⟨-⟩⁴.

Printed gray-tan paper wrapper.

LC NYPL Y

14227. Summary of the Annual Report of the Library Committee of the College of Physicians of Philadelphia for the Year 1904

⟨Philadelphia, 1904⟩

Cover-title. Printed paper wrapper.

Signed at p. 3 by Mitchell and other members of the committee.

NYPL

14228. CONSTANCE TRESCOT A NOVEL ...

NEW YORK THE CENTURY CO. 1905

⟨i-iv⟩, ⟨1⟩-384. 7⁹⁄₁₆″ × 5⅛″ full.

⟨-⟩², ⟨1⟩-24⁸.

V cloth: blue. Flyleaf at front.

"Dr. Mitchell has rewritten *Constance Trescot* three times in the past three years. The manuscript was put into type for the first time two years ago, and a single set of page proofs was struck off on 'large paper' and bound up for the author, who worked for a year on these page proofs. So many changes were made that the book was entirely reset before issue."———PW April 29, 1905.

Noted for *March* PW Jan. 21, 1905. Deposited March 1, 1905. Advertised PW March 18, 1905. Listed PW March 25, 1905. On copyright page: *Published March, 1905*

H   NYPL   Y

14229. Mark Twain's Seventieth Birthday Record of a Dinner Given in His Honor . . .

Harper & Brothers, Publishers New York and London ⟨1905; *i.e.,* 1906⟩

Unpaged. Contains a letter, Nov. 15, 1905; and, a neat quatrain.

For comment see entry No. 770A.

14230. ADDRESS . . . DELIVERED AT THE COMMENCEMENT EXERCISES, CLASS OF '05 OF THE SCHOOL OF NURSING THE PRESBYTERIAN HOSPITAL IN THE CITY OF NEW YORK FLORENCE NIGHTINGALE HALL MAY ELEVENTH, NINETEEN HUNDRED AND FIVE

⟨NEW YORK, 1905⟩

Cover-title.

⟨1⟩-11. 9¼″ × 5⅞″.

⟨-⟩⁶.

Printed greenish-tan laid paper wrapper.

H   NYPL   Y

14231. Dinner to Dr. William Osler Previous to His Departure for England to Assume the Regius Professorship of Medicine in the University of Oxford May Second, Nineteen Hundred and Five Waldorf-Astoria New York

⟨Philadelphia: Patterson & White Co., n.d., 1905⟩

"Presentation of Cicero de Senectute," pp. 26–28.

Printed paper wrapper.

LC   Y

14232. OF AILUROPHOBIA . . .

1905

Two printings noted. Sequence not determined. The designations are for identification only. The texts vary slightly.

PRINTING A

. . . OF AILUROPHOBIA AND THE POWER TO BE CONSCIOUS OF THE CAT AS NEAR, WHEN UNSEEN AND UNHEARD . . .

⟨n.p., PHILADELPHIA, 1905⟩

Caption-title. The above at head of p. ⟨1⟩. At head of title: [*Reprinted from American Medicine, Vol. IX, No. 21, pages 851-853, May 27, 1905.*]

⟨1⟩-10; blank, p. ⟨11⟩; advertisement for *American Medicine*, p. ⟨12⟩. 8″ full × 5⁵⁄₁₆″.

⟨-⟩⁶.

Printed self-wrapper.

PRINTING B

OF AILUROPHOBIA AND THE POWER TO BE CONSCIOUS OF THE CAT AS NEAR, WHEN UNSEEN AND UNHEARD . . . FROM THE TRANSACTIONS OF THE ASSOCIA- TION OF AMERICAN PHYSICIANS 1905

⟨n.p., PHILADELPHIA, 1905⟩

Cover-title.

⟨1⟩-11. 9⅛″ full × 5⅞″.

⟨-⟩⁶.

Printed gray paper wrapper.

Also appears in *Transactions of the Association of American Physicians. Twentieth Session, Held at Washington, D.C., May 16 and 17, 1905. Volume XX*, Philadelphia, 1905.

UV (both)   Y (both)

14233. . . . SOME PERSONAL RECOLLEC- TIONS OF THE CIVIL WAR . . . READ APRIL 5, 1905.

⟨n.d., PHILADELPHIA, 1905⟩

Caption-title. The above at head of p. ⟨1⟩. At head of title: *Reprinted from the Transactions of the College of Physicians of Philadelphia, 1905.*

⟨1⟩-8. 9³⁄₁₆″ full × 5¹⁵⁄₁₆″.

⟨-⟩⁴.

Printed self-wrapper.

Appears also in *Transactions of the College of Physi- cians of Philadelphia. Third Series. Volume the Twenty- Seventh*, Philadelphia, 1905.

LC   NYPL   Y

14234. . . . BOOKS AND THE MAN READ TO THE CHARAKA CLUB OF NEW YORK MARCH 4, 1905

⟨n.p., n.d., 1905⟩

Cover-title. At head of title: *William Osler from S. Weir Mitchell*

⟨1⟩-⟨13⟩, blank leaf. Printed on rectos only. Laid paper watermarked: *Old Berkshire Mills 1893* 9½″ × 6¹⁄₁₆″.

⟨-⟩⁸.

According to NYPL fifty copies only were printed. Collected in *The Comfort of the Hills*, 1910.

B   NYPL   Y

14235. Author's Definitive Edition

New York: The Century Co. 1905–1914

Certain of the volumes went into two or more printings with the imprint date appropriately altered. The dates here given are the earliest located by BAL. The order of issue of the separate volumes is not known to BAL and the titles are here presented alphabetically. For another set see under year 1903 in *Section Two*.

The Adventures of François. 1905.

The Autobiography of a Quack and Other Stories. 1905.

Characteristics. 1905.

Circumstance. 1905.

The Complete Poems. 1914.
    For a comment see below under *The Complete Poems*, 1914.

Constance Trescot. 1905.

Dr. North and His Friends. 1905.

Far in the Forest. 1905.

Hugh Wynne, Free Quaker. 1910.

In War Time. 1905.

John Sherwood, Ironmaster. 1914.

The Red City. 1910.

Roland Blake. 1905.

Westways, a Village Chronicle. 1914.

When All the Woods Are Green. 1905.

The Youth of Washington. 1910.
    Revised. See above under 1904 for first edition.

The present entry on the basis of mixed sets in: BPL, NYPL, Y.

14236. PEARL RENDERED INTO MODERN ENGLISH VERSE . . .

NEW YORK   THE CENTURY CO. 1906

See under 1908 for an extended edition.

⟨i-ii⟩, ⟨1⟩-67; blank leaf (used as pastedown); blank leaf (excised or pasted under the end paper). Laid paper. 7¾″ full × 5⁵⁄₁₆″.

⟨1-4⟩⁸. ⟨4⟩₇ used as a pastedown; ⟨4⟩₈ excised or pasted under the end paper.

S cloth: green. True end paper (book stock) at front. Flyleaf (book stock) at front. At back: ⟨4⟩₇ used as pastedown. Top edges gilt.

The following note inserted in the Y copy: "In a letter to Wm. Osler dated April 5, 1906, a copy of which is found in Harvey Cushing's Collection . . . S.W.M. states that 500 copies . . . were printed and if the book is printed again he will add nine more verses as too many stanzas were left out . . . Mitchell printed *Pearl* to give away."

Deposited Feb. 17, 1906. Listed PW April 14, 1906.

AAS   B   Y

14237. A DIPLOMATIC ADVENTURE . . .

NEW YORK   THE CENTURY CO. 1906

⟨i-iv⟩, ⟨1⟩-166, blank leaf. Laid paper. Frontispiece inserted. 7″ × 4½″.

⟨1⁶, 2-11⁸⟩.

V cloth: blue. White laid end papers. Laid paper flyleaf at front.

Advertised PW March 17, 1906. Deposited March 21, 1906. Noted for the *14th* PW April 7, 1906. Listed PW April 14, 1906. On copyright page: *Published April, 1906*

H   LC   NYPL   Y

14238. . . . THE SONG OF THE FLAGS ON THEIR RETURN TO THE STATES OF THE CONFEDERACY . . .

⟨n.p., 1906⟩

Caption-title. The above at head of text. At head of title: *Collier's for April 21 1906* . . .

Single cut sheet. Printed on recto only. 15¹¹⁄₁₆″ × 11″.

Issued as a separate offprint? Proof only?

Collected in *The Comfort of the Hills*, 1910, under the title "The Song of the Captured Confederate Battle-Flags."

Y

14239. . . . Henry Mills Alden's 70th Birthday Souvenir of its Celebration . . .

⟨New York⟩ . . . 1906 . . . Harper & Brothers

Letter, Oct. 25, 1906, p. 1814.

For fuller entry see No. 6613.

14240. ADDRESS . . . TO THE NURSE-GRADUATES OF THE PHILADELPHIA

ORTHOPAEDIC HOSPITAL AND INFIRMARY FOR NERVOUS DISEASES NOVEMBER 16, 1906

⟨PHILADELPHIA, 1906⟩

Cover-title.

⟨1⟩-17, blank leaf. Paper watermarked *Old Stratford USA* 9″ scant × $6\frac{5}{16}$″.

⟨-⟩^{10}.

Printed self-wrapper.

LC NYPL Y

14241. Dinner of the Trustees of the University of Pennsylvania to Provost Charles Custis Harrison ⟨at⟩ The Bellevue-Stratford Philadelphia, May 23, 1906

⟨n.p., n.d., Philadelphia, 1906⟩

"Remarks ... in Response to the Toast 'The Commercial Value of the University to the City'," pp. 4-44.

Boards, printed paper label on front cover. 300 numbered copies only.

UV

14242. THE MEMORY OF FRANKLIN ... READ AT A DINNER ON THE 20TH OF APRIL, 1906, IN COMMEMORATION OF THE 200TH ANNIVERSARY OF THE BIRTH OF FRANKLIN

⟨n.p., n.d., PHILADELPHIA, 1906⟩

Cover-title.

⟨1-4⟩. Laid paper. 9″ × $5\frac{9}{16}$″.

Single cut sheet folded to make four pages.

LC NYPL Y

14243. Jamestown Tributes and Toasts ⟨Edited by⟩ Julia Wyatt Bullard ...

⟨Lynchburg, Virginia: J. P. Bell Company, Printers, 1907⟩

"A Shirk's Toast," p. 157.

H

14244. SOME MEMORANDA IN REGARD TO WILLIAM HARVEY ...

NEW YORK 1907

⟨i-ii⟩, ⟨1⟩-45. Laid paper. $9\frac{1}{16}$″ × $7\frac{7}{16}$″.

⟨1-6^{4}⟩.

V cloth: blue. White laid end papers.

Two states noted; the sequence has not been determined:

A

Leaves ⟨6⟩$_{1\text{-}4}$ are cancels.

B

Leaves ⟨6⟩$_{1\text{-}4}$ are not cancels.

Does the above represent a correction of misimposition?

Also appears in *Transactions of the Association of American Physicians. Twenty-Second Session ... Volume XXII*, Philadelphia, 1907.

NYPL (A) Y (A, B)

14245. TOAST: TO THE SURVIVING MEMBERS OF THE PATHOLOGICAL SOCIETY ... REPRINTED FROM THE PROCEEDINGS OF THE PATHOLOGICAL SOCIETY OF PHILADELPHIA, 1907 ...

OFFICE OF THE JOURNAL OF MEDICAL RESEARCH BOSTON, MASS., U.S.A. ⟨1907⟩

Cover-title.

63-66. $9\frac{5}{8}$″ × $6\frac{1}{4}$″.

⟨-⟩^{2}.

Printed gray paper wrapper.

Also appears in: *Proceedings of the Pathological Society of Philadelphia New Series, Volume X.* (*Old Series, Volume XXVIII.*) ..., Boston ⟨1907⟩.

LC NYPL Y

14246. Pearl: Rendered into Modern English Verse ...

Portland Maine Thomas Bird Mosher MDCCCCVIII

Extended edition. For first edition see above under 1906.

Printed gray laid paper wrapper, folded over flexible white boards.

"60 copies ... printed on Van Gelder hand-made paper for presentation only, and the type distributed"---P. ⟨iii⟩.

Deposited June 24, 1908.

H Y

14247. A VENTURE IN 1777 ...

PHILADELPHIA GEORGE W. JACOBS & COMPANY PUBLISHERS ⟨1908⟩

Title-page in black and blue.

⟨1⟩-120, 4 blank leaves. Frontispiece and 3 plates inserted, all plates tinted with blue. $7\frac{5}{8}$″ × $5\frac{3}{4}$″ full. Watermarked *Suede Finish*

⟨1-8^{8}⟩.

Two bindings noted; the order is presumed correct:

BINDING A

Yellow buckram. Stamped in gold and colors. White end papers imprinted in blue with garlands, boxes, bouquets. Illustrations tinted with blue.

BINDING B

V cloth: orange-yellow. Stamped in black and blue. The plates are not tinted with blue.

Noted as *in preparation* PW May 16, 1908. On copyright page: *Published September, 1908* Deposited Oct. 1, 1908. Advertised for Oct. 3 PW Oct. 3, 1908. Listed PW Oct. 17, 1908. ·

AAS (B)   H (A)   LC (A)   NYPL (A, B)   UV (A) WR (B)   Y (A)

14248. The Great Fight Poems and Sketches by William Henry Drummond . . .

New York and London G. P. Putnam's Sons The Knickerbocker Press 1908

Cloth, print pasted to front cover.

"In Memory of William Henry Drummond," p. v. Collected in *The Comfort of the Hills,* 1910.

NYPL copy received Oct. 2, 1908. Listed PW Oct. 10, 1908.

H   NYPL   UV

14249. THE RED CITY A NOVEL OF THE SECOND ADMINISTRATION OF PRESIDENT WASHINGTON . . .

NEW YORK THE CENTURY CO. 1908

Two printings noted:

FIRST PRINTING

⟨i-viii⟩, ⟨1⟩-421, 2 blank leaves. Frontispiece inserted; 9 plates inserted and reckoned in the printed pagination. $7\frac{9}{16}$″ × $5\frac{5}{16}$″ scant.

⟨-⟩⁴, ⟨1⟩-24⁸, 25⁴, 26⁸.

SECOND PRINTING

⟨1⟩-26⁸.

V cloth: yellow. Color print pasted to front cover. White wove paper end paper at front; leaf 26₈ used as terminal pastedown.

Noted for *late this month* PW Oct. 10, 1908. Advertised for Oct. 28 PW Oct. 24, 1908. On copyright page: *Published October, 1908* The BA copy received Nov. 3, 1908. Listed PW Nov. 7, 1908. "Went into a second edition before issue"---PW Dec. 5, 1908. The London (Macmillan) edition advertised as *shortly* Bkr Nov. 1908; listed Ath Nov. 21, 1908.

Originally titled *René Vicomte de Courval.* A set of early proofs (in NYPL) of the periodical appearance

(*The Century Magazine,* Jan.-Dec. 1908) gives the early title.

AAS (1st)   H (1st, 2nd)   NYPL (1st, 2nd)   Y (1st, 2nd)

14250. Hugh Wynne Free Quaker . . . ⟨Nineteenth Edition⟩

Published by the Century Co. New York: 1908

For first edition see above under 1897.

"Preface to Nineteenth Edition," pp. vii-xi, dated at end *August, 1908.*

". . . I use a desired opportunity to rectify some mistakes in names, dates, and localities . . ."---P. vii.

Noted PW Dec. 5, 1908.

Y

14251. . . . To the Committee on Ways and Means, Washington, D.C. . . .

⟨At head of the preceding:⟩ The Library Company of Philadelphia . . . December 30, 1908

Not seen. Entry on the basis of a photographic copy.

Single leaf. Printed on both sides. $9\frac{5}{8}$″ × $6\frac{3}{16}$″.

A protest, signed at end by Mitchell and others, on the subject of an effort to increase the duty levied on books and other printed matter.

LCP

14252. . . . ADDRESS DELIVERED . . . TO THE GRADUATING CLASS OF THE NEW YORK HOSPITAL TRAINING SCHOOL FOR NURSES FEBRUARY 28th, 1908

⟨NEW YORK, 1908⟩

At head of title: *The Society of the New York Hospital* . . .

⟨i-ii⟩, ⟨1⟩-⟨28⟩, blank leaf. Laid paper. $9\frac{7}{16}$″ × $6\frac{1}{4}$″.

⟨-⟩¹⁶.

Printed tan paper wrapper.

Note: In some copies the preliminary and terminal blank leaves (⟨-⟩₁,₁₆) are not present.

NYPL   Y

14253. ADDRESS TO THE GRADUATING CLASS AT THE ANNUAL COMMENCEMENT OF THE TRAINING SCHOOL FOR NURSES OF THE HOSPITAL OF THE UNIVERSITY OF PENNSYLVANIA . . . NOVEMBER 24, 1908

PHILADELPHIA THE JOHN C. WINSTON COMPANY
1908

⟨1⟩-20. 9″ × 6″.

⟨-⟩¹⁰.

Printed gray paper wrapper.

H   Y

14254. THE TREATMENT BY REST,
SECLUSION, ETC., IN RELATION TO
PSYCHOTHERAPY ... REPRINTED
FROM THE JOURNAL OF THE AMERI-
CAN MEDICAL ASSOCIATION, JUNE 20,
1908, VOL. L, pp. 2033–2037.

... 1908.   AMERICAN MEDICAL ASSOCIATION.
ONE HUNDRED AND THREE DEARBORN AVENUE.
CHICAGO.

Cover-title.

⟨1⟩-15. 8⁷⁄₁₆″ × 5⁹⁄₁₆″ scant.

⟨-⟩⁸.

Printed blue-green paper wrapper.

NYPL   Y

14255. AVE PENNSYLVANIA

1909

Noted in the following forms; publication dates of
B and C unknown to BAL.

A

AVE. ⟨sic⟩ PENNSYLVANIA DEDICATED
TO PROVOST C. C. HARRISON BY S. WEIR
MITCHELL AND H. A. CLARKE

⟨n.p., PHILADELPHIA, 1909⟩

Sheet music. Cover-title.

Deposited Feb. 6, 1909. Note: A setting by E. M.
Dilley, not seen by BAL, was deposited for copyright April 23, 1909.

Location: Y

B

AVE PENNSYLVANIA! (WORDS BY S.
WEIR MITCHELL. MUSIC BY HUGH A.
CLARKE.) ...

⟨n.p., n.d.⟩

Single leaf. Printed on recto only. 6⁹⁄₁₆″ × 4″.

Text only; music not present.

Location: Y

C

AVE PENNSYLVANIA BY S. WEIR MIT-
CHELL ...

⟨n.p., n.d.⟩

The above on p. ⟨1⟩.

Single leaf folded to make four pages. Off-white
linen-weave paper. Watermarked with a scales
device and a circle enclosing the monogram BT.

⟨1-3⟩. 5³⁄₄″ × 3³⁄₄″. P. ⟨4⟩ blank.

Location: Gd

14256. THE COMFORT OF THE HILLS ...

PRIVATELY PRINTED 1909

For published edition see under 1910.

⟨i-viii⟩, 1-31; DeVinne Press device, p. ⟨32⟩.
Laid paper. 7¹⁄₁₆″ × 4½″.

⟨1-5⟩⁴.

Flexible V cloth: green. White laid end papers.
Double flyleaves.

"... Fifty Copies Printed ... January, Nineteen
Hundred And Nine, Of Which This Is No. ..."
–––P. ⟨iii⟩.

Deposited Feb. 11, 1909. Listed PW March 27,
1909.

B   H   NYPL   Y

14257. ADDRESS ... DELIVERED ON THE
OPENING OF THE NEW HALL OF THE
COLLEGE OF PHYSICIANS OF PHILA-
DELPHIA NOVEMBER 11th, 1909

⟨NEW YORK, n.d., 1909?⟩

⟨i-iv⟩, ⟨1⟩-18, blank leaf. 8⁷⁄₈″ scant × 5½″. Laid
paper watermarked Old Stratford

⟨1-3⁴⟩.

Printed gray-brown linen weave stiff paper wrapper folded over the first and last leaves.

Also appears in:

Transactions of the College of Physicians of Philadelphia
Third Series Volume the Thirty-First, Philadelphia,
1909. Also contains "Memoir of William Thomson, M.D.," pp. ⟨lxi⟩-lxxi.

1787 1909 Exercises on the Occasion of the Dedication
of the New Hall of the College of Physicians of Philadelphia November Tenth and Eleventh MDCCCCIX
⟨Philadelphia, 1909⟩. Also contains "remarks,"
pp. 87–91.

LC   Y

14258. ... ADDRESS DELIVERED BEFORE
THE MEDICAL AND CHIRURGICAL
SOCIETY OF MARYLAND. ON THE OC-
CASION OF THE DEDICATION OF ITS
BUILDING ...

⟨BALTIMORE, 1909⟩

Preceding at head of p. ⟨220⟩. At head of title:
Reprinted from the Bulletin of the Medical and Chirurgi-
cal Faculty of Maryland, June, 1909.

⟨219⟩-227. 9$\frac{11}{16}$″ × 6$\frac{5}{8}$″ full.

Five single leaves, stapled.

Printed self-wrapper.

LC   NYPL   Y

14259. ADDRESS TO THE AMERICAN NEU-
ROLOGICAL ASSOCIATION BY THE
PRESIDENT S. WIER⟨*sic*⟩ MITCHELL . . .
REPRINTED FROM THE JOURNAL OF
NERVOUS AND MENTAL DISEASE, NO.
36, VOL. 7 JULY, 1909.

⟨n.p., CHICAGO, 1909⟩

Cover-title.

⟨i-ii⟩, 385-401. 10″ × 6$\frac{13}{16}$″.

⟨-⟩^{10}.

Printed gray-green paper wrapper.

LC   NYPL   Y

14260. Annual Report of the Library Committee
of the College of Physicians of Philadelphia for
the Year 1909 Reprinted from the Transactions
Third Series, XXXI, 1909

⟨Philadelphia, 1909⟩

Cover-title.

Signed at p. 11 by Mitchell and others.

Printed paper wrapper.

NYPL

14261. . . . Small-Pox as Found and Treated in
Cuba during the Spanish-American War.
Including Correspondence between Dr. S.
Weir Mitchell and Gen'l Leonard Wood . . .

⟨Harrisburg, Penna., 1909⟩

Printed self-wrapper. P. ⟨1⟩ as above. At head of
title: *Commonwealth of Pennsylvania   Department of
Health*

Letter to Dr. Samuel G. Dixon, July 21, 1909,
pp. ⟨1⟩-3.

H   Y

14262. THE COMFORT OF THE HILLS AND
OTHER POEMS . . .

NEW YORK   THE CENTURY CO. 1910

For prior publication of the title poem see above
under 1909.

⟨i⟩-⟨xii⟩, ⟨1⟩-98, blank leaf. 6$\frac{15}{16}$″ × 4$\frac{13}{16}$″.
Wove paper watermarked THE CENTURY CO
arranged in a circle enclosing an open book.

⟨-⟩^{6}, ⟨1⟩-5^{8}, 6^{10}.

V cloth: green-blue. End papers of book stock;
single flyleaves of book stock. Top edges gilt.

Note: A variant has been seen: Blue FL-like
cloth; the publisher's spine imprint stamped from
a face $\frac{3}{32}$″ tall. On normal copies the spine imprint is stamped from a face a trifle less tall.

NYPL copy received Feb. 21, 1910; BA copy Feb.
23, 1910. Deposited Feb. 24, 1910. On copyright
page: *Published February, 1910* Listed PW March 5,
1910.

B   BA   BPL   LC   NYPL   Y

14263. THE   GUILLOTINE   CLUB   AND
OTHER STORIES . . .

NEW YORK   THE CENTURY CO. 1910

⟨i-viii⟩, ⟨1⟩-285. Frontispiece; and, 13 plates
inserted and reckoned in the printed pagination.
7$\frac{1}{2}$″ × 5$\frac{1}{8}$″.

⟨1-16^{8}, 17^{6}⟩. *Signed:* ⟨1⟩^{12}, 2^{9}, 3^{7}, 4-16^{8}, 17^{2}.

V cloth: green.

Advertised PW Sept. 24, 1910. Listed PW Oct. 8,
1910. BA copy received Oct. 18, 1910; NYPL
copy Oct. 19, 1910. Deposited Oct. 27, 1910. On
copyright page: *Published October, 1910*

BA   H   LC   NYPL   Y

14264. Annual Report of the Library Committee
of the College of Physicians of Philadelphia for
the Year 1910 Reprinted from the Transactions
Third Series, XXXII, 1910

⟨Philadelphia, 1910⟩

Printed paper wrapper. Cover-title.

Signed at p. 10 by Mitchell and others.

NYPL

14265. JOHN SHERWOOD, IRONMASTER
. . .

NEW YORK   THE CENTURY CO. 1911

Two printings noted:

FIRST PRINTING

⟨i-viii⟩, ⟨1⟩-316, 2 blank leaves. 7$\frac{1}{2}$″ full × 5$\frac{1}{8}$″.

⟨1^{4}, 2-11^{16}⟩. *Signed:* ⟨-⟩^{4}, ⟨1⟩-14, ⟨15-20⟩^{8}.

SECOND PRINTING

⟨-⟩^{4}, ⟨1⟩-14, ⟨15-20⟩^{8}.

Binding on first printing: V cloth: green. Stamped
in gold. White end paper at front; at back the
pastedown is ⟨11⟩$_{16}$.

Note: Copies in printed paper wrapper are presumed to be advance copies.

Also note: Second printing sheets have been seen
in tan V cloth, stamped in brown.

Announced for spring publication PW Feb. 18, 1911. Announced for *May* PW March 18, 1911. Noted for *May 20* PW May 13, 1911. Listed PW May 20, 1911. Deposited May 26, 1911. On copyright page: *Published, May, 1911*

BA (2nd) H (1st) NYPL (1st) Y (1st; 2nd in variant cloth binding)

14266. Annual Report of the Library Committee of the College of Physicians of Philadelphia for the Year 1911 Reprinted from the Transactions Third Series, XXXIII, 1911

⟨Philadelphia, 1911⟩

Cover-title.

Signed at p. 11 by Mitchell and others.

Printed paper wrapper.

NYPL

14267. President Taft and the Medical Profession Banquet and Reception to President Taft and Invited Guests Given by the Medical Club of Philadelphia at the Bellevue-Stratford, May 4, 1911 Reprinted, with Additions, from the Journal of the American Medical Association, May 13, 1911, Vol. LVI

... 1911 American Medical Association Five Hundred and Thirty-Five Dearborn Avenue Chicago

Cover-title. Printed paper wrapper.

"The Debt of the Country to Physicians," pp. 10-11.

Y

14268. Commemoration Day 1912

Baltimore The Johns Hopkins Press 1912

Printed paper wrapper. Issued as *The Johns Hopkins University Circular 1912 No. 3.*

"George Washington in Biography, Fiction, the Drama, and Verse," pp. 8-29.

Issued March, 1912.

NYPL Y

14269. A BRIEF HISTORY OF TWO FAMILIES THE MITCHELLS OF AYRSHIRE AND THE SYMONS OF CORNWALL ...

PRIVATELY PRINTED PHILADELPHIA 1912

⟨1⟩-45; blank, p. ⟨46⟩; Dornan imprint, p. ⟨47⟩. 9″ scant × 7⁷⁄₁₆″.

⟨1-6⟩⁴.

Mottled gray paper boards, printed paper label. Mottled gray end papers. Flyleaf at front.

Y

14270. THE MEDICAL TREATMENT OF EPILEPSY READ BEFORE THE COLLEGE OF PHYSICIANS OF PHILADELPHIA FEBRUARY 7, 1912 ... REPRINTED FROM THE THERAPEUTIC GAZETTE MARCH 15, 1912

DETROIT, MICH. E. G. SWIFT, PUBLISHER 1912

Cover-title.

⟨1⟩-12. 7¹¹⁄₁₆″ × 5³⁄₁₆″ scant.

⟨-⟩⁶.

Printed gray-blue paper wrapper.

Appears also in: *Transactions of the College of Physicians of Philadelphia Third Series Volume the Thirty-Fourth*, Philadelphia, 1912. Also contains "remarks," pp. 102-103.

Y

14271. ... SOME RECENTLY DISCOVERED LETTERS OF WILLIAM HARVEY WITH OTHER MISCELLANEA BY S. WEIR MITCHELL ... WITH A BIBLIOGRAPHY OF HARVEY'S WORKS BY CHARLES PERRY FISHER ...

PHILADELPHIA 1912

At head of title: *Transactions of the College of Physicians of Philadelphia*

⟨i-ii⟩, ⟨1⟩-59; blank, p. ⟨60⟩; Dornan imprint, p. ⟨61⟩. 9″ × 7⁷⁄₁₆″. 2 illustrations, each with printed protective tissue, inserted.

⟨1-4⟩⁸.

Printed stiff blue paper wrapper. Printed white paper label on front. Blue paper end papers.

B Y

14272. WESTWAYS A VILLAGE CHRONICLE ...

NEW YORK THE CENTURY CO. 1913

⟨i-viii⟩, ⟨1⟩-510, blank leaf. 7½″ × 5³⁄₁₆″.

⟨1⁴, 2-33⁸⟩.

V cloth: green.

Note: According to contemporary notices (see publication notes below) there were three printings in the year 1913. BAL has been unable to identify these.

Listed PW Sept. 13, 1913. Noted for Sept. 12 PW Sept. 13, 1913. BA copy received Sept. 17, 1913. On copyright page: *Published, September, 1913* "Third large edition now ready" ———PW Nov. 29,

1913. The London (Unwin) edition noted for *next week* Bkr Jan. 9, 1914; listed Bkr Jan. 23, 1914.

B BA BPL H NYPL Y

14273. . . . An Account of the Exercises on the Occasion of the Opening of the New Building of the Henry Phipps Institute . . . Philadelphia May 10, 1913

⟨n.p., n.d., Philadelphia, 1913⟩

Printed paper wrapper. At head of title: *The University of Pennsylvania*

Remarks, pp. 45-46.

NYPL

14274. The Semi-Centennial Anniversary of the National Academy of Sciences 1863–1913

Washington 1913

"Speech," pp. 86-90.

Y

14275. The Complete Poems . . .

New York The Century Co. 1914

Printed paper label on spine.

Reprint with the exception of:

"Barabbas"

"An Old Man to an Old Madeira"

"Verses in Honor of William H. Welch"

"Vesperal," here reprinted. Otherwise "Evening," *The Wager and Other Poems*, 1900.

Also issued as a volume in the *Author's Definitive Edition*. Sequence, if any, not established.

Listed PW Oct. 10, 1914. Deposited Oct. 19, 1914. BA copy received Oct. 20, 1914. On copyright page: *Published, October, 1914.*

AAS BA H LC NYPL Y

14276. THE MEDICAL DEPARTMENT IN THE CIVIL WAR . . .

⟨CHICAGO: AMERICAN MEDICAL ASSOCIATION, 1914⟩

⟨1⟩-19. 8⁷⁄₁₆″ × 5½″. Wove paper watermarked: *Anglo-Saxon/JWP Co*

⟨-⟩¹⁰.

Printed blue-gray paper wrapper.

"Reprinted from the Journal of the American Medical Association May 9, 1914, Vol. LXII, pp. 1445-1450."---From the front wrapper.

UV Y

14277. . . . Biographical Memoir of John Shaw Billings 1838-1913 by S. Weir Mitchell with the Scientific Work of John Shaw Billings by Fielding H. Garrison . . .

City of Washington Published by the National Academy of Sciences August, 1917

Printed paper wrapper. At head of title: *National Academy of Sciences of the United States of America Biographical Memoirs Part of Volume VIII*

"Memoir of John Shaw Billings," pp. 375-383.

H LC NYPL Y

14278. The Autobiography of Ethel Newcome by Mary Cadwalader with Verses by S. Weir Mitchell . . .

⟨n.p., n.d., Philadelphia, 1919⟩

Cover-title. Printed self-wrapper. Unpaged. 7 pp.

"The Two Ethels," p. ⟨3⟩. Dated at end: *Christmas, 1897*

Published for the benefit of the Exhibition of Celebrated Dolls at the Emergency Aid Shop, Philadelphia, March 10, 1919.

Query: Is the above first publication of the poem?

HSP

14279. WEIR MITCHELL HIS LIFE AND LETTERS BY ANNA ROBESON BURR

DUFFIELD & COMPANY NEW YORK CITY 1929

Title-page in black and red.

⟨i⟩-⟨xiv⟩, 1-424, blank leaf. Laid paper watermarked: *Kingsley* Frontispiece and 26 plates inserted. 8¹⁵⁄₁₆″ full × 6¼″ full.

⟨1-27⁸, 28⁴⟩.

Red T cloth sides, black CM cloth shelfback. Black end papers printed in gold with a wavy square and star pattern. Flyleaves of book stock.

Note: Leaf ⟨1⟩₅ (the illustrations leaf) is a cancel in all examined copies.

Published Oct. 9, 1929 (date taken from a review copy). Deposited Oct. 11, 1929.

AAS BA H Y

14280. Future Perfect American Science Fiction of the Nineteenth Century ⟨by⟩ H. Bruce Franklin

New York Oxford University Press 1966

"Was He Dead?," pp. 221-247. Reprinted from *The Atlantic Monthly*, Jan. 1870.

LC

SILAS WEIR MITCHELL

SECTION II

In this section are listed reprints of Mitchell's own books. For a list of books by authors other than Mitchell containing material by him see *Section Three*.

14281. Wear and Tear, or Hints for the Overworked . . . Fourth Edition.

Philadelphia: J.B. Lippincott & Co. 1872.

Cursory examination indicates that this is a reprint of the 1871 edition. Reprinted and reissued under date ⟨1871⟩.

14282. Fat and Blood: And How to Make Them . . . Second Edition, Revised.

Philadelphia: J. B. Lippincott & Co. London: 16 Southampton Street, Covent Garden. 1879.

14283. Hephzibah Guinness; Thee and You; and a Draft on the Bank of Spain . . . Second Edition.

Philadelphia: J. B. Lippincott Company. 1887.

Cursory examination indicates that this is a reprint of the first printing, 1880.

14284. Fat and Blood: An Essay on the Treatment of Certain Forms of Neurasthenia and Hysteria . . . Fifth Edition.

Philadelphia: J. B. Lippincott Company. London: 10 Henrietta Street, Covent Garden. 1888.

Cursory examination indicates that this is a reprint of the *Fourth Edition*, 1885. Deposited Oct. 15, 1891.

14285. Songs by Charles Dennée . . . Goodnight . . .

Arthur P. Schmidt. Boston. Leipzig. New York . . . ⟨1894⟩

Sheet music. Cover-title. Plate mark (high voice): APS 3326-4; (low voice): APS 3327-4. For other settings see below under 1903, 1912; and, next entry. Reprinted from *The Mother and Other Poems*, 1893. For an unpublished setting see in *References and Ana* under the year 1934.

14286. Three Songs with Piano Accompaniment . . . Good Night . . . ⟨Music⟩ by C. B. Hawley . . .

New-York, G. Schirmer . . . 1894 . . .

Sheet music. Cover-title. See preceding entry.

14287. The Collected Poems . . .

New York The Century Co. 1896

Cloth, printed paper label on spine.

Deposited May 4, 1896. Advertised for May 9 and noted as *just ready* PW May 9, 1896. Listed PW May 16, 1896.

14288. Hephzibah Guinness; Thee and You; and a Draft on the Bank of Spain . . .

New York The Century Co. 1899

Cursory examination indicates that this is a reprint of the *Third Edition*, 1897.

Copyright notice (press-printed) dated 1880. Also present on the copyright page of the only located copy (Y) is a rubber-stamped notice: *Copyright Renewed 1908 By S. Weir Mitchell*. Presumably not all copies carry the rubber-stamped notice.

14289. Hugh Wynne Free Quaker . . . Continental Edition Illustrated

Published by the Century Co. New York: M·DCCC·XC·IX

2 Vols. Cursory examination indicates that this is a reprint. Deposited Oct. 4, 1899.

14290. Wear and Tear or Hints for the Overworked . . . Ninth Edition Thoroughly Revised

Philadelphia J. B. Lippincott Company London: 36 Southampton Street, Covent Garden 1899

Cursory examination indicates that this is a reprint of the 1887 edition save for a minor alteration in the preface: ". . . It is now but twenty-five years since this little book was written . . ."; in the 1887 edition the reading is *fifteen years*.

Deposited June 7, 1899. For first edition see under year 1871.

14291. Fat and Blood: An Essay on the Treatment of Certain Forms of Neurasthenia and Hysteria . . . Eighth Edition. Edited, with Additions, by John K. Mitchell, M.D.

Philadelphia: J. B. Lippincott Company. London: 36 Southampton Street, Covent Garden. 1902.

14292. Author's Edition . . .

New York The Century Co. 1903

Save for the statement *Author's Edition* at the head of each title-page, and on the spine label, there is no indication that these volumes were issued as a set.

Noted in green T cloth only, goldstamped leather label on spine. Possibly issued in a variety of custom bindings.

BAL has not collated the texts of these volumes *vs* the first printings and assumes that each volume is a reprint. The order of presentation is alphabetical by title:

The Adventures of François

The Autobiography of a Quack and Other Stories

Characteristics

Circumstance

Dr. North and His Friends

Far in the Forest

Hugh Wynne Free Quaker

In War Time

Roland Blake

When All the Woods are Green

14293. Good-Night . . . Music by Aline Fredin . . .

New York G. Schirmer . . . 1903 . . .

Sheet music. Cover-title. For earlier setting see above under 1894.

14294. Fat and Blood: An Essay on the Treatment of Certain Forms of Neurasthenia and Hysteria . . . Eighth Edition. Edited, with Additions, by John K. Mitchell, M.D.

Philadelphia: J. B. Lippincott Company. London: 5 Henrietta Street, Covent Garden 1911.

Cursory examination indicates that this is a reprint of the 1902 printing.

14295. Love's Good Night . . . Music by James Francis Cooke . . .

Philadelphia Theo. Presser Co. 1712 Chestnut St. ⟨1912⟩

Sheet music. Cover-title. For earlier settings see above under *Goodnight* ⟨1894⟩.

14296. ⟨Extract from *The Comfort of the Hills*. Six verses in twelve lines. Text:⟩ "*The years that come as friend | and leave as foe . . .*

⟨n.p., Copyright 1917 Martha Louise Andrews⟩

Single cut sheet. Folded to make four pages. Page: $5\frac{9}{16}''$ × $3\frac{7}{8}''$. Text, with hand-colored illustration, on p. ⟨1⟩; imprint on p. ⟨4⟩. Otherwise blank. Pale buff paper watermarked *Cranes;* in unprinted envelope of the same stock. Issued as a greeting card.

14297. A Madeira Party . . . Printed by Permission of the Century Company

New York Privately Printed Christmas, 1922

Brown paper boards, white paper vellum shelfback, printed paper label on spine.

250 copies printed for Thomas Nast Fairbanks at the Marchbanks Press, 1922.

Reprinted from *A Madeira Party*, 1895.

14298. The Memory of Franklin . . . a Poem Read at the Franklin Dinner, Philadelphia, 1906

⟨New York, 1923⟩

Single leaf. Issued with *The American Printer, Franklin Bi-Centennial Number*, Jan. 20, 1923.

For prior publication see above in *Section One* under year 1906.

SILAS WEIR MITCHELL

SECTION III

In this section are listed books by authors other than Mitchell containing material by him reprinted from earlier books. See *Section Two* for a list of reprints issued under Mitchell's name.

An Old Scrap-Book. With Additions . . .

⟨Cambridge⟩ February 8, 1884.

For comment see entry No. 7763.

Medical Rhymes . . . Selected and Compiled from a Variety of Sources, by Hugo Erichsen . . .

J. H. Chambers & Co., St. Louis, Mo., Chicago, Ill. Atlanta, Ga. 1884.

July Edited by Oscar Fay Adams . . .

Boston . . . ⟨1886⟩

For comment see entry No. 65.

Smithsonian Contributions to Knowledge. Vol. XXVI . . .

City of Washington: Published by the Smithsonian Institution. 1890

Songs of Three Centuries Edited by John Greenleaf Whittier . . .

Boston . . . 1890

For fuller entry see No. 11384.

Memoirs of the National Academy of Sciences. Volume VI.

Washington: Government Printing Office. 1893.

Printed paper wrapper.

Quaker Poems A Collection of Verse Relating to the Society of Friends. Compiled by Charles Francis Jenkins.

Philadelphia: John C. Winston & Co. 1893.

. . . Biographical Memoirs. Vol. III.

Published by the Academy. Washington City. 1895.

At head of title: *National Academy of Sciences.*

Printed paper wrapper.

The Doctor's Window . . . Edited by Ina Russelle Warren . . .

Buffalo . . . Eighteen-Hundred-Ninety-Eight

For comment see BAL, Vol. 2, p. 275.

Anthology of Living American Poets, 1898. Arranged by Deborah Ege Olds.

Cincinnati. The Editor Publishing Company. 1898.

The International Library of Famous Literature . . . Introductions by Donald G. Mitchell . . . and Andrew Lang . . .

New York . . . ⟨1898⟩

For fuller entry see BAL, Vol. 5, p. 204.

Hero Tales of the American Soldier and Sailor . . .

⟨n.p., 1899⟩

For fuller description see in *Thomas Nelson Page* list.

The International Library of Famous Literature . . . Edited by Dr. Richard Garnett . . . in Twenty Volumes . . .

London . . . 1899

For comment see entry No. 10638.

The Memory of Lincoln Poems Selected with an Introduction by M. A. DeWolfe Howe

Boston Small Maynard & Company 1899

An American Anthology . . . Edited by Edmund Clarence Stedman . . .

Boston . . . M DCCCC

For comment see entry No. 3082.

Smithsonian Contributions to Knowledge Vol. XXIX . . .

City of Washington Published by the Smithsonian Institution 1903

Recital of Compositions by Alexander MacFayden . . . at Madam Louise Finkel's Vocal

Studio 1748 Broadway, New York Wednesday Afternoon, March the Fourth . . .

⟨n.p., n.d., after 1903⟩

Program 4 pp.

American Familiar Verse . . . by Brander Mathews . . .

. . . New York . . . 1904

For fuller entry see in James Russell Lowell list, *Section Three.*

Complete Works of Abraham Lincoln Edited by John G. Nicolay and John Hay . . . New and Enlarged Edition . . .

New York Francis D. Tandy Company ⟨1905⟩

12 vols. Presumably issued in a variety of bindings and formats.

Listed PW Nov. 11, 1905.

The Proceedings of the Charaka Club Volume II . . .

New York   William Wood and Company MDCCCCVI

Paper boards, vellum shelf back, printed paper label on front. 315 numbered copies only.

The Home Medical Library Volume VI . . .

New York The Review of Reviews Company 1907

Listed PW June 1, 1907.

Through Italy with the Poets   Compiled by Robert Haven Schauffler . . .

New York . . . 1908

For comment see BAL, Vol. 4, p. 446.

The Proceedings of the Charaka Club Volume III . . .

New York   William Wood and Company MDCCCCX

Paper boards, cloth shelf back, printed paper label on front. 370 numbered copies only.

A Merry Christmas and a Happy New Year to the Sons of the University of Pennsylvania

⟨n.p., 1911⟩

A calendar consisting of a series of seven leaves tied together with red and black cord. Cover-title.

On the card for February is an extract from "The Birthday of Washington," *The Comfort of the Hills* . . . , 1910.

The Poetical Works of William Henry Drummond with an Introduction by Louis Fréchette and an Appreciation by Neil Munro

G. P. Putnam's Sons New York and London The Knickerbocker Press 1912

Listed Bkr Oct. 11, 1912. Noted as *about to publish* Bkr Oct. 18, 1912.

300 Latest Stories by 300 Famous Story Tellers as Told by. . .O. Henry Jack London . . . ⟨and Others⟩

. . . New York ⟨1914⟩

For fuller entry see entry No. 12001.

Modern Short Stories . . . by Frederick Houk Law . . .

New York . . . 1918

For comment see BAL, Vol. 2, p. 427.

The Joy of Life An Anthology . . . by E. V. Lucas . . .

. . . London ⟨1927⟩

For comment see BAL, Vol. 5, p. 258.

Old Madeiras ⟨Edited by⟩ F. Gray Griswold

Duttons, Inc. New York 1929

Printed paper boards, vellum shelf back and corners. 200 copies only.

Deposited Dec. 28, 1929.

REFERENCES AND ANA

The Intestinal Gases. Thesis.

Jefferson Medical College. 1850.

Entry from Burr, p. 397. Presumably unpublished. Prepared by Mitchell as his thesis for his medical degree.

Muscular Phenomena following Blow from Percussion Hammer.

1858.

Entry from Burr, p. 397. No separate publication found. Perhaps a reference to *The Proceedings of the Academy of Natural Sciences*, March, 1858.

⟨Printed letter urging defeat of House of Representatives "A Bill to Amend the Act Respecting Copyrights."⟩

New York . . . 1862.

For fuller description see BAL, Vol. 4, p. 33.

A List of the Original Memoirs of S. Weir Mitchell
. . .

Philadelphia: J. B. Lippincott & Co. 1868.

A list of Mitchell's contributions to learned publications. It is to be observed that BAL has not found offprints of all the papers listed; it is possible that offprints, although unlocated, were done.

For fuller entry see above in *Section One.*

Anonymous. Presumably compiled by Mitchell.

Thee and You.

Philadelphia: J. B. Lippincott & Co., 1876.

Entry from Burr, p. 403. Not located as a separate. Burr's reference is probably to the periodical appearance (*Lippincott's Magazine*, under the pseudonym Edward Kearsley, June-July, 1876). Collected in *Hephzibah Guinness . . .*, 1880.

Also listed (copied from Burr?) by Walter, p. 221, as entry No. 291.

Letter of Bequest: Giving copies of portraits of Harvey and Junter.

College of Physicians, January, 1878.

Thus Burr, p. 403.

The Library of the College of Physicians, Philadelphia, reports that this is a manuscript, not a printed text.

On the Limitations of the So-called "Weir Mitchell Treatment." By W. S. Playfair . . . Reprinted from the "Lancet," January 7, 1888.

⟨London: Ballantyne Press, n.d., 1887⟩

Cover-title. Printed self-wrapper.

Haroun, the Caliph. By Ferid el din Attar.

New York: Century Co., 1891.

Listed in Burr, p. 407.

Mitchell "quotes appreciatively from his own verse and illustrates remarks with quotations from El Din Attar, a reputed contemporary of Omar's. This is of course Mitchell himself, but it caused people to try to buy the works of the mysterious poet. The book department of Wanamaker's, unable to find him listed, asked Mitchell where to obtain the work of El Din Attar."---Earnest, p. 132.

A Catalogue of the Scientific and Literary Work of S. Weir Mitchell . . .

⟨n.p., n.d., Philadelphia, 1894⟩

Caption-title. For fuller description see above in *Section One.*

⟨Menu⟩ December 27th, 1894. Maryland Club . . .

⟨Baltimore: Guggenheimer-Weil, Prs., 1894⟩

Heavy card, folded to make four pages. Edges bevelled and gilded. P. ⟨1⟩ as above.

On p. ⟨1⟩: 15 lines of text: "In that land the wise men, known as Siphograuntes, meet in 'sweet societies', and earnestly bestowe their vacaunte and spare hours in seeking a knoweledg . . . ⟨to⟩ . . . For herein they suppose the felicitie of liffe to consiste." At end of text: *The Yle Utopia Revisited, by Weir Mitchell, 1895.*

Each entry in the menu is accompanied by an extract credited to an author, each extract being dated; the latest being credited to Chas. Sedgwick Minot's *Autobiography*, Boston, 1920. Minot died in 1914 and so far as BAL can determine left no autobiography. The extracts are clearly meant to be humorous and presumably were not contributed by the authors to whom they are assigned.

The Influence of the Poet's Time on the Poet. A Lecture Delivered before the Graduate Club of the University of Pennsylvania, December 3, 1898 . . .

⟨n.p., 1898?⟩

Caption-title. The above at head of p. 85. Paged: 85-108. Laid paper. Leaf: $8^{11}/_{16}'' \times 5^5/_8''$.

Almost certainly not issued thus. Obviously leaves extracted from a larger work, as yet unidentified. At end of text, p. 108, is a brief piece (complete?) titled "Grant's 'Difference' Engine," presumably not by Mitchell. Location: Y.

Sins of the Father

⟨Philadelphia⟩ Lippincott and Co., 1902.

Burr, p. 410, as though a separate publication. In fact, a short story published in *Lippincott's Magazine*, March, 1902.

S. Weir Mitchell . . . by Guy Hinsdale . . . Reprinted from International Clinics, Vol. I., Twelfth Series.

Copyright, 1902, by J. B. Lippincott Company, Philadelphia, Pa.

Cover-title. Printed paper wrapper.

To Doctor Osler in Regard to His Book on "Science and Immortality."

1904.

At one time catalogued in National Union Catalog as though a printed production; in fact, a typescript in the College of Physicians of Philadelphia.

Pretty Poll by S. Weir Mitchell January Sixth 1908

⟨n.p., probably Philadelphia: George W. Jacobs & Co., 1908⟩

A four-page program. Possibly a hoax.

Motor Ataxia from Emotion.

1909.

Entry from Burr, p. 412. Not located. Issued as a separate? Noted only in *The Journal of Nervous and Mental Disease*, Vol. 36, No. 5, May, 1909, pp. 257–260.

The Hospitals at Gettysburg. Letter.

Philadelphia, 1912.

Entry from Burr, p. 412. Not a printed production but a typescript owned by The College of Physicians of Philadelphia. Probably prepared for *The Transactions of the College of Physicians of Philadelphia*, Series 3, Vol. 35, 1913.

Vote of Thanks from the College of Physicians of Philadelphia.

Philadelphia, 1912

At one time catalogued in National Union Catalog as though a printed publication; in fact, a typescript in the College of Physicians of Philadelphia.

Lists of Medical Cadets during War of Rebellion.

Philadelphia, 1913.

Entry from Burr, p. 412. No located. Presumably unpublished.

The "Annual Report of the Library Committee for 1914," in the *Transactions of the College of Physicians of Philadelphia*, Series 3, Vol. 36, 1914, p. 367, lists the following among works of special interest received during the year:

Mitchell, S. Weir. *List of Medical Cadets in Service during the War of the Rebellion*, Philadelphia, 1913. Typewritten. Presented by Dr. S. Weir Mitchell.

Lists of Medical Cadets Who Obtained Rank of Assistant-Surgeon.

Philadelphia, 1913.

Entry from Burr, p. 413. Not located. Presumably unpublished.

Note: In addition to assigning the date 1913 to this piece, Burr also adds the date, 1907.

A Brief Address in Memory of Weir Mitchell by James Cornelius Wilson . . . Read at a Meeting of the Medical Club of Philadelphia, June 26, 1914.

⟨n.p., n.d., 1914⟩

Printed paper wrapper.

S. Weir Mitchell . . . Memoir Read at the Quarterly Meeting of the St. Andrew's Society of Philadelphia, February 28, 1914, by John Gordon Gray . . .

⟨Philadelphia, n.d., 1914⟩

Printed paper wrapper.

In Memory of Silas Weir Mitchell . . . by James J. Putnam . . . Reprinted from the Boston Medical and Surgical Journal . . . May 28, 1914

Boston W. M. Leonard 101 Tremont Street 1914

Cover-title. Printed paper wrapper.

S. Weir Mitchell A Brief Sketch of His Life with Personal Recollections by Beverley R. Tucker

Boston: Richard G. Badger The Copp Clark Co., Limited, Toronto ⟨1914⟩

Paper boards sides, cloth shelf back, printed paper labels.

Silas Weir Mitchell . . . His Place in Neurology by Charles K. Mills . . . Reprinted from the Journal of Nervous and Mental Disease, Vol. 41, No. 2, 1914.

⟨n.p., Chicago, 1914⟩

Cover-title. Printed paper wrapper.

S. Weir Mitchell . . . 1829–1914 Memorial Addresses and Resolutions

Philadelphia 1914

Silas Weir Mitchell A Personal Impression by Edward Jackson . . . Read before the Medical Society of the City and County of Denver, Feb. 3rd, 1914 Reprinted from Colorado Medicine November, 1914

⟨n.p., n.d., 1914⟩

Cover-title. Printed self-wrapper.

The S. Weir Mitchell Oration S. Weir Mitchell Physician Man of Science Man of Letters Man of Affairs by Charles W. Burr . . .

⟨Philadelphia⟩ Published by the College 1920

Hugh Wynne Free Quaker . . . with Introduction and Notes by Vincent B. Brecht . . .

The Century Co. New York ⟨1922⟩

The Weir Mitchell Rest Cure Forty Years Ago and Today* ⟨by⟩ T. H. Weisenburg . . .

⟨Chicago: American Medical Association, 1925⟩

Printed self-wrapper.

Caption-title. The above at head of p. ⟨1⟩. The asterisk refers to a footnote, p. ⟨1⟩: *Read at the Fortieth Anniversary Meeting of the Philadelphia Neurological Society, Nov. 29, 1924.*

At foot of p. 6: *Reprinted from the Archives of Neurology and Psychiatry September, 1925, Vol. 14, pp. 384-389 . . . American Medical Association . . . Chicago*

. . . Silas Weir Mitchell . . . Personal Recollections by W. W. Keen . . .

⟨n.p., 1925⟩

Caption-title. The above at head of p. ⟨644⟩. At head of title: *Reprinted from the Proceedings of the American Academy of Arts and Sciences, Vol. 59, No. 17. January, 1925.*

Pp. ⟨643⟩-649. Printed self-wrapper.

Weir Mitchell His Life and Letters by Anna Robeson Burr

Duffield & Company New York City 1929

Referred to in these lists as *Burr*. Contains a bibliography. For fuller description see entry No. 14279.

Reminiscences of Dr. S. Weir Mitchell ⟨by⟩ Irving Wilson Voorhees

⟨Offprinted from⟩ Bulletin of the New York Academy of Medicine January, 1931, Second Series, Vol. VII, No. 1. pp. 40-48

Cover-title. Printed self-wrapper. Paged ⟨39⟩-48, blank leaf.

Silas Weir Mitchell the Versatile Physician . . . a Sketch of His Life and His Literary Contributions by Nolie Mumey . . .

The Range Press Denver 1934

Paper boards, cloth shelf back. Facsimile letter in envelope inserted.

100 numbered copies signed by Mumey. All issued?

Good Night. By S. Weir Mitchell. Music by N. L. Miller.

Sheet music. Deposited March 9, 1934. Manuscript. Here for the record only. For published settings see in *Section Two* under the years 1894 (two settings), 1903, 1912.

Catalogue ⟨of⟩ the S. Weir Mitchell Collection of Books, Autographs, Prints, and Historical Relics . . . to be Sold at Unrestricted Public Auction . . . May 19th, 1941 . . .

Wm. D. Morley, Inc. Auctioneers-Appraisers . . . Philadelphia . . . ⟨1941⟩

Printed paper wrapper.

Reflex Paralysis Circular No. 6 Surgeon General's Office March 10, 1864 by S. Weir Mitchell Geo. R. Morehouse W. W. Keen, Jr. A Reprint: With Introduction ⟨by John F. Fulton⟩

Historical Library Yale University School of Medicine 1941

Printed paper wrapper. For first printing see in *Section One* under the year 1864.

S. Weir Mitchell Novelist and Physician by Ernest Earnest

Philadelphia University of Pennsylvania Press 1950

S. Weir Mitchell As a Psychiatric Novelist by David M. Rein Preface by C. P. Oberndorf

International Universities Press, Inc. New York New York ⟨1952⟩

. . . Biographical Memoirs Volume XXXII

Published in 1958 for the National Academy of Sciences of the United States of America by Columbia University Press, New York

At head of title: *National Academy of Sciences of the United States of America*

"Silas Weir Mitchell . . . ," by Percival Bailey, pp. ⟨334⟩-353. Contains Mitchell's "Scientific Bibliography," pp. 341–353.

. . . Injuries of Nerves and Their Consequences by S. Weir Mitchell . . . with a New Introduction by Lawrence C. McHenry, Jr.

Dover Publications, Inc., New York ⟨1965⟩

At head of title: *American Academy of Neurology Reprint Series*

Printed paper wrapper.

". . . An unabridged and unaltered republication of the work first published . . . in 1872, to which have been added a new Preface by the Publications Advisory Committee of the American Academy of Neurology and a new

Introduction by Lawrence C. McHenry, Jr. . . . published as Volume II in the American Academy of Neurology Reprint Series."---P. ⟨iv⟩.

S. Weir Mitchell, M.D.---Neurologist   A Medical Biography by Richard D. Walter . . .

Charles C Thomas Publisher   Springfield Illinois U.S.A. ⟨1970⟩

"Bibliography" of Mitchell, pp. 207–225.

NOTE

The following titles are unknown to BAL and inquiry has failed to produce any information.

All are from *S. Weir Mitchell . . . a Medical Biography*, by Richard D. Walter, M.D., Springfield, Illinois ⟨1970⟩. The numbers are those in Dr. Walter's bibliography.

No. 270. Address to the Students of the University of Pennsylvania on the Occasion of Their Receiving the Degree of A.B. Philadelphia, 1907.

No. 292. In Memorium ⟨*sic*⟩: Major General George Cadwalader. (Late President of the Mutual Assurance Co. for Insuring Houses from Loss by Fire. Died Feb. 3, 1879), 1879.

No. 298. *Little Stories*. New York, The Century Co., 1891. *See entry No. 14217.*

WILLIAM VAUGHN STOY MOODY

1 8 6 9 – 1 9 1 0

14299. Cap and Gown Some College Verse Chosen by Joseph La Roy Harrison

Boston Joseph Knight Company 1893

"The Serf's Secret," p. 32. Otherwise unlocated.

H copy received May 22, 1893. Listed PW June 10, 1893.

H NYPL

14300. Harvard College Class of 1893 Baccalaureate Sermon . . . Hymn, Class Day Oration . . . Poem, Ivy Oration, Ode

Cambridge, Mass. Printed by Edward W. Wheeler 1894

Printed paper wrapper.

"Class Poem," pp. ⟨26⟩-30. Uncollected. Under the title "The Song of the Elder Brothers" portions were reprinted in *Some Letters* . . . , 1913.

B H

14301. . . . The Pilgrim's Progress from this World to that Which is to Come . . . by John Bunyan . . . Edited, with Introduction and Notes by William Vaughn Moody

Houghton, Mifflin and Company Boston: 4 Park Street; New York: 11 East Seventeenth Street Chicago: 158 Adams Street The Riverside Press, Cambridge ⟨1896; *i.e.*, 1897⟩

At head of title: *The Riverside Literature Series*

"Introduction," pp. ⟨iii⟩-xiv.

Printed cloth; also, according to contemporary notices, printed paper wrapper. Issued as No. 109 of the series.

Deposited April 3, 1897. Listed, as in *The Riverside Literature Series*, PW April 3, 1897. Published March 20, 1897 (publisher's records).

NOTE

The publication record of this production is both contradictory and confusing. According to the publisher's records the book was published March 20, 1897; the book was issued with an 1896 copyright notice. The following notes are from the publisher's records: *March 18, 1897:* Text for the *Riverside Literature Series* cover composed and electrotyped; cloth; wrapper? both? *March 22, 1897:* 1000 copies printed, *Riverside Literature Series*, presumably for the cloth format. *March 24, 1897:* On this date entry made for composition and electrotyping of the book, *Riverside Literature Series. March 26, 1897:* 1500 copies printed, presumably for the wrappered format. *March 27, 1897:* Title-page for the *Riverside School Library* issue composed and electrotyped. *April 5, 1897:* 500 copies printed of the *Riverside School Library* issue; published in cloth, leather shelf back.

On the basis of the preceding, and examination of five copies of the book, the following statement appears correct:

Features, First Printing (Printings?)

At head of title: *The Riverside Literature Series*

Terminal end paper (cloth binding): The last *numbered* entry is Bunyan's *Pilgrim's Progress*, followed by a single unnumbered entry: De Quincey's *Flight of a Tartar Tribe.*

Imprint: In the imprint the Chicago street address is given as *158 Adams Street.* New York street address: *11 East Seventeenth Street.*

Cloth binding: Two horizontal rules not present.

Features, Later Printings

One or more of the following features present in known reprints:

At head of title: *The Riverside School Library*

Terminal end paper (cloth binding): The list of *The Riverside Literature Series* is extended to 155 numbers, followed by *Extra Numbers*, A to U.

Final page of terminal advertisements dated *August 15, 1900.*

Imprint: In the imprint the Chicago street address is given as: *378-388 Wabash Avenue.* New York street address: *85 Fifth Avenue.*

Cloth binding: Two horizontal rules are present.

H (1st, cloth; reprints) LC (1st, cloth, being a deposit copy)

14302. . . . The Rime of the Ancient Mariner ⟨by⟩ Samuel Taylor Coleridge and the Vision of Sir Launfal ⟨by⟩ James Russell Lowell Edited for School Use by William Vaughn Moody . . .

Chicago Scott, Foresman & Co. 1898

At head of title: *The Lake English Classics*

"Life of Coleridge," pp. 5-18.

"Critical Comment ⟨*The Ancient Mariner*⟩," pp. 19-24.

"Notes ⟨*The Ancient Mariner*⟩," pp. 61-64.

"Introduction ⟨*The Vision of Sir Launfal*⟩," pp. 67–80.

"Notes ⟨*The Vision of Sir Launfal*⟩," pp. 99-103.

Deposited Aug. 25, 1898.

LC

14303. . . . The Lay of the Last Minstrel by Sir Walter Scott with an Introduction by William Vaughn Moody . . .

Chicago Scott, Foresman and Company 1899

At head of title: *The Lake English Classics*

"Life of Scott," pp. 9-38.

"Scott's Place in the Romantic Movement," pp. 39-45.

Two printings noted:

FIRST PRINTING

P. ⟨3⟩: *Lake English Classics. For College Entrance, 1899* . . .

Printer's imprint not present on the copyright page.

SECOND PRINTING

P. ⟨3⟩: *Lake English Classics under the Editorial Supervision of Lindsay Todd Damon* . . .

On copyright page: Imprint of *The Henry O. Shepard Co.*

Deposited April 14, 1899.

H (1st)   LC (1st)   NYPL (2nd)

14304. The Complete Poetical Works of John Milton Cambridge Edition . . .

Boston and New York Houghton, Miffin and Company The Riverside Press, Cambridge ⟨1899⟩

Cloth; half calf; tree calf; levant.

"Editor's Note," pp. ⟨v⟩-vi.

"The Life of Milton," pp. ⟨ix⟩-xxxiv.

According to the publisher's records 2001 copies were printed April 11, 1899; bound during the

period April 11, 1899-May 7, 1900. Listed PW April 22, 1899. *Second printing:* Jan. 18, 1900; for the second printing there are recorded charges of one and a half hours for corrections, and a seven hour charge for alteration of plates; BAL has been unable to identify two printings. Reissued not before 1908 with the *Houghton Mifflin Company* imprint.

UV

14305. . . . The Lady of the Lake by Sir Walter Scott Edited for School Use by William Vaughn Moody . . .

Chicago Scott, Foresman and Company 1899

At head of title: *The Lake English Classics*

Introduction, pp. 9-58.

Deposited Sept. 7, 1899(?).

H   LC

14306. . . . Marmion by Sir Walter Scott with an Introduction by William Vaughn Moody . . .

Chicago Scott, Foresman and Company 1899

At head of title: *The Lake English Classics*

Introduction, pp. 9-57.

Deposited Sept. 25, 1899.

H

14307. . . . The Iliad of Homer Books I., VI., XXII., XXIV. Translated by Alexander Pope Edited for School Use by Wilfred Wesley Cressy . . . and William Vaughn Moody . . .

Chicago Scott, Foresman and Company ⟨1899⟩

Query: Should the date *1899* be present in the imprint?

At head of title: *The Lake English Classics*

". . . The text and synopses were prepared by Mr. Cressy, and the editorial work of the volume was outlined, and in part executed by him. Illness having prevented him from giving final form to the work, it was taken up by Mr. Moody . . ."---P. 8

Listed PW Feb. 24, 1900.

UV

14308. THE MASQUE OF JUDGMENT A MASQUE-DRAMA IN FIVE ACTS AND A PRELUDE . . .

BOSTON SMALL, MAYNARD & COMPANY M C M

⟨i-vi⟩, ⟨1⟩-127, blank leaf. $7\frac{1}{4}'' \times 4^{11}\!/_{16}''$ full; but see below.

⟨1-8⁸, 9⁴⟩.

T cloth: blue. White laid end papers. Edges stained blue. Stamped in gold and black.

Also issued in a so-called large-paper format. Leaf: $7^{13}\!/_{16}'' \times 5^{3}\!/_{16}''$. Bound in tan paper boards, printed paper label on spine. White laid paper end papers. Double flyleaves of laid paper. On copyright page: *One Hundred and Fifty copies of the first edition bound entirely uncut, with paper labels.*

Also occurs in a remainder binding: T cloth: gray; tan. Edges plain. Stamped in silver and black. The Houghton Mifflin reissue of 1902 also thus.

Note: Unsold sheets were issued with the cancel title-page of *Houghton, Mifflin and Company, 1902.* See below under year 1902, in *Section Two* of this list.

Reprinted and reissued by Houghton Mifflin Company not before 1908 under date ⟨1900⟩.

Deposited Nov. 13, 1900. BPL copy received Nov. 15, 1900; H copy received Dec. 11, 1900. Listed PW Dec. 15, 1900.

AAS (trade)   B (trade; variant; untrimmed)   BA (trade)   BPL (trade)   H (trade; untrimmed; 1902)   LC (trade)   Y (trade; variant; untrimmed)

14309. Liberty Poems Inspired by the Crisis of 1898-1900 . . .

Boston   The James H. West Co.   1900

Printed paper wrapper; and, cloth.

Extract from "An Ode in Time of Hesitation," pp. 104–106. Collected in *Poems,* 1901.

Listed PW Dec. 22, 1900.

H

14310. POEMS . . .

BOSTON AND NEW YORK   HOUGHTON, MIFFLIN AND COMPANY   THE RIVERSIDE PRESS, CAMBRIDGE 1901

⟨i⟩-⟨viii⟩, ⟨1⟩-106; blank, p. ⟨107⟩; printer's imprint, p. ⟨108⟩. Laid paper. $7^{7}\!/_{16}'' \times 5''$; but see below.

Three printings issued under date 1901:

FIRST PRINTING

(Also Second?)

⟨1⁴, 2-10⁶⟩. The surviving copyright deposit copy thus; also untrimmed copies.

THIRD PRINTING

(Also Second?)

⟨1-9⁶, 10⁴.⟩

T cloth: green. White laid end papers. Laid paper flyleaf at front. Top edges gilt.

Also issued in a so-called large paper format. Leaf: $7^{5}\!/_{8}'' \times 5^{1}\!/_{8}''$. Bound in tan paper boards, printed paper label on spine. White laid paper end papers. Laid paper flyleaf at front. Pasted to the front pastedown is a paper label printed in green: *This Is One Of A Special Issue Of One Hundred And Fifty Copies Bound In Boards Uncut*

The publisher's records show that 778 copies were printed April 22, 1901; bound during the period April 24-July 12, 1901. On April 24 eight copies were bound in paper. On April 25 and 29, 150 copies were bound untrimmed. *Second printing:* 264 copies printed Aug. 15, 1901; bound Aug. 17, 1901. *Third printing:* 274 copies printed Sept. 26, 1901. *Fourth printing:* 492 copies printed Dec. 17, 1901; imprint date altered to 1902. Reissued as *Gloucester Moors* . . . ⟨1901; *i.e.,* 1908⟩. See below in *Section Two* of this list.

Advertised PW March 16, 1901. Deposited April 29, 1901. A copy of the trade printing (in H) inscribed by the author May 3, 1901. A copy of the untrimmed format received at H May 7, 1901. Listed PW May 11, 1901. Noted as *on our table* Ath Aug. 23, 1902.

AAS (3rd)   B (1st; untrimmed)   BPL (1st)   H (1st; untrimmed)   LC (1st)   UV (untrimmed)   Y (1st; untrimmed; third)

14311. A HISTORY OF ENGLISH LITERA-TURE BY WILLIAM VAUGHN MOODY . . . . . . AND ROBERT MORSS LOVETT . . .

NEW YORK   CHARLES SCRIBNER'S SONS 1902

Two printings noted:

FIRST PRINTING

⟨iii⟩-⟨x⟩, 1-433; blank, pp. ⟨434-436⟩. $7^{13}\!/_{16}'' \times 5^{3}\!/_{16}''$.

⟨1⁴, 2-28⁸, 29²⟩.

SECOND PRINTING

⟨iii⟩-⟨x⟩, 1-433; blank, pp. ⟨434-436⟩; 2 leaves excised.

⟨1-28⁸⟩. ⟨28⟩₇₋₈ excised.

T cloth: green. Double flyleaf at front.

See *A First View of English Literature,* 1905; *A First View of English and American Literature,* 1909.

Presumably all the posthumous editions were revised by either Robert Morss Lovett or Fred B. Millett.

Noted as *soon* PW March 1, 1902. Listed PW May 10, 1902.

AAS (2nd)   B (2nd)   BA (1st)   H (2nd)   UV (2nd)

14312. THE FIRE-BRINGER . . .

BOSTON AND NEW YORK   HOUGHTON, MIFFLIN AND COMPANY   THE RIVERSIDE PRESS, CAMBRIDGE 1904

⟨i-x⟩, ⟨1⟩-107; printer's imprint, p. ⟨108⟩; blank leaf. Laid paper. $7\frac{7}{16}'' \times 5''$; but see below.

⟨1-10⁶⟩.

Buckram: green, both olive-green and grass-green noted. White laid end papers. Laid paper flyleaf at front. Top edges gilt.

Also issued in a so-called large paper format. Leaf: $7\frac{5}{8}'' \times 5\frac{1}{16}''$. Bound in tan paper boards, printed paper label on spine. White laid end papers. Laid paper flyleaf at front. On copyright page: *One Hundred And Fifty Copies Of The First Edition Bound Entirely Uncut, With Paper Label*

Publisher's records: 1010 copies printed March 21, 1904. Bound during the period March 22, 1904–March 1, 1905. Ten copies bound in paper March 22, 1904. 175 labels printed March 25, 1904. 152 untrimmed copies bound March 26, 1904. The second printing was done on Feb. 5, 1906; 276 copies.

Advertised PW March 19, 1904. Deposited March 26, 1904. A copy in H inscribed by Moody March 28, 1904. Noted for *to-day* PW April 2, 1904. Listed PW April 9, 1904. On copyright page: *Published April, 1904*

The London (Gay &) Bird edition listed Ath May 14, 1905. Reprinted not before 1908 and issued with the Houghton Mifflin Company imprint, dated ⟨1904⟩.

AAS (trade)   B (trade; untrimmed)   BA (trade)   H (trade; untrimmed)   NYPL (trade)   UV (trade; untrimmed)   Y (trade; untrimmed)

14313. A First View of English Literature by William Vaughn Moody and Robert Morss Lovett . . .

New York   Charles Scribner's Sons   1905

"This volume is based upon the author's more advanced *History of English Literature* ⟨1902⟩ . . ." ———P. v. See *A History of English Literature*, 1902; and, *A First View of English and American Literature*, 1909.

Issued as a school text; there were various later printings and revisions. A reprint issued under date ⟨1905⟩ was published *ca.* 1910.

Deposited May 26, 1905. Listed PW June 10, 1905.

AAS   B   H   LC   Y

14314. The Poems of Trumbull Stickney

Boston and New York   Houghton, Mifflin & Co. MDCCCCV

Edited by Moody, George Cabot Lodge, John Ellerton Lodge.

On copyright page: *Published November 1905*

Deposited Nov. 9, 1905.

B   H   LC   Y

14315. . . . Verses from the Harvard Advocate Third Series 1886–1906 . . .

Cambridge   The Harvard Advocate   1906 . . .

At head of title: *Dulce est periculum*

"Song," p. 99; *I saw a knight fare gaily in the sun* . . .

Listed PW Oct. 27, 1906.

H   NYPL

14316. THE FAITH HEALER   A PLAY IN FOUR ACTS . . .

BOSTON AND NEW YORK   HOUGHTON MIFFLIN COMPANY THE RIVERSIDE PRESS CAMBRIDGE 1909

⟨i-viii⟩, ⟨1⟩-160; blank, p. ⟨161⟩; printer's imprint, p. ⟨162⟩; blank leaf. $7\frac{3}{4}''$ full $\times 5\frac{3}{16}''$ scant.

⟨1-2⁴, 3-15⁶⟩.

T cloth: brown. White laid end papers. Flyleaf at front.

According to the publisher's records 2019 copies were printed Dec. 29, 1908. On Dec. 22 ⟨sic⟩, 1908, 6 (?) copies were sent to Constable's, London; *see below.* 1255 copies bound during the period Jan. 5–May 12, 1909. The plates were sent to the author Sept. 9, 1909; and on Sept. 11, 1909, 742 sets of unbound sheets.

On the basis of the publisher's records and Moody's letters (in H) to the publisher, on Dec. 2 ⟨sic⟩, 1908, six copies were prepared for purposes of British copyright, three copies being put in binding. These copies may be distinguished by the totally blank verso of title-leaf; and the presence of the spine imprint: CONSTABLE / LONDON

Noted for Dec. 15 in PW Dec. 5, 1908. Deposited Jan. 8, 1909. Noted for the *20th inst.*, PW Jan. 16, 1909. On copyright page: *Published January 1909* Listed PW Feb. 13, 1909. For a revision see below under 1910.

AAS   B   BA   BPL   NYPL   UV   Y

14317. . . . Selections from De Quincey . . . Edited for School Use by William Vaughn Moody . . .

Chicago Scott, Foresman and Company ⟨1909⟩

At head of title: *The Lake English Classics*

Note: In the only located copy the *Contents* leaf is an insert.

"Life of De Quincey," pp. 7-21.

"Joan of Arc," pp. 22-24.

"The English Mail Coach," pp. 24-29.

"De Quincey's Peculiar Distinction as a Writer," pp. 29-31.

"Suggestions for Reading," p. 32.

"Notes," pp. ⟨177⟩-186.

Deposited June 21, 1909.

UC

14318. A First View of English and American Literature by William Vaughn Moody Robert Morss Lovett and Percy H. Boynton . . .

New York Charles Scribner's Sons 1909

For earlier editions see above under 1902, 1905.

According to the publisher's records issued in June, 1909.

CSS

14319. THE GREAT DIVIDE A PLAY IN THREE ACTS . . .

NEW YORK THE MACMILLAN COMPANY 1909 . . .

Note: Copyright notice dated *1906*.

⟨i-vi⟩, ⟨1⟩-167; blank, p. ⟨168⟩; 4 pp. advertisements. Laid paper. $7\frac{1}{4}''$ full × $4\frac{7}{8}''$.

⟨1-11⁸; plus: 12¹⟩.

T cloth: blue.

Under the title *A Sabine Woman a Play in Three Acts* deposited for copyright April 14, 1906; typescript only. Advertised as *nearly ready* PW Sept. 11, 1909. Noted as *published this week* PW Oct. 2, 1909. Listed PW Oct. 16, 1909; Bkr Nov. 12, 1909; Ath Nov. 13, 1909.

AAS B BA H UV Y

14320. The Faith Healer a Play in Three Acts . . .

New York The Macmillan Company 1910 . . .

A revision of the 1909 publication.

Two bindings noted; the sequence is presumed correct:

A: T cloth: blue. Stamped in gold and blind.

B: V cloth: green. Stamped in green.

On copyright page: *Published March, 1910*.

Listed PW March 12, 1910. Advertised as though published Ath April 8, 1910.

AAS (*Binding B*) B (*Bindings A, B*) H (*Binding A*) LC (*Binding A*) UV (*Binding B*) Y (*Binding A*)

14321. Selected Poems from the Harvard Monthly 1885–1910

Published by the Graduate Council of the Harvard Monthly (Incorporated) Cambridge, Mass. 1910

Printed paper wrapper.

Reprint with the exception of: "Daffodils," p. 30.

H

14322. The Poems and Plays . . . with an Introduction by John M. Manly . . .

Boston and New York Houghton Mifflin Company The Riverside Press Cambridge 1912

Two volumes.

1: *Poems and Poetic Dramas.* Reprint save for:

"The Counting Man"

"The Death of Eve"

"The Fountain"

"I am the Woman"

"The Moon-Moth"

"Musa Meretrix"

"Old Pourquoi"

"A Prairie Ride"

"Second Coming"

"Song," *My love is gone into the East* . . .

"Thammuz"

"The Three Angels"

2: *Prose Plays.* Reprint.

According to the publisher's records 1035 copies of Vol. 2 were printed Oct. 26, 1912; 1038 copies of Vol. 1 were printed Oct. 31, 1912. Copies, both volumes, were first bound Nov. 9, 1912. Deposited Nov. 19, 1912.

Note: Reprints were issued without the date *1912* in the imprint. The copyright notice in Vol. 2 is dated 1906, 1909, 1910. The reprint, lacking the date 1912 in the imprint, is therefore apt to be erroneously taken for a 1910 publication. Vol. 1 was issued with a 1912 copyright notice.

B H NYPL UV

14323. SOME LETTERS OF WILLIAM VAUGHN MOODY EDITED WITH AN INTRODUCTION BY DANIEL GREGORY MASON

BOSTON AND NEW YORK HOUGHTON MIFFLIN COMPANY THE RIVERSIDE PRESS CAMBRIDGE 1913

⟨i⟩-⟨xxviii⟩, ⟨1⟩-⟨171⟩; printer's imprint, p. ⟨172⟩. Frontispiece and 1 plate inserted; one double-leaf facsimile inserted. $7\frac{3}{4}''$ × $5\frac{1}{16}''$ scant.

⟨1-12⁸, 13⁴⟩.

T cloth: green. Top edges gilt. *Note:* The spine imprint occurs as follows; the order of B and C uncertain:

A

Stamped from a serifed face. A period present after *CO.*

B

Stamped from a serifed face. No period present after *CO*

C

Stamped from a sans serif face. A period present after *CO.*

According to the publisher's records 1577 copies were printed July 3, 1913. Bound during the period July 21, 1913 to Sept. 7, 1928. 190 sets of sheets discarded May 1, 1929. Plates melted Jan. 3, 1939.

Deposited (*Binding A*) Oct. 13, 1913. BA copy (*Binding B*) received Oct. 15, 1913. H copy (*Binding A*) received Oct. 17, 1913. Listed PW Oct. 25, 1913. On copyright page: *Published October 1913*

B (*Bindings A, C*)   BA (*Binding B*)   H (*Binding A*) LC (*Binding A*, being a deposit copy)   UV (*Bindings A, C*)   Y (*Binding C*)

14324. William Vaughn Moody a Study by David D. Henry . . .

Boston   Bruce Humphries, Inc. Publishers ⟨1934⟩

"New Letters," pp. 223-238. ". . . For the present study, Mrs. Moody has graciously allowed the use of twenty letters, sixteen not heretofore published, four having had a limited circulation in *The Play Book* . . . of the Wisconsin Dramatic Society, March 1915 . . ."---P. 223.

"Early Poems," pp. 239–261. "Those poems . . . which are not available in any of the printed editions of his work and which in this volume have not been quoted at length or epitomized are reproduced in the following pages . . ."---P. 239. The poems are:

"The Amber-Witch," "Angelle," "The Answer," "Applause," "The Briar Rose," "A Chorus of Wagner," "Dance Music," "The Lady of the Fountain," "Life and Death, from the German," "The Picture," "A Sick Room Fancy." Also an early version of "Old Pourquoi"; for a revised version see in Moody's *Poems and Plays*, 1912.

H copy received Nov. 13, 1934.

H   LC   NYPL   Y

14325. LETTERS TO HARRIET . . . EDITED, WITH INTRODUCTION AND CONCLU-SION, BY PERCY MACKAYE

BOSTON AND NEW YORK   HOUGHTON MIFFLIN COMPANY THE RIVERSIDE PRESS CAMBRIDGE 1935

⟨i⟩-⟨x⟩, ⟨1⟩-⟨458⟩. Laid paper watermarked *Flemish Book* . . . Frontispiece and 1 plate inserted. 8¹/₁₆″ full × 5½″ full.

⟨1-28⁸, 29¹⁰⟩.

Green balloon cloth. Laid end papers.

Deposited Dec. 30, 1935. BPL copy received Dec. 30, 1935.

B   BPL   H   LC   NYPL   UV   Y

WILLIAM VAUGHN MOODY

SECTION II

In this section are listed Moody's books containing no material here first published or collected. For a list of books by authors other than Moody containing reprinted Moody material see *Section Three*.

Gloucester Moors and Other Poems . . .

    Boston . . . ⟨1901⟩

See below under 1909.

14326. The Masque of Judgment . . .

    Boston and New York Houghton, Mifflin and Company The Riverside Press, Cambridge 1902

Sheets of the Small, Maynard & Company, 1900, printing with newly printed and inserted front matter.

Issued in both a trade format (trimmed edges, bound in cloth); and, a so-called large paper format (untrimmed edges, presumably bound in paper boards, paper label on spine).

Publisher's record:

May 8, 1902: 20 copies in binding and 361 sets of sheets received from Small, Maynard & Company.

May 29, 1902: 275 title-leaves printed.

June 2, 1902: Two and a half hours of alterations. 150 copies of a four-page cancel (presumably title-leaf and conjugate) printed for the so-called large paper format. *But see entry below, June 27, 1902.*

June 12, 1902: 175 jackets and spine labels printed.

June 27, 1902: 150 copies of a four-page cancel printed for the so-called large paper format. *But see entry above, June 2, 1902.*

Binding: 100 copies bound June 10, 1902. 150 untrimmed copies bound July 2, 1902. 111 copies bound Sept. 18, 1902.

A second printing, 271 copies, recorded July 27, 1904.

Listed PW Oct. 4, 1902.

14327. Gloucester Moors and Other Poems . . .

    Boston and New York Houghton Mifflin Company The Riverside Press Cambridge ⟨1901; *i.e.,* 1909⟩

A reprint of *Poems*, 1901.

278 copies printed Feb. 26, 1909. Bound during the period April 7, 1909 to May 28, 1910.

Two printings noted. The sequence has not been established and the designations are for identification only:

A: Opposite the title-page three titles, unpriced, are listed.

B: Opposite the title-page five titles, priced, are listed.

14328. Good Friday Night . . .

    ⟨The Unbound Anthology Published by the Poets' Guild, 147 Avenue B, New York City, N.Y., n.d., *ca.* 1922⟩

3 sheets, printed on one side only, within a folder. Reprinted from *Poems*, 1901.

14329. Pandora's Song (From the Fire-Bringer) . . .

    ⟨The Unbound Anthology Published by the Poets' Guild, 147 Avenue B, New York City, N.Y., n.d., *ca.* 1922⟩

Single sheet, printed on recto only, within a folder.

14330. Songs by Constance Herreshoff Of Wounds and Sore Defeat . . .

    J. Fischer & Bro., New York 119 West 40th Street . . . ⟨1928⟩

Sheet music. Cover-title. Plate number 0234-5. Reprinted from *The Fire-Bringer*, 1904.

14331. ⟨Pandora's Song⟩ United States of America

    The International Unbound Anthology Consuls' Series ⟨New York: The Poets' Guild, 1930⟩

Not seen. Entry on the basis of a photographic copy.

Cover-title. 4 pp. 500 numbered copies. Reprinted from *The Fire-Bringer*, 1904. For an earlier separate printing see above under *ca.* 1922.

14332. Selected Poems . . . Edited, with Introduction, by Robert Morss Lovett

Boston and New York   Houghton Mifflin Company The Riverside Press 1931

Cloth, printed paper label on spine. Deposited April 2, 1931.

14333. . . . Selected Poems . . . Edited by Robert Morss Lovett . . .

Houghton Mifflin Company   Boston . . . The Riverside Press Cambridge ⟨1931⟩

At head of title: *Riverside College Classics*

WILLIAM VAUGHN MOODY

SECTION III

The following publications contain material by Moody reprinted from earlier books.

A Book of American Humorous Verse . . .

Chicago . . . 1904

For comment see BAL, Vol. 1, p. 411.

Through Italy with the Poets   Compiled by Robert Haven Schauffler . . .

New York . . . 1908

"At Assisi," pp. 168-170, is a reprint of *Part II* of "Song-Flower and Poppy," *Poems*, 1901.

For fuller entry see BAL, Vol. 4, p. 446.

Poems of American History Collected . . . by Burton Egbert Stevenson

Boston . . . 1908

For a fuller entry see in Joaquin Miller, *Section One.*

Chief Contemporary Dramatists . . . Edited by Thomas H. Dickinson . . .

Boston . . . ⟨1915⟩

For a fuller entry see BAL, Vol. 4, p. 362.

The Chicago Anthology   A Collection of Verse from the Work of Chicago Poets Selected and Arranged by Charles G. Blanden and Minna Mathison . . .

Chicago   The Roadside Press   1916

American Poets   An Anthology of Contemporary Verse by Leonora Speyer

Kurt Wolff Verlag   München ⟨1923⟩

American Mystical Verse . . . Selected by Irene Hunter . . .

D. Appleton and Company New York MCMXXV

Poetic Drama . . . Edited by Alfred Kreymborg

Modern Age Books   New York ⟨1941⟩

Deposited Dec. 11, 1941.

REFERENCES AND ANA

A Sabine Woman   A Play in Three Acts . . .

⟨Chicago, n.d., 1906⟩

Typescript. Prepared for copyright purposes. Deposited April 14, 1906. Published in 1909 under the title *The Great Divide;* see above in *Section One.*

The Death of Eve, a Poetic Drama

1909-1910

". . . Never finished . . ."---DAB.

Collected in *Poems and Plays*, 1912.

William Vaughn Moody by Edwin Herbert Lewis

Chicago Literary Club 1914

Printed paper wrapper. 275 copies only.

Moody's The Fire Bringer for To-Day by Martha Hale Shackford

Reprinted from the October Number of The Sewanee Review 1918

Printed paper wrapper.

Commemorative Tributes to Thomas Wentworth Higginson   Julia Ward Howe   Francis Marion Crawford   William Vaughn Moody by Bliss Perry Read at Public Session following Annual Meeting of the American Academy of Arts and Letters New York City December 13, 1912 Reprinted from Vol. VI Proceedings of the Academy

⟨New York⟩ American Academy of Arts and Letters 1922

Printed paper wrapper.

William Vaughn Moody   A Study by David D. Henry . . .

Boston   Bruce Humphries, Inc. Publishers ⟨1934⟩

Bibliography, pp. 263–272.

Concerning William Vaughn Moody with Notes Taken from a Class-Room Note-Book Kept... during the Autumn Quarter of 1896 at the University of Chicago.

Grace Neahr Veeder   Waukesha, Wisconsin
June, 1941

Cover-title. Printed self-wrapper.

William Vaughn Moody by Martin Halpern...

Twayne Publishers, Inc. New York ⟨1964⟩

Printed paper boards. Also issued in printed flexible paper boards with the imprint: *College & University Press Publishers New Haven, Conn. Distributed by Grosset & Dunlap New York ⟨1964⟩.*

CLEMENT CLARKE MOORE

(A Citizen of New-York, Columella, A Landholder, Philalethes)

1 7 7 9 – 1 8 6 3

Note: In the following list BAL has ignored all post-1824 printings of "Account of a Visit from St. Nicholas" save for the earliest known separate printing of *ca.* 1830.

14334. OBSERVATIONS UPON CERTAIN PASSAGES IN MR. JEFFERSON'S NOTES ON VIRGINIA, WHICH APPEAR TO HAVE A TENDENCY TO SUBVERT RELIGION, AND ESTABLISH A FALSE PHILOSOPHY.

NEW-YORK. 1804.

Anonymous. Authorship in doubt. Credited to Moore in *Bibliotheca Jeffersoniana A List of Books Written by or Relating to Thomas Jefferson*, by Hamilton Bullock Tompkins, New York and London, 1887, p. 137. Also credited to Moore by H, LC, UV and others. Sabin (No. 50336) credits the publication to Moore, but in a later entry (No. 72717) credits the publication to one Nicholas(?) Rogers. BAL has found no evidence of authorship.

⟨1⟩-32. 8⅞″ × 5⅝″.

⟨A⟩-D⁴.

Unprinted blue-gray laid paper wrapper.

In all examined copies the word *not* omitted, p. 13, line 11 from bottom, between the words *did* and *occur*.

AAS B BPL H LC NYHS NYPL UV Y

14335. A New Translation with Notes, of the Third Satire of Juvenal. To Which Are Added, Miscellaneous Poems, Original and Translated.

New-York:———Printed for E. Sargeant, No. 39 Wall-Stret ⟨*sic*⟩, opposite the United-States Bank. 1806.

Three binder's states noted; the order of presentation is all but arbitrary.

STATE A

⟨iii⟩-xxvi, ⟨1⟩-⟨191⟩; *Errata*, p. ⟨192⟩. 7¾″ × 4¹¹⁄₁₆″. No table of contents in the front matter; no leaf of *Additional Errata* at back.

⟨A⟩-B, ⟨C⟩, D-I, K-S⁶.

STATE B

⟨iii⟩-xxvi, ⟨1⟩-⟨191⟩; *Errata*, p. ⟨192⟩; *Additional Errata*, pp. ⟨193-194⟩. No table of contents in the front matter.

⟨A⟩-B, ⟨C⟩, D-I, K-S⁶, ⟨T⟩¹.

STATE C

⟨i⟩-xxvi, ⟨1⟩-⟨191⟩; *Errata*, p. ⟨192⟩; *Additional Errata*, pp. ⟨193-194⟩. Table of contents present in the front matter.

⟨A⟩⁷, B-⟨C⟩, D-I, K-S⁶, ⟨T⟩¹. ⟨A⟩₃ (table of contents) inserted.

Mottled pink paper boards, white paper shelf back. Flyleaves.

⟨A⟩₁ᵣ: ⟨*double rule*⟩ | THIRD SATIRE / OF/ JUVENAL. | ⟨*double rule*⟩ | ⟨*rule*⟩ | S. GOULD, PRINTER.

Note: The translation is by John Duer. Those poems herein signed *L* are by Moore.

The prefatory prose "Letter from a Friend," pp. ⟨vii⟩-xxvi, unsigned, is by Moore.

"Lines Addressed to the Fashionable Part of My Young Countrywomen," pp. ⟨106⟩-110.

"Lines Addressed to the Young Ladies who Attended Mr. Chilton's Lectures in Natural Philosophy . . . ," pp. ⟨111⟩-115.

"Lines on Cowper the Poet, Written after Reading the Life of Him by Hayley," pp. ⟨116⟩-118.

"Verses Addressed to a Lady, who Maintained that There is More Happiness in General at an Advanced Period of Life, than in Childhood," pp. ⟨122⟩-127.

"Lines to Petrosa," pp. ⟨128⟩-130.

"Translation of One of the Choruses in the Prometheus of Æschylus," pp. ⟨139⟩-141.

The above six poems collected in *Poems*, 1844.

Listed MA Aug. 1806. Reviewed MA Nov. 1806.

AAS (C) B (C) H (A) UV (B, C)

14336. AN INQUIRY INTO THE EFFECTS OF OUR FOREIGN CARRYING TRADE UPON THE AGRICULTURE, POPULATION, AND MORALS OF THE COUNTRY, BY COLUMELLA...

NEW-YORK: PRINTED BY D. AND G. BRUCE, FOR E. SARGEANT, NO. 39 WALL-STREET, OPPOSITE THE BRANCH BANK. 1806.

⟨1⟩-61; blank, p. ⟨62⟩; blank leaf. 8⅞″ × 5¹¹⁄₁₆″.

⟨A⟩-H⁴.

Paper wrapper?

Listed MA Oct. 1806. Reviewed PF Dec. 6, 1806.

AAS H LC NYPL Y

14337. A LETTER TO SAMUEL OSGOOD, ESQ. OCCASIONED BY HIS LETTER UPON THE SUBJECT OF EPISCOPACY; ADDRESSED TO A YOUNG GENTLEMAN OF THIS CITY. BY PHILALETHES.

NEW-YORK: PRINTED BY COLLINS AND PERKINS. 1807.

Attributed to Moore by Patterson, pp. 49, 165.

Cover-title?

⟨1⟩-14, blank leaf. 9″ × 5⅝″.

⟨A⟩-B⁴.

Paper wrapper?

H

14338. A COMPENDIOUS LEXICON OF THE HEBREW LANGUAGE. IN TWO VOLUMES...

NEW-YORK: PRINTED AND SOLD BY COLLINS & PERKINS, NO. 189, PEARL-STREET. 1809.

1: *Containing an Explanation of Every Word Which Occurs in the Psalms; with Notes.*

⟨i⟩-⟨xvi⟩, ⟨1⟩-474; *Errata*, p. ⟨475⟩. 7⅛″ × 4⁵⁄₁₆″.

2: *Being a Lexicon and Grammar of the Whole Language.*

⟨i-iv⟩, ⟨1⟩-540; *Errata*, p. 541; blank leaf.

1: ⟨a⟩⁶, b², A-I, K-U, X-Z, Aa-Ii, Kk-Qq⁶, Rr⁴.

2: ⟨a⟩², A-I, K-U, X-Z, Aa-Ii, Kk-Uu⁶, Xx⁴, Yy⁶, Zz², ⟨Aaa⟩².

Note: In some copies of Vol. 1 leaf b₂ (pp. ⟨xv-xvi⟩, a blank) is excised.

Probably issued in leather.

In the press---P May 1808. Listed MA Nov. 1809. Again listed MA Jan. 1810. Reviewed MA March 1810.

AAS B H LC NYPL UV

14339. A SKETCH OF OUR POLITICAL CONDITION. ADDRESSED TO THE CITIZENS OF THE UNITED STATES, WITHOUT DISTINCTION OF PARTY. BY A CITIZEN OF NEW-YORK.

NEW-YORK: PRINTED FOR THE AUTHOR, AND FOR SALE AT THE PRINCIPAL BOOKSTORES. C. S. VAN WINKLE, PRINTER. 1813.

⟨1⟩-47. 9¼″ full × 5¹³⁄₁₆″.

⟨1⟩-6⁴.

Paper wrapper?

Listed under "New Publications from January to July," GRR July, 1813.

AAS B BA H NYHS NYPL

14340. A PLAIN STATEMENT, ADDRESSED TO THE PROPRIETORS OF REAL ESTATE, IN THE CITY AND COUNTY OF NEW-YORK. BY A LANDHOLDER...

NEW-YORK: PUBLISHED BY J. EASTBURN AND CO. LITERARY ROOMS, BROADWAY. CLAYTON & KINGSLAND, PRINT. 1818.

⟨1⟩-62, blank leaf. 8¹⁵⁄₁₆″ × 5¾″.

⟨1⟩-8⁴.

Paper wrapper?

AAS LC NYHS UV Y

14341. Journal of the Proceedings of the Bishops, Clergy, and Laity of the Protestant Episcopal Church in the United States of America, in a General Convention, Held in St. Peter's Church ... Philadelphia ... 20th to the 26th Day of May Inclusive ... 1823.

New-York: Printed by T. & J. Swords, No. 99 Pearl-Street. 1823.

Issued in paper?

Report, pp. 94-95.

Location: General Theological Seminary, N.Y.

14342. ACCOUNT OF A VISIT FROM ST. NICHOLAS (Otherwise: "A Visit from St. Nicholas," "The Night before Christmas")

First published in *The Troy Sentinel* (N.Y.), Dec. 23, 1823; other periodical appearances here ignored. Post-1824 publication, save for the earliest known separate printing of *ca.* 1830, also ignored. Noted in the following 1824 publications; sequence not determined. The order of presentation is alphabetical by title.

Citizens & Farmers' Almanack for the Year of Our Lord 1825 . . . Calculated by Joshua Sharp . . .

Philadelphia: Printed and Published by Griggs & Dickinson. ⟨n.d., 1824⟩

Printed self-wrapper. Cover-title.

Unpaged.

Contains "Account of a Visit from St. Nicholas."

Locations: B

Grigg's Almanack, for the Year of Our Lord 1825 . . . Calculated by Joshua Sharp.

Philadelphia: Printed and Published by Griggs & Dickinson, for John Grigg, No. 9, N. Fourth Street, ⟨n.d., 1824⟩

Printed self-wrapper. Unpaged.

Contains "Account of a Visit from St. Nicholas."

Locations: AAS

New Brunswick, (N.J.) Almanack, for the Year of Our Lord 1825 . . . Calculated by Joshua Sharp . . .

Philadelphia: Printed and Published by Griggs & Dickinson, for Joseph C. Griggs, New Brunswick, (New Jersey.) ⟨n.d., 1824⟩

Printed self-wrapper. Unpaged.

Contains "Account of a Visit from St. Nicholas."

Locations: AAS

. . . The United States National Almanac. Comprising Calculations for the Latitudes and Meridians of the Northern, Southern, and Western States; with a Variety of Public Information and Interesting Masonic Matter . . . by David M'Clure.

Philadelphia: R. Desilver, 110, Walnut Street. 1825.

Probably issued in printed paper wrapper. At head of title: *To Be Continued Annually.*

"Account of a Visit from St. Nicholas," p. 34.

Title-page deposited Aug. 27, 1824.

Locations: H

Note: See below under *ca.* 1830 for earliest located separate publication; under 1837 for earliest located formal book publication. Collected in *Poems,* 1844.

14343. Sermons, by Benjamin Moore . . . in Two Volumes . . .

New-York: Printed and Sold by T. and J. Swords, No. 99 Pearl-Street. 1824.

Edited by Moore.

"Advertisement," Vol. 1, p. ⟨iii⟩, dated at end: *New-York, August, 1824.*

Leather?

UP

14344. ADDRESS DELIVERED BEFORE THE ALUMNI OF COLUMBIA COLLEGE, ON THE 4th OF MAY, 1825, IN THE CHAPEL OF THE COLLEGE . . .

NEW-YORK: PUBLISHED BY E. BLISS & E. WHITE. J. SEYMOUR PRINTER, 1825.

⟨1⟩-37, blank leaf. 9" full × 5⅞".

⟨1⟩-5⁴.

Printed paper wrapper?

Listed USLG June 15, 1825; NYR Aug. 1825.

For a facsimile printing see *The Early History of Columbia College . . . ,* 1940, below, in the list of *References and Ana.*

H   LC   NYPL   UV

14345. A LECTURE INTRODUCTORY TO THE COURSE OF HEBREW INSTRUCTION IN THE GENERAL THEOLOGICAL SEMINARY OF THE PROTESTANT EPISCOPAL CHURCH IN THE UNITED STATES, DELIVERED IN CHRIST CHURCH, NEW-YORK, ON THE EVENING OF NOVEMBER 14th, 1825 . . .

NEW-YORK: PRINTED BY T. AND J. SWORDS, NO. 99 PEARL-STREET. 1825.

⟨1⟩-28. 9¼" × 5⅞".

⟨1⟩⁴, 9⁴ ⟨sic⟩, 3⁴, 4².

Paper wrapper?

Listed USLG Jan. 15, 1826.

AAS   B   UV

. . . The United States National Almanac . . .

Philadelphia . . . 1825.

See above under 1824.

14346. ACCOUNT OF A VISIT FROM ST. NICHOLAS, OR SANTA CLAUS . . .

⟨TROY, N.Y.⟩ PRINTED BY N. TUTTLE, AT THE OFFICE OF THE DAILY TROY SENTINEL, 225 RIVER-STREET ⟨n.d., *ca.* 1830⟩

Not seen. Entry from *"The Night before Christmas" an Exhibition Catalogue*, by George H. M. Lawrence, Pittsburgh, 1964, p. 3.

"This is the first known illustrated publication, and first broadside, of the poem. Myron King, the artist-engraver . . ."---*op. cit.*

For prior publication see above under year 1824. Collected in *Poems*, 1844.

An undated broadside, printed in blue and red, was issued *ca.* 1842 by John M. Wolff, Philadelphia.

14347. The New-York Book of Poetry . . .

New-York: George Dearborn, Publisher, No. 38 Gold Street. 1837.

"From a Father to His Children, after Having Had His Portrait Taken for Them," pp. 215-216.

"From a Husband to His Wife," pp. 221-224.

"To a Lady," pp. 211-213.

All the above collected in *Poems*, 1844.

Also contains the earliest located formal book publication of "A Visit from St. Nicholas," pp. 217-219. For an earlier printing see above under 1824: "Account of a Visit from St. Nicholas."

"Never before, we believe" has Moore's "A Visit from St. Nicholas" appeared "under the name of the real author."---AMM Jan. 1837.

For fuller entry see No. 3272.

14348. POEMS . . .

NEW YORK: BARTLETT & WELFORD, 7 ASTOR HOUSE 1844.

⟨i⟩-⟨xiv⟩, ⟨15⟩-216. 7⅝₁₆″ full × 4¾″.

⟨A⟩⁶, 1-17⁶.

Brown paper boards, printed paper label on spine. Flyleaves.

Deposited July 9, 1844. Listed ALB July, 1844; WPLNL Aug. 1844.

H UV Y

14349. George Castriot, Surnamed Scanderbeg, King of Albania. ⟨Edited⟩ by Clement C. Moore . . .

New York: D. Appleton & Company, 200 Broadway. Philadelphia: Geo. S. Appleton, 164 Chesnut-Street. M DCCC L.

A revised edition of *The Historie of George Castriot . . . by Jaques de Lavardin . . . Newly Translated out of French into English by Z. I. . . .*, London, 1596.

⟨1⟩-367; blank, p. ⟨368⟩; advertisements, paged: 2-6, 13-22, 36. 7⅜″ full × 4¹¹₁₆″.

T cloth: slate. TB cloth: green. Pale buff end papers. Flyleaves.

Deposited Sept. 7, 1850. Advertised for *Thursday* (Sept. 12? 19?) LW Sept. 14, 1850. Listed LW Sept. 21, 1850.

AAS H NYHS Y

14350. The Woodbine: A Holiday Gift. Edited by Caroline May . . .

Philadelphia: Lindsay and Blakiston. ⟨1851⟩

"On Finery of Style," pp. ⟨140⟩-145. Otherwise unlocated.

Reviewed USDR Dec. 1851.

B Y

REPRINTS

The following publications contain material by Moore reprinted from earlier books. Printings of "A Visit from St. Nicholas," including publication under variant titles, are here ignored.

The Gems of American Poetry, by Distinguished Authors.

New-York: A. & C. B. Edwards. 1840.

The Poets of America . . . Edited by John Keese.

New York . . . 1840.

For comment see BAL, Vol. 1, pp. 232–233.

The Poets and Poetry of America . . . by Rufus W. Griswold . . .

Philadelphia . . . MDCCCXLII.

For comment see entry No. 6644.

The Poets of the Nineteenth Century . . . Edited by . . . Rev. Robert Aris Willmott . . .

New York . . . 1858.

For comment see entry No. 1663.

The Poets of the West . . .

London . . . 1859.

For comment see BAL, Vol. 1, p. 101.

Golden Leaves from the American Poets Collected by John W. S. Hows . . .

New York: George Routledge and Sons, 416 Broome Street. ⟨1864; *i.e.*, not before 1866⟩

Golden Leaves from the American Poets Collected by John W. S. Hows

New York James G. Gregory 540 Broadway
M DCCC LXV

Reprinted with the imprint: *New York Bunce and Huntington M DCCC LXV*

The Poets and Poetry of America. By Rufus Wilmot Griswold . . .

New York . . . 1873.

For comment see BAL, Vol. 4, p. 60.

REFERENCES AND ANA

A Complete Treatise on Merinos and Other Sheep . . . Recently Published at Paris, by Order of the Government, Compiled by Mr. Tessier . . . and Others . . . Translated from the French . . .

Printed at the Economical School Office, New-York. 1811.

Sometimes credited to Moore. BAL has been unable to find any evidence to support the attribution.

The Visit of Saint Nicholas . . . Facsimile of the Original Manuscript with Life of the Author by William S. Pelletreau . . .

New York: Copyright, 1897, by G. W. Dillingham Co., Publishers. MDCCCXCVII . . .

Listed PW Oct. 2, 1897.

The Christmas Grab-Bag by Clement C. Moore

New York: Cheshire House 1930

Cloth, printed paper label. 750 copies only.

Not by the subject of this list. References in text indicate that the story could not have been written prior to 1873; Moore died in 1863. See p. 8 for a reference to Mark Twain's scrapbook which was patented in 1873.

The Night before Christmas The True Story of a Visit from St. Nicholas With a Life of the Author . . . Written by Arthur N. Hosking

New York Dodd, Mead & Company MCMXXXIV

Printed paper boards. "Bibliography of the Works of Clement Clarke Moore," pp. 34-36.

The Early History of Columbia College an Address . . . by Clement Clarke Moore . . . A Facsimile Edition with an Introduction by Milton Halsey Thomas

New York: Morningside Heights Columbia University Press 1940

Deposited Dec. 9, 1940. For first printing of Moore's address see above in *Section One* his *Address Delivered before the Alumni of Columbia College* . . . , 1825.

The Poet of Christmas Eve A Life of Clement Clarke Moore . . . by Samuel White Patterson

Morehouse-Gorham Co., New York ⟨1956⟩

"The Night Before Christmas" An Exhibition Catalogue Compiled by George H. M. Lawrence Foreword by Anne Lyon Haight

The Pittsburgh Bibliophiles Pittsburgh, Pa. 1964

Printed paper wrapper.

GEORGE POPE MORRIS

1 8 0 2 – 1 8 6 4

Compiled in the following sections:

Section One: Books by Morris, or books containing earliest located appearances of Morris's works.

Section Two: Handbills, sheet music, and like material.

Section Three: Reprints of Morris's own books.

Section Four: Books by authors other than Morris containing reprinted Morris material.

Section Five: References and ana.

SECTION I

Books by Morris, or books containing the earliest located appearance of Morris's works.

14351. Specimens of American Poetry . . . in Three Volumes. By Samuel Kettell . . .

Boston,-S. G. Goodrich and Co. MDCCCXXIX.

"The Miniature," Vol. 3, p. 352.

"What Can it Mean?," Vol. 3, pp. 352-353.

"Woman," Vol. 3, p. 351.

All three collected in *The Deserted Bride*, 1838.

For fuller entry see No. 3251.

14352. The Atlantic Club-Book: Being Sketches in Prose and Verse, by Various Authors . . . in Two Volumes . . .

New-York: Harper and Brothers, 82 Cliff Street. 1834.

According to Foley (p. 223) edited by Morris.

Reprint with the exception of:

"The Dismissed," Vol. 1, pp. 248–249. Collected in *The Deserted Bride*, 1838.

"Sketches from the Springs," Vol. 1, pp. ⟨152⟩-175. Collected in *The Little Frenchman and His Water Lots*, 1839, as "Letters from the Springs."

For fuller description see entry No. 1151.

14353. The American Juvenile Keepsake, for 1835 . . . Edited by Mrs. Hofland.

Brookville, U.C. Published by Horace Billings & Co. ⟨1834⟩

Noted only in publisher's leather.

"Stanzas, Written among the Highlands of the Hudson River," pp. ⟨234-235⟩. Collected in *The Deserted Bride*, 1838, as "Lines for Music."

Also issued with the imprint: *New York: T. Illman* ⟨*1834*⟩.

NYHS

14354. The New-York Book of Poetry . . .

New-York: George Dearborn, Publisher, No. 38 Gold Street. 1837.

*"The Deserted Bride," pp. 168-170.

"Lines for Music," pp. 59-60. Here reprinted. Previously in *The American Juvenile Keepsake, for 1835*, under the title "Stanzas, Written among the Highlands of the Hudson River."

*"Rhyme and Reason. An Apologue," pp. 144-145.

*"Song.–––When Other Friends Are round Thee," p. 238. Previously issued as sheet music, 1836.

*Collected in *The Deserted Bride*, 1838.

For fuller entry see No. 3272.

14355. THE DESERTED BRIDE; AND OTHER POEMS . . .

NEW-YORK: ADLARD & SAUNDERS, BROADWAY, MDCCCXXXVIII.

Contents: Thirty poems and notes. For other editions see below under 1843, 1853.

⟨1⟩-80. 8⅝″ × 5½″.

⟨A⟩-I, K⁴.

Noted in three styles of binding; the sequence, if any, has not been determined and the designations are wholly arbitrary.

BINDING A

H cloth: black. T cloth, damasked with a leafy pattern: black.

T cloth, embossed with a floral pattern: blue; green.

Ornament on front cover measures 2¾″ tall.

Ornament on back cover measures 2¾″ tall.

End papers: buff-coated; peach-coated; salmon-coated; yellow-coated.

Flyleaves: Four at front, four at back. Also issued without flyleaves.

BINDING B

H cloth: black. LP-like cloth: black.

Ornament on front cover measures 2¾″ full tall.

Ornament on back cover measures 1⁷⁄₁₆″ tall.

End papers: yellow-coated.

Flyleaves: Four at front, four at back.

BINDING C

T cloth, embossed with a floral pattern: green.

Ornament on front cover measures 1⁷⁄₁₆″ tall.

Ornament on back cover measures 1⁷⁄₁₆″ tall.

End papers: buff-coated.

Flyleaves: Four at front, four at back.

Noted as *in press* AMM Jan. 1838. Title-page deposited March 1, 1838. A copy (in UV, *Binding B*) inscribed by the author April 2, 1838. Reviewed by *New-Yorker* April 7, 1838. *Recently given to the public*---K May, 1838. Reviewed AMM May, 1838. Listed AMM June, 1838.

B (*Binding A*)   BA (*Binding A*)   BPL (*Binding A*) H (*Binding A*)   LC (*Binding C*)   NYPL (*Bindings A, B*)   UV (*Bindings A, B*)   Y (*Binding A*)

14356. THE LITTLE FRENCHMAN AND HIS WATER LOTS, WITH OTHER SKETCHES OF THE TIMES . . .

PHILADELPHIA: LEA & BLANCHARD, SUCCESSORS TO CAREY & CO. 1839.

⟨1⟩-155. Illustrated. 8″ scant × 4⅞″.

⟨1⟩⁶, A, ⟨B⟩, C-I, K-M⁶.

CM-like cloth: brown; purple. Orange-coated end papers. Yellow-coated end papers. 7 flyleaves at front, 7 flyleaves at back. Also noted with 3 flyleaves at front, 3 flyleaves at back. Also: 2 flyleaves at front, 2 flyleaves at back. Also: 6 flyleaves at front, 6 flyleaves at back.

Deposited April 16, 1839. Noted NYLG April 20, 1839. Reviewed by K May, 1839. For another edition see below under year 1844.

AAS   B   BPL   H   UV   Y

14357. American Melodies; Containing a Single Selection from the Productions of Two Hundred Writers. Compiled by George P. Morris . . .

New-York: Published by Linen and Fennell, No. 229 Broadway. 1841.

"Woodman, Spare that Tree," pp. 93-94 here reprinted; previously in *The Deserted Bride*," 1838, under the title "The Oak."

For comment see entry No. 997.

14358. The Poets of America . . . Edited by John Keese. [Volume Second of the Series.]

New York: Published by Samuel Colman . . . 1842.

Reprint save for "The Chieftain's Daughter. Pocahontas," pp. 313-314. Collected in *The Deserted Bride*, 1843. For publication as sheet music see *The Chieftain's Daughter*, 1841.

For fuller entry see No. 3280.

14359. The Poets and Poetry of America . . . by Rufus W. Griswold . . .

Philadelphia: Carey and Hart, Chesnut Street. MDCCCXLII.

Reprint save for "Land, Ho!," p. 441. Collected in *The Deserted Bride*, 1843. For publication as sheet music see *Land, Ho! A Nautical Song*, 1840.

For fuller entry see No. 6644.

14360. SONGS, DUETTS AND CHORUSSES IN THE NEW OPERA OF THE MAID OF SAXONY . . . THE LIBRETTO, BY GEORGE P. MORRIS . . . THE MUSIC . . . BY C. E. HORN . . .

NEW YORK: J. C. HOUSE, PRINTER, 88 BARCLAY-ST. 1842.

Cover-title?

⟨1⟩-16. 6¾″ scant × 4⅛″ full.

⟨-⟩⁸.

Printed self-wrapper?

Title entered May 23, 1842.

B   Y

14361. Gems from American Poets . . .

New-York: D. Appleton and Company, 200 Broadway. ⟨1842⟩

Reprint with the possible exception of:

a b-"From My Fate There's No Retreating," p. 132. In *The Deserted Bride*, 1843, as "All Should Wed for Love."

a b-"The Gentle Bird on Yonder Spray," p. 145.

a b-"Hark! Tis the Deep-Toned Midnight Bell," p. 155. In *The Deserted Bride*, 1843, as "The Midnight Bell."

a b-"Love is Not a Garden Flower," p. 119.

a-"The Seasons of Love," pp. 31-33.

b-"We Were Boys Together," pp. 104-105. For prior publication as sheet music see *We Were Boys Together*, 1841.

b-"Well-a-Day," pp. 98-99.

a b-"When I Behold that Lowering Brow," pp. 111-112.

a-Also in *Songs, Duetts and Chorusses . . .* , 1842; see preceding entry.

b-Collected in *The Deserted Bride*, 1843.

Deposited Nov. 4, 1842. For fuller entry see No. 5193.

14362. The Legion of Liberty! And Force of Truth, Containing the Thoughts, Words, and Deeds, of Some Prominent Apostles, Champions and Martyrs. Second Division . . .

1842. Sold at the Office of the American A. S. Society, 143 Nassau-St. New York, and at the Offices of the Other Anti-Slavery Periodicals and Depositories. Price 12 1-2 Cents Single, $1.25 per Dozen, $8 per Hundred.

Printed paper wrapper. Unpaged. Contains an eight-verse stanza: *Our hearts are bounding with delight, | 'Tis freedom's jubilee . . .*

Also in *Songs, Duetts and Chorusses . . .* , 1842. Here reprinted?

HM

14363. THE DESERTED BRIDE; AND OTHER POEMS . . .

NEW-YORK: D. APPLETON & CO. 200 BROADWAY. MDCCCXLIII.

Contains 74 poems and notes. For other editions see under 1838, 1853.

⟨1⟩-172. Illustrated. 8″ × 5⁷⁄₁₆″. *Note:* Pp. ⟨109-144⟩ are engraved and printed on recto only; p. ⟨109⟩ is a divisional title-page, dated 1843, for "The Whip-Poor-Will."

Two printings noted. The following variations are sufficient for ready identification. The order given is probable:

PRINTING A

⟨a⟩, b-c, ⟨d⟩, e, F-M⁴, N²; 18 single leaves; T-V⁴, W². Note use of upper and lower case in the signing.

Pp. 16-17: The stanzas are numbered I-III.

P. 169: NOTES. "*Woodman, spare that tree.*" . . .

PRINTING Aa

Same as the preceding but signature mark *b* not present.

PRINTING B

⟨A-B⟩, C, ⟨D⟩, E-M⁴, N²; 18 single leaves; T-V⁴, W². Note use of upper case letters in the signing.

Pp. 16-17: The stanzas are not numbered.

P. 169: NOTES. *a* "*Janet McRea.*" . . .

Pale green paper boards, printed in gold, gray paper shelf back. Goldstamped leather label on spine. Yellow-coated end papers. Flyleaves.

About to publish–––USDR Oct. 1842. Reviewed BJ Dec. 24, 1842.

AAS (B, rebound) H (Aa, rebound) NYPL (A, rebound; B, rebound) Y (B, rebound)

14364. THE WHIP-POOR-WILL. RESPECTFULLY INSCRIBED TO MORTON McMICHAEL, ESQ. . . .

D. APPLETON & Cº NEW YORK. 1843

Engraved throughout. Illustrated. 18 unpaged leaves. Leaf: 7¹¹⁄₁₆″ × 5³⁄₁₆″.

Issued thus? Or extracted from *The Deserted Bride*, 1843?

A separate edition, in illuminated paper wrapper, was issued by E. Ferrett and Co., Philadelphia and New York, n.d., 1846.

H NYPL

14365. . . . THE SONGS AND BALLADS OF GEORGE P. MORRIS . . .

NEW-YORK: MORRIS, WILLIS, & CO: PUBLISHERS, NO. 4 ANN-STREET. 1844. G. W. WOOD & CO., PRINTERS, 45 GOLD ST.

Cover-title. At head of title: *Price 12½ Cents. New Mirror Extra, No. IV.*

⟨1⟩-16. 11¹⁄₁₆″ full × 7½″.

⟨-⟩⁸.

Printed fawn paper wrapper.

The following poems here first collected:

"Life in the West"

"The Main-Truck; or, a Leap for Life"

"Margaretta"

"Not Married Yet"

"O'er the Mountains"

"Oh, Boatman Haste"

"The Pastor's Daughter"

"The Rock of the Pilgrims"

"The Star of Love"

"The Sweep's Carol"

"The Sword and the Staff"

Deposited Jan. 17, 1844. Listed WPLNL March, 1844.

AAS   B   BPL   LC   NYPL   UV   Y

14366. ... The Little Frenchman and His Water Lots, and Other Tales of the Times ...

New-York: Morris, Willis & Co., Publishers, Ann-Street, Near Broadway. 1844. G. W. Wood & Co., Printers, 45 Gold St.

Cover-title. At head of title: *Price*,] [*12½ Cents. New Mirror———Extra Number Five.*

A reprint of *The Little Frenchman and His Water Lots* ..., 1839, with some textual alterations, a few added paragraphs, and alterations of titles.

Printed tan paper wrapper.

AAS   BPL   H   UV

14367. Statement. ⟨Second Edition⟩

⟨Berlin, July 16, 1845⟩

Contains letters to Theodore Sedgwick Fay.

For fuller description see entry No. 5705.

14368. Morris's Melodies. Six of the Most Popular Melodies of Gen. Geo. P. Morris ...

E. Ferrett & Co. No. 68 South Fourth Street, Philadelphia. No. 237 Broadway, New York. No. 30 Cornhill, Boston. 1845 ...

Printed paper wrapper.

Reprint save for "The Heart that Owns Thy Tyrant Sway" and "One Balmy Summer Night, Mary."

Two issues noted; the order of presentation is presumed correct:

ISSUE A

Imprint as above.

ISSUE B

Imprint: E. Ferrett & Co. No. 68 South Fourth Street, Philadelphia. No. 237 Broadway, New York. S. Coleman, No. 30 Cornhill, Boston. 1845.

Deposited Oct. 31, 1845.

B (B)   LC (A)

14369. A Library of the Prose and Poetry of Europe and America ... Compiled by G. P. Morris and N. P. Willis. Complete in One Volume.

New-York: Paine and Burgess. 1846.

Co-edited by Morris; contains no material signed by him.

Reissued 1848 as *The Prose and Poetry of Europe and America.*

Title deposited Dec. 6, 1845. Listed ALB Jan. 1846.

H   Y

14370. The Songs and Ballads of George P. Morris. First Complete Edition.

New-York: Paine & Burgess, 62 John-Street. 1846.

Reprint with the possible exception of the following poems:

"The Days that Are Gone." For prior publication as sheet music see *The Indian and His Bride*, 1844.

"The Prairie on Fire."

"Tis Now the Promised Hour." For prior publication as sheet music see *Tis now the Promis'd Hour,* 1844.

"The Welcome and Farewell."

Two variants (printings?) have been noted. The sequence is all but arbitrary and the designations are for identification only.

VARIANT A

⟨i-ii⟩, ⟨i⟩-xiv, ⟨17⟩-126, blank leaf. $4\frac{5}{8}''$ × $3\frac{3}{16}''$.

The dedication is on ⟨1⟩$_{6r}$; conjugate ⟨1⟩$_3$ is a blank.

The ornament on the sides is a filigree about $3\frac{1}{2}''$ tall. Edges gilt.

VARIANT B

⟨i⟩-⟨xvi⟩, ⟨17⟩-126, blank leaf. $4\frac{1}{2}''$ × $3''$.

The dedication is on ⟨1⟩$_{8r}$; conjugate ⟨1⟩$_1$ is a blank.

It will be observed that the variation in the position of the dedication may have been caused at the bindery rather than at press.

The ornament on the sides is a decoration about $\frac{3}{4}''$ high of a book and musical instruments. Edges plain; or, gilt.

Noted as *soon* USDR Nov. 1845. Noted as *just published* USDR Dec. 1845.

AAS (A)   B (B)   LC (B)   NYHS (A)   Y (A,B)

14371. The Opal: A Pure Gift for the Holy Days. MDCCCXLVIII. Edited by Mrs. Sarah J. Hale.

New York: J. C. Riker, 129 Fulton Street. 1848.

"Walter Gay," pp. ⟨235⟩-236. Collected in *The Deserted Bride*, 1853.

For fuller entry see No. 1030.

14372. Golden Leaflets: A Selection of Poetry . . . Edited by J. M. Fletcher . . .

Boston: Published by J. Buffum. ⟨1848⟩

"Poetry," p. 92. Collected in *The Deserted Bride*, 1853. For prior publication as sheet music see *Poetry*, 1846.

CH

14373. Report of the Proceedings of the Joint Committee Appointed to Make Suitable Arrangements for Bringing on the Bodies of the Officers of the New York Regiment of Volunteers, from Mexico . . . Presented October 2d, 1848.

New York: McSpedon & Baker, Printers to the Common Council, 25 Pine St. 1848.

"The Ode: Prepared for the Occasion . . . ," pp. 47-48. Collected in *The Deserted Bride*, 1853, as "The Fallen Brave."

B

14374. The Opal: A Pure Gift for All Seasons. Edited by Mrs. Sarah Josepha Hale.

New-York: J. C. Riker, 129 Fulton Street. 1849.

"Rhyme of the Ancient Troubadour. A Legend Balladized," pp. ⟨29⟩-30. Collected in *The Deserted Bride*, 1853, as "Song of the Troubadour."

For fuller entry see No. 6866.

14375. Voices from the Press; a Collection of Sketches, Essays, and Poems, by Practical Printers. Edited by James J. Brenton.

New-York: Charles B. Norton, 71 Chambers-Street, (Irving House.) 1850.

Reprint save for "The Human Voice," p. 63; uncollected.

Listed LW Jan. 19, 1850.

H

14376. The Immortal; a Dramatic Romance; and Other Poems. By James Nack. With a Memoir of the Author, by George P. Morris.

New York: Stringer and Townsend, 222 Broadway. 1850.

"Memoir of James Nack," pp. ⟨1⟩-7.

Deposited Oct. 18, 1850.

AAS   B   BPL   H   LC   Y

14377. The Memorial: Written by Friends of the Late Mrs. Osgood and Edited by Mary E. Hewitt . . .

New-York: George P. Putnam, 155 Broadway. 1851.

"Song," *Fare thee well, love———we must sever . . . ,* p. 274. Collected in *The Deserted Bride*, 1853.

The vignette title-page occurs with the date *1851;* and, with some evidence of reengraving, *1852.*

For further comment see entry No. 1187.

14378. History of the Issues of Paper-Money in the American Colonies, Anterior to the Revolution, Explanatory of the Historical Chart of the Paper Money of That Period.

St. Louis: Union, Print, 35 Locust Street, 1851.

Printed paper wrapper. Anonymous. By Adolphus M. Hart.

Three-line comment, p. ⟨3⟩, signed: *Messrs. Morris & Willis.*

AAS

14379. The Odd-Fellows' Offering, for 1852 . . .

New York: Published by Edward Walker, 114 Fulton-Street. M DCCC LII.

Leather.

"Lord of the Castle," p. 170. Collected in *The Deserted Bride*, 1853.

H

14380. "The Soldier's Welcome Home"

For prior publication as sheet music see "The Soldiers Return," 1848.

Collected in *The Deserted Bride*, 1853.

The above poem has been noted in the following two publications; sequence not known.

... Life and Services of General Winfield Scott ... by Edward D. Mansfield ...

New York: Published by A. S. Barnes & Co. ... 1852.

At head of title: *The Only Authentic Edition.*

"The Soldier's Welcome Home," pp. 503-504.

Location: H

Scott and Graham Melodies; Being a Collection of Campaign Songs for 1852. As Sung by the Whig Clubs throughout the United States.

Published by Huestis & Cozans, 104 & 106 Nassau-Street. New York. ⟨n.d., 1852⟩

Printed paper wrapper.

The poem is here titled "Welcome Home" and appears on pp. 5-6.

Location: H

14381. The Odd-Fellows' Offering, for 1854 ...

New York: Edward Walker, 114 Fulton-Street. M DCCC LIV. ⟨*i.e.,* 1853⟩

"Lines on the Burial of Mrs. Mary L. Ward ... ," p. 198. Collected in *The Deserted Bride*, 1853 (Nov.); see next entry.

Deposited Oct. 18, 1853.

NYPL

14382. THE DESERTED BRIDE, AND OTHER PRODUCTIONS ...

NEW YORK: CHARLES SCRIBNER, 145 NASSAU ST. 1853.

Contains 114 poems; "The Maid of Saxony," see above under 1842; and, notes. For other editions see under 1838, 1843.

⟨1⟩-365. Frontispiece, vignette title-page, and 11 plates inserted. 9″ full × 5¹⁵⁄₁₆″ full.

⟨1⟩-30⁶, ⟨31⟩², ⟨32⟩¹.

A cloth: blue; red. T cloth: red. Cream-coated end papers; yellow-coated end papers. Flyleaves. Edges gilt. Also issued in morocco according to listing in NLG Nov. 1853.

Two bindings, presumably simultaneous, noted:

GILT

The ornamental frame on the sides is stamped in blind.

EXTRA GILT

The ornamental frame on the sides is stamped in gold.

Noticed LW Nov. 5, 1853. Listed NLG Nov. 1853.

AAS H NYHS NYPL Y

14383. Book of Words of the Hutchinson Family.

New York: Baker Godwin & Co., Printers, Tribune Buildings, Cor. Nassau and Spruce-Sts. 1853.

Printed paper wrapper.

"Riding in a Stage," p. 55. Elsewhere unlocated.

H

The Odd-Fellows' Offering, for 1854 ...

New York ... M DCCC LIV.

See above under year 1853.

14384. The Knickerbocker Gallery: A Testimonial to the Editor of the Knickerbocker Magazine from Its Contributors ...

New-York: Samuel Hueston, 348 Broadway. MDCCCLV.

Edited by Morris and others; see p. xiv.

"Jeannie Marsh of Cherry Valley," p. ⟨209⟩. For publication as sheet music see *Jeannie Marsh of Cherry Valley*, 1855. Collected in *Poems*, 1860.

For fuller entry see No. 1033.

14385. An Appeal to the People of the United States in Behalf of Lamartine ...

⟨New York: D. Appleton & Co., 1856⟩

Signed by Morris and others.

For fuller entry see No. 10193.

14386. ... The (Old) Farmer's Almanack ... for the Year of Our Lord 1857 ... by Robert B. Thomas ...

Boston: Published by Hickling, Swan & Brown ... 1856 ...

Printed paper wrapper. At head of title: *Number Sixty-Five.*

"Our Land and Flag," p. 39. Otherwise unlocated. Extract?

H NYPL

14387. Wheeler & Wilson M'f'g' Co's Sewing Machines.

Office 343 Broadway, N. Y. ⟨n.d., not before 1856⟩

Cover-title. Printed paper wrapper.

"Song of the Sewing Machine" on the inner front wrapper. Here reprinted?

For publication as sheet music see *Song of the Sewing Machine*, n.d., *ca.* 1860. Collected in *Poems*, 1860. See *The American Reader* . . . , below under year 1860.

B

14388. Memorial of Jessie Willis: Prepared for Her Little Daughters, Annie, Blanche and Jessie, by Their Father.

New York: April, 1858. [For Private Circulation.] John F. Trow, Printer, 377 & 379 Broadway.

"Lines on the Death of Mrs. Jessie Willis," p. 26. Collected in *Poems*, 1860.

H   NYPL

14389. Gifts of Genius: A Miscellany of Prose and Poetry, by American Authors.

New York: Printed for C. A. Davenport. ⟨1859⟩

"Words for Music," pp. 191-192. Collected in *Poems*, 1860, as "The Sycamore Shade."

For comment see entry No. 3717.

14390. Poems . . . with a Memoir of the Author ⟨by Horace Binney Wallace⟩.

New York: Charles Scribner, 124 Grand Street. ⟨1860⟩

Contains thirty poems here first collected.

In all examined copies p. 229 is mispaged 329.

Advertised for Oct. 10 BM Sept. 15, 1859. Advertised for Sept. 1 BM Aug. 15, 1860. Deposited Sept. 7, 1860. Listed BM Sept. 15, 1860; PC Oct. 16, 1860. The tenth printing advertised BM Nov. 15, 1860.

AAS   H   LC

14391. The Campaign of 1860. Republican Songs for the People, Original and Selected . . . Compiled by Thomas Drew . . .

Boston: Published by Thayer & Eldredge. 1860.

Printed paper wrapper.

"Union," pp. 36-37. Also in (reprinted from?) *Poems*, 1860.

Issued after May, 1860.

H

14392. The American Reader of Prose and Poetry. Designed for the Academies and Schools of America . . . by Augustus DeKalb Tarr . . .

Philadelphia: Published by the Author. 1860.

Cloth, leather shelf back.

"The Sewing Machine," pp. 161-162. *Here reprinted?* For other appearances see in *Section Two*, below, *Song of the Sewing Machine*, n.d., *ca.* 1860. Also see above: *Wheeler & Wilson M'f'g' Co's Sewing Machines*, New York, n.d., not before 1856. Collected in *Poems*, 1860.

B

14393. The Poetical Works of Samuel Woodworth. Edited by His Son ⟨Frederick A. Woodworth⟩. In Two Volumes . . .

New York: Charles Scribner, Grand Street. 1861.

"Introductory Notice . . . Prepared from Various Sources," Vol. 1, pp. ⟨11⟩-30.

Title-page deposited July 13, 1860. Listed APC April 6, 1861; PC May 1, 1861.

H   NYHS   Y

14394. The Rebellion Record: A Diary of American Events . . . Edited by Frank Moore . . . First Volume . . .

New York: G. P. Putnam. C. T. Evans, General Agent. 1861.

"The Union, Right or Wrong. A Song for the Volunteers," p. 86. Uncollected. For publication in handbill form see *Our Union, Right or Wrong* in *Section Two*.

For comment see No. 11531.

14395. Poetical Pen-Pictures of the War: Selected from Our Union Poets. By J. Henry Hayward . . .

New York: Published by the Editor. 13 Park Row. 1863.

"The Refugees," pp. 388-389. Otherwise unlocated.

For comment see entry No. 1037.

14396. Actors and Actresses of Great Britain and the United States . . . Edited by Brander Matthews and Laurence Hutton . . . ⟨Vol. 3⟩ Kean and Booth; and Their Contemporaries

Cassell & Company, Limited 739 & 741 Broadway, New York ⟨1886⟩

Poem on Henry Placide, p. 144.

Listed PW Oct. 2, 1886.

For a comment see entry No. 1904.

14397. ... The Magazine of History ... Extra Number---No. 194. A Sketch of the Olden Time ... ⟨and⟩ Briar Cliff or Scenes of the Revolution ⟨by⟩ George P. Morris

New York, N.Y. Reprinted William Abbatt 1935 ...

Printed paper wrapper. At head of title: *Vol. 49 No. 2*

"Briar Cliff," pp. ⟨71⟩-101. "... It was never printed, although as a play it was quite successful."---P. ⟨47⟩.

B H NYPL

SECTION II

Sheet music, handbills, and like material. Arranged alphabetically by title. Obvious reprints (*i.e.*, because of date) are here ignored. Also ignored are all undated British printings. For a comment on the problem of sheet music, and British sheet music in particular, see BAL, Vol. 5, p. 617.

Publications issued prior to collection are set in capital letters. Publications reprinted from the author's books are set in capital and lower case letters.

Song books are listed in *Section One*.

14398. AN ADDRESS, SPOKEN BY MRS. SHARPE, AT THE PARK THEATRE, ON THE EVENING OF THE DRAMATIC FESTIVAL IN HONOR OF WILLIAM DUNLAP, ESQ. WRITTEN BY GEORGE P. MORRIS ...

⟨n.p., n.d., NEW YORK, 1833?⟩

Single leaf. Printed on recto only. $9\frac{3}{8}$″ × $5\frac{7}{16}$″. Collected in *The Deserted Bride*, 1838, as "Address for the Dunlap Benefit."

B

14399. ... THE AMERICAN STANDARD ... MUSIC ... BY A. BAGIOLI ...

NEW YORK ... FIRTH, POND & CO. 547 BROADWAY ... 1862 ...

Sheet music. Cover-title. At head of title: *Dedicated to the Army of the Union*.

Plate number 5268. Elsewhere unlocated.

B

14400. ANNA ⟨ANNIE⟩ OF THE VALE

⟨n.d.⟩

Noted in the following forms. No sequence has been established and the designations are for identification only. Uncollected.

A

Anna of the Vale ...

⟨n.p., n.d.⟩

Single leaf. Printed on recto only. 8″ scant × $4\frac{7}{8}$″ full. Text enclosed by an ornate frame. Anonymous.

B

B

... Annie of the Vale. The Music ... Published by Firth, Pond & Co., No. 547 Broadway, N. Y. ...

A. W. Auner's Card and Job Printing Rooms, Tenth and Race Streets, Philadelphia, Pa. ... ⟨n.d.⟩

Single leaf. Printed on recto only. $7\frac{5}{8}$″ full × $4\frac{9}{16}$″. Anonymous. At head: *A. W. Auner* ...

B

C

Annie of the Vale ... Music by J. R. Thomas, to Be Had at Firth, Pond and Co. 547 Broadway ...

H. De Marsan, Publisher, 60 Chatham Street, New-York. ⟨n.d., not before 1864⟩

Single leaf. Printed on recto only. $10\frac{1}{8}$″ × $6\frac{5}{8}$″.

B   HEH

D

Annie of the Vale ... Music by J. R. Thomas. The Music to be Had at Firth, Pond & Co. 547 Broadway ...

H. De Marsan ... No. 54 Chatham, N. Y. ⟨n.d., not before 1861⟩

Single leaf. Printed on recto only. $10\frac{1}{16}$″ × $6\frac{3}{8}$″.

B

E

Annie of the Vale ... Music by J. R. Thomas. The Music to be Had at Firth, Pond & Co. 547 Broadway ...

H. De Marsan. Dealer in Songs, Toy Books &c. No. 54 Chatham St. N. Y. ⟨n.d., 186-?⟩

Single leaf. Printed on recto only. $9\frac{13}{16}$″ × $6\frac{3}{16}$″.

B

F

Annie of the Vale, Solo & Chorus ... Music by J. R. Thomas ...

Richmond, Va. ... Geo. Dunn & Company, P. O. Box 991 Columbia, S. C. Julian A. Selby. ⟨n.d.⟩

Sheet music. Cover-title.

BA

G

Annie of the Vale . . . Music by J. R. Thomas . . .

New-York . . . Firth, Pond & Co., 547 Broadway . . . 1861 . . .

Sheet music. Cover-title. Plate number: 5148.

The earliest printings do not note arrangement for the guitar on the front cover. Known reprints were printed from plates lacking the plate number. Reprinted and reissued by William A. Pond & Co.

B

H

. . . Annie of the Vale. Printed by Permission of Firth, Pond & Co., Music Publishers, No. 547 Broadway, N. Y., Owners of the Copyright . . .

Firth, Pond & Co. . . . No. 547 Broadway, New York. A. W. Auner, Song Publisher, 110 North 10th St., ab., Arch, Philadelphia. ⟨n.d.⟩

Single leaf. Printed on recto only. $8\frac{7}{8}''$ full × $5\frac{13}{16}''$ full.

At head: *Auner's Printing Office* . . . Anonymous.

B

I

Annie of the Vale. The Music for This Beautiful Song is Published by Firth, Pond & Co., No. 547 Broadway, New York. Send Them 25 Cents and They Will Send You the Music by Return of Mail . . .

⟨n.p., n.d.⟩

Single leaf. Printed on recto only. $6\frac{5}{8}''$ full × 5″.

Decorated with seated female figure. Anonymous.

Note: Possibly an incomplete copy, with the imprint trimmed off. At bottom is the vestige of a wavy rule.

B

J

Annie of the Vale . . .

. . . Charles Magnus, No. 12 Frankfort Street, New York . . . ⟨n.d.⟩

Single leaf. Printed in blue on recto only. At head, in hand-colored lithograph: Portrait of Annie, captioned: *Published by Chs. Magnus, 12 Frankfort St. N.Y.* $7\frac{15}{16}''$ full × $4\frac{15}{16}''$ full. Anonymous.

Laid paper; stationer's embossed seal at lower left: *Pierce ⟨Venice?⟩ Mills* Paper ruled lightly in blue.

B

K

. . . Annie of the Vale . . . Music by J. R. Thomas. Music to be Had at Firth, Pond & Co.'s, 547 Broadway . . .

. . . Horace Partridge . . . No. 27 Hanover Street, Boston. ⟨n.d.⟩

Single leaf. Printed on recto only. At head of title: *522*

$8\frac{7}{16}''$ scant × $6\frac{1}{4}''$.

B

L

. . . Annie. Of the Vale . . .

. . . Horace Partridge . . . 27 Hanover Street, Boston. ⟨n.d.⟩

Single leaf. Printed on recto only. $8\frac{1}{8}''$ × $5\frac{9}{16}''$.

Anonymous. At head of title: *522*

B

14401. . . . ANSWER TO WAIT FOR THE WAGON . . . ARRANGED BY W. WALLACE.

. . . LOUISVILLE   G. W. BRAINARD & CO. 117 FOURTH STREET . . . CLEVELAND S. BRAINARD & CO. OLIVER DITSON BOSTON . . . ⟨1852⟩

Sheet music. Cover-title. At head of title: *A Son Ami Joseph Benedict.* Plate number 572-5. Elsewhere unlocated.

AAS

14402. AU REVOIR. MUSIC BY CHARLES E. HORN.

NEW YORK: JAMES L. HEWITT & CO.

Not seen. Entry based on information taken from *The Songs and Ballads,* 1844. The poem appears also in *The Deserted Bride,* 1843. Further information wanting.

14403. The Ball-Room Belle. Music by Charles E. Horn.

New York: Samuel C. Jollie.

Not seen. Entry based on information taken from *The Songs and Ballads,* 1844. The poem also appears in *The Deserted Bride,* 1843. For another setting see *The Moon and All Her Starry Train,* sheet music, 1839. Further information wanting.

14404. THE BATTLE OF LIBERTY! A PATRIOTIC SONG & CHORUS . . . MUSIC BY RICH. CULVER

PHILADELPHIA: LEE & WALKER, NO. 722 CHESTNUT STREET. ⟨1862⟩

Sheet music. Cover-title. Plate number 8744.5. Uncollected.

B   BA

14405. The Beam of Devotion. Music by George Loder.

Boston: William H. Oakes.

Not seen. Entry based on information taken from *The Songs and Ballads*, 1844. The poem also appears in *The Deserted Bride*, 1843.

Further information wanting. Probably a reference to *The Spirit of Beauty*, issued by Oakes, 1842; see below.

14406. BURRIED ⟨sic⟩ FAITH . . . MUSIC . . . BY CHARLES E. HORN . . .

NEW YORK   PUBLISHED BY JAMES L. HEWITT & CO 239 BROADWAY ⟨n.d., 1836–1843⟩

Sheet music. Cover-title. Also in *The Deserted Bride*, 1838, as "Silent Grief."

B

14407. . . . The Carrier Dove   A Lay of the Minstrel . . . Composed for Mrs. Emma Gillingham Bostwick by Wm. Vincent Wallace . . .

New York . . . Wm. Hall & Son 239 Broadway . . . 1852 . . .

Sheet music. Cover-title. Plate number: 1863. At head of title: *To Miss Louisa Pyne.* Reprinted from *The Deserted Bride*, 1843.

AAS

14408. THE CARRIERS OF THE NEW-YORK MIRROR, TO THEIR PATRONS, ON THE FIRST OF JANUARY, 1834 . . .

PRINTED BY GEORGE P. SCOTT & CO. CORNER OF NASSAU AND ANN STREETS, NEW-YORK. ⟨Jan. 1, 1834⟩

Single cut sheet. Printed on recto only. 13$^{11}/_{16}$″ × 10$^{5}/_{16}$″. Anonymous. Attributed to Morris. Elsewhere unlocated.

Y

The Celebrated Croton Ode . . .

See *The Croton Ode*, below.

14409. Celebration at Portsmouth, N. H., of the 100th Anniversary of the Initiation of Washington   November 4, A. L. 5852. Order of Exercises . . .

Morning Chronicle Job Printing Office. ⟨1852⟩

Single leaf. Laid paper. 9$^{13}/_{16}$″ × 7$^{13}/_{16}$″. Printed on recto only. Issued as a program. Contains "Masonic Ode." For prior publication as sheet music see *Our Order*, 1844, in *Section Two*, below. Collected in *The Deserted Bride*, 1853.

AAS

14410. Cheerly oer the Mountains . . . Music Arranged . . . by George Loder . . .

Atwill, Publisher, 201 Broadway, New York . . . 1844 . . .

Sheet music. Cover-title, Deposited March 30, 1844. Reprinted from *Songs and Ballads*, 1844 (Jan.), where the poem appears as "Oer the Mountains." Title, p. 3: *O'er the Mountains.*

AAS   B   BPL   H   LC

14411. THE CHIEFTAIN'S DAUGHTER . . . MUSIC . . . BY HENRY RUSSELL.

NEW YORK, PUBLISHED BY FIRTH & HALL, NO. 1, FRANKLIN-SQUARE . . . 1841 . . .

Sheet music. Cover-title. Also in (reprinted from?) *The Poets of America* . . . , 1842 (Dec. 1841). Collected in *The Deserted Bride*, 1843.

NYPL

14412. CLEAR THE TRACK! AS SUNG BY THE DEMOCRATIC CLUBS. A SERIOUS SONG AND CHORUS, IN WHICH ALL GOOD DEMOCRATS WILL UNITE . . .

⟨n.p., n.d., 1856⟩

Single cut sheet. Printed on recto only. Blue-gray laid paper. 8$^{3}/_{8}$″ scant × 5$^{3}/_{8}$″.

Anonymous. Credited to Morris by Yale. Otherwise unlocated.

Y

14413. THE COLONEL, A BALLAD . . . MUSIC BY AUSTIN PHILLIPS.

BOSTON. PUBLISHED BY PRENTISS JOYS BUILDING 81 WASHINGTON ST. . . . 1841 . . .

Sheet music. Cover-title. Plate number: 4. Collected in *The Deserted Bride*, 1843.

B   NYPL

14414. COME, COME TO ME LOVE . . . MELODY BY CHARLES E. HORN . . .

NEW YORK   PUBLISHED BY FIRTH & HALL   1 FRANKLIN SQ., JAMES L. HEWITT & CO. 239 BROADWAY ⟨n.d., ca. 1835–1840⟩

Sheet music. The above at head of first page of text and music. Plate number: 160. Also occurs with plate number 2; sequence not determined.

Collected in *The Deserted Bride*, 1843, as "Venetian Serenade."

For another printing see *Venetian Serenade*, 1839; sequence not determined.

B

14415. COME TO ME IN CHERRY TIME ... COMPOSED ... BY MRS. F. H. HUN-SICKER.

NEW YORK. PUBLISHED BY S. T. GORDON, 706 BROADWAY ... 1859 ...

Sheet music. Cover-title. Collected in *Poems*, 1860.

Note: The copyright notice is in the name of Beck & Lawton; did they issue this publication prior to S. T. Gordon?

AAS

14416. THE COOPER BENEFIT. ADDRESS TO THE PUBLIC.

NEW YORK, 1833.

Not seen. Not located. Broadside. 12¼″ × 7¾″. Entry on the basis of a letter received from the late Oscar Wegelin, March 31, 1945.

An open letter addressed to the "ladies and gentlemen of the theatrical profession" asking them to appear for Thomas Abthorpe Cooper's benefit at the Bowery Theatre, New York, Nov. 7, 1833. Signed by Morris, Henry Ogden and William T. McCoun.

14417. ... THE COT NEAR THE WOOD ... MUSIC ... BY SIGNOR DE BEGNIS

NEW YORK ... FIRTH & HALL, NO. I FRANKLIN SQUARE ... 1842 ...

Sheet music. Cover-title. At head of title: *Pr. 25 Cts. Nett.* Deposited Aug. 24, 1842. Collected in *The Deserted Bride*, 1843.

AAS   LC   NYPL

14418. THE CROTON ODE: WRITTEN AT THE REQUEST OF THE CORPORATION OF THE CITY OF NEW-YORK ... AND SUNG IN FRONT OF THE PARK FOUN-TAIN, BY THE MEMBERS OF THE N. Y. SACRED MUSIC SOCIETY, ON THE COMPLETION OF THE CROTON AQUE-DUCT ... OCTOBER 14th, 1842 ...

THIS ODE WAS PRINTED DURING THE PROGRESS OF THE PROCESSION, UPON A PRESS ERECTED ON A MOVEABLE STAGE. NESBITT, PRINTER. ⟨NEW YORK, 1842⟩

Single sheet. Printed on recto only. 13⁹⁄₁₆″ × 5³⁄₈″. Collected in *The Deserted Bride*, 1843.

"At the head of the Typographical Society was a most interesting relic ... It was the press on which Franklin ... worked. Col. Stone ... pre-sided over the typographical performances ... Copies of the Ode of Gen. Morris were worked off and distributed through the crowd as the pro-cession moved along the street."---*New York Weekly Tribune*, Oct. 22, 1842.

It seems unlikely that an antique press, operated on a moving platform, could have produced a sufficiently large quantity of the hand-bills for distribution. It is probable that copies were printed prior to the procession and were tossed from the moving wagon together with copies produced in sight of the crowd.

Printed from three settings. Sequence, if any, has not been determined and the designations are wholly arbitrary.

SETTING A

Penultimate line of text: *When Posterity* ... ⟨note the capital P⟩ Printer's imprint: ... *erected on* / *a* ...

Text enclosed by a chain-like frame, each "link" enclosing an asterisk-like floret.

Location: NYPL

SETTING B

Penultimate line of text: *When Posterity* ... ⟨note the capital P⟩ Printer's imprint: ... *erected on a* / *moveable* ...

Text enclosed by an ornate frame; at each corner a small unit consisting of a cannon and two flags.

Location: H

SETTING C

Penultimate line of text: *When posterity* ... ⟨note the lower case p⟩

Printer's imprint: ... *erected on a* / *moveable* ...

Text enclosed by an ornate frame; at each corner a small unit consisting of a cannon and two flags.

Location: B

Also issued as sheet music:

THE CELEBRATED CROTON ODE WRITTEN AT THE REQUEST OF THE CORPORATION OF THE CITY OF NEW YORK BY GEORGE P. MORRIS, ESQ, AND SUNG IN FRONT OF THE PARK FOUNTAIN BY MRS. STRONG, MISS J. PEARSON, MR. J. PEARSON, AND THE MEMBERS OF THE NEW YORK SACRED MUSIC SOCIETY, ON THE COMPLETION OF THE CROTON AQUE-DUCT, OCT. 14, 1842. THE MUSIC ... ADAPTED FROM ROSSINI'S OPERA OF AMIDA BY SIDNEY PEARSON.

ATWILL, PUBLISHER 201 BROADWAY NEW YORK. ⟨1842⟩

The above at head of first page of text and music. Issued on both white, and on blue, papers.

Location: H

14419. Day Is Now Dawning, Love. A Popular Duett . . . Music . . . by Austin Phillips . . .

New York Atwill, Publisher, 201, Broadway . . . 1840 . . .

Sheet music. Cover-title. Reprinted from *The Deserted Bride*, 1838.

AAS   Y

14420. The Deserted Bride . . . Composed by M. W. Balfe.

New York Published by Wm. Hall & Son 239 Broadway . . . ⟨n.d., *ca.* 1850⟩

Sheet music. Cover-title. Plate number: 4274. Reprinted from *The Deserted Bride*, 1838.

EM

14421. The Dismissed . . . Music by Henry Russell . . .

New York . . . Firth & Hall, No. 1, Franklin Square. ⟨1841⟩

Sheet music. Cover-title. No plate number. Reprinted from *The Deserted Bride*, 1838. Also in *The Atlantic Club-Book*, 1834.

Contains a refrain that does not appear in the collected version. The refrain (*I suppose she was right in rejecting my prayers, But why tell me why did she kick me downstairs*) is only in part original and is derived of Kemble, Debrett or Bickerstaffe.

As above deposited for copyright Jan. 26, 1842. Another printing, presumed later, occurs with plate number *305* and a somewhat varying imprint.

B (without plate number)   H (with plate number) LC (without plate number, being a deposit copy) NYPL (with plate number)

14422. DOWN BY THE RIVER SIDE I STRAY. BALLAD . . . MUSIC . . . BY J. R. THOMAS . . .

NEW YORK   PUBLISHED BY FIRTH, POND & CO 547 BROADWAY . . . 1861 . . .

Sheet music. Cover-title. Plate number: 5132. Uncollected.

The following reprints (in H):

Reprint A: Publisher's imprint: *New York: Firth, Son & Co., 563 Broadway* Issued not before 1863.

Reprint B: Publisher's imprint: *Oliver Ditson & Co., 277 Washington Street* Issued not after 1876. Two printings with this imprint have been seen. In all likelihood the earlier of the two is the one issued with pictorial lithographed cover; the later issue has a typographic cover.

Reprint C: Publisher's imprint: *Oliver Ditson & Co., 451 Washington Street.* Issued not before 1877.

See next entry.

B   H   Y

14423. . . . DOWN BY THE RIVER SIDE. WHERE WATER-LILIES GROW . . . MUSIC BY HERM. TH. KNAKE. WORDS AND MUSIC OF THIS SONG WILL BE SENT POSTPAID TO ANY ADDRESS ON RECEIPT OF 30 CTS., IN STAMPS . . .

A. W. AUNER'S CARD AND JOB PRINTING ROOMS TENTH AND RACE STS., PHILADELPHIA, PA. ⟨n.d., not before 1862?⟩

At head: *A. W. Auner* . . .

Single leaf. Printed on recto only. $7^{13}/_{16}$″ × $4^{1}/_{2}$″. Uncollected. Also issued as sheet music; see preceding entry.

B

14424. THE EVERGREEN . . . MUSIC COMPOSED . . . BY ELIZA MARTYN . . .

NEW-YORK. PUBLISHED BY FIRTH & HALL, I FRANKLIN SQR. . . . 1840 . . .

Sheet music. Cover-title. Deposited Nov. 4, 1840. Collected in *The Deserted Bride*, 1843.

LC   NYPL

14425. The Exile to His Sister, Ballad . . . Composed . . . by W. V. Wallace . . .

New York Published by William Hall & Son, 239 Broadway. London . . . Paris . . . Vienna . . . St Petersburg . . . 1851 . . .

Sheet music. Cover-title. Plate number: 969. Reprinted from *The Deserted Bride*, 1843.

B   NYPL

14426. The Family Bible . . . Music . . . by Miss Augusta Browne . . .

Boston Published by W. H. Oakes & for Sale by E. H. Wade 197 Washington St . . . 1846 . . .

Sheet music. Cover-title. Plate number: 202.5. Deposited Feb. 19, 1847. Reprinted from *The Deserted Bride*, 1843, where the poem appears under the title "My Mother's Bible."

Also noted: A setting by T. Richard, Boston: Oliver Ditson ⟨n.d.⟩. Presumed to be a reprint of an English issue. The earliest noted printing has the publisher's address: *135 Washington St., Boston;* the later printing: *115 Washington St., Boston.*

For an earlier setting see *My Mother's Bible,* below.

AAS H LC

14427. FAREWELL

1859

Two printings of unknown sequence noted. The order of presentation is completely arbitrary.

Collected in *Poems,* 1860, as "We Part Forever."

A

... FAREWELL FOREVER ... FROM THE NEW YORK LEDGER MUSIC BY DR. J. HAYNES ...

BOSTON ... OLIVER DITSON & CO 277 WASHINGTON ST ... 1859 ...

Sheet music. Cover-title. At head of title: *To Mrs. J. H. Long.*

Plate number: 19450.

B

B

FAREWELL, WE PART FOREVER ... FROM THE NEW YORK LEDGER AND PUBLISHED BY PERMISSION MUSIC BY J. B. LIVINGSTON ...

BOSTON PUBLISHED BY OLIVER DITSON & CO 277 WASHINGTON ST ... 1859 ...

Sheet music. Cover-title. Plate number: 19724.

B H

14428. THE FLAG OF OUR UNION

1851

Noted in the following forms. The sequence of A and B is uncertain; printings C and D are almost certainly later. Collected in *The Deserted Bride,* 1853.

A

THE FLAG OF OUR UNION A NATIONAL SONG ... MUSIC BY WM. VINCENT WALLACE ...

NEW JORK ⟨*sic*⟩. PUBLISHED BY WM. HALL & SON 239, BROADWAY. NEW ORLEANS W. I. MAYO. ⟨1851⟩

Sheet music. Cover-title. Plate number: 1022.

Three printings noted:

FIRST PRINTING

Pictorial front cover. Lithograph (on front cover) carries a copyright notice dated 1851. Plate number 1022.

SECOND PRINTING

Lettered (lithographic) front cover: *The Popular Compositions of Wm. Vincent Wallace* ... ⟨*8 numbered titles*⟩ Plate number: 1072.

THIRD PRINTING

Printed from new plates. Publisher's address in the imprint: *543 Broadway.* No plate number.

AAS (2nd) B (1st, 2nd, 3rd)

B

FROM THE HOME JOURNAL. THE FLAG OF OUR UNION ...

⟨n.p., n.d., 1851?⟩

Single cut sheet. Blue-gray wove paper. Printed on recto only. $8\frac{1}{2}'' \times 5\frac{3}{8}''$.

Y

C

... Flag of Our Union for Ever ...

⟨At head:⟩ Johnson, Song Publisher, No. 7 N. 10th St. Phila. ⟨n.d., probably 1858 or later⟩

Single cut sheet. $9\frac{7}{8}'' \times 5\frac{13}{16}''$. Printed on recto only.

B NYPL

D

The Flag of Our Union ...

... Charles Magnus, No. 12 Frankfort Street, New York ... ⟨n.d., not before 1854⟩

Single cut sheet. $8\frac{3}{16}'' \times 5\frac{1}{16}''$. Printed in blue on recto only on lightly ruled note paper. At head, in colors, female figures, American flag lettered *For the Union;* seal of Connecticut. Probably issued during the Civil War. Anonymous.

B

14429. A Fragrant Rose There Grew. Sung by Mr. Keene. Written by George Pope Morris. Composed by W. Blondell.

New York: Thomas Birch, 235 Chapel, near Canal Street, 1824.

Not located. Not seen. Entry on the basis of a notice in NYM Dec. 11, 1824.

Freedom Spreads Her Downy Wings ...

New York ... ⟨n.d.⟩

See below: *God Has Made Us Free!*

14430. GEN. SIEGEL'S CELEBRATED CAMP SONG. WRITTEN BY J. ⟨*sic*⟩ P. MORRIS. MUSIC COMPOSED . . . BY DAVID A. WARDEN.

ENTERED . . . 1862, BY DAVID A. WARDEN . . . EASTERN DISTRICT OF PENNSYLVANIA . . .

Presumably by George Pope Morris. Elsewhere unlocated.

Single leaf. The only copy located has been trimmed and measures 7⅞″ × 4¹⁵⁄₁₆″. Presumably printed on recto only.

Hark! the loud reveille of the artillery / *Echoes in answering shouts from the hills* . . .

Issued as an advertisement for the unlocated sheet music.

H

14431. God Has Made Us Free . . .

1840

For prior printing see "Anniversary Hymn," *The Deserted Bride*, 1838.

Noted in the following forms. Sequence not known; the designations are all but wholly arbitrary.

A

God Has Made Us Free, a National Anthem . . . Music . . . by C. E. Horn . . .

New York . . . C. E. Horn No. 367 Broadway . . . 1840 . . .

Sheet music. Cover-title. Deposited Jan. 7, 1841.

LC

B

God Has Made Us Free! A National Anthem . . . Music Composed . . . by Charles E. Horn . . .

C. E. Horn, 367 Broadway. ⟨n.d., 1840⟩

Single leaf. Text only; music not present. Printed on recto only. 7¹³⁄₁₆″ × 4¹⁵⁄₁₆″ scant. Issued as an advertisement for the sheet music; see above.

EM

C

Freedom Spreads Her Downy Wings, an Anniversary Hymn . . . Arranged with Accompaniment to a Celebrated Cossack Melody and Sung on the Last National Jubilee by Charles E. Horn.

New York Firth & Hall 1 Franklin Sq. ⟨n.d., 1832–1847⟩

Sheet music. The above at head of p. ⟨1⟩. Plate number 3.

AAS

14432. Going o'er the Mountains . . .

1844? 1847?

Sheet music. *Not located*. See *Cheerly oer the Mountains*, 1844; and, *Merrily o'er the Mountains*, 1847.

14433. The Heart that Owns Thy Tyrant Sway.

1845?

Sheet music. *Not seen*. Entry on the basis of information in *Morris's Melodies*, 1845.

14434. The Hours We Dedicate to Thee . . . Music . . . by Joseph Phillip Knight . . .

New York . . . C. Holt Jr.'s Music Store 156 Fulton St. . . . 1847 . . .

Sheet music. Cover-title. Otherwise "The Star of Love," *Songs and Ballads*, 1844.

AAS

14435. The Hunter's Life . . . Composed by Arthur Henshaw . . .

Boston . . . G. D. Russell . . . ⟨1879⟩

Sheet music. Cover-title. Otherwise "The Hunter's Carol," *The Deserted Bride*, 1853. For an earlier setting see *A Life in the Woods* . . . , 1841.

AAS

14436. I LOVE THE NIGHT. AN ORIGINAL SONG AS SUNG BY MRS. BAILEY, LATE MISS WATSON . . . MUSICK . . . BY HENRY RUSSELL . . .

ENTERED . . . 1837, BY CHARLES M'DEVITT . . . NEW-YORK.

Sheet music. Single sheet. Printed on recto only. 13¼″ × 10⅜″. Collected in *The Deserted Bride*, 1838.

Reprints noted:

New York: Firth & Hall ⟨1837⟩. In the earlier of these reprints the text reads: *I love the night when the moon streams bright;* in later reprints the word *streams* is altered to *beams*. Copies in B.

New York: Firth Pond & Co., No. 1 Franklin Sq. ⟨1837⟩. Copy in AAS.

B LC

14437. I Love Thee Still . . . ⟨Music⟩ by Theodore T. Barker.

Boston . . . G. P. Reed 17 Tremont Row . . . 1843

Sheet music. Cover-title. Plate number: 325. Reprint. For an earlier printing see next entry.

AAS B

14438. I NEVER HAVE BEEN FALSE TO THEE . . .

BOSTON. PUBLISHED BY HENRY PRENTISS, 33 COURT ST. . . . 1842 . . .

Sheet music. Cover-title. Pagination: ⟨1⟩-6, blank leaf. Plate number: 200. Music by Charles E. Horn. Collected in *The Deserted Bride*, 1843.

Two states noted; sequence undetermined. The designations are for identification only.

A: Front cover printed in black and buff.

B: Front cover printed in black only.

A presumed reprint (in B) has altered pagination as follows: ⟨1⟩-5; blank, p. ⟨6⟩. Copy in B.

A setting by Philip P. Werlein, issued not before 1854, by Ph. P. Werlein, 5 Camp Street New Orleans, n.d. Copy in B.

B   H   NYPL

14439. I TAKE YOUR HAND IN MINE WILLIE . . . MUSIC BY HENRY KLEBER . . .

NEW YORK . . . FIRTH. POND & CO. 1 FRANKLIN SQUARE . . . 1854 . . .

Sheet music. Cover-title. Plate number: 2981. Elsewhere unlocated.

B

14440. I'm with You Once Again . . . Music . . . by William R. Dempster . . .

Boston. Published by Oliver Ditson, 135 Washington St. . . . 1843 . . .

Sheet music. Cover-title. Reprinted from *The Deserted Bride*, 1843.

AAS   B

14441. THE INDIAN AND HIS BRIDE . . . MUSIC . . . BY . . . FRANCIS H. BROWN . . .

NEW YORK . . . FIRTH, HALL & POND, 239 BROADWAY, COR. PARK PL. & 1 FRANKLIN SQUARE . . . 1844 . . .

Sheet music. Cover-title. Collected as "The Days That Are Gone," *Songs and Ballads*, 1846.

Two states (probably printings) noted:

1: Plate number 669 on pp. 2-6.

2: No plate numbers present.

B (both)   H (1st)

14442. JEANNIE MARSH OF CHERRY VALLEY . . . MUSIC BY THOMAS BAKER . . .

NEW YORK PUBLISHED BY HORACE WATERS 333 BROADWAY . . . 1855 . . .

Sheet music. Cover-title. Also in (reprinted from?) *The Knickerbocker Gallery*, New York, 1855, *q.v.* Collected in *Poems*, 1860.

Two states (printings?) noted. The sequence has not been determined and the designations are for identification only:

A: No advertisements, p. ⟨6⟩.

B: P. ⟨6⟩ imprinted with advertisements.

Reissued, 1858, by Oliver Ditson & Co., Boston.

AAS   B   H

14443. LADY OF ENGLAND! . . . MUSIC . . . BY CHARLES T. MARTYN . . .

NEW-YORK . . . FIRTH & HALL, 1 FRANKLIN SQR. . . . 1840 . . .

Sheet music. Cover-title. Deposited Sept. 10, 1840. Collected in *The Deserted Bride*, 1843.

LC

14444. LAND, HO! A NAUTICAL SONG . . . MUSIC . . . BY JOSEPH PHILLIP KNIGHT . . .

NEW YORK. PUBLISHED BY FIRTH & HALL, 1 FRANKLIN SQR. . . . 1840 . . .

Sheet music. Cover-title. Deposited Oct. 2, 1840.

Issued in a lithographed wrapper; wrapper title: *Euterpean Lyre No. 1 . . . Land Ho . . .*

Also in *The Poets and Poetry of America*, 1842. Collected in *The Deserted Bride*, 1843. Under the title *Land Ho or Fill High the Brimmer, a Quartette*, music by John M. White, issued by Henry Prentiss, Boston, 1840; deposited for copyright Feb. 8, 1841.

AAS   H   LC

14445. . . . Land of Washington . . .

Boston . . . Oliver Ditson 115 Washington St. . . . 1856 . . .

Sheet music. Cover-title. At head of title: *National Songs of America, Arranged for the Piano Forte by Francis H. Brown . . .*

Plate number: 8609. Reprinted from *The Deserted Bride*, 1843, where the poem appears as "Our Patriot Sires."

B   BA

14446. THE LARK SINGS BLITHELY IN THE SKY . . . ADAPTED TO A POPULAR MELODY . . . BY WILLIAM J. LEMON . . .

PHILADELPHIA LEE & WALKER 120 WALNUT ST. . . . 1848 . . .

Sheet music. Cover-title. Plate number: 580. Deposited Dec. 7, 1848. Elsewhere unlocated.

B LC

14447. The Last Words of Washington . . . Composed by J. R. Thomas . . .

New York . . . Firth, Pond & Co. 547 Broadway . . . 1862 . . .

Sheet music. Cover-title. Plate number: 5298. Reprint of "The Hero's Legacy," *The Deserted Bride*, 1853. Reprinted and reissued with the imprint of Thaddeus Firth, New York.

B BPL

14448. The Leap for Life . . . Music . . . by Bernard Covert . . .

⟨n.p.⟩ Published by B. Covert . . . 1850 . . .

Sheet music. Cover-title. Reissued with the imprint of Oliver Ditson, Boston. For an earlier setting see *The Main Truck* . . . , below.

B H

14449. A LIFE IN THE WEST

1844

Sheet music. Also in (reprinted from?) *Songs and Ballads*, 1844.

Two printings noted. The sequence has not been determined and the order of presentation is purely arbitrary. The designations are for identification only.

A

"A LIFE IN THE WEST" THE WORDS BY G. P. MORRIS ESQR. THE MUSIC COMPOSED FOR, AND DEDICATED TO MISS ANNE MARY BACON BY HENRY RUSSELL.

PUBLISHED BY W. C. PETERS LOUISVILLE, KY. . . . 1844 . . .

Cover-title. Front printed in green. Note presence of dedication. Plate number: 51.

AAS B H

B

A LIFE IN THE WEST. SONG THE WORDS BY G. P. MORRIS ESQ. MUSIC BY HENRY RUSSELL . . .

W. C. PETERS. LOUISVILLE PETERS & WEBSTER PETERS & FIELD CINCINNATI, O. . . . 1844 . . .

Cover-title. Front printed in black. Note absence of dedication. Plate number: 51.

AAS B H

14450. A LIFE IN THE WOODS . . . A HUNTING SONG . . . MUSIC . . . BY FRANCIS H. BROWN . . .

NEW YORK . . . ATWILL, 201 BROADWAY . . . 1841 . . .

Sheet music. Cover-title. Deposited Dec. 29, 1841. Collected in *The Deserted Bride*, 1853, as "The Hunter's Carol."

LC

14451. Long Time Ago. A Glee, Arranged for Four Voices . . . by S.P.T.

Boston . . . Henry Prentiss, No. 33 Court St. . . . 1839 . . .

Sheet music. Cover-title. Anonymous. For an earlier setting see *On the Lake where Droop'd the Willow*, below.

B

14452. Look from Thy Lattice Love . . . Music by Theo. M. Brown . . .

New York. Wm. A. Pond & Co. 547 & 865 Broadway . . . 1868 . . .

Sheet music. Cover-title. Plate number: 6873. Otherwise "Open Thy Lattice, Love," *The Deserted Bride*, 1843.

B

14453. LOVE . . . MUSIC . . . BY T. V. GIUBILEI.

NEW-YORK . . . C. E. HORN, 367 BROADWAY . . . 1840 . . .

Sheet music. Caption-title. The above at head of p. ⟨1⟩. Plate number: 190. Deposited Aug. 17, 1840. Otherwise unlocated.

LC

14454. ⟨LOVE AND DOUBT⟩ The Apollo. Containing Sacred, Moral, Sentimental and Other Songs, Duetts, Trios &c. in Seventy-five Numbers . . . No. ⟨*space for number*⟩

New York Published by T. Birch. 190. Chaple ⟨*sic*⟩ near Canal St. . . . Novr. 17th. 1825 . . .

Sheet music. Cover-title. On pp. ⟨2-3⟩: Text and music of "Love and Doubt," music by William Blondell. Elsewhere unlocated.

According to a note in NYM Dec. 11, 1824, "Love and Doubt" was also (?) issued as a separate; further information wanting.

B

14455. LOVE, HONOUR, AND OBEY. A SOUTHERN MELODY . . . ARRANGEMENT . . . BY CHARLES E. HORN . . .

NEW YORK PUBLISHED BY DAVIS & HORN 411 BROADWAY ... 1839 ...

Sheet music. Cover-title. Deposited March 9, 1839. Collected in *The Deserted Bride*, 1843.

Two states (probably printings) noted.

1

Front cover priced 38 cents.

2

Front cover priced 50 cents.

H (2nd) NYPL (1st)

14456. Love Thee, Dearest ... Music by Charles E Horn. Published by Permission of the Editors of the New York Mirror.

New York, Published by James L. Hewitt & Co. 239 Broadway. ⟨n.d., 1836–1837⟩

The above at head of p. ⟨2⟩. Sheet music. For another setting see *Wilt Thou Give Thy Hand?*

H

14457. LOVE'S A TELL-TALE NA ⟨sic⟩ ADMIRED SONG ... MUSIC ... BY FRANCIS H. BROWN ...

NEW YORK ... ATWILL'S, 201, BROADWAY ... 1843 ...

Sheet music. Cover-title. Elsewhere unlocated.

B

14458. ... The Main Truck or, a Leap for Life: A Nautical Ballad ... Music ... by Henry Russell ...

... Peters & Co., Cincinnati, O. Louisville: W. C. Peters, Apollo Hall ... 1845 ...

Sheet music. Cover-title. At head of title: *Peters & Co's Collection of Musical Publications* ...

Plate number: 90. Previously in *Songs and Ballads*, 1844.

H

14459. ... Margaretta ...

Published by National Music Co. Chicago. ⟨n.d., 18--⟩

Sheet music. Cover-title. At head of title: *Soprano or Tenor Songs* ...

Plate number: 993. Music by M. W. Balfe. Presumably a reprint of an English publication.

Reprinted from *Songs and Ballads*, 1844, where it is stated that the poem had been set to music by George Loder but unpublished as sheet music. See *When I Was in My Teens*, below.

B

14460. MARY'S BEAUTY ...

PUBLISHED BY HORACE WATERS 333 BROADWAY NEW YORK. ⟨1853⟩

Sheet music. Cover-title. Elsewhere unlocated.

B

14461. THE MAY QUEEN. BALLAD ... COMPOSED ... BY H. C. WATSON.

BOSTON PUBLISHED BY HENRY PRENTISS 33 COURT STREET. ⟨1842⟩

Sheet music. Cover-title: *Rose Queen*. The above on p. ⟨2⟩. Plate number: 214. Collected in (reprinted from?) *The Deserted Bride*, 1843.

B NYPL

14462. MEETA, A BALLAD ... COMPOSED ... BY CHAS. E. HORN ...

NEW YORK ... DAVIS & HORN 411 BROADWAY ... 1839 ...

Sheet music. Cover-title. Deposited Jan. 19, 1839.

AAS H LC NYPL

14463. Merrily o'er the Mountains. Music by George Loder.

New York: J. Atwill, 201 Broadway, 1847.

Not located. Reviewed NYM June 12, 1847, as a "new edition of a very popular song, *Going o'er the Mountains* ... lithographed frontispiece." For an earlier appearance see above: *Cheerly oer the Mountains.*

14464. MILD IS THINE EYE OF BLUE SWEET MAID ... MUSIC ... BY MR. DE LUCE.

PHILADELPHIA ... GEORGE WILLIG CHESNUT ST. ⟨n.d.⟩

Sheet music. The above at head of p. ⟨2⟩. Text and music on pp. ⟨2-3⟩; pp. ⟨1⟩ and ⟨4⟩ blank. Elsewhere unlocated.

AAS

14465. THE MINIATURE ... COMPOSED BY THOS. COMER.

... 1832 ... THOS. BIRCH ... NEW YORK.

Sheet music. The above at head of p. ⟨1⟩. The text had prior publication in *Specimens of American Poetry*, 1829; see above. Collected in *The Deserted Bride*, 1838.

AAS LC

14466. ... THE MISSING SHIP ...

CHICAGO ... H. M. HIGGINS 117 RANDOLPH ST. ⟨1859⟩

Sheet music. Cover-title. Music by R. T. Curtis. At head of title: *Stray Leaves A Selection of Popular Songs from Various Authors* ...

Collected in *Poems*, 1860.

B

14467. The Missing Star ... Music by Zel' ...

Boston ... Oliver Ditson & Co. 277 Washington St. ... 1862 ...

Sheet music. Cover-title. Plate number: 21679. For an earlier setting see *On the Lake where Droop'd the Willow*, below.

B

14468. THE MOON AND ALL HER STARRY TRAIN ... COMPOSED ... BY CHARLES E. HORN ...

NEW YORK   PUBLISHED BY DAVIS & HORN   411 BROADWAY ... 1839 ...

Sheet music. Cover-title. Title at head of p. 2: *The Ball-Room Belle*. Collected in *The Deserted Bride*, 1843, as "The Ball-Room Belle."

AAS   H

Morris's Melodies ...

... Philadelphia ... New York ... Boston. 1845 ...

See above in *Section One*.

14469. Murmuring Saone ... Music by T. M. Brown ...

Boston   White, Smith & Perry   298, 300 Washington St ... 1871 ...

Sheet music. Cover-title. Plate number: 528. Reprint of "Starlight Recollections," *The Deserted Bride*, 1838.

B

14470. MY BARK IS OUT UPON THE SEA. THE POETRY AND MELODY WRITTEN, COMPOSED ... BY GEORGE P. MORRIS ... ARRANGED BY CHARLES E. HORN.

BOSTON   WM. H. OAKES ... 1840 ...

Sheet music. Cover-title. Collected in *The Deserted Bride*, 1843.

Three states noted; the sequence has not been determined and the designations are for identification only.

A: No publisher's imprint below the flowery decoration on the front.

B: The imprint of *John Ashton & Co.* below the flowery decoration on the front.

C: The imprints of *John Ashton & Co.*, and, *Firth & Hall* below the flowery decoration on the front.

AAS (A,B,C)

14471. MY HOOSIER GIRL ... MUSIC ... BY NATHAN BARKER ...

INDIANAPOLIS ... A. E. JONES & CO. ... 1854 ...

Sheet music. Cover-title. Elsewhere unlocated.

B

14472. ... MY LADY WAITS FOR ME ... MUSIC BY CHAS. J. MERZ.

BOSTON   PUBLISHED BY OLIVER DITSON   WASHINGTON ST ... 1856 ...

Sheet music. Cover-title. Plate number: 8584. At head of title: *To Miss Marie Scheurer*

Collected in *Poems*, 1860. Also issued as a quartet, music by Theo. M. Brown, published by Henry S. Mackie, Rochester, N. Y., 1867.

H

14473. MY MOTHER'S BIBLE, A BALLAD ... MUSIC ... BY HENRY RUSSELL ...

NEW YORK ... FIRTH & HALL   NO. 1 FRANKLIN SQ. ... 1841 ...

Sheet music. Cover-title. Collected in *The Deserted Bride*, 1843.

Reprinted and reissued by William Hall & Son.

H

14474. MY WOODLAND BRIDE ... MUSIC ... BY CHARLES E. HORN ...

NEW YORK ... ATWILL'S MUSIC SALOON   201 BROADWAY ... 1838 ...

Sheet music. The above at head of p. ⟨2⟩. Text and music on pp. ⟨2-3⟩; pp. ⟨1⟩ and ⟨4⟩ blank. Also in (reprinted from?) *The Deserted Bride*, 1838, as "My Mountain Bride."

AAS   B

14475. Near the Banks of That Lone River

ca. 1854

For an earlier setting see below under *Years Ago*.

Noted in the following forms. The order is alphabetical by place of publication:

A

Sheet music. Music by J. T. Gosden. Published by Henry McCaffrey, Baltimore ⟨1854⟩. Locations: AAS   B

B

Sheet music. Music by Theo. La Hache. Published by Oliver Ditson & Co., Boston, 1854. Location: AAS

C

Single leaf. Printed on recto only. Issued as No. 573 in a series. Issued by Horace Partridge, 27 Hanover Street, Boston, n.d., not before 1860. Location: B

D

Sheet music. Music by Theo. La Hache. Published by Blackmar & Co., New Orleans, 1854. Location: AAS

E

Single leaf. Printed on recto only. Published by Charles Magnus, 12 Frankfort St., New York, n.d., not before 1854. Locations: B H

F

Single leaf. Printed on recto only. Published by A. W. Auner, Philadelphia, n.d., not before 1853. Locations: B NYPL

G

Single leaf. Printed on recto only. Published by Johnson, Philadelphia, n.d., not before 1859. Text printed together with "The Harp that Once thro Tara's Hall." Location: B

14476. Near the Lake where Drooped the Willow

1839

For an earlier setting see *On the Lake where Droop'd the Willow.*

Noted in the following forms. The sequence has not been established and the designations are for identification only.

A

Harmonised for Three Voices by Charles E. Horn. Published by Hewitt & Jaques, N. Y., 1839. Locations: AAS B NYPL

B

Arranged as a Quartette by J. M. White. Published by Hewitt & Jaques, N. Y., n.d., not before 1839. Locations: B NYPL

C

Arranged for the Spanish Guitar by I. A. Faulac. Published by Hewitt & Jaques, N. Y., n.d., not before 1839. Location: LC

14477. ⟨NEW-YORK IN 1826⟩ THE NEW-YORK MIRROR, AND LADIES' LITERARY GAZETTE. FOR THE FIRST OF JANUARY, 1826 . . .

[G. F. HOPKINS, PRINTER, NO. 9 NASSAU-STREET.]

Single cut sheet. Printed on recto only. A trimmed example measures $11\frac{7}{8}''\times 9\frac{7}{16}''$.

Collected in *The Deserted Bride,* 1853, as "New-York in 1826."

Y

14478. . . . NOBODY KNOWS A SONG FOR THE TIMES WRITTEN BY GEO. MORRIS. COMPOSED BY JOHN HOSKINS . . .

LOUISVILLE G. W. BRAINARD & CO. 109 FOURTH ST. . . . ⟨1845⟩

Sheet music. Cover-title. Plate number: 872.4. At head of title: *To* ⟨*dash*⟩

Elsewhere unlocated. Presumed to be by the subject of this list.

B

14479. A NORTHERN REFRAIN, SUGGESTED FROM A WELL KNOWN NEW YORK CAROL, SUNG WITH ENTHUSIASTIC APPLAUSE BY MRS. C. E. HORN . . . THE MELODY . . . BY CHARLES E. HORN . . .

NEW YORK PUBLISHED BY DAVIS & HORN 411 BROADWAY . . . 1838 . . .

Sheet music. Cover-title. Deposited Dec. 21, 1838. Collected in *Songs and Ballads,* 1844, as "The Sweep's Carol." According to a note in *Songs and Ballads,* 1844, published as sheet music by James L. Hewitt, New York, under the title "The Sweep's Carol"; further information wanting.

AAS B H LC NYPL

14480. NOT MARRIED YET! . . . MUSIC . . . BY HENRY RUSSELL.

NEW-YORK . . . ATWILL, 201 BROADWAY . . . 1841 . . .

Sheet music. Cover-title. Deposited Dec. 29, 1841. Collected in *Songs and Ballads,* 1844.

Reprinted and reissued by Jollie, New York.

AAS LC

14481. O Sing Once More . . . Music by Camille . . .

Boston . . . G. D. Russell . . . ⟨1880⟩

Sheet music. Cover-title. Reprint of "The Songs of Home," *The Deserted Bride,* 1853. For another setting see *The Song of Home,* below.

AAS

14482. O Think of Me My Own Beloved! . . . Music . . . by Austin Phillips . . .

New-York . . . John F. Nunns, 240 Broadway . . . 1843 . . .

Sheet music. Cover-title. Otherwise "Think of Me," *The Deserted Bride*, 1843.

AAS

14483. O Would That She Were here a Ballad ... The Music ... by F. W. Rosier.

Boston. Published by Henry Prentiss, 33 Court St. ... 1841 ...

Sheet music. Cover-title. Plate number: 12. Otherwise "Lines for Music," *The Deserted Bride*, 1838.

Two issues noted, distinguishable by the lithographed front cover which was done from two different stones. Sequence not determined. A principal variation is the price; in one it is *38 cts;* in the other *50 cts.*

AAS   B   H

Oer the Mountains

See *Cheerly oer the Mountains.*

14484. OFT IN A STILLY NIGHT, A FAVORITE BALLAD ... ARRANGED FOR THE PIANO FORTE BY SIR JOHN STEVENSON.

BOSTON   PUBLISHED BY OLIVER DITSON   115 WASHINGTON ST. ⟨n.d., 1844–1857⟩

Sheet music. The above at head of p. ⟨1⟩.

Thomas Moore's poem with two added stanzas by Morris. Elsewhere unlocated.

B

14485. OH! BOATMAN HASTE! A POPULAR WESTERN REFRAIN ... MUSIC ARRANGED FROM THE WELL KNOWN MELODY OF "DANCE, BOATMEN DANCE," BY GEORGE LODER ...

NEW YORK ... ATWILL'S   201 BROADWAY. NEW ORLEANS ... CHARLES HORST, 19 ST. CHARLES ST. ... 1843 ...

Sheet music. Cover-title. Collected in *Songs and Ballads*, 1844.

AAS   B   H

14486. "OH! I REMEMBER WELL THE TIME" ... COMPOSED ... BY H. SWIFT ...

BOSTON   PUBLISHED BY G. P. REED   17 TREMONT ROW. ⟨1847⟩

Sheet music. Cover-title. Otherwise unlocated.

Three states noted; the following sequence is suggested:

A

P. 7, line 3 of stanza 4: ... *brow and hope,* |

No plate number.

B

P. 7, line 3 of stanza 4: ... *brow and hopes,* |

No plate number.

C

P. 7, line 3 of stanza 4: ... *brow and hopes,* |

Plate number *316* present.

AAS (A)   B (C)   H (A,C)   Y (B)

14487. ... Oh! Think of Me ... Composed by T. Martin Towne ...

... H. N. Hempsted, Milwaukee, Wis. ... ⟨1875⟩

Sheet music. Cover-title. Otherwise "Think of Me," *The Deserted Bride*, 1843.

AAS

14488. OH! THIS LOVE! ... MUSIC ... BY HENRY RUSSELL.

NEW-YORK ... ATWILL   201 BROADWAY ... 1841 ...

Sheet music. Cover-title. Deposited Dec. 29, 1841. Collected in *The Deserted Bride*, 1843.

AAS   B   LC

14489. OH, WE WERE GIRLS TOGETHER ... MUSIC ... BY WILLIAM CLIFTON ...

... 1841 ... THOMAS BIRCH ... NEW YORK.

The above on p. ⟨1⟩. Sheet music. Deposited July 17, 1841. This is an altered version of *We Were Boys Together*, see below.

LC

14490. THE OLD CHURCH BELL, A POPULAR SONG   WORDS BY GEO. R. ⟨sic⟩ MORRIS ... MUSIC ... BY ... FRANCIS H. BROWN.

NEW YORK. PUBLISHED BY FIRTH & HALL, 1 FRANKLIN SQ AND FIRTH, HALL & POND, 239 BROADWAY ... 1844 ...

Sheet music. Cover-title. Deposited Dec. 28, 1844.

Two states noted; the following sequence is presumed correct:

A

No plate number. A deposit copy thus.

B

Plate number: 1255.

Reissued not before 1848 by William Hall & Son, 239 Broadway, N. Y.

Presumably by the subject of this list. Elsewhere unlocated.

B (A,B)   H (A)   LC (A)

14491. Old Ironsides at Anchor Lay . . . Music by B. Covert.

> Boston. Published by Oliver Ditson   115 Washington St. . . . 1850 . . .

Sheet music. Cover-title. Plate number: 2118. Otherwise "The Main-Truck; or, a Leap for Life," *Songs and Ballads*, 1844.

B   BPL   H

14492. ON THE LAKE WHERE DROOP'D THE WILLOW, A SOUTHERN REFRAIN . . . COMPOSED . . . BY CHARLES E. HORN . . .

> NEW YORK . . . PUBLISHED BY JAMES L. HEWITT & CO. 239 BROADWAY . . . 1837 . . .

Sheet music. Cover-title.

Two states noted:

A

Morris's name not present on the front cover.

B

Morris's name present on the front cover.

Collected in *The Deserted Bride*, 1838, as "Southern Refrain."

For later printings see *Long Time Ago, The Missing Star, Near the Lake Where Drooped the Willow.*

AAS (A)   B (A)   NYPL (A,B)   Y (B)

14493. ONE BALMY SUMMER NIGHT, MARY.

> 1845

According to a note in *Morris's Melodies*, 1845, this was issued in separate form as sheet music; not located.

14494. OPEN THY LATTICE, LOVE. A SERENADE . . . COMPOSED . . . BY JOSEPH PHILLIP KNIGHT . . .

> NEW YORK. PUBLISHED BY C. E. HORN, 367 BROADWAY . . . 1840 . . .

Sheet music. Cover-title. Plate number: 192. Collected in *The Deserted Bride*, 1843.

AAS   NYPL

14495. OUR ORDER, LIKE THE ARK OF YORE. A MASONIC HYMN, AS PERFORMED AT THE NEW YORK TABERNACLE SEP. 16 1841 . . . MUSIC . . . BY C. E. HORN.

> NEW YORK   PUBLISHED FOR THE COMPOSER BY WM. HORN & CO. 309 BROADWAY . . . 1844 . . .

Sheet music. Cover-title. Collected in *The Deserted Bride*, 1853, as "Masonic Hymn."

NYPL

14496. OUR UNION, RIGHT OR WRONG. A SONG FOR THE VOLUNTEERS . . . MUSIC BY SIGNOR MUZIO . . .

> H. DE MARSAN, PUBLISHER . . . 38 & 60 CHATHAM STREET, N.Y. ⟨n.d., not before 1860⟩

Single leaf. Printed on recto only. $9^{15}/_{16}''$ full × $6^{3}/_{8}''$ full.

In Freedom's name, our blades we draw . . .

Issued as an advertisement for a sheet music printing; not located as sheet music. Uncollected.

Two printings noted:

A

Publisher's address given as *38 & 60 Chatham Street*. Issued not before 1860.

B

Publisher's address given as *60 Chatham Str.* Issued not before 1864.

For dated publication see *The Rebellion Record*, 1861, in *Section One*.

B (A)   H (B)

14497. Over the Mountain away . . . Music by Theo. M. Brown . . .

> New York   William A. Pond & Co. 547 Broadway . . . 1870 . . .

Sheet music. Cover-title. Plate number: 7720. Otherwise "Oer the Mountains," *Songs and Ballads*, 1844.

AAS

14498. . . . OVER THE WATERS I'LL WANDER WITH THEE A CAROL . . . COMPOSED BY J. R. THOMAS . . .

> NEW YORK . . . FIRTH, SON & CO 563 BROADWAY . . . 1861 . . .

Sheet music. Cover-title. At head of title: *To Mr. Robt. D. Snodgrass.* Plate number: 5199. Uncollected.

Query: Was this preceded by a Firth, Pond & Company printing?

A reprint was issued with the imprint of Oliver Ditson & Company, Boston, 1861.

B

14499. The Pastor's Daughter. A Rural Ballad ... Arranged from the Well Known Melody of Old Dan Tucker by George Loder.

Atwill ... 201 Broadway, New York ... 1844 ...

Sheet music. Cover-title. Previously in *Songs and Ballads*, 1844 (deposited Jan. 17, 1844). As sheet music deposited April 22, 1844.

LC   NYPL

14500. POETRY ... THE MELODY COMPOSED ... BY MRS. LUTHER B. WYMAN ...

NEW YORK, PUBLISHED BY FIRTH & HALL, NO. I, FRANKLIN SQ. AND FIRTH, HALL & POND, NO. 239, BROADWAY ... 1846 ...

Sheet music. Cover-title. Plate number: 3932.

For book publication see *Golden Leaflets* ..., in *Section One*, under year ⟨1848⟩. Collected in *The Deserted Bride*, 1853.

AAS   B

14501. REQUIEM: ON THE DEATH OF GENERAL WILLIAM HENRY HARRISON, LATE PRESIDENT OF THE UNITED STATES. WRITTEN ... AT THE REQUEST OF THE CORPORATION OF THE CITY OF NEW-YORK ...

WM. C. MARTIN, PRINTER. ⟨n.d., 1841⟩

Single cut sheet. Printed on recto only. 12⅝″ full × 5³⁄₁₆″.

Note: On March 31, 1945, the late Oscar Wegelin reported a handbill printing measuring 4″ × 3½″. Further information wanting.

Uncollected.

B

14502. The Retort ... Music by Henry C. Watson.

Boston. Published by Henry Prentiss, 33 Court St. ... 1842 ...

Sheet music. Cover-title. Plate number: 183. Reprinted from *The Deserted Bride*, 1838.

NYPL

14503. ROCK OF THE PILGRIMS, FROM THE CANTATA OF THE PILGRIM FATHERS. COMPOSED BY BENJ. WYMAN ...

NEW YORK ... FIRTH & HALL, I FRANKLIN SQ. AND 239 BROADWAY ... 1844 ...

Sheet music. Cover-title. Collected in *Songs and Ballads*, 1844, where the poem is reported "published by Firth & Hall."

B

14504. ... "The Rocky Mountain Boys" ... Composed by Chas. Zeuner ...

Philadelphia Lee & Walker ... 1849 ...

Sheet music. Cover-title. At head of title: *American Glees No. 3*. Otherwise "Oer the Mountains," *Songs and Ballads*, 1844. For an earlier setting see *Cheerly oer the Mountains*.

AAS   B

14505. Rosabel. Ballad ... Music ... by Joseph Philip Knight ...

New York Published by Hewitt & Jaques 239 Broadway ... 1839 ...

Sheet music. Cover-title. Reprinted from *The Deserted Bride*, 1838.

AAS   B   H

Rose Queen ...

See *The May Queen*.

14506. Sally St. Clair ... Music by Bernard Covert ...

Boston ... Oliver Ditson 115 Washington St. ... N York ... Louisville ... Boston ... 1858 ...

Sheet music. Cover-title. Plate number: 6067. Reprinted from *The Deserted Bride*, 1843. According to a notice in LW March 5, 1853, first published as sheet music in 1853. According to a note in *Songs and Ballads*, 1844, a setting by Charles E. Horn was issued not after 1844; further information wanting.

NYPL

14507. SEARCHER OF HEARTS (THY WILL BE DONE.) HYMN ... COMPOSED ... BY W. V. WALLACE ...

NEW YORK ... WM. HALL & SON 239 BROADWAY ... 1851 ...

Sheet music. Cover-title. Plate number: 1264. Collected in *The Deserted Bride*, 1853, as "Thy Will Be Done." Noted by K Dec. 1851.

Several printings noted. The first printing (printings?) may be distinguished from the later by the following features.

Earliest Form	Later Form

Cover

Price given as: *50 ¢net* ⟨*sic*⟩

Price given in code; *i.e.*, the figure 5 in a star.

P. 4

...Heaven of pray'r ...

...Hearer of pray'r ...

P. 7

Unpaged.   Imprinted with text only.

Folio 7 absent or present. Imprinted with text and music.

Intermediates have been seen.

AAS (later)   B (1st; also later)   BPL (later)

14508. SHE LOVED HIM! BUT SHE KNEW IT NOT. A BALLAD ...

NEW YORK, PUBLISHED BY FIRTH & HALL, NO. I, FRANKLIN-SQ. .... 1842 ...

Sheet music. Cover-title. Also in (reprinted from?) *The Deserted Bride*, 1843.

NYPL

14509. The Shepherds Cottage ... Music by Charles E. Horn.

New-York: Published by C. Holt Jr. Music Publishing Warehouse 156, Fulton St. ... 1847 ...

Sheet music. Cover-title. For an earlier setting see *The Cot near the Wood*, above. Noticed by K May, 1847.

Two states noted; the following sequence is probable:

A: In the title (on front cover): SHEPHERDS

B: In the title (on front cover): SHEPHERD'S

B (B)   H (A,B)

14510. The Seasons of Love. Music by Charles E. Horn.

Unpublished in sheet music form? According to a note in *Songs and Ballads*, 1844, set to music by Horn but unpublished as sheet music at the time *Songs and Ballads* was issued. The poem appears also in *Maid of Saxony*, 1842.

14511. Silent Grief. Music by Charles E. Horn.

New York: James L. Hewitt & Co.

Not seen. Entry based on information taken from *Songs and Ballads*, 1844. The poem also appears in *The Deserted Bride*, 1838. BAL has seen Horn's setting of this poem issued under the title *Burried* ⟨*sic*⟩ *Faith;* see above.

14512. A SOBER SPOUSE FOR ME. A TEMPERANCE FIRE SIDE SONG FOR THE LADIES ... MUSIC ... BY HENRY RUSSELL.

NEW-YORK. PUBLISHED BY FIRTH & HALL I FRANKLIN SQ. & J. L. HEWITT & CO. 239 BROADWAY ... 1844 ...

Cover-title. Sheet music. Collected in *The Deserted Bride*, 1853, as "Temperance Song."

AAS   H

14513. THE SOLDIER AND HIS BRIDE ... MUSIC ... BY HENRY RUSSELL ...

NEW YORK ... FIRTH & HALL, NO. I FRANKLIN SQ. .... 1841 ...

Sheet music. Cover-title. Deposited July 21, 1841. Collected in *The Deserted Bride*, 1843, as "Janet McRea."

Also issued (reprinted) with the publisher's address: *239 Broadway & I Franklin Sq.* Copy in B.

LC (deposit copy)

14514. THE SOLDIERS RETURN ... ENTERED ... 1848 ... A SONG FOR THE PEOPLE ...

NEW YORK ... FIRTH POND & CO. NO. I FRANKLIN SQUARE.

Sheet music. Cover-title. Plate number: 86. Collected in *The Deserted Bride*, 1853, as "The Soldier's Welcome Home." See "The Soldier's Welcome Home," under year 1852, in *Section One*.

Caution: The only example located has been trimmed. Is the imprint complete as here transcribed?

B

14515. SONG, TUNES ---LIGHT, IMANDRA ...

⟨n.p., n.d., *ca.* 1840⟩

Printed in blue. Single leaf. 4$\frac{5}{16}$″ full × 4″. Printed on recto only. Anonymous.

First separate printing? For notes and publication as sheet music see below: *When Other Friends Are Round Thee.*

The only located copy is tipped into the Y copy of Morris's *Deserted Bride*, 1843.

Y

14516. A SONG FOR BUCK AND BRECK ...

⟨n.p., n.d., 1856⟩

Single cut sheet. White wove paper. Stationer's embossed stamp at upper left corner. 9$\frac{3}{4}$″ × 7$\frac{11}{16}$″. Printed on recto only.

Anonymous. Credited to Morris by Yale University Library.

Issued as campaign material, national election of 1856.

Y

14517. ... THE SONG OF HOME ... MUSIC BY J. GASPARD MAEDER.

NEW YORK ... WILLIAM HALL & SON, 239, BROADWAY ... 1850 ...

Sheet music. The above on p. 3. At head of title: *To Mrs. George B. Mathew.* Plate number: 933. Collected in *The Deserted Bride,* 1853, as "The Songs of Home."

AAS   BPL

14518. SONG OF THE SEWING MACHINE ... SET TO MUSIC AND DEDICATED TO THE WHEELER & WILSON SEWING-MACHINE COMPANY, BY H. C. WATSON.

MUSICAL WORLD PRINT: OFFICE 379 BROADWAY, CORNER OF WHITE STREET. ⟨n.d., *ca.* 1860⟩

Sheet music. Cover-title.

First separate printing? See the following entries in *Section One:*

Wheeler & Wilson M'f'g' Co's Sewing Machines, under year *ca.* 1856.

The American Reader of Prose and Poetry ... , under year 1860.

Collected in *Poems,* 1860.

AAS

14519. The Spell That Hath Bound Me

Reprinted from *The Deserted Bride,* 1853, where it appears as "Thou Hast Woven the Spell." Noted as follows; sequence not known.

A

... The Spell That Hath Bound Me ... Music ... by Stephn. Massett ...

Boston ... Oliver Ditson & Co. ... 1858 ...

Sheet music. Cover-title.

AAS

B

New Ballad First Time To Night!! "The Spell That Has Bound Me." Words by Georgr ⟨*sic*⟩ P. Morris, Music ... by Stephen Massett ...

⟨New York⟩ Keech, Printer, 23 Ann Street. ⟨n.d., not before 1858⟩

Single leaf. Pale yellow paper. 9¾″ × 6″. Printed on recto only.

H (Received Aug. 30, 1859)

14520. THE SPIRIT OF BEAUTY ... MUSIC BY, ⟨*sic*⟩ GEO. LODER.

BOSTON ... W. H. OAKES, & FOR SALE BY JOHN ASHTON & CO. 197 WASHINGTON ST. ... 1842 ...

The above on p. ⟨1⟩. Sheet music. Also in (reprinted from?) *The Deserted Bride,* 1843, where it appears under the title "The Beam of Devotion."

See above: *The Beam of Devotion.*

B

14521. ... The Star of Love ... Composed ... by W. V. Wallace ...

New York ... William Hall & Son, 239 Broadway ... 1851 ...

Sheet music. Cover-title. At head of title: *Serenade*

Noted LW Feb. 15, 1851. Reprinted from *Songs and Ballads,* 1844.

Many printings noted, the earliest issued with imprint as given above.

H

Star of Memory

Otherwise *Years Ago!,* q.v., below.

14522. Star-Light Recollections. Music by Charles E. Horn.

New York: James L. Hewitt & Co.

Not seen. Not located. Entry based on a note in *Songs and Ballads,* 1844. The poem also appears in *The Deserted Bride,* 1838.

14523. The Suitors ... Music ... by Charles E. Horn ...

New York ... James L. Hewitt & Co. 239 Broadway ... Firth & Hall, 1 Franklin Square ... 1843 ...

Sheet music. Cover-title. Reprinted from *The Deserted Bride,* 1843.

H

14524. THE SUN NOW GILDS THE MOUNTAIN TOPS ... COMPOSED ... BY J. WATSON ...

PHILADELPHIA. A. FIOT ... NO. 196 1/2 CHESNUT ST. ... 1839 ...

Sheet music. Cover-title. Deposited Aug. 6, 1839. Elsewhere unlocated.

LC

14525. The Sweep's Carol. Music by Charles E. Horn.

New York: James L. Hewitt & Co.

Not seen. Not located. Entry based on a note in *Songs and Ballads*, 1844. See *A Northern Refrain*, sheet music, above.

14526. THE SWORD AND THE STAFF, A NATIONAL ANTHEM ... MUSIC ... BY W. VINCENT WALLACE.

NEW-YORK ... J. L. HEWITT & CO. 239 BROADWAY AND FIRTH & HALL, I FRANKLIN SQ. ... 1843 ...

Sheet music. Cover-title. Listed as *new* BJ Sept. 9, 1843. Collected in *Songs and Ballads*, 1844.

AAS   B

14527. 'TIS NOW THE PROMIS'D HOUR ... MUSIC ... BY FRANCIS H. BROWN.

NEW YORK, PUBLISHED BY ATWILL, 201 BROADWAY ... 1844 ...

Sheet music. Cover-title. Collected in *Songs and Ballads*, 1846.

Note: In some copies the copyright date is altered by hand to *1845.* In quite late printings the alteration is in the stone.

H

14528. TWENTY YEARS AGO, A BALLAD ... MUSIC ... BY AUSTIN PHILLIPS ...

NEW YORK ... ATWILL, 201 BROADWAY ... 1840 ...

Sheet music. Cover-title. Collected in *The Deserted Bride*, 1843.

AAS   B

14529. A VENETIAN SERENADE THE WORDS & MELODY BY GEORGE P. MORRIS ... ARRANGED BY CHARLES E. HORN ...

NEW YORK ... DAVIS & HORN 411 BROADWAY ... 1839 ...

Sheet music. The above at head of p. ⟨1⟩. Deposited Feb. 21, 1839. Collected in *The Deserted Bride*, 1843. For another printing as sheet music see above, *Come, Come to Me Love.*

AAS   LC   UV

14530. THE WATCHWORD "LIBERTY OR DEATH!" ... COMPOSED ... BY J. R. THOMAS ...

NEW YORK ... WM. HALL & SON 543 BROADWAY ... 1860 ...

Sheet music. Cover-title. Plate number: 4595. Otherwise unlocated.

B

14531. WE WERE BOYS TOGETHER. A BALLAD ... MUSIC ... BY HENRY RUSSELL ...

NEW YORK. PUBLISHED BY FIRTH & HALL. NO. I FRANKLIN SQ. ... 1841 ...

Sheet music. Cover-title. Deposited May 6, 1841. Collected in *The Deserted Bride*, 1843. An altered version, under the title "Oh, We Were Girls Together," was deposited July 17, 1841.

NYPL

14532. WEARIES MY LOVE OF MY LETTERS? ... MUSIC ... BY CHARLES E. HORN ...

NEW YORK ... DUBOIS & BACON 167 BROADWAY ... 1836 ...

Sheet music. Cover-title. Collected in *The Deserted Bride*, 1838.

AAS   H

14533. ... WELCOME HOME. BY GEOGE ⟨*sic*⟩ P. MORRIS ...

J. WRIGLEY ... NO. 27 CHATHAM STREET ... NEW YORK. ⟨n.d., not before 1860⟩

Single leaf. 9¹³⁄₁₆″ × 6⁷⁄₁₆″. Printed on recto only. At head of title: *No. 314*

Also in (reprinted from?) *Poems*, New York ⟨1860⟩.

LCP

14534. ... Well-a-Day ... ⟨Music by Alberto Randegger⟩

Boston ... Oliver Ditson & Co. 277 Washington St ... 1872 ...

Sheet music. Cover-title. Plate number: 26666. At head of title: *Songs of Miss Addie S. Ryall* ...

Reprinted from *The Deserted Bride*, 1843.

BPL

14535. A WESTERN REFRAIN, WESTWARD HO! ... COMPOSED ... BY CHARLES E. HORN ...

NEW YORK ... DAVIS & HORN 411 BROADWAY ... 1839 ...

Sheet music. Cover-title. Deposited Feb. 13, 1839. Collected in *The Deserted Bride*, 1843, as "Western Refrain."

AAS   LC   NYPL

14536. What Can it Mean? A New Ballad . . . Composed by Joseph Philip Knight . . .

Philada. Osbourn's Music Saloon, 30 S. 4th. St. . . . 1839 . . .

Sheet music. Cover-title. Plate number: 179. Deposited June 21, 1839. Previously in *The Deserted Bride*, 1838.

LC NYPL

14537. When I Was in My Teens.

Sheet music. *Not seen.* Entry on the basis of information in *Morris's Melodies*, 1845. Otherwise "Margaretta," *Songs and Ballads*, 1844. See *Margaretta*, above.

14538. WHEN OTHER FRIENDS ARE ROUND THEE . . . MUSIC . . . BY CHARLES E. HORN . . .

NEW YORK PUBLISHED BY JAMES L. HEWITT & CO. 239 BROADWAY . . . 1836 . . .

Sheet music. Cover-title.

For earliest book publication see *The New-York Book of Poetry*, 1837.

Collected in *The Deserted Bride*, 1838. For leaflet publication see above: *Song. Tunes———Light, Imandra . . .*

Reprinted and reissued by Firth, Pond & Company, 1 Franklin Square, New York, 1836, *i.e.,* not before 1854.

Also set to music by C.R.W., and issued by F. D. Benteen, Baltimore; W. T. Mayo, New Orleans, 1846.

H

14539. WHERE HUDSONS WAVE . . . IDA, A SCENA . . . MUSIC COMPOSED BY JOSEPH PHILIP KNIGHT.

NEW-YORK PUBLISHED BY FIRTH & HALL, NO. I, FRANKLIN SQ. ⟨1839⟩

Sheet music. Cover-title. Collected in *The Deserted Bride*, 1843.

Two issues (printings?) noted:

1: The cover-title reads: *Where Hudsons Wave . . .*

2: The cover-title reads: *Where Hudson's Wave . . .*

AAS (B) NYPL (A)

14540. WILL NOBODY MARRY ME? . . . MUSIC . . . BY HENRY RUSSELL.

NEW-YORK . . . ATWILL, 201 BROADWAY . . . 1841 . . .

Sheet music. Cover-title. Noticed by K Aug. 1841. Deposited Dec. 29, 1841. Collected in *The Deserted*

Bride, 1843. Reissued not before 1849 by Samuel C. Jollie, New York.

Also issued as a handbill, words only, by Charles Magnus, 12 Frankfort Street ⟨n.d., not before 1854⟩. In B.

AAS (Atwill) B (Atwill) H (Atwill) LC (Atwill) NYPL (Jollie)

14541. THE WILLOW AT THE WELL . . . COMPOSED . . . BY WM. J. WETMORE . . .

NEW YORK . . . MILLETS MUSIC SALOON 329 BROADWAY . . . 1847 . . .

Sheet music. Cover-title Otherwise unlocated.

B

14542. WILT THOU GIVE THY HAND? A POPULAR BALLAD . . . ⟨Music by⟩ W. A. KING.

NEW YORK . . . ATWILL'S MUSIC SALOON 201 BROADWAY . . . 1835 . . .

Sheet music. The above at head of first page of text and music. Collected in *The Deserted Bride*, 1838, as "Love Thee, Dearest."

B

14543. WOODMAN! SPARE THAT TREE!

First published under the title, "The Oak," NYM Jan. 7, 1837. Collected as "The Oak," *The Deserted Bride*, 1838; in the edition of 1843 the poem appears under the more familiar title "Woodman, Spare that Tree."

Several printings have been noted. See below.

WOODMAN! SPARE THAT TREE! A BALLAD . . . THE WORDS COPIED FROM THE NEW YORK MIRROR . . . THE MUSIC BY HENRY RUSSEL. ⟨*sic*⟩

NEW YORK, PUBLISHED BY FIRTH & HALL, N.O. I, FRANKLIN-SQ ⟨1837⟩

Sheet music. Cover-title. Pp. ⟨1⟩-7. Plate numbers as follows: 5 (on pp. 3-6), 4 (on p. 7).

There were many printings. The first printing (printings?) has the following features:

FRONT COVER

No frame or border.

A BALLAD (in a single line)

In the vignette: Weathercock not present on the shed. Vignette signed: *Litho.ʸ. of Endicott N.Y*

As a single line: THE WORDS COPIED FROM THE NEW YORK MIRROR, WRITTEN BY

The line BENJAMIN M. BROWN, ESQ. from an ornate face, the counters of the *O* and the *Q* decorated.

Composer's name misspelled: *Henry Russel.*

Price not present.

PAGE ⟨2⟩

P. ⟨2⟩ devoted to a letter, Morris to Russell, dated *February 1, 1837. Note:* The letter appears also in *The Little Frenchman and His Water Lots,* 1839, pp. ⟨89⟩-92.

PAGE 7

Line 1, stanza 4: . . . *thee* . . . ⟨which is correct⟩

Line 4, stanza 4: . . . *branches* . . . ⟨which is correct⟩

REPRINTS

Reprints have one or more of the above features but also one or more of the following features:

FRONT COVER (REPRINTS)

Frame or border present on quite late printings.

A / BALLAD (set in two lines)

a / BALLAD (set in two lines)

A Ballad (set in one line)

A BALLAD (set in one line)

In the vignette: Weathercock present in quite late printings.

Signed:

Endicott's Lith. 152 Foulten ⟨sic⟩ *St. N. Y.*

Litho. of Endicott N.Y.

Endicott's Lith.

Lithographer's imprint absent.

The Words / COPIED FROM THE NEW YORK MIRROR or: The lines are absent.

The line of the dedicatee's name noted as follows:

BENJAMIN M. BROWN, ESQ. set in an ornate face, the counters in the *O* and *Q* not decorated.

The dedicatee's name printed in upper and lower case script.

Composer's name correctly spelled: *Henry Russell.*

Price (when present):

Pr. 38 cts. nett.

Price 38 cts. nett.

Price 37 1/2 cts Nett.

P. ⟨2⟩

Blank; letter not present. In early reprints the letter is not present; in quite late reprints the letter appears at the head of the first page of text and music.

P. 7

Line 1, stanza 4: . . . *the* . . . ⟨incorrectly⟩ In late printings: *thee*

Line 4, stanza 4: . . . *brances* . . . ⟨for *branches*⟩ In quite late printings: *branches*

PLATE NUMBERS

Plate number 5 present, pp. 3-7.

Plate number 5 present, pp. 3-6; plate number 4 present, p. 7.

It will be noted that the first and early printings are paged ⟨1⟩-7. Quite late reprints are paged ⟨i-ii⟩, 1-5.

Reprinted and reissued by S. T. Gordon, New York ⟨1837; *i.e.*, not before 1858⟩. Copy in H.

The present entry made on the basis of copies in AAS (reprints); H (1st; and, reprints); B (1st); UV (reprints).

LEAFLET PRINTINGS NOTED

Noted as follows. The order of presentation is alphabetical by place of publication.

A

Woodman Spare that Tree.

> J. Catnach, Printer, 2 & 3, Monmouth-Court, Seven Dia,s. ⟨*sic*⟩ . . . ⟨n.p., London, n.d., probably not later than 1838⟩

Single leaf. Printed on recto only. 9¾″ scant × 7⅛″.

Printed together with (at the left of Morris's poem), "The Angel's Whisper." Presumably the two pieces were intended to be cut apart and sold separately.

B

B

Woodman, Spare that Tree . . .

> H. De Marsan, Publisher. Songs, Ballads, Toy Books, &c. 54 Chatham Street, N. Y. ⟨n.d., 1861-1864⟩

Single leaf. Printed on recto only. 10″ × 6¼″.

B H

C

. . . Woodman Spare that Tree . . .

> cJ. ⟨*sic*⟩ H. Johnson . . . No. 7 North Tenth St., Three Doors above Market, Phila. . . . ⟨n.d., not before 1859⟩

Single leaf. Printed on recto only. 9⅝″ × 6⅛″. At head of leaf: *J. H. Johnson, Song Publisher* . . .

B

D

. . . Woodman, Spare that Tree. The Music Will Be Sent, Postpaid, on Receipt of 25 Cents, by the Firm That Sent You This . . .

> ⟨n.p., n.d., *ca.* 1860⟩

Single leaf. 8³⁄₁₆″ × 4⅝″ (a trimmed example).
At head: [*187*]

B

E

Woodman Spare that Tree . . . ⟨and⟩ The Flaunting Flag of Liberty . . .

⟨n.p., n.d., *ca.* 1840⟩

Single leaf. Printed on recto only. 10″ × 7½″.
Probably not an American production. The sense
of "The Flaunting Flag of Liberty" indicates that
this was printed in England.

B

. . . "YANKEE DOODLE." . . . ⟨Music⟩ BY
FRANCIS H. BROWN . . .

NEW YORK . . . ATWILL, 201 BROADWAY . . .
1843 . . .

Sheet music. Cover-title. At head of title: *Atwill's
Collection of National Songs of America. No. 6.* Otherwise unlocated.

AAS

. . . YEARS AGO . . .

BOSTON . . . OLIVER DITSON, 115 WASHINGTON
ST. . . . 1845 . . .

Sheet music. Cover-title. At head of title: *Songs &
Glees of the Baker Family of New Hampshire. Composed
. . . by John C. Baker . . .*

Collected in *The Deserted Bride,* 1853.

Also set to music and reissued under the following
titles: *Near the Banks of that Lone River;* and, *Star of
Memory.*

B

Reprints of Morris's own books.

14544. American Melodies ... Compiled by George P. Morris ...

Philadelphia: Henry F. Anners. ⟨1840; *i.e., ca.* 1845⟩

For first edition see in *Section One* under year 1841.

14545. The Whip-Poor-Will. Respectfully Inscribed to Morton McMichael ...

E. Ferrett and Co. Philadelphia and New York. ⟨1846⟩ ...

Illuminated paper wrapper. Front wrapper dated 1846; back wrapper dated 1845.

Previously in *The Deserted Bride*, 1843. Listed WPLNL Dec. 1845.

14546. The Prose and Poetry of Europe and America ... Compiled by G. P. Morris and N. P. Willis. Complete in One Volume. Ninth Edition.

New-York: Leavitt, Trow and Co., 191 Broadway. 1848.

A reprint, under altered title, of *A Library of the Prose and Poetry of Europe and America* ... , 1846.

14547. The Whip-Poor-Will ...

D. Appleton & Co New York. 1848

Reprinted from *The Deserted Bride*, 1843.

14548. The Prose and Poetry of Europe and America ... Compiled by G. P. Morris and N. P. Willis ...

New-York: Leavitt & Allen, (Successors to Leavitt & Co.), No. 27 Dey-Street. 1852.

A reprint of *A Library of the Prose and Poetry of Europe and America* ... , 1846.

14549. The Songs and Ballads ... First Complete Edition.

New-York: Cady & Burgess, 60 John-Street. 1852.

14550. The Gift Book of American Melodies ... Compiled by George P. Morris.

Philadelphia: Henry F. Anners, No. 48 North Fourth Street. 1854.

Reprint of *American Melodies*, 1841. Advertised as *ready* LW Aug. 13, 1853.

14551. Poems ... Third Edition.

New York: Charles Scribner, 145 Nassau St. MDCCCLIV.

Cloth; and, leather. Reprint of *The Deserted Bride*, 1853.

14552. Poems ... with Illustrations by Weir and Darley ... Fourth Edition.

New York: Charles Scribner, 145 Nassau St. MDCCCLIV.

Reprint of *The Deserted Bride*, 1853.

14553. The Prose and Poetry of Europe and America ... Compiled by G. P. Morris and N. P. Willis ...

New-York: Leavitt & Allen, (Successors to Leavitt & Co.), No. 27 Dey-Street. 1855.

A reprint of *A Library of the Prose and Poetry of Europe and America* ... , 1846.

GEORGE POPE MORRIS

SECTION IV

Books by authors other than Morris containing reprinted Morris material.

The Gems of American Poetry, by Distinguished Authors.

New-York: A. & C. B. Edwards. 1840.

The Household Book of Select Songs, with Numerous Critical Explanatory Observations . . .

Philadelphia: Printed & Published at Young's Office, Black Horse Alley. For Sale at the Principal Book Stores in the United States. 1842.

Songs, Odes, and Other Poems, on National Subjects; Compiled . . . by Wm. McCarty. Part First——Patriotic . . .

Philadelphia: Published by Wm. McCarty, No. 27 North Fifth Street. 1842.

"Pocahontas," pp. 287-288. Previously in *The Poets of America . . . Volume Second . . .*, 1842 (copyrighted 1841) under the title "The Chieftain's Daughter. Pocahontas."

Deposited Nov. 29, 1842.

A Memoir of the Construction, Cost, and Capacity of the Croton Aqueduct . . . by Charles King.

New-York: Printed by Charles King. 1843.

The Ladies' Companion; or, Peoples' Annual: Embellished with Elegant Steel Engravings and Choice Music.

New York: Published at 109 Fulton Street. 1845.

Reprints twenty-three of Morris's poems including the following:

"Bessy Bell," here reprinted under the title "When Life Looks Drear."

"Silent Grief," here reprinted under the title "Concealed Grief."

"A Fragment of an Indian Poem," here reprinted under the title "Indian Songs."

"What Can it Mean?," here reprinted under the title "Seventeen."

"Lines after the Manner of the Olden Time," here reprinted under the title "The Boy-God, Love."

The Poet's Gift . . . Edited by John Keese.

Boston . . . 1845.

For fuller entry see BAL, Vol. 1, p. 206.

The Southern Warbler: A New Collection of . . . Old, and New Songs . . .

Charleston ⟨S. C.⟩. Published by Babcock & Co. 1845.

"Long Time Ago," p. 231; otherwise "Southern Refrain," *The Deserted Bride*, 1843.

The Snow Flake . . . Edited by T. S. Arthur. MDCCCXLVI.

. . . New York . . . 1846.

"One Balmy Summer Night, Mary," (*Morris's Melodies*, 1845) here reprinted, pp. ⟨37⟩-38, under the title "The Memory of the Past." For fuller entry see No. 10016.

National Songs, Ballads, and Other Patriotic Poetry, Chiefly Relating to the War of 1846. Compiled by William M'Carty.

Philadelphia: Published by William M'Carty. 1846.

"National Anthem," *The Deserted Bride*, 1843, here reprinted under the title "God Has Made Us Free," pp. 59-60; and, again, pp. 111-112 under the title "Arm On! Arm On! Ye Brave and Free!"

Dempster's Original Ballad Soirees.

Boston . . . 1847.

For fuller entry see BAL, Vol. 5, p. 595.

The Granite Songster. Containing the Poetry as Sung by the Hutchinson Family . . .

Boston . . . 1847.

For fuller entry see BAL, Vol. 5, p. 594.

The Granite Songster; Comprising the Songs of the Hutchinson Family . . .

> Boston . . . 1847.
>
> For fuller entry see BAL, Vol. 5, p. 594.

The Philopoena, or Friendship's Offering, for 1847 . . . Edited by a Lady.

> New-York: John Levison, 196 Chatham Square. ⟨n.d., 1847⟩

The Marriage Offering: A Compilation of Prose and Poetry. ⟨Edited by Abiel A. Livermore⟩

> Boston: Wm. Crosby and H. P. Nichols, 111 Washington Street. 1848.

The Evergreen; or, Gems of Literature, for MDCCCL. Edited by Rev. Edward A. Rice.

> New York: J. C. Burdick, 162 Nassau Street. J. J. Reed, Printer, 16 Spruce Street. 1850.
>
> Magazine sheets bound as an annual. "The Christian's Daughter---Pocahontas," pp. ⟨137⟩-138. Previously in *The Poets of America . . . Volume Second . . .*, 1842, under the title "The Chieftain's Daughter. Pocahontas."

The Gem of the Season, for 1850. Edited by N. Parker Willis . . .

> New-York . . . MDCCCL.
>
> For comment see entry No. 3169.

The Little Gem, a Christmas, New Year's, and Birth-Day Present . . .

> Hartford: Silas Andrus and Son. 1850.
>
> Reprinted with the imprint: *New York: H. Dayton, No. 29 Ann Street.* ⟨n.d.⟩

The Irving Offering: A Token of Affection, for 1851.

> New-York . . . 1851.
>
> For comment see entry No. 3171.

The Moss Rose, for 1852. Edited by Mrs. Emeline P. Howard.

> New York . . . ⟨1851⟩
>
> For fuller entry see BAL, Vol. 1, p. 373.

Book of Words of the Hutchinson Family.

> New York: Baker, Godwin & Co., Printers, Tribune Buildings, Cor. Nassau and Spruce-Sts. 1851.
>
> Printed paper wrapper.

Municipal Celebration of the Seventy-Seventh Anniversary of American Independence. Order of Exercises at the First Baptist Church, Monday, July 4, 1853.

> ⟨Providence, R. I., Knowles, Anthony & Co., Printers, 1853⟩
>
> 4 pp. Cover-title. "Introductory Anthem," p. ⟨2⟩; otherwise "National Anthem," *The Deserted Bride*, 1843.
>
> Also appears in *An Oration Delivered before the Municipal Authorities and Citizens of Providence, on the Seventy-Seventh Anniversary of American Independence, July 4, 1853*, by Thomas Durfee, Providence, 1853.

The Ladies' Souvenir . . .

> New York . . . ⟨1853; *i.e.*, not before 1856⟩
>
> See below under 1856.

The Odd-Fellows' Offering, for 1853 . . .

> New York: Edward Walker, 114 Fulton-Street. M DCCC LIII.

The Winter Wreath . . .

> New York . . . ⟨1853; *i.e.*, not before 1856⟩
>
> See below under 1856.

Laurel Leaves . . . Edited by Mary E. Hewitt . . .

> New York . . . 1854.
>
> For fuller entry see BAL, Vol. 2, p. 496.

The Thought-Blossom: A Memento. Edited by N. Parker Willis . . .

> New York: Leavitt and Allen, 27 Dey-Street. 1854.
>
> Leather.

The White Veil: A Bridal Gift. Edited by Mrs. Sarah Josepha Hale . . . ⟨Edition B⟩

> Philadelphia . . . 1854.
>
> For comment see entry No. 6883.

Cyclopædia of American Literature . . . by Evert A. Duyckinck and George L. Duyckinck. In Two Volumes . . .

> New York . . . 1855.
>
> For fuller entry see No. 11092A.

The Humorous Poetry of the English Language, from Chaucer to Saxe . . . with Notes . . . by J. Parton.

New York: Published by Mason Brothers, 108 and 110 Duane Street. 1856.

Advertised as *this day* CRN July 12, 1856.

The Harp of Freedom ... by Geo. W. Clark ...

New-York ... 1856.

For fuller entry see No. 1660.

The Ladies' Souvenir: Edited by N. Parker Willis, ⟨*sic*⟩

New York: Leavitt and Allen, 379 Broadway. ⟨1853; *i.e.*, not before 1856⟩

Leather.

The Winter Wreath: Edited by N. Parker Willis, ⟨*sic*⟩

New York: Leavitt and Allen, 379 Broadway. ⟨1853; *i.e.*, not before 1856⟩

Leather.

Memoir and Eulogy of Dr. Elisha Kent Kane, Pronounced by Bro. E. W. Andrews, before the Grand Lodge of ... Free and Accepted Masons in the State of New York, June 5, 1857 ...

New York: Dexter & Brother, 14 & 16 Ann Street. 1857.

Printed paper wrapper? "A Hymn," p. ⟨31⟩; otherwise "Funeral Hymn," *The Deserted Bride*, 1853.

The Poets of the Nineteenth Century ... Edited by ... Rev. Robert Aris Willmott ...

New York ... 1858.

For comment see entry No. 1663.

The Atlantic Souvenir, for 1859 ...

New York: Derby & Jackson, 119 Nassau Street. 1859.

Leather.

A Gallery of Famous English and American Poets. With an Introductory Essay, by Henry Coppée ...

Philadelphia: Published by E. H. Butler & Co. 1859.

Leather.

The Poets of the West ...

London ... 1859.

For comment see BAL, Vol. 1, p. 101.

The Romance of the Ring, and Other Poems. By James Nack.

New York: Delisser & Procter, 508 Broadway, 1859.

Morris's memoir herein had prior publication in Nack's *The Immortal* ..., New York, 1850. See above in *Section One*.

Deposited March 12, 1859.

The Poets of the West ...

London ... New York ... 1860.

For fuller entry see BAL, Vol. 1, p. 374.

The Boy's Banner Book.

James G. Gregory. New York ⟨n.d., *ca.* 1860⟩

Cover-title. Printed paper wrapper.

The Star Spangled Banner ...

⟨n.p., n.d., *ca.* 1860⟩

Caption-title. The above at head of p. ⟨1⟩. Pp. ⟨1⟩-⟨8⟩.

Extracted from a larger work? On pp. 2 and 6 the running head is: *The Banner Book;* further information wanting.

The Patriotic Glee Book ...

... 1863 ... H. M. Higgins ⟨117 Randolph St., Chicago⟩ ...

Printed boards, leather shelfback. "Take Your Harps, from Silent Willows," pp. 71-75. Otherwise "The Union," *Poems*, 1860.

Lyrics of Loyalty ... Edited by Frank Moore

New York ... 1864

For comment see entry No. 1203.

The School-Girl's Garland ... by Mrs. C. M. Kirkland. First Series ...

New York ... 1864.

For comment see entry No. 4837.

Autograph Leaves of Our Country's Authors.

Baltimore ... 1864.

For comment see entry No. 2418.

... Ballads of the War.

New York ... ⟨1864⟩

For comment see BAL, Vol. 1, p. 248.

Life-Lights of Song. Songs of Love & Brotherhood. Edited by David Page . . .

Edinburgh: William P. Nimmo. 1864.

Golden Leaves from the American Poets Collected by John W. S. Hows . . .

New York . . . ⟨1864; *i.e.,* not before 1866⟩

See below under 1866.

Home Ballads by Our Home Poets . . .

New York . . . 1865.

For comment see BAL, Vol. 1, p. 248.

Golden Leaves from the American Poets Collected by John W. S. Hows

New York James G. Gregory 540 Broadway
M DCCC LXV

Reprinted and reissued with the imprint: *New York Bunce and Huntington* M DCCC LXV

The Book of Rubies . . .

New York . . . 1866.

For comment see entry No. 5522.

The Flower of Liberty. Edited . . . by Julia A. M. Furbish.

Boston . . . 1866.

For fuller entry see No. 1424.

Golden Leaves from the American Poets Collected by John W. S. Hows . . .

New York: George Routledge and Sons, 416 Broome Street. ⟨1864; *i.e.,* not before 1866⟩

A Thousand and One Gems of English Poetry . . . Arranged by Charles Mackay . . .

London . . . New York . . . 1867.

For fuller entry see BAL, Vol. 5, pp. 604-605.

The Grant Campaign Songster . . .

New-York . . . ⟨1868⟩

For fuller entry see No. 7025.

Lyra Sacra Americana: Or, Gems from American Sacred Poetry. Selected . . . by Charles Dexter Cleveland . . .

New York: Charles Scribner and Company. London: Sampson Low, Son, and Marston. 1868.

The Masonic Token. A Gift Book. Edited by William T. Anderson . . .

New York: Masonic Publishing Company, No. 2 Bleeker Street. ⟨1868⟩

Household Masonic Library, Book III.

"Requiem," p. ⟨34⟩; otherwise "Funeral Hymn," *The Deserted Bride,* 1853.

The Flower of Liberty. Edited and Illustrated by Julia A. M. Furbish.

Cincinnati, Ohio: White, Corbin, Bouve & Company, No. 124 Walnut Street. 1869.

The Poets of the Nineteenth Century . . . Edited by . . . Robert Aris Willmott . . .

New York . . . 1872.

For comment see BAL, Vol. V, p. 318.

A Hand-Book of English Literature. Intended for the Use of High Schools . . . by Francis H. Underwood . . . American Authors.

Boston: Lee and Shepard, Publishers. New York: Lee, Shepard and Dillingham. 1873.

The Poets and Poetry of America. By Rufus Wilmot Griswold . . . Revised . . .

New York . . . 1873.

For fuller entry see No. 9565. "Life in the West," *Songs and Ballads,* 1844, appears herein under the title "The West."

One Hundred Choice Selections No. 8 . . .

. . . Philadelphia . . . 1874.

For fuller entry see BAL, Vol. 1, p. 84.

Poets and Poetry of Printerdom . . . Edited by Oscar H. Harpel . . .

Cincinnati . . . 1875.

For comment see BAL, Vol. 3, p. 370.

One Hundred Choice Selections No. 13 . . .

. . . Philadelphia . . . Chicago . . . 1877.

For comment see entry No. 3372.

The Fireside Encyclopædia of Poetry . . . Compiled . . . by Henry T. Coates.

. . . Philadelphia. ⟨1878⟩

For fuller entry see in the James Russell Lowell list, *Section Three.*

Golden Thoughts on Mother, Home and Heaven . . . with an Introduction by Rev. Theo. L. Cuyler . . .

> New-York . . . ⟨1878⟩
>
> For fuller entry see BAL, Vol. 5, p. 112.

Poems of Places Edited by Henry W. Longfellow . . . Southern States.

> Boston . . . 1879.
>
> For fuller entry see No. 12213.

Poems of Places Edited by Henry W. Longfellow . . . Western States.

> Boston . . . 1879.
>
> For fuller entry see No. 12214.

Poems of Places Edited by Henry W Longfellow . . . British America . . .

> Boston . . . 1879.
>
> For fuller entry see No. 12215.

The Children's Book of Poetry: Carefully Selected . . . by Henry T. Coates . . .

> Porter & Coates. Philadelphia. ⟨1879⟩

Franklin Square Song Collection . . . by J. P. McCaskey . . .

> New York . . . 1881
>
> For comment see BAL, Vol. 1, p. 86.

Gems for the Fireside . . . ⟨Compiled by⟩ Rev. O. H. Tiffany . . .

> Boston . . . 1881.
>
> For comment see BAL, Vol. 5, p. 610.

Gems for the Fireside . . . ⟨Compiled by⟩ Rev. O. H. Tiffany . . .

> Springfield, Mass. . . . ⟨1883⟩
>
> For comment see BAL, Vol. 5, p. 611.

No. 4. Standard Recitations . . . Compiled . . . by Frances P. Sullivan . . . June, 1884 . . .

> . . . N.Y. . . . ⟨1884⟩
>
> For comment see BAL, Vol. 4, p. 60.

Young People's Scrap-Book: Containing Choice Selections . . . Illustrated Poems . . . ⟨Compiled by Daniel Curry⟩

> Cincinnati . . . 1884.
>
> For fuller entry see BAL, Vol. 5, p. 612.

Half-Hours with the Best Humorous Authors. Selected . . . by Charles Morris . . .

> Philadelphia: J. B. Lippincott Company. 1889.
> 4 Vols.

Occasional Addresses Edited by Laurence Hutton and William Carey

> New-York . . . 1890
>
> For comment see entry No. 5655.

Werner's Readings and Recitations. No. 5 . . . Compiled . . . by Sara Sigourney Rice.

> New York . . . 1891.
>
> For fuller entry see No. 3433.

An American Anthology 1787–1899 . . . Edited by Edmund Clarence Stedman . . .

> Boston . . . M DCCCC
>
> For fuller entry see No. 3082.

The Lawyer's Alcove . . . Edited by Ina Russelle Warren . . .

> New York . . . 1900
>
> For comment see entry No. 4933.

A Book of American Humorous Verse . . .

> Chicago . . . 1904
>
> For comment see BAL, Vol. 1, p. 411.

Our Girls   Poems in Praise of the American Girl . . .

> New York . . . 1907
>
> For comment see entry No. 1945.

Poems of American History Collected . . . by Burton Egbert Stevenson

> Boston . . . 1908
>
> For fuller entry see in Joaquin Miller list.

REFERENCES AND ANA

The Political Mirror: Or Review of Jacksonism . . .

> New-York: Published by J. P. Peaslee, No 49 Cedar Street. 1835.
>
> Anonymous. Sometimes attributed to Morris. BAL has been unable to establish Morris's authorship.

Poems. Illustrated by Weir and Chapman.

> New York: Appleton, 1840.

Not seen. Not located. Entry from Allibone. Presumably an erroneous entry. "Several times reprinted."---Allibone.

Old King Time ... a Ballad ... Music ... by Henry Russell.

New-York ... Atwill 201 Broadway ... 1841 ...

Sheet music. Cover-title. Deposited June 26, 1841. Dedicated to Morris. Anonymous.

The Maid of Saxony [an opera.].

New York, 1842.

Thus Foley. Presumably an abbreviated entry for *Songs, Duetts and Chorusses in the New Opera of the Maid of Saxony* ..., New York, 1842, *q.v.*

Prospectus of the International Art-Union 1849.

Oliver & Brother, Printers, New-York ⟨1849⟩

Cover-title. Printed paper wrapper. Noted by SLM Feb. 1849 as *received*.

On pp. ⟨7⟩-8 is a note "from the *Home Journal*, edited by N. P. Willis and Geo. P. Morris." By Morris? By Willis?

Poems. By James Nack. With Introduction by George Pope Morris.

New York, 1852.

Thus Foley, p. 207. Not found by BAL. Presumably an erroneous entry. Perhaps related to Nack's *The Immortal* ..., New York, 1850, which contains a memoir by Morris; see in *Section One* of this list.

... Our Union, Right or Wrong ...

J, ⟨*sic*⟩ Wrigley. Publisher ... 27 Chatham Street ... New York ⟨n.d., *ca.* 1860–1864⟩

Single leaf. $9^{11}/_{16}''$ full × $6^{3}/_{8}''$. Printed on recto only. At head: *No. 743*

Anonymous.

Rouse, hearts of freedom's only home! | Hark to Disunion's cry ...

Sometimes credited to Morris. Author not known to BAL. Probably credited to Morris because of title similarity; see in *Section Two* Morris's *Our Union, Right or Wrong*, which begins: *In Freedom's name, our blades we draw* ...

The Song-Writers of America.

Further information wanting. Entry from Allibone who states that Morris edited a work of this name. Presumably a book. No such title found in *Union List of Serials*.

SARAH WENTWORTH APTHORP MORTON

(Philenia, a Lady of Boston)

1 7 5 9 – 1 8 4 6

14554. OUÂBI: OR THE VIRTUES OF NATURE. AN INDIAN TALE. IN FOUR CANTOS. BY PHILENIA, A LADY OF BOSTON ...

PRINTED AT BOSTON, BY I. THOMAS AND E. T. ANDREWS, AT FAUST'S STATUE, NO. 45, NEWBURY STREET. MDCCXC.

⟨i⟩-viii, ⟨9⟩-⟨52⟩. Laid paper. Frontispiece inserted. 9⅜″ × 5¹³⁄₁₆″.

⟨A⟩-F⁴, G².

Unprinted blue-gray laid paper wrapper.

Note on p. ⟨iv⟩ dated *October 16th, 1790.* Reviewed by UA Feb. 1791.

AAS   BPL   H   MHS   NYPL   UV   Y

14555. REANIMATION. A HYMN FOR THE HUMANE SOCIETY

Two printings noted; sequence not determined. The designations are completely arbitrary. Date on the basis of W. C. Ford's *Broadsides, Ballads &c. Printed in Massachusetts 1639–1800,* p. 360.

A

⟨fillet⟩ / REANIMATION. / A HYMN for the HUMANE SOCIETY. / BY MRS. MORTON. / [The last stanza is to be sung by those who have been / restored to life from apparent death.] / ⟨text: Six quatrains, numbered I-VI⟩ / ⟨fillet⟩ / ⟨n.p., n.d., 1791⟩

Single cut sheet. Laid paper. Printed on recto only. 11³⁄₁₆″ × 4⅝″.

B   BPL

B

⟨fillet⟩ / REANIMATION. / A HYMN for the HUMANE SOCIETY. / BY MRS. MORTON. / (The last stanza is to be sung by those who have been / restored to life from apparent death.) / ⟨text: Six quatrains, numbered I-VI⟩ / ⟨fillet⟩ / ⟨n.p., n.d., 1791⟩

Single cut sheet. Laid paper. Printed on recto only. 10⅜″ × 4⅛″.

Not seen. Entry on the basis of a photographic copy and correspondence.

HSP

Four versions of the hymn have been seen:

1: As above.

2: 1807. "Hymn. Composed by Mrs. Morton." See below under 1807.

3: 1809: "Mrs. Morton's Hymn. Originally intended to be sung by reanimated persons only." See below under 1809.

4: Collected in *My Mind . . .* , 1823 as "Reanimation. Written at the Request of the Boston Humane Society . . . ," pp. ⟨237⟩-238.

The text of 1791 was reprinted in 1813. See in reprint section below under year 1813.

14556. American Poems, Selected and Original. Vol. I.

   Litchfield: Printed by Collier and Buel. (The Copy-Right Secured As the Act Directs.) ⟨1793⟩

Leather?

Contains the following poems by Mrs. Morton credited to *Philenia.*

a-"Descriptive Lines, Written at the Request of a Friend, upon the Surrounding Prospect from Beacon-Hill in Boston," pp. 176-179. In altered form collected in *Beacon Hill,* 1797.

a-"Invocation to Hope," p. 182.

b-"Lines, Addressed to the Inimitable Author of the Poems under the Signature of Della Crusca," pp. 184-185. Reprinted from *Ouâbi,* 1790.

a,c-"Ode to the President, on His Visiting the Northern States," pp. 180-181. Collected in *My Mind,* 1823, as "Ode for Music."

a-"Philenia to Alfred," pp. 187-188. *Alfred! the heaven lent muse is thine . . .*

a-"Philenia to Alfred," pp. 190-192. *"Pen'ry"* *no Alfred! 'tis not thine . . .*

a,c-"Prayer to Patience," pp. 183-184.

a-Earliest located book publication.
b-Reprinted from *Ouâbi*, 1790.
c-Collected in *My Mind*, 1823.

H NYPL Y

14557. "Rear'd midst the war-empurpled Plain, &c." The Death Song of an Indian Chief. [Taken from Ouâbi, an Indian Tale, in Four Cantos, by Philenia, a Lady of Boston.] Set to Musick by Mr. Hans Gram, of Boston.

⟨n.p., n.d., 1793?⟩

Single cut sheet. Laid paper. Printed on both sides. Caption-title. The above at head of p. ⟨1⟩. 8⅜″ × 10⅞″.

Dated 1793 by Evans.

Reprinted from *Ouâbi*, 1790.

LC

14558. BEACON HILL. A LOCAL POEM, HISTORIC AND DESCRIPTIVE. BOOK I . . .

BOSTON. PRINTED BY MANNING & LORING FOR THE AUTHOR. 1797.

Anonymous. At end of "Apology for the Poem," the initials *S.M.*

⟨i⟩-⟨x⟩, ⟨11⟩-56. Printed on wove paper watermarked: *B 1795; B 1796; 1795; 1796.* 11⅛″ × 8¹³⁄₁₆″.

⟨A⟩-G⁴.

Unprinted gray-blue laid paper wrapper.

All published.

Entered for copyright Sept. 9, 1797.

AAS BA H MHS NYPL UV Y

14559. THE VIRTUES OF SOCIETY. A TALE, FOUNDED ON FACT. BY THE AUTHOR OF THE VIRTUES OF NATURE . . .

BOSTON. PRINTED BY MANNING & LORING, FOR THE AUTHOR. 1799.

⟨1⟩-46, blank leaf. Printed on wove paper watermarked: *1795; 1796; B1796.* 11¹⁄₁₆″ × 8⅞″.

⟨A⟩², B-F⁴, G².

Probably issued in unprinted blue-gray laid paper wrapper.

Entered for copyright July 19, 1799.

B H NYPL Y

14560. An Address Delivered before the Members of the Massachusetts Charitable Fire Society, at Their Anniversary Meeting, June 1, 1804. By Edward Gray, Esq.

Boston. Printed by Russell and Cutler, 1804.

Cover-title? Issued in printed paper wrapper? Printed self-wrapper?

"Ode, for the Ninth Anniversary of the Massachusetts Charitable Fire Society, May 31, 1803," pp. 27-28. Much revised and collected in *My Mind*, 1823, under the title "Ode for the Element of Fire . . ."

AAS H

14561. DEDICATORY HYMN. COMPOSED FOR, AND TO BE SUNG AT THE OPENING OF THE WEST-BOSTON MEETING-HOUSE, ON THURSDAY, NOVEMBER 27, 1806 . . .

⟨n.p., n.d., BOSTON, 1806⟩

Anonymous.

Single leaf. Laid paper. 6⅛″ full × 3¾″. Printed on recto only.

Collected in *My Mind*, 1823.

BPL

14562. Order of Performances on the 22d Anniversary ⟨*sic*⟩ of the Massachusetts Humane Society . . .

⟨n.p., n.d., Boston, 1807⟩

Single leaf. Printed on recto only.

Contains a "Hymn," *Who from the closing shade of night . . .*

See above under 1791 for another version of this hymn.

Two issues noted. The order of presentation is presumed correct:

A

Line 2: . . . ANIVERSARY . . . Printed on wove paper watermarked *J Boies & Co.* 11″ × 9⅜″; trimmed?

B

Line 2: . . . ANNIVERSARY . . . Printed on laid paper. 12¼″ × 9¾″.

AAS (A) UV (B)

14563. Order of Performances at the Chapel Church on the 24th Anniversary of the Massachusetts Humane Society, June 13, 1809 . . .

⟨n.p., Boston, 1809⟩

OUÂBI:

OR THE

VIRTUES OF NATURE.

AN

INDIAN TALE.

IN FOUR CANTOS.

BY PHILENIA, a Lady of Boston.

" Fierce Wars and faithful Loves ſhall moralize my Song."
Spenſer's Fairy Queen.

PRINTED AT *BOSTON*,
BY I. THOMAS AND E. T. ANDREWS,
At *FAUST's* STATUE, No. 45, Newbury Street.

MDCCXC.

Single cut sheet. Printed on recto only. Contains a printing of Mrs. Morton's hymn, *Who, from the closing shades of night* . . .

See above under 1791 for comment and another version of this hymn.

AAS

14564. The Works, in Verse and Prose, of the Late Robert Treat Paine, Jun. Esq. with Notes . . .

Boston: Printed and Published by J. Belcher. 1812.

Boards, printed paper label on spine.

"Philenia to Menander," pp. 132-133.

H

14565. MY MIND AND ITS THOUGHTS, IN SKETCHES, FRAGMENTS, AND ESSAYS . . .

BOSTON: WELLS AND LILLY–––COURT-STREET. 1823.

⟨i⟩-xx, ⟨1⟩-289; blank, p. ⟨290⟩; list of subscribers, pp. ⟨291⟩-295. $9^{11}/_{16}''$ full $\times$ $5^{13}/_{16}''$.

⟨A⟩-B⁴, C², 1-37⁴. Signature mark 6 absent from some copies.

Drab paper boards sides, buff (or peach) paper shelfback, printed paper label on spine. Also brown paper boards, printed paper label on spine. Flyleaves.

AAS   BPL   MHS

14566. The Memorial, a Christmas, New Year's and Easter Offering for 1828. Edited by Frederic S. Hill . . .

Boston: Published by True and Greene, and Richardson and Lord ⟨n.d., after Nov. 3, 1827⟩

According to the preface this publication contains a contribution by Mrs. Morton. Further information wanting.

For comment see entry No. 4586.

14567. My Mind and its Thoughts . . .

New-York: J. P. Peaslee   49 Cedar Street, 1835.

Reprints, with some slight textual alterations, seventy-four of the "Thoughts" previously in *My Mind and its Thoughts* . . . , 1823.

Noted only as part of an omnibus volume, bound together with *A Guide to Domestic Happiness. In a Series of Letters*, by the author of *The Refuge*, ⟨i.e., William Giles⟩ New York, 1835; and, *Essays on Various Subjects* . . . , by Hannah More, New York, 1835.

Binder's title: *Cabinet of Literature.*

Note: In this 1835 reprinting the numbering of the "Thoughts" is extensively altered.

EM

REPRINTS

The following publications contain material ⊢ Morton reprinted from other publications.

Humane Society. The Anniversary of the Massachusetts Humane Society Will Be Celebrated this Day, at 4, o'clock, P.M. in the Chapel Church. Order of Performances . . .

⟨n.p.⟩ June 8, 1813.

Single cut sheet. $12^7/_8''$ full $\times$ $7^{15}/_{16}''$. Printed on recto only.

Contains "Hymn LXXV. For the Humane Society." A reprint of the 1791 version; see above under 1791.

The Columbian Muse . . .

New-York . . . 1794.

For comment see BAL, Vol. 1, p. 184.

The Cypress Wreath, or Mourner's Friend . . .

Greenfield, Mass. Printed and Published by Phelps & Clark. 1828.

Title deposited Dec. 12, 1827. Cloth?

Specimens of American Poetry . . . in Three Volumes. By Samuel Kettell . . .

Boston . . . MDCCCXXIX.

For comment see entry No. 3251.

Songs, Odes, and Other Poems, on National Subjects; Compiled . . . by Wm. McCarty. Part Third–––Military . . .

Philadelphia . . . 1842.

For comment see entry No. 4830.

The American Female Poets . . . by Caroline May.

Philadelphia . . . 1848.

For comment see BAL, Vol. 1, p. 300.

Specimens of Newspaper Literature . . . by Joseph T. Buckingham . . .

Boston . . . 1850.

For comment see entry No. 4645.

Cyclopædia of American Literature . . . by Evert
A. Duyckinck and George L. Duyckinck . . .

New York . . . 1855.

For fuller entry see No. 11092A.

The Liberty Bell. By Friends of Freedom . . .

Boston . . . MDCCCLVIII.

For fuller entry see No. 3185.

Poems of American History Collected . . . by
Burton Egbert Stevenson

Boston . . . 1908

For fuller entry see in Joaquin Miller list.

REFERENCES AND ANA

Occurrences of the Times. Or, the Transactions of
Four Days . . . a Farce. In Two Acts . . .

⟨n.p., n.d., presumably Boston, 1789⟩ Printed
for the Purchasers.

Anonymous. Sometimes ascribed to Mrs.
Morton. See Pendleton-Ellis, p. 38. For fuller
entry see BAL No. 1519.

The Power of Sympathy . . .

. . . Boston . . . MDCCLXXXIX.

Formerly attributed to Mrs. Morton.   By
William Hill Brown. For fuller entry see No.
1518.

The American Indian; or, Virtues of Nature. A
Play. In Three Acts . . . by James Bacon . . .

London: Printed for the Author, by Messrs.
Harrison and Co. No. 18, Paternoster Row.
M DCC XCV.

Printed paper wrapper. Founded on *Ouâbi*,
1790.

Nature: On Freedom of Mind: And Other
Poems.

Boston: Dutton & Wentworth, 1839.

Anonymous. Sometimes attributed to Mrs.
Morton. Dismissed by Pendleton-Ellis, p. 101.

"Though Mrs. Morton doubtless continued to
write verses after 1823, nothing from her pen is
known to have been preserved. A small volume
containing about a half dozen poems, published
anonymously at Boston in 1839 by Dutton and
Wentworth, is attributed to Mrs. Morton con-
jecturally, in a handwritten note in the Columbia University Library copy, probably on the
basis of one of the poems contained, which has
to do with a grave near the monument of Judge
Morton at Taunton. The collection, entitled
Nature: On Freedom of Mind and Other Poems,
shows no similarity, in sentiments or verse style,
to Philenia's poetry."---Pendleton-Ellis, p.
101.

. . . The Power of Sympathy: Or, the Triumph of
Nature. Founded in Truth. By Mrs. Perez Morton
(Sarah Wentworth Apthorp) . . .

Boston: Printed by Cupples & Patterson and
Published by Them at the Back Bay Bookstore
250 Boylston Street ⟨1894⟩

At head of title: *Edited by Walter Littlefield*.

550 numbered copies only.

Not by Mrs. Morton. For comment see entry No.
1518.

Philenia   The Life and Works of Sarah Wentworth Morton . . . by Emily Pendleton and Milton
Ellis

Printed at the University Press Orono, Maine
1931

Printed paper wrapper. *The Maine Bulletin*, Vol.
XXXIV, No. 4, December, 1931.

JOHN LOTHROP MOTLEY

1 8 1 4 – 1 8 7 7

Motley's principal works, *The Rise of the Dutch Republic* and *The History of the United Netherlands*, are here described in their first English and American editions. Not described are the several revised editions.

The present list is offered in four sections:

Section One: Motley's own works; or, works containing earliest located book publication of a Motley contribution.

Section Two: Official and like publications.

Section Three: Reprints of Motley's works issued under his name.

Section Four: Compilations containing Motley material reprinted from earlier books.

14568. MORTON OF MORTON'S HOPE; AN AUTOBIOGRAPHY ... IN THREE VOLUMES ...

LONDON: HENRY COLBURN, PUBLISHER; GREAT MARLBOROUGH STREET. 1839.

Anonymous. See next entry for first American edition.

1: ⟨i⟩-viii, ⟨1⟩-287; printer's imprint, p. ⟨288⟩. 7⅞″ × 4⅞″.

2: ⟨i-iv⟩, ⟨1⟩-322, blank leaf.

3: ⟨i-iv⟩, ⟨1⟩-300; plus: Publisher's catalog, pp. ⟨1-6⟩; a fourth leaf excised; thus in all copies?

1: ⟨A⟩⁴, B-I, K-N¹².

2: ⟨A⟩², B-I, K-O¹², P⁶.

3: ⟨A⟩², B-I, K-N¹², O⁶; plus: ⟨P⟩⁴. *Note:* In the copy here collated ⟨P⟩₄ has been excised; all thus?

Tan-gray paper boards, black H cloth shelfback. Printed paper label on spine.

P. ⟨1⟩ of terminal catalog, Vol. 3, dated *June 1839*. Listed Ath Aug. 31, 1839; LG Aug. 31, 1839; PC Sept. 2, 1839. Advertised PC Sept 2, 1839, as *just published*. Advertised Ath Sept. 7, 1839, with extracts from reviews.

Note: The texts of the British and the American editions vary. The H copy (of the London edition), uncollatable, was presented to Longfellow by Motley and bears the following inscription in Motley's hand: "The marked & erased passages are omitted in the American edition———and wd have been in the English, if there had been time & opportunity to correct the press."

Y

14569. MORTON'S HOPE: OR THE MEMOIRS OF A PROVINCIAL. IN TWO VOLUMES ...

NEW-YORK: PUBLISHED BY HARPER & BROTHERS, 82 CLIFF-STREET. 1839.

Anonymous. See preceding entry for first edition.

Note: The texts of the British and American editions vary.

1: ⟨1⟩-247. 7⅝″ × 4½″.

2: ⟨1⟩-298; 2 pp. advertisements.

1: ⟨1⟩-20⁶, 21⁴.

2: ⟨1⟩², 2-25⁶, 26⁴.

CM cloth: brown; slate. Printed paper label on spine. Flyleaves.

Noted as *in press* NYR July, 1839. Deposited Sept. 23, 1839. Reviewed NYR Oct. 1839.

AAS   B   H   Y

14570. The Boston Book. Being Specimens of Metropolitan Literature.

Boston: George W. Light, 1 Cornhill. 1841.

"Westward Movement of Civilization," pp. ⟨213⟩-217.

For fuller entry see No. 631.

14571. The New World. Park Benjamin, Editor ... a Gift for the Holydays.

New-York, Friday, January 1, 1841 ...

Caption-title. A special issue of *The New World*.

Contains Motley's "Blue Beard, a Story in Five Acts, Translated from the German ⟨of Lewis Tieck⟩ for the New World," p. ⟨3⟩.

H

14572. Characteristics of Men of Genius; a Series of Biographical, Historical, and Critical Essays, Selected, by Permission, Chiefly from the North American Review . . .

London: Chapman, Brothers, 121, Newgate Street. M.DCCC.XLVI.

"Peter the Great," Vol. 2, pp. ⟨257⟩-317. For first American edition see under 1877.

For fuller comment see entry No. 5208.

14573. MERRY-MOUNT; A ROMANCE OF THE MASSACHUSETTS COLONY . . .

BOSTON AND CAMBRIDGE: JAMES MUNROE AND COMPANY. M DCCC XLIX.

Anonymous.

1: ⟨1⟩-8, ⟨1⟩-222; blank leaf. 7^{11}/$_{16}$″ full × 5^1/$_8$″ scant. See below under *Binding* for a comment on inserted advertisements.

2: ⟨1⟩-4, ⟨1⟩-252.

1: ⟨-⟩⁴, 1-18⁶, 19⁴. Leaf 19₄ excised in the two-volumes-in-one format.

2: ⟨-⟩², 1-21⁶.

Occurs in a variety of bindings. The following designations are for identification only and no sequence is suggested.

BINDING A --- TWO VOLUMES

T cloth: black. TB cloth: red. Sides stamped in blind with a triple rule frame, a filigree at each inner corner. At center an ornament 3^1/$_8$″ tall × 1^7/$_8$″. Spine stamped in gold save as noted: MERRY- / MOUNT / ⟨*simple rule*⟩ / VOL. I. ⟨II.⟩ / MUNROE & CO. Spine decorated with an arrangement of blindstamped rules. Yellow end papers. Flyleaves.

Inserted at back of Vol. 1: Publisher's catalog, undated, 4 pp., 22 numbered titles.

UV   Y (inscribed by early owner Jan. 1, 1849)

BINDING B --- TWO VOLUMES

A cloth: green; purple. TB cloth: red. Sides blindstamped with a rules frame, a filigree at each inner corner, a filigree at the center. Spine lettered in gold: MERRY- / MOUNT / ⟨*lozenge rule*⟩ / VOL. I. ⟨2.⟩ / MUNROE & CO. Spine decorated with an arrangement of blindstamped rules. Yellow end papers. Flyleaves.

Inserted at front of Vol. 1: Publisher's catalog, undated, 4 pp., 22 numbered titles.

Note: BAL has seen four copies in this binding bearing presentation inscriptions by Motley, the earliest date being Dec. 20, 1848.

BPL H UV Y

BINDING C --- TWO VOLUMES IN ONE

A cloth: black; red. TB cloth: black. Sides blindstamped with a rules frame, a filigree at each inner corner, a filigree at the center. Spine lettered in gold: MERRY-MOUNT / A ROMANCE / OF THE / MASSACHUSETTS / COLONY / JAMES MUNROE & CO. Pale yellow end papers. Flyleaves.

Inserted at front: Publisher's catalog, undated, 4 pp., 22 numbered titles.

Note: The publisher's spine imprint measures ^{3}/$_{16}$″ tall.

NYPL UV Y

BINDING Ca --- TWO VOLUMES IN ONE

Same as binding C but with one variation: The publisher's spine imprint measures ^{1}/$_8$″ tall.

The UV copy inscribed by an early owner Jan. 1849.

NYPL UV Y

BINDING D --- TWO VOLUMES IN ONE

BD cloth: greenish-tan. HC cloth: Dark purple. TR cloth: dark purple. Sides blindstamped with an ornamented rules frame, at center: An upright ovoid frame. Spine stamped in gold save as noted: MERRY- / MOUNT / ⟨*filigree*⟩ At top and at bottom of spine: A blindstamped triple rule. Yellow end papers. Flyleaves.

Inserted at back: Publisher's catalog, undated, 4 pp., 22 numbered titles.

AAS MHS Y

BINDING E --- TWO VOLUMES IN ONE

TB cloth: red. Sides blindstamped with a triple rule frame, a filigree at each inner corner. At center an ornament 3^1/$_8$″ tall × 1^7/$_8$″. Spine stamped in gold save as noted: MERRY-MOUNT / A ROMANCE / OF THE / MASSACHUSETTS / COLONY. / JAMES MUNROE & CO. ⟨spine imprint presumed to be as here given⟩ Spine decorated with an arrangement of blindstamped rules. Yellow end papers. Flyleaves.

Inserted at front: Publisher's catalog, undated, 4 pp., 22 numbered titles.

BA

BINDING F --- TWO VOLUMES IN ONE

BD cloth: purple. Sides blindstamped with a rules frame. At center of each side, also in blind, an angular ornament measuring 3^1/$_4$″ × 3^1/$_4$″. Spine goldstamped: ⟨*triple rule*⟩ / MERRY / MOUNT /

⟨*simple rule*⟩ | *Motley* | ⟨*filigree*⟩ | ⟨*rules*⟩ Pale yellowish end papers. No inserted catalog. Flyleaves.

Presumably a remainder.

Y

Noted as *just published* LW Dec. 23, 1848. Deposited Dec. 28, 1848. A Boston letter, dated Dec. 21, notes the book as *just published* (LW Dec. 30, 1848). Listed LW Dec. 30, 1848. Reviewed Ath May 5, 1849: *This tale comes from America;* and the reviewer looks forward to *the mails of June* for more copies to arrive. Not found in PC's annual catalog.

14574. THE RISE OF THE DUTCH REPUB-LIC. A HISTORY . . . IN THREE VOL-UMES . . .

LONDON: JOHN CHAPMAN, 8, KING WILLIAM ST., STRAND. CHAPMAN & HALL, 193, PICCADILLY. MDCCCLVI.

For first American edition see next entry.

1: ⟨i⟩-xii, ⟨1⟩-579; printer's imprint, p. ⟨580⟩. 8⁹/₁₆″ × 5½″.

2: ⟨i⟩-iv, ⟨1⟩-582; printer's imprint, p. ⟨583⟩.

3: ⟨i⟩-iv, ⟨1⟩-664. Printer's imprint at foot of p. 664.

1: *Signed:* ⟨A⟩⁶, B-I, K-U, X-Z, AA-II, KK-OO⁸, PP².

2: *Signed:* ⟨A⟩², B-I, K-U, X-Z, AA-II, KK-OO⁸, PP⁴.

3: *Signed:* ⟨A⟩², B-I, K-U, X-Z, AA-II, KK-TT⁸, UU⁴.

Presumably issued in cloth. Inserted at back of Vol. 1 is a publisher's catalog, pp. ⟨1⟩-32.

Advertised for *this day* Ath Feb. 16, 1856. Listed Ath Feb. 16, 1856. Reviewed Ath March 1, 1856. Listed PC March 1, 1856. Reviewed LG March 8, 1856.

NYPL   Y

Later British Printings

The following list is based on trade periodical listings and advertisements. The order of presentation is chronological.

Routledge: 1857 and later.

Beeton: 1858 and later.

Strahan (Edinburgh); and Hamilton, Adams (London): 1859 and later.

George Manwaring: 1860 (?).

Bickers: 1864 and later.

Warne: 1886.

Ward, Lock & Co.: 1888.

W. Swan Sonnenschein: 1889.

W. W. Gibbings: 1889 and later.

14575. THE RISE OF THE DUTCH RE-PUBLIC. A HISTORY . . . IN THREE VOL-UMES . . .

NEW YORK: HARPER & BROTHERS, 329 & 331 PEARL STREET. 1856.

For prior publication see preceding entry.

1: ⟨i⟩-xii, ⟨1⟩-579. 9⁵/₈″ full × 6″.

2: ⟨i-iv⟩, ⟨i⟩-iv, ⟨1⟩-582, blank leaf.

3: ⟨i-iv⟩, ⟨i⟩-iv, ⟨1⟩-664.

1: ⟨1⟩⁶, B⁸, 2-36⁸, ⟨37⟩².

2: ⟨-⟩⁴, 1-36⁸, 37⁴.

3: ⟨-⟩⁴, 1-41⁸, 42⁴.

T cloth: black; purple; slate. TR-like cloth: brown. TZ cloth: black. Yellow-coated end papers. The flyleaves (front and back) comprise a gathering of four leaves used as follows: One used as lining for the end-paper; one excised or pasted under the pastedown; two present as free blanks. According to an advertisement in CRN March 22, 1856, available in cloth; sheep; half-calf.

Noted as *in a few days* CRN March 15 1856. Advertised as *just ready* CRN March 22, 1856. Deposited April 15, 1856. Listed CRN April 19, 1856.

AAS   BA   BPL   H   Y

14576. HISTORY OF THE UNITED NETHER-LANDS: FROM THE DEATH OF WIL-LIAM THE SILENT TO THE SYNOD OF DORT. WITH A FULL VIEW OF THE ENGLISH-DUTCH STRUGGLE AGAINST SPAIN, AND OF THE ORIGIN AND DESTRUCTION OF THE SPANISH AR-MADA . . .

LONDON: JOHN MURRAY, ALBEMARLE STREET. 1860. THE RIGHT OF TRANSLATION IS RESERVED.

In some copies of Vol. 1 the colon following *Netherlands* is lacking.

Note: Entry tentative. For American edition see below under year 1861. For Vols. 3-4 see below under year 1867.

2 Vols. Title-pages in black and orange.

1: ⟨i⟩-xii, ⟨1⟩-532. Frontispiece and 1 folded plate inserted. 8½″ × 5½″.

2: ⟨i⟩-⟨viii⟩, ⟨1⟩-563. Frontispiece inserted.

1: ⟨a⟩⁴, b², B-I, K-U, X-Z, 2A-2I, 2K-2L⁸, 2M².

2: ⟨A⟩⁴, B-D⁸, E⁶, F-I, K-U, X-Z, 2A-2I, 2K-2N⁸, 2O⁴.

Cloth?

Announced BM Aug. 15, 1860. Noted as *forthcoming* Ath Oct. 13, 1860. Noted for *Nov. and Dec.* Ath Nov. 10, 1860. Noted as *just ready* Ath Nov. 24, 1860; Ath Dec. 1, 1860; PC Dec. 1, 1860. Noted in the *New Book List* Ath Dec. 8, 1860. *Now ready* Ath Dec. 15, 1860; PC Dec. 15, 1860. Listed Ath, LG, PC, Dec. 15, 1860. "Mudie, the proprietor of the celebrated Circulating Library in London, took fifteen hundred copies of Motley's *History of the United Netherlands* for his subscribers. The work will be issued immediately by Harpers." ---BM Feb. 1, 1861.

Note: Published in Holland by Martinus Nijhoff, The Hague, 1860; precise date of publication not known. Copy in BPL.

LC   Y

14577. Proceedings of the Massachusetts Historical Society. 1858–1860 . . .

Boston: Printed for the Society. M.DCCC.LX.

Letter to William Amory, *26th February, 1859*, pp. 266-271. For a longer version of this letter see *Autograph Leaves of Our Country's Authors*, 1864, below.

BA   H

14578. HISTORY OF THE UNITED NETHERLANDS: FROM THE DEATH OF WILLIAM THE SILENT TO THE SYNOD OF DORT. WITH A FULL VIEW OF THE ENGLISH-DUTCH STRUGGLE AGAINST SPAIN, AND OF THE ORIGIN AND DESTRUCTION OF THE SPANISH ARMADA . . .

NEW YORK: HARPER & BROTHERS, PUBLISHERS, 327 TO 335 PEARL STREET. 1861.

For prior publication see above under year 1860. For Vols. 3-4 see below under year 1868.

2 Vols.

1: ⟨i⟩-xii, ⟨1⟩-532. Frontispiece and 1 folded plate inserted. $9\frac{3}{16}'' \times 5\frac{13}{16}''$.

2: ⟨i⟩-⟨viii⟩, ⟨1⟩-563; blank, p. ⟨564⟩; advertisements, pp. ⟨1⟩-4. Frontispiece inserted.

1: ⟨A⟩⁶, B-I, K-Z⁸, 2A-2I⁸, 2K².

2: ⟨A⟩⁴, B-I, K-U, X-Z⁸, 2A-2I, 2K-2N⁸, 2O⁴.

TZ cloth: black. Brown-coated on white end papers. Double flyleaves. Advertised in BM April 1, 1861, as in muslin; sheep; half-calf.

Announced BM Nov. 15, 1860. It "has at last made its appearance from the press"---BM Feb. 15, 1861. BA copy received Feb. 19, 1861. Listed BM March 1, 1861. "The sale of Motley's *History of the Netherlands* is something remarkable. Before

the day of publication, the Harpers had, on their books, orders for more than 5,000 copies. In one day 2,000 copies were subscribed for by booksellers and libraries in New York and Brooklyn. The New York Mercantile Library purchased, for circulation, 250 copies . . ."---BM March 1, 1861.

AAS   BA   H   NYPL

14579. CAUSES OF THE CIVIL WAR IN AMERICA . . . REPRINTED, BY PERMISSION, FROM "THE TIMES."

LONDON: GEORGE MANWARING, 8, KING WILLIAM STREET, STRAND. MDCCCLXI. THE RIGHT OF TRANSLATION IS RESERVED.

For first American edition see next entry.

⟨1⟩-30, blank leaf. $8\frac{7}{16}'' \times 5\frac{1}{2}''$.

⟨A⟩-B⁸.

Printed self-wrapper?

Advertised as *this day* Ath June 8, 1861. Noticed by Ath June 15, 1861. Listed PC June 17, 1861.

LC   Y

14580. THE CAUSES OF THE AMERICAN CIVIL WAR

For prior publication in London see preceding entry.

Two editions noted; the sequence has not been determined and the order of presentation is completely arbitrary.

A

THE CAUSES OF THE AMERICAN CIVIL WAR. BY JOHN LATHROP ⟨*sic*⟩ MOTLEY . . .
NEW YORK: D. APPLETON & COMPANY, 443 & 445 BROADWAY. 1861.

Cover-title.

⟨1⟩-24. $9'' \times 5\frac{3}{4}$.

⟨-⟩¹².

Printed self-wrapper.

Listed APC June 15, 1861.

AAS   B   BPL   H   LC   MHS   NYPL   Y

B

LETTERS OF JOHN LOTHROP MOTLEY, AND JOSEPH HOLT. FOR GRATUITOUS DISTRIBUTION . . .

NEW-YORK: HENRY E. TUDOR, PRINTER, 44 ANN STREET. 1861.

On the title-page of all examined copies: . . . *followiug* . . . for . . . *following* . . .

⟨1⟩-34. $7\frac{13}{16}'' \times 5\frac{5}{16}''$. Motley's text pp. ⟨3⟩-27. Holt's statement, pp. 27-34.

⟨1⟩-2⁸, ⟨3⟩¹·

Printed tan paper wrapper.

Issued after May 31, 1861; before July 31, 1861, a copy in Y so inscribed.

Note: See below in *Section Three* for later printings, issued by H. H. Lloyd & Co., New York; and, James G. Gregory, New York. According to Sabin (entry 51103) also issued by G. P. Putnam, New York; not located by BAL.

H   Y

14581. Autograph Leaves of Our Country's Authors.

Baltimore, Cushings & Bailey 1864.

"To William Amory Esq., brother-in-law of Mr. Prescott on Mr. Prescott's death," pp. 182-188. For a shorter version see *Proceedings of the Massachusetts Historical Society. 1858–1860*, Boston, 1860, above.

For fuller entry see No. 2418.

14582. Memorial RGS ⟨Robert Gould Shaw⟩

Cambridge University Press 1864

Letter, September 8, 1863, pp. 156-158.

For comment see entry No. 3197.

14583. The Drum Beat

Published by the Brooklyn and Long Island Fair, for the Benefit of the U.S. Sanitary Commission . . . Brooklyn . . . 1864 . . .

Letter, Feb. 2, 1864, No. XI, p. ⟨1⟩.

For comment see entry No. 148.

14584. HISTORY OF THE UNITED NETH-ERLANDS: FROM THE DEATH OF WILLIAM THE SILENT TO THE TWELVE YEARS' TRUCE---1609 . . . IN FOUR VOLUMES.---VOL. III. ⟨IV⟩ 1590–1600 ⟨1600-9.⟩ . . .

LONDON: JOHN MURRAY, ALBEMARLE STREET. 1867. THE RIGHT OF TRANSLATION IS RESERVED.

For Vols. 1-2 see above under 1860. For American edition of Vols. 3-4 see next entry. Title-pages in black and red.

3: ⟨i⟩-x, ⟨1⟩-599. Frontispiece inserted. 8½″ × 5½″.

4: ⟨i⟩-⟨viii⟩, ⟨1⟩-632. Frontispiece inserted.

3: *Signed:* ⟨a⟩⁴, b¹, B-I, K-U, X-Z, 2*A-2I*, 2*K*-2*P*⁸, 2*Q*⁴.

4: *Signed:* ⟨a⟩⁴, B-I, K-U, X-Z, 2*A-2I*, 2*K*-2*R*⁸, 2*S*⁴.

Presumably issued in cloth.

Announced PC April 15, 1867; Aug. 1, 1867. "Murray will publish before Christmas"---PC Oct. 1, 1867. Advertised as *forthcoming* Ath Oct. 12, 1867; PC Oct. 15, 1867. In *List for Nov. and Dec.* PC Nov. 1, 1867. Advertised as *forthcoming* Ath Nov. 2, 1867. Advertised as *new* PC Nov. 15, 1867. Listed Ath Nov. 16, 1867. Reviewed Ath Nov. 16, 1867. Advertised as *ready* Ath Nov. 23, 1867. Listed ALG Dec. 2, 1867; PC Dec. 10, 1867; Bkr Dec. 12, 1867.

Another edition, presumably revised, was noted by PC Oct. 15, 1868, as *forthcoming; to be published monthly and completed in 4 vols.* Listed by Ath Nov. 21, 1868; PC Dec. 10, 1868. *This day*---PC Dec. 18, 1868. *Now ready*---Ath Feb. 6, 1869, "with the author's latest corrections and additions."

H   NYPL   Y

14585. HISTORY OF THE UNITED NETH-ERLANDS: FROM THE DEATH OF WILLIAM THE SILENT TO THE TWELVE YEARS' TRUCE---1609 . . . IN FOUR VOLUMES.---VOL. III. ⟨IV.⟩ 1590–1600. ⟨1600-9.⟩ . . .

NEW YORK: HARPER & BROTHERS, PUBLISHERS, 327 TO 335 PEARL STREET. 1868.

For Vols. 1-2 see above under 1861. For prior publication of Vols. 3-4 see preceding entry.

3: ⟨i-ii⟩, ⟨i⟩-x, ⟨1⟩-599. Frontispiece. 9¼″ × 5⅞″.

4: ⟨i-iv⟩, ⟨i⟩-⟨viii⟩, ⟨1⟩-632; plus: advertisements, pp. ⟨1⟩-4. Frontispiece.

3: ⟨A⟩⁶, B-I, K-U, X-Z⁸, 2*A-2I*, 2*K*-2*P*⁸, 2*Q*⁴.

4: ⟨A⟩⁶, B-I, K-U, X-Z⁸, 2*A-2I*, 2*K*-2*R*⁸, 2*S*⁴; plus: ⟨2*T*⟩².

Note: In some copies leaf B₁, Vol. 4, (pp. ⟨1⟩-2) is a cancel. BAL has been unable to determine the reason.

TZ cloth: black. Pale peach end papers. Double flyleaves. *Note:* The spine stamping of Vol. 3 occurs in two states of unknown sequence, if any. The designations are completely arbitrary:

A: A period present after NETHERLANDS and after MOTLEY

B: The periods cited are not present.

Note: Sig. P, Vol. 3, occurs on both thick and on thin papers; significance, if any, not known.

"The conclusion of the *History of the United Nether-lands* will appear, this autumn, simultaneously in London and New York."---ALG Sept. 16, 1867. Vol. 3 received by BA Jan. 21, 1868. Vol. 3 listed ALG Feb. 1, 1868. Vol. 4 received by BA Feb. 8, 1868. Vol. 4 listed ALG Feb. 15, 1868.

AAS   H   NYPL

14586. FOUR QUESTIONS FOR THE PEOPLE, AT THE PRESIDENTIAL ELECTION. ADDRESS OF JOHN LOTHROP MOTLEY, BEFORE THE PARKER FRATERNITY, AT THE MUSIC HALL, OCTOBER 20, 1868.

BOSTON: TICKNOR AND FIELDS. 1868.

⟨1⟩-75. 9″ × 5¾″.

⟨1-4⁸, 5⁶⟩. *Signed:* ⟨1⟩-9⁴, 10².

Printed salmon paper wrapper.

Note: All examined copies have *disintregration* for *disintegration* p. 17, line 4 from the bottom.

According to the publisher's records 1000 copies were printed Oct. 1868; bound Oct. 23, 1868. And: "20 copies ⟨printed⟩ on one side for ⟨the use of news⟩papers & one letter copy."

AAS BPL H LC MHS UV Y

14587. HISTORIC PROGRESS AND AMERICAN DEMOCRACY: AN ADDRESS DELIVERED BEFORE THE NEW-YORK HISTORICAL SOCIETY, AT THEIR SIXTY-FOURTH ANNIVERSARY, DECEMBER 16, 1868 . . .

NEW-YORK: CHARLES SCRIBNER AND CO., 654 BROADWAY. 1869.

⟨i-iv⟩, ⟨1⟩-74, blank leaf. 10″ × 6¼″.

⟨1-5⁸⟩.

Printed paper wrapper: blue-green; peach. *Note:* Front repeats letterpress of the title-page save for (on some copies) absence of the period after *Broadway*.

Entered for copyright Jan. 13, 1869. MHS copy received Jan. 29, 1869; BPL copy Feb. 1, 1869; BA copy Feb. 2, 1869. Listed ALG Feb. 2, 1869; PC March 15, 1869. Advertised PC June 15, 1869; Ath July 3, 1869.

AAS B BA BPL H LC MHS NYPL UV Y

14588. Sixty-Third Anniversary Celebration of the New-England Society in the City of New York at Delmonico's Dec. 22, 1868.

⟨n.p., n.d., New York, 1869⟩

Printed paper wrapper.

"Speech," pp. 32-35.

H NYPL Y

14589. Tribute to Henry Hart Milman . . . Dean of St. Paul's, London. [From the Proceedings of the Massachusetts Historical Society.] . . .

⟨n.p., Boston, 1869⟩

Caption-title. The above at head of p. ⟨1⟩. Single cut sheet folded to make four pages.

Comments, pp. 2-4.

Appears also in *Proceedings of the Massachusetts Historical Society. 1867–1869 . . .* , Boston, M.DCCC.-LXIX.

AAS

14590. THE LIFE AND DEATH OF JOHN OF BARNEVELD, ADVOCATE OF HOLLAND; WITH A VIEW OF THE PRIMARY CAUSES AND MOVEMENTS OF THE THIRTY YEARS' WAR . . . IN TWO VOLUMES . . .

LONDON: JOHN MURRAY, ALBEMARLE STREET. 1874. THE RIGHT OF TRANSLATION IS RESERVED.

Title-pages in black and red.

For first American edition see next entry.

1: ⟨i⟩-⟨xvi⟩, ⟨1⟩-389. Frontispiece and 1 plate inserted. 8⁷⁄₁₆″ × 5⅜″.

2: ⟨i⟩-⟨viii⟩, ⟨1⟩-475. 2 plates inserted.

1: ⟨A⟩-I, K-U, X-Z⁸, 2A-2B⁸, 2C³.

2: ⟨A⟩⁴, B-I, K-U, X-Z⁸, 2A-2G⁸, 2H⁴, 2I².

Cloth? Inserted at back of Vol. 2 is a publisher's catalog, pp. ⟨1⟩-20, dated *January, 1874*.

Announced PC July 16, 1873. Advertised as *forthcoming* Ath Oct. 18, 1873; PC Nov. 1, 1873. Advertised as *nearly ready* PC Dec. 8, 1873, Dec. 18, 1873. Advertised for *next week* Ath Jan. 17, 1874. Listed Ath Jan. 31, 1874. Reviewed Ath Jan. 31, 1874. Listed Bkr Feb. 1, 1874. Listed PC Feb. 1, 1874. Advertised without comment PC Feb. 16, 1874. In a letter dated Jan. 31, 1874 (in PC Feb. 16, 1874) R.R.B., from New York, writes: "Motley's new work you will have before me." A *Popular Edition* listed PC Nov. 16, 1875; Ath Nov. 20, 1875.

BA H NYPL Y

14591. THE LIFE AND DEATH OF JOHN OF BARNEVELD, ADVOCATE OF HOLLAND; WITH A VIEW OF THE PRIMARY CAUSES AND MOVEMENTS OF THE THIRTY YEARS' WAR . . . IN TWO VOLUMES . . .

NEW YORK: HARPER AND BROTHERS, PUBLISHERS, FRANKLIN SQUARE. 1874.

For prior publication see preceding entry.

1: ⟨i⟩-⟨xvi⟩, ⟨1⟩-389, blank leaf. Integral frontispiece; and, 1 inserted plate. 9³⁄₁₆″ × 5¹³⁄₁₆″ full.

2: ⟨i⟩-⟨viii⟩, ⟨1⟩-475; blank, p. ⟨476⟩; plus: 6 pages advertisements, blank leaf. Two plates, integral parts of their respective gatherings, are not reckoned in the printed pagination.

1 : ⟨A⟩-I, K-U, X-Z, 2A-2B⁸, 2C⁴.

2 : ⟨A⟩⁴, B-I, K-U, X-Z, 2A-2H⁸ ; plus : ⟨-⟩⁴.

FL cloth: black. TZ cloth: black. Buff end papers; yellow end papers. Flyleaves. An errata slip inserted in some copies of Vol. 2, pp. ⟨viii⟩-⟨1⟩.

Listed PW June 6, 1874.

B   BA   H   NYPL

14592. PETER THE GREAT . . .

NEW YORK: HARPER & BROTHERS, PUBLISHERS, FRANKLIN SQUARE. 1877.

For prior London publication see above under year 1846.

⟨1⟩-106; 14 pp. advertisements. 4¹³⁄₁₆″ × 3⅛″.

⟨1⟩-7⁸; plus : ⟨8⟩⁴.

Printed tan-gray paper wrapper.

It will be observed that the book was issued without a copyright notice; presumably because the text was taken from NAR Oct. 1845 and so in the public domain. Reprinted without the date *1877* on the title-page; copy in Y.

Listed PW Aug. 11, 1877. Issued in London and Edinburgh by T. Nelson & Sons; listed PC July 1, 1887.

LC   UV

14593. 1830. H. U. Memoirs.

Boston: Press of Rockwell and Churchill, 39 Arch Street. 1886.

Memorial of John Bryant, "written soon after Mr. Bryant's decease ⟨1847⟩," pp. ⟨19⟩-21. Earliest located book publication.

H   Y

14594. THE CORRESPONDENCE OF JOHN LOTHROP MOTLEY . . . EDITED BY GEORGE WILLIAM CURTIS. IN TWO VOLUMES . . .

LONDON: JOHN MURRAY, ALBEMARLE STREET. 1889.

For first American edition see next entry.

1 : ⟨i⟩-x, ⟨1⟩-395. Frontispiece inserted. 8¹¹⁄₁₆″ × 5⁹⁄₁₆″.

2 : ⟨i⟩-⟨x⟩, ⟨1⟩-423; printer's imprint, p. ⟨424⟩.

1 : ⟨a⟩⁴, b¹, B-I, K-U, X-Z, 2A-2B⁸, 2C⁶.

2 : ⟨a⟩⁴, b¹, B-I, K-U, X-Z, 2A-2C⁸, 2D⁴, 2E⁸.

V cloth: black. White end papers printed in yellow with an all-over pattern of flowers, griffins, etc., incorporating the initials JM.

"Will be published in the latter part of Feb."——Ath Jan. 26, 1889. Advertised as *this day* PC Feb.

15, 1889. Advertised for the *20th* Ath Feb. 16, 1889. Listed Ath Feb. 23, 1889; PC March 1, 1889. Reviewed Ath March 2, 1889. The second edition advertised Ath May 4, 1889; PC Dec. 31, 1889.

H

14595. THE CORRESPONDENCE OF JOHN LOTHROP MOTLEY . . . EDITED BY GEORGE WILLIAM CURTIS . . . IN TWO VOLUMES . . .

NEW YORK   HARPER & BROTHERS, FRANKLIN SQUARE 1889

For prior publication see preceding entry.

1 : ⟨i-ii⟩, ⟨i⟩-x, ⟨1⟩-395. Portrait frontispiece inserted. 10¹⁄₁₆″ × 6½″. *Note:* The book occurs on both laid and on wove papers; priority, if any, not known.

2 : ⟨i-ii⟩, ⟨i⟩-⟨x⟩, ⟨1⟩-423; blank, p. ⟨424⟩; advertisements, pp. ⟨1⟩-8.

1 : ⟨A⟩⁶, B-I, K-U, X-Z, 2A-2B⁸, 2C⁶.

2 : ⟨A⟩⁶, B-I, K-U, X-Z, 2A-2E⁸.

S cloth: olive green. White laid end papers. Laid paper flyleaves. Top edges gilt.

A copy on laid paper deposited for copyright March 2, 1889. Noted as *just ready* PW March 2, 1889. Advertised for March 12 PW March 9, 1889. The B copy (laid paper) received March 15, 1889. The BA copy (laid paper) received March 19, 1889. Listed PW March 23, 1889.

AAS   B   BA   BPL   H   LC   NYPL   Y

14596. Modern Eloquence . . . ⟨Edited by⟩ Thomas B. Reed . . .

John D. Morris and Company   Philadelphia ⟨1900; *i.e.*, 1901⟩

"The Poets' Corner," Vol. 2, pp. 842-844; delivered at the 84th annual banquet of the Royal Literary Fund, London, May 28, 1873.

Deposited April 19, 1901. Listed PW June 8, 1901, as with the imprint of the University Society.

For fuller comment see entry No. 3467.

14597. John Lothrop Motley and His Family Further Letters and Records Edited by His Daughter and Herbert St John Mildmay . . .

London John Lane The Bodley Head New York John Lane Company MCMX

Contains some letters here first in book form.

"The *Correspondence of . . . John Lothrop Motley . . .* was published in 1889. The favour with which it was received . . . encouraged my sisters and me to draw upon further stores of letters which seemed to us, worthy to appear in print . . . Unfortunately . . . still unpublished letters, are few in number . . . Among those available, however, are several fresh letters . . ."---P. v.

Also issued in the United States, the same sheets being bound for that purpose. The London and American issues may be distinguished:

London

Blue V cloth. Spine imprint: *The Bodley Head.* Leaf X_2 (imprinted with publisher's advertisements) present; publisher's catalog inserted at back of some copies. Also inserted at back of some copies: A prospectus of Anatole France's works.

New York

Red T cloth. Spine imprint: *John Lane Company.* Leaf X_2 excised; neither terminal catalog nor prospectus present.

London issue listed Bkr April 22, 1910. New York issue listed PW May 21, 1910.

AAS (New York)   B (London)   BA (London)   H (both)   MHS (London)   Y (both)

JOHN LOTHROP MOTLEY

SECTION II

OFFICIAL PUBLICATIONS

As Minister to Austria, 1861–1867, and as Minister to Great Britain, 1869–1870, Motley's name is attached to certain official documents. No attempt has been made to locate and to describe such material. The following is a representative selection.

14598. . . . Correspondence Concerning Questions Pending between Great Britain and the United States. Transmitted to the Senate in Obedience to a Resolution.

Washington: Government Printing Office. 1870.

Printed paper wrapper. At head of title: *Department of State.*

Correspondence, pp. 3-19.

NYPL

14599. . . . Correspondence Relating to the Recall of Mr. Motley, Transmitted to the Senate January 9, 1871 . . .

Washington: Government Printing Office. 1871.

Printed paper wrapper. At head of title: *Department of State.*

Contains Motley correspondence. Appears also in: . . . *Message of the President of the United States, Communicating, in Compliance with the Resolution of the Senate of the 5th Instant, the Last Correspondence between Mr. Motley . . . , and the Department of State . . .* ⟨Washington: Government Printing Office, 1871⟩. At head of title: *41st Congress, 3d Session. Senate. Ex. Doc. No. 11.* Copy in H.

BPL   NYPL   Y

14600. . . . Second Annual Report of the State Board of Health of Massachusetts January, 1871.

Boston: Wright & Potter, State Printers, 79 Milk Street (Corner of Federal). 1871.

At head of title: *Senate No. 50.*

Letter, dated London, April 21, 1870, pp. 295-296.

H

Reprints of Motley's works issued under his name. For reprints issued in the books of others see *Section Four*.

14601. No. 20. Serial. Price, 10 Cents. The Pulpit and Rostrum. Sermons, Orations, Popular Lectures, &c. The Causes of the American Civil War: A Paper Contributed to the London Times . . .

New York: H. H. Lloyd & Co., 25 Howard St. London: Trubner & Co., 60 Paternoster Row. July 1st, 1861.

Cover-title. Pp. ⟨207⟩-230. Printed paper wrapper. Listed APC July 20, 1861.

B   BA   H   NYPL

14602. The Causes of the American Civil War. A Letter to the London Times . . .

New York: James G. Gregory, (Successor to W. A. Townsend & Co.,) No. 46 Walker Street. 1861.

Printed paper wrapper, both cream-colored and salmon-colored noted.

At least four printings have been noted. BAL has not attempted to establish a sequence.

Listed APC July 20, 1861.

AAS   BPL   H   LC   MHS   NYPL   UV   Y

14603. Democracy: The Climax of Political Progress and the Destiny of Advanced Races: A Historical Essay . . . Second Edition.

Glasgow: Cameron & Ferguson. London: Charles Griffin & Co. 1869.

Printed paper wrapper.

Query: Does this occur without the statement *Second Edition?*

Note: Erroneously listed in Foley: *Democracy, the Climax of Political Progress. An Historical Essay, Glasgow* ⟨*1875*⟩.

Also occurs in a printing issued Glasgow, n.d.

Reprint of *Historic Progress and American Democracy* . . . , New York, 1869.

o

14604. . . . Prose Passages from the Works of John Lothrop Motley . . . Compiled by Josephine E. Hodgdon . . .

New York   Harper & Brothers, Franklin Square 1883

Printed paper wrapper. At head of title: *Leaflets from Standard Authors* . . .

Deposited Oct. 29 ⟨27?⟩, 1883. Listed PW Nov. 3, 1883.

LC   NYPL

14605. ⟨The Writings of John Lothrop Motley⟩

New York and London   Harper and Brothers Publishers 1900

Issued in a variety of formats and bindings. The *Netherlands Edition*, limited to 500 numbered sets, deposited for copyright on the dates given. For comment on other formats see below.

1: *The Rise of the Dutch Republic*, Vol. 1.

Deposited Jan. 18, 1900.

2: ——, Vol. 2.

Deposited Jan. 18, 1900.

3: ——, Vol. 3.

Deposited Feb. 24, 1900.

4: ——, Vol. 4.

Deposited March 1, 1900.

5: ——, Vol. 5.

Deposited May 1, 1900.

6: *History of the United Netherlands*, Vol. 1.

Deposited May 1, 1900.

7: ——, Vol. 2.

Deposited June 6, 1900.

8: ——, Vol. 3.

Deposited June 20, 1900.

9: ——, Vol. 4.

Deposited Aug. 30, 1900.

10: ——, Vol. 5.

Deposited Sept. 1, 1900.

11: ——, Vol. 6.

> Deposited Nov. 17, 1900.

12: *The Life and Death of John of Barneveldt,* Vol. 1.

> Deposited Nov. 17, 1900.

13: ——, Vol. 2.

> Deposited Dec. 4, 1900.

14: ——, Vol. 3.

> Deposited Dec. 4, 1900.

15: *The Correspondence of John Lothrop Motley, Edited by George William Curtis,* Vol. 1.

> Deposited Dec. 27, 1900.

16: ——, Vol. 2.

> Deposited Dec. 27, 1900.

17: ——, Vol. 3.

> Deposited Dec. 27, 1900.

Noted in the following formats:

Netherlands Edition, limited to 500 numbered sets. Deposited thus.

Library Edition, limited to 1000 sets.

Edition de Luxe, limited to 1000 sets. Issued with the imprint of the *Society of English and French Literature,* New York.

Almost certainly issued in other formats and so-called editions.

B   H   LC   NYPL   Y

The following publications contain material by Motley reprinted from earlier books.

The Boston Book . . .

Boston . . . MDCCCL.

"The Solitary of Shawmut," pp. ⟨72⟩-81. Reprinted from *Merry-Mount* . . . , 1849. For fuller entry see No. 5929.

[New Series. No. 27] New England Loyal Publication Society. Office, No. 8 Studio Building, Boston. October 24, 1868.

Single sheet. Printed on recto only.

Essays from the North American Review. Edited by Allen Thorndike Rice.

New York . . . 1879.

For comment see entry No. 679.

. . . Harper's Fifth Reader American Authors

New York Harper & Brothers, Franklin Square 1889

Note: Reprinted and reissued by The American Book Company not before 1890. For fuller entry see No. 7917.

REFERENCES AND ANA

The Constitution and Mr. Motley. ⟨By Rowland E. Evans⟩

Philadelphia: Published for the Author. 1861.

Printed paper wrapper.

Remarks on Mr. Motley's Letter in the London Times on the War in America.

Charleston: Steam-Power Presses of Evans & Cogswell, Nos. 3 Broad and 103 East Bay Streets. 1861.

Printed paper wrapper.

⟨The Last Will and Testament of John Lothrop Motley⟩

⟨Boston, July 29, 1875⟩

Single cut sheet folded to make four pages. Paged: ⟨1⟩-3; p. ⟨4⟩ blank. 10″ scant × 6¹¹⁄₁₆″.

". . . Signed, sealed, published . . . in the presence of . . . J. P. Healy. James R. Carret. H. W. Putnam."

Motley's Appeal to History; by John Jay. (Reprinted from the International Review.)

A. S. Barnes & Company, Publishers, 111 & 113 William Street, N. Y. ⟨n.d., 1877⟩

Printed paper wrapper. Cover-title.

Tribute of the Massachusetts Historical Society to the Memory of Edmund Quincy and John Lothrop Motley

Boston Massachusetts Historical Society 1877

Printed paper wrapper.

Holland and Her Heroes to the Year 1585. Being an Adaptation of Motley's "Rise of the Dutch Republic." By Mary Albert.

London: C. Kegan Paul & Co., 1 Paternoster Square. 1878.

Presumably Motley had no hand in this production. ". . . Abridged from Mr Motley's Rise of the Dutch Republic . . ."---P. ⟨v⟩. Listed Ath March 2, 1878.

John Lothrop Motley. A Memoir. By Oliver Wendell Holmes.

Boston: Houghton, Osgood and Company. The Riverside Press, Cambridge. 1879.

For fuller description see entry numbers 8928, 8933.

A Biographical Introduction to Motley's Dutch Republic by Moncure D. Conway

London George Bell and Sons . . . New York 1896 . . .

Printed paper wrapper. Prepared for copyright only? Pp. ⟨v⟩-liii. Deposited in the Copyright Office, Library of Congress, March. 11, 1896

The Life and Writings of John Lothrop Motley

⟨New York and London: Harper & Brothers, 1900⟩

Printed paper wrapper, printed paper label on front. Cover-title. Issued as a prospectus.

The Siege of Leyden Condensed from Motley's "The Rise of the Dutch Republic" Edited . . . by William Elliot Griffis . . .

Boston . . . D. C. Heath & Co., Publishers 1901

Deposited Jan. 9, 1901.

Motley's Dutch Nation Being the Rise of the Dutch Republic . . . Condensed . . . by William Elliot Griffis . . .

New York and London   Harper & Brothers Publishers MCMVIII

On copyright page: *Published March, 1908.* Deposited April 2, 1908. Listed PW April 11, 1908.

Heroes of Holland. A Condensation of Motley's Works on Dutch History by C. K. True

New York: Methodist Book Concern, *ca.* 1912.

Not located. Entry from *The United States Catalog of Books in Print January 1, 1912* . . .

Query: Was this publication deposited for copyright May 21, 1883?

The Boy's Motley or the Rise of the Dutch Republic by Helen Ward Banks . . .

New York   Frederick A. Stokes Company Publishers ⟨1914⟩

On copyright page: *August, 1914*

A condensation of *The Rise of the Dutch Republic.*

Literary Pioneers   Early American Explorers of European Culture by Orie William Long

Cambridge, Massachusetts   Harvard University Press 1935

"John Lothrop Motley," pp. ⟨199⟩-224.

John Lothrop Motley   Representative Selections, with Introduction, Bibliography, and Notes by Chester Penn Higby . . . and B. T. Schantz . . .

American Book Company   New York   Cincinnati Chicago Boston Atlanta ⟨1939⟩

On copyright page of first printing: *W.P.I*

. . . The Diplomatic Mission of John Lothrop Motley to Austria 1861–1867 by Sister M. Claire Lynch, O.S.B. A Dissertation . . .

The Catholic University of America Press Washington, D.C. 1944

At head of title: *The Catholic University of America*

Printed paper wrapper.

ELLEN LOUISE CHANDLER MOULTON

(Ellen Louise, A Lady)

1 8 3 5 – 1 9 0 8

Presented in three sections as follows:

Section One: Books by Mrs. Moulton; or, books containing first located publication of Mrs. Moulton's work.

Section Two: Reprints of Mrs. Moulton's own books; sheet music, the text being reprinted from Mrs. Moulton's books.

Section Three: Books by authors other than Mrs. Moulton containing Moulton material reprinted from earlier books.

SECTION I

14606. The Waverley Garland, A Present for All Seasons. Edited by "Ellen Louise." ...

Boston: Published by Moses A. Dow. New York: Dexter & Bro. Philadelphia: A. Winch. Baltimore: Burgess, Taylor & Co. 1853.

"Editress' Preface," pp. ⟨vii⟩-viii.

"Invocation to the Spirit of Poesy," pp. ⟨9⟩-10.

"December," pp. ⟨150⟩-151.

"Elmwood Cottage," pp. ⟨152⟩-157.

"Love's Dream Twice Told," pp. ⟨304⟩-332.

The UV copy inscribed by early owner Dec. 25, 1852.

Reissued as *The Book of the Boudoir* ... , Boston ⟨1853⟩; New York ⟨n.d.⟩.

AAS   B   BPL   UV   Y

14607. The Ladies' Wreath: An Illustrated Annual. Edited by Helen Irving.

New-York: J. C. Burdick, 143 Nassau-Street. ⟨n.d., 1853?⟩

Sheets of Vol. 7 (?) of a periodical bound as an annual. Leather.

"The Parting," pp. 387-388. Elsewhere unlocated.

H

14608. THIS, THAT, AND THE OTHER. BY ELLEN LOUISE CHANDLER ...

BOSTON: PHILLIPS, SAMPSON, AND COMPANY. NEW YORK: JAMES C. DERBY. 1854.

⟨i⟩-x, ⟨11⟩-412; plus: Advertisements, pp. ⟨413-416⟩. Vignette title-page and 8 plates inserted. $7\frac{1}{2}'' \times 4\frac{7}{8}''$.

⟨1⟩-34⁶, 35²; plus: ⟨36⟩².

T cloth: brown; purple-brown; slate-blue. Pale buff end papers; yellow end papers. Flyleaves.

Announced NLG April 1, 15, 1854. Deposited May 15, 1854. Listed NLG June 1, 1854. *Second edition* advertised as *now ready* NLG June 1, 1854. Reviewed NLG June 15, 1854. A copy in B inscribed by early owner July 25, 1854. *Seventh edition* advertised as *now ready* NLG Aug. 1, 1854. Listed PC Oct. 16, 1854.

AAS   B   UV   Y

14609. JUNO CLIFFORD. A TALE. BY A LADY.

NEW YORK: D. APPLETON AND COMPANY, 346 AND 348 BROADWAY. M.DCCC.LVI.

⟨1⟩-408. Frontispiece and vignette title-page inserted. $7\frac{5}{16}''$ scant $\times 4\frac{5}{8}''$ full.

⟨1⟩-2, 4, 4-17¹².

On all examined copies: Superfluous signature mark 5 on p. 87; signature 3 missigned 4 on p. 49.

A cloth: orange. T cloth: brown; green. Blue-coated end papers; green-coated end papers; yellow-coated end papers. Flyleaves.

Noted as *in a few days* CRN Nov. 3, 1855. Noted as *published* APC Nov. 3, 1855. A copy in Y inscribed by early owner Nov. 15, 1855. Listed APC Nov. 17, 1855. Advertised as *recently imported* PC Jan. 1, 1856; listed PC Jan. 16, 1856.

AAS   NYPL   UV   Y

14610. MY THIRD BOOK. A COLLECTION OF TALES . . .

NEW YORK: HARPER & BROTHERS, PUBLISHERS, FRANKLIN SQUARE. 1859.

⟨1⟩-434, 2 pp. advertisements. 7⅜″ × 4¹⁵⁄₁₆″.

⟨A⟩-I, K-S¹², T².

Signature T occurs in the following forms; sequence not determined. The designations are completely arbitrary.

A

P. ⟨435⟩: . . . *The Brontë ⟨sic⟩ Novels* . . .

P. ⟨436⟩: . . . *Miss Muloch's Novels* . . . ⟨*8 titles*⟩

A cloth: blue. P cloth: brown. T cloth: brown. Yellow end papers. Yellow-coated end papers. Brown-coated end papers. Flyleaves.

B

P. ⟨435⟩: *Miss Muloch's Novels* . . . ⟨*7 titles listed. A Life for a Life described as* Shortly⟩

P. ⟨436⟩: *Miss Muloch's Novels* . . . ⟨*2 titles*⟩

A-like cloth: red. BD cloth: green. Yellow-coated end papers. Flyleaves.

C

P. ⟨435⟩: . . . *Harper's Magazine* . . .

P. ⟨436⟩: *Harper's Weekly* . . .

A-like cloth: red. Yellow-coated end papers. Flyleaves.

Deposited Aug. 19, 1859. Advertised among Harper's latest publications BM Sept. 1, 1859. Advertised by Sampson Low as *new* PC Sept. 15, 1859. Listed (as an American book) PC Sept. 15, 1859. Listed BM Oct. 1, 1859. Reviewed LG Dec. 3, 1859.

AAS (A, B)   B (A)   H (A)   NYPL (B)   UV (C)   Y (C)

14611. Looking toward Sunset. From Sources Old and New, Original and Selected. By L. Maria Child . . .

Boston: Ticknor and Fields. 1865.

"The Old Couple," 18 4-line stanzas, pp. ⟨149⟩-151. Anonymous. *See next entry.*

For fuller entry see No. 3198.

14612. Looking toward Sunset. From Sources Old and New, Original and Selected. By L. Maria Child . . . ⟨Fourth Edition⟩

Boston: Ticknor and Fields. 1866.

On copyright page: *Fourth Edition*

"The House in the Meadow," pp. ⟨149⟩-151. Credited to Louise Chandler Moulton. *Note:* This is a revision, in 19 4-line stanzas, of "The

Old Couple," which appears in the preceding entry. Collected in *Poems*, 1878.

H

14613. Stories and Sketches by Our Best Authors.

Boston: Lee and Shepard. 1867.

"Dr. Huger's Intention," pp. 105–118.

Listed ALG July 1, 1867.

AAS

14614. . . . The Lady's Almanac, for the Year 1868.

Boston. Issued by George Coolidge, 3 Milk St. . . . ⟨1867⟩

"Out in the Snow," pp. ⟨22⟩-23. Collected in *Poems*, 1878.

For fuller description see BAL, Vol. 2, p. 246.

14615. The Sunday-School Speaker . . . Collected and Arranged by O. Augusta Cheney.

Loring, Publisher, Corner Bromfield and Washington Streets, Boston. ⟨1869⟩

"Lost Margery," p. 43.

For comment see entry No. 1433A.

14616. BED-TIME STORIES . . .

BOSTON: ROBERTS BROTHERS. 1873.

⟨1⟩-239. Frontispiece and 5 plates inserted. 6¹³⁄₁₆″ × 4⅞″.

⟨1-10¹²⟩. *Signed:* ⟨1⟩-10, ⟨11⟩, 12-13, ⟨14⟩, 15⁸.

C cloth: blue; orange. Brown-coated end papers; gray-coated end papers; green-coated end papers. Flyleaves.

Advertised for Oct. 1 PW Sept. 6, 1873. BA copy received Oct. 8, 1873. Listed PW Oct. 11, 1873. Advertised by Low as a *new American book* PC Dec. 31, 1873; reviewed Ath Jan. 31, 1874.

AAS   H   Y

14617. . . . VIOLETS BLOSSOMED WHERE SHE TROD . . . MUSIC BY THOMAS RYAN . . .

BOSTON. OLIVER DITSON & CO. 277 WASHINGTON ST. . . . 1873 . . .

Sheet music. Cover-title. At head of title: *To the Pupils of the National College of Music*

Plate number: 27552.

Otherwise unlocated.

EM

14618. Little People of God and What the Poets Have Said of Them Edited by Mrs George L Austin

Boston Shepard and Gill 1874

"Somebody's Child," pp. 165-166. Collected in *Poems*, 1878.

Listed PW Dec. 20, 1873.

NYPL

14619. Sea and Shore. A Collection of Poems . . .

Boston: Roberts Brothers. 1874.

"A Quest," pp. 133-134. Collected in *Poems*, 1878.

For fuller entry see No. 4043.

14620. SOME WOMEN'S HEARTS . . .

BOSTON: ROBERTS BROTHERS. 1874.

⟨i-viii⟩, ⟨1⟩-364. Laid paper. 6⅞″ × 4⁹⁄₁₆″.

⟨-⟩⁴, 1-8, 9*, 10-15¹², 16². *Also signed:* ⟨-⟩⁴, A-V⁸, W⁶.

Ecru linen. P cloth: tan. S cloth: green; terracotta. Brown-coated end papers. Laid paper; also, wove paper, flyleaves.

Two states of the binding have been noted. Sequence, if any, has not been determined and the designations are for identification only.

A: The s in SOME on the front cover is blackstamped on a gold field. A copyright deposit copy thus.

B: The s in SOME on the front cover is in intaglio on a gold field.

Listed PW May 16, 1874. Noticed by Ath Aug. 29, 1874.

AAS (A)   BPL (A)   LC (A, being a deposit copy) NYPL (B)   UV (A)   Y (B)

14621. The Hospital Bazaar . . .

Chicago . . . 1874 . . .

"On the Shore," No. 4, p. 54. Otherwise unlocated.

For fuller comment see entry No. 7274.

14622. MORE BED-TIME STORIES . . .

BOSTON: ROBERTS BROTHERS. 1875.

⟨1⟩-238, 2 pp. advertisements. Frontispiece and 3 plates inserted. 6¹³⁄₁₆″ × 4¹³⁄₁₆″.

⟨1-10¹²⟩. Signed: ⟨1⟩-15⁸.

Note: Two states (probably printings) noted.

1: As above. A copyright deposit copy thus.

2: With an additional gathering of six leaves at the back devoted to advertisements.

C cloth: blue; red-orange. FL cloth: green. Brown-coated on white end papers. Flyleaves.

Advertised for Nov. 4 PW Oct. 31, 1874. Listed PW Nov. 7, 1874. Reviewed Ath March 20, 1875.

AAS (1st)   H (1st)   NYPL (2nd)

14623. The Echo. A Journal of the Fair . . .

New York . . . April 10, 1875 . . . ⟨to⟩ April 24, 1875 . . .

An occasional newspaper issued in thirteen parts for the benefit of the Homœopathic Fair.

"An Apology," No. 2, p. 5. Otherwise unlocated.

GD

14624. Ballads of Home. Edited by George M. Baker . . .

Boston Lee and Shepard, Publishers New York Charles T. Dillingham ⟨1875⟩

Pictorial paper boards.

"A Woman's Waiting," pp. 101-105. Collected in *Poems*, 1878.

EM

14625. 1875–1876. Third Season in the United States. . . Mr. Sidney Woollett Will Accept Appointments from Managers of Lecture Courses . . .

Milton on the Hudson, Ulster Co., N. Y. No. 27 West 34th Street, New York . . .

Caption-title. The above at head of p. ⟨1⟩.

A four-page prospectus.

Testimonial, p. ⟨4⟩.

AAS

14626. Two Fortune-Seekers; and Other Stories. By Rossiter Johnson and Other Famous Writers.

Boston: Published by D. Lothrop & Co. Dover, N. H.: G. T. Day & Co. ⟨1875; *i.e.,* 1876⟩

"The White Chrysanthemums," pp. 57-69. Also in *Wide Awake Pleasure Book* ⟨Vol. 1⟩, Boston ⟨1875⟩, a twilight book; see BAL, Vol. 1, p. 73. Collected in *Jessie's Neighbor* . . . ⟨1877⟩.

"Jessie's Neighbor," pp. 209-228. Also appears in (reprinted from?) *Wide Awake Pleasure Book* ⟨Vol. 2⟩, Boston ⟨1876⟩, a twilight book; see BAL, Vol. 1, p. 73. Collected in *Jessie's Neighbor* . . . ⟨1877⟩.

Listed PW Aug. 5, 1876. Advertised as *just ready* PW Sept. 16, 1876.

LC

14627. Songs of Three Centuries. Edited by John Greenleaf Whittier.

Boston: James R. Osgood and Company, Late Ticknor & Fields, and Fields, Osgood, & Co. 1876.

Reprint save for "The Late Spring," p. 291. Collected in *Poems*, 1878, as "The Spring is Late."

For fuller entry see No. 11341.

14628. Laurel Leaves. Original Poems, Stories, and Essays . . .

Boston: William F. Gill and Company, 309 Washington Street. 1876.

"Woe unto the Pitcher," pp. 107-117.

"Waiting for the Children. A Poem for Thanksgiving," pp. 297-304.

For fuller entry see No. 116.

14629. Golden Treasures of Poetry, Romance, and Art by Eminent Poets, Novelists, and Essayists . . .

Boston   William F. Gill and Company   309 Washington Street   1876

"Looking into the Well," pp. 169-171. Collected in *Poems*, 1878.

For comment see entry No. 1749.

14630. Autumn Leaves. ⟨Edited by L. R. Swain?⟩

⟨n.p., n.d., 1876?⟩

"A Child of Earth," pp. 12-13. Collected in *Poems*, 1878.

Copy in the possession of JB inscribed by early owner Jan. 1, 1877.

H

14631. Poems for Our Darlings.

Boston: D. Lothrop & Co., Publishers, 30 and 32 Franklin Street. ⟨1877⟩

Unpaged.

Contains "Wide Awake." The poem also appears in *Wide Awake Pleasure Book* ⟨Vol. 1⟩, Boston ⟨1875⟩; for comment see BAL, Vol. 1, p. 73.

Listed PW Sept. 8, 1877.

B

14632. JESSIE'S NEIGHBOR, AND OTHER STORIES. BY LOUISE CHANDLER MOULTON.

BOSTON: D. LOTHROP AND COMPANY. FRANKLIN ST., CORNER OF HAWLEY. ⟨1877⟩

Not to be confused with another publication of like title issued ⟨1900⟩.

⟨1-60⟩. Illustrated. $6^{13}/_{16}''\times4^{11}/_{16}''$.

⟨1², 2-4⁸, 5⁴⟩.

Pictorial V cloth, printed in colors.

Contents:

"Jessie's Neighbor." Here first collected. Previously in *Two Fortune-Seekers* ⟨1875⟩.

"Two Burial Places of Florence."

"The White Chrysanthemums." Here first collected. Previously in *Two Fortune-Seekers* ⟨1875⟩.

LC

14633. POEMS . . .

BOSTON: ROBERTS BROTHERS. 1878.

Title-page in black and red.

⟨3⟩-153, blank leaf. Illustrated. $5^{3}/_{4}''\times4^{1}/_{8}''$ full.

⟨-⟩³ (2 inserted), ⟨1⟩⁴, 2-9⁸, 10⁶.

S cloth: green; terra-cotta. V cloth: black. Green-coated end papers. White end papers printed in brown with a fern-like pattern. Fly-leaves. Edges stained red.

BPL copy received Dec. 14, 1877. Listed PW Dec. 15, 1877. For a "new edition" see *Swallow Flights* . . . , 1892, below.

AAS   B   BPL   H   NYPL   Y

14634. . . . A Masque of Poets. Including Guy Vernon, a Novelette in Verse.

Boston: Roberts Brothers. 1878.

"A Fallen House," p. 85. Collected in *In the Garden of Dreams*, 1890.

For fuller entry see No. 118.

14635. NEW BED-TIME STORIES . . .

BOSTON: ROBERTS BROTHERS. 1880.

⟨1⟩-230, 10 pp. advertisements. Frontispiece and 3 plates inserted. $6^{3}/_{4}''$ full $\times4^{7}/_{8}''$.

⟨1⟩-15⁸.

CM cloth: blue. FL cloth: green. S cloth: gold; orange-red. Blue-gray end papers printed in ecru with an all-over leafy pattern. White end papers printed in green with an all-over leafy pattern. White end papers printed in brown with an all-over leafy pattern. Flyleaves.

Noted for Oct. 1 PW Sept. 25, 1880. Advertised for Oct. 9 PW Oct. 2, 1880. Listed PW Oct. 16, 1880.

AAS   B   H   NYPL   UV   Y

14636. Sketches and Reminiscences of the Radical Club of Chestnut Street, Boston. Edited by Mrs. John T. Sargent.

Boston: James R. Osgood and Company. 1880.

"To ——," p. 399. *Friend of the weary-hearted and the sad . . .* ; otherwise unlocated.

For fuller entry see No. 8950.

14637. Childhood's Appeal . . .

⟨Boston, 1880–1881⟩

"From Afar," No. III, p. ⟨1⟩. Collected in *At the Wind's Will*, 1899, as "The Mood of a Man."

"To One Who Has Loved Often," No. x, p. 2. Collected in *In the Garden of Dreams*, 1890.

For fuller description see No. 3783.

14638. RANDOM RAMBLES . . .

BOSTON: ROBERTS BROTHERS. 1881.

⟨i⟩-vi, ⟨7⟩-282, 6 pp. advertisements. $5\frac{3}{4}'' \times 4\frac{1}{8}''$ full.

⟨1⟩-18⁸.

⟨1⟩-18^8.

S cloth: brown; green; mauve; mustard. Edges stained red; yellow. White end papers printed in green with an all-over leafy pattern. Also: White end papers printed in brown with a bird and leaf decoration. Flyleaves.

Two binding issues noted:

1: With the spine imprint of *Roberts Bros.*

2: With the spine imprint of *Little, Brown & Co.* A copy in AAS.

BA copy received May 24, 1881; BPL copy May 26, 1881. Deposited May 26, 1881. Listed PW May 28, 1881.

AAS   B   BA   BPL   H   LC   Y

14639. The Sword and the Pen . . .

Boston . . . 1881 . . .

An occasional newspaper. For comment see entry No. 123.

"Long Weeping," translated from Heine, No. 2, p. ⟨1⟩.

"To a New-Born Child," No. 3, p. 6. Repeated in No. 8, p. 9.

14640. Sonnets of Three Centuries: A Selection . . . Edited by T. Hall Caine.

London: Elliot Stock, 62 Paternoster Row. 1882.

"Inter Manes," p. 258. Collected in *At the Wind's Will*, 1899.

Listed PC April 1, 1882.

H

14641. . . . Pen Pictures of Modern Authors

New York   G. P. Putnam's Sons   27 and 29 West 23d Street   1882

"An Evening with Swinburne," pp. 207-209.

For fuller entry see No. 1249.

14642. The Cambridge Book of Poetry and Song . . . by Charlotte Fiske Bates . . .

New York: Thomas Y. Crowell & Co., No. 13 Astor Place. ⟨1882⟩

*"At Sea," p. 845.

"From a Window in Chamouni," p. 846. Otherwise unlocated.

*"Hic Jacet," p. 846.

*"Left Behind," pp. 845-846.

*"My Saint," p. 845.

*Collected in *In the Garden of Dreams*, 1890.

For fuller description see entry Nos. 7887, 11490.

14643. Hearts and Homes, by Emilie Searchfield, Louise Chandler Moulton and Others.

London: F. E. Longley, 1883.

Not located. Not seen. Title-page postulated. Entry from listing in PC June 1, 1883; and, editorial comment, *ibid.*, p. 479.

14644. FIRELIGHT STORIES . . .

BOSTON: ROBERTS BROTHERS. 1883.

⟨1⟩-232; 8 pp. advertisements. Frontispiece and 4 plates inserted. $6^{13}\!/_{16}'' \times 4\frac{7}{8}$ scant.

⟨1⟩-15⁸.

⟨1⟩-15^8.

Two bindings of undetermined sequence noted; the designations are completely arbitrary.

BINDING A

C cloth: blue. FL cloth: green. The title on the spine is goldstamped. White end papers printed in tan with an all-over leafy pattern in intaglio. Also white end papers printed in green with a leafy pattern. Flyleaves. This binding has been seen on a deposit copy; also noted on a reprint of 1887.

BINDING B

S cloth: brown; gold. The title on the spine is stamped in intaglio. White end papers printed in green with an all-over pattern of leaves and blossoms. Flyleaves.

Deposited Oct. 19, 1883. Listed PW Oct. 20, 1883.

AAS (B)   BPL (B)   H (A)   LC (A)   Y (A)

14645. Our Famous Women. Comprising the Lives and Deeds of American Women . . . by . . . Harriet Beecher Stowe. Rose Terry Cooke. Harriet Prescott Spofford. Elizabeth Stuart Phelps . . . Louise Chandler Moulton. Lucy Larcom. Julia Ward Howe . . .

Hartford, Conn.: A. D. Worthington and Company. Chicago: A. G. Nettleton & Co. Cleveland: C. C. Wick & Co. 1883.

"Louisa May Alcott," pp. ⟨29⟩-52.

Reprinted and reissued 1884 with slightly altered title: *Our Famous Women. An Authorized Record* . . . ; for fuller comment see entry No. 11365.

14646. 1884 The Independent Almanac

⟨New York: The Independent, 1883⟩

Printed wrapper. Cover-title.

"Sonnet on Life," p. 8. Collected in *At the Wind's Will*, 1899.

H

14647. Some Noted Princes, Authors, and Statesmen of Our Time . . . Edited by James Parton.

New York: Thomas Y. Crowell & Co., 13 Astor Place. ⟨1885⟩

"Carlyle: His Work and His Wife," pp. 183-187.

"Charles H. Spurgeon," pp. 242-246.

"Mr. Gladstone in the House," pp. 272-276.

"Queen Victoria," pp. 336-346.

"Sir Walter Scott's Home," pp. 225-229.

For comment see entry No. 207.

14648. December Edited by Oscar Fay Adams . . .

Boston D. Lothrop and Company Franklin and Hawley Streets ⟨1885⟩

"In Winter," pp. 70-71. Collected in *In the Garden of Dreams*, 1890.

For fuller comment see entry No. 57.

14649. March Edited by Oscar Fay Adams . . .

Boston D. Lothrop and Company Franklin and Hawley Streets ⟨1886⟩

"By March Wind Led," p. 32. Collected in *In the Garden of Dreams*, 1890.

For fuller comment see entry No. 60.

14650. June Edited by Oscar Fay Adams . . .

Boston D. Lothrop and Company Franklin and Hawley Streets ⟨1886⟩

Reprint save for "She Was Won in an Idle Day," p. 102. Collected in *Swallow Flights*, 1892.

For fuller entry see No. 64.

14651. July Edited by Oscar Fay Adams . . .

Boston D. Lothrop and Company Franklin and Hawley Streets ⟨1886⟩

"Midsummer in New England," p. 87. Collected in *Swallow Flights*, 1892.

For fuller entry see No. 65.

14652. August Edited by Oscar Fay Adams . . .

Boston D. Lothrop and Company Franklin and Hawley Streets ⟨1886⟩

"Eros," p. 79. Collected in *In the Garden of Dreams*, 1890.

For fuller entry see No. 66.

14653. Belford's Annual 1886-7. Edited by Thomas W. Handford . . .

Chicago and New York: Belford Clarke & Co. ⟨1886⟩

"Fain Would I Climb," p. 20. Collected in *At the Wind's Will*, 1899, as "Afar from God."

"The Two Bells," p. 204; credited to *Bessie Chandler Moulton*. By the subject of this list? Not located in the collected works.

See next entry. For fuller entry see No. 10467.

14654. Belford's Chatterbox December, 1886. Edited by Thomas W. Handford . . .

Chicago and New York: Belford Clarke & Co. ⟨1886⟩

"Fain Would I Climb," p. 20.

"The Two Bells," p. 204; credited to *Bessie Chandler Moulton*.

See preceding entry for comment. For fuller entry see No. 10468.

14655. Library Festival at Wellesley College, June 4, 1886.

Cambridge: John Wilson and Son. University Press. 1886.

Printed paper wrapper.

"To the Discoverer of Norumbega," p. 58.

H

14656. OURSELVES AND OUR NEIGH-
BORS: SHORT CHATS ON SOCIAL
TOPICS . . .

BOSTON: ROBERTS BROTHERS. 1887.

Two printings noted:

FIRST PRINTING

⟨1⟩-213; blank, p. ⟨214⟩; advertisements, pp.
⟨1⟩-2. Laid paper. 6¾″ × 4⁹⁄₁₆″. Sheets bulk
⅝″ full.

⟨1-18⁸·⁴⟩. Signed: ⟨1⟩-13⁸, 14⁴.

SECOND PRINTING

⟨1⟩-213; blank, p. ⟨214⟩; blank leaf. Wove
paper. Sheets bulk ½″ scant.

⟨1⟩-13⁸, 14⁴.

V cloth: green. Brown-coated end papers. Laid
paper flyleaves. *Note:* A copy of the second printing
(in B) has been seen bound in white V cloth,
golden-yellow sateen shelf back.

Noted as *at once* PW May 21, 1887. Deposited June
6, 1887. BPL copy (first printing) received June
25, 1887. Listed PW July 2, 1887. A copy of the
second printing in BPL inscribed by the author
Christmas 1887. The London (Ward & Downey;
American sheets) announced for *October* PC Oct.
1, 1887; listed Ath Oct. 29, 1887.

AAS (1st)   B (2nd)   BA (1st),   BPL (1st, 2nd)
H (2nd)   LC (1st)   UV (2nd)   Y (1st)

14657. Garden Secrets. By Philip Bourke Marston
. . . with Biographical Sketch by Louise Chandler Moulton . . .

Boston: Roberts Brothers. 1887.

"Philip Bourke Marston: A Sketch," pp. ⟨9⟩-32.
For another sketch see below under 1891: *A
Last Harvest.*

Deposited Oct. 5, 1887. Advertised for Oct. 8
PW Oct. 1, 1887. Listed PW Oct. 15, 1887.

AAS   B   BA   BPL   H   LC   Y

14658. . . . EDUCATION FOR THE GIRLS.
LOUISE CHANDLER MOULTON TELLS
WHAT TO DO WITH OUR DAUGHTERS
. . . [COPYRIGHT, 1888.] [WRITTEN FOR
THE WORLD.] . . .

⟨NEW YORK, 1888⟩

Caption-title. The above at head of text. At head
of title: *A-3 60 Slips. Return Copy. Regular New York
Syndicate Bureau Article for March 4.*

Not published in this form. Prepared for the use
of subscribers to the New York Syndicate.

Two galley proofs; 17⅝″ × 4¹¹⁄₁₆″ scant; 11¹³⁄₁₆″
× 4⅝″ respectively.

Deposited Feb. 28, 1888.

LC

14659. Report of the Proceedings at the Dinner
Given by the Society of Authors to American
Men and Women of Letters at the Criterion
Restaurant, on Wednesday, July 25, 1888.

London: Society of Authors, 4, Portugal
Street, Lincoln's Inn Fields, W. C. 1888.

Cover-title. Printed paper wrapper.

Brief comment, p. 41.

H

14660. Souvenir of Venice . . .

Boston, December, 1888. Published by the
Women's Educational and Industrial Union . . .

Printed paper wrapper. Unpaged. Tied with tape.

"In Venice." Collected in *At the Wind's Will,*
1899, as "In Venice Once."

"The Shadow Dance." Collected in *In the Garden
of Dreams,* 1890.

AAS   B

14661. The Woman's Story As Told by Twenty
American Women . . . ⟨Edited⟩ by Laura C.
Holloway . . .

New York   John B. Alden, Publisher 1889

"Nan," pp. 245-258.

Deposited Jan. 21, 1889. Also issued with the
cancel title-leaf of Nims & Knight, Troy, N.Y.,
1889.

H   LC

14662. American Sonnets. Selected . . . by William
Sharp.

London   Walter Scott, 24 Warwick Lane   New
York and Toronto: W. J. Gage & Co. ⟨n.d.,
1889⟩

Contains the following by Moulton; each collected
in *In the Garden of Dreams,* 1890.

"After Death," p. 166.

"Beyond Sight and Sound," p. 167.

"A Cry," p. 163.

"In the Court of the Lions by Moonlight," p. 169.

"The Last Good-Bye," p. 164.

"Love's Empty House," p. 162.

"A Parable," p. 168.

"A Silent Guest," p. 165.

For comment see BAL, Vol. 3, p. 101.

H

14663. MISS EYRE FROM BOSTON, AND OTHERS . . .

BOSTON: ROBERTS BROTHERS. 1889.

Two printings noted:

FIRST PRINTING

⟨1⟩-339; blank, p. ⟨340⟩; 12 pp. advertisements. 7″ × 4¾″. Sheets bulk ¾″.

⟨1⟩-22⁸.

Terminal advertisements:

P. ⟨7⟩: . . . *Travels with a Donkey* . . .

P. ⟨10⟩: . . . *Prisoners of Poverty* . . .

SECOND PRINTING

⟨1⟩-339; blank, p. ⟨340⟩; 12 pp. advertisements. 7″ × 4¾″. Sheets bulk ⅞″.

⟨1⟩-22⁸.

Terminal advertisements:

P. ⟨7⟩: . . . *Prisoners of Poverty* . . .

P. ⟨10⟩: . . . *Travels with a Donkey* . . .

S cloth: yellow. V cloth: gray; green. White end papers printed in brown with an all-over leafy pattern. Printed mustard-yellow laid paper wrapper.

Note: Two binding (cloth) patterns noted; the sequence has not been established and the designations are for identification only.

A: The fillet on the front and on the spine measures about 2″ in depth. Initials RB at foot of spine.

B: The fillet on the front and on the spine measures about 1½″ in depth. The initials RB are not present at foot of spine.

Also note: Copies of the second printing have been seen bearing the spine monogram of Little, Brown & Company.

Deposited June 10, 1889. Advertised as in cloth and paper and as *just published* PW June 15, 1889. Listed (cloth only) PW June 22, 1889. Reviewed by Bkr July, 1889.

AAS (1st, *Binding A;* 1st, *Binding B*) B (1st, *Binding A*) BPL (2nd, *Binding A*) H (1st, *Binding A*) NYPL (1st, *Binding A;* 1st, *Binding B*) UV (1st, *Binding A*)

14664. IN THE GARDEN OF DREAMS: LYRICS AND SONNETS . . .

BOSTON: ROBERTS BROTHERS. 1890.

⟨i-iv⟩, ⟨i⟩-⟨x⟩, ⟨11⟩-170; tailpiece, p. ⟨171⟩. Illustrated. 7″ scant × 4¹³⁄₁₆″ scant.

⟨1-22⁴⟩.

White V cloth sides, green V cloth shelf back. Top edges gilt.

Noted as *just ready* PW Dec. 7, 1889. BA copy received Dec. 10, 1889. Deposited Dec. 12, 1889. Listed PW Dec. 21, 1889. The London (Macmillan; American sheets) edition listed Ath Dec. 21, 1889. See below under 1891 for the *Fourth Edition.*

AAS B BA H UV Y

14665. The Art of Authorship . . . Compiled . . . by George Bainton.

London: James Clarke & Co., 13 & 14, Fleet Street. 1890.

Contribution, p. 16.

For comment see entry No. 1271.

14666. The Art of Authorship . . . Compiled . . . by George Bainton

New York D. Appleton and Company 1890

Contribution, p. 16.

For comment see entry No. 1272.

14667. . . . Stepping-Stones, by Marion Harland and Other Stories by Virginia F. Townsend and Louise Chandler Moulton.

New York: Street & Smith ⟨1890⟩

Not located. Entry from *A Catalog of Books Represented by Library of Congress Printed Cards Issued to July 31, 1942,* Vol. 146.

The Select Series. No. 57. Printed paper wrapper. Deposited Sept. 11, 1890. Listed PW Sept. 13, 1890.

Further information wanting.

14668. STORIES TOLD AT TWILIGHT . . .

BOSTON: ROBERTS BROTHERS. 1890.

⟨i-ii⟩, ⟨1⟩-229; blank, p. ⟨230⟩; 8 pp. advertisements. Frontispiece and 3 plates inserted. 6¾″ × 4⅞″.

⟨1-15⁸⟩. *Signed:* ⟨-⟩¹, ⟨1⟩-14⁸, 15⁷.

S cloth: blue; blue-green; gold; red. White end papers printed in lavender with a pattern of circles, filigrees, etc. Also: White end papers printed in tan with a pattern of branch-like units, rules, etc. Flyleaves.

Note: All examined copies (save one) have the author's name present on both the front cover and spine. The exception is the surviving copyright deposit copy which does not carry the author's name. Presumed to be an experimental issue.

Deposited June 30, 1890. Advertised for Sept. 25 PW Sept. 27, 1890. The London (David Stott) edition listed Ath Oct. 24, 1891; PC Nov. 14, 1891.

AAS BPL H LC UV Y

14669. American Sonnets Selected and Edited by T. W. Higginson and E. H. Bigelow

Boston and New York Houghton, Mifflin and Company The Riverside Press, Cambridge 1890

Reprint save for "Robert Browning," p. 167. Collected in *At the Wind's Will*, 1899.

For fuller entry see No. 8373.

14670. Younger American Poets 1830–1890 Edited by Douglas Sladen . . .

Griffith, Farran, Okeden & Welsh Newbery House, Charing Cross Road London and Sydney 1891

For American edition see next entry.

Reprint save for "Wife to Husband," pp. 445-446. Collected in *Swallow Flights*, 1892.

"Laus Veneris," *In the Garden of Dreams*, 1890, appears herein under the altered title, "The Venus of Burne Jones."

For fuller entry see No. 6557.

14671. Younger American Poets 1830–1890 Edited by Douglas Sladen . . .

The Cassell Publishing Company New York 1891

For prior British publication see preceding entry.

Reprint save for "Wife to Husband," pp. 445-446. Collected in *Swallow Flights*, 1892.

"Laus Veneris," *In the Garden of Dreams*, 1890, appears herein under the title, "The Venus of Burne Jones."

For fuller entry see No. 6558.

14672. A Last Harvest . . . by Philip Bourke Marston . . . with Biographical Sketch by Louise Chandler Moulton . . .

London Elkin Mathews, Vigo Street 1891

"Biographical Sketch of Philip Bourke Marston," dated at end *July, 1891*, pp. ⟨1⟩-31. For another sketch of Marston see above under year 1887: *Garden Secrets*. For a revised version of the 1891 sketch see *The Collected Poems of Philip Bourke Marston*, Boston, 1892.

500 small paper copies: 7″ × 4¹³⁄₁₆″; and, 50 numbered large paper copies signed by Mrs. Moulton; not seen by BAL.

Noted for *next week* PC Oct. 17, 1891. Both formats advertised Ath Oct. 24, 1891; Nov. 21, 1891. Listed PC Nov. 21, 1891; PW Jan. 23, 1892.

AAS (1 of 500) BA (1 of 500) BMU (1 of 50; not seen by BAL) BPL (1 of 500) NYPL (1 of 500)

14673. In the Garden of Dreams: Lyrics and Sonnets . . . ⟨Fourth Edition⟩

Boston: Roberts Brothers. 1891.

For first edition see above under 1890. On copyright page: *Fourth Edition*.

Reprint with the exception of "In the Garden of Dreams," which appears herein opposite the title-page.

H

14674. Swallow Flights. New Edition of "Poems," Published in 1877, with Ten Additional Poems . . .

Boston: Roberts Brothers. 1892.

For first edition see *Poems*, 1878, above.

Contains the following added poems:

a-"At a Window"

a-"Down the River"

a-"For Me Alone"

a-"Long Is the Way

b-"Midsummer in New England"

a-"My Birthday"

c-"She Was Won in an Idle Day"

a-"Some Day or Other"

a-"To a Lady in a Picture"

d-"Wife to Husband"

a-Here first located.
b-Previously in *July* . . . , 1886.
c-Previously in *June* . . . , 1886.
d-Previously in *Younger American Poets* . . . , 1891.

Deposited April 7, 1892. Advertised for April 25 PW April 16, 1892. Listed PW May 7, 1892.

AAS B BPL LC NYPL Y

14675. Fair Topics . . . Organ of the Actors' Fund Fair . . .

New York . . . 1892 . . .

"To Hope," No. 6, p. 4.

For fuller description see entry No. 359.

14676. The Collected Poems of Philip Bourke Marston . . . with Biographical Sketch by Louise Chandler Moulton . . .

Boston Roberts Brothers 1892

"Biographical Sketch of Philip Bourke Marston,"
pp. ⟨xxi⟩-xxxviii. For another version of this
sketch see above: *A Last Harvest . . .* , 1891.

"To Philip Bourke Marston," p. ⟨v⟩.

Deposited Aug. 29, 1892. A copy in BPL received
Nov. 5, 1892. Listed PW Nov. 12, 1892.

BA   BPL

14677. Bazaar Book of the Boston Teachers'
    Mutual Benefit Association. Bazaar Held at
    Music Hall, December 5th to 10th, 1892.

Alfred Mudge & Son, Printers, Boston. ⟨1892⟩

Printed paper wrapper.

"A Birthday Wish: For a Very Fortunate Girl,"
p. 49.

SG

14678. Fame's Tribute to Children . . . ⟨Edited
    by Martha S. Hill⟩

Chicago A. C. McClurg and Company 1892

"As Little Children," p. 121.

For fuller entry see BAL, Vol. 1, p. 76.

14679. Quabbin The Story of a Small Town with
    Outlooks upon Puritan Life by Francis H.
    Underwood . . .

Lee and Shepard Publishers Boston . . . ⟨n.d.,
1893⟩

Single cut sheet. For fuller description see entry
No. 9044.

Letter of commendation, p. 3. *Note:* The letter
also appears (reprinted in?) in the terminal
matter of *The Poet and the Man Recollections and
Appreciations of James Russell Lowell,* by Francis
H. Underwood, Boston, 1893; listed PW March 6,
1893.

14680. Memorial to John Greenleaf Whittier, by
    the Citizens of Amesbury. December 17, 1892.

Amesbury: Fred A. Brown, Publisher, 1893.

Printed paper wrapper.

"For the Heavenly Birthday of John Greenleaf
Whittier," p. 36.

H   NYPL

14681. ⟨Lights and Shadows. A Composite Poem⟩

⟨n.p., n.d., 1894⟩

A poem written in collaboration with Thomas
Wentworth Higginson, Julia Ward Howe and
others. For comment see entry No. 8405.

14682. Selections for Supplementary Reading
    from the Youth's Companion. No. 2. Glimpses
    of Europe . . .

Copyright, 1894. Perry Mason & Co., Boston.

Printed paper wrapper.

"Toledo and Cordova," pp. ⟨27⟩-32. Collected in
Lazy Tours in Spain, 1896.

Deposited March 26, 1894.

LC

14683. Arthur O'Shaughnessy His Life and His
    Work with Selections from His Poems by
    Louise Chandler Moulton

MDCCCXCIV Cambridge and Chicago Published
by Stone & Kimball London: Elkin Mathews
& John Lane

Editorial note, *March, 1894,* p. ⟨7⟩.

"Arthur O'Shaughnessy His Life and His Work,"
pp. 13-46.

*The first small-paper edition for America is limited to
five hundred copies, of which four hundred and fifty are
for sale. There is also an edition of sixty copies on hand-
made paper.*---P. ⟨1⟩ of the so-called small-paper
format. Bound in cloth. $6^{11}/_{16}'' \times 4^{3}/_{8}''$.

*Sixty copies are printed on hand-made paper, only
fifty of which are for sale. This is No.*---P. ⟨1⟩ of the
so-called large-paper format. Paper boards,
printed paper label. $6^{15}/_{16}'' \times 4^{3}/_{8}''$.

P. ⟨121⟩: The De Vinne Press device and the
statement: *The Book ends here. February, March,
April, M.DCCC.XC.IV.*

Nearly ready---PW March 31, 1894. Advertised
for May 15 *The Chap-Book,* May 15, 1894. Deposited (small paper) June 15, 1894. Listed Ath
Oct. 6, 1894; PW Feb. 23, 1895.

AAS   BA   BPL   H   LC   NYPL   UV   Y

14684. Great Men and Famous Women A Series
    of Pen and Pencil Sketches . . . Copyright,
    1894 . . . Edited by Charles F. Horne

New-York: Selmar Hess Publisher

"Michel Ney, Marshal of France," Vol. 2, pp.
255-261.

For fuller description see entry No. 10980A.

14685. Notable Single Poems American Authors
    Edited by Ina Russelle Warren

Buffalo Charles Wells Moulton Publisher ⟨n.d.,
1895⟩

"'Bend Low and Hark,'" p. 43. Collected in
At the Wind's Will, 1899.

For comment see entry No. 5672.

14686. Famous Stories Gems of Literature and Art . . .

Boston Lothrop Publishing Company ⟨1895⟩

Unpaged. Contains "To April. (A Rondel of Salutation.)"

For fuller entry see No. 6731.

14687. Press Notices of Songs from Vagabondia . . . Seaward . . . Plays of Maeterlinck . . . Quest of Merlin . . . Marriage of Guenevere . . . Gandolfo.

⟨n.p., n.d., *ca.* 1895⟩

Cover-title. Printed paper wrapper.

Brief comment, p. 29.

B

14688. Tea-Table Chat Gems of Literature and Art . . .

Boston Lothrop Publishing Company ⟨1896⟩

Pictorial boards, cloth shelf back. Unpaged.

Contains "In June"; collected in *At the Wind's Will*, 1899, as "The Birds Come Back."

Deposited July 6, 1896.

LC

14689. LAZY TOURS IN SPAIN AND ELSE-WHERE . . .

BOSTON ROBERTS BROTHERS 1896

⟨i-ii⟩, ⟨i⟩-x, ⟨1⟩-377; blank, p. ⟨378⟩; 2 pp. advertisements. Laid paper. 8¹⁄₁₆″ scant × 5³⁄₈″.

⟨-⟩⁶, ⟨1⟩-3, ⟨4⟩, 5-23⁸, 24⁴, ⟨25⟩².

V cloth: blue-green; brown; green. A laid paper flyleaf at back of some copies.

Deposited July 27, 1896. H copy received Sept. 26, 1896. Listed PW Oct. 10, 1896; Ath (Ward, Lock) Oct. 27, 1896.

AAS BA BPL H LC UV Y

14690. Essays from the Chap-Book . . .

Chicago. Printed for Herbert S. Stone & Company . . . 1896

"The Man Who Dares," pp. 177-191.

For fuller entry see No. 1291.

14691. IN CHILDHOOD'S COUNTRY . . . THE YELLOW HAIR LIBRARY II

BOSTON COPELAND AND DAY LONDON JAMES BOWDEN M DCCC XCVI

Title-page in black and orange.

⟨i⟩-⟨xii⟩, 13-69; blank, p. ⟨70⟩; colophon, p. ⟨71⟩. Laid paper. Illustrated. 8⁵⁄₈″ × 6¹³⁄₁₆″ full.

⟨1², 2-9⁴, 10²⟩. *Signed:* ⟨1⟩-4⁸, ⟨5⟩⁴.

Two states of the binding noted. The order of presentation is presumed correct. The following variations are sufficient for identification:

BINDING A

Rough light tan linen. Sides bordered with a single rule frame. A surviving deposit copy thus.

BINDING B

Smooth light tan linen. Sides not bordered by a single rule frame.

White laid paper end papers printed in blue with a pattern of girls in tree branches. Quadruple laid paper flyleaves.

Note: According to the publisher's catalog for 1896-1897 the book was issued in a trade format; and, a limited printing of 25 copies. BAL has not located an example of the limited format.

". . . Printed . . . November, 1896 . . ."–––Colophon.

Noted as *shortly* PW Dec. 5, 1896. Deposited Dec. 11, 1896. Listed PW Dec. 19, 1896. The London (Bowden) issue listed Ath Feb. 20, 1897. An Allenson (London) issue listed by Bkr Aug. 1902; presumably unsold copies of the Bowden issue. A "new edition" was advertised by Small, Maynard, PW Sept. 29, 1906; not located by BAL.

AAS (Binding B) B (Binding B) H (Binding A) LC (Binding A) UV (Binding A) Y (Binding A)

14692. The Treasury of American Sacred Song . . . Selected and Edited by W. Garrett Horder . . .

London Henry Frowde Oxford University Press Warehouse Amen Corner, E. C. New York: 91 & 93 Fifth Avenue 1896

Cloth, vellum shelf back.

Reprint save for:

"For Easter Morning," p. 212. Otherwise unlocated save as sheet music, 1946.

"The Song of the Stars," p. 213. Collected in *At the Wind's Will*, 1899.

Listed PW Dec. 19, 1896.

BPL

14693. Tales from McClure's Romance . . .

New York Doubleday & McClure Co. 1897

"When She Was Thirty," pp. 81-104.

Deposited Aug. 6, 1897. Noted as *just issued* PW Aug. 14, 1897. Listed PW Aug. 14, 1897; PC May 14, 1898.

AAS   H   Y

14694. An Account of the Exercises at the Dedication and Presentation to the City of Boston of the O'Reilly Monument June 20, 1896

Boston   Printed by Order of the City Council 1897

4 lines of verse, p. 36.

NYPL

14695. The Literature of America and Our Favorite Authors ... Choice Selections from Their Writings ... Compiled and Edited by William Wilfred Birdsall ... Rufus M. Jones ... and Others ...

John C. Winston & Co., Philadelphia Chicago Toronto ⟨1897⟩

Reprint save for "Next Year," p. 270.

Issued as a subscription book with varying imprints; a copy as above was deposited for copyright Jan. 18, 1898.

H   LC

14696. FOUR OF THEM ...

BOSTON: LITTLE, BROWN, AND COMPANY. ⟨1899⟩

⟨i-ii⟩, ⟨1⟩-78. Frontispiece and 1 plate inserted. 7⁵⁄₁₆″ × 5″.

⟨1-5⁸⟩. *Signed:* ⟨-⟩¹, ⟨1⟩-4⁸, 5⁷.

T cloth: green.

Deposited Oct. 7, 1899.

AAS   BPL

14697. AT THE WIND'S WILL LYRICS AND SONNETS ...

BOSTON LITTLE, BROWN, AND COMPANY 1899

Title-page in black and orange.

⟨i-ii⟩, ⟨i⟩-⟨xiv⟩, ⟨1⟩-171; blank, p. ⟨172⟩; advertisements, pp. 1-⟨4⟩, plus: ⟨5-7⟩. 6⁷⁄₈″ × 4³⁄₄″.

⟨-⟩⁸, 1-⟨5⟩, 6-11⁸; plus: ⟨12⟩². *Note:* Leaf ⟨-⟩₃ (the title-leaf) is a cancel.

V cloth: green; white. Flyleaf at back. Top edges gilt.

Announced PW Aug. 5, 1899. Deposited Oct. 26, 1899. Advertised PW Nov. 4, 1899. AAS has a copy inscribed by the author Nov. 4, 1899. Listed PW Dec. 2, 1899. The London edition (Macmillan, American sheets) advertised as though published Ath Nov. 11, 1899; listed Ath Nov. 11, 1899.

AAS   B   BPL   LC   NYPL   UV   Y

14698. JESSIE'S NEIGHBOR ...

BOSTON LITTLE, BROWN, AND COMPANY ⟨1900⟩

Not to be confused with another book of like title issued ⟨1877⟩.

⟨i-ii⟩, 1-64; 2 pp. advertisements. Frontispiece and 2 plates inserted. 7³⁄₈″ × 5″.

⟨1-4⁸, 5²⟩.

T cloth: green. Flyleaves in some copies.

Deposited Sept. 28, 1900.

Contents:

"Jessie's Neighbor." Here reprinted. For prior publication see *Jessie's Neighbor ...*, Boston ⟨1877⟩.

"Sung in the Twilight: A Story of Richard Wagner."

"The Surgeon of the Dolls' Hospital."

BPL   LC

14699. ... THE AMERICAN UNIVERSITY COURSE (STATE REGISTERED)   SECOND MONTH CONDUCT OF LIFE ...

AMERICAN UNIVERSITY SOCIETY NEW YORK ST. LOUIS CHICAGO ⟨n.d., *ca.* 1900⟩

Cover-title. Printed paper wrapper. At head of title: *Register No. 28M. 33,076 B.*

⟨1-12⟩. 5¹⁵⁄₁₆″ × 3¹⁵⁄₁₆″. Laid paper.

⟨-⟩⁶.

A series of questions and answers designed for the use of students of The American University Course.

"... The estimable lady who has undertaken this series of Questions brings to the work a vast amount of experience ..."———Inner front wrapper.

EM

14700. HER BABY BROTHER ...

BOSTON LITTLE, BROWN, AND COMPANY ⟨1901⟩

⟨i-ii⟩, ⟨1⟩-62; plus: 2 pp. advertisements. Frontispiece and two illustrations inserted. 7⁵⁄₁₆″ × 4¹⁵⁄₁₆″.

⟨1-4⁸; plus: 5¹⟩. *Signed:* ⟨-⟩¹, 1-4⁸.

T cloth: ecru.

Deposited Aug. 14, 1901.

BPL

14701 Recent English Dramatists Course XVI: Booklovers Reading Club Books Selected for This Reading Course by Professor Brander Matthews

⟨The Booklovers Library, Philadelphia, 1901⟩

Printed paper wrapper.

The Booklovers Reading Club Hand-Book to Accompany the Reading Course Entitled, Recent English Dramatists ———P. 7.

"Stephen Phillips," pp. 87-98.

Deposited Jan. 21, 1902.

LC

14702. . . . The Wide World

Boston, U.S.A. Ginn & Company, Publishers
The Athenæum Press 1902

At head of title: *Youth's Companion Series*

"A Turkish Debt. A True Story," pp. 52-56. Presumably by Moulton; signed at end: *L.C.M.*

Note: The above may have had prior book publication in one of the *Selections for Supplementary Reading from the Youth's Companion,* ca. 1895.

Deposited Feb. 14, 1902.

H   LC

14703. . . . Love Triumphant A Book of Poems by Frederic Lawrence Knowles . . .

⟨Boston: Dana Estes & Company, n.d., 1904⟩

Caption-title. The above on p. ⟨1⟩. At head of title: *Just Ready Order Now!*

Single cut sheet folded to make four pages.

"A Letter," Jan. 23, 1904, "quoted by permission," pp. ⟨2-3⟩.

Issued as an advertisement for *Love Triumphant.*

H (in original envelope postmarked Oct. 3, 1904)

14704. Birthday Tributes to Mrs. Julia Ward Howe May 27, 1905

⟨Boston: Winthrop B. Jones, for the Authors Club, 1905⟩

Untitled 15-line poem, p. 11.

For comment see entry No. 96.

14705. INTRODUCTION TO THE VALUE OF LOVE AND ITS COMPILER FREDERIC LAWRENCE KNOWLES . . .

BOSTON COPYRIGHT 1906, BY H. M. CALDWELL CO.]

Cover-title. The above decorated in green with classical female figure, etc.

Prepared for copyright? As promotion for Knowles's books?

v-xi; p. ⟨xii⟩ blank save for (in green) female figure, roses, etc. 8½″ full × 5¾″. Each page decorated in green.

⟨-⟩⁴.

Printed cream paper wrapper. Two issues of the wrapper noted:

1ST ISSUE WRAPPER

Preliminary square bracket not present, last line of imprint.

Outer back wrapper headed: UNIFORM WITH THE VALUE OE ⟨*sic*⟩ LOVE

2ND ISSUE WRAPPER

Preliminary square bracket present, last line of imprint.

Outer back wrapper headed: UNIFORM WITH THE VALUE OF LOVE

The introduction also appears in: *The Value of Love Edited by Frederic Lawrence Knowles . . . ,* Boston: H. M. Caldwell Company, 1906. *Note:* A copy of this book (in B) has a cancel title-leaf and Mrs. Moulton's introduction is not present; status not known to BAL. Noted for *before July* PW April 14, 1906. Advertised PW Sept. 29, 1906. Listed PW Nov. 10, 1906. Copies in AAS, B.

AAS (2nd)   BPL (1st)

14706. The Poems and Sonnets of Louise Chandler Moulton . . .

Boston Little, Brown, and Company 1909

Reprint save for the following poems which are here first collected:

"All in One"

"'Beyond'"

"The Bold Ghost"

"For Easter Morn"

"If Once, Just Once"

"Life's Seasons"

"Once More"

"One Day"

"To Julia Ward Howe"

"Why?"

Noted for *this month* PW Nov. 7, 1908. Deposited Dec. 7, 1908. BA copy received Dec. 22, 1908. Noted as *just . . . out* PW Dec. 26, 1908. Listed PW Jan. 16, 1909. The London (Macmillan) edition listed Bkr May 21, 1909.

AAS B BA H LC NYPL

14707. . . . FOR EASTER MORNING FOR FULL CHORUS . . . ⟨Words by⟩ LOUISE

CHANDLER MOULTON ⟨Music by⟩ H. A. SCHIMMERLING ...

COPYRIGHT, 1946, BY G. SCHIRMER, INC. ...

Sheet music. The above on p. ⟨2⟩. At head of title: *G. Schirmer Octavo No. 9557 To the Riverside Church Choir*

Cover-title: *G. Schirmer's Choral Church Music* ...

Plate number 41263.

Previously in *The Treasury of American Sacred Song*, London and New York, 1896.

NYPL

Reprints of Moulton's own books including sheet music. See in *Section Three* for books of other authors containing reprinted Moulton material.

14708. The Book of the Boudoir; or, Memento of Friendship. A Gift for All Seasons. Edited by Ellen Louise . . .

Boston: Phillips, Sampson and Company, Publishers. ⟨1853⟩

Reprint of *The Waverley Garland* . . . , 1853. See next two entries.

14709. The Book of the Boudoir; or, Memento of Friendship. A Gift for All Seasons. Edited by Ellen Louise . . .

New York: Published by Leavitt and Allen. ⟨n.d., 1853?⟩

Leather. Reprint of *The Waverley Garland* . . . , 1853. See preceding entry; see next entry.

14710. The Book of the Boudoir; or, Memento of Friendship A Gift for All Seasons. Edited by Ellen Louise . . .

New York: Published by W. H. Appleton, 92 & 94 Grand St. ⟨n.d., not before 1864⟩

Leather. Reprint of *The Waverley Garland* . . . , 1853. See preceding two entries.

14711. Swallow-Flights . . .

London: Macmillan and Co. 1878 . . .

Advertised *this day* Ath Jan. 12, 1878; PC Jan. 18, 1878. Listed PC Feb. 1, 1878. Advertised with extracts from review Ath Feb. 9, 1878.

14712. The New England Story-Book. Stories by Famous New England Authors . . . Louise Chandler Moulton . . . Etc.

Boston: D. Lothrop and Company, Franklin Street, Corner of Hawley. ⟨1880⟩

For fuller entry see No. 10877.

14713. Jessie's Neighbor. By Louise Chandler Moulton. (With Other Stories by Favorite Authors.)

Boston: D. Lothrop & Company. Franklin St., Corner of Hawley. ⟨n.d., *ca.* 1881⟩

Reprint of *Jessie's Neighbor* ⟨1877⟩ with additional stories by other authors including Ella Farman Pratt, Clara F. Guernsey, Nora Perry. On front: *Out of School Series.*

14714. Illustrated Stories by American Authors . . . The White Chrysanthemums, ⟨by⟩ Louise Chandler Moulton . . .

Boston D. Lothrop and Company Franklin and Hawley Streets ⟨1884⟩

Unpaged. Deposited Oct. 4, 1884.

14715. Illustrated Stories by American Authors . . . Jessie's Neighbor, ⟨by⟩ Louise Chandler Moulton. Two Burial Places in Florence, ⟨by⟩ Louise Chandler Moulton . . .

Boston D. Lothrop and Company Franklin and Hawley Streets ⟨1884⟩

Unpaged. Deposited Nov. 3, 1884.

14716. Our Famous Women. An Authorized Record of the Lives and Deeds of Distinguished American Women of Our Times . . . by . . . Elizabeth Stuart Phelps. Harriet Beecher Stowe . . . Louise Chandler Moulton . . . Sold Only by Subscription.

Hartford, Conn.: A. D. Worthington & Co., Publishers. A. G. Nettleton & Co., Chicago, Ills. 1884.

A subscription book; probably issued with varying imprints and styles of cloth and leather.

14717. The New England Story-Book. Stories by Famous New England Authors: Mrs. A. D. Whitney ⟨sic⟩ . . . Sarah O. Jewett . . . Elizabeth Stuart Phelps, Celia Thaxter . . . E. L. Bynner . . . Louise Chandler Moulton, Etc, ⟨sic⟩ Etc.

Boston: D. Lothrop and Company, Franklin Street, Corner of Hawley. ⟨1886⟩

Pictorial boards. Unpaged.

Deposited July 23, 1886.

14718. The Favorite Story-Book Stories by Famous Authors Mrs. A. D. T. Whitney . . . Sarah O. Jewett . . . Elizabeth Stuart Phelps . . . Celia Thaxter . . . E. L. Bynner . . . Louise Chandler Moulton . . . Etc.

Boston   D Lothrop Company   Washington Street opposite Bromfield ⟨1889⟩

Pictorial boards. Unpaged.

14719. In the Garden of Dreams: Lyrics and Sonnets . . . ⟨Second Edition⟩

Boston: Roberts Brothers. 1890.

Not located.

Presumably a reprint since the *Third Edition*, 1890, contains no material not present in the *First Edition*, 1890.

14720. In the Garden of Dreams: Lyrics and Sonnets . . . ⟨Third Edition⟩

Boston: Roberts Brothers. 1890.

On copyright page: *Third Edition.*

14721. . . . Night . . .

Boston: Arthur P. Schmidt. ⟨1891⟩

Sheet music. Cover-title. At head of title: *Three Songs of the Night by Margaret Ruthven Lang . . .*

Plate number: *A.P.S. 2799.* Otherwise "To Night," *In the Garden of Dreams*, 1890.

14722. In the Garden of Dreams: Lyrics and Sonnets . . . ⟨Fifth Edition⟩

Boston: Roberts Brothers. 1892.

On copyright page: *Fifth Edition.*

14723. The Collected Poems of Philip Bourke Marston . . . with Biographical Sketch by Louise Chandler Moulton . . .

Ward, Lock, Bowden and Co. London: Warwick House, Salisbury Square, E.C. Melbourne: 3 and 5, St. James's Street. 1892 . . .

American sheets with cancel title-leaf. See Boston edition, *Section One*, under year 1892.

Advertised as *immediately* Ath Oct. 22, 1892. Listed Ath Nov. 5, 1892; PC Nov. 12, 1892; Bkr Dec. 1892 (as a November publication).

14724. . . . Fickle Love . . .

Boston. H. B. Stevens Company . . . 1893 . . .

Sheet music. Cover-title. At head of title: *Two Songs by Horatio W. Parker.* Plate number: *H.B.S.Co. 418.*

Otherwise "Eros," in *August*, 1886; *In the Garden of Dreams*, 1890.

14725. Swallow Flights. New Edition of "Poems," Published in 1877, with Ten Additional Poems . . . ⟨Third Edition⟩

Boston: Roberts Brothers. 1893.

On copyright page: *Third Edition.*

14726. Swallow Flights. New Edition of "Poems," Published in 1877, with Ten Additional Poems . . .

London: Macmillan and Co. 1893.

14727. . . . O Sweetest Maid ⟨Music⟩ by Robert A. Stearns . . .

White-Smith Music Publishing Co., Boston . . . ⟨1894⟩

Sheet music. Cover-title. At head of title: *Song*

Plate number: *9409–3* (contralto, baritone). Reprinted from *In the Garden of Dreams*, 1890.

14728. To Night . . . Music by John Francis Gilder . . .

Oliver Ditson Company. Boston . . . ⟨1896⟩

Sheet music. Cover-title. Plate number: *4-1-59471-4.* For an earlier setting see "Night," 1891.

14729. Against Wind and Tide . . .

Boston: Little, Brown, and Company. ⟨1899⟩

According to a "sample copy" in Y 3000 copies were printed Aug. 21, 1899. Deposited Oct. 7, 1899.

14730. . . . A Summer Wooing . . .

The Boston Music Company   Boston, Mass. Copyright, 1898, G. Schirmer, Jr. ⟨1902⟩

Sheet music. Cover-title. At head of title: *Compositions by James H. Rogers . . .*

Note: Copyright notice dated 1902 at foot of first page of text and music.

Plate number: *B.M.Co.716* (mezzo); *B.M.Co.715* (soprano, tenor). Reprinted from *At the Wind's Will*, 1899. Deposited Nov. 25, 1902.

14731. . . . The Voice of Spring . . .

Arthur P. Schmidt   Boston . . . 120 Boylston St. . . . ⟨1904⟩

Sheet music. Cover-title. At head of title: *Arthur Foote . . .*

Plate number: *A.P.S.6352-4.* Reprinted from *At the Wind's Will*, 1899.

14732. . . . To-Night . . .

Chicago   Clayton F. Summy Co. 64 E. Van Buren St. . . . ⟨1914⟩

Sheet music. Cover-title. Plate number: *C.F.S.Co. 1487.* For an earlier setting see "Night," 1891.

The following publications contain material by Moulton reprinted from earlier books.

Declamations and Dialogues for the Sunday-School. By Prof. J. H. Gilmore . . .

> Boston . . . ⟨1871⟩

> For comment see BAL, Vol. 5, p. 318.

A Hand-Book of English Literature. Intended for the Use of High Schools . . . by Francis H. Underwood . . . American Authors.

> Boston: Lee and Shepard, Publishers. New York: Lee, Shepard and Dillingham. 1873.

The Palace of the King . . . Compiled by the Editor of "The Changed Cross;" . . .

> New York . . . 1880.

> For fuller entry see BAL, Vol. 2, p. 105.

Papyrus Leaves . . . Edited by William Fearing Gill . . .

> New York . . . 1880.

> Deposited Dec. 26, 1879. For comment see entry No. 2477.

Flower Songs for Flower Lovers. Compiled by Rose Porter . . .

> New York: Anson D. F. Randolph & Company, 900 Broadway, Cor. 20th Street. ⟨1880⟩

> All Moulton material herein reprinted from other books. The untitled lines beginning *Harold, on a summer day* . . . , extracted from "Roses," *Poems*, 1878.

Poems for Our Darlings.

> Boston: D. Lothrop & Co., Publishers, 30 and 32 Franklin Street. ⟨1880⟩

> Pictorial boards. Cloth shelf back. Unpaged.

The Union of American Poetry and Art . . . by John James Piatt . . .

> Cincinnati . . . 1880

> For fuller entry see in James Russell Lowell, *Section Three*.

Harper's Cyclopædia of British and American Poetry Edited by Epes Sargent

> New York . . . 1881

> For comment see entry No. 4336.

Echoes of the Aesthetic Society of Jersey City

> New-York   Thompson & Moreau, Printers Nos. 51 & 53 Maiden Lane MDCCCLXXXII.

Flowers from Hill and Dale Poems Arranged . . . by Susie Barstow Skelding . . .

> New York . . . 1883

> For fuller entry see No. 11363.

Surf and Wave: The Sea as Sung by the Poets. Edited by Anna L. Ward . . .

> New York: Thomas Y. Crowell & Co. 13 Astor Place. ⟨1883⟩

Flowers from Glade and Garden Poems Arranged . . . by Susie Barstow Skelding . . .

> New York . . . 1884

> For comment see BAL, Vol. 2, p. 39.

An Old Scrap-Book. With Additions . . .

> ⟨Cambridge⟩ February 8, 1884.

> For comment see entry No. 7763.

Flowers for Winter Days . . . Arranged . . . by Susie Barstow Skelding . . .

> New York . . . 1885

> For fuller entry see BAL, Vol. 4, p. 444.

Flowers from Sunlight and Shade . . . Arranged . . . by Susie Barstow Skelding . . .

> New York . . . 1885

> For fuller entry see BAL, Vol. 5, p. 113.

Flowers from Here and There Poems Arranged and Illustrated by Susie Barstow Skelding . . .

> New York White, Stokes, & Allen 1885

April Edited by Oscar Fay Adams . . .

Boston . . . ⟨1886⟩

For comment see entry No. 61.

May Edited by Oscar Fay Adams . . .

Boston . . . ⟨1886⟩

For comment see entry No. 63.

September Edited by Oscar Fay Adams . . .

Boston . . . ⟨1886⟩

For comment see entry No. 67.

November Edited by Oscar Fay Adams . . .

Boston . . . ⟨1886⟩

For comment see entry No. 69.

Birds and Blossoms and What the Poets Sing of Them . . . Edited by Susie Barstow Skelding . . .

New York   Frederick A. Stokes   Successor to White, Stokes, & Allen   1887

Deposited July 29, 1887.

Sea Vistas . . . Edited . . . by Susie Barstow Skelding . . .

New York . . . 1888

For fuller entry see BAL, Vol. 5, p. 113.

Buds and Blossoms . . .

Philadelphia   Peterson Magazine Co.   1889

The Poets' Year . . . Edited by Oscar Fay Adams . . .

Boston . . . ⟨1890⟩

For comment see entry No. 80.

Representative Sonnets by American Poets . . . by Charles H. Crandall

Boston . . . 1890

For comment see entry No. 8374.

Garde Joyeuse . . . by Gleeson White

London . . . 1890

For comment see BAL, Vol. 1, p. 18.

The Lover's Year-Book of Poetry . . . ⟨Compiled⟩ by Horace Parker Chandler Vol. II. July to December

Boston . . . 1892

For fuller entry see BAL, Vol. 4, p. 61.

Werner's Readings and Recitations No. 9 Compiled and Arranged by Jean Carruthers

Edgar S. Werner Publishing & Supply Co. (Incorporated) New York . . . 1892 . . .

Printed paper wrapper?

The Lover's Year-Book of Poetry ⟨Second Series⟩ . . . Married-Life and Child-Life ⟨Compiled⟩ by Horace Parker Chandler . . .

Boston . . . 1893

For comment see entry No. 10903.

The untitled sonnet, Vol. 2, p. 254, had prior publication in *Poems*, 1878, under the title "One Dread."

For Afternoon Readers . . .

Boston . . . ⟨1896⟩

For fuller entry see BAL, Vol. 3, p. 317.

Later American Poems Edited by J. E. Wetherell . . .

Toronto: The Copp, Clark Company, Limited. 1896.

The Lover's Year-Book of Poetry   A Collection of Love Poems for Every Day in the Year   The Other Life by Horace Parker Chandler   Vol. I. January to June

Boston   Roberts Brothers   1896

Library of the World's Best Literature Ancient and Modern   Charles Dudley Warner Editor . . . Thirty Volumes Vol. XXVIII

New York . . . ⟨1898⟩

Deposited Feb. 23, 1898. For fuller comment see entry No. 10624.

Lothrop's Annual . . .

Boston . . . ⟨1898⟩

For fuller entry see BAL, Vol. 1, p. 19.

The International Library of Famous Literature . . . Compiled . . . by Nathan Haskell Dole, Forrest Morgan and Caroline Ticknor . . .

New York . . . ⟨1898⟩

For fuller entry see BAL, Vol. 5, p. 204.

Dew Drops and Diamonds . . .

. . . 1898 . . . Chicago . . .

For comment see BAL, Vol. 1, p. 77.

Anthology of Living American Poets, 1898. Arranged by Deborah Ege Olds.

Cincinnati. The Editor Publishing Company. 1898.

Nature Pictures by American Poets Selected and Edited by Annie Russell Marble . . .

New York The Macmillan Company London: Macmillan & Co., Ltd. 1899 . . .

Deposited Nov. 17, 1899.

Best Things from American Literature Edited by Irving Bacheller . . .

New York . . . 1899

For comment see entry No. 4086.

The International Library of Famous Literature . . . Edited by Dr. Richard Garnett . . . in Twenty Volumes . . .

London . . . 1899

For comment see entry No. 10638.

Wide Awake Story Book for Our Boys and Girls . . .

Boston Lothrop Publishing Company ⟨1899⟩

Pictorial boards, cloth shelf back. Unpaged.

An American Anthology 1787–1899 . . . Edited by Edmund Clarence Stedman . . .

Boston . . . M DCCCC

For fuller entry see No. 3082.

. . . By Land and Sea

1900 Perry Mason & Company Boston, Mass.

At head of title: *The Companion Series*

. . . Under Sunny Skies

Boston, U.S.A. Ginn & Company, Publishers The Athenæum Press 1902

At head of title: *Youth's Companion Series*

Deposited June 2, 1902.

Is this a reprint of a publication issued *ca.* 1895 ? Contains "Granada," pp. 11-18; previously in *Lazy Tours in Spain*, 1896.

Carlyle's Laugh and Other Surprises by Thomas Wentworth Higginson

Boston . . . MDCCCCIX

For fuller entry see No. 8495.

Three Unpublished Poems by Louisa M. Alcott . . .

⟨n.p., Boston?, 1919⟩

For fuller entry see No. 243.

American Mystical Verse . . . Selected by Irene Hunter . . .

D. Appleton and Company New York MCMXXV

REFERENCES AND ANA

Stories. By Mrs. L. C. Moulton, E. Stuart Phelps, Ella Farman, Rossiter Johnson, and Other Story-Tellers.

Boston: Lothrop, 1875.

Not located. Entry from PW Dec. 25, 1875, where the above title is listed. Further information wanting. Possibly a printing of *Two Fortune-Seekers* . . . ⟨1875⟩.

In the Garden of Dreams.

Boston, 1894.

Not located. Entry from Foley. Further information wanting. For the first edition of this title see above under 1890.

The Christmas Garland: A Miscellany of Verses, Stories, and Essays.

Chicago: Herbert S. Stone & Company, 1901

Not located. For comment see BAL, Vol. 3, p. 186. According to an advertisement in PW (Sept. 28, 1901) this was to contain a contribution by Louise Chandler Moulton.

A List of the Books Forming the Gift of Louise Chandler Moulton to the Public Library of the City of Boston

Boston Published by the Trustees 1909

Printed paper wrapper.

Louise Chandler Moulton Poet and Friend by Lilian Whiting

Boston Little, Brown, and Company 1910

On copyright page: *Published, September, 1910*

Advertised for *today* PW Sept. 17, 1910. Deposited Sept. 22, 1910. Listed PW Oct. 1, 1910.

JOHN MUIR

1 8 3 8 – 1 9 1 4

14733. The Wonders of the Yosemite Valley, and of California. By Samuel Kneeland . . . Third Edition, Revised and Enlarged.

Boston: Alexander Moore. Lee & Shepard. New York: Lee, Shepard & Dillingham. 1872.

Muir's comments on "The Yosemite Glaciers," pp. 90-91.

LWC

14734. Proceedings of the Boston Society of Natural History. Vol. xv. 1872–1873.

Boston: Printed for the Society. 1873.

Printed paper wrapper?

Extracts from letters, pp. 148-151; 185-186.

"Professor Kneeland, Secretary Boston Institute of Technology, gathered some letters I sent to Runkle and that *Tribune* letter, and hashed them into a compost called a paper for the Boston Historical Society ⟨*sic*⟩, and gave me credit for all of the smaller sayings and doings and stole the broadest truth to himself . . ."––*Letters to a Friend* . . . , by John Muir, Boston, 1915, pp. 134-135. The material referred to appears on pp. 36-47 of the *Proceedings* . . . , Boston, 1873, under the title "On the Glaciers of the Yosemite Valley," by Dr. Samuel Kneeland.

H

14735. Proceedings of the American Association for the Advancement of Science. Twenty-Third Meeting, Held at Hartford, Conn. August, 1874.

Salem ⟨Mass.⟩: Published by the Permanent Secretary. 1875.

Printed paper wrapper.

"Studies in the Formation of Mountains in the Sierra Nevada, California," Part II, pp. 49-64.

BA   H

14736. ON THE POST-GLACIAL HISTORY OF SEQUOIA GIGANTEA . . .

⟨SALEM, MASS.: SALEM PRESS, 1877⟩

Not seen. Information from Mr. Lloyd W. Currey.

Cover-title.

242-253.

Off-print from *Proceedings of the American Association for the Advancement of Science, Twenty-Fifth Meeting . . . Buffalo, N. Y., August, 1876*, Salem ⟨Mass.⟩, 1877. In H.

14737. Contemporary Biography of California's Representative Men . . . by Alonzo Phelps . . .

San Francisco: A. L. Bancroft and Company, Publishers. 1882.

"The Glaciers and Snow-Banners of California," pp. 104-112.

Query: Was this contribution also issued as a separate? An entry in NUC for the following title: *Snow Banners of the California Alps* suggests the possibility. The NUC locates the title in The United States Weather Bureau Library but the library (Aug. 1969) reported the piece as "not owned." Further information wanting.

Note: Although not so marked the above publication is the second of a two-volume work; the first volume is dated 1881. Possibly issued in a variety of formats; noted in cloth; and, leather.

HEH   Y

14738. Sport with Gun and Rod in American Woods and Waters Edited by Alfred M. Mayer . . .

New York The Century Co ⟨1883⟩

"The Wild Sheep of the Sierra," pp. ⟨280⟩-302. Collected in *The Mountains of California*, 1894.

For comment see BAL, Vol. I, p. 446.

14739. Cruise of the Revenue-Steamer Corwin in Alaska . . .

Two printings noted. Sequence, if any, not determined. The order of presentation is purely arbitrary.

A

Cruise of the Revenue-Steamer Corwin in Alaska and the N. W. Arctic Ocean in 1881. Notes and Memoranda . . .

Washington: Government Printing Office. 1883.

"Botanical Notes on Alaska," pp. 47-53. Collected in *The Cruise of the Corwin*, 1917.

Issued as Treasury Department Document, No. 429; see notice, p. 3.

B

. . . Cruise of the Revenue-Steamer Corwin in Alaska and the N.W. Arctic Ocean in 1881. Notes and Memoranda . . .

Washington: Government Printing Office. 1883.

At head of title: *47th Congress, 2d Session. House of Representatives. Ex. Doc. No. 105.*

"Botanical Notes on Alaska," pp. 47-53. Collected in *The Cruise of the Corwin*, 1917.

Copies of the immediate preceding have been noted bound together with other House of Representatives documents and issued as *The Executive Documents of the House of Representatives for the Second Session of the Forty-Seventh Congress . . . Volume 23*, Washington, 1883.

See below under 1884.

B (B)   BA (A)   H (A,B)   LC (A,B)   Y (A)

14740. History of Tulare County, California, with Illustrations, Descriptive of Its Scenery . . . with Biographical Sketches.

Wallace W. Elliott & Co, Publishers, 609 Montgomery Street, San Francisco, Cal. 1883.

Cloth, leather shelf back.

"The California Alps," p. 73.

Under the heading "Grand Mountains and Glaciers," Muir quoted, pp. 115-116.

Note: The Muir material appears also in *History of Kern County, California . . .*, San Francisco, 1883, pp. 115-136. Prior to publication in the above? Not seen by BAL; information supplied by Mr. Lloyd W. Currey.

LWC

14741. A Southern California Paradise, (In the Suburbs of Los Angeles.) Being a Historic and Descriptive Account of Pasadena, San Gabriel, Sierra Madre, and La Cañada . . .

Edited and Published by R. W. C. Farnsworth, Pasadena, California. 1883.

Cloth; and, printed paper wrapper.

"The Sierra Madre Mountains," pp. 64-66. Extracted from "The Bee-Pastures of California,"

Century Magazine, July, 1882. Collected in *The Mountains of California*, 1894.

EM   LWC

14742. . . . Report of the Cruise of the U. S. Revenue Steamer Thomas Corwin, in the Arctic Ocean, 1881. By Captain C. L. Hooper . . .

Washington: Government Printing Office. 1884.

At head of title: *48th Congress, 1st Session. Senate. Ex. Doc. No. 204.*

"On the Glaciation of the Arctic and Subarctic Regions Visited by the United States Steamer Corwin in the Year 1881," pp. 135-147. Collected in *The Cruise of the Corwin*, 1917.

Also occurs as *The Executive Documents of the Senate of the United States for the First Session of the Forty-Eighth Congress . . . Volume 8 --- No. 204*, Washington, 1884.

Issued in printed paper wrapper?

See above under 1883.

H

14743. Descriptive and Historical Sketch of the Great Salt Lake, (Utah Territory). Issued by Passenger Department the Utah & Nevada Railway.

Salt Lake: J. C. Parker, Printer and Binder. 1886.

Printed paper wrapper.

"Graphic Description of a Bath in the Lake," pp. 21-25.

EM   LWC

14744. Picturesque California

Issued by subscription in a variety of formats. BAL has been unable to establish a sequence. The parts first issued were published by *The J. Dewing Company;* later parts were issued by the successor firm, *J. Dewing Publishing Company.* Later still the firm name reverted to *The J. Dewing Company.* See under 1894 for a revised edition.

Noted in the following formats:

INDIA PROOF EDITION

⟨Printing A⟩

Vol. 1

Picturesque California and the Region West of the Rocky Mountains, from Alaska to Mexico. Edited by John Muir . . . ⟨Volume 1⟩

The J. Dewing Company, Publishers. San Francisco and New York. MDCCCLXXXVII. ⟨Copyright 1887⟩

Vol. 2

Title-page for Vol. 2 issued with *Part 10*.

. . . Picturesque California: The Rocky Mountains and the Pacific Slope . . . ⟨Volume II⟩

J. Dewing Publishing Company New York and San Francisco ⟨1888⟩

At head of title: *Edited by John Muir*

10 portfolios, each in a printed paper wrapper, each within a printed cloth folder.

"Peaks and Glaciers of the High Sierra," Part 1, pp. ⟨1⟩-18.

"The Passes of the High Sierra," Part 1, pp. ⟨19⟩-34.

"The Yosemite Valley," Part 2, pp. ⟨49⟩-88.

"Mount Shasta," Part 4, pp. ⟨145⟩-174.

"Alaska," Part 5, pp. ⟨193⟩-218.

"Washington and Puget Sound," Part 6, pp. ⟨265⟩-288.

"The Basin of the Columbia River," Part 9, pp. ⟨385⟩-414.

Issued in a limited edition, each part numbered; the total number issued not given.

Wrappers of Parts 1-2 imprinted: *The J. Dewing Company* Wrappers of Parts 3-10 imprinted: *The J. Dewing Publishing Company*

Also issued in a trade printing of 32 paper-covered parts.

Part 1 (of the *India Proof Edition*) inscribed by an early owner Nov. 29, 1888; in LC.

Location: LC

INDIA PROOF EDITION

⟨Printing B⟩

. . . Picturesque California: The Rocky Mountains and the Pacific Slope . . .

J. Dewing Publishing Company New York and San Francisco ⟨1887–1888⟩

At head of title: *Edited by John Muir*

2 Vols. Also issued in parts?

In this form deposited for copyright Aug. 22, 1889 ⟨sic⟩. The printed copyright notice in Vol. 1 is dated 1887 and is in the name of *J. Dewing Publishing Co.* Vol. 2 is copyrighted in the name of *J. Dewing Publishing Co.*, dated 1888.

A presumed reprint.

Location: LC

INDIA PROOF EDITION

⟨Printing C⟩

. . . Picturesque California: The Rocky Mountains and the Pacific Slope . . . ⟨Volume 1⟩

J. Dewing Publishing Company New York and San Francisco ⟨1888⟩

At head of title: *Edited by John Muir*

Noted only as an incomplete set. Originally issued in ten paper-covered parts, each part in a cloth folder.

All parts noted (Parts 1-7) are in the printed paper wrapper of the *J. Dewing Publishing Company*.

Issued in a limited printing, each part numbered, but the total number of copies printed not specified.

On the basis of the publisher's name style presumably a reprint.

Location: LC

IMPERIAL JAPAN EDITION

. . . Picturesque California: The Rocky Mountains and the Pacific Slope . . .

Philadelphia George Barrie & Son, Publishers ⟨n.d.⟩

At head of title: *Edited by John Muir*

Limited to 100 numbered copies.

Issued in ten portfolios.

Status not known.

Location: LC

UNKNOWN FORMAT A

Vol. 1

Picturesque California and the Region West of the Rocky Mountains, from Alaska to Mexico. Edited by John Muir . . . Volume I.

The J. Dewing Company, Publishers. San Francisco and New York. MDCCCLXXXVIII. ⟨Copyright notice dated 1887⟩

2 Vols. Issued in ⟨32?⟩ paper-covered parts.

Vol. 2

. . . Picturesque California: The Rocky Mountains and the Pacific Slope . . . ⟨Volume 2⟩

J. Dewing Publishing Company New York and San Francisco ⟨1888⟩

At head of title: *Edited by John Muir*

A reprint.

Location: LC

UNKNOWN FORMAT B

Vol. 1

Picturesque California and the Region West of the Rocky Mountains, from Alaska to Mexico. Edited by John Muir . . . Volume I.

J. Dewing Publishing Company, New York and San Francisco. MDCCCLXXXVIII. ⟨Copyright J. Dewing Publishing Company, 1887⟩

2 Vols. Also issued in 32 paper-covered parts?

Vol. 2

... Picturesque California: The Rocky Mountains and the Pacific Slope ... ⟨Volume 2⟩

J. Dewing Publishing Company New York and San Francisco ⟨1888⟩ ⟨Copyright J. Dewing Publishing Company, 1888⟩

At head of title: *Edited by John Muir*

A reprint.

Location: H

Reported, not seen, in the *Connoisseur Edition* format. Status not known.

14745. ALASKA via NORTHERN PACIFIC

⟨ST. PAUL, MINN.: THE NORTHERN PACIFIC RAIL-ROAD, 1891⟩

Single cut sheet, 13⅞″ × 31¼″, folded to make 36 pages. Page: 7″ × 3⁷⁄₁₆″ full.

Cover-title.

An advertising folder, not a pamphlet. Folded in the manner of a road map.

"Alaska," pp. 3-17. Map on reverse of sheet.

At foot of p. 17: *Poole Bros. Chicago.*

Issued for the season of 1891, June 1st to Oct. 1st, 1891, according to advertisements herein.

Y

14746. THE MOUNTAINS OF CALIFORNIA ...

NEW YORK THE CENTURY CO. 1894

⟨i⟩-⟨xvi⟩, 1-381; leaf, excised or pasted under the end paper. Pp. ⟨i-ii⟩ excised or pasted under the end paper. 7⁹⁄₁₆″ full × 5⅛″.

⟨-⟩⁸, ⟨1⟩-24⁸. Leaves ⟨-⟩₁ and 24₈ excised or pasted under the end paper.

V cloth: tan. Top edges gilt.

Note: The copies first printed, not necessarily the copies first circulated, have folio 1 present on the first page of text.

Deposited Sept. 21, 1894. Noted as *just ready* PW Oct. 3, 1894. Advertised for Oct. 10 in PW Sept. 29, 1894. Listed PW Oct. 20, 1894. The London (Fisher Unwin) edition listed Ath Oct. 20, 1894; PC Nov. 17, 1894. See below under 1911 for an "enlarged" edition.

AAS BA H Y

14747. ... Picturesque California: The Rocky Mountains and the Pacific Slope ...

The J. Dewing Company New York and San Francisco ⟨1894⟩

At head of title: *Edited by John Muir*

An abbreviated version of the 1887-1888 edition, *q.v.*

Issued serially in 32 paper-covered parts, Jan. 1, 1894-Oct. 8, 1894.

Title-page issued with Part 32.

AAS HEH

14748. California Early History: Commercial Position: Climate: Scenery ... July 1897

California State Board of Trade San Francisco, Cal.

Printed paper wrapper.

"The Scenery of California," pp. 16-21.

H

14749. Library of the World's Best Literature Ancient and Modern Charles Dudley Warner Editor ... Thirty Volumes ...

New York R. S. Peale and J. A. Hill Publishers ⟨1897⟩

"Linnaeus," Vol. 16, pp. 9077-9083. Deposited Aug. 9, 1897.

Vol. 18 reprints an extract from Muir's *The Mountains of California*, 1894.

For fuller entry see No. 10624.

14750. Pacific Coast Steamship Co. California British Columbia Washington Alaska Oregon Mexico

San Francisco: Goodell, Perkins & Co., General Agents, May, 1898.

Not seen. Entry furnished by Mr. Lloyd W. Currey.

Single cut sheet, folded to make 32 panels. Contains Muir's "Pathless Treasure Fields of the Frozen Northland," reprinted from *The San Francisco Examiner*, Oct. 11, 1897.

14751. ... Alaska Volume 1 Narrative, Glaciers, Natives by John Burroughs, John Muir and George Bird Grinnell

New York Doubleday, Page & Company 1901

"Notes on the Pacific Coast Glaciers," pp. 119-135.

For fuller entry see No. 2168.

14752. OUR NATIONAL PARKS ...

BOSTON AND NEW YORK HOUGHTON, MIFFLIN AND COMPANY THE RIVERSIDE PRESS, CAMBRIDGE 1901

For extended edition see under year 1909.

⟨i-x⟩, ⟨1⟩-370; blank, p. ⟨371⟩; printer's imprint, p. ⟨372⟩. Laid paper. Frontispiece and 11 plates inserted. 8¹⁄₁₆″ × 5³⁄₁₆″ full.

⟨1¹, 2⁴, 3-25⁸, 26²⟩.

Three printings were issued under date 1901; a fourth printing was issued under date 1902. See publisher's records below.

FIRST PRINTING

(Also a later printing?)

As collated above. A surviving copyright deposit copy, now rebound, and defective, appears to collate thus; received Nov. 2, 1901; the second printing was not done until Nov. 14, 1901.

REPRINT (REPRINTS?)

⟨1-24⁸⟩.

V cloth: green. White laid paper end papers. Top edges gilt. Flyleaf at front.

According to the publisher's records:

1st Printing

Oct. 23, 1901: 992 copies printed. Four copies bound in paper not later than Oct. 24, 1901. Sheets bound Oct. 31-Nov. 18, 1901.

2nd Printing

Nov. 14, 1901: 500 copies printed.

3rd Printing

Dec. 4, 1901: 494 copies printed.

4th Printing

Dec. 20, 1901; 498 copies. Date altered to *1902*.

Note: There were several later reprints issued under date ⟨1901⟩.

On copyright page: *Published November, 1901.*

Deposited Nov. 2, 1901. Copies of the first printing received by both BA and Y on Nov. 12, 1901. Listed PW Nov. 16, 1901. The London edition (Gay & Bird; an importation?) not listed by either Ath or Bkr; advertised as though published Bkr Aug. 1902; Ath Oct. 4, 1902.

AAS (reprint)   BA (1st)   H (1st)   Y (1st)

14753. The Man Shakespeare and Other Essays by Catherine Merrill . . . with Some Words of Appreciation from John Muir

The Bowen-Merrill Company Publishers, Indianapolis ⟨1902⟩

"Words from an Old Friend," pp. 32-38.

H

14754. The Encyclopedia Americana . . . in Sixteen Volumes . . . Volume VIII.

The Americana Company New York Chicago ⟨1904⟩

Unpaged. Noted only in three quarters leather.

Contains "Glacier." Written by Muir; based on his "Notes on the Pacific Coast Glaciers," in *Alaska* . . . , 1901, above.

This volume deposited for copyright March 18, 1904.

H

14755. John Muir Home from a Year of World-Circling His Telepathic Search for Prof. J. D. Butler . . .

⟨n.p., n.d., 1904⟩

Not seen. Entry on the basis of correspondence and photographic copy.

Single leaf. Printed on one side only. 13½″ × 7″.

A news account containing two letters by John Muir:

Addressed to James Davie Butler, *Martinez, California, July 20, 1904.*

Addressed to Mrs. James Davie Butler, *Headquarters of the Tuolumne, Near Castle Peak, August, 1869.*

Presumably an offprint.

The original is in The State Historical Society of Wisconsin, Madison, Wis.

14756. MR. JOHN MUIR'S REPLY TO A LETTER RECEIVED FROM HON. JAMES R. GARFIELD IN RELATION TO THE DESTRUCTIVE HETCH-HETCHY SCHEME . . .

⟨n.p., n.d., 1908?⟩

Caption-title. The above at head of p. ⟨1⟩.

Letter, addressed to Hon. Jas. R. Garfield, Secretary of Interior, Washington, D. C.

⟨1⟩-4. 8½″ × 5⁷⁄₁₆″.

Single leaf, folded to four pages. Text on pp. ⟨1⟩-3; map on p. ⟨4⟩.

Issued after May 14, 1908.

H

14757. San Francisco and the Hetch Hetchy Reservoir Hearing Held before the Committee on the Public Lands of the House of Representatives December 16, 1908 on H. J. Res. 184

Washington Government Printing Office 1908

Cover-title. Printed self-wrapper.

"Memorandum . . . received May 14, 1908 . . . Hetch Hetchy Damming Scheme," pp. 32-33.

"The Endangered Valley–––The Hetch Hetchy Valley in the Yosemite National Park," pp. 38-40. Printed from advance sheets of *The Century Illustrated Monthly Magazine*, Jan. 1909.

Letter, Dec. 16, 1908, signed by Muir and others, p. 42.

See next entry. Also see *Hetch-Hetchy* . . . ⟨n.p., n.d., *ca.* 1909⟩ below.

H

14758. Let All the People Speak and Prevent the Destruction of the Yosemite Park To the Editor: . . .

⟨n.p., n.d., 1909⟩

Caption-title. The above at head of p. ⟨1⟩. Pp. 32. Printed self-wrapper.

Contains the following material by Muir:

Letter, Jan. 12, 1908, p. ⟨1⟩.

Letter, Dec. 21, 1908, signed at end by Muir and others, pp. 2-3. An extended version of the letter dated Dec. 16, 1908, published in the preceding entry.

"The Endangered Valley: The Hetch-Hetchy Valley in the Yosemite National Park," pp. 14-18. An extended version of the piece as published in the preceding entry.

Two editions noted:

First Edition

P. ⟨1⟩: The fourth line reads: *To the Editor: |*

P. 19, last line reads: *private interest. |*

p. 20: Illustration present.

P. 32: Note beginning: *These views have been indorsed* . . .

Second Edition

P. ⟨1⟩: The fourth line reads: *To the Editors and the Public: |*

P. 19, last line reads: *San Francisco Merchants' Association Review, July, 1908. |*

P. 20: Note beginning: *These views have been indorsed* . . .

P. 32: Illustration present.

H (2nd)   UMn (1st)

14759. STICKEEN . . .

BOSTON & NEW YORK   HOUGHTON MIFFLIN COMPANY 1909

⟨i-x⟩, ⟨1⟩-⟨74⟩; blank, p. ⟨75⟩; printer's imprint, p. ⟨76⟩; blank leaf. 7⁷⁄₁₆″ × 4¹¹⁄₁₆″.

⟨1-11⁴⟩.

T cloth: tan.

On copyright page: *Published March 1909*

Note: Also issued as No. 231 in *Riverside Literature Series;* printed paper wrapper; under date ⟨1909⟩. On the basis of the advertisements on the wrapper could not have issued prior to 1914. Copy in LC.

Publisher's Records

Feb. 8, 1909: *First printing;* 2024 copies. Bound during the period Feb. 24 to April 14, 1909.

April 24, 1909: *Second printing;* 1020 copies. Reprint notice present?

April 27, 1909: *Third printing. Third Impression* statement present.

For another version see *My Favorite Stories of the Great Outdoors* . . . , under the year ⟨1950⟩.

Deposited Feb. 26, 1909. Listed PW April 3, 1909.

AAS   H   Y

14760. Our National Parks by John Muir New and Enlarged Edition Fully Illustrated

Boston and New York   Houghton Mifflin Company   The Riverside Press   Cambridge MDCCCCIX

Title-page in black and green.

Although not so marked this is the *Holiday Edition.* See under 1901 for the first edition.

On copyright page: *Published October 1909*

Enlarged by the addition of an "Appendix," pp. 368-376; and, a brief note (probably by the publisher), p. ⟨iii⟩, referring to the appendix.

Publisher's Records

Oct. 11, 1909: "Appendix" composed and electro-typed.

Oct. 19, 1909: 2037 copies printed.

Oct. 19, 1909: 2000 copies of a 2-page cancel were printed; significance not determined.

Oct. 22, 1909-March 3, 1916: The above sheets bound.

Advertised for *to-day* PW Oct. 30, 1909. Y copy received Nov. 2, 1909. BPL copy received Nov. 3, 1909. Deposited Nov. 8, 1909. Listed PW Nov. 13, 1909.

BA   USC   UV   Y

14761. Let Everyone Help to Save the Famous Hetch-Hetchy Valley and Stop the Commercial Destruction Which Threatens Our National Parks . . .

⟨San Francisco, 1909⟩

Caption-title. The above at head of p. 1.

Letter from Muir, *November, 1909*, p. 1.

H   LC   NYPL   UV

14762. HETCH-HETCHY---THE TUO-
LUMNE YOSEMITE...

⟨n.p., n.d., *ca.* 1909?⟩

Not seen. Entry on the basis of a photographic copy.

Caption-title. The above at head of p. ⟨1⟩ of text.

⟨1⟩-9. 7⅝″ × 4⅜″.

Printed self-wrapper.

"Hetch-Hetchy---The Tuolumne Yosemite,"
pp. ⟨1⟩-7. Another version of "The Endangered
Valley..."; see *San Francisco and the Hetch Hetchy
Reservoir...*, 1908; and, *Let All the People Speak...*
⟨n.p., n.d., 1909⟩.

Pp. 8-9 are devoted to "Extracts from State
Geologist Professor J. D. Whitney's Yosemite
Guide-Book..."; *i.e., The Yosemite Guide-Book...
New Edition, Revised and Corrected*, by J. D. Whitney,
1874, to which extracts Muir added the final two
lines.

Issued thus?

UCB

14763. A NATIONAL ISSUE THE HETCH
HETCHY TO BE SAVED TO ALL WHO
ARE INTERESTED IN THE CONSERVA-
TION OF OUR NATIONAL PARKS...
MAY, 1910...

⟨SAN FRANCISCO: SOCIETY FOR PRESERVATION OF
NATIONAL PARKS, 302 MILLS BUILDING, 1910.⟩

Single leaf. Some copies watermarked ⟨--- ?⟩
Bond. Printed on recto only. 8½″ × 5½″.

UV

14764. The Mountains of California... New
and Enlarged Edition...

New York The Century Co. 1911

For first edition see under year 1894.

Cursory examination indicates that the only
additions to this edition are: A dedication, in
which this is identified as the "ninth edition ⟨*i.e.*,
printing⟩"; and, the addition of an index; plus
certain illustrations including revised maps.

Deposited May 26, 1911.

AAS BPL H LC NYPL

14765. MY FIRST SUMMER IN THE
SIERRA... WITH ILLUSTRATIONS
FROM DRAWINGS MADE BY THE
AUTHOR IN 1869...

BOSTON AND NEW YORK   HOUGHTON MIFFLIN
COMPANY   THE RIVERSIDE PRESS   CAMBRIDGE
1911

⟨i-ii⟩, ⟨i⟩-⟨viii⟩, ⟨1⟩-⟨354⟩; blank, p. ⟨355⟩;
printer's imprint, p. ⟨356⟩; blank leaf. Frontispiece and 11 plates (each with printed tissue)
inserted; other illustrations in text. 8⅛″ × 5½″
full.

⟨1-23⁸⟩.

V cloth: green. Top edges gilt.

On copyright page: *Published June 1911*

According to the publisher's records 2863 copies
with the Houghton Mifflin imprint were done May
19, 1911; on the same date the records show 170
copies done with the London (Constable) imprint.
Bound during the period May 24, 1911–Jan. 20,
1913.

NYPL copy received June 2, 1911. Advertised for
today PW June 3, 1911. BA copy received June 6,
1911. Deposited June 15, 1911. Listed PW June
17, 1911. The London (Constable) edition listed
Bkr Sept. 29, 1911.

AAS BA H LC NYPL Y

14766. EDWARD HENRY HARRIMAN...

GARDEN CITY NEW YORK DOUBLEDAY, PAGE &
COMPANY 1911

⟨i-vi⟩, ⟨1⟩-⟨39⟩; blank, pp. ⟨40-42⟩. 7⁵⁄₁₆″ ×
4⁹⁄₁₆″.

⟨1-3⁸⟩.

T cloth: cream. Also tan suède.

A copy in AAS inscribed by early owner Nov. 1911.
Deposited April 22, 1912. Listed PW May 18,
1912.

AAS LC UV

14767. THE YOSEMITE...

NEW YORK THE CENTURY CO. MCMXII

Title-page in black and blind.

⟨i-ii⟩, ⟨i⟩-x, ⟨1⟩-284. Frontispiece, 31 plates, 3
folded maps inserted. 8³⁄₁₆″ × 5½″.

⟨-⟩⁶, ⟨1⟩-17⁸, ⟨18⟩⁶.

V cloth: green-black. Top edges gilt.

On copyright page: *Published, April, 1912*

NYPL copy received April 19, 1912. Listed PW
April 27, 1912. Deposited May 4, 1912.

H NYPL Y

14768. THE STORY OF MY BOYHOOD AND
YOUTH... WITH ILLUSTRATIONS
FROM SKETCHES BY THE AUTHOR

BOSTON AND NEW YORK   HOUGHTON MIFFLIN
COMPANY   THE RIVERSIDE PRESS   CAMBRIDGE
1913

⟨i-ii⟩, ⟨i⟩-⟨viii⟩, 1-⟨294⟩; blank, p. ⟨295⟩; print-er's imprint, p. ⟨296⟩. Frontispiece and 8 plates inserted. 8⅛″ × 5½″ full.

⟨1¹, 2⁴, 3-20⁸, 21⁴⟩

T cloth: green; both grass-green and olive-green noted. Top edges gilt.

On copyright page: *Published March 1913*

Publisher's records show that 3562 copies were printed Feb. 28, 1913; bound during the period Feb. 26 ⟨sic⟩, 1913-Jan. 28, 1914.

Advertised PW March 15, 1913, as *My Boyhood and Youth*. Deposited March 17, 1913. BA copy received March 18, 1913. Listed PW March, 22, 1913.

A letter in H (Houghton Mifflin Company to John Muir; carbon copy; March 17, 1914) indicates that in 1914 the plates were altered, specifically the passage regarding the life and death of half-witted Charlie, pp. 214-217.

For another version see below: *Atlantic Harvest* . . . , 1947.

AAS   BA   H   Y

14769. Anecdotes of the Hour by Famous Men As Told by Winston Churchill . . . Jack London . . . and about 100 Other Notable Men . . .

New York Hearst's International Library Co. 1914

Anecdote, p. 127.

Deposited April 13, 1914.

H

14770. LETTERS TO A FRIEND WRITTEN TO MRS. EZRA S. CARR 1866-1879 . . .

BOSTON AND NEW YORK   HOUGHTON MIFFLIN COMPANY   THE RIVERSIDE PRESS   CAMBRIDGE 1915

⟨i-viii⟩, 1-⟨194⟩; blank, p. ⟨195⟩; printer's im-print, p. ⟨196⟩. Laid paper watermarked with a chained gate. 8⁹⁄₁₆″ × 5⁹⁄₁₆″.

⟨1⁴, 2-12⁸, 13¹⁰⟩.

Slate-green laid paper boards, printed paper label on spine. White laid paper end papers.

"This Edition Consists Of 300 Copies"--- Certificate of issue.

The publisher's records show that 330 copies were printed March 8, 1915; bound during the period March 16-25, 1915. Deposited March 22, 1915.

AAS   BA   H   NYPL   Y

14771. TRAVELS IN ALASKA

TRADE FORMAT

TRAVELS IN ALASKA . . .

BOSTON AND NEW YORK   HOUGHTON MIFFLIN COMPANY   THE RIVERSIDE PRESS   CAMBRIDGE 1915

Title-page printed in black.

⟨i-ii⟩, ⟨i⟩-⟨xii⟩, ⟨1⟩-⟨329⟩; printer's imprint, p. ⟨330⟩. Frontispiece and 11 plates inserted. 8¹⁄₁₆″ full × 5½″.

⟨1-21⁸, 22⁴⟩.

V cloth: gray. Color print pasted to front cover. Top edges gilt.

On copyright page: *Published November 1915*

The publisher's records show there were four printings during the year 1915; BAL has been unable to distinguish more than one printing.

Nov. 24, 1915. *First printing*. 2640 copies. Six copies bound Nov. 24, 1915. Save for the pre-ceding six copies the sheets were bound during the period Nov. 26-Dec. 10, 1915.

Dec. 9, 1915. *Second printing*. 1044 copies. Bound during the period Dec. 13-17, 1915.

Dec. 18⟨?⟩, 1915. *Third printing*. 1040 copies. Bound during the period Dec. 17⟨?⟩-22, 1915.

Dec. 15⟨?⟩, 1915. *Fourth printing*. 1003 copies. Bound during the period Dec. 22, 1915-March 31, 1916.

April 7, 1916. *Fifth printing*. 1050 copies.

Advertised for fall publication PW Sept. 25, 1915. Advertised for Nov. 11 PW Oct. 30, 1915. Adver-tised for *November* PW Nov. 6, 1915. Deposited Dec. 8, 1915. Listed PW Dec. 11, 1915. *Note:* The preceding dates refer to the *trade format* only.

LARGE PAPER FORMAT

TRAVELS IN ALASKA . . .

BOSTON AND NEW YORK   HOUGHTON MIFFLIN COMPANY   1915

Title-page printed in black, green, blind.

⟨i⟩-⟨xii⟩, ⟨1⟩-⟨329⟩; blank leaf. Frontispiece with printed tissue and 16 plates inserted. 9³⁄₁₆″ × 6⅜″.

⟨1², 2⁶, 3-22⁸, 23⁴⟩.

Green laid paper boards sides, green buckram shelf back, brown leather label on spine. Flyleaf at front.

Four Hundred And Fifty Copies Of This Large-Paper Edition . . . Printed . . . November 1915 . . . This Is Number . . .---Certificate of issue.

According to the publisher's records 490 copies were printed Nov. 19, 1915. Bound during the period Nov. 24-Dec. 17 ⟨18?⟩, 1915.

AAS (Trade) B (Trade) BA (Trade) H (both) LC (Trade)   Y (Large Paper)

14772. EDWARD TAYLOR PARSONS
MARCH 15, 1861 MAY 22, 1914

⟨n.p., n.d., probably San Francisco, 1915⟩

Not seen. Entry on the basis of a photographic copy.

Cover-title. Printed paper wrapper.

"Edward Taylor Parsons," pp. ⟨3-5⟩.

Reprinted from *The Sierra Club Bulletin*, Vol. IX, No. 4, Jan. 1915.

UCB

14773. A THOUSAND-MILE WALK TO THE GULF

TRADE FORMAT

A THOUSAND-MILE WALK TO THE GULF ... EDITED BY WILLIAM FREDERIC BADÈ ...

BOSTON AND NEW YORK   HOUGHTON MIFFLIN COMPANY   THE RIVERSIDE PRESS   CAMBRIDGE 1916

Title-page printed in black.

⟨i-iv⟩, ⟨i⟩-⟨xxviii⟩, 1-⟨220⟩; blank, p. ⟨221⟩; printer's imprint, p. ⟨222⟩; blank leaf. Frontispiece and 12 plates inserted. 8 3/16″ full × 5 1/2″.

⟨1^10, 2-15^8, 16^6⟩.

V cloth: green. Top edges gilt.

On copyright page: *Published November 1916*

First trade printing: Nov. 22, 1916. 5218 copies. Bound during the period Nov. 25-Dec. 20, 1916.

Second trade printing: Dec. 19, 1916. 1054 copies. *Dated 1917?* The copies first bound were done on March 15, 1917; other copies put in binding as late as Aug. 14, 1929.

For trade notices see below.

LARGE PAPER FORMAT

A THOUSAND-MILE WALK TO THE GULF BY JOHN MUIR

BOSTON AND NEW YORK   HOUGHTON MIFFLIN COMPANY 1916

Title-page in black, green, blind.

⟨i⟩-⟨xxviii⟩, 1-⟨220⟩. Frontispiece with printed tissue, and 17 plates inserted. 9 3/16″ × 6 5/16″.

⟨1^2, 2^4, 3-16^8, 17^6⟩.

Green laid paper boards sides, green buckram shelf back, green leather label on spine. End papers of book stock. Flyleaves.

Five Hundred And Fifty Copies ... Large-Paper Edition ... Printed ... October, 1916 ... This Is Number ... –––Certificate of issue.

According to the publisher's records 555 large paper copies were printed Nov. 10, 1916. Bound during the period Nov. 20-Dec. 4, 1916.

Both formats advertised PW Sept. 23, 1916; Oct. 28, 1916. Trade format advertised PW Nov. 18, 1916. Large paper format deposited for copyright Nov. 24, 1916. Trade format listed PW Dec. 2, 1916. A copy of the trade format received at H Dec. 5, 1916.

AAS (Large Paper) B (Trade) BA (Trade) LC (Large Paper) H (Both) NYPL (Large Paper) Y (Both)

14774. ⟨The Writings of John Muir. Manuscript Edition⟩

Boston and New York   Houghton Mifflin Company MDCCCCXVI ⟨-MDCCCCXXIV⟩

10 Vols. Limited to 750 numbered sets. Probably issued in a variety of bindings.

Listed in PW March 24, 1917, as though in ten volumes; but note that the listing was on the basis of supplied information, not actual examination.

1: *The Story of My Boyhood and Youth and a Thousand-Mile Walk to the Gulf.* MDCCCCXVI. Reprint. Deposited Dec. 26, 1916.

2: *My First Summer in the Sierra.* MDCCCCXVI. Reprint. Deposited Dec. 26, 1916.

3: *Travels in Alaska.* MDCCCCXVI. Reprint. Deposited Dec. 26, 1916.

4-5: *The Mountains of California.* MDCCCCXVI. Reprint. Deposited Dec. 26, 1916.

6: *Our National Parks.* MDCCCCXVI. Reprint. Deposited Dec. 26, 1916.

7: *The Cruise of the Corwin.* MDCCCCXVIII. No record of copyright deposit found. According to the publisher issued on Nov. 27, 1917. Reprint? See *The Cruise of the Corwin*, 1917.

8: *Steep Trails.* MDCCCCXVIII. No record of copyright deposit found. According to the publisher issued Sept. 28, 1918. Reprint? For trade publication see below under 1918.

9: *The Life and Letters of John Muir. Vol. 1.* MDCCCCXXIII. For trade publication see below under 1924. Deposited March 5, 1924. Reprint? First printing?

10: *The Life and Letters of John Muir. Vol. 2.* MDCCCCXXIV. For trade publication see below under 1924. Deposited Dec. 1, 1924. Reprint? First printing?

B LC NYPL Y

14775. THE CRUISE OF THE CORWIN

"During the cruise Muir kept a daily record of his experiences and observations. He also wrote a series of letters to the *San Francisco Evening Bulletin* in which he turned to account the contents of his journal ..."---P. xxvi. The present work is based on the journal and the letters, plus the addition, in the appendix, of the two pieces earlier published in 1883 and 1884 as government publications, *qq. v.*

TRADE FORMAT

THE CRUISE OF THE CORWIN JOURNAL OF THE ARCTIC EXPEDITION OF 1881 IN SEARCH OF DE LONG AND THE JEANNETTE... EDITED BY WILLIAM FREDERIC BADÈ

BOSTON AND NEW YORK   HOUGHTON MIFFLIN COMPANY   THE RIVERSIDE PRESS   CAMBRIDGE 1917

Title-page in black.

⟨i-iv⟩, ⟨i⟩-⟨xxxii⟩, ⟨1⟩-⟨279⟩; printer's imprint, p. ⟨280⟩. Frontispiece and 21 plates inserted. $8\frac{1}{16}''$ full × $5\frac{1}{2}''$.

⟨1^{10}, 2-19^8, 20^4⟩.

V cloth: gray. Top edges gilt.

On copyright page: *Published November 1917*

The following notes refer to the trade format only. Advertised PW Sept. 22, 1917; Nov. 17, 1917. Deposited Dec. 1, 1917. Listed PW Dec. 8, 1917. Noted as *just ... published* PW Dec. 8, 1917. BA copy received Dec. 11, 1917.

LARGE PAPER FORMAT

THE CRUISE OF THE CORWIN BY JOHN MUIR

BOSTON AND NEW YORK   HOUGHTON MIFFLIN COMPANY 1917

Title-page in black, green, blind.

⟨i-ii⟩, ⟨i⟩-⟨xxxii⟩, ⟨1⟩-⟨279⟩. Frontispiece with printed tissue and 26 plates inserted. $9\frac{1}{8}'' × 6\frac{5}{16}''$.

⟨1^2, 2^6, 3^1, 4-21^8, 22^4⟩.

Green laid paper boards sides, green V cloth shelfback, black leather label on spine. Flyleaf at front.

Five hundred and fifty copies ... printed ... October, 1917 ... This is number ...---Certificate of issue.

Note: Also published as Vol. 7, *Manuscript Edition* of Muir's writings, 1918; and, as Vol. 7, *Sierra Edition* of Muir's writings, 1918. Sequence not known.

AAS (Trade) BA (Trade) H (Large Paper) NYPL (Trade) UV (Large Paper)

14776. ⟨The Writings of John Muir. Sierra Edition⟩

Boston and New York   Houghton Mifflin Company 1917 ⟨-MDCCCCXXIV⟩

1: *The Story of My Boyhood and Youth* ⟨*with: A Thousand Mile Walk*⟩.
1917
Reprint.

2: *My First Summer in the Sierra.*
1917
Reprint.

3: *Travels in Alaska.*
1917
Reprint.

4: *The Mountains of California. Vol. 1.*
1917
Reprint.

5: *The Mountains of California. Vol. 2.*
1917
Reprint.

6: *Our National Parks.*
1917
Reprint.

7: *The Cruise of the Corwin.*
1918
Reprint? See *The Cruise of the Corwin*, 1917, above.

8: *Steep Trails.*
MDCCCCXVIII
Reprint? Also issued as a trade book; see below under 1918.

9: *The Life and Letters. Vol. 1.*
MDCCCCXXIII
Reprint? Also issued as a trade book; see below under 1924.

10: *The Life and Letters. Vol. 2.*
MDCCCCXXIV
Reprint? Also issued as a trade book; see below under 1924.

H

14777. STEEP TRAILS

TRADE FORMAT

STEEP TRAILS BY JOHN MUIR EDITED BY WILLIAM FREDERIC BADÈ WITH ILLUSTRATIONS

BOSTON AND NEW YORK   HOUGHTON MIFFLIN COMPANY MDCCCCXVIII

Title-page printed in black.

⟨i-ii⟩, ⟨i⟩-⟨xii⟩, ⟨1⟩-⟨391⟩; printer's imprint, p. ⟨392⟩, blank leaf. Frontispiece and 11 plates inserted. $8\frac{1}{16}'' × 5\frac{1}{2}''$.

⟨1-24^8, 25-26^6⟩.

V cloth: gray. Top edges gilt. Color-print pasted to front. *Note:* Spine decorated with an ornament stamped in white of pine trees in silhouette. The ornament on the deposit copies depicts palm fronds backed by a rising sun; presumably an experimental binding.

On copyright page: *Published September 1918*

LARGE PAPER FORMAT

STEEP TRAILS CALIFORNIA UTAH NEVADA WASHINGTON OREGON THE GRAND CAÑON BY JOHN MUIR

BOSTON AND NEW YORK   HOUGHTON MIFFLIN COMPANY 1918

Title-page in black, green, blind.

⟨i⟩-⟨xii⟩, ⟨1⟩-⟨391⟩; printer's imprint, p. ⟨392⟩; blank leaf. Frontispiece with printed tissue and 16 plates inserted. 8¹⁵⁄₁₆″ full × 6″.

⟨1², 2⁴, 3¹, 4-27⁸, 28⁴⟩.

Green laid paper boards sides, green V cloth shelf back. Green-black leather label on spine. Double flyleaf at front.

Three hundred and eighty copies . . . printed . . . September, 1918. Three hundred and fifty copies are for sale. This is number———. . . Certificate of issue.

BA copy of the trade format received Oct. 1, 1918. Deposited (trade) Oct. 2, 1918. Trade format listed PW Oct. 5, 1918.

Note: Also published as Vol. 8, *Manuscript Edition* of Muir's writings, 1918; and, as Vol. 8, *Sierra Edition* of Muir's writings, 1918. Sequence not known.

AAS (Trade) BA (Trade) H (Trade) NYPL (Trade) UV (Large Paper)

14778. SAVE THE REDWOODS . . .

⟨SAN FRANCISCO, 1920⟩

Cover-title.

⟨1-8⟩. Illustrated. 9″ × 6″.

⟨-⟩⁴.

Printed stiff gray paper wrapper.

"Reprinted from the *Sierra Club Bulletin*, Volume XI, Number 1, San Francisco, 1920, for the Save the Redwoods League."——Inner front wrapper.

"Found among Muir's papers after his death and now published for the first time."——P. ⟨3⟩.

HEH

14779. THE LIFE AND LETTERS OF JOHN MUIR BY WILLIAM FREDERIC BADÈ . . .

BOSTON AND NEW YORK   HOUGHTON MIFFLIN COMPANY   THE RIVERSIDE PRESS   CAMBRIDGE 1924

1: ⟨i-ii⟩, ⟨i⟩-⟨x⟩, ⟨1⟩-⟨399⟩. Frontispiece with printed tissue inserted. 8¹⁄₁₆″ × 5½″ full.

2: ⟨i-viii⟩, ⟨1⟩-216; ⟨ix-x⟩; 217-⟨454⟩. Frontispiece inserted. 1 plate in text, pp. ⟨ix-x⟩.

1: ⟨1-25⁸, 26⁶⟩.

2: ⟨1-29⁸⟩.

Green buckram, brown leather label on spine. End papers of book stock.

Noted in PW Dec. 13, 1924.

Note: Also published as Vols. 9-10, *Manuscript Edition* of Muir's writings, 1923-1924; and, as Vols. 9-10, *Sierra Edition* of Muir's writings, 1923-1924. Sequence not known.

AAS   H   NYPL   Y

14780. The Letters of Western Authors A Series of Letters . . . in Facsimile . . .

. . . Book Club of California   San Francisco 1935

Includes a letter to ⟨Charles Warren⟩ Stoddard, Feb. 2d ⟨n.y.⟩

For fuller entry see No. 4488.

14781. JOHN OF THE MOUNTAINS THE UNPUBLISHED JOURNALS OF JOHN MUIR EDITED BY LINNIE MARSH WOLFE . . .

BOSTON   HOUGHTON MIFFLIN COMPANY   THE RIVERSIDE PRESS CAMBRIDGE 1938

⟨i⟩-⟨xxiv⟩, ⟨1⟩-459. Frontispiece and 7 plates inserted. 8⁷⁄₁₆″ × 5⅝″ full.

⟨1-29⁸, 30¹⁰⟩.

Coarse tan cloth.

NYPL copy received May 4, 1938. Deposited May 6, 1938.

AAS   B   BPL   H   LC   NYPL   Y

14782. Proposed John Muir-Kings Canyon National Park Including a Summary of a Rival of the Yosemite . . . by John Muir . . . Which Appeared in the Century Magazine November, 1891 . . . Reprinted from Planning and Civic Comment January-March, 1939

American Planning and Civic Association 901 Union Trust Building   Washington, D. C. ⟨1939⟩

Printed self-wrapper.

"A Rival of the Yosemite The Canyon of the South Fork of King's River, California," pp. 8-17.

LWC

14783. A Souvenir of Western Summits

Berkeley, California 1947

Paper wrapper, printed label on front.

"Half Dome," pp. ⟨5⟩-7. "John Muir, in *Daily Evening Bulletin*, San Francisco, November 18, 1875."

"100 copies printed at the Grabhorn Press San Francisco for Francis and Marjory Farquhar for presentation to members of the Sierra Nevada Section of the American Alpine Club at a meeting held at 2930 Avalon Avenue Berkeley, California, March 17, 1947."---Certificate of issue.

H

14784. Atlantic Harvest Memoirs of the Atlantic ... Compiled by Ellery Sedgwick ...

Little, Brown and Company Boston 1947

"Out of the Wilderness," pp. 164-179. For a revised version see *The Story of My Boyhood and Youth*, 1913.

On copyright page: *First Edition Published September 1947*

BA H NYPL

14785. My Favorite Stories of the Great Outdoors ... Selected ... by Roy Chapman Andrews ...

Greystone Press New York ⟨1950⟩

"An Adventure with a Dog and Glacier," pp. 353-367. Reprinted from *The Century Illustrated Monthly Magazine*, New York, Sept. 1897. As a separate, with text revised, issued as *Stickeen*, 1909.

Listed PW Feb. 25, 1950.

NYPL

14786. JOHN MUIR'S STUDIES IN THE SIERRA WITH AN INTRODUCTION BY WILLIAM E. COLBY FOREWORD BY JOHN P. BUWALDA

THE SIERRA CLUB. SAN FRANCISCO. 1950

Title-page in black and blue.

⟨i-ii⟩, ⟨i⟩-⟨xxx⟩, ⟨1⟩-103. 1 plate inserted, other illustrations in text. 9¼″ × 6⅛″.

⟨1-3⁸, 4¹², 5-8⁸⟩.

Orange-buff paper boards, printed.

"... Originally appeared in 1874 and 1875 as a series of seven articles in the *Overland Monthly* ... later (1915 to 1921) reprinted in the *Sierra Club Bulletin* ..."---P. xi.

Deposited April 11, 1950. See below under 1960 for a revised edition.

HEH LC

14787. Gentlemen, Scholars and Scoundrels A Treasury of the Best of Harper's Magazine from 1850 to the Present Edited by Horace Knowles

Harper & Brothers New York ⟨1959⟩

"The New Sequoia Forests of California," pp. 426-437. Originally in *Harper's Monthly*, Nov. 1878.

Note: The text as here given is that of original periodical publication. With extensive revisions collected as part of Chapter VIII, *The Mountains of California*, 1894.

Code letters *I-I* (signifying *printed Sept. 1959*) on the copyright page.

BA H

14788. John Muir's Studies in the Sierra Edited by William E. Colby Foreword by John P. Buwalda

Sierra Club San Francisco ⟨1960⟩

Printed paper boards, cloth shelf back.

On copyright page: *Revised edition*

"... This revised edition ... has nothing to correct, and has been reproduced for the most part photographically from the first edition ... Necessary changes have been made in the preliminaries, and a new section of illustrations ... has been added ..."---P. xii.

For first edition see above under year 1950.

BA LC UV Y

14789. Selected Writings by John Muir South of Yosemite Edited bv ⟨sic⟩ Frederic R. Gunsky ...

Published for the American Museum of Natural History The Natural History Press Garden City, New York ⟨1968⟩

Contains material here first in book form.

"... In selecting the text ... every effort has been made to present Muir's original version, even when, as often occurred, he revised the material and used it again in his books ... Newspaper and magazine articles have been transcribed directly. Paragraphs and sometimes longer passages have been omitted, but the structure of the writing is otherwise unchanged ..."---P. ⟨xii⟩.

On copyright page: *First Edition*

LC UV

14790. THE TREASURES OF THE YOSE-
MITE...

LEWIS OSBORNE ASHLAND, 1970

Edited by L. W. Lane, Jr.

⟨i-ii⟩,⟨1⟩-⟨60⟩, blank leaf. Laid paper water-marked *Utopian*. Illustrated. $10\frac{7}{16}''$ × $6\frac{15}{16}''$.

⟨1-4^8⟩.

Olive-green buckram. Laid paper end papers im-printed (at front) with *Map of the Yosemite Valley;* (at back) with engraving of *The Yosemite.*

Reprinted from *Century Magazine*, Aug. 1890.

"This Special Edition was distributed by advance subscription only."—––P. ⟨3⟩. All copies thus?

LWC

In this section are listed collections of reprinted material issued under Muir's name.

14791. Climb the mountains and get their good tidings . . .

Impressions Broadside----No. 5 ⟨n.p., n.d., San Francisco: Paul Elder & Company, 1904⟩

Reprinted from *Our National Parks*, 1901, p. 56.

Noted in the following forms:

1

4 pp. Printed on p. ⟨1⟩ only. Deposited March 28, 1904. *Location:* LC.

2

Single leaf. Printed on recto only. Used as the frontispiece of *Impressions Quarterly*, San Francisco, June, 1904. *Location:* LC.

3

Not seen. 4 pp.? Issued as *Impression* ⟨*sic*⟩ *Leaflets*, No. 37. Entry from *The United States Catalog Supplement . . . 1902–1905;* 10¢, as though issued in 1905 by Paul Elder & Co., San Francisco.

4

Not seen. 4 pp.? Entry from *The United States Catalog . . . 1912;* 10¢, as though issued by Paul Elder & Co., San Francisco. If issued as part of a series not identified as such.

14792. In American Fields and Forests Henry D. Thoreau, John Burroughs, John Muir . . .

Boston and New York   Houghton Mifflin Company   The Riverside Press   Cambridge 1909

On copyright page: *Published March 1909*

Listed PW March 20, 1909. Deposited May 10, 1909.

Also noted with the imprint: *Boston, New York, and Chicago Houghton Mifflin Company The Riverside Press Cambridge 1909;* status not determined.

According to the publisher's records the first printing, Feb. 15, 1909, consisted of 442 copies for Houghton Mifflin Company and 57 copies for The Reading Circle; bound during the period Feb. 15 to May 17, 1909. *Second printing:* March 31,

1909, 506 copies. *Third printing:* May 26, 1909, 507 copies. On May 24, 1909, 5100 copies printed for The Reading Circle.

14793. . . . The Boyhood of a Naturalist . . . Being Selected Chapters from "The Story of My Boyhood and Youth"

Boston New York Chicago San Francisco Houghton Mifflin Company The Riverside Press Cambridge ⟨1913⟩

Printed paper wrapper. At head of title: *The Riverside Literature Series*

Issued as No. 247 of the series.

Also noted with the following imprint; sequence not determined: *Boston New York Chicago Houghton Mifflin Company   The Riverside Press Cambridge ⟨1913⟩*

14794. The Story of My Boyhood and Youth ⟨*and:* A Thousand-Mile Walk to the Gulf⟩

Boston and New York   Houghton Mifflin Company ⟨1916; *i.e.*, 1917 or later⟩

The Out-of-Door Library, School Edition, Vol. 13. Paged: ⟨iii⟩-⟨xviii⟩, ⟨1⟩-⟨428⟩.

Printed from the plates of *The Writings of John Muir*, 1916–1924.

14795. The California Literary Pamphlets: Number Five Afoot to Yosemite a Sketch by John Muir in Eighteen Seventy-Four with a Foreword by Aurelia Henry Reinhardt . . .

Published for its Members by the Book Club of California October, 1936

Printed paper wrapper. 500 copies only. The text had prior publication, the text varying somewhat, in *Life and Letters*, 1924.

14796. Yosemite and the Sierra Nevada Photographs by Ansel Adams Selections from the Works of John Muir Edited by Charlotte E. Mauk

Published by Houghton Mifflin Company Boston The Riverside Press Cambridge 1948

Published Dec. 13, 1948 (publisher's statement to BAL).

14797. The Wilderness World of John Muir with an Introduction and Interpretive Comments by Edwin Way Teale . . .

Houghton Mifflin Company Boston The Riverside Press Cambridge 1954

Reprint with the possible exception of a series of extracts, pp. ⟨311⟩-323, titled "The Philosophy of John Muir." Certain of these extracts may be here first in book form. BAL has not attempted to trace the source of the extracts but presumes they were selected from Muir's published writings. "Throughout his books Muir's philosophy of life is an important feature of his writings. It is reflected in the following random thoughts set down at various times and in various places . . ." ———Note, p. ⟨311⟩.

Deposited Sept. 7, 1954.

14798. Gentle Wilderness   The Sierra Nevada Text from John Muir Photographs by Richard Kauffman Edited by David Brower

Sierra Club San Francisco ⟨1964⟩

Drawn almost entirely from Muir's *My First Summer in the Sierra*, 1911; contains no material by Muir here first published.

14799. The Story of My Boyhood and Youth . . . with a Foreword by Vernon Carstensen

The University of Wisconsin Press   Madison and Milwaukee 1965

The "Foreword" is somewhat confusing and suggests that the book consists of material from various sources. A cursory examination indicates that the book is a reprint of *The Story of My Boyhood and Youth*, 1913.

JOHN MUIR

SECTION III

The following books contain material by Muir reprinted from earlier books.

... Granting Use of Hetch Hetchy to City of San Francisco ...

⟨n.p., 1909; Washington: The Government Printing Office⟩

Caption-title. The above at head of p. ⟨1⟩. At head of title: *6oth Congress, 2d Session. House of Representatives. Report No. 2085.*

Contains an abbreviated printing of the statement published in *San Francisco and the Hetch Hetchy Reservoir* . . . , 1908.

300 Latest Stories by 300 Famous Story Tellers ...

... New York ⟨1914⟩

For fuller entry see No. 12001.

Century Readings for a Course in American Literature Edited ... by Fred Lewis Pattee ... Third Edition ...

New York The Century Co. ⟨1926⟩

REFERENCES AND ANA

New-York Tribune. Extra No. 21 Scientific Series ...

New-York, September 3, 1874 ...

A digest of Muir's "Glacial Phenomena in the Sierra Nevada," p. 6; "read by Prof. Moore."

Great Evils Resulting from the Destruction of Forests

San Francisco Real Estate Circular, 1876.

Not seen. Entry from *List of the Published Writings of John Muir* ⟨1891⟩. Presumably reference to a periodical, not a separate publication.

I Would Be More to Thee! ... Music ... by Rudolf King ...

Boston ... 1889 ... Oliver Ditson Company ...

Sheet music. Cover-title. Plate number: 53775-4. Presumably not by the subject of this list. Similarly: *On Summer Seas*, music by S. Claude Ridley, Boston: White-Smith Music Publishing Co., n.d.

List of the Published Writings of John Muir.

⟨Martinez, Cal., November, 1891⟩

Printed wrapper. Cover-title.

This publication consists of a printed wrapper enclosing a four-page list; the list is printed in black. A facsimile of the list (4 pp. only, without wrapper) was done and may be distinguished by the fact that the facsimile is printed in bluish-green ink.

Reference List to the Published Writings of John Muir. ⟨By⟩ Cornelius B. Bradley. From the University of California Magazine, Issue of December, 1897.

⟨Berkeley, Cal. 1897⟩

Self-wrapper. Cover-title.

Two California Neighbors A Suggestion for the English Class ...

⟨Sacramento, Cal.⟩ Issued by Edward Hyatt, Supt. of Public Instruction. ⟨1912⟩

Printed paper wrapper. Cover-title.

Alaska Days with John Muir by S. Hall Young ...

New York   Chicago ... Fleming H. Revell Company ... ⟨1915⟩

Listed PW Sept. 11, 1915.

John Muir Memorial Number Sierra Club Bulletin ...

San Francisco January 1916 ...

Cover-title. Printed paper wrapper. *Publications of the Sierra Club Number Fifty-One.*

Contains a bibliography.

Commemorative Tributes to ... John Muir by Robert Underwood Johnson ... Read in the 1915–1916 Lecture Series ... Reprinted from Vol. IX Proceedings of the Academy

⟨New York⟩ American Academy of Arts and Letters 1922

"John Muir," by Robert Underwood Johnson, pp. 21-37.

... John Muir Friend and Interpreter of Nature ... by Linnie Marsh Wolfe ...

⟨Boston: Houghton Mifflin Company, n.d., 1924?⟩

Printed paper wrapper. Cover-title.

Personal Recollections of John Muir by Samuel Merrill

Reprinted from Sierra Club Bulletin Annual Number 1928

Printed paper wrapper. Cover-title.

John Muir Little Stories of His Boyhood and University Years ... ⟨by⟩ Charles E. Brown ...

Madison, Wisconsin 1938

Self-wrapper. Cover-title.

Redwood Mountain Illustrated with Five Original Drawings by John Muir

The John Muir Association Berkeley California ⟨n.d., 1938⟩

Self-wrapper. Cover-title.

Sierra Nevada The John Muir Trail by Ansel Adams

The Archetype Press Berkeley California MCM XXX VIII

500 numbered copies only.

... Suggestions for Observance of Centennnial of the Birth of John Muir ...

United States Department of the Interior, Washington, D. C. April 1, 1938

At head of title: *United States Department of the Interior National Park Service Washington*

Mimeographed. Self-wrapper. Cover-title. Contains a "Bibliography of Periodicals. Articles about John Muir."

Son of the Wilderness The Life of John Muir by Linnie Marsh Wolfe

1945 Alfred A Knopf New York

On copyright page: *First Edition*

John Muir Father of Our National Parks by Charles Norman

Julian Messner, Inc. New York ⟨1957⟩

John Muir and the Sierra Club The Battle for Yosemite by Holway R. Jones

Sierra Club San Francisco ⟨1965⟩

MARY NOAILLES MURFREE

(Charles Egbert Craddock; R. Emmet Dembry)

1 8 5 0 – 1 9 2 2

14800. IN THE TENNESSEE MOUNTAINS
BY CHARLES EGBERT CRADDOCK

BOSTON HOUGHTON, MIFFLIN AND COMPANY NEW
YORK: II EAST SEVENTEENTH STREET THE
RIVERSIDE PRESS, CAMBRIDGE 1884

Two printings noted:

FIRST PRINTING

⟨i-iv⟩, ⟨1⟩-322; leaf excised; plus advertisements:
pp. ⟨1⟩-12. Laid paper. 7″ × 4⅝″ full.

⟨1², 2-14¹², 15⁶; plus: 16⁴, 17²⟩. Leaf ⟨15⟩₆
excised. *Signed:* ⟨-⟩², 1-21⁸.

SECOND PRINTING

⟨i-iv⟩, ⟨1⟩-322; advertisements, pp. ⟨1⟩-10; plus:
pp. 11-12.

⟨1-14¹²; plus: 15¹⟩. *Signed:* ⟨-⟩², 1-20⁸, 21⁷.

V cloth: brown; orange-brown. Gray-coated end
papers. Laid paper flyleaves.

Publisher's Records

First printing. April 14, 1884. 1012 copies printed.
Bound during the period April 16-May 5, 1884.

Second printing. April 29, 1884. 514 copies printed.

Third printing. May 23, 1884. 514 copies printed.
Prepared for the London market with the *Longmans*
imprint.

Fourth printing. Aug. 27, 1884. Not identified by
BAL. Probably printed with a reprint notice on the
title-leaf. 512 copies printed.

Fifth printing. Nov. 10, 1884. 520 copies printed.
Statement *Fifth Edition* on the title-leaf.

Listed PW April 26, 1884. The Longmans printing
listed Ath June 28, 1884.

AAS (2nd)   H (1st)   NYPL (1st, 2nd)   UV (2nd)
Y (1st)

14801. WHERE THE BATTLE WAS FOUGHT
A NOVEL BY CHARLES EGBERT
CRADDOCK . . .

BOSTON JAMES R. OSGOOD AND COMPANY 1884

⟨i-viii⟩, 1-423. 7⁹⁄₁₆″ scant × 4⅞″ full.

⟨1⁴, 2-36⁶, 37²⟩.

S cloth: blue; blue-green; brown; yellow. Leaf
⟨1⟩₁ used as front pastedown; true end paper at
back.

According to the publisher's records there were
two printings in the year 1884; BAL has noted a
single printing only.

First printing. June 28, 1884. 1518 copies printed.
Bound during the period July 11, 1884–Sept.
11, 1884.

Second printing. Sept. 20, 1884. 1018 copies printed.

Third printing. March 28, 1885.

Noted for *this week* PW Sept. 6, 1884. Listed PW
Sept. 13, 1884. The London (Trübner) edition
advertised as *immediately* Ath Oct. 3, 1885; listed
Ath Oct. 3, 1885.

AAS   BPL   NYPL   UV

14802. DOWN THE RAVINE BY CHARLES
EGBERT CRADDOCK . . .

BOSTON HOUGHTON, MIFFLIN AND COMPANY NEW
YORK: II EAST SEVENTEENTH STREET THE RIVER-
SIDE PRESS, CAMBRIDGE 1885

There were four printings in the year 1885. On
the basis of the publisher's records and of dated
inscriptions the following sequence is correct. It is
probable that for the fourth printing (Dec. 24,
1885) the imprint date was altered to 1886; but
whether so or not the records indicate that the
fourth printing was issued with a reprint notice.

FIRST PRINTING

⟨i-iv⟩, ⟨1⟩-196; plus: blank leaf; publisher's
catalog, 4 pp.; blank leaf. Laid paper. Frontispiece and 5 plates inserted. 7″ × 4⅝″. It will be
observed that the blank leaves in the terminal
matter are appreciably lighter in weight than the
paper in the rest of the book.

⟨1², 2-17⁶, 18²; plus: 19⁴⟩. *Signed:* ⟨-⟩², ⟨1⟩-12⁸, 13⁶. See note above under pagination for comment on leaves ⟨19⟩₁,₄

V cloth: brown; green; red. White laid end papers. Front cover decorated in black with a mountain scene.

Note: The spine imprint has been seen in two forms; sequence, if any, not known. The designations are completely arbitrary.

A: HOVGHTON ⟨*sic*⟩ / MIFFLIN ⟨*dot*⟩ & ⟨*dot*⟩ CO

B: HOUGHTON / MIFFLIN ⟨*dot*⟩ & ⟨*dot*⟩ CO Also noted on the third printing.

P. ⟨iv⟩: *Down the Ravine* is priced at $1.25; *The Prophet of the Great Smoky Mountains* is described as *In Press.*

P. ⟨199⟩: ... *Out-Door Books* ... *A Week on the Concord and Merrimack Rivers* ... ⟨to⟩ ... *Country By-Ways* ...

Publisher's records: 2540 copies printed May 22, 1885. Bound during the period May 23 to July 17, 1885. On June 9, 1885 three copies were bound "uncut."

SECOND PRINTING

Not identified. P. ⟨iv⟩ will have *Down the Ravine* priced at $1.25; pagination and signature collation will probably vary from the above.

Publisher's records: 516 copies printed Aug. 13, 1885.

THIRD PRINTING

⟨i-ii⟩, ⟨1⟩-196; blank, pp. ⟨197-198⟩; advertisements, pp. ⟨199-202⟩. Laid paper. Frontispiece and 5 plates inserted. 6¹⁵⁄₁₆″ × 4⁹⁄₁₆″.

⟨1-8¹², 9⁶⟩. *Signed:* ⟨-⟩¹, ⟨1⟩-12⁸, 13⁵.

P. ⟨ii⟩: *Down the Ravine* is priced at $1.00; *The Prophet of the Great Smoky Mountains* is described as *In Press.*

P. ⟨199⟩: *Books for Young Folks* ... *Aesop* ... ⟨to⟩ ... *Down the Ravine* ...

Publisher's records: 514 copies printed Oct. 14, 1885.

FOURTH PRINTING

Not identified. Possibly issued under date 1886; probably carries the statement *Fourth Edition.* According to the publisher's records an edition statement was added Dec. 24, 1885.

Deposited May 27, 1885. Listed PW June 6, 1885. Issued in London by Ward, Lock & Co.; probably in printed paper wrapper. Listed and reviewed by PC and Bkr, both of Sept. 1, 1886.

AAS (1st; 3rd) BA (1st) BPL (1st) H (1st) UV (3rd) Y (1st)

14803. THE PROPHET OF THE GREAT SMOKY MOUNTAINS BY CHARLES EGBERT CRADDOCK

BOSTON AND NEW YORK   HOUGHTON, MIFFLIN AND COMPANY THE RIVERSIDE PRESS, CAMBRIDGE 1885

There were four printings in the year 1885. According to the publisher's records the title-leaf of the fourth printing was altered; was the date *1885* changed to *1886?* Was a reprint notice inserted?

FIRST PRINTING

⟨i-iv⟩, ⟨1⟩-308; blank leaf; plus: publisher's catalog, pp. ⟨1⟩-12. 6¹⁵⁄₁₆″ full × 4⅝″.

⟨1¹, 2-14¹²; plus: 15⁶⟩. *Signed:* ⟨-⟩², 1-19⁸, ⟨20⟩³, ⟨21⟩⁶.

Publisher's records: 2538 copies printed Sept. 11, 1885. Bound during the period Sept. 15–Oct. 1, 1885.

SECOND PRINTING

(Also third?)

⟨i-iv⟩, ⟨1⟩-308; plus: blank leaf; publisher's advertisements, pp. ⟨1⟩-12; blank leaf.

⟨1-13¹²; plus: 14⁸⟩. *Signed:* ⟨-⟩², 1-18⁸, 19¹⁰, ⟨20⟩⁸.

Publisher's records: 1552 copies printed Sept. 16, 1885. Bound Oct. 3, 1885.

THIRD PRINTING

Not identified. 2568 copies printed Oct. 7, 1885.

FOURTH PRINTING

Not identified. 1018 copies printed Nov. 28, 1885. For this printing the title-leaf was altered; date changed? Reprint notice added?

V cloth: green; red. White laid end papers. Flyleaves.

Advertised for Oct. 3 PW Oct. 3, 1885. H copy (rebound; 1st printing) received Oct. 3, 1885. BA copy (rebound; 1st printing) received Oct. 5, 1885. Listed PW Oct. 17, 1885. The London (Chatto & Windus) edition advertised as *shortly* Ath Sept. 5, 1885; listed Ath Oct. 10, 1885.

AAS (1st) B (2nd) BPL (1st) LC (1st) NYPL (1st; 2nd) UV (1st) Y (2nd)

14804. IN THE CLOUDS BY CHARLES EGBERT CRADDOCK ...

BOSTON AND NEW YORK   HOUGHTON, MIFFLIN AND COMPANY THE RIVERSIDE PRESS, CAMBRIDGE 1887

Two printings noted:

FIRST PRINTING

⟨i-viii⟩, ⟨1⟩-452; blank leaf; advertisements, pp. ⟨1⟩-2; plus: pp. 3-12; 3 blank leaves. *Note:* In some copies the final blank leaf is either excised or pasted under the end paper. $7'' \times 4^{11}/_{16}''$.

$\langle 1\text{-}14^{16}, 15^8;$ plus: $16^8 \rangle$.

On p. 12 of the terminal advertisements the last title under Whitney is *Seed-Down* which is listed without price.

SECOND PRINTING

Pagination and signature collation as above. On p. 12 of the terminal advertisements the last title under Whitney is *Home-Spun Yarns* which is listed at $1.50.

V cloth: brown; gray; gray-brown; terra-cotta. White laid end papers.

Note: The binding occurs as follows:

A: Last line of spine imprint reads: MIFFLIN $\langle dot \rangle$ & $\langle dot \rangle$ CO

B: Last line of spine imprint reads: MIFFLIN & CO.

Publisher's Records

First printing: 5048 copies printed Nov. 23, 1886. Bound during the period Nov. 22(?)-Dec. 10, 1886.

Second printing: 2552 copies printed Dec. 9, 1886. Bound during the period Dec. 21, 1886-Aug. 24, 1892.

Deposited Nov. 24, 1886. BA copy (rebound, 1st) received Dec. 1, 1886. H copy (rebound, 1st) received Dec. 9, 1886. Listed PW Dec. 11, 1886.

The London (Ward, Lock) edition announced PC Oct. 1, 1886. Advertised Ath Nov. 27, 1886. Listed Ath Dec. 4, 1886. Noted as *just ready* Ath Dec. 4, 1886. The Ward, Lock & Bowden printing listed PC June 9, 1894.

B (1st) BPL (1st) NYPL (1st; 2nd) NYSL (1st) UV (1st) Y (1st)

14805. THE STORY OF KEEDON BLUFFS BY CHARLES EGBERT CRADDOCK . . .

BOSTON AND NEW YORK HOUGHTON, MIFFLIN AND COMPANY THE RIVERSIDE PRESS, CAMBRIDGE 1888

Two printings noted:

FIRST PRINTING

$\langle i\text{-}iv \rangle$, $\langle 1 \rangle$-257; blank, p. $\langle 258 \rangle$; advertisements, pp. $\langle 1 \rangle$-2; plus: pp. 3-14. $7^1/_{16}''$ scant $\times$ $4^3/_4''$ scant.

$\langle 1\text{-}15^8, 16\text{-}17^6;$ plus: $18^6 \rangle$.

Publisher's records: 3060 copies printed Nov. 23, 1887. Bound during the period Nov. 23, 1887 to Nov. 6, 1888. On Dec. 13, 1887 138 copies were bound "Fancy"; on Dec. 20, 1887, 1 more copy bound "Fancy."

SECOND PRINTING

$\langle i\text{-}iv \rangle$, $\langle 1 \rangle$-257; blank, p. $\langle 258 \rangle$; advertisements, pp. $\langle 1 \rangle$-2; plus: pp. 3-15; blank, p. $\langle 16 \rangle$; blank leaf.

$\langle 1\text{-}16^8, 17^4;$ plus: $18^8 \rangle$.

Publisher's records: 516 copies printed Oct. 25, 1888.

V cloth: brown; green; olive-brown; terra-cotta. White laid end papers. Flyleaves.

Note: Two bindings have been seen; the order of presentation is arbitrary. The following variations are sufficient for identification:

BINDING A

Front lettered in black: THE STORY $\langle dot \rangle$ OF / KEEDON $\langle dot \rangle$ BLUFFS / CHARLES $\langle dot \rangle$ EGBERT $\langle dot \rangle$ CRADDOCK Noted on first printing sheets only.

BINDING B

Front lettered in black: THE $\langle dot \rangle$ STORY / OF / KEEDON / BLVFFS / CHARLES / EGBERT / CRADDOCK Noted on both first and second printing sheets.

Deposited Dec. 1, 1887. Noted as *just ready* PW Dec. 3, 1887. Listed PW Dec. 17, 1887. The London (Ward, Lock) edition listed Ath Dec. 10, 1887; announced $\langle sic \rangle$ PC March 1, 1888.

AAS (1st) BPL (2nd) H (1st) LC (1st) NYPL (1st) NYSL (1st) UV (1st) Y (1st, 2nd)

14806. THE DESPOT OF BROOMSEDGE COVE BY CHARLES EGBERT CRADDOCK . . .

BOSTON AND NEW YORK HOUGHTON, MIFFLIN AND COMPANY THE RIVERSIDE PRESS, CAMBRIDGE 1889

$\langle i\text{-}iv \rangle$, $\langle 1 \rangle$-490; blank leaf; plus: publisher's catalog, pp. $\langle 1 \rangle$-12. $7^1/_{16}''$ full $\times$ $4^{11}/_{16}''$ full.

$\langle 1^2, 2\text{-}31^8, 32^6;$ plus: $33^6 \rangle$.

V cloth: brown; gray-green; green; red. White laid end papers. Flyleaves.

According to the publisher's records 3540 copies were printed Dec. 11, 1888; bound during the period Dec. 14, 1888 to Sept. 23, 1890. The second printing was recorded March 12, 1891. Deposited Dec. 17, 1888. The BA copy (rebound) received Dec. 18, 1888. Listed PW Dec. 29, 1888. The London (Sampson Low) edition advertised for *next week* PC March 1, 1889; listed Ath April 6, 1889.

AAS BPL NYPL UV Y

14807. IN THE "STRANGER PEOPLE'S" COUNTRY A NOVEL BY CHARLES EGBERT CRADDOCK . . .

NEW YORK HARPER & BROTHERS, FRANKLIN SQUARE 1891

⟨i-iv⟩, ⟨1⟩-360, 4 pp. advertisements. Frontispiece and 6 plates inserted; 1 illustration in text. 7¼″ scant × 4⅞″.

⟨-⟩², 1-22⁸, 23⁶.

Two printings noted:

FIRST PRINTING

As above. P. ⟨2⟩ of terminal advertisements lists five titles by Constance Fenimore Woolson.

SECOND PRINTING

Pagination and signature collation as above. P. ⟨2⟩ of terminal advertisements lists six titles by Constance Fenimore Woolson.

S cloth: orange. Laid paper end papers.

Deposited Nov. 7, 1891. The BA copy (rebound) received, 1st printing, Nov. 9, 1891. Listed PW Nov. 14, 1891. The London edition (Osgood; simultaneously issued?) advertised as *forthcoming* PC Nov. 7, 1891; listed Ath Nov. 7, 1891.

AAS (1st)   BPL (1st)   LC (1st)   NYPL (1st; 2nd)   NYSL (1st)   UV (1st)

14808. HIS VANISHED STAR BY CHARLES EGBERT CRADDOCK

BOSTON AND NEW YORK   HOUGHTON, MIFFLIN AND COMPANY   THE RIVERSIDE PRESS, CAMBRIDGE 1894

⟨i-iv⟩, ⟨1⟩-394, blank leaf. 6¹⁵⁄₁₆″ scant × 4⅝″.

Two printings noted:

FIRST PRINTING

⟨1², 2-25⁸, 26⁶⟩.

According to the publisher's records 2526 copies were printed May 18, 1894. Bound during the period May 18 to June 9, 1894.

SECOND PRINTING

⟨1-25⁸⟩.

According to the publisher's records 1014 copies were printed June 7, 1894. Bound during the period June 11, 1894 to Oct. 2, 1895.

V cloth: green; tan. Tan buckram. Gray-coated on white end papers. Flyleaf at front.

Advertised for May 26 "or soon thereafter" PW May 19, 1894. Deposited May 21, 1894. Listed PW June 9, 1894. The London (Chatto & Windus) edition advertised as *shortly* Ath Sept. 22, 1894; listed Ath Oct. 6, 1894.

AAS (1st)   B (1st)   BA (1st)   BPL (2nd)   H (1st)   NYPL (1st)   UV (1st)   Y (1st)

14809. THE PHANTOMS OF THE FOOT-BRIDGE AND OTHER STORIES BY CHARLES EGBERT CRADDOCK…

NEW YORK   HARPER & BROTHERS PUBLISHERS 1895

⟨i-viii⟩, ⟨1⟩-353; blank, p. ⟨354⟩; 4 pp. advertisements; blank leaf. Frontispiece and 13 plates inserted. 7¼″ scant × 4⅞″ scant.

⟨-⟩⁴, ⟨1⟩-18, ⟨19⟩, 20-22⁸, ⟨23⟩⁴.

V cloth: green. White laid paper end papers.

Note: The binding occurs in two states; sequence, if any, not determined:

BINDING A

The ornaments on the spine are stamped in brown and blind; *i.e.*, the pine needles are in brown, the pine cones are in blind. A surviving copyright deposit copy thus.

BINDING B

The ornaments on the spine are stamped in brown and black; *i.e.*, the pine needles are in brown, the pine cones are in black.

Advertised for *about February 15* PW Feb. 9, 1895. Deposited Feb. 15, 1895. Noted as *just ready* PW Feb. 16, 1895. BA copy received Feb. 19, 1895. Listed PW Feb. 23, 1895.

AAS (A)   BPL (A)   H (A)   LC (A)   NYSL (B)

14810. THE MYSTERY OF WITCH-FACE MOUNTAIN AND OTHER STORIES BY CHARLES EGBERT CRADDOCK

BOSTON AND NEW YORK   HOUGHTON, MIFFLIN AND COMPANY   THE RIVERSIDE PRESS, CAMBRIDGE 1895

⟨i-vi⟩, ⟨1⟩-279, blank leaf. 6⅞″ full × 4½″ full.

⟨1-18⁸⟩.

V cloth: brown; green; red. White laid end papers. Flyleaf at front.

According to the publisher's records 2554 copies were printed Nov. 12, 1895; bound during the period Nov. 15, 1895 to April 2, 1896. For the second printing, Sept. 9, 1896, the date in the imprint was altered.

Copies received by H, NYSL Nov. 23, 1895. Listed PW Dec. 7, 1895.

AAS   BA   H   NYPL   NYSL   UV   Y

14811. THE YOUNG MOUNTAINEERS SHORT STORIES BY CHARLES EGBERT CRADDOCK…

BOSTON AND NEW YORK HOUGHTON, MIFFLIN AND COMPANY   THE RIVERSIDE PRESS, CAMBRIDGE 1897

⟨i-viii⟩, ⟨1⟩-262; printer's imprint, p. ⟨263⟩. Frontispiece and 3 plates inserted. Laid paper. 7³⁄₈″ full × 5″.

⟨1-17⁸⟩.

V cloth: green. Laid paper end papers. Laid paper flyleaves.

According to the publisher's records there were three printings in 1897; BAL has been unable to distinguish more than a single printing:

First printing: 1528 copies printed April 23, 1897. With the printing entry is a charge for printing six copies with the imprint of A. P. Watt & Son; Watt copies bound April 24, 1897; presumably for purposes of British copyright. American copies bound during the period May 22 to Sept. 28, 1897.

Second printing: 504 copies printed Oct. 1, 1897. Bound Oct. 4-5, 1897.

Third printing: 512 copies printed Nov. 8, 1897. Date altered to 1898 for this printing.

Deposited May 26, 1897. A copy in UV carries a rubber-stamped date: Sept. 28, 1897; significance not known. The BA, NYPL copies received Sept. 29, 1897. Listed PW Oct. 2, 1897. Noted as *published last week* PW Oct. 2, 1897. *The English Catalogue* lists the title as *London: Gay & Bird, 1898.* Further information wanting; presumably an import distributed by Gay & Bird.

AAS   BA   H   NYPL   UV   Y

14812. THE JUGGLER BY CHARLES EGBERT CRADDOCK

BOSTON AND NEW YORK   HOUGHTON, MIFFLIN AND COMPANY THE RIVERSIDE PRESS, CAMBRIDGE 1897

⟨i-iv⟩, ⟨1⟩-405; printer's imprint, p. ⟨406⟩; blank leaf. 6¹⁵⁄₁₆″ × 4½″ full.

⟨1², 2-26⁸, 27⁴⟩.

Buckram: green; old rose. V cloth: green; mottled tan. White laid end papers. Flyleaf at front.

Note: According to the publisher's records 12 copies of the July installment (*Atlantic Monthly*) were printed June 9, 1897. Similarly, 12 copies of the August installment were printed July 7, 1897. No copies located. *Query:* Were all installments similarly printed? Prepared for British copyright?

According to the publisher's records 2994 copies were printed Nov. 1, 1897; bound during the period Nov. 3–Dec. 30, 1897; one copy bound June 2, 1898. The second printing was done April 5, 1898; 504 copies; date altered to 1898.

Deposited Nov. 5, 1897. BA copy received Nov. 9, 1897. Listed PW Nov. 20, 1897. The London (Gay & Bird) edition noted as *ready May 9* Ath May 7, 1898; listed Ath May 14, 1898.

AAS   B   BA   H   LC   NYPL   UV   Y

14813. THE STORY OF OLD FORT LOUDON BY CHARLES EGBERT CRADDOCK . . .

NEW YORK   THE MACMILLAN COMPANY   LONDON: MACMILLAN & CO., LTD. 1899 ALL RIGHTS RESERVED

⟨i-vi⟩, 1-409; blank, p. ⟨410⟩; plus: 2 pp. advertisements, blank leaf. Frontispiece and 7 plates inserted. 7½″ × 5³⁄₁₆″. *Note:* In some copies the final blank leaf is not present; it is present in both of the copyright deposit copies.

⟨1-26⁸; plus: 27²⟩. See note above regarding leaf ⟨27⟩₂. *Signed:* ⟨A⟩³, B-I, K-U, X-Z, 2A-2C⁸, ⟨2D⟩⁷.

Note: Leaf ⟨27⟩₁ occurs in two states. The sequence has not been determined and the following designations are for identification only.

A: The leaf is imprinted with advertisements on both sides. The deposit copies thus.

B: The leaf is imprinted with advertisements on the recto only.

V cloth: tan.

Deposited Jan. 9, 1899. Listed PW Feb. 11, 1899; Ath March 11, 1899.

AAS (A)   BA (B)   BPL (both)   LC (A)   NYSL (B) UV (A)   Y (A)

14814. THE BUSHWHACKERS & OTHER STORIES BY CHARLES EGBERT CRADDOCK . . .

HERBERT S. STONE & COMPANY   CHICAGO & NEW YORK MDCCCXCIX

Title-page in black, orange and blind.

⟨i-x⟩, ⟨1⟩-312; printer's imprint, p. ⟨313⟩; blank, p. ⟨314⟩; 2 blank leaves. 6¾″ × 4⁵⁄₁₆″. Laid paper. Watermarked with the publisher's circular device.

⟨1⁴, 2-21⁸⟩.

Printed gray paper boards. Laid end papers.

Deposited June 26, 1899. Listed PW July 22, 1899.

AAS   UV

14815. THE CHAMPION BY CHARLES EGBERT CRADDOCK

BOSTON AND NEW YORK   HOUGHTON, MIFFLIN AND COMPANY THE RIVERSIDE PRESS, CAMBRIDGE 1902

⟨i-iv⟩, ⟨1⟩-257; printer's imprint, p. ⟨258⟩; blank leaf. Frontispiece inserted. 7⁷⁄₁₆″ × 4¹⁵⁄₁₆″.

⟨1², 2-17⁸, 18²⟩.

V cloth: green. White laid end papers. Flyleaves; or, flyleaf at front only.

Note: According to the publisher's records (see below) there were two printings during the year 1902. BAL has been unable to distinguish one from the other. The records indicate that corrections were made in the plates prior to the second printing; also, there is indication that the copyright page was altered, but whether the alteration was done prior to the second printing is uncertain.

According to the publisher's records 2010 copies were printed June 2, 1902; bound during the period June 4 to Nov. 13, 1902. A second printing, 516 copies, was done Dec. 16, 1902. The third printing was done Jan. 11, 1905, 275 copies.

On copyright page: *Published September, 1902.*

Deposited June 10, 1902. Listed PW Sept. 13, 1902.

AAS B BA H LC NYPL NYSL UV Y

14816. A SPECTRE OF POWER ⟨by⟩ CHARLES EGBERT CRADDOCK

BOSTON AND NEW YORK   HOUGHTON, MIFFLIN AND COMPANY THE RIVERSIDE PRESS, CAMBRIDGE 1903

⟨i-viii⟩, ⟨1⟩-415; printer's imprint, p. ⟨416⟩. 7³⁄₄″ × 4¹⁵⁄₁₆″.

⟨1⁴, 2-27⁸⟩.

V cloth: blue. White laid paper end papers. Flyleaves.

According to the publisher's records there were two printings in 1903; BAL has been unable to identify the two.

First printing: 2514 copies printed May 18, 1903. Bound during the period May 18 to June 23, 1903.

Second printing: 503 copies printed Sept. 4, 1903. Bound during the period Sept. 17, 1903 to Jan. 1, 1904.

On copyright page: *Published May, 1903*

Deposited May 21, 1903. H copy received May 27, 1903; BA copy June 2, 1903. Listed PW June 6, 1903.

AAS B BA BPL H LC NYPL UV Y

14817. THE FRONTIERSMEN BY CHARLES EGBERT CRADDOCK . . .

BOSTON AND NEW YORK   HOUGHTON, MIFFLIN AND COMPANY THE RIVERSIDE PRESS, CAMBRIDGE 1904

Two printings noted:

FIRST PRINTING

⟨i-viii⟩, ⟨1⟩-364; blank, p. ⟨365⟩; printer's imprint, p. ⟨366⟩; blank leaf. 7¹¹⁄₁₆″ × 4¹⁵⁄₁₆″.

⟨1⁴, 2-24⁸⟩.

According to the publisher's records 2036 copies were printed March 24, 1904. Bound during the period March 25 to April 5, 1904.

SECOND PRINTING

As above save for the signature collation which is: ⟨1-23⁸, 24⁴⟩.

According to the publisher's records 506 copies were printed April 27, 1904. Bound May 5, 1904.

V cloth: blue-gray; blue-green; green. White laid end papers. Flyleaf at front.

Note: The spine imprint varies as follows:

A: HOUGHTON / MIFFLIN & CO. Noted on first printing sheets.

B: HOUGHTON / MIFFLIN ⟨dot⟩ & ⟨dot⟩ CO Noted on second printing sheets.

On copyright page: *Published April 1904*

Advertised for spring publication PW March 19, 1904. Deposited March 29, 1904. Noted for *to-day* PW April 2, 1904. BA copy (1st printing) received April 5, 1904. Listed PW April 9, 1904.

AAS (1st) BA (1st) BPL (1st) H (1st) LC (1st) NYPL (1st) UV (2nd) Y (1st)

14818. THE STORM CENTRE A NOVEL BY CHARLES EGBERT CRADDOCK . . .

NEW YORK THE MACMILLAN COMPANY LONDON: MACMILLAN & CO., LTD. 1905 ALL RIGHTS RESERVED

⟨i-vi⟩, 1-351; blank, p. ⟨352⟩; 4 pp. advertisements; blank leaf. Laid paper. 7½″ × 5³⁄₁₆″.

⟨1-22⁸, 23⁶⟩. *Signed:* ⟨A⟩³, B-I, K-U, X-Z⁸, ⟨a⟩³.

V cloth: green. Top edges gilt.

On copyright page: *Published June, 1905.*

Deposited June 19, 1905. Published June 21, 1905 according to *The United States Catalog of Books in Print.* BA copy received June 28, 1905. Listed PW July 1, 1905; Ath July 29, 1905.

AAS BA H NYPL UV Y

14819. THE AMULET A NOVEL BY CHARLES EGBERT CRADDOCK . . .

NEW YORK THE MACMILLAN COMPANY LONDON: MACMILLAN & CO., LTD. 1906 ALL RIGHTS RESERVED

⟨i-vi⟩, 1-356; 4 pp. advertisements; blank leaf. Laid paper. 7⁷⁄₁₆″ full × 5⅛″ full.

⟨1-23⁸⟩. *Signed:* ⟨A⟩³, B-I, K-U, X-Z⁸, 2A⁵.

T cloth: tan-gray.

On copyright page: *Published October, 1906.*

Deposited Oct. 23, 1906. NYSL copy received Oct. 27, 1906; BA copy received Oct. 30, 1906. Listed PW Nov. 17, 1906; Ath Nov. 24, 1906.

AAS   B   BA   H   LC   NYSL   UV   Y

14820. THE WINDFALL A NOVEL BY CHARLES EGBERT CRADDOCK . . .

NEW YORK   DUFFIELD & COMPANY   1907

⟨i-vi⟩, 1-450. Laid paper. $7\frac{1}{2}''$ full × $5\frac{3}{16}''$.

⟨1⁴, 2-29⁸⟩.

T cloth: blue.

On copyright page: *Published, March, 1907*

Deposited April 12, 1907. NYSL copy received April 17, 1907; BA copy received April 23, 1907. Listed PW April 27, 1907. The London (Chatto & Windus) edition advertised for Oct. 24 Ath Sept. 21, 1907; listed Ath Nov. 2, 1907.

AAS   B   BA   BPL   H   LC   NYSL   UV   Y

14821. THE FAIR MISSISSIPPIAN A NOVEL BY CHARLES EGBERT CRADDOCK

BOSTON AND NEW YORK   HOUGHTON MIFFLIN COMPANY   THE RIVERSIDE PRESS   CAMBRIDGE 1908

⟨i-viii⟩, 1-⟨429⟩; printer's imprint, p. ⟨430⟩; 4 pp. advertisements; blank leaf. Frontispiece inserted. $7\frac{13}{16}''$ full × $5\frac{1}{2}''$ full.

⟨1-27⁸, 28⁶⟩.

V cloth: blue.

On copyright page: *Published October 1908*

According to the publisher's records 2497 copies were printed Oct. 6, 1908. Bound during the period Oct. 6-13, 1908. Further according to the publisher's records the second printing, so marked, was done Oct. 13, 1908; 991 copies. Also according to the publisher's records some copies were made up of mixed sheets, sheets of the first and second printings being bound together.

Deposited Oct. 9, 1908. The NYSL copy received Oct. 23, 1908. Listed PW Oct. 24, 1908.

AAS   BA   BPL   H   NYPL   NYSL   UV   Y

14822. THE RAID OF THE GUERILLA AND OTHER STORIES BY CHARLES EGBERT CRADDOCK . . .

PHILADELPHIA & LONDON   J. B. LIPPINCOTT COMPANY 1912

Title-page in black and orange.

⟨i-ii⟩, ⟨1⟩-334; blank, p. ⟨335⟩; advertisement, p. ⟨336⟩. Frontispiece and 3 plates inserted. $7\frac{1}{2}''$ × $5\frac{1}{16}''$.

⟨1⟩⁹, 2-21⁸. ⟨1⟩₂ inserted.

V cloth: gray-blue.

On copyright page: *Published May, 1912*

Deposited June 24, 1912.

H   LC   NYSL   Y

14823. THE ORDEAL A MOUNTAIN ROMANCE OF TENNESSEE BY CHARLES EGBERT CRADDOCK . . .

PHILADELPHIA & LONDON   J. B. LIPPINCOTT COMPANY 1912

⟨1⟩-⟨281⟩; blank, p. ⟨282⟩; 6 pp. advertisements. Frontispiece inserted. $7\frac{1}{2}''$ scant × $5\frac{1}{16}''$ full.

⟨1⟩-18⁸.

V cloth: gray.

On copyright page: *Published September, 1912*

BA copy received Oct. 22, 1912. Deposited Oct. 23, 1912.

AAS   BA   H   LC   NYPL   NYSL   UV   Y

14824. THE STORY OF DUCIEHURST A TALE OF THE MISSISSIPPI BY CHARLES EGBERT CRADDOCK . . .

NEW YORK   THE MACMILLAN COMPANY   1914

⟨i-vi⟩, 1-439; blank, p. ⟨440⟩; publisher's catalog, 8 pp., blank leaf. $7\frac{9}{16}''$ × $5\frac{1}{8}''$ full.

⟨1-28⁸, 29⁴⟩.

Two bindings noted; the order of presentation is presumed correct:

BINDING A

V cloth: blue. Stamped in gold and black. Deposit copies thus.

BINDING B

V cloth: brown. Stamped in brown. Presumably a remainder binding.

On copyright page: *Published July, 1914.*

Deposited July 9, 1914. NYSL copy (*Binding A*) received July 21, 1914; BA copy (*Binding A*) received July 22, 1914. Listed PW Aug. 15, 1914; Bkr Nov. 6, 1914.

AAS (*Binding A*)   BA (*Binding A*)   BPL (*Binding B*) H (*Binding A*)   LC (*Binding A*)   NYPL (*Binding B*) NYSL (*Binding A*)   UV (*Binding A*)   Y (*Bindings A, B*)

14825. Youth's Companion   Edited by Lovell Thompson with Three Former Companion

Editors, M. A. DeWolfe Howe, Arthur Stanwood Pier, and Harford Powel . . .

Houghton Mifflin Company   Boston   The
Riverside Press Cambridge 1954

"A Warning," pp. 654-660. Reprinted from *The
Youth's Companion*, March 6, 1879. Revised and
collected in *The Young Mountaineers*, 1897.

Deposited Oct. 11, 1954.

H

REFERENCES

Charles Egbert Craddock (Mary Noailles Murfree)
by Edd Winfield Parks

Chapel Hill The University of North Carolina
Press ⟨1941⟩

Mary N. Murfree by Richard Cary . . .

Twayne Publishers, Inc. New York ⟨1967⟩

PETER HAMILTON MYERS

1 8 1 2 – 1 8 7 8

14826. ENSENORE. A POEM . . .

NEW-YORK: WILEY AND PUTNAM, 161 BROADWAY. 1840.

Anonymous.

⟨i⟩-⟨viii⟩, ⟨9⟩-104. 9³⁄₁₆″ full × 5¹¹⁄₁₆″.

⟨1⟩-13⁴.

T cloth: black; blue; brown; purple. Flyleaves in some copies.

Deposited Oct. 31, 1840. Reviewed κ Nov. 1840. See under 1875 for another edition.

AAS   B   BPL   H   LC   NYPL   Y

14827. SCIENCE. A POEM: DELIVERED BEFORE THE EUGLOSSIAN SOCIETY OF GENEVA COLLEGE, AUGUST 4, 1841 . . .

GENEVA, N.Y. PRINTED BY STOW & FRAZEE. 1841.

⟨1⟩-20. 9³⁄₁₆″ × 5³⁄₄″.

⟨1-2⁴, 3²⟩.

Printed yellow paper wrapper.

Noted by κ Nov. 1841.

B   H   NYPL   Y

14828. THE FIRST OF THE KNICKERBOCKERS: A TALE OF 1673 . . .

NEW-YORK: GEORGE P. PUTNAM, 155 BROADWAY. LONDON: PUTNAM'S AMERICAN AGENCY, REMOVED FROM PATERNOSTER ROW TO J. CHAPMAN, 142 STRAND. 1848.

See below under 1849 and 1866.

Anonymous.

⟨i-ii⟩, ⟨i⟩-vi, ⟨9⟩-221; blank leaf. 7⁹⁄₁₆″ full × 4¹⁵⁄₁₆″ full.

⟨1⟩⁴, 2-10¹².

TB cloth: green. Pale peach end papers. Off-white end papers. Flyleaves.

Deposited Nov. 29, 1848. Reviewed USDR Dec. 1848. The Chapman importation advertised as

just received Ath Dec. 9, 1848; listed PC Dec. 15, 1848.

AAS   B   H   NYPL   UV   Y

14829. ELLEN WELLES: OR, THE SIEGE OF FORT STANWIX. A TALE OF THE REVOLUTION . . .

ROME ⟨N.Y.⟩: PUBLISHED BY W. O. M'CLURE. A. J. ROWLEY & CO., PRINTERS. 1848.

⟨1⟩-48. 8½″ × 5⅛″ full.

⟨A⟩-B, B, D⁶.

Printed buff paper wrapper.

UV   Y

14830. THE YOUNG PATROON; OR, CHRISTMAS IN 1690. A TALE OF NEW-YORK. BY THE AUTHOR OF THE "FIRST OF THE KNICKERBOCKERS."

NEW-YORK: GEORGE P. PUTNAM, 155 BROADWAY. LONDON: PUTNAM'S AMERICAN AGENCY, REMOVED FROM PATERNOSTER ROW TO J. CHAPMAN, 142 STRAND. MDCCCXLIX.

⟨i⟩-⟨vi⟩, ⟨5⟩-142. 7½″ full × 5″.

⟨1⟩⁴, 2-6¹², 7⁸.

EXTRA GILT BINDING

A cloth: salmon. Fine-grained TR cloth: greenish slate-blue. Sides stamped in gold. Pale peach end papers. Flyleaf at back; or, flyleaves. Edges gilt.

GILT BINDING

T cloth: blue. TB cloth: green; purple. Fine-grained TR cloth: green; purple. Sides stamped in blind. Pale peach end papers. Flyleaves. Edges plain.

Deposited Dec. 30, 1848. Reviewed USDR Jan. 1849. Advertised as *recently published* LW Feb. 17, 1849. Advertised LW March 17, 1849.

B (gilt)   BA (gilt)   H (gilt)   LC (gilt)   NYPL (extra-gilt)   UV (extra-gilt)   Y (gilt)

ELLEN WELLES;

OR,

THE SIEGE

OF

FORT STANWIX.

A TALE OF THE REVOLUTION.

BY P. HAMILTON MYERS, ESQ.

ROME:
PUBLISHED BY W. O. M'CLURE.
A. J. ROWLEY & CO., PRINTERS.
——
1848.
Price 12½ Cents.

14831. The First of the Knickerbockers: A Tale of 1673 . . . Second Edition.

New-York: George P. Putnam, 155 Broadway. London: Putnam's American Agency, Removed from Paternoster Row to J. Chapman, 142 Strand. MDCCCXLIX.

Revised.

For first edition see above under 1848. See below under 1866.

AAS H UV Y

14832. THE KING OF THE HURONS. BY THE AUTHOR OF "THE FIRST OF THE KNICKERBOCKERS" AND "THE YOUNG PATROON."

NEW YORK: GEORGE P. PUTNAM, 155 BROADWAY. LONDON: PUTNAM'S AMERICAN AGENCY, 49 BOW LANE, CHEAPSIDE. MDCCCL.

Three binding variants noted. The designations are completely arbitrary and are not intended to suggest a sequence.

BINDING VARIANT A

⟨i-xii⟩, ⟨1⟩-319; blank, pp. ⟨320-324⟩; plus: Publisher's catalog, dated *July, 1849*, pp. 1-36. *Note:* Pp. ⟨i-ii⟩, ⟨321-324⟩, excised. 7¼″ full × 5″ scant.

⟨-⟩⁶, 1-13¹², 14⁶; plus: ⟨15⟩¹², ⟨16⟩⁶. Leaves ⟨-⟩₁ and 14₅₋₆ excised.

H cloth: slate-purple. Sides blindstamped with a single rule frame, publisher's monogram at center. Spine goldstamped save as noted: ⟨*blindstamped fillet*⟩ / THE / KING / OF THE / HURONS / ⟨*six blind-stamped filigrees*⟩ / PUTNAM / ⟨*blindstamped fillet*⟩ Yellow end papers.

BINDING VARIANT B

⟨i-xii⟩, ⟨1⟩-319; blank, pp. ⟨320-324⟩. Pp. ⟨i-ii⟩ and ⟨323-324⟩ excised. No terminal catalog present.

⟨-⟩⁶, 1-13¹², 14⁶. Leaves ⟨-⟩₁ and 14₆ excised.

A cloth: slate-green. Sides blindstamped with a single rule frame, publisher's monogram at center. Spine goldstamped save as noted: ⟨*blindstamped rule*⟩ / THE KING / OF THE / HURONS / ⟨*spine decorated with an arrangement of blindstamped rules and three blindstamped filigrees*⟩ Yellow end papers.

BINDING VARIANT C

⟨i-xii⟩, ⟨1⟩-319; blank, pp. ⟨320-324⟩; plus: Publisher's catalog, pp. 1-36, dated *July, 1849*. *Note:* Pp. ⟨i-ii⟩ and ⟨321-324⟩ excised. 7⁵⁄₁₆″ × 4¹⁵⁄₁₆″.

⟨-⟩⁶, 1-13¹², 14⁶; plus: ⟨15⟩¹², ⟨16⟩⁶. Leaves ⟨-⟩₁ and 14₅₋₆ excised.

H cloth: slate-purple. Sides blindstamped with a single rule frame, publisher's monogram at center.

Spine goldstamped save as noted: THE KING / OF THE / HURONS / ⟨*4 goldstamped florets*⟩ Spine decorated in blind with an arrangement of rules and boxes. Yellow end papers.

Noted as issued LW Dec. 15, 1849. Reviewed LW Dec. 22, 1849. Listed LW Dec. 22, 1849. Deposited Feb. 2, 1850.

London Publication

Advertised by Delf as an importation PC Jan. 1, 1850; Ath Jan. 19, 1850. Listed Ath Jan. 5, 1850; LG Jan. 5, 1850; PC Jan. 15, 1850. Reviewed Ath March 23, 1850. Under the title *Blanche Montaigne* listed PC March 1, 1850, as a Routledge publication.

AAS (A,B)   H (A)   UV (C)   Y (A)

14833. BELL BRANDON; AND THE WITHERED FIG TREE. A PRIZE NOVEL . . .

PHILADELPHIA: T. B. PETERSON, NO. 98 CHESNUT STREET ONE DOOR ABOVE THIRD. ⟨1851⟩

Anonymous.

⟨5⟩-114; 2 pp. advertisements(?). 9³⁄₁₆″ × 5¾″. ⟨1⟩-7⁸.

Note: Leaf 7₈ lacking in the only copies examined.

Warning: Pagination and signature collation tentative.

Binding: Probably issued in printed yellow paper wrapper.

"Bell Brandon. A Tale of New York in 1810," pp. 7-68.

"The Withered Fig Tree; a Story of the Affections," pp. 69-114.

Reprinted and reissued not before 1854 with the following imprint: *Philadelphia: T. B. Peterson, No. 102 Chestnut Street, above Third, Girard Stores.* ⟨1851; *i.e.*, not before 1854⟩

UV (incomplete)   Y (lacking 7₈)

14834. . . . Morrell's Pocket Miscellany of Choice, Entertaining, and Useful Reading for Travelers and the Fireside . . .

New York: Arthur Morrell, 25 Park Row; Printed at Morrell's Steam Blank-Book Manufacturing and Printing Establishment, 196 Fulton-St. 1852.

3 parts. For comment see entry No. 8134.

"Lodoiska, the Daughter of Pulaski. Translated from the French, for Morrell's Miscellany," Vol. 2, pp. 127-164.

"The Fortunes of Pulaski; a Sequel to Lodoiska," Vol. 3, pp. 58-80. Translated from the French.

14835. THE EMIGRANT SQUIRE . . .

PHILADELPHIA: T. B. PETERSON, NO. 98 CHESNUT STREET. ⟨1853⟩

⟨5⟩-109; advertisements, pp. ⟨110-116⟩. 9¾″ × 6″.

⟨1⟩-7⁸.

Printed fawn paper wrapper.

Noted as a February publication NLG March 15, 1853. Listed LW April 9, 1853. Reprinted and reissued with the imprint: *Philadelphia: T. B. Peterson and Brothers, 306 Chestnut Street.* ⟨1853; *i.e.*, not before 1866⟩

AAS   LC

14836. THE MISER'S HEIR; OR, THE THE ⟨*sic*⟩ YOUNG MILLIONAIRE . . .

PHILADELPHIA: T. B. PETERSON, NO. 102 CHESTNUT STREET, ⟨*sic*⟩ ⟨1854⟩

Note: The copyright notice is in the name of *A. H. Simmons & Co.* Is there another (earlier?) printing with the Simmons imprint?

⟨5⟩-222; advertisement, pp. 1-22; plus: advertisements, pp. 23-44, 54, 53. 7⁷⁄₁₆″ × 4½.

⟨1-10¹²; plus: 11¹²⟩. *Signed:* ⟨1⟩-19⁶, ⟨S⟩⁶, T¹².

"The Miser's Heir; or, the Young Millionaire," pp. 9-166.

"Ellen Welles; or, the Siege of Fort Stanwix," pp. 167-222. For a separate printing of this story see above under 1848.

A cloth: brown; gray-green; slate-purple. Pale yellow end papers. Flyleaves. Also isued in printed paper wrapper?

Deposited March 23, 1854. Listed NLG April 1, 1854 as in paper.

AAS   B   BPL   UV

14837. The Knickerbocker Gallery: A Testimonial to the Editor of the Knickerbocker Magazine from its Contributors . . .

New-York: Samuel Hueston, 348 Broadway. MDCCCLV.

"A Dutch Belle. From an Unpublished Manuscript," pp. ⟨235⟩-246. In the table of contents this is erroneously listed as at p. 233.

For fuller entry see No. 1033.

14838. THE PRISONER OF THE BORDER; A TALE OF 1838 . . .

NEW YORK: DERBY & JACKSON, 119 NASSAU ST. 1857.

⟨i-iv⟩, 5, vi-viii, 9-378; 6 pp. advertisements. Frontispiece and 3 plates inserted. 7¼″ × 4⅞″.

⟨1⟩-5, ⟨6-7⟩, 8-11, ⟨12⟩, 13-16¹².

T cloth: blue-black; purple; slate. Yellow end papers. Flyleaves. *Note:* The binding occurs in two forms; sequence, if any, not known:

BINDING A

The sides decorated with a double-rule frame.

BINDING B

The sides decorated with a triple-rule frame.

The Y copy (*Binding B*) inscribed by early owner Aug. 24, 1857. Listed Ath Nov. 7, 1857, as an importation. Listed as an American book PC Nov. 16, 1857.

AAS (*Binding B*)   B (*Binding A*)   H (*Binding A*) UV (*Binding B*)   Y (*Binding B*)

14839. Thrilling Adventures of the Prisoner of the Border . . .

New York: Derby & Jackson, 119 Nassau Street. 1860.

Reprint of *The Prisoner of the Border* . . . , 1857.

Two printings noted:

1: Imprint as above.

2: With the publisher's later address in the imprint: *498 Broadway.*

NYPL (1st)   UV (1st, 2nd)

14840. Fort Stanwix: A Tale of the Mohawk in 1777 . . .

New York: American News Co., Publisher's Agent, 119 and 121 Nassau Street. ⟨1865⟩

Reprint of *Ellen Welles* . . . , 1848. Also contains "A Day in the Life of a Rich Man," pp. ⟨76⟩-100; anonymous; presumably not by Myers.

Printed paper wrapper.

NYPL

14841. THE GOLD CRUSHERS. A TALE OF CALIFORNIA . . .

NEW YORK: IRWIN & CO., PUBLISHERS, 102 NASSAU STREET. ⟨1866⟩

⟨5⟩-100. Frontispiece. 6⅜″ × 4″.

⟨1-3¹⁶⟩.

Printed paper wrapper, orange on the outer side, white on the inner.

NYPL

14842. The First of the Knickerbockers: A Tale of 1673 . . .

New York: Chapman & Co., 116 Nassau Street, The American News Co., General Agents, 119 and 121 Nassau Street. 1866.

For earlier editions see above under 1848, 1849.

"Preface," pp. ⟨v⟩-vi, dated at end Sept. 1866. *Note:* The preface is basically a reprint of the 1848 version.

Pictorial paper wrapper. *American Novels*, No. 30.

LC NYPL

14843. Bell Brandon: Or, the Great Kentrips Estate. A Tale of New York in 1810 . . .

New York: Irwin & Co., Publishers, 102 Nassau Street. ⟨1867⟩

Reprint. See *Bell Brandon* . . . ⟨1851⟩.

Pictorial paper wrapper. *Irwin's American Novels*, No. 32.

H NYPL

14844. Nick Doyle, the Gold-Hunter. A Tale of California . . .

New York: Beadle and Company, Publishers, 98 William Street. ⟨1870⟩.

Reprint of *The Gold Crushers* . . . ⟨1866⟩.

Printed orange paper wrapper. *Beadle's Dime Novels*, No. 220.

Reprinted and reissued by Beadle and Adams.

UV

14845. The Red Spy: A Tale of the Mohawk in 1777 . . .

New York Frank Starr & Co., Publishers, 41 Platt Street. ⟨1871⟩

Reprint of *Fort Stanwix* . . . ⟨1865⟩.

Printed buff paper wrapper. *Frank Starr's American Novels*, No. 79.

NYS

14846. ENSENORE, AND OTHER POEMS . . .

NEW YORK: DODD & MEAD, PUBLISHERS, 751 BROADWAY. ⟨1875⟩

A revised version of *Ensenore*, 1840, with other poems.

⟨i-iv⟩, ⟨1⟩-196; blank leaf; leaf excised or pasted under the end paper. 6¹³⁄₁₆″ × 4⁷⁄₁₆″.

⟨1-7¹², 8-10⁶⟩. Leaves ⟨1⟩₁ and ⟨10⟩₆ excised or pasted under the end papers. *Signed:* ⟨1⟩⁸, 2-7, ⟨8⟩, 9-15, ⟨16⟩⁶, ⟨17⟩⁴.

FL cloth: terra-cotta. T cloth, moiréd: green. Covers bevelled. Brown-coated end papers.

Listed PW Aug. 14, 1875.

H LC UV

14847. THE GREAT MOGUL. A NOVEL . . .

NEW YORK: STREET & SMITH, PUBLISHERS. FRANCIS S. STREET. FRANCIS S. SMITH. MDCCC-LXXVIII.

⟨1⟩-61; ⟨70⟩-100; advertisements, pp. ⟨101-106⟩. 1 illustration in text. 7³⁄₁₆″ × 4³⁄₄″. Text of Myers's *The Great Mogul*, Chapters 1-8 only, pp. ⟨9⟩-61. At end of text, p. 61: "The continuation of *The Great Mogul* will be found in No. 3 of the *New York Weekly*, now ready and for sale by every Newsdealer." Text of Bertha M. Clay's *A Thorn in Her Heart*, Chapter 1-8 only, pp. 74-100. At end of text, p. 100: "The continuation of *A Thorn in Her Heart* will be found in No. 51 ⟨Nov. 4, 1878⟩ of Street & Smith's *New York Weekly*, now ready and for sale by every news dealer."

⟨1-2¹², 3¹³, 4¹²⟩. Leaf ⟨3⟩₉ inserted. Leaf ⟨3⟩₉ᵣ imprinted with the table of contents for *A Thorn in Her Heart*; and, on the verso: *Please send us the name and address of all your Country Friends and we will send them one copy of this Book. Street & Smith, Proprietors of New York Weekly, 31 Rose Street, N. Y.*

S cloth: mauve; terra-cotta. Yellow end papers.

BAL has not found full book publication of *The Great Mogul*.

Also appears in the following publication; sequence not known:

"In 1878, Street & Smith issued, with its own title page, the first three chapters of *Carried by Storm* ⟨by May Agnes Early Fleming⟩ divided into eight chapters, to advertise the current serial in their *New York Weekly*. With it was bound 'eight chapters' of Peter Hamilton Myers' *The Great Mogul*, also running as a serial. The latter apparently was never published in book form." Not seen by BAL. Information from *American Fiction 1876-1900* . . . , by Lyle H. Wright, San Marino, Cal., 1966, pp. 191-192. The first three chapters of *Carried by Storm* appeared in the *New York Weekly* Dec. 9, 1878.

UV

14848. . . . THE TREASURE SHIP. A TALE OF NEW YORK . . .

⟨At head of title:⟩ THE SEASIDE LIBRARY . . . VOL. CX. DOUBLE NUMBER . . . NO. 1813 . . . MARCH 29, 1884.

⟨1⟩-46; advertisements, pp. IX-⟨X⟩. 12⅛″ full × 8½″. P. ⟨2⟩ paged I.

⟨-⟩²⁴.

Printed self-wrapper.

Deposited April 4, 1884.

LC

14849. ... ROXY HASTINGS; OR, A RAF-
FLE FOR LIFE ...

NEW YORK: STREET & SMITH, PUBLISHERS, 31
ROSE STREET. ⟨1890⟩

At head of title: *The Select Series. A Weekly Publication . . . No. 55. August 20, 1890 . . .*

⟨1⟩-242; advertisements, pp. ⟨243-256⟩. $7\frac{1}{2}''$ ×
$5\frac{5}{16}''$.

⟨1-8⟩^{16}.

Printed paper wrapper.

Presumed to be the first book publication. Myers
is credited with *Roxy Hastings* on the title-page of
his *The Great Mogul*, 1878.

Deposited Aug. 29, 1890.

LC

14850. ... THE SKY TRAVELER ...

⟨NEW YORK: STREET & SMITH, 1890⟩

Cover-title. The above at head of p. ⟨1⟩. At head
of title: *Log Cabin Library . . . No. 93. Street &
Smith, Publishers. New York . . .*

⟨1⟩-31; p. 32: Lists of *The Nugget Library*, Nos.
1-74; *The Log Cabin Library*, Nos. 1-94. $12\frac{1}{16}''$ ×
$8\frac{7}{8}''$.

⟨-⟩^{16}.

Printed self-wrapper.

Issued under date Dec. 25, 1890.

Presumed to be the first book publication. Myers
is noted as the author of *The Sky Traveler* on the
title-pages of *Nick Doyle . . . ⟨1870⟩; and, The
Great Mogul . . . , 1878.*

IU

REPRINTS

The Atlantic Souvenir, for 1859 ...

New York: Derby & Jackson, 119 Nassau
Street. 1859.

Leather. A partial reprint of *The Knickerbocker
Gallery . . . , 1855, above.*

REFERENCES AND ANA

A Tale of 1673. The Brigantine; or, Admiral
Lowe's Last Cruise. By Decatur Paulding,
U.S.N.

New York: Beadle and Company, Publishers,
118 William Street. ⟨1864⟩

Printed paper wrapper. *Beadle's Dime Novels,*
No. 68.

Sometimes credited to Myers. BAL has found
no evidence to support the attribution. Johannsen does not credit the book to Myers.

The book is an altered printing of *The Brigantine; or, Admiral Lowe, a Tale of the 17th Century,
by an American*, New York: Crowen & Decker,
1839. Listed in Wright anonymously. Author
not known to BAL.

Iron Fist.

ca. 1870.

Myers is credited with the authorship of the
above on the title-pages of *Nick Doyle . . .
⟨1870⟩; and, The Great Mogul, 1878.* Further
information wanting. Periodical publication
only?

JOHN NEAL

(Jehu O'Cataract; A New Englander Over-Sea; Somebody, M.D.C.)

1793 – 1876

14851. THE SAILOR'S GRAVE (MUSIC COMPOSED FOR THE PORTICO BY C. MEINEKE) . . .

⟨n.p., n.d., BALTIMORE: THE PORTICO, JUNE, 1817⟩

Sheet music. Single sheet. Printed on recto only. Issued as a supplement to *The Portico* (Baltimore) in which Neal's poem, "The Sailor's Grave," was published in full, issue of June, 1817. The sheet music prints only the first of eight stanzas.

Anonymous.

H

14852. KEEP COOL, A NOVEL. WRITTEN IN HOT WEATHER. BY SOMEBODY, M.D.C. &c. &c. &c. . . . IN TWO VOLUMES

BALTIMORE: PUBLISHED BY JOSEPH CUSHING. WM. WOODDY, PRINTER. 1817.

1: ⟨i⟩-⟨xviii⟩, 19-239. 7⅛″ × 4¼″.

2: ⟨1⟩-196.

1: ⟨A⟩-I, K-U⁶.

2: ⟨A⟩-I, K-Q⁶, R².

Two issues noted:

1: P. 50, Vol. 2, mispaged 30.

2: P. 50, Vol. 2, correctly paged.

Printed gray-green paper boards.

According to Neal's *Wandering Recollections* . . . , pp. 173, 198, respectively, "appeared June 17, 1817" and published June 27, 1817; Neal in error. Title-page deposited June 27, 1817. Noted in *The Portico*, Baltimore, July-August, 1817, as *just published*.

H (1st)   NYPL (1st)   Y (2nd)

14853. BATTLE OF NIAGARA, A POEM, WITHOUT NOTES; AND GOLDAU, OR THE MANIAC HARPER . . . BY JEHU O'CATARACT . . .

BALTIMORE: PUBLISHED BY N. G. MAXWELL. FROM THE PORTICO PRESS. GEO. W. GRATER, PRINTER. 1818.

See under 1819 for an extended edition.

⟨i⟩-⟨xiv⟩, ⟨15⟩-143. 6¾″ × 4⅛″. Printed on mixed papers, both laid and wove being used.

⟨1⟩-18⁴.

Two issues noted:

1: P. vi mispaged iv.

2: P. vi correctly paged vi.

Printed tan paper boards. White laid paper end papers, laid paper flyleaf at front. *Also:* White wove paper end papers, wove paper flyleaves.

Title-page deposited Aug. 22, 1818. Listed AMM Nov. 1818.

Note: Appleton's reference to a book titled *Goldan* is probably an erroneous entry for *Battle of Niagara . . . Goldau*.

Also note: Pattee (*American Writers . . . John Neal . . .*, 1937), gives the title as *A Poem without Notes; and Goldau, or the Maniac Harper*.

AAS (2nd)   B (1st; 2nd)   H (2nd)   NYPL (2nd)   UV (2nd)   Y (2nd)

14854. General Index to the First Twelve Volumes, or First Series, of Niles' Weekly Register Being a Period of Six Years: From September, 1811, to September, 1817 . . .

Baltimore: Printed and Published by the Editor, at the Franklin Press. Price in Sheets, Three Dollars. 1818.

Edited, for the most part, by Neal.

H

14855. A HISTORY OF THE AMERICAN REVOLUTION; COMPREHENDING ALL THE PRINCIPAL EVENTS BOTH IN THE FIELD AND IN THE CABINET. BY PAUL ALLEN, ESQ. . . . IN TWO VOLUMES . . .

BALTIMORE: PRINTED FOR JOHN HOPKINS. THOMAS MURPHY, PRINTER. 1819.

Paul Allen (1775–1826) "projected a *History of the American Revolution*, the most of which, owing to his irresponsibleness, was written by his friends Neal and Watkins."———DAB. Watkins was Tobias Watkins (1780–1855). For an account of the writing of the book see Neal's *Wandering Recollections . . .*, pp. 201-204.

1: ⟨i⟩-⟨xii⟩, ⟨1⟩-592. $8^7/_{16}'' \times 5^3/_{16}''$.

2: ⟨i⟩-⟨xvi⟩, ⟨1⟩-510, blank leaf.

1: ⟨1⟩⁴, 2², 1-74⁴.

2: ⟨-⟩⁴, *⁴, ⟨1⟩-64⁴.

Two issues of Vol. 1 noted:

1: Vol. 1, p. 457 signed: VLO. 1

2: Vol. 1, p. 457 signed: VOL. 1

Issued in paper boards?

Note: Unsold sheets were issued with a cancel title-leaf imprinted: *Baltimore: Printed for Franklin Betts. Wm. Wooddy, Jr. Printer. 1822.* Copy in H.

Title deposited for copyright "on the Fifteenth Day of March, in the forty first ⟨*sic*⟩ year of the Independence . . ." Published March, 1819, according to Neal's *Wandering Recollections . . .*, 1869, p. 219.

AAS (2nd) B (2nd) BPL (2nd) H (2nd) LC (1st) MHS (2nd) NYPL (2nd)

14856. THE BATTLE OF NIAGARA: SECOND EDITION———ENLARGED: WITH OTHER POEMS . . .

BALTIMORE: PUBLISHED BY N. G. MAXWELL. B. EDES, PRINTER. 1819.

For first edition see above under 1818. Contains much new material.

⟨i⟩-⟨lxviii⟩, ⟨69⟩-272. $6^7/_{16}'' \times 3^7/_8''$. Vignette title-page inserted.

⟨-⟩¹, A-I, K-P⁹. *Note:* A-I, K-P₅ inserted. *Also note:* In the signing the inserted leaves are each misnumbered 4.

Blue paper boards, white paper shelf back. Printed paper label on spine. Flyleaves?

Title deposited July 1, 1819. Advertised and reviewed *Baltimore Patriot*, Aug. 6, 1819. Reviewed by AM Sept. 1819.

According to Neal's list of errata, pp. ⟨271⟩-272, in itself not free of error, the copies first printed have the following errors. BAL has located no copy with all the errors present. To quote Neal: "The following errors occur in a few copies only; most of them having been discovered before the form was entirely worked off." In preparing this note BAL has revised some of Neal's line designations.

a-Dedication: For *your's* read *yours*

a-P. ⟨vii⟩, line 12: For *its* read *their* (Neal erroneously gives line 9)

a-P. xvii: For *we have worn the opinions of her criticism on all subjects* read *we have worn the opinions of Rome ———her criticism on all subjects*

a-P. xxxviii, line 25: For *it* read *them*

b-P. xlv: For *they pass like thoughts o'er a clear blue sky* read *they pass like thoughts o'er a clear-blue eye*

b-P. lvi, line 3: For *glittered* read *glittering*

b-P. lvi, line 20: For *filicitous* read *felicitous*

b-P. 98, line 6: For *quits* read *visits*

a-P. 110, line 11: Substitute a comma for the semicolon, at the end of the line

a-P. 116, line 3 up: Substitute a period for a comma

a-P. 154, line 8: For *give* read *given*

a-P. 235, line 7 up: For *were* read *we're*

a-P. 236, line 9: For *angels' wings* read *angel-wings* (Neal erroneously gives *angel's* for *angels'*.)

Key:

a:-Noted only in the original reading.

b:-Noted only in the revised reading.

H Y (incomplete)

14857. OTHO: A TRAGEDY, IN FIVE ACTS . . .

BOSTON: PUBLISHED BY WEST, RICHARDSON AND LORD. JOHN H. A. FROST, PRINTER, CONGRESS-STREET. 1819.

⟨i⟩-⟨xxiv⟩, ⟨25⟩-120. $6^3/_8'' \times 3^3/_4''$.

⟨1⟩-10⁶. *Note:* In some copies signature mark 9 is absent.

Issued in unprinted paper wrapper?

Title deposited Nov. 13, 1819.

Erroneously dated 1818 by Neal in his *Wandering Recollections . . .*, 1869, p. 219.

B H NYPL UV Y

14858. LOGAN, A FAMILY HISTORY . . . IN TWO VOLUMES . . .

PHILADELPHIA: H. C. CAREY & I. LEA CHESNUT ST. 1822.

1: ⟨1⟩-317, blank leaf. $8'' \times 4^3/_4''$.

2: ⟨1⟩-341; blank, p. ⟨342⟩; *Errata*, p. ⟨343⟩. P. 175 mispaged 157.

1: ⟨A⟩-I, K-U, X-Z, Aa-Cc⁶, Dd⁴.

2: ⟨1⟩-28⁶, 29⁴.

THE SAILOR'S GRAVE

(Music Composed for the PORTICO by C. MEINEKE)

waters are cold and dark, And they swim as still a—round our bark, And as smooth as the heaven a—bove us: And the watery tide is as dis——tant too, As the ai———ry tide with its slee——py blue, The battle is near and our moments few, Let us think of the hearts that love us, Let us think of the hearts that love us.

Drab brown (also blue?) paper boards. Printed paper label on spine. Flyleaves.

Copyright notice in Vol. 1 only.

Title deposited April 1, 1822. *In the press*–––NAR April, 1822. In list of published works (erroneously?) LSR May, 1822. *In the press*–––M Aug. 10, 1822. Listed NAR Jan. 1823. The London (A. K. Newman) edition listed in *British Critic*, March, 1823.

AAS   B   H   NYPL   UV

A History of the American Revolution ... by Paul Allen ... in Two Volumes ...

Baltimore: Printed for Franklin Betts. Wm. Wooddy, Jr. Printer. 1822.

Sheets of the 1819 printing (see above) with cancel title-leaves.

BA   H   UV   Y

14859. SEVENTY-SIX. BY THE AUTHOR OF LOGAN ... IN TWO VOLS. ...

BALTIMORE: PUBLISHED BY JOSEPH ROBINSON, ⟨.⟩ CIRCULATING LIBRARY AND LITERARY ROOMS; AND J. ROBINSON ⟨,⟩ & CO. FREDERICK, MD. 1823.

1: ⟨i⟩-⟨viii⟩, ⟨13⟩-268. $7^{11}/_{16}"$ × $4^{9}/_{16}"$. *Note:* In some copies folio *vi* is not present. *Also note:* The list of errata, Vol. 1, pp. ⟨vii-viii⟩ (*i.e.*, leaf ⟨1⟩₄), in some copies is excised and bound in at the end of either volume. The pagination and signature collation in some copies vary to this extent.

2: ⟨i-iv⟩, ⟨13⟩-260.

1: ⟨1⟩⁴, 2-22⁶, 23².

2: ⟨1⟩², 2⁴, 3-22⁶.

Printed paper boards: gray-blue; tan. Flyleaves.

Dedication dated *January 1, 1823*. Title deposited Feb. 20, 1823. In the quarterly list of NAR July, 1823. The London edition (*Baltimore: Printed. London: Reprinted for G. and W. B. Whittaker*) listed BC May, 1823. Advertised LG July 26, 1823. Reviewed MR Oct. 1823.

B   H   UV   Y

14860. RANDOLPH, A NOVEL ... BY THE AUTHOR OF LOGAN ... IN TWO VOLUMES ...

PUBLISHED FOR WHOM IT MAY CONCERN. 1823.

"... Published in Philadelphia, under the superintendence of Mr. Simpson ..."–––*Wandering Recollections*, p. 229. "... Mr. Stephen Simpson, the real *publisher*..."–––*ib.*, p. 236. "The publisher was really Stephen Simpson of Philadelphia."––– *The Life and Works of Edward Coote Pinkney* ..., prepared by Thomas Ollive Mabbott

and Frank Lester Pleadwell, New York, 1926, note, p. 25. Irving Trefethen Richards, in his unpublished thesis, *The Life and Works of John Neal* ..., Cambridge, 1932, Vol. 1, p. 383, appears not to accept Simpson as the publisher and points out that in the copyright notice Charles I. Jack is named as "proprietor."

1: ⟨i⟩-vi, ⟨7⟩-339. $7^{11}/_{16}"$ × $4^{5}/_{8}"$.

2: ⟨1⟩-346; *Errata*, p. ⟨347⟩.

P. 4, Vol. 2, occurs in two states:

1: Folio 4 inverted.

2: Folio 4 properly set.

1: ⟨A⟩², B-I, K-U, W-Z, AA-EE⁶.

2: ⟨A⟩-I, K-U, W-Z, AA-EE⁶.

Copyright notice in Vol. 1 only.

Blue-gray paper boards sides, white wove paper shelf back. Brown paper boards sides, white laid paper shelf back. Printed paper label on spine; orange, white, yellow papers noted. Flyleaves.

"We have been favoured with some proof sheets ..."–––M July 5, 1823. M July 26, 1823, prints a letter from the author requesting no further publication of extracts until formal book publication "which will be in a few days." Title-page deposited July 28, 1823. Listed NAR Jan. 1824.

AAS   H   NYPL   Y

14861. ERRATA; OR, THE WORKS OF WILL. ADAMS. A TALE BY THE AUTHOR OF LOGAN ... IN TWO VOLUMES ...

NEW-YORK: PUBLISHED FOR THE PROPRIETORS; AND FOR SALE AT THE PRINCIPAL BOOKSTORES IN THE UNITED STATES. 1823.

1: ⟨i⟩-⟨xvi⟩, ⟨17⟩-64; 63-73; ⟨76⟩-325; blank, p. ⟨326⟩; blank leaf. $7^{13}/_{16}"$ × $4^{11}/_{16}"$.

2: ⟨1⟩-364; *Errata*, p. ⟨365⟩.

1: ⟨A⟩², B-I, K-U, W-Z, AA-DD⁶.

2: ⟨-⟩¹, A-I, K-U, W-Z, AA-FF⁶, GG².

The following mispagination noted in Vol. 2:

P. 39 mispaged 93 in some copies.

P. 74 mispaged 47 in all examined copies.

P. 146 mispaged 164 in all examined copies.

Gray-blue paper boards, white paper shelf back. Gray-blue paper boards, tan muslin shelf back. Printed paper label on spine. Flyleaves.

Title-page deposited Nov. 10, 1823. "... Published Nov. 18, 1823 ..."––– *Wandering Recollections*, p. 238. Listed NAR April, 1824.

AAS   UV

14862. BROTHER JONATHAN: OR, THE NEW ENGLANDERS. IN THREE VOL-UMES . . .

WILLIAM BLACKWOOD, EDINBURGH: AND T. CADELL, STRAND, LONDON. MDCCCXXV.

Anonymous.

1: ⟨i-iv⟩, ⟨1⟩-421; printer's imprint, p. ⟨422⟩; leaf excised or pasted under the end paper. Ribbed paper. $7^{15}/_{16}'' \times 4^{7}/_{8}''$.

2: ⟨i-iv⟩, ⟨1⟩-451; printer's imprint, p. ⟨452⟩.

3: ⟨i-iv⟩, ⟨1⟩-452.

1: ⟨A⟩², B-I, K-U, X-Z, AA-DD⁸, EE⁴. EE₄ excised or pasted under the end paper.

2: ⟨A⟩², B-I, K-U, X-Z, AA-FF⁸, GG².

3: ⟨A⟩², B-I, K-U, X-Z, AA-FF⁸, GG².

Salmon paper boards, printed paper label on spine.

Advertised LG May 28, 1825, as *in the press*; repeated June 18. Described as *preparing* BMLA June 1825. Reviewed LG July 9, 1825. Advertised as *now first published* BMLA July 1825. Listed as a July publication BMLA Aug. 1825.

B   H   LC   UV   Y

14863. RACHEL DYER: A NORTH AMERI-CAN STORY . . .

PORTLAND: PUBLISHED BY SHIRLEY AND HYDE. 1828.

⟨i⟩-xx, ⟨21⟩-276. $7^{15}/_{16}'' \times 4^{11}/_{16}''$.

⟨1⟩-23⁶.

Brown paper boards sides, linen shelf back. Shelf-back noted in the following colors: black; brown; purple. Flyleaves. Printed paper label on spine noted in the following colors: green; orange; yellow; white.

Title deposited Oct. 8, 1828. The UV copy in-scribed by Neal Nov. 29, 1828.

H   NYPL   UV   Y

14864. The Token; A Christmas and New Year's Present. Edited by N. P. Willis.

Boston: S. G. Goodrich, 141 Washington Street. MDCCCXXIX.

"Otter-Bag, the Oneida Chief," pp. ⟨221⟩-284.

For fuller entry see No. 6781.

14865. ADDRESS FOR THE NEW YEAR. BY THE EDITORS OF THE YANKEE AND BOSTON LITERARY GAZETTE. JANU-ARY 1 ⟨3 dots⟩ 1829 . . .

⟨BOSTON, 1829⟩

Single cut sheet. Printed on recto only. $9^{3}/_{4}'' \times 7^{3}/_{4}''$.

For earliest located book publication see next entry.

Y

14866. Specimens of American Poetry . . . in Three Volumes. By Samuel Kettell . . .

Boston,-S. G. Goodrich and Co. MDCCCXXIX.

Reprint save for:

"The Birth of a Poet," Vol. 3, p. 99. Elsewhere unlocated.

"Ode to Peace," Vol. 3, pp. 109-111. For prior publication see preceding entry, *Address for the New Year*.

"The Sleeper," Vol. 3, pp. 100-109. Elsewhere unlocated.

For fuller entry see No. 3251.

14867. ADDRESS DELIVERED BEFORE THE PORTLAND ASSOCIATION, FOR THE PROMOTION OF TEMPERANCE, FEB-RUARY 11, 1829 . . .

PORTLAND   DAY & FRASER. 1829.

⟨i-ii⟩, ⟨1⟩-18. $9^{3}/_{16}'' \times 5^{3}/_{4}''$.

⟨1¹, 2-3⁴, 4¹⟩. *Signed:* ⟨1⟩-2⁵.

Printed tan paper wrapper.

AAS   B   H   NYPL

14868. THIRTY-ONE UNANSWERABLE REASONS---ANSWERED

PORTLAND, MAINE, 1829

Unlocated. Entry based on the following extracted from Neal's *Wandering Recollections*, 1869, p. 345: ". . . Meanwhile, I issued a sort of manifesto, on a single page, headed, substantially, in this way: *Thirty-one unanswerable reasons---answered* . . . This I followed up with a pamphlet of about fifty octavo pages, with tables, petitions, on both sides, and statistics . . ." The pamphlet referred to is presumed to be *City of Portland* . . .; see next entry.

14869. CITY OF PORTLAND: BEING A GENERAL REVIEW OF THE PROCEED-INGS HERETOFORE HAD, IN THE TOWN OF PORTLAND, ON THE SUB-JECT OF A CITY GOVERNMENT; WITH THE PETITIONS AND SIGNATURES, AND REMARKS THEREON . . .

PORTLAND: SHIRLEY AND HYDE, PRINTERS. 1829.

Cover-title.

⟨1⟩-47. 8½″ × 5⅞″.

⟨1⟩-4⁶.

Printed self-wrapper.

B   Y

14870. A Practical Grammar of the English Language, in Which the Principles Established by Lindley Murray, Are Inculcated . . . by Roscoe G. Greene . . .

Portland ⟨Maine⟩. Printed by T. Todd, Union St. Published by Shirley & Hyde, 7, Exchange St. 1829.

Boards, leather shelf back.

"Language," p. 52. Otherwise unlocated.

Title deposited Oct. 9, 1828.

UP

14871. The Token; a Christmas and New Year's Present. Edited by S. G. Goodrich . . .

Boston: Published by Carter and Hendee. MDCCCXXX.

"The Utilitarian," pp. ⟨299⟩-318. Otherwise unlocated.

For fuller entry see No. 3102.

14872. THE NEW-ENGLAND ADVENTURER. / ⟨rule⟩ / [We give the following article as it was received. Whether / it is a genuine piece of autobiography from the pen of JOHN / DUNN HUNTER himself, or only a probable sketch of his life by / some one who knew him well, we leave to the reader's decision. / It came to us in a handwriting, much resembling that of our / friend, J. Neal. Should it prove to have been written by him, / that would in our opinion contribute rather to strengthen than / diminish its authenticity, as he has had better opportunities than / any other man, to learn the real history of the singular individual / to which it refers. ED.] / ⟨text⟩

The preceding on p. ⟨1⟩.

⟨1-24⟩. Printed on pp. ⟨1⟩, ⟨4⟩, ⟨5⟩, ⟨8⟩, ⟨9⟩, ⟨12⟩, ⟨13⟩, ⟨16⟩, ⟨17⟩, ⟨20⟩, ⟨21⟩, ⟨24⟩ only. 7¾″ × 4⅛″.

⟨-⟩¹².

Unprinted paper wrapper.

Signed and dated at end, on p. ⟨24⟩: *J.D.H. April 1, 1830.*

Probably the proof sheets of a periodical.

"I think Neal wrote it as an attack on Hunter. It is in Neal's style rather than Hunter's, I should think, and anyhow, no author would so deliberately make himself out a fraud and a liar." R. W.

G. Vail, quoted in a letter from Oscar Wegelin to BAL, June 26, 1945.

NYHS

14873. Principles of Legislation: From the Ms. of Jeremy Bentham; Bencher of Lincoln's Inn. By M. Dumont . . . Translated from the Second Corrected and Enlarged Edition . . . by John Neal.

Boston: Wells and Lilly—Court-Street. G. & C. & H. Carvill, and E. Bliss, New York; E. L. Carey & A. Hart, Philadelphia; W. & J. Neal, Baltimore; P. Thompson, Washington; W. Berrett, Charleston, S. C.; Mary Carrol, New Orleans; W. C. Little, Albany; H. Howe, New Haven, and S. Colman, Portland. 1830.

⟨i⟩-viii, ⟨9⟩-310, blank leaf. Frontispiece inserted. 10¹/₁₆″ × 6¹/₁₆″. P. viii paged at inner margin.

"Preface," pp. ⟨iii⟩-v. At end: *J. N. Portland, April 1, 1830.*

Cloth, printed paper label on spine.

Title deposited April 9, 1830. *Literary Port Folio,* (Phila.) June 3, 1830, reprints a review from the *National Gazette.*

NYPL   UV   Y

14874. AUTHORSHIP, A TALE. BY A NEW ENGLANDER OVER-SEA.

BOSTON: PUBLISHED BY GRAY AND BOWEN. 1830.

⟨i⟩-iv, ⟨1⟩-267. 7¾″ scant × 4¾″ full.

⟨a⟩², 1-22⁶, 23².

Brown paper boards sides. Brown, purple muslin shelf back. Printed paper label on spine. Flyleaves.

Title deposited July 15, 1830. Reviewed AMM Aug. 1830. With the added imprint: *London: Rich,* reviewed LG April 23, 1831. Reviewed MR July, 1831, with the Boston imprint only.

AAS   B   NYPL   Y

14875. OUR COUNTRY. AN ADDRESS DELIVERED BEFORE THE ALUMNI OF WATERVILLE-COLLEGE, JULY 29, 1830 . . .

PORTLAND. PUBLISHED BY S. COLMAN. 1830.

Cover-title?

⟨1⟩-36. 9⁵/₁₆″ × 5⁹/₁₆″.

⟨1⟩-4⁴, 5².

Issued in printed paper wrapper? Self-wrapper?

Listed NAR Oct. 1830.

AAS   B   BPL   H   NYPL   Y

14876. The Token; a Christmas and New Year's Present. Edited by S. G. Goodrich . . .

Boston: Published by Gray and Bowen. MDCCCXXXI.

"The Adventurer," pp. ⟨189⟩-212. For a comment on the authorship of this see entry No. 7572.

For comment see entry No. 6790.

14877. AN ADDRESS DELIVERED BEFORE THE M. C. ⟨MAINE CHARITABLE⟩ MECHANIC ASSOCIATION, THURSDAY EVENING, JAN. 13, 1831 . . .

PORTLAND: PRINTED BY DAY & FRASER. 1831.

Cover-title?

⟨1⟩-17. 9⅛″ × 5¹³⁄₁₆″.

⟨1⟩-2⁴, ⟨3⟩¹.

Issued in printed paper wrapper? Self-wrapper?

NYPL Y

14878. The Token; a Christmas and New Year's Present. Edited by S. G. Goodrich . . .

Boston. Published by Gray and Bowen. MDCCCXXXII.

"David Whicher. A North American Story," pp. ⟨349⟩-372. Possibly by John Neal.

For a discussion of the authorship of this story see "The Authorship of 'David Whicher': The Case for John Neal," by Benjamin Lease, in: Jahrbuch für Amerikastudien . . . , Vol. 12, Heidelberg, 1967. Also see "A Note on the Authorship of 'David Whicher'," by Irving T. Richards; and, "The Authorship of 'David Whicher'," by H. J. Lang, both in: Jahrbuch für Amerikastudien . . . , Vol. 7, Heidelberg, 1962.

For fuller entry see. No. 3256.

14879. The Atlantic Souvenir for MDCCCXXXII.

Philadelphia: Published by Carey and Lea. 1832.

Printed paper boards(?).

"The Haunted Man," by John Neale ⟨sic⟩, pp. ⟨221⟩-246.

H NYPL

14880. THE DOWN-EASTERS . . . IN TWO VOLUMES . . .

NEW-YORK: PUBLISHED BY HARPER & BROTHERS, 82 CLIFF STREET, AND SOLD BY THE PRINCIPAL BOOKSELLERS THROUGHOUT THE UNITED STATES. 1833.

1: ⟨i⟩-⟨viii⟩, ⟨1⟩-206; blank leaf. 7¹¹⁄₁₆″ × 4⅝″.

2: ⟨1⟩-204.

1: ⟨-⟩⁴, A-I, K-R⁶, S².

2: ⟨A⟩-I, K-R⁶.

Blue muslin. Printed paper label on spine. Flyleaves.

Deposited Nov. 29, 1833. Listed AMM Jan. 1834. Reviewed (as an American book) Ath Feb. 21, 1835.

AAS   B   BPL   NYPL   UV   Y

14881. The Token and Atlantic Souvenir. A Christmas and New Year's Present. Edited by S. G. Goodrich.

Boston. Published by Charles Bowen. MDCCC-XXXV.

"Children———What Are They?" pp. ⟨280⟩-298.

For fuller entry see No. 6799.

14882. The Token and Atlantic Souvenir. A Christmas and New Year's Present. Edited by S. G. Goodrich.

Boston. Published by Charles Bowen. MDCCC-XXXVI.

"The Young Phrenologist," pp. ⟨156⟩-169.

For fuller entry see No. 6804.

14883. Charter and By-Laws of the Maine Quarrying Association. Capital 350,000 Dollars. Incorporated March 7, A. D. 1836.

Portland: A. Shirley Printer, 1836.

Anonymous. Presumably compiled by Neal.

⟨1⟩-21, blank leaf. 5⁵⁄₁₆″ × 3¹³⁄₁₆″. Printed green paper wrapper.

Issued after April 9, 1836.

AAS

14884. The Portland Sketch Book. Edited by Mrs. Ann S. Stephens

Portland: Colman & Chisholm. Arthur Shirley, Printer. 1836.

"The Unchangeable Jew," pp. ⟨168⟩-182.

"A War-Song of the Revolution," pp. ⟨183⟩-184.

Deposited Nov. 23, 1836.

H NYPL

14885. The Boston Book. Being Specimens of Metropolitan Literature. Edited by B. B. Thatcher.

Boston: Light & Stearns, 1 Cornhill. 1837 ⟨i.e., 1836?⟩

"Women," pp. ⟨240⟩-244.

For fuller entry see No. 8730.

14886. BANKS AND BANKING. A LETTER TO THE BANK-DIRECTORS OF PORT-LAND . . .

PORTLAND: PRINTED AT THE ORION OFFICE. 1837.

Cover-title?

⟨1⟩-8. 9⅛″ × 5⅝″.

⟨-⟩⁴.

Printed self-wrapper?

Dated at end *July 22, 1837.*

H

14887. ORATION . . . PORTLAND, JULY 4, 1838.

PORTLAND: ARTHUR SHIRLEY ⟨7 dots⟩ PRINTER. 1838.

⟨1⟩-25. 8⅝″ × 5⅜″.

⟨1-3⁴, 4¹⟩.

Printed paper wrapper; green, blue, mauve, yellow noted.

AAS BPL H Y

14888. MAN. A DISCOURSE, BEFORE THE UNITED BROTHERS' SOCIETY OF BROWN UNIVERSITY, SEPTEMBER 4, 1838 . . .

PROVIDENCE: KNOWLES, VOSE & COMPANY. 1838.

⟨i-ii⟩, ⟨1⟩-25. 9⅛″ × 5¾″.

⟨-⟩¹, ⟨1⟩-3⁴, ⟨5⟩¹.

Printed paper wrapper; blue, green noted.

Listed NAR Jan. 1840.

BPL H NYPL Y

14889. First Exhibition and Fair of the Maine Charitable Mechanic Association, Held at the City Hall, in the City of Portland, from Sept. 24 to Oct. 6, 1838.

Portland: Published by the Board of Managers, for the Association. 1838.

Printed paper wrapper.

"Address," pp. ⟨61⟩-80.

Note: P. ⟨61⟩ is a divisional title-page for the address: *An Address before the Maine Charitable Mechanic Association, September 26, 1838 . . .* , Portland: Printed by Charles Day & Co. for the Association. 1838. *Query:* Was the address also issued as a separate?

AAS B H UV

14890. Second Report on the Geology of the State of Maine. By Charles T. Jackson . . .

Augusta: Luther Severance, Printer. 1838.

Printed paper wrapper?

"Some statistical matter . . . furnished through the kindness of John Neal . . ."---P. 111.

H

14891. Tales of the Grotesque and Arabesque. By Edgar A. Poe . . . in Two Volumes . . .

Philadelphia: Lea and Blanchard. 1840.

One-sentence opinion, Vol. 2, p. ii.

For fuller entry see No. 10154.

14892. APPEAL FROM THE AMERICAN PRESS TO THE AMERICAN PEOPLE. IN BEHALF OF JOHN BRATISH ELIOVICH, LATE A MAJOR GENERAL IN THE SERVICE OF HER MOST CATHOLIC MAJESTY, THE QUEEN OF SPAIN . . . AND NOW AN AMERICAN CITIZEN . . .

PRINTED AT THE ARGUS OFFICE, PORTLAND MAINE. 1840.

Cover-title.

⟨1⟩-48. 9½″ × 6¼″.

⟨1⟩-6⁴.

Printed self-wrapper.

Issued after April 27, 1840; see p. 16.

AAS H NYPL

14893. The Envoy. From Free Hearts to the Free . . .

Pawtucket, R.I. Published by the Juvenile Eman. Society. 1840.

Edited anonymously by Mrs. Frances H. W. G. McDougall.

"The Instinct of Childhood," pp. 42-53.

Issued after Aug. 25, 1840. See p. 68.

H

14894. Logan, the Mingo Chief. A Family History. By the Author of "Seventy-Six." . . .

London: Published by J. Cunningham, Crown-Court, Fleet-Street, and Sold by All Booksellers. 1840.

Printed paper wrapper?

A reprint of *Logan, a Family History,* 1822.

BPL UP

14895. American Melodies . . . Compiled by George P. Morris . . .

New-York: Published by Linen and Fennell, No. 229 Broadway. 1841.

"Woman! I've Held Thy Hand in Mine," pp. 142-143.

For fuller entry see No. 997.

14896. John Beedle's Sleigh Ride, Courtship, and Marriage. Attributed to ⟨*i.e.*, by⟩ Capt. ⟨William L.⟩ M'Clintock . . .

New York: Published by C. Wells. 1841.

Printed paper boards, cloth shelf back. Also issued in printed paper wrapper.

Revised by Neal. For comment see Neal's *Wandering Recollections*, p. 342.

AAS   H   LC   MHS   NYPL

14897. Songs, Odes, and Other Poems, on National Subjects; Compiled from Various Sources. By Wm. McCarty. Part Third--- Military . . .

Philadelphia: Published by Wm. McCarty, No. 27 North Fifth Street. 1842.

Reprint save for "Bunker's Hill," pp. 95-97.

For fuller entry see No. 4830.

14898. The Sinless Child, and Other Poems, by Elizabeth Oakes Smith. Edited by John Keese.

Wiley & Putnam, New York. W. D. Ticknor, Boston. M DCCC XLIII.

"Elizabeth Oakes Smith," pp. ⟨xv⟩-xxvi.

Boards, paper label on spine.

BPL   H

14899. The Works of Jeremy Bentham, Published under the Superintendence of His Executor, John Bowring . . .

Edinburgh: William Tait, 107, Prince's Street; Simpkin, Marshall, & Co., London. MDCCCXL-III.

11 Vols.

Brief contributions, Vol. 9, pp. 648, 661-662; letter, *Portland, Maine, 25th July, 1827*, Vol. 10, pp. 573-574, Neal to Bentham.

H

14900. A Pictorial History of England by S. G. Goodrich . . .

Philadelphia: Published by Sorin & Ball, and Samuel Agnew, No. 42 North Fourth Street. 1846.

Boards, leather shelf back.

Two testimonials, dated Feb. 21, 1845; and, May 14, 1845, p. 8 of the second series of terminal advertisements.

Deposited Oct. 25, 1845.

NYPL

14901. The Mayflower. For M DCCC XLVII . . . Edited by Mrs. E. Oakes Smith . . .

Boston: Published by Saxton & Kelt. 1847.

"My Child! My Child!," pp. 112-113.

For fuller entry see No. 8561.

14902. Friendship's Gift: A Souvenir for MDCCC-XLVIII. Edited by Walter Percival.

Boston: Published by John P. Hill. 1848.

Leather?

"Will the Wizard," pp. ⟨16⟩-36.

Reissued as *The Lady's Gift*, Nashua, 1849.

H   NYPL

14903. The Memorial: Written by Friends of the Late Mrs. Osgood and Edited by Mary E. Hewitt . . .

New-York: George P. Putnam, 155 Broadway. 1851.

"Inscription," p. ⟨iii⟩.

The vignette title-page occurs with the date 1851; and, with some evidence of reengraving present, dated 1852. For further comment see entry No. 1187.

14904. The Dew-Drop: A Tribute of Affection. For MDCCCLII.

Philadelphia: Lippincott, Grambo & Co. 1852.

"Phantasmagoria," pp. ⟨153⟩-170. Listed in the table of contents as at p. 152.

For comment see entry No. 1188.

14905. The Proceedings of the Woman's Rights Convention, Held at Syracuse, September 8th, 9th & 10th, 1852.

Syracuse: Printed by J. E. Masters, No. 26, Malcolm Block. 1852.

Printed paper wrapper.

Letter, obviously meant for publication, dated *Portland, July 28, 1852*, pp. 24-28.

H   NYPL

14906. ONE WORD MORE

Noted in the following forms. The order is presumed correct.

TENTATIVE ISSUE A

ONE WORD MORE : / INTENDED FOR / THE REASONING AND THOUGHTFUL / AMONG / UNBELIEVERS. / ⟨*rule*⟩ /

⟨*3 (sic) lines from Ezekiel*⟩ | ⟨*rule*⟩ | BY JOHN NEAL./ ⟨*rule*⟩ | PORTLAND, MAINE: | PRINTED FOR THE AUTHOR, AND FOR SALE AT THE BOOKSTORES. | 1854.

⟨1⟩-211. $7\frac{7}{16}''$ × $4\frac{1}{2}''$. Note presence of folio 211.

⟨-⟩², 1-17⁶, 81² ⟨*sic*⟩. P. 57 missigned 4*; should be 5*.

T cloth: black. Sides blindstamped with a rules frame, a floral filigree at each inner corner. Spine stamped in gold save as noted: ONE | WORD | MORE. | ⟨*rule*⟩ | JOHN NEAL Spine decorated with an arrangment of blindstamped rules. Yellow end papers. Flyleaves.

On copyright page: *Ira Berry, Printer.*

P. 9: Running head: ATL . . .

Location: AAS

TENTATIVE ISSUES B and Ba

ONE WORD MORE: | INTENDED FOR | THE REASONING AND THOUGHTFUL | AMONG | UNBELIEVERS. | ⟨*rule*⟩ | *3 (sic) lines from Ezekiel*⟩ | ⟨*rule*⟩ | BY JOHN NEAL. | ⟨*rule*⟩ | BOSTON: | PUBLISHED BY CROCKER & BREWSTER, | 47 WASHINGTON STREET. | 1854.

⟨1⟩-211. $7\frac{3}{8}''$ scant × $4\frac{9}{16}''$. Note presence of folio 211.

⟨-⟩², 1-17⁶, 18². Signature 18 so signed; the signature is set below the *low* in *lowliest.* P. 57 missigned 4*; should be 5*.

T cloth: black; brownish-black. Sides blindstamped with a rules frame, a floral filigree at each inner corner. Spine stamped in gold save as noted: ONE | WORD | MORE. | ⟨*rule*⟩ | JOHN NEAL Spine decorated with an arrangement of blindstamped rules. Yellow end papers. Flyleaves.

On copyright page: *Ira Berry, Printer.*

Issue B: P. 9, running head: ATL . . .

Issue Ba: P. 9, running head: ALL . . .

H (Issue B) UV (Issue Ba, inscribed by Neal *Jany 1/56*)

TENTATIVE ISSUE C

ONE WORD MORE: | INTENDED FOR | THE REASONING AND THOUGHTFUL | AMONG | UNBELIEVERS. | ⟨*rule*⟩ | *4 (sic) lines from Ezekiel*⟩ | ⟨*rule*⟩ | BY JOHN NEAL. | ⟨*rule*⟩ | PORTLAND, MAINE. | ⟨1854⟩

⟨1⟩-211. $7\frac{3}{8}''$ × $4\frac{1}{2}''$ scant. Note presence of folio 211.

⟨-⟩², 1-17⁶, 18². Signature 18 so signed; the signature is set below the *st*⟨*space*⟩ of *lowliest.* P. 57 missigned 4*; should be 5*.

Brown morocco. Sides blindstamped with a rules frame, a floral filigree at each inner corner. *Note:* The side stamping is identical with that on the cloth binding of *Tentative Issue A.* Spine stamped in gold: ONE | WORD | MORE | J. NEAL Spine also

stamped with an arrangement of rules in gold and blind. White end papers printed in red and gold with an all-over pattern. Double flyleaves. Edges stained red.

On copyright page: *Ira Berry, Printer, Portland.*

P. 9: Running head: ALL . . .

H (inscribed by Neal to Longfellow July 22, 1854. In the inscription Neal states, in part, *not yet published.*)

TENTATIVE ISSUE D

ONE WORD MORE: | INTENDED FOR | THE REASONING AND THOUGHTFUL | AMONG | UNBELIEVERS. | ⟨*rule*⟩ | ⟨*4 (sic) lines from Ezekiel*⟩ | ⟨*rule*⟩ | BY JOHN NEAL. | ⟨*rule*⟩ | PORTLAND, MAINE. | ⟨1854⟩

⟨1⟩-⟨211⟩. $7\frac{3}{8}''$ × $4\frac{1}{2}''$ scant. *Note:* Folio 211 is absent or present as a ghost.

⟨-⟩², 1-17⁶, 18². Signature 18 so signed; the signature is set below the *st*⟨*space*⟩ of *lowliest.* P. 57 missigned 4*; should be 5*.

Special binding for the author? TR-like blackish-green cloth sides, black morocco shelf back and corners. Spine lettered in gold: ONE | WORD | MORE Edges sprinkled. White end papers printed in metallic green (oxidized gold?) with an all-over pattern. Double flyleaves.

On copyright page: *Ira Berry, Printer, Portland.*

P. 9: Running head: ALL . . .

UV (Inscribed by Neal *June 24/54*)

For second edition see next entry.

14907. One Word More: An Appeal to the Reasoning and Thoughtful among Unbelievers . . . Second Edition.

New York: Published by M. W. Dodd, Brick Church Chapel, City Hall Square, 1856.

Extended edition. For first edition see preceding entry.

Cloth?

Deposited Nov. 28, 1855. Listed APC Dec. 22, 1855.

LC

14908. Consistent Democracy. The Elective Franchise for Women. Twenty-Five Testimonies of Prominent Men . . .

Worcester . . . Boston . . . New York . . . Salem, O. . . . Rochester, N. Y. . . . Worcester, Mass. 1858.

Single cut sheet, folded to make four pages.

Statement, p. 3. *Note:* Part of the statement had prior publication in Neal's letter of July 28, 1852;

see *The Proceedings of the Woman's Rights Convention … 1852*, above, under year 1852.

LC

14909. The Past, Present and Future of the City of Cairo, in North America: With Reports, Estimates and Statistics. By a Committee of the Shareholders, September 29, 1858.

Portland: Printed by Brown Thurston. 1858.

Printed paper wrapper.

Neal's name appears on p. 52 as a member of the committee.

H

14910. TRUE WOMANHOOD: A TALE …

BOSTON: TICKNOR AND FIELDS. M DCCC LIX.

⟨i⟩-iv, ⟨5⟩-487. 7⅝″ full × 4¹⁵/₁₆″.

⟨1⟩-30⁸, 31⁴.

BD cloth: purple. L-like cloth: brown. TZ cloth: blue. Brown-coated end papers. Flyleaves. In some copies there is an inserted terminal catalog, pp. 16, dated *November, 1859*.

According to the publisher's records 2000 copies were printed Nov. 17, 1859; by May 30, 1860 1700 copies had been put in binding; the remaining 300 copies were bound June 1, 1864.

Under the title *Womanhood* announced BM July 1, 1859. Deposited Nov. 17, 1859. Listed BM Dec. 1, 1859. Listed as an American book PC Dec. 31, 1859; Feb. 15, 1860.

B NYPL UV Y

14911. The Rebellion Record: A Diary of American Events … Edited by Frank Moore … First Volume …

New York: G. P. Putnam. C. T. Evans, General Agent. 1861.

"Battle Anthem," p. 119.

For comment see entry No. 11531.

14912. … Why the Shoe Pinches; a Contribution to Applied Anatomy, by Hermann Meyer … Translated from the German by John Stirling Craig …

American Edition: By J. C. Plumer, M. D., Boston, Mass. ⟨1861⟩

Probably issued in printed paper wrapper.

At head of title: *Procrustes Ante Portas.*

Pp. 24, plus an appendix paged 1-8.

Testimonial reprinted from the *Portland Transcript* of Jan. 26, 1861, p. 6 of the appendix.

Letter of recommendation, addressed to Dr. John C. Plumer, dated Portland, Maine, Dec. 21, 1861, p. 7 of the appendix.

EM

14913. THE WHITE-FACED PACER: OR, BEFORE AND AFTER THE BATTLE …

NEW YORK: BEADLE AND COMPANY, PUBLISHERS, 118 WILLIAM STREET. ⟨1863⟩

⟨5⟩-100. 6⅜″ × 4³/₁₆″.

⟨1⟩-3¹⁶.

Beadle's Library of Choice Fiction, No. 1.

Printed pale buff paper wrapper.

Published Jan. 12, 1864 (Johannsen). Listed ALG Jan. 15, 1864. Reissued 1883 as No. 535 in *Beadle's New Dime Novels* series. According to Johannsen (Vol. 1, p. 339) reissued 1890 as *Beadle's Boy's Library of Sport*, No. 319, under the title *Deacon Hale's Grit; or, Ebenezer Day's Mad Ride*.

H

14914. Cloud Crystals; a Snow-Flake Album. Collected and Edited by a Lady ⟨Mrs. Frances E. Chickering⟩ …

New York: D. Appleton & Company, 443 & 445 Broadway. London: 16 Little Britain. 1864.

"The Blossoming Skies," p. ⟨42⟩.

Cloth; cloth, gilt extra; morocco.

Listed ALG Dec. 1, 1863.

H NYPL

14915. Autograph Leaves of Our Country's Authors. ⟨Compiled by John Pendleton Kennedy and Alexander Bliss⟩

Baltimore, Cushings & Bailey 1864.

"Our Battle-flag———Hurrah!," pp. 175-176.

For fuller entry see No. 2418.

14916. THE MOOSE-HUNTER; OR, LIFE IN THE MAINE WOODS …

NEW YORK: BEADLE AND COMPANY, PUBLISHERS, 118 WILLIAM STREET. ⟨1864⟩

Two printings noted; the sequence presented is presumed correct:

PRINTING A

⟨5⟩-125; blank, p. ⟨126⟩; advertisements, pp. ⟨127-132⟩. The advertisements paged 19-24. Frontispiece. 6⅜″ × 4³/₁₆″.

⟨1⟩-4¹⁶. *Note:* Sig. 2 is erroneously marked 73 (of the series) for 72.

PRINTING B

⟨5⟩-100. Frontispiece. 6⅜″ × 4⅛″ full.

⟨1⟩-3¹⁶. *Note*: Sig. 2 is erroneously marked 73 (of the series) for 72.

Printed orange paper wrapper. Inner front: . . . *Beadle's Dime Novels, No. 73, to Issue Tuesday, September 27th* . . .

Listed ALG Sept. 15, 1864, *100 pages*. Listed Bkr Sept. 30, 1864, *125 pages*. A Clarke (London) edition listed Bkr May 31, 1865.

Also reprinted and reissued *ca.* 1880 imprinted: *New York: Beadle and Adams, Publishers, No. 98 William Street.* ⟨*1864*⟩. Issued as *Beadle's New Dime Novels*, No. 162 (New Series); No. 483 (Old Series). 100 pp.

AAS (*Printing B*) H (*Printing A*) UV (*Printing B*) Y (*Printing B*)

14917. The Boatswain's Whistle. Published at the National Sailors' Fair . . .

Boston, November 9-19, 1864.

"The Men of the Sea," No. 8, p. 62.

For comment see entry No. 1416.

14918. The Emerald. A Collection of Graphic and Entertaining Tales, Brilliant Poems and Essays, Gleaned Chiefly from Fugitive Literature of the Nineteenth Century.

Boston: John L. Shorey, 13 Washington Street. New York: W. I. Pooley. Philadelphia: J. B. Lippincott & Co. 1866.

Edited by Epes Sargent. Issued in both cloth; and, paper.

"Goody Gracious! And the Forget-Me-Not," pp. ⟨19⟩-33. "Published originally in 1839, this charmingly told tale has been revised by the author for the *Library Series*." Originally in *New-York Mirror*, March 23, 1839.

Advertised for May 15, 1866, ALG May 15, 1866, as in paper and cloth. Listed (cloth only) ALG June 15, 1866.

H UV

14919. LITTLE MOCCASIN; OR, ALONG THE MADAWASKA. A STORY OF LIFE AND LOVE IN THE LUMBER REGION . . .

NEW YORK: BEADLE AND COMPANY, PUBLISHERS, 118 WILLIAM STREET. ⟨1866⟩

⟨5⟩-100. Frontispiece. 6⁵⁄₁₆″ × 4⅛″.

⟨1⟩-3¹⁶.

Issued as *Beadle's Dime Novels*, No. 96.

Printed orange paper wrapper. Inner front: . . . *No. 97, to Issue Tuesday, May 15th* . . . *The Doomed Hunter* . . .

The front wrapper noted with the following added imprints:

American News Co., 121 Nassau St., N. Y.

Irving & Thompson, Toronto, C. W.

Near & Co., Albany, N. Y.

L. J. Noros, 25 So. Main St., Fall River, Mass.

Augustus Robinson, Portland, Me. (A deposit copy imprinted thus.)

A. Williams & Co., 100 Wash'n St., Boston.

Winter Bros., Rondout and Kingston, N. Y.

Announced ALG May 1, 1866. Deposited June 27, 1866. Listed PC Dec. 31, 1866. Reissued in London, 1867, as *Beadle's American Library*, No. 71. Reissued 1879 as No. 451 in *Beadle's New Dime Novels* series.

AAS H LC UV Y

14920. ACCOUNT OF THE GREAT CONFLAGRATION IN PORTLAND, JULY 4th & 5th, 1866, BY JOHN NEAL; AND A NEW BUSINESS GUIDE, GIVING REMOVALS, CHANGES IN BUSINESS, &c.

PORTLAND: COMPILED AND PUBLISHED BY STARBIRD & TWITCHELL. 1866. MONITOR PRINT., 174 MIDDLE ST.

⟨1⟩-32; advertisements, pp. 33-64; *Business Guide and Advertising Index*, pp. ⟨i⟩-viii. 9¼″ × 5⅝″.

⟨1⁸, 2-8⁴⟩.

Printed paper wrapper: faun; gray. Inserted at front is a leaf of salmon paper imprinted with advertisements; inserted at back are two leaves of salmon paper imprinted with advertisements.

Note: In all examined copies the advertisement for Benson & Houghton, p. 53, is inverted.

Also note: In a copy in H there is an inserted folded map of "The Great Fire at Portland July 4th 1866." Imprinted: *Published by Bufford Brothers Boston & New York & S. B. Beckett Portland. Query:* Were some copies issued with the map? Or is the single copy noted the result of an insertion by the original owner of the publication?

Issued during the period Sept. 10-Oct. 22, 1866.

AAS B H MHS NYPL Y

14921. WANDERING RECOLLECTIONS OF A SOMEWHAT BUSY LIFE. AN AUTOBIOGRAPHY . . .

BOSTON: ROBERTS BROTHERS. 1869.

⟨i⟩-viii, ⟨1⟩-431. Laid paper. 6¹³⁄₁₆″ × 4⅝″ scant.

⟨1⁴, 2-19¹²⟩. *Signed:* ⟨-⟩⁴, ⟨1⟩-27⁸.

C cloth: green; purple; terra-cotta. Brown-coated end papers. Laid paper flyleaves.

Deposited June 25, 1869. BA copy received June 29, 1869. Listed ALG July 15, 1869.

AAS B UV Y

14922. GREAT MYSTERIES AND LITTLE PLAGUES . . .

BOSTON: ROBERTS BROTHERS. 1870.

⟨i⟩-⟨vi⟩, 7-271. Frontispiece inserted. 6$\frac{9}{16}$″ × 4$\frac{3}{8}$″.

⟨1⟩-17^8.

C cloth: green; purple; terra-cotta. Brown-coated on white end papers. Flyleaves.

Announced ALG Aug. 2, 1869. Advertised for November ALG Nov. 1, 1869. Listed ALG Dec. 1, 1869. Deposited Dec. 28, 1869.

AAS B H Y

14923. The Pellet . . .

Boston: Published by the Fair. 1872 . . .

An occasional newspaper. For fuller comment see entry No. 169.

"Language," No. 1, p. 10.

14924. PORTLAND ILLUSTRATED . . .

PORTLAND: W. S. JONES, PUBLISHER. 1874.

⟨1⟩-⟨151⟩; advertisements, pp. 152-160. Frontispiece inserted; other illustrations in text. 8$\frac{1}{16}$″ × 5$\frac{3}{4}$″ (paper). 8$\frac{1}{8}$″ × 5$\frac{3}{4}$″ (cloth).

⟨1⟩-3, ⟨4-5⟩, 6-7, ⟨8-10⟩^{8}.

Printed gray-blue paper wrapper. S cloth: brown; green; purple; terra-cotta; green-coated end papers; flyleaves. Inserted at the front of the paper-bound copies is a 2-leaf advertisement.

B BPL H LC Y

14925. Edgar Allan Poe A Memorial Volume by Sara Sigourney Rice.

Baltimore: Turnbull Brothers. 1877.

Letter, Nov. 3, 1875, p. 89.

For comment see entry No. 1757.

14926. The Poets of Maine . . . Compiled by George Bancroft Griffith

Portland, Maine Elwell, Pickard & Company Transcript Job Print Edward Small, Binder 1888

Reprint save for "Cape Cottage," pp. 41-42.

Listed PW June 23, 1888.

H NYPL UV

14927. Bob Gage's Crew; or, the Boys of Logger-Camp.

New York: Beadle and Adams, 1889.

Not located. Not seen. Entry from Johannsen, Vol. 1, p. 337.

Printed paper wrapper. *Beadle's Boy's Library of Sport*, No. 256. Issued March 9, 1889.

A reprint of *Little Moccasin* . . . ⟨1866⟩.

14928. Uncle Jerry, the Quaker; or, the Schoolmaster's Trial.

New York: Beadle and Adams, 1889.

Not located. Not seen. Entry from Johannsen, Vol. 1, p. 337.

Printed paper wrapper. *Beadle's Boy's Library of Sport*, No. 264. Issued May 4, 1889.

A reprint of *The Moose-Hunter* . . . ⟨1864⟩.

14929. Deacon Hale's Grit; or, Ebenezer Day's Mad Ride.

New York: Beadle and Adams, 1890.

Not located. Not seen. Entry from Johannsen, Vol. 1, p. 339.

Printed paper wrapper. *Beadle's Boy's Library of Sport*, No. 319. Issued May 24, 1890.

A reprint of *The White-Faced Pacer* . . . ⟨1863⟩.

14930. The Eighth Year Book 1909 The Bibliophile Society Printed for Members Only

⟨Boston, 1909⟩

Boards, printed paper label on spine.

500 copies only.

Extracts from Neal's contributions to the *Yankee and Literary Gazette*, pp. 32-33.

H NYPL

14931. A Down-East Yankee from the District of Maine by Windsor Daggett

Published by A. J. Huston, Portland, Maine 1920

Printed paper wrapper.

All selections from Neal are here reprinted with the possible exception of:

"Rights of Women. The Substance of a Lecture Delivered by John Neal at the Broadway Tabernacle, January 24, 1843," pp. 41-51. Originally in *Brother Jonathan* (N.Y.) June 17, 1843.

"Sketches of the Five American Presidents and of the Five Presidential Candidates," pp. 24-27. Originally in *Blackwood's Edinburgh Magazine*, May, 1824.

B BA H NYPL

14932. William Cullen Bryant Representative Selections, with Introduction, Bibliography, and Notes by Tremaine McDowell . . .

American Book Company New York Cincinnati Chicago Boston Atlanta ⟨1935⟩

On copyright page of first printing: W. P. I.

Section on Bryant from an article, "American Writers," pp. 365-366; originally in *Blackwood's Edinburgh Magazine*, Sept. 1824. Collected in *American Writers* . . . , 1937, pp. 42-43.

Deposited June 15, 1935.

H Y

14933. AMERICAN WRITERS   A SERIES OF PAPERS CONTRIBUTED TO BLACK-WOOD'S MAGAZINE (1824–1825) BY JOHN NEAL EDITED . . . BY FRED LEWIS PATTEE

DURHAM NORTH CAROLINA DUKE UNIVERSITY PRESS 1937

⟨i⟩-viii, ⟨1⟩-261, blank leaf. 9″ × 6″ full. Wove paper watermarked *Suede Finish*.

⟨1-17⁸⟩.

V cloth: tan.

BPL copy received April 6, 1937. Deposited June 22, 1937.

B BPL H LC NYPL Y

14934. JOHN NEAL TO EDGAR A. POE

YSLETA EDWIN B. HILL 1942

⟨1-5⟩, blank leaf. Laid paper watermarked *Clear Spring Text*. 7½″ × 5″ full.

⟨-⟩⁴.

Printed yellow laid paper wrapper. *Note:* The sheets are either laid in loosely; or, sewn in. *Also:* Unprinted blue paper wrapper. Flyleaves in some copies.

A letter to Poe dated *Portland, June 8, '40*, p. 4.

H LC NYPL Y

14935. OBSERVATIONS ON AMERICAN ART   SELECTIONS FROM THE WRITINGS OF JOHN NEAL (1793–1876) EDITED . . . BY HAROLD EDWARD DICKSON . . .

THE PENNSYLVANIA STATE COLLEGE STATE COLLEGE, PENNSYLVANIA ⟨1943⟩

⟨i⟩-⟨xxviii⟩, 1-115. Frontispiece and 5 double-faced plates inserted. 8¹¹⁄₁₆″ × 5¹³⁄₁₆″ full.

⟨1-9⁸⟩.

Printed cream-yellow paper wrapper. On front: *The Pennsylvania State College Bulletin   The Pennsylvania State College Studies No. 12* . . .

". . . From a scholarly point of view the most worth while of Neal's writings on art are his early pieces in *Randolph, Blackwood's* and *The Yankee*. All of these have been included in the present selection except certain fragmentary items scattered through *The Yankee* of 1828. I have not searched exhaustively for later work. The paper *Brother Jonathan*, for example, contains other art material, particularly exhibition reviews that are probably Neal's . . ."–––P. iii.

AAS B BPL H NYPL Y

REPRINTS

The following publications contain material by John Neal reprinted from earlier books.

Stories of American Life; by American Writers. Edited by Mary Russell Mitford. In Three Vols. . . .

London: Henry Colburn and Richard Bentley, New Burlington Street. 1830.

Advertised for publication "in the course of a few days" LG July 17, 24, 31, 1830. Advertised as "nearly ready" LG Aug. 14, Nov. 20, Nov. 27, 1830. Listed MR Sept. 1830. Reviewed LG Nov. 27, 1830. Advertised as "just published" LG Dec. 4, 1830. Listed LG Dec. 4, 1830. Reviewed Ath Feb. 19, 1831.

Note: Pattee (*American Writers . . . John Neal . . .* , 1937, p. 253) gives the following title: *Lights and Shadows of America*, by Mary Russll ⟨sic⟩ Mitford, 1832. Not found by BAL. A reissue of *Stories of American Life?*

A Practical Grammar of the English Language . . . Second Edition, Improved. By Roscoe G. Greene.

Portland: Published by Shirley and Hyde, Exchange-Street. 1830.

Paper boards, leather shelf back.

The American Common-Place Book of Poetry . . . by George B. Cheever.

Boston . . . 1831.

For fuller entry see No. 1330.

A Practical Grammar of the English Language . . . Third Edition, Revised and Improved. By Roscoe G. Greene.

Portland: G. Hyde and Company, Exchange-Street. 1832.

Lights and Shadows of America. By Mary Russll ⟨sic⟩ Mitford.

1832.

Not located. See *Stories of American Life . . .* , 1830, above.

A Grammatical Text-Book . . . by Roscoe G. Greene.

Boston . . . 1833.

For fuller entry see No. 12052.

Readings in Poetry . . .

London . . . MDCCCXXXIII.

For comment see BAL, Vol. 1, p. 370.

"Day-Break," pp. 389-390, extracted from *Battle of Niagara* . . . , 1818.

The Rosary . . .

Boston . . . 1834.

"Ordination Hymn," p. 167; otherwise "Hymn, (Sung at the Late Ordination of Mr. Pierpont in Boston)," in *The Battle of Niagara: Second Edition*, 1819.

For fuller entry see No. 3263.

Selections from the American Poets . . .

Dublin . . . 1834.

For comment see BAL, Vol. 2, p. 397.

The Columbian Bard . . . by the Editor of "The Bard," etc.

London . . . 1835.

For comment see BAL, Vol. 5, p. 591.

"Night," pp. 197-198, extracted from *Battle of Niagara* . . . , 1818.

A Practical Grammar of the English Language . . . Fourth Edition, Improved. By Roscoe G. Greene.

Portland: Published by William Hyde, for Z. Hyde. 1835.

Paper boards, leather shelf back. Copyright notice dated 1833.

The Laurel . . .

Boston . . . 1836.

For comment see entry No. 984.

Gems from American Poets.

London . . . M DCCC XXXVI.

For comment see BAL, Vol. 2, p. 397.

The Poets of America . . . Edited by John Keese.

New York . . . 1840.

For comment see BAL, Vol. 1, pp. 232-233.

Selections from the American Poets. By William Cullen Bryant.

New-York . . . 1840.

For comment see entry No. 1617.

"The Soldier's Visit to His Family," pp. 246-248, reprinted from *Battle of Niagara* . . . , 1818.

The Poets of America . . . Edited by John Keese. [Volume Second of the Series.]

New York . . . 1842.

For comment see entry No. 3280.

The Poets and Poetry of America . . . by Rufus W. Griswold . . .

Philadelphia . . . MDCCCXLII.

For comment see entry No. 6644.

Gems from American Poets . . .

New-York . . . ⟨1842⟩

For comment see entry No. 5193.

The Anti-Slavery Picknick: A Collection of Speeches, Poems, Dialogues and Songs . . . by John A. Collins.

Boston: H. W. Williams, 25 Cornhill. New-York . . . Philadelphia . . . MDCCCXLII.

Printed paper wrapper.

Songs, Odes, and Other Poems, on National Subjects; Compiled from Various Sources. By Wm. McCarty. Part Second––– Naval . . .

Philadelphia: Published by Wm. McCarty, No. 27 North Fifth Street. 1842.

"Perry's Victory," pp. 346-347, extracted from *Battle of Niagara: Second Edition* . . . , 1819.

Voices of the True-Hearted . . .

Philadelphia . . . ⟨1844–1846⟩

For fuller description see entry No. 12072.

The Poet's Gift . . . Edited by John Keese.

Boston . . . 1845.

For fuller entry see BAL, Vol. 1, p. 206.

The Prose Writers of America . . . by Rufus Wilmot Griswold . . .

Philadelphia . . . 1847.

For comment see entry Nos. 3158, 6676.

Note: F. L. Pattee in Neal's *American Writers* . . . , 1937, p. 253, comments: "The biographical introduction perhaps written by Neal himself;" further information wanting.

The Young Ladies' Oasis: Or, Gems of Prose and Poetry. Edited by N. L. Fergurson ⟨sic⟩ . . .

    Lowell: Nathaniel L. Dayton. 1851.

    "Friendship," p. 117, extracted from "Delphian Ode," *Battle of Niagara: Second Edition* . . . , 1819, p. 237.

The Young Ladies' Oasis: Or, Gems of Prose and Poetry. Edited by N. L. Fergurson ⟨sic⟩ . . . Second Edition.

    Lowell: Nathaniel L. Dayton, 1851.

    Leather.

The Young Ladies' Oasis: Or, Gems of Prose and Poetry. Edited by N. L. Fergurson ⟨sic⟩ . . . Third Edition.

    Lowell: Nathaniel L. Dayton. 1851.

The Oasis: Or, Golden Leaves of Friendship. Edited by N. L. Ferguson . . .

    Lowell: Nathaniel L. Dayton. 1852.

The Oasis: Or, Golden Leaves of Friendship. Edited by N. L. Ferguson . . .

    Boston: Dayton and Wentworth, 86 Washington Street. 1853.

The Native Poets of Maine. By S. Herbert Lancey . . .

    Bangor . . . 1854.

    For fuller entry see No. 12107.

Laurel Leaves . . . Edited by Mary E. Hewitt . . .

    New York . . . 1854.

    For comment see BAL, Vol. 2, p. 496.

The Oasis: Or, Golden Leaves of Friendship. Edited by N. L. Ferguson . . .

    Boston: Dayton and Wentworth, 86 Washington Street. 1854.

Lilies and Violets . . . by Rosalie Bell . . .

    New York . . . 1855.

    For comment see entry No. 1658.

    "The Lesson of Childhood," pp. 301-303; extracted from "Children . . . ," *The Token*, 1835.

The Oasis . . . Edited by N. L. Ferguson . . .

    Boston . . . 1855.

    For fuller entry see BAL, Vol. 5, p. 598.

The Gift Book of Gems . . .

    Bangor David Bugbee & Co. ⟨1856⟩

    All Neal material herein reprinted from other books. "Shakespeare's Tomb," p. ⟨132⟩, extracted from "Will the Wizard," *Friendship's Gift*, 1848.

War Songs of the American Union . . .

    Boston . . . ⟨1861⟩

    For fuller entry see No. 8804.

    "The American Eagle," pp. 55-56, extracted from *Battle of Niagara* . . . , 1818.

Songs of the War . . .

    Albany . . . 1863.

    For comment see entry No. 259.

    "Battle Anthem," p. 55; attributed here to *John Neil*.

Lyrics of Loyalty . . . Edited by Frank Moore

    New York . . . 1864

    For comment see entry No. 1203.

Golden Leaves from the American Poets Collected by John W. S. Hows . . .

    New York: George Routledge and Sons, 416 Broome Street. ⟨1864; *i.e.*, not before 1866⟩

Golden Leaves from the American Poets Collected by John W. S. Hows

    New York James G. Gregory 540 Broadway M DCCC LXV

    Reprinted with the imprint: *New York Bunce and Huntington* M DCCC LXV

    All Neal material herein reprinted from other books. "Music of the Night," pp. 117-118, extracted from *Battle of Niagara: Second Edition* . . . , 1819.

The Flower of Liberty. Edited . . . by Julia A. M. Furbish.

    Boston . . . 1866.

    For comment see entry No. 1424.

    "The War-Eagle," pp. 64-65, extracted from *Battle of Niagara* . . . , 1818.

Anecdotes, Poetry and Incidents of the War . . . Arranged by Frank Moore . . .

    New York . . . 1866.

    For comment see entry No. 3202.

The Golden Gift A Book for the Young . . .

Edinburgh . . . ⟨1868⟩

For comment see entry No. 4257.

"What Are Children?," pp. 104-108; extracted from "Children . . . ," *The Token*, 1835.

The Golden Gift A Book for the Young . . .

New York . . . ⟨1868⟩

For comment see entry No. 4258.

"What Are Children?," pp. 104-108; extracted from "Children . . . ," *The Token*, 1835.

The Flower of Liberty. Edited and Illustrated by Julia A. M. Furbish.

Cincinnati, Ohio: White, Corbin, Bouve & Company, No. 124 Walnut Street. 1869.

Public and Parlor Readings . . . Humorous. Edited by Lewis B. Monroe.

Boston . . . 1871.

For comment see entry No. 1550.

"A Dry Experiment," pp. 154-156; extracted from *Wandering Recollections*, 1869, p. 45.

Public and Parlor Readings . . . Miscellaneous. Edited by Lewis B. Monroe.

Boston . . . 1872.

For fuller entry see BAL, Vol. 5, p. 318.

"My Experience in Elocution," pp. 268-271; extracted from *Wandering Recollections*, 1869, p. 29.

The Poets and Poetry of America. By Rufus Wilmot Griswold . . . Revised . . .

New York . . . 1873.

For fuller entry see No. 9565.

A Hand-Book of English Literature. Intended for the Use of High Schools . . . by Francis H. Underwood, A. M. American Authors.

Boston: Lee and Shepard, Publishers. New York: Lee, Shepard and Dillingham. 1873.

. . . Little Classics. Edited by Rossiter Johnson. Childhood . . .

Boston: James R. Osgood and Company, Late Ticknor & Fields, and Fields, Osgood, & Co. 1875.

At head of title: *Tenth Volume.*

BA copy received April 29, 1875. Listed PW May 1, 1875.

Songs of Three Centuries. Edited by John Greenleaf Whittier.

Boston . . . 1876.

For comment see entry No. 11341.

Poems of Places Edited by Henry W. Longfellow . . . Switzerland and Austria.

Boston . . . 1877.

For fuller entry see No. 12190.

Poems of Places Edited by Henry W. Longfellow . . . America. Middle States.

Boston . . . 1879.

For fuller entry see No. 12211.

"Lake Ontario," pp. 177-178; extracted from *Battle of Niagara*, 1818, p. 39.

Harper's Cyclopædia of British and American Poetry Edited by Epes Sargent

New York . . . 1881

For comment see entry No. 4336.

An Old Scrap-Book. With Additions . . .

⟨Cambridge⟩ February 8, 1884.

For comment see entry No. 7763.

Mountain, Lake, and River . . . by N. P. Willis . . .

Boston . . . 1884.

For comment see BAL, Vol. 3, p. 253.

Half-Hours with the Best Humorous Authors. Selected and Arranged by Charles Morris . . .

Philadelphia: J. B. Lippincott Company. 1889.

4 Vols.

An American Anthology . . . Edited by Edmund Clarence Stedman . . .

Boston . . . M DCCCC

For comment see entry No. 3082.

REFERENCES AND ANA

Poems Written by Somebody; Most Respectfully Dedicated (By Permission) to Nobody; and Intended for Everybody Who Can Read!!!

London: Published at the Request of Several Persons of Distinction, by Baldwin and Co. 1818.

Unprinted paper boards. Paper label on spine? The only located copy lacks spine.

Sometimes attributed to Neal. Halkett & Laing attribute to Byron. Author not known to BAL.

Our Ephraim. A Play.

1821.

Thus Allibone. Further information wanting.

A Sketch of Old England, by a New-England Man . . .

New York, 1822.

Sabin (No. 52158) erroneously credits this publication to John Neal. The author was James Kirke Paulding.

⟨Craven Notice. By Edward Coote Pinkney⟩

Single leaf. Printed on recto only. 2¾″ full × 5″. Wove paper.

"The undersigned, having entered into some correspondence with the reputed author of *Randolph;* who is, or is not, sufficiently described as John Neal, a gentleman by indulgent courtesy . . . Edward C. Pinkney. Baltimore, Oct. 11, 1823." The only located copy is in UV.

See facsimile in BAL, Vol. 6. For comment see *Wandering Recollections,* 1869, pp. 229–235.

The Theatrical Mince Pie, Entirely Original. Containing a Correct Account of the Several Appearances of Mr. Kean amd ⟨sic⟩ Miss Foote, Since Their Late Actions in the Court of King's Bench; together with a Comical History of the Drama for the Last Eight Weeks, and Divers Diverting Articles. By Somebody, Gent.

London. 1825.

General title-page, as above, for a periodical issued in eight numbers, Jan. 1 to Feb. 19, 1825.

Sometimes attributed to Neal. BAL has found no evidence to support the suggestion.

⟨hand⟩ Bulletin Extra. Arrived, at Portland, on Saturday evening last, in the Steam-Boat, in a short passage from London, via New-York, the celebrated author of "Keep Cool," . . . July 12 ⟨1827⟩.

Handbill. 9¾″ × 8″. Text exclusive of heading and date at end, set in 14 lines. Printed on recto only. *See next entry.*

⟨hand⟩ Bulletin Extra. Arrived at Portland, on Saturday evening last, in the Steam Boat, in a short passage from London, via New-York, the infamous author of "Keep Cool," . . . July 12, 1827 . . .

Handbill. 9¾″ × 7⅞″. Text, exclusive of heading, in 21 lines. Printed on recto only. *See preceding entry.*

Both of the preceding are in the Neal collection in H. For Neal's comment on these handbills see his *Wandering Recollections,* 1869, pp. 329-330.

Authorship of these handbills not known to BAL. "Of course, I know the author of these two handbills; but, inasmuch as we have been on good terms for the last forty years, and I have never called him to account, holding that *tit-for-tat* is allowable in such controversies, I shall not give up his name . . ."--- *Wandering Recollections,* 1869, p. 330.

Popular Tracts. No. 7. Containing Effects of Missionary Labours; by Robert Dale Owen. And Religious Revivals; by John Neale ⟨sic⟩.

New-York: Published at the Office of the Free Enquirer. 1830.

Cover-title. Printed self-wrapper.

"Religious Revivals," pp. 8-10. First published under the title "Dr. Beecher," in *The Yankee: And Boston Literary Gazette,* Sept. 17, 1828, p. 301. Authorship assigned to James W. Miller, *The Yankee . . . ,* Oct. 8, 1828, p. 323.

. . . The Butchers of Ghent; or, el Maestro del Campo. A Romance of the Reign of Philip II. From the French of Felix Borgaerts. First American Edition. Translated by the Editor of the Brother Jonathan . . .

⟨New York⟩ Published by Wilson & Company, 162 Nassau-Street. ⟨July 9, 1842⟩

At head of title: *Double Sheet. Butchers of Ghent, Complete. Brother Jonathan . . .*

Printed yellow paper wrapper. At head of p. ⟨iii⟩: *Supplement to Brother Jonathan . . .* Issued as a supplement to Vol. II, No. 4.

Sometimes credited to John Neal. BAL has found no evidence to support the claim. According to LC the translation was done by H. Hastings Weld.

Ruth Elder: A Novel

Listed by Allibone as though issued in book form. Noted only in serial form as follows: In part only (Parts 1-3) in *The New Mirror,* New York, during the period June 3-17, 1843; complete, Parts 1-16, in *Brother Jonathan,* New York, during the period June 17 to Dec. 9, 1843.

Fimbleton Fumbleton, Esq., or the Nobleman Incog. A Mixtum, Gatherum, Omnium, in Twenty Chapters of Foolscap. By "Jim Nale, Gent." Author of Nothing.

Hanover, Pa., Printed by Joseph S. Gitt. 1844.

Unprinted paper boards, leather shelf back.

Sometimes attributed to John Neal. BAL has found no evidence to support the claim. Dr. William Kable, University of South Carolina, dismisses the attribution as "absurd."

Read! Read! The State Temperance Committee of Massachusetts, respectfully ask their fellow citizens of this Commonwealth, to read carefully the following document. Rev. Mr. Hadley, its author, is a Clergyman, and his integrity and veracity is unimpeachable. As will be seen, this paper utterly refutes the statements of John Neal, and others, who are endeavoring to persuade the people of this State that the Maine Law is a failure in the State of its birth . . .

⟨Boston (?), Mass. State Temperance Committee 1853⟩

Broadside. Printed on recto only. Prints a letter from Rev. W. H. Hadley to T. W. Higginson, arguing for the Maine Law. Also prints a circular of the State Temperance Committee.

The Spectre Ship of Salem   A Tale of a Naval Apparition of the Seventeenth Century . . .

Salem, Massachusetts December, 1907

Paper wrapper, printed paper label on front.

"Seventy-Six Copies Printed For George Francis Dow"---P. ⟨ii⟩.

". . . Published in *Blackwood's Magazine* (Edinburgh) for March, 1830, over the pseudonym *Nantucket* . . . Some authorities . . . have attributed the production to Hawthorne, but without specifying on what grounds . . . The sketch, if the work of an American writer,

might with a greater appearance of probability be attributed to John Neal, because of his long connection with *Blackwood's* . . ."---P. K. Foley in a prefatory note, pp. iv-v.

A Down-East Yankee from the District of Maine by Windsor Daggett

Published by A. J. Huston, Portland, Maine 1920

Printed paper wrapper. For fuller entry see above in *Section One*.

The Life and Works of John Neal   A Thesis Presented to the Faculty of Harvard University in Partial Fulfillment of the Requirements for the Degree of Doctor of Philosophy by Irving Trefethen Richards in Four Volumes . . .

Cambridge, Massachusetts 1932

Unpublished *ms* in H. See next entry.

Jahrbuch für Amerikastudien im Auftrag der Deutschen Gesellschaft für Amerikastudien Herausgegeben von Ernst Fraenkel, Hans Galinsky, Dietrich Gerhard und H. J. Lang Band 7

Heidelberg 1962 Carl Winter Universitätsverlag

"John Neal: A Bibliography," by Irving T. Richards, pp. 296-319. See preceding entry.

Rachel Dyer . . . by John Neal   A Facsimile Reproduction with an Introduction by John D. Seelye

Gainesville, Florida   Scholars' Facsimiles & Reprints 1964

THE undersigned, having entered into some correspondence with the reputed author of "Randolph;" who is, or is not, sufficiently described as JOHN NEAL, a gentleman by indulgent courtesy ;—informs honourable men, that he has found him unpossessed of courage to make satisfaction for the insolence of his folly.

Stating thus much, the undersigned commits this Craven to his infamy.

EDWARD C. PINKNEY,

Baltimore, Oct. 11, 1823.

PINKNEY'S CRAVEN NOTICE
(Alderman Library)

JOSEPH CLAY NEAL

1 8 0 7 - 1 8 4 7

14936. CHARCOAL SKETCHES; OR, SCENES IN A METROPOLIS . . .

PHILADELPHIA: E. L. CAREY AND A. HART. 1838.

⟨1⟩-222, blank leaf. Frontispiece and 3 plates inserted. $7\frac{5}{16}'' \times 4\frac{1}{2}''$ full.

⟨1⟩-18⁶, 19⁴.

T cloth embossed with an all-over floral pattern: brownish-purple; green. Also in cloth (black, green) embossed wall-paper fashion with an arrangement of vertical wavy rules which form ovals, the ovals enclosing a pebbled area. Printed paper label on spine. Flyleaves.

Deposited March 7, 1838. Reviewed by K April, 1838. Listed AMM June, 1838.

B   BPL   H   UV   Y

14937. Tales of the Grotesque and Arabesque. By Edgar A. Poe . . . in Two Volumes . . .

Philadelphia: Lea and Blanchard. 1840.

Opinion, Vol. 2, p. iii.

For fuller entry see No. 10154.

14938. IN TOWN & ABOUT OR PENCIL-LINGS & PENNINGS. DESIGNED & DRAWN BY FELIX O. C. DARLEY. WITH ILLUSTRATIVE DESCRIPTIONS BY JOSEPH C. NEAL . . .

PHILADELPHIA. PUBLISHED BY GODEY & MC-MICHAEL, 101, CHESNUT ST. N⁰. I. PRICE, 50 CTS. LITH OF THOˢ SINCLAIR 79, S⁰ THIRD ST. ⟨1843⟩

⟨1⟩-12. $10\frac{1}{2}'' \times 13\frac{7}{8}''$. Title-page and three plates inserted.

1-3² (so-signed).

Printed tan paper wrapper.

Listed NAR April, 1844.

All issued?

AAS   H

14939. PETER PLODDY, AND OTHER ODDITIES . . .

PHILADELPHIA: CAREY & HART, CHESNUT ST. 1844.

⟨1⟩-181; blank leaf; plus: 8 pp. advertisements. Frontispiece and 9 illustrations inserted. $7\frac{5}{8}''$ scant × $4\frac{9}{16}''$.

⟨1⟩-14⁶, 15⁸; plus: ⟨16⟩⁴. All examined copies missigned 9 on p. 101.

Printed tan-orange paper wrapper.

Listed as an October publication in WPLNL Nov. 1844.

UV

14940. The Gift: A Christmas, New Year, and Birthday Present. MDCCCXLV.

Philadelphia: Carey and Hart. 1845.

"The Moral of Goslyne Greene, Who Was Born to a Fortune," pp. ⟨64⟩-76. Collected in *Charcoal Sketches. Second Series*, 1848.

For fuller entry see No. 4024.

14941. CHARCOAL SKETCHES. SECOND SERIES . . .

NEW YORK: BURGESS, STRINGER, & COMPANY, 222 BROADWAY. 1848.

Edited by Alice B. Neal (Mrs. Joseph Clay Neal).

⟨1⟩-192. Two frontispieces and 8 plates inserted. $8\frac{11}{16}'' \times 5\frac{3}{8}''$ scant.

⟨1⟩, 2-5, ⟨6⟩, 7-8, ⟨9⟩, 10-11, ⟨12⟩⁸.

Printed off-white paper wrapper.

Reviewed LW Jan. 1, 1848; K Jan. 1848. Deposited Feb. 25, 1848.

AAS

14942. Gems for You; from New Hampshire Authors. By F. A. Moore.

Manchester, N. H. William H. Fisk. 1850.

"The Green Mountain Maid," pp. 214-216.

For fuller entry see No. 5932.

Reprints of Neal's own books.

Charcoal Sketches . . .

> Philadelphia: Getz, Buck & Co., No. 4 Hart's Buildings. ⟨1837; *i.e., ca.* 1853⟩

See below under 1853.

14943. Charcoal Sketches; or, Scenes in a Metropolis . . . Second Edition.

> Philadelphia: E. L. Carey and A. Hart. 1838.

A cursory examination indicates that this was printed from the plates of the 1838 (*i.e.,* the first) edition.

Cloth, paper label on spine.

14944. Charcoal Sketches; or, Scenes in a Metropolis . . . Third Edition.

> Philadelphia: E. L. Carey and A. Hart. 1839.

A cursory examination indicates this was printed from the plates of the 1838 edition.

Cloth, printed paper label on spine.

14945. Charcoal Sketches; or, Scenes in a Metropolis . . . Fourth Edition.

> Philadelphia: E. L. Carey and A. Hart. 1839.

Cursory examination indicates this was printed from the plates of the 1838 edition.

Cloth, printed paper label on spine.

14946. Charcoal Sketches; or, Scenes in a Metropolis . . . Fifth Edition.

> Philadelphia: E. L. Carey and A. Hart. 1840.

Cursory examination indicates this was printed from the plates of the 1838 edition.

Cloth, printed paper label on spine.

14947. Charcoal Sketches; or, Scenes in a Metropolis . . . Sixth Edition.

> Philadelphia: E. L. Carey and A. Hart. 1841.

Cursory examination indicates this was printed from the plates of the 1838 edition.

Cloth, printed paper label on spine.

14948. The Pic Nic Papers. By Various Hands. Edited by Charles Dickens . . . in Three Volumes . . .

> London: Henry Colburn, Publisher, Great Marlborough Street. MDCCCXLI.

Vol. 2 is a reprint of Neal's *Charcoal Sketches,* 1838.

For a discussion of this book see John C. Eckel's *The First Editions of the Writings of Charles Dickens . . . Revised . . .,* New York and London, 1932. Eckel (p. 145) reports that the copies first printed have the error *publisher young,* Vol. 1, p. ⟨iii⟩, line three; later: *young publisher.*

The Neal material does not appear in the Philadelphia (Lea and Blanchard), 1841, edition of *The Pic Nic Papers.*

A one-volume reprint was issued by Ward & Lock, London, n.d., 1862.

14949. Charcoal Sketches; or, Scenes in a Metropolis . . . New Edition.

> Philadelphia: Carey & Hart, Chesnut Street. 1843.

Cursory examination indicates that this was printed from the plates of the 1838 edition.

Cloth? Probably issued in printed paper wrapper.

14950. *Entry cancelled.*

Charcoal Sketches . . .

> Philadelphia: T. B. Peterson, 102 Chesnut Street. ⟨1843; *i.e.,* 1854⟩

> See below under 1854.

14951. Charcoal Sketches; or, Scenes in a Metropolis . . . New Edition.

> Philadelphia: Carey & Hart, Chesnut Street. 1844.

Cursory examination indicates this was printed from the plates of the 1838 edition.

Printed paper wrapper.

14952. Charcoal Sketches; or, Scenes in a Metropolis . . . New Edition.

> Philadelphia: Carey & Hart, Chesnut Street. 1845.

JOSEPH CLAY NEAL
Entry No. 14936
(Harvard University Library)

Cursory examination indicates this was printed from the plates of the 1838 edition.

Probably issued in printed paper wrapper.

14953. Charcoal Sketches; or, Scenes in a Metropolis . . . New Edition.

Philadelphia: Carey & Hart, Chesnut Street. 1846.

Cursory examination indicates this was printed from the plates of the 1838 edition.

Issued in cloth?

14954. Charcoal Sketches, or Scenes in a Metropolis . . . New Edition.

New-York: Stringer & Townsend. 222 Broadway. 1849.

Cursory examination indicates this was printed from the plates of the 1838 edition.

Cloth?

14955. Charcoal Sketches. Second Series . . .

New York: Stringer & Townsend. 222 Broadway, Cor. Ann-Street. 1850.

Cursory examination indicates this was printed from the plates of the 1848 edition.

Cloth?

14956. Charcoal Sketches; or, Scenes in a Metropolis . . .

Philadelphia: Getz, Buck & Co., No. 4 Hart's Buildings. ⟨1837; i.e., ca. 1853⟩

Printed from the plates of the 1838 edition.

Pictorial paper wrapper.

14957. Peter Ploddy, and Other Oddities . . .

Philadelphia: Getz, Buck & Co., No. 4 Hart's Buildings. ⟨n.d., 1853⟩

Illuminated paper wrapper.

14957A. Charcoal Sketches; or, Scenes in a Metropolis . . .

Philadelphia: T. B. Peterson, 102 Chestnut Street. ⟨1843; i.e., 1854⟩

Cursory examination indicates this was reprinted from the plates of the 1838 edition.

Pictorial paper wrapper.

14958. "Boots:" Or, the Misfortunes of Peter Faber, and Other Sketches . . .

Philadelphia: Henry S. Getz, (Late Getz & Buck.) 1855.

Copyright notice dated 1844.

Printed paper wrapper.

Reprint of Charcoal Sketches. Second Series, 1848.

14959. The Misfortunes of Peter Faber, and Other Sketches . . .

Philadelphia: T. B. Peterson, 102 Chestnut Street. ⟨1856⟩

Reprint of Charcoal Sketches. Second Series, 1848, the editor's introduction revised.

Illuminated paper wrapper.

Reprinted and reissued by T. B. Peterson & Brothers, 306 Chestnut Street ⟨1856; i.e., not before 1858⟩

14960. Neal's Charcoal Sketches. Three Books Complete in One . . .

Philadelphia: T. B. Peterson & Brothers, 306 Chestnut Street. ⟨1865⟩

14960A. A Pocket Book of the Early American Humorists Selections from the Best Writings of Benjamin Franklin, Joseph C. Neal . . . and Others

Boston   Small, Maynard & Company   1907

The following publications contain material by Joseph Clay Neal reprinted from earlier books.

The Prose Writers of America ... by Rufus Wilmot Griswold ...

Philadelphia ... 1847.

For comment see entry Nos. 3158, 6676.

The Book of Gems ... by Eugene Sinclair.

Manchester ... 1854.

For comment see BAL, Vol. 3, p. 155.

Friendship's Offering ... by Eugene Sinclair.

Manchester ... 1858.

For fuller entry see BAL, Vol. 3, p. 156.

A Gift for You ... by Eugene Sinclair.

Boston ... 1858.

Reprint of the preceding entry.

Mark Twain's Library of Humor ...

New York ... 1888

For comment see entry No. 9636.

Half-Hours with the Best Humorous Authors. Selected and Arranged by Charles Morris ...

Philadelphia: J. B. Lippincott Company. 1889. 4 Vols.

"Corner Loungers," Vol. 1, pp. 481-484, extracted from *Peter Ploddy* ..., 1844.

"Undeveloped Genius," Vol. 2, pp. 282-287, extracted from *Charcoal Sketches* ..., 1838.

REFERENCES AND ANA

Scenes in Indian Life, a Series of Original Designs Portraying Events in the Life of an Indian Chief, Drawn and Etched on Stone by F. O. C. Darley ...

Philadelphia, 1843.

Not seen. Not located. Entry from Sabin (No. 18583). Issued in five parts.

An old Library of Congress card for a copy of this work (reported "lost" in 1969) credits the authorship to Neal. Further information wanting. BAL has been unable to establish authorship. Theodore Bolton in *American Book Illustrators* ..., New York, 1938, lists the work as though Darley's.

Sketches Abroad with Pen and Pencil.

New York: Hurd & Houghton, 1868.

Thus an old, temporary, entry in LC catalog, crediting the above title to Neal. The cataloger was in error. The author of the book was Felix O. C. Darley.

Not located by BAL.

ROBERT HENRY NEWELL

(Orpheus C. Kerr)

1 8 3 6 – 1 9 0 1

14961. THE ORPHEUS C. KERR PAPERS.
⟨FIRST SERIES⟩

NEW YORK: BLAKEMAN & MASON, 21 MURRAY
STREET. 1862.

⟨i⟩-viii, ⟨9⟩-382, blank leaf. 7¼″ full × 5″.
Illustrated. *Note:* In some copies the final leaf is
excised.

⟨1⟩, 2-3, ⟨4-5⟩, 6, ⟨7-8⟩, 9-16¹². *Also signed:* ⟨-⟩²,
⟨1⟩⁶, 2⁴, ⟨3⟩⁶, 4⁸, ⟨5⟩⁶, 6⁴, 7-10⁶, ⟨11-12⟩⁶, 13⁶,
⟨14-32⟩⁶.

A cloth: brown. BD cloth: brown; red; slate. HC
cloth: blue. TR cloth: blue-green; salmon. Brown-
coated end papers. Buff end papers. Flyleaves; or,
flyleaf at front only.

Deposited Aug. 23, 1862. Advertised in *Boston
Daily Evening Transcript*, Aug. 25, 1862. Listed (as
an importation) PC Nov. 1, 1862. A Hotten edition
listed by Ath Oct. 14, 1865; Routledge edition
listed PC June 1, 1867; Ward, Lock, & Tyler
edition advertised PC Dec. 8, 1873.

B   BA   H   LC   NYPL   UV   Y

14962. THE ORPHEUS C. KERR PAPERS.
SECOND SERIES.

NEW YORK: CARLETON, PUBLISHER, 413 BROAD-
WAY. (LATE RUDD & CARLETON.) M DCCC LXIII.

⟨i⟩-viii, ⟨9⟩-367; blank, p. ⟨368⟩; advertisements,
pp. ⟨3⟩-6. Folio 330 at inner right corner of all
examined copies. P. 366 mispaged 266. One
illustration in text. 7⁵⁄₁₆″ × 4¹⁵⁄₁₆″.

⟨1⟩-6, ⟨7-8⟩, 9-15¹², 16⁶.

Two states noted:

1: Terminal advertisements paged: ⟨3⟩, 4, 5, 6.

2: Terminal advertisements paged: ⟨3⟩, 5, 4, 6.
Folios 5 and 4 improperly placed.

Note: The book occurs on two weights of paper;
priority, if any, not determined. The designations
are for identification only.

A: Sheets bulk ¹³⁄₁₆″.

B: Sheets bulk 1″ scant.

HC cloth: purple. TR cloth: purple; slate. TZ
cloth: purple. Brown-coated end papers. Flyleaves.

Listed APC May 1, 1863. *Another thousand* advertised
as *just ready* APC May 1, 1863. Listed PC May 15,
1863.

B (1st state)   H (1st state)   LC (1st state)   NYPL
(both states)   Y (both states)

14963. Beadle's Dime American Speaker...
Revised and Enlarged Edition.

New York: Beadle and Company, Publishers,
118 William Street. ⟨1863⟩

Printed paper wrapper.

"Alone," pp. 92-94. Does not appear in the
unrevised, first, edition of this publication. Collected in *The Palace Beautiful*, 1865.

B

14964. The Railway Anecdote Book...

New York: D. Appleton & Co., 443 & 445
Broadway. M.DCCC.LXIV.

"Wonderful Effect of the Draft," p. 227.

For fuller entry see No. 1525.

14965. THE PALACE BEAUTIFUL, AND
OTHER POEMS. BY ORPHEUS C. KERR.

NEW YORK: CARLETON, PUBLISHER, 413 BROAD-
WAY. M DCCC LXV.

Two printings noted:

FIRST PRINTING

⟨i-ii⟩, ⟨i⟩-viii, ⟨11⟩-⟨179⟩. Frontispiece portrait
and 9 plates inserted. 7″ full × 4⁵⁄₈″ full.

⟨1⟩-7¹², 8⁶.

"In Capite," p. ⟨179⟩.

SECOND PRINTING

⟨i⟩-⟨x⟩, ⟨11⟩-178, blank leaf. Laid paper. Frontispiece portrait inserted; no other illustrations.

"In Capite," p. ⟨ix⟩. P. ⟨179⟩ blank.

HC cloth: brown. TR cloth: gray-green; purple. V cloth: black; purple. Green-coated end papers. Flyleaves. Top edges gilt.

Advertised for *this week* ALG Dec. 1, 1864. Listed ALG Dec. 15, 1864. BPL copy (first printing) received Dec. 20, 1864. Listed PC April 1, 1865.

AAS (1st)   H (1st)   B (1st, 2nd)   BPL (1st)   LC (1st)   NYPL (1st, 2nd)   Y (1st, 2nd)

14966. THE MARTYR PRESIDENT.

NEW YORK: CARLETON, PUBLISHER. M DCCC LXV.

Anonymous.

⟨1⟩-43. 7½″ full × 4¹¹⁄₁₆″.

⟨1⟩-3⁶, 4⁴.

Printed white glazed paper wrapper.

Listed ALG May 15, 1865.

According to a letter from the author (in NYPL) 500 copies only were printed.

AAS   B   BPL   H   LC   NYPL   Y

14967. THE ORPHEUS C. KERR PAPERS. THIRD SERIES . . .

NEW YORK: CARLETON, PUBLISHER, 413 BROADWAY. MDCCCLXV.

⟨i-ii⟩, ⟨i⟩-vi, 7-300; advertisements, pp. ⟨301-310⟩. See note below regarding advertisements. 1 illustration in text. 7¼″ × 4⅞″ full.

⟨1⟩-13¹², *Also signed:* ⟨-⟩¹, ⟨1⟩-2, ⟨3⟩-4, ⟨5-23⟩, 24-25⁶, ⟨26⟩⁵. P. 7 erroneously signed 2*; should be 1*; p. 31 erroneously signed 2; should be 2*. All examined copies, both Printings A and B, thus. In some copies signature mark 25 (p. 289) is not present.

TERMINAL ADVERTISEMENTS

The terminal advertisements in the first printings are as follows:

P. ⟨301⟩: *Just Published* . . . *The Palace Beautiful* . . .

P. ⟨302⟩: Blank

P. ⟨303⟩: Divisional title-page dated *1865*.

P. ⟨304⟩: Extract from Butler.

P. ⟨305⟩: *New Books* . . . ⟨to⟩ . . . *Beulah* . . .

P. ⟨306⟩: Paged 4. . . . *Darkness and Daylight* . . . ⟨to⟩ . . . *Peculiar* . . .

P. ⟨307⟩: Paged 5. . . . *A Long Look Ahead* . . . ⟨to⟩ . . . *A New Novel.*–––*In Press* . . .

P. ⟨308⟩: Paged 6; but see below. . . . *The Cloister and the Hearth* . . . ⟨to⟩ . . . *The Squibob Papers* . . .

P. ⟨309⟩: Paged 7. . . . *The Autobiography of a New England Farm-House* . . . ⟨to⟩ . . . *Notes and Comments on Shakspeare* . . .

P. ⟨310⟩: Paged 8. . . . *John Guilderstring's Sin* . . . ⟨to⟩ . . . *Rural Architecture* . . .

Note: BAL suspects that this book went into two or more printings without alteration. The following sequence is suggested:

FIRST PRINTING (PRINTINGS?) A

P. ⟨308⟩ paged 6.

LATER PRINTINGS B

P. ⟨308⟩ unpaged.

Three bindings have been noted. The sequence has not been determined and the designations are for identification only.

BINDING A

C cloth: purple. TR cloth: blackish-blue. Covers bevelled. Sides blindstamped with (at the center) the publisher's circular *Carleton* device; sides bordered with an ornate rules frame, at each inner corner a floret; the innermost section of the frame is squared, not decorated. The frame encloses nothing but the *Carleton* device. Spine stamped in gold save as noted: ⟨*blindstamped heavy rule*⟩ / The / Orpheus C. Kerr / Papers. / ⟨*3 stars*⟩ / CARLETON / ⟨*blindstamped heavy rule*⟩ Blue end papers. Flyleaves.

BINDING B

TR cloth: bluish-slate. Covers not bevelled. Sides blindstamped with (at the center) the publisher's circular *Carleton* device; sides bordered with an ornate rules frame, at each corner an ornament consisting of four ovoids quartering a square; at each innermost corner of the frame is an ornament resembling two crossed squared paper clips. Spine stamped in gold save as noted: ⟨*blindstamped heavy rule*⟩ / The / Orpheus C. Kerr / Papers. / ⟨*3 stars*⟩ / CARLETON / ⟨*blindstamped heavy rule*⟩ Blue end papers. Flyleaves.

BINDING C

TR cloth: purplish-slate. Covers not bevelled. Sides blindstamped with (at center) the publisher's circular *Carleton* device; sides bordered with an ornate frame; at each inner corner an arrangement of three hollow interlocking squares. Spine stamped in gold save as noted: ⟨*blindstamped heavy rule*⟩ / The / Orpheus C. Kerr / Papers. / ⟨*3 stars*⟩ / CARLETON / ⟨*blindstamped heavy rule*⟩ Blue end papers. Flyleaves.

A KNOWN REPRINT, BINDING D

A known reprint has been seen, distinguishable by the following features:

P. ⟨303⟩: Divisional title-page dated 1865. Note that in this reprint the letterpress is not enclosed by an ornate circular frame; in the earlier printings the letterpress is enclosed by an ornate circular frame.

P. ⟨304⟩: Blank. In the earlier printings an extract from Butler is present.

P. ⟨305⟩: *New Books . . . Les Miserables . . . ⟨to⟩ . . . The Art of Conversation . . .*

P. ⟨306⟩: Paged 4. *. . . Marian Grey . . . ⟨to⟩ . . . The Life of Jesus . . .*

P. ⟨307⟩: Paged 5. *. . . A Long Look Ahead . . . ⟨to⟩ . . . Beatrice Cenci . . .*

P. ⟨308⟩: Paged 6. *. . . The Sparrowgrass Papers . . . ⟨to⟩ . . . The Game Fish of the North . . .*

P. ⟨309⟩: Paged 7. *. . . Doesticks; What He Says . . . ⟨to⟩ . . . The Spirit of Hebrew Poetry . . .*

P. ⟨310⟩: Paged 8. *. . . Husband & Wife . . . ⟨to⟩ . . . Hartley Norman . . .*

The binding varies considerably from that noted on earlier printings. In the earlier printings (among other variations) the spine title is stamped in gold. In the reprint here described the spine title is goldstamped in intaglio. Sides blindstamped with the publisher's circular *Carleton* device at center, enclosed by an upright oval frame (about 6¼″ tall), the whole enclosed by a rules frame.

Advertised for *this week* ALG June 1, 1865. Listed ALG June 15, 1865; Bkr July 31, 1865.

AAS (*Printing B, Binding C*)   B (*Printing A, Binding A; Printing B, Binding A*)   H (*Printing A, Binding A; Printing B, Binding B*)   LC (*Printing B, Binding A*)   UV (*Printing B, Binding B; Reprint in Binding D*)   Y (*Printing A, Binding A; Reprint in Binding D*)

14968. The Orpheus C. Kerr Papers . . . with Notes and Introduction by Edward P. Hingston . . .

London: John Camden Hotten, Piccadilly. 1866 . . .

Not seen. Entry on the basis of a photographic reproduction of the BMU copy; and, a reprint issued *ca.* 1870 imprinted: *London: John Camden Hotten, Piccadilly. [All rights reserved.] ⟨n.d.⟩.*

On the basis of the imprint date the book is a complete reprint with the exception of:

"Alliteration," p. ⟨215⟩. Otherwise unlocated.

"The Hairess———A Romance," pp. ⟨216⟩-219. Collected in *Smoked Glass,* 1868.

14969. RECONSTRUCTION. BY ORPHEUS C. KERR . . .

NEW-YORK: THE AMERICAN NEWS COMPANY, GENERAL WHOLESALE AGENTS, 119 & 121 NASSAU STREET. ⟨n.d., 1866? 1867?⟩

Cover-title.

⟨3⟩-46; advertisements, pp. ⟨47-50⟩. Illustrated. 7⅜″ × 4⁹⁄₁₆″. Laid paper.

⟨-⟩²⁴.

Printed self-wrapper.

Contents:

"Reconstruction," comprising four letters from *Taikatchaw Court House, Accomac,* pp. ⟨5⟩-38. Also in (*reprinted from?*) the next entry.

"The Balloon of the Future; a Peep from This Here World into that Air," pp. ⟨39⟩-46.

WR

14970. COMICALITIES; BY ORPHEUS C. KERR, AND OTHER FUNNY FELLOWS. AN AMUSING AND ENTERTAINING MEDLEY FOR LEISURE HOURS, AND TWENTY-FIVE CENTS.

NEW YORK: J. C. HANEY & CO., PUBLISHERS, OFFICE OF MERRYMAN AND THE COMIC MONTHLY, 119 NASSAU STREET. ⟨n.d., 1866? 1867?⟩

⟨3⟩-98. Illustrated. 7¹¹⁄₁₆″ × 4½″ full.

⟨1-4¹²⟩.

Printed green paper wrapper.

Contents: "Reconstruction," comprising four letters from *Taikatchaw Court House, Accomac,* pp. ⟨5⟩-38. Also in (*reprinted from?*) the preceding entry. All after p. 38 anonymous and presumably not by Newell.

B Y

14971. AVERY GLIBUN; OR, BETWEEN TWO FIRES. A ROMANCE. BY ORPHEUS C. KERR.

NEW YORK: G. W. CARLETON & CO., PUBLISHERS. LONDON: S. LOW, SON, & CO. M DCCC LXVII.

⟨i⟩-x, 11-301; leaf excised or pasted under the end paper. 9⁵⁄₁₆″ scant × 5⅞″ scant.

⟨1-19⁸⟩. Leaf ⟨19⟩₈ excised or pasted under the end paper. *Signed:* ⟨1-2⟩, 3-37⁴, 38³.

C cloth: green; purple. LI-like cloth: purple; terra-cotta. RH cloth: green. Blue end papers. Flyleaf at front.

BPL copy received Aug. 1867. Listed ALG Sept. 2, 1867. Advertised ALG Sept. 2, 1867, as in both cloth; and, printed paper wrapper.

AAS BPL NYPL UV Y

14972. SMOKED GLASS. BY ORPHEUS C. KERR . . .

NEW YORK: G. W. CARLETON, PUBLISHER. LONDON: S. LOW, SON, & CO. MDCCCLXVIII.

⟨i⟩-viii, 9-277; blank, p. ⟨278⟩; 10 pp. advertisements paged: ⟨i-ii⟩, ⟨1⟩-8. Frontispiece and 5 plates inserted; other illustrations in text. 7¼″ × 4⅞″.

⟨1-12¹²⟩. *Signed:* ⟨1⟩-24⁶.

C cloth: green; purple; terra-cotta. Blue end papers. Flyleaves.

Advertised for *this week* ALG Sept. 1, 1868. BPL copy received Sept. 8, 1868. Listed ALG Sept. 15, 1868; PC Nov. 2, 1868.

AAS   B   H   LC   NYPL   UV   Y

14973. The Piccadilly Annual of Entertaining Literature . . .

London: John Camden Hotten, 74 & 75, Piccadilly. ⟨1870⟩

"Dickens," p. 72. Collected in *The Cloven Foot*, 1870.

"The Mystery of Mr. E. Drood, Specimen of an Adaptation," pp. 59-62. Collected in *The Cloven Foot*, 1870.

For fuller entry see No. 3323.

14974. THE CLOVEN FOOT: BEING AN ADAPTATION OF THE ENGLISH NOVEL "THE MYSTERY OF EDWIN DROOD," (BY CHARLES DICKENS,) TO AMERICAN SCENES, CHARACTERS, CUSTOMS, AND NOMENCLATURE. BY ORPHEUS C. KERR . . .

NEW YORK: CARLETON, PUBLISHER, MADISON SQUARE. LONDON: S. LOW, SON & CO. MDCCCLXX.

⟨i⟩-vi, ⟨7⟩-279; blank, p. ⟨280⟩; advertisements, pp. ⟨1⟩-8. 7³⁄₁₆″ × 4⅞″.

⟨1-2⟩, 3-9, 19 ⟨sic⟩, 11, ⟨12⟩¹². P. 225 missigned 8*; p. 263 missigned 4.

C cloth: green; purple. Purple end papers. Flyleaves.

Listed ALG Jan. 2, 1871; PC Feb. 1, 1871.

AAS   H   Y

14975. VERSATILITIES . . .

BOSTON: LEE AND SHEPARD, PUBLISHERS. NEW YORK: LEE, SHEPARD, AND DILLINGHAM. 1871.

⟨i-ii⟩, ⟨i⟩-⟨x⟩, ⟨1⟩-266. 6¹⁵⁄₁₆″ × 4⁹⁄₁₆″.

⟨-⟩⁶, 1-3, ⟨4⟩-11¹², ⟨12⟩¹. *Also signed:* ⟨-⟩⁶, A-I, ⟨J⟩, K-⟨L⟩, M-P⁸, Q⁵.

C cloth: green. FL cloth: blue; purple; terra-cotta. P cloth: green; purple; terra-cotta. Coated end papers: brown, green, purple noted. Covers bevelled. Flyleaves.

BA copy received May 13, 1871. Noted as *just ready* ALG May 15, 1871. Listed ALG June 1, 1871; PC July 15, 1871.

AAS   B   BA   BPL   H   LC   NYPL   Y

14976. The Orpheus C. Kerr Papers: Being a Complete Contemporaneous Military History of the Mackerel Brigade . . .

New York: G. W. Carleton & Co., Publishers, Madison Square. London: S. Low, Son & Co. M.DCCC.LXXI.

A revision of *The Orpheus C. Kerr Papers*, first, second and third series. "Introduction," dated 1870, pp. xiii-xviii.

Listed LW June 1, 1871.

B   H

14977. THE WALKING DOLL; OR, THE ASTERS AND DISASTERS OF SOCIETY . . .

NEW YORK: FRANCIS B. FELT & COMPANY, 91 MERCER STREET. 1872.

⟨1⟩-391; blank, p. ⟨392⟩; advertisements, pp. ⟨393-394⟩; blank leaf. 7¼″ × 4⅞″ full.

⟨1⟩-16¹², 17⁶.

C cloth: green; purple. FL cloth: terra-cotta. Brown-coated on white end papers. Flyleaves.

Y copy inscribed Dec. 10, 1871. ". . . Will publish before Christmas"––-ALG Dec. 1871. Listed ALG Jan. 1, 1872.

AAS   BPL   H   UV   Y

14978. The Similibus A Paper Published by the Managers of the Fair for the Benefit of the Homoeopathic Surgical Hospital . . .

New-York . . . 1872 . . .

"Similia Similibus Curantur," No. 5, p. 5. Collected in *Studies in Stanzas*, 1882.

For fuller entry see No. 7745.

14979. Tales of the Chesapeake by Geo. Alfred Townsend . . .

New York: American News Company, 39 and 41 Chambers Street. 1880.

Contains, on an inserted leaf, testimonial by Newell and others.

For fuller description see entry No. 8945.

14980. STUDIES IN STANZAS BY ORPHEUS C. KERR

NEW YORK   THE USEFUL KNOWLEDGE PUBLISHING COMPANY NO. 18 VESEY STREET 1882

⟨1⟩-228. $6\frac{5}{16}''$ × $4\frac{1}{2}''$ full (cloth). $6\frac{11}{16}''$ × 5″ scant (paper).

⟨1⟩-2, ⟨3⟩, 4, ⟨5⟩, 6-7^{16}, 8^2.

S cloth: blue-green; brown; salmon. Front cover stamped in gold and black. Mottled gray-blue paper end papers. Edges gilt. Flyleaves. Also in printed paper wrapper, double flyleaves, edges plain.

Note: A surviving copyright deposit copy (in LC) is in what may be an experimental binding: S cloth: green; front unstamped.

Deposited May 15, 1882.

AAS   B   NYPL   UV

14981. ... THERE WAS ONCE A MAN. A STORY ...

NEW YORK. FORDS, HOWARD, & HULBERT, FOR OUR CONTINENT PUBLISHING CO. 1884

At head of title: "OUR CONTINENT" LIBRARY.

⟨i⟩-⟨x⟩, 7-526; blank leaf. Frontispiece and 16 plates inserted. 7″ full × $4\frac{7}{8}''$ scant.

⟨1^2, 2-34^8⟩.

H cloth: yellow. Gray paper end papers imprinted with advertisements. Flyleaves.

Deposited May 17, 1884. Noted as *just ready* PW May 24, 1884. Listed PW May 24, 1884.

AAS   H

14982. In Bohemia: By John Boyle O'Reilly.

Boston: The Pilot Publishing Co. 597 Washington Street. ⟨1886⟩

Part of Newell's review of O'Reilly's *Songs from the Southern Seas*, reprinted from the *Catholic Review* (N.Y.), p. 9. Earliest located book publication.

Listed PW Oct. 9, 1886.

H   NYPL

14983. Werner's Readings and Recitations. No. 5. American Classics. Compiled and Arranged by Sara Sigourney Rice.

New York: Edgar S. Werner. 1891.

"The Calmest of Her Sex," pp. 75-77.

NYPL

14984. ... Masterpieces of Wit and Humor with Stories and an Introduction by Robert J. Burdette ...

⟨n.p.⟩ Copyright, 1902, by E. J. Long

"His Ancestry Somewhat in Doubt," p. 176.

For comment see entry No. 2013.

Reprints of Newell's own books. For a list of books by authors other than Newell containing reprinted Newell material see *Section III*.

14985. The Orpheus C. Kerr Papers. First Series.

New York: Blakeman & Mason, 21 Murray Street. 1863.

14986. The Orpheus C. Kerr Papers. By R. H. Newell. First Series. ⟨Second Series.⟩ ⟨Third Series.⟩

London: John Camden Hotten, Piccadilly. 1866.

3 Vols. American sheets with altered front and terminal matter.

14987. The Orpheus C. Kerr Papers. With an Introduction by George Augustus Sala. Reprinted from the Original.

London: George Routledge & Sons, the Broadway, Ludgate. ⟨n.d., 1867⟩

Not seen. Entry on the basis of correspondence.

14988. The Mystery of Mr. E. Drood. An Adaptation by Orpheus C. Kerr.

London: John Camden Hotten, 74 & 75, Piccadilly . . . ⟨n.d., 1871⟩

Pictorial paper wrapper. Reprint of *The Cloven Foot*, New York, 1870.

Listed Ath July 29, 1871.

In this section are listed books by authors other than Newell which contain material by him reprinted from earlier books. See *Section Two* for a list of collections of reprinted material issued under Newell's name.

Songs of the War . . .

    Albany . . . 1863.

    For fuller entry see No. 259.

Beadle's Dime Comic Speaker: Comprising Gems of Wit, Humor and Drollery . . .

    New York: Beadle and Company, Publishers, 118 William Street. ⟨1863⟩

    Printed paper wrapper. Published Nov. 28, 1863 (Johannsen).

The Rebellion Record . . . Edited by Frank Moore . . . Sixth Volume . . .

    New-York . . . 1863.

    For fuller entry see No. 11531.

Lyrics of Loyalty . . . Edited by Frank Moore

    New York . . . 1864

    For comment see entry No. 1203.

The Lincoln Memorial: A Record of the Life, Assassination, and Obsequies of the Martyred President. Edited by John Gilmary Shea . . . ⟨Second Edition⟩

    New York: Bunce & Huntington, 540 Broadway. 1865.

    Also issued with a cancel title-leaf imprinted: *New York: Bunce and Huntington. Chicago: S. M. Kennedy, 194 Clark Street. 1865.*

    Untitled eight lines of verse, p. ⟨74⟩. These lines do not appear in the earlier printings of this publication.

    This publication occurs as follows:

FIRST PRINTING

Imprint: *New York: Bunce & Huntington, 540 Broadway. 1865.* Note presence of the period following date.

Editor's name not present on the title-page.

On the copyright page are the copyright notice and the imprints of *Alvord* (printer); and, *Rennie, Shea & Lindsay* (stereotypers and electrotypers).

Table of contents on p. ⟨5⟩; *i.e.*, on a single page.

Does not contain the intercalary poems which appear first in the second edition.

SECOND PRINTING

Imprint: *New York: Bunce & Huntington, 540 Broadway. 1865* Note absence of period following date.

Editor's name not present on the title-page.

On the copyright page is the copyright notice only; the names of printer and stereotyper not present.

Table of contents on p. ⟨5⟩; *i.e.*, on a single page.

Does not contain the intercalary poems which appear first in the second edition.

SECOND EDITION

Imprint: *New York: Bunce & Huntington, 540 Broadway. 1865.* Note presence of the period following the date. Also occurs with cancel title-leaf imprinted: *New York: Bunce and Huntington. Chicago: S. M. Kennedy, 194 Clark Street. 1865.*

Editor's name present on the title-page.

On copyright page is the copyright notice only; the names of printer and stereotyper not present.

Table of contents extended and printed on pp. ⟨5⟩-6.

Contains intercalary poems by Halpine, J. W. Howe, H. T. Tuckerman and others. In the earlier printings the pages on which these poems appear are blank.

It is probable that the earliest form of p. ⟨224⟩ has the name *Julia Ward Howe* correctly spelled; that during the course of printing battering of the types causes the reading to appear thus: *Julia Ward How.*

No record of copyright deposit found save for deposit of the title-page on June 19, 1865. Announced ALG June 1, 1865. Listed ALG June 15, 1865.

The Flower of Liberty. Edited . . . by Julia A. M. Furbish.

> Boston . . . 1866.

> For comment see entry No. 1424.

Yankee Drolleries . . . with Introductions by George Augustus Sala.

> London . . . ⟨n.d., 1868⟩

> For fuller entry see BAL, Vol. 5, p. 429.

The Flower of Liberty. Edited and Illustrated by Julia A. M. Furbish.

> Cincinnati, Ohio: White, Corbin, Bouve & Company, No. 124 Walnut Street. 1869.

One Hundred Choice Selections No. 4 . . . by Phineas Garrett . . .

> . . . Philadelphia . . . 1871.

> For comment see entry No. 2461.

Humorous Poems . . . Edited by William Michael Rossetti . . .

> London . . . ⟨n.d., 1872⟩

> For comment see BAL, Vol. 1, p. 207.

The Comic Poets of the Nineteenth Century . . . by W. Davenport Adams . . .

> London . . . ⟨n.d., 1875⟩

> For comment see BAL, Vol. 3, p. 471.

Yankee Drolleries. The Most Celebrated Works of the Best American Humourists . . . with Introductions by George Augustus Sala.

> London: Chatto and Windus, Piccadilly. 1876.

West Point Tic Tacs . . .

> . . . New York. 1878.

> For comment see entry No. 7299.

One Hundred Choice Selections No. 16 . . . ⟨Compiled⟩ by ⟨Phineas Garrett⟩ . . .

> . . . Philadelphia . . . 1878.

> For comment see entry No. 1554.

Bohemian Days . . . by Geo. Alfred Townsend . . .

> . . . New York. ⟨1880⟩

> For fuller entry see BAL, Vol. 5, p. 610.

One Hundred Choice Selections No. 20 . . .

> . . . Philadelphia . . . 1881.

> For comment see entry No. 5120.

Mark Twain's Library of Humor . . .

> New York . . . 1888

> For comment see entry Nos. 1982, 9636.

Half-Hours with the Best Humorous Authors. Selected and Arranged by Charles Morris . . .

> Philadelphia: J. B. Lippincott Company. 1889.
> 4 Vols.

Martial Recitations . . . Collected . . . by James Henry Brownlee . . .

> Chicago . . . ⟨1896⟩

> For fuller entry see BAL, Vol. 5, p. 338.

The Poetry of American Wit and Humor Selected by R. L. Paget . . .

> Boston . . . MDCCCXCIX

> For fuller entry see No. 1580.

An American Anthology . . . Edited by Edmund Clarence Stedman . . .

> Boston . . . M DCCCC

> For fuller entry see No. 3082.

. . . Gems of Modern Wit and Humor with . . . Introduction by Robert J. Burdette . . .

> ⟨n.p., n.d., 1903⟩

> See entry No. 2013.

Mark Twain's Library of Humor   A Little Nonsense . . .

> . . . New York . . . MCMVI

> For comment see entry No. 3669.

A Pocket Book of the Early American Humorists Selections from the Best Writings of Benjamin Franklin, Joseph C. Neal . . . and Others

> Boston Small, Maynard & Company 1907

. . . Masterpieces of American Humor

> Haldeman-Julius Company   Girard, Kansas
> ⟨n.d., *ca.* 1925⟩

> Printed paper wrapper. At head of title: *Little Blue Book No. 959 Edited by E. Haldeman-Julius*

REFERENCES AND ANA

Fun for the Million . . . by Jerrold . . . Orpheus C. Kerr . . .

> London . . . ⟨n.d., 1873⟩

> Although the name *Orpheus C. Kerr* appears on the title-page, BAL has been unable to identify any material herein as his.

> For fuller entry see BAL, Vol. 2, p. 247.

MORDECAI MANUEL NOAH

1 7 8 5 – 1 8 5 1

14989. THE FORTRESS OF SORRENTO: A PETIT HISTORICAL DRAMA, IN TWO ACTS . . .

NEW-YORK: PUBLISHED BY D. LONGWORTH, AT THE DRAMATIC REPOSITORY, SHAKSPEARE-GAL-LERY. 1808

Anonymous. "Taken from the French opera of Leonora."–––*Early American Plays 1714–1830 . . .*, by Oscar Wegelin, N. Y., 1900, p. 74.

⟨1⟩-28; plus: 4-page list of the *English and American Stage*. 6⅛″ × 3⅞″.

⟨A⟩⁴, B⁶, C⁴; plus: ⟨D⟩².

Probably issued in printed paper wrapper.

Title-page deposited Dec. 4, 1808.

Note: Also seen bound together with other Longworth publications and issued with the general title-page: *. . . The English and American Stage. Volume XXVI . . . Published by D. Longworth, at the Dramatic Repository, Shakspeare-Gallery. 1809.* Copy in AAS.

AAS B BPL H NYHS NYPL Y

14990. Shakspeare Illustrated: Or, the Novels and Histories on Which the Plays of Shakspeare Are Founded. Collected and Translated from the Originals, by Mrs. Lenox . . . with Critical Remarks, and Biographical Sketches of the Writers, by M. M. Noah. In Two Volumes. Vol. I.

Published by Bradford & Inskeep, Philadelphia; Inskeep & Bradford, New York; William M'Ilhenney, Jun., Boston; Coale & Thomas, Baltimore; and E. Morford, Charleston. Printed by T. & G. Palmer, Philadelphia. 1809.

All published.

Paper boards, printed paper label on spine.

AAS H

14991. CORRESPONDENCE AND DOCU-MENTS RELATIVE TO THE ATTEMPT TO NEGOTIATE FOR THE RELEASE OF THE AMERICAN CAPTIVES AT AL-GIERS; INCLUDING REMARKS ON OUR RELATIONS WITH THAT REGENCY . . .

WASHINGTON CITY: PRINTED. 1816.

⟨1⟩-128. 8¾″ × 5½″.

⟨1⟩-16⁴.

Printed paper wrapper?

LC USCA

14992. ORATION, DELIVERED BY AP-POINTMENT, BEFORE TAMMANY SO-CIETY OF COLOMBIAN ⟨*sic*⟩ ORDER, HIBERNIAN PROVIDENT SOCIETY, CO-LUMBIAN SOCIETY UNION SOCIETY OF SHIPWRIGHTS AND CAULKERS, TAILORS', HOUSE CARPENTERS', AND MASONS' BENEVOLENT SOCIETIES. UNITED TO CELEBRATE THE 41st AN-NIVERSARY OF AMERICAN INDEPEN-DENCE . . .

PUBLISHED BY REQUEST OF THE GENERAL COM-MITTEE OF ARRANGEMENTS. NEW-YORK: PRINTED BY J. H. SHERMAN, 85 NASSAU-STREET. 1817.

Cover-title?

⟨1⟩-24. 7⅞″ × 4⅞″.

⟨A⟩-C⁴.

Printed paper wrapper? Self-wrapper?

AAS LC

14993. DISCOURSE, DELIVERED AT THE CONSECRATION OF THE SYNAGOGUE OF ⟨*in Hebrew: Holy Congregation, Remnant of Israel*⟩ IN THE CITY OF NEW-YORK, ON FRIDAY, THE 10TH OF NISAN, 5578, CORRESPONDING WITH THE 17TH OF APRIL, 1818 . . .

NEW-YORK: PRINTED BY C. S. VAN WINKLE, NO. 101 GREENWICH-STREET. 1818.

⟨1⟩-47. 9¼″ × 5¹⁵⁄₁₆″.

⟨1⟩-6⁴. *Note:* In some copies signature mark 4 is not present.

Printed brown paper wrapper.

Reviewed AMM July, 1818.

AAS   B   BPL   H   NYPL   Y

14994. TRAVELS IN ENGLAND, FRANCE, SPAIN, AND THE BARBARY STATES, IN THE YEARS 1813-14 AND 15 . . .

NEW-YORK: PUBLISHED BY KIRK AND MERCEIN, WALL-STREET. LONDON: BY JOHN MILLER, NO. 25 BOW-STREET, COVENT-GARDEN. 1819.

⟨i⟩-⟨viii⟩, ⟨1⟩-431; blank, p. ⟨432⟩; *Appendix,* pp. ⟨i⟩-xlvii. Inserted: Frontispiece, 3 plates, 1 folded plate. 9⅛″ × 5¾″.

⟨-⟩⁴, 1-54⁴, A-F⁴.

Blue-gray paper boards sides, white paper shelf-back. Printed paper label on spine?

Errata, p. ⟨vii⟩.

Title deposited Jan. 25, 1819. Listed by AMM March, 1819, as *recently published.*

AAS   BA   H   NYHS   NYPL   UV   Y

14995. SHE WOULD BE A SOLDIER, OR THE PLAINS OF CHIPPEWA; AN HISTORICAL DRAMA, IN THREE ACTS . . . PERFORMED FOR THE FIRST TIME ON THE 21ST OF JUNE, 1819.

NEW-YORK: PUBLISHED AT LONGWORTH'S DRAMATIC REPOSITORY, SHAKSPEARE GALLERY. G. L. BIRCH & CO. PRINTERS. 1819.

⟨1⟩-73. 6³⁄₁₆″ × 4″.

⟨A⟩-F⁶, G¹.

Issued in printed paper wrapper?

Preface dated *July, 1819.* Listed NAR Sept. 1819.

AAS   B   BPL   H   NYPL   Y

14996. Selections of a Father for the Use of His Children. In Prose and Verse. By Isaac Gomez, Jun. . . .

New-York: Printed by Southwick and Pelsue, No. 9 Wall-Street. 1820.

"Recommendation," *New-York, Sept. 13, 1819,* p. ⟨v⟩.

Note: In the only copy examined a recommendation from *Ph. Milledoler,* dated *New-York, March 3, 1820,* is pasted to p. ⟨iv⟩. Are all copies thus?

Noted only in leather.

Title deposited Sept. 30, 1819.

H

14997. ESSAYS OF HOWARD, ON DOMESTIC ECONOMY. ORIGINALLY PUB-

LISHED IN THE NEW-YORK NATIONAL ADVOCATE. "EYE NATURE'S WALKS."

NEW YORK: PRINTED BY G. L. BIRCH & CO. NO. 39 1/2 FRANKFORT-STREET. 1820.

Anonymous.

⟨1⟩-214, blank leaf. 5⅝″ full × 3⅝″.

⟨A⟩-I, K-S⁶.

Issued in paper boards?

Listed LSR June, 1820. See *Gleanings from a Gathered Harvest,* 1845.

BPL   H   Y

14998. The Wandering Boys: Or, the Castle of Olival. A Melo Drama. In Two Acts.

Boston: Published by Richardson and Lord. Printed by J. H. A. Frost, Congress-St. 1821.

Anonymous.

⟨1⟩-44. 6⅜″ × 4⅛″. Printed self wrapper?

"First played at Charleston, S. C., in 1812, under the title of *Paul and Alexis; or, the Orphans of the Rhine.* Under the new title it was performed at Covent Garden in 1814 and in New York at the Park Theatre in 1820."---*Early American Drama, a Guide to an Exhibition in The William L. Clements Library,* by Ada P. Booth, Ann Arbor, The William L. Clements Library, 1945, p. 16.

". . . I soon produced the little piece, which was called *Paul and Alexis, or the Orphans of the Rhine* . . . After three years' absence in Europe and Africa, I saw the same piece performed at the Park, under the title of the *Wandering Boys,* which even now holds possession of the stage. It seems Mr. ⟨Charles⟩ Young sent the manuscript to London, where the title was changed, and the bantling cut up, altered, and considerably improved."---Noah to William Dunlap in Dunlap's *A History of the American Theatre,* N. Y., 1832, p. 382.

". . . *Paul and Alexis, or the Orphans of the Rhine* . . . was founded on Pixerécourt's *Le Pèlerin Blanc ou les Orphelins du Hameau* (1801), a play which seems to have been the most popular of all Pixerécourt's melodramas . . . Noah follows his original in the plot . . ."---Arthur Hobson Quinn: *A History of the American Drama . . . Second Edition,* N. Y., 1943, p. 193.

Le Pèlerin Blanc was "founded on a romance, *Les Petits Orphelins du Hameau,* by Ducray-Dumesnil, based in its turn on Marsollier's opera of *Les Petits Savoyards* . . ."---ibid.

"This was also played under the name *Paul and Alexis; or, the Orphans of the Rhine.* It was written for Mrs. Young's benefit, and played at Charleston in 1812."---Oscar Wegelin: *Early American Plays 1714-1830* . . . , N. Y., 1900, p. 75.

Other editions noted; arranged alphabetically by publisher:

The Wandering Boys: A Melo-Drama, in Three Acts, the Music by Mr. Nicholson . . ., London: John Cumberland, 6, Brecknock Place, Camden New Town. ⟨n.d., not before *ca.* 1829⟩ Locations: H Y

. . . *The Wandering Boys! or, the Castle of Olival!* . . . *by John Kerr* . . ., London: Printed and Published by John Duncombe, 10, Middle Row, Holborn, ⟨n.d., not before 1835⟩ At head of title: *Duncombe's Edition* "Between his ⟨Kerr's⟩ version and Noah's as printed the differences are so slight as to be negligible . . ."———Arthur Hobson Quinn: *A History of the American Drama* . . . *Second Edition*, N. Y., 1943, p. 193. Location: Y

. . . *The Wandering Boys* . . . *By Anon* . . ., New York: Samuel French, 122 Nassau Street, (Up Stairs.) ⟨n.d., not before 1858⟩ At head of title: *French's Standard Drama   The Acting Edition. No. CLXXXIII.* Location: Y

. . . *The Wandering Boys; or, Castle of Olival, a Melo Drame in Three Acts. Freely Translated and Adapted to the English Stage, from the French of "Le Pelerin Blanc," of Mr. R. C. G. Piexerécourt ⟨sic⟩, by John Kerr. The Original Produced at the Theatre de l'Ambigu-Comique, Paris 1810*, London: Printed by Havell and Co. 79, Newman Street, Oxford Street; and Published by the Author, Theatre, Tottenham Street, Fitzroy Square. ⟨n.d., *ca.* 1825⟩ At head of title: *Dedicated, by Permission, to the Right Honourable the Earl of Fife.* For comment on the authorship see above under the *Duncombe* entry. Locations: H UV

The Wandering Boys . . . *by John Kerr* . . ., Thomas Hailes Lacy, 89, Strand, (Opposite Southampton Street, Covent Garden Market.) London. ⟨n.d., not before 1849⟩ For comment on the authorship see above under the *Duncombe* entry. Location: Y

AAS   B   H   LC   NYHS

14999. AN ADDRESS DELIVERED BEFORE THE GENERAL SOCIETY OF MECHANICS AND TRADESMEN OF THE CITY OF NEW-YORK, ON THE OPENING OF THE MECHANIC INSTITUTION; BY M. M. NOAH . . . TO WHICH IS ADDED, THE REMARKS MADE AT THE REQUEST OF THE MECHANICS' SOCIETY, ON LAYING THE CORNER STONE OF THAT EDIFICE, BY THOMAS R. MERCEIN. A MEMBER OE ⟨sic⟩ THE SOCIETY.

NEW-YORK; WILLIAM A. MERCEIN, PRINTER, NO. 93 GOLD-STREET. 1822

Cover-title?

⟨1⟩-28. 8″ full × 5³⁄₁₆″.

⟨-⟩², 1-⟨3⟩⁴.

Printed paper wrapper? Self-wrapper?

Noah's address, pp. ⟨5⟩-20; Mercein's remarks, with separate title-page, pp. ⟨23⟩-28.

Listed LSR Jan. 1822; NAR April, 1822.

BPL   LC

15000. MARION; OR, THE HERO OF LAKE GEORGE: A DRAMA, IN THREE ACTS, FOUNDED ON EVENTS OF THE REVOLUTIONARY WAR . . .

NEW-YORK: PUBLISHED BY E. MURDEN, CIRCULATING LIBRARY AND DRAMATIC REPOSITORY, NO. 4 CHAMBER ⟨sic⟩ STREET. JAN. 1822.

Cover-title?

⟨1⟩-70; advertisements, p. ⟨71⟩. 6³⁄₈″ × 4″.

⟨1⟩-6⁶.

Printed paper wrapper? Self-wrapper?

Listed LSR Jan. 1822.

B   BPL   H   Y

15001. THE GRECIAN CAPTIVE, OR THE FALL OF ATHENS . . . AS PERFORMED AT THE NEW-YORK THEATRE.

NEW-YORK: PUBLISHED BY E. M. MURDEN, CIRCULATING LIBRARY AND DRAMATIC REPOSITORY, NO. 4 CHAMBERS-STREET. JUNE, 1822.

Cover-title?

⟨i⟩-⟨vi⟩, ⟨1⟩-48. 6⁷⁄₁₆″ × 4¹⁄₈″.

⟨A⟩², ⟨-⟩¹, B-D, ⟨E⟩⁶.

Note: In some copies leaf ⟨-⟩ is inserted in signature ⟨A⟩ and to this extent the pagination and signature collation are altered. Leaf ⟨-⟩ is the *Dramatis Personae.*

Printed paper wrapper? Self-wrapper?

"Will be performed for the first time on the 17th" ———M June 8, 1822. M June 15, 1822, gives an outline of the plot, adding that "a printed copy ⟨of the play⟩ is gratuitously presented to . . . the Boxes and Pit." Listed NAR July, 1822.

AAS   B   H   LC   NYPL   UV   Y

15002. Report of the Trial of an Action on the Case, Brought by Silvanus Miller . . . against Mordecai M. Noah . . . for an Alleged Libel. Tried . . . the 12th Day of December, 1823. By L. H. Clarke.

New-York: Printed by J. W. Palmer and Co. 30 William-Street. 1823.

"To the Editors of the Albany Argus," pp. ⟨3⟩-5.

"Extract of a Letter . . . Dated Albany, February 1, 1823," pp. 5-6.

Issued in unprinted paper wrapper?

Listed NAR April, 1824.

AAS   BA   LC   NYPL   Y

15003. A STATEMENT OF FACTS RELA-
TIVE TO THE CONDUCT OF HENRY
ECKFORD, ESQ. AS CONNECTED WITH
THE NATIONAL ADVOCATE . . .

NEW-YORK, PRINTED BY J. W. BELL & CO.   70
BOWERY. 1824.

Cover-title.

⟨1⟩-12. 9⅛″ × 5¹⁵⁄₁₆″.

⟨1⁴, 2²⟩.

Printed self-wrapper.

AAS   BA   LC   NYHS

15004. A Mirror for Politicians. Moral Beauty of
Consistency Illustrated by sundry extracts fron
⟨sic⟩ the leading prints now engaged in advocating the election of General Jackson to the Presidency. A Warning to Unprincipled Politicians
. . .

⟨n.p., n.d., 1828⟩

Caption-title. The above at head of sheet.

Broadside. Printed on recto only. 22⅝″ × 18¾″.

An attack on Noah, with extracts from his attack
on Jackson uttered during the presidential campaign of 1824. During the campaign of 1828 Noah
was pro-Jackson and this broadside, quoting
Noah's earlier views, was issued by the anti-
Jackson Republicans.

". . . Here is what M. M. Noah wrote in 1824, and
who now daily abuses every one who will not join
in huzza for Jackson . . ."

Two issues noted:

A: Line 3 of heading: . . . *fron* . . .

B: Line 3 of heading: . . . *from* . . .

MHS (A)   UV (B)

15005. A History of the American Theatre. By
William Dunlap . . .

New-York: Printed and Published by J. & J.
Harper, No. 82 Cliff-Street, Sold by the Principal
Booksellers throughout the United States. 1832.

Letter to William Dunlap, July 11, 1832, pp. 380-
384. Reprinted in *Publications of the American Jewish
Historical Society No. 6,* 1897.

For fuller description see entry No. 5025.

15006. PROSPECTUS OF THE EVENING
STAR: A NEW DAILY AND SEMI-
WEEKLY PAPER, TO BE PUBLISHED IN

THE CITY OF NEW-YORK, BY M. M.
NOAH AND THOMAS GILL.

NEW-YORK: CLAYTON & VAN NORDEN, PRINTERS,
NO. 49 WILLIAM-STREET. 1833.

⟨1⟩-16. 7⅞″ × 4¹³⁄₁₆″.

⟨1⟩-2⁴.

Printed self-wrapper? Cover-title?

At end of text: *M. M. Noah.*

LC

15007. DISCOURSE ON THE EVIDENCES
OF THE AMERICAN INDIANS BEING
THE DESCENDANTS OF THE LOST
TRIBES OF ISRAEL. DELIVERED
BEFORE THE MERCANTILE LIBRARY
ASSOCIATION, CLINTON HALL . . .

NEW-YORK: JAMES VAN NORDEN, NO. 27 PINE-
STREET. 1837.

⟨1⟩-40. 9⅛″ × 5¾″.

⟨1⟩-5⁴.

Printed tan paper wrapper.

Reviewed by K June, 1837.

AAS   B

15008. Tales of the Grotesque and Arabesque. By
Edgar A. Poe . . . in Two Volumes . . .

Philadelphia: Lea and Blanchard. 1840.

One-sentence opinion, Vol. 2, p. ii.

For fuller entry see No. 10154.

15009. ⟨In Hebrew: *Book of Jasher*⟩ or the Book
of Jasher; Referred to in Joshua and Second
Samuel. Faithfully Translated from the Original
Hebrew into English.

New York: Published by M. M. Noah & A. S.
Gould, at 144 Nassau-Street. 1840.

"Preface," pp. ⟨iii⟩-vii.

Note: Noah is sometimes credited with the
translation of this work; BAL has been unable to
find any evidence to support the claim.

Two states noted:

FIRST STATE

⟨-⟩1: Blank

⟨-⟩2r: CERTIFICATES . . .

Leaf ⟨-⟩2r is imprinted with recommendations
variously dated April 10-30, 1840; no reviews
present.

T cloth: plum. At center of sides is a blindstamped
filigree, 5⅜″ tall, consisting of eight leafy scrolls.
Flyleaves.

SECOND STATE

⟨-⟩1r: ADVERTISEMENT TO THE SECOND EDITION . . .

⟨-⟩ is devoted to recommendations variously dated April 10–30, 1840; and, extracts from reviews.

T cloth: black. At center of sides is a filigree ornament measuring 4¼″ tall, blindstamped. Flyleaves.

Deposited May 23, 1840. Listed NAR July, 1840. Advertised by Wiley & Putnam as an importation PC July 15, 1840.

AAS (1st)   H (2nd)

15010. DISCOURSE ON THE RESTORATION OF THE JEWS: DELIVERED AT THE TABERNACLE, OCT. 28 AND DEC. 2, 1844 . . .

NEW-YORK: HARPER & BROTHERS, 82 CLIFF-STREET. 1845.

⟨i⟩-viii, ⟨9⟩-55. Folded map inserted. 9¾″ × 6″ scant.

⟨1-3⁸, 4⁴⟩. Signed: ⟨A⟩-G⁴.

Noted in printed white paper wrapper; printed on front only. Also noted in blue paper wrapper; title on p. ⟨1⟩; advertisements on pp. ⟨2-4⟩ of wrapper.

AAS   H   Y

15011. Sir, / ⟨letter, 28 lines, beginning:⟩ An established firm of this City, propose publishing / on the first day of next January, in a style of suitable magnificence / as far as may relate to typography and embellishments, a work to be / called "The National Volume." / ⟨etc., etc., being a request for manuscripts to be published in a projected book. Signed at end:⟩ New York 1st Feby. 1845. M. M. Noah.

Lithographed. Printed on the first page of a single cut sheet of pale gray-blue paper folded to make four pages. Size of page: 10¾″ × 8⅜″. Pp. ⟨2-4⟩ blank. The whole in holograph facsimile.

An abandoned project. See illustration.

H

15012. Gleanings from a Gathered Harvest . . .

New York: Charles Wells, 56 Gold-Street 1845.

⟨i⟩-iv, ⟨5⟩-216. 6⅞″ full × 4¼″ full. White paper boards, printed paper label on spine.

A revised edition of *Essays of Howard* . . . , 1820.

Listed WPLNL Oct. 1845. Deposited Nov. 8, 1845(?). Reissued with cancel title-leaf dated 1847.

AAS   NYHS   Y

15013. The Lives and Opinions of Benj'n Franklin Butler . . . and Jesse Hoyt . . . by William L. Mackeinzie ⟨sic⟩ . . .

Cook & Co., Publishers, Washington-Street, Boston: For Sale by All Periodical Booksellers throughout the United States. 1845.

Letter to Major Swartwout, *March 31, 1829*, p. 38.

Letter to Jesse Hoyt, *23d Feb., 1823*, pp. 39-40.

Comments on Martin Van Buren, pp. 43-44.

Issued in printed paper wrapper?

Two states noted; the order is presumed correct:

1: Author's name on the title-page is misspelled *Mackeinzie.*

2: Author's name on the title-page correctly spelled *Mackenzie.*

H (2nd)   Y (both)

15014. Gleanings from a Gathered Harvest . . .

New-York: H. Long & Bro., 32 Ann Street. 1847.

Sheets of the 1845 printing with cancel title-leaf.

LC

15015. A LETTER ADDRESSED TO THE SOUTHERN DELEGATES OF THE BALTIMORE DEMOCRATIC CONVENTION, ON THE CLAIMS OF THE "BARN-BURNERS" TO BE ADMITTED TO SEATS IN THAT CONVENTION . . .

NEW YORK. 1848.

⟨i-ii⟩, ⟨1⟩-13. 8⅜″ × 5½″.

⟨-⟩⁸.

Printed self-wrapper. Pp. ⟨i-ii⟩ blank; title-page, p. ⟨1⟩.

Dated at end *New York, May 17, 1848.*

H

15016. Friendship's Gift: A Souvenir for MDCCC-XLVIII. Edited by Walter Percival.

Boston: Published by John P. Hill. 1848.

"Attending Auctions," pp. ⟨143⟩-146   Listed in the table of contents as at p. 141.

For fuller entry see above in the John Neal list.

15017. Inconsistency and Hypocrisy of Martin Van Buren. On the Question of Slavery.

⟨n.p., n.d., 1848⟩

Caption-title. The above at head of p. ⟨1⟩.

Issued without wrapper?

Pp. ⟨1⟩-16.

On p. 2 is an extract from Noah:

M. M. Noah in 1834, speculating upon the then impending Presidential election, writes as follows, "every paper almost that we open, speaks contemptuously of Van Buren's prospects for the Presidency; but they speak without knowledge of the labors of the man, and the vast machine of intrigue ... ⟨to⟩ ... he buys the *leaders*, and makes them *accountable for the rank and file*."

H

15018. The Jews, Judea, and Christianity. A Discourse on the Restoration of the Jews ...

London: Hugh Hughes, 15, St. Martin's-le-Grand. 1849.

Printed paper wrapper.

Reprint of *Discourse* ... , 1845.

BPL

15019. ... ADDRESS DELIVERED AT THE RE-OPENING OF THE APPRENTICES' LIBRARY, AND READING ROOMS, AT THE MECHANICS' HALL, 472 BROADWAY, SEPTEMBER 23d, 1850 ...

NEW-YORK: VAN NORDEN & AMERMAN, PRINTERS, NO. 60 WILLIAM-STREET. 1850.

At head of title: GENERAL SOCIETY OF MECHANICS AND TRADESMEN.

Cover-title?

⟨1⟩-16. 8⅝″ × 5⅜″.

⟨-⟩⁸.

Printed paper wrapper? Self-wrapper?

Issued after Oct. 7, 1850.

AAS

15020. History of the Issues of Paper-Money in the American Colonies, Anterior to the Revolution, Explanatory of the Historical Chart of the Paper Money of that Period.

St. Louis: Union, Print, 35 Locust Street, 1851.

Printed paper wrapper. Anonymous. The author was Adolphus M. Hart.

4-line recommendation, p. ⟨3⟩.

AAS

15021. The Odd-Fellows' Offering, for 1851 ...

New York: Published by Edward Walker, 114 Fulton-Street. M DCCC LI.

Leather.

"The Joy of the Law," pp. 40-43.

H

15022. The Odd-Fellows' Offering, for 1852 ...

New York: Published by Edward Walker, 114 Fulton-Street. M DCCC LII.

Leather.

"The Day of Vengeance," pp. 294-298.

H

15023. Publications of the American Jewish Historical Society Number 21   The Lyons Collection Volume I

Published by the Society 1913

Cloth; and, printed paper wrapper.

"Address ... from the *New York Evening Post*, Saturday, September 24, 1825," pp. 230-252.

"... The address delivered ... at the laying of the cornerstone of the City of Ararat, a Zionist project, originated in 1825 ... and the address now published, though repeatedly quoted, has never before been given in the complete form in which it appeared in the daily press at the time." ---P. xi.

H   LC

Sir,

Messrs C. Wells & Co.

An established firm of this City, propose publishing on the first day of next January, in a style of suitable magnificence as far as may relate to typography and embellishments, a work to be called "The National Volume".

The object is to present to the American public a work comprising an essay, paper, or literary offering, from every distinguished Statesman, Historian, Poet or writer of eminence or reputation in the Country, and thus to present to the world an array of names and contributions which may serve to illustrate the ability, taste, and peculiar style of the writers, as well as to perpetuate the names of a confederacy of Men of letters sustaining a high rank in the estimation of their Countrymen.

The direction and management of this work have been entrusted to me by the publishers, and I respectfully solicit from you a contribution in the furtherance of this interesting National object, on any subject you may deem proper.

The publishers assign no limits to the length of the paper, but among other inducements to aid in accomplishing the proposed object, would respectfully suggest that each contribution should be as brief as the nature of the subject will allow, as the list it is supposed will be numerous, although the application is to be confined to those of distinguished talents and reputation.

It is desirous that all the contributions should be received by the first of July, in order that the proper embellishments and designs may be matured and adopted, and I shall be happy to learn from you as soon as possible, whether it will be convenient or desirable to favor the publisher with a paper on any subject which may be agreeable to you.

I have the honor to be

very respectfully
Your obedient servant

M. M. Noah.

New York March 1st 1845.

MORDECAI MANUEL NOAH
Entry No. 15011
Reduced
(Harvard University Library)

Unpublished and misnamed works. Arranged alphabetically by title.

The Grand Canal

Listed in *A History of the American Theatre*, by William Dunlap, 1832, p. 409. Also listed by Friedman, 1942.

Natalie, or the Frontier Maid

Listed by Friedman, 1942.

Oh Yes, or the New Constitution

Listed in *A History of the American Theatre*, by William Dunlap, 1832, p. 409. Also listed by Friedman, 1942. Unlocated by Rosenbach; see his *An American Jewish Bibliography* ..., 1926, p. 205.

The Orphans of the Rhine

Thus *Publications of the American Jewish Historical Society*, Number 21, 1913, p. 229. An erroneous entry. See *The Wandering Boys*, 1821.

Paul and Alexis; or, the Orphans of the Rhine

See *The Wandering Boys*, 1821. *Publications of the American Jewish Historical Society Number 21*, 1913, p. 229, gives this as two titles: thus; *Paul and Alexis;* and, *The Orphans of the Rhine*. Listed by Friedman, 1942.

The Plains of Chippewa

Listed in *Publications of the American Jewish Historical Society Number 21*, 1913, p. 229. See *She Would Be a Soldier*, 1819, for which this is a subtitle.

The Siege of Tripoli

Thus *Publications of the American Jewish Historical Society Number 21*, 1913, p. 229. See *Yusef Caramalli*, below.

"... Afterwards presented as *Yusef Caramalli*" ---Friedman, 1942.

The Siege of Yorktown

Listed in *A History of the American Theatre*, by William Dunlap, 1832, p. 409. Also listed by Friedman, 1942.

Wall Street, or Ten Minutes before Three

Listed by Friedman, 1942.

Yusef Caramalli, or the Siege of Tripoli, a Dramatic Spectacle

Thus LSR June, 1820, p. 265, with title and author given under *List of American, and Important European Late Publications*.

"*The Siege of Tripoli*, first produced in 1820, later played in Philadelphia under the title *Yuseff* ⟨sic⟩ *Caramalli*, has not been preserved."--- DAB.

The title is given as *Yesef Caramatti* by William Dunlap in his *A History of the American Theatre*, N. Y., 1832, p. 409.

Oscar Wegelin, in his *Early American Plays 1714–1830* ..., N. Y., 1900, p. 75, gave the title as *The Siege of Tripoli* and reported the piece as unpublished; Wegelin repeated the statement in the second edition (1905) of his work.

"New-York Theatre.--- *Yusef Caramalli, or the Siege of Tripoli* ... was performed at the New-York theatre on Monday evening, May 15th ..."---*New York Literary Journal*, May, 1820.

"We have not been able to find any copy ..." ---*An American Jewish Bibliography* ..., by A. S. W. Rosenbach, 1926, p. 205.

Noah credited with the authorship of *Yusef Caramalli* on the title-page of *Marion* ..., 1822.

REFERENCES AND ANA

A Letter Addressed to the Members of the Legislature of South-Carolina, Examining the Claims and Qualifications of DeWitt Clinton, to the Presidency of the United States ...

Charleston, S. C. Printed at the Office of the Investigator, by John Mackey & Co. Oct. 1, 1812.

Cover-title. Printed self-wrapper.

At end of text, p. 33: *Diodorus Siculus.*

Sometimes attributed to Noah. BAL has found no evidence to support the claim. *Bibliography of South Carolina 1563–1950*, by Robert J. Turnbull, Vol. 1, p. 484, Charlottesville ⟨1956⟩, states: "Probably ⟨by⟩ William Henry Drayton."

City of New-York---SS. Mordecai M. Noah, of No. 57, Franklin-Street, Being Duly Sworn, Deposeth and Saith, that on the 20th Day of June 1828, at the 2d Ward of the City of New-York, He Was Violently Assaulted, by Elijah J. Roberts, Who Attacked Him on the Steps, and Cow-Skinned Him!! Without Any Just Justification on the Part of the Said Assailant, Wherefore this Deponent Prays, that the Said Elijah J. Roberts, May Be Bound by Recognizance to Be of Good Behaviour and Keep the Peace . . .

⟨n.p., New York, 1828⟩

Broadside. Printed on recto only. Illustrated. 25¼″ × 20⅜″.

The American Biographical Sketch Book. By William Hunt. Vol. I.

Albany: Published by the Author, No. 58 State Street. 1848.

All published? Noted only in leather.

A short sketch of Noah, p. 402; portrait inserted.

Thomas' Buffalo City Directory for 1867. To Which Is Prefixed . . . Early History of Grand Island and the City of Ararat by Lewis F. Allen . . .

Buffalo: Published by Thomas, Howard & Johnson. Franklin Printing House. 1867.

Cloth?

"Early History of Grand Island. The City of Ararat---Its Corner Stone. Mordecai M. Noah. Read before the Buffalo Historical Society Club, Mar. 5, 1866," by Lewis F. Allen, pp. 25-37. For Noah's address on Ararat see above, *Publications of the American Jewish Historical Society*, No. 21, 1913, pp. 230-252.

A Literary Autobiography of Mordecai Manuel Noah. With an Introduction, by George Alexander Kohut. From the Publications of the American Jewish Historical Society, No. 6, 1897.

⟨Press of the Friedenwald Company, Baltimore, 1897⟩

Cover-title. Printed paper wrapper. For prior publication of Noah's letter see *A History of the American Theatre*, by William Dunlap, 1832, above.

Mordecai Manuel Noah a Biographical Sketch by Simon Wolf

Philadelphia   The Levytype Company Publishers 1897

Printed paper wrapper.

Mordecai M. Noah's Discourse on the Restoration of the Jews Republished in Extract with an Introductory Note by D. S. Blondheim

The Lord Baltimore Press   The Friedenwald Company Baltimore, Md., U.S.A. ⟨1905⟩

Printed paper wrapper. Cover-title.

Mordecai Manuel Noah   Zionist, Author and Statesman. By the Rev. Max Raisin . . . Published by the "Achiasaf" Society.

"Verlags-Druckerei", Warsaw. 5666–1905.

Printed paper wrapper. Text in Hebrew.

At end is a section with a divisional title-page in Hebrew and Russian; translated: *Travels in England, France, Spain and the Barbary States in the Years 1813, 1814, 1815, by Mordecai Manuel Noah . . . Selected, Arranged, Abridged and Translated into Hebrew by M. Raisin*. See under year 1819 in main list.

Mordecai M. Noah . . . by A. B. Makover

New York Bloch Publishing Company 1917

Printed paper wrapper.

Major Noah: American-Jewish Pioneer by Isaac Goldberg . . .

Philadelphia The Jewish Publication Society of America 1936

Mordecai Manuel Noah As Playwright by Lee M. Friedman . . . Reprinted from Historia Judaica Vol. IV, No. 2

New York, 1942 Historia Judaica 40 West 68th Street . . .

Printed paper wrapper.

⟨Translation from Yiddish⟩ Mordecai Emanuel Noah Dreamers of Redemption in America A Romance by S. Erdberg

New York Buenos Aires 5712/1951

Colophon dated *14 de Noviembre de 1952.*

⟨Translation from Hebrew⟩ Where Is the Land of Ararat? A Novel of the Life of Mordecai Emanuel Noah by Yochanan Twersky

Tel Aviv, Ayanut, 1953/1954

BENJAMIN FRANKLIN (FRANK) NORRIS

(Justin Sturgis, Marmaduke Masters, Norrys)

1 8 7 0 – 1 9 0 2

15024. YVERNELLE A LEGEND OF FEUDAL FRANCE...

PHILADELPHIA J. B. LIPPINCOTT COMPANY 1892

Title-page in black, blue, gold, rose.

⟨i-ii⟩, ⟨1⟩-116. 11 plates inserted; other illustrations and decorations in text. $9\frac{1}{16}''$ × $6\frac{7}{16}''$.

Inferior numerals indicate inserted leaves. ⟨1^{5}3, 2^4, 3^{4}2-3, 4-5^4, 6^{4}1,4, 7^{4}2-3, 8^{4}1,4, 9^{4}1,4, 10^{4}1,4, 11^4, 12^{4}1,4, 13-14^4, 15-16^1⟩.

V cloth: blue; green; mauve; old rose; orange; white. Leather. Silver-coated end papers with an all-over pattern of roses in intaglio. Gold-coated end papers with an all-over pattern of roses in intaglio. Top edges gilt. Flyleaves.

Advertised for fall publication PW Sept. 26, 1891. Deposited Nov. 19, 1891. Listed PW Dec. 12, 1891.

B   H   LC   NYPL   UV

15025. Blue and Gold.

Published by the Junior Class of the University of California, Berkeley, California. San Francisco: H. S. Crocker Co. 1892.

"The Class of '94," pp. 46-49. Signed: *Historian*. Illustrations by Norris, pp. ⟨50⟩, ⟨51⟩, 231.

NYPL   UV

15026. The Blue and Gold

Published by the Junior Class of the University of California ⟨Berkeley⟩ Press of H. S. Crocker Company 1893

"History of the Class of '94," pp. 28-29.

"Two Pair. A Farce in One Act," pp. 183-192. Written and illustrated by Norris.

"The Story of the Seven Sports; or, the Genie of the Barrel. An Arabian Nights' Tale," pp. 218-222. Anonymous. Credited to Norris by Lohf & Sheehy, p. 50 (entry No. 120): "Illustrated with pen-and-ink sketches by Norris. Unsigned, but attributed to Norris by Harvey Taylor."

Other illustrations by Norris on pp. ⟨57⟩, ⟨81⟩, 104, 114, ⟨133⟩, ⟨155⟩, ⟨194⟩ and ⟨246⟩.

AAS   NYPL   UV

15027. The Story of the Files   A Review of Californian Writers and Literature by Ella Sterling Cummins.

Issued under the Auspices of the World's Fair Commission of California, Columbian Exposition, 1893 ... ⟨San Francisco⟩

"Crepusculum," p. 360. Collected in *Two Poems*, 1930.

For fuller entry see No. 1113.

15028. Christmas Wave

San Francisco 1897

Printed paper wrapper. Cover-title.

Issued as a supplement to *The Wave*, a periodical issued in San Francisco.

"Perverted Tales," pp. 5-7, comprising the following: "The 'Ricksha that Happened," a burlesque of Kipling; "The Green Stone of Unrest," a burlesque of Stephen Crane; "A Hero of Tomato Can," a burlesque of Bret Harte; "Van Bubble's Story," a burlesque of Richard Harding Davis; "Ambrosia Beer," a burlesque of Ambrose Bierce; "I Call on Lady Dotty," a burlesque of Anthony Hope Hawkins.

California State Library, Sacramento

15029. MORAN OF THE LADY LETTY   A STORY OF ADVENTURE OFF THE CALIFORNIA COAST...

NEW YORK DOUBLEDAY & McCLURE CO. 1898

⟨i-viii⟩, 1-293, blank leaf. Laid paper. $7\frac{1}{4}''$ × $4\frac{13}{16}''$.

⟨1-19^8⟩. *Signed:* ⟨-⟩^{4}, ⟨1⟩-18^8, 19^4.

T cloth: green. White laid end papers.

Note: Johnson (p. 399) states "with or without top edges stained; no known priority." Lohf & Sheehy (p. 22) state "some copies have top edges stained." Further information wanting. Thus far (July, 1971) all copies examined by BAL have top edges plain.

Deposited Sept. 19, 1898. Announced PW Sept. 24, 1898. Listed PW Oct. 1, 1898. Issued in London by Grant Richards under the title *Shanghaied;* listed Ath March 25, 1899.

AAS   B   H   LC   Y

15030. Mariposa

   Published by the Ladies Relief Society of Oakland ⟨n.d., 1898⟩

Cover-title. Printed paper wrapper. At head of p. ⟨1⟩: *Mariposa Magazine   One Issue Only   For the Benefit of Ladies Relief Society of Oakland, Cal.*

"After Strange Gods," pp. ⟨28⟩-33. Collected in *Collected Writings Hitherto Unpublished . . .* , 1928.

HM

15031. McTEAGUE   A   STORY   OF   SAN FRANCISCO . . .

   NEW YORK   DOUBLEDAY & McCLURE CO.   1899

⟨i-vi⟩, 1-442; plus: 4 pages: *A New American Author . . .* Laid paper. 7¾″ × 5⅛″ scant.

⟨1-28⁸; plus: 29²⟩. *Signed:* ⟨-⟩³, ⟨1⟩-20, ⟨21⟩, 22-27⁸, 28⁷.

T cloth: red. White laid end papers.

Note: The last word on p. 106 is *moment.* See next entry for a revised printing.

Deposited Feb. 27, 1899. Advertised in PW March 11, 1899. Listed PW March 18, 1899. The London (Grant Richards) edition listed Ath Nov. 4, 1899.

A copy has been reported with signature 25 paged: 385, 388, 385, 388-400. Further information wanting.

H   NYPL   UV

15032. McTeague   A Story of San Francisco ⟨Second Printing, Revised⟩ . . .

   New York   Doubleday & McClure Co.   1899

Title-page decoration printed on a blindstamped diamond.

⟨i-vi⟩, 1-442; 4 pp. devoted to *A New American Author . . .* Laid paper. 7¾″ × 5¹⁄₁₆″ full.

⟨1², 2-29⁸⟩. *Signed:* ⟨1⟩¹¹, 2-20, ⟨21⟩, 22-27⁸, 28⁷.

Revised. P. 106 ends: *for him.* For first (unrevised) printing see preceding entry.

Note: The second printing advertised PW June 10, 1899; the third printing advertised PW June 24, 1899. BAL has been unable to distinguish two printings of the revised edition.

Joseph Katz, University of South Carolina

15033. BLIX . . .

   NEW YORK   DOUBLEDAY & McCLURE CO.   1899

Title-page printed in black and blind.

⟨i-viii⟩, ⟨1⟩-339. 7⅜″ × 4¹³⁄₁₆″.

⟨-⟩⁴, 1-⟨2⟩, 3-21⁸, 22².

V cloth: tan. White end papers, either wove or laid.

Note: The publisher's spine imprint occurs as follows: DOUBLEDAY / & McCLURE Cᵒ̣ / It also occurs in the following form; status not known: DOUBLEDAY / AND / McCLURE Cᵒ̣ / Variant in UV.

Advertised for *next week* PW Sept. 9, 1899. Deposited Sept. 15, 1899. Listed PW Sept. 23, 1899. The London (Grant Richards) edition listed Ath June 23, 1900.

AAS   H   LC   UV   Y

15034. A MAN'S WOMAN . . .

   NEW YORK   DOUBLEDAY & McCLURE CO.   1900

⟨i-viii⟩, 1-286; advertisements, pp. ⟨287⟩. Laid paper. 7¾″ scant × 5⅛″.

⟨-⟩⁴, ⟨1⟩-18⁸. The title-leaf (⟨-⟩₃) is a cancel; the reason therefor not known to BAL. The note on p. viii may hold a clue: "The following novel was completed March 22, 1899, and sent to the printer in October of the same year. After the plates had been made notice was received that a play called *A Man's Woman* had been written by Mrs. Crawford Flexner . . . As it was impossible to change the name of the novel at the time this notice was received, it has been published under its original title."

Two printings noted:

FIRST PRINTING

As above. The title-page is a cancel.

P. 64, last line: *. . . of the bone pro-* /

P. 65, first line: *truding. While Lloyd . . .*

Spine imprint: DOUBLEDAY / & McCLURE CO.

SECOND PRINTING

The title-leaf is integral, not a cancel.

P. 64, last line: *. . . picnickers "grouped"* /

P. 65, first line: *on a hotel . . .*

Spine imprint: DOUBLEDAY / & McCLURE CO.

Also noted in a binding unlike that on the first printings; a most notable variation being the spine

YVERNELLE

A LEGEND OF
FEUDAL FRANCE
BY
FRANK NORRIS

"Cui me moribundam deseris, hospes?"
ÆNEID

ILLUSTRATED

PHILADELPHIA
J. B. Lippincott Company
1892

imprint which reads: DOUBLEDAY / PAGE & / COMPANY

T cloth: red. White laid end papers.

Note: A "special limited" printing, issued in printed paper wrapper, listed PW Oct. 5, 1901; issued by A. Wessels Company, New York.

Deposited Jan. 31, 1900. Advertised for *to-day* PW Feb. 3, 1900. Listed PW Feb. 10, 1900. The London (Grant Richards) edition listed Ath and PC Oct. 20, 1900.

AAS (2nd) BPL (2nd) H (1st) LC (1st) UV (1st, 2nd) Y (1st)

15035. Under the Berkeley Oaks   Stories by Students of the University of California . . .

A. M. Robertson San Francisco 1901

"Travis Hallett's Half-back," pp. ⟨9⟩-36. Collected in *Collected Writings Hitherto Unpublished . . .* , 1928.

Deposited Dec. 19, 1900.

H   UV

15036. . . . THE OCTOPUS   A STORY OF CALIFORNIA . . .

NEW YORK DOUBLEDAY, PAGE & CO. 1901

At head of title: THE EPIC OF THE WHEAT

Five printings noted; for textual variations see chart below.

FIRST PRINTING

⟨i-viii⟩, ⟨1⟩-652, 2 blank leaves. $7^{11}/_{16}''$ × $5^{1}/_{8}''$.

⟨1-8^8, 9-24^{16}, 25^{12}⟩. *Signed:* ⟨-⟩^{4}, ⟨1⟩-41^8.

T cloth: red. Publisher's spine imprint stamped from a sans serif face.

On copyright page: *J. J. Little* device.

SECOND AND THIRD PRINTINGS

See chart below for textual variations.

⟨i-viii⟩, ⟨1⟩-652, 2 blank leaves.

⟨1-2^{16}, 3-20^8, 21-29^{16}, 30^{12}⟩. *Signed:* ⟨-⟩^{4}, ⟨1⟩-41^8.

T cloth: red. Publisher's spine imprint stamped from a modified black letter face.

On copyright page: *Manhattan Press* imprint.

FOURTH PRINTING

⟨i-viii⟩, ⟨1⟩-652, 2 blank leaves. *Note:* In some copies the final blank leaves are excised.

⟨1-20^{16}, 21^{12}⟩. *Signed:* ⟨-⟩^{4}, ⟨1⟩-41^8. *Note:* In some copies the blank leaves are excised.

T cloth: red. Publisher's spine imprint stamped from a modified black letter face.

On copyright page: *Manhattan Press* imprint.

FIFTH PRINTING

⟨i-viii⟩, ⟨1⟩-652, 2 blank leaves.

⟨1-2^{16}, 3-14^8, 15-26^{16}, 27^{12}⟩. *Signed:* ⟨-⟩^{4}, ⟨1⟩, 2-3, ⟨4⟩, 5-8, ⟨9-11⟩, 12-14, ⟨15-17⟩, 18-20, ⟨21-23⟩, 24-25, ⟨26⟩, 27-28, ⟨29⟩, 30, ⟨31⟩, 32-33, ⟨34⟩, 35-36, ⟨37⟩, 38, ⟨39-40⟩, 41^8. *Note:* Certain of the signature marks are present as vestiges only.

T cloth: red. Publisher's spine imprint stamped from a modified black letter face. Also noted in blue-gray paper boards, printed paper label on spine; leaf ⟨1⟩$_1$ excised; location: UV.

On copyright page: *Manhattan Press* imprint.

Note: Joseph Katz in *A Frank Norris Collection*, 1970, p. 14, entry No. 55, reports a copy as follows: "A reprinting of the first edition. The Manhattan Press imprint is on the copyright page. Red cloth stamped in gold . . ." BAL has seen no such form of the book. Mr. Katz, in reply to BAL's query, reported inability to find such a copy in his collection. In short, BAL's studies indicate that the first printing, unrevised text, carries the *J. J. Little* device on the copyright page; that the *Manhattan Press* imprint occurs only on reprints, text revised, of the date 1901.

Shortly---PW March 2, 1901. Noted for the *23d inst.*---PW March 9, 1901. Advertised for March 23 PW March 9, 1901. *In preparation*---PW March 23, 1901. *At once*---PW March 30, 1901. Advertised for *to-day* PW March 30, 1901. Deposited April 1, 1901. Listed PW April 6, 1901. The *10th thousand* advertised PW April 20, 1901. A copy of the third printing (in H) presented by Norris to W. D. Howells under date *May, 1901*. A copy of the fourth printing (in AAS) inscribed by an early owner Oct. 7, 1901. The London (Grant Richards) edition listed Ath Sept. 14, 1901; the Alex. Moring edition advertised as *new* Ath April 13, 1907. The Leipzig (Tauchnitz) edition, Nos. 3542-3543 of the series, issued not before Dec. 1901.

AAS (4th) BPL (4th) H (1st, 3d, 4th, 5th) NYPL (1st) UV (2nd, 4th, 5th) Y (1st)

TEXTUAL ALTERATIONS

The alterations here listed are representative; others are present.

Text	1st Printing	2nd Printing	3d Printing	4th & 5th Printings
P. 49, line 11 from bottom:				
. . . *Lnng/*	x	x	x	
. . . *Long/*				x
P. 278, line 17:				
. . . *never." "Sign* . . .	x			
. . . *never. Sign* . . .		x	x	x

	1st Printing	2nd Printing	3d Printing	4th & 5th Printing
P. ⟨283⟩				
BOOK II in gothic	x			
BOOK II in roman		x	x	x
P. ⟨285⟩ heading				
In gothic	x			
In roman		x	x	x
P. 287, line 14 from bottom:				
consider small ...	x			
consider serious ...		x	x	x
P. 294, line 13:				
Ruggles's offices ...	x			
Ruggles's office ...		x	x	x
P. 393, line 8:				
... sowest it not ...	x			
... sowest is not ...		x	x	x
P. 395, line 2 from bottom:				
Magnus and Lyman ...	x			
Magnus and Harran ...		x	x	x
P. 434, line 11:				
... There's /	x			
... with. /		x	x	x
P. 447, line 6 from bottom:				
stepped on ...	x			
stepped out on ...		x	x	x
P. 494, line 6:				
... mobilized, /	x			
... immobilized, /		x	x	x
P. 497, line 18:				
... lips, from ...	x			
... lips. From ...		x	x	x
P. 500, line 9:				
... jumped high ...	x			
... jumped fair ...		x	x	x
P. 503, line 8 from bottom:				
cork-screw ...	x			
with a ...		x	x	x
P. 504, line 4 from bottom:				
... hills contestants ...	x			
... hills the contestants /		x	x	x
P. 520, line 2 from bottom:				
from ...	x			
behind. /		x	x	x
P. 555, line 3:				
... clamour broke ...	x			
... confusion broke ...		x	x	x

	1st Printing	2nd Printing	3d Printing	4th & 5th Printing
P. 587, line 12:				
wore a rather ...	x			
wore a hat ...		x	x	x
P. 596, line 8 from bottom:				
... bestirred, /	x			
... bestirred her- /		x	x	x
P. 617, line 21:				
... clamouring machinery ...	x			
... bellowing machinery ...		x	x	x
P. 621, line 6:				
... blue eyes ...	x			
... brown eyes ...		x	x	x
P. 631, line 8 from bottom:				
wife and ...	x	x	x	
mother and ...				x
P. 632, line 18:				
... of a ---; ...	x			
... of an outcast; ...		x	x	x
P. 646, line 9:				
... trousers legs ...	x	x		
... trouser legs ...			x	x

15037. The Author's Year Book for 1902. Gathered and Arranged by W. E. Price.

New York The Book-Lover Press, 1902.

"The 'Volunteer Manuscript.' Plain Talk to the Ambitious Amateur," pp. ⟨24⟩-34. Collected in *Responsibilities of the Novelist*, 1903.

Issued in paper boards?

Deposited March 15, 1902.

JC

15038. ... THE PIT A STORY OF CHICAGO ...

NEW YORK DOUBLEDAY, PAGE & CO. 1903

At head of title: THE EPIC OF THE WHEAT

Five printings noted:

FIRST PRINTING, BINDING A

⟨i-viii⟩, ⟨1⟩-421; blank, p. ⟨422⟩; blank leaf. Frontispiece portrait inserted. *Note:* The frontispiece is not present in the surviving copyright deposit copy. 7⅞" full × 5¼".

⟨1-27⁸⟩. Signed: ⟨-⟩⁴, ⟨1⟩-11, ⟨12⟩, 13-22, ⟨23⟩, 24-26⁸, 27⁴.

Gray laid paper boards, printed paper label on spine. Gray laid paper end papers. Top edges stained gray. P. ⟨iii⟩ of the front end paper imprinted: SPECIAL PRESENTATION EDITION / With the compliments of the Publishers / To

On copyright page: *Published February, 1903* / FIRST EDITION / ⟨J. J. Little device⟩

P. 34, line 3: . . . *envelope* . . .

P. 82, line 16: *burnng* . . .

P. 250, line 23: . . . *beyound* . . .

Note: A copy as above was seen at EM (Sept. 1951) inscribed: *This is the first copy printed and was received at office Nov. 20, 1902. F. N. Doubleday.* It differs from the above in that the printed notice is not present on p. ⟨iii⟩ of the front end paper.

FIRST PRINTING, BINDING Aa

Sheets of the above issued for trade use.

Leaf: $7\frac{3}{4}'' \times 5\frac{1}{16}''$. No frontispiece.

T cloth: red. The spine imprint stamped from a sans serif face.

SECOND PRINTING

⟨i-viii⟩, ⟨1⟩-421; blank, p. ⟨422⟩; blank leaf. No frontispiece.

⟨1-27^8⟩. *Signed:* ⟨-⟩^{4}, ⟨1⟩-11, ⟨12⟩, 13-22, ⟨23⟩, 24-26^8, 27^4.

T cloth: red. The spine imprint stamped from a sans serif face.

On copyright page: *Published February, 1903* and J. J. Little device. The statement FIRST EDITION is not present.

P. 34, line 3: . . . *envelope* . . .

P. 82, line 16: *burnng* . . .

P. 250, line 23: . . . *beyound* . . .

THIRD PRINTING

⟨i-viii⟩, ⟨1⟩-421; blank, p. ⟨422⟩; blank leaf. No frontispiece.

⟨1-27^8⟩. *Signed:* ⟨-⟩^{4}, ⟨1⟩-11, ⟨12⟩, 13-22, ⟨23⟩, 24-26^8, 27^4.

T cloth: red. The spine imprint stamped from a modified black letter face.

The *Third Printing* has been noted in the following *Tabard Inn* bindings; see BAL, Vol. 1, pp. xxii-xxiii.

Tabard Inn Binding A: Maroon T cloth. Gold-stamped save as noted. Front: THE PIT / FRANK NORRIS / ⟨*front bordered by a blindstamped rule*⟩ Spine: ⟨*rule*⟩ / THE / PIT / BY / FRANK / NORRIS / ⟨*rule*⟩ Leaf ⟨27⟩$_8$ excised.

Tabard Inn Binding B: Maroon T cloth. Gold-stamped. Front: THE PIT Spine: ⟨*rule*⟩ / THE / PIT / BY / FRANK / NORRIS / ⟨*rule*⟩ Leaf ⟨27⟩$_8$ excised.

Tabard Inn Binding C: Maroon T cloth. Gold-stamped save as noted. Front: THE PIT / FRANK NORRIS / ⟨*front bordered by a blindstamped rule, decorated with dots*⟩ Spine: ⟨*rule*⟩ / THE / PIT / BY / FRANK / NORRIS / ⟨*rule*⟩ Leaf ⟨27⟩$_8$ excised.

Note: Sequence, if any, of the *Tabard Inn* bindings not known; the designations are for identification only.

On copyright page: *Published February, 1903* The statement FIRST EDITION is not present; printer's imprint not present.

P. 34, line 3: . . . *envelope* . . .

P. 82, line 16: *burning* . . .

P. 250, line 23: . . . *beyound* . . .

FOURTH PRINTING

⟨i-viii⟩, ⟨1⟩-421; blank, p. ⟨422⟩; blank leaf. No frontispiece.

⟨1-27^8⟩. *Signed:* ⟨-⟩^{4}, ⟨1⟩-11, ⟨12⟩, 13-22, ⟨23⟩, 24-26^8, 27^4.

T cloth: red. The spine imprint stamped from a modified black letter face.

On copyright page: *Published February, 1903* The statement FIRST EDITION not present; printer's imprint present: *Manhattan Press.*

P. 34, line 3: . . . *envelope* . . .

P. 82, line 16: *burning* . . .

P. 250, line 23: . . . *beyond* . . .

FIFTH PRINTING

⟨i-viii⟩, ⟨1⟩-421, blank, p. ⟨422⟩, blank leaf. No frontispiece.

⟨1-27^8⟩. *Signed:* ⟨-⟩^{4}, ⟨1⟩-11, ⟨12⟩, 13-16, ⟨17⟩, 18-22, ⟨23⟩, 24-26^8, 27^4.

T cloth: red. The spine imprint stamped from a modified black letter face.

On copyright page: *Published February, 1903* The statement FIRST EDITION not present; printer's imprint present: *Manhattan Press.*

P. 34, line 3: . . . *envelop* . . .

P. 82, line 16: *burning* . . .

P. 250, line 23: . . . *beyond* . . .

On copyright page: *Published February, 1903* A copy of the first printing has been seen in paper boards inscribed by the publisher "received . . . Nov. 20, 1902"; see above under *Binding A.* Listed PW Jan. 3, 1903, as in boards, frontispiece portrait. "Doubleday . . . have just ready a special presentation edition ⟨in paper boards⟩ . . . The trade edition ⟨in cloth⟩ will be ready for delivery January 15."---PW Jan. 3, 1903. "Doubleday . . . have now ready . . . *The Pit*, of which 20,000 copies were exhausted a month before the book appeared, and of which two more large editions

were printed before the day of publication . . . "
---PW Jan. 24, 1903. "Three large advance
editions . . . placed before publication last Thursday. Yet we had four different orders for a thousand copies each, besides dozens of smaller
ones . . . "---Advertisement, PW Jan. 24, 1903.
"*The Pit* has come into popularity with great
bounds, and notwithstanding that the advance
sale was very large, the publishers have not been
able to keep up with the orders. In seven days the
fourth edition was ready, and preparations were
made to print a fifth edition of twenty thousand
copies as quickly as several ⟨*sic*⟩ establishments
could manufacture them."---PW Feb. 7, 1903.
Query: Was the book produced from two or more
sets of plates? The London (Grant Richards)
edition promised for Feb. 11, 1903, Ath Jan. 31,
1903. The De la More Press edition advertised
as *new* Ath April 13, 1907.

AAS (1st, *Binding A*)   B(4th)   BA (3d)   BPL (5th)
H (1st, *Binding A;* 2d; 3d; 5th)   JB (3d in Tabard
Inn bindings A-C)   LC (1st, *Binding A*, being a
deposit copy)   UV (1st, *Binding A;* 1st, *Binding Aa;*
3d; 5th)   Y (2d; 3d; 4th)

15039. A DEAL IN WHEAT AND OTHER
STORIES OF THE NEW AND OLD
WEST . . .

NEW YORK DOUBLEDAY, PAGE & COMPANY 1903

⟨i-viii⟩, ⟨1⟩-272. Laid paper. Frontispiece and 3
plates inserted. $8\frac{1}{16}'' \times 5\frac{5}{16}''$.

⟨1-17^8, 18^4⟩.

Noted on two weights of paper; sequence, if any, not
known:

A: Sheets bulk $\frac{7}{8}''$. Copyright deposit copies thus.

B: Sheets bulk $\frac{3}{4}''$.

T cloth: maroon. Stamped in gold. White laid or
wove end papers. Top edges gilt.

Note: A copy has been seen in red T cloth, stamped
in white and green, print pasted to front cover.
Sheets bulk $\frac{7}{8}''$. Leaves $7\frac{5}{8}''$ scant $\times 5\frac{1}{8}''$ scant.
Status unknown. Location: In the collection of
Mr. Joseph Katz, Columbia, S. C.

Advertised for Sept. 3 PW Aug. 1, 1903. Deposited
Sept. 4, 1903. Advertised as *just ready* PW Sept. 5,
1903. Listed PW Sept. 19, 1903. The London
(Grant Richards) edition listed Ath Oct. 17, 1903.

AAS H LC Y

15040. THE RESPONSIBILITIES OF THE
NOVELIST AND OTHER LITERARY
ESSAYS . . .

NEW YORK DOUBLEDAY, PAGE & COMPANY 1903

⟨i-viii⟩, ⟨1⟩-311; blank, p. ⟨312⟩; blank leaf. Laid
paper. Portrait frontispiece inserted. $7\frac{7}{8}''$ full ×
$5\frac{5}{16}''$.

⟨1^9, 2-20^8⟩. Leaf ⟨1⟩$_4$ inserted.

Green sateen. Goldstamped. White laid end
papers. Top edges gilt, otherwise untrimmed.

A variant of unknown status has been seen:

⟨i-vi⟩, ⟨1⟩-311; blank, p. ⟨312⟩; blank leaf. Laid
paper. Portrait frontispiece inserted. $7\frac{5}{8}'' \times$
$5\frac{1}{8}''$ scant.

⟨1-20^8⟩. The sheets appear to be the same as
those described above save for the absence of
leaf ⟨1⟩$_4$, the table of contents leaf.

V cloth: green. Stamped in white on front, printed
paper label on spine. Publisher's imprint stamped
in white at foot of spine. All edges trimmed; top
edges plain. White laid end papers. An imperfect
copy (in Y) shows no evidence of a spine label;
possibly issued with stamped spine. Remainder?
Locations: HM, Y.

On copyright page: *Published, September, 1903*
Advertised for Sept. 17 PW Aug. 1, 1903. Noted
as *just ready* PW Sept. 19, 1903. Advertised for Sept.
22 PW Sept. 19, 1903. Deposited Sept. 21, 1903.
Listed PW Oct. 3, 1903. The London edition
(Grant Richards) listed Ath Oct. 31, 1903.

Query: Issued simultaneously as Vol. 7 of *The
Golden Gate Edition . . . Complete Works of Frank
Norris,* New York, 1903?

AAS H LC Y

15041. Argonaut Stories . . . Selected from the
Argonaut Jerome Hart, Editor

San Francisco: Payot, Upham & Company
Agents for Pacific Coast 1906

"A Caged Lion," pp. 13-23. Collected in *The
Third Circle,* 1909.

For fuller entry see No. 11893.

15042. THE JOYOUS MIRACLE . . .

NEW YORK   DOUBLEDAY, PAGE & COMPANY
MCMVI

Title-page printed in black and pale orange.

Two printings noted:

FIRST PRINTING

⟨i-iv⟩, 1-27; tailpiece, p. ⟨28⟩. Frontispiece and
printed protective tissue inserted. Laid paper.
$7\frac{7}{16}'' \times 4\frac{7}{8}''$.

⟨1-4^4⟩.

SECOND PRINTING

⟨i-viii⟩, 1-27; tailpiece, p. ⟨28⟩. Frontispiece and
printed protective tissue inserted. Laid paper.
$7\frac{7}{16}'' \times 4\frac{7}{8}''$.

⟨1^2, 2-5^4⟩.

Tan linen weave paper boards sides, white imitation vellum shelf back. Laid paper end papers. Top edges gilt.

On copyright page: *Published, October, 1906* Deposited May 28, 1906. Advertised for Oct. 11 PW Sept. 29, 1906. Advertised PW Oct. 6, 1906. Listed PW Oct. 20, 1906. The London (Harper) printing listed PC Oct. 6, 1906; *see next entry.*

H (2d)   LC (1st, being a deposit copy)

15043. THE JOYOUS MIRACLE . . .

LONDON   HARPER AND BROTHERS   MCMVI

Title-page printed in black and pale orange.

⟨i-iv⟩, 1-27; tailpiece, p. ⟨28⟩. Laid paper. Frontispiece and printed protective tissue inserted. 7⅜″ × 4⅞″.

⟨1-4⁴⟩.

Note: The title-leaf (⟨1⟩₂) is a cancel.

V cloth: white.

On verso of title-leaf: *Printed In Cambridge Mass., U.S.A.*

Issued prior to the preceding? Listed PC Oct. 6, 1906.

Y

15044. The Spinners' Book of Fiction by ⟨16 authors⟩ . . . with a Dedicatory Poem by George Sterling . . .

Paul Elder and Company San Francisco and New York ⟨1907⟩

"A Lost Story," pp. 221-242. Collected in *Collected Writings Hitherto Unpublished,* 1928.

For fuller entry see No. 11999.

15045. THE THIRD CIRCLE . . .

NEW YORK: JOHN LANE COMPANY   LONDON: JOHN LANE, THE BODLEY HEAD   MCMIX

⟨i-ii⟩, ⟨1⟩-298; 4 pp. advertisements. Portrait frontispiece inserted. 7⅜″ × 4¹⁵⁄₁₆″.

⟨1-19⁸⟩.

T cloth: red.

Deposited May 27, 1909. BA copy received June 2, 1909. Listed PW June 5, 1909; Bkr July 23, 1909.

AAS   B   BA   H   NYPL   Y

15046. VANDOVER AND THE BRUTE . . .

DOUBLEDAY, PAGE & COMPANY   GARDEN CITY   NEW YORK   1914

Edited by Charles G. Norris; see the foreword to the 1928 edition of this work.

⟨i⟩-⟨x⟩, ⟨1⟩-354; printer's imprint, p. ⟨355⟩; blank, pp. ⟨356-358⟩. 7⅜″ × 5¹⁄₁₆″.

⟨1-23⁸⟩.

T cloth: orange-brown. *Note:* Advance copies were issued in gray paper boards, unbleached linen shelf back, printed paper label on spine.

"Ready April 9"––-PW March 14, 1914. Under date April 3, 1914, Charles G. Norris sent a copy in boards, cloth shelf back, label on spine, to John O'Hara Cosgrave; letter in UV. BA copy in cloth received April 14, 1914. Listed PW April 24, 1914. A "second large printing," not identified by BAL, noted in PW June 27, 1914. The London (Heinemann) edition noted for June 17, 1914, Bkr June 12, 1914; listed Bkr June 19, 1914.

AAS (cloth)   BA (cloth)   H (both)   UV (both)   Y (both)

15047. THE SURRENDER OF SANTIAGO AN ACCOUNT OF THE HISTORIC SURRENDER OF SANTIAGO TO GENERAL SHAFTER JULY 17, 1898 . . .

SAN FRANCISCO   PAUL ELDER AND COMPANY NINETEEN SEVENTEEN

⟨i-vi⟩, ⟨1⟩-24; blank, p. ⟨25⟩; *Published for the Benefit of the Red Cross* . . . , p. ⟨26⟩. Portrait of Gen. Shafter tipped to p. ⟨vi⟩. 6³⁄₁₆″ × 4¹³⁄₁₆″.

⟨-⟩¹⁶.

Printed tan stiff paper wrapper.

" . . . Issued . . . May, nineteen seventeen"––-p. ⟨26⟩.

AAS   H   NYPL   UV

15048. COLLECTED WRITINGS HITHERTO UNPUBLISHED IN BOOK FORM . . . WITH AN INTRODUCTION BY CHARLES G. NORRIS   VOLUME X

1928   DOUBLEDAY, DORAN & COMPANY, INC. GARDEN CITY, NEW YORK

Title-page in black and orange.

⟨i-ii⟩, ⟨i⟩-⟨xiv⟩, ⟨1⟩-335, blank leaf. 8⁹⁄₁₆″ × 5¹³⁄₁₆″. Laid paper.

⟨1⁹, 2-22⁸⟩. Leaf ⟨1⟩₃ inserted.

White imitation vellum and orange paper. Top edges gilt.

Issued as Vol. 10 of *The Argonaut Manuscript Limited Edition,* limited to 245 copies. According to the publisher's prospectus (in NYPL) issued on Nov. 16, 1928. Deposited Feb. 15, 1929. Reissued in black V cloth, printed on wove paper. Pagination and signature collection as above. Leaf: 8⁹⁄₁₆″ × 5¾″. According to Katz issued July 29, 1929. (Mr. Katz's information on the basis of correspondence with the publisher.)

On copyright page of both printings: *First Edition*

H (cloth)   LC (vellum)   NYPL (cloth)   Y (vellum)

15049. ⟨Complete Works of Frank Norris⟩

1928   Doubleday, Doran & Company, Inc. Garden City, New York

Issued in two formats: *The Argonaut Manuscript Limited Edition*, bound in white imitation vellum and orange paper, limited to 245 sets, with a leaf of the *ms* of *McTeague* bound in Vol. I. And, a trade format bound in black V cloth; on the spine: *Collected Writings*

According to a prospectus issued by the publisher (in NYPL) the limited edition was to be published Nov. 16, 1928; it was deposited for copyright Feb. 15, 1929. For further comment on publication see preceding entry.

1-2: *The Octopus.*

3: *Blix. Moran of the Lady Letty.*

4: *The Third Circle. A Deal in Wheat.*

5: *Vandover and the Brute.*

6: *A Man's Woman. Yvernelle.*

7: *The Responsibilities of the Novelist. The Joyous Miracle.*

8: *McTeague.*

9: *The Pit.*

10: *Collected Writings Hitherto Unpublished in Book Form.* See preceding entry.

Reissued 1967 by The Kennikat Press, Inc., Port Washington, N. Y.

NYPL

15050. FRANK NORRIS: TWO POEMS AND "KIM" REVIEWED. WITH A BIBLIOG-RAPHY BY HARVEY TAYLOR.

HARVEY TAYLOR   SAN FRANCISCO 1930

⟨1-46⟩, blank leaf. For the most part printed on one side of leaf only. Wove paper watermarked *Buckeye.* 8″ × 5⅜″. Frontispiece portrait tipped to p. ⟨4⟩.

⟨1-6⁴⟩.

Blue paper boards, white V cloth shelf back. Printed paper label on front. White wove end papers watermarked *Warren's Olde Style.*

" . . . Two hundred copies . . . printed . . . numbered, and signed by the publisher, and the artist . . . "---Colophon.

According to Taylor (*ca.* 1932) 25 copies were issued with an original Charles G. Norris letter inserted.

Contents:

"Crepusculum," p. ⟨9⟩. Previously in *The Story of the Files*, 1893; see above.

"Brunhilde," pp. ⟨11-13⟩. Here first in book form.

"Mr. Kipling's *Kim*," pp. ⟨15-19⟩. Here first in book form.

"The First Editions of Frank Norris. A Bibliography," by Harvey Taylor, pp. ⟨21-45⟩.

B   H   NYPL   Y

15051. Stories and Sketches by Frank Norris from *The Wave* 1893-1898

⟨n.p., n.d., San Francisco: The Westgate Press, 1931⟩

Not seen. Entry on the basis of a photographic copy.

Cover-title. The above on p. ⟨1⟩. Pp. ⟨1⟩-⟨16⟩.

On pp. ⟨3⟩-15: "Unequally Yoked: A Short Story from *The Wave* of December 23, 1893." Previously published in *The Third Circle*, 1909, under the title "Toppan."

On p. ⟨16⟩: The first page of a story titled "Bandy Callaghan's Girl: A Short Story from *The Wave* of April 18, 1896."

Intended for publication in *Frank Norris of "The Wave"* . . . , 1931, *q.v.* Suppressed. The only surviving copy (Stanford University Libraries) is cataloged as follows: "This signature is a short story for which permission was not obtained for inclusion in . . . *Frank Norris of the Wave.* According to the binder of the book, all copies of this signature were destroyed but this one . . . "

See next entry.

15052. FRANK NORRIS OF "THE WAVE" STORIES & SKETCHES FROM THE SAN FRANCISCO WEEKLY, 1893 TO 1897. FOREWORD BY CHARLES G. NORRIS. INTRODUCTION BY OSCAR LEWIS.

1931   SAN FRANCISCO   THE WESTGATE PRESS

Title-page in black and orange. *See preceding entry.*

⟨i-xii⟩, ⟨1⟩-250; colophon, p. ⟨251⟩. 9¼″ × 6⁵⁄₁₆″. Illustrated.

⟨1⁶, 2-16⁸, 17⁶⟩.

Ornamented buff paper boards, rough red-brown cloth shelf back, printed paper label on spine. At front and at back: A gathering of four leaves of book stock used as end papers, one leaf being used as the pastedown, the other three leaves free. Also issued in marbled boards sides, unbleached canvas shelf back; otherwise as the preceding.

"Copy Number . . . of 500 copies printed . . . February 1931"---Colophon.

AAS   H   NYPL   Y

15053. The Letters of Western Authors A Series of Letters . . . in Facsimile . . .

. . . Book Club of California San Francisco 1935

Letter to Harry ⟨Wright⟩, April 5, 1899. Edited by Franklin Walker.

For fuller entry see No. 4488.

15054. TWO UNCOLLECTED ESSAYS BY FRANK NORRIS ⟨Edited⟩ BY WILLARD E. MARTIN, JR.

REPRINTED FROM AMERICAN LITERATURE, VOL. VIII, NO. 2, MAY, 1936

Cover-title.

⟨189⟩-198, blank leaf. Wove paper watermarked *Town Crier Text Made in USA* 9″ × 5⅞″.

6 leaves.

Running head: . . . *Uncollected Verses* . . .

H

15055. THE LETTERS OF FRANK NORRIS EDITED BY FRANKLIN WALKER

SAN FRANCISCO THE BOOK CLUB OF CALIFORNIA MCMLVI

Title page in black and orange.

⟨i⟩-⟨xiv⟩, ⟨1⟩-⟨99⟩; blank, p. ⟨100⟩; colophon, p. ⟨101⟩; blank, pp. ⟨102-110⟩. Frontispiece and 1 facsimile inserted. Laid paper watermarked *Curtis Rag* 11¹/₁₆″ × 8″.

⟨1⁸, 2-10⁶⟩. Leaf ⟨10⟩₆ used as terminal pastedown.

Printed paper boards sides, printed wallpaper fashion in black and red; red-orange V cloth shelf back. Printed paper label on spine. At front: A gathering of four leaves of book stock, the first leaf used as the pastedown; at back: ⟨10⟩₆ used as pastedown.

"Three Hundred And Fifty Copies Printed By Edwin & Robert Grabhorn For The Colt Press ---" Colophon.

Deposited April 18, 1956.

H LC Y

15056. Years of Conscience The Muckrakers An Anthology . . . Edited . . . by Harvey Swados

Meridian Books The World Publishing Company Cleveland and New York ⟨1962⟩

"Life in the Mining Region," pp. ⟨173⟩-182. Reprinted from *Everybody's* (N.Y.), Sept. 1902.

Printed paper wrapper. On copyright page: *First Printing February 1962*

Meridian Books, No. M129.

LC

15057. THE LITERARY CRITICISM OF FRANK NORRIS EDITED BY DONALD PIZER

UNIVERSITY OF TEXAS PRESS, AUSTIN ⟨1964⟩

⟨i⟩-xxiv, ⟨1⟩-247. 8¹⁵/₁₆″ full × 5¹⁵/₁₆″.

⟨1-7¹⁶, 8⁸, 9¹⁶⟩.

V cloth: tan-gray. Top edges stained gray.

" . . . The only collection of ⟨Norris's⟩ . . . criticism available has been the posthumous *The Responsibilities of the Novelist* . . . 1903 and thereafter republished unchanged . . . Its essays were neither selected nor arranged by Norris, but rather were haphazardly thrown together by his publisher . . . Moreover, the volume contains no selections from two important sources---Norris' extensive critical writing for the San Francisco *Wave* during 1896-1897, and his 'Weekly Letter' to the *Chicago American Literary and Art Review* during the summer of 1901 . . . The essays from these two sources as well as additional material omitted from the *Responsibilities* . . . In all, this new material constitutes approximately 40 percent of the present volume . . . "---From the *Preface*.

Y

15058. FRANK NORRIS PETITIONS THE PRESIDENT AND FACULTY OF THE UNIVERSITY OF CALIFORNIA

ISSUED ON THE OCCASION OF THE CENTENNIAL OF THE BIRTH OF FRANK NORRIS THE FRIENDS OF THE BANCROFT LIBRARY ⟨BERKELEY, CAL.⟩ MCMLXX

Cover-title. Single cut sheet of heavy, laid, cream-colored paper, folded to make four pages. Title-page printed in red and black.

⟨1-4⟩. 9¹⁵/₁₆″ × 8¹³/₁₆″. A pocket pasted to p. ⟨3⟩ contains a facsimile of the original petition, 4 pp., blue wove paper, dated *Nov. 1891*. Tipped to the third page of the petition is a facsimile of a printed review of *Yvernelle* "extract⟨ed⟩ from the last issue of Lippincott's magazine." Text, pp. ⟨2-3⟩ by Franklin Walker.

Published in April 1970 by the Council of the Friends of the Bancroft Library . . .---P. ⟨4⟩.

H

15059. A Novelist in the Making A Collection of Student Themes and the Novels Blix and

Vandover and the Brute . . . Edited by James D. Hart . . .

The Belknap Press of Harvard University Press Cambridge, Massachusetts 1970

In addition to reprinting *Blix* and *Vandover and the Brute*, contains "the publication for the first time of forty-four themes that Norris wrote at Harvard, most of which were early versions or studio sketches for his novels *Blix*, *McTeague*, and *Vandover and the Brute* . . . "---P. ix.

H

BENJAMIN FRANKLIN (FRANK) NORRIS

SECTION II

Reprints of Norris's own works.

15060. Shanghaied A Story of Adventure off the California Coast . . .

London Grant Richards 9, Henrietta Street, Covent Garden, W.C. 1899

Otherwise *Moran of the Lady Letty, q.v.,* above, under year 1898.

15061. Golden Gate Edition . . . Complete Works of Frank Norris

Published at New York by Doubleday, Page & Co. 1903

Printed paper boards, cloth shelf back, printed paper label on spine.

"This Edition Consists Of One Hundred Sets, On Strathmore Paper, Of Which This Is No."—Certificate of issue.

1: *Blix. Moran of the Lady Letty.*

2: *A Deal in Wheat.* Reprint? The trade edition listed PW Sept. 19, 1903. As part of the set listed PW Oct. 3, 1903.

3: *McTeague.*

4: *A Man's Woman.*

5: *The Octopus.*

6: *The Pit.*

7: *Responsibilities of the Novelist.* Issued simultaneously with the trade edition? The trade edition was deposited for copyright Sept. 21, 1903; listed PW Oct. 3, 1903. The set was listed in PW Oct. 3, 1903.

15062. The Panic Episode from . . . "The Pit" . . . William A. Brady's Magnificent Production, in Which Wilton Lackaye Appears As Curtis Jadwin

⟨New York(?), 1903 (1904?)⟩

Printed paper wrapper. Reprinted from *The Pit,* 1903.

15063. The Complete Works of Frank Norris . . .

New York P. F. Collier & Son Publishers ⟨v.d., 1899–1903; *i.e.,* 1905⟩

1: *The Octopus.*

2: *The Pit. A Deal in Wheat.*

3: *McTeague. A Man's Woman.*

4: *Blix. Moran of the Lady Letty. Essays on Authorship.*

In a letter to BAL (Sept. 3, 1970) Mr. Joseph Katz, Norris's bibliographer, states: The date "1905 comes from a private communication from Doubleday. The traditional 1903 is impossible . . ."

15064. A Review of Kim . . .

⟨n.p., n.d., 1934⟩

Cover-title. ⟨1-7⟩. 7″ × 5″. Noted on three types of paper; sequence, if any, not known; the designations are completely arbitrary:

A: Off-white wove paper.

B: White wove paper.

C: White wove paper watermarked *Strathmore Broadcaster U.S.A.*

"Of this edition 275 copies were printed of which this is number ⟨space⟩"—Certificate of issue, p. ⟨7⟩.

For prior publication see *Frank Norris . . . "Kim" Reviewed,* 1930.

15065. . . . Six Essays on the Responsibilities of the Novelist

Yonkers, New York 1949 The Alicat Bookshop Press

At head of title: *Frank Norris*

Printed paper wrapper. *Outcast Chapbooks, No. XV.* Reprint of six essays from *The Responsibilities of the Novelist,* 1903.

On copyright page: . . . *This edition of 1,000 copies was . . . printed . . . in April, 1949 . . .*

BENJAMIN FRANKLIN (FRANK) NORRIS

SECTION III

Books containing material by Norris reprinted from earlier books.

California Story Book

Published by the English Club of the University of California Berkeley California 1909

Pathway to Western Literature ⟨Edited⟩ by Nettie S. Gaines . . .

Stockton, California Nettie S. Gaines All Rights Reserved ⟨1910⟩

California Play and Pageant

⟨The English Club, University of California, Berkeley, Cal. 1913⟩

Printed paper boards. Unpaged.

Literary California . . . ⟨Compiled⟩ by Ella Sterling Mighels . . .

. . . San Francisco . . . 1918

For comment see BAL, Vol. 1, p. 226.

Masterpieces of Adventure in Four Volumes . . . Edited by Nella Braddy

Garden City . . . 1921

"The Ship that Saw a Ghost," Vol. 3, pp. 3-26. Reprinted from *A Deal in Wheat*, 1903. For fuller entry see BAL, Vol. 5, p. 462.

Songs and Stories Selected . . . by Edwin Markham . . .

Powell Publishing Company San Francisco Los Angeles Chicago ⟨1931⟩

Our Lives American Labor Stories Edited by Joseph Gaer

Boni and Gaer New York ⟨1948⟩

Deposited Oct. 18, 1948.

A Cavalcade of Collier's Edited by Kenneth McArdle

A. S. Barnes & Company, Inc. New York ⟨1959⟩

The Californians: Writings of Their Past and Present Edited by Robert Pearsall ⟨and⟩ Ursula Spier Erickson . . .

San Francisco Hesperian House ⟨1961⟩

2 Vols.

REFERENCES AND ANA

The Responsibilities of the Novelist . . . by Frank Norris . . .

New York Doubleday, Page & Company 1903

A brief bibliography, pp. 305-311.

For fuller entry see above in *Section One*.

Frank Norris ⟨by Charles G. Norris⟩ . . .

⟨Garden City, N.Y.: Doubleday, Page & Co., n.d., 1914⟩

Cover-title. Printed paper wrapper.

Frank Norris: Two Poems and "Kim" Reviewed. With a Bibliography by Harvey Taylor.

Harvey Taylor San Francisco 1930

For fuller entry see above in *Section One*.

Frank Norris a Biography by Franklin Walker

MCMXXXII Doubleday, Doran & Company, Inc. Garden City, New York

On copyright page: Publisher's monogram and the statement: *First Edition*

. . . Frank Norris (Benjamin Franklin Norris) Bibliography and Biographical Data . . . Joseph Gaer, Editor

Abstract from the SERA Project 2-F2-132 (3-F2-197) California Literary Research ⟨n.d., 1935?⟩

Cover-title. Printed self-wrapper. At the head of title: *Monograph #3*

Mimeographed. 100 numbered copies only.

Frank Norris a Study by Ernest Marchand

Stanford University Press Stanford University, California London: Humphrey Milford Oxford University Press ⟨1942⟩

Frank Norris   A Bibliography   Compiled by Kenneth A. Lohf & Eugene P. Sheehy

The Talisman Press Los Gatos, California 1959

Frank Norris by Warren French . . .

Twayne Publishers, Inc. New York ⟨1962⟩

Printed paper boards.

For the New Year by Frank Norris

⟨These lines are in a copy of *Moran of the Lady Letty* in the collection of Joseph Katz. They are first published in one hundred copies, January 1969, for the friends of Mr. and Mrs. Joseph Katz, with their best wishes for the New Year.⟩

Cover-title. Single cut sheet French-folded to make 4 pp. Page: 5½″ × 4¼″ scant. Tan laid paper watermarked *Beckett*. Not by Frank Norris. A garbled quotation from Lewis Carroll's *Through the Looking-Glass* . . . , Chapter v.

The Merrill Studies in The Octopus Compiled by Richard Allan Davison . . .

Charles E. Merrill Publishing Company   A Bell & Howell Company   Columbus, Ohio ⟨1969⟩

Printed paper wrapper.

Frank Norris (1870-1902) An Exhibition Marking the Centenary of His Birth 5 March–12 March 1970 from the Collection of Joseph Katz at the McKissick Library University of South Carolina

⟨Columbia, S.C., 1970⟩

Cover-title. Paper wrapper. "One Hundred And Fifty Copies Published."–––Certificate of issue. Mimeographed.

A Frank Norris Collection by Joseph Katz

Department of English Bibliographical Series No. 5 University of South Carolina Columbia 1970

Printed paper wrapper. Limited to 350 numbered copies   "This is the catalogue of an exhibition mounted 5-12 March 1970 at the McKissick Library, University of South Carolina, to mark the one hundredth anniversary of Frank Norris' birth. One hundred and fifty copies were published first in mimeograph for distribution at the exhibition. Since then a few items have been added, entries renumbered, and slight revisions made . . . "–––From the preface.

The Merrill Checklist of Frank Norris Compiled by John S. Hill . . .

Charles E. Merrill Publishing Company   A Bell & Howell Company   Columbus, Ohio ⟨1970⟩

Printed paper wrapper.

. . . The Pit Introduced by James D. Hart . . .

Charles E. Merrill Publishing Company   A Bell & Howell Company   Columbus, Ohio ⟨1970⟩

At head of title: *Frank Norris*

"This text . . . is a facsimile of the first state, first impression, first edition . . . "–––P. ⟨iv⟩.

EDGAR WILSON (BILL) NYE

1 8 5 0 – 1 8 9 6

15066. A HOWL IN ROME

CHICAGO MILWAUKEE & ST PAUL RY. ⟨n.d., *ca.* 1880⟩

Cover-title.

Note: Printed throughout in black on buff.

⟨1⟩-14; advertisements, pp. ⟨15-16⟩. Illustrated. 6⅝″ × 4⅞″.

⟨-⟩⁸.

Printed self-wrapper.

Revised and collected in *Bill Nye and Boomerang*, 1881, as "Speech of Spartacus."

H

15067. Puck's Annual for 1881 . . .

New York: Published by Keppler & Schwarzmann. 1881.

"Entomologist," pp. ⟨61⟩-63. Collected in *Forty Liars*, 1882.

For fuller entry see No. 1882.

15068. Dick's Recitations and Readings No. 12 . . . Edited by Wm. B. Dick . . .

New York: Dick & Fitzgerald, Publishers, No. 18 Ann Street. ⟨1881⟩

Cloth; and, printed paper wrapper.

"The Language of the Rail," pp. 116-118.

Listed PW Feb. 19, 1881.

LC

15069. BILL NYE AND BOOMERANG; OR, THE TALE OF A MEEK-EYED MULE, AND SOME OTHER LITERARY GEMS . . .

CHICAGO: BELFORD, CLARKE, & CO., 1881.

Six printings noted:

FIRST PRINTING

⟨i-iv⟩, ⟨i⟩-⟨vi⟩, 7-286, blank leaf. Illustrated. 7⅛″ × 4¹³⁄₁₆″.

⟨-⟩², ⟨1-2⟩ *3-*10, *10, *12-*16, ⟨17-18⟩⁸.

FL cloth: terra-cotta. S cloth: green. Front blackstamped save as noted: BILL NYE / & / BOOMERANG / ⟨*preceding 3 lines decorated with rules, flourishes, etc., the whole enclosing a goldstamped vignette of a mule*⟩ Spine goldstamped: ⟨*fillet*⟩ / BILL NYE / AND / ⟨*mule*⟩ / BOOMERANG. / BELFORD, CLARKE & CO / ⟨*fillet*⟩ Yellow end papers.

Copyright page: Imprinted with copyright notice only, the notice set in three lines and dated 1880.

SECOND PRINTING

⟨i-ii⟩, ⟨i⟩-⟨vi⟩, 7-286. 7″ × 4¾″. Illustrated.

⟨1-18⁸⟩. *Signed:* ⟨-⟩¹, ⟨1-2⟩, *3-*10, *10, *12-*16, ⟨17⟩⁸, ⟨18⟩⁷.

S cloth: mustard. Front: Same as on the first printing, above. Spine: ⟨*blackstamped fillet*⟩ / BILL NYE / AND / ⟨*mule*⟩ / BOOMERANG. / ⟨*preceding 4 lines in gold; all the following in black:*⟩ / ⟨*kimonoed Japanese figure*⟩ / ⟨*horizontal ornament*⟩ / ⟨*parrot in a suspended hoop*⟩ / ⟨*fillet*⟩ Yellow end papers.

Copyright page: Imprinted with copyright notice dated 1881 in two lines; and, 3-line imprint of Donohue & Henneberry.

THIRD PRINTING

⟨i-ii⟩, ⟨i⟩-⟨vi⟩, 7-286. 7⅛″ × 4¹³⁄₁₆″ scant. Illustrated.

⟨1-18⁸⟩. *Signed:* ⟨-⟩¹, ⟨1-2⟩, *3-*10, *10, *12-*16, ⟨17⟩⁸, ⟨18⟩⁷.

S cloth: blue; dark maroon. Front: Same as on the first printing, above. Spine: ⟨*blackstamped triple rule*⟩ / BILL NYE / AND / ⟨*mule*⟩ / BOOMERANG. / ⟨*preceding 4 lines in gold*⟩ / ⟨*all the following in black:*⟩ / ⟨*kimonoed Japanese figure*⟩ / ⟨*triple rule*⟩ / ⟨*ornament*⟩ / ⟨*triple rule*⟩ Yellow end papers.

Copyright page: Imprinted with copyright notice only, the notice set in 3 lines and dated 1880.

FOURTH PRINTING

⟨i-ii⟩, ⟨i⟩-⟨vi⟩, 7-286. 7³⁄₁₆″ × 4¹³⁄₁₆″. Illustrated.

⟨1-18⁸⟩. *Signed:* ⟨-⟩¹, ⟨1-2⟩, *3-*10, *10, *12-*16, ⟨17⟩⁸, ⟨18⟩⁷.

On reverse of title-page: Copyright notice not present. Present only is the imprint of Donohue & Henneberry, set in 3 lines.

Printed tan paper wrapper.

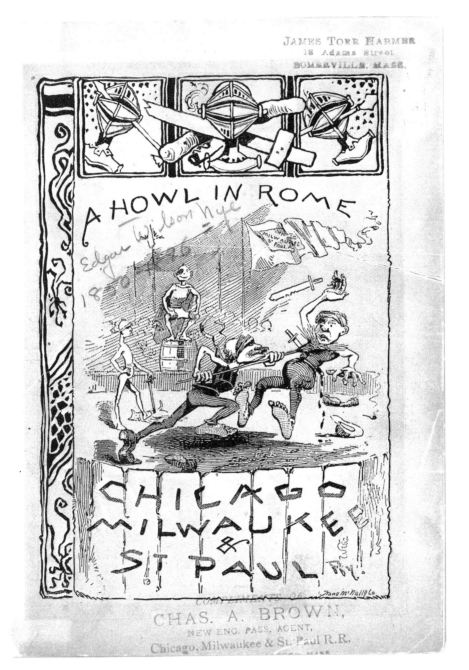

EDGAR WILSON NYE
Entry No. 15066
(Harvard University Library)

FIFTH PRINTING

⟨i-ii⟩, ⟨i⟩-⟨vi⟩, 7-286; plus: publisher's catalog, 16 pp. 7″ full × 4¹³⁄₁₆″ full. Illustrated.

⟨1-18⁸; plus: 19⁸⟩. *Signed:* ⟨-⟩¹, ⟨1-2⟩, *3-*10, *10, *12-*16, ⟨17⟩⁸, ⟨18⟩⁷, ⟨19⟩⁸.

FL cloth: terra-cotta. S cloth: green. Front: Same as on first printing, above. Spine: ⟨*blackstamped fillet*⟩ / BILL NYE / AND / ⟨*mule*⟩ / BOOMERANG. / ⟨*preceding 4 lines goldstamped*⟩ / ⟨*all of the following blackstamped:*⟩ / ⟨*ornament*⟩ / ⟨*fillet*⟩ White end papers printed in brown with a floral pattern.

Note: In the earlier printings the gatherings are sewn with thread; in this fifth printing the gatherings are saddle-stitched with wire; *i.e.,* stapled.

Note: Issued *ca.* 1883. P. ⟨5⟩ of the terminal advertisements: An advertisement for *Peck's Bad Boy and His Pa* of which the publishers state *this will be the most popular book of 1883.* P. ⟨14⟩ of the terminal advertisements is devoted to *A History of Our Own Times,* described as *In press, ready July 1st, 1883.*

Copyright page: No copyright notice present. Present only is the imprint of Donohue & Henneberry, set in three lines.

SIXTH PRINTING

⟨i-ii⟩, ⟨i⟩-⟨vi⟩, 7-286; plus publisher's catalog, 16 pp. 7¹⁄₁₆″ × 4¾″ scant. Illustrated.

⟨1-18⁸; plus: 19⁸⟩. *Signed:* ⟨-⟩¹, ⟨1-2⟩, *3-*10, *10, *12-*16, ⟨17⟩⁸, ⟨18⟩⁷, ⟨19⟩⁸.

Copyright page: Copyright notice, 3 lines, set within horizontal rules; dated 1883 (the type so battered that one is obliged to guess the final digit). At foot of page, under a single horizontal rule: Imprint of Donohue & Henneberry set in a single line.

S cloth: yellow. Front stamped as on the first printing described above. Spine: Presumably the same as that on the fifth printing. White end papers printed in brown with a floral pattern.

Issued *ca.* 1883. P. ⟨5⟩ of the terminal advertisements says of *Peck's Bad Boy and His Pa:* "this will be the most popular book of 1883." P. ⟨15⟩ of the terminal advertisements says of *A History of Our Own Times:* "In press, ready July 1st, 1883."

Listed PW Feb. 26, 1881, as in both cloth; and, printed paper wrapper.

BPL (6th)   H (1st, 2nd, 3d, 5th)   UV (1st, 4th) Y (1st)

15070. Puck on Wheels. No. II. For the Summer of 1881 . . .

New York: Published by Keppler & Schwarzmann. 1881.

"Patrick Oleson," pp. ⟨107⟩-111. Collected in *Forty Liars,* 1882.

For fuller entry see No. 1883.

15071. Dick's Recitations and Readings No. 13 . . . Edited by Wm. B. Dick . . .

New York: Dick & Fitzgerald, Publishers, No. 18 Ann Street. ⟨1881⟩

"Bill Nye on Childhood," pp. 79-81. Otherwise "Some Thoughts of Childhood," in *Bill Nye and Boomerang,* 1881.

"The True Tale of William Tell," pp. 82-83. Collected in *Forty Liars,* 1882.

For fuller entry see No. 3394.

15072. . . . The Reading Club and Handy Speaker . . . Edited by George M. Baker. No. 10.

Boston: Lee and Shepard, Publishers. New York: Charles T. Dillingham. ⟨1882⟩

"Autumn Thoughts," pp. 18-19. Collected in . . . *Cordwood,* 1887.

For fuller entry see No. 3790.

15073. FORTY LIARS, AND OTHER LIES . . .

CHICAGO: BELFORD, CLARKE & CO., ST. LOUIS: BELFORD & CLARKE PUBLISHING CO. MDCCCLXXXII.

⟨3⟩-6, ⟨3⟩-⟨6⟩, ⟨9⟩-124; ⟨i-ii⟩, 125-202; ⟨iii-iv⟩, 203-264, 2 blank leaves. 7⅛″ × 4¹³⁄₁₆″ full. Illustrated.

⟨1-17⁸⟩.

C cloth: blue. S cloth: blue; mustard; purple. Yellow end papers. *Note:* The spine occurs in two states; the order of presentation is presumed correct.

A

Stamped in gold save as noted: ⟨*double rule*⟩ / FORTY / LIARS / AND OTHER / LIES / ⟨*rule*⟩ / BILL NYE. / ⟨*two blackstamped filigrees*⟩ / ⟨*double rule*⟩ A deposit copy thus.

B

Stamped in gold: ⟨*double rule*⟩ / FORTY / LIARS / AND OTHER / LIES / ⟨*rule*⟩ / BILL NYE. / ⟨*double rule*⟩

Deposited May 11, 1882. See next entry.

H (B)   LC (A)   UV(A)   Y (B)

15074. Forty Liars, and Other Lies . . . ⟨Second Edition⟩

Chicago: Belford, Clarke & Co., St. Louis: Belford & Clarke Publishing Co. MDCCCLXXXII.

For first edition see preceding entry.

Pp. ⟨1⟩-⟨6⟩, ⟨5⟩-6, ⟨9⟩-122, ⟨i-ii⟩, 123-202, ⟨iii-iv⟩, 203-301.

Extended edition. Contains the following pieces not present in the first edition:

"Apostrophe Addressed to O. Wilde"; "Brass Knuckles and Phrenology"; "A Cruel Stab"; "He Wanted Blood"; "How Great Men Dance"; "A Masculine Kettle Drum"; "Maxwell's Death"; "The Ready Letter Writer"; "A Reminiscence"; "The Siamese Twins"; "Sic Semper Gloria Colorow"; "Sleeping with a Rocky Mountain"; "Trouble in a Silver Mine"; "Uncle Tom's Cabin"; "Wants to Come"; "Women Wanted."

H   UV

15075. St. Jacobs Oil Family Calendar 1883-4 and Book of Health and Humor for the Million Containing Original Sketches by the Greatest Humorists of the Day

The Charles A. Vogeler Co. Baltimore, Md. ⟨1882? 1883?⟩

Printed paper wrapper. Cover-title.

"Bill Nye's Cat," p. 3. Collected in *Baled Hay*, 1884. "Written for the St. Jacobs Oil Family Calendar . . . "

AAS

15076. Second Annual St. Jacobs Oil Family Calendar . . . 1884-5 and Book of Health & Humor for the Million Containing Original Humorous Prize Sketches and Illustrations, by the Leading Humorists of America

The Charles A. Vogeler Co. Baltimore, Md. U.S.A. ⟨1883⟩

Printed wrapper. Cover-title.

"Bill Nye Shaved by a Sioux," p. 5. "Written for the St. Jacobs Oil Family Calendar . . . "

AAS

15077. Wit and Humor of the Age . . . by Mark Twain, Robt. J. Burdette, Josh Billings, Alex. Sweet, Eli Perkins. With the Philosophy of Wit and Humor, by Melville D. Landon . . .

Chicago: Western Publishing House. 1883.

"Bill Nye Condemns Liars," p. 207. Otherwise "Our Compliments," *Forty Liars*, 1882.

"Dutch Idea of Insurance," pp. 528-529.

"Simple Faith," pp. 362-364. Collected in *Baled Hay*, 1884.

For fuller entry see No. 11220.

15078. . . . American Fun for Grave and Gay. The Best Things from Mark Twain . . . Josh Billings . . . Bill Nye . . .

F. M. Lupton, Publisher, 27 Park Place, New York. ⟨n.d., 1883-1886⟩

Cover-title. At head of title: *Price Twenty-Five Cents.*

Printed paper wrapper.

Reprint with the possible exception of:

"Chipeta's Address to the Utes," p. 4. Also in (reprinted from?) *Baled Hay*, 1884.

"Fraternal Sparring," p. 7. Also in (reprinted from?) *Baled Hay*, 1884.

"Health Food," p. 18. Also in (reprinted from?) *Baled Hay*, 1884.

"My Cabinet," p. 17. Also in (reprinted from?) *Baled Hay*, 1884.

"Strabismus and Justice," p. 16. Also in (reprinted from?) *Remarks*, 1887.

"Why We Blush," p. 38. Not elsewhere located.

HM

15079. BALED HAY. A DRIER BOOK THAN WALT WHITMAN'S "LEAVES O' GRASS." . . .

NEW YORK AND CHICAGO: BELFORD, CLARKE & CO. 1884.

⟨1⟩-320. Frontispiece inserted; other illustrations in text. 7 1/16″ × 4 3/4″.

⟨1⟩-20⁸.

S cloth: blue; brown; green. White end papers printed in brown with a leafy pattern. *Also:* Plain green end papers. Also issued in printed paper wrapper; two printings of the wrapper noted; contemporary advertisements suggest the following sequence. The following is sufficient for identification.

WRAPPER A

Fawn paper. Outer back wrapper: *Over One Million Sold* . . .

WRAPPER B

Mottled green paper. Outer back wrapper: *Best Editions of Popular Standards* . . .

Deposited Feb. 4, 1884. Advertised as in cloth and paper *The American Bookseller* (N.Y.) April 15, 1884.

H (cloth; wrapper B)   LC (cloth)   UV (wrapper A)   Y (wrapper A)

15080. . . . BOOMERANG SHOTS . . .

WARD, LOCK, AND CO. LONDON: WARWICK HOUSE, SALISBURY SQUARE, E.C. NEW YORK: 10, BOND STREET. ⟨n.d., 1884⟩

Printed paper wrapper. At head of title: *Though quite erratic seem the weapon's throws . . .*

Pp. 124.

BAL regrets its inability to do a full collation of this sixpenny pamphlet publication. The only located copy (Michigan State University Library) is in such fragile state that it cannot be collated. The publication comprises material by Nye, some of it perhaps here first collected, together with material by other authors.

Listed by PC and Bkr May 1, 1884. Advertised PC and Bkr June 1, 1884. Again listed PC July 15, 1887; Bkr Aug. 1, 1887.

15081. . . . HITS AND SKITS . . .

WARD, LOCK, AND CO. LONDON: WARWICK HOUSE, SALISBURY SQUARE, E.C. NEW YORK: 10, BOND STREET. ⟨n.d., 1884⟩

At head of title: *You've but to choose your special bit . . .*

Not seen. Entry on the basis of a photographic copy of the title-page and table of contents of the BMU copy.

Examination of the table of contents indicates that some of the material herein was reprinted from earlier books; that some of the material was later collected in *Remarks . . .* , 1887; and that much of the material, on the basis of titles only, remains otherwise unpublished in book form. Further checking indicated.

Listed PC May 15, 1884; Bkr June, 1884. Advertised under *New Sixpenny Volume* in Bkr June, 1884. According to contemporary notices issued in printed paper wrapper. Pp. 124.

15082. Third Annual St. Jacobs Oil Family Calendar 1885 and Book of Health and Humor for the Million Containing Original Humorous Articles & Illustrations by the Leading Humorists of America.

The Charles A. Vogeler Company Baltimore, Maryland, U.S.A. Copyright. ⟨1884⟩

Printed paper wrapper. Cover-title.

According to the prefatory notes the Nye contributions were written for publication herein:

"An August Dog-Tail," p. 16.

"Big Steve," p. 25. Collected in *Thinks*, 1888.

"Calf-Beesness," p. 10.

"The Day We Celebrate," p. 14.

"Never Got the Appointment," p. 29.

"A November Picnic," p. 22.

"An October Idyl," p. 20.

"The Rhubarb-Pie," p. 12. Collected in *Thinks*, 1888.

"Solemn Thoughts," p. 18.

"Three American Saints," p. 4.

"Vanity and Vexation," p. 6.

AAS

15083. Brother Jonathan's Jokes, Funny Stories, and Laughable Sketches. An Everlasting Encyclopedia of Wit and Humor . . .

New York: Excelsior Publishing House, 29 & 31 Beekman Street. ⟨1885⟩

Printed paper wrapper.

"Everything is Lovely. The Beautiful Story of Damon and Pythias as Retold by Bill Nye," pp. 12-13.

EM

15084. . . . St. Jacobs Oil Family Calendar 1886 and Book of Health and Humor for the Million Containing Original Humorous Articles and Illustrations by the Leading Humorists of America

The Charles A. Vogeler Company. Baltimore, Maryland, U.S.A. ⟨1885⟩

Printed paper wrapper. Cover-title. At head of title: *United States Edition.*

All of the following "written for the St. Jacobs Oil Family Calendar . . . "

"Bill Nye on Cyclones," p. 3. Collected in *Remarks . . .* , 1887, as "On Cyclones."

"Bill Nye's Dog," p. 31. Collected in *Remarks . . .* , 1887, as "My Dog."

"Care of House Plants," p. 23. Collected in *Remarks . . .* , 1887.

"Mush and Melody," p. 17. Collected in *Remarks . . .* , 1887.

"The Sedentary Hen," p. 9. Collected in *Remarks . . .* , 1887.

AAS

15085. Third Crop. Pickings from Puck. Being a Choice Collection of . . . Pieces, Poems and Pictures from Puck . . .

New York: Keppler & Schwarzmann. ⟨1886⟩

Pictorial paper wrapper.

"Business is Business," p. 16. Signed *B.N.* Elsewhere unlocated. Presumably by Nye.

"Drunk in a Plug-Hat," p. 45. Collected in *Remarks . . .* , 1887.

"Woodtick William's Story," p. 5. Collected in *Remarks* . . . , 1887.

Deposited Sept. 23, 1886.

LC

15086. No. 14. Standard Comic Recitations by Best Authors . . . Compiled . . . by Frances P. Sullivan . . . December, 1886 . . .

J. M. ⟨*sic*⟩ Ivers & Co., Publishers, 86 Nassau Street, N.Y. . . . ⟨1886⟩

"Bill Nye on the Bronze Goddess," pp. 42-43. Collected in *Thinks*, 1888.

For fuller entry see No. 11451.

15087. Short Stories by Sam Davis.

Golden Era Company, San Francisco, Cal. 1886.

"Bill Nye's Speech ⟨at the Quill Driver's Council⟩," pp. 155-157.

H Y

15088. REMARKS . . .

CHICAGO: A. E. DAVIS & COMPANY. 1887.

A subscription book and as such issued with varying imprints. The deposit copies imprinted as above.

Also noted with the following imprints:

CHICAGO: / A. E. DAVIS & COMPANY. / MINNEAPOLIS: / BUCKEYE PUBLISHING CO. / 1887.

NEW YORK CITY: / THE M. W. HAZEN COMPANY, / 64 and 66 W. Twenty-Third St., / 1887. The title-leaf is a cancel.

⟨i⟩-⟨x⟩, 11-504. Illustrated. 8⅝" × 6⅝" full.

⟨1-31⁸, 32⁴⟩.

S cloth: green. White end papers printed in yellow; or, green; or, brown, with an all-over floral pattern. Flyleaves. Also noted in three-quarters brown morocco, cloth sides. Presumably issued in a variety of subscribers' bindings.

Deposited Jan. 31, 1887.

AAS H JSK NYPL Y

15089. Beecher Memorial   Contemporaneous Tributes to the Memory of Henry Ward Beecher Compiled and Edited by Edward W. Bok

Privately Printed Brooklyn, New York 1887

Contribution, pp. 69-70.

For comment see entry No. 2148.

15090. BILL NYE'S CORDWOOD . . .

CHICAGO: RHODES & McCLURE PUBLISHING CO. 1887.

⟨7⟩-161, 2 blank leaves. Illustrated. 7⅝" × 5⁵⁄₁₆" scant.

⟨1-10⁸⟩.

S cloth: red. Bevelled covers. White end papers printed in yellow with an all-over squared pattern.

The following five pieces contained herein also appear in *Remarks*, 1887 (January):

"Bill Nye Attends a Western Theatre . . ."; "The Bronco Cow"; "Favored a Higher Fine"; "How Bill Nye Failed to Make the Amende Honorable . . ."; "Mr. Sweeney's Cat."

Deposited July 1, 1887.

H Y

15091. Fourth Crop. Pickings from Puck. Being a Choice Collection of . . . Pieces, Poems and Pictures from Puck . . .

Keppler & Schwarzmann, New York. ⟨1887⟩

Reprint save for the following:

"An Artillery Ride," p. 54.

"Mr. Mardigras O'Malley," p. 24.

"They Do Not Speak As They Pass By," p. 30.

"A Tradition. More Light on the History of G. W.," p. 14.

For fuller entry see No. 696.

15092. . . . Broad Grins by Captain Heartyman . . .

Chicago Laird & Lee Publishers Clark and Adams Streets ⟨1887⟩

At head of title: *The Merry Folks Illustrated Library.*

Pictorial paper wrapper.

"Bill Nye's Red Pup," pp. ⟨5⟩-7.

EM

15093. The Fun Library . . . Humorous Stories . . . from Brightest Sources of Current Wit and Humor.

Boston: J. H. & A. L. Brigham, 179 Milk Street. ⟨n.d., *ca.* 1887⟩

"A Fond Father's Letter," p. ⟨2⟩. Also in (reprinted from?) *Remarks* . . . , 1887, above.

For fuller entry see BAL, Vol. 2, p. 249.

15094. BILL NYE'S CHESTNUTS OLD AND NEW. LATEST GATHERING . . .

CHICAGO AND NEW YORK: BELFORD, CLARKE & CO. 1888.

⟨i⟩-x, 11-286, blank leaf. Illustrated. 7⁵⁄₁₆″ × 4³⁄₄″.

⟨1⟩-2, ⟨3⟩, 4-6, ⟨7⟩, 8-11, ⟨12⟩, 13, ⟨14⟩, 15-18⁸. *Note:* Signatures 10, 11, missigned on leaf 2 of gathering.

S cloth: blue-green. White end papers printed in pale brown with an arrangement of dots, florets, etc. Flyleaf at front.

Note: Contains much material reprinted from earlier books with the addition of 44 pieces here first collected.

Deposited Feb. 20, 1888.

H

15095. What American Authors Think about International Copyright

New-York American Copyright League 1888

One-paragraph statement, pp. 7-8.

For comment see entry No. 218.

15096. ... AN ARISTOCRAT IN AMERICA: EXTRACTS FROM THE DIARY OF THE RIGHT HONORABLE LORD WILLIAM HENRY CAVENDISH - BENTINCK - PELHAM - CLINTON - ST. MAUR - BEAUCHAMP-DEVERE, K.G.

NEW YORK: M. J. IVERS & CO., PUBLISHERS, 86 NASSAU STREET; 326 AND 328 PEARL STREET. ⟨1888⟩

At head of title: AMERICAN SERIES.

⟨1⟩-128. 7¼″ × 5″.

⟨1-8⁸⟩.

Issued in printed paper wrapper as *American Series*, No. 71, under date March 25, 1888.

Contents:

"An Aristocrat in America," pp. ⟨3⟩-59. By Nye?

"Mr. Weller in America," pp. ⟨61⟩-79. By Nye?

"Some Things from Nye," pp. ⟨81⟩-128, as follows:

*"Bill Nye Goes a-Shopping. He Traffics in Red Suspenders with Blue Ends"

*"Bill Nye's New Operetta. Something Entirely New and Recherche in the Musical Line"

*"Bill Nye Meets a Citizen. He Draws from Him a Sad Story of Modern Journalism"

*"Bill Nye in a Bobtail. He Takes a Cheap Excursion without Going out of Town"

"Bill Nye's Horrorscope. He Pays a Brief Visit to a Professional Star Reader." Here reprinted.

Also in *Chestnuts . . .* , 1888, as "Bill Nye Pays a Brief Visit to a Professional Star Reader." Also in *Railway Guide*, 1888, as "Prying open the Future."

"Bill Nye and J. Caesar. Some of the Peculiarities of Julius Caesar—Politics in Rome at an Early Period." Also in *Railway Guide*, 1888, as "Julius Caesar in Town."

*"Bill Nye Takes a Man into His Confidence and Educates Him. Value to Ardent Truth-Seekers"

"Some Confidential Advice. Bill Nye Diagnosticates the Plaint of a Country Cousin." Here reprinted. Also in *Chestnuts . . .* , 1888, as "Bill Nye Diagnosticates the Plaint of a Country Cousin."

*"Bill Nye on the Tariff. He Labors to Show How Little He Knows about the Issues"

Deposited May 7, 1888.

Here first located.

LC Y

15097. NYE AND RILEY'S RAILWAY GUIDE BY EDGAR W. NYE AND JAMES WHITCOMB RILEY ...

CHICAGO THE DEARBORN PUBLISHING COMPANY 88 AND 90 LA SALLE STREET NEW YORK 1888 SAN FRANCISCO

Two printings noted:

FIRST PRINTING

⟨iii⟩-xvi, ⟨1⟩-203; blank, p. ⟨204⟩; advertisements, pp. ⟨205-206⟩; 2 blank leaves. Illustrated. 7⁵⁄₈″ × 5¼″.

⟨1-14⁸⟩.

SECOND PRINTING

⟨v⟩-xvi, ⟨1⟩-203; blank, p. ⟨204⟩; advertisements, pp. ⟨205-206⟩. Illustrated. Leaf (cloth): 7⁵⁄₈″ × 5¼″. Printed paper wrapper: 7⁹⁄₁₆″ × 5³⁄₁₆″.

⟨1¹, 2-14⁸, 15⁴⟩. *Note:* ⟨1⟩ᵥ is a portrait of Nye; ⟨2⟩₁ᵣ is a portrait of Riley.

S cloth: golden yellow; noted on both printings. White end papers printed in pink with a pattern of snowflake-like ornaments. The second printing has also been seen in printed laid green paper wrapper.

Note: Copies of the second printing have been seen (in cloth) with cancel title-leaf imprinted: CHICAGO. / F. T. NEELY, / 1889. Pp. ⟨205-206⟩, the advertisements, excised. Copies in AAS, H, UV.

Noted for Nov. 5, PW Nov. 3, 1888. Advertised as in both cloth; and, paper, PW Nov. 3, 1888. Deposited Nov. 30, 1888. Listed PW Dec. 15, 1888 as in both cloth and paper.

H (2nd)   LC (1st)   NYPL (2nd)   UV (1st; 2nd)

15098. BILL NYE'S THINKS PREPARED AT THE INSTIGATION OF THE AUTHOR IN RESPONSE TO A LOUD, PIERCING AND POPULAR DEMAND

CHICAGO THE DEARBORN PUBLISHING CO 88 AND 90 LaSALLE ST NEW YORK 1888 SAN FRANCISCO

⟨i-iv⟩, ⟨1⟩-181; blank, p. ⟨182⟩; 3 blank leaves. 1 illustration in text. $5^{11}/_{16}'' \times 4^{5}/_{16}''$.

⟨1-12⁸⟩.

Printed white paper wrapper.

Advertised (paper only) PW Nov. 3, 1888. Noted for Nov. 5 PW Nov. 3, 1888. Deposited Dec. 8, 1888. Listed PW Dec. 15, 1888. Reissued as *Neely's Series*, Vol. 1, No. 3, under date *July, 1889;* copy in BPL. Noted as *on our table* Ath Nov. 9, 1889.

LC

15099. . . . "Out West;" Being Puck's Best Things about the Wild and Wooly Wilderness . . .

Keppler & Schwarzmann, New York, 1888.

At head of title: *Puck's Library, No. XVIII.*

Pictorial paper wrapper.

"The Amateur Cow-Boy," p. 4.

"Brave Brady.—A Tale Founded on Fact," p. ⟨6⟩.

"Bronco Sam," p. 26. Previously in *Remarks,* 1887.

Deposited Dec. 17, 1888.

LC NYPL

15100. A Library of American Literature . . . Edited by Edmund Clarence Stedman and Ellen Mackay Hutchinson . . .

New-York . . . 1888–1890.

11 Vols. For fuller comment see entry No. 1350.

"The Pass Came Too Late," Vol. 10, pp. 609-613.

Listed PW Dec. 22, 1888.

15101. . . . Some Famous Pseudonyms. Well-Known Authors Tell the Stories of Their Nom de Plumes . . .

. . . Copyrighted . . . 1889, by the Bok Syndicate Press of New York . . .

Contains an autobiographical statement by Nye.

For fuller entry see No. 11224.

15102. Looking Forward ⟨by Frank⟩ Tennyson ⟨Neely⟩ . . . Copyrighted by F. T. Neely, 1889.

F. T. Neely, Publisher and Wholesale Bookseller, Bill Nye's Publisher. Chicago, New York. ⟨1890⟩

On front: . . . *150th Thousand . . . Neely's Series—Vol. 1, No. 9. February, 1890* . . .

Printed paper wrapper.

"Autobiography of James Whitcomb Riley . . . ," pp. 196-199. Not by Riley but by Nye.

"Autobiography of Bill Nye. (Edgar Wilson Nye.)," pp. 200-203. Not by Nye but by Riley.

Note: The above is a reprint of an unlocated earlier publication. The running head is: *My Visit to the World's Fair* which may be the title of the true first printing of the book.

"Riley's publishers, the Bowen-Merrill Company, used *The Autobiography of James Whitcomb Riley* on circulars issued in the early '90's."—*A Bibliography of James Whitcomb Riley,* by Anthony J. Russo and Dorothy R. Russo, 1944, p. 170.

The "autobiographies" appear also in *Eccentricities of Genius* . . . , by J. B. Pond ⟨1900⟩, pp. 240-246, where an account of the circumstances of their writing is given. See entry No. 15104.

B IU

15103. . . . His Fleeting Ideal. A Romance of Baffled Hypnotism. The Joint Work of P. T. Barnum . . . Bill Nye . . . ⟨and Others⟩ The Red Cover Series. No. 87. Issued Quarterly . . . July, 1890 . . .

New York: J. S. Ogilvie, Publisher, 57 Rose Street.

At head of title: *The Great Composite Novel.*

Cloth; and, printed paper wrapper.

"Chapter XII. Conclusion," by Bill Nye, pp. 169-187.

Deposited July 18, 1890.

H LC

15104. . . . Kings of the Platform and Pulpit by Melville D. Landon . . .

Chicago F. C. Smedley & Co., Publishers. 1890

"Bill Nye," pp. 306-330. The section consists of anecdotes; letters; speeches and extracts from speeches (some here in their earliest located book appearance) and:

"Bill Nye Makes Rome Howl!" Otherwise "The Speech of Spartacus" in *Bill Nye and Boomerang,* 1881. Same as *A Howl in Rome,* n.d., ca. 1880, above.

"Bill Nye Writes His Autobiography." Written by James Whitcomb Riley. For an account of the writing of this "autobiography" see J. B. Pond's *Eccentricities of Genius,* New York ⟨1900⟩, p. 241.

For fuller entry see BAL, Vol. 2, p. 249; and, entry No. 11225. Also see entry No. 15102.

15105. ⟨Facsimile letter⟩ New York Sept. 1. 1891 Dear Sir I take pleasure in announcing that on the 21 of Sept. at the Union Square Theatre in this city. The Cadi, a new play, will be produced....

Facsimile of a letter written by Nye as promotion for his play. Printed on p. ⟨1⟩ of a single leaf of paper folded to make 4 pp. Laid paper. Page: 9¼″ × 5¾″. Pp. ⟨2-4⟩ blank.

H

15106. Odds and Ends, by John Ernest McCann and Ernest Jarrold (Mickey Finn), with an Introduction by Bill Nye.

The Alliance Publishing Company. New York. ⟨1891⟩

Introductory letter, New York, Dec. 3, 1891, addressed to Jarrold and McCann, p. 5.

UV

15107. THE PRODIGAL SON

A song in Nye's *The Cadi, a Three Act Play*. For a comment on *The Cadi* see below in section of *References and Ana*.

Two forms noted; sequence not determined. The order of presentation is completely arbitrary.

SHEET MUSIC

...THE PRODIGAL SON A COMICAL BALLAD MUSIC ARRANGED BY JOSEPHINE GRO.

NEW-YORK; HITCHCOCK AND McCARGO PUBLISHING CO., LTD. 385 SIXTH AVENUE ABOVE 23RD STREET. 11 PARK ROW OPP. ASTOR HOUSE. 283 SIXTH AVE. BELOW 18TH STREET. 249 GRAND ST. NEAR ALLEN ST. ⟨1891⟩

Sheet music. Cover-title. At head of title: *The Latest Success. As Sung In Bill Nye's Cadi, For 125 Nights In New-York. By Thomas Q. Seabrooke*

Reprints have been seen with the following imprints; no effort has been made to establish a sequence and the designations are wholly arbitrary.

REPRINT A

New York: Hitchcock Publishing House, 385 Sixth Avenue. 11 Park Row. 262 W. 125 Street. Chicago: National Music Co., 215 Wabash Avenue. ⟨1891⟩ Copy in H.

REPRINT B

New York: Benjamin W. Hitchcock, 385 Sixth Avenue; Chicago: National Music Co., 215 Wabash Avenue ⟨1891⟩ Copy in USC.

REPRINT C

New York: Hitchcock Publishing Company, 49 Eighth Avenue. 7 Barclay Street, Near Broadway ⟨1891⟩ Copy in H.

HANDBILL

1272 THE PRODIGAL SON COPYRIGHT, 1891, BY HITCHCOCK & McCARGO PUBLISHING COMPANY (LIMITED). THE WORDS AND MUSIC OF THIS SONG WILL BE SENT TO ANY ADDRESS ...

...H. J. WEHMAN, 130 PARK ROW, NEW YORK CITY ...

Single leaf. 9½″ × 6″. Printed on recto only.

H (both)

15108. With the Wits ...

Philadelphia J. B. Lippincott Company. 1891.

Pictorial paper wrapper.

"Kink II," pp. 81-87.

H

15109. ...BILL NYE LETTER...NYE AT THE PLAY ...

⟨AMERICAN PRESS ASSOCIATION: SYNDICATE DEPARTMENT ... 1892⟩

Caption-title. At head of title: AMERICAN PRESS ASSOCIATION. SYNDICATE DEPARTMENT ... *This Matter is Not to Be Published Before Saturday Afternoon, Nov. 19, 1892.*

Prepared for the use of subscribers to the syndicate; press release.

Single sheet. Printed on recto only. 12⅜″ × 10⁷⁄₁₆″. Illustrated.

Deposited Nov. 15, 1892.

LC

15110. The First Book of the Authors Club Liber Scriptorum ...

New York Published by the Authors Club M DCCC XCIII

"The Lex Loci of the Hired Girl," pp. ⟨433⟩-435.

For fuller entry see No. 1283.

15111. ... St. Jacobs Oil Family Almanac and Book of Health and Humor for the Million, 1893. Containing Original Humorous Articles and Illustrations by the Leading Humorists of America

The Charles A. Vogeler Co. Baltimore, Maryland, U.S.A. ... 1893 ...

Printed paper wrapper. Cover-title. At head of title: ⟨Hand⟩ *Pull out this wire loop* . . .

"Bill Nye's Cow," p. 27. "Written for the St. Jacobs Oil Family Almanac . . ."

AAS

15112. "The Story of My First Watch" . . .

⟨New York⟩ The New York Standard Watch . . . ⟨1893⟩

Cover-title. Printed paper wrapper.

"From the Celebrated 'Bald-Headed Humorist'," pp. 13-14.

EM

15113. BILL NYE'S HISTORY OF THE UNITED STATES . . .

J. B. LIPPINCOTT CO., PHILADELPHIA ⟨1894⟩

Three printings noted:

FIRST PRINTING

⟨1⟩-329. Pp. ⟨1-2⟩ excised or pasted under the end paper. Illustrated. 8³⁄₁₆″ × 5⁹⁄₁₆″.

⟨a⟩-i, k-u⁸, v⁴, ⟨w⟩¹. Leaf ⟨a⟩₁ excised or pasted under the end paper. *Also signed:* ⟨1⟩-5, ⟨6⟩-13, ⟨14⟩-26, ⟨27⟩⁶, 28³. *Also signed:* ⟨A⟩-I, K-N¹², ⟨O⟩⁹.

Sheets bulk 1³⁄₁₆″.

On copyright page: PRINTED BY J. B. LIPPINCOTT COMPANY, PHILADELPHIA, PA., U.S.A. Note presence of the abbreviation PA.

P. 81: Signature mark *f* present but in battered state.

P. 101: Signature *9** present.

Spine imprint: J. B. LIPPINCOTT CO.

SECOND PRINTING

⟨1⟩-329, blank leaf. Illustrated.

⟨a⟩-i, k-u⁸, v⁶. *Also signed:* ⟨1⟩-5, ⟨6⟩-13, ⟨14⟩-26, ⟨27⟩⁶, 28⁴. *Also signed:* ⟨A⟩-I, K-N¹², ⟨O⟩¹⁰.

Sheets bulk 1³⁄₈″.

On copyright page: PRINTED BY J. B. LIPPINCOTT COMPANY, PHILADELPHIA, PA., U.S.A. Note presence of the abbreviation PA.

P. 81: Signature mark *f* present as a fragment.

P. 101: Signature mark *9** present but in battered state.

Spine imprint: J. B. LIPPINCOTT CO.

Note: In the only examined copy the title-leaf appears to be a cancel.

THIRD PRINTING

⟨1⟩-329, blank leaf. Illustrated.

Signature collation as in *Second Printing* but see references to pp. 81, 101, below.

Sheets bulk 1¼″.

On copyright page: PRINTED BY J. B. LIPPINCOTT COMPANY, PHILADELPHIA, U.S.A. Note absence of abbreviation PA.

P. 81: Signature mark *f* totally gone.

P. 101: Signature mark *9** totally gone.

Spine imprint: LIPPINCOTT

Note: The error *advaced* for *advanced*, p. 283, line 2 from bottom, is present in all examined copies, including the ⟨1906⟩ reprint issued by Thompson & Thomas.

Advertised as *just issued* PW March 3, 1894. Noted as *shortly* PW March 10, 1894. Listed PW March 17, 1894; Ath Sept. 8, 1894.

AAS (1st) H (1st, 2nd, 3rd) UV (1st, 3rd) Y (1st)

15114. BILL NYE'S HISTORY OF ENGLAND FROM THE DRUIDS TO THE REIGN OF HENRY VIII . . .

PHILADELPHIA   J. B. LIPPINCOTT COMPANY MDCCCXCVI

⟨i-ii⟩, ⟨1⟩-⟨10⟩, 13-⟨214⟩, blank leaf. Illustrated. 8³⁄₁₆″ × 5½″ full.

⟨a⟩-i, ⟨k⟩, l-m, ⟨n⟩⁸, ⟨o⟩⁴. *Also signed:* ⟨1⟩-2, ⟨3-4⟩, 5-7, ⟨8⟩, 9, ⟨10⟩, 11-12, ⟨13-14⟩, 15-16, ⟨17-18⟩⁶. *Also signed:* ⟨A-B⟩, C-F, ⟨G⟩, H, ⟨I⟩¹².

Blue H cloth sides, red C cloth shelfback. Fly-leaves in some copies.

Note: The spine imprint occurs in two states; sequence not known; the designations are completely arbitrary:

A: In roman capitals of equal size. The J ⟨dot⟩ B ⟨dot⟩ thus.

B: In a fancy roman, large and small capitals. The *L* is a swash, etc. The J ⟨period⟩ B ⟨period⟩ thus.

Advertised PW Sept. 26, 1896. Deposited Sept. 28, 1896. Listed PW Oct. 17, 1896; PC Feb. 20, 1897.

AAS B H LC UV Y

15115. Werner's Readings and Recitations No. 15 Compiled and Arranged by Caroline Earnest Dickenson

New York   Edgar S. Werner & Company . . . 1896 . . .

"If I Were a Boy Again," pp. 133-135.

Probably issued in both cloth; and, printed paper wrapper.

NYPL

15116. A GUEST AT THE LUDLOW AND OTHER STORIES ...

INDIANAPOLIS AND KANSAS CITY   THE BOWEN-MERRILL COMPANY   M DCCC XCVII

Title-page in black and red.

⟨i-xvi⟩, 1-262; "An Article on the Writings of James Whitcomb Riley," by *Chelifer*, pp. ⟨263⟩-272. Frontispiece and 20 plates inserted. 7¼" × 4⅞".

⟨-⟩⁸, ⟨1⟩-17⁸.

Red linen. Top edges gilt.

Deposited Oct. 16, 1896. Listed PW Nov. 7, 1896. Reissued with the Bobbs-Merrill imprint.

B   H   NYPL   UV   Y

15117. The Literature of America and Our Favorite Authors ... Choice Selections from Their Writings ... Compiled and Edited by William Wilfred Birdsall ... Rufus M. Jones ... and Others ...

John C. Winston & Co., Philadelphia Chicago Toronto ⟨1897⟩

Reprint save for "Mr. Whisk's True Love," p. 369.

Issued as a subscription book with varying imprints; a copy as above was deposited for copyright Jan. 18, 1898.

H   LC

15118. Werner's Readings and Recitations No. 20 Compiled and Arranged by Pauline Phelps

New York   Edgar S. Werner & Company Copyright, 1899 ...

"The Legend of the Knot-Hole," pp. 159-161.

NYPL

15119. Voigtländer and I in Pursuit of Shadow Catching ... by James F. Ryder

Cleveland, O.: The Cleveland Printing & Publishing Co. The Imperial Press 1902

Review of Mrs. Julia A. Moore's poems, pp. 158-164.

Deposited Oct. 28, 1902. Listed PW Dec. 6, 1902.

H

15120. THE FUNNY FELLOWS GRAB-BAG. BY BILL NYE AND OTHER FUNNY MEN.

... 1903 ... NEW YORK: J. S. OGILVIE PUBLISHING COMPANY 57 ROSE STREET.

⟨1⟩-123; blank, p. ⟨124⟩; 4 pp. advertisements. Illustrated. 7¼" × 5⅛".

⟨1-4¹⁶⟩.

Printed pale orange on white paper wrapper.

So much material herein is credited to Nye that the book is, virtually, a one-man production.

H

15121. BILL NYE HIS OWN LIFE STORY CONTINUITY BY FRANK WILSON NYE ...

THE CENTURY CO. NEW YORK LONDON ⟨1926⟩

⟨i⟩-xx, ⟨1⟩-412. Frontispiece and 15 plates inserted; other illustrations in text. 8¹⁵⁄₁₆" × 6".

⟨1¹⁰, 2-26⁸, 27⁶⟩.

B cloth: blue.

Deposited Sept. 27, 1926. The London (Werner, Laurie) edition listed Bkr Feb. 11, 1927.

AAS   BA   H   LC   NYPL   UV   Y

15122. LETTERS OF EDGAR WILSON NYE NOW IN THE UNIVERSITY OF WYOMING LIBRARY EDITED BY NIXON ORWIN RUSH

LARAMIE UNIVERSITY OF WYOMING LIBRARY 1950

Title-page in black and orange.

⟨i-ii⟩, ⟨1⟩-29; blank, pp. ⟨30-32⟩; colophon, p. ⟨33⟩. Wove paper watermarked *Beckett* 7⅜" scant × 4¹¹⁄₁₆".

⟨1-4⁴, 5²⟩.

V cloth: green. Pale buff end papers printed in brown with an arrangement of florets.

Two hundred copies ... printed by the Southpass Press, the University of Wyoming Library, Laramie, Wyoming.---Colophon.

Deposited May 7, 1951.

H   LC   UV   Y

15123. Bill Nye's Western Humor Selected and with an Introduction by T. A. Larson ...

University of Nebraska Press Lincoln ⟨1968⟩

Contains some material here first in book form.

"The selections appearing in this volume have been taken from Laramie, Cheyenne, and Denver newspapers, and from six books ..."---P. xii.

LC

EDGAR WILSON (BILL) NYE

SECTION II

Reprints of Nye's own books; and, books containing reprinted Nye material issued with Nye's name on the title-page. For books containing Nye reprints issued without Nye's name on the title-page see *Section III*.

15124. Baled Hay ...

New York: Frank F. Lovell & Company, 83 Elm Street. ⟨1884; *i.e.,* 1887⟩

Printed paper wrapper. Issued in *Lovell's Household Library,* under wrapper date *March 31, '87.*

Remarks ...

...F. T. Neely. Chicago ... ⟨1886⟩

See entry No. 15128.

15125. Illustrated Book of American Humour. Containing Selections from Mark Twain, Nye & Others.

London: Saxon, 1888.

Not located. Entry made for the record only. Listed PC Sept. 1, 1888, pp. 192, sewed, 1/-.

15126. Forty Liars, and Other Lies ...

Chicago, New York, San Francisco: Belford, Clarke & Co. 1889.

Cloth; also in printed paper wrapper: *The Household Library,* Vol. 5, No. 17, Sept. 11, 1889.

15127. Selections from Bill Nye, Bob Burdette, & Other American Humorists.

London: Saxon, 1889.

Not located. Entry made for the record only. Listed PC Nov. 15, 1889, pp. 160, 1/-. Reviewed by Bkr Dec. 14, 1889.

15128. Remarks ...

Published by F. T. Neely. Chicago. New York. ⟨1886; *i.e.,* 1889?⟩

15129. Three of a Kind Choice Selections from the Boundless Humor of America's Favorite Humorists ... Bill Nye ...

Chicago Belford-Clarke Company 1890

Printed paper wrapper.

15130. Bill Nye's Chestnuts Old and New. Latest Gathering ...

New York John W. Lovell Company 150 Worth Street, Corner Mission Place ⟨n.d., *ca.* 1890⟩

15131. Bill Nye's Grim Jokes Ready to Read ...

Publishers W. B. Conkey Company Chicago ⟨n.d., not before 1890⟩

Bill Nye's Red Book ...

... Chicago ⟨1891⟩

See below under 1907.

Bill Nye's Remarks ...

... Chicago ⟨1891⟩

See below under *ca.* 1900.

15132. Poems by James Whitcomb Riley Yarns by Bill Nye ...

1891 ... Published by F. T. Neely Chicago and New York

Printed paper wrapper dated *December, 1891.* Reprint of *Nye and Riley's Railway Guide,* 1888. Also issued in cloth,

15133. Sparks from the Pen of Bill Nye ...

F. T. Neely Publisher for Bill Nye Chicago and New York 1891

Printed pink paper wrapper. Reprinted from *Bill Nye's Thinks,* 1888.

Two printings noted:

1: P. ⟨1⟩: *Chicago and North-Western Railway* ...

2: P. ⟨1⟩: ... *Neely's Great Historical Chart* ...

15134. Remarks ...

Chicago Laird & Lee, Publishers 1892

A Neely edition listed PW March 18, 1893.

15135. Forty Liars and Other Lies ...

Chicago: Morrill, Higgins & Co., 1892.

Printed paper wrapper. *The Midland Series*, Vol. II, No. 2. Issued under date May 27, 1892. Deposited May 2, 1892.

15136. American Wit and Humor Choice Selections from the Boundless Humor of America's Favorite Humorists . . . Bill Nye . . .

Chicago: Morrill, Higgins & Co. ⟨1892⟩

Printed paper wrapper. *The Midland Series*, Vol. IV, No. 2. Issued under date Aug. 28, 1892.

15137. Poems by James Whitcomb Riley Yarns by Bill Nye . . .

. . . 1891 . . . Published by F. Tennyson Neely, Chicago New York ⟨1892⟩

Issued in printed paper wrapper dated *September, 1892*.

15138. Poems by James Whitcomb Riley Yarns by Bill Nye . . .

Chicago Laird & Lee, Publishers 1892

Printed paper wrapper.

15139. Baled Hay . . .

Chicago W. B. Conkey Company ⟨1893⟩

Printed paper wrapper. Also issued in cloth imprinted: *Chicago W. B. Conkey Company Publishers* ⟨*1893*⟩

15140. Bill Nye and Boomerang, or the Tale of a Meek-Eyed Mule . . .

Chicago W. B. Conkey Company ⟨1893⟩

A slightly truncated printing of the first printing, 1881. Pp. 284.

Printed paper labels. It is probable that the book was issued in salvage cases and the labels conceal the original stamping covering a title other than *Bill Nye and Boomerang*.

15141. Baled Hay . . .

Chicago: W. B. Conkey Company, Publishers. 1894.

Printed paper wrapper. *The White City Series*, Vol. I, No. 9. Issued under date *June, 1894*. Deposited Sept. 14, 1894.

15142. Bill Nye's Chestnuts Old and New Latest Gathering . . .

Chicago: W. B. Conkey Company, 1894.

Printed paper wrapper. *The White City Series*, Vol. I, No. 11. Issued under date *Aug. 1894*. Deposited Sept. 14, 1894.

15143. American Wit and Humor Choice Selections from the Boundless Humor of America's Favorite Humorists . . . Bill Nye . . .

Chicago   Homewood Publishing Company Publishers ⟨1895⟩

15144. Nye and Riley's Wit and Humor (Poems-Yarns) by Bill Nye and James Whitcomb Riley . . . Neely's Popular Library. No. 57. Jan. 15, 1896. Issued Semi-Monthly . . .

F. Tennyson Neely   Publisher   New York Chicago

Printed paper wrapper; and, cloth.

15145. Bill Nye's Remarks . . .

F. Tennyson Neely New York Chicago 1896

Also issued under date ⟨1896⟩.

15146. Nye and Riley's Wit and Humor (Poems and Yarns) . . .

Chicago Thompson & Thomas ⟨1900⟩

Also noted with the imprint: *Thompson & Thomas Chicago* ⟨*1900*⟩.

15147. Bill Nye's Remarks . . .

Thompson & Thomas Chicago ⟨1891; *i.e., ca.* 1900⟩

A reprint of the first 196 pp. of *Remarks* . . . , 1887, Running heads: *Bill Nye's Red Book*.

Also issued with the imprint: *The Charles C. Thompson Co. Chicago* ⟨1891; *i.e., ca.* 1909⟩

15148. Bill Nye's Sparks . . .

Copyright, 1891, by E. W. Nye. Copyright, 1896, by F. Tennyson Neely. Copyright, 1901, by Hurst & Company.

Pictorial paper boards, cloth shelfback. Does not have the statement *Knickerbocker Classics* or *Cosmos Series* on binding.

15149. Bill Nye's Sparks . . . Copyright, 1891 . . . 1896 . . . 1901 . . .

New York Hurst & Company Publishers

Cloth, color print pasted to front. On binding: *Knickerbocker Classics* Also issued in the *Cosmos Series;* front cover so stamped.

15150. Library of Wit and Humor . . . Bill Nye . . . with "Philosophy of Wit and Humor" by Melville D. Landon . . .

1901 . . . Chicago   M. A. Donohue & Co. 407-429 Dearborn St.

15151. Library of Wit and Humor from the Writings of . . . Bill Nye . . . with "Philosophy of Wit and Humor" by Melville D. Landon . . .

. . . 1901 . . . Chicago   Thompson & Thomas 262 Wabash Avenue

15152. Nye and Riley's Wit and Humor (Poems-Yarns) . . . Neely's Popular Library. No. 57. Jan. 15, 1896 . . .

Chicago: Thompson & Thomas ⟨1902?⟩

Note: The copyright notice is rubber-stamped on the reverse of the title-page; it is not wholly legible. However, 1902 appears reasonable. Printed from the plates of the Neely, 1896, printing.

Contains an obituary of Nye, died Feb. 22, 1896.

15153. On the "Shoe-String" Limited with Nye and Riley James Whitcomb Riley's Poems and Bill Nye's Yarns . . .

Thompson & Thomas Chicago ⟨1905⟩

Printed paper wrapper. Reprint of *Nye and Riley's Railway Guide*, 1888, with the addition of a publisher's introduction and an unsigned biographical sketch of Nye.

Deposited Feb. 23, 1905.

15154. Nye and Riley's Wit and Humor . . .

Thompson & Thomas Chicago ⟨1905⟩

15155. Bill Nye's Red Book . . .

Thompson & Thomas Chicago 1906

15156. American Lecturers and Humorists by Melville D. Landon . . . and Lectures of . . . Bill Nye . . . and Others . . .

The Saalfield Publishing Company   Akron, Ohio New York ⟨1906⟩

15157. Bill Nye's Comic History of England . . .

Thompson & Thomas Chicago, Ill. ⟨1906⟩

15158. Bill Nye's History of the United States . . .

⟨Chicago: Thompson & Thomas, 1906⟩

15159. Bill Nye's Red Book . . .

Thompson & Thomas Chicago ⟨1891; *i.e.*, 1907⟩

Deposited Aug. 8, 1907. Listed PW Sept. 14, 1907. Reprinted and reissued by Willey Book Co., New York, under date ⟨1891⟩.

15160. Stories of Humor in Two Parts by Oliver Wendell Holmes Bill Nye . . . and Others

New York   Doubleday, Page & Company Publishers ⟨1908⟩

Deposited Oct. 13, 1908. Printed from the plates of an unidentified two-volume work.

15161. Suggestions for a School of Journalism by Bill Nye Himself As Found in Bill Nye and Boomerang . . . 1881.

Los Angeles: 1950

Printed paper wrapper. Colophon, p. ⟨11⟩: *To recognize . . . the opening in February, 1950, of the Graduate Department of Journalism at the University of California at Los Angeles, this booklet has been presented by the Department of Journalism at Los Angeles City College and printed by the Los Angeles City College Press. 350 copies for the Typophiles, New York*

In this section are listed books by authors other than Nye which contain material by him reprinted from earlier books. See *Section II* for a list of collections of reprinted material issued under Nye's name.

. . . Fun Burst   A Book for All Seasons, for Both Sexes, and for Every Country . . . Edited by Henry L. Williams

> London   John & Robert Maxwell, Publishers   Milton House, Shoe Lane, Fleet Street [All Rights Reserved] ⟨n.d., 1882⟩

> *Not seen.* Entry on the basis of a photographic copy of the title-page and table of contents of the BMU copy.

> A series of 32-page pamphlets (Nos. 27-39 of the series) issued with general title-page as above. One of the pamphlets (presumably) by Nye.

> Listed PC April 1, 1882, as in both cloth; and, printed paper boards. It is only in an advertisement in PC June 15, 1886 ⟨*sic*⟩ that one hears it contains Nye material.

> *Presumably* contains nothing by Nye first in book form, but precise information is wanting.

. . . Comic Conceits   The Cheeriest of Companions for Dull Days . . . Edited by Henry L. Williams

> London   John & Robert Maxwell, Publishers   Milton House, Shoe Lane, Fleet Street . . . ⟨n.d., 1883⟩

> For fuller entry see BAL, Vol. 3, pp. 399-400. Also see *Sprightly Banter* ⟨n.d., *ca.* 1883⟩ in the section of *References and Ana*, below.

. . . The Reading Club and Handy Speaker . . . Edited by George M. Baker. No. 16.

> Boston . . . ⟨1885⟩

> For fuller entry see BAL, Vol. 2, p. 95.

. . . St. Jacobs Oil Family Calendar and Book of Health and Humor for the Million Containing Original Humorous Articles and Illustrations by the Leading Humorists of America

> The Charles A. Vogeler Company. Baltimore, Maryland, U.S.A. ⟨1886⟩

> At head of title: *United States Edition.*

> Cover-title. Pictorial paper wrapper.

Mark Twain's Library of Humor . . .

> New York . . . 1888

> For comment see entry No. 9636.

One Hundred Choice Selections No. 28 . . .

> Published by P. Garrett & Co., 708 Chestnut Street, Philadelphia, Pa., and 130 E. Adams Street, Chicago, Ill. 1888.

> Cloth; and, printed paper wrapper. Deposited Dec. 18, 1888.

Fifth Crop. Pickings from Puck . . .

> . . . New York. ⟨1889⟩

> For fuller description see entry No. 77.

Fenno's Favorites, No. 9. 100 Choice Pieces for Reading and Speaking . . . ⟨Compiled⟩ by Frank H. Fenno . . .

> Philadelphia: John E. Potter & Company, 1111 and 1113 Market Street. ⟨1890⟩

> Printed paper wrapper.

American Lecturers and Humorists by Melville D. Landon . . .

> . . . Akron . . . ⟨1893⟩

> See below under *ca.* 1898.

Authors' Readings Compiled . . . by Art Young . . .

> New York   Frederick A. Stokes Company   Publishers ⟨1897⟩

> Listed PW Sept. 11, 1897.

American Lecturers and Humorists by Melville D. Landon . . .

> . . . New York ⟨1893; *i.e., ca.* 1898⟩

> For fuller entry see No. 11228.

. . . Masterpieces of Wit and Humor . . . Introduction by Robert J. Burdette . . .

Copyright, 1902 . . .

For comment see entry No. 2013.

. . . Gems of Modern Wit and Humor with . . . Introduction by Robert J. Burdette . . .

⟨n.p., n.d., 1903⟩

See entry No. 2013.

Mark Twain's Library of Humor   Men and Things . . .

. . . New York . . . MCMVI

For comment see entry No. 3666.

Mark Twain's Library of Humor   A Little Nonsense . . .

. . . New York . . . MCMVI

For comment see entry No. 3669.

Masters of Mirth and Eloquence by Melville D. Landon . . .

The Golden West Publishing Company Seattle, Washington ⟨1906⟩

REFERENCES AND ANA

Sprightly Banter. By Bill Nye.

London: John and Robert Maxwell, Milton House, Shoe Lane, Fleet Street ⟨n.d., *ca.* 1883⟩

Not seen. Not located.

Presumably a 32-page pamphlet containing material by Nye. Examination of the text (as published in *Comic Conceits* ⟨n.d., 1883⟩, for which see above in *Section Three*) has failed to produce any material identified as by Nye. Issued as No. 51 of a series. Reprinted in *Comic Conceits*, London: John & Robert Maxwell, listed in PC May 1, 1883.

Bill Nye's Blossom Rock.

Chicago, 1885.

Not located. Entry from CHAL, 1921, Vol. 4, p. 643. Presumably a ghost.

The Cadi. A Three Act Play.

San Francisco: Francis, Valentine & Co., 1891.

No copy located. Possibly not printed. A manuscript copy was deposited for copyright March 23, 1891.

For printings of "The Prodigal Son," a song in this production, see above in *Section One* under the year 1891.

The Stag Party.

Ca. 1895–1896.

No copy located. No record of publication found. A play. ". . . Completed under pressure shortly before his last illness, which was a failure."——— DAB.

Eccentricities of Genius . . . by Major J. B. Pond

G. W. Dillingham Company Publishers   New York ⟨1900⟩

Excerpts from letters, pp. 252-258.

"The Autobiography of Bill Nye," pp. 241-244. "Autobiography of James Whitcomb Riley," pp. 244-246. See *Looking Forward* . . . ⟨1890⟩, in *Section One* above.

Deposited Nov. 19, 1900. Listed PW Dec. 8, 1900.

The American Press Humorists' Book. ("Bill" Nye Monument Edition.) Edited and Published by Frank Thompson Searight

. . . Los Angeles, California . . . 1907.

Bill Nye His Own Life Story Continuity by Frank Wilson Nye . . .

The Century Co. New York London ⟨1926⟩

For fuller entry see above in *Section One*.

FITZ-JAMES O'BRIEN

1 8 2 8 - 1 8 6 2

15162. SIR BRASIL'S FALCON, A POEM . . .

PUBLISHED IN SEPTEMBER NO. OF THE UNITED STATES REVIEW. 1853.

Cover-title.

⟨1⟩-10. 9″ × 5¾″.

1⁴, 2¹.

Printed gray paper wrapper.

Collected in *Poems and Stories*, 1881.

H

15163. . . . BEGINNING THE WORLD WORDS BY FITZ JAMES O'BRIEN, MUSIC BY THOMAS BAKER . . .

NEW YORK PUBLISHED BY HORACE WATERS, 333 BROADWAY. BOSTON, PHILA, CINCINNATI . . . 1853 . . .

Sheet music. Cover-title. At head of title: *Bleak House Ballads N.° 1*

Deposited Nov. 22, 1853.

B NYPL

15164. ONCE A YEAR BALLAD . . . MUSIC BY THOMAS BAKER . . .

NEW-YORK . . . HORACE WATERS 333 BROADWAY . . . 1853 . . .

Sheet music. Cover-title.

Deposited Dec. 27, 1853.

EM

15165. The Ballads of Ireland; Collected and Edited, by Edward Hayes . . .

A. Fullarton & Co. London, Edinburgh, and Dublin. 1855.

For first American edition see next entry.

2 Vols. *Note:* The punctuation of the title-pages varies.

"The Boatmen of Kerry," Vol. 1, pp. 15-17. Uncollected.

"Irish Castles," Vol. 2, pp. 355-356. Collected in *Poems and Stories*, 1881.

"Loch Ina . . . ," Vol. 1, pp. 21-22. Collected in *Poems and Stories*, 1881.

NYPL

15166. The Ballads of Ireland; Collected and Edited by Edward Hayes . . .

Boston: Patrick Donahoe, 23 Franklin Street. 1856.

For first edition see preceding entry.   First American edition.

2 Vols.

"The Boatmen of Kerry," Vol. 1, pp. 53-55. Uncollected.

"Irish Castles," Vol. 2, p. 321. Collected in *Poems and Stories*, 1881.

"Loch Ina . . . ," Vol. 1, pp. 58-59. Collected in *Poems and Stories*, 1881.

H

15167. Tales and Sketches for the Fire-Side, by the Best American Authors. Selected from Putnam's Magazine.

New York: A. Dowling, 36 Beekman Street 1857.

"Mrs. Macsimum's Bill," in the issue of Dec. 1854. Elsewhere unlocated.

"Sea," in the issue of Dec. 1854. Collected in *Poems and Stories*, 1881.

"The Three Gannets," in the issue of Nov. 1854. Collected in *Poems and Stories*, 1881.

Irregular pagination. For comment see entry No. 8239.

15168. . . . A GENTLEMAN FROM IRELAND. A COMEDY, IN TWO ACTS . . . AS PERFORMED AT WALLACK'S THEATRE.

ENTERED . . . 1858 . . . NEW YORK: SAMUEL FRENCH, 122 NASSAU STREET, (UP STAIRS.)

At head of title: THE MINOR DRAMA. THE ACTING EDITION. NO. CLVI.

Query: Does this publication occur with an earlier imprint: *121 Nassau Street?*

⟨1⟩-20. 7⁷⁄₁₆″ × 4⁵⁄₈″.

⟨1⁸, 2²⟩.

Printed tan paper wrapper.

Note: The earliest printing (the first?) located collates as above; the following features present on the wrapper:

Inner front: French's Standard Drama . . . ⟨Vols. I-XXIV⟩

Inner back: ⟨the preceding concluded; Vols. XXV-XXVI⟩ . . . Plays in French and English . . . Massey's Exhibition Reciter . . .

Back: French's Minor Drama . . . ⟨Vols. I-XX; 2 numbers only, 153-154, listed under XX⟩

Reprints have been seen with one or more of the following features:

Inner front wrapper: French's Standard Drama . . . ⟨Vols. I-XL⟩

Outer back wrapper: French's Minor Drama . . . ⟨Vols. I-XXXVI⟩

A printing issued *ca.* 1885 has the publisher's street address in the imprint: *28 West 23d Street.*

A printing issued *ca.* 1900 does not bear the name of the publisher; copyright notice present in the name of Samuel French, dated 1858.

H

15169. Folk Songs Selected and Edited by John Williamson Palmer . . .

New York: Charles Scribner, 124 Grand Street. London: Sampson Low, Son and Company. M DCCC LXI.

"The Cave of Silver," pp. 338-340. Elsewhere unlocated.

For fuller entry see No. 11312.

15170. The Rebellion Record: A Diary of American Events . . . Edited by Frank Moore . . . First Volume . . .

New York: G. P. Putnam. C. T. Evans, General Agent. 1861.

"The Seventh," pp. 17-18 (*Poetry and Incidents* section). Uncollected. For earliest located formal book publication see *John Brown* . . . , 1863.

"The Seventh Regiment," pp. 148-154 (*Documents and Narratives* section). Uncollected. For earliest located formal book publication see *Anecdotes* . . . , 1866.

For comment see entry No. 11531.

15171. . . . Tales of the Time. By Fitz-Hugh Ludlow . . . Fitz-James O'Brien . . . Thomas Bailey Aldrich, and Miss C. M. Sedgwick.

New-York: H. Dexter & Co., and Ross & Tousey. Boston: A. Williams & Co., and J. J. Dyer & Co. ⟨n.d., 1861⟩

Cover-title. At head of title: *Price, Twenty-Five Cents.*

Printed paper wrapper.

"Bob o' Link," pp. 62-66. Uncollected.

Printed from the plates of K.

Y

15172. Poetical Pen-Pictures of the War: Selected from Our Union Poets. By J. Henry Hayward . . .

New York: Published by the Editor. 13 Park Row. 1863.

"The Countersign," pp. 255-256. Anonymous. Collected in *Poems and Stories*, 1881.

For fuller entry see No. 1037.

15173. John Brown, and "The Union Right or Wrong" Songster . . .

San Francisco: D. E. Appleton & Co., Publishers, 508 Montgomery Street, East Side, between Sacramento and Commercial Sts. 1863.

Printed paper wrapper.

"The Seventh," pp. 37-38. Uncollected. Earliest formal book publication located. For prior publication see above: *The Rebellion Record* . . . , 1861.

H NYPL

15174. Atlantic Tales. A Collection of Stories from the Atlantic Monthly.

Boston: Ticknor and Fields. 1866.

"The Diamond Lens," pp. ⟨21⟩-49. Collected in *Poems and Stories*, 1881.

For comment see entry No. 3775.

15175. Anecdotes, Poetry and Incidents of the War: North and South. 1860-1865. Collected and Arranged by Frank Moore . . .

New York: Printed for the Subscribers. 1866.

"The March of the Seventh Regiment," pp. 228-233. Uncollected. Earliest located formal book publication. For prior publication see *The Rebellion Record* . . . , 1861, above, where the piece appears under the title "The Seventh Regiment."

For fuller entry see No. 3202.

15176. One Hundred Choice Selections in Poetry and Prose, Both New and Old . . . ⟨Compiled⟩ by Nathaniel K. Richardson . . .

Philadelphia: Published by P. Garrett & Co., 702 Chestnut Street. 1866.

"Kane———Died February 16, 1857," pp. 19-21. Collected in *Poems and Stories*, 1881.

For fuller entry see No. 1425.

15177. Good Stories. Part III . . .

Boston: Ticknor and Fields. 1868.

Printed paper wrapper.

"Three of a Trade; or, Red Little Kriss Kringle," pp. ⟨119⟩-125. Uncollected.

BPL NYPL

15178. Good Stories. Part IV . . .

Boston: Ticknor and Fields. 1868.

Probably issued in printed paper wrapper.

"From Hand to Mouth," pp. ⟨3⟩-49. Uncollected.

BA

15179. What I Know about Joking; or, the White-House Jester . . .

⟨n.p., n.d., New York?, 1872⟩

Printed paper wrapper. Unpaged. Very probably printed from the plates of a periodical.

"The Irish Prince and the Mysterious Barber. A Legend of Old." Uncollected.

HM

15180. One Hundred Choice Selections No. 12 . . . by Phineas Garrett . . .

Published by P. Garrett & Co., 708 Chestnut Street, Philadelphia, Pa., and 116 E. Randolph Street, Chicago, Ill. 1876.

"Minot's Ledge," pp. 28-29. Collected in *Poems and Stories*, 1881.

For fuller entry see No. 5530.

15181. One Hundred Choice Selections No. 14 . . . ⟨Compiled⟩ by ⟨Phineas Garrett⟩ . . .

Published by P. Garrett & Co., 708 Chestnut Street, Philadelphia, Pa., and 116 E. Randolph Street, Chicago, Ill. 1877.

"The Lost Steamship," pp. 45-47. Collected in *Poems and Stories*, 1881.

For fuller entry see No. 7098.

15182. The Knapsack   A Daily Journal of the Seventh Regiment New York Armory Fair . . .

New York . . . November 17, 1879 . . . ⟨to⟩ . . . December 6, 1879

An occasional newspaper. Complete in 18 numbers. No. 16 erroneously numbered 15.

"The Midnight March," No. 18, Dec. 6, 1879, p. 14. Uncollected.

Earliest located book publication: *History of the Seventh Regiment of New York 1806-1889*, by Col. Emmons Clark, New York, 1890.

H

15183. THE POEMS AND STORIES OF FITZ-JAMES O'BRIEN. COLLECTED AND EDITED, WITH A SKETCH OF THE AUTHOR, BY WILLIAM WINTER.

BOSTON: JAMES R. OSGOOD AND COMPANY. 1881.

⟨i-ii⟩, ⟨i⟩-lxii, ⟨1⟩-485; leaf excised or pasted under the end paper. Frontispiece, 3 plates and 1 2-page facsimile inserted; other illustrations in text. $7\frac{3}{8}'' \times 4\frac{3}{4}''$.

⟨1-2¹², 3⁸, 4-23¹², 24⁴⟩. ⟨24⟩₄ excised or pasted under the end paper. *Signed:* ⟨-⟩¹, ⟨a⟩, b-d⁸, ⟨1⟩⁷, 2-30⁸, ⟨31⟩⁴.

S cloth: blue, brown; green; maroon; purple. Brown-coated on white end papers. Flyleaf at front.

Publisher's records:

Jan. 26, 1881. 1530 copies printed.

Feb. 3–March 15, 1881: 994 copies bound.

April 25, 1884: Plates sold at a trade sale; delivered to Rand, Avery & Company for delivery to Charles Scribner's Sons.

May 27, 1884: 516 copies (in sheets) sold as junk.

Noted as *just ready* PW Feb. 12, 1881. BA copy received Feb. 14, 1881. Listed PW Feb. 26, 1881.

BA H NYPL UV Y

15184. One Hundred Choice Selections No. 19 . . .

Published by P. Garrett & Co., 708 Chestnut Street, Philadelphia, Pa., and 116 E. Randolph Street, Chicago, Ill. 1881.

"Ormolu's Tenement House," pp. 8-11. Uncollected.

For fuller entry see No. 3392.

15185. The Sword and the Pen . . .

Boston . . . 1881 . . .

"Amy Scudder. (A Fragment.)," No. 9, pp. 8-9.

An occasional newspaper. For fuller entry see No. 123.

15186. . . . Swinton's Fourth Reader

Copyright, 1883, by Ivison, Blakeman, Taylor, and Company Publishers New York and Chicago

Cloth, leather shelfback. At head of title: *The Reader the Focus of Language-Training*

"Independence Bell," pp. 337-340. Anonymous. Uncollected.

Earliest located book publication. BAL cannot believe that this popular poem remained unanthologized for so long. The poem was first published in *Harper's Weekly*, July 4, 1857, under the title "How the Bell Rang." For further comment see Wolle, pp. 148-149.

Reprinted *ca.* 1890 with the following imprint: *New York Cincinnati Chicago American Book Company from the Press of Ivison, Blakeman & Company ⟨1883⟩*.

NYPL

15187. History of the Seventh Regiment of New York 1806–1889 by Colonel Emmons Clark . . .

New York Published by the Seventh Regiment 1890

2 Vols.

"The Midnight March," Vol. 2, p. 3. For prior publication see *The Knapsack* . . . , 1879, above.

Also contains reprinted extracts.

Deposited Feb. 26, 1890.

H

15188. Library of the World's Best Mystery and Detective Stories Edited by Julian Hawthorne English Irish . . .

New York The Review of Reviews Company 1907

Reprint save for "A Terrible Night," pp. 48-55.

Deposited Aug. 11, 1908.

H

FITZ-JAMES O'BRIEN

SECTION II

Reprints issued under O'Brien's name. For books containing O'Brien reprints issued without O'Brien's name on the title-page see *Section III*.

15189. The Diamond Lens with Other Stories . . . Collected and Edited, with a Sketch of the Author by William Winter A New Edition

New York Charles Scribner's Sons 1885

Published April 4, 1885 (publisher's records). Listed PW April 11, 1885. The London (Ward & Downey) edition listed Ath Nov. 12, 1887 ⟨*sic*⟩.

15190. What Was It? And Other Stories . . .

London: Ward & Downey, 12, York Street, Covent Garden. 1889.

Not seen. Entry on the basis of a photographic copy. Listed PC Aug. 1, 1889.

15191. The Diamond Lens with Other Stories . . . Edited . . . by William Winter A New Edition

New York Charles Scribner's Sons 1893

15192. The Golden Ingot, The Diamond Lens, A Terrible Night. What Was It? A Mystery

New York: Reynolds Publishing Company ⟨1921⟩

Unlocated. Entry from Wolle, p. 252.

Reprinted from *The Poems and Stories* . . . , 1881; and, *Library of the World's Best Mystery and Detective Stories*, 1907, above. Wolle (p. 252) reports a 1923 reissue in the *Famous Authors' Handy Library*.

15193. Collected Stories . . . Edited with an Introduction by Edward J. O'Brien

Albert & Charles Boni New York 1925

Two bindings have been seen; the order of presentation is presumed correct:

A: Blue buckram, device blindstamped on front cover. Copy in H.

B: Red V cloth, sides unstamped. Copy in H.

Deposited Oct. 12, 1925.

15194. The Diamond Lens and Other Stories . . . with an Introduction by Gilbert Seldes . . .

New York William Edwin Rudge 1932

Limited to 750 copies. BPL copy received May 18, 1932; deposited May 25, 1932.

FITZ-JAMES O'BRIEN

SECTION III

In this section are listed books by authors other than O'Brien which contain material by him reprinted from earlier books. See *Section Two* for collections of reprinted material issued under O'Brien's name.

"What Was It?," one of O'Brien's most popular tales, was first published in *Harper's New Monthly Magazine*, March, 1859, and appears in numerous anthologies issued after *The Poems and Stories of Fitz-James O'Brien*, 1881, the earliest located book publication of the story. BAL has ignored all such later appearances.

"The Diamond Lens" has received similar treatment. It was first published in *The Atlantic Monthly*, Jan. 1858; earliest located book appearance: *Atlantic Tales*, 1866; first collected in *The Poems and Stories of Fitz-James O'Brien*, 1881. All anthological appearances, save the 1866, have been ignored.

Songs of the Soldiers . . . Edited by Frank Moore

New York . . . 1864

For comment see entry No. 261.

Modern Classics . . . and Other Stories from the "Atlantic Monthly."

Philadelphia . . . ⟨1865; *i.e.,* 1876⟩

For fuller entry see BAL, Vol. 2, p. 273.

Poetry Lyrical, Narrative, and Satirical of the Civil War . . . Edited by Richard Grant White

New York . . . 1866

For comment see entry No. 4604.

History of the Seventh Regiment, National Guard, State of New York, during the War of the Rebellion . . . by William Swinton . . .

New York and Boston: Fields, Osgood, & Co. 1870.

Reprint save for extract from a letter, p. 463.

Deposited Dec. 21, 1869.

A Library of Poetry and Song . . . by William Cullen Bryant

New York . . . 1871

For fuller entry see No. 1722.

Illustrated Library of Favorite Song . . . Edited by J. G. Holland . . .

New York . . . ⟨1873⟩

For comment see entry No. 2853.

Songs of Nature Selected from Many Sources . . .

New York . . . 1873.

For fuller entry see No. 4760.

Modern Classics . . . and Other Stories from the "Atlantic Monthly."

Philadelphia . . . ⟨1865; *i.e.,* 1876⟩

For fuller entry see BAL, Vol. 2, p. 273.

Hillside and Seaside in Poetry . . . Edited by Lucy Larcom

Boston . . . 1877

For fuller entry see No. 11345.

The Reading Club and Handy Speaker . . . Edited by George M. Baker. No. 4.

Boston . . . 1877.

For comment see entry No. 8303.

Famous Stories by De Quincy ⟨*sic*⟩, Hawthorne . . . and Others . . . in Two Vols. . . .

New York: R. Worthington, 750 Broadway. 1878.

The Fireside Encyclopædia of Poetry . . . Compiled . . . by Henry T. Coates.

. . . Philadelphia. ⟨1878⟩

For fuller entry see in the James Russell Lowell list, *Section Three*.

... A Century of American Literature 1776–1876 Edited by Henry A. Beers ...

New York Henry Holt and Company 1878

At head of title: *Leisure Hour Series.*---*No. 100*

Advertised PW Sept. 14, 1878, as *nearly ready.* Listed PW Dec. 7, 1878.

Poems of Places Edited by Henry W. Longfellow ... New England. Vol. II.

Boston ... 1879.

For fuller entry see No. 12209.

Poems of Places Edited by Henry W. Longfellow ... Oceanica ...

Boston ... 1879.

For fuller entry see No. 12216.

The Union of American Poetry and Art ... by John James Piatt ...

Cincinnati ... 1880

For fuller entry see in James Russell Lowell, *Section Three.*

Gems for the Fireside ... ⟨Compiled by⟩ Rev. O. H. Tiffany ...

Boston ... 1881.

For fuller entry see BAL, Vol. 5, p. 610.

Harper's Cyclopædia of British and American Poetry Edited by Epes Sargent

New York ... 1881

For comment see entry No. 4336.

Famous Stories by DeQuincy ⟨*sic*⟩, Hawthorne ... and Others ...

Boston: DeWolfe, Fiske and Company, 365 Washington Street. ⟨n.d., not before 1881⟩

One Hundred Choice Selections No. 22 ...

... Philadelphia ... 1883.

For comment see entry No. 4738.

Gems for the Fireside ... ⟨Compiled by⟩ Rev. O. H. Tiffany ...

Springfield ... ⟨1883⟩

For fuller entry see BAL, Vol. 5, p. 611.

Brilliant Diamonds of Poetry and Prose ... ⟨Compiled by⟩ Rev. O. H. Tiffany ...

Published for the Trade. ⟨n.p., 1883⟩

A truncated printing of the preceding entry.

No. 4. Standard Recitations ... Compiled ... by ... Frances P. Sullivan ... June, 1884 ...

... N. Y. ... ⟨1884⟩

For comment see BAL, Vol. 4, p. 60.

Life and Letters of Bayard Taylor Edited by Marie Hansen-Taylor and Horace E. Scudder in Two Volumes ...

Boston Houghton, Mifflin and Company New York: 11 East Seventeenth Street The Riverside Press, Cambridge 1884

"The Helmet," Vol. 1, p. 284. Otherwise "The Challenge," *The Poems and Stories*, 1881, p. 107.

The Household Library of Ireland's Poets, with Full and Choice Selections from the Irish-American Poets ... Collected and Edited by Daniel Connolly.

Published by the Editor, 28 Union Square, New York. 1887

Deposited Jan. 12, 1888.

A Library of American Literature ... Edited by Edmund Clarence Stedman and Ellen Mackay Hutchinson ...

New-York ... 1888–1890.

For comment see entry No. 1350.

Library of the World's Best Literature Ancient and Modern Charles Dudley Warner Editor ... Vol. XVIII

New York ... ⟨1897⟩

For comment see entry No. 10624.

An American Anthology 1787–1899 ... Edited by Edmund Clarence Stedman ...

Boston ... M DCCCC

"The Second Mate," pp. 303-304; otherwise "The Lost Steamship," *The Poems and Stories*, 1881.

For fuller entry see No. 3082.

Irish Literature Justin McCarthy M.P. Editor ...

... Philadelphia ⟨1904⟩

For comment see BAL, Vol. 1, p. 399.

American Familiar Verse   Vers de Société Edited ... by Brander Matthews ...

... New York ... 1904

For fuller entry see in James Russell Lowell, *Section Three.*

The Golden Treasury of Irish Songs and Lyrics Edited by Charles Welsh . . .

New York Dodge Publishing Company 40-42 East 19th Street ⟨1907⟩

2 Vols. Deposited March 15, 1907. Listed PW April 13, 1907.

Poems of American History Collected . . . by Burton Egbert Stevenson

Boston . . . 1908

For fuller entry see in Joaquin Miller, *Section One.*

Great Ghost Stories Selected by Joseph Lewis French with a Foreword by James H. Hyslop . . .

New York Dodd, Mead and Company 1918

Masterpieces of Mystery in Four Volumes . . . Edited by Joseph Lewis French

Garden City New York Doubleday, Page & Company 1920

Future Perfect American Science Fiction of the Nineteenth Century ⟨by⟩ H. Bruce Franklin

New York Oxford University Press 1966

REFERENCES AND ANA

Carrier's New Years Address for New York Times

New York, *ca.* 1860.

Not located. Entry from Wolle, p. 261.

Wolle, p. 202, quotes from Maverick (see below) who gives an account of the composition of the address but does not identify O'Brien as the 'author'. Wolle, p. 129, presents evidence identifying O'Brien as the unnamed 'author'.

"An illustration of this Bohemian trickery was given, several years ago, in the office of the New York *Times.* One of the brightest, best-read, and most reckless of the Bohemians of the city, suddenly nipped by evil fortune, secluded himself for a day from the gaze of his fellows, and then appeared in the editorial room with a roll of manuscript. It was a Carrier's Address in verse, intended for the first of January, admirably written, full of local hits, crackling with fun. It was gladly accepted. 'Could you let me have forty dollars?' asked the poet. In violation of a rule in force in newspaper offices, which prohibits prepayment for literary contributions, the money was given, and in the evening there was high revel at Pfaff's,—an underground saloon on Broadway much frequented by the Bohemians of the day. The New Year arrived; and the *Times* Carriers' Address was widely

distributed and generally read. It was a creditable literary performance,—in fact, far superior to the average character of these annual inflictions. But a stray copy was found by a reader of the *Times* in a western town; and this person, struck by lines in the poem which seemed familiar, made some investigations. It then appeared that the dishonest poet had 'adopted' an old Address, changing the order of the verses, adding bits of local color, interjecting a few allusions to the principal events of the year, and then successfully passing it off as an original production."—*Henry J. Raymond and the New York Press for Thirty Years . . . ,* by Augustus Maverick, Hartford, 1870, p. 251.

Stories by American Authors III . . .

New York Charles Scribner's Sons 1884

"The Spider's Eye," pp. ⟨5⟩-29; credited to O'Brien.

". . . It has been attributed to O'Brien, may not be his; the weight of evidence, which at best is slight, could be made to throw the balance in favor of O'Brien or of Lucretia P. Hale . . ."—Wolle, p. 117.

The 1885 and 1898 printings attribute the story to Lucretia P. Hale.

Two bindings noted; for comment see entry No. 10567.

Rosedale, or the Rifle Ball.

Printed but Not Published. ⟨n.p., n.d., *ca.* 1890⟩

Copy in H.

Printed paper wrapper. ⟨i-ii⟩, 1-69. 8¹¹⁄₁₆″ × 5³⁄₈″.

"Lester ⟨*i.e.,* John Johnstone⟩ Wallack allowed himself to be credited with the authorship of it for twenty-five years. He paid Fitz James O'Brien $100 to dramatize it from a novel, *Lady Lee's Widowhood,* in *Blackwood's Magazine.*"—From a clipping, *The New York Dramatic Mirror,* date unknown; tipped in the H copy.

A *ms* of the play (in H) appears to be in Lester Wallack's hand, and is accompanied by a letter from Wallack's son, Arthur, to Evart Jansen Wendell (Oct. 30, 1900), in which the handwriting is identified as Lester Wallack's. The letter reads in part: ". . . I have the original MS of *Rosedale* as written by my father & all in his own hand . . ."

"The author of *Rosedale* was not Lester Wallack, as the playbills always said. At a dinner given in this city ⟨New York⟩ in 1890 it was stated by Charles Gayler that Fitz James O'Brien . . . was paid $100 by Lester Wallack to write it. For a quarter of a century Lester Wallack was credited with the authorship of that drama . . ." ———T. Allston Brown: *A History of the New York Stage* . . . , New York, 1903, Vol. 2, p. 252.

"The actual authorship of *Rosedale* has been much, and unjustly, questioned . . . I know nothing about any statement relative to *Rosedale*, made by Charles Gayler . . . two years after the death of Wallack. I knew not only Wallack but Gayler and O'Brien, however, intimately well. I know that Gayler,———an able and genial man, esteemed by many friends, of whom I was one,———was not entirely amicable in his feeling toward Lester Wallack. I was the literary executor of O'Brien . . . and the only collection of O'Brien's writings . . . is one made by me . . . Among all O'Brien's papers that came into my possession, and in all the inquiries and searches made by me relative to his life and work (and they were diligent and thorough), I never came upon an intimation, or saw or heard even a single word, in any way suggestive of O'Brien's authorship of *Rosedale*, ———although I ascertained his authorship of seven plays, namely, *A Gentleman from Ireland, The Sisters, My Christmas Dinner, Duke Humphrey's Dinner, The Cup and the Lip, The Two Ophelias,* and *Blood Will Tell.* Lester Wallack had a sincere and deep regard for Fitz-James O'Brien, and it was not in his nature to appropriate and publish as his own the work of his dead friend, ———or of anybody else. It is *possible,* though *not likely,* that Wallack may have paid O'Brien for doing some slight hack work on an early draft of the play . . ."———William Winter: *Vagrant Memories* . . . , New York, 1915, pp. 88, 90-91.

"On September 30, 1863, Wallack's Theatre was opened for the season with a new play, *Rosedale, or the Rifle Ball.* This was a great success, being acted 125 times during the season . . . Lester Wallack was posted on the playbills as its author; but Charles Gayler, the prolific playwright and something of a rival of O'Brien's, at a dinner given in New York in 1890, stated that Wallack had paid O'Brien $100 to dramatize it from a novel, *Lady Lee's Widowhood,* which had some years previously appeared in *Blackwood's Magazine.* Such a course of action seems unlike Lester Wallack, but there is no evidence either way."——— Francis Wolle: *Fitz-James O'Brien* . . . , 1944, p. 230.

Fitz-James O'Brien A Literary Bohemian of the Eighteen-Fifties by Francis Wolle . . .

University of Colorado Studies Series B. Studies in the Humanities Vol. 2, No. 2 Boulder, Colorado May, 1944 Price $2.00

Deposited for copyright Aug. 28, 1944.

NOTE

The following plays are listed by Wolle, pp. 265-266, as unpublished:

Blood Will Tell

The Cup and the Lip. A Three Act Play. 1856.

Duke Humphrey's Dinner. A Dramatic Sketch. 1856.

My Christmas Dinner. A Farce. 1852.

Samson.

The Sisters. A Drama in Two Acts Adapted from the French, Ange ou Diable. 1854.

The Two Ophelias.

The Tycoon, or Young America in Japan. A Burlesque. 1860. In collaboration with Charles G. Rosenberg.

15195. SONGS FROM THE SOUTHERN SEAS, AND OTHER POEMS . . .

BOSTON: ROBERTS BROTHERS. 1873.

⟨1⟩-227. 6⅞″ × 4⅝″ full.

⟨1⟩-9¹², 10⁶.

FL cloth: brown; green. S cloth: green; purple; terra-cotta. Brown-coated on white end papers. Flyleaves. Top edges gilt.

Advertised for Nov. 1 PW Oct. 25, 1873. Listed PW Nov. 1, 1873.

AAS BPL H NYPL UV Y

15196. Proceedings of the Franklin Typographical Society, at the Observance of the Semi-Centennial of its Institution, January 17, 1874: With a Brief Historical Sketch.

Boston: Published by the Society. 1875.

Printed paper wrapper.

Remarks, pp. 50-51.

H

15197. Laurel Leaves. Original Poems, Stories, and Essays . . .

Boston: William F. Gill and Company, 309 Washington Street. 1876.

Cloth; and, morocco.

"A Nation's Test. Read at the O'Connell Centennial in Boston, on August 6, 1875," pp. 391-397. Collected in *Songs, Legends, and Ballads*, 1878.

Note: This is the earliest located book appearance of the poem. It may have had earlier publication in one of those publications devoted to the O'Connell centenary but such an appearance has not been found by BAL.

For fuller entry see No. 116.

15198. The Reading Club and Handy Speaker . . . Edited by George M. Baker. No. 3.

Boston: Lee and Shepard, Publishers. 1876.

Cloth. Also issued in printed paper wrapper?

"Bone and Sinew and Brain," pp. 25-27. Collected in *Songs, Legends, and Ballads*, 1878.

Advertised PW Dec. 18, 1875. Listed PW Dec. 25, 1875. Advertised as *just published* PW Jan. 1, 1876. Again advertised PW Jan. 8, 1876.

H

15199. Solomon. By Constance Fenimore Woolson.

Odessa, Ontario: James Neish & Sons, Publishers. ⟨n.d., *ca.* 1876⟩

Printed paper wrapper.

"Macarius the Monk," pp. ⟨95⟩-96. Collected in *Songs, Legends, and Ballads*, 1878.

The H copy inscribed by early owner April 12, 1876.

H NYPL Y

15200. One Hundred Choice Selections No. 13 . . . ⟨Compiled⟩ by ⟨Phineas Garrett⟩ . . .

Published by P. Garrett & Co., 708 Chestnut Street, Philadelphia, Pa., and 116 E. Randolph Street, Chicago, Ill. 1877.

"The Ride of Collins Graves," pp. 16-18. Collected in *Songs, Legends, and Ballads*, 1878.

For fuller entry see No. 3372.

15201. SONGS, LEGENDS, AND BALLADS . . .

BOSTON: THE PILOT PUBLISHING COMPANY, 1878.

⟨i⟩-⟨x⟩, ⟨1⟩-318; blank leaf; *Opinions of the Press*, pp. ⟨1⟩-14. Laid paper. 6⅞″ scant × 4⅝″ scant. ⟨1-21⁸, 22⁴⟩.

S cloth: purple. Brown-coated on white end papers. Laid paper flyleaves. Top edges gilt.

A copy (in H) presented by O'Reilly to Longfellow Sept. 30, 1878. Noticed by Ath Oct. 19, 1878. Listed PW Nov. 2, 1878.

AAS B BPL H UV Y

15202. MOONDYNE: A STORY FROM THE UNDER-WORLD . . .

BOSTON: THE PILOT PUBLISHING COMPANY. 1879.

See next entry for revised edition.

⟨i⟩-⟨viii⟩, ⟨1⟩-327. 7⅟₁₆″ full × 4¾″.

⟨1-14¹²⟩.

S cloth: purple. Brown-coated on white end papers. Flyleaves.

Published serially in *The Pilot* (Boston), Nov. 30, 1878–May 10, 1879. "Now ready in book form" ––– *The Pilot*, May 10, 1879.

AAS   BA   BPL   MHS   Y

15203. Moondyne: A Story from the Under-World . . . Third Edition.

Boston: Roberts Brothers. 1879.

Revised. For first edition see preceding entry.

Query: Is this the first Robert Brothers printing? Did the publisher consider original serial publication the first printing; and first book publication (above) the second edition? See publication notes below which indicate that the *third edition* is in fact the second book publication.

PW Sept. 6, 1879, announced the "third edition from new plates." PW Oct. 4, 1879, carried an advertisement offering the book for "this week." Listed PW Oct. 11, 1879. A copy in BPL inscribed by O'Reilly Oct. 31, 1879. Reviewed Bkr Nov. 1879.

BPL

15204. The Union of American Poetry and Art A Choice Collection of Poems by American Poets Selected . . . by John James Piatt . . .

Cincinnati W. E. Dibble, Publisher 1880

"A Savage," p. 586. Collected in *The Statues in the Block,* 1881.

For fuller entry see James Russell Lowell, *Section Three.*

H

15205. THE STATUES IN THE BLOCK, AND OTHER POEMS . . .

BOSTON: ROBERTS BROTHERS. 1881.

⟨1⟩-110, blank leaf. Laid paper. 6⅝″ × 4¼″ scant.

⟨1-14⁴⟩. Signed: ⟨1⟩-7⁸.

S cloth: gold; green. White end papers printed in tan and brown with an all-over bird and leaf pattern. Laid paper flyleaves. Top edges stained yellow.

BA copy received April 6, 1881. Listed PW April 9, 1881.

BA   H   UV   Y

15206. The Poets' Tributes to Garfield   The Collection of Poems Written for the Boston Daily Globe, and Many Selections . . . ⟨First Edition⟩

Cambridge, Mass. Published by Moses King Harvard Square 1881

For fuller entry see No. 8955.

"Midnight. September 19, 1881," pp. 33-35. Collected in *In Bohemia,* 1886, with one stanza omitted.

Note: The poem was first published on the front page of *The Boston Daily Globe,* Vol. xx, No. 89, Sept. 27, 1881. The *Globe* also published a printing of the first page on satin, printed on recto only, with the statement in the heading: *Vol. IX, No. 39* ⟨*sic*⟩. A copy of the separate printing on satin is in Y.

15207. The Sword and the Pen . . .

Boston . . . 1881 . . .

An occasional newspaper. For comment see entry No. 123.

"The Priceless Things," No. 10, p. 6. Collected in *In Bohemia,* 1886.

15208. THE   THREE   QUEENS . . . [READ BEFORE THE PHI BETA KAPPA SOCIETY, AT DARTMOUTH COLLEGE, JUNE 29, 1881.] . . .

⟨n.p., n.d., probably Boston, 1881⟩

Caption-title. The above at head of p. ⟨1⟩.

⟨1⟩-4. Single sheet folded to make four pages. Size of page: 10¹³⁄₁₆″ × 8½″. Laid paper.

Collected in *In Bohemia,* 1886. Also published in *Anniversary of the New Hampshire Alpha of the Phi Beta Kappa Society at Dartmouth College, June 29th, 1881. Oration, Governor Charles H. Bell. Poem, John Boyle O'Reilly, LL.D.,* ⟨Hanover, N. H.⟩ Published by the Society ⟨1881⟩.

BPL   UV

15209. Human Life in Shakespeare by Henry Giles . . . with Introduction by John Boyle O'Reilly

Boston Lee and Shepard, Publishers New York Charles T. Dillingham 1882

"Introductory Note," pp. ⟨iii⟩-vi.

Listed PW May 20, 1882.

B   BPL

15210. AMERICA . . . READ AT THE RE-UNION OF THE ARMY OF THE POTO-MAC, AT DETROIT, ON JUNE 14, 1882 . . .

⟨n.p., 1882?⟩

Caption-title. The above at head of text.

Single cut sheet of laid paper (see below for comment) folded to make four pages. Text on pp. ⟨1⟩ and ⟨3⟩. Pp. ⟨2⟩ and ⟨4⟩ blank. Size of page: $10^{15}/_{16}'' \times 8^{1}/_{2}''$.

Noted on two types of paper; sequence, if any, unknown:

A: Paper watermarked *Whiting Paper Co*

B: Paper watermarked *Old Berkshire Mills 1882*

Collected in *In Bohemia*, 1886. Also in: *The Society of the Army of the Potomac. Report of the Thirteenth Annual Re-Union . . .* , New York, 1882. The *Report* also contains a "Response" by O'Reilly, p. 68.

BPL (A)   LC (B)   MHS (A)

15211. THE CITY STREETS . . .

⟨n.p., n.d., 1883?⟩

Caption-title. The above at head of p. ⟨1⟩. Single cut sheet folded to make four pages. Text on pp. ⟨1⟩ and ⟨3⟩. Pp. ⟨2⟩ and ⟨4⟩ blank. Page: $10^{5}/_{8}'' \times 8^{1}/_{2}''$ full.

"In January, 1883, he wrote another of his great poems, challenging the inequalities and injustices of the social system, *The City Streets*."---Roche, p. 224.

Collected in *In Bohemia*, 1886. Also in *Representative Poems . . .* , 1886, q.v.

B

15212. The Elocutionist's Annual Number 12 . . . Compiled by Mrs. J. W. Shoemaker.

Publication Department, National School of Elocution and Oratory. Philadelphia. 1884.

"Wendell Phillips," pp. 41-44. Collected in *In Bohemia*, 1886.

For fuller entry see No. 10454.

15213. THE KING'S MEN A TALE OF TO-MORROW BY ROBERT GRANT JOHN BOYLE O'REILLY J. S. OF DALE ⟨F. J. Simpson⟩ AND JOHN T. WHEELWRIGHT . . .

NEW YORK   CHARLES SCRIBNER'S SONS   1884

⟨i-vi⟩, ⟨1⟩-270; 10 pp. advertisements; blank leaf. $6^{13}/_{16}'' \times 4^{3}/_{4}''$.

⟨1-18⁸⟩.

Noted in the following two states of binding:

BINDING A

S cloth: brown; maroon; tan. Front cover both lettered and decorated. Cream end papers. Laid paper flyleaves. The publisher's file copy thus; the surviving deposit copy thus.

BINDING B

S cloth: tan. Front cover decorated only, not lettered. White end papers.

Published Aug. 9, 1884 (publisher's records). BA copy (rebound) received Aug. 11, 1884. Deposited (*Binding A*) Aug. 14, 1884. Listed PW Aug. 16, 1884.

B (B)   BPL (B)   LC (A)   NYPL (A)   Y (A)

15214. Excelsior Recitations and Readings No. 2 . . . Edited by T. J. Carey.

New York: Excelsior Publishing House, 29 and 31 Beekman Street. ⟨1884⟩

"What Made Him Glad," pp. 109-110. Collected in *In Bohemia*, 1886, as "An Old Vagabond."

For fuller entry see No. 5546.

15215. "THE LEOPARD CAN'T CHANGE HIS SPOTS." GREAT SPEECH OF JOHN BOYLE O'REILLY . . . DELIVERED AT WILKES-BARRE, PA., SEPT. 10, 1884 . . .

⟨n.p., n.d., presumably 1884⟩

Caption-title. The above at head of p. ⟨1⟩.

⟨1⟩-4. Text printed in two columns. $8^{1}/_{2}'' \times 5^{3}/_{4}''$.

Single cut sheet folded to make four pages.

MHS

15216. Representative Poems of Living Poets American and English Selected by the Poets Themselves with an Introduction by George Parsons Lathrop

Cassell & Company, Limited   739 & 741 Broadway, New York   1886

Reprint with the possible exception of "The City Streets," pp. 484-489. The poem also appears as an undated separate; see above under 1883 (?). Collected in *In Bohemia*, 1886 (October).

For comment see entry No. 436.

15217. HEADQUARTERS $5 PARLIAMENTARY FUND, / 252 Washington St., Boston, Mass. / You are cordially invited to attend a public meeting to be / held in Tremont Temple, on Wednesday, July 7th, at 8 o'clock / P.M., in aid of the Parliamentary contest for Home Rule in / Ireland ⟨etc., etc.⟩

At end: JOHN BOYLE O'REILLY, *Chairman* . . .

Issued in 1886. Single leaf. Printed on recto only. 8⅜″ × 5⁹⁄₁₆″.

BPL

15218. IN BOHEMIA...

BOSTON: THE PILOT PUBLISHING CO.   597 WASH-
INGTON STREET. ⟨1886⟩

⟨1⟩-97; blank, p. ⟨98⟩; blank leaf; advertisements, pp. ⟨1⟩-6, ⟨1⟩-6, plus: 7-⟨21⟩. Laid paper.
7⅜″ full × 4⅞″.

⟨1-7⁸, plus: 8⁸⟩.

Noted in the following bindings; the sequence has not
been determined and the order of presentation is
arbitrary. However, *Binding A* has been seen inscribed by the author, the earliest inscription
noted being Sept. 20, 1886.

BINDING A

V cloth: green.

End papers: White laid or wove.

Flyleaves: White laid or wove.

Top edges: Gilded.

Frontispiece: Not present.

BINDING B

S cloth: green.

End papers: White laid or wove.

Flyleaves: None.

Top edges: Plain.

Frontispiece: Not present.

BINDING C

S cloth: green.

End papers: White laid or wove.

Flyleaves: None.

Top edges: Gilded.

Frontispiece: Portrait present.

BINDING D

S cloth: green.

End papers: White printed in brown with an all-
over leafy pattern.

Flyleaves: Wove paper.

Top edges: Plain.

Frontispiece: Portrait present.

BINDING E

V cloth: blue.

End papers: Printed in brown with an all-over leafy
pattern.

Flyleaves: Wove paper.

Top edges: Gilded.

Frontispiece: Portrait present.

A copy of *Binding A* (in LC) has been seen inscribed by the author Sept. 20, 1886. Listed PW
Oct. 9, 1886.

AAS (A)   BA (A)   BPL (A)   H (A, C)   LC (A)
NYPL (B)   UV (A, E)   Y (A, D)

15219. Woman Suffrage Unnatural and Inexpedient. Views of Rev. O. B. Frothingham...
John Boyle O'Reilly...Richard H. Dana...

Boston: 1886.

Cover-title. Printed self-wrapper.

"Letter from John Boyle O'Reilly," pp. ⟨12⟩-13;
dated *February 11, 1886.*

MHS

15220. THE IRISH QUESTION: ITS COM-
MERCIAL AND INDUSTRIAL ASPECTS.
ADDRESS   BEFORE   THE   BEACON
SOCIETY OF BOSTON, SATURDAY, FEB-
RUARY 28, 1886...

⟨n.p., n.d., probably Boston, 1886⟩

Caption-title. The above on p. ⟨1⟩.

⟨1⟩-10, blank leaf. 8⅝″ × 5¾″.

⟨-⟩⁶.

Printed self-wrapper.

BPL

15221. The Poetry and Song of Ireland. With
Biographical Sketches of Her Poets. Compiled
and Edited by John Boyle O'Reilly...

New York: Gay Brothers & Co., 14 Barclay
Street. ⟨1887⟩

The title-leaf is a cancel. All copies thus?

"Introduction," pp. ⟨v⟩-xiv. Also contains a
selection of O'Reilly's poems, all here reprinted.

Deposited Jan. 27, 1887. Reprinted and reissued
with the publisher's later address in the imprint:
30, 32, 34 Reade Street. See under 1889 for another
edition.

LC

15222. Elocutionary Studies and New Recitations, ⟨Edited⟩ by Mrs. Anna Randall-
Diehl...

New York: 48 University Place, Edgar S.
Werner, 1887...

Flexible cloth.

"The Press Evangel," pp. 61-62. Collected in
Life...⟨1891⟩.

Listed PW Nov. 5, 1887.

JN

15223. Ireland's Cause in England's Parliament by Justin McCarthy, M.P. With Preface by John Boyle O'Reilly

Boston Ticknor and Company 211, Tremont Street 1888

Cloth; and, printed paper wrapper.

"Preface," pp. v-vi.

Listed PW Jan. 21, 1888.

NYPL Y

15224. What American Authors Think about International Copyright

New-York American Copyright League 1888

Statement, p. 8.

For comment see entry No. 218.

15225. The Crime against Ireland by J Ellen Foster with a Preface by John Boyle O'Reilly

Boston D Lothrop Company Franklin and Hawley Streets ⟨1888⟩

"Preface," pp. ⟨iii-iv⟩.

Listed PW March 31, 1888. Advertised as in both cloth; and, paper, PW May 5, 1888.

NYPL

15226. ETHICS OF BOXING AND MANLY SPORT . . .

BOSTON TICKNOR AND COMPANY 211, TREMONT STREET 1888

⟨i-ii⟩, ⟨i⟩-xviii, 1-358, blank leaf; advertisements, pp. 1-4; plus: 5-20. Frontispiece and 5 plates inserted; other illustrations in text. $7\frac{5}{8}'' \times 5\frac{3}{8}''$ full.

⟨1², 2-23⁸, 24⁶, 25⁸; plus: 26⁸⟩.

V cloth: blue; green; tan.

Deposited April 21, 1888. Noted for *today* PW April 21, 1888. Listed PW April 28, 1888; PC (Trübner, American sheets) May 15, 1888. See under 1890 for an extended edition.

AAS BPL H NYPL Y

15227. The Elocutionist's Annual Number 16 . . . Compiled by Mrs. J. W. Shoemaker

Publication Department The National School of Elocution and Oratory Philadelphia 1888

Cloth; and, printed paper wrapper.

"The Wonderful Country," pp. 149-150. Collected in *Life* . . . ⟨1891⟩.

Deposited Oct. 1, 1888.

LC

15228. Arbor Day . . . Edited and Compiled by Robert W. Furnas.

Lincoln, Neb.: State Journal Company, Printers. 1888.

Bound in imitation leather.

Letter, April 9, 1888, p. 106.

BA

15229. A Memorial of Crispus Attucks, Samuel Maverick James Caldwell, Samuel Gray and Patrick Carr from the City of Boston . . .

Boston Printed by Order of the City Council 1889

"Crispus Attucks," pp. ⟨51⟩-56. Collected in *Life* . . . ⟨1891⟩.

BA Y

15230. The Poetry and Song of Ireland. Edited by John Boyle O'Reilly . . . with the Publisher's Supplement to the Second Edition . . .

New York: Gay Brothers & Co., 30, 32 & 34 Reade Street. ⟨1889⟩

For first edition see above under 1887.

The edition of 1887 "as prepared by Mr. O'Reilly . . . is retained unaltered in the present volume. . ." ———From the "Publisher's ⟨prefatory⟩ Announcement." Extended by the addition of a supplement (not by O'Reilly). In the front matter is a facsimile of O'Reilly's agreement with the publishers for publication of the first edition.

Deposited March 10, 1891. Reissued with the publisher's later address *21 Warren Street*.

H Y

15231. The Proceedings at the Celebration by the Pilgrim Society at Plymouth, August 1st, 1889 of the Completion of the National Monument to the Pilgrims.

Plymouth: Avery & Doten, Book and Job Printers. 1889.

Printed flexible cloth wrapper.

"The Pilgrim Fathers," pp. 107-115. Collected in *Life* . . . ⟨1891⟩.

AAS H

15232. Athletics and Manly Sport . . .

Boston Pilot Publishing Company 597 Washington Street 1890.

An extended edition of *Ethics of Boxing* . . . , 1888. Contains "Canoeing in the Dismal Swamp," pp. 351-452, not present in the original work.

Deposited Feb. 24, 1890. Listed PW April 12, 1890.

BPL H Y

15233. Joel Chandler Harris' Life of Henry W. Grady Including His Writings and Speeches. A Memorial Volume . . . Edited by Joel Chandler Harris . . .

New York: Cassell Publishing Company, 104 & 106 Fourth Avenue. ⟨1890⟩

"The Death of Henry W. Grady," pp. 499-501.

For fuller entry see No. 7120.

15234. The Art of Authorship . . . Compiled . . . by George Bainton.

London: James Clarke & Co., 13 & 14, Fleet Street. 1890.

Contribution, pp. 331-334.

For fuller entry see No. 1271.

15235. No. 27. Standard Recitations by Best Authors . . . Compiled . . . by Frances P. Sullivan . . . March, 1890 . . .

M. J. Ivers & Co., Publishers, 86 Nassau Street, N. Y. . . . ⟨1890⟩

"The Wonderful Country," pp. 24-25. Collected in *Life* . . . ⟨1891⟩

For fuller entry see No. 4161.

15236. The Art of Authorship . . . Compiled . . . by George Bainton

New York D. Appleton and Company 1890

Contribution, pp. 331-334.

For comment see entry No. 1272.

15237. Best Selections for Readings and Recitations Number 18 Compiled by Silas S. Neff . . .

Philadelphia The Penn Publishing Company 1890

Cloth; and, printed paper wrapper.

"The Good," p. 39. Collected in *Life* . . . ⟨1891⟩, as "What is Good."

Deposited July 28, 1890.

Also appears in *One Hundred Choice Selections No. 30* . . . , 1890, p. 117. Precise publication date not determined; deposited for copyright Nov. 23, 1892 ⟨*sic*⟩.

LC

15238. Songs of Three Centuries Edited by John Greenleaf Whittier . . .

Boston and New York Houghton, Mifflin and Company The Riverside Press, Cambridge 1890

Reprint save for "The Cherry-Stone Artist," pp. 355-356. Collected in *Life* . . . ⟨1891⟩, as "An Art Master."

H

15239. LIFE OF JOHN BOYLE O'REILLY, BY JAMES JEFFREY ROCHE: TOGETHER WITH HIS COMPLETE POEMS AND SPEECHES, EDITED BY MRS. JOHN BOYLE O'REILLY . . .

NEW YORK: CASSELL PUBLISHING COMPANY, 104 & 106 FOURTH AVENUE. ⟨1891⟩

Two printings (with the above imprint) noted:

FIRST PRINTING

⟨i-ii⟩ (excised); ⟨i⟩-⟨xxii⟩, 1-790; blank leaf. Frontispiece and 7 plates inserted. $9\frac{1}{8}''$ full × $6\frac{5}{16}''$ full.

⟨1^4, 2-51^8, 52^4⟩. Leaf ⟨1⟩$_1$ excised.

P. 790, the first entry reads: *Public Farewell to Politics, 333* /

SECOND PRINTING

Pagination: As above.

⟨1-51^8⟩.

P. 790, the first entry reads: *Public Life, Farewell to Politics, 333* /

P cloth: brown. White end papers printed in green with a floral pattern. Flyleaves. As a subscription book issued in a variety of bindings. According to an advertisement in PW May 2, 1891, also issued in full morocco; and, half morocco.

Noted for Jan. 1, 1891, PW Dec. 13, 1890. The London (Unwin; American printing?) listed Ath April 11, 1891.

REPRINTS

The following reprints have been noted. The order of presentation is completely arbitrary:

New York The Mershon Company Publishers ⟨1891⟩ Copy in BPL

Philadelphia, Pa.: John J. McVey ⟨*1891*⟩ Probably issued *ca.* 1915. Locations: BPL UV

Copies issued with the Cassell imprint having the street address as *31 East 17th Street* were issued not before 1894. Copies in B, MHS, Y.

AA3 (2nd)   H (1st)   MHS (2nd)   Y (2nd)

Reprints of O'Reilly's own books; musical settings of poems reprinted from O'Reilly's books. See *Section III* for a list of books by authors other than O'Reilly containing material by him.

15240. Songs from the Southern Seas, and Other Poems . . .

Boston: Patrick Donahoe. 1874.

15241. Songs, Legends and Ballads . . . Second Edition.

Boston: The Pilot Publishing Company. 1880.

15242. The Statues in the Block, and Other Poems . . . Fourth Edition.

Boston: Roberts Brothers. 1887.

15243. Jacqueminots . . . Music by Max Eliot . . .

White, Smith &. Co. Boston   New York
Chicago . . . ⟨1888⟩

Sheet music. Cover-title. Plate number 7298-3. Reprinted and reissued by White-Smith Music Publishing Company. Reprinted from *The Statues in the Block*, 1881.

15244. Moondyne Joe . . .

Philadelphia H. L. Kilner & Co. Publishers ⟨n.d., not before 1890⟩.

A reprint of *Moondyne* . . . , 1879.

Other reprints noted; the order of presentation is alphabetical by publisher:

New York: P. J. Kenedy & Sons ⟨1879; *i.e.*, not before 1905⟩

London: George Routledge & Sons, Limited ⟨n.d., not before 1889⟩

Philadelphia: Sunshine Publishing Company ⟨n.d., before 1900⟩

Note: Issued as *The Golden Secret or Bond and Free, a Tale of Bush and Convict Life in Western Australia,* Melbourne: E. W. Cole ⟨n.d.⟩

15245. "The Old School Clock" . . . Music by Francis Marsena.

Published by F. L. Hodgdon & Co., Everett Square, Hyde Park, Mass. . . . ⟨1890⟩

Sheet music. Cover-title. Reprinted from *Songs from the Southern Seas*, 1873.

15246. Watchwords from John Boyle O'Reilly Edited by Katherine E Conway

Boston: Printed by Joseph George Cupples and Published by Him at the Back Bay Bookstore 250 Boylston Street ⟨1891⟩

A series of extracts from O'Reilly. BAL presumes that all the material herein was extracted from the author's books but this is an assumption only; and, perhaps, some of the material was taken from periodicals.

Small paper format: Cloth, leaf: 6⅞″ full × 3⅞″.

Large paper format: Green silk stamped in gold and blind. Also three-quarters cloth, marbled paper boards sides. *Edition de luxe. Only five hundred copies . . . printed, of which this is No. . . .*———Certificate of issue. 7¹⁵⁄₁₆″ full × 5⁷⁄₁₆″ full.

Both formats listed as *not seen* PW Feb. 13, 1892. Small paper copies deposited Aug. 29, 1892.

15247. Woman Suffrage Unnatural and Inexpedient . . .

Boston: 1894.

Cover-title, printed self-wrapper. See in *Section One* under year 1886.

15248. . . . A White Rose . . .

Boston H. B. Stevens Company . . . ⟨1900⟩

Sheet music. Cover-title. At head of title: *A Group of Rose Songs by Homer A Norris* . . .

Plate number: H.B.S.CO.864. Reprinted from *In Bohemia* ⟨1886⟩.

15249. Selected Poems . . . Introduction by William A. Hovey

H. M. Caldwell Co. New York and Boston. ⟨1904⟩

According to *The United States Catalog* . . . issued in cloth; leather; and, limp chamois.

Deposited Oct. 26, 1904.

Also noted with the imprint of Paul Elder & Company, San Francisco.

15250. Selections from the Writings of John Boyle O'Reilly and Father Abram J. Ryan.

Chicago: Ainsworth & Company, 1904?

Not seen. Not located.

Issued as *Lakeside Series of English Readings*, No. 103. Printed paper wrapper. Presumably contains no material here first collected.

Entry from *The American Catalog 1900–1905* . . .

15251. A Tragedy . . . Composed by J. W. Bischoff . . .

Arthur P Schmidt Leipzig Boston New York . . . 1906 . . .

Sheet music. Cover-title. Plate number: A.P.S. 7304-4. Reprinted from *In Bohemia* ⟨1886⟩.

15252. Selected Poems . . . ⟨Edited by William A. Hovey⟩

H. M. Caldwell Co. New York and Boston. ⟨1907⟩

Cloth, pictorial paper label.

15253. Love Was True to Me . . . Music by Frederic G. Shattuck . . .

The William Maxwell Music Co. 8 East Sixteenth Street New York ⟨1908⟩

Sheet music. Cover-title. Reprinted from *Life* . . . ⟨1891⟩.

15254. Two Roses . . . ⟨Music by⟩ Chester B. Searle . . .

The H. W. Gray Company 21 E. 17th St: New York . . . ⟨1909⟩

Sheet music. Cover-title. Plate number: G 113-13. Previously in *In Bohemia* ⟨1886⟩.

15255. The Old School Clock. Saint Macarius . . .

Chicago: Ainsworth & Company, *ca.* 1912.

Lakeside Classics, No. 114. Presumably issued in printed paper wrapper.

Not seen. Not located. Title and imprint postulated. Entry taken from *The United States Catalog Books in Print January 1, 1912* . . .

Presumably contains no material here first in book form.

15256. The Story of Saint John Berchmans, the Story of Father Marquette, etc.

Chicago: Ainsworth & Company, *ca.* 1912.

Not seen. Not located. Entry taken from *The United States Catalog Books in Print January 1, 1912* . . .

Presumably contains no material here first in book form.

15257. Selected Poems . . .

New York P. J. Kenedy & Sons 1913

15258. . . . A Cream-White Rose-Bud . . .

Boston: Oliver Ditson Company . . . ⟨1916⟩

Sheet music. Cover-title. At head of title: *Louis Victor Saar Songs* . . .

Plate number: 5-132-71218-3.

Otherwise "A White Rose," *In Bohemia* ⟨1886⟩.

15259. . . . A White Rose . . .

J. Fischer & Bro. New York. ⟨1916⟩

Sheet music. Cover-title. At head of title: *Complimentary Copy Fischer Edition* . . . ⟨All copies thus?⟩

Plate number: J.F.&B.4034-3 (high voice).

Reprinted from *In Bohemia* ⟨1886⟩.

15260. . . . Roses . . .

Boston: Oliver Ditson Company . . . ⟨1917⟩

Sheet music. Cover-title. At head of title: *Songs by Josef A. Pasternack* . . .

Plate number: 5-144-71790-4.

Otherwise "A White Rose," *In Bohemia* ⟨1886⟩.

15261. . . . The Red Rose Whispers of Passion . . . Music by Arthur Foote . . .

The Arthur P. Schmidt Co. Boston . . . ⟨1919⟩

Sheet music. Cover-title. At head of title: *Professional Copy To John McCormack* ⟨All copies thus?⟩

Plate number: A.P.S.11648-4.

Otherwise "A White Rose," *In Bohemia* ⟨1886⟩.

15262. Songs and Ballads by American Composers Three Songs . . . by Louis Adolphe Coerne . . . A White Rose . . .

New York G. Schirmer Boston ⟨1919⟩

Sheet music. Cover-title. Plate numbers: 28978c and 28978.

Reprinted from *In Bohemia* ⟨1886⟩.

15263. Roses-Red and White . . . Music by G. S. White . . .

G. Ricordi & Co., 14 East 43rd Street New York . . . ⟨1921⟩

Sheet music. Cover-title. Plate number: N.Y. 113. Otherwise "A White Rose," *In Bohemia* ⟨1886⟩.

JOHN BOYLE O'REILLY

SECTION III

In this section are listed books by authors other than O'Reilly which contain material by him reprinted from earlier books. See *Section II* for a list of reprints issued under O'Reilly's name.

The Family Library of British Poetry . . . Edited by James T. Fields and Edwin P. Whipple . . .

> Boston . . . 1878.
>
> For fuller entry see No. 5971.

Poems of Places Edited by Henry W. Longfellow . . . Africa.

> Boston . . . 1878.
>
> For fuller entry see No. 12206.

One Hundred Choice Selections No. 16 . . . ⟨Compiled⟩ by ⟨Phineas Garrett⟩ . . .

> . . . Philadelphia . . . 1878.
>
> For comment see entry No. 1554.

The Elocutionist's Annual Number 6 . . . Edited by J. W. Shoemaker . . .

> Philadelphia . . . 1878.
>
> For comment see BAL, Vol. 2, p. 248.

O'Connell Centenary Record, 1875. Published by Authority of the O'Connell Centenary Committee.

> Dublin: Joseph Dollard, 13 & 14 Dame-Street. 1878 . . .

Poems of Places Edited by Henry W. Longfellow . . . New England. Vol. 1.

> Boston . . . 1879.
>
> For fuller entry see No. 12208.

Poems of Places Edited by Henry W. Longfellow . . . Western States.

> Boston . . . 1879.
>
> "Chicago . . . ," pp. 61-62. Otherwise "The Wail of Two Cities . . . ," *Songs from the Southern Seas*, 1873. For fuller comment see entry No. 12214.

Poems of Places Edited by Henry W. Longfellow . . . Oceanica . . .

> Boston . . . 1879.
>
> For fuller entry see No. 12216.

Papyrus Leaves . . . Edited by William Fearing Gill . . .

> New York . . . 1880.
>
> Deposited Dec. 26, 1879. For comment see entry No. 2477.

Warne's Illustrated International Annual . . . Edited by Joseph Hatton

> London . . . 1880 . . .
>
> For fuller entry see No. 10443.

One Hundred Choice Selections No. 19 . . .

> . . . Philadelphia . . . 1881.
>
> For comment see entry No. 3392.

Harper's Cyclopædia of British and American Poetry Edited by Epes Sargent

> New York . . . 1881
>
> "At Best" is here mistitled "At Rest." For comment see entry No. 4336.

In Memoriam. Gems of Poetry and Song on James A. Garfield . . .

> Columbus . . . 1881.
>
> For comment see entry No. 122.

The Household Library of Catholic Poets . . . Edited by E. P. Ryder . . .

> Joseph A. Lyons. The University of Notre Dame: Notre Dame, Indiana. 1881.

The Poets' Tributes to Garfield . . . ⟨Second Edition⟩

> Cambridge . . . 1882
>
> For comment see entry No. 1248.

In the Saddle A Collection of Poems on Horse-back-Riding ⟨Edited by Annie Allegra Long-fellow⟩ . . .

> Boston Houghton, Mifflin and Company New York: 11 East Seventeenth Street The River-side Press, Cambridge 1882
>
> Advertised PW June 24, 1882, as for *June 24.* Listed PW July 22, 1882.

The Cambridge Book of Poetry and Song . . . by Charlotte Fiske Bates . . .

> New York . . . ⟨1882⟩
>
> For comment see entry Nos. 7887 and 11490.

One Hundred Choice Selections No. 21 . . .

> . . . Philadelphia . . . 1882.
>
> For comment see entry No. 2486.

. . . Selections for School Exhibitions and Private Reading . . . Nos. 1, 2, 3 . . .

> Boston . . . 1882.
>
> For comment see BAL, Vol. 2, p. 472.

Parker's Choice Selections No. 1 . . . Compiled . . . by C. C. Parker . . .

> Sedalia, Mo. . . . 1884.
>
> For comment see BAL, Vol. 1, p. 75.

Surf and Wave: The Sea as Sung by the Poets. Edited by Anna L. Ward . . .

> New York: Thomas Y. Crowell & Co. 13 Astor Place. ⟨1883⟩

No. 9. Standard Recitations by Best Authors . . . Compiled . . . by Frances P. Sullivan . . . Sept. 1885 . . .

> . . . N. Y. . . . ⟨1885⟩
>
> For comment see entry No. 331.

One Hundred Choice Selections No. 27 . . .

> Published by P. Garrett & Co., 708 Chestnut Street, Philadelphia, Pa., and 130 E. Adams Street, Chicago, Ill. 1887.
>
> Cloth; and, printed paper wrapper. Deposited Oct. 14, 1887.

No. 19. Standard Recitations by Best Authors . . . Compiled . . . by Frances P. Sullivan . . . March, 1888 . . .

> . . . N. Y. . . . ⟨1888⟩
>
> For fuller entry see in *James Russell Lowell* list, *Section One.*

Poems of Wild Life . . . Edited by Charles G. D. Roberts . . .

> London . . . 1888
>
> For comment see BAL, Vol. 1, p. 380.

American Sonnets. Selected . . . by William Sharp.

> London . . . ⟨n.d., 1889⟩
>
> For comment see BAL, Vol. 3, p. 101.

. . . Harper's Fifth Reader American Authors

> New York . . . 1889
>
> Copies imprinted *New York . . . American Book Company* ⟨1889⟩ were issued not before 1890. For fuller comment see entry No. 7917.

The Elocutionist's Annual Number 17 . . . Compiled by Mrs. J. W. Shoemaker

> Philadelphia . . . 1889
>
> For comment see entry No. 1270.

Buds and Blossoms . . .

> Philadelphia Peterson Magazine Co. 1889

Golden Lays for Youthful Days. Selected Poems from the Best Poets . . .

> . . . Chicago . . . 1889.
>
> For comment see entry No. 7899A.

Werner's Readings and Recitations. No. 2. Compiled . . . by Elsie M. Wilbor.

> New York . . . 1890.
>
> For comment see BAL, Vol. 1, p. 249.

No. 29. Standard Recitations by Best Authors . . . Compiled . . . by Frances P. Sullivan . . . September, 1890 . . .

> . . . N. Y. . . . ⟨1890⟩
>
> For fuller entry see No. 9026.

Souvenir Dramatic Entertainment for the Bene-fit of John Boyle O'Reilly Memorial Fund Given by the Adelphi Dramatic Club . . .

> Union Hall, 18 Boylston Street, Boston. ⟨n.d., Oct. 28, 1890⟩
>
> Printed paper wrapper. Cover-title.

Local and National Poets of America . . . Edited . . . ⟨by⟩ Thos. W. Herringshaw . . .

> Chicago . . . 1890.
>
> For fuller entry see BAL, Vol. 2, p. 391.

The Speakers' Library . . . Edited by Daphne Dale.

> 1890 . . . Chicago Philadelphia.
>
> For comment see entry No. 6324.

No. 30. Standard Recitations by Best Authors . . . Compiled . . . by Frances P. Sullivan . . . December 1890 . . .

> . . . N. Y. . . . ⟨1890⟩
>
> For comment see BAL, Vol. 5, p. 114.

Younger American Poets 1830–1890 Edited by Douglas Sladen . . .

> . . . London . . . 1891
>
> For fuller entry see No. 6557.

Younger American Poets 1830-1890 Edited by Douglas Sladen . . .

> . . . New York 1891
>
> For fuller entry see No. 6558.

No. 31. Standard Recitations by Best Authors . . . Compiled . . . by Frances P. Sullivan . . . March 1891 . . .

> . . . N. Y. . . . ⟨1891⟩
>
> For comment see BAL, Vol. 2, p. 275.

Souvenir Program of the Entertainment in Aid of the Sick Benefit Fund of the Franklin Typographical Society Tremont Temple, Tuesday Evening, December 1, 1891.

> The Rockwell & Churchill Press. Boston, Mass.
>
> Printed paper wrapper. Cover-title.

One Hundred Choice Selections No. 30 . . .

> Published by P. Garrett & Co., 708 Chestnut Street, Philadelphia, Pa., and 130 E. Adams Street, Chicago, Ill. 1892.
>
> Cloth; and, printed paper wrapper. Deposited Nov. 23, 1892.

The Lover's Year-Book of Poetry . . . ⟨Compiled⟩ by Horace Parker Chandler Vol. II. July to December

> Boston . . . 1892
>
> For fuller entry see BAL, Vol. 4, p. 61.

No. 38. Standard Recitations by Best Authors . . . Compiled . . . by Frances P. Sullivan . . . December 1892 . . .

> . . . N. Y. . . . 1893 . . .
>
> For comment see entry No. 364.

Shoemaker's Best Selections for Readings and Recitations Number 21 Compiled by Austin H. Merrill

> Philadelphia . . . 1893
>
> For comment see BAL, Vol. 3, pp. 138-139.

Dick's Recitations . . . No. 18 . . . Edited by Harris B. Dick . . .

> New York . . . ⟨1893⟩
>
> For comment see entry No. 715.

Random Rhymes. ⟨Edited by Roland R. Conklin⟩

> ⟨n.p., Kansas City, Mo., 1893⟩

The Hamilton Declamation Quarterly Edited by Professors Oren Root and Brainard G. Smith of Hamilton College, Clinton, N. Y. Vol. 1, No. 1 April, 1895

> Syracuse, N. Y. C. W. Bardeen, Publisher . . . 1895 . . .
>
> Printed paper wrapper.

Library of the World's Best Literature Ancient and Modern Charles Dudley Warner Editor . . . Thirty Volumes Vol. XIX

> New York . . . ⟨1897⟩
>
> For fuller entry see No. 10624.

The International Library of Famous Literature . . . Compiled . . . by Nathan Haskell Dole, Forrest Morgan and Caroline Ticknor . . . in Twenty Volumes . . .

> New York . . . ⟨1898⟩
>
> For comment see BAL, Vol. 5, p. 204.

Dew Drops and Diamonds . . .

> . . . 1898 . . . Chicago . . .
>
> For comment see BAL, Vol. 1, p. 77.

The Poetry of American Wit and Humor Selected by R. L. Paget . . .

> Boston . . . MDCCCXCIX
>
> For fuller entry see No. 1580.

The International Library of Famous Literature . . . Edited by Dr. Richard Garnett . . . in Twenty Volumes . . .

> London Issued by the Standard 1899
>
> For comment see entry No. 10638.

An American Anthology 1787–1899 . . . Edited by Edmund Clarence Stedman . . .

> Boston . . . M DCCCC
>
> For fuller entry see No. 3082.

Modern Eloquence . . . ⟨Edited by⟩ Thomas B. Reed . . . Vol. II . . .

     . . . Philadelphia ⟨1900; *i.e.,* 1901⟩

For comment see entry No. 3467. Vol. 2 deposited April 19, 1901.

Papyrus Club   Thirtieth Anniversary Dinner Held at the Revere House February Fourteenth Mcmiii

     ⟨n.p., n.d., Boston, 1903⟩

Printed paper wrapper.

American Familiar Verse   Vers de Société Edited . . . by Brander Matthews . . .

     . . . New York . . . 1904

For fuller entry see in James Russell Lowell, *Section Three.*

A Book of American Humorous Verse . . .

     Chicago . . . 1904

For comment see BAL, Vol. 1, p. 411.

Irish Literature Justin McCarthy M.P. Editor . . .

     . . . Philadelphia ⟨1904⟩

For comment see BAL, Vol. 1, p. 399.

The Golden Treasury of Irish Songs and Lyrics Edited by Charles Welsh . . .

     New York . . . ⟨1907⟩

For fuller entry see BAL, Vol. 3, p. 371.

Poems of American History Collected . . . by Burton Egbert Stevenson

     Boston . . . 1908

For fuller entry see in Joaquin Miller, *Section One.*

Dreams and Images An Anthology . . . Edited by Joyce Kilmer

     . . . New York 1917

For comment see entry No. 11115.

Papyrus Club   Forty-Fifth Anniversary Dinner Held at Young's Hotel December First Mcmxvii

     ⟨n.p., Boston, 1917⟩

Printed paper wrapper, illustration pasted to front.

The Catholic Anthology by Thomas Walsh . . .

     New York . . . 1927 . . .

For fuller entry see No. 11130.

Silver Linings   Poems of Hope and Cheer Collected by Joseph Morris and St. Clair Adams . . .

     New York   George Sully & Company ⟨1927⟩

REFERENCES AND ANA

Stories and Sketches . . .

Boston, 1888

Not seen. Not located. Entry from Allibone (where it is reported a *16mo*) ; and, *English Catalogue* . . . , 1889, (where it is reported as a Boston publication, *12mo* at *7s/6d*).

Presumably a ghost.

Souvenir   Dramatic Entertainment for the Benefit of John Boyle O'Reilly Memorial Fund Given by the Adelphi Dramatic Club . . .

     Union Hall, 18 Boylston Street, Boston. ⟨n.d., Oct. 28, 1890⟩

Printed paper wrapper. Cover-title.

Life of John Boyle O'Reilly, by James Jeffrey Roche . . .

     New York . . . ⟨1891⟩

For fuller description see above in *Section 1.*

A Memorial of John Boyle O'Reilly from the City of Boston . . .

     Boston   Printed by Order of the City Council 1890

An Account of the Exercises at the Dedication and Presentation to the City of Boston of the O'Reilly Monument June 20, 1896

     Boston   Printed by Order of the City Council 1897

A Tenth Anniversary ⟨by Henry Munroe Rogers⟩

     ⟨n.p., n.d., Boston: The Papyrus Club, 1908⟩

Cover-title. Printed self-wrapper. Pp. 12.

   "This Poem ⟨*An Irish Invasion!*⟩ was read at a dinner given by John Boyle O'Reilly . . . to a few friends on the 22nd day of November, 1879, to commemorate the Tenth Anniversary of his arrival in America, by its author, Henry M. Rogers.

"It was read again by him at a meeting of the Papyrus Club, December, 1879, and read again by him at a meeting of the Papyrus Club, February 1, 1908 . . ."

Seek for a Hero by William G. Schofield The Story of John Boyle O'Reilly

P. J. Kenedy & Sons New York ⟨1956⟩

. . . The American Years of John Boyle O'Reilly 1870-1890   Abstract of a Dissertation . . . by Francis G. McManamin . . .

The Catholic University of America Press Washington, D. C. 1959

At head of title: *The Catholic University of America*

Printed paper wrapper.

FRANCES SARGENT LOCKE OSGOOD

(Florence)

1811–1850

15264. SKETCHES FOR THE FAIR.

⟨n.p., n.d., Boston, 1833⟩

Anonymous.

⟨1⟩-18, blank leaf. 9⅛″ × 5⅝″.

⟨1⁸, 2²⟩.

Printed blue paper wrapper.

Issued for the benefit of the Perkins Institute Fair, Boston, 1833.

Attributed to Mrs. Osgood by Cornelia Walter Richards in *The Boston Evening Transcript*, Dec. 8, 1887, p. 6.

AAS   BPL

15265. The Token and Atlantic Souvenir. A Christmas and New Year's Present. Edited by S. G. Goodrich.

Boston. Published by Charles Bowen.
MDCCCXXXIV.

"To Jane," by *Florence*, p. ⟨336⟩. Collected in *Wreath*, 1838.

For fuller entry see No. 12055.

15266. The Oasis. Edited by Mrs. Child . . .

Boston: Allen and Ticknor. 1834.

"An Infant Abolitionist," by *Florence*, pp. ⟨201⟩-202.

For fuller description see No. 3118.

15267. Youth's Keepsake. A Christmas and New Year's Gift for Young People . . .

Boston: Published by E. R. Broaders. 1835.

"'My Mother's Kiss Made Me a Painter,'" by *Florence*, pp. ⟨121⟩-122. Collected in *Wreath*, 1838.

For comment see entry No. 981.

15268. The Token and Atlantic Souvenir. A Christmas and New Year's Present. Edited by S. G. Goodrich.

Boston. Published by Charles Bowen.
MDCCCXXXVI.

"Anna's Picture," by *Florence*, p. ⟨32⟩. Collected in *Wreath*, 1838.

For comment see entry No. 6804.

15269. Youth's Keepsake. A Christmas and New Year's Gift for Young People . . .

Boston: Published by John Allen & Co. 1836.

"Matilde's Picture," by *Florence*, pp. ⟨151⟩-154. Collected in *Wreath*, 1838.

Boards, leather shelfback; and, cloth.

H copy inscribed by early owner Dec. 24, 1836.

H   NYPL

15270. The Ladies' Wreath; a Selection from the Female Poetic Writers of England and America. With Original Notices and Notes: Prepared Especially for Young Ladies. A Gift-Book for All Seasons. By Mrs. Hale . . .

Boston: Marsh, Capen & Lyon. New York: D. Appleton & Co. 1837.

a "The Blind Girl," pp. 327-330.

a "A Fragment," p. 336.

"Lines on a Picture of a Young Girl Weighing Cupid and a Butterfly," p. 334. Collected in *Poems*, 1846, as "On a Picture."

a "My Mother's Sigh," pp. 330-331.

a "Stanzas," pp. 331-332. *When the warm blessed spirit that lightens the sky* . . .

b "The Star of Promise," pp. 335-336.

b "To a Young Friend," pp. 332-333.

a. Elsewhere unlocated.
b. Collected in *Wreath*, 1838.

For fuller entry see No. 6812.

15271. The Boston Book. Being Specimens of Metropolitan Literature. Edited by B. B. Thatcher.

Boston: Light & Stearns, 1 Cornhill. 1837.

"The Spell of Love," pp. ⟨245⟩-246.

For comment see entry No. 8730.

15272. The English Annual, for MDCCCXXXVII ...

London: Published by Edward Churton, 26, Holles Street, Cavendish Square, and Desilver, Thomas, and Co., Philadelphia. MDCCCXXXVII.

"The Language of Gems," pp. 119-121. Collected in *Wreath*, 1838.

Cloth? Leather?

NYPL

15273. The Token and Atlantic Souvenir, a Christmas and New Year's Present. Edited by S. G. Goodrich.

Boston: Otis, Broaders, and Company. M DCCC XXXIX. ⟨*i.e.,* 1838⟩

"Leonor," pp. ⟨172⟩-173.

"Off with the old love and on with the new," pp. ⟨94⟩-95.

Both collected in *Wreath*, 1838.

For comment see entry No. 9936.

15274. A WREATH OF WILD FLOWERS FROM NEW ENGLAND

LONDON ISSUE

A WREATH OF WILD FLOWERS FROM NEW ENGLAND ...

LONDON: EDWARD CHURTON, 26, HOLLES STREET, CAVENDISH SQUARE. 1838.

⟨i⟩-⟨xvi⟩, ⟨1⟩-368. $7\frac{13}{16}'' \times 4\frac{7}{8}''$.

⟨A⟩[8], B-I, K-Q[12], R[4].

Note: In some copies the list of subscribers (leaves R₃₋₄) is excised.

T cloth: blue; purple-brown. Yellow coated end papers. Spine gold-stamped save as noted: A / Wreath / of / Wild Flowers / BY / MRS OSGOOD Spine decorated with an arrangement of blind-stamped rules.

AMERICAN ISSUE

Sheets of the London issue bound in T cloth, brownish-black and purple noted. Spine gold-stamped save as noted: ⟨*double rule*⟩ / Mrs. OSGOOD'S / POEMS / ⟨*double rule*⟩ Spine decorated with an arrangement of blindstamped rules. Brown end papers. Flyleaves.

Inserted at front: *Notices of the Work,* being a series of extracts from British reviews; 2 pp.

The final two leaves (list of subscribers) excised.

On inner back cover is the blindstamped device of *Bradley, Binder, Boston.*

London publication: Advertised LG Nov. 24, 1838. Published in November, 1838, according to *The English Catalogue of Books.* Listed LG, Dec. 1, 1838; PC Dec. 1, 1838. Advertised as *just published* Ath Dec. 1, 1838. Listed Ath Dec. 8, 1838. Issued during the period Nov. 8–Dec. 7 according to BMLA Dec. 1838. Reviewed Ath Jan. 12, 1839; LG March 9, 1839.

American publication: Reviewed, place or publisher not stated, K Nov. 1839: "reaches us from ... Weeks, Jordan & Co., Boston." Reviewed NAR Jan. 1840, with London imprint given.

B (London) H (both) UV (American) Y (London)

15275. THE CASKET OF FATE ...

LONDON, 1839.

For Boston printing see under 1840.

⟨1⟩-79. $2\frac{9}{16}'' \times 2\frac{1}{4}''$ scant.

⟨A⟩-E[8].

Brown moiréd silk T cloth. Yellow end papers. Edges gilt. Also issued in cream-white paper boards?

Note: In this printing the dedication is "to Mrs. Bates" and begins *The dazzling diamond binds thy hair* ... The Boston edition is dedicated "to My Mother"; the dedicatory verses begin: *Thou'lt cherish, sweet mother* ...

AAS B

15276. Finden's Tableaux of the Affections; a Series of Picturesque Illustrations of the Womanly Virtues ... Edited by Mary Russell Mitford ...

London: Charles Tilt, Fleet Street. MDCCCXXXIX.

"Zulette," pp. ⟨43⟩-45.

Note: In the table of contents the author's name appears thus: *Frances A. Osgood.*

LC

The Token and Atlantic Souvenir ...

Boston ... M DCCC XXXIX. ⟨*i.e.,* 1838⟩

See above under *1838.*

15277. Selections from the American Poets. By William Cullen Bryant.

New-York: Harper & Brothers, 82 Cliff-Street. 1840.

"The Morning Walk, or the Stolen Blush," pp. 252-253. Appears also in *Wreath*, 1838. Collected in *Poems*, 1846.

For fuller entry see No. 1617.

15278. THE CASKET OF FATE . . . SECOND EDITION.

BOSTON, WEEKS, JORDAN AND CO. 1840.

Presumably the first American edition. For prior London publication see above under 1839.

⟨1⟩-67; blank, pp. ⟨68-70⟩; leaf excised or pasted under the end paper. 2⅝″ × 2 1/16″.

⟨A⟩-D¹².⁶.

A cloth: green. S cloth: blue. Edges gilt. Cream-coated end papers. Triple flyleaves at front.

Under the title *The Cataract of Fate* it is noted as *in press* NYR July, 1839; no further mention found.

B   Y

15279. American Melodies . . . Compiled by George P. Morris . . .

New-York: Published by Linen and Fennell, No. 229 Broadway. 1841.

"Your Heart Is a Music-Box, Dearest!," p. 36. Previously in *Wreath*, 1838; earliest located American book printing.

For fuller entry see No. 997.

15280. The Boston Book. Being Specimens of Metropolitan Literature.

Boston: George W. Light, 1 Cornhill. 1841.

"A Fable," pp. ⟨218⟩-220. Collected in *The Floral Offering*, 1847.

For fuller entry see No. 631.

15281. THE POETRY OF FLOWERS AND FLOWERS OF POETRY: TO WHICH ARE ADDED, A SIMPLE TREATISE ON BOT-ANY, WITH FAMILIAR EXAMPLES, AND A COPIOUS FLORAL DICTIONARY. EDITED BY FRANCES S. OSGOOD.

NEW YORK: J. C. RIKER, 15 ANN STREET. 1841.

Note: This volume contains so much Osgood material that it must be considered one of her primary productions. In addition to poetry here first located, it contains at least thirteen poems which had prior London publication in *A Wreath of Wild Flowers* . . . , 1838.

"Most of the prose portions of the following pages have been adopted from an English work, entitled *The Sentiment of Flowers*. The editor has made a few alterations and additions, in order to adapt it to American readers, and has illustrated the whole

with poetical sentiments, original and selected." ---P. ⟨3⟩.

Two editions (simultaneously issued?) noted. The texts vary. The following is sufficient for identification:

FIRST EDITION, FIRST PRINTING

⟨1⟩-276. Frontispiece, vignette title-page, 11 plates inserted. 7¼″ scant × 4½″.

⟨A⟩-I, K-X⁶.

Red levant. Pale salmon end papers. Flyleaves. Edges gilt.

On copyright page: Imprints of *J. S. Redfield*, stereotyper; and, *Piercy and Reed*, printers.

P. ⟨26⟩: Blank.

P. ⟨272⟩: List of twelve numbered plates.

FIRST EDITION, SECOND PRINTING

On copyright page: Imprint of *J. S. Redfield*, stereotyper. Printer's imprint not present.

P. ⟨26⟩: Untitled poem by Lucy Hooper present.

P. ⟨272⟩: List of twelve numbered plates.

Noted in both cloth; and, printed paper boards.

SECOND EDITION, FIRST PRINTING

On copyright page: Imprints of *J. S. Redfield*, stereotyper; and, *Piercy and Reed*, printers.

P. ⟨26⟩: Present is an untitled poem by Lucy Hooper.

P. ⟨272⟩: List of four numbered plates.

SECOND EDITION, SECOND PRINTING

On copyright page: Imprint of *J. S. Redfield*, stereotyper. Printer's imprint not present.

P. ⟨26⟩: Untitled poem by Lucy Hooper present.

P. ⟨272⟩: List of four numbered plates.

Title-page deposited Dec. 23, 1840. Listed NAR Jan. 1841.

BPL (Second edition, second printing) H (First edition, first printing; First edition, second printing) LC (Second edition, first printing) NYPL (First edition, second printing) Y (Second edition, second printing)

15282. The Token and Atlantic Souvenir, an Offering for Christmas and the New Year.

Boston: Published by David H. Williams . . . 1842.

"A Song," p. ⟨278⟩; *They tell me I was false to thee* . . . Collected in *Poems*, 1846.

For comment see entry No. 1005.

15283. The Gift: A Christmas and New Year's Present for 1842.

Philadelphia: Carey & Hart. ⟨1841⟩

"The Cottage Where We Dwell," pp. 321-322.

"A Wreath of Riddles," pp. 163-164.

For comment see entry No. 1002.

15284. The Child's Gem, for 1842. Edited by a Lady.

New-York: Published by S. Colman, for the Proprietors, 14 John Street. ⟨1841⟩

Leather.

"Edward's Trial, a True Story," pp. ⟨44⟩-47.

Listed NAR Jan. 1842.

JN

15285. The Poets of America . . . Edited by John Keese. [Volume Second of the Series.]

New York: Published by Samuel Colman . . . 1842.

"The Child Playing with a Watch," pp. ⟨93⟩-94. Also in *Wreath*, 1838; collected in *Poems*, 1846.

"To Miss M-----," pp. ⟨69⟩-71. Also in *Wreath*, 1838.

For comment see entry No. 3280.

15286. THE SNOW-DROP; A NEW-YEAR'S GIFT FOR CHILDREN . . .

PROVIDENCE: HIRAM FULLER. M DCCC XLII.

⟨i⟩-viii, ⟨1⟩-88. 4½″ full × 3⁹⁄₁₆″ full (cloth). 4½″ scant × 3¹¹⁄₁₆″ (wrapper).

⟨-⟩⁴, 1-7⁸·⁴.

T cloth: purple, pale yellow end papers. Printed cream paper wrapper, white paper pastedowns.

Just published---BJ Jan. 14, 1843.

AAS   B

15287. MAY QUEEN . . .

BOSTON . . . HENRY PRENTISS, 33 COURT ST. . . . 1842 . . .

Sheet music. Cover-title. Plate number 518.

The text had prior publication under the title "A May-Day Song," in *Wreath*, 1838.

B

15288. The Hare-Bell; a Token of Friendship. Edited by Rev. C. W. Everest . . .

Hartford: Henry S. Parsons. 1844.

"To Little Henry, Listening to a Poem by the Author," p. 91.

For comment see entry No. 1014.

15289. The Poetry of Love. Edited by Rufus W. Griswold . . .

Boston: Gould, Kendall & Lincoln. 1844.

"First Affection," pp. 114-117. Collected in *Poems*, 1850, where it appears with added preliminary verses.

An unspecified edition listed WPLNL March, 1844. For further comment see entry No. 1017.

15290. PUSS IN BOOTS, AND THE MARQUIS OF CARABAS, RENDERED INTO VERSE . . .

NEW-YORK: BENJAMIN & YOUNG, 62 JOHN-STREET. MDCCCXLIV.

⟨1⟩-43. Vignette title-page and 11 plates inserted. 6¹¹⁄₁₆″ × 5⁹⁄₁₆″.

⟨-⟩², ⟨1⟩-2⁸, 3⁴. *Note:* Signature collation tentative.

H cloth: brown; green. T cloth: red. Buff end papers. Triple flyleaves, one being used as lining for the end paper. Edges gilded.

Listed as a May publication WPLNL June, 1844.

AAS   B   UV

15291. American Tales, for Children. By Miss A. A. Gray. Lydia Maria Child. Miss Colman. Mr. Solyman Brown. ⟨ditto marks⟩ Frances S. Osgood. ⟨ditto marks⟩ C. D. Macleod.

Boston:---Otis Clapp. Glasgow:---J. & G. Goyder. MDCCCXLIV.

Printed paper wrapper.

"Little Josephine's Three Wishes. A Fairy Tale," pp. 25-29. The tale embodies a poem, "The Fairy Boat-Song."

Note: The contribution appears also in *The Boys' and Girls' Annual*, Boston: T. H. Carter and Company, n.d. In B. Sequence not known.

Location: Mr. Benjamin Tighe, Athol, Mass.

15292. ECHO SONG   I KNOW A NOBLE HEART! THE WORDS BY MRS. FRANCIS ⟨*sic*⟩ S. OSGOOD MUSIC . . . BY HERMAN S. SARONI.

PHILADELPHIA, GEORGE WILLIG, 171 CHESNUT ST. . . . 1845 . . .

Sheet music. The above at head of p. ⟨2⟩. Words and music, pp. ⟨2-3⟩; pp. ⟨1⟩ and ⟨4⟩ blank.

Collected in *Poems*, 1850.

Deposited Nov. 22, 1845.

LC

15293. LULU . . . COMPOSED & ARRANGED FOR THE PIANO FORTE . . .

. . . F. D. BENTEEN, BALTIMORE. ⟨1845⟩

Sheet music. Cover-title. Plate number 691. Composer's name not present.

Collected in *Poems*, 1846.

Deposited Dec. 12, 1845.

B

15294. THE FLOWER ALPHABET, IN GOLD AND COLORS . . .

BOSTON, PUBLISHED BY S. COLMAN, NO. 30 CORN-HILL. ⟨1845⟩

Title-page in red, blue and black.

⟨1-16⟩. Printed on one side of leaf only save for the title-leaf. Pp. ⟨15-16⟩ blank. Vignette title-page and 24 plates inserted. The letters *U* and *X* not present in copies examined; all thus? 7⅜″ × 5½″.

⟨-⟩⁸.

Black paper boards, blue paper boards, embossed with an all-over leafy scroll. Printed in gold. Lavender-coated end papers decorated in gold; or, plain white end papers. Flyleaves. Edges gilt. Also: blue paper boards embossed with a wood-grain pattern; white end papers decorated in gold; flyleaves.

Three-line errata slip inserted between pp. ⟨4-5⟩.

Vignette title-page: *The Floral Alphabet Little May's First Lesson.*

Note: A variant of unknown status is in AAS. The text appears to be composed of singletons, not an 8vo gathering. The vignette title-page is not present; instead there is a floral chromolithograph which appears also in *The Floral Year . . .* , edited by Mrs. Anna Peyre Dinnies, Boston, 1847. Bound in red A cloth. Remainder?

Announced WPLNL Sept. 1845. Notes as *in preparation* K Sept. 1845.

AAS   B

15295. The Ladies' Companion; or, Peoples' Annual . . .

New York: Published at 109 Fulton Street. 1845.

Sheets of *The Ladies' Companion; a Monthly Magazine*, New York, Vols. 17-18, 1842-1843, bound as a single volume, cloth, with title-page as above. A twilight book; see BAL, Vol. 1, p. xxi, for comment.

Reprint with the possible exception of:

"Ellen Ardelle: A Song," p. 88, Vol. 2.

"The Flower and the Brook," p. 218, Vol. 2.

"Love Will Not Stay to Be Weighed," p. 253, Vol. 1.

"The Lutin. A Fairy Legend," p. 299, Vol. 2. Collected in *Poems*, 1846, as "The Lutin-Steed."

"Purity's Pearl; or, the History of a Tear," p. 28, Vol. 2.

"The Triumph of the Spiritual over the Sensual. ———An Allegory," pp. 116-117, Vol. 1.

All of the above collected in *Poems*, 1846.

HM

15296. The Memento: A Gift of Friendship. Edited by C. W. Everest . . .

New-York: Wiley & Putnam, 161 Broadway. 1845.

"Little May," pp. 122-123.

"'Under the Rose,'" p. 203.

For fuller entry see No. 1567.

15297. The Opal: A Pure Gift for the Holy Days. MDCCCXLVI. Edited by John Keese . . .

New-York: J. C. Riker, 129 Fulton-Street. 1846.

"The Soul-Flower," pp. ⟨252⟩-253. Collected in *The Floral Offering*, 1847.

For fuller entry see No. 8557.

15298. Scenes in the Life of the Saviour: By the Poets and Painters. Edited by Rufus W. Griswold . . .

Philadelphia: Lindsay and Blakiston. 1846.

"The Daughter of Herodias," pp. 83-91. Collected in *Poems*, 1850.

For fuller entry see No. 6672.

15299. POEMS . . .

NEW YORK: PUBLISHED BY CLARK & AUSTIN. M DCCC XLVI.

⟨1⟩-252. Frontispiece and vignette title-page inserted. For leaf size see below under bindings.

⟨1⟩-21⁶. Signature mark 21* (p. 245) lacks the numeral 2.

Two states (printings?) noted:

1: Printer's and stereotyper's imprint not present on the copyright page. Copyright deposit copy thus.

2: Imprint of Richard C. Valentine, stereotyper; and, Peck & Stafford, printers, on the copyright page.

The following bindings listed in *Blake's American Bookseller's Complete Reference Trade List*, 1847:

Muslin, gilt edges

Imitation morocco, gilt edges

Imitation morocco, gilt edges and sides (*i.e.*, extra gilt).

Turkey morocco, gilt edges.

Silk, gilt edges.

The following bindings have been seen. The designations are completely arbitrary and are for identification only:

BINDING A

A cloth: green. Fine ribbed T cloth, moiréd, red. T cloth: blue; purple.

Sides: Blindstamped with a triple rule frame, enclosing a filigree frame.

At center of front: In gold, a basket-like ornament decorated with leaves and flowers, measuring $2^5/_{16}''$ tall.

Spine: Goldstamped. ⟨*filigree*⟩ / MRS. OSGOOD's / POEMS / ⟨*filigree extending to foot of spine*⟩ The word POEMS stamped from a face $3/_{16}''$ tall.

Edges: Plain.

End papers: White, printed in green with an all-over pattern of small ornaments. Also: Plain unprinted buff end papers. Flyleaves.

Leaf: $6^{15}/_{16}''$ full × $4^7/_{16}''$.

LC (*1st state; being a deposit copy*) UV (*1st state*) Y (*1st state*)

BINDING Aa

Fine ribbed T cloth, damasked with a wood-grain pattern, red.

Sides: Blindstamped with a triple rule frame enclosing a filigree frame.

At center of front: In gold, a basket-like ornament decorated with leaves and flowers measuring $2^5/_{16}''$ tall.

Spine: Goldstamped. ⟨*filigree*⟩ / MRS. OSGOOD's / POEMS / ⟨*filigree extending to foot of spine*⟩ The word POEMS stamped from a face $5/_{32}''$ tall.

Edges: Plain.

End papers: Undecorated off-white. Flyleaves.

Leaf: $6^7/_8''$ full × $4^7/_{16}''$ scant.

Y (*1st state*)

BINDING B

T cloth: green, decorated in black with an all-over pattern of clover leaves.

Sides: Blindstamped with a triple rule frame enclosing a filigree frame.

At center of front: In gold, a basket filled with fruit, corn, etc. The ornament measures $2^7/_{16}''$ tall.

Spine: Goldstamped. ⟨*ornament*⟩ / MRS. OSGOOD's / POEMS / ⟨*ornament extending to foot of spine*⟩ The word POEMS stamped from a face $5/_{32}''$ tall.

Edges: All edges gilt.

End papers: White, printed in blue and red with a plaid-like pattern. Flyleaves.

Leaf: $7''$ full × $4^7/_{16}''$.

Y (*2nd state*)

NOTE

Also occurs in black morocco, stamped as above. Leaf: $6^7/_8''$ full × $4^3/_8''$. White end papers printed in blue-green with an all-over pattern of small crosses and dots. Flyleaves. Copy in BPL, 2nd state sheets.

BINDING C

T cloth: dull grayish-purple.

Sides: Blindstamped with a rule frame enclosing a strapwork filigree frame.

At center of front: Goldstamped: A fruit-filled urn measuring $1^3/_8''$ tall.

Spine: Goldstamped. ⟨*ornament*⟩ / MRS. OSGOOD's / POEMS / ⟨*ornament extending to foot of spine*⟩ The word POEMS stamped from a face $3/_{16}''$ tall.

Edges: Plain.

End papers: Yellow. Flyleaves.

Leaf: $6^{15}/_{16}''$ full × $4^7/_{16}''$.

AAS (*2nd state*) H (*2nd state*)

BINDING D

Imitation brown morocco.

Sides: Wholly goldstamped with a triple rule frame enclosing filigree ornaments.

Spine: Goldstamped. ⟨*ornament*⟩ / MRS. OSGOOD's / POEMS / ⟨*ornament extending to foot of spine*⟩ The word POEMS stamped from a face $5/_{32}''$ tall.

Edges: All edges gilt.

End papers: White, printed in blue with an arrangement of small crosses and dots. Flyleaves.

Leaf: $6^{15}/_{16}''$ × $4^5/_{16}''$.

AAS (*2nd state*)

Deposited Dec. 17, 1845. Noted as received K Dec. 1845. Reviewed NAR Dec. 1845.

15300. CALL ME PET NAMES . . .

⟨n.p., n.d., 1846?⟩

Single leaf. $7^7/_8''$ × $4^3/_4''$. Printed on one side of leaf only.

Reprint? Also appears in *Poems*, 1846.

NYPL

15301. THE CRIES OF NEW-YORK, WITH FIFTEEN ILLUSTRATIONS, DRAWN FROM LIFE BY A DISTINGUISHED ARTIST. THE POETRY BY FRANCES S. OSGOOD.

NEW YORK: JOHN DOGGETT, JR., DIRECTORY ESTABLISHMENT, NO. 156 BROADWAY. 1846.

⟨1⟩-32. Illustrated. 9″ × 5¾″.

⟨1-4⁴⟩.

Printed tan paper wrapper. Two printings of the wrapper noted. The following is sufficient for identification. Sequence not certain.

WRAPPER A

Outer back: On The 12Th Of October, 1845, Will Be Issued . . . The Great Metropolis . . . For 1846 . . .

WRAPPER B

Outer back: Price Twenty-Five Cents, The Great Metropolis . . . For 1846 . . .

AAS (Wrapper A)   H (Wrapper B)

15302. The Floral Gift, from Nature and the Heart Edited by Mary Chauncey.

Worcester: Published by Jonathan Grout, Jr. 203 Main Street. 1846

Reprint save for "Pride," p. 35.

Two printings noted. For comment see BAL, Vol. 5, p. 594.

15303. The Pioneer: Or Leaves from an Editor's Portfolio. By Henry Clapp, Jr. . . .

Lynn: Printed by J. B. Tolman, 12 Exchange-St. 1846.

"Labor," pp. 94-95; five stanzas. Here reprinted? For another printing see next entry. Collected as "Laborare est Orare," *Poems*, 1850, extended to six stanzas.

"Slander," pp. 84-85. Collected in *Poems*, 1850, as "Calumny."

AAS   H

15304. Voices of the True-Hearted . . .

Philadelphia . . . J. Miller M'Kim, No. 31 North Fifth Street . . .

"Labor," p. ⟨257⟩; in five stanzas. See preceding entry. Here reprinted?

For fuller entry see No. 12072.

15305. Sibylline Verses; or, the Mirror of Fate. ⟨Compiled⟩ By Miss H. J. Woodman . . .

Boston: Published by Abel Tompkins, 38 Cornhill. 1846.

Untitled poem, p. 128: *Turn to thy books, my gentle girl--- . . .*

Untitled poem, p. 142: *As smiles with glory, soft but warm . . .*

H

15306. The Opal: A Pure Gift for the Holydays. MDCCCXLVII. Edited by John Keese . . .

New-York: J. C. Riker, 129 Fulton-Street. 1847.

"Nature's Pet," pp. ⟨195⟩-196.

"Unrest," pp. ⟨13⟩-14.

Both collected in *Poems*, 1850.

For comment see entry No. 6853.

15307. The Mirror of Life. Edited by Mrs. L. C. Tuthill . . .

Philadelphia: Lindsay and Blakiston. ⟨1847⟩

"Boyhood," pp. ⟨34⟩-35.

For comment see entry No. 6855.

15308. The Fountain. A Gift: "To Stir up the Pure Mind by Way of Remembrance." . . . Edited by H. Hastings Weld.

Philadelphia: William Sloanaker. 1847.

"Le Porte-Bouquet, or Genius and Ingenuity; an Incident in Fashionable Life," pp. 119-125.

For comment see entry No. 9296.

15309. THE FLORAL OFFERING, A TOKEN OF FRIENDSHIP. EDITED BY FRANCES S. OSGOOD . . .

PHILADELPHIA: CAREY AND HART, 126 CHESNUT STREET. 1847.

Contains so much material by Mrs. Osgood that in spite of the statement "edited by" it must be considered one of her primary books.

⟨1-124⟩. 10⁹⁄₁₆″ × 8¹¹⁄₁₆″. 10 plates inserted.

⟨2⟩-32².

H cloth: greenish-gray. S cloth: white. T cloth: greenish-gray. Edges gilt. Pale buff end papers. Triple flyleaves.

Deposited Dec. 4, 1846. Listed WPLNL Jan. 1847. Distributed in London by Chapman; advertised PC Nov. 15, 1848; listed Ath Nov. 18, 1848; listed PC Dec. 1, 1848.

B   BA   LC

15310. The Golden Gift: A Token for All Seasons. Edited by J. M. Fletcher.

Nashua, N. H. Published by J. Buffum, Main Street. 1847.

Reprint save for "Rely on Right," p. 91.

Reprinted *ca.* 1850 imprinted: *Boston: Published by J. Buffum.* ⟨*1846*⟩

DE V   EM

15311. The Mayflower. For M DCCC XLVIII . . . Edited by Mrs. E. Oakes Smith . . .

Boston: Published by Saxton and Kelt. 1848.

"Confidence and Affection," pp. 139-140.

For comment see entry No. 6498.

15312. The American Female Poets: With Biographical and Critical Notices, by Caroline May.

Philadelphia: Lindsay & Blakiston. 1848.

Reprint save for:

"Little Children," pp. 397-398.

"Stanzas for Music," pp. 392-394.

Both collected in *Poems,* 1850.

Issued Sept. 30–Oct. 6, 1848, according to LW Oct. 7, 1848. Reissued as *Pearls from the American Female Poets* ⟨1869⟩.

NYPL

15313. The American Gallery of Art, from the Work of the Best Artists, with Poetical and Prose Illustrations, by Distinguished American Authors. Edited by J. Sartain.

Philadelphia: Lindsay and Blakiston. ⟨1848⟩

"The Peasant Girl of Frascati," pp. 87-88.

Deposited Oct. 26, 1848. Reviewed by H Nov. 11, 1848.

H

15314. The Opal: A Pure Gift for the Holy Days. MDCCCXLVIII. Edited by Mrs. Sarah J. Hale.

New York: J. C. Riker, 129 Fulton Street. 1848.

"To One Who Said 'You Will Weary of Me,'" p. ⟨130⟩. Collected in *Poems,* 1850, as "Weary of You."

For comment see entry No. 1030.

15315. Lays of the Western World . . .

New York: Putnam. ⟨n.d., 1848⟩

Unpaged. Contains "The Mother of Moses."

For fuller entry see No. 1639.

15316. The Lover's Gift; or Tributes to the Beautiful. American Series. Edited by Mrs. E. Oakes Smith . . .

Hartford: Henry S. Parsons. 1848.

Reprint save for "Had We But Met," pp. 56-58.

Collected in *Poems,* 1850.

B

15317. The Female Poets of America. With Portraits, Biographical Notices, and Specimens of Their Writings. By Thomas Buchanan Read.

Philadelphia: Published by E. H. Butler & Co. 1849.

Reprint save for:

"Eurydice," pp. 83-86.

"A Sermon," pp. 80-81.

Both collected in *Poems,* 1850.

Note: Sabin incorrectly states that this book was published in August, 1848.

American Publication: Advertised for *Saturday next* LW Oct. 7, 1848, at prices ranging from $4 to $6.50, depending on binding. A limited issue of 100 copies with proofs on India paper offered at the same time at $15. Listed LW Oct. 14, 1848. Reviewed LW Oct. 21, 1848. Deposited Nov. 25, 1848. Reviewed NAR April, 1849. A fourth edition "with additions and alterations" reviewed USDR Dec. 1850. A revised edition was advertised in NLG Dec. 15, 1854.

British Publication: Advertised by John Chapman as *just received* Ath Nov. 4, 1848, but since the title does not appear in other similar advertisements published soon after that date there is a possibility that Chapman did not distribute the book. As a John Wiley importation advertised in Ath Dec. 2, 1848. The *Third Edition* listed by PC Dec. 15, 1849, as a John Chapman importation, with *additions* and *corrections*.

H

15318. The Female Poets of America. By Rufus Wilmot Griswold . . .

Philadelphia: Carey and Hart, Chesnut Street. MDCCCXLIX.

Reprint save for:

"Ashes of Roses," pp. 284-285.

"Beauty's Prayer," p. 281.

"Caprice," p. 287.

"The Cocoa-Nut Tree," p. 275.

"Dream Music, or the Spirit-Flute," pp. 282-283.

"A Farewell to a Happy Day," p. 273.

"The Flower Love-Letter," p. 280.

"Ida's Farewell," p. 279.

"Lady Jane," p. 278.

"Music," p. 285.

"No!," p. 286.

"Reflections," p. 274.

"Song," p. 286. *Should all who throng with gift and song* . . .

"To My Pen," p. 283.

"To Sleep," p. 281.

All of the above, save one, collected in *Poems*, 1850. The exception is "Reflections" which is otherwise unlocated.

For comment see entry No. 6681.

15319. A LETTER ABOUT THE LIONS . . .

NEW YORK: GEORGE P. PUTNAM, 155 BROADWAY; LONDON: PUTNAM'S AMERICAN AGENCY, REMOVED FROM PATERNOSTER ROW TO J. CHAPMAN, 142 STRAND. 1849.

⟨1⟩-24. $5\frac{1}{8}'' \times 3\frac{1}{4}''$.

⟨1⟩-3⁴.

Unprinted white paper wrapper. Issued in an envelope done in imitation of a postmarked envelope.

Advertised as *recently published* LW Jan. 6, 1849. Listed LW Jan. 13, 1849.

H

15320. The Brilliant; a Gift Book for 1850. Edited by T. S. Arthur.

New York: Baker and Scribner, 145 Nassau Street and 36 Park Row. 1850. ⟨*i.e.*, 1849⟩

"The Soul's Appeal," pp. ⟨291⟩-292. Collected in *Poems*, 1850.

For fuller entry see No. 4864.

15321. I WANDERED IN THE WOODLAND . . . MUSIC BY HERRMAN S. SARONI.

NEW YORK . . . WM. HALL & SON, 239 BROADWAY OPPOSITE THE PARK. ⟨1849⟩

Sheet music. Cover-title. Plate number: 486.

Deposited Nov. 28, 1849. Collected in *Poems*, 1850.

AAS

15322. The Forget-Me-Not, for 1850. Edited by Mrs. Emeline S. Smith.

New York: Published by Nafis & Cornish. St. Louis, Mo.: Van Dien & MacDonald. ⟨1849⟩

"The Hidden Rill," pp. ⟨20⟩-21.

For fuller entry see No. 6869.

15323. The Odd-Fellows' Offering, for 1849 . . . Edited by Paschal Donaldson.

New York: Published by Edward Walker, 114 Fulton-Street. M DCCC XLIX.

"Violet Vere's Vacation," pp. 53-62.

H

The Brilliant . . . for 1850 . . .

New York . . . 1850.

See above under 1849 (Sept.).

15324. The Odd-Fellows' Offering, for 1850 . . . Contributed Chiefly by Members of the Order.

New York: Published by Edward Walker, 114 Fulton Street. M DCCC L.

"The Israelites Crossing the Red Sea," pp. 55-57.

Leather.

Reviewed K Dec. 1849. Listed LW Dec. 1, 1849.

H

15325. The Literati: Some Honest Opinions about Autorial Merits and Demerits . . . by Edgar A. Poe . . .

New-York: J. S. Redfield, Clinton Hall, Nassau-Street. Boston: B. B. Mussey & Co. 1850.

Recollections of Edgar Allan Poe, written at the editor's request, pp. xxxvi-xxxviii.

For fuller description see entry No. 6687.

15326. POEMS . . .

PHILADELPHIA: CAREY AND HART. 1850.

Edited anonymously by Rufus Wilmot Griswold.

⟨1⟩-466; advertisements, pp. ⟨467-472⟩. Frontispiece, vignette title-page, 10 plates inserted. $8\frac{15}{16}'' \times 5\frac{3}{4}''$.

⟨A⟩-I, K-U, X-Z, 2A-2I, 2K-2P⁶, 2Q⁸. *Note:* 2Q₆₋₇ are inserted conjugates.

Note: P. 341 incorrectly signed *3F2*. All examined copies thus.

Noted in the following bindings. Sequence, if any, not known. According to the advertisement on p. ⟨471⟩ the book was available in scarlet cloth; calf; Turkey morocco. The designations are for identification only.

BINDING A

Fine-ribbed T cloth, red, damasked with a woodgrain pattern. Buff end papers. Flyleaves. All edges gilt. Note that the two curved flourishes immediately below the spine lettering curve down; *i.e.*, a waning moon effect. Copy in AAS (lacking 2Q₆₋₇).

Same as *Binding A* but the flourishes noted above curve up; *i.e.*, a waxing moon effect. Copy in Y.

Red morocco. A principal feature of the stamping on the sides is the presence of a heavy goldstamped filigree at top and another at bottom. ECT for ETC on spine. Copy in Y.

Morocco: black, brown, red. A principal feature is the presence of a large (7¹⁄₁₆″ tall) goldstamped ornament on the sides. A copy in BPL inscribed by early owner Jan. 1, 1850. Occurs with edges plain; and, edges gilded. Copies in BPL, UV.

Reviewed by *Literary American* (N.Y.) Dec. 29, 1849. BPL copy (binding C) inscribed by early owner Jan. 1, 1850. Listed LW Jan. 5, 1850. Distributed in London by Chapman; listed PC Aug. 1, 1850.

15327. The Gem of the Season, for 1850. Edited by N. Parker Willis . . .

New-York: Leavitt and Company, 191 Broadway. MDCCCL.

Cloth; and, leather.

"The Indian Maiden's Reply," pp. ⟨15⟩-16. Here reprinted? Also in the preceding entry.

The Copyright Office reports: "No exact date given in District Court records . . . entered . . . in the year 1849 . . ."

H   HEH   P   Y

15328. The Irving Offering: A Token of Affection, for 1851.

New-York: Leavitt and Company, No. 191 Broadway. 1851.

"The Magic Lute," pp. ⟨89⟩-99. Prose. Embodies four poems, three of which had prior book publication. The fourth, "The Crimson Plume," is here in its only located book appearance.

For fuller entry see No. 3171.

15329. The Gem of the Western World, for 1851 . . . Edited by Mary E. Hewitt.

New-York: Published by Cornish, Lamport & Co. ⟨1851⟩

Leather.

"To Sarah, on Her Birthday," p. ⟨292⟩.

DU

15330. . . . ANNIE RAMSAY   BALLAD BY THE AUTHOR OF CALL ME PET NAMES.

PHILADELPHIA, A. FIOT   196 CHESNUT ST. . . . 1852 . . .

Sheet music. Cover-title. Plate number: None. At head of title: *To Miss Julia Gans*

B

15331. The Odd-Fellows' Offering, for 1852 . . .

New York: Published by Edward Walker, 114 Fulton-Street. M DCCC LII.

Leather.

"The Artist in the Burning Ship: A Posthumous Poem," p. ⟨4⟩.

H

15332. The Thought-Blossom: A Memento. Edited by N. Parker Willis . . .

New York: Leavitt and Allen, 27 Dey-Street. 1854.

Leather.

Reprint save for "Leonora L'Estrange," pp. ⟨212⟩-224.

UV

15333. Harper's Cyclopædia of British and American Poetry Edited by Epes Sargent

New York Harper & Brothers, Franklin Square 1881

Reprint save for "The Author's Last Verses," p. 708.

Note: Eight lines titled "Little Things," p. 708, here erroneously credited to Osgood; the lines were written by Julia A. Fletcher Carney.

For fuller entry see No. 4336.

15334. LINES TO MR. DODSON, ENGRAVER OF THE PLATE OF FEMALE CONTRIBUTORS TO GRAHAM'S MAGAZINE . . .

BROOKLYN: N.Y. 1885.

Title in black, gold and red.

8 leaves numbered ⟨i-ii⟩, ⟨1⟩-5, blank leaf. Except for the title-page printed on rectos only. Japan vellum. Frontispiece inserted. 10⁷⁄₁₆″ × 7³⁄₄″. *Also:* Printed on wove paper watermarked *J Whatman 1881*. Leaf 9¹³⁄₁₆″ × 7¹¹⁄₁₆″.

Printed paper wrapper of book stock.

Elzevir Press. 10 Copies Printed No . . .

Issued by Paul Leicester Ford and his brother, Worthington Chauncey Ford.

A copy of the Whatman issue in Y inscribed by Paul Leicester Ford April 16, 1885.

NYPL (vellum)   Y (paper)

15335. Actors and Actresses of Great Britain and
the United States ... Edited by Brander
Matthews and Laurence Hutton ...

Cassell & Company, Limited 739 & 741 Broadway, New York ⟨1886⟩

"Mrs. Mowatt," Vol. 4, p. 156.

For fuller entry see No. 1904.

15336. A Memoir of T. Buchanan Read ...

Printed for Private Circulation   Philadelphia
1889

"Read's Genevieve," p. 43.

For comment see entry No. 1231.

15337. Passages from the Correspondence and
Other Papers of Rufus W. Griswold ...

Cambridge, Mass., W: M. Griswold, 1898.

Letter, dated ⟨1850⟩, p. 256.

Sonnet addressed to Griswold, March 3, 1849,
(*For one, whose being is to mine a star* . . .), p. 218.

For comment see entry No. 6712.

FRANCES SARGENT LOCKE OSGOOD

SECTION II

Reprints of Osgood's own books; musical settings of poems reprinted from Osgood's own books.

15338. Flower Gift, a Token of Friendship for All Seasons. With a Complete Floral Dictionary.

Chambersburg, Pa.: Shryock, Reed & Co ⟨1840; *i.e.*, after 1841⟩

Edited by Osgood and with material by her herein.

Reprinted from the plates of *The Poetry of Flowers* ..., 1841. *Note:* In producing this book the publishers used plates from each of two editions and thus produced a garbled version.

15339. A Wreath of Wild Flowers from New England ... Second Edition.

London: Edward Churton, Cavendish Square. Boston: Saxton & Peirce 133 1-2 Washington St. 1842.

15340. Happy at Home ... ⟨Music⟩ by J. A. Getze ...

Boston ... George P. Reed 17 Tremont Row. ⟨1846⟩

Sheet music. Cover-title. No plate number. Reprinted from *Poems*, 1846.

15341. Look! How the Stars Like Jewels Glisten ... Adapted to a French Melody ... by Charles Grobe ...

Philadelphia Lee & Walker 120 Walnut St. ... 1848 ...

Sheet music. Cover-title. Plate number: 554. Deposited Nov. 3, 1848. Reprinted from *The Poetry of Flowers* ..., 1841.

15342. Beneath Italias Laughing Skies ... Music ... by C.F.I.

New York, Published by F. Riley & Co. 297, Broadway ... 1848 ...

Sheet music. The above at head of p. ⟨2⟩. Plate number: None, save for *Mina dolce. 2* on p. ⟨3⟩. Pp. ⟨1⟩ and ⟨4⟩ blank; text and music pp. ⟨2⟩-3. Previously in *Poems*, 1846.

15343. Poems ...

New York: Published by Clark & Austin. 205 Broadway. 1848.

15344. Poems ...

New York: Published by Clark & Austin. 205 Broadway. 1849.

Poems ...

New York: Riker, Thorne & Co. ... ⟨1849; *i.e.*, not before 1854⟩

See below under 1854.

15345. ... I Have Something Sweet to Tell You or "I'm talking in my sleep!" ... Music by James E. Magruder ...

... W. C. Peters, Baltimore ... ⟨1850⟩

Sheet music. Cover-title. At head of title: *To Miss Elizabeth Stanforth*. Plate number: 1617–4 (piano arrangement); 1618-3 (guitar arrangement). Reprinted from *Poems*, 1850.

Later settings and printings noted; the arrangement is alphabetical by name of publisher:

Baltimore: F. D. Benteen. Composer: F. W. Barbour. 1851.

Philadelphia: Couenhoven, Scull & Co. Composer: James Couenhoven. 1851.

Boston: Oliver Ditson. Composer: Charles C. Converse. 1855.

Louisville: David P. Faulds. Composer: S. W. Stone. 1851.

Boston: G. P. Reed & Co. Composer: T. S. Lloyd. 1853.

Boston: E. H. Wade. Composer: Henry Stanley. 1851.

Undated reprints were issued by: Century Music Publishing Company, New York; J. E. Ditson & Company, Philadelphia; T. B. Harms & Company, New York; Benjamin W. Hitchcock, New York; G. D. Russell, Boston; Richard A. Saalfield, New York; White-Smith Music Publishing Company, Boston.

Under the title "I'm Talking in My Sleep," music by Beckel, issued by John A. Janke, Philadelphia, 1852.

15346. Poems . . .

New York: Published by Clark, Austin & Co., 205 Broadway. 1850.

15347. Call Me Pet Names . . . ⟨Music⟩ Composed . . . by H. R. Harris

Published by F. D Benteen Baltimore W. T. Mayo New Orleans . . . 1851 . . .

Sheet music. The above on p. ⟨2⟩. Plate number: 2094. Pp. ⟨1⟩ and ⟨4⟩ blank. Text and music on pp. ⟨2-3⟩.

Previously in *Poems*, 1846.

Also noted in another setting; sequence not determined: Composer's name not present; published by Lee & Walker, Philadelphia, 1851.

Later settings noted:

Music by J. C. Woodman; published by Oliver Ditson, 1853.

Music by Giovanni Sconcia; published by Russell & Richardson, 1858, under the title *Call Me Sweet Names*.

15348. . . . Your Heart Is a Music Box, Dearest! . . . Music by James E. Magruder . . .

Published by F. D. Benteen Baltimore W. T. Mayo New Orleans. ⟨1851⟩

Sheet music. Cover-title. At head of title: *To Miss Mary J. Zaveille*. Plate number: 2093. Previously in *A Wreath of Wild Flowers from New England*, 1838; *American Melodies . . .* , 1841.

15349. . . . "I'm Talking in My Sleep" or I Have Something Sweet to Tell You . . . Music by Beckel.

Philadelphia   John A. Janke   258 Market St. . . . 1852 . . .

Sheet music. Cover-title. At head of title: *To Miss Ruth Anna Atkins*. For an earlier setting see *I Have Something Sweet to Tell You*, 1850.

15350. Poems . . .

New York: Published by Clark, Austin & Co., 205 Broadway. 1852.

15351. Poems . . . Illustrated . . .

Philadelphia: A. Hart, Late Carey & Hart. MDCCCLIII.

15352. Poems . . . Illustrated . . .

New York: Riker, Thorne & Co. 129 Fulton Street. ⟨1849; *i.e.*, not before 1854⟩

15353. Call Me Sweet Names . . . Music by Giovanni Sconcia . . .

Boston. Russell & Richardson 291 Washington St. . . . 1858 . . .

Sheet music. Cover-title. For an earlier setting see *Call Me Pet Names*, 1851.

15354. The Poetry of Flowers and Flowers of Poetry . . . Edited by Frances S. Osgood.

New York: Derby & Jackson, 119 Nassau Street. 1858.

Leather.

15355. Poems . . .

New York: Clark, Austin, Maynard & Co., 3 Park Row and 3 Ann Street. 1861.

15356. Poems . . . Illustrated . . .

World Publishing House, 139 Eighth Street, New York. 1876.

15357. . . . Osgood's Poetical Works . . .

Philadelphia: John E. Potter and Company, 617 Sansom Street. ⟨n.d., *ca.* 1886⟩

At head of title: *The Large Type Edition*.

15358. . . . Osgood's Poetical Works . . .

Philadelphia: The Keystone Publishing Co. 1890.

At head of title: *The Large Type Edition*.

FRANCES SARGENT LOCKE OSGOOD

SECTION III

In this section are listed books by authors other than Osgood which contain material by her reprinted from earlier books. See *Section II* for a list of collections of reprinted material issued under Osgood's name.

Gems from American Female Poets . . . by Rufus W. Griswold.

> Philadelphia . . . 1842.
>
> For comment see No. 6643.

The Poets and Poetry of America. With an Historical Introduction. By Rufus W. Griswold . . .

> Philadelphia . . . MDCCCXLII.
>
> For fuller entry see No. 6644.

Gems from American Poets . . .

> New-York . . . ⟨1842⟩
>
> For comment see entry No. 5193.

The Flower Vase . . . by Miss S. C. Edgarton . . .

> Lowell . . . 1843.
>
> For comment see entry No. 8540.

The Poet's Gift . . . Edited by John Keese.

> Boston . . . 1845.
>
> For fuller entry see BAL, Vol. 1, p. 206.

A Book of Hymns for Public and Private Devotion.

> Cambridge . . . 1846.
>
> For fuller entry see No. 1630.

Flora's Album, Containing the Language of Flowers Poetically Expressed. Edited by John S. Adams . . .

> Boston: Published by Elias Howe. 1847.

Golden Leaflets: A Selection . . . Edited by J. M. Fletcher . . .

> Boston . . . ⟨1848⟩
>
> For a fuller entry see No. 12094.

Gift-Leaves of American Poetry. Edited by Rufus W. Griswold.

> New-York . . . ⟨1849⟩
>
> For comment see entry No. 6682.

The Crocus . . . Edited by Sarah Josepha Hale . . .

> New York . . . ⟨1849⟩
>
> For fuller entry see No. 6868.

The Boston Book . . .

> Boston . . . MDCCCL.
>
> For comment see entry No. 5929.

Gems from the Spirit Mine . . .

> London . . . MDCCCL.
>
> For fuller entry see BAL, Vol. 5, p. 596.

The Present . . . Edited by F. A. Moore . . .

> Manchester . . . 1850.
>
> For fuller description see No. 2800.

Memory and Hope.

> Boston: Ticknor, Reed, and Fields. MDCCCLI.
>
> Cloth; and, leather. Noticed LW Jan. 18, 1851.

The Chaplet of Roses. By Park Moody.

> New York . . . ⟨1851⟩
>
> For comment see entry No. 2885.

The Gem of the Western World, for All Seasons . . . Edited by Mary E. Hewitt.

> New York . . . ⟨n.d., *ca.* 1853–1854⟩
>
> For fuller entry see BAL, Vol. 3, p. 155.

The Ladies' Wreath . . . Edited by Mrs. S. T. Martyn.

> New-York . . . 1851.
>
> For fuller entry see No. 8571.

The Female Prose Writers of America. With Portraits, Biographical Notices, and Specimens of Their Writings. By John S. Hart . . .

Philadelphia: Published by E. H. Butler & Co. 1852.

The Illustrated Souvenir   A Gift Book for the Holidays . . . "Edited ⟨sic⟩ by the Author of the "Glory and Downfall of Edom," &c.

Boston: Published by Stone & Co., 11 Cornhill. ⟨1852⟩

"To One Who Feared She Would Interrupt Me," p. 76; otherwise "Interrupt Me, Little Darling," Poems, 1850.

The String of Diamonds . . . by a Gem Fancier.

Hartford . . . 1852.

For fuller entry see No. 1190.

The Gem of the Season: A Souvenir for 1853 . . .

New-York: Leavitt & Allen, 27 Dey Street. MDCCCLIII.

Listed NLG Nov. 15, 1852. See next entry.

The Gem of the Season. A Souvenir for All Seasons . . .

New-York: Leavitt and Allen, 27 Dey Street. 1853.

Sheets of the preceding with cancel title-leaf.

The Ladies' Souvenir . . .

New York . . . ⟨1853; i.e., not before 1856⟩

See below under 1856.

The Winter Wreath . . .

New York . . . ⟨1853; i.e., not before 1856⟩

See below under 1856.

The White Veil . . . Edited by Mrs. Sarah Josepha Hale . . .

Philadelphia . . . 1854.

For comment see entry No. 6883.

The Young Lady's Cabinet of Gems: A Choice Collection of . . . Poetry and Prose. ⟨Edited⟩ By Virginia De Forrest.

Boston: Kelley & Brother. 1854.

The Ladies' Souvenir: Edited by N. Parker Willis, ⟨sic⟩

New York: Leavitt and Allen, 379 Broadway. ⟨1853; i.e., not before 1856⟩

Leather.

The Winter Wreath: Edited by N. Parker Willis, ⟨sic⟩

New York: Leavitt and Allen, 379 Broadway. ⟨1853; i.e., not before 1856⟩

Leather.

Cyclopædia of American Literature . . . by Evert A. Duyckinck and George L. Duyckinck. In Two Volumes . . .

New York . . . 1855.

For fuller entry see No. 11092A.

The Psalms of Life . . . ⟨Compiled⟩ by John S. Adams . . .

Boston . . . ⟨1857⟩

For fuller entry see No. 11306.

The Poets of the West . . .

London . . . 1859.

For comment see BAL, Vol. I, p. 101.

A Gallery of Distinguished English and American Female Poets. With an Introduction by Henry Coppée . . .

Philadelphia: Published by E. H. Butler & Co. 1860.

Leather. Advertised as now ready APC Nov. 12, 19, 1859. Listed APC Dec. 3, 1859.

Fading Flowers. By Meta Lander ⟨i.e., Margaret Oliver Lawrence⟩ . . .

Boston: J. E. Tilton and Company. 1860.

Listed APC Dec. 24, 1859.

. . . The (Old) Farmer's Almanack . . . for the Year of Our Lord 1861 . . . by Robert B. Thomas . . .

Boston: Published by Swan, Brewer & Tileston . . . 1860 . . .

Printed paper wrapper   At head of title: Number Sixty-Nine.

The Poets of the West . . .

London . . . New York . . . 1860.

For fuller entry see BAL, Vol. I, p. 374.

The School-Girl's Garland. A Selection . . . By Mrs. C. M. Kirkland. Second Series. Parts Third and Fourth.

> New York . . . 1864.
>
> For fuller entry see No. 11185.

Golden Leaves from the American Poets Collected by John W. S. Hows . . .

> New York . . . ⟨1864; *i.e.*, not before 1866⟩
>
> See below under 1866.

Lyra Americana . . . Selected . . . by the Rev. George T. Rider . . .

> New York . . . 1865.
>
> For comment see entry No. 2827.

Golden Leaves from the American Poets Collected by John W. S. Hows

> New York   James G. Gregory   540 Broadway   M DCCC LXV
>
> Reprinted with the imprint: *New York   Bunce and Huntington*   M DCCC LXV

The Sunday Book of Poetry Selected and Arranged by C. F. Alexander . . .

> Cambridge . . . 1865
>
> For fuller entry see BAL, Vol. 5, p. 603.

The Book of Rubies . . .

> New York . . . 1866.
>
> For comment see entry No. 5522.

Golden Leaves from the American Poets Collected by John W. S. Hows . . .

> New York: George Routledge and Sons, 416 Broome Street. ⟨1864; *i.e.*, not before 1866⟩

Christ and the Twelve . . . Edited by J. G. Holland . . .

> . . . Springfield . . . 1867.
>
> For comment see entry No. 8604.

Chimes for Childhood . . . ⟨Edited by Dana Estes⟩

> Boston . . . ⟨1868⟩
>
> For comment see entry No. 11325.

A Collection of Songs of the American Press, and Other Poems Relating to the Art of Printing. Compiled by Charles Munsell.

> Albany, N. Y. 1868.
>
> Cloth?

A Mother's Souvenir. Compiled from the Writings of Some of the Most Distinguished Poets and Poetesses of the Day. By Mrs. H. W. T. Sayers . . . Edited by Rev. D. A. Pierce . . .

> Pittsburgh: A. A. Anderson & Sons, Book and Job Printers, No. 67 Fifth Ave. 1872.
>
> "Yes, Take Them First, My Father," pp. 101-102. Otherwise "A Mother's Prayer in Illness," *Poems*, 1846.

American Poems. Selected and Edited by William Michael Rossetti . . .

> London: E. Moxon, Son, & Co., Dover Street, and 1 Amen Corner, Paternoster Row. ⟨n.d., after Nov. 1872⟩
>
> Cloth?

One Hundred Choice Selections No. 7 . . . Compiled . . . by Phineas Garrett . . .

> . . . Philadelphia . . . 1873.
>
> For comment see entry No. 2465.

Little People of God . . . Edited by Mrs George L Austin

> Boston . . . 1874
>
> For fuller entry see in *Louise Chandler Moulton* list.

Songs of Three Centuries. Edited by John Greenleaf Whittier.

> Boston . . . 1876.
>
> For fuller entry see No. 11341.

The Elocutionist's Annual Number 5 . . . Edited by J. W. Shoemaker . . .

> Philadelphia: J. W. Shoemaker & Co., Publishers. 1877
>
> Cloth; and, printed paper wrapper.

The Fireside Encyclopædia of Poetry . . . Compiled . . . by Henry T. Coates.

> . . . Philadelphia. ⟨1878⟩
>
> For fuller entry see in James Russell Lowell list, *Section Three.*

Garnered Treasures from the Poets . . .

> Philadelphia . . . 1878.
>
> For fuller entry see No. 4772.

. . . The Reading Club and Handy Speaker . . . Edited by George M. Baker. No. 8.

> Boston . . . 1880.
>
> For comment see entry No. 7316.

The Union of American Poetry and Art A Choice Collection . . . Selected . . . by John James Piatt . . .

>Cincinnati . . . 1880

>For fuller entry see in *James Russell Lowell* list, *Section Three.*

Gems for the Fireside . . . ⟨Compiled by⟩ Rev. O. H. Tiffany . . .

>Boston . . . 1881.

>For comment see BAL, Vol. 5, p. 610.

Gems for the Fireside . . . ⟨Compiled by⟩ Rev. O. H. Tiffany . . .

>Springfield, Mass. . . . ⟨1883⟩

>For comment see BAL, Vol. 5, p. 611.

Opening Addresses Edited by Laurence Hutton

>New-York . . . 1887

>For comment see entry No. 1045.

The Poets of Maine . . . Compiled by George Bancroft Griffith

>Portland . . . 1888

>For comment see BAL, Vol. 1, p. 87.

Belford's Annual. 1888–9. Edited by Thomas W. Handford . . .

>Chicago . . . ⟨1888⟩

>For comment see entry No. 5735.

No. 32. Standard Recitations by Best Authors . . . Compiled . . . by Frances P. Sullivan . . . June 1891 . . .

>. . . N. Y. . . . ⟨1891⟩

>For comment see No. 5563.

An American Anthology 1787–1899 . . . Edited by Edmund Clarence Stedman . . .

>Boston . . . M DCCCC

>All Osgood poems herein reprinted from other books. "The Hand That Swept the Sounding Lyre," *Poems*, 1850, appears herein under the revised title "On a Dead Poet." For fuller entry see No. 3082.

The Lawyer's Alcove . . . Edited by Ina Russelle Warren . . .

>New York . . . 1900

>For comment see entry No. 4933.

American Familiar Verse   Vers de Société Edited . . . by Brander Matthews . . .

>. . . New York . . . 1904

>For fuller entry see in James Russell Lowell, *Section Three.*

REFERENCES AND ANA

Philosophical Enigmas; a Series of Poetical Enigmas on Scientific Subjects, Chiefly Original, with Accompanying Solutions in Prose, by the Author of "Poetry of Flowers," &c., Designed for the Amusement & Instruction of Youth.

>London: Published by William & Henry Rock, Card Makers & Fancy Stationers ⟨n.d., 183-⟩

>*Not seen. Not located.* Entry on the basis of a card in The Charles Patterson Van Pelt Library, University of Pennsylvania.

>The publication is reported lost. On the basis of the library's records the publication consisted of 42 separate cards; a game.

>*Note:* The date assigned by UP is faulty. *The Poetry of Flowers* was issued in late 1840, not later than Jan. 1841.

Interpretation of Flora.

>Philadelphia, 1841.

>*Not located. Not seen.* Entry from Foley, p. 215, where the publication is described as a *12mo.*

>Presumably a ghost.

The Rose.

>Providence, 1842.

>*Not located. Not seen.* Presumably a ghost. Entry from Foley, p. 215, where the publication is described as an *18mo.*

The Memorial: Written by Friends of the Late Mrs. Osgood and Edited by Mary E. Hewitt . . .

>New-York . . . 1851.

>For fuller entry see No. 1187; also see in the *John Neal* list.

Gems.

>New York: Clark, Austin & Co., before Oct. 1852.

>*Not located. Not seen.* Entry from Roorbach (New York, 1852) where this publication is listed at *19¢.* Probably an erroneous entry for *Poems*, 1852.

Laurel Leaves: A Chaplet Woven by the Friends of the Late Mrs. Osgood. Edited by Mary E. Hewitt . . .

New York . . . 1854.

Reprint of *The Memorial* . . . , 1851; see above.

For fuller entry see BAL, Vol. 2, p. 496.

The School-Girl's Garland . . . By Mrs. C. M. Kirkland. First Series . . .

New York . . . 1864

"Little Things," p. 17. Here erroneously credited to Mrs. Osgood; the author was Julia A. Fletcher Carney. For further comment see No. 4837.

15359. Dick's Recitations and Readings No. 6 . . . Edited by Wm. B. Dick . . .

New York: Dick & Fitzgerald, Publishers, No. 18 Ann Street. ⟨1877⟩

"Uncle Gabe's White Folks," pp. 32-34. Collected in *Befo' de War*, 1888.

For fuller entry see No. 3375.

15360. Stories by American Authors IX . . .

New York Charles Scribner's Sons 1885

"Marse Chan," pp. ⟨5⟩-41. Collected in *In Ole Virginia*, 1887.

Listed PW Jan. 24, 1885. BA copy received Jan. 26, 1885.

Two bindings noted; for comment see entry No. 10567.

AAS H NYPL UV

15361. IN OLE VIRGINIA OR MARSE CHAN AND OTHER STORIES . . .

NEW YORK CHARLES SCRIBNER'S SONS 1887

Three printings noted:

FIRST PRINTING

⟨i-viii⟩, ⟨1⟩-230; blank leaf; plus: advertisements, pp. ⟨i-xii⟩. Laid paper. 7¼″ × 4⅞″.

⟨-⟩⁴, 1-14⁸, 15⁴; plus: ⟨16⟩⁶.

Terminal Advertisements

⟨i⟩: Popular Books . . . Old Creole Days . . . Popular Edition . . . Mrs. Burnett's Earlier Stories . . . Rudder Grange . . .

⟨ii⟩: Popular Books . . . The Lady, or the Tiger . . . That Lass o' Lowrie's . . . Saxe Holm s ⟨*sic*⟩ Stories . . .

⟨iii⟩: Stories by American Authors . . . ⟨Nos. I-X⟩

⟨iv⟩: Chronicle of the Coach . . .

⟨v⟩: . . . Stockton's Stories The Lady, or the Tiger ? . . . ⟨to⟩ . . . The Cloverfield's Carriage . . .

⟨vi⟩: New Editions . . . Saxe Holm's Stories. First Series . . . Second Series . . .

⟨vii⟩: Three Delightful Novels. The Midge . . . Face to Face . . . The Late Mrs. Null . . .

⟨viii⟩: A Beautiful New Edition. Rudder Grange . . .

⟨ix⟩: Uniform Library Edition / Mrs. Frances Hodgson Burnett's Novels. That Lass o' Lowrie's . . . ⟨to⟩ . . . Surly Tim . . .

⟨x⟩: New Dollar Novels . . . Valentino . . . ⟨to⟩ . . . Color Studies . . .

⟨xi⟩: Books by Andrew Lang . . .

⟨xii⟩: A New Book . . . The Merry Men . . . ⟨to⟩ . . . A Child's Garden of Verses . . .

SECOND PRINTING

⟨i-viii⟩, ⟨1⟩-230; blank leaf; plus: advertisements, pp. ⟨i-vi⟩, ⟨1⟩-⟨6⟩, blank leaf; leaf excised. Laid paper. 7⁵⁄₁₆″ × 4⅞″.

⟨-⟩⁴, 1-14⁸, 15⁴; plus: ⟨16⟩⁸. Leaf ⟨16⟩₈ excised.

Terminal Advertisements

⟨i⟩: Weird Tales . . .

⟨ii⟩: By the Author of Dr. Jekyll. Kidnapped . . .

⟨iii⟩: Chronicle of the Coach . . .

⟨iv⟩: Just Published . . . Underwoods . . . The Merry Men . . .

⟨v⟩: Three Delightful Novels. The Midge . . . Face to Face . . . The Late Mrs. Null . . .

⟨vi⟩: Stories by American Authors . . . ⟨Nos. I-X⟩

⟨1⟩: New Dollar Novels . . . Valentino . . .

2: . . . The Last Meeting . . . Within the Capes . . .

3: . . . A Wheel of Fire . . . Roses of Shadow . . . Across the Chasm . . .

4: . . . A Desperate Chance . . . Color Studies . . .

⟨5⟩: A New and Uniform Edition. George W. Cable's Writings . . .

⟨6⟩: . . . A Child's Garden of Verses . . .

THIRD PRINTING

⟨i-viii⟩, ⟨1⟩-230; blank, pp. ⟨231-232⟩; plus advertisements: pp. ⟨i-iv⟩, ⟨1⟩-⟨10⟩, blank leaf. 7¼″ × 4⅞″. Laid paper.

⟨-⟩⁴, 1-14⁸, 15⁴; plus: ⟨16⟩⁸.

Terminal Advertisements

⟨i⟩: Author's Editions. Robert Louis Stevenson's Books . . .

⟨ii⟩: . . . Thirty-Eighth Thousand. Strange Case . . .

⟨iii⟩: . . . New Arabian Nights . . .

⟨iv⟩: . . . Memories and Portraits . . .

⟨1⟩: New Dollar Novels . . . Valentino . . .

2: . . . The Last Meeting . . . Within the Capes . . .

3: . . . A Wheel of Fire . . . ⟨to⟩ . . . Across the Chasm . . .

4: . . . A Desperate Chance . . . Color Studies . . .

⟨5⟩: Popular Books in Paper . . . The Christmas Wreck . . . ⟨to⟩ . . . An Apache Campaign in the Sierra Madre . . .

⟨6⟩: Stories by American Authors . . . ⟨Nos. 1-x⟩

⟨7⟩: Frank R. Stockton's Writings . . . The Bee-Man of Orn . . . ⟨to⟩ . . . Tales Out of School . . .

⟨8⟩: . . . Mrs. Frances Hodgson Burnett's Novels. That Lass o' Lowrie's . . . ⟨to⟩ . . . Surly Tim . . .

⟨9⟩: . . . George W. Cable's Writings. The Grandissimes . . . Old Creole Days . . . Popular Edition of Old Creole Days . . .

⟨10⟩: A New Book by Joel Chandler Harris. Free Joe . . .

V cloth: green. Pale yellow end papers. Laid paper flyleaves.

Published May 21, 1887, 3000 copies; publisher's records. Listed PW May 28, 1887. A copy of the first printing (in AAS) inscribed by early owner June 8, 1887.

AAS (1st)   BPL (3d)   UV (1st; 2nd; 3d)   Y (1st)

15362. BEFO' DE WAR ECHOES IN NEGRO DIALECT BY A. C. ⟨Armistead Churchill⟩ GORDON AND THOMAS NELSON PAGE

NEW YORK CHARLES SCRIBNER'S SONS 1888

⟨i-ii⟩, ⟨i⟩-⟨viii⟩, ⟨1⟩-131; blank leaf; leaf excised or pasted under the end paper. 7¼″ × 4⅞″ scant. *Note:* In some copies pp. ⟨vii-viii⟩ are excised; a blank leaf.

⟨-⟩⁴, ⟨*⟩¹, 1-8⁸, 9⁴. *Note:* In some copies leaf ⟨*⟩ is not present; in all examined copies leaf 9₄ is excised or pasted under the end paper.

V cloth: mottled pink sides, light brown buckram shelfback. Cream end papers printed in olive with a pattern of dandelion seeds. Also: plain yellow end papers. Flyleaf at front.

Published April 14, 1888, 1500 copies; publisher's records. Advertised for *today* PW April 14, 1888. Deposited April 16, 1888. Listed PW April 21, 1888.

AAS   B   BPL   H   NYPL   UV   Y

15363. No. 21. Standard Comic Recitations by Best Authors . . . Compiled . . . by Frances P. Sullivan . . . September, 1888 . . .

M. J. Ivers & Co., Publishers, 86 Nassau Street, N. Y. . . . ⟨1888⟩

"The April Face," pp. 22-23. Collected in *The Coast of Bohemia*, 1906.

For fuller entry see BAL, Vol. 5, p. 272.

LC

15364. TWO LITTLE CONFEDERATES . . .

NEW YORK CHARLES SCRIBNER'S SONS 1888

Two printings noted:

FIRST PRINTING

⟨i-x⟩, 1-156, 2 pp. advertisements, plus: 8 pp. advertisements. Illustrated. 8¼″ × 6⅝″.

⟨1-21⁴; plus: 22⁴⟩. *Signed:* ⟨-⟩⁵, ⟨1⟩-9⁸, 10⁷; ⟨11⟩⁴.

SECOND PRINTING

⟨i-x⟩, 1-156; blank, pp. ⟨157-158⟩; plus: 8 pp. advertisements. Illustrated.

⟨1-21⁴; plus: 22⁴⟩. *Signed:* ⟨-⟩⁵, ⟨1⟩-9⁸, 10⁷; ⟨11⟩⁴.

V cloth: blue-gray. Yellow end papers. Flyleaves.

Published Oct. 10, 1888, 2835 copies; publisher's records. Deposited Oct. 11, 1888. Listed PW Oct. 20, 1888. The second printing advertised PW Nov. 10, 1888. The London (Unwin) edition advertised for Dec. 8 in Ath Dec. 1, 1888; listed Ath Dec. 15, 1888.

AAS (2nd)   LC (1st)   NYPL (2nd)   UV (2nd)   Y (both)

15365. The Parnell Movement Being the History of the Irish Question from the Death of O'Connell to the Present Time by T. P. O'Connor . . . with Sketch of the Author by Thomas Nelson Page.

New York Cassell Publishing Company 104 & 106 Fourth Avenue ⟨1891⟩

"Sketch of the Author," pp. v-xiv.

Deposited April 23, 1891. Listed PW May 2, 1891.

BPL   UV   Y

15366. ON NEWFOUND RIVER . . .

NEW YORK CHARLES SCRIBNER'S SONS 1891

For an extended edition see below under year 1906.

⟨i-vi⟩, 1-240, blank leaf. Laid paper. 7¼″ × 4¹³⁄₁₆″.

⟨1-15⁸, 16⁴⟩.

V cloth: light green.

Deposited June 2, 1891. Published June 4, 1891, 5000 copies; publisher's records. Advertised for

June 4 PW May 23, 1891. Noted as *just issued* PW June 6, 1891. Listed PW June 13, 1891. The London (Osgood) edition advertised for *this day* Ath June 6, 1891; listed Ath June 13, 1891.

AAS H NYPL Y

15367. . . . PAPER READ BY THOMAS NELSON PAGE, AT THE THIRD ANNUAL MEETING, HELD AT WHITE SULPHUR SPRINGS, W. VA., JULY 28th, 29th and 30th, 1891.

RICHMOND, VA.: EVERETT WADDEY CO., PUBLISHERS AND PRINTERS, 1891.

At head of title: THE VIRGINIA STATE BAR ASSOCIATION

Caption-title, p. ⟨3⟩: *The Old Virginia Lawyer.*

⟨1⟩-11. 9³⁄₁₆″ scant × 5⅞″.

⟨1⟩⁴, 2².

Printed gray paper wrapper.

Collected in *The Old South*, 1892.

UV

15368. ELSKET AND OTHER STORIES . . .

NEW YORK CHARLES SCRIBNER'S SONS 1891

⟨i⟩-⟨viii⟩, 1-208; advertisements, pp. ⟨1⟩-8. Laid paper. 7³⁄₁₆″ × 4¹³⁄₁₆″.

⟨1-14⁸⟩.

V cloth: green; maroon.

Deposited Oct. 7, 1891. Noted and advertised as *just published* PW Oct. 10, 1891. Listed PW Oct. 17, 1891. The London (Osgood) edition advertised for March 18 in Bkr March 18, 1892; listed Ath March 19, 1892.

AAS BPL H NYPL UV Y

15369. AMONG THE CAMPS OR YOUNG PEOPLE'S STORIES OF THE WAR . . .

NEW YORK CHARLES SCRIBNER'S SONS 1891

⟨i-xvi⟩, ⟨1⟩-163; blank, p. ⟨164⟩; 4 pp. advertisements. Illustrated. 8³⁄₁₆″ full × 6⅝″ scant.

⟨-⟩⁸, 1-⟨2⟩, 3-4, ⟨5⟩-10⁸, 11⁴.

V cloth: gray-blue. Cream white end papers. Flyleaf at back.

Deposited Nov. 6, 1891. Published Nov. 9, 1891; publisher's records. Listed PW Dec. 5, 1891. The London (Walter Scott) edition listed PC Oct. 1, 1892.

AAS H LC UV Y

15370. THE OLD SOUTH ESSAYS SOCIAL AND POLITICAL . . .

NEW YORK CHARLES SCRIBNER'S SONS 1892

⟨i⟩-⟨x⟩, ⟨1⟩-344; pp. ⟨345-346⟩ excised; publisher's catalog, pp. ⟨1⟩-12. Portrait frontispiece inserted. 7³⁄₁₆″ full × 4⅞″ scant.

⟨1-23⁸⟩. Leaf ⟨23⟩₂ excised.

V cloth: blue-gray.

Published May 19, 1892, 2000 copies; publisher's records. Deposited May 20, 1892. H copy received May 20, 1892. Advertised in PW May 21, 1892. Listed PW June 4, 1892. For another edition see under 1919.

AAS BPL H LC UV Y

15371. ADDRESS . . . ON THE NECESSITY FOR A HISTORY OF THE SOUTH. DELIVERED BEFORE THE GRAND CAMP OF CONFEDERATE VETERANS OF THE STATE OF VIRGINIA. AT ITS ANNUAL MEETING IN THE CITY OF ROANOKE, JUNE 22, 1892. PUBLISHED BY WILLIAM WATTS CAMP, OF ROANOKE, VA., AT WHOSE REQUEST THE ADDRESS WAS DELIVERED.

ROANOKE, VA., HAMMOND'S PRINTING WORKS. 1892.

Cover-title.

1-⟨26⟩. 8⅞″ × 5¾″.

⟨1-3⁴, 4¹⟩.

Printed blue-gray laid paper wrapper. Inserted at front: A pink slip, 2⁹⁄₁₆″ × 5¼″: *The object in view in having Dr. Page deliver this address was to arouse a widespread interest in securing the writing and publishing of a history of the South . . .*

LC UV

15372. Fame's Tribute to Children . . . ⟨Edited by Martha S. Hill⟩

Chicago A. C. McClurg and Company 1892

A sentiment, p. 71.

For fuller entry see BAL, Vol. 1, p. 76.

LC

15373. From Dixie. Original Articles Contributed by Southern Writers for Publication as a Souvenir of the Memorial Bazaar for the Benefit of the Monument to the Private Soldiers and Sailors of the Confederacy . . . with Heretofore Unpublished Poems, by Some Who Have "Crossed over the River."

Richmond, Va.: West, Johnston & Co., MDCCCXCIII.

"To a Saxon Woman," p. ⟨104⟩.

AAS copy inscribed by early owner April 27, 1893. Deposited Sept. 9, 1893.

AAS H NYPL

15374. PASTIME STORIES...

NEW YORK   HARPER & BROTHERS PUBLISHERS
1894

⟨i-ii⟩, ⟨i⟩-x, ⟨1⟩-220; 4 pp. advertisements.
$7\frac{1}{16}'' \times 4\frac{7}{8}''$. 21 plates inserted; 1 illustration in text.

⟨-⟩⁶, ⟨1⟩-14⁸.

S cloth: blue. White laid paper end papers.

Deposited May 29, 1894. Listed PW June 2, 1894.

AAS H LC Y

15375. THE BURIAL OF THE GUNS...

NEW YORK CHARLES SCRIBNER'S SONS 1894

Two printings noted:

FIRST PRINTING

⟨i-viii⟩, ⟨1⟩-258. Laid paper. $7\frac{3}{16}'' \times 4\frac{13}{16}''$.

⟨1⁴, 2-17⁸, 18¹⟩.

SECOND PRINTING

⟨i-viii⟩, ⟨1⟩-258, blank leaf. Laid paper.

⟨1-16⁸, 17⁶⟩.

V cloth: cream. Front lettered in gold: THE
BURIAL / OF THE GUNS / THOMAS / NELSON / PAGE /
⟨all the preceding within a decoration stamped
in pale green and rose⟩ Noted on both first and
second printings.

A remainder binding has been noted; seen only on
second printing sheets. V cloth: maroon; front not
lettered.

According to the publisher's records published
Oct. 27, 1894; 3000 copies. Deposited Oct. 27,
1894. BA copy (first printing) received Oct. 30,
1894. Listed PW Nov. 3, 1894. The London edition
(Ward, Lock & Bowden) advertised as *just ready*
Ath Nov. 24, 1894; listed Ath Nov. 24, 1894.

AAS (1st)   H (both)   UV (both)   Y (2nd)

15376. Thought Blossoms from the South   A
Collection of Poems, Essays, Stories, etc. By
Southern Writers, with an Introduction by
Hon. John Temple Graves. Compiled by Louise
Threete Hodges, Assisted by Gertrude Eloise
Bealer. A Souvenir of the Cotton States and
International Exposition.

⟨Atlanta, Ga., The Foote & Davies Company,
1895⟩

"Sleep," p. 132. Collected in *The Coast of Bohemia*,
1906.

Deposited Sept. 21, 1895.

B

15377. THE OLD GENTLEMAN OF THE
BLACK STOCK...

NEW YORK CHARLES SCRIBNER'S SONS 1897

In *The Ivory Series.*

⟨i-vi⟩, ⟨1⟩-137. $6\frac{3}{8}'' \times 3\frac{13}{16}''$ full.

⟨1-18⁴⟩.

White buckram. Top edges gilt.

Deposited June 12, 1897. BA copy received June
15, 1897. Listed PW June 19, 1897. Noted as *just
ready* PW June 19, 1897.

AAS BA BPL H NYPL UV Y

15378. Social Life in Old Virginia before the
War...

New York Charles Scribner's Sons M DCCC-
XCVII

Reprinted from *The Old South*, 1892, save for the
"Introduction," written for this separate printing,
pp. 1-5.

Published Nov. 27, 1897, 5000 copies; publisher's
records. Advertised for Nov. 27 PW Nov. 20, 1897.
Deposited Nov. 29, 1897. Listed PW Dec. 11, 1897.

AAS BA BPL H UV Y

15379. The Authors Club Dinner to Richard
Henry Stoddard. At the Savoy, New York,
March 25, 1897... Reprinted from the Mail and
Express, New York, Issue of March 26, 1897.

⟨n.p., n.d., New York, 1897⟩

Remarks, p. 16.

For comment see entry No. 6581.

15380. TWO PRISONERS...

NEW YORK R. H. RUSSELL MDCCCXCVIII

For a revised edition see below under 1903.

Two printings noted; the sequence has not been
firmly established and the designations are for
identification only.

PRINTING A

⟨1⟩-82; blank, pp. ⟨83-92⟩. Laid paper. Frontis-
piece inserted. $7\frac{1}{2}''$ full × $5\frac{1}{4}''$. See under signature collation for comment on the terminal blank
leaves.

⟨1⁶, 2², 3-6⁸, 7⁶⟩. ⟨1⟩₂₋₃ are inserted conjugates
and comprise the fly-title-page and the acknowledgments. ⟨7⟩₃₋₄, are inserted blank conjugates
and are present in some copies only. ⟨7⟩₆ is used
as the terminal pastedown.

PRINTING B

⟨1⟩-82. Laid paper. Frontispiece inserted. $7\frac{1}{2}''$
full × $5\frac{1}{4}''$.

⟨1-5⁸, 6¹⟩.

V cloth: green. Top edges gilt. See below for comment on end papers.

End Papers, Printing A

Leaf ⟨7⟩₆ used as terminal pastedown. Laid paper end paper at front. No flyleaves.

End Papers, Printing B

Laid paper end papers. Triple flyleaves of laid paper at front and at back; or, no flyleaves at front, triple flyleaves of laid paper at back.

Noted as *just published* PW April 16, 1898. Deposited April 21, 1898. Listed PW April 23, 1898. A copy of *Printing B* (NYPL) inscribed by Page *May, 1898*.

AAS (B)   BPL (A)   LC (A, being a deposit copy) NYPL (B)   UV (B)   Y (A, B)

15381. RED ROCK   A CHRONICLE OF RECONSTRUCTION BY THOMAS NELSON PAGE   ILLUSTRATED

NEW YORK   CHARLES SCRIBNER'S SONS   1898

Two printings noted:

FIRST PRINTING

Title-page as above.

⟨i⟩-⟨xvi⟩, 1-584; advertisements, pp. ⟨1⟩-4. Frontispiece and 10 plates inserted. 7⁷⁄₁₆″ × 4¹⁵⁄₁₆″.

⟨-⟩⁸, ⟨1⟩-36⁸, 37⁶.

V cloth: green. Stamped in black, gold, terracotta. Top edges plain.

SECOND PRINTING

Title-page: As above but extended to read: ILLUSTRATED BY B. WEST CLINEDINST

⟨i⟩-⟨xvi⟩, 1-584; blank, pp. ⟨585-586⟩; advertisements, pp. ⟨1⟩-4; blank leaf.

⟨-⟩⁸, ⟨1⟩-37⁸.

V cloth: green. Stamped in black, gold, terracotta. Top edges plain. Also noted stamped in gold only.

Note: BAL suspects that two or more printings are described under *Second Printing.*

Note: The publishers report that "a very few copies ⟨were⟩ bound for the author for presentation." A copy thus in UV has the following features: First printing sheets; top edges gilt, other edges untrimmed. Leaf: 7¹¹⁄₁₆″ × 5¼″. Binding stamped in gold only. The UV copy inscribed to Robert Bridges by the author *Novr. 1898*. Another copy (in Y), rebound but with the original binding preserved, inscribed by Page Oct. 29, 1898.

Advertised PW Sept. 24, 1898. Deposited Oct. 28, 1898. Published Oct. 29, 1898, 10,000 copies;

publisher's records. Noted for *today* PW Oct. 29, 1898. Advertised for *today* PW Oct. 29, 1898. Listed PW Nov. 5, 1898. "First edition (10,000) exhausted before publication. Second edition ready immediately."———Advertisement, PW Nov. 12, 1898. "Fifth Edition. 30th Thousand"——— Advertised PW March 11, 1899. "Fortieth Thousand" advertised PW April 8, 1899. 84th thousand advertised PW March 17, 1900. The London (Heinemann) edition advertised for Jan. 16, 1899, Ath Jan. 14, 1899; listed PC Jan. 21, 1899.

AAS (1st)   BPL (2nd)   UV (both)   Y (both)

15382. Spanish-American War Songs   A Complete Collection of Newspaper Verse during the Recent War with Spain   Compiled . . . by Sidney A. Witherbee.

Sidney A. Witherbee, Publisher, Detroit, Mich. 1898.

"The Dragon of the Sea," pp. 731-732. Collected in *The Coast of Bohemia*, 1906.

For fuller entry see No. 738.

15383. SANTA   CLAUS'S   PARTNER . . . ⟨tinted vignette⟩

NEW YORK   CHARLES SCRIBNER'S SONS   1899 COPYRIGHT, 1899, BY CHARLES SCRIBNER'S SONS

Two printings noted:

FIRST PRINTING

⟨i-xii⟩, 1-⟨177⟩; blank, p. ⟨178⟩; *Merrymount Press* imprint, p. ⟨179⟩; blank, p. ⟨180⟩; blank leaf. The title-leaf (pp. ⟨vii-viii⟩) is an inserted leaf, printed on coated paper; the body of the book is printed on uncoated paper. Seven plates, on coated paper, inserted. 7¼″ × 5³⁄₁₆″.

⟨1⁹, 2-12⁸⟩. Leaf ⟨1⟩₄ (the title-leaf) inserted.

SECOND PRINTING

⟨i-viii⟩, 1-⟨177⟩; blank, pp. ⟨178-182⟩. The title-leaf (pp. ⟨iii-iv⟩) is an insert, printed on coated paper; the body of the book is printed on uncoated paper. Seven plates, on coated paper, inserted.

⟨1⁷, 2-12⁸⟩. Leaf ⟨1⟩₂ (the title-leaf) inserted.

BINDING

First Printing Sheets

C cloth: orange-red. Sides identically stamped with a blindstamped ornate frame. Lettering in gold. Top edges gilt. No flyleaves.

EXTRA GILT BINDING

C cloth: orange-red. Stamped as above but all stamping gold, not blind and gold. Top edges gilt. No flyleaves.

BINDING

Second Printing Sheets

C cloth: red. Sides identically stamped with a blindstamped ornate frame. Lettering in gold. Top edges gilt. Double flyleaf at front.

Deposited Oct. 27, 1899. The publisher's records show that 10,400 copies, of which 500 were shipped to William Briggs, Toronto, were published Oct. 28, 1899. BA copy (1st printing) received Oct. 31, 1899. Listed PW Nov. 4, 1899.

London publication: The BMU catalog lists a Sands & Company (London) edition of 1899; further information wanting. The Grant Richards edition listed Ath Sept. 14, 1901. A Chatto & Windus edition listed Ath Oct. 15, 1910.

AAS (1st; 1st extra gilt) BA (1st) BPL (1st extra gilt) H (1st) LC (1st, being a deposit copy) NYPL (1st) UV (1st; 1st extra gilt; 2nd) Y (1st; 1st extra gilt)

15384. Envion and Other Tales of Old and New Virginia. By Armistead C. Gordon. With a Preface by Thomas Nelson Page.

F. Tennyson Neely, Publisher, London. New York. Chicago. ⟨1899⟩

Noted in the following printings; sequence not determined; the designations are arbitrary.

A

Pp. ⟨1⟩-171; blank, pp. ⟨172-176⟩. Front matter misimposed, causing the first page of text to appear on the verso of the first page of Page's preface. Noted in printed paper wrapper of The Syndicate Purchasers, New York. Title-page: Leaf ⟨1⟩3r.

Note: The publisher of this book, F. Tennyson Neely, filed a petition in bankruptcy Oct. 21, 1899; see PW Oct. 28, 1899. The book appears not to have been issued by Neely although sheets bearing the Neely imprint were produced. Not advertised by Neely who appears to have stopped advertising in PW after June, 1897. No PW listing found.

Further note: The Syndicate Purchasers were in business (this on the basis of contemporary notices and listings) from about 1900 to 1905. In PW of Aug. 11, 1900, Oct. 27, 1900, they offered for sale the plates and copyrights purchased at the Neely sale.

A copy of the above in UV is bound in cloth. Rebound? Status not known.

B

Pp. ⟨5⟩-171; blank, pp. ⟨172-176⟩. Front matter correctly imposed. Noted in cloth only, printed paper label on spine. In red on the copyright page is the following notice: *This edition is limited to*

twenty-four numbered and signed copes . . . Title-page: ⟨1⟩1r.

". . . Many years ago he ⟨Thomas Nelson Page⟩ wrote an introduction to a little volume of stories. The book was accepted by a publisher who failed before its publication. I secured the plates, and had privately printed twenty four copies for distribution among my friends . . ."———Letter, Armistead C. Gordon to Charles Scribner, Nov. 25, 1922. Letter in H.

H (B)   UV (A in wrapper; A in cloth; B)

15385. Hero Tales of the American Soldier and Sailor As Told by the Heroes Themselves and Their Comrades   The Unwritten History of American Chivalry

⟨n.p.,⟩ Hero Publishing Co. ⟨1899⟩

Edited by J. W. Buel. Copyright notice in the name of A. Holloway.

"The Answer," p. 120. Collected in *The Coast of Bohemia,* 1906, as "The Old Lion."

Note: A subscription book and as such occurs with a variety of imprints. The following have been noted; sequence, if any, not known:

A: *Hero Publishing Co.* ⟨1899⟩ Location: H.

B: *Century Manufacturing Company | Philadelphia, Pa. | ⟨1899⟩* Location: H

C: *Elliott Publishing Company | Philadelphia, Pa. | ⟨1899⟩* Location: H.

15386. The Peace Cross Book   Cathedral of SS. Peter and Paul   Washington

Published by R. H. Russell   New York MDCCCXCIX

Edited by Henry Yates Satterlee.

Boards, printed paper label on front.

"The Peace Cross at Washington," pp. 29-37.

Printed at the Caslon Press, New York, in March Mdcccxcix.———Colophon.

LC

15387. The Old Gentleman of the Black Stock . . .

New York   Charles Scribner's Sons 1900 . . .

For another version see under year 1897. "Preface," written for this edition, pp. vii-viii.

". . . I have availed myself of the opportunity offered by the publication of this new edition . . . to enlarge the story . . ."———P. vii.

Note: Copies occur with a leaf of laid paper (watermarked *d's | Linen*; watermark incomplete) printed in blue: *The Author's First Edition | ⟨rule⟩ | The Author's Best Wishes | for a | Happy New Year | Copy in* Y.

Deposited Oct. 5, 1900. BPL copy received Oct. 9, 1900. Listed PW Oct. 13, 1900.

AAS   BA   BPL   H   NYPL   Y

15388. Favorite Food of Famous Folk . . .

. . . John P. Morton & Company . . . Louisville, Kentucky . . . MCM

Contribution, p. 43.

For fuller entry see No. 470.

15389. Proceedings at the Twentieth Annual Meeting and Twentieth Annual Festival of the New England Society in the City of Brooklyn . . .

Borough of Brooklyn. 1900.

Printed paper wrapper.

"Address," in response to the toast "The Debt Each Part of the Country Owes the Other," pp. 40-50.

H

15390. Second Annual Report of Old Home Week in New Hampshire August 11 to 18, 1900 . . .

Manchester, N. H.   Arthur E. Clarke, Public Printer   1900

Printed paper wrapper.

Address, pp. 58-68.

B

15391. GORDON KEITH . . .

CHARLES SCRIBNER'S SONS   NEW YORK   1903

⟨i⟩-⟨x⟩, ⟨1⟩-548, blank leaf. Frontispiece and 7 plates inserted. $7\frac{9}{16}'' \times 5\frac{1}{8}''$ (trade format). $7\frac{3}{4}'' \times 5\frac{5}{16}''$ ("special edition").

⟨1-35⁸⟩.

V cloth: blue. Stamped in gold and blue-white. *Note:* Two states of the front cover have been noted; priority not established and the designations are for identification only:

A: With the designer's monogram, *MA*, to the right of and below the lettering.

B: Monogram not present.

Note: In addition to the trade format, copies were prepared for the author's use: Binding stamped in gold only (not gold and blue-white) *MA* monogram present. Top edges gilt, other edges untrimmed. Leaf: $7\frac{3}{4}'' \times 5\frac{5}{16}''$. Two copies have been seen (UV, Y) each inscribed by the author and dated *May 29, 1903.* According to the publisher's records fifty copies were prepared thus.

On copyright page: *Published May, 1903*

Advertised for *May* PW March 21, 1903. Noted for *May* PW March 28, 1903. Advertised for *this month* PW April 11, 1903. Noted for *next month* PW April 11, 1903. Noted for *May 29* PW May 2, 1903. According to the publisher's records published May 29, 1903, 50,000 copies, of which 50 were specially bound for the author. Advertised for *May 29* PW May 30, 1903. BA copy received June 2, 1903. Listed PW June 27, 1903. The London (Heinemann) edition listed Ath Aug. 15, 1903; reviewed Ath Aug. 29, 1903.

AAS   (A)   B   (B)   BPL   (A)   H   (A, B)   LC   (B)   UV   (B)   Y   (B)

15392. Two Prisoners . . .

New York   R. H. Russell   MCMIII

A revision of the 1898 edition.

Deposited Sept. 18, 1903. "Have brought out this week"---PW Sept. 19, 1903. Listed PW Oct. 10, 1903.

AAS   B   H   LC   Y

15393. BRED IN THE BONE . . .

CHARLES SCRIBNER'S SONS   NEW YORK   MCMIV

⟨i-x⟩, ⟨1⟩-274, 4 pp. advertisements. Frontispiece and 7 plates inserted. $7\frac{5}{8}'' \times 4\frac{7}{8}''$ full.

⟨1-18⁸⟩.

Noted in the following bindings:

A

T cloth: green. Front lettered in gold. Top edges gilt. The publisher's file copy thus.

B

T cloth: green. Front unstamped. Top edges plain.

C

Not seen. According to the publisher's records 3500 copies were remaindered in red cloth with white stamping. Further information wanting.

On copyright page: *Published, May, 1904*

Advertised PW Feb. 13, 1904; March 19, 1904. Noted as *shortly* PW March 26, 1904. Noted as *in preparation* PW May 7, 1904. Advertised as *immediately* PW May 14, 1904. Noted for *the 21st inst* PW May 14, 1904. Advertised as *now ready* PW May 21, 1904. BA copy received May 24, 1904. Listed PW June 4, 1904.

Note: According to the publisher's records published May 21, 1904. A total of 20,500 copies were printed of which 3500 were later bound as a "cheap edition" in red cloth with white stamping. Not seen in "red cloth".

BA   (A)   BPL   (A)   H   (A)   NYPL   (B)   UV   (A)   Y   (A)

15394. THE NEGRO: THE SOUTHERNER'S
PROBLEM . . .

CHARLES SCRIBNER'S SONS   NEW YORK   1904

Three printings noted:

FIRST PRINTING

⟨i-ii⟩, ⟨i⟩-⟨xiv⟩, ⟨1⟩-316, 4 pp. advertisements.
$7^{7}/_{16}'' \times 4^{15}/_{16}''$.

⟨1-21⁸⟩.

P. 73 ends: . . . *risen to $14,- |*

Index not present.

SECOND PRINTING

⟨i-ii⟩, ⟨i⟩-⟨xiv⟩, ⟨1⟩-324, 4 pp. advertisements.

⟨1-20⁸, 21¹²⟩

P. 73 ends: . . . *in the year |*

Index present.

THIRD PRINTING

Imprinted: *Young People's Missionary Movement of
the United States and Canada   New York* ⟨1904;
i.e., 1909⟩

⟨i-ii⟩, ⟨i⟩-⟨xiv⟩, ⟨1⟩-324.

⟨1², 2-22⁸⟩.

P. 73 ends: . . . *in the year |*

Index present.

According to the publisher's records 498 copies
bearing the above imprint were manufactured in
the year 1909.

On copyright page: *Published, November, 1904*

T cloth: maroon. Flyleaf at back.

Deposited Nov. 29, 1904. Published Nov. 30, 1904;
publisher's records. H and NYPL copies (first
printing) received Dec. 3, 1904. Listed PW Dec. 10,
1904.

AAS (1st)   B (1st)   BA (1st)   H (1st, 2nd)   NYPL (1st)
UV (1st)   Y (1st, 3d)

15395. . . . Two Hundred and Fiftieth Anniversary of the Town ⟨York, Maine⟩ . . . August 5,
1902

Published by the Old York Historical and
Improvement Society, York, Maine   1904

At head of title: *Agamenticus, Bristol, Georgeana,
York an Oration . . . by . . . James Phinney Baxter . . .*

Printed paper wrapper.

"Address," pp. 113-118.

Y

15396. On Newfound River . . .

New York   Charles Scribner's Sons   1906

". . . In preparing a new edition for the press, the
author has enlarged the work by certain additions
. . ."---From the preface. See above under year
1891 for original book publication.

Deposited Oct. 5, 1906. Published Oct. 6, 1906;
publisher's records. Noted as *just ready;* and:
". . . A re-written and enlarged edition of Thomas
Nelson Page's excellent story . . ."---PW Oct. 6,
1906. Listed PW Oct. 20, 1906. As Vol. 3 of the
works deposited Oct. 31, 1906.

BPL   H   LC   Y

15397. ⟨Plantation Edition of the Works of
Thomas Nelson Page⟩

⟨New York: Charles Scribner's Sons, 1906–
1912⟩

Issued in a *trade format;* leaf size $7^{7}/_{16}'' \times 5''$;
printed on laid paper watermarked with the TNP
monogram. Also issued in a *limited edition* of 230
numbered copies; leaf size $8^{1}/_{16}'' \times 5^{1}/_{8}''$; printed
on hand-made paper watermarked *Ruisdael.*

Vols. 1-12 deposited Oct. 31, 1906; Vols. 13-14
deposited Nov. 12, 1909; Vols. 15-16 deposited
Dec. 21, 1909; Vols. 17-18 deposited Nov. 5,
1912. Vols. 1-12 listed PW April 6, 1907.

Vol. 1. *In Ole Virginia.* 1906.

"Introduction to the Plantation Edition," pp. vii-
xiii. Dated at end *August 11, 1906.*

Vol. 2. *The Burial of the Guns.* 1906.

Reprint.

Vol. 3. *On Newfound River.* 1906.

Reprint.

Vol. 4. *Red Rock   A Chronicle of Reconstruction I.* 1906.

Reprint.

Vol. 5. *Red Rock   A Chronicle of Reconstruction II.*
1906.

Reprint.

Vol. 6. *Gordon Keith I.* 1906.

Reprint.

Vol. 7. *Gordon Keith II.* 1906.

Reprint.

Vol. 8. *The Old Gentleman of the Black Stock   Santa
Claus's Partner.* 1906.

Reprint.

Vol. 9. *Bred in the Bone.* 1906.

Reprint.

Vol. 10. *Pastime Stories   Poems.* 1906.

Reprint with the possible exception of "L'Envoy,"
p. 313.

Vol. 11. *Two Little Confederates Among the Camps Two Prisoners.* 1906.

Reprint.

Vol. 12. *The Old South Essays Social and Political.* 1906.

Reprint with the possible exception of "The Old-Time Negro"; elsewhere unlocated.

Vol. 13. *The Old Dominion Her Making and Her Manners.* 1909.

Reprint.

Vol. 14. *Under the Crust Tommy Trot's Visit to Santa Claus.* 1909.

Reprint.

Vol. 15. *John Marvel Assistant I.* 1909.

Reprint.

Vol. 16. *John Marvel Assistant II.* 1909.

Reprint.

Vol. 17. *Robert E. Lee Man and Soldier I.* 1912.

Reprint.

Vol. 18. *Robert E. Lee Man and Soldier II.* 1912.

Reprint.

BA BPL LC Y

15398. What's Next or Shall a Man Live Again? ... Compiled by Clara Spalding Ellis ...

Boston Richard G. Badger The Gorham Press 1906

Statement, p. 41.

Listed PW Nov. 3, 1906.

EM

15399. THE COAST OF BOHEMIA ...

NEW YORK CHARLES SCRIBNER'S SONS 1906

Title-page in black and red.

⟨i⟩-⟨x⟩, ⟨1⟩-126. Laid paper. $7\frac{9}{16}''$ full × $5\frac{3}{16}''$.

⟨1^4, 2-9^8⟩.

V cloth: red. White laid paper end papers. Laid paper flyleaves. Top edges gilt.

Noted as *shortly* PW Oct. 27, 1906. Advertised for Nov. 10 PW Nov. 3, 1906. Noted for *the 10th inst.* PW Nov. 3, 1906. Deposited Nov. 3, 1906. Published Nov. 10, 1906; publisher's records. BPL copy received Nov. 12, 1906. Listed PW Dec. 1, 1906.

AAS BPL H LC NYPL UV Y

15400. ... Arguments before the Committees on Patents of the Senate and House of Representatives ... December 7, 8, 10 and 11, 1906.

Washington: Government Printing Office. 1906.

Statement, pp. 96-97.

For fuller entry see No. 3494.

15401. UNDER THE CRUST ...

NEW YORK CHARLES SCRIBNER'S SONS 1907

Title-page in black and red.

Three printings noted:

FIRST PRINTING

⟨i⟩-⟨viii⟩, ⟨1⟩-307. Wove paper. Frontispiece and 7 plates inserted. $7\frac{9}{16}''$ × $5\frac{3}{16}''$.

⟨1-19^8, 20^6⟩.

SECOND (THIRD?) PRINTING

⟨i⟩-⟨viii⟩, ⟨1⟩-307. Wove paper. Title-leaf, a cancel, printed on laid paper. Frontispiece and 7 plates inserted.

⟨1-19^8, 20^6⟩.

THIRD (SECOND?) PRINTING

⟨i⟩-⟨viii⟩, ⟨1⟩-307; blank, p. ⟨308⟩; 4 pp. advertisements. Wove paper. Title-leaf, a cancel, printed on laid paper. Frontispiece and 7 plates inserted.

⟨1-20^8⟩.

At p. ⟨309⟩ is an advertisement for 5 titles, the first being *The Old Dominion*, which was published Feb. 29, 1908 (publisher's records); the second title is *Under the Crust*, with extracts from two reviews.

V cloth: green. Top edges gilt.

On copyright page: *Published, November, 1907*

Advertised PW Sept. 28, 1907. Advertised for Nov. 9 PW Oct. 26, 1907. Noted for Nov. 8 PW Nov. 2, 1907. Deposited Nov. 7, 1907. Published Nov. 9, 1907; publisher's records. Advertised as *just published* PW Nov. 9, 1907. BA copy (1st printing) received Nov. 13, 1907. Listed PW Nov. 23, 1907.

AAS (1st) B (1st) BA (1st) H (2nd) NYPL (3rd) UV (1st) Y (1st)

15402. Jamestown Tributes and Toasts ⟨Edited by⟩ Julia Wyatt Bullard ...

⟨Lynchburg, Virginia: J. P. Bell Company, Printers, 1907⟩

"The Old South," p. 177. A 2-line sentiment: "Her ivory palaces have been destroyed; but Myrrh, Aloes and Cassia still breathe among her dismantled ruins."

"A Vision of Raleigh," p. 32. "From his poem written for the Virginia Day Celebration at the Jamestown Exposition, June 12, 1907." Extracted from the longer poem. For full publication see below under 1909.

H

15403. THE LOSS OF THE FIDUCIARY PRINCIPLE. A PAPER PRESENTED BY THOMAS NELSON PAGE... AT THE THIRTIETH ANNUAL MEETING OF THE NEW YORK STATE BAR ASSOCIATION, HELD AT THE CITY OF ALBANY, N.Y., ON THE 15th AND 16th OF JANUARY, 1907, AND REPRINTED FROM THE THIRTIETH ANNUAL REPORT OF THE PROCEEDINGS OF THE ASSOCIATION.

⟨n.p., n.d., ALBANY, N.Y., 1907⟩

⟨1⟩-31. 9$\frac{1}{16}$″ × 6″.

⟨-⟩^{16}.

Printed gray laid paper wrapper.

Also appears in *New York State Bar Association Proceedings of the Thirtieth Annual Meeting Held at Albany January 15–16 1907 . . .* , Albany, 1907. Copy in NYPL.

H NYPL

15404. THE OLD DOMINION HER MAKING AND HER MANNERS...

CHARLES SCRIBNER'S SONS NEW YORK 1908

⟨i⟩-⟨xii⟩, ⟨1⟩-394; 4 pp. advertisements, blank leaf. 7$\frac{1}{2}$″ full × 5$\frac{3}{16}$″.

⟨1^6, 2-26^8⟩.

T cloth: green. Top edges gilt.

On copyright page: *Published February, 1908*

Noted for Feb. 29 in PW Feb. 22, 1908. Advertised for Feb. 29 in PW Feb. 22, 1908. NYPL copy received Feb. 28, 1908. Published Feb. 29, 1908; publisher's records. Deposited Feb. 29, 1908. Listed PW April 4, 1908.

AAS BA BPL H NYPL UV Y

15405. TOMMY TROT'S VISIT TO SANTA CLAUS...

NEW YORK CHARLES SCRIBNER'S SONS 1908

⟨i-viii⟩, 1-94, blank leaf. Frontispiece and 5 plates inserted. 8″ × 5$\frac{5}{8}$″.

⟨1^4, 2-7^8⟩.

V cloth: blue-gray.

On copyright page: *Published October, 1908*

Advertised for Oct. 10 PW Oct. 3, 1908. Published Oct. 10, 1908, 22,900 copies; publisher's records. Noted for *this week* PW Oct. 10, 1908. Advertised for Oct. 10 PW Oct. 10, 1908. Listed PW Oct. 24, 1908.

AAS BA H NYPL Y

15406. ROBERT E. LEE THE SOUTHERNER ...

CHARLES SCRIBNER'S SONS NEW YORK 1908

⟨i-ii⟩, ⟨i⟩-⟨xiv⟩, ⟨1⟩-312, 4 pp. advertisements. Portrait frontispiece and printed tissue inserted. Laid paper. 7$\frac{1}{2}$″ × 4$\frac{7}{8}$″.

⟨1-20^8, 21^6⟩.

T cloth: green. Top edges gilt.

On copyright page: *Published October, 1908*

Advertised PW Sept. 26, 1908. Published Oct. 24, 1908; 5000 copies; publisher's records. Deposited Oct. 24, 1908. Noted as *today* PW Oct. 24, 1908. BPL copy received Oct. 27, 1908. Listed PW Dec. 19, 1908. The London (Laurie) edition listed Bkr Feb. 19, 1909.

AAS BA NYPL Y

15407. JOHN MARVEL ASSISTANT...

NEW YORK CHARLES SCRIBNER'S SONS 1909

⟨i⟩-⟨x⟩, 1-573; blank, p. ⟨574⟩; 4 pp. advertisements. Frontispiece and 7 plates inserted. 7$\frac{7}{16}$″ scant × 4$\frac{15}{16}$″.

⟨1^8, 2-18^{16}, 19^{14}⟩.

Two states (probably printings) noted:

1

P. ⟨578⟩: The first title listed is *A Captured Santa Claus.*

2

P. ⟨578⟩: The first title listed is *Tommy Trot's Visit to Santa Claus.*

T cloth: green.

On copyright page: *Published October, 1909*

Advertised PW Sept. 25, 1909. Advertised for Oct. 16 PW Oct. 2, 1909. Noted for Oct. 16 PW Oct. 2, 1909. Published Oct. 16, 1909, 50,000 copies; publisher's records. BPL copy of the first state received Oct. 16, 1909. Advertised as *now ready* PW Oct. 16, 1909. Listed PW Oct. 16, 1909. The second printing advertised PW Oct. 30, 1909. The third printing advertised PW Dec. 18, 1909. As Vols. 15-16 of Page's collected works deposited Dec. 21, 1909. The London (Laurie) edition listed Bkr Feb. 25, 1910.

AAS (1st) BA (2nd) BPL (2nd) H (1st) UV (both) Y (both)

15408. The Official Blue Book of the Jamestown Ter-Centennial Exposition A D 1907 The Only Authorized History of the Celebration... ⟨Edited by Charles Russel Keiley⟩

The Colonial Publishing Company, Inc. Norfolk, Virginia, U.S.A. ⟨1909⟩

"The Vision of Raleigh," pp. 205-208. For a partial printing of this poem see *Jamestown Tributes and Toasts* ⟨1907⟩, above.

Eulogy of "the victor of Yorktown," p. 310.

UV

Works

1909

See above under 1906.

15409. The Old Virginia Gentleman and Other Sketches by George W. Bagby Edited with an Introduction by Thomas Nelson Page

New York Charles Scribner's Sons 1910

"Preface A Virginia Realist," pp. v-⟨xiii⟩.

For fuller entry see No. 576.

15410. ... ADDRESS ... WEST VIRGINIA MINING ASSOCIATION WASHINGTON, D.C. DECEMBER 16, 1910.

⟨n.p., n.d., 1910⟩

Not seen. Entry on the basis of a photographic copy.

Cover-title. At head of title: *No. 15*

⟨1⟩-7.

⟨-⟩⁴.

Printed paper wrapper.

VSL

15411. The Cliff-Dwellers An Account of Their Organization ...

Chicago 168 Michigan Avenue MCMX

Printed wrapper.

Letter of greeting, p. 48.

H NYPL

15412. MOUNT VERNON AND ITS PRES-ERVATION 1858-1910 THE ACQUISI-TION, RESTORATION, AND CARE OF THE HOME OF WASHINGTON BY THE MOUNT VERNON LADIES' ASSOCIA-TION OF THE UNION FOR OVER HALF A CENTURY ...

⟨THE KNICKERBOCKER PRESS, N.Y., FOR THE MOUNT VERNON LADIES' ASSOCIATION OF THE UNION, 1910⟩

⟨i⟩-⟨xii⟩, 1-84. Frontispiece and 15 plates inserted. Laid paper. 7⁷⁄₁₆″ × 5¹⁄₁₆″ full.

⟨-⟩⁶, ⟨1⟩-5⁸, 6².

Two printings noted:

FIRST PRINTING

As above.

SECOND PRINTING

Pagination as above but with the following variations: Printed on wove paper. In the copies examined the color prints of George and Martha Washington, which are present in the first printing, are not present.

⟨1⁶, 2-5⁸, 6¹⁰⟩. *Signed:* ⟨-⟩⁶, ⟨1⟩-5⁸, 6².

S cloth: red. Double laid paper flyleaves. Top edges gilt.

BPL (2nd) LC (1st) UV (2nd) Y (both)

15413. THOMAS NELSON PAGE ON THE CASE OF THE SOUTHERN APPALACH-IAN MOUNTAINEER EXTRACT FROM THE REPORT OF THE NINETEENTH CONTINENTAL CONGRESS OF THE NATIONAL SOCIETY OF THE DAUGH-TERS OF THE AMERICAN REVOLUTION APRIL 18, 1910, pp. 29-35 ...

⟨n.p., n.d., 1910?⟩

Caption-title. The above on p. ⟨1⟩.

Single cut sheet folded to make four pages.

⟨1⟩-3; blank, p. ⟨4⟩. 9⁷⁄₁₆″ full × 6¹⁄₈″. Laid paper.

Offprinted from *Proceedings of the Nineteenth Continental Congress of the Daughters of the American Revolution*, Washington, D. C., April 18th to 23rd, 1910; printed paper wrapper. Copy in LC.

For another (and briefer) version see *Thirteenth Report of the National Society of the Daughters of the American Revolution October 11, 1909, to October 11, 1910 ...*, Washington, 1911. Issued as Senate Document, No. 856, 61st Congress, 3d session; ordered printed March 2, 1911.

Y

15414. ROBERT E. LEE MAN AND SOLDIER ...

NEW YORK CHARLES SCRIBNER'S SONS 1911

⟨i⟩-xviii, ⟨1⟩-734. Inserted: Portrait frontispiece with printed tissue; 2 folded maps; 6 1-page maps; 1 2-page map. 8¼″ × 5¹¹⁄₁₆″.

⟨1-23¹⁶, 24⁸⟩.

T cloth: maroon. Top edges gilt.

On copyright page: *Published December, 1911*

Listed PW Nov. 16, 1911.

H Y

Works

1912

See above under 1906.

15415. THE LAND OF THE SPIRIT ...

CHARLES SCRIBNER'S SONS NEW YORK 1913

⟨i-ii⟩, ⟨i⟩-⟨xii⟩, ⟨1⟩-257. Frontispiece and 7 plates inserted. 7$\frac{7}{16}$" full × 5$\frac{1}{8}$" full.

⟨1-17⁸⟩.

V cloth: blue. Flyleaf at front.

On copyright page: *Published April, 1913*

Noted for April PW March 15, 1913. Noted as *published* PW April 12, 1913. Published April 19, 1913; publisher's records. Deposited April 22, 1913. Listed PW April 26, 1913. The London (Laurie) edition listed Bkr Aug. 29, 1913.

AAS H NYPL UV Y

15416. The Shepherd Who Watched by Night ... Reprinted from Scribner's Magazine by the Courtesy of the Author and the Publishers for the Board of Ministerial Relief and Sustentation of the Presbyterian Church in the United States ...

Charles Scribner's Sons, Publishers New York ⟨1913⟩

Printed drab brown paper wrapper.

The piece had prior publication in *The Land of the Spirit;* see preceding entry. Contains, not present in *The Land of the Spirit,* a letter by Page. p. ⟨2⟩.

Published May 9, 1913; publisher's records. Deposited May 14, 1913.

LC UV

15417. The Novels, Stories and Sketches of F. Hopkinson Smith ⟨Vol. 22⟩ Felix O'Day With an Introduction by Thomas Nelson Page

Charles Scribner's Sons New York 1915

"Introduction," pp. ix-xv.

H

15418. ... TOMMASO JEFFERSON APOS-TOLO DELLA LIBERTÀ (1743-1826) ... CON PREFAZIONE DEL SEN. MAG-GIORINO FERRARIS ...

R. BEMPORAD & FIGLIO, EDITORI FIRENZE MILANO ROMA PISA NAPOLI PALERMO ⟨n.d., 1918⟩

At head of title: AMERICANI ILLUSTRI RACCOLTA BIOGRAFICA DIRETTA DA H. NELSON GAY N.º 1-2

⟨I⟩-III. Frontispiece inserted. Laid paper. 7$\frac{5}{8}$" × 4$\frac{3}{4}$" full.

⟨1⟩-7⁸.

Printed white paper wrapper.

B H LC NYPL

15419. GREETINGS TO THE AMERICAN SOLDIERS IN ITALY FROM THOMAS NELSON PAGE AMERICAN AMBAS-SADOR TO ITALY

⟨n.p., n.d., ROME, 1918?⟩

Cover-title. Printed in black and colors.

⟨1⟩-7. 6$\frac{3}{4}$" × 4$\frac{5}{8}$".

⟨-⟩⁴.

Printed self-wrapper.

H NYPL

15420. The Old South Essays Social and Political With a New Preface ...

The Chautauqua Press Chautauqua, New York MCMXIX

Reprint save for "Preface to New Edition," pp. vii-viii. For first edition see under year 1892.

Deposited Aug. 6, 1919. Listed PW June 19, 1920; again listed July 3, 1920.

AAS Y

15421. ADDRESS AT THE THREE HUN-DREDTH ANNIVERSARY OF THE SET-TLEMENT OF JAMESTOWN ...

RICHMOND, VA. WHITTET & SHEPPERSON, PRINT-ERS 1919 ⟨i.e., 1920⟩

⟨1⟩-28, 2 blank leaves. Paper watermarked: WM. PENN BOOK 8$\frac{13}{16}$" × 5$\frac{3}{4}$".

⟨-⟩¹⁶.

Noted in the following states. The order is presumed correct.

A

No copyright notice present save for the following rubber stamped at the foot of the title-page: *Copyright 1920 by* / THE SOCIETY OF THE COLONIAL DAMES OF AMERICA / *in the State of Virginia*

Blue-gray paper wrapper. Front: ⟨ *fillet* ⟩ / *Address* / AT THE / *Three Hundredth Anniversary* / OF THE SETTLEMENT OF / JAMESTOWN / *By* / HON. THOMAS NELSON PAGE / ⟨*ornament*⟩ / 1607–1907 / ⟨ *fillet* ⟩

B

Rubber stamped copyright notice not present on title-page. Wrapper imprinted: ⟨ *fillet* ⟩ / *Address* / AT THE / *Three Hundredth Anniversary* / OF THE SETTLEMENT OF / JAMESTOWN / *By* / HON. THOMAS NELSON PAGE / COPYRIGHT, 1920, BY THE COLONIAL

DAMES OF AMERICA, IN THE STATE OF VIRGINIA / ⟨ornament⟩ / 1607–1907 / ⟨fillet⟩

Note: Dated 1907 by Johnson. Johnson almost surely in error.

Deposited March 3, 1920. MHS copy (state A) received March 17, 1920. BA copy (state A) received March 23, 1920. AAS copy (state A) received May 12, 1920. NYPL copy (state B) received May 15, 1920.

AAS (A)   BA (A)   MHS (A)   NYPL (B)   UV (A)

15422. Uncle Remus His Songs and His Sayings by Joel Chandler Harris with an Introduction by Thomas Nelson Page . . .

D. Appleton and Company New York MCMXX London

"Introduction to the Gift Edition," pp. v-vii.

Symbol (*1*) below text, p. 265.

Advertised PW Sept. 25, 1920; Oct. 9, 1920. Listed PW Nov. 13, 1920; Bkr Jan. 1921.

UV

15423. ITALY AND THE WORLD WAR . . .

NEW YORK CHARLES SCRIBNER'S SONS 1920

⟨i-ii⟩, ⟨i⟩-⟨xiv⟩, 1-422, blank leaf. Inserted: 5 1-page maps, 1 2-page map. 9″ × 6″.

⟨1-27⁸, 28⁴⟩.

T cloth: maroon.

On copyright page: *Published November, 1920*

Published Nov. 26, 1920; publisher's records. BPL copy received Nov. 26, 1920. Deposited Nov. 29, 1920. Listed PW Dec. 4, 1920. The London (Chapman & Hall) edition listed NA March 5, 1921; Bkr April, 1921. Advertised as *ready* NA March 12, 1921. Reviewed NA May 21, 1921.

AAS   BA   H   LC   UV   Y

15424. From the Rapidan to Richmond and the Spottsylvania Campaign . . . by William Meade Dame . . .

Baltimore Green-Lucas Company 1920

"Introduction," pp. xi-xii.

Deposited Feb. 9, 1921.

NYPL

15425. . . . DANTE AND HIS INFLUENCE STUDIES . . .

NEW YORK CHARLES SCRIBNER'S SONS 1922

At head of title: UNIVERSITY OF VIRGINIA FLORENCE LATHROP PAGE-BARBOUR FOUNDATION

⟨i⟩-xvi, 1-239. Frontispiece and 1 plate inserted. 7½″ × 5⅛″ scant.

⟨1-16⟩⁸.

T cloth: maroon. *Note:* All examined copies have the spine stamped in gold. A surviving copyright deposit copy (in LC) has the spine stamped in what may be black. Oxidization only?

On copyright page: *Published October, 1922*

Published Oct. 20, 1922; publisher's records. Deposited Oct. 23, 1922. H copy received Oct. 23, 1922. BA copy received Oct. 25, 1922. Listed PW Nov. 11, 1922. The London (Chapman & Hall) edition listed by NA Feb. 10, 1923.

AAS   BA   H   LC   UV   Y

15426. WASHINGTON AND ITS ROMANCE . . .

DOUBLEDAY, PAGE & COMPANY 1923 NEW YORK

⟨iii⟩-⟨xxxiv⟩, 1-196, 2 blank leaves. Frontispiece, title-page, and 6 plates inserted. 8¹³⁄₁₆″ × 6¾″.

⟨1-12⁸, 13⁴, 14-15⁸⟩.

T cloth: green. Color print pasted to front. Top edges gilt.

On copyright page: *First Edition*

BPL copy received Oct. 30, 1923. BA copy received Nov. 6, 1923. Deposited Nov. 23, 1923. The London (Heinemann) edition listed by PC Jan. 19, 1924.

AAS   B   BA   LC   NYPL   Y

15427. Virginian Writers of Fugitive Verse by Armistead C. Gordon . . .

New York James T. White & Co. ⟨1923⟩

"Introduction," pp. xiii-xv.

"The Shepherd of the Seas," p. 335, reprinted from *The Coast of Bohemia*, 1906.

H   UV

15428. THE RED RIDERS . . .

NEW YORK CHARLES SCRIBNER'S SONS 1924

⟨i-ii⟩, ⟨i⟩-⟨x⟩, ⟨1⟩-338, blank leaf. 7½″ scant × 5⅛″.

⟨1-22⁸⟩.

T cloth: red.

BA copy received Sept. 16, 1924. Deposited Sept. 19, 1924. Listed PW Sept. 27, 1924.

AAS   BA   H   NYPL   Y

15429. ON LINCOLN ... A SPEECH DE-
DELIVERED ... AT THE MASONIC
TEMPLE IN WASHINGTON ... AT THE
LINCOLN MEMORIAL CELEBRATION
ON FEBRUARY 14, 1909 A PAPER READ
BEFORE THE MASSACHUSETTS HIS-
TORICAL SOCIETY ON NOVEMBER 13,
1947 BY FREDERIC HAINES CURTISS

1949 T. O. METCALF CO. BOSTON

⟨1⟩-23. 9$\frac{1}{16}$″ × 6″. Wove paper watermarked
Strathmore Text USA

⟨-⟩¹².

Printed tan paper wrapper.

BA   MHS   UV

SECTION II

IN THIS SECTION are listed collections of reprinted material issued under Page's name; sheet music; separate editions. See *Section III* for a list of books by others containing material by Page reprinted from earlier books.

15430. In Ole Virginia or Marse Chan and Other Stories . . .

Ward, Lock and Co., London: Warwick House, Salisbury Square, E. C. New York: Bond Street ⟨n.d., 1889⟩

Pictorial paper boards.

Listed Ath Feb. 9, 1889; PC Feb. 15, 1889. A new edition, with an introduction by T. P. O'Connor, listed PC March 11, 1893, with Ward, Lock, Bowden & Co., as publisher.

Under the title *In Ole Virginia and the Burial of the Guns* announced as a Heinemann publication PC Sept. 30, 1899; no further word seen; presumably unpublished.

15431. In Ole Virginia or Marse Chan and Other Stories . . . with an Etching by W. L. Sheppard

New York Charles Scribner's Sons 1890

Cloth, cameo-like ornament on the front cover.

15432. Works.

New York: Charles Scribner's Sons, 1891–1894.

Not seen. Not located. Entry on the basis of Foley, p. 216, and *The American Catalogue . . . 1890–1895 . . . ;* see below.

Presumably contains no material here first collected.

Described by Foley as the *Library Edition*, in 4 volumes, issued 1893.

Described by *American Catalogue* as in five volumes, designated the *New Uniform Edition*, comprising the following volumes: *The Burial of the Guns; Elsket and Other Stories; In Ole Virginia; The Old South; On Newfound River.* Issued 1891–1894.

See entry No. 15397 for Page's collected works.

15433. Marse Chan A Tale of Old Virginia . . .

Charles Scribner's Sons New York, 1892

Deposited Oct. 14, 1892. Published Oct. 15, 1892; publisher's records. Listed PW Oct. 29, 1892. The London (Sampson Low) edition listed Ath Feb. 18, 1893. Reprinted from *In Ole Virginia . . . ,* 1887.

15434. Meh Lady A Story of the War . . .

Charles Scribner's Sons New York, 1893

Listed PW Oct. 21, 1893. The London (Sampson Low) edition listed Ath Nov. 4, 1893. Reprinted from *In Ole Virginia . . . ,* 1887.

15435. Polly A Christmas Recollection . . .

Charles Scribner's Sons New York, 1894

Deposited Oct. 5, 1894. Published Oct. 6, 1894; publisher's records. BA copy received Oct. 9, 1894. Listed PW Oct. 13, 1894. Reprinted from *In Ole Virginia . . . ,* 1887.

15436. Unc' Edinburg A Plantation Echo . . .

Charles Scribner's Sons New York, 1895

Deposited Sept. 28, 1895. Published Sept. 28, 1895; publisher's records. Reprinted from *In Ole Virginia . . . ,* 1887.

15437. In Ole Virginia . . . Illustrated . . .

New York Charles Scribner's Sons MDCCCXCVI

Deposited Oct. 10, 1896. Listed PW Oct. 17, 1896.

15438. Pastime Stories . . .

New York Charles Scribner's Sons 1898

Deposited May 14, 1898.

15439. A Captured Santa Claus . . .

Charles Scribner's Sons New York 1902

On copyright page: *Published, October, 1902*

Advertised as *published to-day* PW Nov. 1, 1902. Listed PW Nov. 8, 1902. Reprinted from *Among the Camps,* 1891.

15440. The Page Story Book Edited by Frank E. Spaulding . . . and Catherine T. Bryce . . .

New York Charles Scribner's Sons 1906

Deposited May 12, 1906. Listed PW May 19, 1906.

15441. Three Poems by Thomas Nelson Page Set to Music by Ernest Schelling "Faded Spray of Mignonette" . . .

New York: G. Schirmer ⟨1907⟩

Sheet music. Cover-title. Plate number: 19404.

A full suite (not seen by BAL) comprises the following titles in addition to the above: "Love-Song" and "The Harbour-Light." All reprinted from *The Coast of Bohemia,* 1906.

15442. The Stranger's Pew . . .

New York Charles Scribner's Sons 1914

Printed boards, cloth shelfback. Reprinted from *The Land of the Spirit,* 1913.

On copyright page: *Published August, 1914*

Received at LC Sept. 1, 1914. Listed PW Sept. 5, 1914.

15443. The Shepherd Who Watched by Night . . .

New York Charles Scribner's Sons 1916

On copyright page: *Published September, 1916*

Published Sept. 9, 1916, 3000 copies; paper boards, and, a few in leather; publisher's records. Received at LC Sept. 14, 1916. Listed PW Sept. 16, 1916. Reprinted from *The Land of the Spirit,* 1913.

15444. Mount Vernon and Its Preservation 1858–1910 . . . ⟨by⟩ Thomas Nelson Page

⟨New York, 1932⟩

On copyright page: *Revised Edition Copyright, 1932* . . .

Page material reprinted from the 1910 edition.

Received at LC May 11, 1932. Deposited for copyright June 15, 1932.

15445. The Stable of the Inn . . .

⟨n.p., 1959⟩

*This limited edition was privately printed for the friends of Aldus Printers . . . Christmas, 1959–––*Colophon.

Printed paper boards. Reprinted from *The Land of the Spirit,* 1913.

The following books by authors other than Page contain material by him reprinted from other books.

Burdett's Negro Dialect Recitations and Readings Edited . . . by . . . James S. Burdett.

New York: Excelsior Publishing House. 29 and 31 Beekman Street. ⟨1884⟩

Pictorial paper wrapper.

. . . Stories of the Railway

New York Charles Scribner's Sons 1893

At head of title: *Stories from Scribner*

Printed paper wrapper; cloth; half calf.

"'Run to Seed,'" pp. ⟨103⟩-148; reprinted from *Elsket* . . . , 1891.

Advertised PW May 13, 1893. BA copy received May 23, 1893. Listed PW June 3, 1893.

. . . Stories of the South

New York . . . 1893

For fuller entry see BAL, Vol. 3, p. 400.

Songs of the South . . . Edited by Jennie Thornley Clarke . . .

Philadelphia . . . 1896

For fuller entry see BAL, Vol. 5, p. 295.

An American Anthology 1787–1899 . . . Edited by Edmund Clarence Stedman . . .

Boston . . . M DCCCC

For fuller entry see No. 3082.

Modern Eloquence . . . ⟨Edited by⟩ Thomas B Reed . . .

. . . Philadelphia ⟨1900; *i.e.,* 1901⟩

For comment see entry No. 3467.

Fifty-Two Stories of School Life and after for Girls . . . Edited by Alfred H. Miles . . .

London: Hutchinson & Co., 34, Paternoster Row. ⟨1903⟩

Listed Ath Nov. 14, 1903.

Short Story Classics (American) . . . Edited by William Patten . . .

. . . New York ⟨1905⟩

5 Vols. For comment see entry No. 6378.

Poems of American History Collected . . . by Burton Egbert Stevenson

Boston . . . 1908

For fuller entry see in Joaquin Miller, *Section One.*

300 Latest Stories by 300 Famous Story Tellers . . .

. . . New York ⟨1914; *i.e.,* not before 1915⟩

For fuller entry see No. 12001.

Headlights and Markers An Anthology of Railroad Stories Edited by Frank P. Donovan, Jr. and Robert Selph Henry

New York Creative Age Press, Inc. ⟨1946⟩

REFERENCES

The Men Who Make Our Novels by George Gordon

New York Moffat, Yard & Company 1919

Thomas Nelson Page A Memoir of a Virginia Gentleman by His Brother Rosewell Page . . .

New York Charles Scribner's Sons 1923

Trade format: Paper boards, cloth shelf back, printed paper label on spine. Leaf: $7\frac{7}{16}''$ × $5\frac{3}{16}''$.

Limited format: Paper boards, paper vellum shelfback, printed paper label on spine. Leaf: $9\frac{1}{16}''$ × $6\frac{1}{16}''$. Certificate of issue: *Of This Edition One Hundred Copies Have Been Printed. This Copy Is No.*

On copyright page: *Published May, 1923*

Commemorative Tributes to Page by Robert
Underwood Johnson Wilson by Bliss Perry Bacon
by Charles A. Platt Prepared for the American
Academy of Arts and Letters 1924

⟨n.p.⟩ American Academy of Arts and Letters
1925 . . .

Academy Publication No. 50. Printed paper
wrapper.

Thomas Nelson Page by Theodore L. Gross . . .
Twayne Publishers, Inc. New York ⟨1967⟩
Printed paper boards.

FRANCIS PARKMAN

1 8 2 3 − 1 8 9 3

Not to be confused with another of the same name, 1788–1852, author of *An Offering of Sympathy to Parents Bereaved of Their Children*, Boston, 1830; *A Sermon Delivered in the New North Church, in Boston, Jan. XXVIII, 1849, on Resigning His Pastoral Charge*, Boston, 1849.

Note: Parkman's histories were reprinted many times, some of the reprints were revised. It is entirely probable that virtually no printing was issued unaltered. Those with added material, or with alterations observed by BAL, are here listed; but it is by no means certain that all altered or revised editions have been seen.

15446. THE CALIFORNIA AND OREGON TRAIL: BEING SKETCHES OF PRAIRIE AND ROCKY MOUNTAIN LIFE...

NEW-YORK: GEORGE P. PUTNAM, 155 BROADWAY. LONDON: PUTNAM'S AMERICAN AGENCY, REMOVED FROM PATERNOSTER ROW TO J. CHAPMAN, 142 STRAND. 1849.

For other editions see below under years 1852, 1872, 1892, 1943.

Three printings noted:

FIRST PRINTING

1-448; plus publisher's catalog. The catalog has been noted in two forms; sequence, if any, not known:

Terminal Catalog A: 2 leaves paged 3-6.

Terminal Catalog B: 4 leaves paged 3-10.

$7\frac{1}{2}'' \times 4\frac{15}{16}''$. Frontispiece and vignette title-page inserted.

⟨1-2⟩, 3-5, ⟨6⟩, 7-8, ⟨9-10⟩, 11-⟨12⟩, 13-14, ⟨15-18⟩^{12}, 19^8. Plus: A final gathering of advertisements; see above under pagination.

Pp. 1-2: Devoted to advertisements.

On copyright page: Imprint of *Leavitt, Trow & Co.*

Terminal catalog: Inserted; either two leaves or four.

No page reference on the frontispiece.

Author's name on spine stamped from a sans-serif face; or, a serifed face; sequence, if any, not known.

SECOND PRINTING

⟨1⟩-448; advertisements, pp. ⟨449-455⟩, paged: 1-6, 8; verso of p. 8 blank. Frontispiece and vignette title-page inserted.

⟨1-2⟩, 3-5, ⟨6⟩, 7-8, ⟨9-10⟩, 11-⟨12⟩, 13-14, ⟨15-18⟩, 19^{12}.

Pp. ⟨1-2⟩: Blank.

On copyright page: Imprint of *Leavitt, Trow & Co.*

Terminal catalog: Integral; not an insert.

No page reference on the frontispiece.

Author's name on spine noted only in a serifed face.

THIRD PRINTING

⟨1⟩-448; advertisements, pp. ⟨449-455⟩, paged: 1-6, 8; verso of p. 8 blank. Frontispiece and vignette title-page inserted.

⟨1-2⟩, 3-5, ⟨6⟩, 7-8, ⟨9-10⟩, 11-⟨12⟩, 13-14, ⟨15-18⟩, 19^{12}.

Pp. ⟨1-2⟩: Blank.

Copyright page: Imprint of *Leavitt, Trow & Co.* not present.

Terminal catalog: Integral; not an insert.

The statement *See page 290* appears on the frontispiece.

Author's name on spine noted only in a serifed face.

T cloth: black; blue; brown; slate. Off-white end papers. Flyleaves. The author's name on the spine occurs in two styles; sequence not determined:

A: Stamped from a sans-serif face. Noted on first printing sheets only.

B: Stamped from a serifed face; noted on first printing sheets; and, also on reprints.

Note: Also reported in printed paper wrapper. Advertised as in both cloth; and, paper, LW March 10, 1849. Not seen by BAL.

Note: The cloth-bound copies above are decorated on the sides with an arabesque ornament, the undecorated central part measuring 6⅞″ tall.

Two copies of the first printing have been seen, perhaps an experimental binding; the central part of the side stamping measures 3⅞″. Neither frontispiece nor vignette title-page present. Bound in black T cloth; no terminal catalog. Yellow end papers. Flyleaves. The copies examined were in the possession of Mr. Howard S. Mott, Sheffield, Mass.; and, Miss Peggy Christian, Los Angeles, Cal.

First published in K Feb. 1847 to Feb. 1849. Advertised as *in press* LW Feb. 17, 1849. Noted as published *this week* LW March 10, 1849. Listed LW March 17, 1849. The second edition advertised LW April 7, 1849. The third edition advertised LW April 21, 1849. Distributed in London (Chapman); noted as *just imported* Ath April 14, 1849.

AAS (3d, binding B) H (1st, binding A; 1st, binding B; 2d, binding B) LC (1st, binding B) Y (1st, binding A; 2d, binding B; 3d, binding B)

15447. HISTORY OF THE CONSPIRACY OF PONTIAC, AND THE WAR OF THE NORTH AMERICAN TRIBES AGAINST THE ENGLISH COLONIES AFTER THE CONQUEST OF CANADA . . . IN TWO VOLUMES . . .

LONDON: RICHARD BENTLEY, NEW BURLINGTON STREET, PUBLISHER IN ORDINARY TO HER MAJESTY. 1851.

For first American edition see next entry.

Note: Collation tentative.

1: ⟨i⟩-xvi, ⟨1⟩-338, 2 pp. advertisements. 2 folded maps inserted. 7½″ × 4¾″.

2: ⟨i⟩-⟨viii⟩, ⟨1⟩-316. Folded map inserted.

1: ⟨A⟩⁸, B-I, K-P¹², Q². *So signed.*

2: ⟨A⟩⁴, B-I, K-O¹², P². *So signed.*

Probably issued in cloth.

Advertised as *in the press* Ath July 19, 1851. Advertised for *the 25th* Ath Aug. 9, 1851. Advertised for *Tuesday* ⟨*the 19th*⟩ Ath Aug. 16, 1851. Advertised for *the 20th* PC Aug. 16, 1851. Advertised for *next week* Ath Aug. 23, 1851. Listed Ath Aug. 23, 1851; LG Aug. 23, 1851. Advertised as *just published* Ath Aug. 30, 1851. Listed PC Sept. 1, 1851. Advertised as *now ready* Ath Sept. 8, 1851; *just published* PC Sept. 16, 1851.

NYPL

15448. HISTORY OF THE CONSPIRACY OF PONTIAC, AND THE WAR OF THE NORTH AMERICAN TRIBES AGAINST THE ENGLISH COLONIES AFTER THE CONQUEST OF CANADA . . .

BOSTON: CHARLES C. LITTLE AND JAMES BROWN. LONDON: RICHARD BENTLEY. 1851.

For prior London publication see preceding entry. Also see below under years 1855, 1868, 1870.

⟨i⟩-xxiv, ⟨1⟩-630, blank leaf. 2 full-page maps and 2 folded maps inserted. 9⅛″ full × 5⅞″.

⟨a⟩-b⁶, A-Z⁶, AA-ZZ⁶, AAA⁴. *Also signed:* ⟨A⟩-C⁴, 1-79⁴.

Three bindings of unknown sequence noted; the designations are wholly arbitrary:

BINDING A

A cloth: black; green; purple-slate. T cloth: brown (faded black?); black; slate. The blindstamped ornament on the sides is 7⁵⁄₁₆″ tall. Publisher's spine imprint: LITTLE AND BROWN. Flyleaves. Peach end papers; yellow end papers.

BINDING B

T cloth: black. The blindstamped ornament on the sides is 7⁵⁄₁₆″ tall. Publisher's spine imprint: LITTLE & BROWN Flyleaves. Peach end papers; yellow end papers.

BINDING C

T cloth: green. The blindstamped ornament on the sides is 4⅞″ tall. Publisher's spine imprint: LITTLE AND BROWN Flyleaves. Yellow end papers.

Reviewed (from advance sheets?) K July, 1851. H copy (rebound) received Sept. 13, 1851. Deposited Sept. 20, 1851. Listed LW Sept. 27, 1851. Listed NLA Oct. 15, 1851. Reviewed NAR Oct. 1851; AWR Nov. 1851.

AAS (A) H (A) NYPL (A,B) UV (A,C) Y (A)

15449. Prairie and Rocky Mountain Life; or, the California and Oregon Trail . . . Third Edition.

New York: George P. Putnam, 155 Broadway 1852.

For first edition see above under year 1849.

"Preface to the Third Edition," dated at end *February 1st, 1852*, pp. ⟨3-4⟩.

Two states of the binding have been seen; the order of presentation presumed correct:

A

Spine lettered in capital letters only. A copyright deposit copy thus.

B

Spine lettered in capital and lower case letters.

Advertised as *now ready* NLG March 15, 1852. Deposited April 26, 1852.

BA (A) LC (A, being a deposit copy) UV (B)

15450. History of the Conspiracy of Pontiac . . .

Boston: Little, Brown and Company. 1855.

For first edition see above under year 1851.

Additions to footnotes on pp. 188, 250, 475; and, to "Appendix F," pp. 624-625.

Advertised as *just published* APC Oct. 20, 1855.

MHS

15451. VASSALL MORTON. A NOVEL . . .

BOSTON: PHILLIPS, SAMPSON AND COMPANY. 1856.

$\langle 1 \rangle$-414, 6 pp. advertisements. $7\frac{3}{8}'' \times 4\frac{3}{4}''$ full.

$\langle 1 \rangle$-35^6.

A cloth: red. T cloth: black; brown; purple. Yellow end papers. Flyleaves.

Advertised for May 24 CRN May 17, 1856. Advertised as *now ready* CRN May 24, 1856. Listed CRN May 24, 1856. Listed PC July 16, 1856. Advertised by Trübner as an importation Ath July 19, 1856.

AAS BA H MHS NYPL

15452. PIONEERS OF FRANCE IN THE NEW WORLD . . .

BOSTON: LITTLE, BROWN AND COMPANY. 1865.

For another edition see below under year 1886.

General title-page, p. $\langle i \rangle$: *France and England in North America. A Series of Historical Narratives . . . Part First . . .*

$\langle i \rangle$-$\langle xxiv \rangle$, $\langle 1 \rangle$-420. Laid paper. Portrait frontispiece and 2 maps inserted. $8\frac{3}{16}''$ full $\times 5\frac{1}{2}''$.

$\langle 1\text{-}2^6, 3\text{-}28^8, 29^2 \rangle$. *Signed:* $\langle a \rangle$-b^6, 1-35^6.

C cloth: reddish-brown; green; dull purple. Brown-coated end papers. Laid or wove flyleaves.

Also a large paper format. Precise date of publication not known. Imprint: *Boston: Little, Brown and Company 1866.* Leaf: $9\frac{11}{16}'' \times 6\frac{1}{2}''$. On verso of title-page: *Seventy-five copies printed. No. $\langle$space for number$\rangle$* Locations: AAS BPL UV

Deposited Sept. 1, 1865? Advertised for Sept. 2 ALG Sept. 1, 1865. MHS copy received Sept. 6, 1865. Noticed ALG Sept. 15, 1865. Listed ALG Sept. 15, 1865. A copy in H presented by Parkman to T. W. Parsons, Oct. 17, 1865. Listed PC Nov. 1, 1865. Advertised by Low as a *recent importation* PC Jan. 17, 1866. The Routledge (London) edition listed Bkr Feb. 1, 1868.

AAS BPL H MHS Y

15453. THE BOOK OF ROSES . . .

BOSTON: J. E. TILTON AND COMPANY. 1866.

$\langle 1 \rangle$-225, blank leaf. Vignette title-page inserted. Also inserted: 2 plates, each reckoned in the printed pagination. $7\frac{1}{2}'' \times 5\frac{1}{16}''$.

$\langle 1^9, 2\text{-}5^8, 6^9, 7\text{-}14^8 \rangle$. $\langle 1 \rangle_6$ and $\langle 6 \rangle_6$ inserted. *Signed:* $\langle 1 \rangle$-14^8, $\langle 15 \rangle^2$.

C cloth: green; purple. V cloth: green. Brown-coated on white end papers. Flyleaves of either laid or wove paper.

BPL copy received April 21, 1866. BA copy received April 24, 1866. Listed ALG May 1, 1866. Deposited May 5, 1866. Listed Bkr May 31, 1866; PC July 2, 1866.

AAS H

PIONEERS OF FRANCE IN THE NEW WORLD . . .

BOSTON . . . 1866.

Large paper edition. See above under year 1865.

15454. Boston Athenæum. Special Meeting of the Proprietors.

Boston, February 25, 1867 . . .

Printed self-wrapper. Cover-title.

Signed at end by Parkman and others.

NYPL

15455. THE JESUITS IN NORTH AMERICA IN THE SEVENTEENTH CENTURY . . .

BOSTON: LITTLE, BROWN, AND COMPANY. 1867.

General title-page, p. $\langle i \rangle$: *France and England in North America. A Series of Historical Narratives . . . Part Second . . .*

$\langle i \rangle$-$\langle xcii \rangle$, $\langle 1 \rangle$-463. Laid paper. Map inserted. $8\frac{3}{16}''$ full $\times 5\frac{1}{2}''$.

$\langle 1\text{-}5^8, 6^6, 7\text{-}35^8 \rangle$. *Signed:* $\langle a \rangle$-g^6, h^4, 1-38^6, 39^4.

C cloth: reddish-brown; green; dull purple. Brown-coated end papers. Laid paper flyleaves.

Also a large paper format. Precise date of publication not known. Imprint: *Boston: Little, Brown, and Company. 1867.* Leaf: $9\frac{9}{16}'' \times 6\frac{1}{2}''$. On p. $\langle iv \rangle$: *Seventy-five copies printed. No. $\langle$space for number$\rangle$* Locations: BPL UV

Advertised for May 25 ALG May 15, 1867. Deposited May 23, 1867? A copy in H inscribed by Parkman May 27, 1867. Listed ALG June 15, 1867. A copy of the *Second Edition*, dated 1867, in BPL. The Routledge (London) edition listed Bkr Feb. 1, 1868.

BA H MHS Y

15456. Historical Account of Bouquet's Expedition against the Ohio Indians, in 1764. $\langle$By William Smith$\rangle$ With Preface by Francis Parkman . . .

Cincinnati, O. Robert Clarke & Co. 1868.

"Prefatory," pp. ⟨xi⟩-xvi.

"Biographical Sketch of Henry Bouquet," pp ⟨xvii⟩-xxiii, translated by Parkman.

H copy presented to Parkman by the publisher Oct. 20, 1868. AAS copy inscribed by the publisher Oct. 26, 1868.

AAS   BA   H   MHS   Y

15457. History of the Conspiracy of Pontiac . . . Fourth Edition, Revised.

  Boston: Little, Brown, and Company. 1868.

Contains revisions, additions, and a brief "Prefatory Note to the Fourth Edition," p. ⟨v⟩, dated at end *September, 1867.*

For first edition see above under 1851.

Two printings have been noted. The sequence has not been established and the designations are for identification only. The following is sufficient for identification:

PRINTING A

P. ⟨i⟩: Title-page

P. ⟨v⟩: *Prefatory Note . . .*

PRINTING B

P. ⟨i⟩: Fly-title-page

P. ⟨vi⟩: *Prefatory Note . . .*

AAS (A)   H (A)   Y (A,B)

15458. THE DISCOVERY OF THE GREAT WEST . . .

  BOSTON: LITTLE, BROWN, AND COMPANY. 1869.

For another edition see below under year 1879.

General title-page, p. ⟨i⟩: *France and England in North America. A Series of Historical Narratives . . . Part Third . . .*

⟨i⟩-⟨xxiv⟩, ⟨1⟩-425, blank leaf. Map inserted. 8⅜" scant × 5⁷⁄₁₆" full.

⟨1⁸, 2⁴, 3-28⁸, 29⁴, 30²⟩. *Signed:* ⟨a⟩⁵, b⁷, 1-2, ⟨3⟩, 4-35⁶, 36⁴.

C cloth: green; dull purple; terra-cotta. C cloth: green, embossed with a scattering of small stars. Brown-coated end papers. Flyleaves.

Also a large paper format. Precise date of publication not known. Imprint: *Boston: Little, Brown, and Company. 1870.* Leaf: 9⅝" scant × 6½". On verso of title-page: *Seventy-five copies printed. No.* ⟨*space for number*⟩ Locations: AAS UV

Deposited Oct. 25, 1869. BPL copy received Oct. 27, 1869. Listed ALG Nov. 1, 1869. The London (Murray) edition advertised as *forthcoming* Ath Nov. 6, 1869; listed PC Dec. 8, 1869.

AAS   BPL   H   MHS   Y

15459. The Conspiracy of Pontiac and the Indian War after the Conquest of Canada . . . Sixth Edition, Revised, with Additions . . .

  Boston: Little, Brown, and Company. 1870.

For first edition see above under year 1851.

2 Vols. Revised.

A copy in MHS inscribed by Parkman Dec. 20, 1870. A copy in BPL received Dec. 21, 1870. Listed ALG Jan. 2, 1871; PC Feb. 1, 1871. Advertised ALG March 1, 1871, as in cloth, half cloth, calf.

H   MHS

THE DISCOVERY OF THE GREAT WEST . . .

  BOSTON . . . 1870.

Large paper edition. See above under year 1869.

15460. To the Alumni. ⟨Text: 22 lines in 3 paragraphs. At end: 10 names including that of Francis Parkman⟩

⟨n.p., n.d., probably Cambridge, Mass., 1871⟩

Single leaf. Printed on recto only. 7¹⁵⁄₁₆" × 4¹⁵⁄₁₆".

Addressed to Harvard alumni on behalf of J. Elliot Cabot, a nominee for post as a Harvard overseer.

Gd

15461. The Oregon Trail . . . Fourth Edition, Revised

  Boston Little, Brown, and Company 1872

For first edition see above under year 1849.

". . . The necessary corrections have been made in the present edition."---P. ⟨v⟩.

"Preface to the Fourth Edition," dated at end *March 30, 1872,* pp. ⟨vii⟩-ix.

Listed WTC May 9, 1872.

H   Y

15462. THE OLD RÉGIME IN CANADA . . .

  BOSTON: LITTLE, BROWN, AND COMPANY. 1874.

For another edition see below under year 1894.

General title-page, p. ⟨i⟩: *France and England in North America. A Series of Historical Narratives . . . Part Fourth . . .*

⟨i⟩-xvi, ⟨1⟩-448. 2-page map inserted between pp. xvi-⟨1⟩. 8³⁄₁₆" × 5½".

⟨-⟩⁸, ⟨1⟩-28⁸.

Note: It is probable that the book went into two printings, distinguishable as follows:

PRESUMED FIRST PRINTING

Sheets bulk 1¹⁄₁₆" more or less.

P. ⟨iii⟩: A comma is present after the word WORLD

P. ⟨iii⟩: A broken comma is present after the name LITTLE

P. ⟨403⟩: Lines 7-9 of the *Extrait* printed from un-battered types.

P. 417: In some copies the 7, in signature 27, is present only as a vestige.

P. 419: In some copies the terminal letters of the last two lines are battered; in other copies the types are unbattered.

PRESUMED SECOND PRINTING

Sheets bulk 1¼″ scant.

P. ⟨iii⟩: Comma not present after the word WORLD

P. ⟨iii⟩: The comma after the name LITTLE is so broken as to seem a period.

P. ⟨403⟩: Lines 7-9 of the *Extrait* printed from battered types.

P. 417: The 7, in signature 27, present in all examined copies; the 7 replaced.

P. 419: In all examined copies the terminal letters of the last two lines are battered.

First printing sheets have been seen in the following three states of binding; sequence not determined. The designations are for identification only:

STATE A BINDING

C cloth: blue; purple. P cloth: green; terra-cotta. Sides stamped in blind with an ornamented rules frame. At center of front, goldstamped, vignette of an Indian warrior. Spine goldstamped: ⟨*fillet*⟩ / THE / OLD RÉGIME / IN / CANADA. / ⟨*diamond rule*⟩ / PARKMAN / ⟨*ornament*⟩ / LITTLE.BROWN & CO. ⟨*sic*⟩ / ⟨*fillet*⟩ Brown-coated end papers. Flyleaves.

STATE B BINDING

P cloth: blue. Sides stamped in blind with an ornamented frame. At center of front, gold-stamped, vignette of an Indian warrior. Spine goldstamped: ⟨*fillet*⟩ / PARKMAN'S / WORKS / ⟨*diamond rule*⟩ / THE / OLD RÉGIME / IN / CANADA. / LITTLE.BROWN & CO. ⟨*sic*⟩ / ⟨*fillet*⟩ Brown-coated end papers. Flyleaves.

STATE C BINDING

P cloth: terra-cotta. Sides stamped in blind with an ornamented rules frame. The Indian vignette not present. Spine goldstamped: ⟨*fillet*⟩ / THE / OLD RÉGIME / IN / CANADA. / ⟨*diamond rule*⟩ / PARKMAN / ⟨*ornament*⟩ / LITTLE.BROWN & CO. ⟨*sic*⟩ / ⟨*fillet*⟩ Brown-coated end papers. Flyleaves.

Also a large paper format. Precise date of publication not known. Imprint: *Boston: Little.* ⟨*sic*⟩ *Brown, and Company. 1874.* Leaf: 9⅝″ × 6⅝″. On p. ⟨iv⟩: *Seventy-five copies printed. No.* ⟨*space for number*⟩ Locations: AAS UV

PW Sept. 5, 1874, noted receipt of a set of sheets. MHS copy (1st) inscribed by Parkman Sept. 22,

1874. H copy (1st, rebound) inscribed by Parkman Sept. 24, 1874. NYPL copy (1st) inscribed by Parkman Sept. 26, 1874. MHS copy (1st) inscribed by Parkman Sept. 29, 1874. A copy in H (1st, rebound) inscribed by Parkman Sept. 29, 1874. Listed PW Oct. 10, 1874. A copy in H (2d) inscribed by Parkman Dec. 1874.

British Publication

Advertised by Low under "new American books now ready" PC Oct. 16, 1874. Boston edition reviewed Ath Oct. 31, 1874. Boston edition listed Bkr Dec. 1, 1874. Boston edition advertised by Trübner Bkr Dec. 1, 1874. Listed (English printing?) Ath Jan. 23, 1875; PC March 16, 1875.

AAS (1st)   BPL (1st)   H (1st, 2nd)   LC (1st, being a deposit copy)   MHS (1st, 2nd)   NYPL (1st)   Y (1st)

15463. COUNT FRONTENAC AND NEW FRANCE UNDER LOUIS XIV...

BOSTON: LITTLE, BROWN, & COMPANY. 1877.

General title-page, p. ⟨iii⟩: *France and England in North America. A Series of Historical Narratives... Part Fifth...*

⟨i⟩-xvi, ⟨1⟩-463. 2-page map inserted between pp. xvi-⟨1⟩. 8¼″ scant × 5⁷⁄₁₆″ full.

⟨-⟩⁸, 1-29⁸.

Two states noted. The sequence has not been firmly established and the designations are for identification only.

A

P. ⟨iii⟩ (the general title-page) reads: ... / "OREGON TRAIL," "THE OLD REGIME IN CANADA," ETC. / ...

B

P. ⟨iii⟩ (the general title-page) reads: ... / "OREGON TRAIL," ETC. / ... *Note:* The *Fourth Edition,* 1877, thus; the *Seventh Edition,* 1880, thus.

P cloth: green; terra-cotta. Brown-coated end papers. Flyleaves.

Also a large paper format. Precise date of publication not known. Imprint: *As above.* Leaf: 9⁹⁄₁₆″ × 6½″. On p. ⟨vi⟩: *Seventy-five copies printed. Note:* The general title-page is in *State B.* Locations: AAS UV

Note: A copy (State B sheets) has been seen with a single leaf of advertisements inserted at the front: *PARKMAN'S WORKS. The Pioneers of France in the New World...*

A copy of *State A* (in H, rebound) inscribed by Parkman Sept. 8, 1877. Advertised for Sept. 12, 1877, PW Sept. 8, 1877. Listed PW Sept. 15, 1877. A copy of *State A* (MHS) received Nov. 15, 1877. Advertised as in cloth; and, half calf, PW Dec. 8, 1877. A copy of *State B* (in BA) received Dec. 20, 1877, inscribed by Parkman Dec. 1877.

British Publication

Advertised as *a new American book* PC Nov. 2, 1877. Boston edition listed PC Nov. 16, 1877. Reviewed Ath Jan. 5, 1878. Advertised as a Trübner importation Bkr Jan. 1878.

AAS (A)   H (A)   MHS (A)   UV (B)   Y (A)

15464. Essays from the North American Review. Edited by Allen Thorndike Rice.

New York: D. Appleton and Company, 549 and 551 Broadway. 1879.

"James Fenimore Cooper," pp. ⟨358⟩-376. Reprinted from NAR Jan. 1852.

For fuller entry see No. 679.

15465. La Salle and the Discovery of the Great West . . . Eleventh Edition. Revised, with Additions.

Boston: Little, Brown, and Company. 1879.

A new edition of *The Discovery of the Great West*, 1869.

"Preface of the Eleventh Edition," dated *10 December, 1878*, pp. ⟨vii⟩-x.

Advertised for Sept. 15 PW Sept. 6, 1879. BA copy received Sept. 16, 1879. MHS copy inscribed by Parkman Sept. 22, 1879. Advertised by Trübner as an importation Bkr Dec. 2, 1879. Listed PW Dec. 18, 1879.

AAS   H   MHS   UV   Y

15466. SOME OF THE REASONS AGAINST WOMAN SUFFRAGE

For another version of this see "The Woman Question" in *Representative Selections . . .* ⟨1938⟩, below.

According to the Riverside Press records there were at least eight printings of this pamphlet; BAL has noted the following. *Printing A* is presumed to be the first printing.

PRINTING A

SOME OF THE REASONS / AGAINST / WOMAN SUFFRAGE. / BY / FRANCIS PARKMAN. / PRINTED AT THE REQUEST OF AN ASSOCIATION / OF WOMEN. / ⟨n.p., n.d., 1883⟩

Cover-title.

⟨1⟩-16. $9\frac{7}{16}''$ × $5\frac{7}{8}''$.

⟨-⟩⁸.

Printed ecru paper wrapper; printed gray-green paper wrapper. On inner front: *Contents* . . . Back wrapper unprinted.

On p. 16: Folio 16 and 28 lines of text.

The H copy received Feb. 27, 1883. Presumably this is the printing noted by PW March 10, 1883, as having been "reprinted 'at the request of an association of women' in and about Boston."

Locations: AAS, B, BA, BPL, H, UV, Y

PRINTING B

SOME OF THE REASONS / AGAINST / WOMAN SUFFRAGE. / BY / FRANCIS PARKMAN. / PRINTED AT THE REQUEST OF AN ASSOCIATION / OF WOMEN. / ⟨n.p., n.d.⟩

Cover-title.

⟨1⟩-16. Laid paper. Also: wove paper. $9\frac{5}{16}''$ × $5\frac{7}{8}''$.

⟨-⟩⁸.

Printed ecru paper wrapper. Printed gray-green paper wrapper. On inner front: *Contents* . . . Back wrapper unprinted.

On p. 16: Folio 16 and 11 lines text only.

Locations: AAS, B, MHS, UV

PRINTING C

SOME OF THE REASONS / AGAINST / WOMAN SUFFRAGE. / BY / FRANCIS PARKMAN. / PRINTED AT THE REQUEST OF AN ASSOCIATION / OF WOMEN. / ⟨n.p., n.d.⟩

Cover-title.

⟨i-ii⟩, ⟨1⟩-16. $9\frac{1}{4}''$ × $5\frac{7}{8}''$.

⟨1⁸, 2¹⟩.

Printed self-wrapper.

On p. 16: Folio 16 and 11 lines of text only.

Locations: H, LC

PRINTING D

SOME OF THE REASONS / AGAINST / WOMAN SUFFRAGE. / BY / FRANCIS PARKMAN. / ISSUED BY MASSACHUSETTS MAN SUFFRAGE ASSOCIATION / 7A PARK STREET, BOSTON. / ⟨n.d., 1904?⟩

Cover-title.

⟨i-ii⟩, ⟨1⟩-16. $9\frac{5}{16}''$ × $5\frac{7}{8}''$.

⟨1⁸, 2¹⟩.

Printed self-wrapper.

On p. 16: Folio 16 and 11 lines of text only.

Paper bulks $\frac{3.5}{1000}''$ thick.

Location: H

PRINTING Da

Same as *Printing D* but printed on paper measuring $\frac{3}{1000}''$ thick.

Location: H

PRINTING Db

Same as *Printing D* but printed on paper measuring ⁴⁄₁₀₀₀″ thick.

Location: AAS

PRINTING E

SOME OF THE REASONS / AGAINST / WOMAN SUFFRAGE. / BY / FRANCIS PARKMAN. / ISSUED BY MASSACHUSETTS MAN SUFFRAGE ASSOCIATION / 7A PARK STREET, BOSTON. / ⟨n.d., 1904?⟩

Cover-title.

⟨i-ii⟩, ⟨1⟩-16. $9\frac{3}{8}″ \times 5\frac{15}{16}″$.

⟨1⁸, 2¹⟩.

Printed self-wrapper.

On p. 16: Folio 16, 11 lines of text; and: *Reprinted by the Massachusetts Association opposed to further Extension of Suffrage to Woman . . . Brookline, Mass. P.O. Box 134.*

Location: Gd

PRINTING F

SOME OF THE REASONS / AGAINST / WOMAN SUFFRAGE. / BY / FRANCIS PARKMAN / AUTHOR OF "THE OREGON TRAIL," "PIONEERS OF FRANCE IN THE NEW WORLD," ETC. / Issued by the Massachusetts Association Opposed to the Further Extension of / Suffrage to Women. / Pamphlets and leaflets may be obtained from the Secretary, / Room 615, / Kensington Building, / 687 Boylston Street, Boston, Mass. / ⟨n.d., 1904?⟩

Cover-title.

⟨i-ii⟩, ⟨1⟩-16. $9\frac{1}{8}″$ scant $\times 5\frac{11}{16}″$.

⟨1⁸, 2¹⟩.

Printed self-wrapper.

Location: AAS

Publication Notes

No record found for the 1883 printing.

April 29, 1884. 1000 copies printed. Charged to Mrs. H. O. Houghton. 18 pp. A wrapper appears to have been printed.

July 3, 1885. 1000 copies printed. 16 pp. A wrapper was printed. Printed for Miss L. P. Sohier.

Jan. 7, 1886. 1000 copies printed. 16 pp. 56 lb. paper. A wrapper was printed. Charged to Miss L. P. Sohier.

May 2, 1894. 500 copies printed; charge for binding 519 copies. 55 lb. paper. 18 pp. Charged to Mrs. J. C. Fisk.

May 14, 1894. 1000 copies printed; charge for binding 1005 copies. 18 pp. Charged to Mrs. J. C. Fisk.

May 18, 1894. 1000 copies printed; charge for binding 987 copies. 55 lb. paper. 18 pp. Charged to Mrs. J. C. Fisk.

May 22, 1894. 1000 copies printed; charge for binding 1034 copies. 50 lb. paper. 18 pp. Charged to Mrs. J. C. Fisk.

Sept. 20, 1894. 500 copies printed. 18 pp. No record of wrapper. 50 lb. paper. Charged to Mrs. J. C. Fisk.

Dec. 15, 1904. Charge for alteration of plates. 500 copies printed; charge for binding 512 copies. Charged to the Massachusetts Association Opposed to Women Suffrage.

15467. Proceedings of the Massachusetts Historical Society. Vol. xx. 1882–1883 . . .

Boston: Published by the Society. M.DCCC.LXXXIV.

Remarks on C. F. Adams, Jr.'s paper on the printing of old manuscripts, p. 183.

BA   H   MHS

15468. The Acadians . . .

⟨Bangor, Maine, 1884⟩

Note IV, p. 8.

For fuller entry see above in *Robert T. S. Lowell* list.

15469. MONTCALM AND WOLFE . . .

BOSTON: LITTLE, BROWN, AND COMPANY. 1884.

2 Volumes. For another edition see below under year 1887.

General title-page, p. ⟨i⟩: *France and England in North America. A Series of Historical Narratives . . . Part Seventh . . .*

1: ⟨i⟩-xvi, ⟨1⟩-514. Portrait frontispiece of Montcalm inserted; also inserted: 1 2-page map; and, 5 1-page maps. $8\frac{3}{16}″$ full $\times 5\frac{7}{16}″$. *Note:* Inserted between pp. 214-215 is a single leaf, printed on both sides, in explanation of the maps.

2: ⟨i-ii⟩, ⟨i⟩-x, ⟨1⟩-502, blank leaf. Portrait frontispiece of Wolfe inserted; also inserted: 3 1-page maps.

1: ⟨-⟩⁸, 1-32⁸, 33¹.

2: ⟨-⟩⁶, 1-31⁸, 32⁴.

C cloth: purple; terra-cotta. P cloth: green. Spine stamped in gold: ⟨*fillet*⟩ / MONTCALM / AND / WOLFE / ⟨*diamond rule*⟩ / PARKMAN / ⟨*ornament*⟩ / VOL. I. ⟨II.⟩ / LITTLE . BROWN & CO. ⟨*sic*⟩ / ⟨*fillet*⟩ Brown-coated end papers. Flyleaves. In some copies of Vol. 1 there is a single flyleaf at front, a double flyleaf at back.

Also noted in a variant binding: C cloth: purple. Spine stamped in gold: ⟨*fillet*⟩ / PARKMAN'S / WORKS / ⟨*diamond rule*⟩ / MONTCALM / AND / WOLFE / I. ⟨II.⟩ / LITTLE.BROWN & CO. ⟨*sic*⟩ / ⟨*fillet*⟩ Brown-coated end papers. Vol. 1: Flyleaf at front; double flyleaf at back; Vol. 2: Flyleaves. Location: UV

Note: In some copies of Vol. 1 there is inserted at the front a single leaf, printed on both sides, advertising Parkman's works.

Also a large paper format. Precise date of publication not known. Imprint: *Boston: Little, Brown, and Company. 1885.* Leaf: 9⅝″ scant × 6½″. On reverse of title-leaves: *Seventy-five copies printed.* Location: AAS

Publication Notes, Vol. 1

Noted for *next week* PW Oct. 18, 1884. MHS copy presented by Parkman Oct. 25, 1884. Noted as *now ready* PW Oct. 25, 1884. Deposited Oct. 27, 1884. H copy presented by Parkman Oct. 27, 1884. Listed PW Nov. 15, 1884, but listed as *not seen.* The London (Macmillan) edition (American printing?) listed Ath Nov. 1, 1884.

Publication Notes, Vol. 2

Noted for *next week* PW Oct. 18, 1884. Listed PW Nov. 15, 1884, but listed as *not seen.* MHS copy presented by Parkman Nov. 22, 1884. H copy presented by Parkman Nov. 24, 1884. Deposited Nov. 26, 1884. The London (Macmillan) edition (American printing?) listed Ath Nov. 29, 1884.

H   MHS   Y

15470. Historic Handbook of the Northern Tour . . .

Boston: Little, Brown, and Company. 1885.

Cloth; and, printed paper wrapper.

"This book is a group of narratives . . . drawn, with the addition of explanatory passages, from *The Conspiracy of Pontiac, Pioneers of France in the New World, The Jesuits in North America, Count Frontenac,* and *Montcalm and Wolfe.*"---P. ⟨v⟩.

Deposited June 5, 1885. Listed PW July 4, 1885.

AAS   BA   H   LC   MHS   NYPL   UV

15471. Addresses at the Complimentary Dinner to Dr. Benjamin Apthorp Gould. Hotel Vendôme, Boston, May 6, 1885.

Lynn, Mass.: Press of Thos. P. Nichols. 1885.

Printed paper wrapper.

Comment, p. 27.

AAS   B   H   NYPL

15472. An Open Letter to a Temperance Friend. / ⟨*rule*⟩ / MY DEAR MADAM: / ⟨*text*⟩ / Yours very truly, / F. PARKMAN. / ⟨n.p., n.d., Boston, *ca.* 1885⟩

Single leaf. 8⅜″ scant × 5½″. Printed on recto only.

"You and I agree in aim though not in methods. You think that license-suffrage for women will help the temperance cause . . ."

H   NYPL

MONTCALM AND WOLFE . . .

BOSTON . . . 1885.

Large paper edition. See above under year 1884.

15473. Pioneers of France in the New World . . . Twenty-Fifth Edition. Revised, with Additions.

Boston: Little, Brown, and Company. 1886.

For first edition see above under year 1865.

"Since this book first appeared some new documentary evidence touching it has been brought to light . . . This added information is incorporated in the present edition, which has also received some literary revision."---From the "Prefatory Note to the Twenty-fifth Edition," p. ⟨vii⟩.

NHSL

15474. Montcalm and Wolfe . . . Tenth Edition.

Boston: Little, Brown, and Company. 1887.

For first edition see above under year 1884.

2 Vols.

The inserted frontispiece portrait, Vol. 2, has a conjugate leaf carrying a note, *The Portrait of Wolfe,* dated at end *15 October, 1887.* "The portrait of Wolfe in the present edition of this book was never before made known to the public . . ."

H

15475. Appletons' Cyclopædia of American Biography Edited by James Grant Wilson and John Fiske . . .

New York D. Appleton and Company 1, 3 and 5 Bond Street 1887 ⟨-1889⟩

"Louis, Count Frontenac," Vol. 2, pp. 553-555.

"Marquis de Montcalm," Vol. 4, pp. 363-365.

"Robert Cavalier de la Salle," Vol. 3, pp. 621-622.

For fuller entry see No. 6020.

15476. The French-War Papers of the Maréchal de Lévis Described by the Abbé Casgrain. With Comments by Francis Parkman and Justin Winsor. Fifty Copies Privately Reprinted from the Proceedings of the Massachusetts Historical Society, April 12, 1888.

Cambridge: John Wilson and Son. University Press. 1888.

Cover-title.

⟨1⟩-11, blank, p. ⟨12⟩. 9¼″ × 5¾″ scant. Printed self-wrapper.

BPL   H   LC   NYPL   Y

15477. Proceedings of the Massachusetts Historical Society. Vol. III.––Second Series. 1886–1887 . . .

Boston: Published by the Society. M.DCCC.LXX-XVIII.

Remarks, pp. 159, 216.

"Report on the Historical Portraits Exhibited by Major Walter," pp. 179-187.

H   MHS   NYPL

15478. Proceedings of the Massachusetts Historical Society. Vol. IV.––Second Series. 1887–1889 . . .

Boston: Published by the Society. M.DCCC.LXX-XIX.

Letter, pp. 92-93.

H   MHS   NYPL

15479. The Romance of Dollard by Mary Hartwell Catherwood . . .

The Century Co. New-York ⟨1889⟩

"Preface," pp. 1-3.

Two printings noted:

First Printing

⟨i-viii⟩, 1-206. Frontispiece and 6 plates inserted. 7¹¹⁄₁₆″ × 4¹⁵⁄₁₆″. Pp. ⟨i-ii⟩ excised or pasted under the end paper.

⟨-⟩⁴, ⟨1⟩-17⁶, 18¹. Leaf ⟨-⟩₁ excised or pasted under the end paper.

Second Printing

⟨i-vi⟩, 1-206. Frontispiece and 6 plates inserted.

⟨1⟩-12⁸, 13², 14⁸.

For further comment see entry No. 2952.

15480. OUR COMMON SCHOOLS . . .

⟨BOSTON: CITIZENS' PUBLIC SCHOOL UNION, 1890⟩

Cover-title.

⟨1⟩-6, blank leaf. 9½″ × 6″.

⟨-⟩⁴.

At end: *Boston, January, 1890.* At head of p. ⟨3⟩: [*Distributed by the Citizens' Public School Union.*]

Printed from two settings; sequence, if any, not known. The designations are for identification only. The following is sufficient for identification.

SETTING A

P. ⟨3⟩: The heading [*Distributed by the Citizens' Public School Union.*] is set (including the brackets) 2¾″ wide.

SETTING B

P. ⟨3⟩: The heading cited is set 2¹³⁄₁₆″ wide.

AAS (B)   BA (B)   BPL (A)   H (B)   MHS (A,B)   NYPL (A)   UV (B)   Y (A,B)

15481. The Art of Authorship . . . Compiled . . . by George Bainton.

London: James Clarke & Co., 13 & 14, Fleet Street. 1890.

Contribution, pp. 181-182.

For comment see entry No. 1271.

15482. The Art of Authorship . . . Compiled . . . by George Bainton

New York D. Appleton and Company 1890

Contribution, pp. 181-182.

For comment see entry No. 1272.

15483. A HALF-CENTURY OF CONFLICT . . .

BOSTON: LITTLE, BROWN, AND COMPANY. 1892.

2 Vols.

General title-page, leaf ⟨-⟩₂ᵣ: *France and England in North America. A Series of Historical Narratives . . . Part Sixth . . .*

1: ⟨i-iv⟩, ⟨i⟩-viii, ⟨1⟩-333, blank leaf. 8³⁄₁₆″ × 5⅜″.

2: ⟨i⟩-viii, ⟨1⟩-395. 3 maps inserted; 2 of the maps have inserted index leaves.

1: ⟨-⟩⁶, 1-21⁸.

2: ⟨-⟩⁴, 1-24⁸, 25⁶.

Two states of Vol. 1 have been noted. The sequence is presumed correct.

STATE A

University Press imprint on the verso of *both* general title-page and true title-page.

STATE B

University Press imprint on verso of true title-page only; not on the verso of general title-page.

C cloth: purple. P cloth: terra-cotta. A copy of *State B* has been seen in green P cloth. Black-coated end papers. Flyleaves; or, double flyleaves in Vol. 2.

Also a large paper format. Precise date of publication not known. Imprint: *Boston: Little, Brown, and Company. 1892.* Leaf: 9¾″ × 6½″. On the verso of the true title-pages: *Seventy-five copies printed.* Locations: AAS Y

Advertised for *May* PW March 5, 1892. MHS copy (*State A*) inscribed by Parkman May 7, 1892. MHS copy (*State A*) received from Parkman May 24, 1892, with inserted presentation slip dated May 20, 1892. BA copy (*State A*) received from Parkman May 25, 1892, with inserted presentation slip dated May 20, 1892. MHS copy (*State A*) inscribed by Parkman May 21, 1892. Deposited May 21, 1892. Listed PW June 4, 1892.

Query: Issued in London (Macmillan) prior to Boston issue? The London issue (American sheets) noted as *immediately* Ath May 14, 1892. Listed Ath May 14, 1892. Noted as *ready* PC May 21, 1892. Listed PC May 28, 1892; Bkr June, 1892.

BA (A)   H (B)   MHS (A)

15484. The Oregon Trail ... Illustrated by Frederic Remington

Boston Little, Brown, and Company 1892

For first edition see under year 1849.

"Preface to the Illustrated Edition," pp. ⟨vii⟩-ix.

Two printings noted:

First Printing

Pagination: ⟨i⟩-xvi, 1-411. *List of Illustrations* not present.

Second Printing

Pagination: ⟨i⟩-xx, 1-411. *List of Illustrations* present.

Noted in: V cloth: both mustard and buff noted; vellum; leather; unbleached linen. All identically stamped.

Deposited Sept. 28, 1892.

AAS (2d)   H (2d)   MHS (1st)   UV (1st)   Y (2d)

15485. ... The Old Régime in Canada ... Revised, with Additions.

Boston: Little, Brown, and Company. 1894.

At head of title: *France and England in North America. Part Fourth.*

For first edition see above under year 1874.

"Prefatory Note to Revised Edition," p. ⟨vii⟩.

Deposited March 8, 1894.

H LC NYPL

15486. ⟨The Works of Francis Parkman⟩

Boston Little Brown and Company ... 1897 ⟨-1898⟩

Edition de Luxe, limited to 300 numbered sets. *The Champlain Edition*, limited to 1200 numbered sets.

"The text used is that of the latest edition of each work prepared for the press by the distinguished author. He carefully revised and added to several of his works ... Thus he rewrote and enlarged *The Conspiracy of Pontiac;* the new edition of *La Salle and the Discovery of the Great West* (1878) and the 1885 edition of *Pioneers of France* included very important additions; and a short time before his death he added to *The Old Régime* fifty pages, under the title of *The Feudal Chiefs of Acadia.* The present edition therefore includes each work in its final state as perfected by the historian, and the indexes have been entirely re-made."---*Publisher's Preface.*

The Champlain Edition was also issued with the joint imprint of Little Brown and Company, Boston; and, J. F. Taylor and Co., New York.

1-2: *Pioneers of France in the New World. France and England in North America. Part First ... in Two Volumes ...*

Boston, 1897.

Deposited June 30, 1897.

3-4: *The Jesuits in North America in the Seventeenth Century. France and England in North America. Part Second ... in Two Volumes ...*

Boston, 1897.

Deposited July 26, 1897.

5-6: *La Salle and the Discovery of the Great West. France and England in North America. Part Third ... in Two Volumes ...*

Boston, 1897.

Deposited Aug. 21, 1897.

7-8: *The Old Régime in Canada. France and England in North America. Part Fourth ... in Two Volumes ...*

Boston, 1897.

Deposited Sept. 30, 1897.

9-10: *Count Frontenac and New France under Louis XIV. France and England in North America. Part Fifth ... in Two Volumes ...*

Boston, 1897.

Deposited Oct. 29, 1897.

11-12: *A Half-Century of Conflict. France and England in North America. Part Sixth ... in Two Volumes ...*

Boston, 1897.

Deposited Nov. 29, 1897.

13-15: *Montcalm and Wolfe. France and England in North America. Part Seventh ... in Three Volumes ...*

Boston, 1897-1898.

Vols. 1-2 dated 1897; Vol. 3 dated 1898. Vols. 1-2 deposited Dec. 31, 1897; Vol. 3 deposited Jan. 24, 1898.

16-18: *The Conspiracy of Pontiac and the Indian War after the Conquest of Canada . . . in Three Volumes . . .*

Boston, 1898.

Vol. 1 deposited Jan. 24, 1898; Vols. 2-3 deposited Feb. 24, 1898.

19-20: *The Oregon Trail . . . in Two Volumes . . .*

Boston, 1898.

Deposited March 21, 1898.

LC   UV

15487. LETTERS FROM FRANCIS PARK-MAN TO E. G. SQUIER WITH BIO-GRAPHICAL NOTES AND A BIBLIOG-RAPHY OF E. G. SQUIER BY DON C. SEITZ

CEDAR RAPIDS, IOWA   THE TORCH PRESS   NINETEEN ELEVEN

⟨1⟩-58, blank leaf. Paper watermarked *Normandy Vellum France.* 9⁹⁄₁₆″ full × 6³⁄₈″.

⟨1-6⁴, 7⁶⟩.

Printed gray laid paper boards, gray S cloth shelf-back. End papers of book stock. In some copies, flyleaves of book stock.

Two hundred copies only . . .---P. ⟨4⟩.

Deposited Oct. 5, 1911.

AAS   H   LC   MHS   NYPL   Y

15488. MR. PARKMAN AND HIS CANADIAN CRITICS FROM "THE NATION" NEW YORK, AUGUST 1, 1878

REPRINTED FOR THE CENTENARY OF FRANCIS PARKMAN SEPTEMBER 16, 1923

Cover-title.

Anonymous. Although written in the third person, presumably by Parkman. Daniel C. Haskell (*The Nation . . . Index of Titles and Contributors,* New York, 1953, Vol. 2, p. 389) credits the piece to Parkman.

⟨1⟩-10, blank leaf. 8″ full × 5⁵⁄₈″.

⟨-⟩⁶.

Printed self-wrapper.

AAS

15489. Francis Parkman   Representative Selections, with Introduction, Bibliography, and Notes by Wilbur L. Schramm . . .

American Book Company   New York   Cincinnati Chicago Boston Atlanta ⟨1938⟩

On copyright page: *W.P.I.*

Reprint save for:

"The Failure of Universal Suffrage," pp. 159-180.

"The New-Hampshire Ranger," pp. 16-25.

"Satan and Dr. Carver," pp. 25-40.

"Studies of Nature," pp. 15-16.

"The Tale of the 'Ripe Scholar,'" pp. 152-159.

"The Woman Question," pp. 180-201. For another version see *Some of the Reasons against Woman Suffrage,* above, under ⟨1883⟩.

Excerpts from Parkman's diary, pp. 47-99.

Reviews, pp. 202-222.

B   H   LC   NYPL

15490. The Oregon Trail . . . Edited from His Notebooks by Mason Wade . . .

Printed for the Members of the Limited Editions Club   New York, 1943

Leather. Limited to 1500(?) copies.

For first edition see above under 1849.

"The present text is based upon the last edition revised by Parkman, that of 1892. In addition, some passages of interest, included in the magazine version but later omitted, have been restored; and new material drawn from the notebooks has been added, by permission of their owner, the Massachusetts Historical Society . . ."---P. xi.

Deposited Aug. 20, 1943.

B   H   LC   Y

15491. THE JOURNALS OF FRANCIS PARK-MAN EDITED BY MASON WADE . . .

NEW YORK AND LONDON   HARPER & BROTHERS PUBLISHERS   MCMXLVII

2 Volumes.

Title-pages in black and red-brown.

1: ⟨i⟩-⟨xxvi⟩, ⟨1⟩-381; colophon, p. ⟨382⟩. Frontispiece and 7 plates inserted; other illustrations in text. 9⁵⁄₁₆″ × 6¼″.

2: ⟨i-viii⟩, ⟨383⟩-718. Frontispiece and 7 plates inserted; other illustrations in text.

1: ⟨1-24⁸, 25⁴, 26⁸⟩.

2: ⟨1-20⁸, 21⁴, 22⁸⟩.

Blue linen. End papers printed in brown with maps.

Note: Reported, not seen: Copies in green cloth. Remainder?

On copyright page of each volume: 10-7; *First Edition;* and code letters I-W (signifying printed Sept. 1947).

Noted for Oct. 29 PW July 26, 1947. A copy was received by *Publishers' Weekly* Nov. 5, 1947. H copy received Nov. 11, 1947. Published Nov. 12, 1947 (publisher's statement).

AAS BA H MHS Y

15492. PARKMAN'S DARK YEARS: LETTERS TO MARY DWIGHT PARKMAN BY HOWARD DOUGHTY

OFFPRINT FROM HARVARD LIBRARY BULLETIN VOLUME IV, NUMBER I WINTER 1950

Cover-title.

53-85. Wove paper watermarked *Warren's Olde Style*. 10¼" scant × 6¹³⁄₁₆".

Sheets extracted from the journal and issued in printed gray paper wrapper, imprinted as above.

MHS

15493. Youth's Companion   Edited by Lovell Thompson with Three Former Companion Editors, M. A. DeWolfe Howe, Arthur Stanwood Pier, and Harford Powel . . .

Houghton Mifflin Company   Boston   The Riverside Press Cambridge 1954

"Adventures of Pierre Radisson," pp. 457-468.

Deposited Oct. 11, 1954.

H

15494. LETTERS OF FRANCIS PARKMAN EDITED AND WITH AN INTRODUCTION BY WILBUR R. JACOBS . . .

PUBLISHED IN CO-OPERATION WITH THE MASSACHUSETTS HISTORICAL SOCIETY NORMAN: UNIVERSITY OF OKLAHOMA PRESS ⟨1960⟩

Title-pages in black and red.

2 Vols.

1: ⟨i⟩-⟨lxvi⟩, ⟨1⟩-204; blank, p. ⟨205⟩; colophon, p. ⟨206⟩. Frontispiece and 6 2-page plates inserted. Wove paper watermarked *Warren's Olde Style*. 9¼" full × 6¹⁄₁₆".

2: ⟨i⟩-xl, ⟨1⟩-286; blank, p. ⟨287⟩; colophon, p. ⟨288⟩. Frontispiece and 6 2-page plates inserted.

1: ⟨1-17⁸⟩.

2: ⟨1-19⁸, 20⁴, 21⁸⟩.

V cloth: brown. Top edges sprinkled red.

On copyright page of each volume: *First Edition*.

Deposited Aug. 22, 1960.

AAS BPL H Y

FRANCIS PARKMAN

SECTION II

Reprints of Parkman's own books.

15495. Pioneers of France in the New World . . . Second Edition.

Boston: Little, Brown and Company. 1865.

Cursory examination indicates that this is a reprint of the first printing but with an erratum notice inserted on p. 420.

15496. The Oregon Trail Sketches of Prairie and Rocky-Mountain Life . . . Fifth Edition, Revised

Boston Little, Brown, and Company 1873

Cursory examination indicates that this is a reprint of the *Fourth Edition*, 1872.

15497. The Conspiracy of Pontiac and the Indian War after the Conquest of Canada . . . Eighth Edition, Revised, with Additions . . .

Boston: Little, Brown, and Company. 1879.

2 Vols. Presumably a reprint of the *Sixth Edition*, 1870.

15498. . . . Mr. Parkman's Histories.

⟨Boston, 1889⟩

Printed self-wrapper. Preceding at head of p. ⟨1⟩. At head of title: *Old South Leaflets. Seventh Series, 1889. No. 3.*

15499. . . . The Capture of Quebec. From Parkman's "Conspiracy of Pontiac."

⟨Boston, 1889⟩

Printed self-wrapper. Preceding at head of p. ⟨1⟩. At head of title: *Old South Leaflets. Seventh Series, 1889. No. 4.*

Extracted from *The Conspiracy of Pontiac*, 1870.

15500. . . . Braddock's Defeat. 1755. The French and English in America . . .

New York: Maynard, Merrill, & Co., Publishers, ⟨*sic*⟩ ⟨1890⟩

At head of title: *Historical Classic Readings.---No. 7.*

Printed paper wrapper.

15501. . . . Champlain and His Associates. An Account of Early French Adventure in North America . . .

New York: Maynard, Merrill, & Co., Publishers, ⟨*sic*⟩ ⟨1890⟩

At head of title: *Historical Classic Readings---No. 6.*

Printed paper wrapper.

15502. . . . The Speech of Pontiac . . . from Parkman's "Conspiracy of Pontiac."

⟨Boston, 1890⟩

Printed self-wrapper. Preceding at head of p. ⟨1⟩. At head of title: *Old South Leaflets. Eighth Series, 1890. No. 5.*

15503. . . . Prose Passages from the Works of Francis Parkman . . . Compiled by Josephine E. Hodgdon . . .

Boston Little, Brown, and Company 1893

Cloth; and, printed paper wrapper. At head of title: *Leaflets from Standard Authors Parkman*

15504. The Oregon Trail . . . Author's Edition

Boston Little, Brown, and Company 1894

15505. . . . Pioneers of France in the New World . . . Revised, with Additions.

Boston: Little, Brown, and Company. 1894.

At head of title: *France and England in North America. Part First.*

15506. ⟨Francis Parkman's Works. New Library Edition⟩

Boston: Little, Brown, and Company. 1898

12 Vols. A thirteenth volume was later added: *A Life of Francis Parkman*, by Charles Haight Farnham, first published in 1900.

Advertised PW Sept. 24, 1898, as in cloth; half calf: half levant. Vols. 1-2 listed PW Oct. 29, 1898. Advertised PW Nov. 5 as *published November 5th.* Vols. 3-12 listed PW Dec. 24, 1898.

15507. ⟨Francis Parkman's Works. Frontenac Edition⟩

Boston Little, Brown, and Company 1899

15 Vols. All published?

15508. ⟨Francis Parkman's Works. La Salle Edition⟩

Boston Little, Brown and Company MDCCCCII

20 Vols. Limited to 500 numbered sets. Noted in cloth, printed paper label on spine. According to PW listing, March 22, 1902, also available in three-quarters levant.

15509. The Struggle for a Continent Edited from the Writings of Francis Parkman by Pelham Edgar . . .

Boston Little, Brown, & Company 1902

Two states (printings?) noted. The sequence has not been determined and the order of presentation is arbitrary.

A

The statement *Published October, 1902* not present on the copyright page. The surviving copyright deposit copy (LC) thus.

B

The statement *Published October, 1902* present on the copyright page. Copies: AAS and Y.

Deposited Sept. 25, 1902. Listed PW Oct. 11, 1902. The London (Macmillan) edition listed Ath Nov. 22, 1902.

15510. The Romance of Canadian History Edited from the Writings of Francis Parkman by Pelham Edgar . . . School Edition

Toronto   George N. Morang & Company Limited 1903

15511. ⟨Francis Parkman's Works. Frontenac Edition⟩

Boston Little, Brown, and Company 1905

13 Vols. All published?

15512. The Struggle for a Continent Edited from the Writings of Francis Parkman by Pelham Edgar . . .

Boston Little, Brown, & Company 1907

15513. The Boys' Parkman Selections from the Historical Works of Francis Parkman Compiled by Louise S. Hasbrouck . . .

Boston Little, Brown, and Company 1912

Two printings noted:

1: On copyright page: *Published, April, 1912* Deposit copy thus.

2: On copyright page: *Published, September, 1912*

15513A. Rivals for America . . . Selections from "France and England in North America" Compiled by Louise S. Hasbrouck . . .

Boston Little, Brown, and Company 1915

On copyright page: *Published, October, 1915*

15514. ⟨Francis Parkman's Works. Frontenac Edition⟩

New York Charles Scribner's Sons 1915

16 Volumes. All published?

15515. The Battle for North America Edited by John Tebbel from the Works of Francis Parkman

1948   Doubleday & Company, Inc. Garden City, New York

On copyright page: *First Edition*

15516. The Parkman Reader From the Works of Francis Parkman Selected and Edited with an Introduction and Notes by Samuel Eliot Morison . . .

Little, Brown and Company Boston Toronto ⟨1955⟩

On copyright page: *First Edition*

". . . I have made these selections from his multi-volumed series on *France and England in North America* . . . The actual *copy* sent to the printer has been taken from pages of the Frontenac or the Centenary Edition, both of which incorporate the last author's revisions . . ."———P. ⟨ix⟩.

15517. . . . The Discovery of the Great West: La Salle Edited by William R. Taylor

Rinehart & Company, Inc. New York Toronto ⟨1956⟩

At head of title: *Francis Parkman* Otherwise *La Salle and the Discovery of the Great West.*

REPRINTS

The following books contain material by Parkman reprinted from earlier books.

The Boston Book . . .

Boston . . . MDCCCL.

"The Chase," pp. ⟨126⟩-133, extracted from *The California and Oregon Trail,* 1849. For fuller entry see No. 5929.

... Harper's Fifth Reader American Authors

New York ... 1889

"The Heights of Abraham," pp. 410-420, extracted from *Montcalm and Wolfe*, 1884. For fuller entry see No. 7917.

REFERENCES AND ANA

Francis Parkman par l'Abbé H. R. Casgrain

Québec C. Darveau, Imprimeur-Éditeur 8, Rue la Montagne 1872 ...

Printed paper wrapper.

The Defences of Norumbega and a Review of the Reconnaissances of Col. T. W. Higginson ... Dr. Francis Parkman ... A Letter to Judge Daly ... by Eben Norton Horsford

Boston and New York Houghton, Mifflin and Company The Riverside Press, Cambridge 1891

Francis Parkman. A Sketch. By O. B. Frothingham. [Written for the Massachusetts Historical Society.]

Boston: John Wilson and Son. University Press. 1894.

Printed paper wrapper. Contains excerpts from "The Failure of Universal Suffrage," pp. 29-30; originally in NAR July–August, 1878. For a reprinting of the whole see *Representative Selections* ⟨1938⟩, pp. 159-180.

Tributes of the Massachusetts Historical Society to Francis Parkman, at a Special Meeting, Nov. 21, 1893.

Cambridge: John Wilson and Son. University Press. 1894.

Cover-title. Printed self-wrapper. Contains material also published in the next entry.

Proceedings of the Massachusetts Historical Society. Second Series. ––– Vol. VIII. 1892–1894 ...

Boston: Published by the Society. M.DCCC.XCIV.

Letter, dated Nov. 28, 1868, p. 350. Autobiographical fragment, pp. 350-360. See preceding entry.

Memoir of Francis Parkman by Edward Wheelwright Reprinted from the Publications of the Colonial Society of Massachusetts Vol. I.

Cambridge John Wilson and Son University Press 1894

Printed paper wrapper.

Francis Parkman. By Barrett Wendell.

[Reprinted from the Proceedings of the American Academy of Arts and Sciences, Vol. XXIX.] ⟨n.d., 1894⟩

Cover-title. Printed paper wrapper.

Francis Parkman

Boston Little, Brown, and Company 1896

Printed paper wrapper. Cover-title.

A Life of Francis Parkman by Charles Haight Farnham ...

Boston Little, Brown, and Company 1900

... Francis Parkman by Henry Dwight Sedgwick

Boston and New York Houghton, Mifflin and Company The Riverside Press, Cambridge 1904

At head of title: *American Men of Letters*

On copyright page: *Published May, 1904*

Trade format: Cloth, stamped in gold. *Limited format:* Cloth, printed paper label on spine; on copyright page: *Of this first edition 150 copies have been bound entirely uncut, with paper label.*

Listed PW June 4, 1904.

Francis Parkman by Henry Cabot Lodge ...

Boston 1923

Printed paper wrapper. *From the Proceedings of the Massachusetts Historical Society for June, 1923* –––P. ⟨2⟩.

... Letters of Francis Parkman to Pierre Margry with Introductory Note by John Spencer Bassett

Northampton, Mass. Published Quarterly by the Department of History of Smith College ⟨1923⟩

Printed paper wrapper. At head of title: *Vol. VIII, Nos. 3 & 4 April–July, 1923 Smith College Studies in History John Spencer Bassett Sidney Bradshaw Fay*

Parkman Centenary Celebration at Montreal 13th November, 1923

Published by the Parkman Centenary Sub-Committee and McGill University Montreal ⟨1923⟩

Printed paper wrapper. *McGill University Publications Series 1, No. 6.*

Francis Parkman, 1823–1923 by Joseph Schafer

Reprinted from the Wisconsin Magazine of History Volume VII, Number 3, March, 1924 ⟨Madison, Wis., 1924⟩

Cover-title. Printed paper wrapper.

Francis Parkman Representative Selections, with Introduction, Bibliography, and Notes by Wilbur L. Schramm . . .

. . . New York . . . ⟨1938⟩

For fuller entry see above in *Section One*.

Francis Parkman Heroic Historian by Mason Wade

Published by the Viking Press New York 1942

On copyright page: *First Published in November 1942* . . .

. . . Parkman's History The Historian As Literary Artist

Yale University Press New Haven 1953

At head of title: *Otis A. Pease*

The Wallace Notestein Essays, Vol. 1.

Francis Parkman by Howard Doughty

New York The Macmillan Company 1962

On copyright page: *First Printing*

THOMAS WILLIAM PARSONS

1 8 1 9 – 1 8 9 2

The Parsons list is presented in five sections as follows:

1: Parsons's primary books; and, books by others containing the earliest located book publication of Parsons contributions.

2: Leaflets; and, sheet music. *Note:* Only that sheet music constituting first publication (periodicals excepted) is included.

3: Reprints of Parsons's own books.

4: Books of authors other than Parsons containing Parsons material reprinted from books.

5: References and ana.

Note: In the preparation of the following list BAL made full use of the unpublished bibliographical notes compiled by the late Charles E. Goodspeed deposited in The Houghton Library.

SECTION ONE

15518. The First Ten Cantos of the Inferno of Dante Alighieri. Newly Translated into English Verse.

Boston: William D. Ticknor. M DCCC XLIII.

⟨1⟩-83. 1 plate inserted. 8⅞″ full × 5½″ full.

Brown paper boards, printed paper label on spine.

Parsons presented a copy to J. L. Motley Aug. 29, 1843; not seen by BAL; information from Myers & Company's (London) catalog, No. 284, March, 1932. H copy received Aug. 30, 1843, gift of the translator. Reviewed K Aug. 1843.

AAS   H

15519. The Bridal Wreath, a Wedding Souvenir. Edited by Percy Bryant.

Boston: William J. Reynolds, 1845.

"The Groomsman to His Mistress," pp. 28-29. Collected in *Poems*, 1854.

CAW

15520. The Boston Book. Being Specimens of Metropolitan Literature.

Boston: Ticknor, Reed, and Fields. MDCCCL.

"July," pp. ⟨82⟩-83. Not to be confused with another poem of the same name in *A Mood of May* . . . (leaflet). Collected (truncated) in *Poems*, 1893.

"To a Lady, with a Head of Pope Pius Ninth," pp. ⟨223⟩-224. Collected in *Poems*, 1854.

For fuller entry see No. 5929.

15521. POEMS . . .

BOSTON: TICKNOR AND FIELDS. M DCCC LIV.

⟨i⟩-⟨x⟩, ⟨11⟩-189; blank leaf. 7½″ × 5¼″.
Note: In some copies the terminal blank leaf has been excised.

Three issues noted:

FIRST ISSUE

Noted as a set of folded sheets only; issued thus?

P. ⟨11⟩: *Epistle to Samuel Rogers, London.*

P. 12: *Good-humored wisdom . . .*

P. ⟨13⟩: *Preface to the Letters.*

P. 14: *Hesperia's muse . . .*

Signature collation: ⟨1⟩-12⁸. Leaf ⟨12⟩₈ excised.

No cancels in signature ⟨1⟩.

SECOND ISSUE

The faulty arrangement corrected by cancelling leaves ⟨1⟩₆₋₇ and inserting the reprinted (corrected) leaves. Text occurs:

P. ⟨11⟩: *Preface to the Letters.*

P. 12: *Good-humored wisdom . . .*

P. ⟨13⟩: *Epistle to Samuel Rogers, London.*

P. 14: *Hesperia's muse . . .*

⟨1⟩-12⁸. Leaves ⟨1⟩₆₋₇ are cancels.

THIRD ISSUE

Same as *Second Issue* but leaves ⟨1⟩₆₋₇ are not cancels; the correction done by reprinting.

A cloth: brown. T cloth: brown. Yellow end papers. Flyleaves.

Note: Remainders have been seen in terra-cotta C cloth; and brown star-sprinkled C cloth. Both of the preceding have been noted with the *Osgood* monogram at foot of spine. Also noted in green C cloth with *Ticknor & Co.* at foot of spine; leaf $7\frac{1}{8}'' \times 4\frac{15}{16}''$.

Deposited Aug. 15, 1854. Advertised as *in press* NLG Aug. 15, 1854. Advertised for Sept. 16 NLG Sept. 15, 1854. Listed NLG Oct. 2, 1854. Advertised as *now ready* NLG Jan. 1, 1855.

BRITISH PUBLICATION

Reviewed LG March 15, 1856, with imprint: *London, Trübner & Co.; Boston, Ticknor & Fields.* Reviewed Ath June 21, 1856, with Boston imprint only. No PC listing found.

Publisher's Records

June 9, 1854. 1000 copies printed. Published Sept. 16, 1854.

By May 30, 1860: 836 copies had been bound. No earlier information found.

March 24, 1864: 49 copies bound.

Aug. 20, 1868: 24 copies bound.

March 22, 1871: 50 copies bound.

March, 1876: Plates (also sheets?) sold to Welch, Bigelow & Company. See PW April 1, 1876, p. 440.

Nov. 29, 1876: Remaining sheets pulped.

AAS (3rd)   B (2nd)   BA (2nd)   BPL (2nd; 3rd) H (1st; 2nd; 3rd; Osgood)   Y (2nd)

15522. Sixteenth Triennial Festival of the Massachusetts Charitable Mechanic Association . . . Oct. 11, 1854.

Boston, Printed for the Association by Isaac R. Butts. 1854.

Printed paper wrapper.

"Ode," pp. 8–9; *Praise Nature for her perfect things* . .

Uncollected. Also issued as a separate; see in *Section Two*, below.

H   NYPL   Y

15523. Transactions of the Norfolk Agricultural Society, for 1854.

Published by the Society. ⟨Dedham, Mass., 1854? 1855?⟩

Printed paper wrapper.

"Autumn Hymn," p. 128; *Should Autumn's golden days depart* . . .

Uncollected. Also issued as a separate; see in *Section Two*, below.

Y

15524. The Knickerbocker Gallery: A Testimonial to the Editor of the Knickerbocker Magazine from its Contributors . . .

New-York: Samuel Hueston, 348 Broadway. MDCCCLV.

"To a Rich Rascal," p. ⟨95⟩; uncollected.

For fuller entry see No. 1033.

15525. An Address Delivered before the Massachusetts Charitable Mechanic Association, at the Celebration of Their Seventeenth Triennial Festival, at Fanueil Hall, October 14, 1857. By Joseph M. Wightman . . .

Boston: Geo. C. Rand & Avery, City Printers, No. 3, Cornhill. 1857.

Printed paper wrapper.

"Ode in Praise of the Useful Arts," pp. 23–24.

Uncollected. Also issued as a separate; see in *Section Two*, below.

B   H   Y

15526. An Oration Delivered before the Municipal Authorities of the City of Boston, July 5, 1858, by John S. Holmes . . .

Boston: Geo. C. Rand and Avery, City Printers, No. 3 Cornhill, 1858.

Printed paper wrapper.

Untitled ode "written expressly for the occasion" beginning: "Call us early in the morning–––call us early, mother mine," p. 99.

Uncollected.

H   Y

15527. The Lady's Almanac, for the Year 1864.

Boston, Published by George Coolidge, No. 3 Milk Street. New York: Sold by H. Dexter, Hamilton & Co. ⟨1861; *i.e.,* 1863⟩

"Mary Booth," p. ⟨121⟩. Collected in *The Rosary*, 1865.

H   NYPL

15528. The Spirit of the Fair . . .

New York . . . 1864.

"Forty Years," No. 15, p. 173. Uncollected.

For fuller entry see No. 11186.

15529. Seventeen Cantos of the Inferno of Dante Alighieri.

Boston: Printed by John Wilson and Son. MDCCCLXV.

⟨i⟩-⟨xii⟩, ⟨1⟩-104. $8\frac{3}{4}'' \times 6\frac{5}{8}''$.

A copy in UV inscribed by Parsons May 1, 1865; a copy in H inscribed by Parsons May 8, 1865. Deposited May 17, 1865. Listed as an American book PC July 1, 1865.

AAS B H LC UV Y

15530. THE ROSARY . . . EIGHTY COPIES PRINTED.

CAMBRIDGE, MASSACHUSETTS: JOHN WILSON AND SONS. 1865.

Title-page in black and red.

⟨3⟩-46, blank leaf. Laid paper.

⟨1⟩³, 2-6⁴. ⟨1⟩₂ inserted.

Noted in the following bindings; sequence (doubtful) not known.

A

Leaf: 8⅞″ full × 6¾″. Unwatermarked laid paper.

Bound in purple C cloth. Blue end papers. Laid paper flyleaves. Top edges gilt.

B

Leaf: 9³⁄₁₆″ × 6¹⁵⁄₁₆″. Unwatermarked laid paper.

Bound in tan-gray paper boards, printed paper label on front. Top edges not gilded. Wove paper flyleaves. Green-coated end papers; blue paper end papers.

C

Leaf: 10⅝″ × 7⅜″. Wove paper watermarked *J Whatman Turkey Mill 1865.*

Bound in red P cloth, goldstamped. Top edges not gilded. Blue paper end papers. Wove paper flyleaves.

A copy of A (in H) inscribed Christmas, 1865. Copies of B (in H, Y) inscribed Christmas, 1865.

AAS (B) H (A,B,C) NYPL (A) Y (A,B)

15531. THE MAGNOLIA . . .

CAMBRIDGE, MASSACHUSETTS: JOHN WILSON AND SON. 1866.

Title-page in black and red.

⟨i-iv⟩, ⟨1⟩-58. 11¹¹⁄₁₆″ × 9⅛″ full.

⟨a-b⟩¹, 1-7⁴, 8¹.

C cloth: green; purple-black; red; terra-cotta. Yellow-coated end papers. Flyleaves; or, single flyleaf at front, double flyleaf at back. Top edges gilt. *Note:* Front stamped with a floral ornament which occurs in two positions of unknown sequence if sequence there is:

A

The stem points to the lower left corner of the front.

B

The stem in a more or less vertical position pointing to bottom center of the front.

Copies in H inscribed by the author Dec. 1866. A copy in H inscribed by the author Jan. 1867. Listed ALG Feb. 1, 1867.

BA BPL H MHS Y

15532. The First Canticle Inferno of the Divine Comedy of Dante Alighieri Translated by Thomas William Parsons

Boston De Vries, Ibarra and Company
MDCCCLXVII

Noted in the following forms. The sequence, if any, has not been established and the designations are all but arbitrary.

A

Title-page as above.

Pagination: ⟨i-iv⟩, ⟨1⟩-216. Not illustrated. Leaf (all edges trimmed, top edges gilt): 8⅞″ full × 6¾″.

⟨-⟩², 1-27⁴. Signature mark 21 present in full; or, with the figure 2 lacking; or, totally absent.

C cloth: purple; red. Covers bevelled. Sides blindstamped with a double rule frame. Front lettered in gold: *Dante. | Inferno. | T. W. Parsons.* ⟨note presence of the periods⟩ Spine stamped in gold save as noted: ⟨double rule⟩ | *The | Divine | Comedy | Boston.* | ⟨double rule⟩ Spine decorated in blind with an arrangement of three quadruple rules. Violet-coated end papers. Wove paper flyleaves.

Note: The dedication set in roman and in old English faces.

Locations: H (4 copies, three being inscribed respectively to Lowell, Emerson, Norton, under date *August, 1867*) Y

B

Title-page: As above save for the imprint which reads: *New York G. P. Putnam and Son* MDCCCLXVII

Pagination: ⟨i-iv⟩, ⟨1⟩-216. Not illustrated. Leaf (all edges trimmed, top edges gilt): 8¹⁵⁄₁₆″ scant × 6¾″.

⟨-⟩², 1-27⁴. Signature mark 21 present either in full or with the 2 lacking.

C cloth: purple; red. Covers bevelled. Sides blindstamped with a double rule frame. Front lettered in gold: *Dante | Inferno | T. W. Parsons |* ⟨note absence of periods in first two lines⟩ Spine stamped in gold save as noted: ⟨double rule⟩ | *The | Divine | Comedy | ⟨double rule⟩* Spine decorated in blind with an arrangement of three quadruple rule. Violet-coated end papers. Wove paper flyleaves; or, laid paper flyleaves.

Note: The dedication set in roman and in old English faces.

Locations: H (2 copies, one being inscribed by Parsons *September, 1867*) Y (Inscribed by Parsons *August, 1867*)

C

Title-page imprinted: Boston De Vries, Ibarra and Company MDCCCLXVII

Pagination: ⟨i-iv⟩, ⟨1⟩-216. Illustrated by the insertion of an engraved frontispiece and 75 numbered plates. Leaf (top edges gilt, other edges trimmed): $8^{15}/_{16}'' \times 6^{11}/_{16}''$.

⟨-⟩², 1-27⁴. The *2* in signature mark 21 lacking.

C cloth: purple. Covers bevelled. Sides blind-stamped with a double rule frame. Front gold-stamped: *The | Divine | Comedy* Spine goldstamped: DANTE'S | INFERNO | ⟨*decorated rule*⟩ | PARSONS | DORE'S ILLUSTRATIONS ⟨*decorated with rules and flourishes*⟩ All of the preceding in a single rule frame. Violet end papers. Wove paper fly-leaves.

Note: The dedication set in roman face only.

Locations: H (Inscribed by Parsons *September-1867*)

D

Title-page imprinted: Boston De Vries, Ibarra and Company MDCCCLXVII

Pagination: ⟨i-iv⟩, ⟨1⟩-216. Illustrated by the insertion of a photograph of a mask of Dante. Leaf (top edges gilt, otherwise untrimmed): $9^{1}/_{4}'' \times 7^{1}/_{8}''$.

⟨-⟩², 1-27⁴. Signature mark 21 either present; or, absent.

C cloth: purple. Covers bevelled. Sides unstamped. Spine stamped in gold save as noted: ⟨*quadruple rule*⟩ | *The | Divine | Comedy* | ⟨*quadruple rule*⟩ Spine decorated in blind with an arrangement of three quadruple rules. Marbled green end papers mounted on white paper. Laid paper flyleaves. Also: Mottled red and black end papers mounted on white paper.

Note: The dedication set in roman face only.

Locations: AAS (Inscribed by Parsons *October 1867*) H (Inscribed by Parsons *October 1867*) UV (Inscribed by Parsons *October 1867*)

E

Title-page imprinted: Boston De Vries, Ibarra and Company MDCCCLXVII

⟨i-iv⟩, ⟨1⟩-216. Not illustrated. Leaf (all edges trimmed, top edges gilt): $8^{15}/_{16} \times 6^{3}/_{4}''$.

⟨-⟩², 1-27⁴. The figure *2* in signature mark 21 lacking.

C cloth: purple-brown. Covers bevelled. Sides blindstamped with a double-rule frame. Front

lettered in gold: *Dante | Inferno | T.W. Parsons* ⟨*note absence of periods in first two lines*⟩ Spine stamped in gold save as noted: ⟨*double rule*⟩ | *The | Divine | Comedy | ⟨*double rule*⟩ Spine decorated in blind with an arrangement of three quadruple rules. Violet-coated end papers. Wove paper flyleaves.

Note: The dedication is set in roman face only.

Locations: UV (Inscribed by Parsons Nov. 4, *1867*)

F

Title-page imprinted: Boston De Vries, Ibarra and Company MDCCCLXVII

⟨i-iv⟩, ⟨1⟩-216. Illustrated by the insertion of a photograph of a mask of Dante. Leaf (top edges gilt, otherwise untrimmed): $9^{1}/_{8}'' \times 7^{3}/_{16}''$.

⟨-⟩², 1-27⁴. Signature mark 21 present in full.

C cloth: purple. Covers bevelled. Sides unstamped. Spine stamped in gold save as noted: ⟨*quadruple rule*⟩ | *The | Divine | Comedy* | ⟨*quadruple rule*⟩ Spine decorated in blind with an arrangement of three quadruple rules. Green-coated end papers mounted on white wove paper. Wove paper flyleaves.

Note: The dedication set in roman and in old English faces.

Locations: B   Y

G

Title-page imprinted: Boston De Vries, Ibarra and Company MDCCCLXVII

⟨i-iv⟩, ⟨1⟩-216. Illustrated by the insertion of an engraved frontispiece and 75 numbered plates. Leaf (top edges gilt, other edges trimmed): $8^{7}/_{8}'' \times 6^{1}/_{2}''$.

⟨-⟩², 1-27⁴. Signature mark 21 lacks the figure *2*.

C cloth: purple. Covers bevelled. Sides blind-stamped with a double rule frame. Front stamped in gold: *The | Divine | Comedy.* Spine stamped in gold: DANTE'S | INFERNO | ⟨*decorated rule*⟩ | PARSONS | DORE'S ILLUSTRATIONS ⟨*decorated with rules and flourishes*⟩ | BOSTON. All the preceding in a single rule frame. Violet-coated end papers. Wove paper flyleaves.

Note: The dedication set in roman only.

Location: AAS

H

Title-page imprinted: Boston De Vries, Ibarra and Company MDCCCLXVII

⟨i-iv⟩, ⟨1⟩-216. Illustrated by the insertion of an engraved frontispiece and 75 numbered plates. Leaf (top edges gilt, other edges trimmed): $8^{7}/_{8}''$ full $\times 6^{11}/_{16}''$.

⟨-⟩², 1-27⁴. Signature mark 21 present.

C cloth: purple. Covers bevelled. Sides blind-stamped with a double rule frame. Spine gold-stamped: DANTE'S / INFERNO / ⟨decorated rule⟩ / PARSONS / DORE'S ILLUSTRATIONS ⟨decorated with rules and flourishes⟩ / DEVRIES IBARRA & CO. / BOSTON. / All the preceding in a single rule frame. Brown-coated end papers. Wove paper flyleaves.

Note: The dedication set in roman only.

Location: H

I

Title-page imprinted: *Boston De Vries, Ibarra and Company* MDCCCLXVII

⟨i-iv⟩, ⟨1⟩-216. Illustrated by the insertion of a photograph of a mask of Dante. Leaf (top edges gilt, otherwise untrimmed): $9\frac{3}{16}''$ × $7\frac{1}{16}''$.

⟨-⟩², 1-27⁴. The figure 2 in signature mark 21 lacking.

C cloth: purple. Covers bevelled. Front gold-stamped: *Dante / Inferno / T.W. Parsons /* Spine stamped in gold save as noted: ⟨*quadruple [?] rule*⟩ / *The / Divine / Comedy / ⟨quadruple [?] rule⟩* Spine decorated in blind with an arrangement of three quadruple rules. Green-coated end papers mounted on white paper. Wove paper flyleaves.

Note: The dedication set in roman and old English.

Location: H (inscribed by Parsons *January 1868*)

Copies of *Form A* (in H) presented to James Russell Lowell, Ralph Waldo Emerson, Charles Eliot Norton *August, 1867*. A copy of *Form B* (in Y) presented to William R. Alger *August, 1867*. Listed ALG Sept. 16, 1867; noted as both with and without illustrations. A copy of *Form C* (in H) presented to George Ticknor Sept. 1867. Copies of *Form D* (in AAS, H, UV) inscribed *October, 1867*. A copy of *Form E* (in UV) presented to Howard M. Ticknor Nov. 4, 1867. Deposited Jan. 25, 1868; no illustrations; the dedication in roman and old English. A copy of *Form I* (in H) inscribed by Parsons *January 1868*.

British Publication

Listed PC as an American book, Nov. 1, 1867, as both illustrated and unillustrated. Again listed PC as an American book, Dec. 10, 1867; unillustrated. Advertised by Low in PC Jan. 16, 1868, without illustrations, as an importation.

15533. A. E. G. . . .

Cambridge: Press of John Wilson and Son. 1869.

A memorial of Ann Eliza Gore Guild, 1826–1868.

"Le Pres so al Mattin' del Ver ci Sogna," p. 137. At end: *T.W.P.* Collected in *The Old House,* 1870, as "When Dreams Are Truest"; and in *The The Shadow of the Obelisk,* 1872, and *Poems,* 1893,

under the title "Morning Dreams." See in *Section Two* for a leaflet printing: *Love, Let's Be Thankful* . . .

B H

15534. THE OLD HOUSE AT SUDBURY . . .

CAMBRIDGE   PRESS OF JOHN WILSON AND SON 1870

Three states (printings?) noted:

FIRST STATE

⟨i⟩-⟨viii⟩, ⟨9⟩-114; tail-piece, p. ⟨115⟩; blank, p. ⟨116⟩; blank leaf; blank leaf excised. Illustrated. 8″ full × $5\frac{3}{16}''$ (untrimmed; *i.e.,* the so-called large paper format). $7\frac{1}{2}''$ scant × $4\frac{15}{16}''$ (trimmed paper format).

⟨1⟩⁴, 2-8⁸. Leaf 8₈ excised.

Untrimmed: C cloth: purple. Gray-coated end papers; cream-coated end papers. Flyleaf at front. *Trimmed:* C cloth: terra-cotta. Cream-coated end papers. Flyleaf at front. *Both:* Bevelled covers. Sides blindstamped with a rule frame, floriated at the corners. Spine stamped in gold: ⟨*double rule*⟩ / *The* / OLD / HOUSE / AT / SUDBURY / ⟨*ornament*⟩ / ⟨*double rule*⟩ Front cover not lettered. In the trimmed paper format all edges stained red.

Note: In some copies there is inserted between pp. ⟨88⟩-89 a 1-page note regarding the illustration on p. ⟨88⟩. At end of note: *B.P.* ⟨*i.e.,* Benjamin Pierce⟩.

P. ⟨v⟩, entry for p. 24: . . . PURO." Note presence of period.

P. vi, entry for p. 95: NATURAL HISTORY OE ⟨*sic*⟩ THE PEACOCK

P. ⟨vii⟩: In the leaders for the *Palm Leaves* entry there is a misplaced (above the line) dot; and, a comma instead of a period (5th point in the line).

P. 41: The vignette is printed in black.

P. ⟨115⟩: The tail-piece is printed in black.

On both p. vi and p. 100: *An Eastern Lesson* for *An Easter Lesson.*

SECOND STATE

Pagination: As above. Leaf $7\frac{5}{8}''$ × $4\frac{15}{16}''$ (trimmed, top edges gilt). $7\frac{5}{8}''$ × $4\frac{7}{8}''$ (trimmed, all edges gilt).

Signature collation: As above.

C cloth: yellow. Brown-coated end papers. Flyleaf at front. Covers bevelled. Sides blind-stamped with a rule frame, floriated at the corners. Front stamped in gold: *The Old* / ⟨*square ornament*⟩ *House at* / *Sudbury* / T. W. PARSONS./ ⟨*floret*⟩ ⟨*square ornament*⟩ 1870. ⟨*square ornament*⟩ Spine stamped in gold: ⟨*double rule*⟩ / *The* / OLD / HOUSE / AT / SUDBURY / ⟨*ornament*⟩ / ⟨*double rule*⟩ All edges trimmed, top edges gilt. *Also:* All edges trimmed and gilded, cream-coated end papers.

P. ⟨v⟩, entry for p. 24: . . . PURO" Note absence of period.

P. vi, entry for p. 95: NATURAL HISTORY OF THE PEACOCK

P. ⟨vii⟩: In the leaders for the *Palm Leaves* entry there is a misplaced (above the line) dot; and, a comma instead of a period (5th point in the line).

P. 41: The vignette is printed in brown.

P. ⟨115⟩: The tail-piece is printed in brown.

Note: The only examined copies do not have the inserted note at pp. ⟨88⟩-89.

On both p. vi and p. 100: The title is given correctly as: *An Easter Lesson.*

THIRD STATE

Pagination: As above. Leaf 7⅝" × 4¹⁵⁄₁₆".

Signature collation: As above.

C cloth: yellow. Cream-coated end papers. Flyleaf at front. Covers bevelled. Sides blind-stamped with a rule frame, floriated at the corners. Front stamped in gold: *The Old* / ⟨*square ornament*⟩ *House at* / *Sudbury* / T. W. PARSONS. / ⟨*floret*⟩ ⟨*square ornament*⟩ *1870.* ⟨*square ornament*⟩ Spine stamped in gold: ⟨*double rule*⟩ / *The* / OLD / HOUSE / AT / SUDBURY / ⟨*ornament*⟩ / ⟨*double rule*⟩ All edges trimmed and gilded. *Also:* Top edges gilt, other edges plain, brown-coated end papers.

P. ⟨v⟩: Entry for p. 24: . . . PURO" Note absence of period.

P. vi, entry for p. 95: NATURAL HISTORY OF THE PEACOCK

P. ⟨vii⟩, the leaders for the *Palm Leaves* entry are normalized.

P. 41: The vignette is printed in brown.

P. ⟨115⟩: The tail-piece is printed in brown.

On both p. vi and 100: The title is given correctly as: *An Easter Lesson.*

Note: Occurs both with and without the inserted note, pp. ⟨88⟩-89.

A copy of the *First State* (in H) inscribed by early owner *Dec. 28, 1869.* A copy of the *Second State* (in H) inscribed by Parsons *Jan. 1870.* A copy of the *Third State* (in Y) inscribed by Parsons *Jan. 1870.*

B (1st, 2nd)   H (1st, 2nd, 3rd)   LC (1st)   MHS (1st) Y (3rd)

15535. Reminiscences of Lucius Manlius Sargent: With an Appendix Containing a Genealogy of His Family, and Other Matters. By John H. Sheppard.

Boston: Printed by David Clapp & Son. 1871.

Printed paper wrapper.

Untitled prefatory poem (*Rest! noble spirit! where thy worth they know*), p. ⟨iii⟩. For a separate printing of the poem see in *Section Two* under *From the Reminiscences . . .*

H

15536. THE SHADOW OF THE OBELISK AND OTHER POEMS . . .

LONDON: HATCHARDS, PICCADILLY. 1872.

Two issues noted; the sequence presented is tentative:

A (B?)

⟨i-ii⟩, ⟨i⟩-⟨x⟩, ⟨1⟩-115. 7⅛" scant × 5⅜".

⟨A⟩⁶, B-H⁸, I². Leaves ⟨A⟩₁,₆ are blank conjugates; inserted by the binder?

Printer's imprint (John Strangeways, London) on reverse of title-leaf and at foot of p. 115.

B (A?)

⟨i⟩-viii, ⟨1⟩-115.

⟨A⟩⁴, B-H⁸, I². Leaf I₂ is a cancel; see below.

The blank leaves present in *Issue A* (see above) are not present.

Printer's imprint (John Strangeways, London) on reverse of title-leaf only; not at foot of p. 115.

Note: Leaf I₂ cancelled. Was the Strangeways imprint (present in *Issue A*) found offensive? The cancellans was printed from duplicate settings. Minute variations (virtually impossible to describe) are present; the most readily apparent variation being the letter *m*, stanza 1, verse 3, in the word *image.* In one setting the letter is unbroken; in the other setting the lower serif of the central vertical is broken. Hence, copies of *Issue B* occur with the leaf printed from one setting or the other. Presumably the settings were used simultaneously.

C cloth: purple. LI cloth: blue. P cloth: brown; purple. T cloth: green. Covers bevelled. An interleaved copy (presumably the author's) is in terra-cotta T cloth. Blue-green coated end papers. Edges plain; or, gilt.

Note: About twenty-five percent of the poems herein are here first collected; the remaining poems had prior book publication.

Advertised for *this day* PC May 1, 1872. Listed Ath May 4, 1872; PC May 16, 1872. Noted Ath June 1, 1872, as *just published*, with extract from a review. A copy of *Issue B* (in H) presented by Parsons to Longfellow, *London, June, 1872.*

AAS (B)   B (B)   H (A,B)   MHS (B)   NYPL (B) UV (B)   Y (A,B)

15537. The Milton Echo.

Milton, June 17, 1873. Published by the Ladies of the First Congregational Parish, Milton ⟨Mass.⟩

Caption-title. The above at head of p. ⟨1⟩. A four-page "newspaper".

"Sonnet by Giusti, to Giambattista del Vico, the Philosopher," p. 3. Collected in *The Willey House*, 1875.

H

15538. AGASSIZ MEMORIAL TEACHERS' AND PUPILS' FUND "THE PRAYER OF AGASSIZ" A POEM BY JOHN G. WHITTIER AND "AGASSIZ" A SONNET BY T. W. PARSONS

CAMBRIDGE   PRINTED AT THE RIVERSIDE PRESS 1874

Cover-title.

⟨1⟩-⟨7⟩; tailpiece, p. ⟨8⟩. Laid paper. 7⁷⁄₁₆″ × 4⅞″ full.

⟨-⟩⁴.

Printed self-wrapper.

Parsons's poem, originally in the *Boston Advertiser*, Jan. 19, 1874. Collected in *The Willey House*, 1875. For separate publication see *Agassiz* in *Section Two*.

AAS   BA   BPL   H   NYPL

15539. THE WILLEY HOUSE AND SONNETS . . .

CAMBRIDGE   PRESS OF JOHN WILSON AND SON 1875

⟨1⟩-42, blank leaf. 4 plates inserted. 7⁹⁄₁₆″ × 5⁵⁄₁₆″.

⟨1-5⁴, 6²⟩.

C cloth: orange-tan; purple; yellow. Bevelled covers. Brown-coated end papers. Flyleaves. Top edges gilt.

A copy in Y inscribed by Parsons *Jan. 1875*. For an extended edition see below under 1875.

H   NYPL   UV   Y

15540. The Ante-Purgatorio of Dante Alighieri Translated by T. W. Parsons

Cambridge   Press of John Wilson and Son August, 1875

⟨1⟩-46, blank leaf. 9½″ scant × 5¹³⁄₁₆″ (in wrapper). 10¹⁄₁₆″ × 5⅞″ (folded sheets).

Printed gray paper wrapper. Also noted as folded sheets.

AAS   H   UV   Y

15541. The Willey House and Sonnets . . . ⟨Extended Edition⟩

Cambridge   Press of John Wilson and Son 1875

For first edition see above under 1875.

Extended by the addition of "Sonnet to Henry W. Longfellow," p. 30; and "To Wendell Phillips," p. *31.

Sheets of the first printing but with the following alterations:

⟨1⟩₂₋₃ (the title-leaf and table of contents) cancelled and reprinted with table of contents extended.

Leaf ⟨4⟩₃ cancelled; leaves ⟨4⟩₃₋₄ inserted.

AAS   BA   H   LC

15542. Benjamin Peirce . . . A Memorial Collection, by Moses King.

Cambridge, 1881. Massachusetts.

Printed paper wrapper; and, cloth.

"Ben Dell' Intelletto," p. 3. Previously in *The Willey House*, 1875.

Two lines of poetry, p. 6: *Peirce! among living men thou morning star! | Shin'st Hesperus now where souls departed are. |* Dated at end *Oct. 9, 1880*. Not elsewhere located.

Four 4-line stanzas beginning *Peirce! who wast ever in our minds*, p. 37. For a leaflet printing of this poem see in *Section Two* under *Benjamin Peirce*.

Listed PW March 12, 1881.

AAS   B   H   NYPL

15543. Wayside Gleanings for Leisure Moments. ⟨Edited by Mrs. Anna L. Beck Möring⟩ Printed for Private Circulation.

⟨University Press: John Wilson and Son, Cambridge⟩ 1882.

Reprint save for:

"To a Lady, [Whose ring bore the motto Dieu est ma Roche.]," p. 10. Uncollected.

"Birth-Day Poem," *The Willey House*, 1875, appears herein under the title "A Plea for January."

H

15544. The Two Hundred and Forty-Seventh Annual Record of the Ancient and Honorable Artillery Co. . . . 1884–1885. Sermon by Rev. William Lawrence . . .

Boston: Alfred Mudge & Son, Printers, 24 Franklin Street. 1885.

Printed paper wrapper.

"To the Hon. Robert C. Winthrop," pp. 126–127. Originally in the *Boston Daily Advertiser* and *Boston Evening Transcript*, Feb. 25, 1885. Uncollected. Also issued as a separate; see in *Section Two* under

To Honourable Robert C. Winthrop . . . , n.p., n.d., 1885?

H

15545. Development of Christianity among the Cultivated Class of Romans, as Imagined by Dante, in the Instance of the Poet Statius, in the Twenty-Second Canto of the Purgatorio, Interpreted by Mr. Parsons . . .

Printed for the Concord School of Philosophy. ⟨n.p., n.d., 1886⟩

See next entry. For another version see in *Section Two*, below: *Canto Twenty-Second* and *Purgatorio. Canto Twenty-Second.* Collected in *The Divine Comedy* . . . , 1893.

⟨1⟩-11; blank, p. ⟨12⟩. 8⅛″ full × 5¾″ scant.

Printed self-wrapper.

P. ⟨1⟩: *Printed for the Use of the Concord School of Philosophy.*

BPL copy inscribed ⟨by Parsons?⟩ *July 1886.*

BPL

15546. Development of Christianity among the Cultivated Class of Romans, as Imagined by Dante, in the Instance of the Poet Statius, in the Twenty-First and Twenty-Second Cantos of the Purgatorio Interpreted by Mr. Parsons . . .

Printed for the Concord School of Philosophy. ⟨n.p., n.d., 1886⟩

Cover-title.

See preceding entry. For another version see in *Section Two*, below: *Canto Twenty-Second*; also, *Purgatorio. Canto Twenty-First*; also, *Purgatorio. Canto Twenty-Second.* Collected in *The Divine Comedy* . . . , 1893.

⟨i-ii⟩, ⟨1⟩-⟨8⟩, ⟨5⟩-11; blank, p. ⟨12⟩. 8⁵⁄₁₆″ × 5¾″. Wrapper of book stock pasted to the publication; front of wrapper being pp. ⟨i-ii⟩; back of wrapper being pp. 11-⟨12⟩.

Note: The text of "Canto Twenty-Second," pp. ⟨5⟩-11, printed from the altered setting of the preceding entry.

H copy inscribed by Parsons Sept. 15, 1886.

H

15547. Memorial Meeting. Proceedings of the Metaphysical Club . . . March 24, 1886, in Memory of Its Late President, Julia Romana Anagnos.

Boston: Press of Henry H. Clark & Co. 1886.

Printed paper wrapper.

"Julia Romana Anagnos," pp. 62-63; uncollected.

For a leaflet printing see *Giulia Romana Anagnos* . . . , in *Section Two*, below.

400 Copies. Printed privately . . . --- Certificate of issue.

H

15548. Opening Addresses Edited by Laurence Hutton

New-York The Dunlap Society 1887

Address, Sept. 11, 1854, pp. 107-110. Collected in *Poems*, 1893, as "Address for the Opening of the Boston Theatre, September 11, 1854."

For comment see entry No. 1045.

15549. Buds and Blossoms Illustrated

Philadelphia Peterson Magazine Co. 1889

"Pilgrim's Isle," p. 12. Collected in *Poems*, 1893.

EM

15550. A Memorial of the American Patriots Who Fell at the Battle of Bunker Hill, June 17, 1775 . . .

Boston: Printed by Order of the City Council. MDCCCLXXXIX.

"Ode for the Dedication of the Bunker-Hill Tablets," pp. 20-23. Uncollected. For publication in leaflet form see in *Section Two* under *Ode for the Dedication* . . .

H Y

15551. No. 27. Standard Recitations by Best Authors . . . Compiled . . . by Frances P. Sullivan . . . March, 1890 . . .

M. J. Ivers & Co., Publishers, 86 Nassau Street, N. Y. . . . ⟨1890⟩

"To a Lady for a Picture of Pansies," p. 23. For another (earlier?) printing see in *Section Two*, leaflet *Benvenuta Lilibœa.*

For fuller entry see No. 4161.

15552. Representative Sonnets by American Poets . . . by Charles H. Crandall

Boston and New York Houghton, Mifflin and Company The Riverside Press, Cambridge 1890

"To a Poet in the City," p. 252. Here reprinted? For comment on other appearances see *A Mood of May* . . . , in *Section Two*.

For fuller entry see No. 8374.

15553. Occasional Addresses Edited by Laurence Hutton and William Carey

New-York The Dunlap Society 1890

"An Address at the Players'," Dec. 31, 1888, pp. 134–135. Collected in *Poems*, 1893. For a separate printing see *Address to the Assembly* . . . in *Section Two*.

For fuller entry see No. 5655.

15554. CIRCUM PRAECORDIA . . .

BOSTON: PRINTED BY JOSEPH GEORGE CUPPLES AND PUBLISHED BY HIM AT THE BACK BAY BOOKSTORE 250 BOYLSTON STREET ⟨1892⟩

Title-page in black and rose.

⟨i-xii⟩, 1-93; blank, p. ⟨94⟩; plus: publisher's catalog, 8 pp. For leaf size see below under bindings.

⟨1⁵, 2-13⁴; plus: 14⁴⟩. ⟨1⟩₃ inserted.

Noted in the following bindings; the sequence, if any, has not been determined. It will be noted that the PW listing records two bindings. The following designations are for identification only.

A

V cloth: white. Stamped in gold only. Front: *Circum* | *Præcordia* | THE COLLECTS | OF THE | CHURCH | ⟨ornament⟩ | ⟨all the preceding in a filigree frame⟩ Spine: THE | COLLECTS | OF THE | CHURCH | ⟨rule⟩ | PARSONS | BOSTON: | CUPPLES White wove paper end papers. Top edges gilt. Leaf: 7¼″ × 4″ scant.

B

S cloth: dark slate gray. Goldstamped save as noted. Front: *Circum Præcordia* | THE COLLECTS | OF THE | CHURCH | ⟨ornament⟩ | ⟨all the preceding in a red-stamped filigree frame⟩ Spine: THE | COLLECTS | OF THE | CHURCH | ⟨rule⟩ | PARSONS | BOSTON: | CUPPLES White wove paper end papers. All edges stained orange. Leaf: 6⅞″ × 3⅞″.

C

S cloth: lavender. Stamped in lavender. Front: *Circum* | *Præcordia* | THE COLLECTS | OF THE | CHURCH | ⟨ornament⟩ | ⟨all the preceding in a filigree frame⟩ Spine: THE | COLLECTS | OF THE | CHURCH | ⟨rule⟩ | PARSONS White wove paper end papers. Top edges gilt. Leaf: 7⅛″ × 4″ scant.

D

V cloth: white. Stamped in gold save as noted. Front: *Circum* | *Præcordia* | THE COLLECTS | OF THE | CHURCH | ⟨ornament⟩ | ⟨the preceding 6 lines in purple enclosed by a goldstamped filigree frame⟩ Spine stamped in gold: THE | COLLECTS | OF THE | CHURCH | ⟨rule⟩ | PARSONS | BOSTON: | CUPPLES White wove paper end papers. Top edges gilt. Leaf: 7⅛″ × 4″.

A copy in BA (*Binding C*) inscribed by Parsons March 27, 1892. Listed in PW, as in two bindings, April 9, 1892.

AAS (D)   B (D)   BA (C)   BPL (B, C)   H (A, C)
Y (D)

15555. No. 36. Standard Recitations by Best Authors . . . Compiled . . . by Frances P. Sullivan . . . June 1892 . . .

M. J. Ivers & Co., Publishers, 379 Pearl Street, N. Y. . . . ⟨1892⟩

"At Fifty-One," p. 37. Otherwise unlocated.

For fuller entry see No. 5748.

15556. The Divine Comedy of Dante Alighieri Translated into English Verse by Thomas William Parsons with a Preface by Charles Eliot Norton and a Memorial Sketch by Louise Imogen Guiney

Boston and New York Houghton, Mifflin and Company   The Riverside Press, Cambridge 1893

⟨i-iv⟩, ⟨i⟩-⟨xx⟩, ⟨1⟩-353; blank, p. ⟨354⟩; advertisement, p. ⟨355⟩. *Trimmed:* 7⅜″ × 4¹⁵⁄₁₆″. *Untrimmed:* 7⁹⁄₁₆″ × 5″ full.

Trimmed: Maroon V cloth stamped in gold and blind. *Untrimmed:* Maroon V cloth, printed paper label on spine. On label: . . . *First Edition*

Publisher's Records

Nov. 13, 1893: 784 copies printed.

Nov. 17, 1893–Feb. ⟨4?⟩ ⟨1894?⟩: Sheets put in binding.

Nov. 29, 1893: 100 back labels printed.

Dec. 1, 1893: 30 copies bound untrimmed.

June 8, 1896: Plates altered.

June 11, 1896: 150 copies printed. Date altered to 1896.

Deposited Nov. 20, 1893. Advertised and noted as *just ready* PW Dec. 2, 1893. Listed PW Dec. 9, 1893.

AAS   H   Y

15557. POEMS . . .

BOSTON AND NEW YORK HOUGHTON, MIFFLIN AND COMPANY THE RIVERSIDE PRESS, CAMBRIDGE 1893

⟨i-ii⟩, ⟨i⟩-viii, ⟨1⟩-250. *Trimmed:* 7⅜″ full × 4¹⁵⁄₁₆″ full. *Untrimmed:* 7⅝″ × 5¹⁄₁₆″ full.

⟨1-15⁸, 16⁶, 17⁴⟩.

Trimmed: Maroon V cloth, stamped in gold and blind. Blue-black-coated end papers. Flyleaves. Top edges gilt. *Untrimmed:* Maroon V cloth. Printed paper label on spine. On label: . . . *First Edition* White laid end papers. Flyleaves. Top edges plain. *Note:* The trimmed copies have been noted in polished V cloth; and, unpolished V cloth.

Publisher's Records

Nov. 20, 1893: 784 copies printed.

Nov. 22, 1893–March 22, 1918: Sheets put in binding.

Nov. 22, 1893: One copy bound in paper cover.

Nov. 29, 1893: 100 back labels printed.

Dec. 1, 1893: 30 copies bound untrimmed.

Nov. 22, 1929: Plates sent to C. C. Birchard & Co., Boston, Mass.

Deposited (trimmed, unpolished cloth) Nov. 27, 1893. Advertised and noted as *just ready* PW Dec. 2, 1893. BA copy received Dec. 5, 1893. Listed PW Dec. 9, 1893.

AAS   BA   BPL   H   LC   UV   Y

15558. History of the Military Company of the Massachusetts Now Called the Ancient and Honorable Artillery Company of Massachusetts. 1637–1888. By Oliver Ayer Roberts . . . Volume III.———1822–1865.

Boston: Alfred Mudge & Son, Printers, 24 Franklin Street. 1898.

"Sicut Patribus Sit Deus Nobis!," pp. 275-276. Written for the 218th anniversary of the company, June 2, 1856. Elsewhere unlocated.

H

15559. . . . Ipswich Dunes by Frank Bolles from the Atlantic Monthly . . . October, 1891 Also Selections from Old Ipswich in Verse . . .

Ipswich, Mass June, 1901 . . .

Unprinted brown paper wrapper.

"Burial of Augustine Heard," pp. 37-38.

FCW

15560. Characters in Tales of a Wayside Inn by John van Schaick, Jr. . . .

Boston   The Universalist Publishing House 16 Beacon Street ⟨1939⟩

"Some Letters of Parsons," pp. ⟨173⟩-195. All the letters are addressed to Longfellow.

BA

15561. LETTERS BY T. W. PARSONS EDITED BY ZOLTÁN HARASZTI . . . WITH AN ESSAY BY AUSTIN WARREN . . .

BOSTON, MASSACHUSETTS   PUBLISHED BY THE TRUSTEES OF THE PUBLIC LIBRARY ⟨1940⟩

⟨1⟩-126; blank, p. ⟨127⟩; Boston Public Library imprint, p. ⟨128⟩. Frontispiece inserted; other illustrations in text. 10⅝″ scant × 7¹¹⁄₁₆″ (wrapper). 10⁹⁄₁₆″ × 7¾″ (boards).

1-8⁸.

Printed gray paper wrapper. Also gray; also, green, laid paper boards sides, black V cloth shelfback.

"Reprinted, with additions, from the September, October, November, December 1938 and January 1939 issues of *More Books*, the Bulletin of the Boston Public Library."———P. ⟨2⟩. The entire printing consisted of 1000 copies in wrapper, 500 copies in boards, cloth shelfback; see p. ⟨128⟩.

B   BA   BPL   H   LC   NYPL   Y

Leaflets; and, sheet music. *Note:* Only that sheet music constituting first publication of the text (periodicals excepted) is here included. The order is alphabetical by title, not by date of publication. Publication dates for certain of these entries not known.

15562. AD SENATOREM ADVENAM IN ORIS PATRUM ADVENARUM

This appears to have evolved as follows:

A

AD SENATOREM ADVENAM IN ORIS / PATRUM AD-VENARUM. / ⟨*diamond rule*⟩ / ⟨*text: 6 lines in Latin*⟩ / SCITUATE, MASSACHUSETTS, / *June 30, 1877.* /

Single leaf. Wove paper. $8^{15}/_{16}'' \times 5^{9}/_{16}''$. Anonymous. *Proof only?*

Line 4: *Gentis, in aeternum, omen posuit Juris.* /

Line 6: *Lucida arena haec sic tibi pax maneat!* /

B

AD SENATOREM ADVENAM IN ORIS / PATRUM AD-VENARUM. / ⟨*text: 6 lines in Latin*⟩ / SCITUATE, MASSACHUSETTS. / *July 9, 1877.* / ⟨*diamond rule*⟩ / TO A SENATOR VISITING THE SHORE OF THE / PILGRIM FATHERS. / ⟨*7 lines of text*⟩ / ⟨*n.p., n.d.*⟩

Single leaf. Printed on recto only. Wove paper. $9'' \times 6^{3}/_{16}''$. *Note:* Size of leaf postulated. Noted only as a proof printing; so marked by both Parsons and the printer, John Wilson & Son. Anonymous.

Line 4: *Gentis, in aeternum, omen posuit Juris.* /

Line 6: *Lucida arena haec sic tibi pax maneat!* /

C

AD SENATOREM ADVENAM IN ORIS / PATRUM AD-VENARUM. / ⟨*text: 6 lines in Latin*⟩ / SCITUATE, MASSACHUSETTS, / July 9, 1877 / T. W. PARSONS. / ⟨*n.p., n.d.*⟩

Single leaf. Printed on recto only. Wove paper. $8^{13}/_{16}'' \times 5^{11}/_{16}''$ scant.

Line 4: *Gentis, in omine grandis posuit populi:* /

Line 6: *Sic tibi pax maneat lucida arena freti!* /

Uncollected.

BPL (A, C)   H (B, C)

15563. ADDRESS TO THE ASSEMBLY AT THE OPENING OF THE PLAYERS' CLUB IN NEW YORK ...

⟨n.p., n.d., 1888–1889⟩

Single leaf folded to make four pages. Laid paper. Watermarked: *Liberty Linen*   Page: $9'' \times 5^{3}/_{4}''$. Pp. ⟨2⟩ and ⟨4⟩ blank. Text on pp. ⟨1⟩ and ⟨3⟩.

Read at The Players by Lawrence Barrett, Dec. 31, 1888. Published in *Atlantic Monthly*, Feb. 1889; *Occasional Addresses*, edited by Laurence Hutton and William Carey, 1890, see above. Collected in *Poems*, 1893.

BPL   H   Y

15564. AFTER THE FUNERAL. H.M.P. MARCH 27, SUNDAY BEFORE PASSION SUNDAY, WHICH IS THE SUNDAY BEFORE PALM SUNDAY ... SCITUATE, LAST OF AUGUST, 1880 ...

⟨n.p., n.d., 1881?⟩

Single leaf. Printed on one side of leaf only. Laid paper. Watermarked: *Raven* ⟨?⟩ $9^{1}/_{8}'' \times 5^{11}/_{16}''$.

Prints two poems: "After the Funeral" and an untitled quatrain beginning *She never came: that shadow fell* ... Both published in *Century Magazine*, Aug. 1884. For another printing of both see below: *In Remembrance*.

"After the Funeral" collected in *Poems*, 1893, as "In Remembrance."

BPL   H

15565. AGASSIZ ... DECEMBER, 1873.

⟨n.p., n.d.⟩

Single leaf. Printed on recto only. $8''$ full $\times 4^{15}/_{16}''$. First published in the *Boston Advertiser*, Jan. 19, 1874. Also published in *Agassiz Memorial* ..., 1874, described above in *Section One*. Collected in *The Willey House*, 1875.

B   BPL   H

15566. ALL' AUGUSTA REGINA MAR-GHERITA DI SAVOJA

Two printings noted. Sequence not determined. The designations are completely arbitrary.

PRINTING A

ALL' AUGUSTA REGINA / MARGHERITA DI SAVOJA. / ⟨rule⟩ / ⟨text⟩ / T. W. PARSONS. / ⟨n.p., n.d.⟩

Single cut sheet folded to make four pages. Page: 7″ × 4½″. Text on p. ⟨1⟩, otherwise unprinted.

Location: BPL

PRINTING B

F.E.R.T. / *Fortitudo Eorum Romam* ⟨sic⟩ *Tenet.* / *The strength of Savoy hath possession of Rome.* / ⟨preceding three lines in a decorated box⟩ / ALL' AUGUSTA REGINA / MARGHERITA DI SAVOJA. / ⟨rule⟩ / ⟨text⟩ / ⟨n.p., n.d.⟩

Single leaf. 6¹¹⁄₁₆″ × 4⁵⁄₁₆″. Anonymous. Printed on one side of leaf only.

Location: BPL   H

15567. ALLE SORELLE . . . T.W.P.

⟨n.p., n.d.⟩

Single leaf. Laid paper. Also: Paper watermarked with a waffle-like pattern. 8¹⁄₁₆″ × 5⁵⁄₁₆″. Printed on recto only. Collected in *The Magnolia*, 1866. First published in *Albion* (N.Y.) June 17, 1865––– Goodspeed.

H

15568. "AND THERE IS NO HEALTH IN US." . . .

⟨n.p., n.d., *ca.* 1888⟩

Single leaf. Printed on one side only. 7¹¹⁄₁₆″ × 4¾″. Uncollected. First published in *Boston Sunday Herald*, April 15, 1888–––Goodspeed.

AAS   B   BPL   H

15569. AN AUTUMN HYMN . . . FOR THANKSGIVING EVENING, WARREN STREET CHAPEL, 1854 . . .

⟨n.p., Boston, 1854⟩

Single leaf. Printed on one side only. 7¼″ × 3⅞″ scant. Uncollected.

Also appears in *Transactions of the Norfolk Agricultural Society, for 1854;* see above under ⟨1854? 1855?⟩

H

15570. BACON AND SHAKESPEARE . . .

⟨n.p., n.d.⟩

Single leaf. Printed on one side only. 6″ full × 4⁷⁄₁₆″. Uncollected. First published in *Century Magazine*, Oct. 1901.

B   H

15571. BEN DELL' INTELLETTO . . .

⟨n.p., n.d., December 23, 1872?⟩

Single leaf. Printed on one side only. 7⅞″ × 5⅜″. First published *Boston Daily Advertiser*, Dec. 23, 1872–––Goodspeed. Collected in *The Willey House*, 1875.

Note: A proof printing (in BPL) does not have the author's name present.

AAS   B   H

15572. BENJAMIN PEIRCE . . .

CHRISTMAS-TIDE, 1880.

Single leaf. Printed on recto only. 6⁵⁄₁₆″ × 5″ full. Also in *Benjamin Peirce . . .*, 1881, described in *Section One.* First published in *Boston Daily Advertiser*, Dec. 18, 1880–––Goodspeed. Uncollected.

H

15573. BENVENUTA LILIBŒA . . .

⟨n.p., n.d., *ca.* 1888⟩

Single leaf. Printed on recto only. 6¹³⁄₁₆″ × 4¹¹⁄₁₆″. Uncollected. First published in *Boston Daily Advertiser*, March 16, 1888–––Goodspeed. For another printing see *No. 27 Standard Recitations . . .* ⟨1890⟩, in *Section One.*

B   H

15574. THE BIRTHDAY OF MICHAEL ANGELO . . .

⟨n.p., n.d., Boston, 1875?⟩

The above on p. ⟨1⟩.

Pp. ⟨1⟩-4. 9⅝″ × 6³⁄₁₆″. Single leaf folded to make four pages.

The above is presumably the first published form. Also exists in a pasted-up galley proof which shows some textual variations as, for example:

Galley proof: Introductory verses read: . . . *One of thy country's . . .*

Published form: Introductory verses read: . . . *One of his country's . . .*

First published in *The Journal of Speculative Philosophy* (St. Louis), April, 1875–––Goodspeed. "This little poem was written for the anniversary of the four hundredth birthday of Michael Angelo, as celebrated by the Woman's Club of Boston."–––Terminal note.

Also issued in book form, London, 1875; see in *Section Three.*

H (both)

15575. CANDLEMAS NIGHT . . .

⟨n.p., n.d., 1884?⟩

Single leaf. Printed on recto only. 10¹⁵⁄₁₆″ × 5⅝″.

Three printings noted; sequence not determined. The designations are for indentification only; no sequence is suggested.

A

Letterpress set 8″ deep. Footnotes present. Noted on both laid and on wove papers.

B

Letterpress set 8⁹⁄₁₆″ deep. Footnotes present. Noted on wove paper only.

C

Footnotes not present. Noted on wove paper only.

Written in memory of Wendell Phillips who died Feb. 2, 1884. First published in *Boston Daily Advertiser*, Feb. 5, 1884———Goodspeed. Collected in *Poems*, 1893.

AAS (C) BPL (A) H (A, B, C,)

15576. CANTO TWENTY-SECOND . . .

⟨n.p., n.d.⟩

Proof only? Single cut sheet. Printed on recto only. 16⅝″ full × 6⁵⁄₁₆″. Anonymous. For another printing see *Purgatorio. Canto Twenty-Second*, below.

Precise date of publication not known. Collected in *The Divine Comedy* . . . , 1893. Also see *Development of Christianity among the Cultivated Class of Romans . . . Twenty-Second Canto* . . . , Printed for the Concord School of Philosophy ⟨n.p., n.d., 1886⟩; and, *Development of Christianity among the Cultivated Class of Romans . . . Twenty-First and Twenty-Second Cantos* . . . , Printed for the Concord School of Philosophy ⟨n.p., n.d., 1886⟩.

H

15577. . . . A CHRISTMAS CAROL . . .

⟨n.p., n.d., *ca.* 1856?⟩

Single leaf. Printed on one side of leaf only. 9⅞″ scant × 7¼″ full. Anonymous.

First published in *Putnam's Monthly Magazine*, Jan. 1856; and, the *Boston Courier*, Dec. 25, 1855. Stanzas 1–2 collected in *The Rosary*, 1865.

At head of title: ⟨7 lines from *Hamlet*, Act 1, Sc. 1⟩

The above consists of four seven-line stanzas. The first two stanzas were reprinted in the following forms. Sequence not known and the designations are for identification only.

REPRINT A

A CHRISTMAS CAROL. | ⟨7 lines from Hamlet⟩ | ⟨text: 2 7-line stanzas⟩ | ⟨n.p., n.d.⟩

Anonymous. Single leaf of wove paper. Printed on recto only. 8½″ × 5⁷⁄₁₆″.

Location: BPL

REPRINT B

A CHRISTMAS CAROL. | ⟨diamond rule⟩ | ⟨7 lines from Hamlet⟩ | ⟨text: 2 7-line stanzas⟩ | T. W. PARSONS. | ⟨n.p., n.d.⟩

Single leaf of wove paper. Printed on recto only. 7″ scant × 4⅜″.

Location: BPL

REPRINT C

Same as *Reprint B* but printed on laid paper watermarked *Royal Irish Linen;* watermark conjectured. 7¾″ scant × 4⅞″.

Location: H

REPRINT D

Same as *Reprint B* but printed on laid paper watermarked *Royal Irish Linen;* watermark conjectured. The whole within a red-rule frame.

Location: H

B H

City of Boston. Ninety-Second Anniversary . . .

See below under *Original Ode.*

15578. A COLLECT FOR ST. BARNABAS'S DAY. A PRAYER FOR THOSE IN THE HOSPITAL . . .

⟨n.p., n.d.⟩

Single leaf. Printed on recto only. Laid paper. The only copy located indicates the presence of an unreadable typographic watermark. 5⁷⁄₁₆″ full × 4³⁄₁₆″.

Collected in *Cirum Praecordia* ⟨1892⟩, as "A Christmas Carol for Patients in the Massachusetts Hospital."

BPL

15579. THE COLLECT FOR THE EIGHTH SUNDAY AFTER TRINITY . . .

⟨n.p., n.d.⟩

Single leaf. Printed on recto only. Laid paper. The only copy located has an unreadable watermark. 4¹⁵⁄₁₆″ × 4½″ scant.

Collected in *Circum Praecordia* ⟨1892⟩, as "The Eighth Sunday after Trinity."

BPL

15580. THE COLLECT FOR THE FIFTH SUNDAY AFTER TRINITY . . .

⟨n.p., n.d.⟩

Single leaf. Laid paper. Watermarked *Old Berkshire*⟨?⟩. 5⁷⁄₁₆″ × 4³⁄₁₆″. Printed on recto only.

Collected in *Circum Praecordia* ⟨1892⟩, as "The Fifth Sunday after Trinity."

BPL

15581. THE COLLECT FOR THE FIFTH SUNDAY IN LENT...A LESSON FOR LENT...

⟨n.p., n.d.⟩

Single leaf. Laid paper. Watermarked *Berkshire Mills 1890*. $5\frac{15}{16}'' \times 4\frac{3}{16}''$. Printed on recto only.

"The Collect," much altered and revised, appears in *Circum Praecordia* ⟨1892⟩, as "The Fifth Sunday in Lent."

"A Lesson for Lent," collected in *Circum Praecordia* ⟨1892⟩. According to Goodspeed first published in the *Boston Post* and the *Boston Transcript*, March 14, 1891. Also in *The Divine Comedy* ..., 1893, p. 351, as "Fragment of Canto the Fifth." Compare with "An Easter Lesson," *The Rosary*, 1865; and *A Lesson for Easter* in *Section Two*.

H

15582. THE COLLECT FOR THE FOURTH SUNDAY BEFORE CHRISTMAS, OR ADVENT SUNDAY...

⟨n.p., n.d., 1890?⟩

Single leaf. Gray-blue linen finish paper. $7\frac{7}{8}''$ scant $\times 4\frac{13}{16}''$.

Collected in *Circum Praecordia* ⟨1892⟩. First published in the *Boston Post*, Dec. 1, 1890——— Goodspeed.

AAS H

15583. THE COLLECT. FOR THE SUNDAY AFTER ASCENSION DAY.

Not seen. Entry from Goodspeed, p. 23. Noted only as published in *Circum Praecordia* ⟨1892⟩ under the title "The Sunday after Ascension Day."

15584. THE COLLECT FOR THE SUNDAY AFTER CHRISTMAS DAY...⟨BY⟩ T. W. PARSONS. THE DYING YEAR...⟨BY⟩ ADELINE TREADWELL LUNT.

⟨n.p., n.d., 1891?⟩

Single leaf. Printed on recto only. $7\frac{1}{2}'' \times 4\frac{1}{8}''$. Parsons's *Collect*, much revised and extended, collected in *Circum Praecordia* ⟨1892⟩, as "Christmas Day."

H

15585. THE COLLECT FOR THE TWENTIETH SUNDAY AFTER TRINITY...

⟨n.p., n.d., 1890⟩

Single leaf. Gray-blue linen finish paper. Printed on one side of leaf only. $4\frac{7}{8}''$ scant $\times 3\frac{7}{8}''$.

First published in *Boston Post*, Oct. 18, 1890. Collected in *Circum Praecordia* ⟨1892⟩, under the title "The Twentieth Sunday after Trinity."

H

15586. THE COLLECT FOR TRINITY SUNDAY

Not seen. According to Goodspeed, p. ⟨1⟩, this was issued as a leaflet; not located by BAL. Begins: *"Almighty Father! everlasting God*... Collected in *Circum Praecordia* ⟨1892⟩, as "Trinity."

15587. THE COLLECT FOR WHITSUNDAY ...COROLLARY FROM DANTE...

⟨n.p., n.d.⟩

Single leaf. Printed on recto only. Watermarked (conjectured) with a shield bearing *H M Co* $7''$ scant $\times 4\frac{15}{16}''$.

"The Collect..." in *Circum Praecordia* ⟨1892⟩, as "Whitsunday."

"Corollary..." in *Circum Praecordia* ⟨1892⟩, as "A Passage from the Paradiso."

BPL

15588. COUNT ERNST VON MANSFELDT THE PROTESTANT

Three printings noted:

FIRST PRINTING

COUNT ERNST VON MANSFELDT THE / PROTESTANT. / ⟨simple rule⟩ / ⟨text⟩ / ⟨n.p., n.d.⟩

P. ⟨1⟩ as above. Anonymous. First published in *Century Magazine*, June, 1884.

Single cut sheet folded to make four pages. Page: $7\frac{7}{8}''$ full $\times 4\frac{15}{16}''$. Wove paper. Watermarked: *Arlington Mills*

Text on pp. ⟨1–3⟩; p. ⟨4⟩ blank.

Stanza 3, line 3: *appoach* for *approach*

Stanza 13, line 1: *While she, all tears, yet kneeling said /*

A copy in H inscribed by Parsons *March, 1882.*

REPRINTS

COUNT ERNST VON MANSFELDT / THE PROTESTANT. / ⟨ornamented rule⟩ / ⟨text⟩ / ⟨n.p., n.d.⟩

P. ⟨1⟩ as above. Anonymous.

Single cut sheet folded to four pages. Page: $8\frac{1}{2}''$ scant $\times 5\frac{11}{16}''$. Laid paper.

Text on pp. ⟨1–3⟩; p. ⟨4⟩ blank.

Two printings of the reprint noted:

Reprint A

The statement (PRIVATE PROOF.) not present at head of title.

Stanza 3, line 3: *approach* correctly spelled.

Stanza 13, line 1: *She, still in tears and kneeling, said |*

Stanza 13, line 4: *. . . hearthy . . .*

Reprint B

The statement (PRIVATE PROOF.) appears at head of title.

Stanza 3, line 3: *approach* correctly spelled.

Stanza 13, line 1: *She, still in tears and kneeling, said |*

Stanza 13, line 4: *. . . hear thy . . .*

B (*Reprint A*) BPL (*Reprints A, B*) H (1st; *Reprints A, B*)

15589. . . . DANTE'S PURGATORIO. CANTO FIFTEENTH. TRANSLATED BY T. W. PARSONS . . .

⟨n.p., n.d.⟩

At head of title: [*Proof.* Three cut sheets, the largest measuring $16\frac{1}{4}'' \times 5\frac{5}{8}''$.

Proof only?

Note: A trimmed copy in Y lacks the word [*Proof.* Collected in *The Divine Comedy . . .* , 1893.

H

15590. DANTE'S PURGATORIO. CANTO XXX . . .

⟨n.p., n.d., 1883?⟩

Single leaf folded to make four pages. P. ⟨1⟩ as above.

⟨1⟩–4. Watermarked *Westlock* Page: $8\frac{7}{16}'' \times 5\frac{7}{16}''$.

Three editions noted:

1: Line 18: *An hundred leaped up to that moving shrine |*

2: Line 18: *An hundred spraug* ⟨sic⟩ *as to a moving shrine |*

3: Line 18: *An hundred sprang* ⟨sic⟩ *as to a moving shrine |*

Collected in *The Divine Comedy . . .* , 1893.

First published in *The Catholic World* (New York), April, 1883.---Goodspeed.

AAS (2d)   B (3d)   H (1st, 2d)   UV (2d)   Y (2d)

15591. DECEMBER FOURTEENTH . . . ANNIVERSARY OF THE DEATH OF PRINCE ALBERT, 1861.

⟨n.p., n.d.⟩

Anonymous.

The above on p. ⟨1⟩. Single leaf folded to four pages. Page: $5\frac{3}{4}'' \times 4\frac{15}{16}''$.

Pp. ⟨1–3⟩ imprinted with title and text; p. ⟨4⟩ blank.

First published in the *Boston Daily Advertiser*, Jan. 17, 1872. Collected in *The Shadow of the Obelisk*, 1872; *Poems*, 1893.

BPL

15592. DIES IRÆ . . . ⟨*Faintness of heart and sinking of the soul*⟩

⟨n.p., n.d.⟩

Single leaf. Laid paper watermarked: ⟨-----⟩n Printed on recto only. $5\frac{7}{16}'' \times 4\frac{1}{4}''$.

Uncollected.

BPL

15593. EASTER HYMN. TO BE SUNG AT THE CHURCH IN WAYLAND, EASTER SUNDAY, APRIL 16th, 1876. CHERUBINI . .

⟨n.p., n.d., 1876?⟩

Single leaf. Printed on recto only. $8'' \times 5''$. Collected in *Poems*, 1893.

BPL H

15594. EASTER SUNDAY ⟨*Breathe soft, O East wind, on our Easter-morn*⟩ . . .

Single leaf. Printed on recto only. $7'' \times 4\frac{5}{8}''$.

An obvious proof; probably of a newspaper setting. For formal (and revised) printing see *In the Church of the Immaculate Conception*; and, *In Remembrance*, both in *Section Two*.

H

15595. EMERSON . . .

⟨n.p., n.d., Boston, 1882?⟩

Single cut sheet. Printed on recto only. $10\frac{1}{2}'' \times 8''$ scant. Watermarked: *Old Reliable Mills*

First published in the *Boston Daily Advertiser*, May 30, 1882.---Goodspeed. Collected in *Poems*, 1893.

B   BPL   H   UV

15596. EPITAPH. FOR A MONUMENT IN LANCASTER, MASS. . . .

⟨n.p., n.d., not before April 20, 1887⟩

Single leaf. Printed on recto only. $7\frac{1}{8}''$ full $\times 4\frac{11}{16}''$.

Uncollected. Written in memory of George A. Parker, died April 20, 1887.

B   BPL   H

15597. EPITHALAMIUM ⟨*Blessed maiden! happy lover!*⟩ ...

⟨n.p., May 16, 1885⟩

Single leaf. Folded to four pages. Laid paper. Watermarked *Royal Irish Linen Marcus Ward & Co*

⟨1-3⟩, p. ⟨4⟩ blank. 5⅞″ × 5″.

Uncollected.

BPL   H

15598. EPITHALAMIUM. F.R. AND G.E.T. OCTOBER 21, 1868 ...

⟨n.p., n.d.⟩

Anonymous. By T. W. Parsons?

Single leaf. Printed on recto only. 8½″ × 5⅜″.

BPL

15599. FANNY READ MONTI. PALERMO, SICILY, JANUARY 11th, 1869 ...

⟨n.p., n.d., Boston?, 1869⟩

Single cut sheet folded to make four pages. Laid paper. Page: 8¹⁄₁₆″ × 4¹⁵⁄₁₆″. Printed on p. ⟨1⟩ only, otherwise blank.

Uncollected. Anonymous.

B   H

15600. FOR MARY DUDLEY'S MARRIAGE DAY: IN REMEMBRANCE OF FOURTEEN YEARS AGONE! AND IN HOPE OF A REMEMBRANCE FOURTEEN YEARS HENCE.

⟨WAYLAND, MASS.?⟩ OCTOBER, 1884.

The above on p. ⟨1⟩.

Single leaf folded to four pages. Text on pp. ⟨1-3⟩; p. ⟨4⟩ blank. 8″ scant × 5¼″. Watermarked: *Park Mills Super* ⟨*Bond?*⟩

Uncollected. Originally in *Our Young Folks* (Boston), Aug. 1870.

H

15601. FOR THE HEADSTONE ...

⟨n.p., n.d.⟩

Anonymous. Single leaf. Printed on one side only. Watermarked: *Whiting Paper Co.* 7⅜″ × 4⁹⁄₁₆″. Uncollected.

H

15602. FROM LONDON TO MILTON HILL ...

23, PALL MALL. JANUARY, 1872.

Single leaf. Printed on recto only. 7¹⁵⁄₁₆″ × 4⅞″. At end: *T.W.P.*

Collected in *The Shadow of the Obelisk*, 1872; *The Willey House*, 1875.

H

15603. FROM THE REMINISCENCES OF THE LATE LUCIUS MANLIUS SARGENT ...

BOSTON, JULY, 1871.

Single leaf folded to make four pages. Text on p. ⟨1⟩. Laid paper. 8″ scant × 5″ scant.

Anonymous. Appears also in John H. Sheppard's *Reminiscences of Lucius Manlius Sargent* ..., 1871, *q.v.*, *Section One*. Uncollected.

H

15604. GARFIELD ... SEPT. 26, 1881.

⟨n.p., n.d.⟩

Single leaf. Watermarked: *Ravelstone* Printed on recto only. 9¹⁄₁₆″ × 5¾″.

Uncollected.

Two printings noted; the sequence has not been established and the designations are for identification only:

Printing A

Stanza 3, line 1: ... *over* ...

Stanza 4, line 2: ... *peace!* ...

Printing B

Stanza 3, line 1: ... *o'er* ...

Stanza 4, line 2: ... *peace* ...

B (A)   BPL (A, B)   H (B)   LC (A)

15605. GIULIA ROMANA ANAGNOS ...

⟨n.p., n.d.⟩

Single leaf folded to four pages. P. ⟨1⟩ as above.

Text on pp. ⟨1⟩ and ⟨3⟩; pp. ⟨2⟩ and ⟨4⟩ blank. 6⅜″ × 5¼″ full.

Uncollected. First published in the *Boston Daily Advertiser*, March 15, 1886.---Goodspeed. For book publication see *Memorial Meeting* ..., 1886, in *Section One*.

BPL   H

15606. GOING TO BORDEAUX ...

IN BORDEAUX, JANNARY ⟨*sic*⟩ 16th, 1871.

Single leaf. Printed on recto only. 9⅛″ × 7⅜″.

Uncollected. Appears also in the *Boston Courier*, Feb. 17, 1871---Goodspeed.

H

15607. A GOLDEN WEDDING. [REPRINT-ED FROM THE "BOSTON COURIER" OF OCTOBER 4, 1867.] ...

⟨Boston, 1867?⟩

The above on p. ⟨1⟩.

Single leaf folded to make four pages. Text on pp. ⟨1⟩-3; p. ⟨4⟩ blank. 9½″ × 7⁷⁄₁₆″.

Text of account signed on p. 3 with the pseudonym *Viaterra*. Parsons's poem, "Our Golden Wedding on the Island," p. 3. Uncollected. Also appears as a separate; see *Our Golden Wedding on the Island*, below.

H

15608. GRAVESTONE OF DAVID STEUART ROBERTSON LANCASTER, MASS. ...

⟨n.p., n.d.⟩

Single leaf. Laid paper. Printed on recto only. 8¾″ × 6¹⁄₁₆″.

Also in *Poems*, 1854, as "Epitaph upon My Friend, David Steuart Robertson."

H

15609. IL GUIDO ROSPIGLIOSI ...

⟨n.p., n.d.⟩

Anonymous. Printed in black and red. Single leaf. Printed on recto only. 8⁹⁄₁₆″ × 6″.

First published in *Atlantic Monthly*, Jan. 1870---Goodspeed. Under the title "Guido's Aurora" appears also in *Shadow of the Obelisk*, London, 1872; *Poems*, Boston, 1893.

B H

15610. HELEN BISHOP ...

⟨n.p., n.d.⟩

Single leaf. Printed on recto only. 5⁷⁄₈″ scant × 4¹¹⁄₁₆″.

Uncollected. First published in the *Boston Post*, Aug. 4, 1890---Goodspeed.

BPL

15611. HYMN FOR THE ORDINATION AT WAYLAND. DATE 1886 ...

⟨Wayland, Mass, 1886?⟩

Single leaf. Printed on recto only. 9″ × 6¾″. Uncollected.

Note: Line 3, stanza 5: *With one great light* ... Also exists in a presumed proof state in which the line cited reads: *With a great light* ...

First published in *Boston Transcript*, Sept. 14, 1886 ---Goodspeed.

BPL (published printing)   H (both)

IL GUIDO ...

See under *Guido* ...

15612. IMPERIUM IN IMPERIO ...

⟨n.p., n.d.⟩

Single leaf folded to four pages. The above on p. ⟨1⟩. Anonymous.

Text on pp. ⟨1⟩ and ⟨3⟩; pp. ⟨2⟩ and ⟨4⟩ blank. 6⅜″ × 5⅛″.

Uncollected. First published in *Boston Daily Advertiser*, Dec. 23, 1878. A copy in H inscribed by Parsons Dec. 30, 1878.

B H LC

15613. ... IN ECLIPSE ...

⟨n.p., n.d.⟩

Single leaf. Laid paper. Printed on recto only. At head of title: *For the Century.* 9⁷⁄₁₆″ × 6¹⁄₁₆″. Watermarked: *Liberty Linen*

Collected in *Cirum Praecordia* ⟨1892⟩.

B BPL H UV Y

15614. IN MEMORY OF J.M.B. MARCH XXIX, MDCCCLXIII ...

⟨n.p., 1863⟩

Anonymous. A single sheet of stationery, laid paper, folded to four pages. Text on p. ⟨1⟩, otherwise blank. At upper left of p. ⟨1⟩: Embossed stamp of *Irving Mills.* 8″ × 4⁷⁄₈″.

Written in memory of J. M. Bowles. Uncollected.

H

15615. IN REMEMBRANCE ... SCITUATE BY THE SEA, LAST OF AUGUST, 1880.

⟨n.p., n.d.⟩

Noted in the following forms. The sequence has not been established and the designations are for identification only.

A(B?)

Pp. ⟨1-3⟩; blank, p. ⟨4⟩. Single cut sheet of wove paper folded to four pages. Page: 10″ × 7″.

The following features are sufficient for identification:

IN REMEMBRANCE. Note presence of the period. Printed from types ⁵⁄₃₂″ high.

Line 6: *Hangs wilted, watching for her wheels;* |

Line 14: *... thoughts* ...

Contents

"In Remembrance." Also appears in leaflet form as "After the Funeral"; see above. First published in *Century Magazine*, Aug. 1884. Collected in *Poems*, 1893.

Untitled quatrain beginning: *She never came. That shadow fell, to last . . .*, dated March 27, 1881. First published *Century Magazine*, Aug. 1884. Also in "After the Funeral" leaflet; see above.

Untitled ten lines beginning: *Into the noiseless country Annie went.* This is a revised form of the poem. For an earlier version see below under *Into the Noiseless Country Annie Went.* Collected in *Poems*, 1893.

Untitled twenty-four lines beginning: *O Rest of God that endeth every pain!* For a separate printing see below: *O Rest of God . . .* First published in *Century Magazine*, Aug. 1884. Collected in *Poems*, 1893.

B(A?)

Not from the same setting as the above.

Pp. ⟨1-3⟩; blank, p. ⟨4⟩. Single cut sheet of laid paper folded to make four pages. Page: 7⅜″ × 4¹¹⁄₁₆″.

The following features are sufficient for identification:

IN REMEMBRANCE   Note absence of period. Printed from types ⅛″ high.

Line 6: *Hangs wilted, watching for her wheels; |*

Line 14: *. . . thought . . .*

Contents: As in *Printing A.*

C

Revised and extended. Done from a completely new setting.

Pp. ⟨1-4⟩. Single cut sheet of wove paper watermarked: *Westlock* Page: 8½″ scant × 6⅞″.

Line 6 of "In Remembrance" reads: *Stands watching, waiting for her wheels; |*

Line 14 of "In Remembrance" reads: *. . . thought . . .*

Added text:

Untitled twenty lines beginning: *Child of light and hope! though fled . . .* Not by Parsons; by Louise Imogen Guiney. See BAL No. 6714.

"Easter Sunday, 1883." For other printings of this see *Easter Sunday*, above; and, *In the Church of the Immaculate Conception*, below.

BPL (A, C)   H (B, C)   UV (A)

15616. IN SAINT JOSEPH'S. AUGUST 10 . . .

⟨n.p., n.d., 1887?⟩

Single leaf. Printed on recto only. 6½″ × 4⅜″.

Written in memory of Adeline A. Parks, d. Aug. 8, 1887. First published in *Boston Daily Advertiser*,

Aug. 27, 1887———Goodspeed. Collected in *Circum Praecordia* ⟨1892⟩.

AAS   BPL   H

15617. IN THE CHURCH OF THE IMMACU-LATE CONCEPTION . . .

⟨n.p., March 27, 1883?⟩

The above on p. ⟨1⟩. Single leaf folded to make four pages. Text on pp. ⟨1⟩ and ⟨3⟩; pp. ⟨2⟩ and ⟨4⟩ blank. 7⅞″ × 4⅞″.

"In the Church of the Immaculate Conception," p. ⟨1⟩. Uncollected.

"Easter Sunday," March 27, 1883, p. ⟨3⟩. Appears also in *In Remembrance* and *Easter Sunday*, see above in *Section Two*. Uncollected.

AAS   B   H

15618. IN THE WOODS AGAIN . . .

⟨n.p., n.d.⟩

Single leaf. Printed on recto only. 8⁹⁄₁₆″ × 5½″.

For comment see below under *A Mood of May . . .*, wherein "In the Woods Again" appears under the title "June."

B   H

15619. INSCRIPTION FOR THE HOUSE LATELY OCCUPIED BY THE HON. GEO. LUNT IN SCITUATE, MASSACHUSETTS

In Latin. Five lines. *Not seen.* Entry from Goodspeed.

15620. THE INTELLECTUAL REPUBLIC

Two printings noted:

FIRST PRINTING

PRIZE POEM. | ⟨*wavy rule*⟩ | *Delivered before the Boston Lyceum.* | ⟨*wavy rule*⟩ | THE INTELLECTUAL REPUBLIC. | BY THOMAS W. PARSONS, JR. | ⟨*double rule*⟩ | ⟨*text: set in two columns divided by a wavy rule*⟩

Single cut sheet. Printed on recto only. 9⅞″ × 6⁵⁄₁₆″.

Line 26, column 2: *. . . Chaldaea's . . .*

SECOND PRINTING

PRIZE POEM | *Delivered before the Boston Lyceum,* | NOVEMBER 19, 1840. | ⟨*wavy rule*⟩ | THE INTELLECTUAL REPUBLIC. | BY THOMAS W. PARSONS, JR. | (*Spoken by Mr. Whiston, of the Elocution Class*) | ⟨*text: set in two columns divided by a wavy rule*⟩

Single cut sheet. Printed on recto only. 9⅞″ × 6⁵⁄₁₆″.

Line 26, column 2: *. . . Chaldæa's . . .*

First published in the *Boston Daily Advertiser*, Nov. 21, 1840----Goodspeed. Collected in *Poems*, 1854, as "The Intellectual Republic . . ."

BPL (1st)   H (2nd)

15621. . . . ⟨Ten-line poem beginning:⟩ INTO THE NOISELESS COUNTRY ANNIE WENT . . . EASTER MONDAY, 1881.

⟨n.p., 1881?⟩

At head of title: Six lines of verse beginning *O earth, so full of weary noises . . .*

Single leaf. Laid paper. 7⅜″ × 5¹¹⁄₁₆″.

Line 7: *Of gathering darkness, as I kneel before |*

Two printings noted:

First Printing

As above.

Second Printing

Single leaf. Laid paper. Watermarked: *Ravelstone* 7⅞″ × 5⅞″.

Line 7: *Of deepening darkness, as I kneel before |*

For another (revised) printing see *In Remembrance* leaflet, in *Section Two*, above. Collected in *Poems*, 1893.

B (2d)   H (1st, 2d)

15622. JAMES RUSSELL LOWELL'S BIRTH-DAY. FEBRUARY 22d, 1889 . . .

⟨n.p., n.d.⟩

Single leaf. Printed on recto only. 8⅛″ × 5″ scant.

Uncollected. First published in *The Critic* (N.Y.), Feb. 23, 1889.

BPL

15623. LAND OF COLUMBUS NATIONAL QUARTET COMPOSED FOR THE CHIL-DREN OF THE WARREN ST CHAPEL WORDS BY DR. T. W. PARSONS MUSIC BY GEO. HEWS.

BOSTON   PUBLISHED BY OLIVER DITSON & CO   277 WASHINGTON ST . . . ⟨n.d.⟩

Sheet music. Single page. The above at head of words and music. 13¹⁵⁄₁₆″ × 10⁹⁄₁₆″.

Otherwise unlocated.

B

15624. A LESSON FOR EASTER. FROM DANTE . . .

⟨n.p., n.d., 1880?⟩

In black and red.

Card. 3½″ × 4⅜″. Printed on recto only. The H copy inscribed (by Parsons?) *1880*. Also appears in *The Rosary*, 1865, as the last four lines of "An Easter Lesson." Compare with *The Collect for the Fifth Sunday in Lent . . .* above in *Section Two*.

B   H

15625. . . . ⟨Twenty lines beginning:⟩ LIKE AS THE LARK THAT SOARING HIGHER AND HIGHER . . .

⟨n.p., n.d., 1891?⟩

Single leaf. Laid paper. Watermarked: *Old Berkshire Mills*   Printed on one side of leaf only. 5⁹⁄₁₆″ × 4⁵⁄₁₆″. It is probable that a complete example of the watermark reads *Old Berkshire Mills 1891*

At head of title: "*Quale allodetta che in aere si spazia . . .*

Written in memory of James Russell Lowell, d. Aug. 12, 1891. First published in the *Boston Post*, Aug. 15, 1891. Collected in *Poems*, 1893, under the title "Like as the Lark."

B   BPL   H

15626. LORD ALFRED

First published in the *Boston Daily Advertiser*, Feb. 1, 1887.

Five separate printings noted. The order is not firmly established but *Form A* is probably the earliest since it contains (stanza 9, line 4): . . . *thy temples bare!*, which is the newspaper reading. All other printings are altered and read: . . . *discrownéd hair* or *discrowned hair*.

Uncollected.

PRINTING A

LORD ALFRED. | AN ELEGY. | ⟨*decorated rule*⟩ | ⟨*2 lines in Latin from Ovid*⟩ | ⟨*decorated rule*⟩ | ⟨*text: Five 4-line stanzas*⟩

At end of text, p. ⟨2⟩: T. W. PARSONS.

Single leaf. 8⁷⁄₁₆″ × 5½″. Possibly originally with blank conjugate. Printed on both sides: 5 quatrains on recto; 7 on verso.

Text

In the Ovid extract: *Meandri*

Stanza 2, line 1: . . . *only in their . . .*

Stanza 2, line 2: *Who hold . . .*

Stanza 3, line 2: . . . *styled: |*

Stanza 4, line 3: *O, who . . .*

Stanza 6, line 3: . . . *today, |*

Stanza 7, line 1: . . . *my Lord, . . .*

Stanza 7, line 4: . . . *baggary . . .*

Stanza 8, line 1: ... *Demos! You* ...

Stanza 9, line 1: *Was there* ...

Stanza 9, line 2: ... *my lord forbear |*

Stanza 9, line 4: ... *thy temples bare! |*

Location: UV

PRINTING B

LORD ALFRED. | *An Elegy.* | ⟨*simple rule*⟩ | ⟨*2 lines in Latin from Ovid*⟩ | ⟨*simple rule*⟩ | ⟨*text: Five 4-line stanzas*⟩

At end of text, p. ⟨3⟩: T. W. PARSONS.

Single leaf folded to make four pages. Page: 7″ full × 4½″. Text on pp. ⟨1⟩ and ⟨3⟩; pp. ⟨2⟩ and ⟨4⟩ blank.

Text

In the Ovid extract: *Mœndri*

Stanza 2, line 1: ... *only in their* ...

Stanza 2, line 2: *Who held* ...

Stanza 3, line 2: ... *styled: |*

Stanza 4, line 3: *Oh, who* ...

Stanza 6, line 3: ... *to-day, |*

Stanza 7, line 1: ... *my lord,* ...

Stanza 7, line 4: ... *beggary* ...

Stanza 8, line 1: ... *Demos! You* ...

Stanza 9, line 1: *Was their* ...

Stanza 9, line 2: ... *my lord, forbear |*

Stanza 9, line 4: ... *discrownéd hair! |*

Locations: B   H

PRINTING C

LORD ALFRED. | *An Elegy.* | ⟨*simple rule*⟩ | ⟨*2 lines in Latin from Ovid*⟩ | ⟨*simple rule*⟩ | ⟨*text: Five 4-line stanzas*⟩

At end of text, p. ⟨3⟩: T. W. PARSONS.

Single leaf folded to make four pages. Page: 7″ full × 4½″. Text on pp. ⟨1⟩ and ⟨3⟩; pp. ⟨2⟩ and ⟨4⟩ blank.

Text

In the Ovid extract: *Mœandri*

Stanza 2, line 1: ... *only to their* ...

Stanza 2, line 2: *Who hold* ...

Stanza 3, line 2: ... *styled; |*

Stanza 4, line 3: *Oh, who* ...

Stanza 6, line 3: ... *to-day, |*

Stanza 7, line 1: ... *my lord,* ...

Stanza 7, line 4: ... *beggary* ...

Stanza 8, line 1: ... *Demos, you* ...

Stanza 9, line 1: *Was there* ...

Stanza 9, line 2: ... *my lord, forbear |*

Stanza 9, line 4: ... *discrownéd hair! |*

Location: BPL

PRINTING D

LORD ALFRED. | *An Elegy.* | ⟨*decorated rule*⟩ | ⟨*2 lines in Latin from Ovid*⟩ | ⟨*decorated rule*⟩ | ⟨*text: Five 4-line stanzas*⟩

At end of text, p. ⟨2⟩: T. W. PARSONS.

Single leaf folded to four pages. Page: 8⁷⁄₁₆″ × 5½″. Text on pp. ⟨1-2⟩; pp. ⟨3-4⟩ blank.

Text

In the Ovid extract: *Meandri*

Stanza 2, line 1: ... *only in their* ...

Stanza 2, line 2: *Who hold* ...

Stanza 3, line 2: ... *styled: |*

Stanza 4, line 3: *O, who* ...

Stanza 6, line 3: ... *today, |*

Stanza 7, line 1: ... *my Lord,* ...

Stanza 7, line 4: ... *baggary* ...

Stanza 8, line 1: ... *Demos! You* ...

Stanza 9, line 1: *Was there* ...

Stanza 9, line 2: ... *my lord forbear |*

Stanza 9, line 4: ... *discrowned hair! |*

Locations: AAS   H

PRINTING E

LORD ALFRED. | *An Elegy.* | ⟨*simple rule*⟩ | ⟨*2 lines in Latin from Ovid*⟩ | ⟨*simple rule*⟩ | ⟨*text: Five 4-line stanzas*⟩

At end of text, p. ⟨4⟩: T. W. PARSONS.

Single cut sheet folded to make four pages. Page: 8″ × 5½″ full. Text on pp. ⟨1⟩ and ⟨4⟩; pp. ⟨2-3⟩ blank.

Text

In the Ovid extract: *Meandri*

Stanza 2, line 1: ... *only to their* ...

Stanza 2, line 2: *Who held* ...

Stanza 3, line 2: ... *styled: |*

Stanza 4, line 3: *Oh, who* ...

Stanza 6, line 3: ... *to-day, |*

Stanza 7, line 1: ... *my lord,* ...

Stanza 7, line 4: ... *beggary* ...

Stanza 8, line 1: ... *Demos! You* ...

Stanza 9, line 1: *Was their* ...

Stanza 9, line 2: ... *my lord, forbear* |

Stanza 9, line 4: ... *discrowned hair!* |

Location: AAS

15627. ... LOVE, LET'S BE THANKFUL WE ARE PAST THE TIME ...

Single cut sheet as follows: ⟨*one line from Dante*⟩ | ⟨*diamond rule*⟩ | ⟨*text: 16 lines*⟩ | T. W. PARSONS.

$5\frac{9}{16}''$ full × 5″. Printed on recto only.

Also in *The Old House at Sudbury*, 1870, under the title: "When Dreams Are Truest." Also in *The Shadow of the Obelisk*, 1872; and, *Poems*, 1893, as "Morning Dreams." For another printing see in *Section One* above *A.E.G.* ..., Cambridge, 1869.

AAS

15628. MARTIAL ODE. WRITTEN FOR THE ANCIENT AND HONORABLE ⟨*sic*⟩ ARTILLERY COMPANY ...

⟨n.p., n.d.⟩

Single leaf. Printed on recto only. $9\frac{1}{4}'' \times 5\frac{1}{4}''$ scant.

Two printings noted:

First Printing

In the heading: *Honorable*

Stanza 6, line 3: ... *eagle's* ...

Stanza 7, line 3: *Sound the State's* ...

Second Printing

In the heading: *Honourable*

Stanza 6, line 3: ... *Eagle's* ...

Stanza 7, line 3: *Speak England* ...

Note: Also appears under the title: "Ode. Ancient of Days," in *Order of Exercises ... June 4, 1888* ... ⟨Boston, 1888⟩, described below, *Section Two*, under title *1638.1888* ... Collected in *Poems*, 1893.

Caution: Not to be confused with another poem written for the Ancient and Honorable Artillery Company, 1856.

B (2d)   BPL (1st)   H (2d)

15629. ... MAY DAY ...

⟨n.p., n.d.⟩

Single leaf. $6\frac{7}{8}'' \times 4\frac{5}{8}''$. Printed on recto only. At head of title: *A Song for the Children.* Anonymous.

Appears also in *The Willey House*, 1875.

BPL

15630. MERCEDES

Two printings noted:

FIRST PRINTING

For the Springfield Republican. | MERCEDES. | ⟨*text*⟩ | T. W. PARSONS. | SCITUATE. | ⟨n.d.⟩

Single leaf. Printed on one side only. White paper. $7\frac{5}{8}'' \times 5\frac{9}{16}''$.

Line 9: *Less dear, less cherished than the tender tale* |

SECOND PRINTING

MERCEDES. | ⟨*text*⟩ | T. W. PARSONS. | BOSTON, 1878.

Single leaf. Printed on one side only. Gray paper watermarked with an all-over waffle pattern. $5\frac{1}{4}''$ scant × $4\frac{1}{4}''$. Also white paper damasked with rules, $6'' \times 4\frac{3}{4}''$.

Line 9: *Less dear a memory than the tender tale* |

First published in the *Springfield* (Mass.) *Republican*, July ⟨June?⟩ 26, 1878---Goodspeed. Collected in *Poems*, 1893.

AAS (1st)   B (2d)   BPL (1st)   H (both)   UV (1st)

15631. A MOOD OF MAY, A FYTTE IN JUNE, A JULY JESTING ...

⟨n.p., n.d.⟩

The above on p. ⟨1⟩.

Single cut sheet folded to make four pages. Page: $8\frac{1}{2}'' \times 5\frac{1}{2}''$.

Text on pp. ⟨1⟩ and ⟨3⟩; pp. ⟨2⟩ and ⟨4⟩ blank.

Contents:

"June." For another printing see leaflet *In the Woods Again.* In *Boston Evening Transcript*, May 21, 1884, under the title "To a Poet in the City." Also in *Atlantic Monthly*, June, 1884, under title "To a Poet in the City." Also in *Representative Sonnets*, 1890, as "To a Poet in the City." Collected in *Poems*, 1893, as "To a Poet in the City."

"July." Not elsewhere located. Not to be confused with another poem of the same name in *The Boston Book* ..., 1850.

"May." Elsewhere unlocated.

BPL

15632. ... O REST OF GOD THAT ENDETH EVERY PAIN! ...

⟨n.p., n.d., 1884?⟩

Untitled. First line as above. Preceding text: *Lo corpo ond' ella fu eacciata giace* ...

Noted in the following forms of unknown sequence; the designations are for identification only:

A

White laid paper. $8\frac{5}{16}''$ scant × $4\frac{3}{4}''$. Single leaf. Printed on recto only.

B

White wove paper. Portion of watermark present: TH $7^{15}\!/_{16}'' \times 4^{15}\!/_{16}''$. Printed on recto only. Single leaf.

C

Lavender laid paper. Watermarked: *A Pirie & Sons | 1866 Note:* It is doubtful that the watermark in its entirety is present in any single example. $7^{1}\!/_{8}'' \times 4^{1}\!/_{2}''$. Printed on recto only. Single leaf.

For a later revised version see *In Remembrance* leaflet in *Section Two.*

First published in *Century Magazine*, Aug. 1884. Collected in *Poems*, 1893.

AAS (A)   BPL (C)   H (A, B)

ODE. ANCIENT OF DAYS.

See entry No. 15657.

15633. ODE FOR THE DEDICATION OF THE BUNKER HILL TABLETS . . .

⟨n.p., n.d.⟩

The above on p. ⟨1⟩. Pp. ⟨1-3⟩; blank, p. ⟨4⟩. $10^{5}\!/_{8}'' \times 8^{1}\!/_{16}''$.

Single leaf folded to make four pages.

First published in the *Boston Transcript*, June 18, 1889———Goodspeed. Also in *A Memorial . . .*, 1889; see in *Section One.* Uncollected.

AAS   B   BPL   H   MHS   Y

15634. ODE IN PRAISE OF THE USEFUL ARTS; WRITTEN FOR THE MASSACHUSETTS CHARITABLE MECHANIC ASSOCIATION . . .

⟨n.p.,⟩ OCTOBER 14, 1857.

Single leaf of gray paper. Printed on recto only. $9^{3}\!/_{4}'' \times 7^{5}\!/_{8}''$.

The following readings present:

Stanza 5, line 3: *Excess . . .*

Stanza 8, line 4: *Who honours Heaven in honouring Art. |*

BPL has a proof printing in which the above readings are:

Stanza 5, line 3: *Except . . .*

Stanza 8, line 4: *Who honors Heaven in honoring Art. |*

Appears also in *An Address . . . by Joseph M. Wightman . . .*, 1857; see above in *Section One.* Also published in *Boston Evening Transcript*, Oct. 24, 1857.

Uncollected.

B   H   MHS

15635. ODE, WRITTEN FOR THE SIXTEENTH TRIENNIAL FESTIVAL OF THE MASSACHUSETTS CHARITABLE MECHANIC ASSOCIATION . . .

DAMRELL & MOORE, PRINTERS, 16 DEVONSHIRE STREET, BOSTON. ⟨n.d, 1854⟩

Single leaf. Laid paper. $10'' \times 7^{13}\!/_{16}''$. Printed on recto only. Small embossed oval wreath enclosing the name *Carew* in upper left corner.

Appears also in *Sixteenth Triennial Festival of the Massachusetts Charitable Mechanic Association . . . Oct. 11, 1854*, Boston, 1854. Originally in *Boston Transcript*, Oct. 12, 1854; *Boston Journal*, Oct. 12, 1854.

Uncollected.

H   MHS

15636. ODE WRITTEN TO COMMEMORATE THE 250th ANNIVERSARY OF THE BOSTON LATIN SCHOOL

Noted in the following forms:

FIRST PRINTING

ODE / WRITTEN TO COMMEMORATE / THE 250th ANNIVERSARY / OF THE / BOSTON LATIN SCHOOL. | ⟨decorated rule⟩ | 1 | ⟨12 lines of text⟩ | 2 | ⟨2 lines of text⟩

P. ⟨1⟩ as above. Anonymous.

Single cut sheet folded to make 4 pages. Unwatermarked wove paper. Page: $7^{7}\!/_{8}'' \times 5^{3}\!/_{8}''$.

Text on pp. ⟨1-3⟩; p. ⟨4⟩ blank.

Line 9 of "Epodos," p. ⟨3⟩: *. . . proud of garlands poorly got! |*

Three footnotes on p. ⟨3⟩.

Location: H

SECOND (THIRD?) PRINTING

ODE / WRITTEN TO COMMEMORATE / THE 250th ANNIVERSARY / OF THE / BOSTON LATIN SCHOOL. | ⟨decorated rule⟩ | ⟨3 lines from Horace⟩ | ⟨diamond rule⟩ | 1 | ⟨12 lines of text⟩ | 2 | ⟨2 lines of text⟩

P. ⟨1⟩ as above. Anonymous.

Single cut sheet folded to make 4 pages. Wove paper. Watermarked *Westlock* $8^{3}\!/_{8}'' \times 6^{3}\!/_{4}''$.

Text on pp. ⟨1-3⟩; p. ⟨4⟩ blank.

Line 9 of "Epodos," p. ⟨3⟩ concealed in part by a pasted cancel; see below.

Footnotes 3-7 on p. ⟨3⟩.

Locations: BPL   H

THIRD (SECOND?) PRINTING

ODE / WRITTEN TO COMMEMORATE / THE 250th ANNIVERSARY / OF THE /

BOSTON LATIN SCHOOL. | ⟨decorated rule⟩ | ⟨3 lines from Horace⟩ | ⟨diamond rule⟩ | 1 | ⟨12 lines of text⟩ | 2 | ⟨2 lines of text⟩

P. ⟨1⟩ as above.

Single cut sheet folded to make 4 pages. Wove paper. Watermarked *Westlock* 8⁷⁄₁₆″ × 6³⁄₄″.

Text on pp. ⟨1-3⟩. On p. ⟨4⟩: *A Committee of the Latin School Association having called upon Mr. Parsons for an Ode . . . he has consented to write one . . . a few copies have been privately printed . . . Little, Brown & Company.*

Line 9 of "Epodos," p. ⟨3⟩ concealed in part by a pasted cancel; see below.

Footnotes 3-7 on p. ⟨3⟩.

Location: H

The Cancel

The cancel present in the second and third printings occurs in two forms; the designations are for identification only and no sequence is either suggested or implied:

Cancel A

garlanded, but gloried not——— |

Noted in the H copies of *Printings Two* and *Three*.

Cancel B

garlanded, but gloried not; |

Noted in the BPL copy of *Printing Two*.

15637. ON A BUSTE OF DANTE . . .

⟨n.p., n.d.; after 1865, before 1893⟩

Single leaf folded to make four pages. Text on pp. ⟨1-3⟩; p. ⟨4⟩ blank.

Two printings noted; sequence undetermined.

PRINTING A

Laid paper. Watermarked *Fine Irish Linen.* 7³⁄₄″ × 5″ scant. 16 lines on p. ⟨1⟩.

PRINTING B

Laid paper. No watermark present in the copy examined. 8″ × 4¹⁵⁄₁₆″. 20 lines on p. ⟨1⟩.

First published in the *Boston Daily Advertiser*, Oct. 7, 1841———Goodspeed. First collected in *The First Ten Cantos . . .*, 1843, and reprinted in several successive books. Some of the later printings contain revisions.

H (A, B)

15638. ON A BUST OF LONGFELLOW . . .

⟨n.p., n.d., 1887?⟩

Anonymous.

Single leaf. Printed on recto only. 7″ full × 4¹⁄₂″ scant.

Uncollected. Originally in the *Boston Daily Advertiser*, June 28, 1887.

BPL   H

15639. ON A FADED PHOTOGRAPH. TO MRS. ANNIE FIELDS . . .

⟨n.p., n.d.⟩

Anonymous.

Single leaf. Printed on recto only. *Wove paper:* 6⁷⁄₈″ × 4⁷⁄₁₆″. Also noted on wove paper, heavily watermarked with vertical and horizontal rules to produce small squares: 7³⁄₁₆″ scant × 4⁵⁄₈″.

Uncollected.

BPL (both)

15640. ON A HEAD OF HERMIONE

Noted in three forms; sequence not determined:

A

ON A HEAD OF HERMIONE, | PAINTED BY WILLIAM WILLARD. | ⟨rule⟩ | ⟨text: 10 lines⟩ | ———T. W. PARSONS. | ⟨n.p., n.d.⟩

Single leaf. Printed on recto only. 7″ full × 4¹⁄₂″. Text set solid.

Line 5: *A face to love, unconscious of its charm,* |

Line 6: *Showing a soul incapable of harm;* |

Location: B

B

ON A HEAD OF HERMIONE, | BY WILLIAM WILLARD. | ⟨rule⟩ | ⟨text: 10 lines⟩ | T. W. Parsons. | ⟨n.p., n.d.⟩

Single leaf. Printed on recto only. Text spaced out; *i.e.,* a break between lines 6 and 7. 8³⁄₁₆″ × 5¹¹⁄₁₆″ full.

Line 5: *A face that could not frown, and if it smile,* |

Line 6: *Reveals a soul incapable of guile;* |

Location: AAS

C

ON A HEAD OF HERMIONE. | PAINTED BY WILLIAM WILLARD. | ⟨rule⟩ | ⟨text: 10 lines⟩ | ———T. W. PARSONS. | ⟨n.p., n.d.⟩

Single leaf. Printed on recto only. Text set solid. 7″ full × 4¹⁄₂″.

Line 5: *A face that could not frown, and if it smile,* |

Line 6: *Reveals a soul incapable of guile;* |

Locations: B   BPL   H

Collected in *Poems,* 1893.

15641. ON A PHOTOGRAPH JUST RECEIVED FROM A FRIEND IN ROME . . .

⟨n.p., n.d.⟩

Single leaf. Printed on recto only. $8^9/_{16}'' \times 5^1/_2''$ full (*Printing A*). $8^1/_{16}'' \times 5^3/_{16}''$ (*Printing B*).

Two printings noted; sequence not established.

A

Verse 9: *Where by Emmanuel* . . .

Verse 15: *Ev'n in this world* . . .

Verse 16: . . . *subject here* |

B

Verse 9: *Where Victor's name* . . .

Verse 15: *In this new world* . . .

Verse 16: . . . *lover here* |

Originally in *Atlantic Monthly*, Dec. 1887.———Goodspeed. Collected (*Printing B*) in *Poems*, 1893.

BPL (A)   H (B)

15642. ON A PICTURE . . .

AUGUST, 1877.

Single leaf. Printed on recto only. $8'' \times 5''$.

First published in *Boston Daily Advertiser*, Sept. 22, 1877———Goodspeed. Collected in *Poems*, 1893, as "Sonnet on a Photograph of an Unknown Lady . . ."

B H

AN OPEN LETTER TO THOMAS B. ALDRICH . . .

See: *La Pineta Distrutta*

15643. ORIGINAL HYMN ⟨in:⟩

Order of Exercises at the Unitarian Festival, at Music Hall, Tuesday, May 24, 1864 . . .

⟨n.p., Boston(?), 1864⟩

Program. Four pages. P. ⟨1⟩ as above.

"Original Hymn," *Ours, as our Father's God*, p. 3. Uncollected.

H

15644. ORIGINAL ODE ⟨in:⟩

City of Boston. Ninety-Second Anniversary of American Independence, July 4, 1868. Order of Exercises in Music Hall.

Alfred Mudge & Son, City Printers, 34 School Street.

Program. Single cut sheet folded to make four pages. On p. ⟨3⟩: "Original Ode," *Dependent man declared, one day* . . . Collected in *The Old House* . . . , 1870, as "Ode."

AAS

15645. OUR GOLDEN WEDDING ON THE ISLAND. ARRANGED FROM MENDELSSOHN, BY MR. F. F. HEARD TO BE SUNG BY MISS MARTHA B. STONE . . .

SEPTEMBER 25, 1867.

Single leaf. Laid paper. Printed on one side only. $7^3/_{16}'' \times 4^7/_8''$.

Anonymous. Uncollected.

For another printing see *A Golden Wedding*, above.

H

15646. OUR OCTOCENARIAN ⟨sic⟩ SCHOLAR, ON HIS BIRTH-DAY, MARCH 5th, 1886 . . .

⟨n.p., n.d.⟩

Single leaf folded to make four pages. P. ⟨1⟩ as above.

⟨1-3⟩; page ⟨4⟩ blank. Page: $6^3/_4'' \times 4^1/_2''$ scant.

Two issues noted:

A

Last stanza, line 1: . . . *are age-worn, blind,* |

B

Last stanza, line 1: . . . *are silent, blind,* |

First published in *Boston Daily Advertiser*, March 5, 1886; *Boston Transcript*, March 5, 1886. Uncollected.

BPL (A)   H (B)

15647. PARADISI GLORIA. WRITTEN AFTER HEARING A SERMON BY THE REV. DR. GEORGE PUTNAM . . .

⟨n.p., n.d., 1862?⟩

The above on p. ⟨1⟩. Single leaf folded to make four pages.

Text on pp. ⟨1⟩ and ⟨3⟩; pp. ⟨2⟩ and ⟨4⟩ blank.

Noted on laid paper watermarked *Royal Irish Linen Marcus Ward & Co* Leaf: $5^{15}/_{16}'' \times 4^{15}/_{16}''$. Also on unwatermarked wove paper; leaf: $6^3/_8'' \times 5^1/_8''$.

Collected in *The Rosary*, 1865.

B (both)   H (both)

15648. LA PINETA DISTRUTTA . . .

⟨n.p., n.d.⟩

Single leaf. $10^{13}/_{16}'' \times 5^9/_{16}''$. Printed on recto only.

First published in *Boston Daily Advertiser*, Nov. 17, 1883. Collected in *Poems*, 1893.

Another (later?) edition noted:

AN OPEN LETTER TO THOMAS B. ALDRICH, POET, IN BEHALF OF THE PHI

BETA KAPPA SOCIETY. LA PINETA DIS-
TRUTTA...

⟨n.p., n.d.⟩

Single leaf. 16⅝″ × 7³⁄₁₆″ full. Printed on recto
only.

Note: The texts vary.

B (presumed first)   BPL (both)   H (both)   Y (presumed first)

PRIZE POEM...

See: *The Intellectual Republic*

15649. PROEM. ⟨*Down by the sea, beside the
pilgrim dunes...*⟩

For publication as sheet music see below under
The Sphinx.

Three forms have been seen. The following order is
presumed correct.

A

PROEM. | ⟨*text: 8 lines, followed by 4 quatrains*⟩ |
⟨*n.p., n.d.*⟩

P. ⟨2⟩ as above. Five quatrains on p. ⟨2⟩.

Anonymous.

Printed on pp. ⟨2-3⟩; pp. ⟨1⟩ and ⟨4⟩ blank.
Leaf: 7¼″ scant × 4¾″.

The following is sufficient for identification:

Line 1 of poem (not of the "Proem"): *And one
day, wandering vacant on the strand,* |

H

B

PROEM. | ⟨*text: 8 lines*⟩ | ⟨*rule*⟩ | ⟨*10 quatrains*⟩ |
⟨*rule*⟩ | ⟨*n.p., n.d.*⟩

Anonymous.

Single cut sheet. Printed on recto only. 8¾″ × 4″
scant.

Line 1 of poem (not of the "Proem"): *And one
day, wandering vacant on the strand,* |

H

C

PROEM. | ⟨*decorated rule*⟩ | ⟨*text: 8 lines*⟩ | ⟨*rule*⟩ |
⟨*4 quatrains*⟩ | ⟨*n.p., n.d.*⟩

P. ⟨3⟩ as above. Five quatrains on p. ⟨4⟩.

Anonymous.

Printed on pp. ⟨3-4⟩ of a 4-page leaflet. Pp. ⟨1-2⟩
blank.

Line 1 of poem (not of the "Proem"): *There, as
we wandered vacant on the strand,* |

Noted on two types of paper; sequence, if any, not
known. The designations are for identification
only.

A: Watermarked with an all-over design of rules,
dashes, stars, leafy ornaments. Size of page:
7⁵⁄₁₆″ × 4¹³⁄₁₆″. *Location:* H

B: Lightly calendered white wove paper. Size of
leaf: 8½″ × 5¼″. *Locations:* B H

Collected in *Poems,* 1893.

15650. PURGATORIO. CANTO TWENTY-
FIRST

Noted in the following printings. Sequence not
determined. Perhaps proofs only.

PRINTING A

PURGATORIO. | CANTO TWENTY-FIRST.
| ⟨19 line prefatory note⟩ | ⟨text: 13 lines⟩ | ⟨n.p.,
n.d.⟩

Single leaf. Printed on one side only. 7⅞ × 5⅜″.
Anonymous.

PRINTING B

PURGATORIO. | CANTO TWENTY-FIRST.
| 'La Sete natural che mai non sazia.' | ⟨text: 90
lines⟩ | ⟨n.p., n.d.⟩

Single leaf. Printed on one side only. 17⅜″ × 6¼″.
Anonymous.

Note: The only examined copy may not be complete. Goodspeed (p. 38) describes a copy containing 91 lines of text.

Collected in *The Divine Comedy,* 1893.

For another version see in *Section One* above:
*Development of Christianity among the Cultivated Class
of Romans... Twenty-First and Twenty-Second Cantos...,* Printed for the Concord School of
Philosophy ⟨n.p., n.d., 1886⟩.

H (both)

15651. PURGATORIO. CANTO TWENTY-
SECOND...

⟨n.p., n.d.⟩

Single cut sheet. Printed on recto only. 18¾″
scant × 6¾″.

Proof only? Anonymous.

For another printing see *Canto Twenty-Second,*
above. Sequence not determined. Collected in
The Divine Comedy..., 1893. Also see in *Section
One* the following: *Development of Christianity among
the Cultivated Class of Romans... Twenty-First and
Twenty-Second Cantos...,* Printed for the Concord
School of Philosophy ⟨n.p., n.d., 1886⟩.

H

15652. PYROLA PATH

Three printings noted. The following sequence is
presumed correct. Uncollected.

A

PYROLA PATH. / ⟨rule⟩ / ⟨2 quatrains⟩ / ⟨n.p., n.d.⟩

Single leaf. Printed on recto only. Wove paper watermarked: *Arlington Mills* 6⅞″ × 4¾″.

Anonymous. Two four-line stanzas only.

Locations: B   BPL   H

B

PYROLA PATH. / ⟨rule⟩ / ⟨3 lines from Paradiso⟩ / ⟨rule⟩ / ⟨2 quatrains⟩ / ⟨rule⟩ / Printed for my niece of Italy, Ellen Parsons Monti; and my | niece of New England, Francesca Monti Lunt. / ⟨n.p., n.d.⟩

Single leaf. Printed on recto only. Wove paper watermarked: *Arlington Mills* 6¹⁵⁄₁₆″ × 4¾″.

Anonymous. Two four-line stanzas only.

Location: B

C

PYROLA PATH. / ⟨rule⟩ / ⟨3 lines from Paradiso⟩ / ⟨rule⟩ / ⟨3 quatrains⟩ / –––T. W. PARSONS. / ⟨rule⟩ / Printed for my niece of Italy, Ellen Parsons Monti; | and my niece of New England, Francesca Monti Lunt. / ⟨n.p., n.d.⟩

Single leaf. Printed on recto only. 7¹⁄₁₆″ × 4½″ full.

Three four-line stanzas.

Locations: AAS   B   BPL   H

15653. QUANDO CANTA ROSALINDA...

⟨n.p., n.d.⟩

Single leaf. Printed on recto only. 8½″ × 5½″.

"The first stanza of this, with several changes, together with the last and next to last stanzas, printed in *Advertiser*, May 31, *Transcript* June 2, 1884, under the title *On Reading a Book of Poems by Louise Imogen Guiney.* It refers to her first book, *Songs at the Start* . . . "–––Goodspeed.

Uncollected.

Two issues noted; the sequence has not been established:

A

Stanza 1, line 1: . . . *her lovely* . . .

Stanza 2, line 1: *Oft, should* . . .

Stanza 2, line 2: *Give the* . . .

Stanza 2, line 3: . . . *house–––by twos* . . .

Stanza 4, line 1: *So, as* . . .

B

Stanza 1, line 1: . . . *the lovely* . . .

Stanza 2, line 1: *If haply* . . .

Stanza 2, line 2: *Gives the* . . .

Stanza 2, line 3: . . . *house, by twos* . . .

Stanza 4, line 1: *So, when* . . .

B (B)   BPL (B)   H (A)

15654. RALPH WALDO EMERSON...

⟨n.p., n.d.⟩

Single leaf. Printed on recto only. 6″ × 7⅞″. Uncollected.

The only located example inscribed by Charles E. Goodspeed: "This proof . . . was printed for me by Mr. Updike many years ago. For some reason which I do not now recall the project ended with this copy. C. E. G. June, 1942."

H

15655. SAINT FRANCIS OF ASSISI. A SKETCH FROM THE PARADISO OF DANTE...

⟨n.p., n.d.⟩

Noted as proof only. Anonymous. Size (approximated) 13″ × 4½″.

At least two forms seen:

1: The word *Proof* does not appear at head.

2: With [*Proof.*] at head.

Collected in *The Divine Comedy*, 1893.

BPL (both)   H (both)

15656. ⟨Untitled 24-line poem beginning:⟩ SING, heavy heart! for heaviness...

⟨n.p., n.d.⟩

Single leaf. 8½″ × 5⁷⁄₁₆″. Printed on recto only.

Appears in *Poems*, 1893, immediately following the text of "Candlemas Night" and as though a part of that poem, but there is no readily apparent connection. The lines are not present in the leaflet printing of "Candlemas Night."

BPL   H

15657. ODE. ANCIENT OF DAYS. ⟨in:⟩

1638. 1888. Order of Exercises on the Two Hundred and Fiftieth Anniversary of the Ancient and Honorable Artillery Company, at New Old South Church, Monday, June 4, 1888, 10 O'Clock A.M.

⟨Boston: Mudge & Son, Printers, 1888⟩

Single leaf folded to make four pages. Cover-title. Printed in brown.

For a separate printing see *Martial Ode* . . . , above. Collected in *Poems*, 1893.

H

15658. SONG. Strike me a note of sweet degrees
––––... December Atlantic.

⟨n.p., n.d.⟩

Single leaf. Gray-blue linen-weave paper. 7⅞″ scant × 4¹³⁄₁₆″.

First published in *Atlantic Monthly*, Dec. 1890. Collected in *Poems*, 1893, as "Song." For publication as sheet music see "Strike Me a Note."

B H

A SONG FOR THE CHILDREN. MAY DAY...

See: *May Day*

15659. SONNET. ⟨*There loomed a great shape lately scarce in sight*⟩

⟨n.p.⟩ 1879.

Single leaf. Printed on recto only. Pale gray wove paper with smooth piqué-like finish. 5⅞″ full × 4¾″.

First published in *Scribner's Monthly Magazine*, Feb. 1879. Collected in *Poems*, 1893.

H

15660. ...A SONNET FOR THE EIGHTH SUNDAY AFTER TRINITY...

⟨n.p., n.d.⟩

Single leaf. Printed on recto only. 5¹¹⁄₁₆″ × 4⅝″ scant. At head of title: [*For the Boston Evening Transcript.*]

At end of text: T. W. PARSONS. / *Oceanside, Scituate.*

Originally in the *Boston Post*, July 18, 1891; the *Boston Evening Transcript*, July 18, 1891. Collected in *Circum Praecordia* ⟨1892⟩.

H

15661. SONNET SUGGESTED BY A THOUGHT OF M. ANGELO...

BEACON HILL PLACE, OCTOBER, 1884.

Single leaf. Printed on recto only. Uncollected.

The following printings noted; sequence not established.

A

Wove paper. Watermarked (in part): ILLS FINE 8″ scant × 5¼″.

Line 2 of heading: Comma present.

Line 1 of text: *The days are near...*

Line 13 of text: ... *way-worn soldiers...*

At end of BEACON HILL PLACE: Inverted comma

B

Laid paper. 6⅜″ scant × 5³⁄₁₆″.

Line 2 of heading: Comma not present.

Line 1 of text: *The days are near...*

Line 13 of text: ... *way-worn soldiers...*

At end of BEACON HILL PLACE: Comma correctly set

C

Wove paper. 6⅜″ full × 5³⁄₁₆″.

Line 2 of heading: Comma not present.

Line 1 of text: *The days draw near...*

Line 13 of text: ... *we tired pilgrims...*

At end of BEACON HILL PLACE: Comma correctly set

T. W. PARSONS set ⁷⁄₃₂″ below the last line of text.

D

Laid paper. A trimmed example measures 6⅜″ × 4½″.

Line 2 of heading: Comma not present.

Line 1 of text: *The days draw near...*

Line 13 of text: ... *we tired pilgrims...*

At end of BEACON HILL PLACE: Comma correctly set

T. W. PARSONS set ⁹⁄₃₂″ below the last line of text.

B (C)   BPL (B)   H (A, C, D)

15662. The Sphinx. Music by Edward Maryon. A Symphonic Poem for Baritone and Orchestra. 1915.

Not seen. Entry from Goodspeed. A reprint of "Proem" (*Down by the sea, beside the pilgrim dunes*); see above in *Section Two.*

15663. ...STRIKE ME A NOTE FROM A SONG BY T. W. PARSONS MUSIC BY F. BOOTT...

BOSTON ... MDCCCXCI ... OLIVER DITSON COMPANY ...

Sheet music. Cover-title. Plate number: 55071-3. At head of title: *To Mrs. F. J. Child...*

Reprint? See *Song. Strike me a note...*, above, in *Section Two.*

B

15664. ⟨Untitled poem beginning:⟩ THINK NOT OF ME AMID THE CROWD...

AUGUST 18, 1886.

Single leaf. Printed on recto only. $8\frac{1}{2}'' \times 5\frac{7}{16}''$. Collected in *Poems*, 1893, as "Think Not of Me amid the Crowd."

B   BPL

15665. . . . TO A HUNGARIAN LADY——— HOMEWARD BOUND . . .

⟨n.p., n.d.⟩

Single leaf. Printed on one side only. Laid paper. Watermarked: *Liberty linen* $7\frac{15}{16}'' \times 4\frac{15}{16}''$. At head of title: *For the March number of the Century.* (PRIVATE PROOF.)

The preliminary statement notwithstanding, not found in *Century Magazine*. Collected in *Poems*, 1893.

B   BPL   H

15666. TO BEATRICE BIDDLE BACHE IN RETURN FOR A BIRTHDAY BASKET OF ROSES . . .

⟨n.p., n.d.⟩

Single leaf. Printed on recto only. $8\frac{7}{16}'' \times 5\frac{7}{16}''$. Uncollected.

B   BPL

15667. TO DR. H. I. BOWDITCH . . . THE CDLLECT ⟨*sic*⟩ FOR THE SECOND SUNDAY AFTER TRINITY . . .

⟨n.p., n.d.⟩

Single leaf. Printed on recto only. $5\frac{13}{16}'' \times 4\frac{11}{16}''$.

"To Dr. H. I. Bowditch," first published in *Boston Post*, June 14, 1890. Uncollected.

"The Collect . . . ," collected in *Circum Praecordia* ⟨1892⟩.

H

15668. TO FRIENDS IN FLORIDA, IN ACKNOWLEDGEMENT OF ORANGE BLOSSOMS . . .

⟨n.p., n.d.⟩

Single leaf. Printed on recto only. $8\frac{15}{16}'' \times 5\frac{5}{8}''$. Uncollected.

Two versions noted; sequence undetermined:

A

Line 2 of text: *In orange groves* . . .

Line 5 of text: *Therefore I sigh* . . .

Line 16 of text: . . . *wonld reveal* |

B

Line 2 of text: *In orange orchards* . . .

Line 5 of text: *Henceforth on Hungary* . . .

Line 16 of text: . . . *would reveal* |

B (B)   BPL (A)   H (A)

15669. TO HARVEY D. PARKER, GREETING . . .

MAY 10, 1881.

Single leaf folded to make four pages. Printed on p. ⟨1⟩ only. Page: $6\frac{3}{8}'' \times 5\frac{1}{4}''$. Uncollected.

BPL (lacking blank conjugate)   H

15670. TO HONOURABLE ROBERT C. WINTHROP, AFTER PERUSAL OF HIS ORATION UPON THE COMPLETION OF THE WASHINGTON MONUMENT . . .

⟨n.p., n.d.⟩

Also in *The Two Hundred and Forty-Seventh Annual Record* . . . , 1885, above, *Section One*. Uncollected.

Single cut sheet of paper, folded to make four pages. Printed on pp. ⟨2-3⟩ only, pp. ⟨1⟩ and ⟨4⟩ blank.

Three printings noted:

1

P. ⟨2⟩, line 14 of text: . . . *towered* . . .

P. ⟨2⟩, line 3 from bottom: . . . *George was* . . .

P. ⟨3⟩, line 26: . . . *Mah'met's* . . .

Printed on wove paper. Proof printing only? Page: $8\frac{11}{16}'' \times 5\frac{3}{4}''$ scant.

2

P. ⟨2⟩, line 14 of text: The word *towered* altered to *towers* by means of erasure and overprinting.

P. ⟨2⟩, line 3 from bottom: *George* altered to *This* by means of erasure and overprinting.

P. ⟨3⟩, line 26: *Mah'met's* reset to *Mahomet's*.

Printed on laid paper. Page: $7\frac{7}{8}'' \times 5\frac{1}{8}''$.

3

P. ⟨2⟩, line 14 of text: The word *towered* altered to *towers* by resetting, not by means of erasure and reprinting.

P. ⟨2⟩, line 3 from bottom: The name *George* altered to *This* by resetting, not by means of erasure and reprinting.

P. ⟨3⟩, line 26: . . . *Mahomet's* . . .

Printed on laid paper. Page: $7\frac{13}{16}'' \times 5\frac{1}{2}''$.

First published in *Boston Daily Advertiser* and *Boston Evening Transcript*, Feb. 25, 1885.

H (1, 2, 3)

15671. TO MILDRED BOOTH GROSS-
MANN, WITH A GIFT OF LILY-BUDS ...

⟨n.p., n.d.⟩

Single leaf. Printed on recto only. $7\frac{1}{16}'' \times 4\frac{1}{2}''$
full. Collected in *Poems*, 1893, as "With a Gift of
Lily-Buds."

AAS B   H   Y

15672. TO MRS. GROSSMANN ...

FEBRUARY FOURTEENTH, 1888.

Single leaf. Laid paper. Printed on recto only.
$7'' \times 4\frac{3}{8}''$. Uncollected.

H   Y

15673. TO MRS. MAY M----. WHO SENT
ME FROM STRATFORD A SCION OF
SHAKESPEARE'S MULBERRY ...

⟨n.p., n.d.⟩

Single leaf. Laid paper. Printed on recto only.
$7\frac{7}{16}'' \times 4\frac{5}{16}''$. Uncollected. Originally in the
Boston Post, Aug. 22, 1890---Goodspeed.

H

15674. TO MRS. WATERSTON. THE SWANS
OF ST. JAMES'S ...

⟨n.p., n.d.⟩

Single leaf. Printed on recto only. Grayish-white
wove paper. $7\frac{3}{4}'' \times 5\frac{1}{8}''$. Uncollected.

BPL   H

15675. TO THE NEW ROYALL PROFES-
SOR ...

⟨n.p., n.d.⟩

Single leaf. Printed on recto only. $8'' \times 5''$. Collected in *The Willey House*, 1875.

AAS   H

15676. TWENTY-FOURTH OF OCTOBER,
1852 ...

⟨n.p., 1852⟩

Anonymous.

Single sheet folded to make four pages. P. ⟨i⟩ as
above.

Pp. ⟨i⟩-iii; p. ⟨iv⟩ blank save for presence of
mourning border. Page: $10\frac{5}{8}'' \times 8\frac{3}{16}''$ full.

Written on the death of Daniel Webster. Dated
at end *November 1st, 1852*.

First published in *Today, a Boston Literary Journal*,
Nov. 20, 1852---Goodspeed. Revised, truncated,
collected in *Poems*, 1854.

AAS   B   BPL   H   Y

15677. THE TWO DAYS. ELECTION OF
ABRAHAM LINCOLN ... NOVEMBER 8th,
1864 ...

⟨n.p., n.d.⟩

Anonymous. By Parsons? Not found in the collected works.

Single leaf. $8'' \times 5''$; measurement approximated.
Printed on recto only. Issued with a blank conjugate?

BPL

15678. THE TWO DAYS. JULY 4th, 1865.
THE FLAG ...

HEARD'S ISLAND. JULY 4, 1865.

Anonymous. Also in *The Rosary*, 1865.

Single leaf. $7\frac{15}{16}'' \times 5''$. Printed on recto only.
Issued with a blank conjugate?

BPL

15679. YESTERDAY ...

⟨n.p., n.d.⟩

Single cut sheet folded to make four pages. P. ⟨1⟩
as above. Text of "To-Day" on p. ⟨3⟩. Pp. ⟨2⟩
and ⟨4⟩ blank. Page: $8'' \times 5\frac{3}{16}''$. Uncollected.

BPL   H

THOMAS WILLIAM PARSONS

SECTION III

Reprints of Parsons's own books.

15680. Versi sopra un Busto di Dante di Thomas W. Parsons Tradotti dall'Inglese da Generale ⟨Luigi⟩ Masi

Palermo Stabilimento Tipografico Lao Premiato con Diverse Medaglie. Via Celso, 31. 1872.

Printed paper wrapper. Pp. ⟨1⟩-9. 9³⁄₁₆″ × 6⅛″ scant.

Translation and text on opposing pages. Parsons's original reprinted from *The First Ten Cantos*, 1843. *Note:* A reprint of the above was done (in Boston?) *ca.* 1887. Paged: ⟨1⟩-7. 8⅛″ × 5⅜″.

B (2nd)   BPL (2nd)   H (1st, 2nd)   LC (2nd)   Y (2nd)

15681. The Birthday of Michael Angelo . . . [For Private Circulation.]

London: Hatchards, Piccadilly. 1875.

⟨1⟩-15; printer's imprint, p. ⟨16⟩. 5⁵⁄₁₆″ × 4³⁄₁₆″. Printed mottled blue-gray paper wrapper.

Two issues noted:

1

As above. On p. 10: Eleven verses. Noted in printed paper wrapper only.

2

As above save for the following variations: On p. 10: Three verses. Leaves 4-5 are reprinted inserted conjugates. Noted in yellow P cloth; mauve S cloth: and, printed mottled blue-gray paper wrapper.

Note: Presumably issued after the Boston, 4-page printing described above in *Section Two*.

AAS (1st)   B (2nd)   BA (2nd)   BPL (1st)   H (1st, 2nd)   Y (2nd)

15682. The Ante-Purgatorio of Dante Alighieri. Translated by T. W. Parsons.

London: Hatchards, Piccadilly. 1876.

B   H   LC   Y

15683. Circum Præcordia . . .

Portland Maine Thomas B Mosher MDCCCCVI

450 copies on Van Gelder handmade paper; printed paper boards, paper vellum shelf back and corners, printed label on spine. Also: 50 numbered copies on Japanese vellum, printed paper wrapper folded over unprinted flexible boards.

Deposited (Van Gelder paper) Nov. 8, 1908 ⟨*sic*⟩.

B   Y

15684. . . . For One Who Fell in Battle   Eight-Part Chorus for Mixed Voices . . .

New York: G. Schirmer   Boston: Boston Music Co.   London . . . Berlin . . . Leipzig . . . Paris . . . ⟨1911⟩

Cover-title. At head of title: *G. Schirmer's Collection of Part-Songs & Choruses for Mixed Voices No. 5536* . . . ⟨*Music by*⟩ *Ch. M. Lœffler*

Plate number 22365. Reprinted from *The Magnolia*, 1866.

BPL

Books of authors other than Parsons containing Parsons material here reprinted.

The Poets and Poetry of Europe . . . by Henry Wadsworth Longfellow . . .

Philadelphia . . . M DCCC XLV.

For fuller entry see No. 12078.

The Estray: A Collection of Poems . . .

Boston . . . 1847.

For fuller entry see No. 12088.

Gift-Leaves of American Poetry. Edited by Rufus W. Griswold.

New-York . . . ⟨1849⟩

For fuller entry see No. 6682.

Cyclopædia of American Literature . . . by Evert A. Duyckinck and George L. Duyckinck . . .

New York . . . 1855.

For fuller entry see No. 11092A.

The Household Book of Poetry . . . Edited by Charles A. Dana.

New York . . . 1858.

"On a Lady Singing," pp. 613-614; otherwise "Upon a Lady Singing," *Poems,* 1854.

For fuller entry see No. 12120.

The Poets of the Nineteenth Century . . . Edited by . . . Rev. Robert Aris Willmott . . .

New York . . . 1858.

For comment see entry No. 1663.

Golden Leaves from the American Poets Collected by John W. S. Hows . . .

New York: George Routledge and Sons, 416 Broome Street. ⟨1864; *i.e.,* not before 1866⟩

Golden Leaves from the American Poets Collected by John W. S. Hows

New York . . . M DCCC LXV

For fuller entry see BAL, Vol. 5, p. 603.

The Flower of Liberty. Edited . . . by Julia A. M. Furbish.

Boston . . . 1866.

"Our Flag," pp. 27-28; otherwise "The Flag," *The Rosary,* 1865.

For fuller entry see No. 1424.

The Flower of Liberty. Edited and Illustrated by Julia A. M. Furbish.

Cincinnati, Ohio: White, Corbin, Bouve & Company, No. 124 Walnut Street. 1869.

See preceding entry for first edition.

The Poets of the Nineteenth Century . . . Edited by . . . Robert Aris Willmott . . .

New York . . . 1872.

For fuller entry see BAL, Vol. 5, p. 318.

American Poems. Selected and Edited by William Michael Rossetti . . .

London: E. Moxon, Son, & Co., Dover Street, and 1 Amen Corner, Paternoster Row. ⟨n.d., after Nov. 1872⟩

Cloth?

The Poets and Poetry of America. By Rufus Wilmot Griswold. With Additions by R. H. Stoddard . . . Revised . . .

New York . . . 1873.

All Parsons material herein reprinted from other books. "Upon a Lady, Singing," *Poems,* 1854, appears herein under the title "On a Lady Singing." "To a 'Magdalen,' a Painting by Guido," *Poems,* 1854, appears herein under the title "On a Magdalen by Guido."

For fuller entry see No. 9565.

A Hand-Book of English Literature. Intended for the Use of High Schools . . . by Francis H. Underwood . . . American Authors.

Boston: Lee and Shepard, Publishers. New York: Lee, Shepard and Dillingham. 1873.

Noted as *forthcoming* PW July, 1873 (*Educational Number*). No further word found.

... Little Classics. Edited by Rossiter Johnson. Minor Poems ...

    Boston ... 1875.

    For fuller entry see BAL, Vol. 5, p. 608.

The Sunny Side ... by Chas. W. Wendté and H. S. Perkins ...

    New York ... ⟨1875⟩

    For fuller entry see No. 178.

Songs of Three Centuries. Edited by John Greenleaf Whittier.

    Boston ... 1876.

    For comment see entry No. 11341.

The Century Plant ... Published in Aid of the Grand Centennial Fair of the Marshfield Agricultural and Horticultural Society, July 4th, 5th and 6th, 1876.

    ⟨Marshfield, Mass., 1876⟩

    An occasional newspaper. All issued. 8pp. Edited by Florence V. R. Browne.

Poems of Places Edited by Henry W. Longfellow ... Scotland. Vol. I.

    Boston ... 1876.

    For fuller entry see No. 12177.

Poems of Places Edited by Henry W. Longfellow ... France and Savoy. Vol. II.

    Boston ... 1877.

    For fuller entry see No. 12183.

Poems of Places Edited by Henry W. Longfellow ... Italy. Vol. II.

    Boston ... 1877.

    For fuller entry see No. 12185.

Poems of Places Edited by Henry W. Longfellow ... Italy. Vol. III.

    Boston ... 1877.

    For fuller entry see No. 12186.

The Fireside Encyclopædia of Poetry ... Compiled ... by Henry T. Coates.

    ... Philadelphia. ⟨1878⟩

    "The Groomsman to the Bride's-Maid," p. 183; otherwise "The Groomsman to His Mistress," *Poems*, 1854.

    For fuller entry see in the James Russell Lowell list, *Section Three*.

Poetry of America ... ⟨Edited⟩ by W. J. Linton.

    London ... 1878.

    All Parsons material herein reprinted from earlier books. "Mary Booth," *The Rosary*, 1865, appears herein as "Dirge."

    For fuller entry see No. 7872.

Poems of Places Edited by Henry W Longfellow ... America. British America ...

    Boston ... 1879.

    "Imperium in Imperio," pp. 50-52. Earliest located book publication. Also appears as a separate, issued not later than Dec. 30, 1878. The separate is described in *Section Two*.

    For fuller entry see No. 12215.

Poems of Places Edited by Henry W. Longfellow ... Oceanica ...

    Boston ... 1879.

    "On the Death of Napoleon," by Manzoni, translated by Parsons, pp. 116-120. Otherwise "Manzoni's Ode on the Death of Napoleon," *Poems*, 1854.

    For fuller entry see No. 12216.

Poems of Places Edited by Henry W. Longfellow ... America. Middle States.

    Boston ... 1879.

    For fuller entry see No. 12211.

The Union of American Poetry and Art A Choice Collection ... Selected ... by John James Piatt ...

    Cincinnati ... 1880

    For fuller entry see in *James Russell Lowell* list, *Section Three*.

Harper's Cyclopædia of British and American Poetry Edited by Epes Sargent

    New York ... 1881

    For comment see entry No. 4336.

Indian Summer Autumn Poems and Sketches ⟨Compiled by⟩ L. Clarkson ...

    New York ... 1881 ...

    For comment see entry No. 10449.

Favorite Poems ...

    New York ... ⟨n.d., after May 1, 1881⟩

    "Bust of Dante," pp. 446-448. Otherwise "On a Bust of Dante," *The First Ten Cantos* ..., 1843.

    For fuller entry see BAL, Vol. 5, p. 320.

The Cambridge Book of Poetry and Song . . .
by Charlotte Fiske Bates . . .

> New York . . . ⟨1882⟩
>
> For comment see entry Nos. 7887, 11490.

Young People's Scrap-Book . . . ⟨Compiled by
Daniel Curry⟩

> Cincinnati . . . 1884.
>
> "September," p. 55. Otherwise "A Song for
> September," *Poems*, 1854.
>
> For fuller entry see BAL, Vol. 5, p. 612.

Belford's Chatterbox. December, 1884. Edited by
Elmo . . .

> Chicago . . .1884.
>
> "September," p. 53. Otherwise "A Song for
> September," *Poems*, 1854.
>
> For fuller description see BAL, Vol. 5, p. 320.

September Edited by Oscar Fay Adams . . .

> Boston . . . ⟨1886⟩
>
> For comment see entry No. 67.

November Edited by Oscar Fay Adams . . .

> Boston . . . ⟨1886⟩
>
> For comment see entry No. 69.

The Sonnets of Europe . . . by Samuel Waddington . . .

> London . . . 1886.
>
> "From the Vita Nuova," p. 14. Otherwise
> "Sonnet XIII," *The Old House at Sudbury*, 1870.
>
> For fuller entry see BAL, Vol. 5, p. 613.

Camp-Fire Sketches and Battle-Field Echoes of
the Rebellion. Compiled by W. C. King, and
W. P. Derby . . .

> . . . Springfield . . . 1887.
>
> For fuller entry see BAL, Vol. 5, p. 613.

Souvenir of Venice . . .

> Boston, December, 1888. Published by the
> Women's Educational and Industrial Union . . .
>
> Printed paper wrapper. Tied with tape. Un-
> paged.

The Poets' Year . . . Edited by Oscar Fay
Adams . . .

> Boston . . . ⟨1890⟩
>
> For fuller entry see No. 80.

The Lovers' Year-Book of Poetry . . . by Horace
Parker Chandler Vol. II. July to December

> Boston . . . 1892
>
> For fuller entry see BAL, Vol. 4, p. 61.

The Lovers' Year-Book of Poetry ⟨Second Series⟩
. . . Married-Life and Child-Life by Horace
Parker Chandler . . .

> Boston . . . 1893
>
> For fuller entry see No. 10903.

Through Love to Light A Selection . . . by John
White Chadwick and Annie Hathaway Chadwick

> Boston . . . 1896
>
> "Civitas Dei," p. 7. Otherwise the first stanza
> of "Paradisi Gloria," *The Rosary*, 1865.
>
> For fuller entry see No. 2633.

The Treasury of American Sacred Song . . .
Edited by W. Garrett Horder . . .

> London . . . 1896
>
> For fuller entry see in the *Louise Chandler Moulton*
> list, *Section One*.

Not Changed but Glorified and Other Verses
Edited . . . by Canon Knowles

> New York   James Pott & Co., Publishers
> Fourth Avenue & 22nd Street 1896

The Doctor's Window . . . Edited by Ina Russelle
Warren . . .

> Buffalo . . . Eighteen-Hundred-Ninety-Eight
>
> For comment see BAL, Vol. 2, p. 275.

An American Anthology 1787–1899 . . . Edited by
Edmund Clarence Stedman . . .

> Boston . . . M DCCCC
>
> For comment see entry No. 3082.

American Familiar Verse Vers de Société Edited
. . . by Brander Matthews . . .

> . . . New York . . . 1904
>
> For fuller entry see in James Russell Lowell,
> *Section Three*.

Through Italy with the Poets   Compiled by
Robert Haven Schauffler . . .

> New York . . . 1908
>
> For comment see BAL, Vol. 4, p. 446.

Poems of American History Collected . . . by
Burton Egbert Stevenson

> Boston . . . 1908

> For fuller entry see in Joaquin Miller, *Section
> One*.

The History of the Boston Theatre 1854–1901 by
Eugene Tompkins . . . ⟨and⟩ Quincy Kilby . . .

> Boston and New York   Houghton Mifflin
> Company The Riverside Press Cambridge 1908

> Boards, cloth shelfback, leather label on spine.
> 160 numbered copies.

> Reprints, pp. 20-21, the concluding portion of
> Parsons's "Address for the Opening of the Boston
> Theatre, September 11, 1854." Previously in
> *Poems*, 1893.

> Noted for Dec. 15, PW Dec. 5, 1908.

The Players   Minutes of the First Meeting,
December 31, 1888, together with the Deed of
Gift from Edwin Booth

> New York   1908

> Printed paper wrapper.

> Poem, pp. 10-12. Otherwise "Address to the
> Assembly . . . Players' Club . . . December 31,
> 1888," in *Poems*, 1893.

REFERENCES AND ANA

Ghetto di Roma

> Boston, 1854

> Both DAB and CHAL list this as a separate.
> Almost certainly a ghost caused by an imperfect

reading of Allibone. The poem appears in
Poems, 1854.

The Weary

> Cambridge, Mass. 1865

> 80 copies privately printed. *Not located. Not seen.*
> Entry on the basis of CHAL, Vol. 4, p. 650.
> Presumably a ghost; erroneous entry for *The
> Rosary*, Cambridge, 1865.

The American Poets: A Review of the Works of
Thomas William Parsons. By W. R. Alger. Reprinted from the "Christian Examiner."

> Cambridge: Press of John Wilson and Son.
> 1869.

> Cover-title. Printed self-wrapper.

Seaward   An Elegy on the Death of Thomas
William Parsons by Richard Hovey

> Boston D. Lothrop Company 1893

> For fuller entry see BAL No. 9376.

. . . Thomas William Parsons Poet and Gentleman
by Joseph Edgar Chamberlin . . .

> Privately Printed for the Chile Club and Mem-
> bers of the Omar Khayyám Club of America
> ⟨1923⟩

> Printed paper wrapper. At head of title:
> *Rosemary Press Brochures*

A Bibliography of the Works of Thomas William
Parsons by Charles E. Goodspeed with Notes by
Allen Herbert Bent.

> Unpublished. Deposited in The Houghton Li-
> brary, Harvard University.

Initials, Pseudonyms, and Anonyms for Volume VI

Ad Senatorem·Advenam in Oris Patrum Advenarum. By Thomas William Parsons

All' Augusta Regina Margherita di Savoja. By Thomas William Parsons

Allen, Paul, Esq. See *A History of the American Revolution . . .*, by John Neal

Anna ⟨Annie⟩ of the Vale. By George Pope Morris. See in the Morris list, *Section Two*

Author of *Behemoth.* Cornelius Mathews

—— *Call Me Pet Names.* Frances Sargent Osgood

—— *Georgia Scenes.* Augustus Baldwin Longstreet

—— *Logan.* John Neal

—— *Logan, the Mingo Chief.* John Neal

—— *My Farm of Edgewood.* Donald G. Mitchell

—— *Reveries of a Bachelor.* Donald G. Mitchell

—— *Seventy-Six.* John Neal

—— *The Betrothed of Wyoming.* Presumably James McHenry

—— *The First of the Knickerbockers.* Peter Hamilton Myers

—— *The New Priest in Conception Bay.* Robert T. S. Lowell

—— *The Virtues of Society.* Mrs. Sarah W. A. Morton

—— *Wet Days at Edgewood.* Donald G. Mitchell

—— *The Wilderness.* James McHenry

Beacon Hill. A Local Poem . . ., 1797. By Mrs. Sarah W. A. Morton

Behemoth: A Legend of the Mound-Builders. By Cornelius Mathews

Bell Brandon; and, the Withered Fig Tree. A Prize Novel. By Peter Hamilton Myers

Betrothed of Wyoming, The, an Historical Tale. Presumably by James McHenry

Biglow Papers, The, Second Series. By James Russell Lowell

Bob Short. See note under *Poetic Effusions*, 1819, in the Augustus Baldwin Longstreet list of *References and Ana.*

Brother Jonathan; or, the New Englanders. By John Neal

Calmstorm, the Reformer. A Dramatic Comment. By Cornelius Mathews

Canto Twenty-Second ⟨of Purgatorio⟩. Translated by Thomas William Parsons

Carriers of the New-York Mirror, The, to their Patrons . . . January, 1834. Attributed to George Pope Morris. See Morris list, *Section Two.*

Caskoden, Edwin. *Pseudonym for Charles Major*

Cavendish-Bentinck-Pelham-Clinton-St. Maur-Beauchamp-Devere, K. G., Right Honorable Lord William Henry. *See in Edgar Wilson Nye under the year 1888.*

Chandler, Ellen Louise. *Later Ellen Louise Chandler Moulton*

Chanticleer: A Thanksgiving Story of the Peabody Family. By Cornelius Mathews

Christ of the Snow, The, a Norwegian Legend. By S. Weir Mitchell. See in Mitchell list under n.d., ca. 1887.

Christmas Carol, A, (Oh bird of dawning! all the night . . .) By Thomas William Parsons

Citizen of New-York, A. 1813. *Pseudonym for Clement Clarke Moore*

Class Poem. 1838. By James Russell Lowell

Clear the Track! as Sung by the Democratic Clubs . . . See in George Pope Morris, *Section Two*

Columella. *Pseudonym for Clement Clarke Moore*

Count Ernst von Mansfeldt the Protestant. By Thomas William Parsons

Craddock, Charles Egbert. *Pseudonym for Mary Noailles Murfree*

Crowquill, Jno. *Pseudonym for Donald Grant Mitchell*

December Fourteenth . . . Anniversary of the Death of Prince Albert, 1861. By Thomas William Parsons

Dedicatory Hymn. Composed for . . . the Opening of the West-Boston Meeting-House . . . 1806. By Mrs. Sarah W. A. Morton

Dembry, R. Emmet. *Pseudonym for Mary Noailles Murfree*

Dies Irae . . . Faintness of heart and sinking of the soul . . . By Thomas William Parsons

Dreamer, A. *Pseudonym for Amy Lowell*

E.W.S. *Elizabeth Wister Stevenson.* See in the S. Weir Mitchell list: *The Children's Hour,* 1864

Editors of the Yankee and Boston Literary Gazette, The. *Pseudonym for John Neal;* Neal's *Address for the New Year, 1829,* issued with the authorship credited thus. The address, titled "Ode to Peace," credited to John Neal, published in *Specimens of American Poetry,* by Samuel Kettell, Boston, 1829

Ellen Louise. *Pseudonym for Ellen Louise Chandler Moulton*

Ensenore. A Poem. By Peter Hamilton Myers

Epithalamium. F. R. and G. E. T. October 21, 1868. See in the Thomas W. Parsons list, *Section Two*

Essays of Howard, on Domestic Economy. By Mordecai M. Noah

Fanny Read Monti. Palermo, Sicily, January 11th, 1869. By Thomas William Parsons

First of the Knickerbockers, The, a Tale of 1673. By Peter Hamilton Myers

Flag of our Union, The. See in the George Pope Morris list, *Section Two*

Florence. *Pseudonym for Frances Sargent Osgood*

For the Headstone. By Thomas William Parsons

Fortress of Sorrento, The; a Petit Historical Drama, in Two Acts. See in the Mordecai M. Noah list under 1808.

From the Reminiscences of the late Lucius Manlius Sargent. By Thomas William Parsons

Greaves, Richard. *Pseudonym for George Barr McCutcheon*

Guido Rospigliosi, Il. By Thomas William Parsons

Homer Wilbur. *Pseudonym for James Russell Lowell*

Howard, Essays of, on Domestic Economy. By Mordecai M. Noah

Ik. Marvel. *Pseudonym of Donald Grant Mitchell*

Il Guido Rospigliosi. By Thomas William Parsons

Il Pesceballo. Opera Seria: In Un Atto. By James Russell Lowell

Imperium in Imperio. By Thomas William Parsons

In Memory of J. M. B. March XXIX, MDCCCLXIII. By Thomas William Parsons

Indian Fairy Book, The. From the Original Legends . . . Edited by Cornelius Mathews

J. R. L. *James Russell Lowell*

Jehu O'Cataract. *Pseudonym for John Neal*

Jno. Crowquill. *Pseudonym for Donald G. Mitchell*

John Marr and Other Sailors . . . By Herman Melville

Kerr, Orpheus C. *Pseudonym for Robert Henry Newell*

L., J. R. *James Russell Lowell*

Lady, A. 1856. *Louise Chandler Moulton*

Landholder, A. *Pseudonym for Clement Clarke Moore*

List of the Original Memoirs of S. Weir Mitchell, A. Presumably compiled by S. Weir Mitchell

Literary Traveller, A. See under the year 1833 in the *Augustus Baldwin Longstreet* list of *References and Ana*

Logan, a Family History. By John Neal

Long Time Ago. A Glee. By George Pope Morris

Louise, Ellen *Pseudonym for Ellen Louise Chandler Moulton*

M., S. *Mrs. Sarah W. A. Morton*

M., S. W. *Silas Weir Mitchell*

Martyr President, The. New York, 1865. By Robert Henry Newell

Marvel, Ik. *Pseudonym for Donald G. Mitchell*

. . . *May Day, a Song for the Children.* By Thomas William Parsons

Merry-Mount; a Romance of the Massachusetts Colony. By John Lothrop Motley

Moneypenny, or, the Heart of the World. A Romance of the Present Day. By Cornelius Mathews

Morton of Morton's Hope; an Autobiography. By John Lothrop Motley

Morton's Hope; or, the Memoirs of a Provincial. By John Lothrop Motley

Mr. Parkman and His Canadian Critics . . . By Francis Parkman

Native Georgian, A. *Pseudonym for Augustus Baldwin Longstreet*

Nature: On Freedom of Mind: And Other Poems, 1839. See in list of *References and Ana*, Sarah
    Wentworth Apthorp Morton

Near the Banks of That Lone River. By George Pope Morris. See in *Section Two* of the Morris list

New Englander Over-Sea, A. *Pseudonym for John Neal*

New Priest in Conception Bay, The. By Robert T. S. Lowell

New Translation with Notes, of the Third Satire Juvenal . . . , New-York, 1806. See in the *Clement
    Clarke Moore* list.

New-York Mirror, The, and Ladies' Literary Gazette. For the First of January, 1826 . . . See in the
    George Pope Morris list, *Section Two*, under *New-York in 1826*.

Observations upon Certain Passages in Mr. Jefferson's Notes on Virginia . . . , 1804. See in *Clement
    Clarke Moore* list.

O'Cataract, Jehu. *Pseudonym for John Neal*

Occurrences of the Times . . . ⟨1789⟩. Sometimes credited to Mrs. Sarah W. A. Morton; see in
    section of Morton *References and Ana*

Ode Written to Commemorate the 250th Anniversary of the Boston Latin School. By Thomas William
    Parsons

On a Bust of Longfellow. By Thomas William Parsons

On a Faded Photograph. To Mrs. Annie Fields. By Thomas William Parsons

Opera Goer, An. *Pseudonym for Donald G. Mitchell*

Orpheus C. Kerr. *Pseudonym for Robert Henry Newell*

Our Golden Wedding on the Island. By Thomas William Parsons

P., T. W. *Thomas William Parsons*

Pesceballo, Il. Opera Seria: In Un Atto. By James Russell Lowell

Philalethes. *Pseudonym for Clement Clarke Moore*

Philenia, a Lady of Boston. *Pseudonym for Mrs. Sarah W. A. Morton*

Poker of Fun, A. *Pseudonym for Amy Lowell*

Political Mirror, The, or Review of Jacksonism . . . See in George Pope Morris, list of *References
    and Ana*

Politicians, The, a Comedy, in Five Acts. By Cornelius Mathews

Prayer, A. By S. Weir Mitchell. Issued without date. See under 1898

Proem. Down by the Sea . . . By Thomas William Parsons

Purgatorio. Canto Twenty-First. Translated by Thomas William Parsons

Purgatorio. Canto Twenty-Second. Translated by Thomas William Parsons

Pyrola Path. By Thomas William Parsons

S., E. W. *Elizabeth Wister Stevenson*

S. M. *Sarah W. A. Morton*

S. W. M. *S. Weir Mitchell*

The Sailor's Grave. (*Music Composed for The Portico by C. Meineke*) . . . Text by John Neal. See in Neal list under the year 1817

Saint Francis of Assisi. A Sketch from the Paradiso of Dante. By Thomas William Parsons

Secondsight, Solomon. Pseudonym for James McHenry

Short Account, A, of the Courtship of Alonzo & Melissa. By Isaac Mitchell

Short, Bob. See note under *Poetic Effusions*, 1819, in the Augustus Baldwin Longstreet list of *References and Ana*

Sketches for the Fair. By Frances Sargent Osgood

Smith, The Late Ben. *Pseudonym for Cornelius Mathews*

Somebody, M. D. C., &c. &c. &c. *Pseudonym for John Neal*

Song for Buck and Breck, A. Said to be by George Pope Morris. See in Morris list, *Section Two*

Song for the Children, A. May Day. By Thomas William Parsons

Song. Tunes——Light, Imandra . . . See in George Pope Morris list, *Section Two*

Song . . . When other friends are round thee . . . See in George Pope Morris list, *Section Two*

Story of Toby, The, a Sequel to "Typee." By Herman Melville

Successful Operator, A. See in *Joaquin Miller*, list of *References and Ana* under year 1881

T. W. P. *Thomas William Parsons*

Their Ostracized Poet. See in *James Russell Lowell* under year 1838

Timoleon, etc. By Herman Melville

Tree by the Well, The. By Joaquin Miller

Twenty-Fourth of October, 1852. By Thomas W. Parsons

The Two Days. Election of Abraham Lincoln. See in the Thomas W. Parsons list, *Section Two*

The Two Days. July 4th, 1865. The Flag. By Thomas W. Parsons

Voice from the South, A. Comprising Letters from Georgia to Massachusetts . . . By Augustus Baldwin Longstreet

Wakondah; the Master of Life. A Poem. By Cornelius Mathews

Wandering Boys, The, or, the Castle of Olival. A Melo Drama. See under the year 1821 in the Mordecai M. Noah list.

Where Rolls the Oregon. By Joaquin Miller, n.d., 1876.

Wilbur, Homer. *Pseudonym for James Russell Lowell*

Wilderness, The, or, Braddock's Times. A Tale of the West. By James McHenry

Wonderful Quiz, A. *Pseudonym for James Russell Lowell*

Wonderful Stories of Fuz-Buz the Fly . . . , The. By S. Weir Mitchell